MARKETING, 10E

MARKETING, 10E

FIND YOUR **BAK**
(**B**OOK **A**CTIVATION **K**EY)
AFTER LAST PAGE OF TEXT

Joel R. Evans
Hofstra University

Barry Berman
Hofstra University

THOMSON

Australia · Canada · Mexico · Singapore · Spain · United Kingdom · United States

Marketing, 10e: Marketing in the 21st Century
Joel R. Evans and Barry Berman

Executive Editors:
Michele Baird, Maureen Staudt, and
Michael Stranz

Marketing Manager:
Mikka Baker

Managing Editor:
Kendra Leonard

Marketing Coordinators:
Lindsay Annett and Sara Mercurio

Production/Manufacturing Manager:
Donna M. Brown

Production Editorial Manager:
Dan Plofchan

Rights and Permissions Specialists:
Kalina Hintz and Bahman Naraghi

Cover Image:
© Getty

The Adaptable Courseware Program consists of products and additions to existing Thomson products that are produced from camera-ready copy. Peer review, class testing, and accuracy are primarily the responsibility of the author(s).

Marketing in the 21st Century / Joel R. Evans and Barry Berman -10th Edition

Preview Guide ISBN: 0-759-39257-9
Book ISBN: 0-759-39155-6
Package ISBN: 0-759-39325-7

LCCN: 2006929382

International Divisions List

Asia (Including India):
Thomson Learning
(a division of Thomson Asia Pte Ltd)
5 Shenton Way #01-01
UIC Building
Singapore 068808
Tel: (65) 6410-1200
Fax: (65) 6410-1208

Australia/New Zealand:
Thomson Learning Australia
102 Dodds Street
Southbank, Victoria 3006
Australia

Latin America:
Thomson Learning
Seneca 53
Colonia Polano
11560 Mexico, D.F., Mexico
Tel (525) 281-2906
Fax (525) 281-2656

Canada:
Thomson Nelson
1120 Birchmount Road
Toronto, Ontario
Canada M1K 5G4
Tel (416) 752-9100
Fax (416) 752-8102

UK/Europe/Middle East/Africa:
Thomson Learning
High Holborn House
50-51 Bedford Row
London, WC1R 4L$
United Kingdom
Tel 44 (020) 7067-2500
Fax 44 (020) 7067-2600

Spain (Includes Portugal):
Thomson Paraninfo
Calle Magallanes 25
28015 Madrid
España
Tel 34 (0)91 446-3350
Fax 34 (0)91 445-621

To

Linda, Stacey, and Jennifer

Linda; Glenna, Paul, Danielle, and Sophie; and Lisa, Ben, Emily, and Philip

Brief Contents

Contents

Part III
Consumer Analysis: Understanding and Responding to Diversity in the Marketplace 221

8 Final Consumers 223

9 Organizational Consumers 255

Part VI
Promotion Planning 517

17 Integrated Marketing Communications 519

18 Advertising and Public Relations 545

19 Personal Selling and Sales Promotion 573

Part VII
Price Planning 607

20 Considerations in Price Planning 609

21 Developing and Applying a Pricing Strategy 631

Preface

With this third Atomic Dog edition, *Marketing* continues its transformation into a state-of-the-art multimedia package. Our subtitle, *Marketing in the 21st Century*, is not just a cute catchphrase. It signifies our focus on the marketing concepts that will be essential for the future success of any organization or person, presented in a technologically advanced pedagogical format. We are proud to lead the principles of marketing textbook market into full reader interactivity—at a value price point.

Marketers in the 21st century, more than ever before, need to understand and properly apply new communication technologies, especially the World Wide Web. Although the media have widely reported on the difficulties associated with *E-commerce* (referring to online sales transactions), the potential uses of *E-marketing* (encompassing any marketing activities conducted through the Internet, from customer analysis to marketing-mix components) are truly enormous.

With this in mind, *Marketing in the 21st Century* not only covers emerging topics in detail, it does so in an interactive, dynamic manner. Here's how: The book can be purchased in two ways: (1) in a four-color print format with access to a full-featured Web site or (2) as a subscription to the full-featured Web site. The print version has all the elements that you expect from *Marketing*: comprehensive topical coverage, colorful design, cases, career material, and so on. The Web site has the complete text, chapter by chapter, in a reader-enticing format. It contains more than 1,800 hotlinks to actual Web sites, distributed throughout the book; more than 100 animated in-chapter figures that visually display flowcharts, bar charts, and so on; a clickable glossary so the reader can immediately see the definitions of key terms; a list of "Web Sites You Can Use" in each chapter (which also appears in the print text); hotlinks to a strategic marketing plan outline, by part of the book; an online Web exercise in each chapter; and a whole lot more!

These are challenging times for all of us. We have seen the true arrival of the PC age and the World Wide Web, the steady movement in the United States and many other nations around the globe toward service- rather than production-driven economies, a growing understanding and interest in customer service and customer satisfaction, more attention to consumer diversity, the emergence of free-market economies in Eastern Europe and elsewhere, business and government grappling with such ethical issues as the consumer's right to privacy, the impact of deregulation on society, and a host of other actions.

The years ahead promise to be even more intriguing, as the European Union adds more member countries, nations in the Americas make their markets more accessible to one another, other foreign opportunities grow, technological advances continue, and we try to cope with slow-growth economies and political uncertainties in various parts of the globe. As we prepare for the coming decade and beyond, an appreciation of marketing (and its roles and activities) becomes critical.

We believe that a 21st-century principles of marketing textbook must incorporate both traditional and contemporary aspects of marketing, carefully consider environmental factors, address the roles of marketing and marketing managers, and show the relevance of marketing for those who interact with or are affected by marketing activities (such as consumers). We also believe such a textbook should describe marketing concepts to readers in a lively, comprehensive, and balanced way. As we indicate at the start of Chapter 1, marketing is "an exciting, fast-paced, and contemporary business discipline."

Although the basic components of marketing (such as consumer behavior, marketing research and information systems, and product, distribution, promotion, and price planning) form the foundation of any introductory-level marketing textbook, contemporary techniques and topics also need to be covered in depth. Among the contemporary topics given full-chapter-length coverage in *Marketing in the 21st Century* are developing and enacting strategic marketing plans; societal, ethical, and consumer issues; global marketing; marketing and the Internet; final consumer demographics, lifestyles, and decision making; organizational—b-to-b—consumers (manufacturers, wholesalers, retailers, government, and nonprofit institutions); goods versus services marketing (including nonprofit marketing); integrated marketing communications; and coordinating and analyzing the marketing plan. Environmental effects are noted throughout the book.

Marketing in the 21st Century explains all major principles, defines key terms, integrates topics, and demonstrates how marketers make everyday and long-run decisions. Examples based on such diverse organizations as Apple, Coca-Cola, eBay, Google, Jet Blue, Metropolitan Life, Nestlé, Sephora, United Parcel Service (UPS), Visa, and Wal-Mart appear in each chapter. The examples build on text material, reveal the dynamic nature of marketing, and involve students in real-life applications of marketing.

The New Tradition of *Marketing in the 21st Century*

We are as dedicated today as in the first edition of *Marketing* to having **the** most contemporary principles of marketing text on the market. We have listened carefully to the feedback from our colleagues, our students, and our team at Atomic Dog, and we have acted on this feedback. The world is evolving and so are we.

Interactive Learning Brings *Marketing* to Life During the time that we have worked on *Marketing in the 21st Century*, we have been amazed by the technological skills of Atomic Dog Publishing. We hope you will be, too. As was already noted, *Marketing* has a full-featured, highly interactive Web site that we believe will motivate students to learn about marketing principles in a way that encourages their participation in the learning process. **Our goal is to move the reader from passive learning to active learning**.

These are just some of the ways in which the online edition of this book brings *Marketing* to life:

- The complete text is online. Material may be accessed via concise, simple instructions. A drop-down screen in every chapter lets the reader easily move between topics in the chapter.
- Animated figures in each chapter illustrate key concepts. For example, in Chapter 1, the reader can see how selling and marketing philosophies differ; in Chapter 10, the difficulties of following the majority fallacy are highlighted through a series of moving images; in Chapter 12, the various types of services are easier to understand through a visual depiction; and in Chapter 22, the stages of integrated marketing planning are enlivened.
- The figures are not only animated—they are also highly interactive. Through the use of "mouseovers" and "clickthroughs," the reader can access more information (such as definitions and examples) about the topics in the figures. This means that the online design of the figures is less cluttered, and that instant self-testing is possible.
- All of the in-chapter key terms are linked to the glossary. With just a click, the definition of a term appears onscreen.
- Through a drop-down screen, the reader can do a key word search for any topic in the book from any chapter in the book.
- Each chapter integrates Quick Checks throughout. These are true-false questions designed to test comprehension.
- The end of each chapter features a full study guide for the chapter, with multiple choice, true-false, and fill-in questions.
- A simple click connects the reader to one of the more than 1,800 hotlinks noted throughout the book. These links deal with a wide range of organizations and information. At the end of every chapter, online and in print, there is a "Web Sites You Can Use" section, as well as a Web-based exercise.
- At the beginning of each part of the online book, there is a hotlink to the relevant section of a strategic marketing plan.
- Eighteen computer exercises (keyed to important marketing topics) are available through an online download.
- There is a comprehensive computerized strategic planning exercise (keyed to Chapter 3).
- Our Web site features a series of Excel spreadsheets that can be used as individual or integrated market planning analyses. They add a financial dimension when used along with *StratMktPlan*.

Content Changes for the 21st Century Here is a synopsis of the content changes we have made for *Marketing in the 21st Century*. We hope you are pleased with them:

1. All of the opening vignettes are new. The vignettes deal with major events in the history of some of the world's leading companies, including Walt Disney, General Electric, Toyota, Boeing, DuPont, Dell, Subway, American Express, Anheuser-Busch, Tiffany, and Microsoft.
2. All chapter boxes are new. The boxes follow three themes: "Ethical Issues in Marketing," "Global Marketing in Action," and "Marketing and the Web." The boxes' thought-provoking nature has been retained.
3. "Web Sites You Can Use" is a very reader-friendly, in-text feature. The end of every chapter lists valuable Web sites related to marketing. These chapter-related sites range from search engines to shopping venues to benchmarking practices.
4. All of the short cases are new.
5. The eight comprehensive part cases are all new.
6. All data and examples are as current as possible.
7. The careers appendix (Appendix A) has been updated and features a number of hotlinks.
8. The 18 computer exercises are summarized in Appendix C. They may be downloaded from the online edition Resource Folder. These exercises are extremely easy to use, are self-contained, and operate in the Windows XP environment. All directions are contained on computer screens and are self-prompting.

Building on the Strong Foundation of *Marketing*

These **general features** have been retained from prior editions of *Marketing*:

- A lively, easy-to-read writing style.
- A balanced treatment of topics by size of firm, goods- and service-based firms, profit-oriented and nonprofit firms, final and organizational consumers, and so on.

- Comprehensive coverage of all important marketing concepts, including 11 chapters on the marketing mix (product, distribution, promotion, and price planning).
- A full-color design throughout the book, including lots of photos and figures. These illustrations are all keyed to the text, as well as visually attractive.
- Part openers that provide integrated overviews of the chapters in every part.
- Many definitions from the American Marketing Association's online *Dictionary of Marketing Terms*.
- Early coverage of societal, ethical, and consumer issues, and global marketing (Chapters 5 and 6).
- Service marketing coverage in the section on product planning (Chapter 12).
- A mix of short and long cases, 38 cases in all (30 short cases and 8 comprehensive cases).
- An appendix on careers in marketing.
- An appendix on marketing mathematics.
- An appendix on computerized exercises that accompany the text. A computer symbol in the relevant chapters keys the exercises to the concepts involved.
- A detailed glossary.
- Separate company, name, and subject indexes.

These features have also been retained and are contained **in each chapter:**

- Chapter objectives that outline the major areas to be investigated.
- An opening vignette that introduces the material through a real-world situation.
- An introductory overview that sets the tone for the chapter.
- Thought-provoking boxed extracts on key marketing topics.
- Descriptive margin notes (in the print version) that highlight major concepts.
- Boldface key terms that identify important definitions.
- Many flowcharts and current figures and tables that explain how marketing concepts operate and provide up-to-date information.
- Numerous footnotes to enable the reader to do further research.
- Chapter summaries keyed to chapter objectives. These summaries are followed by a listing of key terms, with text page references.
- End-of-chapter questions divided into separate "review" and "discussion" categories.

The *Marketing in the 21st Century* Package

A complete package accompanies *Marketing in the 21st Century*. For students, there are online computerized exercises, a study guide, and numerous hotlinks to career information, current events, and so on. To aid the classroom learning experience, the following instructor supplements are available on CD:

- Test Bank—includes over 3,500 items comprised of multiple-choice, true-false, and essay questions. The multiple-choice and true-false questions are categorized as terminology/concept and applied/comprehensive/integrative. All multiple-choice and true-false questions are classified by degree of difficulty. The Test Bank is available in the ExamView Pro® format, which enables instructors to quickly create printed tests using either a Windows or Macintosh computer. Instructors can enter their own questions and customize the appearance of the tests they create.
- Instructor's Resource Manual—includes sample syllabi, answers to end-of-chapter review and discussion questions, answers to part-ending short and comprehensive case questions, answers to marketing mathematics questions, answers to computer-based marketing exercises, suggested term paper topics, and a listing of professional and trade associations.
- Instructor's Lecture Manual—contains teaching goals, chapter overviews, key terms, suggested discussion topics, class exercises, and complete lecture notes for each chapter in the text, Appendix A (Careers in Marketing), and Appendix B (Marketing Mathematics).
- PowerPoint presentations.

How *Marketing in the 21st Century* is Organized

Marketing in the 21st Century is divided into eight parts. Part 1 presents marketing in today's society, describes its environment, presents strategic planning from a marketing perspective, and discusses marketing information systems and the marketing research process. Part 2 covers the broad scope of marketing: societal, ethical, and consumer issues; global marketing; and marketing and the Internet. Part 3 deals with marketing's central thrust: understanding final and organizational (b-to-b) consumers in a diverse marketplace. It examines demographics, lifestyle factors, consumer decision making, target market strategies, and sales forecasting. Both final consumers and organizational consumers are included.

Part 4 covers product planning, branding and packaging, goods versus services marketing, the product life cycle, new products, and mature products. Part 5 deals with distribution planning, value chain management, logistics, wholesaling, and retailing. Part 6 examines integrated promotion planning, the communication channel, advertising, public relations, personal selling, and sales promotion. Part 7 looks at price planning, price strategies, and applications of pricing. Part 8 integrates marketing planning—including benchmarking and customer satisfaction measurement—and looks to the future.

We are pleased that previous editions of *Marketing* were adopted at hundreds of colleges and universities nationwide and around the world. We hope the third Atomic Dog edition, *Marketing in the 21st Century*, is satisfying to continuing adopters and meets the needs of new ones. Thanks for your support and encouragement.

Please feel free to communicate with us. We welcome comments regarding any aspect of *Marketing in the 21st Century* or its package: Joel R. Evans or Barry Berman, Department of Marketing and International Business, Hofstra University, Hempstead, N.Y., 11549. You can E-mail us at **mktjre@hofstra.edu** or **mktbxb@ hofstra.edu**. We promise to reply to any correspondence we receive.

Joel R. Evans
Barry Berman
Hofstra University

A Brief Walk Through

Marketing, 10e: Marketing in the 21st Century

You will find an overview of several distinctive features of *Marketing in the 21st Century* in this walking tour. Through these features, we present the most complete coverage possible of the field of marketing—and do so in an interesting, interactive, and contemporary way.

It's all covered—from absolute product failure to yield management pricing.

Marketing in the 21st Century introduces and integrates key marketing concepts, many of which have grown in importance, such as strategic planning, database marketing, marketing and the Internet, integrated marketing communications, and value chain management.

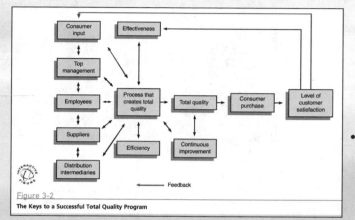

Figure 3-2

The Keys to a Successful Total Quality Program

We look at total quality from a marketing perspective.

Figure 17-1

Integrated Marketing Communications and FedEx Kinko's

"Make it. Print it. Pack it. Ship it."

Source: Reprinted by permission.

The value of integrated marketing communications Is an underlying theme in *Marketing*.

7-3 THE MULTIFACETED POTENTIAL MARKETING ROLES FOR THE INTERNET

After reviewing the company benefits of the Internet in marketing, it should be clear that the Web has the potential to serve several marketing roles, as shown in Figure 7-5 and discussed next. Each firm must determine which roles to pursue and how to prioritize their importance.

Projecting an image—A firm can project an image at its Web site through the site's design (colors, graphics, etc.) and the content presented. Have you ever heard of Accenture (http://www.accenture.com)—formerly Andersen Consulting? No? Well, you can learn a lot about the firm and the image it is striving to project by visiting its

The Internet can serve many roles besides generating sales.

The Internet can serve many marketing roles for farsighted firms.

Table 14-1 Selected Distribution Goals by Party

Party	Distribution Goals
Suppliers/ Manufacturers	To gain access to the distribution channel
	To ensure that all distribution functions are performed by one party or another
	To hold down distribution and inventory costs
	To foster relationship marketing with distribution intermediaries and customers
	To obtain feedback from distribution intermediaries and customers
	To have some control over the distribution strategy
	To optimize production runs and achieve economies of scale

The importance of the value chain and the value delivery chain are highlighted.

We believe marketing's vital role should be shown in varied situations. So, we have worked especially hard to present a balance of examples on domestic and international marketing, large and small firms, goods and services, and final consumers and organizational consumers.

Figure 4-2

Marketing Information Systems: Playing at an Airport Near You

With the advent of powerful, fast, and inexpensive computer terminals and networks, firms in any industry and of any size can easily set up a marketing information system. The airline industry is in the forefront with state-of-the-art MIS programs, such as that used by Japan Airlines (http://www.jal.co.jp/en).

Source: Reprinted by permission of Susan Berry, Retail Image Consulting, Inc.

This exemplifies our extensive coverage of global marketing.

Small firms, as well as large ones, are involved with marketing and strategic planning.

3-6b Moonstruck Chocolate Company: A Strategic Marketing Plan by a Small Specialty Firm[25]

In 1993, Bill Simmons and his wife Deb opened Moonstruck Chocolate Company (then known as Moonstruck Chocolatier) in Portland, Oregon. When it began, Moonstruck was exclusively a maker of truffles for the wholesale market. It sold to retailers such as Neiman Marcus, Marshall Field, and Starbucks. The firm introduced it first retail store in 1996 and sales rose rapidly. Today, Moonstruck is a successful firm specializing in chocolate-based products, with annual sales approaching $4 million and high-powered goals for the future. Why? The firm has created, implemented, and monitored a solid strategic marketing plan. Let's look at the highlights of Moonstruck's plan.

Although a small company, Moonstruck Chocolate has a detailed strategic marketing plan.

Chapter 12 ("Goods Versus Services Planning") integrates services marketing into product planning.

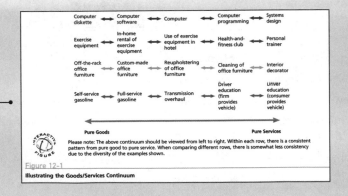

Figure 12-1

Illustrating the Goods/Services Continuum

Please note: The above continuum should be viewed from left to right. Within each row, there is a consistent pattern from pure good to pure service. When comparing different rows, there is somewhat less consistency due to the diversity of the examples shown.

Both final and organizational consumers are important to marketers.

Final consumers buy for personal, family, or household use; organizational consumers buy for production, operations, or resale.

decision making. *Final consumers* buy goods and services for personal, family, or household use. Chapter 9 looks at *organizational consumers*, those buying goods and services for further production, usage in operating the organization, or resale to other consumers. Chapter 10 explains how to devise a target market strategy and use sales forecasts.

For *Marketing in the 21st Century*, we have three thought-provoking boxes in every chapter:

- "Ethical Issues in Marketing."
- "Global Marketing in Action."
- "Marketing and the Web."

Each box presents a real-life situation and asks the reader to be a decision maker and state a position or make suggestions.

Ethical Issues in Marketing

Chapter	Title
1	The Ethics of Monitoring Customer Service Calls
2	Disneyland: Corporate Philanthropist
3	Profitable Corporate Social Responsibility
4	The Bill of Rights for Survey Respondents
5	American Entrepreneurs Seek to Help Solve Social Problems
6	Battling Corruption and Bureaucracy in Nigeria
7	Business Schools 1, Hackers 0
8	Marketing to Children: The Controversy Rages On
9	Nike Promotes the Good Practices of Its Suppliers
10	Dr Pepper Recognizes the Importance of the Hispanic Market
11	Addressing the Flood of Counterfeit Products
12	Improving the Integrity of Bankers
13	Do Consumers Care About "Ethical" Products?
14	Chargebacks and Markdown Money: An Intensifying Battle Between Channel Members
15	Protecting the Distribution Rights of Legitimate Film Wholesalers
16	Should Barnes & Noble Have Moved New Writers Off a Power Aisle?
17	A Failure to Communicate Honestly: Fatal Errors in the Job Search
18	Using Ads to Overcome Negative Publicity: A Proper Approach?
19	Are Frequent Flier Programs a Good Deal for Consumers?
20	Fighting Against Below-Cost Gas Prices: A Good Idea?
21	Merchants Take on Visa and MasterCard over Credit-Card Fees
22	Meeting Ethical Responsibilities in a Tough Marketplace

Global Marketing in Action

Chapter	Title
1	NBA Europe Live: Marketing U.S. Sports on the Global Stage
2	Procter & Gamble in Germany: Succeeding Where Others Have Failed
3	Chevron: Introducing a New Gasoline Additive Worldwide
4	Neuromarketing Experiments Come to Marketing Research
5	The Evolution of Marketing Practices in India
6	Avon Calling: A Global Star Shines Brighter Than Ever
7	Live 8: The Global Power of the Internet
8	Body Shop: Using "Masstige" Marketing to Attract New Customers
9	Specialty Malls for Wholesale Buyers
10	Japanese Consumers Love U.S.-Made Coach Bags
11	Chinese Brands Go Global
12	The Kenya Tourist Board Ramps Up Its Marketing Efforts
13	Brand Extendibility on the Global Stage
14	Lenovo's Distribution Network a Key Asset After Acquisition of IBM's PC Division
15	Capacitor Industries: Wholesaling Electronic Components from China
16	Russia: Appealing But Sometimes Scary for Western Retailers
17	Cadbury's Dairy Milk: Sending Inconsistent Messages
18	Advertising on MTV: Reaching a Worldwide Audience
19	The Best Salespeople in Hong Kong Are Millionaires
20	EasyGroup: An Anti-Luxury Approach
21	The $100 Computer
22	Maintaining a Leading Position Around the Globe

Marketing and the Web

Chapter	Title
1	Craigslist: Building a Proper User-Driven Online Community
2	What Wireless Technology Customers Want Online
3	Print Media and Broadcast Media Refashion Their Strategies
4	Tips for Doing Marketing Research Online
5	Making the Can-Spam Act Work Better
6	Europe on the Web
7	Why Amazon, eBay, and Google Are Opening Their Data Bases to Others
8	Blogging: An Emerging Form of Consumer Communications
9	Designing a Super B-to-B Web Site
10	Getting Inside Shoppers' Minds
11	Using the Internet to Strengthen Brand Popularity
12	Online Reservations: An Effective Tool for Hotels
13	Photo-Sharing Web Sites Revolutionize Picture Taking
14	eBay and Its Sellers: Not Always on the Same Page
15	Electrical Distributors Flock to the Internet
16	The Lifestyle Center: A Bricks-and-Mortar Response to the Internet
17	How Spyware and Adware Can Undermine Online Communications Efforts
18	The Boom in Web-Based Advertising
19	Online Coupons Come of Age
20	Looking for the Best Deal? Check Out Comparison Shopping Web Sites
21	Online Music Pricing: Pay per Download Versus a Yearly Subscription
22	Benchmarking E-Commerce

Marketing in the 21st Century has 30 short cases and eight comprehensive part cases. These cases cover a wide range of companies and scenarios. All are extremely current.

Case 3: Southwest Airlines: Retooling While on Top[c1-3]

During its nearly four decades of service, Southwest Airlines' (http://www.southwest.com) operating strategy has been a simple one. In return for its mechanics, pilots, and flight attendants out-hustling its competitors, Southwest would provide job security and reward employees with company stock. Yet, even though Southwest has never laid off an employee and its stock is valued at $11 billion (almost three times that of the other major airlines combined), Southwest's May 2005 stock price was down by more than 30 percent as compared with 2001. Much of its 2005 profits were due to Southwest's hedging fuel costs better than competitors. As a result, its fuel cost for 85 percent of its needs was $26 per barrel versus an industry average cost of over $50. Without the fuel cost advantage, Southwest would have lost money in four of the past nine quarters as of March 2005.

Southwest Airlines' overall strategy has focused on several components: operational simplicity due to the use of one type of aircraft (this keeps mechanic training and parts inventory low), a company-wide devotion to keeping costs and fares low, and an emphasis on efficiency (due to the fast turnaround of its aircraft between arrival and departure). Southwest's strategy was distinctive in the past, but today, it has been copied by airlines such as JetBlue (http://www.jetblue.com) and AirTran (http://www.airtran.com). According to current chief executive, "Hey, I can admit it, our competitors are getting better. Sure, we have an enormous cost advantage. Sure, we're the most efficient. The problem is, I just don't see how that can be indefinitely sustained without some sacrifice."

Southwest is increasingly facing competition from new upstarts, as well as the entrenched legacy carriers. Upstarts such as JetBlue initially borrowed Southwest's one-airplane model and added such goodies as leather seats, individual TV screens, and fancy snacks. JetBlue's costs are lower than Southwest's. And the legacy carriers such as Delta (http://www.delta.com) and United (http://www.united.com) have cut their cost of flying a passenger mile to 8.4 cents versus Southwest's 6.3 cents. The recent bankruptcies of Delta, Northwest (http://www.nwa.com/), United, and US Airways (http://www.usairways.com) enabled these airlines to cut unprofitable routes, reduce interest payments for aircraft, reduce pension obligations, and lower employee wages.

One way that Southwest is seeking to better compete is by expanding its routes. This lets Southwest lower its personnel costs by hiring new, lower-paid employees and spreading its administrative overhead costs over more seats. Southwest recently increased its presence in the Chicago market by raising the number of flights at Midway airport. Its purchase of a share in ATA (http://www.ata.com), a bankrupt carrier, also gave Southwest's customers greater access to such cities as Boston, Denver, Minneapolis, and Honolulu. Southwest also started flying to Philadelphia and Pittsburgh.

Southwest is seeking to improve its efficiency through employee, attrition, a hiring freeze, and generous severance packages to longtime employees. It reduced the number of employees per aircraft from 89 in 2002 to 74 in 2005. Another source of savings is through technology that automates certain functions or provides self-service opportunities to customers. Among Southwest's high-technology applications are its Southwest Web site (responsible for over $3 billion in annual bookings), its self-service kiosks, and the Gate Reader software that keeps gate agents up-to-date on a passenger's status and special needs. As Southwest's chief information officer says, "As our airline scales, for us to provide the same kind of high-touch customer service, we have to automate a lot of things we've been able to do without technology previously. The challenge is doing that without conceding the customer touch."

Questions

1. Discuss the strategic benefits of Southwest Airlines' low-cost strategy.
2. Describe how the bankruptcy filings of Delta and United are reducing Southwest's low-cost advantage.
3. How can Southwest sustain its low-cost strategy?
4. Explain how Southwest Airlines can retain its corporate culture as it expands further.

End-of-part cases integrate the material discussed in the group of chapters in particular parts of the text.

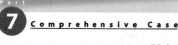

Part 7 — Comprehensive Case

Making "Cents" of Pricing[PC-7]

INTRODUCTION

Considering all the elements of the marketing mix, price has the most direct effect on profitability. Price is also the most easily controlled of the elements. Yet properly setting prices and measuring their impact on the entire organization is seldom done properly, or in a manner that optimizes long-term market share and profitability. Pricing strategy must focus on overall category profitability and consider the strategic implications of price changes on brand equity, product positioning, product cannibalization, and competitive response. In addition, the impact of price changes needs to be evaluated in the context of both return on marketing investment and impact on the remaining elements of the marketing mix.

Marketing departments traditionally provide insights into market acceptance of new offerings and prices but have had limited impact on building business cases for changing prices. At a recent American Marketing Association (http://www.marketingpower.com) Research Conference, Sally Dancer, a senior practice expert at consulting firm McKinsey & Co. (http://www.mckinsey.com), indicated that CEOs want marketing to become a full business partner. She then went on to challenge marketers to become more involved in developing business cases that directly link marketing initiatives with profits.

Based on what Dancer and others are saying, there is a big incentive for marketing departments to expand their traditional role of providing insights and become a more active partner in building a financial model, especially when it comes to developing pricing strategy. In order for marketing departments to make the transition from simply providing business insights to developing full-blown business cases, they need to redesign their research studies to reflect actual marketplace behavior, incorporating inputs for all items in the marketing mix.

CURRENT PARADIGMS

Traditionally, the role of marketing in developing pricing strategy has been the ability to understand market acceptance of price changes to new and existing goods and services. Through the use of various experiments, market researchers have learned about the trade-offs between brands, prices, features, and channels for leveraging customer value propositions and developing pricing strategies. This is valuable information, but this type of research does not do a good job of replicating the complexity of current marketplaces and extracting the real impact of price and price sensitivity. For example, many studies create an artificial marketplace that forces competitive offerings to contain similar features and prices when, in reality, many competitive offerings have features and prices that are unique to a single brand. In addition, some experiments typically underestimate the impact of price and provide price sensitivity in aggregate, rather than by brand.

Pricing research typically focuses on a customer's preference for specific offerings and reports findings in terms of percentages. Given the lack of a complete set of competitive offerings and prices in the marketplace, it's difficult to align preference measures with current market conditions and then accurately project how changes in the marketing mix will affect the marketplace, especially in financial terms. Furthermore, this process tends to lower the value of research because management can only make decisions on a relative "percentage" basis, rather than on an absolute "profit" basis. To develop a meaningful pricing strategy, marketers must integrate customer input on a complete competitive marketplace with all the other business variables that affect pricing decisions.

Many organizations make pricing decisions based on secondary or syndicated data sources, internal costs, or competitive factors. Although each of these items needs to be considered, profit potential and brand equity can erode significantly with strategies based on these items alone. Some companies get input on customers' willingness to pay from measurements based on observed marketplace behavior. Such measurements are limited because they only reflect existing product characteristics. In addition, observational data doesn't involve controls, so it can be difficult to separate the trends and sensitivities in the observed data from external phenomena such as product availability, promotion, and advertising for both the company and competitors.

Because internal costs have a major impact on profitability, not linking them to market input on competitive pricing and customer willingness to pay can affect profits dramatically. It's unwise to develop a reactive pricing strategy based on customers leveraging one supplier over another to get the best possible price. It's equally unwise to develop a pricing strategy in reaction to competitive price changes, internal sales goals, or inventory levels. These factors need to be considered but basing pricing strategies only on such inputs can damage long-term profitability and product equity. Pricing strategy must also take into account long-term market response and impact on sales channels and profitability.

BUSINESS CASE DEVELOPMENT

Figure 1 shows a comprehensive approach to developing a financial model from market insight. The key is to be able to report the

[PC-7] Adapted by the authors from David M. Feldman, "Making Cents of Pricing," *Marketing Management* (May-June 2005), pp. 21–25. Reprinted by permission of the American Marketing Association.

Table of Cases

All of the short cases, as well as the eight comprehensive part cases are new:

When Anne M. Mulcahy, a Xerox (http://www.xerox.com) executive with 30 years of experience at the firm, was chosen chief executive officer of Xerox, the company was in horrific shape. The Securities and Exchange Commission was examining Xerox's accounting practices, the company had $14 billion in debt, and it faced tough competition from Hewlett-Packard (http://www.hp.com), Canon (http://www.canon.com), and other copier companies.

Mulcahy repositioned Xerox from a firm that just sold copiers to all kinds of consumers to an "information flow" provider that scans and stores documents in a digital format for large corporate clients. One tough decision Mulcahy made was to discontinue Xerox's marketing of consumer printers, a business Mulcahy had started years ago. To financially stabilize Xerox, she reduced Xerox's debt to less than $10 billion. She also managed Xerox so that it has regularly met financial analysts' earnings projections. Despite spinning off its Palo Alto Research Center (http://www.parc.xerox.com), Xerox still gets two-thirds of its $16 billion in annual revenues from goods and services that are less than two years old.

One way Xerox was able to return to profitability was by carefully studying the needs of its key customers. After analyzing a large insurance company that was a major customer, Xerox learned that the information-related costs in acquiring new business were very high. Xerox showed the client how it could tag the information early on so it could be reused on an automated basis. This process cut the cost of getting a new client for the insurer by 40 to 50 percent.

Mulcahy is also investing in color printing. Xerox wants to increase the percent of material that is printed in color (instead of black and white) from 4 percent to 10 percent within 10 years. New digital technology has reduced the costs of color printing, so low-production volumes can be efficiently printed. Diagnostics for color printers also enable Xerox engineers to notify customers when their machines need servicing. Xerox makes 15 times as much profit from a color page as from one that is black and white.[1]

In this chapter, we will study the complex environment in which marketing decisions are made. We will see that an organization's level of success (or failure) is related not only to its marketing efforts, but also to the external environment in which it operates and its ability to adapt to environmental changes.

Chapter Objectives

1. To examine the environment within which marketing decisions are made and marketing activities are undertaken
2. To differentiate between those elements controlled by a firm's top management and those controlled by marketing, and to enumerate the controllable elements of a marketing plan
3. To enumerate the uncontrollable environmental elements that can affect a marketing plan and study their potential ramifications
4. To explain why feedback about company performance and the uncontrollable aspects of its environment and the subsequent adaptation of the marketing plan are essential for a firm to attain its objectives

[1] Various company and other sources.

A key goal is to reinforce the principles in *Marketing in the 21st Century* in a real-world, lively way. So, we've got all the in-text pedagogy you could want: part openers, chapter outlines, chapter objectives, chapter vignettes, highlighted key terms and marginal notes, photos and line art, bottom-of-page footnotes, useful Web links, summaries linked to chapter objectives, review and discussion questions, appendixes, and more!

Chapter-opening vignettes engage students in marketing in a very reader-friendly manner. These vignettes cover diverse organizations and situations.

Web Sites You Can Use

The U.S. government has the most comprehensive collection of Web sites in the world. It makes available all sorts of information on a free or nominal-fee basis. What a wealth of data! One general-access site (http://www.firstgov.gov) provides access to several hundred million government Web pages. Here are the addresses of several specialized U.S. government sites:

- Bureau of Economic Analysis (http://www.bea.doc.gov)
- Bureau of Labor Statistics (http://www.stats.bls.gov)
- Census Bureau (http://www.census.gov)
- Consumer Product Safety Commission (http://www.cpsc.gov)
- Department of Commerce (http://www.commerce.gov)
- Department of Labor (http://www.dol.gov)
- Economic and Statistics Administration (http://www.esa.doc.gov)
- Environmental Protection Agency (http://www.epa.gov)
- Federal Communications Commission (http://www.fcc.gov)
- Federal Reserve Board (http://www.federalreserve.gov)
- Federal Trade Commission (http://www.ftc.gov)
- Fedstats (http://www.fedstats.gov)
- Fed World (http://www.fedworld.gov)
- Food and Drug Administration (http://www.fda.gov)
- International Trade Administration (http://www.ita.doc.gov)
- Library of Congress (http://www.loc.gov)
- Securities and Exchange Commission (http://www.sec.gov)
- Small Business Administration (http://www.sba.gov)
- Technology Administration (http://www.technology.gov)
- Women's Bureau—Department of Labor (http://www.dol.gov/wb)

In each chapter, there is a feature entitled "Web Sites You Can Use," which lists valuable Web resources specifically related to marketing.

About the Computer Supplements Accompanying

Marketing, 10e: Marketing in the 21st Century

Online and in Print

Marketing, 10e: Marketing in the 21st Century is available online as well as in print. The online version demonstrates how the interactive media components of the text enhance presentation and understand. For example,

- Animated illustrations help clarify concepts and bring them to life.
- QuickCheck interactive questions and chapter quizzes test students knowledge of various topics and provide immediate feedback.
- Clickable glossary terms provide immediate definitions of key concepts.
- References and footnotes "pop up" with a click.
- Highlighting capabilities allow students to emphasize main ideas. They can also add personal notes in the margin.
- The search function allows students to quickly locate discussions of specific topics throughout the text.
- An interactive study guide at the end of each chapter provides tools for learning, such as interactive key-term matching and the ability to review customized content in one place.

Students may choose to use just the online version of the text or both the online and print versions together. This gives them the flexibility to choose which combination of resources works best for them. To assist those who use the online and print versions together, the primary heads and subheads in each chapter are numbered the same. For example, the first primary head in Chapter 1 is labeled 1-1, the second primary head in this chapter is labeled 1-2, and so on. The subheads build from the designation of their corresponding primary head: 1-1a, 1-1b, etc. This numbering system is designed to make moving between the online and print versions as seamless as possible.

Finally, next to a number of figures and exhibits in the print version of the text, you will see an icon similar to those below. This icon indicates that this figure or exhibit in the online edition is interactive in a way that applies, illustrates, or reinforces the concept.

Computer-Based Marketing Exercises

As noted in the preface, *Marketing* has a series of computer exercises that may be downloaded from our Web site. These exercises are extremely easy to use, are self-contained, and operate in the Windows environment, including Windows XP. All directions are contained on computer screens and are self-prompting.

The *Computer-Based Marketing Exercises* are designed to apply and reinforce specific individual concepts in *Marketing*. The exercises are explained in Appendix C; and throughout *Marketing*, a computer symbol signifies which concepts are related to the exercises:

1. Marketing Orientation
2. Boston Consulting Group Matrix
3. Questionnaire Analysis
4. Ethics in Action
5. Standardization in International Marketing Strategy
6. Vendor Analysis
7. Segmentation Analysis
8. Product Positioning
9. Services Strategy
10. Product Screening Checklist
11. Economic Order Quantity
12. Wholesaler Cost Analysis
13. Advertising Budget
14. Salesperson Deployment
15. Price Elasticity
16. Key Cost Concepts
17. Performance Ratios
18. Optimal Marketing Mix

There is also a detailed computer exercise, *StratMktPlan*, that encompasses all major elements of a strategic marketing plan. It is explained in the Chapter 3 appendix and is linked to the part openers throughout *Marketing*. This exercise may be downloaded separately from our Web site.

For professors who like to demonstrate how Excel may be applied in marketing situations, there is a special download at the Web site with a variety of simple Excel-based exercises.

Acknowledgments

Throughout our professional lives and during the period of time that the various editions of this book have been researched and written, a number of people have provided us with support, encouragement, and constructive criticism. We would like to publicly acknowledge and thank many of them.

In our years as graduate students, we benefited greatly from the knowledge transmitted from professors Conrad Berenson, Henry Eilbirt, and David Rachman, and colleagues Elaine Bernay, William Dillon, Stanley Garfunkel, Leslie Kanuk, Michael Laric, Kevin McCrohan, Leon Schiffman, and Elmer Waters. We learned a great deal at the American Marketing Association's annual consortium for doctoral students, the capstone of any marketing student's education.

At Hofstra University, colleagues Benny Barak, Andrew Forman, Jing Hu, William James, Songpol Kulviwat, Keun Lee, Anil Mathur, Charles McMellon, Rusty Mae Moore, James Neelankavil, Ralph Polimeni, Elaine Sherman, Shawn Thelen, Boonghee Yoo, and Yong Zhang have provided the collegial environment needed for a book of this type.

We would especially like to thank the following colleagues who have reviewed this or previous editions of *Marketing* and *Principles of Marketing*. These reviewers have made many helpful comments that have contributed greatly to this book:

Wayne Alexander (Moorhead State University)
Rolph Anderson (Drexel University)
Julian Andorka (DePaul University)
Kenneth Anglin (Mankato State University)
Thomas Antonielli, Sr. (Strayer College)
Harold Babson (Columbus State Community College)
Ken Baker (University of New Mexico)
John Bates (Georgia Southern University)
Stephen Batory (Bloomsburg University)
Richard Behr (Broome Community College)
Kurt Beran (Oregon State University)
Wanda Blockhus (San Jose State University)
John Boos (Ohio Wesleyan University)
Jeff Bradford (Drake University)
Donald Bradley, III (University of Central Arkansas)
James Brock (Susquehanna University)
Harvey Bronstein (Oakland Community College)
Sharon Browning (Northwest Missouri State University)
John Bunnell (Broome Community College)
Jim Burrow (North Carolina State University)
Gul Butaney (Bentley College)
Stephen Calcich (Hampton University)

Robert Chapman (Orlando College)
Yusef Choudhry (University of Baltimore)
Gloria Cockerell (Collin County College)
Barbara Coe (University of North Texas)
Linda Jane Coleman (Salem State College)
Kenneth Crocker (Bowling Green State University)
James Cronin, Jr. (Cape Cod Community College)
John Cronin (Western Connecticut State University)
Richard Cummings (College of Lake County)
Benjamin Cutler (Bronx Community College)
Homer Dalbey (San Francisco State University)
Betty Diener (University of Massachusetts, Boston)
Peter Doukas (Westchester Community College)
Rebecca Elmore-Yalch (University of Washington)
Mort Ettinger (Salem State University)
Roland Eyears (Central Ohio Technical College)
Frank Falcetta (Middlesex Community College)
Lawrence Feick (University of Pittsburgh)
Benjamin Findley, Jr. (University of West Florida)
Frank Franzak (Virginia Commonwealth University)
Stanley Garfunkel (Queensborough Community College)
Betsy Gelb (University of Houston)
Donald Gordon (Illinois Central College)
Jill Grace (University of Southern California)
Harrison Grathwohl (California State University at Chico)
Blaine Greenfield (Bucks County Community College)
Thomas Greer (University of Maryland)
Charles Gulas (Wright State University)
Gregory Gundlach (University of Notre Dame)
Robert Gwinner (Arizona State University)
Rita Hall (Sullivan Junior College)
Robert Hammond (Lexington Community College)
G. E. Hannem (Mankato State University)
Nancy Hansen (University of New Hampshire)
William Harris, III (Quinnipiac University)
Douglas Hawes (University of Wyoming)
Jon Hawes (University of Akron)
Dean Headley (Wichita State University)
Allen Heffner (Lebanon Valley College)
Thomas Hickey (State University of New York at Oswego)
Nathan Himmelstein (Essex County College)
Patricia Hopkins (California State Polytechnic University at Pomona)
Jerry Ingram (Auburn University at Montgomery)
Laurence Jacobs (University of Hawaii)
Rajshekhar Javalgi (Cleveland State University)
Norma Johansen (Scottsdale Community College)

Edna Johnson (North Carolina Agricultural and Technical State University)

Paul Joice, Sr. (Walla Walla College)

Mary Joyce (Emerson College)

Albert Kagan (University of Northern Iowa)

Ruel Kahler (University of Cincinnati)

Bernard Katz (Oakton Community College)

J. Steven Kelly (DePaul University)

John Kerr (Florida State University)

Bettie King (Central Piedmont Community College)

Gail Kirby (Santa Clara University)

Charles Knapp (Waubonsee Community College)

John Krane (Community College of Denver)

R. Krishnan (University of Miami)

Darwin Krumrey (Kirkwood Community College)

J. Ford Laumer (Auburn University)

William Layden (Golden West College)

Marilyn Liebrenz-Himes (George Washington University)

Robert Listman (Valparaiso University)

James Littlefield (Virginia Polytechnic Institute and State University)

Yusen Liu (University of St. Thomas)

John Lloyd (Monroe Community College)

William Locander (University of South Florida)

Kenneth Lord (Niagara University)

Robert Lorentz (Florida Institute of Technology)

William Lovell (Cayuga Community College)

Keith Lucas (Ferris State College)

Jacob Manakkalathil (University of North Dakota)

Scott Marzluf (National College)

Michael Mayo (Kent State University)

Ken McCleary (Virginia Polytechnic Institute and State University)

Elaine McGivern (Bucknell University)

James McMillan (University of Tennessee)

H. Lee Meadow (Eastern Illinois University)

John Mentzer (University of Tennessee)

Jim Merrill (Indiana University)

James Meszaros (County College of Morris)

Ronald Michael (University of Kansas)

Ronald Michman (Shippensburg State University)

John Milewicz (Jacksonville State University)

Howard Mills (Ulster City Community College)

Edward Moore (State University of New York College at Plattsburgh)

Linda Morable (Richland College)

John Morgan (West Chester University)

Linda Morris (University of Idaho)

Ed Mosher (Laramie County Community College)

Carol Stewart Mueller (Nassau Community College)

Paul Murphy (John Carroll University)

Margaret Myers (Northern Kentucky University)

Donald Nagourney (New York Institute of Technology)

Peter Nye (Northeastern University)

Kenneth Papenfuss (Ricks College)

Dennis Pappas (Columbus State Community College)

Terry Paul (Ohio State University)

William Perttula (San Francisco State University)

Michael Peters (Boston College)

Ann Pipinski (Northeast Institute of Education)

Robert Pollero (Anne Arundel Community College)

Edward Popper (Bellarmine University)

William Qualls (University of Illinois)

S. R. Rao (Cleveland State University)

Lloyd Rinehart (Michigan State University)

Edward Riordan (Wayne State University)

David Roberts (Virginia Polytechnic Institute and State University)

Mary Lou Roberts (University of Massachusetts at Boston)

Scott Roberts (Old Dominion University)

Donald Robin (University of Southern Mississippi)

John Rogers (California Polytechnic State University at San Luis Obispo)

Randall Rose (University of South Carolina)

Barbara Rosenthal (Miami Dade Community College)

Thomas Rossi (Broome Community College)

Nancy Ryan-McClure (Texas Tech University)

Barbara Samuel (University of Scranton)

Peter Sanchez (Villanova University)

Alan Sawyer (University of Florida)

Robert Schaffer (California State Polytechnic University at Pomona)

Martin Schlissel (St. John's University)

Stanley Scott (University of Alaska at Anchorage)

Donald Self (Auburn University at Montgomery)

Mohamad Sepehri (Sheperd College)

Rajagopalan Sethuraman (Southern Methodist University)

Reshma Shah (University of Pittsburgh)

Richard Sielaff (University of Minnesota at Duluth)

M. Joseph Sirgy (Virginia Polytechnic Institute and State University)

Richard Skinner (Ashland University)

Michael Smith (Temple University)

Norman Smothers (California State University at Hayward)

Gregory Snere (Ellsworth Community College)

Michael Solomon (Auburn University)

Patricia Sorce (Rochester Institute of Technology)

A. Edward Spitz (Eastern Michigan University)

Thomas Stafford (Texas Women's University)

Gary Stanton (Erie Community College)

Margery Steinberg (University of Hartford)

Jeffrey Stoltman (Wayne State University)

Robert Swerdlow (Lamar University)

Richard Szecsy (St. Mary's University)

Donna Tillman (California State Polytechnic University at Pomona)

Ed Timmerman (Abilene Christian University)

Frank Titlow (St. Petersburg Junior College)

Charles Treas (University of Mississippi)

David Urban (Virginia Commonwealth University)

Anthony Urbaniak (Northern State University)

Richard Utecht (University of Texas at San Antonio)

William Vincent (Santa Barbara City College)
Gerald Waddle (Clemson University)
Donald Walli (Greenville Technical College)
John Walton (Miami University)
J. Donald Weinrauch (Tennessee Technological University)
Colleen Wheeler (St. Cloud University)
Mildred Whitted (St. Louis Community College at Forest Park)
Jack Wichert (Orange Coast College)
David Wills (Sussex County Community College)
George Winn (James Madison University)
Martin Wise (Harrisburg Area Community College)
Joyce Wood (Northern Virginia Community College)
Gene Wunder (Washburn University)
Richard Yalch (University of Washington)
Anthony Zahorik (Vanderbilt University)
William Ziegler (Seton Hall University)

To the many students at Hofstra who have reacted to the material in *Marketing in the 21st Century*, we owe a special thanks, because they represent the true constituency of any textbook authors.

Our appreciation is extended to the fine people at Atomic Dog and Thomson Custom Publishing. We expressly thank (in alphabetical order) the outstanding team that worked on *Marketing in the 21st Century, 10e*: Christine Abshire, Mikka Baker, Joe Devine, Kendra Leonard, Chris Morgan, Dan Plofchan, Victoria Putman, Steve Scoble, Maureen Staudt, and Dreis VanLanduyt.

We are pleased to recognize the contributions of Diane Schoenberg, our editorial associate; and Jody Longshore, our graduate research assistant. Our appreciation and thanks are extended to Chip Galloway for his continued outstanding work on the computer exercises and Mid Semple for her initial work on many of the PowerPoint® slides that accompany this book. We also thank the American Marketing Association, Retail Forward, and Susan Berry for their cooperation and the right to reproduce case materials and photos.

To our families, this book is dedicated—out of respect, love, and appreciation.

Joel R. Evans
Barry Berman

About the Authors

Joel R. Evans, Ph.D., is the RMI Distinguished Professor of Business and Professor of Marketing and International Business at Hofstra University. Before joining Hofstra, he worked for a *Fortune 500* firm, owned a business, and taught at Baruch College and New York University. Dr. Evans is author or editor of numerous books and articles and is active in various professional associations. At Hofstra, he has received three Dean's Awards and the School of Business Faculty Distinguished Service Award. Dr. Evans has also been honored as Teacher of the Year by the Hofstra M.B.A. Association.

Barry Berman, Ph.D., is the Walter H. "Bud" Miller Distinguished Professor of Business and Professor of Marketing and International Business at Hofstra University. He also serves as the Director of Hofstra University's Executive Master of Business Administration program. Dr. Berman is author or editor of numerous books and articles and is active in various professional associations. At Hofstra, he has received two Dean's Awards. Dr. Berman has also been honored as Teacher of the Year by the Hofstra M.B.A. Association.

Joel R. Evans and Barry Berman are co-authors of several best-selling texts, including *Marketing in the 21st Century* and *Retail Management: A Strategic Approach* (Prentice Hall). They have co-chaired numerous prestigious conferences, including an American Marketing Association Faculty Consortium on "Ethics and Social Responsibility in Marketing" and the Academy of Marketing Science/American Collegiate Retailing Association Triennial Retailing Conference. Each has a chapter in Dartnell's *Marketing Manager's Handbook*. Drs. Evans and Berman have been consultants for such firms as Fortunoff, NCR, Olympus USA, and Simon Properties. Both regularly teach undergraduate and graduate marketing courses to a wide range of students.

About Atomic Dog

Atomic Dog is faithfully dedicated to meeting the needs of today's faculty and students, offering a unique and clear alternative to the traditional textbook. Breaking down textbooks and study tools into their basic "atomic parts," we were able to recombine them and utilize rich digital media to create a "new breed" of textbook.

This blend of online content, interactive multimedia, and print creates unprecedented adaptability to meet different educational settings and individual learning styles. As part of Thomson Custom Solutions (**http://www.thomson custom.com**), we offer even greater flexibility and resources in creating a learning solution tailor-fit to your course.

Atomic Dog is loyally dedicated to our customers and our environment, adhering to three key tenets:

- **Focus on Essential and Quality Content**: We are proud to work with our authors to deliver you a high-quality textbook at a lower cost. We focus on the essential information and resources students need and present them in an efficient but student-friendly format.
- **Value and Choice for Students**: Our products are a great value and provide students more choices in 'what and how' they buy-often at a savings of 30–40 percent versus traditional textbooks. Students who choose the online edition may see even greater savings compared to a print textbook. Faculty play an important and willing roll-working with us to keep costs low for their students by evaluating texts online and supplementary material.
- **Reducing Our Environmental 'Paw-Print'**: Atomic Dog is working to reduce its impact on our environment in several ways. Our textbooks and marketing materials are printed on recycled paper and we will continue to explore environmentally friendly methods. We encourage faculty to review text materials online instead of requesting a print review copy. Students who buy the online version do their part by going 'paperless' and eliminating the need for additional packaging or shipping. Atomic Dog will continue to explore new ways that we can reduce our 'paw print' in the environment and hope you will join us in these efforts.

Atomic Dog is dedicated to faithfully serving the needs of faculty and students—providing a learning tool that helps make the connection. [We know that after you try our texts Atomic Dog, like a great dog, will become your faithful companion.]

Part 1

An Introduction to Marketing in the 21st Century

In Part 1, we begin our study of marketing and discuss concepts that form the basis for the rest of the text.

1 Marketing Today

To begin our journey, we look at marketing's dynamic nature, broadly define "marketing," and trace the evolution of marketing. Special attention is paid to the marketing concept, a marketing philosophy, customer service, and customer satisfaction and relationship marketing. We also examine the importance of marketing, as well as marketing functions and performers.

2 The Environment in Which Marketing Operates

This chapter covers the complex environment within which marketing functions, with an emphasis on both the factors that can be controlled and those that cannot be controlled by an organization and its marketers. We show that without adequate environmental analysis, a firm may function haphazardly or be shortsighted.

3 Developing and Enacting Strategic Marketing Plans

Here, we first differentiate between strategic business plans and strategic marketing plans, and present the total quality approach to planning. Next, we examine different kinds of strategic plans and the relationships between marketing and other functional areas. We then present the steps in the strategic planning process. A sample outline for a strategic marketing plan is presented and the actual strategic marketing plan of a small firm is highlighted.

4 Information for Marketing Decisions

In this chapter, we discuss why marketing decisions should be based on sound information. We describe the role and importance of the marketing information system, which coordinates marketing research, continuous monitoring, and data storage and provides the basis for decision making. We also cover the steps in the marketing research process, and show that marketing research may involve surveys, observation, experiments, and/or simulation.

After reading Part 1, you should understand elements 1–5 of the strategic marketing plan outlined in Table 3-2 (page 76).

Chapter 1

Marketing Today

The Walt Disney Company (**http://www.disney.com**) is a huge media conglomerate that owns the ABC television network and more than 70 radio stations. Its Walt Disney Studios produces films under various brands (including Walt Disney Pictures, Hollywood Pictures, and Miramax). And Disney's Walt Disney World and Disneyland are among the most popular family resort destinations in North America.

One of Disney's hidden jewels is Disney University, a training facility with 20 instructors who teach Disney's obsession for customer service to other firms. As a Disney spokesperson says, generating a passion for customer service requires "creating the ultimate guest experience," one that reaches consumers on an emotional level. Although Disney University does not release data on its profitability or the number of attendees, a typical program costs $2,400 per person for a two-and-a-half day program (not including hotel-related expenses or theme park admission fees).

Among the strategies taught at Disney University are the following:

- Customer satisfaction is based on well-trained and dedicated "cast members," as the firm refers to its employees. "You can build, create, and design the most wonderful place in the world, but it takes people to make it work," states a Disney University programming director.
- Disney is a great believer in the cross-utilization of employees and managers. In peak periods, a high-level executive may sell popcorn or even stock shelves. This facilitates a corporate-wide message among all Disney employees as to the importance of their jobs.
- Disney invests heavily in training. Sweepers are trained in body language so they can offer help before being asked. They also receive training in recognizing signs of child abuse.
- All of Disney's staff members, not just those playing Snow White or Mickey Mouse, are taught to think of themselves as characters playing to an audience: If staff members smile, so will customers.
- "Every guest receives the V.I.P. treatment. We roll out the red carpet for the Jones family from Joliet just as we would (with a few embellishments) for the Eisenhowers from Palm Springs."[1]

In this chapter, we will learn more about the importance of service in generating customer loyalty. We will also look at the roles of marketing, see how marketing has evolved, and look at its scope.

Chapter Objectives

1. To illustrate the exciting, dynamic, and influential nature of marketing
2. To define marketing and trace its evolution—with emphasis on the marketing concept, a marketing philosophy, customer service, and customer satisfaction and relationship marketing
3. To show the importance of marketing as a field of study
4. To describe the basic functions of marketing and those who perform these functions

1-1 OVERVIEW

Marketing is a fast-paced, contemporary, seldom-boring business discipline. We engage in marketing activities or are affected by them on a daily basis, both in our

---

[1] Various company and other sources.

business-related roles and as consumers. Okay, but what exactly does "marketing" mean? Well, it is not just advertising or selling goods and services, although these are aspects of marketing. And it is not just what we do as supermarket shoppers every week, although this, too, is part of marketing.

"Marketing"—as formally defined in Section 1-2,—is involved with anticipating, managing, and satisfying demand via the exchange process. As such, marketing encompasses all facets of buyer/seller relationships. Specific marketing activities (all discussed later in this chapter) include environmental analysis and marketing research, broadening an organization's scope, consumer analysis, product planning, distribution planning, promotion planning, price planning, and marketing management.

In a less abstract manner, here are two examples of real-world marketing—one from a business perspective and one from a consumer perspective:

Business perspective: Donna Noville, a 2001 BBA with a finance major, is an agent for a large insurance broker. The firm specializes in insurance for businesses of all sizes and types. Noville is now ready to open her own firm, but must make a number of decisions: Who should her clients be? What kinds of insurance should she offer? Where should she open her office? How will she attract her clients? What fee schedule should she set? Is it ethical to try to attract clients she worked with at her old firm? *Each of these questions entails a business-related marketing decision.*

Let's look at some of Donna Noville's marketing options:

- *Clients*—Noville could target small or medium businesses (consistent with her work experience) and/or individuals (for personal insurance needs).
- *Kinds of insurance*—Noville could be a full-service insurance broker for her clients and offer a wide array of insurance options, including property, casualty, liability, fire, health, and so on; she could offer selected kinds of insurance; or she could specialize in particular insurance, such as property.
- *Office location*—Noville could open an office in a professional building, a small shopping center, or her home. She could also do client visits, thus making the choice of office location less important.
- *Attracting clients*—Noville must determine the best way to reach her potential clients, such as running ads in local newspapers, sending out direct mail pieces to prospective clients, making appearances at civic events (such as a community forum on elder care insurance), and so on.
- *Fee schedule*—Noville must rely on her own experience with her previous firm and look at what competitors are doing. Then, she could price similar to others or lower/higher than them (depending on her desired image and a realistic reading of the marketplace).
- *Ethics*—Noville must weigh the personal dilemma of "stealing" clients from her old firm against the difficulty of starting a business from scratch without any client base.

Consumer perspective: At the same time that Donna Noville is making decisions about her new insurance firm, James Nash is reappraising his status as an insurance client. He owns a restaurant and has been a client of a mid-sized insurance broker for 10 years. That firm has been responsible for James Nash's business and personal insurance. Yet, he is now unhappy. He feels the broker takes him for granted. But before switching insurance firms, these questions must be answered: What kind of firm should he select? What insurance services should he seek? Where should the new broker be located? How will he learn more about possible firms? What fees should he be willing to pay? Is it ethical to show prospective firms the insurance policies developed by his present broker? *Each of these questions addresses a consumer-related marketing decision.*

Let's look at some of James Nash's marketing options:

- *Kind of firm*—Nash could select a small, medium, or large insurance broker. Given his current dissatisfaction, he might want to avoid medium and large firms.
- *Insurance services*—Nash could continue having one broker for all of his business and personal insurance needs; or he could use a different broker for his business and

> Marketing is a dynamic field, encompassing many activities.

Marketing and the Web

Craigslist: Building a Proper User-Driven Community

In 1995, Craig Newmark, a computer security architect at a brokerage firm, began using the Internet to tell readers about interesting events in San Francisco. Responding to his viewers' suggestions, Newmark started including other services such as job listings. Soon, the listings were changed from an E-mail to a Web site format that could automatically add E-mail postings to the craigslist (http://www.craigslist.org) site. Newmark began to devote himself full-time to craigslist as of early 1999.

Each month, craigslist is used by 10 million people, lists more than 5 million classified ads, and receives over 2.5 billion page views. According to a recent report by an Internet marketing research firm, craigslist is the most effective job site in the San Fran-

cisco area. There are now 175 craigslist sites across all 50 states and about 35 countries. The parts of craigslist sites with the most page views (in order) are jobs, housing, items for sale, personals, and forums.

In addition to craigslist being free in most markets, the Web site does not accept banner advertising. It only charges for employer job listings in Los Angeles, New York City, and San Francisco and may soon charge for New York City apartment listings. When Craig Newmark was asked about not charging for most listings, his response was: "How much money do you need to make?"

Source: Based on material in April Y. Pennington, "Craigslist: Middleman," *Entrepreneur* (May 2005), p. 160; and "About Craigslist," http://www.craigslist.org (March 19, 2006).

personal accounts. He must also consider what medical insurance policy best suits his future needs, as well as those of his family.

- *Office location*—Nash could look for an insurance broker that makes on-site visits (as his present firm does) or seek a firm that has an office near to his restaurant or residence.
- *Learning about firms*—Nash could ask prospective firms for references, check out credentials and certifications, interview candidates, and/or require firms to perform a sample task.
- *Fee schedule*—Nash knows he must get "fair" quotes, not "low ball" ones. He recognizes that you get what you pay for; and he wants better service.
- *Ethics*—Nash believes he, as the client, has the right to show any current insurance policies to prospective firms.

> We are all involved with or affected by marketing.

A marketing match? For "marketing" to operate properly, buyers and sellers need to find and satisfy each other (conduct exchanges). Do you think that Donna Noville and James Nash would make a good marketing match? We do—but only if their strategy (Noville) and expectations (Nash) are in sync.

As these examples show, goods and service providers ("sellers") make marketing-related decisions such as choosing who their customers are, what goods and services to offer, where to sell these goods and services, the features to stress in ads, and the prices to charge. They also determine how to be ethical and socially responsible, and whether to sell products globally in addition to domestically. Marketing-related activities are not limited to large corporations or people called "marketers." They are taken on by all types of companies and people.

As consumers ("buyers"), the marketing practices of goods and service providers affect many of our choices, as well as those made by our parents, spouses, other family members, and friends and associates. For virtually every good and service we purchase, the marketing process affects whom we patronize, the assortment of models and styles offered in the marketplace, where we shop, the availability of knowledgeable sales personnel, the prices we pay, and other factors. Marketing practices are in play when we are born (which doctor our parents select, the style of furniture they buy), while we grow (our parents' purchase of a domestic or foreign car or sports utility vehicle, our choice of a college), while we conduct our everyday lives (the use of a particular brand of toothpaste, the purchase of status-related items), and when we retire (our consideration of travel options, a change in living accommodations).

An in-depth study of marketing requires an understanding of its definition, evolution (including the marketing concept, a marketing philosophy, and customer service), importance and scope, and functions. These principles are discussed throughout Chapter 1.

1-2   MARKETING DEFINED

In 2004, the American Marketing Association introduced a 21st-century definition of marketing, calling it "an organizational function and a set of processes for creating, communicating, and delivering value to customers and for managing customer relationships in ways that benefit the organization and its stakeholders."[2]

For purposes of clarity, this shorter, more direct definition of marketing forms the basis of our text:

> *Marketing* is the anticipation, management, and satisfaction of demand through the exchange process.

> **Marketing** includes anticipating demand, managing demand, and satisfying demand.

It involves goods, services, organizations, people, places, and ideas.

Anticipation of demand requires a firm to do consumer research on a regular basis so it can develop and introduce offerings desired by consumers. *Management of demand* includes stimulation, facilitation, and regulation tasks. Stimulation motivates consumers to want a firm's offerings due to attractive product designs, distinctive promotion, fair prices, and other strategies. Facilitation is the process whereby the firm makes it easy to buy its offering by having convenient locations, accepting credit cards, using informed salespeople, and enacting other strategies. Regulation is needed when peak demand periods exist rather than balanced demand throughout the year or when demand exceeds supply. Then, the goal is to spread demand throughout the year or to demarket a good or service (reduce overall demand). *Satisfaction of demand* involves product availability, actual performance upon purchase, safety perceptions, after-sale service, and other factors. For consumers to be satisfied, goods, services, organizations, people, places, and ideas must fulfill their expectations. See Figure 1-1.

Marketing can be aimed at consumers or at publics. **Consumer demand** refers to the attributes and needs of final consumers, industrial consumers, wholesalers and retailers, government institutions, international markets, and nonprofit institutions. A firm may appeal to one or a combination of these. **Publics' demand** refers to the attributes and needs of employees, unions, stockholders, the general public, government agencies, consumer groups, and other internal and external forces that affect company operations.

> **Demand** is affected by both **consumers** and **publics**.

The marketing process is not concluded until consumers and publics *exchange* their money, their promise to pay, or their support for the offering of a firm, institution, person, place, or idea. Exchanges must be done in a socially responsible way, with both the buyer and the seller being ethical and honest—and considering the impact on society and the environment.

> **Exchange** completes the process.

A proper marketing definition should not be confined to economic goods and services. It should cover organizations (Big Brothers and Big Sisters), people (politicians), places (Hawaii), and ideas (the value of seat belts). See Figures 1-2 and 1-3. A consumer orientation must be central to any definition. And from a societal perspective, a firm should ask if a good or service *should* be sold, in addition to whether it can be sold.

---

[2] "Marketing Redefined," *Marketing News* (September 15, 2004), p. 1.

Figure 1-1

At Steward Leonard's, the Customer Is Always Right

Source: Reprinted by permission of Susan Berry, Retail Image Consulting, Inc.

Figure 1-2

The Societal Perspective of Marketing

Marketing is not only conduct by profit-driven firms but by nonprofit entities, such as the Make-a-Wish Foundation (**http://www.wish.org**).

Source: Reprinted by permission.

greater FORT LAUDERDALE
800-22-SUNNY

Get a sunny state of mind in Greater Fort Lauderdale.
Call 800-22-SUNNY or visit www.sunny.org to get your
journey started.

Figure 1-3

Marketing Ft. Lauderdale, Florida, as a Tourist Attraction

Source: Reprinted by permission.

1-3 THE EVOLUTION OF MARKETING

Marketing's evolution in an industry, country, or region of the world often entails a sequence of stages: barter era→production era→sales era→marketing department era→marketing company era. In some industries, nations, and regions, marketing practices have evolved through each stage and involve a good consumer orientation and high efficiency; in others, marketing practices are still in infancy.

Marketing can be traced to the **barter era**.

In the **production era**, output increases to meet demand.

In the **sales era**, firms sell products without first determining consumer desires.

The **marketing department era** occurs when research is used to determine consumer needs.

The **marketing company era** integrates consumer research and analysis into all efforts.

The **marketing concept** is consumer-oriented, market-driven, value-driven, integrated, and goal-oriented.

Marketing's origins can be traced to people's earliest use of the exchange process: the **barter era**. With barter, people trade one resource for another—such as food for animal pelts. To accommodate exchanges, trading posts, traveling salespeople, general stores, and cities evolved along with a standardized monetary system. In the least developed nations of the world, barter is still widely practiced.

The modern system of marketing begins with the industrialization of an industry, country, or region. For the world's most developed nations, this occurred with the Industrial Revolution of the late 1800s. For developing nations, efforts to industrialize are now under way. Why is industrialization so important? Without it, exchanges are limited because people do not have surplus items to trade. With the onset of mass production, better transportation, and more efficient technology, products can be made in greater volume and sold at lower prices. Improved mobility, densely populated cities, and specialization also let more people share in the exchange process: They can turn from self-sufficiency (such as making their own clothes) to purchases (such as buying clothes). In the initial stages of industrialization, output is limited and marketing is devoted to products' physical distribution. Because demand is high and competition is low, firms typically do not have to conduct consumer research, modify products, or otherwise adapt to consumer needs. The goal is to lift production to meet demand. This is the **production era** of marketing.

At the next stage, companies expand production capabilities to keep up with consumer demand. Many firms hire a sales force and some use advertising to sell their inventory. Yet, because competition is still rather low, when firms develop new products, consumer tastes or needs receive little consideration. The role of the sales force and advertising is to make consumer desires fit the features of the products offered. Thus, a shoe manufacturer might make brown wingtip shoes and use ads and personal selling to persuade consumers to buy them. That firm would rarely determine consumer tastes before making shoes or adjust output to those tastes. This is the **sales era** of marketing. It still exists where competition is limited, such as in nations recently converting to free-market economies.

Supply begins to exceed demand as competition grows. Firms cannot prosper without marketing input. They create marketing departments to conduct consumer research and advise management on how to better design, distribute, promote, and price products. Unless firms react to consumer needs, competitors might better satisfy demand and leave the firms with surplus inventory and falling sales. Although marketing departments share in decisions, they may be in a subordinate position to production, engineering, and sales departments. This is the **marketing department era**. It still exists where marketing has been embraced, but not as the driving force in an industry or company.

Over the last several decades, firms in a growing number of industries, nations, and regions have recognized marketing's central role; marketing departments at those firms are now the equal of others. The firms make virtually all key decisions after thorough consumer analysis: Because competition is intense and sophisticated, consumers must be aggressively drawn and kept loyal to a firm's brands. Company efforts are well integrated and regularly reviewed. This is the **marketing company era**. Figure 1-4 indicates the key aspects of each era in marketing's evolution.

The marketing concept, a marketing philosophy, customer service, and customer satisfaction and relationship marketing are the linchpins of the marketing company era. Each topic is examined in the following subsections.

1-3a   The Marketing Concept

As Figure 1-5 shows, the **marketing concept** is a consumer-oriented, market-driven, value-based, integrated, goal-oriented philosophy for a firm, institution, or person.[3] Here is an example of it in action:

[3] For an analysis of the marketing concept and its applications, see Frederick E. Webster, Jr., "Defining the New Marketing Concept," *Marketing Management*, Vol. 2 (Number 2, 1994), pp. 23–31; Dave Webb, Cynthia Webster, and Areti Krepapa, "An Exploration of the Meanings and Outcomes of a Customer-Defined Market Orientation," *Journal of Business Research*, Vol. 48 (May 2000), pp. 101–112; Geraldine Fennell and Greg M. Allenby, "Specifying Your Market's Boundaries," *Marketing Research* (Summer 2003), pp. 32–37; Alan R. Andreasen, Ronald C. Goodstein, and Joan W. Wilson, "Transferring 'Marketing Knowledge' to the Nonprofit Sector," *California Management Review*, Vol. 47 (Summer 2005), pp. 46–67; and Alan R. Andreasen, "Marketing Scholarship, Intellectual Leadership, and the Zeitgeist," *Journal of Public Policy & Marketing*, Vol. 24 (Spring 2005), pp. 133–136.

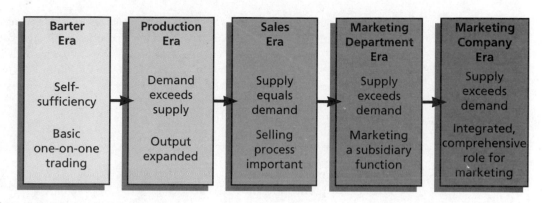

Figure 1-4

How Marketing Evolves

Offering a $5,000 warranty on a $50 product sounds insane, especially when you know plenty of customers will take you up on it. But for Matthew Smith, whose shoe company has honored that warranty for nearly a decade, that gutsy promise was the smartest move he ever made. Shoes For Crews (**http://www.shoesforcrews.com**), which is based in West Palm Beach, Fla., and has 160 employees, makes work shoes that are guaranteed not to slip. It was a blip in the industry before offering its gonzo warranty, which covers medical expenses and workers' comp costs. Last year, the company took in revenue of more than $100 million. Offering refunds to unhappy customers is as old as selling itself. But the supercharged guarantee offered by Smith is something new. Advertising insiders call it "risk-reversal marketing." The idea is to think about what a potential customer's biggest fear is about doing business with you, and assume some or all of that risk yourself. "It's a powerful way to set yourself apart," says David Frey, a Houston marketing consultant.[4]

The marketing concept's five elements are crucial to the long-term success of a good, service, organization, person, place, or idea: A *consumer orientation* means examining consumer needs, not production capability, and devising a plan to satisfy them. A *market-driven approach* means being aware of the structure of the marketplace, especially the attributes and strategies of competing firms. A *value-based philosophy* means offering goods and services that consumers perceive to have superior value relative to their costs and the offerings of competitors. With an *integrated marketing focus*, all the activities relating to goods and services are coordinated, including finance, production, engineering, inventory control, research and development, and marketing. A *goal-oriented firm* employs marketing to achieve both short- and long-term goals— which may be profit, funding to find a cure for a disease, increased tourism, election

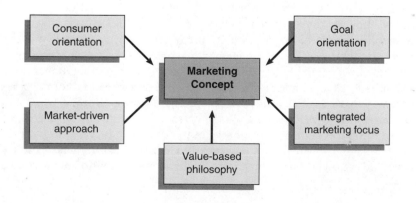

Figure 1-5

The Marketing Concept

[4] Dee Gill, "... Or Your Money Back," *Inc.* (September 2005), p. 46.

of a political candidate, a better company image, and so on. Marketing helps attain goals by orienting a firm toward pleasing consumers and offering desired goods, services, or ideas.

Following are some of the many things that managers can do to adhere to the spirit of the marketing concept:

- Create a customer focus throughout the firm.
- Listen to customers.
- Define and cultivate distinctive competencies.
- Define marketing as market intelligence.
- Target customers precisely.
- Manage for profitability, not sales volume.
- Make customer value the guiding star.
- Let the customer define quality.
- Measure and manage customer expectations.
- Build customer relationships and loyalty.
- Define the business as a service business.
- Commit to continuous improvement and innovation.
- Manage the company culture along with strategy and structure.
- Grow with partners and alliances.
- Destroy marketing bureaucracy.[5]

Through the marketing concept, a firm analyzes, maximizes, and satisfies consumer demand. Yet, it is only a guide to planning. A firm must also consider its strengths and weaknesses in production, engineering, and finance. Marketing plans need to balance goals, customer needs, and resource capabilities. The impact of competition, government regulations, and other external forces must also be evaluated. These factors are discussed in Chapters 2 and 3.

1-3b Selling Versus Marketing Philosophies

Figure 1-5 highlights the differences in selling and marketing philosophies. The benefits of a marketing, rather than a sales, orientation are many. Marketing stresses consumer analysis and satisfaction, directs the firm's resources to making goods and services consumers want, and adapts to changes in consumer traits and needs. Under a marketing philosophy, selling is used to communicate with and understand consumers; consumer dissatisfaction leads to changes in policy, not a stronger or different sales pitch. Marketing looks for real differences in consumer tastes and devises offerings to satisfy them. Marketing is geared to the long run, and marketing goals reflect overall company goals. Finally, marketing views customer needs broadly (such as heating), not narrowly (such as fuel oil).

As a case in point, consider Wahl Clipper Corporation (**http://www.wahlclipper.com**), which makes electric shavers, hair trimmers, and other personal care products. The company was founded in 1919 and now operates around the world. How has it been able to prosper for so long? According to former company president Jack Wahl, "I realized the difference between sales and marketing. That's a big thing for a small company. Sales means simply presenting the product and collecting money. Marketing means stepping back and looking for the needs of the customer, and for the best way to get through to that user." The firm is now led by Jack's son Gregory, who knows that "To maintain our leadership position in the personal care categories we serve, we must have vision. Vision to continually improve our existing products. Vision to bring new products to market which meet the wants and needs of consumers. Vision to stay innovative and ahead of our competitors, and vision to support our customers, the

> With a marketing orientation, selling helps to communicate with and understand consumers.

---

[5] Frederick E. Webster, Jr., "Executing the New Marketing Concept," *Marketing Management*, Vol. 3 (Number 1, 1994), pp. 9–16.

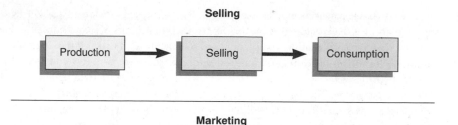

Selling

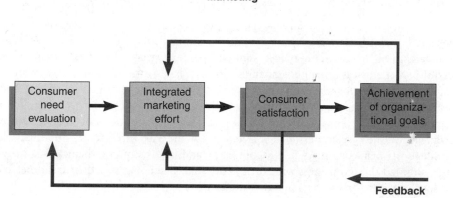

Marketing

Figure 1-6

The Focus of Selling and Marketing Philosophies

retailers, with sales and marketing programs that make it easy, fun, and profitable for them to sell more Wahl products. Leading with vision means constantly being alert to new opportunities. By sharing the vision, we can make tomorrow absolutely extraordinary."[6]

1-3c Customer Service

Customer service involves the identifiable, but rather intangible, activities undertaken by a seller in conjunction with the basic goods and/or services it offers.[7] In today's highly competitive marketplace, the level of customer service a firm provides can greatly affect its ability to attract and retain customers. Nonetheless, firms often have to make customer service trade-offs. For instance, supermarkets must weigh the potential loss of business if waiting lines are too long versus the cost of hiring more cashiers.

Unless a consumer is happy with *both* the basic good (such as a new PC) or service (such as the installation of computer software) offered by a seller *and* the quality of customer service (such as polite, expert sales personnel and on-time appointments), he or she is unlikely to patronize the seller—certainly not in the long run. Imagine your reaction to this situation:

> For our new shower, we choose an acrylic enclosure with a glass door. But getting the shower from Tubs to working in my second-floor bathroom proves to be a most frustrating chore. We buy a floor model, hoping to save a few dollars. Big mistake. The salesperson checks and insists the massive shower will fit through the 24-inch bathroom door. Tubs would deliver the unit in three parts and reconstruct it on site, he promises. A week before delivery day, Tubs workers rip the glass door from its hinges while moving the unit in the store. Against my better judgment, I allow them to fix the damage, instead of buying a new one. The delivery guys show up with the unit already assembled. And no one told them it had to be delivered to the bathroom. They only do curbside drop-off. Only when I threaten to return the shower do they

Customer service tends to be intangible, but quite meaningful, to many consumers.

[6] Jerry Flint, "Father Says, 'Jump,'" *Forbes* (August 14, 1995), p. 144; and "About Wahl," http://www.wahl.com/aboutus.html (February 27, 2006).

[7] "Dictionary of Marketing Terms," http://www.marketingpower.com/mg-dictionary.php (May 3, 2006).

relent. E-mail to management goes unanswered. The salesperson is slow to act. Finally, they agree to do what they promised in the first place. After three hours of scratched walls, smashed fingers, groaning and swearing, and pushing and pulling, the unit makes it through the door—but only after we rip the casings off the entry and say a prayer or two. It would be weeks later before the handset and shower head arrive. The halogen light unit showed up after months of telephone badgering. The wooden seat replacement for the damaged original sat under the salesperson's desk for a couple of weeks before someone found it. As I write, one of the body sprays isn't working. And the promised owner's manual hasn't arrived yet."[8]

According to consumer surveys, perceptions about the overall level of customer service at U.S. businesses is declining. Why? As one marketing expert says, "Customers don't want to be 'managed'; they just want companies to make their lives easier and less stressful." Nonetheless, many companies do not have a good handle on customer satisfaction. As another marketing expert puts it, "Given the potential impact of losing a customer, you would think that having a well-engineered service recovery system would be standard operating procedure. Yet it is not. Most organizations do not know what percentage of their customers had a problem in the last three to six months; what percentage of their customers had a complaint and didn't contact them about it; why people stopped doing business with them; and what percentages of their customer base were loyal, restless, or on the verge of switching."[9]

Despite the preceding comments, lots of firms do positively address the issue of customer service: "The new customer service is a process of turning power over to the customer—allowing the customer to tell us what he or she is interested in and not interested in, what kind of information he or she wants, what level of service is desired, and how he or she wants us to communicate (where, when, and how often)." Such companies as Ritz-Carlton, Kroger, Federal Express, and Blockbuster are *empowering employees*, whereby workers are given broad leeway to satisfy customer requests. With empowerment, employees are encouraged and rewarded for showing initiative and imagination. They can "break the rules" if, in their judgment, customer requests should be honored. For example, all Ritz-Carlton hotel (**http://www.ritz-carlton.com**) employees (including housekeepers) are trained to listen for customer complaints and to be familiar with possible solutions: "We are ladies and gentlemen serving ladies and gentlemen." At Kroger supermarkets (**http://www.kroger.com**), "We will satisfy consumer needs better than the best of our competitors. Operating procedures will reflect our belief that the organizational levels closest to the consumer are best positioned to respond to changing consumer needs." Similarly, Federal Express (**http://www.fedex.com**) drivers can help customers pack breakable items; and Blockbuster (**http://www.blockbuster. com**) actively promotes employee empowerment.[10]

SAS (**http://www.scandinavian.net**), the Scandinavian airline, has ATM-like video stations outside many arrival gates for passengers to communicate feedback about good and bad customer service experiences. Caterpillar (**http://www.caterpillar.com**), the maker of agricultural and heavy-construction equipment, monitors customer equipment remotely, by sending an electronic "warning" signal to its own service technicians, and indicating the parts and tools needed to make repairs. Westfield America (**http://www.westfield.com**), the shopping center operator, has its concierges walk through the centers and take a more assertive customer service role: "A shopper looking for a particular retailer will not just be given directions; a concierge will accompany the

> To offer better customer service, some firms are **empowering employees.**

customer service helps create stats to be able to improve →

---

[8] Royson James, "One Cold Blast of Reality," *Toronto Star Online* (May 5, 2005).

[9] Frederick Newell, "Who's the Boss?" **http://www.destinationcrm.com/articles/default.asp?ArticleID=3107** (May 2003); and Bob Stiefbold, "Dissatisfied Customers Require Recovery Plans," *Marketing News* (October 27, 2003), p. 4. See also Roger Bougie, Rik Pieters, and Marcel Zeelenberg, "Angry Customers Don't Come Back, They Get Back: The Experience and Behavioral Implications of Anger and Dissatisfaction in Services," *Journal of the Academy of Marketing Science*, Vol. 31 (Fall 2003), pp. 377–393.

[10] Newell, "Who's the Boss?" **http://www.destinationcrm.com/articles/default.asp?ArticleID=3107**; Marilyn Adams, "When Something Is Wrong, Those Who Care Make It Right," *USA Today* (September 12, 2000), p. E11; and company Web sites. See also "2005 Customer Champions," *1to1 Magazine* (April 2005), pp. 17–23.

shopper to the store and introduce him or her to the manager."[11] PARKnSHOP (**http://www.parknshop.com**), Hong Kong's leading supermarket chain, has a strong customer service approach—including a delivery policy that says: "With PARKnSHOP, you carry what's fresh. We deliver the rest. Free."

1-3d Customer Satisfaction and Relationship Marketing

Customer satisfaction is a crucial element in successful marketing. It is the degree to which there is a match between a customer's expectations of a good or service and the actual performance of that good or service, including customer service.[12] As two experts note: "Successful firms know that the customer is the ultimate judge of the quality of a shopping experience. Consumers enjoy more choice than before—in stores, brands, and channels—and have access to an ever-increasing amount of information upon which to base their buying decisions. Capturing the purchasing power of these sophisticated consumers is a difficult and constant challenge."[13] Figure 1-7 shows 11 representative factors that affect overall customer satisfaction.

This is how daunting it can be to keep customers satisfied:

> Customer satisfaction is doing what your customer expects—in a sense, being adequate. Most organizations provide adequate service. They do precisely what they say they are going to do— no less and, usually, no more. Unfortunately, people don't talk about adequate service. Instead, they tell anyone who will listen about really bad service or really delightful service.

> Firms cannot usually prosper without a high level of **customer satisfaction**.

Figure 1-7

Factors That Affect Customer Satisfaction

Source: Steven Hokanson, "The Deeper You Analyze, the More You Satisfy Customers," *Marketing News* (January 2, 1995), p. 16. Reprinted by permission of the American Marketing Association.

[11] Stephen W. Brown, "Practicing Best-in-Class Service Recovery," *Marketing Management* (Summer 2000), pp. 8–9; and Debra Hazel, "May I Help You?" *Shopping Centers Today* (November 2003), pp. 25–26.

[12] "Dictionary of Marketing Terms," **http://www.marketingpower.com/mg-dictionary.php** (May 3, 2006). See also Chatura Ranaweera and Jaideep Prabhu, "On the Relative Importance of Customer Satisfaction and Trust as Determinants of Customer Retention and Positive Word of Mouth," *Journal of Targeting, Measurement & Analysis for Marketing*, Vol. 12 (September 2003), pp. 82–90; Andy Taylor, "Rediscovering Customer Satisfaction," *Business Horizons*, Vol. 46 (September-October 2003), pp. 3–14; and Timothy L. Keiningham, Tiffany Perkins-Munn, and Heather Evans, "The Impact of Customer Satisfaction on Share-of-Wallet in a Business-to-Business Environment," *Journal of Service Research*, Vol. 6 (August 2003), pp. 37–50.

[13] Theresa Williams and Mark J. Larson, "Preface," *Creating the Ideal Shopping Experience* (Bloomington, Indiana: Indiana University, 2000), p. 1.

Ethical Issues in Marketing

The Ethics of Monitoring Customer Service Calls

Although just 2 percent of customer service calls are monitored by outside auditing firms, call-monitoring firms have the capability to tap their clients' phone lines and capture what is on each operator's screen during his or her conversation with a customer. Most such calls are monitored without the need to enter a client's office.

Those who favor using "professional eavesdroppers" say it's a good way to determine how well a company's service personnel interact with their customers. According to one call-monitoring firm, "We have no agenda other than making sure they're providing quality service." Many clients use the data from call-monitoring firms—such as how often a service representative repeats a customer's name and whether a service representative takes the time to verify that he or she is talking to the customer (as

opposed to a spouse)—to reward excellent callers. Call-monitoring firms also provide training sessions to service people based on their specific call-monitoring experiences with the particular firm.

Those who are concerned about call-monitoring feel that consumers need to know that their conversations are being taped and that their identities may be shared with others. Some clients are even concerned that having too much information about their customers may be harmful to good long-term relationships. They wonder whether customers should be able to opt out of having their conversations monitored and whether customers' knowledge that conversations are being monitored inhibits the conversations.

Source: Based on material in Jennifer Gill, "This Call May Be Monitored," *Inc.* (June 2005): p. 29-30.

Customer delight goes beyond satisfaction. It ensures that each contact with your customers reinforces their belief that your organization is truly special, the best at what you do. It involves an element of the unexpected. Pleasant surprises are found in the small details of a customer interaction.[14]

If a customer becomes upset, several actions can be taken: (1) "If you have answered the phone on behalf of the company, you have accepted 100-percent responsibility. So get off the 'It's not my fault' syndrome." (2) "Saying you're sorry won't fix the problem, but it definitely does help to defuse it immediately." (3) "When someone is angry or frustrated with your company, the one thing he or she needs is someone to agree with him or her—or at least show understanding." (4) "Don't make a customer wait for good service. Get him or her whatever is needed immediately." (5) "Ask the customer what would make him or her happy." (6) "Service recovery is not just fixing the problem. It's making sure it won't happen again." (7) "After you feel the problem has been fixed, follow-up on it."[15]

> Through **relationship marketing,** companies try to increase long-term customer loyalty.

Companies with satisfied customers have a good opportunity to convert them into loyal customers, who purchase from those firms over an extended period. From a consumer-oriented perspective, when marketing activities are performed with the conscious intention of developing and managing long-term, trusting customer relations, *relationship marketing* is involved.[16] Why is this so important? "Several years ago, in *The Loyalty Effect*, Bain & Company documented the outstanding financial results you can achieve by cultivating customer loyalty: A 5 percent increase in customer retention increases profits by 25 to 95 percent. It costs so much to acquire customers that many of them are unprofitable in the early years. Only later, when the cost of serving loyal customers falls and the volume of their purchases rises, do relationships generate big returns."[17] See Figure 1-8.

---

[14] John Paul, "Are You Delighting Your Customers?" *Nonprofit World* (September-October 2000), pp. 34-35.

[15] Nancy Friedman, "Check Out These Seven Steps to a Service Recovery," *Tire Business* (June 6, 2005), p. 9.

[16] "Dictionary of Marketing Terms," http://www.marketingpower.com/mg-dictionary.php (May 3, 2006).

[17] Darrell K. Rigby, Frederick Reichheld, and Chris Dawson, "Winning Customer Loyalty Is the Key to a Winning CRM Strategy," *Ivey Business Journal*, Vol. 67 (July-August 2003), pp. 1-5.

Figure 1-8

Baskin-Robbins: Bringing a Relationship Marketing Philosophy to Ice Cream

Offering special pricing is one of the many tactics used by Baskin-Robbins (**http://www.baskinrobbins.com**) to generate repeat business and very loyal shoppers.

Source: Reprinted by permission.

Office Depot (**http://www.officedepot.com**), the giant chain retailer of office-supplies, and equipment, is one of many firms that has mastered relationship marketing, especially with its Web sites. For example,

Tech Depot (**http://www.techdepot.com**) is a direct marketer of computer and technology products. We have over 100,000 business, government, and education customers. Our account management team, combined with our robust online catalog, saves customers time and money. We offer qualified customers many advantages such as flexible credit terms, dedicated account managers, and Extranets. *Multibillion Dollar Buying Power*: As a subsidiary of Office Depot, we have direct relationships with leading manufacturers and distributors to ensure that our customers obtain the most competitive prices each and every day. *Broad Selection*: 100,000+ products, including PC hardware, software, networking, and supplies. *Total Purchasing Convenience*: Security and privacy are assured; bill-when-ship policy; powerful search engine. *Incomparable Service*: Personalized, one-on-one account management; dedicated customer care teams; free-sales technical support; no restocking fees.[18]

Saturn, one of the auto divisions of General Motors, is another leader in relationship marketing. It has won several awards in this area due to its hassle-free sales process, its customer-friendly Web site (**http://www.saturn.com**), and other factors: "It's no secret that most people dread shopping for a car, which is why Saturn retailers are continually finding ways to make buying and servicing your vehicle more pleasant. In addition to the

---

[18] "About Us," **http://www.techdepot.com/static/aboutus.asp?iid=211** (March 11, 2006).

now famous no-hassle, no-haggle sales policy, many Saturn retailers continue to improve the retail experience with additions like family-room-style waiting areas, computer terminals, and children's play areas."[19]

Sephora (**http://www.sephora.com**) is a retail concept intent on generating loyal customers. Founded in France, Sephora is one of the world's leading chains of perfume and cosmetics stores. In addition to France, it has stores in Canada, China, the Czech Republic, Greece, Italy, Luxembourg, Monaco, Poland, Portugal, Romania, Russia, and Spain; and it is growing rapidly. Sephora came to the United States in mid-1998 with its New York and Miami stores. There are now about 100 U.S. stores nationwide. The key to Sephora's success is its unique selling approach: "When you enter Sephora, you meet the creative spirit driving the concept, a spirit that now offers you an entirely new way of shopping for beauty. *Freedom* comes to you in a hands-on, self-service shopping environment. Feel free to touch, smell, and experience each and every product. You are also free to choose the level of assistance you desire, from individual experience and reflection, to detailed expert advice. *Beauty* comes to you through a splendid international array of unique and luxurious beauty products. *Pleasure* comes through an environment designed to stimulate the senses—a blend of expert advice, personal freedom, and special service displays brings you the latest beauty tips and treatment breakthroughs."[20]

Many Web sites exist that can help client firms improve their level of customer satisfaction and relationship marketing. Some of the available sites include: Business Research Lab (**http://www.busreslab.com/consult/custsat.htm**), CustomerSat.com (**http://www.customersat.com**), Customer Value, Inc. (**http://www.cval.com**), and Triversity (**http://www.triversity.com**).

1-4   THE IMPORTANCE OF MARKETING

This section discusses several reasons why the field of marketing should be studied. First, because marketing stimulates demand, a basic task for it is to generate consumer enthusiasm for goods and services. Worldwide, $60 trillion of goods and services are produced annually (expressed in purchasing-power-parity), with the United States accounting for 21 percent of that sum.[21]

> Marketing stimulates consumers, constitutes a large part of sales costs, employs many people, supports industries, affects all consumers, and plays a major role in our lives.

A large portion of each sales dollar goes to cover the costs related to such marketing activities as product development, packaging, distribution, advertising and personal selling, price marking, and administering consumer credit programs. Some estimates place the costs of marketing as high as 50 percent or more of sales in certain industries. Yet, it should not be assumed that the performance of some marketing tasks by consumers would automatically lead to lower prices. Could a small business really save money by having the owner fly to Detroit to buy a new truck directly from the maker rather than from a local dealer? Would a family be willing to buy clothing in bulk to reduce a retailer's transportation and storage costs?

Tens of millions of people work in marketing-related jobs in the United States alone. They include those employed in the retailing, wholesaling, transportation, warehousing, and communications industries and those involved with marketing jobs for manufacturing, service, agricultural, mining, and other industries. Projections indicate future employment in marketing will remain strong.

Marketing activities also involve entire industries, such as advertising and marketing research. Total annual worldwide advertising expenditures approximate $500 billion. Many agencies, such as Omnicom Group (**http://www.omnicomgroup.com**) and Interpublic Group

---

[19] "About Us," **http://www.saturn.com/saturn/aboutus** (March 14, 2006).

[20] "Sephora.com," **http://www.optimall.org/links/sephora.htm** (April 3, 2006).

[21] "The World Economic Outlook Data Base," **http://www.imf.org/external/pubs/ft/weo/2005/02/data/index.htm** (September 2005).

Global Marketing in Action

NBA Europe Live: Marketing U.S. Sports on the Global Stage

As part of a two-year agreement, four NBA (http://www.nba.com) teams are competing against top European basketballs clubs in October 2006 and 2007 and conducting their training camps as part of NBA Europe Live. The competition ends with a final event in a fifth European country featuring games with the NBA teams, the Euroleague (http://www.euroleague.net) Basketball champion, and the Euroleague Basketball runner-up.

According to the NBA commissioner, "NBA Europe Live exemplifies how sports leagues around the world can work together for the long-term growth of their sport. As the relevance of basketball continues to grow globally, the NBA and EA Sports [http://www.easports.com] share a vision to deliver basketball, entertainment, music, and technology to our fans around the world."

The NBA has 30 teams in the United States and Canada and is one of the largest suppliers of sports television and Internet programming in the world. Euroleague Basketball includes 24 clubs from 12 or more countries. Euroleague has expanded its television reach to now include Africa, the Middle East, North America, and South America.

As a forerunner to its current activities, the NBA visited Europe in 2003 to host the NBA Europe Games, which featured a pre-season game between NBA champion of the year San Antonio Spurs and the Memphis Grizzlies in Paris. The Memphis Grizzlies also played an exhibition game against Euroleague champion FC Barcelona in Barcelona, Spain.

Source: Based on material in "NBA and Euroleague Basketball Announce NBA Europe Live Presented by EA SPORTS," *Business Wire* (June 14, 2005).

(http://www.interpublic.com) of the United States, WPP Group (http://www.wpp.com) of Great Britain, Japan's Dentsu (http://www.dentsu.com), and France's Publicis Groupe (http://www.publicis.com/corporate/en), have worldwide billings of several billion dollars each. More than $20 billion worldwide is spent yearly on various types of commercial marketing research. Firms such as VNU (http://www.vnu.com) of the Netherlands, which owns A.C. Nielsen (http://www.acnielsen.com); IMS Health (http://www.imshealth.com) and Information Resources Inc. (http://www.infores.com) of the United States; Taylor Nelson Sofres (http://www.tnsofres.com) of Great Britain; and GfK Group (http://www.gfk.com) of Germany each generate yearly worldwide revenues of more than one-half billion dollars.

All people and organizations serve as consumers for various goods and services. By understanding the role of marketing, consumers can become better informed, more selective, and more efficient. Effective channels of communication with sellers can also be established and complaints resolved more easily and favorably. Consumer groups have a major impact on sellers.

Because resources are scarce, marketing programs and systems must function at their peak. Thus, by optimizing customer service, inventory movement, advertising expenditures, product assortments, and other areas of marketing, firms will better use resources. Some industries may even require demarketing (lowering the demand for goods and services). The latter often include energy consumption.

Marketing impacts strongly on people's beliefs and lifestyles. In fact, it has been criticized as fostering materialistic attitudes, fads, product obsolescence, a reliance on gadgets, status consciousness, and superficial product differences—and for wasting resources. Marketers reply that they merely address the desires of people and make the best goods and services they can at the prices people will pay.

Marketing has a role to play in our quality of life. For example, marketing personnel often encourage firms to make safer products, such as child-proof bottle caps. They create public service messages on energy conservation, AIDS prevention, driver safety, alcohol abuse, and other topics. They help new goods, ideas, and services (such as Apple's iPods [http://www.ipod.com], improved nutrition, and HBO [http://www.hbo.com]) to be recognized and accepted by people and organizations.

A knowledge of marketing is extremely valuable for those not directly involved in a marketing job. Marketing decisions must be made by:

- *Doctors*—What hours are most desirable to patients?
- *Lawyers*—How can new clients be attracted?
- *Management consultants*—Should fees be higher, lower, or the same as competitors' fees?
- *Financial analysts*—What investments should be recommended to clients?
- *Research and development personnel*—Is there demand for a potential "breakthrough" product?
- *Economists*—What impact will the economy have on how various industries market their offerings?
- *Statisticians*—How should firms react to predicted demographic shifts?
- *Teachers*—How can students become better consumers?
- *City planners*—How can businesses be persuaded to relocate to the city?
- *Nonprofit institutions*—How can donor contributions be increased?

Each profession and organization must address patient, client, consumer, student, taxpayer, or contributor needs. And more of them than ever before are performing marketing tasks such as research, advertising, and so on.

1-5   MARKETING FUNCTIONS AND PERFORMERS

There are eight basic *marketing functions*: environmental analysis and marketing research, broadening the scope of marketing, consumer analysis, product planning, distribution planning, promotion planning, price planning, and marketing management. They are shown in Figure 1-9, which also notes where they are discussed in the text.

Here are brief descriptions of the functions:

- *Environmental analysis and marketing research*—Monitoring and adapting to external factors that affect success or failure, such as the economy and competition, and collecting data to resolve specific marketing issues.
- *Broadening the scope of marketing*—Deciding on the emphasis on and approach to societal/ethical issues and global marketing, as well as the role of the Web in a marketing strategy.
- *Consumer analysis*—Examining and evaluating consumer characteristics, needs, and purchase processes, and selecting the group(s) of consumers at which to aim marketing efforts.
- *Product planning (including goods, services, organizations, people, places, and ideas)*—Developing and sustaining products, product assortments, product images, brands, packaging, and optional features; deleting faltering products.
- *Distribution planning*—Forming logistical relations with distribution intermediaries, physical distribution, inventory management, warehousing, transportation, the allocation of goods and services, wholesaling, and retailing.
- *Promotion planning*—Communicating with customers, the general public, and others through some form of advertising, public relations, personal selling, and/or sales promotion.
- *Price planning*—Determining price levels and ranges, pricing techniques, terms of purchase, price adjustments, and the use of price as an active or passive factor.
- *Marketing management*—Planning, implementing, and controlling the marketing program (strategy) and individual marketing functions, appraising the risks and benefits in decision making, and focusing on total quality.

Typically, a firm should first study its environment and gather relevant marketing information. The firm should determine how to act in a socially responsible and ethical manner, consider whether to be domestic and/or global, and decide on the proper use of

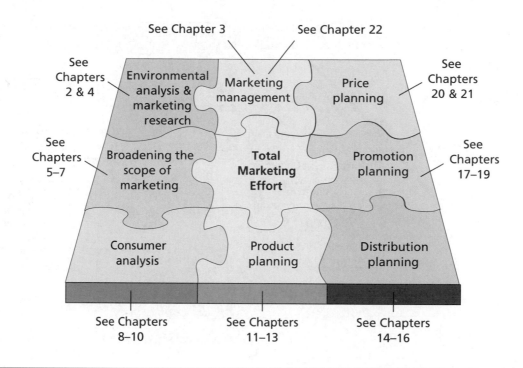

Figure 1-9

The Basic Functions of Marketing

the Web. At the same time, the firm should analyze potential customers to learn their needs and select the group(s) on which to focus. It should next plan product offerings, make distribution decisions, choose how to communicate with customers and others, and set proper prices. These four functions (in combination, known as the *marketing mix*) should be done in a coordinated manner, based on environmental, societal, and consumer analysis. Through marketing management, the firm's overall marketing program would be planned and carried out in an integrated manner, with fine-tuning as needed.

Although many marketing transactions require the performance of similar tasks, such as being ethical, analyzing consumers, and product, distribution, promotion, and price planning, they can be enacted in many ways (such as a manufacturer distributing via full-service retailers versus self-service ones, or a financial-services firm relying on telephone contacts by its sales force versus in-office visits to potential small-business clients by salespeople).

Marketing performers are the organizations or individuals that undertake one or more marketing functions. Included are manufacturers and service providers, wholesalers, retailers, marketing specialists, and organizational and final consumers. As Figure 1-10 shows, each performer has a distinct role. Although responsibility for marketing tasks can be shifted in various ways, basic marketing functions usually must be done by one performer or another. They often cannot be omitted.

Sometimes, one marketing performer decides to carry out all, or virtually all, marketing functions (such as Boeing analyzing the marketplace, acting ethically, operating domestically and globally, having a detailed Web site [**http://www.boeing.com**], seeking various types of customers, developing aerospace and related products, distributing products directly to customers, using its own sales force and placing ads in select media, and setting prices). Yet, for the following reasons, one performer often does not undertake all marketing functions:

- Many firms do not have the financial resources to sell products directly to consumers. They need intermediaries to share in the distribution process.

> Usually at least one **marketing performer** must undertake each basic marketing function.

Figure 1-10

Who Performs Marketing Functions

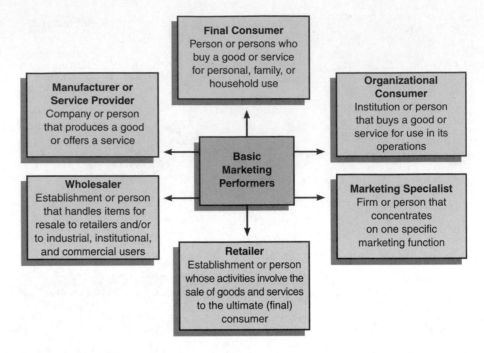

- Marketing directly to customers may require goods and services producers to offer complementary products or sell the complementary products of other firms so distribution is carried out efficiently.
- A performer may be unable or unwilling to complete certain functions and may seek a marketing specialist to fulfill them.
- Many performers are too small to do certain functions efficiently.
- For numerous goods and services, established distribution methods are in force and it is difficult to set up other methods (such as bypassing independent soda distributors to sell directly to retail stores).
- Some consumers may want to buy in quantity, visit self-service outlets, and pay cash to save money.

1-6 FORMAT OF THE TEXT

Marketing in the 21st Century has eight parts. The balance of Part 1 focuses on the marketing environment, developing marketing plans, and the information needed for marketing decisions. Part 2 covers the key topics related to the broadened scope of marketing: societal, ethical, and consumer issues; global marketing; and the Web. The discussion in Parts 1 and 2 sets the foundation for studying the specific aspects of marketing.

Part 3 deals with marketing's central orientation: understanding consumers. It looks at the demographics, social and psychological traits, and decision process of final consumers; organizational consumer attributes and decision making; and developing a target market and sales forecasting. Parts 4 to 7 discuss the marketing mix (product, distribution, promotion, and price planning) and the actions needed to enact a marketing program in depth. Part 8 considers the marketing management implications of the topics raised throughout *Marketing* and discusses how to integrate and analyze an overall marketing plan.

Numerous illustrations of actual marketing practices by a variety of organizations and individuals are woven into our discussions. And although such topics as marketing and society, global marketing, marketing and the Web, organizational consumers, and goods versus service marketing get separate chapter coverage to highlight certain points, applications in these areas are presented throughout the text.

Web Sites You Can Use

In every chapter of *Marketing in the 21st Century*, we present a variety of links to worthwhile Web sites related to that chapter.

An important tool for any Web "surfer" looking for information about a topic related to marketing is a search engine. This tool enables the user to generate a clickable list of links on virtually any subject imaginable, from advertising to zero-based budgeting. Dozens of free search engines are available on the Web. Because each one has a slightly different method of searching, you should rely on multiple search engines if you want to do comprehensive research on a subject. After experimenting with various search engines, many users settle on a few that they really like.

Here are some of the most popular and useful search engines. Visit them and see what they offer:

- 1st Headlines (http://www.1stheadlines.com)
- About.com (http://www.about.com)
- Alexa (http://www.alexa.com)
- All the Web (http://www.alltheweb.com)
- AltaVista (http://www.altavista.com)
- Ask (http://www.ask.com)
- Dogpile (http://www.dogpile.com)
- Excite (http://www.excite.com)
- ExpressFind (http://www.expressfind.com)
- Fagan Finder (http://www.faganfinder.com)
- Fazzle (http://www.fazzle.com)
- Findspot (http://www.findspot.com)
- Go.com (http://www.go.com)
- Google (http://www.google.com)

- HighBeam Research (http://www.highbeam.com/library/index.asp)
- HotBot (http://www.hotbot.com)
- IcySpicy (http://www.icyspicy.com)
- Inbox Robot (http://www.inboxrobot.com)
- Internet Archive (http://www.archive.org)
- iTools (http://www.itools.com)
- Iwon (http://www.iwon.com)
- Ixquick (http://www.ixquick.com)
- Looksmart (http://search.looksmart.com)
- Lycos (http://www.lycos.com)
- Lycos Multimedia (http://multimedia.lycos.com)
- Mamma (http://www.mamma.com)
- Metacrawler (http://www.metacrawler.com)
- MSN Search (http://search.msn.com)
- My Way (http://www.myway.com)
- NBCi (http://nbci.msnbc.com/nbci.asp)
- ProFusion (http://www.profusion.com)
- Scrub the Web (http://www.scrubtheweb.com)
- Search Bug (http://www.searchbug.com)
- Search.com (http://www.search.com)
- Vivisimo (http://www.vivisimo.com)
- Webcrawler (http://www.webcrawler.com)
- WiseNut (http://www.wisenut.com)
- WorldPages (http://www.worldpages.com)
- Yahoo! (http://www.yahoo.com)
- Zenith Optimedia Marketer's Portal (http://www.marketersportal.com)

Summary

In every chapter, the summary is linked to the objectives stated at the beginning of that chapter.

1. *To illustrate the exciting, dynamic, and influential nature of marketing* Marketing may be viewed from both business and consumer perspectives, and it influences us daily. As goods and service providers, we make such marketing-related decisions as choosing who customers are, what goods and services to offer, where to sell them, what to stress in promotion, what prices to charge, how to be ethical and responsible, and whether to operate globally. As consumers, the marketing process affects whom we patronize, choices in the marketplace, where we shop, the availability of sales personnel, the prices we pay, and other factors.

2. *To define marketing and trace its evolution—with emphasis on the marketing concept, a marketing philosophy, customer service, and customer satisfaction and relationship marketing* Marketing involves anticipating, managing, and satisfying demand via the exchange process. It includes goods, services, organizations, people, places, and ideas.

Marketing's evolution can be traced to the earliest use of barter in the exchange process (the barter era); but, it

has truly developed since the Industrial Revolution, as mass production and improved transportation have enabled more transactions to occur. For many firms, modern marketing has evolved via these eras: production, sales, marketing department, and marketing company. Yet, in developing nations, marketing is still in its early stages.

The marketing concept requires an organization or individual to be consumer-oriented, market-driven, and value-based; have an integrated effort; and be goal-oriented. A marketing philosophy means assessing and responding to consumer wants—to real differences in consumer tastes and to long-run opportunities and threats—and engaging in coordinated decision making.

For a company to do well, emphasis must be placed on customer service: the identifiable, rather intangible, acts performed by a seller in conjunction with the basic goods and/or services it offers. A number of firms now empower employees so as to improve the level of customer service. Customer satisfaction occurs when consumer expectations are met or exceeded. After customer satisfaction is established, firms then have opportunities to attract loyal customers by paying attention to relationship marketing.

3. *To show the importance of marketing as a field of study* Marketing is a crucial field because it stimulates demand; marketing costs can be high; a large number of people work in marketing positions; it involves entire industries, such as advertising and marketing research; all organizations and people are consumers in some situations; it is necessary to use scarce resources efficiently; marketing impacts on people's beliefs and lifestyles; and marketing influences the quality of our lives. Some marketing knowledge is valuable to all of us, regardless of occupation.

4. *To describe the basic functions of marketing and those who perform these functions* The key marketing functions are environmental analysis and marketing research; broadening the scope of marketing; consumer analysis; product, distribution, promotion, and price planning; and marketing management. Responsibility for doing tasks can be shifted and shared among manufacturers and service providers, wholesalers, retailers, marketing specialists, and consumers. Due to costs, assortment requirements, specialized abilities, company size, established distribution methods, and consumer interests, one party usually does not perform all functions.

Key Terms

marketing (p. 7)

consumer demand (p. 7)

publics' demand (p. 7)

exchange (p. 7)

barter era (p. 10)

production era (p. 10)

sales era (p. 10)

marketing department era (p. 10)

marketing company era (p. 10)

marketing concept (p. 10)

customer service (p. 13)

empowering employees (p. 14)

customer satisfaction (p. 15)

relationship marketing (p. 16)

marketing functions (p. 20)

marketing performers (p. 21)

Review Questions

1. Explain the
   a. anticipation of demand.
   b. management of demand.
   c. satisfaction of demand.
   d. exchange process.
2. Give an example of a good, service, organization, person, place, and idea that may be marketed.
3. Describe the five eras of marketing.

4. What is the difference between a selling orientation and a marketing orientation?
5. What are the five components of the marketing concept? Give an example of each component.
6. What is customer service? Why is it so important to any firm?
7. What is customer satisfaction? Why is it so important to any firm?
8. What are the basic functions performed by marketing?

Discussion Questions

1. a. As Donna Noville, insurance broker, what business-related marketing decisions would you make? Why?
   b. As James Nash, insurance company client, what consumer-related marketing decisions would you make? Why?
   c. Develop a plan for Donna Noville to attract James Nash as a client.

2. As the manager of an upscale grocery store, how would your customer services differ from those offered by a more price-oriented grocery store? Why?
3. Develop a seven-item questionnaire to assess the quality of a firm's customer satisfaction efforts.
4. What would a nonmarketing major learn by studying marketing? Give examples for three distinct majors (including at least two nonbusiness majors).

Web Exercise

Visit **http://www.catapultsystems.com/careers/ empowerment.htm** and learn more about employee empowerment. (a) Comment on Catapult's Rules of Empowerment. (b) Could these rules be applied by your college bookstore? Explain your answer.

Chapter 2

The Environment in Which Marketing Operates

When Anne M. Mulcahy, a Xerox (**http://www.xerox.com**) executive with 30 years of experience at the firm, was chosen chief executive officer of Xerox, the company was in horrific shape. The Securities and Exchange Commission was examining Xerox's accounting practices, the company had $14 billion in debt, and it faced tough competition from Hewlett-Packard (**http://www.hp.com**), Canon (**http://www.canon.com**), and other copier companies.

Mulcahy repositioned Xerox from a firm that just sold copiers to all kinds of consumers to an "information flow" provider that scans and stores documents in a digital format for large corporate clients. One tough decision Mulcahy made was to discontinue Xerox's marketing of consumer printers, a business Mulcahy had started years ago. To financially stabilize Xerox, she reduced Xerox's debt to less than $10 billion. She also managed Xerox so that it has regularly met financial analysts' earnings projections. Despite spinning off its Palo Alto Research Center (**http://www.parc.xerox.com**), Xerox still gets two-thirds of its $16 billion in annual revenues from goods and services that are less than two years old.

One way Xerox was able to return to profitability was by carefully studying the needs of its key customers. After analyzing a large insurance company that was a major customer, Xerox learned that the information-related costs in acquiring new business were very high. Xerox showed the client how it could tag the information early on so it could be reused on an automated basis. This process cut the cost of getting a new client for the insurer by 40 to 50 percent.

Mulcahy is also investing in color printing. Xerox wants to increase the percent of material that is printed in color (instead of black and white) from 4 percent to 10 percent within 10 years. New digital technology has reduced the costs of color printing, so low-production volumes can be efficiently printed. Diagnostics for color printers also enable Xerox engineers to notify customers when their machines need servicing. Xerox makes 15 times as much profit from a color page as from one that is black and white.[1]

In this chapter, we will study the complex environment in which marketing decisions are made. We will see that an organization's level of success (or failure) is related not only to its marketing efforts, but also to the external environment in which it operates and its ability to adapt to environmental changes.

Chapter Objectives

1. To examine the environment within which marketing decisions are made and marketing activities are undertaken
2. To differentiate between those elements controlled by a firm's top management and those controlled by marketing, and to enumerate the controllable elements of a marketing plan
3. To enumerate the uncontrollable environmental elements that can affect a marketing plan and study their potential ramifications
4. To explain why feedback about company performance and the uncontrollable aspects of its environment and the subsequent adaptation of the marketing plan are essential for a firm to attain its objectives

[1] Various company and other sources.

2-1 OVERVIEW

The environment within which marketing decisions are made and enacted is depicted in Figure 2-1. The ***marketing environment*** consists of five elements: controllable factors, uncontrollable factors, the organization's level of success or failure in reaching objectives, feedback, and adaptation.

Controllable factors are those directed by an organization and its marketers. First, several broad decisions are made by top management. Then, marketing managers make specific decisions based on the guidelines. In combination, these factors lead to an overall offering (*A* in Figure 2-1). The *uncontrollable factors* are beyond an organization's control, but they affect how well it does (*B* in Figure 2-1).

The interaction of controllable factors and uncontrollable factors determines an organization's level of success or failure in reaching its goals. Feedback occurs when a firm makes an effort to monitor uncontrollable factors and assess its strengths and weaknesses. Adaptation refers to the changes in a marketing plan that an organization makes to comply with the uncontrollable environment. If a firm is unwilling to consider the entire environment in a systematic manner, it increases the likelihood that it will have a lack of direction and not attain proper results.

When analyzing the environment, an organization should consider it from two perspectives: The ***macroenvironment*** includes the broad demographic, societal, economic, political, technological, and other forces that an organization faces. The ***microenvironment*** includes the forces close to an organization that directly impact its

> The **marketing environment** consists of controllable factors, uncontrollable factors, organizational performance, feedback, and adaptation.

> Both the **macroenvironment** and the **microenvironment** must be understood.

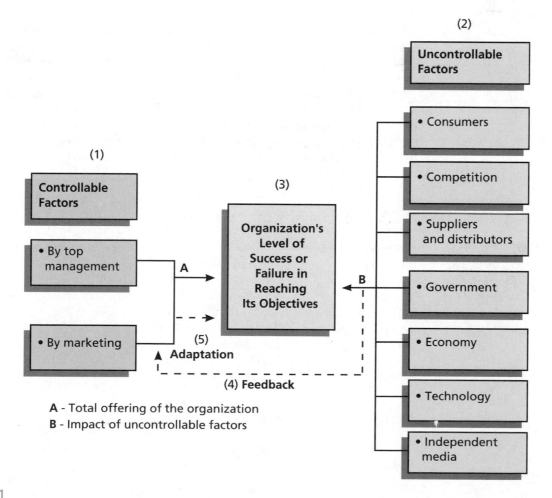

A - Total offering of the organization
B - Impact of uncontrollable factors

Figure 2-1

The Environment Within Which Marketing Operates

Marketing and the Web

What Wireless Technology Customers Want Online

TNS Telecoms (http://www.tnstelecoms.com) regularly surveys 30,000 households to determine their attitudes and actions concerning telecommunications. In one recent study, 20 percent of wireless phone users reported that they want to access local content such as local weather and/or traffic alerts via text messaging. Those people interested in local content are among the highest-spending wireless customers. Despite this, only 2 percent of respondents receive any kind of local service. According to a vice-president at TNS Telecoms, "There is apparently some level of disconnect." There is the question of whether customers can't find local content or aren't willing to pay. "More than likely, there are not enough services out there drawing customers."

These are the features that wireless users most desire:

- 18 percent want to be able to download ringtones.
- 16 percent desire a ringback service whereby they can hear a song clip instead of a basic ring.
- 16 percent want to use a wireless phone to make dinner or hotel reservations.
- 13 percent want to access the latest news, sports, and other information from newspapers and other periodicals.
- 13 percent would like to make small purchases (such as soda in a vending machine or public transportation fares) by entering a code number into their wireless phone.

Source: Based on material in Enid Burns, "Wireless Users Want Local Content," http://www.clickz.com/stats/sectors/wireless/article.php/3520196 (July 14, 2005).

ability to serve customers, including distribution intermediaries, competitors, consumer markets, and the capabilities of the organization itself.[2] The Business Owner's Toolkit gives a good overview of the macroenvironment (**http://www.toolkit.cch.com/text/P03_8023.asp**).

Throughout this chapter, the various parts of Figure 2-1 are described and tied together so that the complex environment of marketing can be understood. In Chapter 3, the concept of strategic planning is presented. Such planning establishes a formal process for developing, implementing, and evaluating marketing programs in conjunction with the goals of top management.

2-2 CONTROLLABLE FACTORS

> The organization and its marketers can manage **controllable factors.**

Controllable factors are internally directed by an organization and its marketers. Some of these factors are directed by top management; these are not controllable by marketers, who must develop plans to satisfy overall organizational (top management) goals. In situations involving small or medium-sized institutions, both broad policy and marketing decisions are often made by one person, usually the owner. Even then, broad policies are often set first and marketing plans adjust to them. A person could decide to open an office-supply store selling products to small businesses (broad policy) and stress convenient hours, a good selection of items, quantity discounts, and superior customer service (marketing plan).

2-2a Factors Directed by Top Management

Top management is responsible for numerous decisions, five of which are quite important to marketers: line of business, overall objectives, role of marketing, role of other

[2] "Dictionary of Marketing Terms," **http://www.marketingpower.com/mg-dictionary.php** (May 3, 2006).

Figure 2-2

Factors Controlled by Top Management

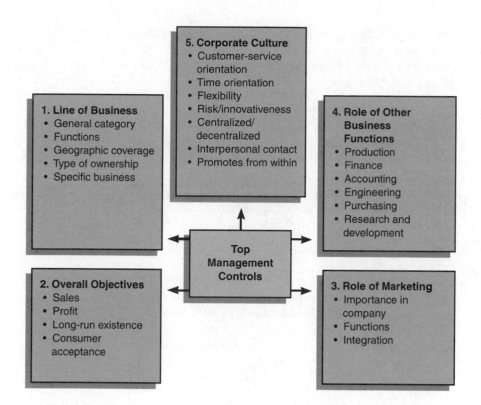

business functions, and corporate culture. They impact on all aspects of marketing. Figure 2-2 shows the types of decisions in these areas.

The *line of business* refers to the general goods/service category, functions, geographic coverage, type of ownership, and specific business of a firm. The general goods/ service category is a broad definition of the industry in which a firm seeks to be involved. It may be energy, transportation, computing, or a host of others. The business functions outline a firm's position in the marketing system—from supplier to manufacturer to wholesaler to retailer—and the tasks it seeks to do. A firm may want to be in more than one position. Geographic coverage can be neighborhood, city, state, regional, national, or international. Ownership ranges from a sole proprietorship, partnership, or franchise to a multiunit corporation. The specific business is a narrow definition of the firm, its functions, and its operations, such as Ben & Jerry's (**http://www.benandjerrys.com**)—the maker and retailer of premium ice cream, frozen yogurt, and sorbets.

Overall objectives are broad, measurable goals set by top management. A firm's success or failure may be determined by comparing objectives with actual performance. Usually, a combination of sales, profit, and other goals is stated by management for short-run (one year to two years or less) and long-run (several years) periods. Most firms cite customer acceptance as a key goal with a strong effect on sales, profit, and long-run existence. The Business Owner's Toolkit gives a good synopsis of the considerations in goal setting (**http://www.toolkit.cch.com/text/p01_0350.asp**).

Top management determines the role of marketing by noting its importance, outlining its activities, and integrating it into company operations. Marketing's importance is evident when marketing personnel have decision-making authority, the rank of the chief marketing officer is equal to that of other areas (usually vice-president), and proper resources are given. It is not considered important by a firm that gives marketing personnel advisory status, places marketing personnel in a subordinate position (like reporting to the production vice-president), equates marketing with sales, and withholds the funds needed for research, promotion, and other marketing tasks. The larger marketing's role, the greater the likelihood that a firm has an integrated marketing organization.

A firm's **line of business** refers to its business category.

The smaller its role, the greater the possibility that a firm undertakes marketing tasks on a project, crisis, or fragmented basis.

The roles of other business functions and their interrelationships with marketing need to be defined clearly to avoid overlaps, jealousy, and conflict. Consider one business expert's observation: "It is traditional in most companies that the operating division is the lead dog on the sled and that other divisions function in supporting roles. Yet, in most companies, it is not the operating division that is charged with growth and success. It is the marketing folks."[3] Production, finance, accounting, engineering, purchasing, and research and development departments each have different perspectives, orientations, and goals. This is discussed further in Chapter 3.

Top management strongly influences a firm's **corporate culture**: the shared values, norms, and practices communicated to and followed by those working for the firm. Corporate culture may be described in terms of:

> **Corporate culture** involves shared values, norms, and practices.

- *A customer-service orientation*—Is the commitment to customer service clear to employees?
- *A time orientation*—Is a firm short- or long-run oriented?
- *The flexibility of the job environment*—Can employees deviate from rules? How formal are relations with subordinates? Is there a dress code?
- *The level of risk/innovation pursued*—Is risk taking fostered?
- *The use of a centralized/decentralized management structure*—How much input into decisions do middle managers have?
- *The level of interpersonal contact*—Do employees freely communicate with one another?
- *The use of promotions from within*—Are internal personnel given preference as positions open?

Nordstrom (**http://www.nordstrom.com**) expects employees to treat customers exceptionally well. Hagberg Consulting Group (**http://w3.hcgnet.com/Services. asp?id=2**) is one of many firms that offers consulting services to enable clients to enhance their corporate cultures; and *Fortune* annually publishes a list of the best firms to work for in the United States (**http://money.cnn.com/magazines/fortune/bestcompanies**). See Figure 2-3.

Advanced Bionics develops, manufactures, and markets implantable neurostimulation devices—bionic technologies that treat neurological conditions. It recently introduced the Clarion Bionic Ear System to restore hearing to the deaf. The firm is also creating other bionic devices for neurological conditions, including chronic pain. At its Web site (**http://www.advancedbionics.com/aboutus/culture.asp**), Advanced Bionics describes its corporate culture and the driving forces behind it:

> Our culture is best described by our people: smart, high-spirited, driven, energetic, and committed. We attract employees who are dedicated to improving the lives of individuals who suffer from neural disorders. The culture of Advanced Bionics is shaped daily by our special mission, the leaders who drive the business, and by the people from all over the world, including 51 different countries, who come here to work. As company president and co-CEO Jeff Greiner says: "We are building a company with a culture where reliability matters most, where innovation and time to market are the keys to our financial success, where crazy ideas are encouraged, where discipline and teamwork are part of our fabric, and where our employees understand the privilege of being engaged together in a business whose mission is to improve the lives of others."

After top management sets company guidelines, the marketing area begins to develop the factors under its control.

---

[3] John Malmo, "Marketing, Not Operations, Makes It Tick," *GoMemphis.com* (May 5, 2003).

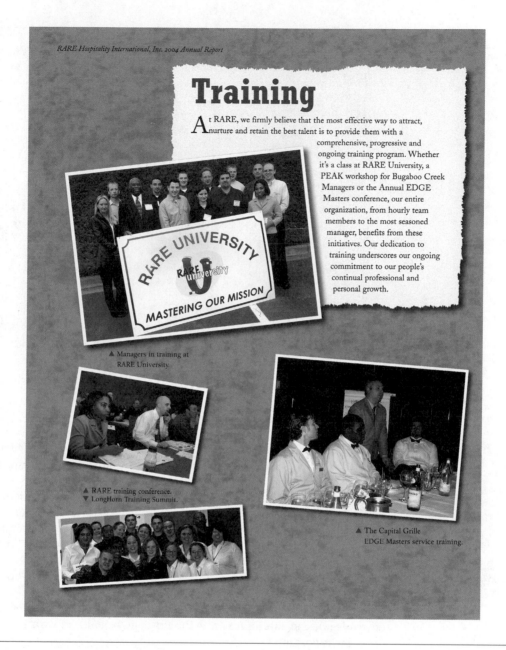

Figure 2-3

A Customer-Friendly Corporate Culture Pays Off

The restaurants of Rare Hospitality International (**http://www.rarehospitality.com**)—LongHorn Steakhouse, Bugaboo Creek Steak House, and Capital Grille—are hit with customers because they train highly motivated and skilled employees.

2-2b Factors Directed by Marketing

The major factors controlled by marketing personnel are the selection of a target market, marketing objectives, the marketing organization, the marketing mix, and assessment of the marketing plan. See Figure 2-4.

One of the most crucial marketing-related decisions involves the choice of a ***target market***, which is the particular group(s) of customers a firm proposes to serve, or whose needs it proposes to satisfy, with a particular marketing program. When selecting a target market, a company usually engages in some form of ***market segmentation***, which involves subdividing a market into clear subsets of customers that act in the same way

> A **target market** is the customer group to which an organization appeals. **Market segmentation** is often used in choosing a target market.

Figure 2-4

Figure 2-4

Factors Controlled by Marketing

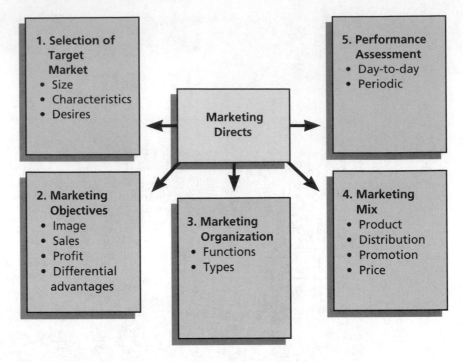

1. Selection of Target Market
- Size
- Characteristics
- Desires

Marketing Directs

5. Performance Assessment
- Day-to-day
- Periodic

2. Marketing Objectives
- Image
- Sales
- Profit
- Differential advantages

3. Marketing Organization
- Functions
- Types

4. Marketing Mix
- Product
- Distribution
- Promotion
- Price

Differential advantages consist of the firm's unique features that attract consumers.

or that have comparable needs.[4] A company can choose a large target market or concentrate on a small one, or try to appeal to both with separate marketing programs for each. As a rule, these questions must be addressed before devising a target market approach: Who are our customers? What kinds of goods and services do they want? How can we attract them to our company? For some interesting insights on target markets, visit the Web site of Brock Henderson & Associates (**http://brockh.win.net/ target.htm**).

At marketing-oriented firms, the choice of a target market affects all other marketing decisions. A book publisher appealing to the high school science market would have a different marketing approach than one appealing to the adult fiction market. The first firm would seek an image as a well-established publisher, specialize product offerings, make presentations to high school book-selection committees, sell in large quantities, and offer books with many photos and line drawings that could be used for several years. The second firm would capitalize on well-known authors or publish books on hot topics to establish an image, have books on a variety of subjects, use newspaper ads and seek favorable reviews, distribute via bookstores, sell in small quantities (except if large chains are involved), and de-emphasize durability, photos, and artwork to produce books as efficiently as possible.

Marketing objectives are more customer-oriented than those set by top management. Marketers are quite interested in the image consumers hold of a firm and its products. Sales goals reflect a concern for brand loyalty (repeat purchases), growth via new-product introductions, and appeal to unsatisfied market segments. Profit goals are related to long-term customer loyalty. Most important, marketers seek to create *differential advantages*, the unique features in a firm's marketing program that cause consumers to patronize that firm and not its competitors. Without differential advantages, a firm would have a "me-too" philosophy and offer the consumer no reasons to select its offerings over competitors' products.

Differential advantages can be based on a distinctive image, new products or features, product quality, customer service, low prices, availability, and other factors. Snapple (**http://www.snapple.com**) is known for its offbeat beverages such as its Mango Madness flavor, Levi's Dockers (**http://www.us.dockers.com**) for their comfortable fit, Cognos Company (**http://www.cognos.com**)—the business software firm—for

[4] "Dictionary of Marketing Terms," **http://www.marketingpower.com/mg-dictionary.php** (May 3, 2006).

Figure 2-5

Edy's Ice Cream: Highlighting Its Differential Advantages

Source: Reprinted by permission.

outstanding customer service, Sony (**http://www.sony.com**) for high-tech consumer electronics, Tiffany (**http://www.tiffany.com**) for high-quality jewelry, Wal-Mart (**http://www.walmart.com**) for selection and prices, and Edy's Slow-Churned ice cream (**http://www.edys.com**) for its great taste with one-half the fat. See Figure 2-5. Build-A-Bear Workshop allows customers to build their own stuffed animals, which they can even do online (**http://www.buildabear.com**): "Shop online for your beary best pal. When you find the pawfect pal, add a Build-A-Sound personal voice greeting by selecting 'Build-A-Sound' under the 'Add Sound' menu options. As you complete your online order, you will be instructed to call a toll-free number and record your beary own

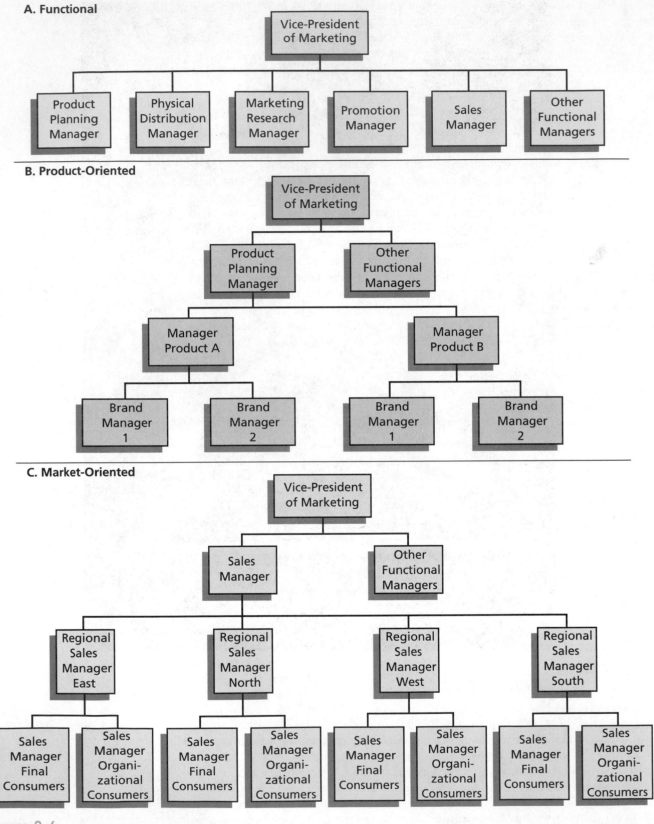

Figure 2-6

Illustrations of Marketing Organizations

personalized 10-second message! Your personalized voice message will play from inside your bear or other furry pal every time it's hugged!"

A *marketing organization* is the structural arrangement that directs marketing functions. It outlines authority, responsibility, and the tasks to be done so that functions are assigned and coordinated. As illustrated in Figure 2-6, an organization may be functional, with jobs assigned in terms of buying, selling, promotion, distribution, and other tasks; product-oriented, with product managers for each product category and brand managers for each brand, in addition to functional categories; or market-oriented, with jobs assigned by geographic market and customer type, in addition to functional categories. A single firm may use a mixture of forms.

A *marketing mix* is the specific combination of marketing elements used to achieve objectives and satisfy the target market. It comprises decisions regarding four major variables: *Product* decisions involve determining what goods, services, organizations, people, places, and/or ideas to market; the number of items to sell and their quality; the innovativeness pursued; packaging; product features; warranties; when to drop existing products; and more. *Distribution* decisions include choosing whether to sell via intermediaries or directly to consumers, how many outlets to sell through, how to interact with channel members, the terms to negotiate, the tasks assigned to others, supplier choice, and more. *Promotion* decisions include selecting a combination of tools (ads, public relations, personal selling, and sales promotion), whether to share promotions with others, the image sought, the level of personal service, media choice, message content, promotion timing, and more. *Price* decisions include choosing overall price levels, the price emphasis, the relation between price and quality, the emphasis to place on price, how to react to competitors, when to offer discounts, how prices are computed, what billing terms to use, and more. A marketing mix is used by all firms, even farmers selling at roadside stands.

When devising a marketing mix, these questions should all be considered:

- Is the target market precisely defined?
- Does the total marketing effort, as well as each element of the mix, meet the target market's needs?
- Are marketing mix elements consistent with one another?
- Do the elements add up to form a harmonious, integrated whole?
- Is each marketing mix element being given its best use?
- Does the marketing mix build on the firm's cultural and tangible strengths? Does the marketing mix imply a way to correct any weaknesses?
- Is a distinctive personality in the competitive marketplace created?
- Is the company protected from the most obvious competitive threats?[5]

Canon (**http://www.canon.com**), a leading maker of cameras and other products, is an example of a firm applying the marketing mix concept well. It has distinct marketing mixes for different target markets. For beginners, it offers simple Sure Shot-model point-and-shoot cameras with automatic focus and a built-in flash. The cameras are sold in all types of stores, including discount stores. Ads appear on TV and in general magazines. The cameras typically sell for $50 to $75. For serious amateur photographers, Canon has more advanced cameras with superior features and attachments. They are found in camera stores and finer department stores. Ads are placed in specialty magazines. The cameras sell for several hundred dollars. For professional photographers, Canon has even more advanced cameras with top-of-the-line features and attachments. They are sold via select camera stores and ads are placed in trade magazines. The cameras are costly

> A **marketing organization** may be functional, product-oriented, or market-oriented.

> The **marketing mix** consists of four elements: product, distribution, promotion, and price.

[5] Benson P. Shapiro, "Rejuvenating the Marketing Mix," *Harvard Business Review*, Vol. 63 (September-October 1985), p. 34. See also Boonghee Yoo, Naveen Donthu, and Sungho Lee, "An Examination of Selected Marketing Mix Elements and Brand Equity," *Journal of the Academy of Marketing Science*, Vol. 28 (Spring 2000), pp. 195–211; Håkan Håkansson and Alexandra Waluszewski, "Developing a New Understanding of Markets: Reinterpreting the 4 Ps," *Journal of Business & Industrial Marketing*, Vol. 20 (No. 3, 2005), pp. 110–117; and Paul S. Hunt, "Seizing the Fourth P," *Marketing Management* (May-June 2005), pp. 40–44.

(the top-of-the-line EOS-1Ds is about $8,000). In sum, Canon markets the right products in the right stores, promotes them in the right media, and has the right prices for its various target markets.

> **Performance assessment involves monitoring and evaluating marketing activities.**

The last, but extremely important, factor directed by marketers involves performance assessment: monitoring and evaluating overall and specific marketing effectiveness. Evaluations need to be done regularly, with both the external environment and internal company data being reviewed. In-depth analysis of performance should be completed at least once or twice each year. Strategy revisions need to be enacted when the external environment changes or the company encounters difficulties.

2-3   UNCONTROLLABLE FACTORS

> **Uncontrollable factors influence an organization and its marketers but are not fully directed by them.**

Uncontrollable factors are the external elements affecting an organization's performance that cannot be fully directed by that organization and its marketers. A marketing plan, no matter how well conceived, may fail if uncontrollable factors have too adverse an impact. Thus, the external environment must be regularly observed and its effects considered in any marketing plan. Contingency plans relating to uncontrollable variables should also be a key part of a marketing plan. Uncontrollable factors that especially bear studying are consumers, competition, suppliers and distributors, government, the economy, technology, and independent media. See Figure 2-7.

2-3a   Consumers

> **Organizations need to understand consumer trends, interpersonal influences, the decision process, and consumer groups.**

Although a firm has control over its target market selection, it cannot control the changing characteristics of its final or organizational consumers. A firm can react to, but not control, consumer trends related to age, income, marital status, occupation, race, education, place and type of residence, and the size and power of organizational customers. For example, health insurers must deal with the fact that many of their largest business customers are downsizing; thus, fewer employees need insurance.

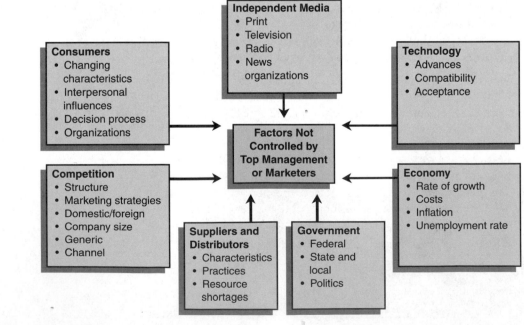

Figure 2-7

Uncontrollable Factors

Ethical Issues in Marketing

Disneyland: Corporate Philanthropist

Fifty years ago, Walt Disney (http://www.disney.com) became involved with its first community philanthropic programs to help the efforts of local nonprofit organizations. Since then, donations by Disneyland Resort and its employees in Anaheim, California, just one of the company's locations, have reached $10 million.

In one recent year, more than $440,000 in grants was given to 30 organizations, and Disneyland's employees contributed 116,000 hours of volunteer service to such community projects and events as teaching in Junior Achievement programs and remodeling facilities at the Boys and Girls Club of Orange County. Disneyland also serves as host for the annual Children's Hospital of Orange County/Disneyland Resort "Walk in the Park" fund raising program, which attracts 12,000 walk participants and generates $1 million in pledges annually.

As part of its 50th anniversary celebration, Disneyland hosted a fundraiser for the Make-A-Wish foundation, sponsored 50 youth-based volunteer projects, and provided 50 $1,000 scholarships to students active in community service. As Anaheim's mayor noted, "All of our residents have benefited from the decision Walt Disney made to locate the Happiest Place on Earth in the City of Anaheim. Disneyland in Anaheim is an integral part of our city's heritage and greatly contributes to the quality of life our residents enjoy." The president and chief executive officer of the Volunteer Center of Orange County stated that the Disneyland Resort "set the standard for others to follow."

Source: Based on material in "Disneyland Resort Contributed Nearly $10 Million to Local Community in 2004," *PR Newswire Association* (March 4, 2005).

Interpersonal influences on consumer behavior need to be understood. People's purchases are affected by the corporate culture at their jobs as purchasing agents; their family, friends, and other social contacts; and the customs and taboos shaping culture and society. For instance, in some states, liquor sales are more regulated (as to outlets, prices, other goods that can be sold, and days open) than they are in others through state liquor boards (http://www.atf.treas.gov/alcohol/info/faq/subpages/lcb.htm).

Because people act differently in buying various types of goods and services, the consumer decision process—the steps people go through when buying products—affects the way that products are marketed. In the case of company cars, a purchasing agent carefully looks for information on a number of models, ranks several alternatives, selects a favorite, negotiates terms, and finally completes the purchase. On the other hand, with an inexpensive meal, a person looks at a watch, sees it is lunch time, and goes to a nearby fast-food outlet.

Consumer rights groups speak on behalf of consumers at public hearings, at stockholder meetings, and with the mass media. To avoid some negative consequences from active consumer groups, a firm must communicate with customers on relevant issues (such as a product recall), anticipate problems (such as order delays), respond to complaints (such as poor service), and be sure it has good community relations (such as sponsoring neighborhood projects). Consumers Union (http://www.consumersunion.org), which publishes *Consumer Reports*, is one of the largest consumer advocacy groups.

2-3b   Competition

The competitive environment often affects a company's marketing efforts and its success in reaching a target market. Thus, a firm should assess its industry structure and examine competitors in terms of marketing strategies, domestic/foreign firms, size, generic competition, and channel competition. Each year, *Business Week* (http://www.business week.com) publishes an overview of the trends occurring in a number of industries. It also makes its forecasts available online.

A company could face one of four possible competitive structures: With a *monopoly*, just one firm sells a given good or service and has a lot of control over its marketing plan. This occurs in the United States when a firm has a patent (exclusive rights to a sell a product it invented for a fixed number of years) or is a public utility, such as a local

> Monopoly, oligopoly, monopolistic competition, and **pure competition** are the main types of competitive structure.

power company. In an ***oligopoly***, a few firms—usually large ones—account for most industry sales and would like to engage in nonprice competition. The U.S. carbonated beverage industry is a good example of this. According to Beverage Digest (**http://www.beveragedigest.com**), Coca-Cola Company, PepsiCo, and Cadbury Schweppes (Dr Pepper/7 Up) account for 90 percent of U.S. soft drink sales. In ***monopolistic competition***, there are several firms in an industry, each trying to offer a unique marketing mix—based on price or nonprice factors. It is the most common U.S. industry structure, followed by oligopoly. Service stations, beauty salons, stationery stores, garment makers, computer-clone makers, and furniture makers are some industry sectors facing monopolistic competition. In ***pure competition***, many firms sell virtually identical goods or services and they are unable to create differential advantages. This occurs rarely in the United States and is most common for selected food items and commodities (and happens if numerous small firms compete with each other).

After analyzing its industry's competitive structure, a firm should study the strategies of competitors. It should look at their target markets and marketing mixes, images, differential advantages, which markets are saturated and which are unfulfilled, and the extent to which consumers are content with the service and quality provided by competitors. See Figure 2-8. Hoover's Online (**http://www.hoovers.com**) is an excellent source of information on thousands of firms around the world. Brief company profiles are free.

Both domestic and foreign competition should be examined. For instance, in the United States, Merrill Lynch (**http://www.ml.com**) competes with Citigroup (**http://www.citigroup.com**), American Express (**http://www.americanexpress.com**), and others—besides traditional brokerage firms—for financial services business. Many U.S. and West European industries are mature; the amount of domestic competition there is rather stable. In some industries, competition is rising due to the popularity of innovations such as notebook PCs. In others, domestic competition is intensifying as a result of government deregulation. For instance, hundreds of companies offer long-distance telephone service in the United States alone.

Foreign competitors now play a major role in many industries. In the United States, foreign-based firms are capturing large market shares for such products as steel, pharmaceuticals, office machines, telecommunications equipment, apparel, consumer electronics, and motor vehicles. At the same time, competition in foreign markets is more intense for U.S.-based firms than before as rivals stress innovations, cost cutting, good distribution and promotion, and other factors. Nonetheless, U.S.-based firms remain globally dominant in such areas as aerospace, chemicals, information technology, transport equipment, scientific instruments, and cereal.[6]

For many industries, there has been a trend toward larger firms due to mergers and acquisitions, as well as company sales growth. Mergers and acquisitions have involved telecommunications firms such as Nextel (**http://www.nextel.com**) being acquired by Sprint (**http://www.sprint.com**) to become Sprint Nextel; technology firms such as Hewlett-Packard (**http://www.hp.com**) acquiring Compaq (**http://www.compaq.com**); food firms such as Nestlé (**http://www.nestle.com**) acquiring San Pellegrino water (**http://www.sanpellegrino.com**); consumer products firms such as Sony (**http://www.sony.com**) buying MGM Studios (**http://www.mgm.com**); retailers such as Kmart (**http://www.kmart.com**) acquiring Sears (**http://www.sears.com**) to become Sears Holding Corporation; media firms such as Movie Gallery (**http://www.moviegallery.com**) acquiring Hollywood Entertainment (**http://www.hollywoodvideo.com**); and many others. Internal sales growth has been great for such firms as Wal-Mart (**http://www. walmart. com**), Microsoft (**http://www.microsoft.com**), Toyota (**http://www.toyota.com**), and Dell (**http://www.dell.com**)—each with annual sales of several billion dollars.

From a small firm's vantage point, personal service, a focus on underserved market segments, an entrepreneurial drive, and flexibility are differential advantages; cooperative ventures and franchising let such firms buy in bulk and operate more efficiently. To large

Foreign competition is intensifying.

Figure 2-8

REI: Succeeding in a Highly Competitive Marketplace

REI (**http://www.rel.com**) is a retailer of high-end gear, clothing, and footwear for camping, bicycling, climbing, paddling, and other outdoor activities. Although it competes with scores of other firms, from Sports Authority to North Face to L.L. Bean to Lone Arrow, REI stands out. Its stores are exciting (as this photo shows), it has strong guarantees, and its members can save money on the products carried.

Source: Reprinted by permission of Retail Forward.

[6] "Foreign Trade Highlights," **http://www.ita.doc.gov/td/industry/otea/usfth/tabcon.html** (February 28, 2006).

firms, widespread distribution, economies of scale, well-known brands, mass-media ads, and low-to-moderate prices are competitive tactics.

Every organization should define competition in generic terms (as broadly as possible). *Direct competitors* are similar to the firm with regard to the line of business and marketing approach. *Indirect competitors* are different, but still compete with it for customers. Both types should be accounted for in a marketing plan. A movie theater not only competes with other theaters—direct competitors—but with indirect competitors such as online firms (i.e., **http://www.netflix.com**), video stores, TV and radio shows, video games, sporting events, live theater, amusement parks, bookstores, restaurants, and schools. A theater owner should ask, "What must I do to compete with a variety of entertainment and recreation forms, in terms of movie selection, prices, hours, customer service, refreshments, and parking?"

A company should also study the competition from its channel members (resellers). Each party in the distribution process has different goals and would like to maximize its control over the marketing mix. Some wholesalers and retailers carry their own brands in addition to those of manufacturers.

> Competition should be defined generically—as widely as possible.

2-3c Suppliers and Distributors

Many firms rely on their suppliers and distributors (wholesalers and retailers) to properly run their own businesses. Without their ongoing support, it would be hard, if not impossible, for a company to succeed.

Suppliers provide the goods and services that firms need to operate, as well as those that the firms resell to their customers. In general, a firm is most vulnerable when there are relatively few suppliers, specific goods and services are needed to run a business or satisfy customer demand, competitors would gain if the firm has a falling-out with a supplier, suppliers are better attuned to the desires of the market place, suppliers informally take care of maintenance and repair services, the turn-around time to switch suppliers is lengthy, and suppliers have exclusive access to scarce resources.

> Suppliers and distributors can have a dramatic impact on an organization.

For firms unable to market products directly to consumers, distributors (whole-salers or retailers) are needed. As a rule, a firm is most vulnerable when there are relatively few distributors in an area, the distributors carry many brands, shelf space is tight, the firm is unknown in the marketplace, particular distributors account for a large part of the firm's revenues, distributors help finance the firm, distributors are better attuned to the marketplace, and competitors are waiting in the wings to stock the distributors.

These are among the supplier/distributor practices that a firm should regularly study: delivery time or requests, product availability, prices, flexibility in handling special requests, marketing support, consistency of treatment, returns policies, and other services. Unsatisfactory performance in one or more of these areas could have a lasting impact on a firm and its competence to enact marketing plans.

A firm's ability to carry out its plans can be affected by the availability of scarce resources—regardless of suppliers' good intentions. Over the past three decades, periodic shortages and volatile price changes have occurred for many basic commodities, such as gasoline, home heating oil, other petroleum-based products, plastics, synthetic fibers, aluminum, chrome, silver, tungsten, nickel, steel, glass, grain, fertilizer, cotton, and wool. And despite efforts at conservation, some raw materials, processed materials, and component parts may remain or become scarce over the next decade.

If resource shortages and/or rapid cost increases occur, one of three actions is possible: (1) Substitute materials might be used to construct products, requiring more research and product testing. (2) Prices might be raised for products that cannot incorporate substitute materials. (3) Firms might abandon products if resources are unavailable and demarket others where demand is greater than can be satisfied.

2-3d Government

Worldwide, governmental bodies have a great impact on marketing practices by placing (or removing) restrictions on specified activities. Rulings can be regional, national, state, and/or local. For example, the European Union sets rules for its member nations.

In the United States, for nearly 120 years, Congress has enacted federal legislation affecting marketing practices, as highlighted in Table 2-1. This legislation can be divided into three groupings: antitrust, discriminatory pricing, and unfair trade practices; consumer protection; and deregulation.

The first group of laws protects smaller firms from anticompetitive acts by larger ones. These laws seek a "level playing field" by barring firms from marketing practices that unfairly harm competitors. The second group of laws helps consumers deal with deceptive and unsafe business practices. These laws protect consumer rights and restrict certain marketing activities (e.g., banning tobacco ads from TV). The third group of laws have deregulated various industries to create more competition. They allow firms greater flexibility in marketing plans. The Federal Trade Commission (FTC) is the major U.S. regulatory agency monitoring restraint of trade and enforcing rules against unfair competition and deceptive practices (**http://www.ftc.gov**).

Besides federal regulation and agencies, each state and local government in the United States has its own legal environment. State and local laws may regulate where a firm can locate, the hours it can be open, the types of items sold, if prices must be marked on every item, how goods must be labeled or dated, the amount of sales tax (**http://www.salestaxinstitute.com/sales_tax_rates.jsp**), and so forth. State and local governments may also provide incentives, such as small business assistance, for firms to operate there.

The political environment often affects legislation. Marketing issues like these are often discussed via the political process prior to laws being enacted (or not enacted): Should certain goods and services be stopped from advertising on TV? Should state governments become more active in handling consumer complaints? Both firms and consumer groups can have input into the process. The goal is to market their positions to government officials. A strength of the U.S. political system is its

> U.S. federal legislation involves interstate commerce; each state and local government has its own regulations, as well.

Global Marketing in Action

Procter & Gamble in Germany: Succeeding Where Others Have Failed

The chairman and chief executive officer of Procter & Gamble (P&G) (**http://www.pg.com**) feels that the German market is extremely important to his firm: "We cannot succeed globally without succeeding in Europe, and we cannot win in Europe unless we are winning in Germany." Germany is P&G's third-largest market in the world and has been a very lucrative market for P&G, whose products have the largest market share of all brands in 11 product categories and are either the number-one or number-two leading brand in 17 categories.

According to P&G's chief executive, a number of reasons account for P&G's status in Germany:

- The company opened its first research and development centers in Germany more than 35 years ago. Its two research centers in Germany now employ close to 700 scientists and researchers. These centers support innovations for

the German market and world markets for baby care, feminine care, and family care.

- Several of the company's major chemical, engineering, and technology suppliers, such as BASF (**http://corporate.basf.com/en**) and Metro-Makro (**http://www.metrogroup.de**), are German-based. This adds an additional Germany-based presence to P&G.

- Many of the firm's products, including Pantene shampoo, Pampers disposable diapers, and Head & Shoulders shampoo, have been rated highly by Stiwa (**http://www.stiwa.com**), the German consumer-product testing institute. This recognition reinforces trust in P&G among German consumers.

Source: Based on material in A. G. Lafley, "Leading Change in Germany," *Vital Speeches of the Day* (January 13, 2005), pp. 242–245.

Table 2-1   Key U.S. Legislation Affecting Marketers

Year	Legislation	Major Purpose
A. Antitrust, Discriminatory Pricing, and Unfair Trade Practices		
1890	Sherman Act	To eliminate monopolies
1914	Clayton Act	To ban anticompetitive acts
1914	FTC Act	To establish the Federal Trade Commission to enforce rules against restraints of trade
1936	Robinson-Patman Act	To prohibit price discrimination toward small distributors or retailers
1938	Wheeler-Lea Amendment	To amend the FTC Act to include more unfair or deceptive practices
1946	Lanham Trademark Act	To protect and regulate trademarks and brands
1976	Hart-Scott-Rodino Act	To require large firms to notify the government of their merger plans
1989	Trademark Revision Act	To revise the Lanham Trademark Act to include products not yet introduced on the market
1990	Antitrust Amendments Act	To raise the maximum penalties for price fixing
1994	International Antitrust Enforcement Assistance Act	To authorize the Federal Trade Commission and the Justice Department to enter into mutual assistance programs with foreign antitrust authorities
1995	Interstate Commerce Communication Termination Act	To require the Federal Trade Commission and the Justice Department to file periodic reports to assess and make recommendations concerning anticompetitive features of rate agreements among common carriers
2002	Sarbanes-Oxley Corporate Responsibility Act	To prevent accounting fraud by requiring greater accountability by companies and their senior executives
2004	Antitrust Criminal Penalty Enhancement and Reform Act	To amend the Sherman Act to increase maximum prison sentences (from 3 to 10 years) and raise the maximum fine for individuals (from $350,000 to $1 million) for restraint of trade among the States, monopolizing trade, and other restraints of trade.
B. Consumer Protection		
1906 1906	Food and Drug Act Meat Inspection Act	To ban adulterated and misbranded food and drugs, and to form the Food and Drug Administration (FDA)
1914 1938	FTC Act Wheeler-Lea Amendment	To establish a commission and provisions for protecting consumer rights
1939 1951 1953 1958	Wool Products Labeling Act Fur Products Labeling Act Flammable Fabrics Act Textile Fiber Identification Act	To require wool, fur, and textile products to show contents and to prohibit dangerous flammables
1958 1960 1962	Food Additives Amendment Federal Hazardous Substances Labeling Act Kefauver-Harris Amendment	To prohibit food additives causing cancer, require labels for hazardous household products, and require drug makers to demonstrate effectiveness and safety
1966	Fair Packaging and Labeling Act	To require honest package labeling and reduce package-size proliferation
1966	National Traffic and Motor Vehicle Safety Act	To set safety standards for autos and tires
1966 1969 1970 1972	Child Protection Act Child Toy Safety Act Poison Prevention Labeling Act Drug Listing Act	To ban hazardous products used by children, create standards for child-resistant packages, and provide drug information
1966 1970	Cigarette Labeling Act Public Health Smoking Act	To require warnings on cigarette packages and ban radio and TV cigarette ads
1967 1968	Wholesome Meat Act Wholesome Poultry Act	To mandate federal inspection standards
1968 1970	Consumer Credit Protection Act Fair Credit Reporting Act	To have full disclosure of credit terms and regulate the use of credit information

(continued)

1970	Clean Air Act	To protect the environment
1972	Consumer Product Safety Act	To create the Consumer Product Safety Commission (CPSC) and set safety standards
1975	Magnuson-Moss Consumer Product Warranty Act	To regulate warranties and set disclosure requirements
1975	Consumer Goods Pricing Act	To disallow retail price maintenance
1980	Fair Debt Collection Practices Act	To eliminate the harassment of debtors and ban false statements to collect debts
1980	FTC Improvement Act	To reduce the power of the FTC to implement industrywide trade regulations
1990	Clean Air Act	To expand the 1970 Clean Air Act
1990	Children's Television Act	To reduce the amount of commercials during children's programs
1990	Nutrition Labeling and Education Act	To have the FDA develop a new system of food labeling
1991	Telephone Consumer Protection Act	To safeguard consumers against undesirable telemarketing practices
1992	Cable Television Consumer Protection and Competition Act	To better protect consumer rights with regard to cable television services
1996	Credit Repair Organizations Act	To prohibit misleading representations associated with credit repair services
1998	Children's Online Protection Act	To protect children's privacy by giving parents the tools to control what information is collected from their children online
1998	Telemarketing Fraud Protection Act	To strengthen penalties for telemarketing fraud
1999	Gramm-Leach-Bliley Act	To protect the privacy of consumers' personal financial information
2002	Best Pharmaceuticals for Children Act	To amend the Federal Food, Drug, and Cosmetic Act to improve the safety and efficacy of pharmaceuticals for children
2003	Do Not Call Registry Act	To authorize the Federal Trade Commission to set up a federal registry of consumers who do not want to be called by telemarketers
2003	Can Spam Act	To make it illegal to send junk E-mail (spam) that fails to meet several conditions
2003	Medicare Prescription Drug, Improvement, and Modernization Act	To provide for a voluntary program for prescription drug coverage under Medicare and to allow a deduction for amounts contributed to health savings accounts
2004	Sports Agent Responsibility and Trust Act	To make it unlawful for an agent to recruit a student athlete by giving any false information, making a false promise, or providing anything of value
2005	Junk Fax Prevention Act	To require that unsolicited faxes include a "clear and conspicuous notice on the first page" explaining how the customer can be removed from that distribution list

C. Industry Deregulation

Over the last 35 years, various laws and regulations have been enacted to make the natural gas, airline, trucking, railroad, banking, electricity, telecommunications, and other industries more competitive.

continuity, which lets organizations and individuals develop strategies for long periods of time.

Internationally, one of the biggest legal and political challenges facing nations that now have free-market economies—after decades of government-controlled markets—is how to privatize organizations that were formerly government-run: "In the short-term, privatization can potentially cause tremendous social upheaval, as privatization is often accompanied by large layoffs. If a single large firm or many small firms are privatized at once and upheaval results, particularly if the state

Privatization is changing the number of businesses in foreign countries.

mishandles the privatization process, a whole nation's economy may plunge into despair."[7]

2-3e The Economy

The rate of growth in a nation's or region's economy can have a huge effect on a firm's marketing efforts. A high growth rate means the economy is strong and the marketing potential is large. Quite important to marketers are consumer perceptions—both in the business and final consumer sectors—regarding the economy. For instance, if people believe the economy will be favorable, they may increase spending; if they believe the economy will be poor, they may cut back.[8] To measure consumer perceptions, the Conference Board (**http://www.conference-board.org/economics/crc.cfm**) and the University of Michigan (**http://www.sca.isr.umich.edu**), among others, perform consumer confidence surveys to see if Americans are optimistic, pessimistic, or neutral about the economy. In uncertain times, many organizational consumers are interested in preserving their flexibility.

A country's economic growth is reflected by changes in its ***gross domestic product (GDP)***, which is the total annual value of goods and services produced in a country less net foreign investment. These are the estimated 2006 GDPs (in U.S. dollars and at purchasing parity) for 10 selected nations: United States, $12.6 trillion; China, $8.4 trillion; Japan, $3.7 trillion; India, $2.7 trillion; Germany, $2.3 trillion; France, $1.7 trillion; Italy, $1.6 trillion; Brazil, $1.4 trillion; Canada, $1.1 trillion; and Mexico, $1.1 trillion.[9] In recent years, the yearly growth in most of these nations has been 3 to 4 percent or so; and when certain industries, such as autos and housing, speed up or slow down, the effects are felt in other areas, such as insurance and home furnishings. The United States is expected to have real GDP growth averaging about 3 to 4 percent annually during the next few years.[10]

> Economic growth is measured by the **gross domestic product.**

Some business costs—such as raw materials, unionized labor wages, taxes, interest rates, and office (factory) rental—are generally beyond any firm's control. If costs rise by a large amount, marketing flexibility may be limited because a firm often cannot pass along all of the increase; it might have to cut back on marketing activities or accept lower profits. If costs are stable, marketers are better able to differentiate products and expand sales because their firms are more apt to invest in marketing activities.

From a marketing perspective, the real income of consumers is critical. Whereas actual income is the amount earned by a consumer (or his/her family or household) in a given year, ***real income*** is the amount earned in a year adjusted by the rate of inflation. For example, if a person's actual income goes up by 4 percent in a year (from $50,000 to $52,000) and the rate of inflation (which measures price changes for the same goods and services over time) is 4 percent for the year, real income remains constant [($52,00) − ($52,000/1.04) = $50,000]. If actual income increases exceed the inflation rate, real income rises and people can buy more goods and services. If actual income goes up by less than the inflation rate, real income falls and people must buy fewer goods and services.[11]

> **Real income** describes earnings adjusted for inflation. Both inflation and unemployment affect purchases.

---

[7] "Privatization," **http://www.en.wikipedia.org/wiki/Privatization** (March 29, 2006).

[8] See James C. Cooper and Kathleen Madigan, "Putting Their Money Where Their Mouths Aren't," *Business Week* (August 8, 2005), pp. 25–26.

[9] "The World Economic Outlook Data Base," **http://www.imf.org/external/pubs/ft/weo/2005/02/data/index.htm** (September 2005)

[10] To obtain ongoing information about the U.S. economy, visit the Web site for the Survey of Current Business: **http://www.bea.doc.gov/bea/pubs.htm.**

[11] For more information on the impact of inflation, visit "Overview of BLS Statistics on Inflation and Consumer Spending," **http://www.bls.gov/bls/inflation.htm.**

A high rate of unemployment can adversely affect many firms because people who are unemployed are likely to cut back on nonessentials wherever possible. Low unemployment often means substantial sales of large-ticket items, as consumers are better off, more optimistic, and more apt to spend earnings.

2-3f Technology

Technology refers to developing and using machinery, products, and processes. Individual firms, especially smaller ones with limited capital, often must adapt to technological advances (rather than control them).

Many firms depend on others to develop and perfect new technology, such as computer microchips; only then can they use the new technology in products, such as automated gasoline pumps at service stations, talking toys, or electronic sensors in smoke detectors for office buildings. With new technology, the inventor often secures patent protection, which excludes competitors from using that technology (unless the inventor licenses rights for a fee).

In several areas, companies have been unable to achieve practical technological breakthroughs. For example, no firm has been able to develop and market a cure for the common cold, a good-tasting nontobacco cigarette, a commercially acceptable electric car, or a truly effective and safe diet pill.

When new technology first emerges, it may be expensive and in short supply, both for firms using the technology in their products and for final consumers. The challenge is to mass produce and mass market the technology efficiently. In addition, some technological advances require employee training and consumer education before they can succeed. Thus, an emphasis on user-friendliness can speed up the acceptance of new technology.

Certain advances may not be compatible with goods and services already on the market or may require retooling by firms wanting to use them in products or operations. Every time an auto maker introduces a significantly new car model, it must invest hundreds of millions of dollars to retool facilities. Each time a firm buys new computer software to supplement existing software, it must see if the new software is compatible (e.g., can the firm's PCs run all the computer programs the firm uses?).

To flourish, technological advances must be accepted by each firm in the distribution process (manufacturer/service provider, wholesaler, retailer). Should any of the firms not use a new technology, its benefits may be lost. If small retailers do not use electronic scanning equipment, cashiers must ring up prices by hand even though packages are computer-coded by manufacturers. In 2000, *Time* magazine selected a list of the 20 most important technological developments of the 20th century, ranging from the automobile to the Internet (**http://www.time.com/time100/builder/tech_supp/tech_supp.html**).

2-3g Independent Media

Independent media are communication vehicles not controlled by a firm; yet, they influence government, consumer, and publics' perceptions of that firm's products and overall image. Media can provide positive or negative coverage when a firm produces a new product, pollutes the air, mislabels products, contributes to charity, or otherwise performs a newsworthy activity. Coverage may be by print media, TV, radio, the Internet, and news organizations. To receive good coverage, a firm should willingly offer information to independent media and always try to get its position written or spoken about.

Although the media's coverage of information about a firm or information released by a firm is uncontrollable, paid advertising is controllable by the firm. Ads may be rejected by the media; but, if they are accepted, they must be presented in the time interval and form stipulated by the firm.

> **Technology** includes machinery, products, and processes.

> **Independent media** affect perceptions of products and company image.

2-4   ATTAINMENT OF OBJECTIVES, FEEDBACK, AND ADAPTATION

An organization's success or failure in reaching objectives depends on both how well it directs its controllable factors and the impact of uncontrollable factors. As shown in Figure 2-1, it is the interaction of an organization's total offering and the uncontrollable environment that determines how it does.

To optimize marketing efforts and secure its long-run existence, a firm must get *feedback*—information about the uncontrollable environment, the organization's perform- ance, and how well the marketing plan is received. Feedback is gained by measuring consumer satisfaction, looking at competitive trends, evaluating relationships with govern- ment agencies, studying the economy and potential resource shortages, monitoring the independent media, analyzing sales and profit trends, talking with suppliers and distrib- utors, and utilizing other methods of acquiring and assessing information.

After evaluating feedback, a company—when necessary—needs to engage in *adap- tation*, thereby fine-tuning its marketing plan to be responsive to the environment, while continuing to capitalize on its differential advantages. The firm should look continually for new opportunities that fit its overall marketing plan and are attainable by it, and respond to potential threats by revising marketing policies.

For instance, many small optical shops are struggling due to the growth of such large chains as LensCrafters (**http://www.lenscrafters.com**), Sterling Optical (**http:// www.sterlingoptical.com**), Pearle Vision (**http://www.pearlevision.com**), and others. The latter advertise extensively, buy in quantity to get special deals, and offer fast service and good prices. To operate in this environment, small optical shops use adaptation strategies like this one by Eyetique (**http://www.eyetique.com**), a four-outlet optical chain in Pennsylvania:

> We could talk about our 21-point vision exams, in-house finishing lab, and fast service but savvy shoppers would say, "So what?" Those services are run-of-the-mill for opticians and eyewear stores everywhere. But if you want to know what makes Eyetique so special, it's personality! And our stores have it. You'll see personality everywhere you look—from our artwork by famed Pittsburgh artist Burton Morris to our rows and rows of glasses from the hottest names in eyewear.
>
> Our opticians pride themselves on relationships and being welcoming, friendly, and most important—inquisitive. Why does inquisitive top the list? The only way we can guide you to the perfect glasses is to take the time to learn about you. Are you artistic? Athletic? A trendsetter or a classic? Are you outgoing or reserved? Do you work in an office? At a construction site? Our staff needs to know who you are to recommend the best choices for your consideration. Eyetique is proud to serve customers who are local and national celebrities, and customers who aren't. Everyone who walks into Eyetique gets treated like they're one of a kind—because they are.
>
> The Eyetique Advantage corporate benefits program for Pittsburgh area businesses, schools, and other organizations of 25 employees or more, provides special rates on vision and hearing exams and eyewear. This program is available at no cost to the employer and requires no paperwork. Employers can get more information by calling (800) 422-5320.[12]

In gearing up for the future, a firm must strive to avoid *marketing myopia*—a shortsighted, narrow-minded view of marketing and its environment. It is a "self- inflicted and avoidable harm caused to an organization due to a lack of attention to and poor implementation of marketing concepts and principles." These are some major warning signs:

Feedback provides information that lets a firm **adapt** to its environment.

Marketing myopia is an ineffective marketing approach.

---

[12] "About Eyetique," http://www.eyetique.com/about.html (April 6, 2006).

- *We-know syndrome*—This is an ongoing assumption that the correct answers to crucial questions are always known.
- *Me-tooism*—This occurs when goods and services are too similar to those of competitors and there is no competitive advantage.
- *Monopricis*—This occurs if a firm's primary (or only) marketing/competitive tool is changing prices.
- *Customerphobia*—This is the fear of having a close relationship with and really caring about consumers and their wants.
- *Fax-me complex*—This occurs when the firm is completely dominated by tasks that require immediate attention (crises).
- *Hypermentis*—This occurs when executives devote too much of their time to thinking, studying, and planning while they take little action.
- *Global idiosis*—This is the lack of ability or willingness to compete internationally.
- *If it works, don't fix it*—This occurs when business is very good, but no one knows why and everyone is hesitant to make changes.
- *Interfunctionalphobia*—This is a lack of mutual understanding, integration, and cooperation among a firm's various functional areas.
- *Short-run fetish*—This occurs when decisions are too biased toward the short run, thus sacrificing long-run performance.[13]

Web Sites You Can Use

The U.S. government has the most comprehensive collection of Web sites in the world. It makes available all sorts of information on a free or nominal-fee basis. What a wealth of data! One general-access site (http://www.firstgov.gov) provides access to several hundred million government Web pages. Here are the addresses of several specialized U.S. government sites:

- Bureau of Economic Analysis (http://www.bea.doc.gov)
- Bureau of Labor Statistics (http://www.stats.bls.gov)
- Census Bureau (http://www.census.gov)
- Consumer Product Safety Commission (http://www.cpsc.gov)
- Department of Commerce (http://www.commerce.gov)
- Department of Labor (http://www.dol.gov)
- Economic and Statistics Administration (http://www.esa.doc.gov)
- Environmental Protection Agency (http://www.epa.gov)

- Federal Communications Commission (http://www.fcc.gov)
- Federal Reserve Board (http://www.federalreserve.gov)
- Federal Trade Commission (http://www.ftc.gov)
- Fedstats (http://www.fedstats.gov)
- Fed World (http://www.fedworld.gov)
- Food and Drug Administration (http://www.fda.gov)
- International Trade Administration (http://www.ita.doc.gov)
- Library of Congress (http://www.loc.gov)
- Securities and Exchange Commission (http://www.sec.gov)
- Small Business Administration (http://www.sba.gov)
- Technology Administration (http://www.technology.gov)
- Women's Bureau—Department of Labor (http://www.dol.gov/wb)

Summary

1. *To examine the environment within which marketing decisions are made and marketing activities are undertaken* The marketing environment comprises controllable factors, uncontrollable factors, the organization's level of success or failure in reaching its objectives, feedback, and adaptation. The macroenvironment includes the broad societal and economic forces facing a firm; the microenvironment includes the more direct forces that affect a firm's ability to serve its customers.

[13] John H. Antil, "Are You Committing Marketcide?" *Journal of Services Marketing*, Vol. 6 (Spring 1992), pp. 45-53. See also Yves Doz, Jose Santos, and Peter J. Williamson, "Marketing Myopia Re-Visited: Why Every Company Needs to Learn from the World," *Ivey Business Journal*, Vol. 68 (January-February 2004), pp. 1–6.

12. When a firm defines its competition in generic terms, it
    a. examines its existing channel relationships.
    b. focuses on patent expiration dates.
    c. analyzes the competitive structure within a specific industry.
    d. looks at competition as broadly as possible.

13. Which type of competition most closely resembles generic competition?
    a. Horizontal competition
    b. Vertical competition
    c. Direct competition
    d. Indirect competition

14. Which statement about technology is true?
    a. Patents provide exclusive rights to sell new products for virtually unlimited time periods.
    b. Small firms must adapt to technological advances rather than control them.
    c. Technology cannot reduce the impact of resource shortages.
    d. Loss of patent protection decreases competition.

15. To attain its objectives, a firm is well advised to
    a. maintain its existing strategies at all costs.
    b. ignore uncontrollable factors.
    c. acquire feedback from the environment.
    d. bypass the independent media entirely.

For the answers to these questions, please visit the online site for this book at **http://www.atomicdog.com.**

Chapter 3

Developing and Enacting Strategic Marketing Plans

General Electric (GE) (**http://www.ge.com**) regularly ranks high on *Fortune*'s "Global Most Admired Companies" list, *Fortune*'s "America's Most Admired Companies" list, and *Financial Times*' "World's Most Respected Companies Survey." Over the years, GE has been a major force in many strategic planning theories that have been adopted by planners worldwide, including the concept of strategic business units as the building blocks of a corporate plan, the need for a strong mix of businesses, and the value of assessing business strength and market opportunities in evaluating an overall strategy.

When John F. Welch, Jr., took over as GE's chief executive, GE had net profits of $1.7 billion on sales of $25 billion. By September 2001, when Jeffrey R. Immelt succeeded Welch, GE's annual earnings were $28 billion on $130 billion in sales. In 2005, GE's revenues exceeded $170 billion. Immelt has promised investors that revenues will grow at least 8 percent yearly from existing operations and that profits will grow at an even faster rate. Unlike Welch—who stressed cost-cutting, efficiency, and buying and selling businesses—Immelt focuses on risk taking, sophisticated marketing strategies, and innovation.

GE comprises six operating segments (down from 11 in July 2005): GE Industrial, GE Commercial Financial Services, NBC Universal, GE Healthcare, GE Consumer Finance, and GE Infrastructure. The reduction in business units saves $200 million to $300 million per year in administrative costs.

GE recently sold $15 billion of its less profitable businesses, such as insurance, and purchased more than $60 billion of businesses in high-growth areas—such as bioscience, security, and wind power. Slow-growth, low-profit-margin businesses now comprise just 10 percent of GE's portfolio.

GE expects that 60 percent of its future revenue growth will come from developing nations. The firm understands that developing economies with a strong demand for power, rail, transportation, health-care services, and consumer finance can turn to GE for all of these needs. Although GE now receives one-half of its revenues from international markets, only 15 percent comes from developing countries.[1]

In this chapter, we will consider strategic planning from a marketing perspective and review, in depth, each of the steps in the strategic planning process. We will also examine the use of strategic planning by both small and large firms.

Chapter Objectives

1. To define strategic planning and consider its importance for marketing
2. To describe the total quality approach to strategic planning and show its relevance to marketing
3. To look at the different kinds of strategic plans and the relationships between marketing and the other functional areas in an organization
4. To describe thoroughly each of the steps in the strategic planning process: defining organizational mission, establishing strategic business units, setting marketing objectives, performing situation analysis, developing marketing strategy, implementing tactics, and monitoring results
5. To show how a strategic marketing plan may be devised and applied

---

[1] Various company and other sources.

3-1 OVERVIEW

As described in Chapter 2, the environment within which marketing operates includes a number of factors directed by top management and others directed by marketing. To coordinate these factors and provide guidance for decision making, it is helpful to engage in a formal strategic planning process. For marketers, such a process consists of two main components: a strategic business plan and a strategic marketing plan.

A ***strategic business plan*** provides "the overall direction an organization will pursue within its chosen environment and guides the allocation of resources and effort. It also provides the logic that integrates the perspectives of functional departments and operating units, and points them all in the same direction." It has (1) an external orientation, (2) a process for formulating strategies, (3) methods for analyzing strategic situations and alternatives, and (4) a commitment to action.[2]

A ***strategic marketing plan*** outlines the marketing actions to undertake, why they are needed, who is responsible for carrying them out, when and where they will be completed, and how they will be coordinated. A marketing plan is carried out within the context of a firm's broader strategic plan.

> Strategic planning includes both a **strategic business plan** and a **strategic marketing plan.**

Our discussion of strategic planning in marketing is presented early in this book for several reasons. The strategic planning process

- gives a firm direction and better enables it to understand the dimensions of marketing research, consumer analysis, and the marketing mix. It is a hierarchal process, moving from company guidelines to specific marketing decisions.
- makes sure each division's goals are integrated with firmwide goals.
- encourages different functional areas to coordinate efforts.
- requires a firm to assess its strengths and weaknesses and consider environmental opportunities and threats.
- outlines the alternative actions or combinations of actions a firm can take.
- presents a basis for allocating resources.
- highlights the value of assessing performance.

Figure 3-1 highlights how a firm can have a clear and directive strategic vision. Marketing's role in strategic planning is a crucial one:

> Marketing should have a key role in strategic planning.

> If you ask senior executives what constitutes business success, profitability and growth are likely to be top of mind. Ask them to define the role of marketing in that success and the question is likely to be met with blank stares. Yet marketing is a key contributor to profitability and growth—more than generally acknowledged. Marketing programs can have a dramatic effect on current customers by continually tilting perception of value toward the firm. Thus, well-constructed long-term marketing programs can meet a dual need: They can entice new customers and reassure those already in place.[3]

For example, mass merchandisers such as Wal-Mart (**http://www.walmart.com**) recognize that each element of their strategy must reflect a customer orientation. Thus, Wal-Mart discount department stores place most sales personnel in product categories where customers want assistance, not evenly throughout the stores.

In Chapter 3, we discuss a total quality approach to strategic planning, various kinds of strategic plans, relationships between marketing and other functional areas, and the strategic planning process—and show how strategic marketing plans may be outlined and applied. Chapter 22, which concludes the text, deals with how marketing plans are integrated and analyzed in a total quality framework.

---

[2] "Dictionary of Marketing Terms," **http://www.marketingpower.com/mg-dictionary.php** (May 3, 2006). For good background information on strategic planning, see Sven Smit, Caroline Thompson, and Patrick Viguerie, "The Do-Or-Die Struggle for Growth," *McKinsey Quarterly* (Number 3, 2005), pp. 34–45; and Jack Welch, "It's All in the Sauce," *Fortune* (April 18, 2005), pp. 138–144.

[3] Ross Goodwin and Brad Ball, "What Marketing Wants the CEO to Know," *Marketing Management* (September-October 2003), pp. 18–23.

About Atomic Dog

Atomic Dog is faithfully dedicated to meeting the needs of today's faculty and students, offering a unique and clear alternative to the traditional textbook. Breaking down textbooks and study tools into their basic 'atomic parts' we were able to recombine them and utilize rich digital media to create a "new breed" of textbook.

This blend of online content, interactive multimedia, and print creates unprecedented adaptability to meet different educational settings and individual learning styles. As part of Thomson Custom Solutions, we offer even greater flexibility and resources in creating a learning solution tailor-fit to your course.

Atomic Dog is loyally dedicated to our customers and our environment, adhering to three key tenets:

Focus on Essential & Quality Content: We are proud to work with our authors to deliver you a high-quality textbook at a lower cost. We focus on the essential information and resources students need and present them in an efficient but student friendly format.

Value and Choice for Students: Our products are a great value and provide students more choices in 'what and how' they buy—often at a savings of 30-40% versus traditional textbooks. Students who choose the online edition may see even greater savings compared to a print textbook. Faculty play an important and willing role—working with us to keep costs low for their students by evaluating texts online and supplementary material.

Reducing Our Environmental 'Paw-Print': Atomic Dog is working to reduce its impact on our environment in several ways. Our textbooks and marketing materials are printed on recycled paper and we will continue to explore environmentally friendly methods. We encourage faculty to review text materials online instead of requesting a print review copy. Students who buy the online version do their part by going 'paperless' and eliminating the need for additional packaging or shipping. Atomic Dog will continue to explore new ways that we can reduce our 'paw print' in the environment and hope you will join us in these efforts.

Atomic Dog is dedicated to faithfully serving the needs of faculty and students—providing a learning tool that helps make the connection. We know that after you try our texts that Atomic Dog—like a great dog—becomes your faithful companion.

Figure 3-1

The Clear Strategic Vision of Atomic Dog

A general planning Web site (**http://www.businessplans.org/topic10.html**) from Business Resource Software provides good planning materials from a small business perspective.

3-2 A TOTAL QUALITY APPROACH TO STRATEGIC PLANNING

> All firms should adopt a **total quality** approach, thereby becoming more process- and output-related in satisfying consumers.

Any firm—small or large, domestic or global, manufacturing or services driven—should adopt a total quality viewpoint when devising a strategic plan. **Total quality** is a process- and output-related philosophy whereby a firm strives to fully satisfy customers in an effective and efficient manner. To flourish, a total quality program needs a customer focus, top management commitment, an emphasis on continuous improvement, and support from employees, suppliers, and distribution intermediaries:

- *Process-related philosophy*—Total quality is based on all the activities that create, develop, market, and deliver a good or service for the customer. A company gains a competitive advantage if it offers better-quality goods and services than competitors or if it offers the same quality at a lower price.
- *Output-related philosophy*—Although process-related activities give a good or service its value, the consumer usually can only judge the total quality of the finished product that he or she purchases. Many consumers care about what they buy, rather than how it was made.

- *Customer satisfaction*—To the consumer, total quality refers to how well a good or service performs. Customer service is a key element in a person's ultimate satisfaction, which is affected by the gap between that person's expectations of product performance and actual performance.
- *Effectiveness*—To a marketer, this involves how well various marketing activities (such as adding new product features) are received by consumers.
- *Efficiency*—To a marketer, this involves the costs of various marketing activities. A firm is efficient when it holds down costs while offering consumers the appropriate level of quality.
- *Customer focus*—With a total quality viewpoint, a firm perceives the consumer as a partner and seeks input from that partner as it creates, develops, markets, and delivers a good or service.
- *Top management commitment*—Senior executives must be dedicated to making a total quality program work and to ensuring that corners are not cut in an attempt to be more efficient. In the best firms, "total quality" becomes ingrained as part of the corporate culture.
- *Continuous improvement*—A firm must continuously improve its quality because, in most cases, today's total quality will become tomorrow's suboptimal quality. A complacent company will be hurt by the dynamics of the marketplace and fast-paced technological and global marketplace trends.
- *Employee support and involvement*—Employees must "buy into" a total quality program for it to work. Empowering employees not only gets them involved in the total quality process, but also assures that customer problems are promptly addressed and resolved in the customer's favor.
- *Supplier and distributor support and involvement*—Suppliers and resellers can greatly affect total quality due to their involvement in creating it. They too must "buy into" a firm's total quality efforts.

Figure 3-2 shows how a total quality program should work. At the left are the participants who create total quality. There is an interchange among the parties and between the parties and the process. In this way, a good's or service's effectiveness and efficiency are influenced. Total quality is the output. The process and total

> For a total quality program to work, every party in the process must participate.

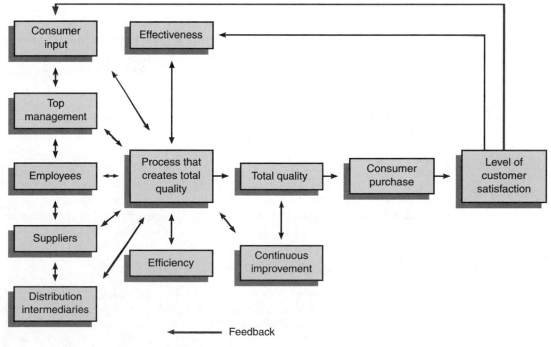

Figure 3-2

The Keys to a Successful Total Quality Program

Marketing and the Web

Print Media and Broadcast Media Refashion Their Strategies

The online world of advertising is rapidly changing. Older tactics whereby advertisers aggressively sought banner ads with the hope of getting clicks from interested viewers are no longer very popular.

Print publishers and television media executives are also increasingly aware that their audiences are spending more time online. Many traditional media are now buying Internet sites and beginning their own initiatives. Rupert Murdoch's News Corporation purchased Myspace.com (http://www.myspace.com), a site with 18 million monthly visitors, for $580 million. Fox Broadcasting Company formed Fox Interactive Media (http://www.fox.com). The Washington Post (http://www.washingtonpost.com) launched two Web sites for its local and global audiences with the plan to increase Internet advertising.

Building or purchasing Web sites is a defensive strategy by traditional media. Many newspapers are facing lower circulations and the loss of real-estate and classified job advertising to the Web. Television networks have significant competition from digital video recorders and on-demand viewing. Traditional radio stations must deal with the millions of paid subscribers to satellite radio programming.

Still, online advertising represents less than 5 percent of total advertising spending, according to one Internet marketing research company. And unlike traditional media, where firms such as Procter & Gamble (http://www.pg.com) are the leading advertisers, the largest online advertisers are firms such as Vonage (http://www.vonage.com), an Internet phone service; LowerMyBills.com (http://www.lowermybills.com), which searches for the best deals on loans and Internet and phone services; and Verizon (http://www.verizon.com).

Source: Based on material in Megan Barnett, "All the News That Clicks," *U.S. News & World Report* (August 1, 2005), pp. 36–38.

quality itself are regularly improved. If a consumer feels a product has superior total quality, a purchase is made. When experience with a purchase is pleasing, customer satisfaction occurs. Because one effectiveness measure is customer satisfaction, there is an impact arrow. Satisfaction is feedback that places consumer input into the process. The consumer's central focus is evident because this party appears three times: consumer input, consumer purchase, and customer satisfaction. At the Ritz-Carlton hotel chain (http://www.ritzcarlton.com), the only two-time service company winner of the Malcolm Baldrige National Quality award, total quality is imperative: "Ritz-Carlton is a place where the genuine care and comfort of our guests is our highest mission. We pledge to provide the finest personal service and facilities for our guests who will always enjoy a warm, relaxed, yet refined ambience. The Ritz-Carlton experience enlivens the senses, instills well-being, and fulfills even the unexpressed wishes and needs of guests. Each employee is empowered. When a guest has a problem or needs something special, you should break away from your regular duties, and address and resolve the issue."[4]

Sometimes, the total quality process breaks down in a way that may be difficult to fix. For example, many firms have had glitches with their Web sites, including heavy traffic causing system overloads, poor inventory and shipping coordination, too long a time for replies to E-mail, and so forth. These problems require expensive and time-consuming solutions. To learn more about the strategic aspects of total quality management (TQM), visit the U.S. Chamber of Commerce Web site (http://www.uschamber.com/sb/business/P03/P03_9000.asp). It highlights the role of marketing in TQM.

3-3   KINDS OF STRATEGIC PLANS

Strategic plans can be categorized by their duration, scope, and method of development. They range from short-run, specific, and department-generated plans to long-run, broad, and management-generated plans.

---

[4] "Gold Standards," http://www.ritzcarlton.com/corporate/about_us/gold_standards.asp (March 19, 2006).

Plans may be short run (typically 1 year), moderate in length (2 to 5 years), or long run (5 to 10 or even 15 years). Many firms rely on a combination: Short-run and moderate-length plans are more detailed and operational in nature than long-run plans.

Japan's Canon (**http://www.canon.com**), the maker of cameras, machines, and optical products, has taken this planning approach:

> The Excellent Global Corporation Plan is a medium- to long-term management plan with the goal of building a corporate group that continues contributing to society through technological innovation, aiming to be a corporation worthy of admiration and respect worldwide. In the first phase of the plan, which began in 1996, Canon inculcated the concepts of profit orientation and total optimization, introducing production reforms and cash flow-based consolidated business performance evaluation. In the second phase, which began in 2001, we aimed to become Number 1 in all our businesses and strengthen our research and development. We achieved great results, including development reforms and in-house manufacturing of key components. While working to conclude Phase II, we also made thorough preparations to pursue healthy growth, our target for Phase III, which began in 2006.[5]

The scope of strategic plans also varies. Separate marketing plans may exist for each of a firm's major products; a single, integrated marketing plan may encompass all products; or a broad business plan with a section devoted to marketing may be used. Separate marketing plans by product line are often used by consumer-goods manufacturers; a single, integrated marketing plan is often employed by service firms; and a broad business plan is often utilized by industrial-goods manufacturers. A firm's diversity and the number of distinct market segments it seeks both have a strong influence in this planning aspect.

Last, plans may be devised by a bottom-up, top-down, or combination approach. In bottom-up planning, input from salespeople, product managers, advertising people, and other marketing areas is used to set goals, budgets, forecasts, timetables, and marketing mixes. Bottom-up plans are realistic and good for morale. Yet, it may be hard to coordinate bottom-up plans and to include different assumptions about the same concept when integrating a company-wide plan. Shortcomings of bottom-up plans are resolved in the top-down approach, whereby senior managers centrally direct planning. A top-down plan can use complex assumptions about competition or other external factors and provide a uniform direction for marketing. Input from lower-level managers is not actively sought and morale may diminish. A combination of the two approaches could be used if senior executives set overall goals and policy, and marketing personnel form plans for carrying out marketing activities.

3-4 STRENGTHENING RELATIONSHIPS BETWEEN MARKETING AND OTHER FUNCTIONAL AREAS IN AN ORGANIZATION

An organization's strategic planning efforts must accommodate the distinct needs of marketing and other functional areas. This is not always simple, due to the different orientations of each area, as shown in Table 3-1. Marketers may seek tailor-made products, flexible budgets, nonroutine transactions, many product versions, frequent purchases, customer-driven new products, employee compensation incentives, and aggressive actions against competitors. This may conflict with goals of other functional areas to seek mass production (production), stable budgets (finance), routine transactions (accounting), limited models (engineering), infrequent orders (purchasing), technology-driven new products (research and development), fixed employee compensation (personnel), and passive actions against competitors (legal).

Top management's job is to ensure that every functional area sees the need for a balanced view in company decision making and has input on decisions. Though some

Short-run plans are precise; long-run plans outline needs.

Consumer-products firms often have plans for each line.

Bottom-up plans foster employee input; top-down plans are set by top management.

The perspectives of marketing and other functional areas need to be reconciled.

---

[5] "Strategies 2005," **http://www.canon.com/about/strategies** (December 14, 2005).

Ethical Issues in Marketing

Profitable Corporate Social Responsibility

Generally speaking, firms can no longer afford to ignore social responsibility or to keep quiet about their efforts in raising funds for charities. According to a director at a British-based ad agency, "It has gotten to the stage where every brand needs to be seen to be putting something back; the wider stakeholders are expecting it. Our research shows consumers think that that as long as the good cause at the end of the CSR [consumer social responsibility] benefits, then it is worth it."

The chief executive of Sainsbury (http://www.sainsbury.co.uk), a major British-based supermarket chain, recently told investors that its charity promotion generated an additional 0.3 percent of same-store sales. Many of the 4 million shoppers that visited a Sainsbury store to purchase a red nose (as part of the chain's Comic Relief charity promotion) purchased more goods on the same trip.

Yet, despite being concerned about socially responsible business practices, most consumers want benefits beyond a company's being simply ethical. As one market analyst noted, "gone are the days when people would buy a product they didn't enjoy just because it was ethical." When Cafédirect (http://www.cafedirect.co.uk), a coffee company that promoted fair dealings with poor coffee growers, was first introduced, its coffee mostly sold to a niche market concerned with the working conditions of coffee growers. After the brand was repositioned as an upscale coffee, its sales increased by 23 percent over prior levels.

Source: Based on material in "Show Them You Care," *Marketing Week* (May 5, 2005), p. 41.

degree of tension among departments is inevitable, conflict can be reduced by encouraging interfunctional contact; seeking personnel with both technical and marketing expertise; forming multifunctional task forces, committees, and management-development programs; and setting goals for each department that take other departments into account.

Table 3-1	The Orientations of Different Functional Areas
Functional Area	**Major Strategic Orientation**
Marketing	To attract and retain a loyal group of consumers through a unique combination of product, distribution, promotion, and price factors
Production	To utilize full plant capacity, hold down per-unit production costs, and maximize quality control
Finance	To operate within established budgets, focus on profitable items, control customer credit, and minimize loan costs for the company
Accounting	To standardize reports, detail costs fully, and routinize transactions
Engineering	To develop and adhere to exact product specifications, limit models and options, and concentrate on quality improvements
Purchasing	To acquire items via large, uniform orders at low prices and maintain low inventories
Research and Development	To seek technological breakthroughs, improvements in product quality, and recognition for innovations
Personnel	To hire, motivate, supervise, and compensate employees in an efficient manner
Legal	To ensure that a strategy is defensible against challenges from the government, competitors, channel members, and consumers

3-5 THE STRATEGIC PLANNING PROCESS

The *strategic planning process* has seven interrelated steps: defining organizational mission, establishing strategic business units, setting marketing objectives, performing situation analysis, developing marketing strategy, implementing tactics, and monitoring results. Because the process encompasses both strategic business planning and strategic marketing planning, it should be conducted by a combination of senior company executives and marketers. The strategic planning process is depicted in Figure 3-3.

This process applies to small and large firms, consumer and industrial firms, goods- and services-based firms, domestic and global firms, and profit-oriented and nonprofit-oriented institutions. Planning at each step in the process may differ by type of firm, but using a thorough strategic plan is worthwhile for any company. Sample plans for three businesses—manufacturer, service provider, and retailer—are available at the Business Owner's Toolkit site (**http://www.toolkit.cch.com/tools/buspln_m.asp**).

The steps in strategic planning are discussed in the following sections.

> The **strategic planning process** includes steps from defining a mission to monitoring results.

3-5a Defining Organizational Mission

Organizational mission refers to a long-term commitment to a type of business and a place in the market. It "describes the scope of the firm and its dominant emphasis and values," based on that firm's history, current management preferences, resources, and distinctive competences, and on environmental factors.[6]

An organizational mission can be expressed in terms of the customer group(s) served, the goods and services offered, the functions performed, and/or the technologies utilized. It is more comprehensive than the line-of-business concept noted in Chapter 2. Organizations that diversify too much may not have a clear sense of direction. The mission is considered implicitly whenever a firm

- seeks a new customer group or abandons an existing one,
- introduces a new product (good or service) category or deletes an old one,

> A firm sets its direction in an **organizational mission**.

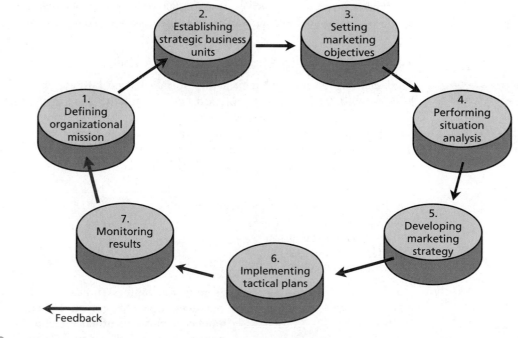

Figure 3-3

The Strategic Planning Process

---

[6] "Dictionary of Marketing Terms," **http://www.marketingpower.com/mg-dictionary.php** (May 3, 2006).

- acquires another company or sells a business,
- engages in more marketing functions (a wholesaler opening retail stores) or in fewer marketing functions (a small innovative toy maker licensing its inventions to an outside company that produces, distributes, and promotes them), or
- shifts its technological focus (a phone manufacturer placing more emphasis on cellular phones).

Here are two diverse illustrations of a clear organizational mission:

Atomic Dog (**http://www.atomicdog.com**)[the publisher of this book] blends online content delivery, interactive multimedia components, and print to form a completely unique learning and teaching tool. Our online textbooks ("New Breed Textbooks") contain interactive elements that allow instructors and students to customize their text to meet course objectives and fit individual learning styles. Identical core content found in the online edition is also available in the print edition with iconic references to interactive material found online. We give authors and instructors a clear content alternative with college textbooks, while providing students superior choice and value. That's our mission. Ultimately, our hope is that our publications, like great dogs, become your best friends.[7]

JetBlue is bucking a trend. We were profitable within our first year of operation, and our product— new planes, leather seats, up to 24 channels of TV programming for every customer, low fares and friendly service—ups the ante at a time when other airlines are cashing in their chips. How have we done it? (1) JetBlue is the best-capitalized airline startup in history. This means we are able to invest in the best product available. You'll see it in our new planes, comfy leather seats, free satellite TV, and fast check-in technology. (2) Our fleet of new Airbus A320s comes with a host of advantages. New aircraft are more reliable, so they spend less time on the ground where they don't make money. They're more efficient, so we spend less on fuel than other carriers. In fact, contrary to what you may have heard, the youngest fleet in the sky belongs to JetBlue. (3) We screen employees rigorously, train them well, and give them the best tools. That means our people are motivated and service-oriented. We love changing the industry for the better! (4) By offering our customers the best experience we can deliver, we find most of them come back regularly and tell their friends and family about us. At JetBlue, we're not perfect, but we do try to do things differently and work hard to be the best. Don't take our word for it. Ask someone who's flown us.[8]

3-5b   Establishing Strategic Business Units

After defining its mission, a firm may form strategic business units. Each ***strategic business unit (SBU)*** is a self-contained division, product line, or product department in an organization with a specific market focus and a manager with complete responsibility for integrating all functions into a strategy. An SBU may include all products with the same physical features or products bought for the same use by customers, depending on the mission of the organization. Each SBU has these general attributes:

> **Strategic business units (SBUs)** are separate operating units in an organization.

- A specific target market
- Its own senior marketing executive
- Control over its resources
- Its own marketing strategy
- Clear-cut competitors
- Distinct differential advantages

The SBU concept lets firms identify the business units with the most earnings potential and allocate to them the resources needed for growth. For instance, at General Electric, every SBU must have a unique purpose, identifiable competitors, and all its major business functions (manufacturing, finance, and marketing) within the control of

---

[7] "About Atomic Dog Publishing," **http://www.atomicdogpublishing.com/AboutUs.asp** (April 6, 2006).
[8] "JetBlue 101," **http://www.jetblue.com/learnmore/air101.html** (April 6, 2006).

that SBU's manager. Units not performing up to expectations are constantly reviewed and, if necessary, consolidated with other units, sold, or closed down.

The proper number of SBUs depends on a firm's organizational mission, its resources, and the willingness of top management to delegate authority. A small or specialized firm can have as few as one SBU; a diversified firm can have one up to 100 or more. Thus, the rather-specialized WD-40 Company (**http://www.wd40.com**) has three main SBUs: multipurpose lubricants (WD-40 and 3-in-One), heavy-duty hand cleaners (Lava and Solvol), and household products (such as Carpet Fresh and Spot Shot). And the highly diversified Johnson & Johnson (**http://www.jnj.com**), with more than 200 SBUs, "is the world's most comprehensive and broadly based manufacturer of health care products, as well as a provider of related services, for the consumer, pharmaceutical, and medical devices and diagnostics markets."[9]

Firms sometimes eliminate SBUs that do not fit for them. After careful consideration, PepsiCo (**http://www.pepsico.com**) spun off its restaurant SBUs—KFC, Pizza Hut, and Taco Bell—to concentrate on three businesses: carbonated beverages, snack foods, and noncarbonated beverages. PepsiCo then acquired Quaker Oats, with its Gatorade drinks and other food products.

3-5c   Setting Marketing Objectives

A firm needs overall marketing objectives, as well as goals for each SBU. Objectives are often described in both quantitative terms (dollar sales, percentage profit growth, market share, etc.) and qualitative terms (image, level of innovativeness, industry leadership role, etc.).

> Marketing objectives may include quantitative and qualitative measures.

For example, Hewlett-Packard (**http://www.hp.com**) is a nearly 70-year-old firm that "is a technology solutions provider to consumers, businesses, and institutions globally. The company's offerings span IT infrastructure, global services, business and home computing, and imaging and printing." It has a solid base of marketing goals that complement its overall corporate objectives:

Customer Loyalty—To provide products, services, and solutions of the highest quality and deliver more value to our customers that earns their respect and loyalty. Underlying beliefs supporting this objective: Our continued success is dependent on increasing the loyalty of our customers. Listening attentively to customers to truly understand their needs, then delivering solutions that translate into customer success is essential to earn customer loyalty. Competitive total cost of ownership, quality, inventiveness, and the way we do business drives customer loyalty.

Growth—To view change in the market as an opportunity to grow; to use our profits and our ability to develop and produce innovative products, services, and solutions that satisfy emerging customer needs. Underlying beliefs supporting this objective: Growth comes from taking smart risks, based on the state of the industry—that requires both a conviction in studying the trends, but also in inducing change in our industry. Our size (and diversity of businesses) gives us an ability to weather economic cycles and turn them to our favor.

Market Leadership—To grow by continually providing useful and significant products, services, and solutions to markets we already serve—and to expand into new areas that build on our technologies, competencies, and customer interests. Underlying beliefs supporting this goal: There are more places we can contribute than we will be capable of contributing. We must focus. To be average is not good enough, we play to win. We must be number 1 or number 2 in our chosen fields.[10]

Small firms' goals may be less ambitious than those set by their larger counterparts, but they are no less important. Goals are necessary to focus the firm and to be able to

---

[9] "Our Company," **http://www.jnj.com** (April 8, 2006).
[10] "HP Corporate Objectives," **http://www.hp.com/hpinfo/abouthp/corpobj.html** (March 11, 2006).

monitor the level of success or failure. Without goals, how can a firm really measure its performance?

3-5d Performing Situation Analysis

In *situation analysis*, also known as SWOT analysis, an organization identifies its internal strengths (*S*) and weaknesses (*W*), as well as external opportunities (*O*) and threats (*T*). Situation analysis seeks to answer: Where is a firm now? Where is it headed? Answers are derived by recognizing both company strengths and weaknesses relative to competitors, studying the environment for opportunities and threats, assessing the firm's ability to capitalize on opportunities and to minimize or avoid threats, and anticipating competitors' responses to company strategies. The Business Owner's Toolkit site (**http://www.toolkit.cch.com/text/p03_8020.asp**) provides an in-depth discussion of many of the factors to be reviewed during a situation analysis.

> **Situation analysis** investigates a firm's strengths, weaknesses, opportunities, and threats.

Situation analysis can, and should be, conducted at any point in a firm's life. Consider these examples:

> The growth target for internal businesses at Procter & Gamble [P&G, **http://www.pg.com**] is 4 to 6 percent annually. With P&G's global consumer goods markets expanding only 2 to 3 percent per year, that's no easy task. Yet, P&G has hit or exceeded its goal year after year under A. G. Lafley's leadership. How? The answer starts with focus: Under previous CEO Durk Jager, rapid-fire product launches distracted managers from old-line franchises like Crest and Pampers. Those big brands suffered. "All businesses had equal rights to capital and people," recalls chief financial officer Clayton Daley, Jr. Lafley had a different idea—channeling resources to the company's areas of strength. "What are you really good at?" he asks. "We're good at building great brands, innovating, and leveraging size." A case in point is P&G's big bet on beauty care. Not long ago, the firm's Olay beauty care brand was affectionately known as "Oil of Old Lady," says Lafley. Today, Olay has emerged as one of the company's fastest-growing brands.[11]

> Although Adidas (**http://www.adidas.com**) and Reebok (**http://www.reebok.com**), the number-two and number-three players in the sneaker and sports-apparel markets, have long been described as being in a war with Nike (**http://www.nike.com**), the truth is that until now they've not really had the leverage to draw the 800-pound gorilla into anything more than the occasional scuffle, and Nike has dominated the business for more than a decade. Now sports marketing experts expect Adidas (with its acquisition of Reebok) to put up more of a fight, particularly in the U.S. market, where it will gain clout and better command of shelf space with such important retailers as Foot Locker and Sports Authority, as well as media-buying discounts. But the true battle ahead lies in endorsements, where new "sole mates" Adidas and Reebok can lure bigger-name stars away from Nike's stable. But athletic endorsements are only the start. Where Reebok has done the better job has been in making inroads into the urban community, with signature shoes from rappers Jay-Z and 50 Cent and an endorsement deal with rapper Nelly. Adidas' best-selling clothing line has come via its affiliation with designer Stella McCartney, and the company is perhaps better-known globally through an endorsement deal with English soccer star David Beckham. Adidas CEO Herbert Hainer said he intends to keep both companies separate—much as Nike does with the companies it purchased, such as Converse.[12]

Here's what an accounting firm's SWOT analysis might look like: *Strengths*: experienced associates, prime location, reputation/image, income tax expertise. *Weaknesses*: seasonality, dependence on senior partner, limited funds. *Opportunities*: idle resources during off-season (offices, computers, employees), joint marketing arrangements with noncompeting firms, fee-based seminars, tax reform. *Threats*: learning required to be

---

[11] Patricia Sellers, "Bigger and BIGGER," *Fortune* (September 5, 2005), pp. 104–107.
[12] Rich Thomaselli, "Deal Sets Stage for Full-Scale War with Nike," *Advertising Age* (August 8, 2005), p. 5.

expert in new regulations, technology (enabling self-preparation), IRS policies that simplify tax returns, competition from newer types of firms (such as online tax preparers).[13]

Sometimes, situation analysis reveals weaknesses or threats that cannot be overcome, and a firm drops or sells a product line or division. About a decade ago, General Mills (**http://www.generalmills.com**) sold its popular restaurant division—comprised of the Red Lobster, Olive Garden, and China Coast chains. Why? Fifty-five percent of General Mills' food profits were used to fund the restaurant business; and the firm decided to focus instead on its leading food brands. This is the firm's focus today: "General Mills gets its Kix as the number 2 U.S. cereal maker. Among its Big G Cereals brands are Cheerios, Chex, Total, Kix, and Wheaties. General Mills is also a brand leader in flour (Gold Medal), baking mixes (Betty Crocker, Bisquick), dinner mixes (Hamburger Helper), fruit snacks (Fruit Roll-Ups), and grain snacks (Chex Mix, Pop Secret). It is also number 1 in branded yogurt (Colombo, Go-Gurt, and Yoplait). Through joint ventures, the company has expanded its cereals and snacks into Europe. Its 2001 acquisition of Pillsbury (refrigerated dough products, frozen vegetables) from Diageo doubled the company's size, making it one of the world's largest food companies."[14]

Figure 3-4 highlights BMW's strong move into "pre-owned" cars, after a SWOT analysis.

3-5e Developing Marketing Strategy

A *marketing strategy* outlines the way in which the marketing mix is used to attract and satisfy the target market(s) and achieve an organization's goals. Marketing-mix decisions center on product, distribution, promotion, and price plans. A separate strategy is necessary for each SBU in an organization; these strategies must be coordinated.

A marketing strategy should be unambiguous to provide proper guidance. It should take into account a firm's mission, resources, abilities, and standing in the marketplace; the status of the firm's industry and the product groups in it (such as light versus regular beer); domestic and global competitive forces; such environmental factors as the economy and population growth; and the best options for growth—and the threats that could dampen it. For instance, IBM does a lot of image advertising as part of its overall marketing strategy in order to enhance its stature in the business community.

> A good **marketing strategy** provides a framework for marketing activities.

Four strategic planning approaches are presented next: product/market opportunity matrix, Boston Consulting Group matrix, General Electric business screen, and Porter generic strategy model.

The Product/Market Opportunity Matrix The *product/market opportunity matrix* identifies four alternative marketing strategies to maintain and/or increase sales of business units and products: market penetration, market development, product development, and diversification.[15] See Figure 3-5. The choice of an alternative depends on the market saturation of an SBU or product and the firm's ability to introduce new products. Two or more alternatives may be combined.

> The **product/market opportunity matrix** involves market penetration, market development, product development, and diversification options.

Market penetration is effective when the market is growing or not yet saturated. A firm seeks to expand the sales of its present products in its present markets through more intensive distribution, aggressive promotion, and competitive pricing. Sales are increased

[13] Adapted by the authors from "How to Develop a Strategic Business Plan," **http://www.peoplestax.com/tax_prac/ strategic_plan.htm** (March 19, 2006).

[14] "General Mills, Inc.," **http://www.hoovers.com/general-mills/--ID__10639--/free-co-factsheet.xhtml** (February 28, 2006).

[15] H. Igor Ansoff, "Strategies for Diversification," *Harvard Business Review*, Vol. 35 (September-October 1957), pp. 113–124. See also "Matrix V4 Quick Guide Step 3: The Ansoff Matrix," **http://www.market-modelling.co.uk/ MATRIX/MATRIX_Step02_2.htm** (March 2, 2006).

Figure 3-4

Profiting from SWOT Analysis

After studying the marketplace, BMW decided to place greater emphasis on the sales of used cars ("certified pre-owned").

Source: Reprinted by permission.

Figure 3-5

The Product/Market Opportunity Matrix

Source: Adapted from H. Igor Ansoff, "Strategies for Diversification," *Harvard Business Review*, Vol. 35 (September-October 1957), pp. 113–124.

Market

	Present	New
Present	Market penetration strategy	Market development strategy
New	Product development strategy	Diversification strategy

Product

by attracting nonusers and competitors' customers and raising the usage rate among current customers.

Market development is effective when a local or regional business looks to widen its market, new market segments are emerging due to changes in consumer lifestyles and demographics, and innovative uses are discovered for a mature product. A firm seeks greater sales of present products from new markets or new product uses. It can enter new territories, appeal to segments it is not yet satisfying, and reposition existing items. New distribution methods may be tried; promotion efforts are more descriptive.

Product development is effective when an SBU has a core of strong brands and a sizable consumer following. A firm develops new or modified products to appeal to present markets. It stresses new models, better quality, and other minor innovations closely related to entrenched products—and markets them to loyal customers. Traditional distribution methods are used; promotion stresses that the new product is made by a well-established firm.

Diversification is used so a firm does not become too dependent on one SBU or product line. The firm becomes involved with new products aimed at new markets. These products may be new to the industry or new only to the company. Both distribution and promotion orientations are different from those usually followed by the firm.

Here is how the product/market opportunity matrix can be applied to United Parcel Service—UPS (**http://www.ups.com**):

- Market penetration—UPS is the world's largest package-delivery firm. It advertises extensively on TV and in magazines. The current slogan is "What Can Brown Do for You?" Daily, it handles more than 14 million packages and documents for 8 million customers.
- Market development—It is stepping up efforts around the world, where client use of delivery services tends to be much less than in the United States. In 1990, UPS International operated in 40 nations; now, it is operative in more than 200 countries and territories. The firm's Web site is accessible in 21 languages and dialects, and has dedicated content for more than 100 countries.
- Product development—UPS now offers more shipping choices than ever before, including SonicAir (same-day service), Next Day Air Early A.M., Next Day Air, Next Day Air Saver, 2nd Day Air A.M., 2nd Day Air, 3 Day Select, Ground, and various Worldwide Express services.
- Diversification—Though the major focus of UPS is on package delivery, it has such subsidiaries as UPS Supply Chain Solutions (**http://www.ups-scs.com**)—offering supply chain support, from transportation to customs; UPS Capital (**http://www.upscapital.com**)—a provider of financial and insurance solutions that lets businesses increase cash flow, limit exposure to loss, and strengthen their credit; UPS Professional Services (**http://www.ups-psi.com**)—a global management consulting group that delivers business solutions; and the UPS Store (**http://www.upsstore.com**), a 4,400-unit chain.[16] See Figure 3-6.

The Boston Consulting Group Matrix The *Boston Consulting Group matrix* lets a firm classify each SBU in terms of market share relative to key competitors and annual industry growth. A firm can see which SBUs are dominant compared to competitors and whether the industries in which it operates are growing, stable, or declining. The matrix comprises stars, cash cows, question marks, and dogs, as well as the strategies for them.[17] See Figure 3-7.

The assumption is that the higher an SBU's market share, the better its long-run marketplace position because of rather low per-unit costs and high profitability (**http://www.bcg.com**). This is due to economies of scale (larger firms can automate or

> The Boston Consulting Group matrix uses market share and industry growth to describe stars, cash cows, question marks, and dogs.

[16] Various sections, **http://www.ups.com** (March 9, 2006).
[17] "The Growth-Share Matrix," **http://www.bcg.com/this_is_bcg/mission/growth_share_matrix.jsp** (March 11, 2006).

Figure 3-6

The UPS Store

After acquiring the Mail Boxes Etc. chain, UPS renamed it under its corporate banner (**http://www.theupsstore.com**).

Source: Reprinted by permission of Susan Berry, Retail Image Consulting, Inc.

standardize production, service tasks, distribution, promotion, and so on), experience (as operations are repeated, a firm becomes more effective), and better bargaining power. At the same time, the industry growth rate indicates a firm's need to invest. A high growth rate means a substantial investment will be needed to maintain or expand the firm's position in a growing market.

A *star* is a leading SBU (high market share) in an expanding industry (high growth). The main goal is to sustain differential advantages despite rising competition. It can generate substantial profits but needs financing to grow. Market share can be kept or increased by intensive advertising, product introductions, greater distribution, and/or price reductions. As industry growth slows, a star becomes a cash cow.

A *cash cow* is a leading SBU (high market share) in a mature or declining industry (low growth). It often has loyal customers, making it hard for competitors. Because sales are rather steady, without high costs for product development and the like, a cash cow produces more cash (profit) than needed to hold its market share. Profits support the growth of other company SBUs. Marketing is oriented to reminder ads, periodic discounts, keeping up distribution channels, and offering new styles or options to encourage repurchases.

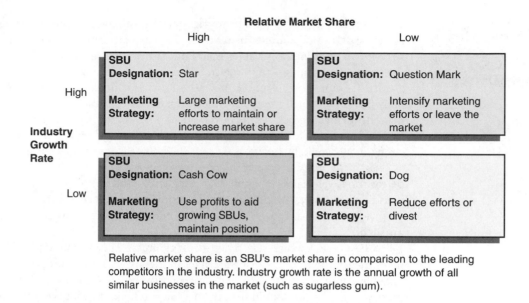

Relative Market Share

Relative market share is an SBU's market share in comparison to the leading competitors in the industry. Industry growth rate is the annual growth of all similar businesses in the market (such as sugarless gum).

Figure 3-7

The Boston Consulting Group Matrix

Source: Adapted from Bruce D. Henderson, "The Experience Curve Reviewed: IV. The Growth Share Matrix of the Product Portfolio" (Boston: Boston Consulting Group , 1973). *Perspectives*, No. 135.

A *question mark* is an SBU that has had little impact (low market share) in an expanding industry (high growth). There is low consumer support, differential advantages are weak, and competitors are leaders. To improve, a big marketing investment is needed in the face of strong competition. A firm must decide whether to beef up promotion, add distributors, improve product attributes, and cut prices—or to abandon the market. The choice depends on whether a firm believes the SBU can compete successfully with more support and what that support will cost.

A *dog* is an SBU with limited sales (low market share) in a mature or declining industry (low growth). Despite time in the marketplace, it has little customer interest—and lags behind competitors in sales, image, and so on. A dog usually has cost disadvantages and few growth opportunities. A firm with such an SBU can appeal to a specialized market, harvest profits by cutting support, or exit the market.

IBM (**http://www.ibm.com**) operates in five segments: global services—technology support and consulting; hardware—mainframe computers, servers, and more; software—mostly for businesses and institutions; global financing—client funding for systems, software, and services; and enterprise investments—which develops industry-specific information technology solutions supporting IBM's hardware, software, and global services segments (such as product life cycle management software that serves the industrial sector and helps customers manage the development and manufacturing of their products). The firm applies the principles suggested by the Boston Consulting Group matrix. It examines SBUs in terms of expected industry growth and market position, and then sets marketing strategies. In recent years, there has been a shift away from hardware—which contributed less than one-third of IBM's overall revenues in 2005 (down from 43 percent in 1998)—and toward global services, which accounted for 48 percent of sales in 2005 (up from 36 percent in 1998). The shift is due to a combination of declining hardware sales in a stagnant industry and the strong opportunities for information technology services.[18]

[18] *IBM Annual Reports.*

> The **General Electric business screen** measures industry attractiveness and company business strengths.

The General Electric Business Screen The *General Electric business screen* ategorizes SBUs and products in terms of industry attractiveness and company business strengths. It uses more variables than both the product/market opportunity matrix and the Boston Consulting Group matrix. Industry attractiveness depends on market size and growth, competition, technological advances, and the social/legal environment. Company business strengths embody differential advantages, market share, patent protection, marketing effectiveness, control over prices, and economies of scale. An SBU may have high, medium, or low industry attractiveness, as well as high, medium, or low business strengths; it would be positioned accordingly on the screen in Figure 3-8.[19]

SBUs in green are investment/growth areas. They are in strong industries and performing well. They are similar to stars in the Boston Consulting Group matrix. Full marketing resources are proper, and high profits are expected. Innovations, product-line extensions, product and image ads, distribution intensity, and solid price margins are pursued.

SBUs in yellow are selectivity/earnings areas. They are not positioned as well as investment/growth SBUs. An SBU may be strong in a weak industry (as a cash cow), okay in a somewhat attractive industry, or weak in an attractive industry (as a question mark). A firm wants to hold the earnings and strength of cash cows, and use marketing to maintain customer loyalty and distribution support. For question marks, a firm must decide whether to raise its marketing investment, focus on a specialized market niche, acquire another business in the industry, or trim product lines. The medium/medium SBU is an opportunity to appeal to underserved segments and invest selectively in marketing.

Figure 3-8

The General Electric Business Screen

Source: Maintaining Strategies for the Future Through Current Crises (Fairfield, CT: General Electric, 1975).

Industry Attractiveness

Invest/grow strategy

Selectivity/ earnings strategy

Harvest/divest strategy

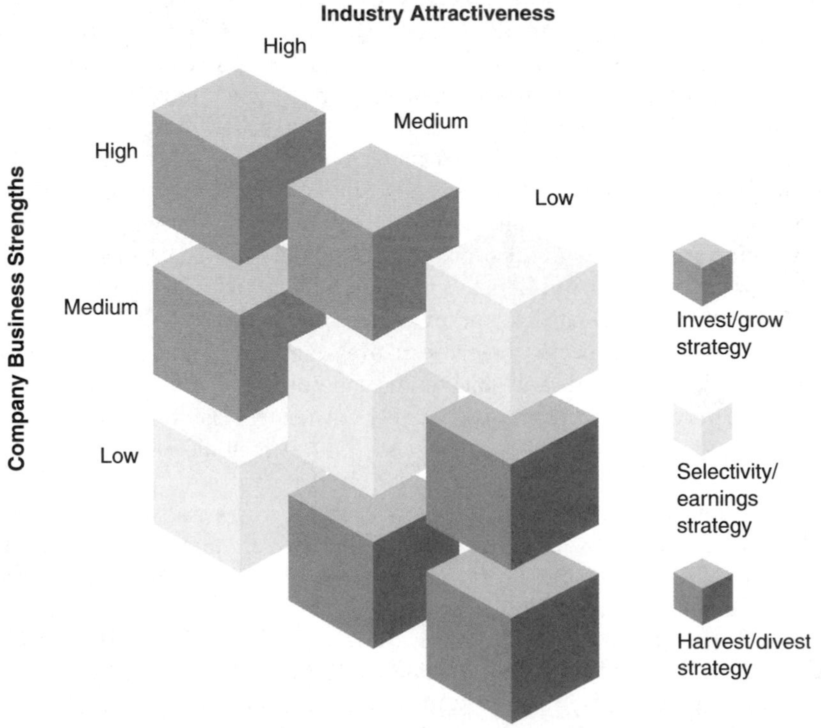

[19] "The GE/McKinsey Matrix," http://www.quickmba.com/strategy/matrix/ge-mckinsey (March 11, 2006); and David A. Aaker, *Strategic Marketing Management*, Seventh Edition (New York: Wiley, 2005).

SBUs in red represent harvest/divest areas. They are similar to dogs in the Boston Consulting Group matrix. A firm can minimize its marketing effort, concentrate on a few products rather than a product line, divest, or close down the SBU. Profits are harvested because investments are minimal.

Bausch & Lomb (**http://www.bausch.com**) applies the fundamentals of the business screen. It is building its current eye care businesses, as well as pursuing new opportunities within the global eye care market: "Bausch & Lomb is the eye health company dedicated to perfecting vision and enhancing life for consumers around the world. Its core businesses include soft and rigid gas permeable contact lenses and lens care products, and ophthalmic surgical and pharmaceutical products. The Bausch & Lomb name is one of the best known and most respected healthcare brands in the world. Founded in 1853, the Company is headquartered in Rochester, New York. It employs approximately 12,400 people worldwide and products are available in more than 100 countries."[20] To concentrate on its main businesses, Bausch & Lomb sold its sunglass SBU (featuring Ray-Ban), its Miracle Ear hearing aid SBU, and its animal research SBU.

Visit "Do You know GE?" (**http://www.ge.com/en/company/companyinfo/at_a_ glance/know_ge.htm**) to learn about the varied major contributions made by the firm that has given us the GE business screen.

The Porter Generic Strategy Model The ***Porter generic strategy model*** identifies two key marketing planning concepts and the options available for each: competitive scope (broad or narrow target) and competitive advantage (lower cost or differentiation). The model pinpoints these basic strategies: cost leadership, differentiation, and focus.[21] See Figure 3-9.

With a *cost-leadership strategy*, an SBU aims at a broad target market and offers goods or services in large quantities. Due to economies of scale, a firm can reduce per-unit costs and have low prices. This gives it higher profit margins than competitors, allows better response to cost rises, and/or lures price-conscious consumers. Among those using cost leadership are UPS (**http://www.ups.com**), DuPont (**http://www. dupont.com**), and Wal-Mart (**http://www.walmart.com**).

> The **Porter generic strategy model** distinguishes among cost leadership, differentiation, and focus strategies.

Competitive Advantage

Competitive Scope

Firm pursues a **COST LEADERSHIP STRATEGY** by targeting the mass market and featuring low prices.	Firm pursues a **DIFFERENTIATION STRATEGY** by targeting the mass market and featuring distinctive attributes in goods and/or services.
Firm pursues a **COST FOCUS STRATEGY** by targeting a niche market and featuring low prices.	Firm pursues a **DIFFERENTIATION FOCUS STRATEGY** by targeting a niche market and featuring distinctive attributes in goods and/or services.

Figure 3-9

The Porter Generic Strategy Model

Source: Tables developed by the authors based on concepts in Michael E. Porter, *Competitive Advantage: Creating and Sustaining Superior Performance* (New York: Free Press, 1985), pp. 11–16.

---

[20] "About Bausch & Lomb," **http://www.bausch.com/us/vision/about/index.jsp** (March 9, 2006).
[21] Michael E. Porter, *Competitive Advantage: Creating and Sustaining Superior Performance* (New York: Free Press, 1985), pp. 11–26; Michael E. Porter, *Competitive Strategy: Techniques for Analyzing Industries and Competitors* (New York: Free Press, 1980), pp. 34–46; and "Porter's Generic Strategies," **http://www.quickmba.com/strategy/ generic.shtml** (March 11, 2006).

In a *differentiation strategy*, an SBU aims at a large market by offering goods or services viewed as quite distinctive. The goods or services have a broad appeal, yet are perceived by consumers as unique by virtue of features, availability, reliability, and so on; price is less important. Among those using differentiation are Federal Express (**http://www.fedex.com**), Seiko (**http://www.seiko.com**), and Caterpillar Tractor (**http://www.cat.com**).

With a *focus strategy*, an SBU (which could be a small firm) seeks a narrow market segment via low prices or a unique offering. It can control costs by concentrating on a few key products aimed at specific consumers (cost focus) or by having a specialist reputation and serving a market unsatisfied by competitors (differentiation focus). Printek Direct! (**http://www.printekdirect.com**) markets refurbished printers to cost-conscious customers, while the Baby Jogger Company (**http://www.babyjogger.com**) makes a line of strollers for those who like jogging with their babies and toddlers. A neighborhood hardware store usually has a good combination of service, convenient location, and long hours; a local radio station may cater to an over-40 audience by playing mostly rock music from the 1960s, 1970s, and 1980s.

The Porter model shows that a small firm can profit by concentrating on one competitive niche, even though its total market share may be low. A firm does not have to be large to do well.

Evaluation of Strategic Planning Approaches The strategic planning approaches just discussed are widely used—at least informally. Many firms assess alternative market opportunities; know which products are stars, cash cows, question marks, and dogs; recognize what factors affect performance; understand their industries; and realize they can target broad or narrow customer bases. Formally, strategic planning models are most apt to be used by larger firms; and the models are adapted to the needs of the specific firms employing them.

The approaches' major strengths are that they let a firm analyze all SBUs and products, study the effects of various strategies, reveal the opportunities to pursue and the threats to avoid, compute marketing and other resource needs, focus on key differential advantages, compare performance with designated goals, and discover principles for improving. Competitors can also be studied.

> **Strategic models have pros and cons, and should be only part of planning.**

The approaches' major weaknesses are that they may be hard to use (particularly by a small firm), may be too simplistic and omit key factors, are somewhat arbitrary in defining SBUs and evaluative criteria (such as relative market share), may not be applicable to all firms and situations (a dog SBU may be profitable and generate cash), do not adequately account for environmental conditions (such as the economy), may overvalue market share, and are often used by staff planners rather than line managers.

These techniques are only planning aids. They do not replace the need for managers to engage in hands-on decisions by studying each situation and basing marketing strategies on the unique aspects of their industry, firm, and SBUs.

3-5f   Implementing Tactical Plans

A *tactical plan* specifies the short-run actions (tactics) that a firm undertakes in implementing a given marketing strategy. At this stage, a strategy is operationalized. A tactical plan has three basic elements: specific tasks, a time frame, and resource allocation.

> **A marketing strategy is enacted via tactical plans.**

The marketing mix (specific tasks) may range from a combination of high quality, high service, low distribution intensity, personal selling emphasis, and above-average prices to a combination of low quality, low service, high distribution intensity, advertising emphasis, and low prices. Each SBU should have a distinct marketing mix, based on its target market and strategic emphasis. The individual mix elements must be coordinated for each SBU, and conflicts among SBUs must be minimized.

Proper timing (time horizon) may mean being the first to introduce a product, bringing out a product when the market is most receptive, or quickly reacting to a competitor's strategy to catch it off guard. A firm must balance its desire to be an industry leader with clear-cut competitive advantages against its concern for the risk of being innovative. Marketing opportunities exist for limited times, and the firm needs to act accordingly.

Marketing investments (resources) may be order processing or order generating. Order-processing costs involve recording and handling orders, such as order entry, computer-data handling, and merchandise handling. The goal is to minimize those costs, subject to a given level of service. Order-generating costs, such as advertising and personal selling, produce revenues. Reducing them may be harmful to sales and profits. A firm should estimate sales at various levels of costs and for various combinations of marketing functions. Maximum profit rarely occurs at the lowest level of expenditure on order-generating costs.

Tactical decisions differ from strategic decisions in these ways. They

- are less complex and more structured.
- have a much shorter time horizon.
- require a considerably lower resource commitment.
- are enacted and adjusted more often.

PepsiCo's Frito-Lay (**http://www.fritolay.com**) "is the undisputed chip champ. The company makes some of the best-known and top-selling snack-food brands, including Cheetos, Doritos, Fritos, Lay's, Rold Gold, Ruffles, SunChips, and Tostitos. Frito-Lay also makes Grandma's cookies, Funyuns onion-flavored rings, Cracker Jack candy-coated popcorn, and Smartfood popcorn."[22] At Frito-Lay, tactical planning means regularly introducing new versions of its products, prepping delivery people and retailers for these products, aggressively promoting products, and maintaining profit margins—while not giving competitors a chance to win market share by maintaining lower prices, advertising heavily, and servicing retail accounts very well. On the other hand, small manufacturers may need to use outside food brokers to gain any access to food retailers. Even then, they may have a tough time getting chains as customers.

3-5g Monitoring Results

Monitoring results involves comparing the actual performance of a firm, business unit, or product against planned performance for a specified period. Actual performance data are then fed back into the strategic planning process. Budgets, timetables, sales and profit statistics, cost analyses, and image studies are just some measures that can be used to assess results.

> Performance is evaluated by **monitoring results**.

When actual performance lags, corrective action is needed. For instance, "When it comes time to implement a strategy, many companies find themselves stymied at the point of execution. Having identified the opportunities within their reach, they watch as the results fall short of their aspirations. Too few companies recognize the reason. Mismatched capabilities, poor asset configurations, and inadequate execution can all play their part in undermining a company's strategic objectives."[23]

Some plans must be revised due to the impact of uncontrollable factors on sales and costs. For this reason, many farsighted firms develop contingency plans to outline their potential responses in advance, should unfavorable conditions arise.

We discuss the techniques for evaluating marketing effectiveness in Chapter 22. The techniques are covered at the end of our book so that the fundamental elements of marketing are thoroughly explored first.

---

[22] "Frito-Lay, Inc.," http://www.hoovers.com/frito-lay/--ID_48009--/free-co-factsheet.xhtml (March 9, 2006).
[23] Tsun-yan Hsieh and Sara Yik, "Leadership as the Starting Point of Strategy," *McKinsey Quarterly* (Number 1, 2005), p. 67.

Global Marketing in Action

Chevron: Introducing a New Gasoline Additive Worldwide

Chevron (http://www.chevron.com) recently began to sell gasoline with the ingredient Techron at its gasoline stations in the United States and at many stations throughout Latin America. This marks the initial phase of Chevron's selling Techron in all of its markets worldwide. Techron will eventually be sold in such major markets as Asia, Africa, and Europe, as well as in all grades of gasoline sold by the company. Chevron will be the first oil company to include a branded additive in all of its global markets. This strategy enables Chevron to use standardized promotions in all countries. It also raises its level of gasoline performance worldwide.

Techron helps prevent deposit build-up on intake valves and fuel injectors that can impact a vehicle's performance and emissions. Techron also cleans an engine's intake system while it minimizes combustion chamber deposits that can cause knocking, the loss of power during acceleration, and higher levels of emissions. According to one Chevron executive, "Not only do gasolines with Techron help keep those engine parts clean, but they also help remove deposits left by gasolines with lower-quality additive packages."

As a result of the merger of Chevron and Texaco that took place in 2001, both Chevron and Shell had the rights to use the Texaco brand in the United States market until July 1, 2006. As of that date, Chevron acquired exclusive rights to the Texaco brand. Only Chevron-supplied stations, however, can sell gasolines with the Techron additive.

Source: Based on material in "ChevronTexaco Launches Techron Globally," *Business Wire* (May 2, 2005).

3-6   DEVISING A STRATEGIC MARKETING PLAN

> Written documents aid strategic marketing planning and are useful for all sorts of firms.

A firm can best create, implement, and monitor a strategic marketing plan when it has a written plan. This encourages executives to carefully think out and coordinate each step in the planning process, better pinpoint problem areas, be consistent, tie the plan to goals and resources, measure performance, and send a clear message to employees and others. A sample outline for a written strategic plan and an application of strategic planning by a small firm are covered next.

3-6a   A Sample Outline for a Written Strategic Marketing Plan

What are the ingredients of a good strategic marketing plan? It should:

- be integrated into an organization's overall business plan.
- affect the consideration of strategic choices.
- press a long-range view.
- make the resource allocation system visible.
- provide methods to help strategic analysis and decision making.
- be a basis for managing a firm or SBU strategically.
- offer a communication and coordination system both horizontally (between SBUs and departments) and vertically (from senior executives to front-line employees).
- help a firm and its SBUs cope with change.[24]

Table 3-2 presents a sample outline for a written strategic marketing plan. This outline may be used by firms of any size or type. *[Please note: There is a comprehensive strategic marketing plan exercise accompanying this book. It is described in the appendix at the end of the chapter. If you are online, you may access the exercise by clicking on the special computer icon. In addition, at the beginning of each part of the text, there is a planning icon.*

---

[24] Adapted by the authors from Aaker, *Strategic Marketing Management.*

If you are online, click on the icon to review the implications of what you learn in that part from a strategic marketing plan perspective.]

3-6b Moonstruck Chocolate Company: A Strategic Marketing Plan by a Small Specialty Firm[25]

In 1993, Bill Simmons and his wife Deb opened Moonstruck Chocolate Company (then known as Moonstruck Chocolatier) in Portland, Oregon. When it began, Moonstruck was exclusively a maker of truffles for the wholesale market. It sold to retailers such as Neiman Marcus, Marshall Field, and Starbucks. The firm introduced it first retail store in 1996 and sales rose rapidly. Today, Moonstruck is a successful firm specializing in chocolate-based products, with annual sales approaching $4 million and high-powered goals for the future. Why? The firm has created, implemented, and monitored a solid strategic marketing plan. Let's look at the highlights of Moonstruck's plan.

> Although a small company, Moonstruck Chocolate has a detailed strategic marketing plan.

Organizational Mission Moonstruck has a clear mission: to bring the higher European standard for chocolate to the American marketplace and to create chocolate cafés that serve as a meeting place in a busy, impersonal world. To do so, Moonstruck is "romancing" the cocoa bean and educating customers, as Starbucks did with coffee.

In 2001, Dave and Sally Bany acquired the firm. They were searching for a small business to take national: "One taste of Moonstruck's products and they were hooked. To make fitting use of a well-worn phrase, they liked it so much they bought the company." The Banys want to grow the cafés, the wholesale business, direct sales (through 1-800-557-MOON), and sales from the Web site.

Organizational Structure Dave and Sally Bany manage the business. They participate in new-product discussions, assist with local deliveries, conduct factory tours, and otherwise run things. The firm has a staff of nearly 100 employees (150 during major holiday seasons), including a team of chocolatiers who "quietly work away on a variety of confections, hand-crafted, dipped, and decorated, ranging from toffee to truffles to chocolate bars. One chocolate can take as much as 36 hours to finish. Head chocolatier Robert Hammond tests new flavors and ideas. And the arduous quest for a tasty sugar-free (or diabetic) chocolate continues."

Marketing Objectives Moonstruck has ambitious goals. Sales have been increasing nicely due to the debut of various popular new chocolate lines, the opening of two new stores, and expansion of the wholesale portion of its business. As Sally Bany says, "We want to be a national brand and we're well on our way to that as long as we keep making great products."

Situation Analysis Founders Bill and Deb Simmons formulated their strategic plan based on Starbucks, the retail coffee giant. They did a comprehensive analysis of Starbucks' business model before opening Moonstruck. As they commented in *Inc.*, "What really lit a fuse under Starbucks was not just its commitment to better beans but its move into retail—selling coffee by the cup. The stores were decorated with bins of coffee beans, photos of coffee trees, and shelves of gleaming coffee paraphernalia. Employees were trained to educate customers about what they were drinking and why it tasted good. For many, the experience was so engaging that Starbucks became a natural

---

[25] The material in this section is based on **http://www.moonstruckchocolate.com** (March 14, 2006); Phil Lempert, "Moonstruck Chocolate," *Gourmet Retailer* (June 2005), p. 143; Elizabeth Fuhrman, "A New Moon," *Candy Industry* (June 2004), pp. 28–33; Gillian Drummond, "Hot Chocolate," *Caterer & Hotelkeeper* (August 14, 2003), pp. 29–30; and Edward O. Welles, "The Next Starbucks," *Inc.* (January 2001), pp. 48–53.

Table 3-2   A Sample Outline for a Written Strategic Marketing Plan

Using as much detail as possible, please address each of these points for your organization:

1. Organizational Mission
   a. In 50 words or less, describe the current mission of your organization.
   b. In 50 words or less, describe how you would like your organizational mission to evolve over the next five years and the next ten years.
   c. How is the organizational mission communicated to employees?

2. Organizational Structure
   a. State and assess the current organizational structure of your organization.
   b. Does your organization have strategic business units? If yes, describe them. If no, why not?
   c. Does each major product or business unit in your organization have a marketing manager, proper resources, and clear competitors? Explain your answer.

3. Marketing Objectives
   a. Cite your organization's overall marketing goals for the next one, three, five, and ten years.
   b. Cite your organization's specific marketing goals by target market and product category for the next one, five, and ten years in terms of sales, market share, profit, image, and customer loyalty.
   c. What criteria will be used to determine whether goals have been fully, partially, or unsatisfactorily reached?

4. Situation Analysis
   a. Describe the present overall strengths, weaknesses, opportunities, and threats (SWOT) facing your organization.
   b. For each of the key products or businesses of your organization, describe the present strengths, weaknesses, opportunities, and threats.
   c. How do you expect the factors noted in your answers to (a) and (b) to change over the next five to ten years?
   d. How will your organization respond to the factors mentioned in the answer for (c)?
   e. Describe the methods your organization uses to acquire, distribute, and store the information necessary to make good marketing decisions.

5. Developing Marketing Strategy
   a. Compare your organization's overall strategy with those of leading competitors.
   b. Describe your organization's use of these strategic approaches: market penetration, market development, product development, and diversification.
   c. Categorize each of your organization's products or businesses as a star, cash cow, question mark, or dog. Explain your reasoning.
   d. For each product or business, which of these approaches is most appropriate: invest/grow, selectivity/earnings, or harvest/divest? Explain your reasoning.
   e. For each of your organization's products or businesses, which of these approaches is most appropriate: cost leadership, differentiation, cost focus, or differentiation focus? Explain your reasoning.

6. Societal, Ethical, and Consumer Issues
   a. What is your organization's view of its responsibilities regarding societal, ethical, and consumer issues?
   b. How are organizational policies developed with regard to societal, ethical, and consumer issues?
   c. Discuss your organization's social responsibility approach in terms of the general public, employees, channel members, stockholders, and competitors.
   d. State your organization's code of ethics and how acceptable ethical practices are communicated to employees.
   e. Describe your organization's strategy for dealing with consumers' basic rights (information and education, safety, choice, and to be heard).

7. Global Marketing
   a. What is the role of global marketing in your organization's overall strategy?
   b. Describe the cultural, economic, political and legal, and technological environment in each major and potential foreign market that your organization faces.
   c. Describe your organization's strategy in terms of which and how many foreign markets your organization should enter.
   d. Develop an appropriate organizational format for each current and potential foreign market.
   e. State the extent to which your organization utilizes a standardized, nonstandardized, or glocal marketing approach in its foreign markets.
   f. Explain how your organization's marketing mix varies by foreign market.

8. Marketing and the Internet
   a. Does your organization use the Internet (Web) in its marketing strategy? If no, why not?
   b. If your organization uses the Web, does it engage in E-marketing rather than just in E-commerce? If no, why not?
   c. If your organization uses the Web, what are the marketing-related goals?
   d. If your organization uses the Web, is a systematic Internet marketing strategy applied? If no, why not?

(continued)

Using as much detail as possible, please address each of these points for your organization:

9. Consumer Analysis and Target Market Strategy
   a. What are the demographic characteristics of the target market segments served or potentially served by your organization?
   b. What are the lifestyle and decision-making characteristics of the target market segments served or potentially served by your organization?
   c. Do you market to final consumers, organizations, or both? How does this approach affect your overall marketing strategy?
   d. Describe the important consumer trends that could have a major effect on your organization.
   e. Explain the demand patterns that exist for your organization's products (homogeneous, clustered, or diffused).
   f. Describe your organization's choice of target market strategy (undifferentiated, differentiated, or concentrated marketing) and target market(s).
   g. Does your organization understand and utilize such concepts as derived demand, the heavy-usage segment, and benefit segmentation? Why or why not?
   h. State how your marketing mix(es) is (are) appropriate for the target market(s) chosen.
   i. What sales forecasting procedures are used by your organization? How are they related to your target market strategy?

10. Product Planning
    a. Describe your organization's products from the perspective of tangible, augmented, and generic product concepts.
    b. Are your organization's products viewed as convenience, shopping, or specialty products by consumers? How does this placement affect the marketing strategy?
    c. Discuss the rationale behind the width, depth, and consistency of your organization's product mix.
    d. Describe your organization's product management organization.
    e. Discuss your organization's competitive and company product positioning for each product/brand.
    f. Describe your organization's use of corporate symbols and its branding strategy.
    g. Outline your organization's overall packaging strategy.
    h. What kinds of goods (durable and/or nondurable) and services (rented-goods, owned-goods, and/or nongoods) are sold by your organization? What are the ramifications of this for the marketing strategy?
    i. How are your organization's products positioned along the goods/service continuum? What are the ramifications of this for the marketing strategy?
    j. Describe your organization's new-product planning process.
    k. In what product life-cycle stage is each of your organization's major product groupings?
    l. How can your organization extend the life-cycle stage for those products now in the introduction, growth, and maturity life-cycle stages?

11. Distribution Planning
    a. How are channel functions allocated among distribution intermediaries and your organization?
    b. Explain how relationship marketing is used in your organization's channel of distribution.
    c. State your organization's distribution approach with regard to channel length (direct or indirect) and channel width (exclusive, selective, or intensive distribution), and whether a dual distribution strategy is appropriate.
    d. Present an approach for your organization's achieving and maintaining channel cooperation.
    e. Describe your organization's overall logistics strategy (including transportation modes, inventory management, and foreign distribution).
    f. Explain your organization's choice of wholesaler type and your choice of specific wholesalers.
    g. Explain your organization's choice of retailer type and your choice of specific retailers.
    h. How are wholesalers and retailers evaluated by your organization?

12. Promotion Planning
    a. State your organization's broad promotion goals and the importance of each one.
    b. Discuss your organization's overall promotion plan from the perspective of integrated marketing communications; and describe the roles of advertising, public relations, personal selling, and sales promotion at your organization.
    c. Describe how your organization determines its overall promotional budget.
    d. For each element of the promotional mix (advertising, public relations, personal selling, and sales promotion):
       ❑ Set specific goals.
       ❑ Assign responsibility.
       ❑ Establish a budget.
       ❑ Develop a strategy (such as themes/messages/selling techniques/promotions, media choice, timing, cooperative efforts).
       ❑ Set criteria for assessing success or failure.
    e. Describe how your organization's promotion efforts vary by target market and product.
    f. At your organization, what is the role for new communications formats and technologies (such as the World Wide Web, electronic in-store point-of-purchase displays, and hand-held computers for salespeople)?

13. Price Planning
    a. Explain your organization's overall pricing approach (price-based versus nonprice-based) and how you determine the "value" your organization provides to consumers.

(continued)

Using as much detail as possible, please address each of these points for your organization:

    b. Categorize your organization's target market(s) in terms of price sensitivity, and state how this affects the pricing strategy.

    c. What is your organization's pricing philosophy for dealing with cost increases or decreases?

    d. What practices does your organization follow to ensure compliance with all government rules about pricing?

    e. Describe the role each channel member (including your organization) plays in setting prices.

    f. Explain the competitive pricing environment your organization faces.

    g. State your firm's specific pricing objectives.

    h. Describe your organization's price strategy with regard to its use of cost-based, demand-based, and/or competition-based pricing.

    i. When your organization implements a price strategy, which of these elements does it use: customary versus variable pricing, one-price versus flexible pricing, odd pricing, the price-quality association, leader pricing, multiple-unit pricing, price lining, price bundling, geographic pricing, purchase terms, and price adjustments?

14. Integrating and Analyzing the Marketing Plan

    a. Describe your organization's processes for integrating and analyzing its marketing plans.

    b. Detail how the long-term, moderate-term, and short-term plans are compatible.

    c. Explain how the elements of the marketing mix are coordinated.

    d. Are ongoing marketing budgets sufficient? Does your organization differentiate between order-generating and order-processing costs? Explain your answers.

    e. How do you expect competitors to react as you implement your organization's strategy?

    f. Discuss how your organization utilizes benchmarking, customer satisfaction research, marketing cost analysis, sales analysis, and the marketing audit.

15. Revising the Marketing Plan

    a. What contingency plans does your organization have in place if there are unexpected results?

    b. Are marketing plans revised as conditions warrant? Explain your answer.

    c. Is your organization reactive or proactive in its approach to revising marketing plans? Explain your answer.

Note: Points 1–5 relate to Part 1 in the text.
    Points 6–8 relate to Part 2 in the text.
    Point 9 relates to Part 3 in the text.
    Point 10 relates to Part 4 in the text.
    Point 11 relates to Part 5 in the text.
    Point 12 relates to Part 6 in the text.
    Point 13 relates to Part 7 in the text.
    Points 14–15 relate to Part 8 in the text.

gathering place, and that made the brand familiar. The more we poked at the Starbucks model, the better it looked." The Banys are following the approach of applying Starbucks' principles to fine chocolate.

Developing Marketing Strategy The two strategic planning approaches with the most relevance for Moonstruck are the product/market opportunity matrix and the Porter generic strategy model. The firm is engaged in both a product development strategy (producing distinctive new chocolate products for current chocolate customers) and a market development strategy (seeking out those who have not thought of chocolate beverages as "must have" drinks). It is a great believer in a differentiation strategy (superior products at a premium price).

Societal, Ethical, and Consumer Issues Moonstruck uses the highest-quality ingredients. It treats employees and customers courteously, honestly, and respectfully. The firm stands behind all of the products it makes and sells, and is socially responsible.

Global Marketing Moonstruck searches the globe for the best cocoa beans, consistent with its organizational mission: "Our chocolate products are made with only the finest, freshest ingredients. The company's chocolate originates from rare cocoa beans that are among the highest quality produced anywhere in the world. When properly fermented and roasted, the cocoa seeds achieve fine profiles of unique flavors with nuances of fresh flowers, ripe fruits, and rich woods."

Marketing and the Internet Moonstruck has a colorful, animated, well-planned Web site (**http://www.moonstruckchocolates.com**) that describes the background of the company and the products it makes. The site also lists the firm's retail locations and permits online ordering.

Consumer Analysis and Target Market Strategy Moonstruck appeals to customers who are interested in quality, uniqueness, assortment, and service—and are willing to pay for it. The firm has two market segments: final consumers (who buy for personal use and in small quantities) and corporate customers (who buy products as gifts and in larger quantities).

Product Planning Moonstruck has greatly expanded its product line since the early days, adding products that complement each other well. Today, the product line includes chocolate truffles, chocolate bars, chocolate pecan clusters, chocolate pops, chocolate mints, toffee, hot cocoa mixes, chocolate and espresso drinks (at its cafés), and lots more.

Distribution Planning As already noted, Moonstruck offers products in many venues: its own cafés, retail stores, telemarketing, and the Web. Its retail cafés are changing. The new prototype features the firm's moon logo, chocolate-colored swirls woven into the ceiling and carpeting, and seating for about 20 to 25 people.

Promotion Planning Moonstruck uses in-store tastings and demonstrations to draw customers into impulse purchases. It also does some print advertising. But its biggest promotion effort revolves around the publicity it receives from newspaper and magazine stories. In 2005, the firm received a lot of publicity by being included in the Annual Academy Award Gift Basket, which is given out to celebrities for attending the awards ceremony ("chocolate for the stars").

Price Planning Moonstruck has above-average prices, reflective of the quality and status accorded its products. Most revenues are from high-margin chocolate truffles and drinks. For example, one 16 piece truffle collection in a special gift box retails for $36.00 and one 9-piece truffle collection in a standard box retails for $18.

Integrating and Analyzing the Plan The Banys constantly keep their eye on the ball. They recognize that every decision they make reflects on the image and performance of Moonstruck Chocolate. The couple regularly monitors performance and looks for ideas that fit within their overall vision for the firm.

Revising the Marketing Plan Unlike Bill and Deb Simmons, the Banys are not big believers in franchising as a mechanism for future growth in Moonstruck Chocolate Cafés. As Dave Bany says, "I understand it's pretty difficult to control quality, and that makes me hesitant." Retail expansion will be funded by the Banys and, perhaps, some outside investors in the company.

Web Sites You Can Use

A variety of Web sites provide step-by-step advice on strategic planning and many even have free, downloadable, easy-to-use templates. Here we present a number of such sites, divided into two categories: strategic business plans and strategic marketing plans:

Strategic Business Plans
- BizMove.com—*Developing a Successful Business Plan* (**http://www.bizmove.com/small-business/business-plan.htm**)
- Bplans.com—*How to Write a Business Plan* (**http://www.bplans.com/dp**)

- Business Owner's Toolkit—*Writing Your Business Plan* (**http://www.toolkit.cch.com/text/p02_5001.asp**)
- Center for Business Planning—*Planning Guidelines* (**http://www.businessplans.org/guide.html**)
- Inc.—*Writing a Business Plan* (**http://www.inc.com/guides/write_biz_plan**)
- Edward Lowe Foundation—*How to Create a Long-Run Plan* (**http://edwardlowe.org/index.peer?page=main&storyid=0054**)
- PlanWare—*Writing a Business Plan* (**http://www.planware.org/bizplan.htm**)

- Tutor2You—*Strategy: What Is a Strategy?* (**http://www.tutor2u.net/business/strategy/what_is_strategy.htm**)

Strategic Marketing Plans
- BizMove.com—*Small Business Marketing* (**http://www.bizmove.com/small-business/marketing.htm**)
- Bplans.com—*Sample Marketing Plans* (**http://www.bplans.com/sp/marketingplans.cfm**)
- Business Resource Software—*Marketing Plan* (**http://www.businessplans.org/Market.html**)
- Inc.—*Marketing Guides* (**http://www.inc.com/guides/marketing**)

- Edward Lowe Foundation—*Marketing Resource Guide* (**http://edwardlowe.org/index.peer?page=ENTstartupguide&part=4**)
- Morebusiness.com—*Marketing Department* (**http://www.morebusiness.com/running_your_business/marketing**)
- Morebusiness.com—*Sample Marketing Plan* (**http://www.morebusiness.com/templates_worksheets/bplans/printpre.brc**)
- U.S. Chamber of Commerce—*Building a Successful Marketing Plan* (**http://www.uschamber.com/sb/business/P03/P03_8000.asp**)

Summary

1. *To define strategic planning and consider its importance for marketing* Strategic planning encompasses both strategic business plans and strategic marketing plans. Strategic business plans describe the overall direction firms will pursue within their chosen environment and guide the allocation of resources and effort. Strategic marketing plans outline what marketing actions to undertake, why those actions are needed, who is responsible for carrying them out, when and where they will be completed, and how they will be coordinated.

   Strategic planning provides guidance via a hierarchical process, clarifies goals, encourages departmental cooperation, focuses on strengths and weaknesses (as well as opportunities and threats), examines alternatives, helps allocate resources, and points out the value of monitoring results.

2. *To describe the total quality approach to strategic planning and show its relevance to marketing* A total quality approach should be used in devising and enacting business and marketing plans. In that way, a firm adopts a process- and output-related philosophy, by which it strives to fully satisfy consumers in an effective and efficient manner. Customer focus; top management commitment; emphasis on continuous improvement; and support and involvement from employees, suppliers, and channel members are all involved.

3. *To look at the different kinds of strategic plans and the relationships between marketing and the other functional areas in an organization* A firm's strategic plans may be short run, moderate in length, or long run. Strategic marketing plans may be for each major product, presented as one company-wide marketing plan, or considered part of an overall business plan. A bottom-up, top-down, or combined management approach may be used.

   The interests of marketing and the other functional areas in a firm need to be accommodated in a strategic plan. Departmental conflict can be reduced by improving communications, employing personnel with broad backgrounds, establishing interdepartmental programs, and blending departmental goals.

4. *To describe thoroughly each of the steps in the strategic planning process* First, a firm defines its organizational mission—the long-term commitment to a type of business and a place in the market. Second, it establishes strategic business units (SBUs), the self-contained divisions, product lines, or product departments with specific market focuses and separate managers. Third, quantitative and qualitative marketing objectives are set. Fourth, through situation analysis, a firm identifies its internal strengths and weaknesses, as well as external opportunities and threats.

   Fifth, a firm develops a marketing strategy—to outline the way in which the marketing mix is used to attract and satisfy the target market(s) and accomplish organizational goals. Every SBU has its own marketing mix. The approaches to strategy planning include the product/market opportunity matrix, the Boston Consulting Group matrix, the General Electric business screen, and the Porter generic strategy model. They should be viewed as planning tools that aid decision making; they do not replace the need for executives to engage in hands-on planning for each situation.

   Sixth, a firm uses tactical plans to specify the short-run actions necessary to implement a given marketing strategy. At this stage, specific tasks, a time horizon, and resource allocation are made operational. Seventh, a firm monitors results by comparing actual performance against planned performance, and this information is fed back into the strategic planning process. Adjustments in strategy are made as needed.

5. *To show how a strategic marketing plan may be devised and applied* Strategic marketing plans work best when they are integrated within the overall strategic business plan, and are prepared systematically and comprehensively—as illustrated in Table 3-2. This is exemplified by Moonstruck Chocolate, a small confectionary firm.

Key Terms

strategic business plan (p. 55)

strategic marketing plan (p. 55)

total quality (p. 56)

strategic planning process (p. 61)

organizational mission (p. 61)

strategic business unit (SBU) (p. 62)

situation analysis (p. 64)

marketing strategy (p. 65)

product/market opportunity matrix (p. 65)

Boston Consulting Group matrix (p. 67)

General Electric business screen (p. 70)

Porter generic strategy model (p. 71)

tactical plan (p. 72)

monitoring results (p. 73)

Review Questions

1. Explain Figure 3-2, which deals with the total quality approach.
2. Distinguish between bottom-up and top-down strategic plans. What are the pros and cons of each?
3. Why are conflicts between marketing and other functional areas inevitable? How can these conflicts be reduced or avoided?
4. Under what circumstances should a company consider reappraising its organizational mission?
5. In situation analysis, what is the distinction between strengths and opportunities and between weaknesses and threats? How should a firm react to each of these factors?
6. Distinguish between the Boston Consulting Group matrix and the Porter generic strategy model.
7. Explain how tactical decisions differ from strategic decisions.
8. What are the ingredients of a good strategic marketing plan?

Discussion Questions

1. Do you think your college or university is following a total quality approach? Why or why not? What total quality recommendations would you make for your school?
2. What issues should a small grocery store chain study during situation analysis? How could it react to those issues?
3. Give a current example of each of these strategic approaches: market development, product development, market penetration, and diversification. Evaluate the strategies.
4. Develop a rating scale to use in analyzing the industry attractiveness and company business strengths of a large travel agency, a small printer manufacturer, or a medium-sized auto parts manufacturer.

Web Exercise

Bplans.com (http://www.bplans.com/sp/marketingplans.cfm) offers several free sample marketing plans at its Web site. Take a look at the sample marketing plan for Soapy Rides Car Wash (http://www.bplans.com/spv/3469/index.cfm?affiliate=pas), a car wash for luxury vehicles, and critique it. What could a prospective competitor learn from studying this plan?

Practice Quiz

1. An organization's direction within its chosen environment and its allocation of resources is usually determined by
   a. strategic planning.
   b. tactics.
   c. diversification.
   d. strategic business units.

2. Separate marketing plans for each product line are often used by
   a. service firms.
   b. industrial-goods manufacturers.
   c. consumer-goods manufacturers.
   d. local governments.

3. Which of these is *not* a way to drop tension among functional departments?
   a. Setting objectives for each department that are completely independent of other departments' goals
   b. Encouraging interfunctional contact
   c. Seeking employees who blend technical and marketing expertise
   d. Establishing interfunctional task forces and committees

4. Organizational mission refers to
   a. specific actions undertaken to implement a given marketing strategy.
   b. a long-term commitment to a type of business and a place in the market.

    c. a strategy in which a firm seeks greater sales of present products or new product uses.

    d. a technique by which an organization individually assesses and positions every strategic business unit.

5. According to the strategic planning process, the next step after a firm defines its organizational mission is to
    a. set marketing objectives.
    b. perform situation analysis.
    c. develop marketing strategies.
    d. establish strategic business units.

6. An example of a qualitative term that can be used to describe objectives is
    a. percentage profit growth.
    b. dollar sales.
    c. market share.
    d. level of innovativeness.

7. Which of the following questions does situation analysis seek to answer?
    a. How will resources be allocated?
    b. Who is responsible for carrying out marketing actions?
    c. In what direction is a firm headed?
    d. What marketing actions should be undertaken?

8. As part of a product development strategy, a firm could
    a. develop new models of existing products to appeal to present markets.
    b. reposition existing products.
    c. become involved with new products aimed at new markets.
    d. seek to attract nonusers of its existing products.

9. A strategic business unit with a high market share in an expanding industry is a
    a. question mark.
    b. star.
    c. dog.
    d. cash cow.

10. The General Electric business screen looks at two major dimensions: industry attractiveness and
    a. company business strengths.
    b. target market features.
    c. market share.
    d. profitability.

11. Strategic business units shown in investment/growth areas of the General Electric business screen are
    a. performing well in unattractive industries.
    b. performing poorly in unattractive industries.
    c. performing well in strong industries.
    d. performing poorly in strong industries.

12. According to the Porter generic strategy model, with a differentiation strategy, a strategic business unit
    a. aims at a large market by offering goods or services viewed as distinctive.
    b. seeks a narrow target segment through low prices or a unique offering.
    c. aims a new product at a new market.
    d. appeals to a broad market and offers products at low prices and in large quantities.

13. A major weakness of the strategic planning approaches discussed in this chapter is that they
    a. prevent a firm from analyzing all its business units and products.
    b. do not focus on creating and keeping key differential advantages.
    c. do not allow a firm to follow competitors' actions.
    d. are sometimes difficult to implement.

14. The level of investment in specific marketing activities and the timing of marketing actions are decisions relating to
    a. establishing SBUs.
    b. developing marketing strategy.
    c. monitoring results.
    d. implementing tactics.

15. Monitoring results involves
    a. establishing strategic business units.
    b. comparing actual performance to planned performance for a specified time period.
    c. setting marketing objectives.
    d. identifying internal strengths and weaknesses, as well as external opportunities and threats.

For the answers to these questions, please visit the online site for this book at **http://www.atomicdog.com.**

3 Appendix

Strategic Marketing Plan

In Chapter 3, we presented a detailed sample outline for preparing a written strategic marketing plan (Table 3-2). Throughout *Marketing*, the part-opening pages refer to the specific sections of the sample plan that apply to each of the eight parts in the book.

To provide you with more insight into strategic marketing plans, we have prepared the special computer exercise that is described in this appendix. It is called *StratMktPlan*. You may access the exercise by clicking on the icon or by going to our Web site (**http://www.atomicdog.com**).

StratMktPlan is based on the sample outline in Chapter 3. From that outline, we have selected a cross section of questions for you to address. You will be assigned to a specific firm and gear your answers toward it. Answers are typed directly into easy-to-use drop-down windows. The exercise outline is shown in Table 1.

By answering all *StratMktPlan* questions, you prepare a comprehensive strategic marketing plan. Depending on your professor's goals, different students or student teams can be assigned to competing companies in the same industry, or assigned to companies with totally different strategies and resources. One student or team can be assigned to a national firm selling mass-appeal products, and another group is assigned to a local firm selling a product for a niche market.

You are encouraged to use secondary sources (including the Web) to devise a marketing plan when working on the *StratMktPlan* computer exercise. SWOT analysis (strengths, weaknesses, opportunities, and threats) should include data derived from secondary sources.

There are two ways in which your professor can assign the *StratMktPlan* exercise: (1) You or a team of students can be

Table 1   *StratMktPlan* Exercise Outline

Develop an integrated strategic marketing plan for the assigned company by addressing each of the questions below.

Organizational Mission
- In 50 words or less, describe the current mission of your organization.

Marketing Goals
- Cite your organization's overall marketing goals for the next one, three, five, and ten years.

Situation Analysis
- Describe the present overall strengths, weaknesses, opportunities, and threats (SWOT) facing your organization.

Developing Marketing Strategy
- Compare your organization's overall strategy with those of leading competitors.

Societal, Ethical, and Consumer Issues
- What is your organization's view of its responsibilities regarding societal, ethical, and consumer issues?

Global Marketing
- What is the role of global marketing in your organization's overall strategy?

Marketing and the Internet
- Does your organization use the Internet (Web) in its marketing strategy? If no, why not?

Consumer Analysis and Target Market Strategy
- What are the demographic characteristics of the target market segments served or potentially served by your organization?
- Do you market to final consumers, organizations, or both? How does this approach affect your overall marketing strategy?
- Describe your organization's choice of target market strategy (undifferentiated, differentiated, or concentrated marketing) and target market(s).

(continued)

Product Planning

- Describe your organization's products from the perspective of tangible, augmented, and generic product concepts.
- Discuss the rationale behind the width, depth, and consistency of your organization's product mix.

Distribution Planning

- Explain how relationship marketing is used in your organization's channel of distribution.
- State your organization's distribution approach with regard to channel length (direct or indirect) and channel width (exclusive, selective, or intensive distribution), and whether a dual distribution strategy is appropriate.

Promotion Planning

- State your organization's broad promotion goals and the importance of each one.
- Discuss your organization's overall promotional plan from the perspective of integrated marketing communications, and describe the roles for advertising, public relations, personal selling, and sales promotion at your organization.

Price Planning

- Explain your organization's overall pricing approach (price-based versus nonprice-based) and how you determine the "value" your organization provides to consumers.
- Categorize your organization's target market(s) in terms of price sensitivity, and state how this affects the pricing strategy.

Integrating and Organizing the Marketing Plan

- How do you expect competitors to react as you implement your organization's strategy?

Revising the Marketing Plan

- What contingency plans does your organization have in place if there are unexpected results?

requested to hand in *StratMktPlan* assignments one part at a time, with submissions spaced out over the term. (2) You or a team of students can be requested to work on *StratMktPlan* as a comprehensive course assignment, with one overall submission at the end of the semester.

We have included in the *StratMktPlan* computer exercise an illustration of a strategic marketing plan for College Logo Clothing and More, based on the Table 1 questions in this appendix. College Logo Clothing and More is a private, profit-oriented store located within 1 mile of your campus. This retailer competes with your campus store in selling merchandise that contains college logos (such as clothing, writing implements, and leather goods). Although the specific answers in this illustration may not be directly applicable to another company, the example should stimulate your thinking and give you a better idea of how to handle the questions.

Chapter 4

Information for Marketing Decisions

About 80 years ago, Arthur C. Nielsen, Sr. pioneered many important concepts in marketing research, including devising a system for rating radio and television programs, as well as measuring retail sales. Nielsen is also credited with developing equipment to determine which radio and TV programs consumers listened to and watched, as well as a scanning device that enables retailers to collect timely data on weekly sales by item. Prior to Nielsen, radio stations would ask listeners to mail in postcards to let the stations know if they enjoyed particular programs. Firms such as Post Cereal and Kellogg would monitor their sales by counting the number of freight cars going in and out of their warehouses.

One of the major initial obstacles to the development of marketing research at A.C. Nielsen (**http://www.acnielsen.com**) was getting retailers to give the firm access to data. Large grocery chains, such as Kroger and Safeway, were initially concerned that competitors would use the data to learn their specific strategies. Nielsen eventually was able to convince these retailers that they needed to know their market share, as well as what was selling in their total market area, while protecting their proprietary data.

Nielsen is now a division of VNU (**http://www.vnu.com**), a Netherlands-based information provider and the world's leading provider of retail sales data. It compiles data from in-store scanners and in-store audits in more than 80 nations. Retailers use the data to assess their market share, pricing levels, and promotions. Nielsen has a consumer panel of more than 125,000 households in about 20 countries. The panel data enables subscribers to review data on brand loyalty, consumer purchases, and consumer demographic characteristics.

Food Lion, a major grocery retailer with over 1,200 stores in 11 states, uses Nielsen's Homescan consumer panel to gain a better understanding of shoppers and Nielsen's ACView service to measure Food Lion's market share on a national basis and within its local markets. According to Food Lion, "Our success is primarily dependent upon how well we serve our shoppers. The Nielsen Homescan consumer panel will give us additional insights we need to keep our focus as consumer-centric as possible."[1]

In this chapter, we will look at the value of marketing information, explain the role of a marketing information system (which gathers, analyzes, disseminates, and stores relevant marketing data), and describe the marketing research process. We will also take a look at sampling methodologies and online surveys.

Chapter Objectives

1. To show why marketing information is needed
2. To explain the role and importance of marketing information systems
3. To examine a basic marketing information system, commercial data bases, data-base marketing, and examples of marketing information systems in action
4. To define marketing research and its components and to look at its scope
5. To describe the marketing research process

4-1 OVERVIEW

> Firms make better decisions when they have good marketing information.

A firm needs to have good information before, while, and after making (and enacting) marketing decisions if its strengths, weaknesses, opportunities, and threats are to be assessed accurately; actions are to be proper for a given marketing environment; and performance is to be maximized. See Figure 4-1.

---

[1] Various company and other sources.

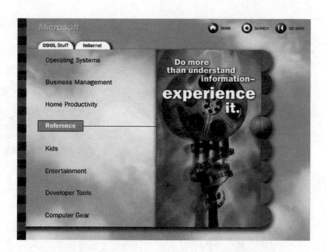

Figure 4-1

Taking a Proactive Approach to Marketing Information

A company's chances for success rise dramatically if it seeks out—and uses—in-depth marketing information.

Source: Reprinted by permission of Retail Planning Associates. Photography by Michael Houghton/STUDIOHIO.

Good information enables marketers to

- gain a competitive edge.
- reduce financial and image risks.
- determine consumer attitudes.
- monitor the environment.
- gather competitive intelligence.
- coordinate strategy.
- measure performance.
- improve advertising credibility.
- gain management support for decisions.
- verify intuition.
- improve effectiveness.

A reliance on "gut feelings," executive judgment, and past experience is not sufficient in making marketing decisions: "To create sustained demand, you have to know your customers and what motivates them to buy from you. Developing that kind of knowledge, and using it effectively, means putting accurate, up-to-date marketing data at the core of every demand-creation program, and every demand-creation strategy."[2]

The *scientific method*—incorporating objectivity, accuracy, and thoroughness— should be followed when collecting and analyzing any marketing information. With *objectivity*, data are gathered in an open-minded way. Judgments are not reached until all data are collected and analyzed. *Accuracy* requires the use of carefully constructed research tools. Each aspect of data gathering, such as the study format, the sample, and tabulations, is well planned and executed. *Thoroughness* deals with the comprehensive nature of information gathering. Mistaken conclusions may be reached if probing is not intense enough.

> The **scientific method** requires objectivity, accuracy, and thoroughness.

In this chapter, two vital aspects of marketing information are covered: marketing information systems and marketing research. A marketing information system guides all of a firm's marketing-related information efforts—and stores and disseminates data—on a continuous basis. Marketing research involves gathering and analyzing information on specific marketing issues:

> Often, it seems that a marketing researcher's passion surfaces only in preventing a firm from making mistakes, earning him or her a reputation as an idea killer rather than a team player. By proactively using data to transform a firm's business, researchers can channel their passion for discovery into growth initiatives that companies desperately need, thereby earning a place at the corporate table.[3]

---

[2] Sheri Taylor Gilchrist, "Six Steps to Data-Driven Demand Creation," http://www.targetonline.com/sics/285665026489051.bsp (July 5, 2005).

[3] John W. Huppertz, "Passion Vs. Dispassion," *Marketing Research* (Summer 2003), p. 18.

Figure 4-2

Marketing Information Systems: Playing at an Airport Near You

With the advent of powerful, fast, and inexpensive computer terminals and networks, firms in any industry and of any size can easily set up a marketing information system. The airline industry is in the forefront with state-of-the-art MIS programs, such as that used by Japan Airlines (**http://www.jal.co.jp/en**).

Source: Reprinted by permission of Susan Berry, Retail Image Consulting, Inc.

4-2 MARKETING INFORMATION SYSTEMS

The collection of marketing information should not be a rare event that occurs only when data are needed on a specific marketing topic. If research is done this way, a firm faces several risks: Opportunities may be missed. There may be a lack of awareness of environmental changes and competitors' actions. It may be impossible to analyze data over several time periods. Marketing plans and decisions may not be properly reviewed. Data collection may be disjointed. Previous studies may not be stored in an easy-to-access format. Time lags may result if a new study is required. Actions may be reactionary rather than anticipatory. Thus, it is essential for any firm, regardless of its size or type, to utilize some form of marketing information system to aid decision making. See Figure 4-2.

A ***marketing information system (MIS)*** is "a set of procedures and methods designed to generate, analyze, disseminate, and store anticipated marketing decision information on a regular, continuous basis."[4] This means that a firm should:

- Actively amass data from internal company documents, existing external documents, and primary studies (when necessary).
- Analyze data and prepare suitable reports—in terms of the mission, strategy, and proposed tactics.
- Distribute analyzed data to the right marketing decision makers in the firm (who will vary based on the particular topics covered).
- Store data for future use and comparisons.
- Seek all relevant data that have either current or future marketing ramifications—not just data with specific short-term implications.
- Undertake data collection, analysis, distribution, and storage in an ongoing manner.

Figure 4-3 shows how an information system can be used operationally, managerially, and strategically for several aspects of marketing.

Next, we present the components of a basic marketing information system, commercial data bases, data-base marketing, and examples of MIS in action.

> A **marketing information system (MIS)** regularly gathers, analyzes, disseminates, and stores data.

---

[4] Adapted by the authors from Robert A. Peterson, *Marketing Research*, 2nd ed. (Dallas: Business Publications, 1988), p 31; and "Dictionary of Marketing Terms," **http://www.marketingpower.com/mg-dictionary.php** (May 3, 2006).

Global Marketing in Action

Neuromarketing Experiments Come to Marketing Research

Neuroco (http://www.neuroco.com), a marketing research firm based in England, is regarded by many industry analysts as being at the forefront of neuromarketing. Neuromarketing integrates neuroscience and clinical psychology to better understand how consumers react to products, brands, and ads. Unlike other neuromarketing researchers that use machinery the size of an SUV (and that weighs 32 tons), Neuroco uses a technology that is much lighter and more portable. This allows Neuroco to study consumer behavior at a store, a mall, or at a consumer's home.

Neuroco's current clients include Royal & Sun-Alliance (http://www.royalsunalliance.com), the second-largest insurance company in Great Britain, and Hewlett Packard (http://www.hp.com). Neuroco evaluated Royal's 30-second TV ads by examining the electroencephalography (EEG) readings—brain waves—of 60 consumers as they watched the ads. Neuroco found that the consumers were most engaged during an ad's most dramatic scene, and that their interest dropped at the ad's tagline "You'd better ring the Royal." As a result of this analysis, Royal withdrew the commercial.

Hewlett Packard used Neuroco to determine which of two ads would give its digital camera advertising campaign the greatest neurological boost with consumers. Although the ads were viewed in a similar fashion in face-to-face interviews, the EEG analysis showed a strong advantage to the ad version where a woman had a warmer expression. According to an executive with Hewlett Packard's ad agency, "The Neuroco data was priceless. It gave us insight that goes beyond normal market research."

Source: Based on material in Thomas Mucha, "This Is Your Brain on Advertising," *Business 2.0* (August 2005), pp. 35–37.

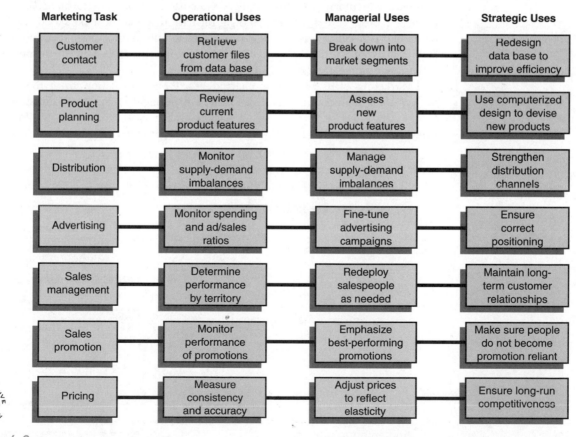

Marketing Task	Operational Uses	Managerial Uses	Strategic Uses
Customer contact	Retrieve customer files from data base	Break down into market segments	Redesign data base to improve efficiency
Product planning	Review current product features	Assess new product features	Use computerized design to devise new products
Distribution	Monitor supply-demand imbalances	Manage supply-demand imbalances	Strengthen distribution channels
Advertising	Monitor spending and ad/sales ratios	Fine-tune advertising campaigns	Ensure correct positioning
Sales management	Determine performance by territory	Redeploy salespeople as needed	Maintain long-term customer relationships
Sales promotion	Monitor performance of promotions	Emphasize best-performing promotions	Make sure people do not become promotion reliant
Pricing	Measure consistency and accuracy	Adjust prices to reflect elasticity	Ensure long-run competitiveness

Figure 4-3

How Marketing Information Can Be Utilized

Source: Adapted by the authors from Rajendra S. Sisodia, "Marketing Information and Decision Support Systems for Services," *Journal of Services Marketing,* Vol. 6 (Winter 1992), pp. 51–64.

4-2a A Basic Marketing Information System

A basic marketing information system is shown in Figure 4-4. It begins with a statement of company objectives, which provide broad guidelines. These goals are affected by environmental factors, such as competition, government, and the economy. Marketing plans involve the choice of a target market, marketing goals, the marketing organization, the marketing mix (product, distribution, promotion, and price decisions), and performance measurement.

After marketing plans are outlined, a firm's total marketing information needs can be specified and satisfied via a *marketing intelligence network*, which consists of continuous monitoring, marketing research, and data warehousing. *Continuous monitoring* is used to regularly study a firm's external and internal environment. It can entail reading trade publications, watching news reports, getting constant feedback from employees and customers, attending industry meetings, observing competitors' actions (competitive intelligence), and compiling periodic company reports. *Marketing research* is used to obtain information on particular marketing issues (problems). Information may be retrieved from storage (existing company data) or acquired by collecting external secondary data and/or primary data. *Data warehousing* involves retaining all types of relevant company records (sales, costs, personnel performance, etc.), as well as information collected through continuous monitoring and marketing research. These data aid decision making and are kept for future reference. Marketing research should be considered as just one part of an ongoing, integrated information system.

Depending on a firm's resources and the complexity of its information needs, a marketing intelligence network may or may not be fully computerized. Small firms can do well if their employees and managers read industry publications, attend trade shows, observe competitors, talk with suppliers and customers, track performance, and store the results of these efforts. In any event, information needs must be stated and regularly reviewed, data sources identified, personnel given information tasks, storage and retrieval facilities set up, and data routed to decision makers. The keys to a good MIS are consistency, completeness, and orderliness.

Marketing plans should be enacted based on information from the intelligence network. Through continuous monitoring, a firm might learn that a competitor intends to cut prices by 7 percent during the next month. This would give the firm time to explore its own marketing options (switch to cheaper materials, place larger orders to get

> A marketing intelligence network includes marketing research, continuous monitoring, and data warehousing.

Figure 4-4

A Basic Marketing Information System

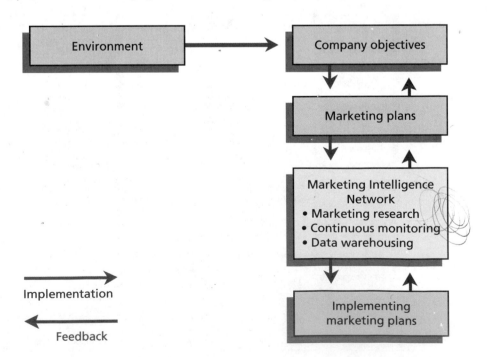

discounts, or ignore the cuts) and select one. If monitoring is not done, the firm might be caught by surprise and forced just to cut prices, without any other choice.

A basic MIS has these advantages: organized data collection, a broad perspective, the storage of vital data, crisis avoidance, coordinated marketing plans, speed in gathering the data to make decisions, data retained over several time periods, and the ability to do cost-benefit analysis. Yet, forming an MIS may not be easy. Initial time and costs may be high, and setting up a sophisticated system may be complex.

4-2b   Commercial Data Bases

Because client companies need current, comprehensive, and relatively inexpensive information about the environment in which they operate, many specialized research firms offer ongoing *commercial data bases* with information on population traits, the business environment, economic forecasts, industry and individual companies' performance, and so forth. Such data bases may include newspaper and magazine articles, business and household addresses culled from Yellow Pages and other sources, industry and company news releases, government reports, conference proceedings, indexes, patent records, and so on. Research firms sell access to their data bases to clients, usually for a rather low fee.

Data bases may be available in printed form, on CDs and DVDs, and as downloads from the Internet. Several commercial data-base firms exist that concentrate on tracking and clipping newspaper and magazine articles on an orderly basis; unlike with computerized data bases, these firms actually look for information on subjects specified by clients. They offer their services for a fee. There are probably 1,000 to 2,000 information brokers around the world (many of them in the United States).

Firms such as InfoUSA (**http://www.infousa.com**) provide business and household addresses and other data in CD, DVD, download, and additional formats. InfoUSA gathers data from phone directories, annual reports, and government agencies; it also makes millions of calls each year to keep data bases current. For $385, a client can buy an InfoUSA data base of 1,275 public U.S. colleges and universities—with addresses, contact names and titles, phone and fax numbers, Web addresses, data on number of employees and number of PCs, public versus private status, and so forth. InfoUSA has more than 4 million customers—from single-person firms to giant corporations. Donnelley Marketing (**http://www.donnelleymarketing.com**), Dun & Bradstreet (**http://www.dnb.com**), and Experian (**http://www.experian.com**) are other popular commercial data-base providers.

Many firms, schools, and libraries subscribe to one or more online data bases, whereby users have free access or are charged a small fee. Among the best-known data-base services are ProQuest (**http://www.infolearning.com**), InfoTrac Web from Gale Group (**http://www.gale.com/pdf/facts/itweb.pdf**), Factiva (**http://www.factiva.com**) from Dow Jones & Reuters, and Lexis-Nexis (**http://www.lexis-nexis.com**) from Reed Elsevier. With these services, the user can do a search on a particular topic or firm. Full articles or reports may also be accessed and printed, sometimes for an additional fee.

4-2c   Data-Base Marketing

In conjunction with their MIS efforts, many firms are using data-base marketing to better identify target markets and more efficiently reach them. *Data-base marketing* is a computerized technique that compiles, sorts, and stores relevant information about customers and potential customers; uses that information to highlight opportunities and prioritize market segments; and enables the firm to profitably tailor marketing efforts for specific customers or customer groups. This process is shown in Figure 4-5.

Among the three steps in data-base marketing described in Figure 4-5, data mining is the most crucial. *Data mining* is an in-depth, computerized search of available information to find profitable marketing opportunities that may otherwise be hidden. The goal is to pinpoint the most attractive customer segments, along with their unique attributes and needs. For example, if a retail store monitors a customer's purchases and

> Commercial data bases can provide useful ongoing information.

> Through data-base marketing and careful data mining, companies can enhance customer interactions.

Structuring the Data Warehouse	Data Mining	Data-Base Marketing
Company compiles, sorts, and stores relevant customer information: • Demographic and lifestyle characteristics • Past purchase behavior • Attitudes • Desired product features • Trends • Etc.	Company: (a) Reviews information in data warehouse to highlight marketing opportunities (b) Derives customer profiles based on most meaningful factors (c) Generates possible market segments with unique needs (d) Prioritizes market segments based on their profit potential	Company pinpoints its marketing efforts to stimulate customer interest, to offer tailored differential advantages, and to maximize customer satisfaction. Relationship marketing is the foundation for all long-run efforts.

Figure 4-5

Applying Data-Base Marketing

notices that he or she buys a lot of silk shirts, a "data mining system will make a correlation between that customer and silk shirts. The sales department will look at that information and may begin direct mail marketing of silk shirts to that customer, or it may alternatively attempt to get the customer to buy a wider range of products. In this case, the data mining system used by the retail store discovered new information about the customer that was previously unknown to the company."[5]

In data mining, a data base

is your own private weapon in the battle for business. It's a source of information compiled about your own customers, past and present, and also about people you have reason to believe are genuine prospects. You place into it as many appropriate specifics as you can, including information about past purchasing patterns and whatever else may be relevant to making a sale. Your data base will help you identify your most responsive targets, and send out tailored messages. Data-base marketing provides a level of targeting and personalization that's been a dream. Thanks to today's sophisticated yet inexpensive computer technology, it can be expedited efficiently, simply, and cost-effectively. It is a superb tool for generating efficient responses, strengthening customer relationships, and settling the foundation for even more powerful marketing programs in the future.[6]

Relationship marketing benefits from data-base marketing. A firm can identify those customers with whom it would most like to have long-term relationships, learn as much as possible about them (such as demographics, purchase behavior, and attitudes), customize marketing efforts toward them, and follow up to learn the level of satisfaction. A firm might even compute a "lifetime value" for specific customers, based on their purchase history, and adjust marketing efforts accordingly. See Figure 4-6.

When setting up a data base, each actual or potential customer gets an identifying code. Then, *contact information* such as name, address, phone number, industry code (if a business customer), and demographic data (when appropriate), and *marketing information* such as source and date of contact(s) with firm, purchase history, product interests, and responses to offers are entered and updated for every customer. Data should be distributed to a firm's marketing decision makers and kept in the MIS. Efforts should be coordinated so customers are not bombarded with mailings and a consistent image is maintained.

---

[5] "Data Mining," **http://en.wikipedia.org/wiki/Data_mining** (May 3, 2006). See also Shawn Thelen, Sandra Mottner, and Barry Berman, "Data Mining: On the Trail to Marketing Gold," *Business Horizons*, Vol. 47 (November-December 2004), pp. 25–32.

[6] "USPS: Data-Base Marketing," **http://www.usps.com/directmail/faqs/dbmrktg.htm** (April 3, 2004).

Figure 4-6

Using Data-Base Marketing to Foster Customer Relationships

Through its store-based computerized checkouts, Menards (**http://www.menards.com**)—a home improvement retailer—employs a data-base marketing strategy, which enables it to better target opportunities by store location and to get feedback about the behavior of its Menards Big Card credit customers.

Source: Reprinted by permission of Susan Berry, Retail Image Consulting, Inc.

Many consulting companies are available to help clients with data-base marketing. One is Database Marketing Solutions (**http://www.database-marketing.com/services/index.html**): "Businesses are striving as never before to make the most of each customer relationship. Thus, marketing data must be managed and interpreted with unprecedented precision and accuracy. With solid information, you can plan, execute, measure, and improve customer-centered initiatives that focus on your most promising targets. That's where our skilled data-base marketing specialists are invaluable. Relying on proven methodology, we unlock the power of your data to drive profitable marketing programs."

In practice, data-base marketing might actually work like this:

(1) No matter how busy you are, be sure to enter every new customer and prospect name into your data base, along with other pertinent information. Every time you touch base with a customer or prospect, make a notation so you'll have a running log. (2) Organize your prospecting list into a pyramid, with the hottest prospects at the top and the coldest ones at the bottom. This way, you can devote the most time to the prospects that are most likely to buy from you and not waste time on those likely to say no. (3) Once you've started mining your data base, you can get a better handle on which customers are going to buy from you and when. To keep track of pending sales, use an Excel spreadsheet. As potential projects come in the door, type the client's name, type of project, and expected dollar value. (4) An easy, cost-effective way to keep in touch with clients is by sending a weekly E-mail newsletter. It should go not only to your existing customers, but also to prospects, previous customers, and people you meet at trade shows or networking events. (5) No matter what else comes up, be sure to set aside time each day for prospecting and data-base management.[7]

---

[7] Rosalind Resnick, "Do-It-Yourself Data-Base Marketing," **http://www.entrepreneur.com/article/0,4621,310778,00.html** (September 1, 2003).

4-2d MIS in Action

Millions of organizations worldwide now use some form of MIS in their decision making, and the trend is expected to continue. In fact, as a result of computer networking, progressive firms (and divisions within the same firm) around the globe are transmitting and sharing their marketing information with each other quickly and inexpensively. The majority of *Fortune 1000* companies and most large retailers engage in data-base marketing.

Among the specific firms using their marketing information systems well are Office Depot, Sears, and the U.S. Postal Service (USPS). Each devotes considerable time and resources to its system. Following are examples of how they apply MIS.

Office Depot (**http://www.officedepot.com**) sells through stores, direct mail, contract delivery, the Internet, and business-to-business E-commerce. To facilitate the flow of information throughout the firm, it recently devised a new marketing information system that combines data from many different sources: "Existing sales data are being integrated into a combined model, while the project team is bringing its customer identification management in-house from a service bureau." This brings together "credit marketing, call center data, and Web site data." As a result, Office Depot now has "an enterprise view" within its marketing information system, "while allowing us to better target customers based on their relationships from the operational system."[8]

Sears (**http://www.sears.com**) is one of the world's largest retailers. It has invested heavily in business-intelligence software so that its marketing information system can be better used by the firm's inventory analysts "to give customers the best possible product selections at each of the retailer's stores." Sears installed AllocationXpert software from Applied Intelligence Solutions (**http://www.aisllc.com**): "Inventory analysts enter parameters into AllocationXpert based on merchandise categories to allocate apparel. The software draws on historical sales data, logic, and decision patterns from previous transactions. It also considers point-of-sale data, promotions, quantities, season, replenishment cycles, product type, and region to make recommendations on where merchandise is needed most."[9]

Every day, the United States Postal Service (**http://www.usps.com**) handles more than 40 percent of the world's mail. This enormous task requires a top-flight marketing information system: "USPS uses a massive system to analyze many areas of its business, including sales at individual post offices, the use of manpower and transportation resources, and the efficiency of mail-processing facilities, all with an eye toward improving customer service and boosting productivity." The system contains "logistical data from mail-processing facilities, package-tracking data, air-transportation data, and customer relationship data." USPS "also collects retail data from 37,000 post offices every night and provides post-office managers with reports about the previous day's sales. Managers even use the data to analyze how often post-office customers use the automated postal centers" located in several thousand post offices.[10]

4-3 MARKETING RESEARCH DEFINED

Marketing research involves systematically gathering, recording, and analyzing information about specific issues related to the marketing of goods, services, organizations, people, places, and ideas. It may be done by an outside party or by the firm itself. As noted earlier, marketing research should be used as one component of a firm's overall marketing information efforts. For example, see Figure 4-7.

---

[8] Jeff Jedras, "Office Depot Builds Data Warehouse to Serve 80 Locations," *Computing Canada* (April 8, 2005), p. 21.

[9] Laurie Sullivan, "Business Intelligence Pays Off for Sears," *Information Week* (May 9, 2005), p. 57.

[10] Rick Whiting, "Data Transformation," *Information Week* (April 18, 2005), p. 75.

For marketing research to be effective, several points need to be kept in mind:

- The research must not be conducted haphazardly.
- The process involves a sequence of tasks: data gathering, recording, and analysis.
- Data may be available from different sources: the firm itself, an impartial agency (such as the government), or a research specialist working for the firm.
- Research may be applied to any aspect of marketing that requires information to aid decision making.
- All results and their implications must be communicated to the right decision maker(s) in a firm.

Just because a firm chooses to use marketing research does not mean it must engage in expensive projects such as test marketing and national consumer attitude surveys. It may get enough data by analyzing internal sales reports or from informal meetings with customer-service personnel. Marketing research does require an orderly approach and adherence to the scientific method. For every marketing issue studied, the amount and cost of research depend on the kinds of data needed to make informed decisions, the risk involved in making those decisions, the potential consequences of the decisions, the importance of the issue to the firm, the availability of existing data, the complexity of the data-gathering process for the issue, and other factors.

As an example, Pulte Homes (**http://www.pulte.com**) is now the top U.S. home-builder, with annual revenues of $12 billion: "Behind much of this success is an old business practice—sophisticated marketing research—that has eluded the notoriously fragmented industry for decades." Pulte Homes pays "as much attention to consumer surveys and demographic data as to the detail work on custom homes." As its chief executive says, "Toyota sells Corollas to entry-level buyers, Camrys to the middle market, and Lexuses to the top. Why can't we do the same in homebuilding?" Through marketing research, Pulte "finds prized land that other builders pass up and better matches home designs with customers' tastes." The firm spends several million dollars each year on its research efforts.[11]

Figure 4-7

Gap: Balancing the Old and the New

Research showed that Gap customers are interested in a combination of basics and fashion. As a recent story by Julie Creswell in *Fortune* noted: "By striking a balance between basics and more stylish items, the company hopes not to scare away its core customers. 'We're not looking to chase every trend,' says the president of Gap stores. 'We hope to add more of a designer's attention to detail and aesthetics to the brand.'"

Source: Reprinted by permission of Susan Berry, Retail Image Consulting, Inc.

---

[11] Diane Brady, "Trying Not to Be A Fashion Victim," *Business Week* (October 6, 2003), p. 112.

4-4 THE SCOPE OF MARKETING RESEARCH

Client companies annually spend more than $16 billion worldwide (40 percent in the United States) for data gathered by marketing research firms. The top 25 research firms (nearly half of which are U.S.-based) account for two-thirds of the total, with more than 1,000 firms responsible for the rest.[12] These amounts are in addition to research sponsored by government and other institutions and to internal research efforts of firms themselves—which run to billions of dollars each year.

These are the topical areas in which companies are most apt to engage in or sponsor marketing research efforts: industry/market characteristics and trends, customer/product satisfaction, market-share analyses, segmentation studies, brand awareness and preference, purchase intentions, competitive intelligence, and concept development and testing. On average, companies spend 1 to 2 percent of their revenues on marketing research. For example, see Figure 4-7.

Five aspects of marketing research merit special discussion. These involve the rapid rise in customer satisfaction studies, the use of the Internet, the application of single-source data collection, ethical considerations, and the complexities of international marketing research.

Companies now participate in more customer satisfaction research than ever before, in keeping with the customer focus noted in Chapter 1. This form of research has more than doubled in recent years, with some firms doing their own studies and others hiring specialists. Whirlpool (http://www.whirlpool.com) sends its own surveys on appliance satisfaction to thousands of consumer households each year. It also pays hundreds of consumers per year to "fiddle" with computer-simulated products at its Usability Lab. Whirlpool's research also extends to its European, Latin American, and Asian marketplaces. On the other hand, Maritz Research (http://www.maritzresearch. com) generates worldwide revenues of several million dollars by doing customer satisfaction studies for clients. As one observer noted, many firms "regularly conduct customer satisfaction studies to gauge perceptions and track changes in satisfaction over time. Sometimes, what is most interesting, however, isn't the level of satisfaction that exists, or even how much that level has risen or fallen over time, but what drives customer satisfaction. Firms that use research to gauge customer satisfaction often express surprise regarding what their studies uncover."[13]

Over the last several years, spending for online marketing research has grown quite rapidly—from $3.5 million in 1996 to a projected $4 billion in 2008.[14] In fact, one of the largest marketing firms in the United States, NPD Group (http://www.npd.com), decided to shift its focus to Web-based research and away from "offline" research. The firm "gleans consumer insight from our online consumer panel, the largest online consumer panel providing ongoing tracking services across a broad range of industries. The NPD online panel has over 2.5 million registered members who have agreed to participate in our surveys and provide information on their purchasing behavior. NPD has selected over 600,000 members for its core sample, from which most studies are performed."[15] Here are other examples of how online marketing research is being employed:

- Many businesspeople start doing their research by checking out competitors' Web sites, using search engines, and accessing online annual reports and trade publications. Information is current, easy to obtain, and often free.
- Hoover's (http://www.hoovers.com): Through online subscriptions, the firm "provides comprehensive, up-to-date, business information for sales, marketing, business development, and other professionals who need intelligence on U.S. and global companies, industries, and the people who shape them." It "offers proprietary

---

[12] Jack Honomichl, "Honomichl Global Top 25," *Marketing News* (August 15, 2005), special section.

[13] Kevin Cacioppo, "Measuring and Managing Customer Satisfaction," http://www.qualitydigest.com (September 2000); and "The Value of Customer Satisfaction Research," *Online Registration* (January 10, 2005), p. 4.

[14] Cambiar Research, "Online Research: The Great Equalizer?" http://www.mrweb.com/drno/news4111.htm (May 26, 2005).

[15] "NPD Group: Consumer Panel," http://www.npd.com/about.consumerpanel.html (April 27, 2006).

information about 40,000 companies, more than 300,000 officers, and 600 industries in an easy-to-read format."[16]

- Greenfield Online (**http://www.greenfield.com**) offers online research capabilities to clients "without their investment in technology and infrastructure. Our proprietary panel recruitment and maintenance strategies give us access to low-incidence groups including business owners, doctors, ailment sufferers, IT professionals—and the list goes on and on."[17]

Due to technological advances, ***single-source data collection*** – whereby research firms track the activities of individual consumer households from the programs they watch on TV to the products they purchase at stores—is now possible. For instance, via its BehaviorScan service, Information Resources Inc. (IRI) (**http://www.infores.com**) monitors the viewing habits and shopping behavior of thousands of households in various markets. Microcomputers are hooked to household TVs and note all programs and ads watched. Consumers shop in supermarkets, drugstores, and other stores with scanning registers and present cashiers with special cards (resembling credit cards). Cashiers enter each consumer's identification code, which is electronically keyed to every item bought. Via computer analysis, viewing and shopping behavior are then matched with such information as age and income.

Because of the unethical practices of some firms, many potential respondents are "turned off" to participating in marketing research projects. In fact, a lot of Americans say they will not answer a survey. To help turn the situation around, the Marketing Research Association (**http://www.mra-net.org**) recently revised its code of ethics. It strongly encourages member firms to adhere to these practices:

> **Single-source data collection** is a result of high-tech advances.

All Marketing Research Association members

1. will ensure that each study is conducted according to the client's exact written or oral specifications as long as they don't contradict the standards herein.
2. will observe confidentiality with all research techniques or methodologies and with information considered confidential or proprietary. Information will not be revealed that could be used to identify clients or respondents without proper authorization.
3. will report research results accurately and honestly.
4. will not intentionally abuse public confidence in opinion and marketing research. At no time is marketing research information to be used to intentionally mislead public opinion.
5. will not misrepresent themselves as having qualifications, experience, skills, resources, or other facility locations that they do not possess.
6. will refrain from referring to membership in the Marketing Research Association as proof of competence, since the MRA does not certify any person's or organization's competency or skill.
7. will not ask those who subcontract research to engage in any activity that is not acceptable as defined in the Code or that is prohibited under any applicable federal, state, local laws, regulations, and/or ordinances.
8. will protect the confidentiality of anything learned about a client's business as a result of access to proprietary information and will require all employees to sign a nondisclosure statement.[18]

With more firms striving to expand their foreign endeavors, international marketing research is now more important. This can be quite challenging. For instance, the language used, respondent selection, and interviewer training are among the areas requiring special consideration.[19] Consider the following example.

---

[16] "Hoover's Company Information," **http://www.hoovers.com/global/corp/index.xhtml?pageid=10617** (April 27, 2006).

[17] "Greenfield: Who We Are," **http://www.greenfield.com/whoweare.htm** (April 27, 2006).

[18] Marketing Research Association, *Code of Marketing Research Standards*, **http://www.mra-net.org/pdf/expanded_code.pdf** (ratified May 12, 2003).

[19] See Cheryl Nakata and Yili Huang, "Progress and Promise: The Last Decade of International Marketing Research," *Journal of Business Research*, Vol. 58 (May 2005), pp. 611–618.

Ethical Issues in Marketing

The Bill of Rights for Survey Respondents

The Council for Marketing and Opinion Research (CMOR) (http://www.cmor.org) has a survey respondents' bill of rights that highlights several important ethical issues that research companies need to address.

Here are some of the areas covered by the CMOR respondents' bill of rights:

- A respondent's privacy should always be maintained. The respondent's name, phone number, and specific responses to a survey are not to be disclosed to anyone outside the research industry.
- Respondents should be told the contact person's name, his or her employer, and the purpose of the research study.
- Respondents' names or other information should not be sold; and respondents should not be contacted unless to confirm their participation.

- Interviewers should be courteous and offer to call back at a more convenient time, if necessary.
- Respondents should be informed in advance if an interview is to be recorded and the intended use of the recording.
- Respondents should not be sold anything under the guise of research.
- A respondent's decision to not participate in the study, not answer specific questions, or to discontinue participation should be politely respected.
- Respondents should be assured that the highest standards of professional conduct will be upheld in the collection and reporting of information they provide.

Source: Based on material in "Respondent Bill of Rights," *CMOR: Promoting & Advocating Survey Research*, http://www.cmor.org/research/rights.cfm (February 9, 2006).

Firms deciding how to best market products to the billions of people in Eastern Europe and Central Asia increasingly do marketing research there. Yet, designing and conducting research is hard. Some people have never been surveyed before. Communications systems, especially phone service, may be subpar by Western standards. Secondary data from government agencies and trade associations may be lacking. Thus, firms must be adaptable. When it did research there, Kodak (**http://www.kodak.com**) could not find relevant consumer data, a photography trade association, or pictures of local cameras for use in a questionnaire. So, to gather data on camera usage and preferences, Kodak took part in a multiclient survey devised by SRG International Ltd. (**http://www.srgicorp.com**). The survey was conducted in nine former Soviet republics; since each had its own language, nine questionnaire versions were prepared.

4-5   THE MARKETING RESEARCH PROCESS

The **marketing research process** consists of steps from issue definition to implementation of findings.

The **marketing research process** consists of a series of activities: defining the issue or problem to be studied; examining secondary data (previously collected); generating primary data (new), if necessary; analyzing information; making recommendations; and implementing findings. InfoTech Marketing's Web site (**http://www.smsource.com/research.htm**) is a useful tool for learning more about the process.

Figure 4-8 presents the complete process. The steps are to be completed in order. For example, secondary data are not examined until a firm states the issue or problem to be studied, and primary data are not generated until secondary data are thoroughly reviewed. The dashed line around primary data means these data do not always have to be generated. Many times, a firm can obtain enough information internally or from published sources to make a marketing decision without gathering new data. Only if secondary data are insufficient should a firm gather primary data. The research process is described next.

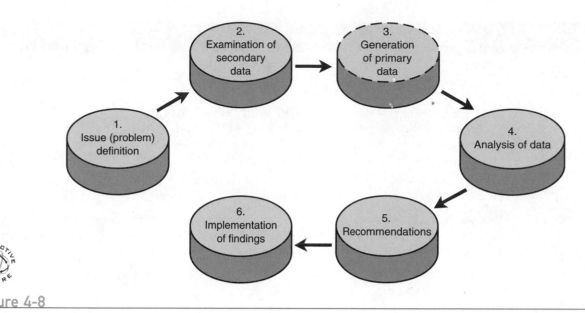

Figure 4-8

The Marketing Research Process

4-5a Issue (Problem) Definition

Issue (problem) definition is a statement of the topic to be looked into via marketing research. Without a focused definition, irrelevant and expensive data—which could confuse rather than illuminate—may be gathered. A good problem definition directs the research process to collect and analyze appropriate data for the purpose of decision making.

When a firm is uncertain about the precise topic to investigate or wants to broadly study an issue, it uses exploratory research. The aim of *exploratory research* is to gain ideas and insights, and to break broad, vague problem statements into smaller, more precise statements.[20] Exploratory research, also called "qualitative research," may involve in-depth probing, small-group discussions, and understanding underlying trends. Once an issue is clarified, conclusive research, also called "quantitative research," is used. *Conclusive research* is the structured collection and analysis of data pertaining to a specific issue or problem. It is more focused than exploratory research, and requires larger samples and more limited questions to provide quantitative data to make decisions. Table 4-1 contrasts the two forms of research.

> Research efforts are directed by **issue definition**.

> **Exploratory research** looks at unclear topics; **conclusive research** is better defined.

4-5b Secondary Data

Secondary data consist of information not collected for the issue or problem at hand but for some other purpose; this information is available within a firm or externally. Whether secondary data fully resolve an issue or problem or not, their low cost and rather fast accessibility mean that primary data should not be collected until a thorough secondary data search is done.

> **Secondary data** have been previously gathered for purposes other than the current research.

[20] "Dictionary of Marketing Terms," http://www.marketingpower.com/mg-dictionary.php (May 3, 2006).

Table 4-1   Examples of Exploratory and Conclusive Research

Vague Research Topic	Exploratory Research	Precise Research Topic	Conclusive Research
1. Why are sales declining?	1. Discussions among key personnel to identify major cause	1. Why is the turnover of sales personnel so high?	1. Survey sales personnel and interview sales managers
2. Is advertising effective?	2. Discussions among key advertising personnel to define effectiveness	2. Do adults recall an advertisement the day after it appears?	2. Survey customers and noncustomers to gauge advertising recall
3. Will a price reduction increase revenues?	3. Discussions among key personnel to determine the level of a price reduction	3. Will a 10 percent price reduction have a significant impact on sales?	3. Run an in-store experiment to determine effects

Advantages and Disadvantages Secondary data have these general advantages and disadvantages:

Advantages
- Many types are inexpensive because primary data collection is not involved.
- Data assembly can be swift, especially for published or company materials.
- Several sources and perspectives may be available.
- A source (such as the government) may obtain data a firm could not get itself.
- Data assembled by independent sources are highly credible.
- They are helpful when exploratory research is involved.

Disadvantages
- Available data may not suit the current research purpose due to incompleteness and generalities.
- Information may be dated or obsolete.
- The methodology used in collecting the data (such as the sample size) may be unknown.
- All the findings of a research study may not be made public.
- Conflicting results may exist.
- Because many research projects are not repeated, the reliability of data may not be proven.

Sources Two major sources of secondary data exist: Internal secondary data are available within a firm. External secondary data are available outside a firm. Most companies use each source in some way.

> A firm's records or past studies comprise internal secondary data.

Internal Secondary Data The information inside a firm should be reviewed before spending time and money searching for external secondary data or collecting primary data. Internal sources include budgets, sales figures, profit-and-loss statements, customer billings, inventory records, prior research reports, and written reports.

At the beginning of the business year, most firms set detailed budgets for the next 12 months. The budgets, based on sales forecasts, outline planned expenditures for every good and service during the year. By examining the sales of each division, product line, item, geographic area, salesperson, time of day, day of week, and so on, and comparing these sales with those of prior periods, performance can be measured. With profit-and-loss statements, actual achievements can be measured against profit goals by department, salesperson, and product. Customer billings provide information on credit transactions, sales by region, peak selling seasons, sales volume, and sales by customer category. Inventory records show the levels of goods bought, manufactured, stored, shipped, and/or sold throughout the year.

Prior research reports, containing the findings of past marketing research efforts, are often stored and retained for future use. When a report is used initially, it is primary data. Later reference to that report is secondary in nature because it is no longer employed for its basic purpose. Written reports (ongoing data stored by a firm) may be compiled by top management, marketing executives, sales personnel, and others. Among the information attainable from such reports are typical customer complaints.

External Secondary Data If a research issue or problem is not resolved through internal secondary data, a firm should use external secondary data sources. Government and nongovernment sources are available.

All levels of government distribute economic and business statistics. Various U.S. government agencies also publish pamphlets on such diverse topics as franchising and deceptive sales practices. These materials are distributed free of charge or sold for a nominal fee. The *Catalog of U.S. Government Publications* (**http://catalog.gpo.gov/f**) lists these items. In using government data, particularly census statistics, the research date must be noted. There may be a lag before government data are released.

> Government and nongovernment sources make available external secondary data.

Three types of nongovernment secondary data exist: regular publications; books, monographs, and other nonregular publications; and commercial research houses. Regular publications contain articles on diverse aspects of marketing and are available in libraries or via subscriptions. Some are quite broad in scope (*Business Week*); others are more specialized (*Journal of Advertising Research*). Periodicals are published by conventional publishing companies, as well as by professional and trade associations. See below for a list of the Web sites of about 50 marketing-related publications.

Examples of Marketing-Related Publications

- *Advertising Age* (http://www.adage.com)
- *American City Business Journals* (http://www.bizjournals.com)
- *Brandweek* (http://www.brandweek.com)
- *BtoB* (http://www.netb2b.com)
- *Business Week* (http://www.businessweek.com)
- *Chain Store Age* (http://www.chainstoreage.com)
- *Consumer Insight* (http://us.acnielsen.com/pubs/index.shtml)
- *Consumer Reports* (http://www.consumerreports.org)
- *Demographic Research* (http://www.demographic-research.org)
- *Direct* (http://www.directmag.com)
- *Display & Design Ideas* (http://www.ddimagazine.com)
- *DM News* (http://www.dmnews.com)
- *Drug Store News* (http://www.drugstorenews.com)
- *DSN Retailing Today* (http://www.dsnretailingtoday.com)
- *E-Commerce News* (http://www.internetnews.com/ec-news)
- *Entrepreneur Magazine* (http://www.entrepreneur.com)
- *Forbes* (http://www.forbes.com)
- *Fortune* (http://money.cnn.com/magazines/fortune.com)
- *Hoover's Online* (http://www.hoovers.com)
- *Inbound Logistics* (http://www.inboundlogistics.com)
- *Inc.* (http://www.inc.com)
- *Incentive* (http://www.incentivemag.com)
- *Industry Standard* (http://www.thestandard.com)
- *Information Week* (http://www.informationweek.com)
- *Journal of Advertising* (http://www.mesharpe.com/mall/results1.asp?acr=joa)
- *Journal of Advertising Research* (http://www.arfsite.org/resources/jar.html)
- *Journal of Business Ethics* (http://www.kluweronline.com/issn/0167-4544)
- *Journal of Consumer Marketing* (http://www.emeraldinsight.com/info/journals/jcm/jcm.htm)
- *Journal of Database Marketing & Consumer Strategy Management* (http://www.palgrave-journals.com/dbm)
- *Journal of Marketing* (http://www.marketingpower.com/live/content1053C362.php)
- *Journal of Marketing Research* (http://www.marketingpower.com/live/content1054C363.php)
- *Journal of Services Marketing* (http://www.emeraldinsight.com/info/journals/jsm/jsm.htm)
- *London Times* (http://www.thetimes.co.uk)
- *Marketing Magazine* (http://www.brandrepublic.com/magazines/marketing/index.cfm)

(continued)

- *Marketing News* (http://www.marketingpower.com/live/content1049C77.php)
- *Marketing Week* (http://www.marketingweek.co.uk)
- *McKinsey Quarterly* (http://www.mckinseyquarterly.com)
- *Multichannel Merchant* (http://www.multichannelmerchant.com)
- *Newsweek International Editions* (http://www.msnbc.msn.com/id/3037881/site/newsweek)
- *New York Times* (http://www.nytimes.com)
- *Nonprofit Times* (http://www.nptimes.com)
- *Progressive Grocer* (http://www.progressivegrocer.com)
- *Promo* (http://www.promomagazine.com)
- *Restaurant Business* (http://www.restaurantbiz.com)
- *Sales & Marketing Management* (http://www.salesandmarketing.com)
- *Selling Power* (http://www.sellingpower.com)
- *Shopping Centers Today* (http://www.icsc.org/srch/sct/199701)
- *Stores* (http://www.stores.org)
- *Target Marketing* (http://www.targetonline.com)
- *USA Today* (http://www.usatoday.com)
- *Value Retail News* (http://www.valueretailnews.com)
- *Wall Street Journal* (http://www.wsj.com)

Books, monographs, and other nonrecurring literature are also published by conventional publishing companies, as well as by professional and trade associations. These materials deal with special topics in depth and are compiled on the basis of interest by the target audience.

Various commercial research houses conduct periodic and ongoing studies and make results available to many clients for a fee. The fee can be low or range into the tens of thousands of dollars (or more), depending on the extent of the data. That kind of research is secondary when the firm purchasing data acts as a subscriber and does not request specific studies pertaining only to itself; in this way, commercial houses provide a number of research services more inexpensively than if data are collected for a firm's sole use. Among the leaders are A.C. Nielsen (**http://www.acnielsen.com**), IMS Health (**http://www.imshealth.com**), Arbitron (**http://www.arbitron.com**), and Maritz Research (**http://www.maritz.com**).

Two excellent online sources of free marketing information on various subjects are About Marketing (**http://marketing.about.com**) and KnowThis.com's *Marketing Virtual Library* (**http://www.knowthis.com**).

4-5c Primary Data

Primary data consist of information gathered to address a specific issue or problem at hand. Such data are needed if secondary data are insufficient for a proper marketing decision to be made.

> **Primary data** relate to a specific marketing issue.

Advantages and Disadvantages Primary data have these general advantages and disadvantages:

Advantages
- They are collected to fit the precise purpose of the current research topic.
- Information is current.
- The methodology of data collection is controlled and known by the firm.
- All findings are available to the firm, which can maintain its secrecy.
- There are no conflicting data from different sources.
- A study can be replicated (if desired).
- When secondary data do not resolve all questions, collecting and analyzing primary data is the only way to acquire information.

Disadvantages
- Collection may be time consuming.
- Costs may be high.
- Some types of information cannot be collected (e.g., Census data).
- The company's perspective may be limited.
- The firm may be incapable of collecting primary data.

Research Design If a firm decides primary data are needed, it must devise a ***research design***, which outlines the procedures for collecting and analyzing data. A research design includes the following decisions.

Who Collects the Data? A company can collect data itself or hire an outside research firm for a specific project. The advantages of an internal research department are the knowledge of company operations, total access to company personnel, ongoing assembly and storage of data, and high commitment. The disadvantages of an internal department are the continuous costs, narrow perspective, possible lack of expertise on the latest research techniques, and potentially excessive support for the views of top management. The strengths and weaknesses of an outside research firm are the opposite of those for an inside department.

What Information Should Be Collected? The kinds and amounts of data to be collected should be keyed to the issue (problem) formulated by the firm. Exploratory research requires different data collection than that for conclusive research.

Who or What Should Be Studied? First, the people or objects to be studied must be stated; they comprise the population. People studies typically involve customers, personnel, and/or distribution intermediaries. Object studies usually center on firm and/or product performance.

Second, the way in which people or objects are selected must be decided. Large and/or dispersed populations usually are examined by ***sampling***, which requires the analysis of selected people or objects in the designated population, rather than all of them. It saves time and money; and when used properly, the sample's accuracy and representativeness can be measured. With *probability (random) sampling*, every member of the designated population has an equal or known probability of being chosen for analysis. For example, a researcher may select every 50th person in a phone directory. With *nonprobability sampling*, members of the population are chosen on the basis of convenience or judgment. For instance, an interviewer may select the first 100 dormitory students entering a college cafeteria. A probability sample is more accurate, but it is more costly and difficult than a nonprobability sample.

Marketing and the Web

Tips for Doing Marketing Research Online

In 2005, companies spent more than $1.1 billion on online marketing research, a 16 percent increase over 2004. Among the advantages of online research are the ability to conduct surveys without having to employ interviewers, the automatic collection of responses, fewer coding errors, and greater respondent anonymity.

Here are some tips for conducing marketing research online:

- Develop specific objectives for data collection. Pre-test your study on a small sample to assure it accomplishes these objectives.
- Define your sample carefully. Survey methodology, content, and incentives need to reflect the sample's characteristics.
- Determine how to contact respondents. Choose among using E-mail notifications, Web links, and pop-up windows.
- Find the optimal balance between brevity and length. Too short a questionnaire may leave some topics uncovered, and overly long questionnaires can affect response rates.
- Show respondents their progress on a questionnaire with a bar chart or percentage completion graph.
- Use open-ended questions to explore respondents' attitudes. New text-mining software facilitates the coding of these questions.
- Carefully monitor responses. Is the response rate low? Is the survey completed in the promised time?
- Use a proper incentive to increase your response rate. Match the incentive to the effort needed to properly complete the survey.

Source: Based on material in Richard Kottler, "Eight Tips Offer Best Practices for Online MR [Market Research]," *Marketing News* (April 1, 2005), pp. 24-25.

Third, the sample size must be set. Generally, a large sample will yield greater accuracy and will cost more than a small sample. Other methods exist for assessing sample size in terms of accuracy and costs, but a description of them is beyond the scope of this text.

One of the leading firms in client sampling support is Survey Sampling International (**http://www.ssisamples.com**).

What Technique of Data Collection Should Be Used?. Four basic methods of primary-data collection are used: survey, observation, experiment, and simulation.

A *survey* gathers information from respondents by communicating with them. It can uncover data about attitudes, purchases, intentions, and consumer traits. Yet, it is subject to incorrect or biased answers. A questionnaire is used to record answers. A survey can be done in person or by phone or mail. At its Web site, Surveypro.com offers a series of free tutorials on how to design surveys (**http://www.surveypro.com/tutorial**) and dozens of sample questions (**http://www.surveypro.com/sample**).

A *personal survey* is face-to-face and flexible, can elicit lengthy replies, and reduces ambiguity. It may be relatively expensive, however, and bias is possible because the interviewer may affect results by suggesting ideas to respondents or by creating a certain mood during the interview. A *phone survey* is fast and relatively inexpensive, especially with the growth of discount telephone services. Responses are usually brief, and non-response may be a problem. It must be verified that the desired respondent is the one contacted. Some people do not have a phone, or they have unlisted numbers. The latter problem is now overcome through computerized, random digit-dialing devices. A *mail survey* reaches dispersed respondents, has no interviewer bias, and is relatively inexpensive. Nonresponse, slowness of returns, and participation by incorrect respondents are the major problems. The technique chosen depends on the goals and needs of the specific research project.

With a *nondisguised survey*, the respondent is told a study's real purpose; in a *disguised survey*, the person is not. The latter may be used to indirectly probe

> A **survey** communicates in person, over the phone, or by mail.

Nondisguised

1. Why are you buying a sports car?
_____
_____
_____

2. What factors are you considering in the purchase of a sports car?
_____
_____
_____

3. Is status important to you in buying a sports car?
_____ Yes
_____ No

4. On the highway, I will drive my sports car
_____ within the speed limit.
_____ slightly over the speed limit.
_____ well over the speed limit.

Disguised

1. Why do you think people buy sports cars?
_____
_____
_____

2. What factors do people consider in the purchase of a sports car?
_____
_____
_____

3. Are people who purchase sports cars status-conscious?
_____ Yes
_____ No

4. On the highway, sports car owners drive
_____ within the speed limit.
_____ slightly over the speed limit.
_____ well over the speed limit.

Figure 4-9

Nondisguised and Disguised Surveys

Figure 4-10

A Semantic Differential for a Color Television

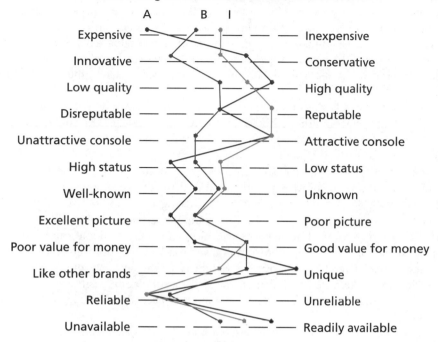

Please mark the blanks that best indicate your feelings about Brand A, your feelings about Brand B, and your ideal rating for a 27" **color console television set**.

	A B I	
Expensive		Inexpensive
Innovative		Conservative
Low quality		High quality
Disreputable		Reputable
Unattractive console		Attractive console
High status		Low status
Well-known		Unknown
Excellent picture		Poor picture
Poor value for money		Good value for money
Like other brands		Unique
Reliable		Unreliable
Unavailable		Readily available

Legend: A = brand of the company
         B = leading competitor
         I = ideal rating for a brand by respondent

attitudes and avoid a person's answering what he or she thinks the interviewer wants to hear or read. The left side of Figure 4-9 is nondisguised and shows the true intent of a study on people's attitudes and behavior about sports cars. The right side shows how the survey can be disguised: By asking about sports car owners in general, a firm may get more honest answers than with questions directed right at the respondent. The intent of the disguised study is to uncover the respondent's actual reasons for buying a sports car.

A **semantic differential** is a list of bipolar (opposite) adjective scales. It is a survey technique with rating scales instead of, or in addition to, traditional questions. It may be disguised or nondisguised, depending on whether the respondent is told a study's true purpose. Each adjective in a semantic differential is rated on a bipolar scale, and average scores for all respondents are computed. An overall company or product profile is then devised. The profile may be compared with competitors' profiles and consumers' ideal ratings. Figure 4-10 shows a semantic differential.

Observation is a research method whereby present behavior or the results of past behavior are observed and noted. People are not questioned and cooperation is unnecessary. Interviewer and question bias are minimized. Observation often is used in actual situations. The major disadvantages are that attitudes cannot be determined and observers may misinterpret behavior.

In disguised observation, a person is unaware he or she is being watched. A two-way mirror, hidden camera, or other device would be used. With nondisguised observation, a person knows he or she is being observed. Human observation is done by people; mechanical observation records behavior by electronic or other means, such as a video camera taping in-store customer behavior or reactions to a sales presentation.

> A nondisguised survey reveals its purpose, whereas a disguised one does not.

> A **semantic differential** uses bipolar adjectives.

> In **observation**, behavior is viewed.

An **experiment** varies marketing factors under controlled conditions.

An *experiment* is a type of research in which one or more factors are manipulated under controlled conditions. A factor may be any element of marketing, from package design to advertising media. In an experiment, just the factor under study is varied; all other factors remain constant. For example, to evaluate a new package design for a product, a manufacturer could send new packages to five retail outlets and old packages to five similar outlets; all marketing factors other than packaging remain the same. After one month, sales of the new package at the test outlets are compared with sales of the old package at similar outlets. A survey or observation is used to determine the reactions to an experiment.

An experiment's key advantage is that it can show cause and effect—such as a new package lifting sales. It is also methodically structured and enacted. Key disadvantages are the rather high costs, frequent use of contrived settings, and inability to control all factors in or affecting a marketing plan.

Simulation enables marketing factors to be analyzed via a computer model.

Simulation is a computer-based method to test the potential effects of various marketing factors via a software program rather than real-world applications. A model of the controllable and uncontrollable factors facing the firm is first built. Different combinations of factors are then fed into a computer to see their possible impact on a marketing strategy. Simulation requires no consumer cooperation and can handle many interrelated factors. Yet, it may be complex and hard to use; does not measure actual attitudes, behavior, and intentions; and is subject to the accuracy of the assumptions made. For an online, interactive demonstration of a simulation, visit Marketplace Business Simulations' Web site (**http://www.marketplace-simulation.com**) and click "demos."

Table 4-2 shows the best uses for each kind of primary data collection.

How Much Will the Study Cost?. The overall and specific costs of a study must be outlined. Costs may include executive time, researcher time, support staff time, pre-testing, computer usage, respondent incentives (if any), interviewers, supplies, printing, postage or phone expenses, special equipment, and marketing expenses (such as ads).

Research costs range from personnel time to marketing expenses.

A study's expected costs should be compared with the expected benefits to be derived. Suppose a consumer survey costing $10,000 would let a firm improve the package design of a new product. With the changes suggested by research, the firm would lift its first-year profit by $30,000. Thus, the net increase due to research is $20,000 ($30,000 profit less $10,000 in costs).

How Will the Data Be Collected?. The people needed to collect the required data must be determined and the attributes, skills, and training of the data-collection force specified. Too often, this important phase is improperly planned, and data are collected by unqualified people.

Interviewers administer surveys or respondents fill them out.

Data collection can be administered by research personnel or it can be self-administered. With *administered data collection*, interviewers ask questions or observers note

Table **4-2**	The Best Uses of Primary Data-Collection Techniques
Technique	**Most Appropriate Uses**
Survey	When determining consumer or distribution intermediary attitudes and motivations toward marketing-mix factors; measuring purchase intentions; relating consumer traits to attitudes
Observation	When examining actual responses to marketing factors under realistic conditions; interest in behavior and not in attitudes
Experiment	When controlling the research environment is essential, and establishing a cause-and-effect relationship is important
Simulation	When deriving and analyzing many interrelationships among variables

behavior; they record answers or behavior and explain questions (if asked) to respondents. With *self-administered data collection*, respondents read questions and write their answers. There is a trade-off between control and interviewer probing (administered) versus privacy and limited interviewer bias (self-administered).

How Long Will the Data-Collection Period Be?. The time frame for data collection must be stipulated, or else a study can drag on. Too long a time frame may lead to inconsistent responses and secrecy violations. Short time frames are easy to set for personal and phone surveys. Mail surveys, observation, and experiments often require much more time to implement; nonetheless, time limits must be defined.

When and Where Should Information Be Collected?. The day and time of data collection must be set. It must also be decided if a study is done on or off a firm's premises. The desire for immediacy and convenience has to be weighed against the need to contact hard-to-reach respondents at the proper time.

Data Collection. After the research design is detailed, data are then collected. Those engaged in data collection must be properly supervised and follow directions exactly. Responses or observations must be entered correctly.

4-5d   Data Analysis

In **data analysis**, the information on questionnaires or answer forms is first coded and tabulated and then analyzed. Coding is the process by which each completed data form is numbered and response categories are labeled. Tabulation is the calculation of summary data for each response category. Analysis is the evaluation of responses, usually by statistical techniques, as they pertain to the specific issue or problem under investigation. The relationship of coding, tabulation, and analysis is shown in Figure 4-11.

> **Data analysis** consists of coding, tabulation, and analysis.

One firm offering data analysis services is 1010data (**http://www.1010data.com**). Visit its site for a "test drive."

4-5e   Recommendations

Recommendations are suggestions for a firm's future actions based on marketing research findings. They are typically presented in written (sometimes oral) form to marketing decision makers. The report must be appropriate for the intended audience. Thus, technical terminology must be defined. Figure 4-11 shows recommendations flowing from completed research.

After recommendations are made to the proper decision makers, the research report should be warehoused in the marketing intelligence network. It may be retrieved in the future, as needed. Sample research reports may be viewed at Envirosell's Web site (**http://www.envirosell.com/case_studies.html**).

4-5f   Implementation of Findings

A research report represents feedback for marketing managers, who are responsible for using findings. If they ignore the findings, research has little value. If they base decisions on the results, then marketing research has great value and the organization benefits in the short and long run.

Marketing managers are most apt to implement research findings if they have input into the research design, broad control over marketing decisions, and confidence that results are accurate. Figure 4-11 provides an illustration of how a firm could implement research findings.

1. Do you drink coffee?	☐ Yes	01	300
	☐ No	02	200
2. In general, how frequently do you drink coffee? (Check only one answer.)	☐ Two or more times per day	03	142
	☐ Once per day	04	84
	☐ Several times per week	05	42
	☐ Once or twice per week	06	20
	☐ One to three times per month	07	12
	☐ Never	08	200
3. During what time of day do you drink coffee? (Check all answers that apply.)	☐ Morning	09	270
	☐ Lunch time	10	165
	☐ Afternoon	11	100
	☐ Dinner time	12	150
	☐ Evening	13	205
	☐ None	14	200

Coding: Questionnaires numbered A001 to A500. Each response is labeled 01 to 14 (e.g., Morning is 09; Evening is 13). Question 3 is a multiple-response question.

Tabulation: Total responses are shown above right.

Analysis: 60% drink coffee. About 28% drink coffee two or more times daily (representing 47% of all coffee drinkers); almost 25% of coffee drinkers (74 people) consume coffee less than once per day. 90% of coffee drinkers consume coffee in the morning; only one-third consume it in the afternoon.

Recommendations: The coffee industry and individual firms need to increase the advertising geared toward noncoffee drinkers, as well as infrequent coffee drinkers. Emphasis should also be placed on lifting coffee consumption during afternoon hours.

Implementation of findings: New, more aggressive advertising campaigns will be developed and the annual media budgets devoted to increasing overall coffee consumption will be expanded. One theme will stress coffee's value as an afternoon "pick-me-upper."

Figure 4-11

Data Analysis, Recommendations, and Implementation of Findings for a Study on Coffee

Web Sites You Can Use

A number of Web sites are valuable for a firm to visit when collecting the information necessary to make the proper marketing decisions. Here is a cross section of general-interest sites:

- Annual Report Gallery (**http://www.reportgallery.com**)— "A free Internet service that will enable interested parties

to review a company's annual report in an easy convenient manner."

- Competitive Intelligence Resource Index (**http://www.bidigital.com/ci**)—"A search engine and listing of sites-by-category for finding competitive intelligence resources."

- Dismal Scientist (**http://www.economy.com/dismal**)— "Provides daily analysis of the global macroeconomic, industry, financial, and regional trends that affect your business, organization, or investments."
- How Stuff Works (**http://www.howstuffworks.com**)— "Widely recognized as the leading source for clear, reliable explanations of how everything around us actually works."
- *Information Please Almanac* (**http://www.infoplease.com**)—"All the knowledge you need."
- Internet Public Library Reference Center (**http:// www.ipl.org**)—"The first public library of and for the Internet community."

- LibrarySpot (**http://www.libraryspot.com**)—"To break through the information overload of the Web and bring the best library and reference sites together."
- Marketingprofs.com (**http://www.marketingprofs.com**)— "Marketing know-how from professionals + professors."
- Marketing Today (**http://www.marketingtoday.com/ news_feeds/index.htm**)—"The Online Guide to Marketing in the Information Age."

Summary

1. *To show why marketing information is needed* With good information, a firm can accurately assess its strengths, weaknesses, opportunities, and threats; operate properly in the marketing environment; and maximize performance. Reliance on gut feelings, judgment, and experience is not sufficient. The scientific method requires objectivity, accuracy, and thoroughness in research projects.

2. *To explain the role and importance of marketing information systems* Collecting marketing information should not be viewed as an infrequent event. Acting in that manner can have negative ramifications, especially with regard to misreading the competition and other external factors that can affect a firm's performance.

   A marketing information system (MIS) is a set of procedures to generate, analyze, disseminate, and store anticipated marketing decision information on a regular, continuous basis. It can aid a company operationally, managerially, and strategically.

3. *To examine a basic marketing information system, commercial data bases, data-base marketing, and examples of marketing information systems in action* The key to a basic MIS is the marketing intelligence network, which consists of continuous monitoring, marketing research, and data warehousing. The intelligence network is influenced by the environment, company goals, and marketing plans, and it affects the implementation of marketing plans. Marketing research should be considered as just one part of an ongoing, integrated information system. An MIS can be used by both small and large firms.

   Specialized research firms offer valuable information via commercial data bases that contain data on the population, the business environment, the economy, industry and company performance, and other factors. Data bases are available in printed form, on CDs and DVDs, and as downloads from the Internet.

   Many firms look to data-base marketing for improving their customer interactions. Data-base marketing involves setting up an automated system to identify and characterize customers and prospects and then

using quantifiable information to better reach them. With data mining, firms seek out hidden opportunities related to specific customers.

Marketing information systems are being used by firms of every size and type.

4. *To define marketing research and its components and to look at its scope* Marketing research entails systematically gathering, recording, and analyzing data about specific issues related to the marketing of goods, services, organizations, people, places, and ideas. It may be done internally or externally.

   Expenditures on marketing research run into the billions of dollars annually. Five aspects of research are noteworthy: customer satisfaction studies, the growth of Web-based research, single-source data collection, ethical considerations, and intricacies of international research.

5. *To describe the marketing research process* This process consists of defining the issue or problem to be studied, examining secondary data, generating primary data (when needed), analyzing data, making recommendations, and implementing findings. Many considerations and decisions are needed in each stage.

   Exploratory (qualitative) research is used to develop a clear definition of the study topic. Conclusive (quantitative) research looks at a specific issue in a structured manner. Secondary data—not gathered for the study at hand but for some other purpose—are available from internal and external (government, nongovernment, commercial) sources. Primary data—collected specifically for the purpose of the investigation at hand—are available through surveys, observation, experiments, and simulation. Primary data collection requires a research design: the framework for guiding data collection and analysis. Primary data are gathered only if secondary data are inadequate. Costs must be weighed against the benefits of research. The final stages of marketing research are data analysis—coding, tabulating, and analysis; recommendations—suggestions for future actions based on research findings; and implementation of findings by management.

Key Terms

scientific method (p. 87)

marketing information system (MIS) (p. 88)

marketing intelligence network (p. 90)

continuous monitoring (p. 90)

marketing research (p. 90)

data warehousing (p. 90)

commercial data bases (p. 91)

data-base marketing (p. 91)

data mining (p. 91)

marketing research (p. 94)

single-source data collection (p. 97)

marketing research process (p. 98)

issue (problem) definition (p. 99)

exploratory research (p. 99)

conclusive research (p. 99)

secondary data (p. 99)

primary data (p. 102)

research design (p. 103)

sampling (p. 103)

survey (p. 104)

semantic differential (p. 105)

observation (p. 105)

experiment (p. 106)

simulation (p. 106)

data analysis (p. 107)

Review Questions

1. Why is marketing information necessary? What may result if managers rely exclusively on intuition?
2. What is the scientific method? Must it be used each time a firm does research? Explain your answer.
3. Describe the elements of a basic marketing information system.
4. Distinguish between commercial data bases and data-base marketing.

5. Differentiate between conclusive and exploratory research. Give an example of each.
6. When is primary data collection necessary?
7. Outline the steps in a research design.
8. Under what circumstances should a firm use observation to collect data? Simulation? Explain your answers.

Discussion Questions

1. A PC manufacturer wants to get information on the average amount that U.S. companies spend annually on PCs, what types of PCs they buy, the characteristics of the companies that buy PCs, the time of year when PC purchases are heaviest and lightest, the sales of leading competitors, and customer satisfaction. Explain how the firm should set up and enact a marketing intelligence network. Include internal and external data sources in your answer.

2. FedEx Kinko's is an internationally oriented copy-and-print chain. Barbara's Copy Center is an independent local business. If both wish to gather data about their respective competitors' marketing practices, how would your research design differ for each?
3. Develop a semantic differential to determine attitudes toward the price of movie DVDs. Explain your choice of adjectives.
4. Comment on the ethics of disguised surveys. When would you recommend that they be used?

Web Exercise

At its Web site, SuperSurvey (http://www.supersurvey.com/demo.htm) provides a demonstration of how its online survey service presents results. Select "Results viewer demo reports."

Describe what you learn from this demonstration. Would you recommend SuperSurvey? Why or why not?

Practice Quiz

1. Which of the following is *not* a reason why a firm should continuously collect and analyze information regarding its marketing plan?
   a. To gain a competitive edge
   b. To monitor the environment
   c. To rely more heavily on executive judgment
   d. To coordinate strategy

2. Which of the following is *not* a component of a marketing intelligence network?
   a. Simulation
   b. Data warehousing
   c. Marketing research
   d. Continuous monitoring

Case 2: Should Customers Ever Be Turned Away?[c1-2]

A recent trend in marketing is for manufacturers and retailers to focus their marketing strategies on their profitable consumers. Some have even tried to reduce purchases by unprofitable customers. Delta (http://www.delta.com) is among the airlines that recently changed their frequent flyer programs to make it more difficult for consumers who continually select the lowest airline fares to earn free trips. Likewise, many retailers have begun to track consumers and refuse to provide refunds to consumers who frequently return merchandise. Some banks have increased usage fees on small and unprofitable accounts.

The electronics chain Best Buy (http://www.bestbuy.com) hired Larry Selden, author of *Angel Customers and Demon Customers*, to help the firm remove unprofitable customers from its mailing list. Most unprofitable customers that Best Buy is targeting have a history of abusive returns (such as returning a good in unsaleable condition or returning a laptop computer he or she purchased for short-term use instead of renting the unit). Best Buy's Reward Zone loyalty program is intended to recruit its most profitable customers instead of trying to maximize customer participation. According to the agency that created the Reward Zone program, "It is controversial to redline customers. But done correctly, it really is simply about saying I have a limited pool of money, and I need as a businessperson to spend that money where I can get the most return." Best Buy's Reward Zone members, on average, spend $844 per year at the chain versus about $400 for its average customer. Same-store sales growth in stores with the Reward Zone program have averaged double that of stores where the program has not yet been established.

Unilever (http://www.unilever.com), has a different viewpoint in dealing with unprofitable customers. Unilever's HomeBasics relationship marketing program is designed to reach Unilever's highest-value consumers with direct mail and online messages and to get them to increase their spending. However, as the head of HomeBasics says, "It may be different in a service industry, but when it comes to us, there are no undesirable customers. There are undesirable marketing tactics. If we can't make money selling a product, that's not the consumer's fault."

Some of difficulties also exist in reducing rewards given to less profitable customers. In December 2002, Delta changed its Skyline program to give passengers paying its lowest fares one-quarter of the miles it gave to its profitable first-class customers. Even before the new program was announced, angry customers started a Web site, SaveSkymiles.com (http://www.saveskymiles.com). As a result of the December 2002 changes, some passengers filed a class-action suit against Delta and even raised money to purchase ads in *USA Today* critical of Delta. Delta subsequently changed its rewards system so that first-class passengers now get 150 percent as many points and upgrades as customers who pay the lowest fares (versus 400 percent before the change).

Another potential problem is that competitors may not follow a firm's strategy in dealing with unprofitable customers. In the early 1990s, Procter & Gamble (P&G) (http://www.pg.com) reduced coupon spending and trade promotions while it increased its advertising and cut list prices. As P&G's chairman and chief executive officer said, "The cost per net extra case [for couponing] is about twice the net sales coupons generate, or about eight to 10 times its profit contribution." Unfortunately for P&G, its competitors did not follow its strategy. Ultimately, P&G lost 18 percent in market share without a significant increase in brand loyalty. And when P&G's competitors followed its coupon-free marketing program in upstate New York, they were subjected to antitrust litigation. The case was settled by P&G's distributing $2 in coupons to affected consumers.

Questions

1. How can the profitability of a customer group be assessed?
2. a. List and describe three examples of unprofitable customers for a retailer of major appliances.
   b. List and describe three examples of unprofitable customers for a local supermarket.
3. Describe three potential pitfalls to a marketer's strategy of reducing purchases by its least profitable customers.
4. Develop a loyalty card program for a hotel chain that reflects the profitability of different customer segments.

[c1-2] The data in the case are drawn from Jack Neff, "Why Some Marketers Turn Away Customers," *Advertising Age* (February 14, 2005): pp. 1, 10.

Case 3: Southwest Airlines: Retooling While on Top[c1-3]

During its nearly four decades of service, Southwest Airlines' (http://www.southwest.com) operating strategy has been a simple one. In return for its mechanics, pilots, and flight attendants out-hustling its competitors, Southwest would provide job security and reward employees with company stock. Yet, even though Southwest has never laid off an employee and its stock is valued at $11 billion (almost three times that of the other major airlines combined), Southwest's May 2005 stock price was down by more than 30 percent as compared with 2001. Much of its 2005 profits were due to Southwest's hedging fuel costs better than competitors. As a result, its fuel cost for 85 percent of its needs was $26 per barrel versus an industry average cost of over $50. Without the fuel cost advantage, Southwest would have lost money in four of the past nine quarters as of March 2005.

Southwest Airlines' overall strategy has focused on several components: operational simplicity due to the use of one type of aircraft (this keeps mechanic training and parts inventory low), a company-wide devotion to keeping costs and fares low, and an emphasis on efficiency (due to the fast turnaround of its aircraft between arrival and departure). Southwest's strategy was distinctive in the past, but today, it has been copied by airlines such as JetBlue (http://www.jetblue.com) and AirTran (http://www.airtran.com). According to current chief executive, "Hey, I can admit it, our competitors are getting better. Sure, we have an enormous cost advantage. Sure, we're the most efficient. The problem is, I just don't see how that can be indefinitely sustained without some sacrifice."

Southwest is increasingly facing competition from new upstarts, as well as the entrenched legacy carriers. Upstarts such as JetBlue initially borrowed Southwest's one-airplane model and added such goodies as leather seats, individual TV screens, and fancy snacks. JetBlue's costs are lower than Southwest's. And the legacy carriers such as Delta (http://www.delta.com) and United (http://www.united.com) have cut their cost of flying a passenger mile to 8.4 cents versus Southwest's 6.3 cents. The recent bankruptcies of Delta, Northwest (http://www.nwa.com/), United, and US Airways (http://www.usairways.com) enabled these airlines to cut unprofitable routes, reduce interest payments for aircraft, reduce pension obligations, and lower employee wages.

One way that Southwest is seeking to better compete is by expanding its routes. This lets Southwest lower its personnel costs by hiring new, lower-paid employees and spreading its administrative overhead costs over more seats. Southwest recently increased its presence in the Chicago market by raising the number of flights at Midway airport. Its purchase of a share in ATA (http://www.ata.com), a bankrupt carrier, also gave Southwest's customers greater access to such cities as Boston, Denver, Minneapolis, and Honolulu. Southwest also started flying to Philadelphia and Pittsburgh.

Southwest is seeking to improve its efficiency through employee, attrition, a hiring freeze, and generous severance packages to longtime employees. It reduced the number of employees per aircraft from 89 in 2002 to 74 in 2005. Another source of savings is through technology that automates certain functions or provides self-service opportunities to customers. Among Southwest's high-technology applications are its Southwest Web site (responsible for over $3 billion in annual bookings), its self-service kiosks, and the Gate Reader software that keeps gate agents up-to-date on a passenger's status and special needs. As Southwest's chief information officer says, "As our airline scales, for us to provide the same kind of high-touch customer service, we have to automate a lot of things we've been able to do without technology previously. The challenge is doing that without conceding the customer touch."

Questions

1. Discuss the strategic benefits of Southwest Airlines' low-cost strategy.
2. Describe how the bankruptcy filings of Delta and United are reducing Southwest's low-cost advantage.
3. How can Southwest sustain its low-cost strategy?
4. Explain how Southwest Airlines can retain its corporate culture as it expands further.

[c1-3] The data in the case are drawn from Barney Gimbel, "Southwest's New Flight Plan," *Fortune* (May 16, 2005), pp. 93-98; and Tony Kontzer, "Wings of Change," *Informationweek* (March 28, 2005): pp. 37-38, 42.

Case 4: Fedex Kinko's: A Creative Collaboration[c1-4]

In January 2004, FedEx purchased Kinko's, a 150-store chain specializing in print and Web access services for final and business consumers. A major advantage of the purchase for FedEx was its ability to quickly add FedEx's full range of shipping services in all of Kinko's locations. FedEx decided to combine its 1,000-plus overnight delivery storefronts with Kinko's stores so that the firm could "make it, print it, pack it, and ship it." According to FedEx Kinko's (**http://www.fedexkinkos.com**) vice-president of field operations, "The branding and logistical elements of the merger have been completed with the customer in mind." FedEx Kinko's now has about 1,450 chain locations with 21,000 employees in 11 countries.

The transition was far from easy. To compete effectively, the combined operations needed an information system that could track labor costs, pricing data, and customer data. Among the challenges that FedEx Kinko's faced were the lack of a uniform data warehouse, the use of different computer systems, the need for duplicate data entry, and aging point-of-sale systems.

FedEx Kinko's new system, called Order-to-Pay, has a number of distinctive attributes. Customer information can be accessed at all FedEx Kinko's locations. A Philadelphia-based customer can revise and print a PowerPoint presentation made in Chicago and then E-mail the presentation to any location. The new marketing information system also contains considerable data on each customer. This data base will enable FedEx Kinko's to better develop new services, as well as to more effectively personalize services to meet each customer's unique needs: "Customer benefits range from faster and easier ordering and checkout to improved order status, tracking, and easy reordering of frequent orders."

FedEx Kinko's serves two distinct groups of business customers, as well as final consumers. Large business consumers typically use FedEx Kinko's to ship merchandise and to outsource printing functions; small and middle-size businesses use it more for creating presentations, printing, and shipping. For each of these segments, FedEx Kinko's also serves as a vital link between a mobile professional and a firm's library of corporate documents. Documents such as sales presentations and marketing materials are stored by FedEx Kinko's and can be printed online when needed.

Both small and large accounts now utilize FedEx for their sign and banner needs. Before the acquisition by FedEx, Kinko's had sign and banner departments in many of its stores. After the acquisition, FedEx Kinko's opened three stores that specialize in producing signs and graphics. These stores are able to utilize advanced graphics in signs ranging from five-foot trade show posters to large outdoor grand-opening banners. Now, FedEx Kinko's also has 380 sign and banner departments that can produce a wide range of signs and banners (except for neon and electric signs). Sign hanging and mounting supplies are also available.

One growing market for business consumers is the shipment of large digital packages: "If someone needs to E-mail a 12 MB presentation to a 12-member sales staff, a company's servers may not be built to handle that load. Ours can handle it. Delivery isn't just limited to air and ground."

Many final users like to use FedEx Kinko's Wi-Fi connections to access the Web and E-mail applications from locations away from home. A large group of job seekers also use FedEx Kinko's for printing resumés and envelopes.

In recognition of its information technology, *Information Week* awarded FedEx Kinko's "*Information Week* 500" status for a top information innovator (2001-2004). FedEx Kinko's recently announced that it will use 30 percent post-consumer recycled paper (instead of 10 percent). This change will conserve roughly 18,850 tons of wood.

Questions

1. Describe FedEx Kinko's line of business.
2. Discuss the synergies between FedEx and Kinko's for final consumers.
3. Discuss the synergies between FedEx and Kinko's for organizational consumers.
4. How can FedEx Kinko's avoid marketing myopia?

[c1-4] The data in the case are drawn from John Gaffney, "FedEx Kinko's Prints Customer Plan," *1to1 Magazine* (May-June 2005): pp. 11-12; Steve Rowen, "Fed Excellence," *Chain Store Age* (July 2005): p. 46A; and "About FedEx" **http://www.fedex.com** (April 30, 2006).

Making Sure That Marketing Decisions Match the Business Strategy[pc-1]

INTRODUCTION

As one chief executive once said, "Strategies most often fail because they aren't executed well. Things that are supposed to happen don't happen." But what is required for successful strategy execution? Our research shows that though some strategies excel under certain conditions, any of the business strategies we describe can succeed in competitive environments if properly implemented. Moreover, conditions in the competitive environment change. We believe that once senior management commits to a business strategy, the execution of the strategy depends on making the appropriate marketing decisions.

CHOOSING STRATEGIES

There are four fundamental business strategies that each organization must choose from and then stick with: Pioneer, Fast Follower, Cost Leader, and Customer Centrics.

Pioneer

The Pioneers' primary goal is to identify and exploit new product and market opportunities by offering innovative products or by viewing the market from a different perspective. For example, W.L. Gore and Associates (http://www.gore.com) innovates on many fronts and boldly follows its inventions into completely different businesses. The company got its start when Bill Gore, a DuPont chemist, envisioned some ways to use Teflon that DuPont (http://www.dupont.com) wasn't pursuing. In 1969, Gore's son, Bob, found a way to stretch the polymer to create Gore-Tex, which became the basis for a host of new products, including the outdoor fabric that is still W.L. Gore's best-selling line. Using Gore-Tex as its springboard, Gore has also become a major player in areas as diverse as guitar strings, dental floss, medical devices, and fuel cells.

Fast Follower

Fast Followers imitate Pioneers' successful product and market development efforts while maintaining a core of traditional products and customers. Because Fast Followers don't have the first-mover advantage of Pioneers, they must improve on the Pioneers' offering.

Followers can be as successful as early entrants if they're committed to learning from customers about their experiences with Pioneers' offerings and if they carefully follow Pioneers' strategic moves.

In 2000, Bill Gates went to the annual Game Developers Conference in San Jose, bearing a blaster aimed at Sony (http://www.sony.com), whose PlayStation 2 had rocked Japan the previous week by selling nearly a million machines in three days. After a year of top-secret development, Gates revealed details about X-Box, a video game machine that could someday be one of Microsoft's (http://www.microsoft.com) most lucrative new products. X-Box would have more speed, better graphics and audio, and more memory than the PlayStation 2. Similar to the situation in operating systems, applications software, and Internet browsers, Microsoft was not a pioneer in video game machines. However, this has not stopped Microsoft from dominating those markets.

Cost Leader

Cost Leaders are usually late entrants that engage in aggressive efforts to protect their market from competitors. They typically achieve cost leadership through comparisons of their value-chain costs with those of competitors. They seek efficiency in many areas of the value chain, enabling them to offer low prices. JetBlue (http://www.jetblue.com) started operations in early 2000 and has exceeded all expectations. An airline can offer low fares only by having a low cost structure. Airline costs are measured in cents per available seat mile (CASM). JetBlue has reported the lowest CASM in the industry, one-third lower than the industry average. JetBlue's operating margins have been comparable to those of Southwest Airlines (http://www.southwest.com), arguably the most successful airline in history. JetBlue was able to achieve this low-cost position by flying point-to-point, using a single aircraft type, realizing high productivity, and having faster turn times, allowing aircraft to spend less time on the ground.

Customer Centrics

Customer Centrics create customer value by offering high-quality products supported by good service at lower prices than Pioneers, yet at higher prices than either Fast Followers or Cost Leaders. This enables them to create value for buyers and achieve superior performance. The Broadmoor Hotel and Spa (http://www.broadmoor.com) in Colorado Springs has received five-star ratings from Mobil Travel Guide for more than 40 consecutive years. The goal of the hotel is simple: to give every guest an outstanding experience. To accomplish this, it provides service above and beyond what is expected, doing everything possible to provide a

[pc-1] Adapted by the authors from Stanley F. Slater, Eric M. Olson, and G. Tomas M. Hult, "Proper Pairs," *Marketing Management* (March-April 2005): pp. 23–28. Reprinted by permission of the American Marketing Association.

superior experience. Employees are recruited and trained with this service philosophy in mind, so that they will provide caring, individualized service to customers.

SUCCESSFUL STRATEGIES

Once you've determined what the most appropriate strategy will be for your organization, you must figure out how to make it successful, as highlighted in Figure 1 and discussed next.

Pioneer

The most successful Pioneers are both customer- and innovation-oriented, patient, and have a decentralized marketing organization with a high proportion of marketing specialists. They use aggressive marketing because they target innovators and early adopters. Of all

of the strategy types, Pioneers are the most proactive in their product and/or market development efforts. They monitor a wide range of market conditions, making them heavy users of marketing research. They target early adopters with innovative products, and so they must educate customers and stimulate demand through advertising. Because products are often "new to the world," they must provide high levels of service to help customers understand these innovative products before and after the sale. It is important for Pioneers to be able to charge premium prices to recoup their investment in these activities.

Newell Rubbermaid (http://www.newellrubbermaid.com), recognized by *Fortune* as a "top 10 innovator," is a prototypical Pioneer. Rubbermaid was formed in 1920 as Wooster Rubber, and in 1934 pioneered the rubber housewares business with the introduction of the first rubber dustpan. In the 1950s, Rubbermaid developed a breakthrough product for the hotel industry—a safety bathmat with suction cups on the bottom. This deceptively simple product

The most successful Pioneers:	The most successful Fast Followers:	The most successful Cost Leaders:	The most successful Customer Centrics:
• Systematically learn about customers.	• Systematically learn about customers.	• Engage in little systematic marketing research.	• Are moderate users of marketing research.
• Systematically collect information about industry trends.	• Analyze competitor objectives and actions.	• Analyze competitors' value chains.	• Systematically study customer needs.
• Learn about unarticulated customer needs with observational techniques.	• Offer a broad product/service line.	• Offer a relatively narrow product line.	• Learn about unarticulated customer needs with observational techniques.
• Use early adopters for new product/service ideas and feedback.	• Develop products/services that have broad market appeal.	• Are process, not product, innovators.	• Focus marketing activities on specific segments.
• Evaluate and focus marketing activities on specific segments.	• Price below industry average.	• Provide adequate product quality.	• Develop innovative products/ services.
• Develop innovative new products/services.	• Use price promotions and discounts.	• Are price competitors.	• Provide durable products/services.
• Quickly move from product/service concept to introduction.	• Distribute broadly.	• Distribute broadly.	• Provide products/services with high reliability.
• Regularly increase technical sophistication of products/services.	• Employ a sales force with general skills.	• Number of advertising impressions is below industry average.	• Achieve or maintain superior product performance.
• Achieve superior product performance.	• Generate sales through external sales force.	• Invest little in high-quality advertising materials.	• Provide service with a high degree of consistency and accuracy.
• Respond quickly to customers' requests and problems.	• Maintain high salesperson-to-sales-manager ratios.	• Use minimal media advertising.	• Respond quickly to customers' requests and problems.
• Provide superior service quality.	• Evaluate salesperson performance based on achievement of targets or quotas.	• Use decentralized (close to the customer) decision making.	• Clearly communicate with customers.
• Develop relationships with key customers.	• Use decentralized (close to customer) decision making.		• Provide superior service quality.
• Price above industry average.	• Employ a high number of marketing specialists.		• Develop long-term relationships with key customers.
• Use selective distribution through best distributors available.			• Employ a highly skilled and knowledgeable sales force.
• Use decentralized (close to the customer) decision making.			• Use internal sales force.
• Employ a high number of marketing specialists.			• Evaluate salesperson performance based on prescribed behaviors.
			• Use decentralized (close to the customer) decision making.

Figure 1

Steps for Success

presented a huge technical challenge: Manufacturing it required a complicated three-layer mold. It also escalated the company's development and ultimately led to the establishment of Rubbermaid Commercial Products (RCP) in 1967. Originally, RCP manufactured and marketed products for commercial and institutional markets. Throughout its history, RCP has demonstrated leadership based on its competence in the materials sciences. In the 1970s, RCP led the technology conversion from metal and wood to plastic, and in the 1980s, it led the development of high-performance industrial and agricultural products. In the 1990s, the commercial product focus turned to globalization and increasing its solution-based new-product focus. As noted on the Newell Rubbermaid Web site: "A new culture has taken shape within our firm due to the values, dedication, and passion our employees bring with them every day. It's a culture of customer focus, marketing prowess, and new product innovation. We're proactive innovators, developing, selling, and quickly implementing new products and programs at retail. Then, we follow through with high-impact marketing activities and store service."

Rubbermaid has beefed up its research and development. A $20 million NASCAR sponsorship and new TV ads (its first in years) have also pumped blood into what had become a stagnant franchise. But the firm considers those defensive moves, describing its new Phoenix Program, as "the single most important thing we're doing." The Phoenix Program is part guerrilla marketing, part corporate culture overhaul, part management training, and part crash course in how to rise from the ashes in the world of retail. Phoenix Program reps have teamed with Wal-Mart (http://www.walmart.com), Home Depot (http://www.homedepot.com), Lowe's (http://www.lowes.com), and other retailers across North America where Rubbermaid products are sold. At those retailers' stores, they do everything from stocking shelves to demonstrating new stain-resistant plastic food containers to organizing in-store scavenger hunts.

To successfully develop new products and markets, Pioneers closely observe customers' use of goods or services in normal routines, work closely with lead users, and conduct and evaluate market experiments. Procter & Gamble's (P&G), (http://www.pg.com) chief executive emphasizes that P&G innovation is driven by understanding customer needs. The firm's chief marketing officer has urged its marketers to spend lots of time with consumers in their homes, watching the ways they wash their clothes, clean their floors, and diaper their babies, and asking consumers about their habits and frustrations.

Pioneers also work closely with lead users—customers or potential customers who have needs that are advanced relative to other market members and who expect to benefit significantly from a solution to their needs. Lead users often reveal unarticulated needs. P&G has reduced its reliance on test marketing and often undertakes market experiments. In this process, the initial offering is the foundation for subsequent, more refined generations that follow.

However, as the chief executive of General Electric (http://www.ge.com) notes, a Pioneer strategy requires patience. He has poured extra money into research while loosening timelines on projects that may not pay off for 10 years or more: "I just see very clearly that unless you're out there pushing the envelope and driving innovation, you're not going to get the kind of margins and the kind of growth that we need."

Because the key to success for Pioneers is the development of innovative new products and entry into new markets, reliance on formal rules and procedures will stifle speed, creativity, and flexibility. *Fortune* has suggested that Nokia (http://www.nokia.com), a leading manufacturer of cell phones from Finland, may be the least hierarchical big firm in the world. Nokia's chief executive explains its organizational philosophy this way: "How do you send a very strong signal that this is a meritocracy, and this is a place where you are allowed to have a bit of fun, to think unlike the norm, where you are allowed to make a mistake?"

Fast Followers

The most successful Fast Followers bridge the chasm between early adopter markets and early majority markets through a mass marketing strategy. As Fast Followers are concerned both with developing new products and venturing into new markets while protecting a stable core of products and markets, they must pursue a relatively broad market with a relatively broad product line. They need less advertising than Pioneers, as Pioneers have already created awareness of the product category. Fast Followers typically use intensive distribution and relatively little promotion, and charge lower prices than Pioneers to induce switching. Microsoft has been very aggressive in its pricing to encourage potential buyers to purchase the X-Box instead of Sony's PlayStation 2. Fast Followers identify opportunities by monitoring customer reactions and competitors' activities, successes, and failures to identify unattended segments or product improvement opportunities.

Fast Followers attempt to limit new product introductions to categories that have shown promise in the marketplace. It is important for these firms to monitor customer reactions to understand their reactions to Pioneers' offerings. The Apple Newton (http://www.apple.com) was the first personal digital assistant (PDA). It used software designed to learn the owner's personal handwriting style, encompassing millions of variations. A *Doonesbury* comic strip captured the essence of the user's experience: A man scrawls "I am writing a test sentence" and the machine throws back "Egg freckles?" Learning from customer experiences with the Newton, Palm Pilot (http://www.palm.com) designers figured it would be more effective to have one style of script that millions of users could easily learn rather than the other way around. It worked, with millions of Palm Pilot users happily learning Graffiti.

To more effectively learn about customer likes and dislikes, Microsoft has moved beyond using researchers, who typically sit in labs behind one-way mirrors watching consumers grapple with software, to using small teams of anthropologists who visit the homes of regular people and study them at their computers. Afterward, they report their findings back to the company, which combines the data with results from focus groups, phone surveys, and Microsoft's usability labs.

Successful Fast Followers also monitor competitors to understand their successes and failures, and to identify competitors' product-market development plans so that they will not be starting from too far behind. Avis (http://www.avis.com) has successfully employed the competitor-oriented philosophy, embodied in the slogan "We Try Harder." By portraying itself as the follower to industry leader Hertz (**http://www.hertz.com**), Avis focused the attention of its employees on providing superior service. This approach had the dual benefit of creating a unique position in the minds of consumers who came to see "No. 2" Avis as both a close rival of Hertz and distinctly separated from the rest of the car rental pack.

Cost Leaders

The most successful Cost Leaders are marketing minimizers. They are internal-cost oriented, place lower emphasis on product innovation, and have decentralized marketing organizations. Marketing minimizers reduce risk by waiting until a product concept is proven in the market before introducing their version. They pursue their market with adequate quality, low prices, and an intensive distribution strategy. They generally have the most focused product line and use the fewest specialist marketing personnel.

Dell Computer (**http://www.dell.com**) is a master of this strategy. Dell machines are made to order and delivered directly to the customer, who gets the exact machine he or she wants at a lower price than the competition. The firm gets paid by the customer weeks before it pays suppliers. Dell is so successful that it ranks very high on the *Fortune 500*, ahead of Coca-Cola (**http://www.cocacola.com**), Microsoft, and DuPont.

Cost Leaders defend their market from competitors by benchmarking their value chain costs against those of competitors. They seek to reduce costs in primary activities such as logistics, operations, and sales and marketing, and reduce costs in support activities such as procurement, R&D, and administration. Continuous improvement in operations lets a firm to realize improvements as it drives down the learning curve. This does not mean that these firms ignore innovation. It means that process innovation that improves production efficiency takes precedence over product innovation. It also does not mean that Cost Leaders ignore customers; it means that customer relationships have a different focus. As Michael Dell says, "We have a relentless focus on our customers. Once we learn directly from our customers what they need, we work closely with partners and vendors to build and ship relevant technologies at a low cost."

Customer Centrics

The best Customer Centrics target narrow segments where they can develop close relationships with customers and provide high-quality, innovative products to them. However, the firms engage in only a moderate amount of marketing research and do not typically charge prices as high as Pioneers do. Their distribution strategy is generally selective and they use ads moderately. Unlike low-cost counterparts, Customer Centrics acquire and retain customers by attention to superior service, product quality, or image. The most successful Customer Centrics firms place a heavy emphasis on understanding customers.

Starbucks (**http://www.starbucks.com**) may be the ultimate Customer Centric. It provides a lifestyle experience, a not-too-trendy community experience wrapped around a steaming cup of coffee in a cozy living room that exists on every block between home and work. Expanding on that concept, Starbucks launched the first of several fully integrated café-music stores, beautiful spaces with warm lighting and wood paneling where customers can buy CDs, or linger with a drink while listening to music and sifting through thousands of songs stored in a computerived data base to create their own personalized, mixed-CD masterpiece. This is customer-driven innovation. "Our customers respond to music," says Starbucks' senior vice-president of marketing. "Part of why they come is as an entertainment destination, for a respite, a break with friends, as a place for community gathering. The idea for the music service is very grounded in why people come to Starbucks."

Good Customer Centrics provide outstanding service and/or high quality products to select sets of customers who value and are willing to pay for them. Because service is ultimately delivered by customer contact personnel, it is imperative that these people be able to make customer relations decisions without having to check with higher level managers on every decision. However, a set of formal policies and rules is important in Customer Centric firms to guide frontline marketers in how to react to and address potential customer relations issues.

According to its chief executive, the most important investment that Starbucks made was in creating a unique relationship with its people and getting them to understand that the battle cry of the company is "to exceed the expectations of our customers." To accomplish this, Starbucks has long emphasized human-resource policies. It offers all frontline employees the same package of health care and other benefits that its most senior executives enjoy, including stock options. Equally important is the extensive training Starbucks gives to its store employees, so they can best handle demanding customers.

Questions

1. Comment on this statement: "Strategies most often fail because they aren't executed well. Things that are supposed to happen don't happen."
2. Distinguish among the four fundamental business strategies described in this case: Pioneer, Fast Follower, Cost Leader, and Customer Centrics.
3. What makes a successful Pioneer? A successful Cost Leader?
4. What are the biggest risks that Fast Followers face? What should they do to minimize these risks?
5. Do you agree that Starbucks is the "ultimate Customer Centric?" Why or why not?
6. How would you compete against Starbucks?
7. Should a company have a different fundamental business strategy for each of its strategic business units (SBUs)? Explain your answer.

Broadening the Scope of Marketing

In Part 2, we present an expanded perspective of marketing—one that is necessary today.

5 Societal, Ethical, and Consumer Issues

In this chapter, we examine the interaction of marketing and society. We begin by exploring the concept of social responsibility and discussing the impact of company and consumer activities on natural resources, the landscape, environmental pollution, and planned obsolescence. Next, ethics is discussed from several vantage points: business, consumer, global, and teachability. We then turn to consumerism and consider the basic rights of consumers: to information, to safety, to choice in product selection, and to be heard. The current trends related to the role of consumerism are also noted.

6 Global Aspects of Marketing

Here, we place marketing into a global context—important for both domestic and international firms, as well as those large and small. We distinguish among domestic, international, and global marketing. Then, we see why international marketing takes place and how widespread it is. Cultural, economic, political and legal, and technological factors are discussed. We conclude by looking at the stages in the development of an international marketing strategy: organization, entry decisions, degree of standardization, and product, distribution, promotion, and price planning.

7 Marketing and the Internet

At this point, we look at the emergence of the Internet and its impact on marketing practices. We show why the Internet is valuable in marketing and look at the many potential marketing roles for the Internet. Next, we cover how the Internet may be used to enhance a marketing strategy and present several examples. We end the chapter with a discussion of the challenges of the Internet in marketing and a forecast about the future of E-marketing.

After reading Part 2, you should understand elements 6–8 of the strategic marketing plan outlined in Table 3-2 (page 76).

Chapter 5

Societal, Ethical, and Consumer Issues

In 1991, Lance Armstrong won the U.S. amateur bicycling championship and then decided to become a professional athlete during 1992. Then, in 1996, Armstrong was diagnosed with testicular cancer and given a 50 percent chance of survival by his doctors. His surgery and chemotherapy were successful; Armstrong returned to training three months after chemotherapy and to professional cycling in 1998.

In one of the greatest comebacks in the history of sports, Lance Armstrong won his first Tour de France race less than three years after his initial diagnosis with cancer. In total, he won seven consecutive Tour de France bicycle races (1999–2005). The Tour de France is widely acknowledged to be bicycle racing's toughest and most prestigious race. In 2005, *Forbes* magazine ranked Armstrong as number 15 in its annual listing of the 100 most powerful celebrities in the world.

As one observer puts it, "Lance Armstrong is the ultimate athletic brand: an extraordinary winner, a cancer survivor who rebuilt his body into an endurance machine, an effective corporate spokesperson, and an outspoken advocate." Others credit Lance Armstrong with generating wider U.S. recognition of cycling as a sport and for garnering acceptance for Trek Bicycle (**http://www.trekbikes.com**), the maker of his bikes. He is also responsible for the sales of tens of millions of yellow Livestrong (**http://www.livestrong.org**) wristbands at $1 each. Proceeds are used for cancer research at the Lance Armstrong Foundation (LAF).

In 1997, Lance Armstrong founded LAF as a nonprofit organization. Its mission is to enhance the quality of life for those living with, through, and beyond cancer by supporting scientific research, educational community programs, after-treatment support for those with cancer and their families, and advocacy efforts. LAF secures contributions from the public by selling silicon bracelets, from direct contributions, and from corporate donors such as Nike, which gives $1 from the sales of selected products to the LAF. Each year, LAF raises as much as $40 million. Due to its high efficiency (it only spends 13 cents, on average, to raise $1) and effectiveness, Charity Navigator (**http://www.charitynavigator.org**) has given LAF a coveted four-star rating.[1]

In this chapter, we will study several issues relating to the interaction of marketing with overall society, as well as with consumers. We will look again at business responses to social responsibility.

Chapter Objectives

1. To consider the impact of marketing on society
2. To examine social responsibility and weigh its benefits and costs
3. To look into the role of ethics in marketing
4. To explore consumerism and describe the consumer bill of rights
5. To discuss the responses of manufacturers, retailers, and trade associations to consumerism and study the current role of consumerism

5-1   OVERVIEW

Individually (at the company level) and collectively (at the industry level), the activities involved with marketing goods, services, organizations, people, places, and ideas strongly

[1] Various company and other sources.

affect society. They have the potential for both positive and negative consequences, regarding such factors as these:

> Marketing can have both a positive and a negative impact on society.

- The quality of life (standard of living)
- Natural resources, the landscape, and environmental pollution
- Consumer expectations and satisfaction with goods, services, and so on
- Consumer choice
- Innovation
- Product design and safety
- Product durability
- Product and distribution costs
- Product availability
- Communications with consumers
- Final prices
- Competition
- Employment
- Deceptive actions

In the United States and many other highly industrialized nations, marketing practices have made a variety of goods and services available at rather low prices and at convenient locations. These include food products, motor vehicles, telecommunications services, clothing, entertainment, books, insurance, banking and other financial services, audio and video equipment, furniture, and PCs.

At the same time, the lesser use of modern marketing practices in some parts of the world has often led to fewer product choices, higher prices, and less convenient shopping. For example,

> The general shortage of commodities in Zimbabwe has created a burgeoning black market, which is limiting access to basic items for most of the poor. A public relations officer for the Consumer Council of Zimbabwe said, "The emergence of the black market is a sad development and will affect the consumer because goods are sold at unbelievably high prices and the cost of living will soar." An informal survey carried out around the capital, Harare, revealed that most shops had run out of basic commodities, such as sugar, maize-meal, flour, cooking oil, toothpaste, and margarine. Almost all these commodities are readily available on the black market and in backyard kiosks, where they are being sold at prices up to three times the official rate.[2]

Yet, even in the United States and other nations where marketing is quite advanced, marketing activities can create unrealistic consumer expectations, result in minor but costly product design changes, and adversely affect the environment. Thus, people's perceptions of marketing are mixed, at best. Over the years, studies have shown that many people feel cheated in their purchases due to deception, the lack of proper information, high-pressure sales pitches, and other tactics. Consumers may also believe they are being "ripped off" when prices are increased. And waiting in store lines and poor customer service are two more key areas of consumer unhappiness.

Consumer displeasure is not always transmitted to companies. People may just decide not to buy a product and privately complain to friends. Usually, only a small percentage of disgruntled consumers take time to complain to sellers. The true level of dissatisfaction is hidden. However, few people who are displeased, but do not complain, buy a product again from the same firm. In contrast, many who complain and have their complaints resolved do buy again:

> At TD Canada Trust (**http://www.tdcanadatrust.com**), Tim Hockey is telling 30,000 personal banking employees they should treat every complaint as a gift. Customers who gripe are

---

[2] UN Integrated Regional Information Networks, "Zimbabwe: Parallel Market Flourishes as Shelves Empty," *Africa News Online* (May 6, 2005).

presenting the bank with an opportunity: "If we don't take that opportunity to fix the problem, they will walk across the street and we have lost a customer. And if we don't fix it for the individual customer, we have lost the chance to fix what might be a more systemic problem. When someone says he or she has a customer who has a problem, that is not an imposition. It can't be, 'OK, I will get to that when I have finished my real job.' " The bank is also empowering staff with dollars: "We're saying it's over to you. If it is to reverse a service charge or in some cases to send flowers and just apologize, that's up to you as to how you want to make it right. We have allocated millions of dollars for this."[3]

In this chapter, we divide our discussion into three broad areas: social responsibility—addressing issues concerning the general public and the environment, employees, channel members, stockholders, and competitors; ethics—knowing and doing what is morally correct, with regard to society in general and individual consumers; and consumerism—focusing on the rights of consumers.

5-2   SOCIAL RESPONSIBILITY

> Social responsibility aids society. The **socioecological view of marketing** considers voluntary and involuntary consumers.

Social responsibility is a concern for "the consequences of a person's or firm's acts as they might affect the interests of others."[4] Corporate social responsibility means weighing the impact of company actions and behaving in a way that balances short-term profit needs with long-term societal needs. This calls for firms to be accountable to society and for consumers to act responsibly—by disposing of trash properly, wearing seat belts, not driving after drinking, and not being abusive to salespeople. See Figure 5-1.

From a marketing perspective, social responsibility also encompasses the *socioecological view of marketing*. According to this view, firms, their customers, and others should consider all the stages in a product's life span in developing, selling, purchasing, using, and disposing of that product. And the interests of everyone affected by a good's or service's use, including the involuntary consumers who must share the consequences of someone else's behavior, should be weighed. For example, how much of a scarce resource should a firm use in making a product? What should be the rights and responsibilities of smokers and nonsmokers (as involuntary consumers) to one another?

As two observers recently noted, social responsibility

calls upon marketers to balance three considerations in setting their marketing policies: company profits, consumer wants satisfaction, and public interest. Originally, companies based their marketing decisions largely on immediate company profit calculations ignoring public interests. They then began to recognize the long-run importance of satisfying consumer wants, and this introduced the marketing concept. Now they are beginning to factor in society's interest in their decision making.[5]

To respond to the socioecological view of marketing, many firms now use "design for disassembly" (DFD), whereby products are designed to be disassembled in a more environmentally friendly manner once they outlive their usefulness. Firms use fewer parts and less materials, and recycle more materials. For example, various consumer electronics companies, such as Panasonic (**http://www.panasonic.com**) and Philips (**http://www.philips.com**) are heavily involved with DFD: "Features like low-lead or no-lead solder, modular electronics boards, snap-fit rather than glued joints, and included instructions for disassembly make it easier for dead products to have a new life. Whether as a repaired item with an easily replaced piece, a consumer disassembled and recycled

---

[3] Michael Kane, "Compounding Satisfaction: Bank Empowers Employees to Address Customer Complaints," *Star Phoenix Online* (August 29, 2005).

[4] "Dictionary of Marketing Terms," **http://www.marketingpower.com/mg-dictionary.php** (May 3, 2006).

[5] Bernadette D'Silva and Stephen D'Silva, "Use of Societal Concept of Marketing in Corporate Image Building," **http://www.indiainfoline.com/bisc/sydfac06.html** (November 11, 2004).

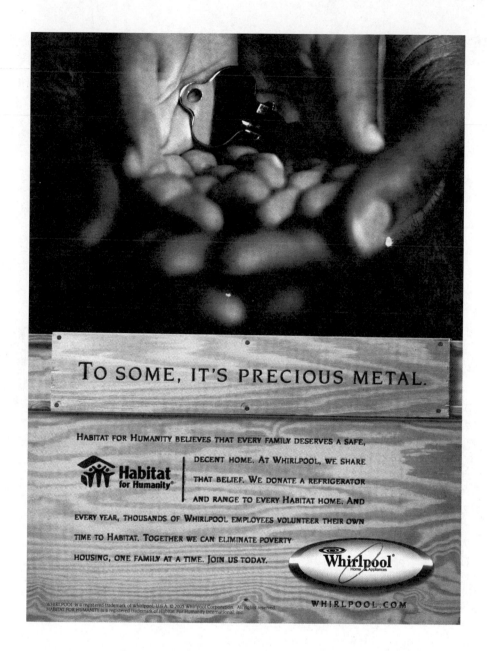

Figure 5-1

Social Responsibility in Action

Source: Reprinted by permission of Habitat for Humanity and Whirlpool Corporation. Photo: Andy Anderson. Woodwork: Hac Job.

piece, or one that can easily be scrapped out by more professional disassemblers, either locally, or in Asia."[6]

At times, social responsibility poses dilemmas for firms and/or their customers because popular goods and services may have potential adverse effects on consumer or societal well-being. Examples of items that pose such dilemmas are tobacco products, no-return beverage containers, food with high taste appeal but low nutritional content, crash diet plans, and liquor.

Until the 1960s, such resources as air, water, and energy were seen as limitless. Responsibility to the general public was rarely considered. Many firms now realize they should be responsive to the general public and the environment, employees, channel members, stockholders, and competitors, as well as customers. Table 5-1 shows socially responsible marketing in these areas.

---

[6] Dominic Muren, "Built For Breakdown," http://www.idfuel.com/index.php?p=374&more=1#more374 (January 24, 2005).

Table 5-1   Illustrations of Socially Responsible Marketing Practices

Regarding the General Public and the Environment

Community involvement

Contributions to nonprofit organizations

Hiring hard-core unemployed

Product recycling

Eliminating offensive signs and billboards

Properly disposing of waste materials

Using goods and services requiring low levels of environmental resources

Regarding Employees

Ample internal communications

Employee empowerment allowed

Employee training about social issues and appropriate responses to them

No reprisals against employees who uncover questionable company policies

Recognizing socially responsible employees

Regarding Channel Members

Honoring both verbal and written commitments

Fairly distributing scarce goods and services

Accepting reasonable requests by channel members

Encouraging channel members to act responsibly

Not coercing channel members

Cooperative programs addressed to the general public and the environment

Regarding Stockholders

Honest reporting and financial disclosure

Publicity about company activities

Stockholder participation in setting socially responsible policy

Explaining social issues affecting the company

Earning a responsible profit

Regarding Competitors

Adhering to high standards of performance

No illegal or unethical acts to hinder competitors

Cooperative programs for the general public and environment

No actions that would lead competitors to waste resources

This is how Johnson & Johnson (http://www.jnj.com) views its societal role, as highlighted in Figure 5-2:

> We believe our first responsibility is to the doctors, nurses, and patients, to mothers and fathers, and all others who use our products and services. In meeting their needs, everything we do must be of high quality. We must constantly strive to reduce our costs in order to maintain reasonable prices. Customers' orders must be serviced promptly and accurately. Our suppliers and distributors must have an opportunity to make a fair profit.

> We are responsible to our employees, the men and women who work with us throughout the world. Everyone must be considered as an individual. We must respect their dignity and recognize their merit. They must have a sense of security in their jobs. Compensation must be fair and adequate, and working conditions clean, orderly, and safe. We must be mindful of

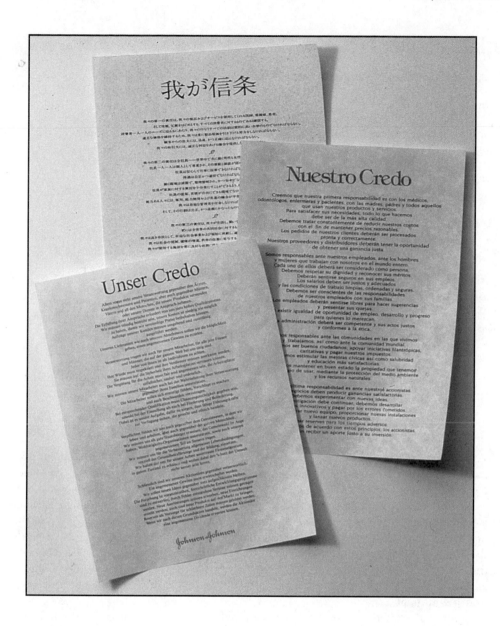

Figure 5-2

Johnson & Johnson's Global Social Responsibility Credo

At Johnson & Johnson, "A shared system of values, known as *Our Credo,* serves as a guide for all who are part of the Johnson & Johnson Family of Companies. The Credo can be found in 36 languages, each expressing the responsibilities we have to our customers, employees, communities, and stockholders." All of the various language versions of the credo are available at the company Web site (**http://www.jnj.com**).

Source: Reprinted by permission.

ways to help our employees fulfill their family responsibilities. Employees must feel free to make suggestions and complaints. There must be equal opportunity for employment, development, and advancement for those qualified. We must provide competent management, and their actions must be just and ethical.

We are responsible to the communities in which we live and work and to the world community as well. We must be good citizens—support good works and charities and bear our fair share of taxes. We must encourage civic improvements and better health and education. We must maintain in good order the property we are privileged to use, protecting the environment and natural resources.

Our final responsibility is to our stockholders. Business must make a sound profit. We must experiment with new ideas. Research must be carried on, innovative programs developed, and mistakes paid for. New equipment must be purchased, new facilities provided, and new products launched. Reserves must be created to provide for adverse times. When we operate according to these principles, the stockholders should realize a fair return.[7]

---

[7] "Our Credo," **http://www.jnj.com/our_company/our_credo** (May 3, 2006).

Ethical Issues in Marketing

American Entrepreneurs Seek to Help Solve Social Problems

During the past several years, a number of American entrepreneurs have invested in businesses that focus on solving the social problems of the poor countries in which they are located. Marketing analysts attribute this trend to increased media attention on social problems in poor countries, the development of foundations by billionaires, and the popularity of *The Fortune at the Bottom of the Pyramid*, a book that focuses on making money by selling to the poor. Let's look at how two U.S. entrepreneurs are making a difference.

Dr. Jordan Kassalow, an eye physician with considerable experience in poor countries, found through experience that most of his patients needed basic reading glasses, not sophisticated eye surgery. With the assistance of a partner, Kassalow founded the Scojo Foundation (**http://www.scojofoundation.org**),

a nonprofit organization, to identify, train, and finance local businesspeople to sell eyeglasses in such countries as El Salvador, Guatemala, and India. The Scojo Foundation has been recognized by the World Bank as a leader in innovation.

KickStart (**http://www.kickstart.org/**) is a San Francisco-based nonprofit group that has developed basic agricultural equipment designed specifically for poor African farmers. KickStart's equipment is made by small manufacturers in Africa and sold by small African retail firms. One of KickStart's founders states that the equipment enables African farmers to earn over $30 million in profits annually.

Source: Based on material in Joshua Kurlantzick, "Rescue Mission: Can American Entrepreneurs Help Solve Social Ills?" *Entrepreneur* (August 2005), pp. 15–16.

Company and consumer activities have a significant impact on natural resources, the landscape, pollution, and planned obsolescence. These areas are discussed next.

5-2a   Natural Resources

Today, we are aware that our global supply of natural resources is not unlimited. Both consumer behavior and marketing practices contribute to some resource shortages. Nonetheless, Americans annually discard 1,610 pounds of trash per person—including large amounts of paper, food, aluminum, plastic, tires, furniture, and clothing. Packaging is an especially big component of trash. How do other nations compare? Australians discard 1,525 pounds per person, the Germans 1,300 pounds, the British 1,280 pounds, the French 1,170 pounds, and the Japanese 905 pounds. In the less-industrialized Mexico, the amount is 710 pounds.[8] The U.S. Environmental Protection Agency (EPA) even has an entire Web site devoted to municipal solid waste (**http://www.epa.gov/epaoswer/non-hw/muncpl**).

Although Americans spend billions of dollars yearly on garbage collection and disposal—and thousands of curbside recycling programs exist nationwide—only 31 percent of U.S. trash is actually recycled (up from 6 percent in 1960). The world's most ambitious formal recycling program is in Germany, where 80 percent of all packaging materials—from aluminum to paper—must be recycled.[9]

> Resource depletion can be slowed by reducing consumption, improving efficiency, limiting disposables, and lengthening products' lives.

Natural resource depletion can be reduced if the consumption of scarce materials is lessened and more efficient alternatives are chosen; fewer disposable items—such as cans, pens, and lighters—are bought; products are given longer life spans; and styles are changed less frequently. Convenient recycling and repair facilities, better trade-in arrangements, such common facilities as apartments (that share laundry rooms, etc.), and simpler packaging can also contribute to better resource use.

Progressive actions require cooperation among business, stockholders, government, employees, the general public, consumers, and others. They also involve changes in lifestyles and corporate ingenuity. As the EPA suggests, businesses and consumers can "produce less waste by practicing the 3Rs: Reduce the amount and toxicity of trash you

---

[8] *OCED in Figures: 2004 Edition* (Paris: OCED Publications, 2004), pp. 48–49.

[9] "Municipal Solid Waste: Basic Facts," **http://www.epa.gov/epaoswer/non-hw/muncpl/facts.htm** (September 16, 2005); and "All About Recycling," **http://www.howtogermany.com/pages/recycling.html** (September 16, 2005).

Figure 5-3

Protecting Scarce Resources

Source: Reprinted by permission of the American Forest & Paper Association.

discard. Reuse containers and products; repair what is broken or give it to someone who can repair it. Recycle as much as possible, which includes buying products with recycled content."[10] See Figure 5-3.

5-2b   The Landscape

Garbage dumps and landfills, discarded beverage containers, and abandoned cars are examples of items marring the landscape.

In the United States, 56 percent of discarded materials are disposed of in dumps and landfills (the rest is recycled or burned). Nonetheless, many communities no longer permit new dumps and landfills, existing ones are closing for environmental reasons (there are now 2,000 landfills, down from 18,000 at their peak), and recycling efforts are being stepped up at existing dumps and landfills. In areas of Europe and Japan, landfills are at capacity—hence, those countries have a greater interest in recycling and incineration.[11]

---

[10] "Reduce, Reuse, and Recycle," http://www.epa.gov/epaoswer/non-hw/muncpl/reduce.htm (May 3, 2006).

[11] "Basic Facts," http://www.epa.gov/epaoswer/non-hw/muncpl/facts.htm (February 20, 2006).

At one time, virtually all beverage containers were recycled. When no-return bottles and cans were developed, littering at roadsides and other areas became a major problem. To reduce litter, several states and localities have laws requiring deposit fees that are refunded when consumers return empty containers. Many manufacturers and retailers feel the laws unfairly hold them responsible for container disposal, as littering is done by consumers—not them. Also, the labor and recycling costs associated with container returns have led to slightly higher beverage prices. Presently, container laws are just moderately effective, and consumers still must be better educated as to the value of proper disposal.

Cars are sometimes abandoned on streets, where they are then stripped of usable parts. One suggestion to cover the disposal of a car is to include an amount in its original price or in a transfer tax. For example, Maryland has a small fee on title transfers to aid in the removal of abandoned cars.

Other ways to reduce the marring of the landscape include limits or bans on billboards and roadside signs, fines for littering, and better trade-ins for autos and appliances. Neighborhood associations, merchant self-regulation, area planning and zoning, and consumer education can also improve appreciation for the landscape. This is a cooperative effort. A merchant cleanup patrol cannot easily overcome pedestrians who throw litter on the street. Here is what Nike (**http://www.nike.com**) is doing to help:

> Nike's Reuse-A-Shoe program was born in 1993, when we began collecting both post-consumer, nonmetal-containing athletic shoes of any brand and Nike shoes that are returned due to a material or workmanship flaw (defectives). That footwear is separated into three main materials—upper fabric, midsole foam and outsole rubber—and then ground up. Nike Grind Rubber, from outsoles and recycled manufacturing material, goes into baseball and soccer fields, as well as golf products, weight room flooring, and running tracks. Nike Grind Foam, from midsoles, is used in synthetic basketball courts, tennis courts, and playground surfacing. Nike Grind Upper Fabric, from textile and leather uppers is used for padding under hardwood basketball floors.[12]

5-2c Environmental Pollution

Dangerous pollutants must be reduced and substitutes found. Environmental pollution can be generated by spray-can propellants, ocean dumping of industrial waste, lead from gas and paint, pesticides, sulfur oxide and other factory emissions, improper disposal of garbage, and other pollutants. Consider this:

> Through improved treatment and disposal, most industrialized countries have greatly reduced the effects of many pollutants, with consequent improvements in water quality. Unfortunately, new contaminants from intensive agriculture and development activities in watersheds have kept the cleanup from being complete. In general, national water cleanup programs have not been effective in reducing pollutants such as nutrients, sediments, and toxics that come in runoff from agriculture, urban and suburban storm water, mining, and oil and gas operations. Meanwhile, in most developing countries, traditional pollution sources like sewage and new pollutants like pesticides have heavily degraded water quality, particularly near urban industrial centers and intensive agricultural areas. An estimated 90 percent of wastewater in developing countries is still discharged directly to rivers and streams without any waste processing treatment.[13]

Government and industry in the United States, Western Europe, and Japan devote a combined total of several hundred billion dollars annually to environmental protection.

---

[12] "Reuse-a-Shoe," **http://www.nike.com/nikebiz/nikebiz.jhtml?page=27&cat=reuseashoe** (April 30, 2006).

[13] Carmen Revenga and Greg Mock, "Dirty Water: Pollution Problems Persist," **http://earthtrends.wri.org/features/view_feature.cfm?theme=2&fid=16** (October 2000).

And antipollution spending has risen considerably in many less-developed nations in Latin America, Asia, and Africa. The EPA (**http://www.epa.gov**) is the major U.S. government agency involved with pollution; a number of state agencies are also active in this area. Numerous other nations have their own government agencies to deal with the issue.

These are among the voluntary activities of companies and associations:

- New PCs, printers, monitors, and other electronic devices automatically "power down" when not in use to reduce air pollution and conserve energy.
- The American Chemistry Council (**http://www.americanchemistry.com**) has been working with the EPA to keep hazardous compounds out of the environment.
- 3M spends a portion of its research-and-development budget on projects involving environmental protection, and its Web site has an environmental section (**http://www.3m.com/about3m/sustainability**).
- Japan's Ebara Corporation (**http://www.ebara.co.jp/en**) uses its own technology to remove harmful sulphur dioxides and nitrogen oxides from power plants more efficiently.
- More than 40 major firms participate in the Global Environmental Management Initiative (**http://www.gemi.org**), designed to foster an exchange of information about environmental protection programs.
- The Coalition for Environmentally Responsible Economies (**http://www.ceres.org**) is a nonprofit group of investors, public pension funds, foundations, unions, and environmental, religious, and public interest groups working with business to enhance corporate environmental responsibility worldwide.

5-2d Planned Obsolescence

Planned obsolescence is a marketing practice that capitalizes on short-run material wearout, style changes, and functional product changes.

> **Planned obsolescence** can involve materials, styles, and functions.

In *material planned obsolescence,* firms choose materials and components that are subject to comparatively early breakage, wear, rot, or corrosion. For example, the makers of disposable lighters and razors use this form of planned obsolescence in a constructive manner by offering inexpensive, short-life, convenient products. However, resistance is growing to material planned obsolescence because of its effects on natural resources and the landscape.

In *style planned obsolescence*, a firm makes minor changes to differentiate the new year's offering from the prior year's. Because some people are style-conscious, they will discard old items while they are still functional so as to acquire new ones with more status. This is common with fashion items and cars.

With *functional planned obsolescence*, a firm introduces new product features or improvements to generate consumer dissatisfaction with currently owned products. Sometimes, features or improvements may have been withheld from an earlier model to gain faster repurchases. A style change may accompany a functional one to raise consumer awareness of a "new" product. This form of planned obsolescence occurs most often with high-tech items such as computers.

Marketers reply to criticism thusly: Planned obsolescence is responsive to people's desires as to prices, styles, and features and is not coercive; without product turnover, people would be disenchanted by the lack of choices; consumers like disposable items and often discard them before they lose their effectiveness; firms use materials that reduce prices; competition requires firms to offer the best products possible and not hold back improvements; and, for such items as clothing, people desire continuous style changes. As Michael Dell said, "There's no such thing at Dell (**http://www.dell.com**) as finished, done, good enough. We believe that we can improve things all the time, so we constantly look for opportunities."[14]

---

[14] Kevin McKean, "Planned Obsolescence," **http://www.Infoworld.com/article/03/09/26/38OPeditor_1.html** (September 26, 2003).

Several firms have enacted innovative strategies with regard to planned obsolescence. Kodak (**http://www.kodak.com**) recycles single-use disposable cameras. Canon (**http://www.canon.com**) has a factory in China to recondition and refill used copier cartridges. SKF of Sweden (**http://www.skf.com**) is a worldwide bearings maker; to increase the life of its products, it has added more preventative maintenance services.

5-2e The Benefits and Costs of Social Responsibility

> Social responsibility has benefits as well as costs; these, need to be balanced.

Socially responsible actions have both benefits and costs. Among the benefits are improved worker and public health, as reflected in fewer and less severe accidents, longer life spans, and less disease; cleaner air; better resource use; economic growth; a better business image; an educated public; government cooperation; an attractive, safe environment; an enhanced standard of living; and self-satisfaction for the firm. Many of these benefits cannot be quantified. Nonetheless, expectations are that the U.S. Clean Air Act (**http://www.epa.gov/oar/caa/contents.html**) and the laws of other nations will ultimately save thousands and thousands of lives each year, protect food crops, reduce medical costs, and lead to clearer skies.

Although some social-responsibility expenditures are borne by a broad cross-section of firms and the general public (via taxes and higher prices), the benefits of many environmental and other programs are enjoyed primarily by those living or working in affected areas. The costs of socially responsible actions can be high; U.S. environmental-protection spending is nearly 2 percent of the annual gross domestic product. Various environmentally questionable products that are efficient have been greatly modified or removed from the marketplace, such as leaded gasoline. Because of various legal restrictions and fears of lawsuits, new-product planning tends to be more conservative; and resources are often allotted to prevention rather than invention. Furthermore, trade-offs have to be made in determining which programs are more deserving of funding. See Figure 5-4.

To be effective, all parties must partake in socially responsible efforts—sharing both benefits and costs. This means business, consumers, government, channel members, and others. Sometimes, tragic events bring people together. For example, in September 2005, after the Hurricane Katrina disaster along the U.S. Gulf Coast, the American Red Cross

Figure 5-4

The Benefits and Costs of Social Responsibility

Benefits	Costs
Worker and public health	Unequal distribution of benefits
Cleaner air	Dollar costs
Efficient use of resources	Removal of some goods from the market
Economic growth	Conservative product planning
Improved business image	Resources allocated to prevention rather than invention
Government cooperation	
Public education	
Attractive environment	
Better standard of living	
Self-satisfaction of firm	

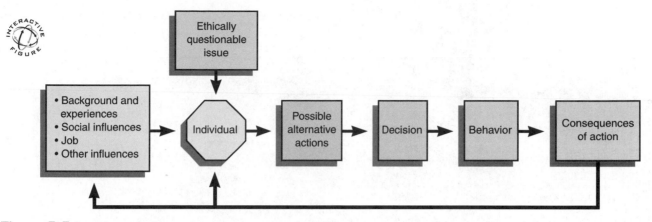

Figure 5-5

A Framework for Ethical/Unethical Decision Making

(**http://www.redcross.org**) received nearly $1 billion in contributions from hundreds of thousands of private citizens around the world and numerous businesses contributed large sums of money, goods, and services for relief, relocation, and rebuilding efforts.

5-3 ETHICS

In any marketing situation, ***ethical behavior*** based on honest and proper conduct ("what is right" and "what is wrong") should be followed. This applies both to situations involving company actions that affect the general public, employees, channel members, stockholders, and/or competitors, and to situations involving company dealings with consumers.

Figure 5-5 outlines a framework for ethical/unethical decision making. An individual is affected by his or her background and experiences, social influences, and the specific job. When an ethical dilemma occurs, these factors come into play (consciously or subconsciously). For each ethically questionable issue, the person considers alternative actions, makes a decision, and acts accordingly. He or she then faces the consequences, which affect future decisions. The recently revised ethics code of the American Marketing Association (**http://www.marketingpower.com/live/content435.php**) is shown in Figure 5-6.

Of great importance in studying ethics are answers to these two questions: How do people determine whether an act is ethical or unethical? Why do they act ethically or unethically?[15] People *determine* (learn) whether or not given actions are ethical through their upbringing, education, job environment, and life-long experiences—and others' responses to their behavior. People may also apply their own cognitive reasoning skills to decide what is morally acceptable. Individuals *act* ethically or unethically based on their expectations of the rewards or punishments—financial, social, and so forth—flowing from their actions. They consider both the magnitude of the rewards or punishments (such as the size of a raise or the maximum fine that could be imposed on a company) and the likelihood of their occurrence (such as the probability of getting a large raise or having a large fine imposed on the firm).

> **Ethical behavior** involves honest and proper conduct.

> **Ethics theories range from egoism to virtue ethics.**

---

[15] Shelby D. Hunt, "Foundations of the Hunt-Vitell Theory of Ethics," presented at the 1995 AMA Faculty Consortium on Ethics and Social Responsibility in Marketing (Hempstead, NY: Hofstra University).

Preamble

We commit ourselves to promoting the highest standard of professional ethical norms and values for our members. Norms are established standards of conduct that are expected and maintained by society and/or professional organizations. Values represent the collective conception of what people find desirable, important, and morally proper. Values serve as the criteria for evaluating the actions of others. Marketing practitioners must recognize that they not only serve their enterprises but also act as stewards of society in creating, facilitating, and executing the efficient and effective transactions that are part of the greater economy. In this role, marketers should embrace the highest ethical norms of practicing professionals and ethical values toward stakeholders (e.g., customers, employees, investors, channel members, regulators, and the host community).

General Norms

1. Marketers must do no harm. This means doing work for which they are appropriately trained or experienced so that they can actively add value to their organizations and customers. It also means adhering to all applicable laws and regulations and embodying high ethical standards in the choices they make.

2. Marketers must foster trust in the marketing system. This means that products are appropriate for their intended and promoted uses. It requires that marketing communications about goods and services are not intentionally deceptive or misleading. It suggests building relationships that provide for the equitable adjustment and/or redress of customer grievances. It implies striving for good faith and fair dealing to contribute toward the efficacy of the exchange process.

3. Marketers must embrace, communicate, and practice the fundamental ethical values that will improve consumer confidence in the integrity of the marketing exchange system. These basic values are intentionally aspirational and include honesty, responsibility, fairness, respect, openness, and citizenship.

Ethical Values

Honesty— to be truthful and forthright in our dealings with customers and stakeholders.
- We will tell the truth in all situations and at all times.
- We will offer products of value that do what we claim in our communications.
- We will stand behind our products if they fail to deliver their claimed benefits.
- We will honor our explicit and implicit commitments and promises.

Responsibility—to accept the consequences of our marketing decisions and strategies.
- We will make strenuous efforts to serve the needs of our customers.
- We will avoid using coercion with all stakeholders.
- We will acknowledge the social obligations to stakeholders that come with increased marketing and economic power.
- We will recognize our special commitments to economically vulnerable market segments such as children, the elderly, and others who may be substantially disadvantaged.

Fairness—to try to balance justly the needs of the buyer with the interests of the seller.
- We will represent our products in a clear way in selling, advertising, and other forms of communication; this includes the avoidance of false, misleading, and deceptive promotion.
- We will reject manipulations and sales tactics that harm customer trust.
- We will not engage in price fixing, predatory pricing, price gouging, or "bait-and-switch" tactics.
- We will not knowingly participate in material conflicts of interest.

Respect—to acknowledge the basic human dignity of all stakeholders.
- We will value individual differences even as we avoid stereotyping customers or depicting demographic groups (e.g., gender, race, sexual orientation) in a negative or dehumanizing way in our promotions.
- We will listen to the needs of our customers and make all reasonable efforts to monitor and improve their satisfaction on an ongoing basis.
- We will make a special effort to understand suppliers, intermediaries, and distributors from other cultures.
- We will appropriately acknowledge the contributions of others, such as consultants, employees, and coworkers, to our marketing endeavors.

Openness—to create transparency in our marketing operations.
- We will strive to communicate clearly with all our constituencies.
- We will accept constructive criticism from our customers and other stakeholders.
- We will explain significant product or service risks, component substitutions, or other foreseeable eventualities that could affect customers or their perception of the purchase decision.
- We will fully disclose list prices and terms of financing, as well as available price deals and adjustments.

Citizenship—to fulfill the economic, legal, philanthropic, and societal responsibilities that serve stakeholders in a strategic manner.
- We will strive to protect the natural environment in the execution of marketing campaigns.
- We will give back to the community through volunteerism and charitable donations.
- We will work to contribute to the overall betterment of marketing and its reputation.
- We will encourage supply chain members to ensure that trade is fair for all participants, including producers in developing countries.

Implementation

Finally, we recognize that every industry sector and marketing subdiscipline has its own specific ethical issues that require policies and commentary. An array of such codes can be accessed through links on the AMA Web site. We encourage all such groups to develop and/or refine their industry and discipline-specific codes of ethics to supplement these general norms and values

Figure 5-6

The American Marketing Association's Code of Ethics

Source: Reprinted by permission.

Various ethical theories seek to explain why people and organizations act in particular ways. Here are four of them, applied to marketing:

- *Egoism*—a theory asserting that individuals act exclusively in their own self-interest. Example: A product manager postpones investing in improvements for a mature product because he or she expects to be promoted within the next six months and wants to maximize short-term profits.
- *Utilitarianism*—a theory asserting that individual and organizational actions are proper only if they yield the greatest good for the most people (the highest net benefit). Example: A pharmaceutical company markets an FDA-approved drug with some side effects as long as it helps more people combat a particular disease than the number affected by the (minor) side effect.
- *Duty-based*—a theory asserting that the rightness of an action is not based on its consequences, but rather is based on the premise that certain actions are proper because they stem from basic obligations. Example: A supermarket chain sets below-average prices in a low-income area even though this adversely affects company profits in that community.
- *Virtue ethics*—a theory asserting that actions should be guided by an individual's or organization's seeking goodness and virtue ("living a good life"). Example: A virtuous firm is totally truthful in its ads, packaging, and selling efforts, and does not use manipulative appeals to persuade customers.[16]

Ethical issues in marketing can generally be divided into two categories: process-related and product-related.[17] **Process-related ethical issues** involve "the unethical use of marketing strategies or tactics." Examples include dishonest advertising, price fixing, selling products overseas that have been found unsafe in the United States, and bribing purchasing agents of large customers. **Product-related ethical issues** involve "the ethical appropriateness of marketing certain products." For example, should tobacco products, sugar-coated cereals, and political candidates be marketed? More specifically, should cigarettes be sold? Should there be restrictions on their sales? Should cigarette ads be allowed? Should cigarette taxes be raised to dampen use? Should smoking be banned in offices, restaurants, and planes?

Marketers need to consider **process-related** and **product-related ethical issues**.

To maintain the highest possible ethical conduct by employees, senior executives must make a major commitment to ethics, communicate standards of conduct to each employee, reward ethical behavior, and discourage unethical behavior. This example sums up the intricacy of many ethical issues for marketers:

> Information may or may not affect consumption, but one ethical justification given for market systems is that they leave final product selections to informed customers. Ethical concerns arise, however, as to how information is presented. What if information is expressed in a persuasive manner? There is no generally accepted theory of ethics with regard to marketing persuasion, and persuasion is prevalent in marketing. Marketing persuasion spreads through competition. In addition, marketers, as experts in their discipline, often know better what will fulfill customers' needs than do the customers. Do customers want to be persuaded by marketers when something is in the marketers' own best interest? Will customers think this ethical? Most people want to feel that their decisions are their own—with no undue influence from others.[18]

Next, we examine ethics from four vantage points: a business perspective, a consumer perspective, a global perspective, and the teachability of ethics.

[16] Gene R. Laczniak and Patrick E. Murphy, *Ethical Marketing Decisions: The Higher Road* (Needham Heights, MA: Allyn & Bacon, 1993), pp. 28–42.

[17] Gene R. Laczniak, Robert F. Lusch, and William A. Strang, "Ethical Marketing: Perceptions of Economic Goods and Social Problems," *Journal of Macromarketing*, Vol. 1 (Spring 1981), p. 49.

[18] Dillard B. Tinsley, "Ethics Can Be Gauged by Three Key Rules," *Marketing News* (September 1, 2003), p. 24.

5-3a A Business Perspective

> Many companies have ethics codes; some have implicit standards.

Most firms in the U.S. *Fortune 500* have formal ethics codes. Some codes are general and resemble organizational mission statements; others are specific and operational. In contrast, French, British, and German firms are less apt to have formal codes; acceptable standards of behavior are more implied. The European Union has been working to clarify the latter situation.

One of the most complex aspects of business ethics is setting the boundaries as to what is ethical. To address this, the following scale was devised and tested with a variety of marketing personnel. The scale suggests that businesspeople make better decisions if they consider whether a marketing action (is):[19]

Fair	_ _ _ _ _ _	Unfair
Just	_ _ _ _ _ _	Unjust
Culturally Acceptable	_ _ _ _ _ _	Culturally Unacceptable
Violates an Unwritten Contract	_ _ _ _ _ _	Does Not Violate an Unwritten Contract
Traditionally Acceptable	_ _ _ _ _ _	Traditionally Unacceptable
Morally Right	_ _ _ _ _ _	Not Morally Right
Violates an Unspoken Promise	_ _ _ _ _ _	Does Not Violate an Unspoken Promise
Acceptable to My Family	_ _ _ _ _ _	Unacceptable to My Family

Here are examples showing business responses to ethical issues:

> Cause-related marketing has good and bad points.

- *Cause-related marketing* is a somewhat controversial practice wherein profit-oriented firms contribute specific amounts to given nonprofit organizations for each consumer purchase of certain goods and services during a special promotion (such as sponsorship of a sport for the Olympics). It has been used by such firms as American Express (**http://www.americanexpress.com**) and MasterCard (**http://www.mastercard.com**), and such nonprofits as the International Red Cross (**http://www.icrc.org**). Advocates feel cause-related marketing stimulates direct and indirect contributions and benefits the images of both the profit-oriented firms and the nonprofit institutions involved in it. Critics say there is too much commercialism by nonprofit groups and implicit endorsements for sponsor products.

- Atlanta-based HomeBanc Mortgage's (**http://www.homebanc.com/Careers/EthicsCode.aspx**) associates must adhere to these standards: "I will act with honesty and integrity and hold fast to the highest standards of ethical conduct, refraining from actual or apparent conflicts of interest in personal and professional relationships. I will report any material transaction or relationship that could give rise to such conflict. I will act in good faith, carefully and responsibly, in a competent and diligent manner. I will not misrepresent material facts or allow my judgment to be subordinated in any way."

- Mary Kay Cosmetics (**http://www.marykay.com**) was one of the first firms to halt product testing on animals: "To signify our commitment, we have signed a document drafted by the Coalition for Consumer Information on Cosmetics, supported by People for the Ethical Treatment of Animals (PETA), the Humane Society of the United States, and the Doris Day Animal League. This contract, commonly known as the 'PETA Pledge,' provides our assurance that, not only do we not conduct any animal testing, we will not use animal testing at any time in the future."[20]

---

[19] R. Eric Reidenbach, Donald P. Robin, and Lyndon Dawson, "An Application and Extension of a Multidimensional Ethics Scale to Selected Marketing Practices and Marketing Groups," *Journal of the Academy of Marketing Science*, Vol. 19 (Spring 1991), p. 84.

[20] "Product Safety," **http://www.marykay.com/Corporate/ProductSafety.aspx** (March 31, 2006).

Global Marketing in Action

The Evolution of Marketing Practices in India

A recently released Conference Board (**http://www. conference-board.org**) study calls for India to continue to break free from its "feudal mind-set" and insular nature to become a bigger player in the world economy. The report notes that many Indian firms have traditionally managed a workforce almost entirely comprised of Indians, run their business almost exclusively in the home market, and sold their products only to Indian customers.

The Conference Board's director of India operations says, "A solid period of domestic economic growth, the perception of India as a premier destination for international outsourcing, the rise of India-based multinationals, and an explosion in direct foreign investment by Indian firms have thrust Indian business practices into the global spotlight."

Here is a brief summary of what Indian business leaders need to do to adopt a global mind-set. These leaders should:

- Think globally in terms of their size of operations, product quality, and use of best practices.
- Recognize that enacting the proper strategy and focusing on its execution are much more difficult than suggested by many textbooks.
- Embrace new technology regardless of where it was developed.
- Recognize and respect differences among people in different regions and countries.
- Be fully prepared to adhere to laws from different countries.
- Benchmark performance against global standards.

Source: Based on material in "Indian Companies Must Discard Traditional Business Practices to Continue Becoming World-Class Players in Global Economy," PR Newswire US (July 6, 2005).

5-3b   A Consumer Perspective

Just as business has a responsibility to act in an ethical and a societally-oriented way, so do consumers. Their actions impact on businesses, other consumers, the general public, the environment, and so on. Ethical standards in marketing transactions can truly be maintained only if both sellers and buyers act in a mutually respectful, honest, fair, and responsible manner.[21]

> Consumers should act as ethically to business as they expect to be treated.

Yet, consumers may find it hard to decide what is acceptable—especially with regard to broad societal issues. Daniel Yankelovich (**http://www.dyg.com**), an expert in the area, says a society goes through seven stages to form a consensus on major issues (such as how to deal with health care for older people):

1. The public becomes aware of an issue, but citizens do not yet feel a pressing need to take action.
2. The public moves beyond awareness to a sense of urgency.
3. The public begins to look at alternatives for dealing with issues, converting free-floating concern into calls for action.
4. The public is resistant to costs and trade-offs.
5. The public considers the advantages and disadvantages of the available alternatives.
6. The public accepts an idea but is not yet ready to act on it.
7. The public accepts an idea both morally and emotionally.[22]

With regard to consumer perceptions about whether specific activities on their part are proper, consider the actions cited in Figure 5-7. Which of them would you, *as a consumer*, deem to be ethically acceptable? Which would be ethically wrong? What should be the ramifications for consumers engaging in acts that are ethically unacceptable?

---

[21] For a good overview of consumer ethics research, see Scott J. Vitell, "Consumer Ethics Research: Review, Synthesis, and Suggestions for the Future," *Journal of Business Ethics*, Vol. 43 (March 2003), pp. 33–47.

[22] Daniel Yankelovich, "The Seven Stages of Public Opinion," **http://www.publicagenda.org/polling/ polling_stages.cfm** (December 12, 2005).

Figure 5-7

Ethical Appropriateness of Selected Consumer Activities

As a consumer, how would you rate these actions in terms of their ethical appropriateness? Use a scale from 1-10, with 1 being fully ethical and 10 being fully unethical.

Activities	Ratings
Being less than truthful on surveys	—
Changing price tags on merchandise in a retail store	—
Drinking a can of soda in a supermarket without paying for it	—
Exaggerating quality at a garage sale	—
Getting too much change and not saying anything	—
Giving misleading price information to a clerk for an unpriced item	—
Inflating an insurance claim	—
Joining a music club just to get some free CDs without any intention of buying	—
Observing someone shoplifting and ignoring it on a given shopping trip	—
Purchasing a counterfeit product	—
Purchasing a product made by underage workers	—
Purchasing a useful product that is environmentally questionable	—
Repeating store visits to buy more merchandise that is available in limited quantity	—
Reporting a lost item as "stolen" to an insurance company in order to collect money	—
Returning merchandise after wearing it and not liking it	—
Selling a frequent flier ticket	—
Stretching the truth on an income-tax return	—
Using a long-distance telephone access code that does not belong to you	—
Using computer software or games you did not buy	—

Sources: Figure devised by the authors using activities listed in James A. Muncy and Scott J. Vitell, "Consumer Ethics: An Investigation of the Ethical Beliefs of the Final Consumer," *Journal of Business Research*, Vol. 24 (June 1992), p. 303; Sam Fullerton, David Taylor, and B. C. Ghosh, "A Cross-Cultural Examination of Attitudes Towards Aberrant Consumer Behavior in the Marketplace: Some Preliminary Results from the USA, New Zealand, and Singapore," *Marketing Intelligence & Planning*, Vol. 15 (April-May 1997), p. 211; and Russell Belk, Timothy Devinney, and Gina Eckhardt, "Consumer Ethics Across Cultures," *Consumption, Markets, and Culture*, Vol. 8 (September 2005), pp. 275–289.

5-3c A Global Perspective

> Ethical decisions can be complicated on an international level

Ethical standards can be hard to apply globally due to several factors: (1) Different societies have their own views of acceptable behavior for interpersonal conduct, communications, and businesses. (2) Misunderstandings may arise due to poor language translations. (3) In less-developed nations, less concern may exist for social and consumer issues than for improving industrialization. (4) Governments in some nations have questionable rules so as to protect domestic firms. (5) Executives are usually more aware of ethical standards in their home nations than in foreign ones. (6) Global ethical disputes may be tough to mediate. Under whose jurisdiction are disagreements involving firms from separate nations?

Here are some perspectives on global ethical challenges:

- "Because ethics are a part of culture, to study ethical choices without explicitly considering the cultural context is not realistic. Differing cultural reactions to consumption practices would be expected to occur, not only because moral values are socially and culturally constructed, but also because there are cultural differences in social roles, gender roles, institutional structures, welfare expectations, laws, and traditional rights, privileges, and obligations. In other words, culture filters our perceptions of what constitutes good or responsible consumption and what are perceived to be the consequences of violating these moral norms. Due to varying conceptions of what is good for the individual and what is good for society, the judgment of what constitutes an ethical breach in the first place would be expected to vary greatly depending on cultural orientation."[23]

- "Ah, the good old days. Back 30, 20, even 10 years ago, companies could run their overseas business pretty much however they wanted. What happened in a land far away bore little consequence to the main operations. If a factory used underage workers in poor countries, well, that's just the way things were done there. Giving and accepting elaborate gifts? Part of the culture. And if your subsidiary didn't adhere to the same pollution control standards as its U.S. counterparts, it was justified on the grounds that environmental laws overseas weren't as strict. But now, global business ethics has become a dilemma for many U.S. firms."[24] The Caux Round Table (**http://www.cauxroundtable.org**) is a group of international business leaders aiming to focus attention on global corporate responsibility.

- "Some foreign officials view public business dealings as profit-making opportunities and exploit them to supplement meager salaries, build personal fortunes, or recoup investments made to 'purchase' their positions. Some multinational firms have complied with questionable payment requests, hoping to trade payoffs and presents for favorable consideration by decision makers in order to win government or state enterprise contracts. The scale of international bribery is immense; the World Bank estimates that $50 billion to $80 billion per year goes to corrupt officials."[25]

Firms that market globally need to keep three points in mind: One, *core business values* provide the basis for worldwide ethics codes. These are company principles "that are so fundamental they will not be compromised" in any foreign markets. These include promise keeping, nondeception, the protection of societal and consumer rights, and to not knowingly do harm. Two, *peripheral business values* are less important to the firm and may be adjusted to foreign markets. These relate to local customs in buyer-seller exchanges, selling practices, and so on. Three, if possible, *ethnocentrism*—perceiving other nations' moral standards in terms of one's own country—must be avoided.[26]

Here are some specific suggestions for companies to properly engage in globally ethical practices: Include international personnel when setting and enacting ethical practices, and listen to diverse views. View globally ethical practices as a competitive advantage that can be communicated to consumers, the general public, and others. Do

---

[23] Russell Belk, Timothy Devinney, and Gina Eckhardt, "Consumer Ethics Across Cultures," *Consumption, Markets, and Culture*, Vol. 8 (September 2005), pp. 275–289.

[24] Meryl Davids, "Ethics: Global Standards, Local Problems," *Journal of Business Strategy*, Vol. 20 (January-February 1999), p. 38.

[25] Wayne Hamra, "Bribery in International Business Transactions and the OECD Convention: Benefits and Limitations," *Business Economics* (October 2000), p. 34.

[26] Gene R. Laczniak "Observations Concerning International Marketing Ethics," presented at the 1995 AMA Faculty Consortium on Ethics and Social Responsibility in Marketing (Hempstead, NY: Hofstra University).

not rely only on the legal statutes in countries where ethical practices are not codified. Deploy ethical compliance officials wherever business is done. Print ethics codes in various languages, not just English. Do not presume that people in other countries are less interested in ethical behavior than those in the home market.[27]

5-3d The Teachability of Ethics

Ethical concepts can be communicated.

Given the impact of societal values, peer pressure, self-interests and personal ambitions (and fear of failure), and other factors on people's sense of ethically acceptable behavior, considerable debate has ensued as to whether ethics can be taught.[28] As one expert noted: "A familiar argument holds that if people haven't learned ethics and values by the time they're adults, it's naive to expect higher education to step in and save their souls. The counterargument says that teaching moral philosophy and various ethical frameworks in universities can help shape students' careers."[29]

Despite the question as to whether ethics can be taught, it is clear that the following can be transmitted to people so that their ethical perceptions can be influenced:

- Clear ethics codes
- Role models of ethical people
- Wide-ranging examples of ethical and unethical behavior
- Specified punishments if ethical behavior is not followed.
- The vigilance of professors and top management regarding such issues as cheating on tests, misleading customers, and other unethical practices
- The notion that ethical actions will never put an employee in jeopardy (thus, a salesperson should not be penalized for losing a customer if he/she is unwilling to exaggerate the effectiveness of a product)

Consider this view of the role of teaching ethical standards to business students:

Business managers today confront unprecedented problems, issues, questions, and predicaments—the likes of which earlier generations never knew. The techniques of the past are not only difficult to apply to today's demands, but they may be inadequate for, or irrelevant to, tomorrow's requirements; business students need to be prepared to deal creatively with the new and unforeseen, for they will rarely confront the traditional and the predictable. Old ethical responses will have to be transformed in unexpected ways and interpreted with imagination. Already many managers in leading internationalized businesses explicitly discuss the merits of other-regarding, and even the benefits of altruistic behavior among their employees, partners, collaborators, and colleagues. The teaching of business ethics, thus, is not likely to be a passing fad, but a long-term and important, though difficult, responsibility for colleges and corporate businesses. The faculties of the former and the managers of the latter had better develop strategies and tactics that help them convince both students and employees that business ethics is an increasingly salient concern in the new, emerging environment of business, as well as in the rapidly changing corporate organization.[30]

For more ethics insights, visit Applied Ethics Resources (**http://www.ethicsweb.ca/resources**), Center for Ethical Business Cultures (**http://www.cebcglobal.org**), Ethics Toolkit (**http://www.ethics.org/toolkit.html**), International Business Ethics Institute (**http://www.business-ethics.org**), and *Business Ethics* magazine (**http://www.business-ethics.com**).

---

[27] International Business Ethics Institute, "10 Mistakes in Global Ethics Programs," *PM Network* (April 2005), p. 51.

[28] In recognition of the importance of this topic, the Fall 2004 issue of *Marketing Education Review* (http://www.marketingeducationreview.com) was devoted to "Ethics and Marketing Education."

[29] Jeffrey Pfeffer, "Teaching the Wrong Lesson," *Business 2.0* (November 2003), p. 60.

[30] James W. Kuhn, "Emotion as Well as Reason: Getting Students Beyond 'Interpersonal Accountability'," *Journal of Business Ethics*, Vol. 17 (February 1998), pp. 297–299.

5-4 CONSUMERISM

In contrast to social responsibility, which involves firms' interfaces with all of their publics, consumerism focuses on the relations of firms and their customers. *Consumerism* encompasses "the wide range of activities of government, business, and independent organizations that are designed to protect people from practices that infringe upon their rights as consumers."[31]

Consumer interests are most apt to be served well in industrialized nations, where their rights are considered important, and governments and firms have the resources to address consumer issues. In less-developed nations and those now turning to free-market economies, consumer rights have not been as suitably honored due to fewer resources and to other commitments; the early stages of consumerism are just now emerging in many of these nations.

U.S. consumerism has evolved through five distinct eras. The first era was in the early 1900s and focused on the need for a banking system, product purity, postal rates, antitrust regulations, and product shortages. Business protection against unfair practices was emphasized. During the second era, from the 1930s to the 1950s, issues were product safety, bank failures, labeling, misrepresentation, stock manipulation, deceptive ads, credit, and consumer refunds. Consumer groups, such as Consumers Union (**http://www.consumersunion.org**), and legislation grew. Issues were initiated but seldom resolved.

The third era began in the early 1960s and lasted to 1980. It dealt with all areas of marketing and had a great impact. Ushering in this era was President Kennedy's *consumer bill of rights*: to information, to safety, to choice in product selection, and to be heard. These rights, cited in Figure 5-8, apply to people in any nation or economic system. Other events also contributed to the era's aggressiveness. Birth defects from the drug thalidomide occurred. Several books—on marketing's ability to influence people, dangers from unsafe autos, and funeral industry tactics—were published. Consumers became more unhappy with product performance, firms' complaint handling, and deceptive and unsafe acts; and they set higher—perhaps unrealistic—expectations. Product scarcity occurred for some items. Self-service shopping and more complex products caused uncertainty for some people. The media publicized poor practices more often. Government intervention expanded, and the FTC (**http://www.ftc.gov**) extended its consumer activities.

The fourth era took place during the 1980s as consumerism entered a more mature phase, due to the dramatic gains of the 1960s and 1970s and an emphasis on business deregulation and self-regulation. Nationally, no major consumer laws were enacted and budgets of federal agencies concerned with consumer issues were cut. Yet, state and local governments became more active. In general, the federal government believed that most firms took consumer issues into account when devising and applying their marketing plans, and fewer firms ignored consumer input or publicly confronted consumer groups. Cooperation between business and consumers was better, and confrontations were less likely.

Since 1990, the federal government has been somewhat more involved with consumer issues. Its goal is to balance consumer and business rights. Some national laws have been enacted and U.S. agencies have stepped up enforcement practices. At the same time, many state and local governments are keeping a high level of commitment. Unfair business tactics, product safety, and health issues are the areas receiving the most attention. Today, more firms address consumer issues and resolve complaints than before.

These key aspects of consumerism are examined next: consumer rights, the responses of business to consumer issues, and the current role of consumerism.

> **Consumerism** protects consumers from practices that infringe upon their rights.

> President Kennedy declared a **consumer bill of rights**: to information, to safety, to choice, and to be heard.

---

[31] "Dictionary of Marketing Terms," **http://www.marketingpower.com/mg-dictionary.php** (May 3, 2006).

Figure 5-8

Consumers' Basic Rights

- To be informed and protected against fraudulent, deceitful, and misleading statements, advertisements, labels, etc.; and to be educated as to how to use financial resources wisely.

- To be protected against dangerous and unsafe products.

- To be able to choose from among several available goods and services.

- To be heard by government and business regarding unsatisfactory or disappointing practices.

5-4a   Consumer Rights

As noted, consumer rights fall into four categories: information and education, safety, choice, and the right to be heard. Each is discussed next.

Consumer Information and Education   The right to be informed includes protection against fraudulent, deceitful, or grossly misleading information, advertising, labeling, pricing, packaging, and so forth—and being given enough information to make good decisions. In the United States, many federal and state laws have been enacted in this area.

The federal Magnuson-Moss Consumer Product Warranty Act requires warranties to be properly stated and enforced (**http://www.ftc.gov/bcp/conline/pubs/buspubs/warranty. htm#Magnuson-Moss**). They must be available prior to purchases, so consumers may read them in advance. A *warranty* is an assurance to consumers that a product meets certain standards. An *express warranty* is explicitly stated, such as a printed form showing the minimum mileage for tires. An *implied warranty* does not have to be stated to be in effect; a product is assumed to be fit for use and packaged properly, and is assumed to conform to promises on the label. The FTC monitors product-accompanying information as to the warrantor's identity and location, exceptions in coverage, and how people may complain. A *full warranty* must cover all parts and labor for a given time. A *limited warranty* may have conditions and exceptions, and a provision for labor charges. Implied warranties may not be disclaimed.

Many states have laws regarding consumer information. For instance, cooling-off laws (allowing people to reconsider and, if they desire, cancel purchase commitments made in their homes with salespeople) exist in about 40 states. Unit-pricing laws that let people compare the prices of products coming in many sizes (such as small, medium, large, and economy) are likewise on a state-by-state basis. Government actions involving consumer information are also increasing internationally.

Unfortunately, the existence of good information does not mean consumers will use it in their decision making. At times, information is ignored or misunderstood, especially by those needing it most (such as the poor); thus, consumer education is needed. Most state departments of education in the United States have consumer education staffs. Such states as Illinois, Oregon, Wisconsin, Florida, Kentucky, and Hawaii require public high school students to take a consumer education course. And hundreds of programs are conducted by all levels of government, as well as by private profit and nonprofit groups.

A **warranty** assures consumers that a product will meet certain standards.

Marketing and the Web

Making the Can-Spam Act Work Better

The 2004 Can-Spam Act regulates the sending of commercial E-mail messages. According to Can-Spam, commercial E-mail messages must contain the full address of the sender and need to have an opt-out mechanism (that will be implemented within 10 days of receipt). Unsolicited E-mails must also clearly disclose that the message is an advertisement.

Two areas relating to the Can-Spam Act require further clarification: what constitutes a commercial E-mail message (in cases of dual-purpose E-mails) and how "refer-a-friend" promotions are treated by the law.

The FTC (http://www.ftc.com) has ruled that whether or not a message is commercial depends on the description in the message's subject line, as well as the placement of commercial and noncommercial content. For dual-content messages, a message is viewed as commercial if the subject line advertises a product or the noncommercial content does not appear at the beginning of the message.

In "refer-a-friend" messages, a consumer is encouraged to forward the message to family members and friends. In this way, the message appears as if it is not an advertisement but a message. Recipients cannot opt-out of these messages. The FTC intends to treat such E-mails as commercial solicitations.

The FTC has clearly stated that E-mail advertisers cannot use technical difficulties as a defense to a Can-Spam violation. E-mail marketers must also verify that their E-mail lists are continually revised to reflect opt-out requests.

Source: Based on material in Linda A. Goldstein, "FTC Intensifies Focus on Can-Spam," *Response* (June 2005), p. 57.

The programs typically cover how to purchase goods and services; key features of credit agreements, contracts, and warranties; and consumer protection laws.

Two good online consumer information sources are Consumer.gov (**http://www. consumer. gov**) and Consumer Affairs.com (**http://www.consumeraffairs.com**).

Consumer Safety Concern continues to grow over consumer safety because every year millions of people worldwide are hurt and thousands killed in incidents involving products other than motor vehicles. People also worry about having a safe shopping environment, one free from crime.

The yearly cost of U.S. product-related consumer injuries is estimated at more than $700 billion. Critics believe up to one-quarter of these injuries could be averted if firms made safer, better-designed products.

The Consumer Product Safety Commission, or CPSC (**http://www.cpsc.gov**), is the federal U.S. agency with major responsibility for product safety. It has jurisdiction over 15,000 types of products—including TVs, bicycles, lamps, appliances, toys, sporting goods, ladders, furniture, housewares, and lawn mowers. It also regulates structural items in homes such as stairs, retaining walls, and electrical wiring. The major products outside the CPSC's authority are food, drugs, cosmetics, tobacco, motor vehicles, tires, firearms, boats, pesticides, and aircraft. Each of these is regulated by other agencies. The Environmental Protection Agency (**http://www.epa.gov**) can recall autos not meeting emission standards; and the Food and Drug Administration (**http://www.fda.gov**) oversees food, drugs, cosmetics, medical devices, radiation emissions, and similar items.

The CPSC has a broad jurisdiction. It can

- develop voluntary standards with industry.
- issue and enforce mandatory standards, banning consumer products if no feasible standard would adequately protect the public.
- obtain the recall of products or arrange for their repair.
- conduct research on potential product hazards.
- inform and educate consumers through the media, state and local governments, and private organizations, and by responding to consumer inquiries.

When the CPSC finds a product hazard, it can issue an order for a firm to bring the product into conformity with the applicable safety rule or repair the defect, exchange the product for one meeting safety standards, or refund the purchase price. Firms found breaking safety rules can be fined, and executives can be personally fined and jailed for up to a year. **Product recall**, whereby the CPSC asks—orders, if need be—firms to recall and modify (or discontinue) unsafe products, is the primary enforcement tool. The CPSC has initiated many recalls (**http://www.cpsc.gov/cpscpub/prerel/prerel.html**), and a single recall may entail millions of units of a product. It has also banned such items as flammable contact adhesives, easily overturned refuse bins, asbestos-treated products, and a flame retardant in children's clothing that was linked to cancer.

The U.S. motor vehicle industry, overseen by the National Highway Traffic Safety Administration, NHTSA (**http://www.nhtsa.gov**), has had many vehicles recalled for safety reasons. Over the last 25 years, there have been thousands of U.S. recalls (often voluntary actions under NHTSA prodding) involving millions of cars, trucks, and other vehicles (some of which have been recalled more than once). NHTSA also makes its vehicular testing data available at its Web site (**http://www.nhtsa.dot.gov/cars/testing/comply**).

Consumers also have the right to sue the maker or seller of an injurious product. A legal action on behalf of many affected consumers is known as a **class-action suit**. Each year in the United States, numerous consumer suits are filed in federal courts and in state courts; these include both individual and class-action suits. Consumer suits have been rarer outside the United States. Yet, this too is changing. For example, until just 15 years ago, Chinese consumers "had little recourse when they were shocked, burned, or dismembered by shoddy state-produced goods. Now they can sue."[32] Since then, millions of product liability lawsuits have been filed in China.

A firm can reduce the negative effects of product recalls, as well as the possibility of costly class-action suits, by communicating properly when it learns a product is unsafe. This means voluntarily telling affected consumers, citing specific models that are unsafe, making fair adjustment offers (repair, replacement, or refund), and quickly and conveniently honoring those offers.

Consumer Choice The right to choose means people have several products and brands from which to select. Figure 5-9 illustrates this. As noted earlier, the lack of goods and services (of any brand) is a key consumer concern in less-developed and newly free-market nations where demand often far outstrips the supply for such items as coffee, bread, jeans, shoes, cosmetics, and fresh meat.

The federal governments in many industrialized countries have taken various actions to enhance the already extensive consumer choices there:

- Patent rights have time limits, after which all firms can use the patents.
- Noncompetitive business practices, such as price fixing, are banned.
- Government agencies review proposed company mergers; in some cases, they have stopped mergers if they felt industry competition would be lessened.
- Restrictions requiring franchisees to purchase all products from their franchisors have been reduced.
- The media are monitored to ensure that ad space or time is available to both small and large firms.
- Imports are allowed to compete with domestic-made items.
- Various service industries have been deregulated to foster price competition and encourage new firms to enter the marketplace.

In the United States and many other highly industrialized nations, consumer choice for certain product categories is so extensive that some experts wonder if there are too many options. For instance, in *The Paradox of Choice: Why More Is Less*, Swarthmore psychology professor Barry Schwartz says that excessive choice can actually make shoppers unhappy: "While it's better to have some choice than no choice, this doesn't mean

[32] Craig S. Smith, "Chinese Discover Product-Liability Suits," *Wall Street Journal* (November 13, 1997), p. B1. See also "Class Action Litigation in China," *Harvard Law Review*, Vol. 111 (April 1998), pp. 1523–1541.

Figure 5-9

Bed Bath & Beyond: Facilitating the Right to Choose

Source: Reprinted by permission of Susan Berry, Retail Image Consulting, Inc.

that more choice is better than less choice. Beyond a certain point, adding more options can paralyze a person's ability to select any one of them. (Think of choosing among the nearly two dozen varieties of chocolate-chip cookies one finds on the shelves of a modern supermarket.) Even when we manage to make a selection, the magnitude of options makes it harder for us to be content. After all, we've forgone so many alternatives that might have turned out to be better."[33]

Consumers' Right to Be Heard The right to be heard means people should be able to voice their opinions (sometimes as complaints) to business, government, and other parties. This gives consumers input into the decisions affecting them. To date, no overall U.S. consumer agency exists to represent consumer interests, although several federal agencies regulate various business practices relating to consumers. Their addresses and phone numbers, as well as those of trade associations, are available from the Federal Consumer Information Center's Consumer Action web Site (**http://www.consumeraction.gov**). Most states and major cities have their own consumer affairs offices, as do many corporations. Each encourages consumer input.

> Various federal, state, and local agencies are involved with consumers.

Consumer groups also exist that represent the general public or specific consumer segments. They publicize consumer opinions and complaints, speak at government and industry hearings, and otherwise generate consumer input into the decision processes of government and industry. Because a single consumer rarely has a significant impact, consumer groups frequently become the individual's voice.

5-4b The Responses of Business to Consumer Issues

Over the past four decades, in many nations, the business community has greatly increased its acceptance of the legitimacy and importance of consumer rights; many firms now have real commitments to address consumer issues in a positive manner. Nonetheless, a number of companies have raised reasonable questions about

> Firms have become much more responsive to consumers, yet questions remain about the effects of consumerism on firms.

---

[33] Mark Dolliver, "Coping with Consequences of Overabundant Choice," *Adweek.com* (January 3, 2005).

consumerism's impact on them. They particularly wonder why there isn't a *business bill of rights* to parallel the consumer's. Here are some of the questions that businesspeople raise:

- Why do various states, municipalities, and nations have different laws regarding business practices? How can a national or global company be expected to comply with each of these laws?
- Don't some government rules cause unnecessary costs and time delays in new-product introductions that outweigh the benefits of these rules?
- Is it really the job of business to ensure that consumers obey laws (such as not littering) and use products properly (such as wearing seat belts)?
- Isn't business self-regulation preferred over government regulation?
- Are multimillion-dollar jury awards to consumers getting out of hand?

Selected responses to these questions by manufacturers, retailers, and trade associations are discussed next.

Manufacturers Many firms have long-standing programs to handle consumer issues. Maytag (**http://www.maytag.com**) introduced Red Carpet Service in 1961 to improve its appliance repair service. Zenith (**http://www.zenith.com**) set up a customer relations department in 1968; Motorola (**http://www.motorola.com**) created an Office of Consumer Affairs in 1970; and RCA (**http://www.rca.com**) opened a corporate consumer affairs office in 1972.

General Electric runs a GE Answer Center (**http://www.geappliances.com/geac**), which handles consumer phone inquiries 24 hours a day, 7 days a week. It processes millions of calls yearly—questions from potential consumers and do-it-yourselfers, complaints from unhappy customers, and suggestions as to improvements. At the Answer Center, GE can satisfy current customers and attract potential ones, gather data about demographics, and gain insights about its marketing strategy and possible new products.

In the area of product recalls, many firms are now doing better. For instance, LifeScan (**http://www.lifescan.com**), a Johnson & Johnson company, makes meters that diabetics use to monitor sugar levels. When a single meter was found to be defective, LifeScan voluntarily recalled its entire product line and notified 600,000 customers within 24 hours. Because of how it handled the recall, LifeScan's market share has risen since that incident.

Some manufacturers have introduced new products or reformulated existing ones to better satisfy consumer concerns about a clean and safe environment for them and their children. One such firm is Shell (**http://www.shell.com**).

Despite manufacturers' interest in consumer issues, there remain times when their performance could be better: "The blinking 12:00 has long been a humorous reminder of the difficulty many of us have had programming and configuring consumer electronics. But there's nothing funny about spending thousands of dollars on a high-definition TV only to wind up watching both programming and DVDs in standard definition. There's plenty of blame to go around: confusing, poorly written manuals; overly complex products; consumer laziness, and ignorant salespeople and inept cable and satellite installers."[34]

Retailers Numerous retailers have expressed a positive concern about consumer issues, some for several decades. J.C. Penney (**http://www.jcpenney.com**) first stated its consumer philosophy in 1913, and Macy's (**http://www.macys.com**) formed a Bureau of Standards to test merchandise in 1927. In the 1970s, the Giant Food (**http://www.giantfood.com**) supermarket chain devised its own consumer bill of rights (paralleling the one articulated by President Kennedy):

---

[34] Michael Fremer, "News to Use: HDTV Setup," *Bergen Record Online* (January 22, 2005).

- Right to safety—no phosphates, certain pesticides removed, toys age-labeled.
- Right to be informed—better labeling, readable dating of perishable items, and nutritional labeling.
- Right to choose—continued sale of cigarettes and food with additives.
- Right to be heard—consumer group meetings, in-house consumer advocate.
- Right to redress—money-back guarantee on all products.
- Right to service—availability of store services and employee attentiveness.

For 20 years, Wal-Mart (**http://www.walmart.com**) has had in-store signs to inform consumers about environmentally safe products. It has also run newspaper ads encouraging suppliers to make more environmentally sound products. At 7-Eleven Japan (**http://www.sej.co.jp/english**), three times a week, top executives sample foods sold at the chain. Target donates more than $100 million per year. See Figure 5-10.

Retailers and consumer groups have opposing views involving ***item price removal***, whereby prices are marked only on shelves or aisle signs and not on individual items. Numerous retailers, particularly supermarkets, advocate item price removal because electronic checkouts let them computer-scan prices through codes on packages. They say this reduces labor costs and that these reductions are passed on to consumers. Consumer groups believe the practice is deceptive and will make it harder for them to guard against misrings. Item price removal is banned in a number of states and local communities. Giant Food is a leading advocate of item price removal; it passes the cost savings along to consumers.

> With **item price removal**, prices are displayed only on shelves or signs.

Trade Associations Trade associations represent groups of individual firms. Many have been quite responsive to consumer issues through such actions as coordinating and distributing safety-related research findings, setting up consumer education programs, planning product standards, and handling complaints.

The Major Appliance Consumer Action Program (MACAP) is an educational and complaint-handling program of the Association of Home Appliance Manufacturers (**http://www.aham.org**). The Direct Marketing Association (**http://www.the-dma.org**) sets industry guidelines and has a consumer action phone line. The National Retail

Figure 5-10

Target: Giving Back to the Community

Source: Reprinted by permission of Susan Berry, Retail Image Consulting, Inc.

Federation (**http://www.nrf.com**) has a Consumer Affairs Committee and offers information to the public. The Alliance Against Fraud in Telemarketing & Electronic Commerce (**http://www.fraud.org/aaft/aaftinfo.htm**) is dedicated to reducing fraudulent practices and consists of consumer groups, trade associations, labor unions, phone companies, federal and state agencies, and telemarketers.

The Better Business Bureau, or BBB (**http://www.bbb.com**), is the largest and broadest business-run U.S. trade association involved with consumer issues. It publishes educational materials, handles complaints, supervises arbitration panels, outlines ethical practices, publicizes unsatisfactory activities and the firms involved, and has nationwide offices. It supports self-regulation. Nationwide, the BBB handles nearly 1 million consumer-business disputes each year. These disputes are sometimes decided by impartial arbitrators, whose rulings are usually binding on participating firms but not on consumers.

Trade associations may vigorously oppose potential government rules. For example, the Tobacco Institute (funded by tobacco firms) lobbied for many years against further restrictions on tobacco sales, promotion, distribution, and use. Today, due to a civil legal settlement, its Web site (**http://www.tobaccoinstitute.com**) disseminates information. As the site notes, it "is designed to provide the public with access to documents produced by the Tobacco Institute in Attorney General reimbursement lawsuits and certain other specified civil actions, and to documents produced after October 23, 1998 through June 30, 2010 in smoking and health actions, and includes certain enhancements, all as provided for by paragraph IV of the Attorneys General Master Settlement Agreement (MSA)."

5-4c   The Current Role of Consumerism

During the 1980s, there was much less U.S. federal government activity on consumer-related issues than during the 1960s and 1970s due to the quality of self-regulation, consumerism's success, increased conservatism by Congress and the American people, and the importance of other issues.

By 1980, many firms had become more responsive to consumer issues. Thus, less pressure existed for government or consumer groups to intervene. A move to industry deregulation also took place as a way to increase competition, encourage innovations, and stimulate lower prices. In addition, consumerism activity was less needed because of the successes of past actions. On all levels, government protection for consumers had improved dramatically since the early 1960s, and class-action suits won big settlements from firms, making it clear that unsafe practices were costly. Consumer groups and independent media publicized poor practices, so firms knew such activities would not go unnoticed. In the 1980s, many members of Congress and sectors of the American public became more conservative about the role of government in regulating business. They felt government had become too big, impeded business practices, and caused unneeded costs; thus, some government agency functions were limited and budgets cut. Consumerism issues were not as important as other factors, including unemployment, the rate of inflation, industrial productivity, and the negative international balance of trade.

After a decade of a "hands-off" approach, many U.S. government leaders, consumer activists, and business leaders felt that the balance between business and consumer rights had tipped a little too much in favor of business. Hence, the federal government has assumed a somewhat more aggressive posture toward consumer-related issues than in the 1980s and states and localities are continuing to be heavily involved.

Here are some indications of the enhanced role of the U.S. government:

> Federal U.S. consumerism efforts have picked up, after a relative lull in the 1980s.

- The U.S. Justice Department (**http://www.usdoj.gov**) has vigorously pursued legal action against several pharmaceutical firms, charging them with civil and criminal violations regarding kickbacks to doctors, overcharging, selling drugs for unapproved uses, and inadequate testing. It has won billions of dollars in settlements and fines.

- In 2005, the Federal Trade Commission (**http://www.ftc.gov/opa/2005/03/ameridebt.htm**) settled a complaint against AmeriDebt, which resulted in the firm's closing "as part of a settlement of Federal Trade Commission charges that it deceived consumers into paying at least $170 million in hidden fees. The FTC charged that the company misrepresented that it was a nonprofit credit counseling organization that would teach consumers how to manage their finances for no up-front fee. The settlement requires AmeriDebt to transfer all current clients' accounts to a third party and bars the company from participating in any aspect of the credit counseling business in the future."
- There is now a comprehensive Web site for product recalls (**http://www.recalls.gov**)—"your online resource for government recalls"—that enables consumers to learn about recalls involving almost any product in one convenient place.
- The FTC promotes its Bureau of Consumer Protection at its Web site (**http://www.ftc.gov/bcp/bcp.htm**).
- The Securities and Exchange Commission has added an Office of Internet Enforcement, OIE (**http://www.sec.gov/divisions/enforce/internetenforce.htm**): "In general, OIE undertakes investigations and initiates SEC prosecutions based on leads culled from the SEC's Complaint Center; performs surveillance for potential Internet securities-related fraud which includes review of public complaints; formulates investigative procedures; provides guidance to Enforcement staff nationwide; organizes and maintains the OIE Computer Lab to aid in the surveillance of the Internet for potential securities fraud and to assist in Internet-related securities fraud investigations; acts as a clearinghouse and repository for Internet-related legal and technical policy and developments; and organizes and presents seminars, training classes, and speeches within the SEC and to other agencies."

Several states have also increased their activities. For example, Arizona, Maryland, Oklahoma, and Texas recently enacted laws to regulate gift cards and gift certificates, thereby joining 17 other states with such laws. Here are key provisions of the Arizona law, which went into effect on October 31, 2005:

In general, the law requires that a gift card that is subject to an expiration date or any fee clearly and conspicuously disclose the expiration date, the amount of the fee, and when it is incurred. Such disclosure must be clearly visible to a consumer before a purchase is made: for a paper gift certificate, the disclosure(s) must be made on the front of the certificate; for telephone sales of gift cards, the disclosure(s) must be made verbally before purchase; and for online purchases, the disclosure(s) must be made online before purchase.[35]

In many nations outside the United States, government, industry, and consumer groups are stepping up efforts relating to consumer rights—as past efforts have often been lacking in foreign markets. Some nations are making real progress, whereas others have a long way to go. No other nation has gone through as many stages or passed as many laws to protect consumer rights as the United States. The worldwide challenge will be for government, business, and consumer groups to work together so the socioecological view of marketing, ethical behavior, consumer rights, and company rights are in balance.

[35] "Four States Enact New Gift Card Laws," **http://www.loeb.com/CM/Alerts/Alerts212.asp** (June 2005).

Web Sites You Can Use

The Federal Citizen Information Center makes the most recent copy of the complete *Consumer Action Handbook* available online (**http://www.consumeraction.gov/viewpdf.shtml**) for free. It contains much useful consumer information, including the names, addresses, phone numbers, Web addresses, and

E-mail addresses for numerous consumer organizations, local Better Business Bureaus, corporations, trade associations, state and local consumer protection offices, military consumer offices, and federal agencies.

Summary

1. *To consider the impact of marketing on society* Marketing actions can have both positive and negative consequences regarding such areas as the quality of life and consumer expectations. Various studies have shown that people's perceptions of marketing are mixed. Firms need to recognize that many dissatisfied consumers do not complain; they simply do not rebuy offending products.

2. *To examine social responsibility and weigh its benefits and costs* Social responsibility involves a concern for the consequences of a person's or firm's acts as they might affect the interests of others. It encompasses the socioecological view of marketing, which looks at all the stages of a product's life and includes both consumers and nonconsumers. Social responsibility can pose dilemmas when popular goods and services have potential adverse effects on consumer or societal well-being.

   Consumers and marketing practices have led to some resource shortages. To stem this, cooperative efforts among business, stockholders, government, employees, the public, consumers, and others are needed. Garbage dumps and landfills, discarded containers, and abandoned autos are marring the landscape. Thus, many areas have laws to rectify the situation. Dangerous pollutants need to be removed and safe alternatives found to replace them; environmental pollution will be an issue for the foreseeable future. Planned obsolescence is a heavily criticized practice that encourages material wearout, style changes, and functional product changes. Marketers say it responds to consumer demand; critics say it increases resource shortages, is wasteful, and adds to pollution.

   Socially responsible actions have such benefits as worker and public health, cleaner air, and a more efficient use of resources. They also have costs, such as the unequal distribution of benefits, dollar expenditures, and conservative new-product planning. Benefits and costs need to be weighed.

3. *To look into the role of ethics in marketing* Ethical behavior, based on honest and proper conduct, comes into play when people decide whether given actions are ethical or unethical and when they choose how to act. Egoism, utilitarianism, duty-based, and virtue ethics theories help explain behavior. Marketing ethics can be divided into two categories: process-related and product-related.

   Ethics may be viewed from four vantage points: a business perspective, a consumer perspective, an international perspective, and teachability. A major difficulty of ethics in business relates to setting boundaries

for deciding what is ethical. For high ethical standards to be kept, both consumers and firms must engage in proper behavior. Ethical standards in a global setting are especially complex. Much debate has ensued as to whether ethics can be taught.

4. *To explore consumerism and describe the consumer bill of rights* Consumerism deals with the relations of firms and their consumers. It comprises the acts of government, business, and independent organizations that are designed to protect people from practices that infringe upon their rights as consumers.

   U.S. consumerism has seen five eras: early 1900s, 1930s to 1950s, 1960s to 1980, 1980s, and 1990 to now. The third era was the most important and began with President Kennedy's stating a consumer bill of rights—to information, to safety, to choice, and to be heard. The interest now is in balancing consumer and business rights in the United States, as well as in other countries.

   The right to be informed includes consumer protection against fraudulent, deceitful, grossly misleading, or incomplete information, advertising, labeling, pricing, packaging, or other practices. Consumer education involves teaching people to spend their money wisely.

   The concern over the right to safety arises from the large numbers of people who are injured or killed in product-related accidents. The U.S. Consumer Product Safety Commission has the power to order recalls or modifications for a wide range of products; other agencies oversee such products as autos and pharmaceuticals.

   The right to choose means consumers should have several products and brands from which to select. In the United States, some observers wonder if there is too much choice.

   The right to be heard means consumers should be able to voice their opinions to business, government, and other parties. Several government agencies and consumer groups provide this voice.

5. *To discuss the responses of manufacturers, retailers, and trade associations to consumerism and study the current role of consumerism* Many firms and associations are reacting well to consumer issues. A small number intentionally or unintentionally pursue unfair, misleading, or dangerous acts.

   The current era of consumerism has witnessed more activism than in the 1980s and less than in the 1960s and 1970s. In the 21st century, government, business, and consumers will continue working together to resolve consumer issues.

Key Terms

social responsibility (p. 126)

socioecological view of marketing (p. 126)

planned obsolescence (p. 133)

ethical behavior (p. 135)

process-related ethical issues (p. 137)

product-related ethical issues (p. 137)

cause-related marketing (p. 138)

consumerism (p. 143)

consumer bill of rights (p. 143)

warranty (p. 144)

product recall (p. 146)

class-action suit (p. 146)

item price removal (p. 149)

Review Questions

1. Define the term *social responsibility*. What are the implications for marketers?
2. Describe the pros and cons of planned obsolescence as a marketing practice.
3. What is ethical behavior? Distinguish among the egoism, utilitarianism, duty-based, and virtue ethics theories.

4. Why is cause-related marketing a controversial practice?
5. Why are ethical standards of conduct particularly complex for international marketers?
6. How does consumerism differ from social responsibility?
7. Explain the consumer bill of rights.
8. Describe the current role of consumerism.

Discussion Questions

1. From a company's perspective, why is hidden consumer dissatisfaction a particular problem? How would you go about making dissatisfaction less hidden?
2. Present a seven-point ethics guide for operating in India.
3. How would you teach marketing ethics to a class of graduate business students? What topics would you discuss? Why?

4. As an executive for a leading apparel manufacturer, how would you implement a product recall if you discover that some of your children's shirts have easily detached buttons that could be swallowed by small children?

Web Exercise

Eaton Corporation has been widely praised for its global ethics practices. Visit the firm's home page (http://www.eaton.com) and scroll down the "Quick Links" toolbar on the left of the screen and select the section called "Global Ethics." (1) Review both the *Code of Ethics* and the *Ethics Guide* and then comment on them. (2) What do you think about Eaton's decision to publish these materials in many different languages? Are there any downsides to this approach? Explain your answer.

Practice Quiz

1. Which of these statements is correct?
   a. Marketing practices rarely encourage unrealistic consumer expectations.
   b. The true level of customer dissatisfaction is usually hidden.
   c. Deceptive actions are okay if no one is physically injured.
   d. Tobacco products are not affected by the socioecological view of marketing.

2. Corporate social responsibility
   a. does not refer to issues such as product availability and innovation.
   b. considers only the needs of society.
   c. balances short-term profit needs with society's long-term needs.
   d. considers only deceptive actions.

3. Which of these countries annually discards the most trash per person?
   a. Mexico
   b. Japan
   c. United States
   d. France

4. A practice that encourages short-run material wearout, style changes, and functional product changes is
   a. planned obsolescence.
   b. a class-action suit.
   c. item price removal.
   d. product recall.

5. An example of a product-related ethical issue is
   a. price fixing.
   b. bait-and-switch advertising.

  c. bribing purchase agents.

  d. cigarette manufacturing.

6. Which of the following statements about cause-related marketing is *not* correct?

  a. Critics say there is too much commercialism by nonprofit groups and implicit endorsements for sponsor products.

  b. Advocates feel it benefits both the profit-oriented firms and nonprofit institutions involved in it.

  c. While its use was once considered somewhat controversial, that is no longer true.

  d. It has been used by such nonprofits as the Red Cross.

7. Which of the following is *not* one of the basic rights outlined in President Kennedy's consumer bill of rights?

  a. Low prices

  b. Information

  c. Safety

  d. Choice

8. During the fourth era of consumerism,

  a. cooperation between business and consumers declined.

  b. state and local governments became less active in environmental issues.

  c. there was a reduction in the emphasis on business deregulation.

  d. the budgets of the federal agencies concerned with consumer issues were cut back.

9. Consumers who need it most

  a. use product information infrequently.

  b. use product information in their decision making.

  c. demand more product information.

  d. use product information to complain to manufacturers.

10. Which of the following products does *not* fall under the jurisdiction of the Consumer Product Safety Commission?

  a. Pesticides

  b. TV sets

  c. Bicycles

  d. Electrical wiring

11. The primary enforcement tool of the Consumer Product Safety Commission is

  a. fines.

  b. product recall.

  c. imprisonment.

  d. purchase-price refunds.

12. Which of these statements is correct?

  a. Consumer lawsuits are rare in the United States.

  b. Japan has more consumer lawsuits than any other country.

  c. Consumers have the right to sue the makers of injurious products.

  d. The CPSC is a legislative branch of the Supreme Court.

13. Which of the following is *not* available to consumers in their quest to be heard?

  a. Industry specialists

  b. A single overall U.S. consumer agency

  c. Consumer groups

  d. A directory of federal agencies regulating business

14. The largest and broadest business-operated U.S. trade association involved with consumer issues is the

  a. National Retail Federation.

  b. Association of Home Appliance Manufacturers.

  c. Better Business Bureau.

  d. Bank Marketing Association.

15. In contrast to the 1980s, currently,

  a. there is a somewhat more aggressive federal government posture toward consumer-related issues.

  b. the Food and Drug Administration is reducing its efforts to curb misleading advertising.

  c. firms are no longer required to report settlements of product-safety lawsuits involving death or disabling injuries to the CSPC.

  d. state and local governments have reduced their involvement in consumer-related issues.

For the answers to these questions, please visit the online site for this book at **http://www.atomicdog.com.**

Chapter 6

Global Aspects of Marketing

When Kiichiro Toyoda, the founder of Toyota Motor Corporation (http://www.toyota.com), worked with his younger cousin, Eiji, to build a factory in central Japan, neither Kiichiro nor Eiji could have ever predicted the firm's subsequent success. Toyota Motor Corporation is now Japan's largest car maker and the world's second largest car maker (after General Motors). The first plant, located in what is now referred to as "Toyota City," was responsible for introducing such key marketing concepts as just-in-time inventory management, the *kanban* system of parts labeling, and *kaizen*, a continuous improvement process.

Toyota has learned much about international marketing since it first exported the Toyota Crown to the United States in 1957. Although the Crown was viewed as too underpowered for the U.S. market, its smaller Corolla model (introduced in the United States in 1968) quickly became popular with American consumers looking for an inexpensive and reliable car. The Corolla became the best-selling car model of all time. And the Toyota Camry was ranked the best-selling car in the United States seven times.

By 1970, Toyota became the world's fourth-largest car manufacturer. In 2003, Toyota overtook Ford Motor Company (http://www.ford.com) as the world's second largest car maker. Its current global market share is 10 percent versus 15 percent for General Motors (http://www.gm.com). However, Toyota has a 15 percent world market share objective for 2010.

Toyota is currently focusing on expanding its global manufacturing capabilities. Its strategy is based on producing cars near to or in the same countries where they will be purchased. Over this past decade, Toyota has opened major vehicle plants in India (1999), France (2001), China (2002), Mexico (2004), and the Czech Republic (2005).

Much of Toyota's global focus is on China, which is expected to become the second-largest car market (behind the United States) by 2010. With a Chinese-based partner, Toyota is building Land Cruisers and Corollas in China. In another partnership, Toyota is building engines. Toyota's fourth car assembly plant is scheduled to open in China in 2006.[1]

In this chapter, we will explore the environment facing international marketers, including data on U.S. imports and exports, and see how to develop an international marketing strategy.

Chapter Objectives

1. To define domestic, international, and global marketing
2. To explain why international marketing takes place and study its scope
3. To explore the cultural, economic, political and legal, and technological environments facing international marketers
4. To analyze the stages in the development of an international marketing strategy

6-1 OVERVIEW

International transactions—including both goods and services—generate $12 trillion in yearly global sales. And virtually every nation engages in significant international business, whether it be the United States with $3 trillion in yearly exports and imports of goods and

---

[1] Various company and other sources.

services, Namibia (in southern Africa) with $3 billion in exports and imports, or Tonga (in the South Pacific) with $140 million in exports and imports. In many areas, the market-place has a wide mix of foreign firms competing with domestic ones.[2]

Whether a company is big or small, operates only in its home nation or both domestically and abroad, markets goods or services, and is profit- or nonprofit-driven, it needs to grasp key international marketing concepts and devise a proper strategy. This means having a broadened marketing perspective:

> The idea that global business is the exclusive purview of large corporations must change. Too many smaller firms are missing opportunities for growth through exports. Promoting goods and services internationally often results in profitable sales for those with the motivation, competency, and willingness to make use of help available from state and federal agencies. Despite increasing opportunities, some businesses are not interested because they are comfortable in the domestic economy. This situation is dangerous because the global economy—with its accelerating pace of change and ever-newer information technology— brings competition from unexpected places. Small U.S. firms have a cultural disadvantage relative to most equivalent-sized firms elsewhere. The immense size of the U.S. market has heretofore provided sufficient opportunity, with little need to learn other languages, other customs, or other ways of doing business. By contrast, European and Asian businesses have acquired the skills, networks, and support needed in the global marketplace, and have been involved in international business for a long time.[3]

Domestic marketing encompasses a firm's efforts in its home country. *International marketing* involves marketing goods and services outside a firm's home country, whether in one or several markets. *Global marketing* is an advanced form of international marketing in which a firm addresses global customers, markets, and competition. It is used by both multinational and global firms.

A company may act domestically, internationally, or both; efforts vary widely. Here is the range of options that may be pursued:

- A *domestic firm* restricts its efforts to the home market. It believes the base market is both large enough and responsive enough to meet its sales and profit goals.
- An *exporting firm* recognizes that the home market is no longer adequate for it fully to meet revenue and profit goals. A firm typically uses exporting when it seeks to sell its traditional products in foreign markets, often via distribution and sales intermediaries. A relatively low percentage of business is outside the domestic market.
- An *international firm* makes modifications in its existing products for foreign markets or introduces new products there; the firm knows it must aggressively cultivate foreign markets. There remains enough strength in the domestic market for that market to remain the dominant one for the company.
- A *multinational firm* is a worldwide player. Although corporate headquarters are in the home nation, the domestic market often accounts for 50 percent or less of sales and profits—and the firm operates in dozens of nations or more. Geographically, the business scope and opportunity search are broad. Many leading U.S. players, such as Boeing (**http://www.boeing.com**), Citigroup (**http://www.citigroup.com**), and McDonald's (**http://www.mcdonalds.com**), are in this category; they market items around the world, but have a distinctly American business culture. See Figure 6-1.
- A *global firm* is also a worldwide player. Yet, because its domestic sales are low, it places even more reliance on foreign transactions. It has the greatest geographic scope. Such firms have been more apt to emerge in smaller nations, where companies have historically needed foreign markets to survive (in contrast to U.S.

Due to its impact, international marketing concepts should be understood by all types of firms.

Domestic marketing involves the home nation, **international marketing** embraces foreign activities, and **global marketing** has a worldwide focus.

A firm may be domestic, exporting, international, multinational, or global.

---

[2] "The World Factbook," **http://www.odci.gov/cia/publications/factbook** (March 31, 2006); "Most Frequently Accessed Tables," **http://www.wto.org** (March 31, 2006); and "U.S. International Trade in Goods and Services," *United States Bureau of Economic Analysis News* (October 13, 2005).

[3] Nadar H. Shooshtari and Jack Reece, "Global Business and the Smaller Company," *Montana Business Quarterly* (Summer 2000), p. 17.

Figure 6-1

McDonald's: A U.S.-Based Multinational Firm

More than one-half of McDonald's sales are from outlets outside the United States. Though it has restaurants in about 120 different nations (such as the Shanghai unit shown here), it has a distinctly American corporate culture and image.

Source: Reprinted by permission of Retail Forward.

firms). A quintessential global firm is Sweden's Ikea furniture store chain (**http://www.ikea.com**), which derives only 8 percent of total sales from its Swedish customers. It has stores in Europe, North America, Asia, Australia, and the Middle East; prints catalogs in 25 languages; and purchases merchandise from suppliers in 55 nations. See Figure 6-2.

It is clear, now that we are in the 21st century, that more domestic firms will need to become exporters and then international in orientation. And multinational firms will need to become more global, thereby acting boundaryless and not dominated by a home-country-based corporate culture.

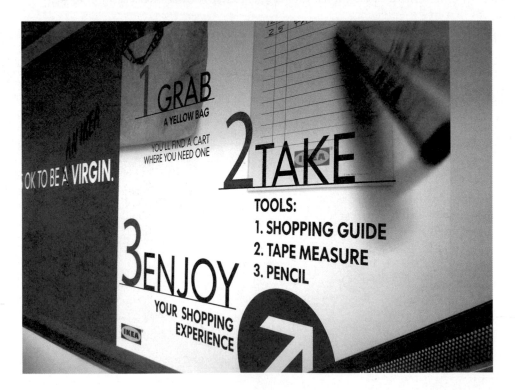

Figure 6-2

Ikea: A Truly Global Firm

Due to the small size of its domestic market (Sweden has a population of just 9 million), Ikea derives well over 90 percent of its sales from outside of Sweden. Therefore, it must think globally and seek expansion in foreign markets.

Source: Reprinted by permission of Susan Berry, Retail Image Consulting, Inc.

This chapter looks at why international marketing occurs, its scope, its environment, and the components of an international marketing strategy.

6-2 WHY INTERNATIONAL MARKETING TAKES PLACE

For several reasons, countries and individual firms are engaging in greater international marketing efforts than ever before.[4] These are shown in Figure 6-3 and are discussed next.

According to the concept of *comparative advantage*, each country has distinct strengths and weaknesses based on its natural resources, climate, technology, labor costs, and other factors. Nations can benefit by exporting the goods and services with which they have relative advantages and importing the ones with which they have relative disadvantages. Comparative advantages may generally be grouped into two categories: (a) those related to the physical environment of a country (such as natural resources and climate) and (b) those related to the socioeconomic development of a country (such as technological advances or low labor costs). Among the best U.S. comparative advantages are its agricultural productivity, the level of technological prowess, and service industry expertise.

Economic and demographic trends vary by country. A firm in a nation with weak domestic conditions (such as high inflation) and/or a small or stagnant population base can stabilize or increase sales by marketing products in more favorable foreign markets. The U.S. market is attractive due to rather low inflation and unemployment, as well as the relative affluence. Developing and less-developed nations are potentially lucrative markets due to their population growth; more than 90 percent of world growth is in such nations. Thus, Heinz (**http://www.heinz.com**) now targets developing and less-developed nations due to their growth and nutrition needs. Its brands are established in Africa, Asia, and the Pacific Rim:

> India, a land with time-honored culinary customs, is an emerging marketplace for Heinz. Indian consumers know the brand as the source of premium Heinz Ketchup and Heinz Chili

> Countries trade items with which they have a **comparative advantage**.

> The domestic economy and demographics affect international efforts.

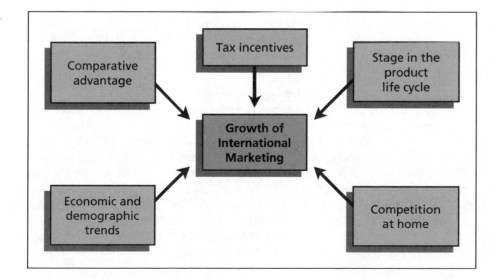

Figure 6-3

Why International Marketing Occurs

Sauce. Heinz began producing tomato ketchup in India in 2000, only six years after entering the country. Since then, an increasing number of families are finding ways to make Heinz Ketchup a regular at their dinner tables. Heinz has established a widespread distribution system and formed profitable partnerships through shops, food stalls, and other outlets. To foster greater consumer loyalty, Heinz is adapting to local cultures and building trust through good taste and nutrition.[5]

Competition in a firm's domestic market may be intense and lead to its expanding internationally, as these examples show:

Home competition may lead to international efforts.

- The U.S. optical-products marketplace is highly competitive. So, U.S.-based Bausch & Lomb (http://www.bausch.com) has increased its activities in regions with expansion opportunities. Its non-U.S. sales represent nearly 60 percent of its total sales, and it markets products in more than 100 nations.
- In Europe, Germany's Henkel (http://www.henkel.com) is a leading maker of detergents, cleansers, and personal-care items, as well as industrial chemicals. Yet, it faces intense European competition from Dutch-British Unilever (http://www.unilever.com) and America's Procter & Gamble (http://www.pg.com), among others. So, it has been pumping up efforts in Asia and Africa.

International marketing may extend the product life cycle or dispose of discontinued items.

Because products are often in different stages of their life cycles in different nations, exporting may be a way to prolong the cycles. For instance, the U.S. market for tobacco products has been falling, for health and social reasons. To stimulate cigarette sales, Philip Morris International (http://www.pmintl.com) and R.J. Reynolds (http://www.rjrt.com) have turned more to foreign sales. The two firms have heightened their efforts in Eastern Europe—where cigarette smoking is popular and shortages of domestic tobacco products occur. International marketing can also be used to dispose of discontinued goods, seconds, and manufacturer remakes (repaired products). These items can be sold abroad without spoiling the domestic market for full-price, first-quality items. However, firms must think carefully about selling unsafe products in foreign markets, a practice that can lead to ill will on the part of the governments there.

Some countries entice new business from foreign firms by offering tax incentives in the form of low property, import, and income taxes for an initial period. In addition, multinational firms may adjust revenue reports so their largest profits are recorded in nations with the lowest tax rates.

6-3 THE SCOPE OF INTERNATIONAL MARKETING[6]

The United States is both the world's largest goods and services exporter and importer.

The world's leading export countries are the United States, Germany, Japan, France, Great Britain, and China. Together, they account for $4.5 trillion annually in goods and services exports (out of the $12 trillion in yearly world exports). In 2005, U.S. merchandise exports were roughly $870 billion, an amount equal to about 7 percent of the U.S. gross domestic product and one-tenth of world merchandise exports. Services accounted for $375 billion in U.S. exports. Among the leading U.S. exports are capital goods, industrial supplies and materials, food grains, medical equipment, and scientific instruments, and such services as tourism, entertainment, engineering, accounting, insurance, and consulting. Although 70 percent of U.S. foreign business revenues are generated by large firms, almost one-quarter million U.S. firms with less than 20 employees engage in some level of international marketing.

---

[5] *Heinz 2005 Annual Report,* http://www.heinz.com/2005annualreport/goodfood_india.html.

[6] The data cited in this section are from "The World Economic Outlook Database," http://www.imf.org/external/pubs/ft/weo/2005/02/index.htm (September 2005); "Most Frequently Accessed Tables;" and "U.S. International Trade in Goods and Services."

The United States is also the world's largest importer, followed by Germany, Great Britain, Japan, France, and China. In 2005, U.S. merchandise imports were about $1.65 trillion—more than one-sixth of total world merchandise imports. Service imports were an additional $320 billion. Leading U.S. imports are petroleum, motor vehicles, raw materials, and clothing.

Due to the high level of imports in 2005, the United States had a merchandise ***trade deficit***—the amount by which the value of imports exceeds the value of exports—of $780 billion. This was far and away the greatest merchandise deficit in the world and set a U.S. record. On the other hand, U.S. services stayed strong, with a service ***trade surplus***—the amount by which the value of exports exceeds the value of imports—of $55 billion in 2005. By a large amount, this was the greatest service surplus of any nation.

The U.S. merchandise trade deficit is due to a variety of factors:

- The attractive nature of the U.S. market. Per-capita consumption is high for most goods and services.
- The slow-growth economies in a number of other countries depressing consumer purchases there.
- Increased competition in foreign markets.
- U.S. dependence on foreign natural resources (including petroleum).
- High U.S. labor costs.
- Trade restrictions in foreign markets.
- U.S. firms virtually exiting such markets as televisions and VCRs.
- Making products in the United States with imported parts and materials.
- The complacency of some U.S. firms in adapting their strategies to the needs of foreign markets.
- The mediocre image of U.S. products in the eyes of many Americans.
- The emphasis of many U.S. firms on profits over market share. In contrast, Japanese firms try to keep prices stable to maximize market share—even if they must reduce profit margins to do so.

Because merchandise trade deficits have been so high, U.S. firms are improving their product quality, focusing on market niches, becoming more efficient, building overseas facilities, and engaging in other tactics to improve competitiveness. Some have called for tighter import controls and more access to restricted foreign markets; one outcome of their efforts is the Omnibus Trade & Competitiveness Act that requires the President to press for open markets. The U.S. government has also negotiated with foreign governments to help matters. For example, China has agreed to amend some practices to improve its trade balance with the United States. Nonetheless, the U.S. trade deficit with China is $175 billion a year.

Despite the trade deficit, the United States is the dominant force globally. Between its imports and exports, the country accounts for more than one-quarter of all global trade.

> The United States has had large merchandise **trade deficits** and large service **trade surpluses**.

6-4 THE ENVIRONMENT OF INTERNATIONAL MARKETING

Although the principles described in this book are applicable to international marketing strategies, there are often major differences between domestic and foreign markets—and marketing practices may have to adapt accordingly. Each market should be studied separately. Only then can a firm decide how much of its domestic marketing strategy can be used in foreign markets and what elements should be modified.

To gain insights about the global marketplace, useful resources such as these may be consulted:

- International Monetary Fund's "IMF Publications" (**http://www.imf.org/external/pubind.htm**).
- OECD Data Online (**http://oecdwash.org/DATA/online.htm**).

Figure 6-4

**The Environment Facing
International Marketers**

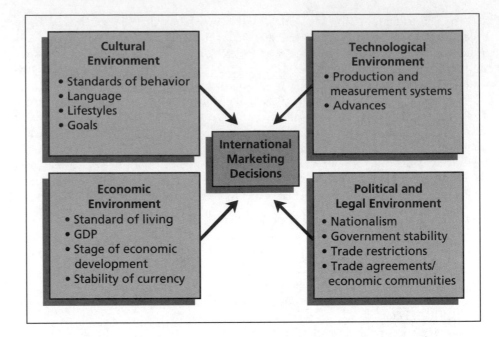

- United Nations' "UN & Business" (**http://www.un.org/partners/business/
index.asp**).
- U.S. Census Bureau's International Programs Center (**http://www.census.gov/ipc/www**).
- U.S. International Trade Administration (**http://www.ita.doc.gov**, 1-800-USA-TRADE).
- World Trade Organization's "Resources" (**http://www.wto.org/english/res_e/res_e.htm**).

The major cultural, economic, political and legal, and technological environments facing international marketers are discussed next. See Figure 6-4.

6-4a The Cultural Environment

International marketers need to be tuned in to each foreign market's cultural environment. A *culture* consists of a group of people sharing a distinctive heritage. It teaches behavior standards, language, lifestyles, and goals; is passed down from one generation to another; and is not easily changed. Almost every country has a different culture; regional and continental differences also exist. A firm unfamiliar with or insensitive to a foreign culture may try to market goods or services that are unacceptable to that culture. For example, beef and unisex products are rejected by some cultures.

Table 6-1 shows the errors a firm engaged in international marketing might commit due to a lack of awareness about foreign cultures. Sometimes, the firm is at fault because it operates out of a domestic home office and gets little local input. Other times, such as when marketing in less-developed nations, information may be limited because a low level of population data exists and mail and phone service are poor. In either case, research—to determine hidden meanings, the ease of pronunciation of brand names and slogans, the rate of product consumption, and reasons for purchases and nonpurchases— may not be fully effective.

Cultural awareness can be improved by employing foreign personnel in key positions, hiring experienced marketing research specialists, locating offices in each country of operations, studying cultural differences, and responding to cultural changes.[7] Table 6-2 shows several cultural opportunities.

Consider this critique regarding the way many Western firms act when dealing with foreign cultures:

> Inadequate information about foreign **cultures** is a common cause of errors.

---

[7] See Allen P. Roberts, Jr., "Mind Your Manners," *Inc.* (September 2005), p. 50.

Table 6-1	Illustrations of Errors in International Marketing Because of a Lack of Cultural Awareness

Many American consumers have considered Nokia cell phones (from Finland) to be less fashionable than other phone brands, which has adversely affected sales.

In the Czech Republic, portable phones did poorly when first introduced because they were perceived as walkie-talkies.

Japanese cars had engine trouble in China, where drivers turn off their motors when stopped at red lights. Because the air-conditioning in these cars kept going with the motors off, the engines malfunctioned.

At the Moscow Pizza Hut, consumers did not purchase the Moscva Seafood pizza, with sardines and salmon. "Russians have this thing. If it's their own, it must be bad."

Pepsodent failed in Southeast Asia when it promised white teeth to a culture where black or yellow teeth are symbols of prestige.

In Quebec, a canned-fish manufacturer promoted a product by showing a woman dressed in shorts, golfing with her husband, and planning to serve canned fish for dinner. These activities violated cultural norms.

Maxwell House advertised itself as the "great American coffee" in Germany, although Germans had little respect for American coffee.

In Mexico, a U.S. airline meant to advertise that passengers could sit in comfortable leather seats; but the phrase used in its Spanish translation ("sentado en cuero") meant "sit naked."

African men were upset by a commercial for men's deodorant that showed a happy male being chased by women. They thought the deodorant would make them weak and overrun by women.

Source: Compiled by the authors from various publications.

The DHL [http://www.dhl.com] Export Barometer recently found that different business and cultural practices were considered by more first-time exporters to be a major barrier to exporting than any other factor. Despite this, businesses often underestimate the importance of culture in international dealings—even though failing to account for cultural differences can lead to minor mix-ups or deal-breaking errors. As one expert illustrated, at one extreme, there is the example of a businessperson who was in China setting up a joint venture. Progress was slow and the person became frustrated. "He got angry in a meeting, very angry, and showed a great deal of emotion in front of two senior Chinese executives. He put the entire relationship at risk." In China, it is considered bad manners and poor business acumen to show emotion at work. "The Westerner saw it as just an emotional outburst and didn't see it effecting the transaction. The Chinese saw it as a major change in the relationship."[8]

One way to learn about a foreign culture is to visit Web-based search engines relating to specific nations or regions. Visit Lycos MultiMania (**http://www.multimania. lycos.fr**)—France; Yahoo! UK & Ireland (**http://www.uk.yahoo.com**), one of about two dozen country-based Yahoo! sites; and Terra (**http://www.terra.com**)—Latin America. Most of these sites are in the languages of the nations they represent.

6-4b The Economic Environment

The economic environment of a nation indicates its present and potential capacities for consuming goods and services. Measures of economic performance include the standard of living, the gross domestic product (GDP), the stage of economic development, and the stability of the currency.

---

[8] Zoe Fielding, "Culture Shock: Confusion Sours Export Deals," *Manufacturers' Monthly (Australia) Online* (June 2005).

Table 6-2   Illustrations of Cultural Opportunities for International Marketers

General Motors is now designing vehicles capable of being manufactured with either right- or left-hand drive to appeal to driving customs around the world.

To accommodate the weak electrical infrastructure in India, as well as the low consumer incomes, Hewlett-Packard created an inexpensive and portable solar charger.

Globally, the greatest growth in ready-to-eat cereal sales is in Latin America, where there is new interest in convenient foods.

After one year of employment, in most European countries, people receive 20 to 25 days of vacation (compared to 10 days for Canadians and Americans). This means an emphasis on travel, summer homes, and leisure wear.

Japanese consumers are attracted by high-tech vending machines—such as those that play music, talk, dispense free products at random, and use splashy rotating signs.

Worldwide, consumers want the "American look" provided by Levi's jeans.

At Domino's outlets in Australia, the favorite pizzas are those with prawns and pineapple.

In China, the most popular color is red—indicating happiness. Black elicits a positive response because it denotes power and trustworthiness.

French Canadians drink more soda, beer, and wine than their English-speaking counterparts.

Nigerians believe "good beer only comes in green bottles."

British consumers insist on cake mixes that require their adding fresh eggs, as Betty Crocker mixes sold there do.

Source: Compiled by the authors from various publications.

> The quality of life in a nation is measured by its **standard of living**.

The **standard of living** refers to the average quantity and quality of goods and services that are owned and consumed in a given nation. United Nations (**http://www.un.org**) and Organization for Economic Cooperation & Development (**http://www.oecd.org**) data show that the United States has the highest standard of living of any major industrialized country. By reviewing a nation's per-capita ownership and consumption across a range of goods and services, a firm can estimate the standard of living there (regarding the average *quantity* of goods and services). Table 6-3 compares data for 11 diverse countries.

> The total value of goods and services produced in a nation is its **gross domestic product**.

As noted in Chapter 2, the **gross domestic product (GDP)** is the total value of goods and services produced in a country each year. Total and per-capita GDP are the most-used measures of a nation's wealth because they are regularly published and easy to calculate and compare with GDP data from other nations. Yet, per-capita GDP may be misleading. The figures are typically means and not income distributions; a few wealthy citizens may boost per-capita GDP, while most people have low income. And due to price and product availability differences, incomes buy different standards of living in each nation. According to the World Bank's (**http://www.worldbank.org**) *World Development Indicators* data base, a U.S. income of $40,000 yields about the same standard of living—purchasing power parity—as $22,150 in Greece, $12,550 in Argentina, $5,575 in China, $3,125 in India, and $800 in the Congo.

Marketing opportunities often can be highlighted by looking at a country's stage of economic growth. One way to classify growth is to divide nations into three main categories: industrialized, developing, and less-developed.[9] See Figure 6-5.

> Countries can be classified as **industrialized, developing,** and **less developed**.

Industrialized countries have high literacy, modern technology, and per-capita income of several thousand dollars. They can be placed into two main subgroups: established free-market economies and newly emerging free-market economies. The former include the United States, Canada, Japan, Australia, and nations in Western Europe; they have a large middle class, annual per-capita GDP of $15,000 and up, and

---

[9] "Dictionary of Marketing Terms," **http://www.marketingpower.com/mg-dictionary.php** (May 3, 2006).

Table 6-3	Ownership and Consumption in 11 Countries					
	Passenger Cars (per 100 People)	TV Sets (per 100 People)	Telephone Land Lines (per 100 People)	Cell Phones (per 100 People)	Daily Newspaper Circulation (per 100 People)	Electricity Consumption (Kilowatt Hours per Year per Person)
United States	80	81	62	54	21	12,385
Brazil	8	22	21	25	4	1,890
Canada	56	71	61	40	16	14,850
China	5	32	20	21	4	1,250
France	57	60	56	69	22	6,830
Great Britain	43	52	58	82	33	5,585
India	1	7	5	3	3	475
Italy	57	53	46	96	10	5,060
Japan	54	69	56	68	58	7,620
Nigeria	0.1	7	1	3	3	150
Russia	12	41	25	12	11	6,235

Source: Computed by the authors from "InfoNation," http://www.cyberschoolbus.un.org/infonation/index.asp (March 3, 2006); and *World Factbook 2005*, http://www.cia.gov/cia/publications/factbook/index.html (updated as of August 9, 2005).

plentiful goods and services to satisfy their needs. The latter include Russia and its former republics, as well as other Eastern European nations; though industrialized, they have a smaller middle class, annual per-capita GDP of $6,000 to $14,000, and insufficient goods and services to satisfy all their needs.

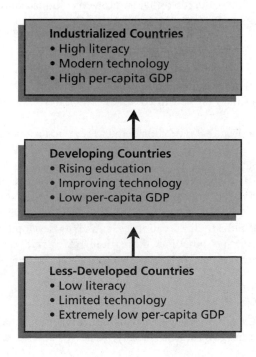

Figure 6-5

The Stages of Economic Development

Marketing and the Web

Europe on the Web

From 2003 to 2005, online sales in Europe more than doubled—to a projected $20 billion in 2005. Some marketing experts attribute the rise in online purchasing to the switch to the euro currency in much of Europe. The euro frees consumers from converting currencies and enables both buyers and sellers to better understand a good's true cost. In contrast to many other European countries, Great Britain still uses the British pound.

The European Interactive Advertising Association (EIAA) (http://www.eiaa.net) reports that more than 20 percent of Europeans make at least six online purchases each year. By country, Great Britain (with 13 million online households) and Germany (with 18 million online households) account for the biggest online spenders, with the average purchase between $35 and $1,500 (in U.S. dollars). The EIAA reports that 91 percent of European consumers are satisfied with their online shopping experience—far higher than in the United States—and that one-third are more confident in online shipping than they were in 2003.

Significant differences exist in online access and purchasing by country. Households in Sweden, Norway, Denmark, and Finland have almost 58 percent online access, whereas online household access is 13 percent for Spain, Portugal, and Italy. Surprisingly, France, which has one of the lowest Internet penetration rates in Europe, leads Europe in time spent online.

Sources: Based on material in Digby Orsmond, "Europeans Crown Online Shopping Aisles," *Response* (June 2005), p. 64; and authors' estimates.

In *developing countries*, education and technology are rising, and per-capita GDP is about $4,000 to $9,000. Included are many Latin American and Southeast Asian nations. Although these countries are striving to build their industries, consumers are limited in what they can buy (due to the scarcity and relatively high prices of goods and services). They account for 20 percent of world population and almost one-third of its income.

Less-developed countries include a number of nations in Africa and Asia. Compared to other nations, literacy is lower and technology is more limited. Per-capita GDP is typically below $2,000 (sometimes less than $1,000). These nations have two-thirds of world population but less than 15 percent of world income. According to United Nations (UN) data, people in the most affluent one-fifth of the world have 65 times greater per-capita GDP than those in the bottom one-fifth.

The greatest marketing opportunities often occur in industrialized nations due to their higher incomes and standards of living. However, industrialized countries tend to have slow rates of population growth, and sales of some product categories may have peaked. In contrast, developing and less-developed nations tend to have more rapidly expanding populations but now purchase few imports. There is long-run potential for international marketers in these nations. For example, Brazilians have only 80 cars per 1,000 population and Indians 13 per 1,000. The 1.3 billion people of China have 65 million cars—far fewer than in the United States, which has less than one-quarter of the population of China.

> Currency stability affects foreign sales and profit.

Currency stability should also be considered in transactions because sales and profits could be affected if a foreign currency fluctuates widely relative to a firm's home currency. For example, should the value of a foreign currency lessen relative to the U.S. dollar, then U.S. products become more expensive to consumers in that foreign country (exports) and that country's products become less expensive for U.S. consumers (imports).

The currencies of industrialized countries, as well as developing and less-developed nations, typically fluctuate—sometimes dramatically. As a rule, established free-market industrialized countries' currencies have been more stable than those of other nations.

6-4c The Political and Legal Environment

Every nation or region has a unique political and legal environment. Among the factors to consider are nationalism, government stability, trade restrictions, and trade agreements and economic communities. These factors can be complex, as the growing European Union has discovered.

Nationalism refers to a country's efforts to become self-reliant and raise its stature in the eyes of the world community. At times, a high degree of nationalism may lead to tight restrictions on foreign firms to foster the development of domestic industry at their expense. In the past, some nations even seized the assets of multinational firms, revoked their licenses to operate, prevented funds transfers from one currency to another, increased taxes, and/or unilaterally changed contract terms.

Government stability must be studied in terms of two elements: consistency of business policies and orderliness in installing leaders. Do government policies regarding taxes, company expansion, profits, and so on remain rather unchanged over time? Is there an orderly process for selecting and installing new government leaders? Firms will probably not function well unless both factors are positive. Thus, although many companies have made large investments in developing nations, others have stayed away from some less-developed and developing countries.

A firm can protect itself against the adverse effects of nationalism and political instability. Prior to entering a foreign market, it can measure the potential for domestic instability (riots, government purges), the political climate (stability of political parties, manner of choosing officials), and the economic climate (financial strength, government intervention)—and avoid nations deemed unsuitable. PRS Group provides political risk assessment of nations around the globe and shows a sample report at its Web site (**http://www.prsonline.com**). The U.S. Overseas Private Investment Corporation, or OPIC (**http://www.opic.gov**), insures American investments in developing and less-developed nations against asset takeovers and earnings inconvertibility; in addition, private underwriters insure foreign investments. Risks can also be reduced by using foreign partners, borrowing money from foreign governments or banks, and/or utilizing licensing, contract manufacturing, or management contracting (which are covered later in the chapter).

Another aspect of the international political and legal environment involves trade restrictions. Most common is the *tariff*, a tax placed on imported products by a foreign government. The second major restriction is a *trade quota*, which sets limits on the amounts of products that can be imported into a country. The strictest form of trade quota is an *embargo*, which disallows entry of specified products into a country. The third major restriction involves *local content laws*, which require foreign-based firms to set up local plants and use locally made components. The goal of tariffs, trade quotas, and local content laws is to protect economies and domestic workers of the nations involved. Embargoes often have political ramifications, such as the United States refusing to trade with Cuba. Here are examples:

- The United States imposes tariffs (**http://www.dataweb.usitc.gov**) on imported clothing, ceramic tiles, rubber footwear, brooms, flowers, cement, computer screens, sugar, candy, trucks, and other items. The tariffs raise import prices relative to domestic items. At its Web site, the U.S. International Trade Administration cites tariffs by other nations (**http://www.trade.gov/td/tic/tariff**).
- China has trade quotas on a variety of agricultural products, including corn, cotton, palm oil, rice, soybean oil, sugar, vegetable seed oil, wheat, and fine wool.
- To stimulate domestic production, for nearly a decade, Brazil placed an embargo on most foreign computer products—thus banning their sales there.
- In Italy, food products cannot be called pasta unless they are made from durum wheat, which is the country's major kind of wheat.

Trade agreements and economic communities have reduced many barriers among nations. In 1948, 23 nations, including the United States, signed the General Agreement on Tariffs and Trade (GATT) to foster multilateral trade. By 1994, 115 nations participated in GATT. From its inception, GATT helped lower tariffs on manufactured goods. But members got bogged down because trade in services, agriculture, textiles, and investment and capital flows was not covered; and GATT let members belong to regional trade

Nationalism involves a host country's attempts to promote its interests.

Tariffs, trade quotas, embargoes, and **local content laws** are forms of trade restrictions.

associations (economic communities), with fewer trade barriers among the nations involved in those associations than with those not involved.

In 1995, after years of tough negotiations, GATT was replaced by the *World Trade Organization, or WTO* (**http://www.wto.org**). About 150 nations have since joined the WTO, whose mission is to open up markets even further and promote a cooperative atmosphere around the globe:

> The World Trade Organization is the only international organization dealing with the global rules of trade between nations. Its main function is to ensure that trade flows as smoothly, predictably, and freely as possible. Consumers and producers know that they can enjoy secure supplies and greater choice of the finished products, components, raw materials, and services that they use. Producers and exporters know that foreign markets will remain open to them. The result is also a more prosperous, peaceful, and accountable economic world. Virtually all decisions in the WTO are taken by consensus among all member countries and they are ratified by members' parliaments. Trade friction is channeled into the WTO's dispute settlement process where the focus is on interpreting agreements and commitments, and how to ensure that countries' trade policies conform with them. By lowering trade barriers, the WTO's system also breaks down other barriers between peoples and nations. At the heart of the system—known as the multilateral trading system—are the WTO's agreements, negotiated and signed by a large majority of the world's trading nations, and ratified in their parliaments. These agreements are the legal ground-rules for international commerce. Essentially, they are contracts, guaranteeing member countries important trade rights. They also bind governments to keep their trade policies within agreed limits to everybody's benefit.[10]

In contrast to the WTO, which promotes free trade around the world, each *economic community* promotes free trade among its member nations—but not necessarily with nonmember nations. As a result, the best interests of the WTO and economic communities may clash.

The two leading economic communities are the European Union (**http://www.europa. eu.int/index_en.htm**) and the North American Free Trade community (**http://www.mac. doc.gov/nafta**). As of mid-2004, the *European Union (EU)*, also called the Common Market, grew to 25 countries: 15 long-standing members (Austria, Belgium, Denmark, Finland, France, Germany, Great Britain, Greece, Ireland, Italy, Luxembourg, the Netherlands, Portugal, Spain, and Sweden) and new 10 ones (Cyprus, the Czech Republic, Estonia, Hungary, Latvia, Lithuania, Malta, Poland, Slovak Republic, and Slovenia). EU rules call for no trade restrictions among members, uniform tariffs with nonmembers, common product standards, and a free flow of people and capital. The aim is for members to have an open marketplace, such as exists among states in the United States. One of the EU's biggest challenges has been installing a common currency, the euro, across all of its members. The combined GDP of the enlarged EU is about that of the United States; the total population is more than 1.5 times that of the United States. And the EU hopes to add even more countries in the future.

The *North American Free Trade Agreement (NAFTA)* was enacted in 1994, creating an economic community that links the United States, Canada, and Mexico; it has sought to remove tariffs and other trade restrictions among the three countries. The population of NAFTA countries is about 95 percent that of the expanded EU, while the NAFTA members' GDP is nearly 20 percent higher. Considerable discussions have occured about forming a U.S.-Central American Free Trade Agreement, which would include the United States and 5 Central American nations (**http://www.wola.org/economic/cafta.htm**).

Other economic communities include the Andean Pact (**http://www.comunidadandina. org**), with 5 Latin American members; Association of Southeast Asian Nations (**http:// www.aseansec.org**), with 10 members; Caribbean Common Market (**http://www.caricom.org**), with more than a dozen members; Central American Common Market (**http://www.imf. org/external/np/sec/decdo/sieca.htm**), with 5 members; Gulf Cooperation Council

---

[10] "The WTO in Brief," **http://www.wto.org/english/thewto_e/whatis_e/inbrief_e/inbr00_e.htm** (March 29, 2006).

(**http://www.imf.org/external/np/sec/decdo/gcc.htm**), with 6 Arabic members; Economic Community of West African States (**http://www.imf.org/external/np/sec/decdo/ecowas.htm**), with 15 members; and Mercosur (**http://www.guia-mercosur.com**), with 4 Latin American members.

The International Monetary Fund gives descriptions of many other economic communities at its Web site (**http://www.imf.org/external/np/sec/decdo/contents.htm**).

6-4d The Technological Environment

International marketing is affected by technological factors such as these:

> International marketing may require adjustments in technology.

- Technology advances vary around the world. For example, outside the United States, cable TV is more limited. Even in Western Europe, only 40 percent of households have cable TV (compared to 70 percent in the United States).
- Foreign workers must often be trained to run equipment unfamiliar to them.
- Problems occur if equipment maintenance practices vary by nation or adverse physical conditions exist, such as high humidity, extreme hot or cold weather, or air pollution.
- Electricity and electrical power needs may vary by nation and require product modifications. For example, U.S. appliances work on 110 volts; European appliances work on 220 volts.
- Although the metric system is used in nations with 95 percent of the world's population, the United States still relies on ounces, pounds, inches, and feet. Thus, auto makers, beverage bottlers, and many other U.S. firms make items using metric standards—and then list U.S. and metric measures side-by-side on labels and packages. For the United States to convert to the metric system (which it has been trying to do since 1866, when Congress passed the first law on the metric system), the American consumer must be better educated about measurement and learn meters, liters, and other metric standards; the process remains slow (**http://www.pueblo.gsa.gov/cic_text/misc/usmetric/metric.htm**).

On the positive side, various technological advances are easing the growth of international marketing. They involve communications (TV satellites, the Internet, fax machines), transactions (automatic teller machines), order processing (computerization), and production (multiplant innovations).

6-5 DEVELOPING AN INTERNATIONAL MARKETING STRATEGY

The vital parts of an international marketing strategy are explored next: company organization, market entry decisions, the degree of standardization, and product, distribution, promotion, and price planning.

6-5a Company Organization

A firm has three organizational formats from which to choose: exporting, joint venture, and direct ownership. They are compared in Figure 6-6.

With **exporting**, a firm reaches international markets by selling products made in its home country directly through its own sales force or indirectly via foreign merchants or agents. In direct selling, a firm situates its sales force in a home office or in foreign branch offices. This is best if customers are easy to locate, concentrated, or come to the seller. With indirect selling, a firm hires outside specialists to contact customers. The specialists may be based in the home or foreign nation. There are 2,000 specialized U.S. export management firms marketing products in foreign nations (**http://www.ita.doc.gov/td/oetca/emcs.html**).

> **Exporting** lets a firm reach international markets without foreign production.

Global Marketing in Action

Avon Calling: A Global Star Shines Brighter Than Ever

While "Ding Dong, Avon calling" was one of the best-known ad phrases of the 1950s in the United States, today's Avon (http://www.avon.com) representative could be British, Russian, or Chinese. One in three British women are Avon customers, Avon is the best-selling cosmetics brand in Russia, and it is the number-two brand in China, after L'Oreal.

Avon's success in the more than 140 countries where its products are sold is due in part to its flexibility. For example, Avon provides Spanish consumers with larger bottles of personal care items than other European consumers to appeal to their preferences. An Avon spokesperson adds, "The Japanese really like technology-driven skincare and our Mediterranean consumers like long-lasting citrus fragrances. Marketers select their product package from a vast global menu."

Another part of Avon's competitive advantage comes from its direct selling channel. According to Avon's vice-president of marketing for Avon in Great Britain, "Competition is fierce; our competitors are the mass brands like L'Oreal [http://www.loreal.com], Olay [http://www.olay.com], and Nivea [http://www.nivea.com]. However, we're set apart by our channel, brand equity, heritage, and high technology at affordable prices. We've got the relationship with customers through our reps and brochures. It's harder for people to have a relationship with a brand on the supermarket shelf." The direct selling model also enables Avon to quickly set up a sales network by using independent representatives.

Source: Based on material in "Avon: Opportunity Knocks," *Brand Strategy Online* (April 5, 2005).

Indirect selling is best if customers are hard to locate or dispersed, if a potential exporter has limited funds, and/or if local customs are unique.

An exporting structure requires minimal investment in foreign facilities. There is no foreign production by the firm. The exporter may modify packages, labels, or catalogs at its domestic facilities in response to foreign market needs. Exporting involves the lowest commitment to international marketing. Most smaller firms that engage in international marketing rely on exporting. For example, Purafil (http://www.purafil.com) is a Georgia-based maker of equipment that removes corrosive, odorous, and toxic gases from commercial and industrial environments, as well as museums, libraries, and archives. It

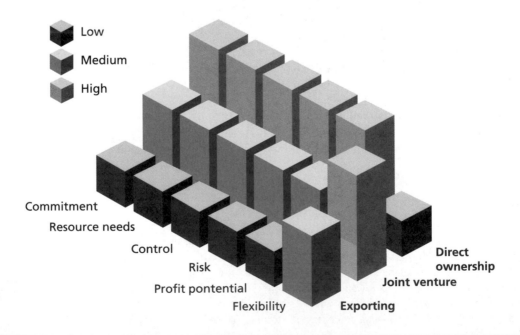

Figure 6-6

Alternate Company Organizations for International Marketing

relies on local distributors to market its products in more than 50 countries around the globe, and foreign business now accounts for 60 percent of the firm's $50 million in annual revenues.[11]

With a *joint venture* (also known as a *strategic alliance*), a firm agrees to combine some aspect of its manufacturing or marketing efforts with those of a foreign company so as to share expertise, costs, and/or connections with key persons. A joint venture may also lead to favorable trade terms from a foreign government if products are made locally and there is some degree of foreign ownership. However, such ventures may not be easy: "Partners must be able to agree on goals and policies, and to renegotiate them in response to changes in the environment. Partners from different countries often have different mother tongues, and this can be expected to cause communication difficulties. Failure by partners to quickly learn about each other may lead to misunderstandings and suspicion, and eventually to lower commitment, poor economic results, and dissolution."[12]

Here are examples of firms engaged in international joint ventures:

- Huachen BMW Automotive Company (**http://www.bmw-brilliance.cn**) is a joint venture between BMW (Germany) and Huachen Automotive Group Holding (China). It is involved with 3-series and 5-series BMW car models.
- Airbus Industrie (**http://www.airbus.com**), a jet maker, is operated by two European aerospace firms: the European Aeronautic Defence and Space Company (arising from the merger of Airbus consortium "partners" Aerospatiale-Matra of France, DaimlerChrysler Aerospace of Germany, and CASA of Spain), and BAE Systems of Great Britain.
- Thailand's Charoen Pokphand (**http://www.cpthailand.com**) has had a telecommunications venture with Verizon (United States), an insurance venture with Allianz AG (Germany), and a food venture with Indo-Aquatics (India).
- Gigante (**http://www.gigante.com.mx/content/gigante/english/group/index.html**) has joint ventures in Mexico with U.S.-based Radio Shack (**http://www.radioshack.com**) and Office Depot (**http://www.officedepot.com**). See Figure 6-7.

Joint ventures operate under several different formats. *Licensing* gives a foreign firm the rights to a manufacturing process, trademark, patent, and/or trade secret in exchange for a commission, fee, or royalty. The Coca-Cola Company (**http://www.cocacola.com/worldwide**) and PepsiCo (**http://www.ambev.com.br/eng/index_en.php**) license products in some nations. In *contract manufacturing*, a firm agrees to have a foreign partner make its products locally. The firm markets the products itself and provides management expertise. This is common in book publishing. In *management contracting*, a firm acts as a consultant to foreign companies. Such hotel chains as Hilton (**http://www.hilton.com**), Hyatt (**http://www.hyatt.com**), and Sheraton (**http://www.starwoodhotels.com/sheraton**) use management contracting. With *joint ownership*, a firm produces and markets products in partnership with a foreign firm so as to reduce costs and spread risk. Sometimes, a foreign government may require joint ownership with local businesses as a condition for entry. In Canada, outsiders must use joint ownership with Canadian firms for new ventures.

With *direct ownership*, a firm owns production, marketing, and other facilities in one or more foreign nations without any partners. The firm has full control over its operations in those nations. Thus, Great Britain's Invensys (**http://www.invensys.com**) owns a factory in Belluno, Italy, that makes electromagnetic timers for washing machines. Sometimes, wholly owned subsidiaries may be established. In the United States, Stop & Shop and Giant Food, the supermarket chains, are subsidiaries of Royal Ahold (**http://www.ahold.com**) of the Netherlands. Similarly, foreign facilities of U.S.-based firms annually yield revenues of hundreds of billions of dollars.

> A **joint venture** can be based on licensing, contract manufacturing, management contracting, or joint ownership.

> **Direct ownership** involves total control of foreign operations and facilities by a firm.

---

[11] Julia Boorstin, "Small & Global: Exporting Cleaner Air," **http://www.fortune.com/fortune/smallbusiness/marketing/articles/0,15114,643698,00.html** (June 2004).

[12] Jean Francois Hennart and Ming Zeng, "Cross-Cultural Differences and Joint Venture Longevity," *Journal of International Business Studies*, Vol. 33 (Winter 2002), p. 700.

Figure 6-7

Gigante: A Good Joint Venture Partner

Mexico's Gigante has joint ventures in that country with various foreign firms, including U.S.-based Radio Shack and Office Depot.

Source: Reprinted by permission of Susan Berry, Retail Image Consulting, Inc.

Under direct ownership, a firm has all the benefits and risks of owning a foreign business. Potential labor savings exist and marketing plans are more sensitive to local needs. Profit potential may be high, although costs may also be high. Nationalistic acts are a possibility, and government restrictions are apt to be stricter. This is the riskiest organization form.

Companies often combine formats. For instance, a firm could export to a country with a history of political unrest and use direct ownership in a country with tax advantages for construction. McDonald's worldwide efforts (**http://www.mcdonalds.com/countries.html**) combine company restaurants, franchised restaurants, and affiliate-operated restaurants (whereby McDonald's owns 50 percent or less of assets, with the rest owned by resident nationals). Company outlets are largely in the United States, Canada, France, Great Britain, and Germany; franchised outlets are mostly in the United States, Canada, France, Germany, and Australia; and affiliate restaurants are common in Latin America, Japan, and other Pacific nations.

6-5b Market Entry Decisions

> A firm needs to determine which and how many foreign markets in which to do business.

Various factors must be considered in deciding which and how many foreign markets a firm should enter. Here are several of them:

Which Market(s) to Enter
- Are there cultural similarities between a foreign nation and a firm's home market? How vital is this?
- Are there language similarities between a foreign nation and a firm's home market? How vital is this?
- Is the standard of living in a foreign market consistent with what a firm would offer there?

- How large is a foreign market for the goods and services a firm would offer there? Is it growing? What is the regional potential (e.g., Eastern Europe)?
- Is the technology in a foreign market sufficient for a firm to do business? Is the country's infrastructure sufficient?
- Are there enough skilled workers in a foreign country?
- Are the media in a foreign country adequate for a firm's marketing efforts?
- What is the level of competition in a foreign market?
- What government restrictions would a firm face in a foreign market? The economic communities?
- How stable are the currency and government in a foreign market?
- Is the overall business climate in a foreign country favorable to a firm?

How Many Markets to Enter
- What are the firm's available resources?
- How many foreign markets could a firm's personnel properly oversee and service?
- How diverse are multiple foreign markets? What is the geographic proximity?
- What are the marketing economies of scale—regional or global?
- Are exporting arrangements possible? Are joint ventures possible?
- What are a firm's goals regarding its mix of domestic and foreign revenues?
- How extensive is competition in a firm's home market?

6-5c Standardizing Plans

A firm engaged in international marketing must determine the degree to which plans should be standardized. Both standardized and nonstandardized plans have benefits and limitations.

With a ***standardized (global) marketing approach***, a firm uses a common marketing plan for all nations in which it operates—because it assumes worldwide markets are becoming more homogeneous due to better communications, more open country borders, the move to free-market economies, and other factors. This approach downplays differences among countries. Marketing and production economies exist—product design, packaging, advertising, and other costs are spread over a large product base. A uniform image is presented, training foreign personnel is easier, and centralized control is applied. Yet, standardization is insensitive to individual market needs, and input from foreign personnel is limited:

> Companies sometimes assume that what works in their home country will work in another country. They take the same product, same advertising campaign, even the same brand names and packaging, and to try to market it the same way in another country. The result in many cases is failure. Why? Well, the assumption that one approach works everywhere fails to consider differences that exist between countries and cultures. While many companies who sell internationally are successful following a standardized marketing strategy, it is a mistake to assume this approach will work without sufficient research that addresses this question.[13]

With a ***nonstandardized marketing approach***, a firm sees each nation or region as distinct and requiring its own marketing plan. This strategy is sensitive to local needs and means grooming foreign managers, as decentralized control is undertaken. It works best if distinctive major foreign markets are involved or a firm has many product lines. Consider T-Mobile's (**http://www.t-mobile.com**) approach: the firm's "heady global strategy is being played out locally with a twist based on each country organization's unique challenges and market. In the face of increased competition in Eastern Europe, the Czech Republic is using

Under a **global approach**, a common marketing plan is used for each nation. Under a **nonstandardized approach**, each country is given a separate marketing plan. A **glocal approach** is a combination strategy.

[13] "Global Marketing," **http://www.knowthis.com/internl.htm** (April 2, 2006).

Ethical Issues in Marketing

Battling Corruption and Bureaucracy in Nigeria

The developers of The Palms, a 215,000-square-foot shopping center in Lagos, Nigeria, have faced a number of difficult challenges. Because the Nigerian government bans many imports, including furnishings for the shops and even carpeting for the movie theater, the store fixtures must be locally manufactured. Some shipments have been delayed because the developers of the center have refused to bribe local officials. A 9-inch-thick, 8-foot-high concrete block wall must be built around the perimeter of the center for riot protection. An electric power generator plant is also necessary to ensure power due to Lagos' frequent electrical outages. Last, the center needs its own sewage and water purification facilities.

Plans for The Palms include 63 smaller shops (most of which are Nigerian owned), two major retailers to serve as traffic generators (a supermarket, and an appliance and electronics store), and a movie theater. The center's target market includes middle-class and wealthy Nigerians, as well as foreigners who work in Nigeria, many of whom work in Nigeria's oil industry.

Currently, Nigeria has no modern shopping center. According to The Palms' manager, "The Palms will serve to lift the whole retail market in Nigeria and serve as the benchmark for retail in the future."

Source: Based on material in Ed McKinley, "Against All Odds," *Shopping Center Today* (April 2005), pp. 55–58.

a multisite, multimedia environment to manage its customer communications within a single infrastructure; T-Mobile in Germany is increasing sales performance and simplifying business processes by centrally managing all information and communications; and T-Mobile USA is keeping pace with the changing U.S. marketplace by arming its contact center agents with the skills and knowledge they need to respond to customers' needs."[14]

In recent years, more firms (such as T-Mobile) have used a *glocal marketing approach*, which stands for *think global and act local*. This approach combines standardized and nonstandardized efforts to enable a firm to attain production efficiencies, have a consistent image, have some home-office control, and still be responsive to local needs. This is how Coca-Cola (**http://www.cocacola.com**)—widely known for its global brands—uses a glocal approach:

> Who is the owner today of Thums Up, that indigenous Indian cola brand? None other than Coca-Cola, which has long recognized the importance of a balanced brand portfolio. In addition to purchasing strategically important local brands, Coca-Cola's homegrown offering has diversified into areas such as bottled water, juices, and iced tea. In fact, the company has for many years marketed canned tea drinks in Japan, responding to a clear local market need.[15]

When choosing a marketing approach, a firm should evaluate whether differences among countries are great enough to warrant changes in marketing plans, which elements of marketing can be standardized, whether the size of each foreign market could lead to profitable adaptation, and if modifications can be made on a regional rather than a country basis.

6-5d   Product Planning

> **Straight extension, product adaptation, backward invention,** and **forward invention** are methods of international product planning.

International product planning (for both goods and services) can be based on straight extension, product adaptation, backward invention, and/or forward invention.

In a *straight extension* strategy, a firm makes and markets the same products for domestic and foreign sales. The firm is confident it can sell items abroad without modifying the products, the brand name, packaging, or ingredients. This simple

[14] Mila D'Antonio, "T-Mobile's Global Strategy Goes Local," *1to1* (July-August 2005), p. 28.

[15] "Local Vs. Global Brands—Who Will Win?" **http://www.brandchannel.com/forum.asp?bd_id=3** (September 23, 2005).

approach capitalizes on economies of scale in production. Apple (**http://www.apple.com**) markets the same PCs in the United States, Mexico, and many other countries. Soda companies use straight extension in many (but not all) countries around the world. Beer makers also use straight extension, and imported beer often has a higher status than domestic beer. Yet, straight extension does not account for differences in customers, laws, customs, technology, and other factors.

With a *product adaptation* strategy, domestic products are modified to meet foreign language needs, taste preferences, climates, electrical requirements, laws, and/or other factors. It is assumed that new products are not needed and minor changes are sufficient. This is the most-used strategy in international marketing: Campbell Soup Company (**http://www.campbellsoupcompany.com/around_the_world.asp**) prints food packages in the languages of the nations in which they are sold, as shown in Figure 6-8. Disneyland Resort Paris (**http://www.disneylandparis.com**) features Mickey Mouse, Cinderella, and other U.S. Disney characters but also has food concessions and hotels that are adapted to European tastes; KFC (**http://www.kfc.co.jp**) has grilled rice balls to go with its fried chicken wings in Japan; PepsiCo's Cheetos cheese-flavored puff snack (**http://www.cheetos.com**) is cheeseless in China (with flavors such as buttered popcorn); gasoline formulations vary according to a nation's weather conditions; and appliances are modified to accommodate different voltage requirements.

With *backward invention*, a firm appeals to developing and less-developed nations by making products less complex than the ones it sells in its domestic market. This includes manual cash registers and nonelectric sewing machines for consumers in areas without widespread electricity and inexpensive washing machines for consumers in low-income countries. Whirlpool (**http://www.whirlpool.com**) affiliates build and sell an inexpensive "world washer" in Brazil, Mexico, and India. It is compact, is specially designed (so it does not tangle a sari), handles about one-half the capacity of a regular U.S. washer, and accommodates variations in component availability and local preferences.

In *forward invention*, a company develops new products for its international markets. This plan is riskier and more time consuming and requires a higher investment than other strategies. It may also provide the firm with great profit potential and, sometimes, worldwide recognition for innovativeness. With nearly three-quarters of its overall sales coming from foreign markets, U.S.-based Colgate-Palmolive (**http://www.colgate.com**) often engages in forward invention. For example, it developed La Croix bleach for Europe and Protex antibacterial soap for Asia, Africa, and Latin America. See Figure 6-9.

6-5e Distribution Planning

International distribution planning encompasses the selection and use of resellers and products' physical movement. A firm may sell direct to customers or hire outside distribution specialists—depending on the traditional relationships in a country, the availability of appropriate resellers, differences in distribution practices from those in the home country, government restrictions, costs, and other factors. For example,

> Channel members and physical distribution methods depend on customs, availability, costs, and other factors.

- Central cities in Europe often have more shopping ambience than central cities in the United States.
- In Brazil, PepsiCo (**http://www.ambev.com/br/eng/index_en.php**) markets soft drinks through the domestic Brahma beer and soda company because of Brahma's extensive distribution network.
- Amway sells its household products in Japan (**http://www.amway.co.jp**) via hundreds of thousands of local distributors (who are also customers); as in the United States, distributors earn commissions on sales.
- In the Philippines, Avon (**http://www.avoncompany.com/world**) uses a special system of branch outlets to service its representatives. See Figure 6-10.

Distribution often requires special planning: Processing marine insurance, government documents, and other papers may take time. Transportation may be inefficient if a nation has limited docking facilities, poor highways, or few vehicles. Distribution by ship

Figure 6-8

Product Modification at Campbell Soup Company: Adapting to Local Markets

Campbell adjusts product ingredients and packaging to reflect cultural differences among countries.

Source: Reprinted by permission.

is slow and may be delayed. Stores may be much smaller than those in the United States. Inventory management must take into account warehousing availability and the costs of

Figure 6-9

Forward Invention by Colgate-Palmolive

The firm has introduced a number of products especially made for its foreign markets and not sold in its home base of the United States.

Source: Reprinted by permission.

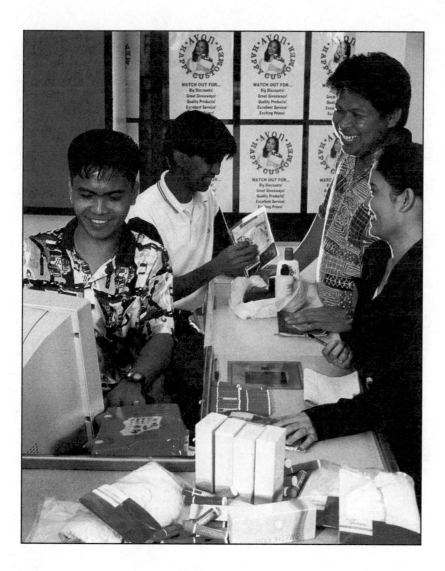

Figure 6-10

Avon: Meeting Local Distribution Needs

For foreign markets where the distribution structure is underdeveloped, Avon uses a system of branches to help sales representatives receive products for delivery to customers. Avon has "branch supermarkets," like the one shown here in the Philippines.

Source: Reprinted by permission.

shipping in small amounts. When Ben & Jerry's entered Russia a decade ago, it had problems due to the lack of refrigerated trucks and freezers. So, it brought in Western trucks and freezers to store its ice cream. The distribution process turned out to be too costly and inefficient, causing Ben & Jerry's to exit the Russian market. The firm still operates in more than 15 other countries.[16]

6-5f   Promotion Planning

Campaigns can be global, nonstandardized, or glocal. Figure 6-11 shows an example of a glocal ad.

> International promotion planning depends on the overlap of audiences and languages and the availability of media.

Firms may use global promotion for image purposes. To celebrate Disneyland's 50th anniversary, Walt Disney Co. (http://www.disney.com) recently introduced its first global campaign: "It's called the Happiest Celebration on Earth—playing off Disneyland's long-time advertising line, the Happiest Place on Earth. As a senior Disney executive put it, 'Disneyland is really a worldwide brand. It is very exportable. When you go market to market, your perception of Disneyland is a similar idea. It is a similar creative execution

---

[16] "Our Company," http://www.benjerry.com/our_company (April 2, 2006).

Figure 6-11

A Glocal Ad from American Express

American Express is a worldwide financial services company. It runs English ads, such as the one here, in various English-speaking countries; and it runs ads in the languages of many of the other countries in which it does business. Its advertising themes—such as security—tend to be universal.

Source: Reprinted by permission.

around the world. It allows us to be more efficient.'"[17] And Gap Inc. (**http://www.gapinc.com**) has run ads around the world featuring Sarah Jessica Parker and Madonna.[18]

Companies marketing in various European nations often find that some standardization is desirable due to overlapping readers, listeners, and viewers. For instance, German TV shows are received by a large percentage of Dutch households and *Paris Match* magazine (**http://www.parismatch.com**) has readers in Belgium, Switzerland, Luxembourg, Germany, Italy, and Holland.

There are also good reasons for using nonstandardized promotion. Many countries have distinctions that are not addressed by a single promotion campaign—including customs, language, the meaning of colors and symbols, and literacy. Appropriate media may be unavailable. In a number of nations, few households own TV sets, ads are restricted, and/or mailing lists are not current. National pride sometimes requires that individual promotions be used. Even within regions that have perceived similarities, such as within Western Europe or within Latin America, differences exist. In both regions, several different languages are used, and many consumers want to receive messages in their own language.

Most firms end up utilizing glocal promotion plans:

Standardized strategies seem most apt if a product is utilitarian and the message is informational. Reasons for buying or using the good or service are rational—and less apt to

---

[17] Wayne Friedman, "Brand Management," *Daily Variety Online* (April 29, 2005).

[18] Jane Wardell, "Global Chains Send Universal Messages to Converging World," *Associated Press Online* (February 28, 2005).

vary by culture. Glue, batteries, and gasoline are such products. A standardized approach would also appear effective if a brand's identity and desirability are integrally linked to a specific national character. Coca-Cola and McDonald's are marketed as "quintessential American products"; Chanel is a "quintessential French product." Yet, it is generally more effective to *glocalize strategies* to local customs and cultures:

- Product usage often varies according to the culture.
- For many products, benefits are more psychological than tangible, requiring an understanding of the psychologies of different cultures.
- Some societies are demonstrative and open; others are aloof or private.
- Advertisers must consider a multicultural and flexible strategy if a brand is in different stages of development or of varying stature across different markets.
- A commercial for a mature market may not work well in a developing one.
- A commercial in a market where the product/brand is unique has quite a different task than a commercial where competition is intense.[19]

The World Advertising Research Center (**http://www.warc.com**) offers much useful information on international promotion planning.

6-5g   Price Planning

The basic considerations in international price planning are whether prices should be standardized, the level at which prices are set, the currency in which prices are quoted, and terms of sale.

Unless a firm operates in an economic community such as the EU (and sometimes, even then), price standardization is hard. Taxes, tariffs, and currency exchange charges are among the costs a firm incurs internationally. For example, a car made in the United States is typically priced at several thousand dollars higher when sold in Japan, due to currency exchange fees, shipping costs, taxes, inspection fees, and so forth. "Homologation" alone (inspections and modifications needed to meet Japan's standards) could add $2,000 to $3,000 to the final selling price.

When setting a price level, a firm would consider such local factors as per-capita GDP. Thus, firms may try to hold down prices in developing and less-developed countries by marketing simpler product versions or employing less-expensive local labor. On the other hand, prices in such industrialized nations as France and Germany can reflect product quality and the added costs of international marketing.

Some firms set lower prices abroad to enhance their global presence and sales or to remove excess supply from their home markets and preserve the prices there. With *dumping*, a firm sells a product in a foreign nation at a price much lower than in its home market, below the cost of production, or both. In the United States and many other nations, duties may be levied on products "dumped" by foreign firms.[20]

If a firm sets prices on the basis of its home currency, the risk of a foreign currency devaluation is passed along to the buyer and there is better control. But this strategy has limitations. Consumers may be confused or unable to convert a price into their own currency, or a foreign government may insist that prices be quoted in its currency. Two easy-to-use currency converter Web sites are Universal Currency Converter (**http://www.xe.net/ucc**) and FXConverter (**http://www.oanda.com/converter/classic**).

Terms of sale also need to be set. This involves such judgments as what fees or discounts channel intermediaries get for the tasks they perform, when ownership is transferred, what payment form is required, how much time customers have to pay bills, and what constitutes a proper refund policy.

> Major decisions in international price planning involve standardization, levels, currency, and sales terms. **Dumping** is disliked by host countries.

---

[19] McCollum Spielman Worldwide, "Global Advertising: Standardized or Multicultural? *Topline* (Number 37, 1992), pp. 3–4.

[20] See "Monitoring of Antidumping and Countervailing Duty Cases Against U.S. Firms in Other Countries," **http://www.ia.ita.doc.gov/foradcvd** (March 15, 2006).

Web Sites You Can Use

Four Web sites pertaining to global marketing are especially noteworthy. The CIA World Factbook (**http://www.odci.gov/cia/publications/factbook**) reports current demographic and economic data on virtually every country in the world. The Center for International Business Education and Research (CIBER) at Michigan State University (**http://www.ciber.msu.edu**), Center for International Business & Travel (**http://www.internationalist.com/business**), and WWW Virtual Library: International Affairs Resources (**http://www2.etown.edu/vl/intlbus.html**) have a number of valuable resources.

Summary

1. *To define domestic, international, and global marketing* Domestic marketing covers a firm's efforts in its home country. International marketing involves goods and services sold outside the home nation. Through global marketing, a firm operates in many nations. A company may be categorized as a domestic firm, exporting firm, international firm, multinational firm, or global firm. For any type of company (whether domestically or internationally oriented) to succeed in today's competitive marketplace, it must grasp key international marketing concepts and act appropriately.

2. *To explain why international marketing takes place and study its scope* International marketing occurs because nations want to exchange goods and services with which they have comparative advantages for those with which they do not. Firms seek to minimize weak economic conditions and attract growing markets, avoid domestic competition, extend the product life cycle, and get tax breaks.

   The United States is the world's largest exporter for both goods and services. Hundreds of thousands of U.S. firms engage in some level of international business. The United States is also the world's leading importer, with a huge merchandise trade deficit. In contrast, the United States has a service trade surplus. Several reasons account for the merchandise trade deficit, ranging from the American market's allure to the emphasis of U.S. firms on profits over market share. Various actions are under way to reduce this deficit; and the United States is the dominant force worldwide.

3. *To explore the cultural, economic, political and legal, and technological environments facing international marketers* The cultural environment includes the behavior standards, language, lifestyles, and goals of a country's citizens. The economic environment incorporates a nation's standard of living, GDP, stage of development, and currency stability. The political and legal environment includes nationalism, government stability, trade rules, and trade agreements and economic communities such as the World Trade Organization, European Union, and North American Free Trade group. The technological environment creates opportunities and problems.

4. *To analyze the stages in the development of an international marketing strategy* In developing a strategy, a firm may stress exporting, joint ventures, or direct ownership of operations. Each approach has a different commitment, resource needs, control, risk, flexibility, and profit range.

   A company should consider several factors in deciding on which and how many foreign markets to enter. These include cultural and language similarities with the home market, the suitability of the standard of living, consumer demand, its own available resources, and so on.

   A firm may use standardized (global), nonstandardized, or glocal marketing. The decision depends on the differences among the nations served, which marketing elements can be standardized, the size of each market, and the possibility of regional adaptation.

   Product planning may extend existing products into foreign markets, modify them, produce simpler items for developing nations, or invent new products for foreign markets. Distribution planning looks at channel relations and sets a network for direct sales or channel intermediaries. Physical distribution features would also be analyzed. Promotion planning would stress global, mixed, or glocal campaigns. Price planning would outline whether prices should be standardized, the price level, the currency for price quotes, and terms of sale.

Key Terms

domestic marketing (p. 157)

international marketing (p. 157)

global marketing (p. 157)

comparative advantage (p. 159)

trade deficit (p. 161)

trade surplus (p. 161)

culture (p. 162)

standard of living (p. 164)

gross domestic product (GDP) (p. 164)

industrialized countries (p. 164)

developing countries (p. 166)

less-developed countries (p. 166)

nationalism (p. 167)

tariff (p. 167)

trade quota (p. 167)

embargo (p. 167)

local content laws (p. 167)

World Trade Organization, or WTO (p. 168)

economic community (p. 168)

European Union (EU) (p. 168)

North American Free Trade Agreement (NAFTA) (p. 168)

exporting (p. 169)

joint venture (p. 171)

direct ownership (p. 171)

standardized (global) marketing approach (p. 173)

nonstandardized marketing approach (p. 173)

glocal marketing approach (p. 174)

straight extension (p. 174)

product adaptation (p. 175)

backward invention (p. 175)

forward invention (p. 175)

dumping (p. 179)

Review Questions

1. Distinguish among domestic, international, and global marketing.
2. How can a firm improve its cultural awareness?
3. Differentiate among industrialized, developing, and less-developed countries.
4. If the value of the Kenyan shilling goes from 75 shillings per U.S. dollar to 65 shillings per U.S. dollar, will U.S. products be more or less expensive in Kenya? Why?
5. Define each of the following:
   a. Local content law
   b. Tariff
   c. Embargo

6. What are the pros and cons of exporting versus joint ventures?
7. Why would a firm use a nonstandardized international marketing strategy? What are the potential disadvantages of this strategy?
8. Distinguish among these product-planning strategies: straight extension, product adaptation, backward invention, and forward invention. When should each be used?

Discussion Questions

1. Cite three basic differences between marketing in the United States and in Europe.
2. In China, there are 5 cars per 100 people, compared with 80 per 100 people in the United States. What are the ramifications of this from a marketing perspective?

3. What are the advantages and disadvantages of a country's belonging to an economic community such as the European Union?
4. Develop a 10-question checklist by which a life insurance company could determine which and how many foreign markets to enter.

Web Exercise

Dell has separate Web sites for customers in the United States, Italy, and Peru. Go to the Dell home page (http://www.dell.com) and select each of these countries from the "Choose A Country/Region" toolbar at the top of the screen. Take a look at the three different countries' sites; then comment on the similarities and differences among the sites. Explain how Dell is using a glocal strategy.

Practice Quiz

1. Companies are more likely to engage in international marketing when
   a. competition in the home country slackens.
   b. the home economy is growing.
   c. the home population base is stagnant.
   d. the home tax rates are lower.

2. Which of these is *not* a contributing factor to the U.S. trade deficit?
   a. Trade restrictions in foreign markets
   b. The high quality control for U.S.-made products
   c. High U.S. labor costs
   d. Increased competition in foreign markets

3. Cultural awareness most clearly requires marketing research on
   a. the stability of currency.
   b. hidden meanings.
   c. trade restrictions.
   d. size of demand.

4. The gross domestic product (GDP)
   a. is difficult to calculate.
   b. refers to the average quantity and quality of goods and services consumed in a country.
   c. gives the United States an index of 100 against which other nations are rated.
   d. does not take into account differences in living standards in different countries.

5. Developing countries have
   a. per-capita income of about $4,000 to $9,000.
   b. two-thirds of the world's population.
   c. widespread modern technology.
   d. less than 15 percent of the world's income.

6. Which of the following is *not* a way in which an international firm can protect itself from the adverse effects of nationalism?
   a. Measuring domestic instability
   b. Taking in foreign partners
   c. Insuring itself
   d. Engaging in direct ownership

7. Which of these disallows entry of specified products into a country?
   a. Embargo
   b. Tariff
   c. Quota
   d. Local content laws

8. Which statement is correct?
   a. NAFTA includes Brazil.
   b. Africa is growing via its Council for Mutual Economic Assistance.
   c. The European Union has a larger population than the United States.
   d. Economic communities are now illegal.

9. The lowest level of commitment to international marketing is
   a. licensing.

b. contract manufacturing.
c. direct ownership.
d. exporting.

10. Which of the following is *not* a type of joint venture?
    a. Indirect selling
    b. Licensing
    c. Management contracting
    d. Contract manufacturing

11. The riskiest form of organization for international marketing is
    a. joint venture.
    b. direct ownership.
    c. exporting.
    d. management contracting.

12. Standardized international marketing plans
    a. are sensitive to local needs.
    b. work best when distinctive foreign markets are involved.
    c. present a uniform image.
    d. involve decentralized control.

13. The international product-planning strategy appropriate for laundry detergent formulation is
    a. forward invention.
    b. backward invention.
    c. straight extension.
    d. product adaptation.

14. In which of the following countries does PepsiCo market soft drinks via the domestic Brahma beer and soda company?
    a. Brazil
    b. Japan
    c. Great Britain
    d. Mexico

15. Dumping refers to selling goods abroad
    a. at high prices.
    b. with prices similar to those in the home market.
    c. so that cheap labor may be used.
    d. to remove excess supply from the home market.

For the answers to these questions, please visit the online site for this book at **http://www.atomicdog.com.**

Chapter 7

Marketing and the Internet

Larry Page and Sergey Brin met as computer science doctoral students who were studying methods for searching and organizing large quantities of data. They developed a formula that would order the results of a data search by relevancy. To Page and Brin, early online search engines, which typically sorted Web pages by analyzing words and their positions within a document, were woefully inadequate as the Web expanded. They were convinced that a Web page pointed to by 100 sites would be more valuable than one referred to by 5 linked sites.

In 1998, Page and Brin presented their findings at the World Wide Web Conference. One year later, after they raised close to $30 million in funding, they launched Google (**http://www.google.com**). Today, Google is the most widely used site for Web searches, on topics ranging from consumer reviews of digital cameras to health-related questions to current events. Google also licenses its search technology to more than 100 companies, including America Online (**http://www. americaonline.com**).

Although the founders initially did not want to accept advertising, Google's ability to attract consumers looking for a "New York City plumber" or a "Miami to Los Angeles flight" has been quite appealing to a large number of advertisers. Today, 95 percent of Google's sales revenue comes from advertising. Google's AdWords (**http://www.google.adwordsstrategy.com**) program enables advertisers to buy words that will trigger their ads. These ads appear in the margin of Google's text listings. Google also has an AdSense program that positions ads on the Web in sites that are not owned by Google (such as a link to a site placed within an article).

In August 2005, Google raised $4 billion in a new stock offering. The filing with the Securities and Exchange Commission stated that Google "may use the proceeds of this offering for acquisitions of complementary businesses, technologies, or other assets." Some analysts viewed this offering as adding capital that would be necessary to better compete with Microsoft and Yahoo. Google also recently introduced a second-generation version of its search tool. This version can be personalized and allows independent programmers to extend Google's capabilities.[1]

In this chapter, we will explore the various marketing roles of the Internet. We will also examine how traditional marketers can use the Internet as a vital part of their overall marketing strategy.

Chapter Objectives

1. To demonstrate why the Internet is a valuable marketing tool
2. To explore the multifaceted potential marketing roles for the Internet
3. To show how to develop an Internet marketing strategy
4. To illustrate how the Internet is being utilized to enhance marketing strategies
5. To consider the challenges of using the Internet in marketing and to forecast the future of E-marketing

---

[1] Various company and other sources.

7-1 OVERVIEW

As an introduction to our discussion of marketing and the Internet, let's define four basic terms.

The *Internet*, also known as "the Net," is a global electronic superhighway of computer networks—a network of networks in which users at one computer can get information from another computer (and sometimes talk directly to users at other computers). It is a public, cooperative, self-sustaining system accessible to hundreds of millions of people worldwide. The *World Wide Web (WWW)*, also known as "the Web," comprises all of the resources and users on the Internet using the Hypertext Transfer Protocol (HTTP). It is a way to access the Internet, whereby people work with easy-to-use Web addresses and pages. Through the Web, users see words, colorful charts, pictures, and video, and hear audio.[2] Although the two terms have somewhat different meanings, they both relate to online activities—and are both used interchangeably by the media and by companies. Thus, in this chapter (and book), both terms have the same connotation: online activities.

E-marketing includes any marketing activity that is conducted through the Internet, from customer analysis to marketing-mix components. *E-commerce* refers to revenue-generating Internet transactions. E-marketing is the broader concept, and it does not necessarily have sales as the primary goal.

By virtue of its rather low costs, its wide geographic reach, and the many marketing roles it can serve, the Internet should be a key part of *any* firm's marketing strategy—regardless of the firm's size or characteristics. In the decades ahead, virtually every firm will have some kind of Web presence, much as they now have a phone, a fax machine, an answering machine, and other technological tools.

Since the Internet's inception as a commercially viable business resource, its importance and value have been misperceived by many. At first, a number of experts talked of how Internet firms would soon overwhelm traditional retailers and drive them out of business. They predicted that annual online retail sales in the United States alone would soon reach hundreds of billions of dollars. They were wrong: Online retail sales are only a fraction of what was predicted. Now, some experts have dismissed the Internet as a short-lived business fad; and they cite the high failure rate of "dot com" firms as evidence of the Internet's fall. Again, they are wrong about the Internet's impact.

These experts have not recognized how long a major new technology takes to permeate the marketplace. The majority of people in the world still do not have a PC, "surf the Web," or shop online. In addition, a lot of people who own a PC, surf, and shop online still prefer shopping at stores due to the purchase immediacy, the hands-on buying experience, the social interaction with others, and so forth.

The true impact of the Internet, and the reason we are devoting a full chapter to this topic, relates to the multiple marketing tasks that can be undertaken, both better and more efficiently—not to the level of sales revenues to be attained. This point underscores why the rush to judge the Internet as a business fad was so wrong. Generating sales revenue is only one of a multitude of benefits that the Internet can achieve for a firm. Most of our focus is on E-marketing, not just on E-commerce.

In this chapter, we will cover several aspects of marketing and the Internet: why the Internet is such a valuable marketing tool, the multifaceted uses of the Internet, developing an Internet marketing strategy, applications of the Internet in marketing strategies, and the challenges and future of E-marketing.

> The **Internet** is a global superhighway of computer networks. Through the **World Wide Web**, people work with easy-to-use Web addresses and pages.

> **E-marketing** involves any marketing activity on the Internet, whereas **E-commerce** is its revenue-generating component.

[2] "Look It Up," http://whatis.techtarget.com (May 3, 2006).

7-2 WHY THE INTERNET IS A VALUABLE TOOL IN MARKETING

Web usage is rising rapidly worldwide.

According to *Computer Industry Almanac*, as of 2007, about 1.35 billion people around the globe are expected to be using the Internet. This signifies great E-marketing opportunities for firms. For just the 10 countries highlighted in Table 7-1, during 2005, there were already almost 290 million active home users; on average, they typically spent 20 to 30 hours monthly online and went online 30 or so times a month. In the near future, it is expected that three-quarters of all U.S. households will be online.[3]

People surf the Internet for many reasons other than shopping. They often seek out entertainment, financial, sports, and news sites. They do product research. They "talk" to one another (many via AOL Instant Messenger, **http://www.aim.com**). They communicate online with companies to register complaints and make suggestions. They send E-mails and greetings cards. The U.S. Postal Service (**http://www.usps.com**) handles 550 million pieces of mail per day; in contrast, billions of E-mail messages are sent every day!

Companies (actually, their employees) also surf the Web for a variety of reasons other than shopping. They see what competitors are doing. They read about industry trends and events. They communicate with suppliers. They exchange data among offices anywhere in the world. They monitor inventory levels. They survey customers and measure satisfaction. They do sophisticated analyses of customer data bases.

Table 7-1	Internet Penetration of the Home Market in 10 Countries			
	Active Home Users (Millions)	**Average Time Spent per Month**	**Average Number of Sessions per Month**	**Active Home Users as a Percentage of Total Population**
United States	141	30 hours, 15 min.	34	48
Japan	38	16 hours, 30 min.	30	30
Germany	30	28 hours, 50 min.	33	36
Great Britain	23	24 hours, 40 min.	30	38
France	15	29 hours, 45 min.	35	25
Brazil	12	30 hours, 55 min.	27	6
Spain	10	25 hours, 20 min.	30	25
Australia	10	31 hours, 5 min.	35	50
Sweden	5	20 hours, 5 min.	25	55
Switzerland	4	27 hours, 20 min.	34	53

Sources: Compiled by the authors from *Nielsen//NetRatings*, http://www.nielsen-netratings.com (August 2005); and U.S. Bureau of the Census, International Data Base.

---

[3] "Population Explosion!" http://www.clickz.com/stats/sectors/geographics/article.php/5911_151151 (July 7, 2005).

Bernie & Phyls Furniture (**http://www.bernieandphyls.com**), a family-run, Boston-area chain with six stores and annual sales of $120 million, is a good illustration of how the Internet presents a variety of E-marketing opportunities beyond E-commerce:

The site accounts for under one percent of direct sales, but the company has no regrets about investing in its Web strategy. "Our goal was not really to derive sales," said CEO Larry Rubin. "It was to drive people into the stores." That's one of the ways the site has proven its worth. Consumers have the option of purchasing online, but the bigger result is that they're coming into showrooms with photos of items they printed out, saying they want to take a closer look. And when a customer calls with a question or problem, the employee can use a computer to call up an image of the very piece the consumer is talking about. "It's often hard for customers to describe what is wrong with something on the phone, but it's much easier when both are looking at the same thing. The goal is to service the customer at the highest level, and having the entire catalog of merchandise on the company's internal site helps accomplish this," said spokeswoman Amy Blumenthal. If a part has to be replaced, it can be ordered before a service technician goes to the house, possibly saving one diagnostic trip.[4]

Likewise, Ikea (**http://www.ikea.com**) devotes a lot of attention to its Web site. It has colorful descriptions and photos of its home-furnishings product lines. There is a worldwide store locator. The firm explains its vision. But mostly, Ikea emphasizes in-store shopping as the way for consumers to get the most out of their home-furnishings shopping experience. The Swedish-based retailer places more emphasis on its E-marketing efforts than on E-commerce.

Let us next examine two specific aspects of marketing and the Internet: the three phases of Internet use by companies and the benefits of using the Internet in marketing.

7-2a Bricks-and-Mortar, Clicks-Only, and Bricks-and-Clicks

E-marketing is evolving through the three phases shown in Figure 7-1. The phases are (1) bricks-and-mortar firms, (2) clicks-only firms, and (3) bricks-and-clicks firms.

Bricks-and-mortar firms are traditional companies that have not gotten involved with the Internet. Until a few years ago, this was very much the predominant business format, as these companies believed the Internet provided too few benefits relative to the costs and complexity of being online. Now, bricks-and-mortar firms are likely to be small in size and scope.

In the 1990s, a number of innovative *clicks-only firms* entered the marketplace. These companies do business just online. They do not have traditional facilities. Many clicks-only firms have generated good revenues, but have had trouble turning a profit. They often expanded too fast and invested quite heavily in their infrastructures. There has been a major shakeup among clicks-only firms, with a number of once-popular companies going out of business. Yet, thousands and thousands of clicks-only firms still exist.

The trend today is more toward *bricks-and-clicks firms* that operate in both a traditional setting and on the Internet. Virtually every large retailer (as well as numerous medium-size and small firms) has a substantial Web presence. The same is true of manufacturers, wholesalers, government organizations, nonprofit organizations, and others. The bricks-and-clicks approach enables companies to appeal to multiple market segments, maximize customer contact points, leverage the strengths of each form of business, and enter into new alliances.

Edmunds, Wal-Mart, and Sephora are traditional firms that have actively become bricks-and-clicks. Edmunds (now **http://Edmunds.com, http://www.edmunds.com**) "was founded in 1966 for the purpose of publishing new and used automotive pricing guides to assist automobile buyers, and Edmunds.com continues to publish automotive

Bricks-and-mortar firms are not involved with the Internet. **Clicks-only firms** do business just online. **Bricks-and-clicks firms** combine traditional and Internet formats.

---

[4] "Clint Engel, "Web Site: Few Sales But Big Payoffs," *Furniture Today* (August 29, 2005), p. 24.

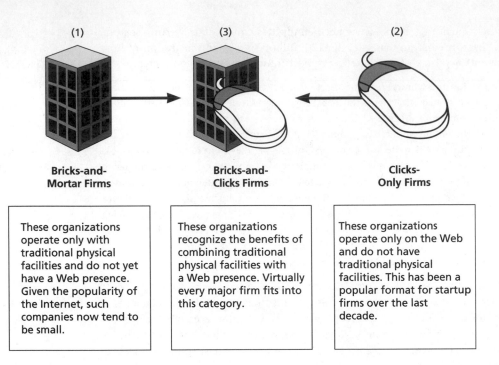

Figure 7-1

The Three Phases of Marketing and the Internet

guides today. In 1994, before the Web had become mainstream, Edmunds.com's new car pricing data was posted on the Internet—the first time consumer automotive information had been provided through the Internet. Today, our Web site consists of more than 340,000 pages accessed by over 200,000 people a day." At Wal-Mart (**http://www. walmart.com**), the world's largest firm, "Walmart.com is a lot like your neighborhood Wal-Mart store. We feature a great selection of high-quality merchandise, friendly service, and, of course, everyday low prices. We also have another goal: to bring you the best shopping experience on the Internet. But we think of ourselves, first and foremost, as a retailer."[5] French-based Sephora (**http://www.sephora.com**) actively promotes its Web site at company beauty stores around the world. See Figure 7-2.

Amazon.com (**http://www.amazon.com**) is one of the increasing number of formerly clicks-only firms that now also operate traditional facilities or have alliances with partners having traditional facilities. It has alliances with Babies "R" Us (**http://www. babiesrus.com**), Office Depot (**http://www.officedepot.com**), Target Stores (**http:// www.target.com**), and Toys "R" Us (**http://www.toysrus.com**), among others. Atomic Dog (**http://www.atomicdog.com**) now markets its texts in college bookstores, as well as online. See Figure 7-3.

7-2b The Benefits of a Company's Using the Internet in Marketing

The value of the Internet in marketing is best conveyed by reviewing the benefits that a company may receive by going online. Several of these benefits are shown in Figure 7-4 and described next.

Communicability—The Web makes it easy for a firm to communicate with each of its constituencies: consumers, suppliers, resellers, employees, the media, government

> The potential marketing benefits of the Internet range from communicability to sales revenues.

---

[5] "Edmunds.com Company Profile and History," **http://www.edmunds.com/help/about/profile.html** (March 29, 2006); and "An Introduction to Walmart.com," **http://www.walmart.com** (March 29, 2006).

Figure 7-2

Sephora Successfully Moves to a Bricks-and-Clicks Strategy

Sephora's Web site (**http://www.sephora.com**) features a huge product selection and most of the popular brands in its beauty care category—just like Sephora's stores.

Source: Reprinted by permission of Susan Berry, Retail Image Consulting, Inc.

bodies, and others. As one observer noted, "The Internet allows you opportunities to talk to people on a continual, dialog basis in a way that we've never had before."[6]

Focus/tailored approach—The Web enables a firm to focus on a specific target market and offer a marketing mix especially devised for that target market The Internet is also especially good for targeted E-mails. For example, "BestBuy.com has debuted an E-mail service where customers can sign up to receive pre-order info the second DVD street dates are available for theatrical films."[7]

Information—A firm can amass information about almost any facet of its business from free Web sites, as well as fee-based ones. Both secondary data and primary data can be garnered via the Internet.

Timeliness—With the Internet, a company can operate in "real time," which means the ability to communicate, gather information, and so forth in a contemporaneous manner. The time lags associated with other marketing tools are much shorter on the Web.

Cost efficiencies—Reduced costs are often a result of Internet usage. Postal costs decrease. Inventory costs can be lowered because there is more efficient communication between companies and their suppliers. Sales personnel can follow-up with clients more efficiently. There are no shipping costs for items such as software that are sold via the Web and downloaded by customers.

Dynamism/flexibility—The Internet is a dynamic and flexible medium that lets a company rapidly adjust its marketing mix. For instance, if a firm sees that a particular

Figure 7-3

Atomic Dog's Clicks-First Strategy

Source: Reprinted by permission.

---

[6] Richard Lennox quote in Beth Snyder Bulik and Jennifer Gilbert, "Digital Marketing Hits the Mainstream," *Business 2.0* (March 20, 2001), p. 68.

[7] Susanne Ault, "Best Buy Boosts Web Presence as Early Lure," Video Business (February 28, 2005), p. 6.

Figure 7-4

Company Benefits of Using the Internet in Marketing

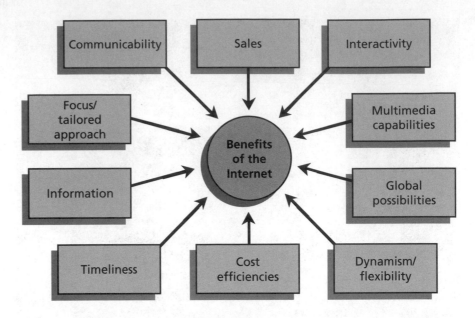

product is not selling well, it can instantly change the advertising at its Web site or lower the price until consumer demand reaches a satisfactory level. Likewise, if a firm runs out of a popular item that it is selling, a reorder can be placed immediately through the Web.

Global possibilities—With the Internet, a company can effectively and inexpensively communicate with its constituencies around the world, thereby increasing the reach of the firm's marketing strategy. The expensive part of operating a global E-commerce Web site is often the distribution costs that result from expanding into new geographic markets.

Multimedia capabilities—The Internet offers huge multimedia possibilities for marketers, especially as many users convert to cable, DSL, or other fast connections. More company Web sites will soon be showing 3-D pictures of products that can be rotated 360 degrees, streaming audio and video, photo galleries of product offerings, and so forth.

Interactivity—Unlike traditional advertising, which is uni-directional (from company to audience), the Internet can be deployed interactively (from company to audience *and* from audience to company)—much like personal selling. A firm can ask people to click on a section of its Web site that they would like to visit and then transport them to that particular section, where more user choices are made. For example, an airline site can gather data on the destination and date a person wants to travel to from his or her home area, and then display the alternative flights that fit the person's criteria.

Sales—For a clicks-only firm, the Internet represents the sole source of revenue. For a bricks-and-clicks firm, the Internet offers the potential for growing the business. As an example, in 1999, 25 percent of Southwest Airlines' (**http://www.southwest.com**) reservations were made online. Today, the company generates 60 percent of its revenues from online transactions. Also consider that 60 percent of those in the United States who use the Internet buy online each year.[8]

[8] Pew Internet & American Lifestyle Project, *Internet: The Mainstreaming of Online Life*, **http://www.pewinternet.org** (2005).

Global Marketing in Action

Live 8: The Global Power of the Internet

The first Live Aid concert, held more than two decades years ago, was viewed by 1 billion people and raised $100 million for African famine relief. In July 2005, entertainers such as U2, Madonna, Paul McCartney, and Stevie Wonder performed at Live 8 concerts to attract more attention to the need for debt relief for third-world countries. The concerts took place in Philadelphia, London, Paris, Berlin, Rome, and Barrie, Canada (near Toronto), and viewers/listeners could access the concert via MTV, traditional radio, satellite radio, and the Internet.

Again, an estimated 1 billion people tuned into Live 8 (http://www.live8live.com) via one medium or another; however, this time, the Internet broadcasts were especially noteworthy. According to an AOL spokesperson, "This has woken up the broader entertainment industry and consumers that online is a really satisfying experience. And from an awareness standpoint, it is a watershed moment for streaming." At noon, AOL alone had 100,000 viewers for Paul McCartney and U2 playing "Sgt. Pepper's Lonely Hearts Club Band," and the number the of simultaneous viewers climbed to 175,000. By the end of the day, over 5 million people had streamed parts of Live 8.

As a result of consumers' experience with Live 8 via AOL, traffic dramatically increased for AOL's *Top 11*, a new online show that targeted MTV's *TRL* audience. As an AOL spokesperson said, traffic "went from tens of thousands to hundred of thousands" of viewers.

Sources: Based on material in Jonathan Takiff, "Live 8 Concerts on TV, Radio, and Internet," *Chattanooga Times Free Press Online* (July 1, 2005); and Bill Werde and Antony Bruno, "Live 8's Other Message," http://Billboard.com (July 16, 2005).

7-3 THE MULTIFACETED POTENTIAL MARKETING ROLES FOR THE INTERNET

After reviewing the company benefits of the Internet in marketing, it should be clear that the Web has the potential to serve several marketing roles, as shown in Figure 7-5 and discussed next. Each firm must determine which roles to pursue and how to prioritize their importance.

> The Internet can serve many roles besides generating sales.

Projecting an image—A firm can project an image at its Web site through the site's design (colors, graphics, etc.) and the content presented. Have you ever heard of Accenture (http://www.accenture.com)—formerly Andersen Consulting? No? Well, you can learn a lot about the firm and the image it is striving to project by visiting its Web site—which explains what Accenture is, what it does, the types of clients it serves, where it does business, and a whole lot more: "Accenture is a global management consulting, technology services, and outsourcing company, with net revenues of $14 billion. Committed to delivering innovation, Accenture collaborates with its clients to help them become high-performance businesses and governments. Using our industry knowledge, service-offering expertise, and technology capabilities, we identify new business and technology trends and develop solutions to help clients around the world."[9]

Customer service—Many firms use the Internet to supplement their traditional customer service. At its Web site, Staples, the office products chain, has a "Staples Rebates" section (http://www.stapleseasyrebates.com/promocenter/staples/promo_search.html)—where a customer can see what rebate offers are available by entering the name of the manufacturer, the product code, a keyword, or a rebate number.

Channel relations—The Internet can help channel members to better understand one another, to coordinate their distribution strategies, to smooth over conflicts, and so forth. WineryExchange (http://www.wineryexchange.com/cgi-bin/wineryexchange/home.jsp) is "the leading global supplier of quality private-label wine brands for global

---

[9] "Company Overview," http://www.accenture.com/xd/xd.asp?it=enweb&xd=aboutus/company/co_company.xml (March 29, 2006).

Figure 7-5

How the Internet May Be Utilized in Marketing

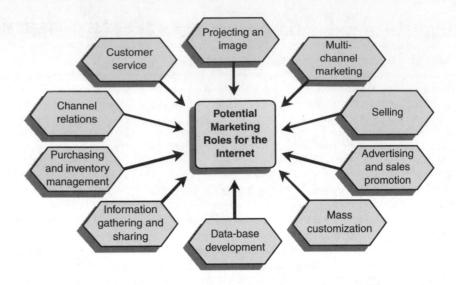

wine retailers. In close consultation with our retail partners, we create the wine blends, brand names, packaging, and marketing plans. We manage all aspects of production, compliance, and distribution to ensure that the highest-quality wines satisfy the needs of our partners. We provide our retailers with an experienced team of winemakers, production specialists, legal compliance experts, and marketing and sales professionals committed to the success of these partners."[10]

Purchasing and inventory management—The Web can greatly facilitate company purchases and inventory management. Procter & Gamble (**http://www.pg.com**), the consumer products manufacturer, has two distinct password-protected Web sites to assist its retailers in making purchases for resale to final consumers: "The P&G Customer Portal (**https://customer.pg.com**) and Web Order Management (**http://order. pg.com/ jsp/login/login_norm.jsp**) systems assist the company's trade partners in purchasing, managing, and promoting P&G products. These Web-based systems are always available. They provide product information, order status, and invoices."[11]

Information gathering and sharing—As previously noted, the Internet has considerable possibilities for providing marketing information. At its Web site (**http://www.quirks. com**), *Quirks Marketing Research Review* "promotes the use, understanding, and value of marketing research across all industries. We feature over 1,000 case history and technique articles in our Article Archive, an interactive researcher forum, free marketing research job postings, and the most comprehensive directories of custom research providers found anywhere—just to name a few of the resources available here!"[12]

Data-base development—Due to the online interactions between a firm and its suppliers and customers, extensive marketing data bases can be developed. Amazon. com's Web site (**http://www.amazon.com**) has millions of registered customers, many of whom regularly shop at **http://Amazon.com**. The firm has purchase data and contact information on these customers.

Mass customization—An extremely attractive feature of the Internet involves companies' ability to engage in ***mass customization***, a process by which mass-market goods and services are individualized to satisfy a specific customer need, at a reasonable price. According to one systems design firm, "Based on the public's growing desire for product

Through online **mass customization**, a company can individualize mass-market goods and services to satisfy a specific customer need, at a fair price.

---

[10] "WineryExchange: Corporate Overview," **http://www.wineryexchange.com/cgi-bin/wineryexchange/about/ aboutus.jsp?hometype=about** (March 29, 2006).

[11] "B2B Directory: Retail Customers," **http://pg.com/b2b/retail_customers.jhtml** (March 30, 2006).

[12] "Welcome," **http://www.quirks.com/index.asp** (March 30, 2006).

personalization, it serves as the ultimate combination of 'custom-made' and 'mass production.' Simply stated, mass customization is about choice; about giving consumers a unique product when, where, and how they want it. The Internet makes it possible for anyone to compile music CDs containing any combination of songs. Or obtain customized home mortgages. Or design a one-of-a-kind friend of Barbie, complete with unique name, clothing, and personality. Mass customization not only benefits the consumer, it offers the manufacturer significant benefits: a high degree of product/service flexibility, reduced inventory risk, and a competitive edge."[13]

Advertising and sales promotion—A company can promote its goods and services, along with its image, through the Internet. It can use banner ads at portal sites, be listed at search engines, and present multimedia messages and special sales promotions at its own Web site. Consider Google's (**http://www.google.com**) AdWords program, which "aims to provide the most effective advertising available for businesses of any size. We pledge to help you meet your customer acquisition needs by enabling you to reach people looking for your good or service, fully control your ad budget, easily create and edit your ads, and see your ads on Google within minutes of creating them. You'll also have 24/7 access to detailed performance reports that help you track the effectiveness of your ad campaigns."[14]

Selling—Generating sales is a key Internet marketing role for many firms. (We've listed it here to re-emphasize that selling is only one role for the Internet.) When engaging in E-commerce, this should be kept in mind: "Creating a satisfying shopping experience online is different from the same task offline because an online shopper is both consumer and co-designer of the shopping experience. Clicking from site to site and page to page, online shoppers have more control over the time, the place, and the way in which they move through a merchandise offering than store shoppers. A site's role isn't simply to create a shopping experience. It is also to develop and share with the consumer the tools (such as information, personalization options, navigational features, opinions of others, help guides, etc.) that can make a great shopping experience possible."[15] See Figure 7-6.

Multichannel marketing—Bricks-and-clicks firms engage in multichannel marketing, whereby they sell their products through more than one distribution format, in this case, the Internet and at least one other format. Barnes & Noble has a Web site (**http://www.barnesandnoble.com**), more than 820 stores, an 800 number, and in-store video kiosks. Its Web site offers free shipping on most orders of $25 or more.

7-4 DEVELOPING AN INTERNET MARKETING STRATEGY

To best use the Internet in marketing, a firm should be systematic in preparing and enacting the proper strategy. Figure 7-7 presents the steps to be followed in this process. The six middle boxes relate to the basic components of an Internet marketing strategy. The four outside boxes are key influences in making strategic decisions. Let us explore each of these factors.

> There are six basic steps in developing an Internet marketing strategy.

1. Goal categories are set, drawn from the factors in Figure 7-5. Both quantitative and qualitative objectives should be enumerated. These are the well-articulated Internet objectives of Zeppelin (**http://www.real-estate-tech.com**), a Hong Kong-based real-estate consulting company: (a) "To share real-estate learning, information, and knowledge via analyses, commentaries, articles, research, statistical tables, charts, technical tutorials, and newsletters including our own Real-Estate Tech." (b) "To create a Real-Estate Forum for

[13] Gerber Scientific, "What Is Mass Customization?" **http://www.mass-customization.com** (March 31, 2006).

[14] "AdWords Advantages," **http://adwords.google.com/select/advantages.html** (March 31, 2006).

[15] Jackie Pollok, "The Online Shopping Experience," *Hot Topics* (Columbus, OH: Retail Forward, August 2000), p. 1.

Figure 7-6

Driving Global E-Commerce

The Internet is transforming the way people work, play, and shop. That is certainly true in Brazil, where Som Livre (assisted by Unisys) is the country's leading online music retailer. It has more than 50,000 Real Audio music files—from 150 recording labels—that customers can sample before buying.

Source: Reprinted by permission. Richard Bowditch, Photographer.

interested parties to express their own views and ideas." (c) "To incorporate professional, academic, institutional, corporate, business, and other useful links for convenience." (d) To introduce our services and our company to interested parties and prospective clients/customers." (e) "To make available and market some of our real-estate products such as financial spreadsheets, tutorials, etc. to prospective users."[16]

2. The target audience is identified and selected, and its desires are studied. Here are some recent research findings about online users:

    • On a daily basis, more than 70 million American adults use the Internet.

    • In comparison with dial-up users, broadband users "spend more time online and do more online activities, especially those that exploit bigger information 'pipelines,' such as accessing streaming video. They are much more likely to create content and share it with the rest of the online population. And they report greater levels of satisfaction with the role of the internet in their lives."

    • Broadband connections (as a percentage of the population) are highest in such countries as South Korea, Hong Kong, and Canada.

    • For every $1 spent on Internet purchases, "Web-to-Store" shoppers spend $1.60 offline at local stores. In addition, "Web-to-Store" shoppers tend to be more satisfied than those who only visit stores without first using the Internet.

    • More than one-half of those buying new cars in the United States obtain information from the Internet before visiting a showroom.

    • Six types of Internet consumers have been identified: newbie shoppers—older first-time Web purchasers who start with small purchases; reluctant shoppers—motivated to buy but worried about security and privacy; frugal shoppers—

[16] "Web Objectives," http://www.real-estate-tech.com/zeppelin_web_objectives.htm (April 3, 2006).

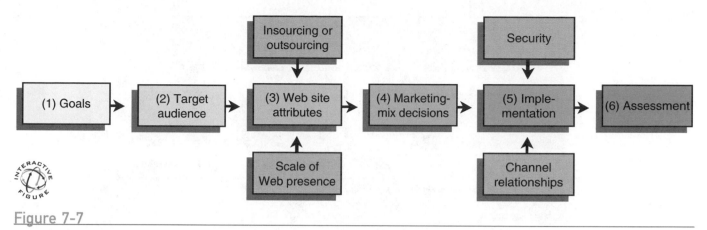

Figure 7-7

The Stages of an Internet Marketing Strategy

active searchers for the lowest prices; strategic shoppers—know what they want before going online and go to specific sites; enthusiastic shoppers—like to shop; and convenience shoppers (the largest group)—buy online to save time.[17]

As shown in Figure 7-8, people have numerous reasons for shopping online. Different target audiences place a different emphasis on these reasons. Thus, consumer desires must be examined carefully before embarking on the specifics of an Internet marketing strategy.

3. Web site attributes are determined. First, the company must decide whether to undertake all Web-related activities itself (insourcing) or to have specialized firms do some or all Web-related activities for it (outsourcing). Most companies outsource technical development and maintenance of their sites; far fewer fully develop sites on their own. Small firms often outsource the entire operation. For an investment of $800 and $75 per month, Hoover Web Design (**http://www.hooverwebdesign.com**) will design, host, and maintain "a custom 10-page site designed to represent your business with a user-friendly interface. Your pages can be home, about, services, location, and contact. You can include a photo gallery, a calendar of events, or any other pages which will advertise your business." Second, the company must choose the scale of its Web presence, especially the weight of the site in its overall marketing strategy, the percent of the marketing budget devoted to the site, and how the site is to be implemented. How is the site to be used for customer service, channel relations, selling, and so on? Are all products to be displayed at the site? Is the site to be simple or have a full range of bells and whistles? How widely is the site to be promoted?

> A company must decide between insourcing and outsourcing Web activities, and determine the scope of its Web presence.

After making decisions as to insourcing or outsourcing and the scale of the Web presence, site attributes are chosen. Here are some factors to consider in designing a marketing-oriented Web site:

> It is critical for a Web site to be designed well.

- *Web address*—The company can have its own Web address or be part of a Web community. It must carefully pick a name to use. This is becoming more

[17] Pew Internet & American Lifestyle Project, *Internet: The Mainstreaming of Online Life*, **http://www.pewinternet.org** (2005); Rob McGann, "Web-to-Store Consumers Spend, Shop More at Local Stores," **http://www.clickz.com/stats/ sectors/retailing/article.php/3461611** (January 19, 2005); "Retail Web Sites Are Powerful Drivers of In-Store Sales, Brand Loyalty, and Customer Satisfaction," *Business Wire* (January 19, 2005); Jean Halliday, "Half Hit Web Before Showrooms," *Advertising Age* (October 4, 2004); and Melinda Cuthbert, "All Buyers Not Alike," *Business 2.0* (December 26, 2000), pp. 134, 137.

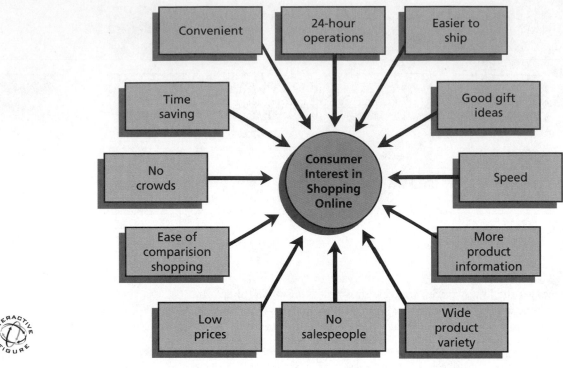

Figure 7-8

Why Consumers Purchase Online

complex due to the addition of new domain suffixes (as designated by ICANN, **http://www.internic.net/faqs/new-tlds.html**): .info and .biz for general use, .pro for professionals, .name for personal sites, .museum for museums, .aero for the aerospace industry, and .coop for business cooperatives.

- *Home page*—The home page is the gateway to the firm. It projects an image, presents information, and routes viewers to other relevant company pages. It must be easy to navigate and laid out well.

- *Site content*—The content can include some or all of these topics: company background, company vision and philosophy, financial performance, product descriptions, where products are sold, community service involvement, customer service, an online shopping cart, career opportunities, press releases, and more.

- *Use of multimedia*—A site can be rather plain with mostly text and a few graphics, or it can involve the heavy use of photos, animations, audio clips, video clips, and so forth.

- *Links*—Web sites can have two types of links. Almost every company has *internal links:* a person clicks on an icon on the home page and he or she is then transported to another section within the company's site. There may also be *external links:* a person clicks on an icon on the home page and he or she is then sent to another site outside of the firm's site, such as a trade association or a search engine. With the latter, the person may or may not return to the company site.

- *Shopping tools*—If a firm engages in E-commerce, there must be a mechanism for directing shoppers through the purchase process, including a secure way of entering personal data. Amazon.com (**http://www.amazon.com**) is widely admired for the "1-Click" shopping option it offers to customers.

- *Electronic data interchange*—A Web site must be able to facilitate the exchange of information among company employees and with channel members. This is especially critical in E-commerce for order shipping and inventory control.

- *Feedback*—Visitors must have a way to communicate with the firm, and there must be a mechanism for the company to respond in a timely manner.

- *Trade-offs*—When designing a site, trade-offs must be weighed. A site with a lot of graphics and photos may take a long time for users to download if they are using a dial-up Internet connection. So, how many bells and whistles should a site have, given the limitations for some users?

4. Internet-based marketing-mix decisions are made while developing the Web site; they must be consistent (synergistic) with offline marketing decisions. These are some examples:

    - *Product decisions*—Which products are listed at the site? Which products are featured at the site? Many firms do not list or describe all items in their product mix. Also, what should be the features of downloadable products (software, music, publications, etc.) that are sold online?

    - *Distribution decisions*—If the company sells at its site, does it ship from one locale or from around the country (world)? How quickly can (should) products be delivered to customers?

    - *Promotion decisions*—Which promotion mix should be used to reach the firm's Internet goals? There are many ways to promote a site and E-marketing efforts, from banner ads to listing Web addresses in traditional ads to E-mail, and more. One highly effective online tool is the ***opt-in (permission-based) E-mail***, whereby Internet users agree to receive targeted E-mail from a firm. It is far more effective than unsolicited E-mail, which turns off a lot of people. As one expert noted: "Given skepticism about E-mail, we know that to earn trust, we must do it intentionally and systematically. In contrast to many marketing campaigns, these customers have already selected themselves as a target audience. Subscribers to permission-based E-mail start out interested in hearing your value proposition."[18]

    - *Pricing decisions*—Engaging in E-commerce requires two fundamental pricing decisions: How should online prices relate to those for offline businesses (including those of the firm itself)? How frequently should prices be changed to reflect market conditions? Because so many Internet shoppers are price-driven, online prices have tended to be lower than offline prices for the same products, and online transactions are often not subject to sales tax. Although the technology exists to adjust online pricing by the minute, firms must be careful not to confuse consumers or to get them upset if they visit a site and then return the next day to purchase, only to find that the price has risen.

> **Opt-in E-mail**, which is sent with the permission of the consumer, is good for both the company and the consumer.

5. At this point, the Internet marketing strategy is implemented. Again, two factors affect a firm's ability to properly enact its strategy: security and channel relationships. A vast number of Internet users are concerned about Web security, and they are hesitant to provide personal information for fear that "hackers" will obtain the data or that firms will resell the data. The security issue can be dealt with by offering a secure section of a Web site, protected by a well-known firm such as VeriSign (**http://www.verisign.com**) or Cybertrust (**http://www.cybertrust.com**), for entering personal data and credit information. The reselling issue can be handled by having a clear, user-friendly privacy policy that is accessible by clicking an icon at the Web site. With regard to channel relationships, a move into E-commerce may place a company into conflict with its suppliers or resellers, which may view this action as a form of competition. So, the trade-offs must be weighed.

    The firm must be sure that its Web strategy runs smoothly, once it is enacted. It must be alert to several possible breakdowns in the system, such as site crashes, out-of-stock conditions, a slow response to customer inquiries, incorrect prices, hacker invasions, and poor coordination with the offline strategy.

> A Web site must be secure, protect privacy, and not be a threat to other channel members.

---

[18] Morgan Stewart, "You've Got Permission, Now Be Relevant: How to Use Segmentation, Targeting, and Personalization to Deliver Relevant E-Mail," **http://email.exacttarget.com/pdf/segmentation-whitepaper.pdf** (2005).

6. The last step in an Internet marketing strategy is to assess performance and make necessary modifications. Assessment should be closely tied to the Web goals (step 1) that have been set in terms of image, customer service, sales, and so forth. These are some measures that can be studied: daily site traffic, average length of the stay at the site, ratings on customer service surveys, sales revenues, costs per transaction, repeat business, the number and type of system breakdowns per time period, and more. The effectiveness of banner ads placed at other sites must be also be judged.

Special attention should be paid to rating the quality of the Web site itself. These are among the factors that should be regularly reviewed from the Internet user's perspective:[19]

- Clarity of site's mission
- Download time
- Time needed to comprehend site characteristics
- Informational value
- Ease of navigability
- Use of graphics/multimedia
- Interactivity
- Currency
- Security
- Simplicity of purchasing
- Printability of site pages
- Creativity

Marketing and the Web

Why Amazon, eBay, and Google Are Opening Their Data Bases to Others

Amazon.com's (http://www.amazon.com) data base contains product descriptions, prices, sales rankings, customer reviews, and other assorted data. For the past several years, through a project titled Amazon Web Services, the company has opened up its data base to over 65,000 programmers and businesses. Similarly, eBay (http://www.ebay.com) has opened its data base of 33 million weekly auction items to 15,000 registered software developers, and Google (http://www.google.com) gives out some of its search results data.

Of the 65,000 programmers and businesses that have signed up to use Amazon's free access, about one-third have developed tools to assist Amazon's 800,000 active sellers. One of these is ScoutPal (http://www.scoutpal.com), a service that converts a cell phone into a mobile barcode scanner. This scan-

ner enables a book dealer who sells books on Amazon to download Amazon's most current prices for books and to calculate the likely profit margin before a purchase is made. ScoutPal now has over 1,000 subscribers who pay $10 per month each for the service.

As with Amazon, many of eBay's applications automate the listing or display of items. According to an eBay executive, "Sellers who use our APIs [application programming interfaces] become at least 50 percent more productive than those who use the Web site itself." One major chain of pawnshops uses eBay's API to automatically upload its most current pawned items from its 46 shops directly to eBay.

Source: Based on material in Erick Schonfeld, "The Great Giveaway," *Business 2.0* (April 2005), pp. 81–86.

[19] See Joel R. Evans and Vanessa E. King, "Business-to-Business Marketing and the Worldwide Web: Planning, Managing, and Assessing Web Sites," *Industrial Marketing Management*, Vol. 28 (July 1999), pp. 343–358; and J. Cox and B. G. Dale, "Key Quality Factors in Web Site Design and Use: An Examination," *International Journal of Quality & Reliability Management*, Vol. 19 (Number 7, 2002), pp. 862–888.

7-5 HOW THE INTERNET IS BEING APPLIED IN MARKETING STRATEGIES

We now present several examples of E-marketing in action.

> Internet marketing is being applied in many ways.

7-5a   Consumer Analysis

As Table 7-2 indicates, in the United States, slightly more females than males use the Internet and Internet usage is highest for young adults. Suburbanites, middle-income people, and college graduates are more apt to use the Internet than older adults, urban dwellers, and high school graduates, respectively. Aside from E-mail, information-related activities are the most popular Internet tasks. Online purchases as a percentage of total category sales (including both offline and online) are growing rapidly in many categories. The average online order is at least $100 for several categories, led by computer hardware.

According to a comScore Networks (**http://www.comscore.com**) study, shopping behavior is greatly affected by the length of time that a person has used the Internet: "Newbie online shoppers tend to cling to the familiar. They are 81 percent more likely than experienced shoppers to shop only at sites they've shopped at in the past. However, willingness to shop at new sites increases among users with more experience online. And, as experience and comfort grow, spending grows. Research data indicate that 75 percent of online shoppers are willing to try a new Internet merchant."[20]

7-5b   Product Planning

Companies are taking a variety of product-planning approaches to the Internet. For example, Atomic Dog (**http://www.atomicdog.com**), the publisher of this text, is involved with Internet-driven texts and print versions of the publications. The online texts feature high-tech graphics, animations, interactivity, and other dynamic attributes not found in traditional printed books.

At Pillsbury's Web site (**http://www.pillsbury.com**), people can download recipes that may use ingredients that the firm markets: "Plan meals in minutes with these quick ideas from the Pillsbury Kitchens! Get recipes and menus for family dinners and get-togethers, as well as handy tips for making mealtime quick, easy and memorable." For example, "Chili Supper for Four: When you can make a pot of chili this easily, there's no excuse! Gather your friends for a chili evening supper."[21]

More firms are also heeding this advice:

> On the Web, all goods are not equal. One important dimension on which items differ is in the ability of consumers to ascertain the quality of products in cyberspace. On one end of the spectrum are commodity products, where quality can be clearly and contractually articulated and conveyed. Products such as oil, paper clips, and stock shares all fall under this category. On the other end of the continuum are products for which the perception of quality differs from consumer to consumer and product to product, such as produce, used cars, and works of art. Understanding how hard it is to convey quality, reliability, or consistency for certain classes of products over the Web enables businesspeople to think strategically about the long-term success of different types of E-commerce.[22]

---

[20] James Maguire, "The State of E-Commerce: Online Shopping Trends," **http://www.ecommerce-guide.com/news/trends/article.php/3524581** (August 2, 2005).

[21] "C'mon Over!" **http://www.pillsbury.com/solve/cmon_over.aspx** (March 11, 2006).

[22] John M. de Figueiredo, "Sustainable Profitability in Electronic Commerce," *Sloan Management Review,* **Vol. 41** (Summer 2000), p. 41.

Table 7-2	Internet Usage: A U.S. Perspective		
Population Attributes	**% Using the Internet**	**Online Activities**	**% of Internet Users Engaging in Activities**
Male/female online ratio	48/52	Use E-mail	98
18 to 29 years old	78	Get health information	80
30 to 49 years old	74	Research products	75
65 years old and over	25	Get news	70
Suburban	68	Buy products	60
Urban	62	Make travel reservations	55
Lower income	44	Use instant messaging	37
Middle income	81	Read blogs	27
High school graduate	52	Participate in online auctions	22
College graduate	88	Download music	15
Selected Products Bought Online	**2010 Projected % of All U.S. Retail Purchases in Category**	**Selected Online Sales by Product Category**	**2005 Average Order Size ($)**
Computer hardware	54	Computer hardware	585
Computer software	53	Event tickets	122
Travel	42	Automotive	120
Event tickets	39	Consumer electronics	100
Books	28	Sporting goods	75
Consumer electronics	22	Home and garden	70
Apparel	12	Shoes and athletic footwear	55
Furniture	10	Computer software	50
Automotive	3	Apparel	45
Food and beverages	3	Toys, games, and hobbies	40

Sources: Table developed by the authors based on data from Pew Internet & American Lifestyle Project, *Internet: The Mainstreaming of Online Life*, http://www.pewinternet.org (2005); Carrie A. Johnson, *Trends: U.S. E-Commerce Overview: 2004 to 2010* (Cambridge, MA: Forrester Research, August 2, 2004); and "Online Report Card," *Nielsen//NetRatings Press Release* (April 7, 2005).

7-5c Distribution Planning

On the one hand, there is Terry Precision Cycling (http://www.terrybicycles.com), a small manufacturer of bicycles and related products for women. The firm does relatively little E-commerce business at its Web site, and relies on independent bicycle shops around the country. On the other hand, there is Office Depot (http://www.officedepot.com), the huge chain. Although its stores generate $11 billion in yearly sales, Office Depot's Web site provides most of its sales growth, with annual online sales hitting $3.5 billion.

One of the most complex aspects of E-distribution involves business-to-business exchanges that connect sellers and potential buyers. The most successful such exchange is Covisint (http://www.covisint.com), initially formed by several auto makers: "Covisint is the leading provider of services that enable the integration of vital business information and processes between partners, customers, and suppliers. Covisint uses an industry-centric approach leveraging deep expertise and state-of-the-art technology to address industry specific needs. Covisint bridges gaps created by dissimilar business systems and adapts businesses to work with the myriad of business processes and technologies used by partners." At present, it services more than 22,000 businesses as customers (in 100 countries) and thousands of suppliers.[23]

With the distribution problems that a number of online firms have faced, they are now more apt to outsource delivery to such industry powerhouses as UPS (**http:// www.ups.com**), which has a significant Internet logistical presence with its UPS OnLine Tools. See Figure 7-9.

7-5d Promotion Planning

With the demise of such prominent E-commerce firms as Pets.com and eToys.com, many Internet-driven firms have scaled back their TV advertising efforts. These efforts

Figure 7-9

Moving at the Speed of E-Logistics

UPS has established an E-logistics division to handle Internet transactions. It dominates the shipments of products purchased online.

Source: Reprinted by permission. Photo by John Huet.

[23] "About Covisint," **http://www.covisint.com/about** (March 12, 2006).

proved too costly and too ineffective. Print and online ads remain popular. In-store kiosks have a role, as illustrated in Figure 7-10. And opt-in E-mail is rising rapidly in popularity.

To learn more about online promotion planning, read these excellent articles: "The Web Marketing Checklist: 31 Ways to Promote Your Web Site" (**http://www.wilson web.com/articles/checklist.htm**) and "How to Attract Visitors to Your Web Site" (**http://www.wilsonweb.com/articles/attract.htm**).

7-5e Price Planning

According to Jupiter Research (**http://www.jupiterresearch.com**), 80 percent of Internet shoppers comparison shop before buying and nearly one-half of Internet shoppers visit three to five sites before making a purchase. Some firms set their online prices similar to—or slightly below—their offline prices, and count on customer loyalty to their brands and the convenience of Web shopping to stimulate business. Other companies such as eBay (**http://www.ebay.com**) and Priceline.com (**http://www.priceline.com**) focus their appeal on people who like to price shop and get bargains.

Still other companies use the Internet to sell close-out merchandise at deep discounts:

Smart Bargains [**http://www.smartbargains.com**] makes it easy for brand-oriented, value-conscious consumers to find wonderful bargains on the products they love. Every day, we offer superior quality goods and top brands at up to 70 percent off retail value. We are dedicated to offering the best possible bargain shopping experience available online. Our commitment to

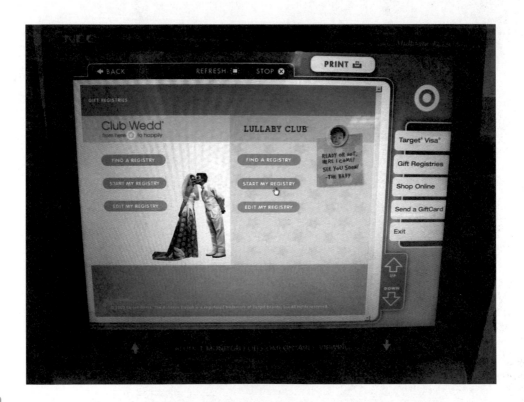

Figure 7-10

A New Job for In-Store Kiosks

With its in-store kiosks, Target's (**http://www.target.com**) customers can place orders through a Club Webb bridal registry and a Lullaby Club registry. This enables shoppers to see items in the store before buying them.

Source: Reprinted by permission of Susan Berry, Retail Image Consulting, Inc.

the customer's experience begins with the Web site and continues through to the purchase with state-of-the-art fulfillment and highly responsive customer service.[24]

7-6 CURRENT CHALLENGES AND FUTURE PROSPECTS FOR E-MARKETING

In this section, we look at the challenges and future prospects for marketing and the Internet.

7-6a The Challenges of Using the Internet in Marketing

Some challenges faced by marketers when using the Internet are beyond their control (such as slow-speed dial-up connections and the complexity of multichannel marketing); others are self-inflicted (such as poor customer service and overly rapid expansion). Before turning to several specific challenges, both uncontrollable and self-inflicted, let us cite some general reasons why E-marketing can be so daunting:

- A company's corporate culture may be hard to adapt to the Internet.
- Internet marketing may not capitalize on a company's core competencies.
- The proper roles for E-marketing may not be specified clearly enough—or be realistic in nature.
- Web users can be very demanding.
- The personal touch may be important to many customers.
- Channel partners may be alienated.
- Online and offline systems may be hard to integrate.
- It may be difficult to determine which Internet functions to insource and which to outsource.
- Investment costs and ongoing expenses may be underestimated.

> Web challenges fall into two categories: uncontrollable and self-inflicted.

Let us now review a number of specific challenges related to marketing and the Internet.

Consumer resistance to online shopping—Despite the rapid growth of online sales, less than 5 percent of U.S. retail revenues and about 8 to 10 percent of U.S. business-to-business revenues are from Internet transactions. Why? Many final consumers still want personal contact, the immediacy of a store purchase, and the ability to touch products before buying. They also often find the online purchase process to be too cumbersome. From a business-to-business perspective, "Many firms must largely redesign important purchasing processes from the ground up to capitalize on technology. Then they must motivate employees to embrace broad changes while training them in new methods. There is a lack of software integration capabilities between purchasers and suppliers."[25]

> These challenges must be reviewed carefully and in-depth.

Customer service—Web users often feel frustrated by what they perceive as inadequate customer service. According to a BenchmarkPortal (**http://www.benchmarkportal.com**) study of small and medium-sized businesses, "Many North American businesses are missing out on revenue opportunities due to poor or nonexistent E-mail customer service. Among key cross-industry findings are: A shocking 51 percent of the companies did not respond at all; 70 percent failed to respond within 24 hours; and 79 percent responded with an inaccurate and/or incomplete answer." In addition, the study found that "the E-business sector performed the best in responsiveness, with 52 percent responding within 24 hours. Surprisingly, financial services and retail companies were least responsive, with 72 percent and 60 percent respectively not sending any response at

---

[24] "Smart Bargains. About Us," **http://www.smartbargains.com/About-Us.aspx** (March 12, 2006).

[25] "E-Commerce & Internet Business Statistics," **http://www.plunkettresearch.com/technology/ecommerce_statistics_1.htm** (2005); and "Online Purchasing Continues to Grow," *Supply House Times* (September 2003), p. 40.

all." As BenchmarkPortal's director of research noted, "Our study serves as a wakeup call to the majority of North American firms who are losing business due to poor online service."[26] Companies must do better, some significantly better.

System breakdowns—Various system breakdowns have occurred and will continue to occur. Some are caused by companies' lack of attention to their sites, but most are due to the sheer complexity of E-marketing with regard to the number of parties involved in a typical Web site (from Internet service provider to content Web master), the amount of traffic on the Web, the number of links that firms have at their sites (which must be checked regularly to be sure they are not broken), the use of multimedia, and other factors. In addition, firms must constantly be vigilant and protect their sites against intrusions from hackers who may corrupt files, steal customer data, and be otherwise destructive.

Speed of site performance—Slow connections are irritating to both users and companies that have Web sites. Users with dial-up telephone connections—still the dominant mode for home users—must wait to log on every time they dial-up, face periodic busy signals, and endure long delays when photos or other multimedia tools are featured at the Web site. Some features, such as video clips, may not work at all with a dial-up connection. Firms are disappointed because they must scale down their sites so that downloads are not excessively slow for dial-up users. With the advent of "always on" cable, DSL, and other high-speed connections (already in use by most businesses and a growing number of homes in the United States), this challenge will not be as daunting in the years ahead as it is today.

Internet connection costs—Although the promise of high-speed connections is great, the prices will have to drop for more users to sign on. As of 2006, Cablevision's Optonline (**http://www.optonline.com**) charged a monthly cable Internet connection fee of $44.95 for those who also subscribed to its cable TV service and $49.95 for those who did not; Verizon's DSL service (**http://www.verizon.net**) promoted a number of monthly pricing plans, including a final consumer plan for $14.95 (with a connect speed much slower than a cable connection), a final consumer plan for $39.95 (with a connect speed somewhat slower than a cable connection) and a business plan for $204.95 (with a connect speed comparable to a cable connection). These services do not require a telephone. For some consumers, even dial-up services are too expensive. In 2006, the AOL (**http://www.aol.com**) standard monthly dial-up fee was $23.90.

Legal issues—Because Internet use is so new, legal precedents often do not yet exist. The legal challenges facing E-marketing fall into two categories: firm versus firm and government activities. In the first category are disputes over copyrights, patents, and business practices. For example, a number of music companies successfully sued Napster (**http://www.napster.com**) to require the firm to stop facilitating the free exchange of copyrighted materials, forcing Napster to change its business strategy. Amazon.com (**http://www.amazon.com**) sued Barnes & Noble.com (**http://www.bn.com**) to prevent the latter from offering one-click shopping, as Amazon.com has a patented process for it. The two firms settled out of court. With regard to government actions, among the most contentious issues are whether to tax items sold over the Internet (in the United States, sales tax is not required unless a firm has a physical presence in a state with a sales tax), whether children should be denied access to undesirable sites, whether there should be rules governing purchase terms and delivery dates, and whether and how to protect individuals' privacy.

Privacy issues—Internet users are willing to provide some personal data. Yet, they are concerned about what information is requested at Web sites and how that information is to be used. According to one study, for sites in which they are interested, 90 percent of people will provide an E-mail address, 82 percent their name, 55 percent their address, 21 percent their employer, and 11 percent their credit-card number. However, they do not

---

[26] "First of Its Kind Benchmarking Study Uncovers Major Shortfalls in E-Mail Customer Service Among Small and Medium-Sized Businesses," *Market Wire* (June 8, 2005). See also Gwo-Guang Lee and Hsiu-Fen Lin, "Customer Perceptions of E-Service Quality in Online Shopping," *International Journal of Retail & Distribution Management*, Vol. 33 (Number 2, 2005), pp. 161–176.

want that data shared with other firms. As a leading privacy advocate notes, "Many times, customers are concerned about handing over personal information, because once they do, they know it's out of their control. All that data can fall into the hands of a computer hacker or a dishonest employee. Some of it can be sold to telemarketers or purveyors of junk mail. Our sense is that customers are more willing to spend their dollars with companies that protect their information and don't pry into their personal lives just so the marketing department can aggregate information and categorize them."[27] To better address consumer online privacy concerns, a number of organizations have formed the nonprofit Online Privacy Alliance (**http://www.privacyalliance.org**).

Communicating without spam—Opt-in (permission-based) E-mail can be very successful. People respond well when they are asked if it is okay for a firm to communicate with them and what kinds of information they would like to get. What most Web users object to is the extensive use of *spam*, which is unsolicited and unwanted E-mail. By 2005, more than 80 percent of all E-mail was spam: "Thanks to the glut of spam, average-quality E-mail marketing isn't doing the trick anymore. The solution? You're going to have to turn your E-mail ads into E-mail newsletters if you want them to get read. Americans complain about advertising, but they also accept a huge amount of it—if it's tied to valuable content."[28] As noted in Chapter 5, a federal anti-spam law was enacted to try to alleviate the spam problem. It has thus far been ineffective because "spammers" have been able to circumvent it.

Clutter—There is a lot of clutter on the Web, given the huge number of companies that are now online. It is becoming much tougher for any one company to be noticed and to stand out. For instance, in Chapter 1, we cited more than 40 search engines; and there are many others. They must work quite hard to differentiate themselves. In general, this means that well-known firms will have an easier time attracting Web visitors and that all firms must keep up their promotion efforts.

Finding a workable business model—Some Internet-based firms have still not earned a profit due to excessive investments, overly rapid expansion, system breakdowns, and overestimates about how quickly people would buy online. They need a more realistic and focused business model. For example, although Webvan spent $1 billion during 1999-2000 to develop an online grocery business (which expanded to include electronics, toys, drugstore items, and other product lines), its 2000 sales were less than $100 million and it suffered enormous losses. It went out of business in mid-2001.

Expectations of free services—A particularly vexing challenge for those that offer online services is how to generate revenues from them. As evidenced by all the free Web sites referenced in this book, thousands of sites allow free access to valuable resources—including newspapers, magazines, encyclopedias, software, consulting advice, and a whole lot more. Thus, users often expect these services to be free; and they will bypass sites that charge a fee. Attempts to generate revenues at these sites by having paid advertising have not proven to be very successful.

Integrating bricks-and-clicks operations—It is not always easy to integrate offline and online strategies. Some leading companies have misfired because of insufficient coordination, such as Barnes & Noble, which did not allow in-store returns of online purchases when it began Internet selling. Today, it does. Due to the price-sensitive nature of Web shoppers, some companies have lower prices online than offline. This may be disturbing to store shoppers who feel they should have the same opportunities for discounts. With store-based transactions, companies need on-premises inventory so products are immediately available. Yet, with Web-based sales, central warehouses can be more efficient.

Global issues—Even though the Internet is a worldwide communications vehicle, cultural, language, currency, legal, and other differences among countries can affect a

> Internet users are really turned off by **spam**, unsolicited and unwanted E-mail.

---

[27] Cyber Dialogue, "Full Disclosure," *Promo* (October 2000), p. 43; and "Privacy Imperatives for Customer Data," *Business Week Online* (January 24, 2005).

[28] Sean Michael Kerner, "Deadly Duo: March 2005," **http://www.clickz.com/stats/sectors/email/article.php/3497256** (April 13, 2005); and Andy Sernovitz, "Content-Centered E-Mail in 6 Steps," *B to B* (November 10, 2003), p. 20.

Ethical Issues in Marketing

Business Schools 1, Hackers 0

In early 2005, a message posted to a BusinessWeek.com discussion board stated that MBA applicants to prestigious schools could determine if they were accepted by pasting a URL message into a Web browser and then typing a password. Almost all of the 100 applicants that followed this procedure saw only a blank page as the security breach was quickly repaired. Despite this, three prestigious MBA programs—Harvard Business School, MIT's Sloan School of Management, and Carnegie Mellon University—decided to reject all of these applicants on ethical grounds. In addition, the company whose online software was broken into that night considered legal action against the applicants for gaining unauthorized entry into its site.

As the dean of the Harvard Business School said, the applicants' efforts were "a serious breach of trust that cannot be countered by rationalization." Yet, not everyone agrees that the actions taken by these schools were proper.

According to the director of the Prudential Business Ethics Center at Rutgers University (**http://www.pruethics.rutgers.edu**), "If this were the worst thing businesspeople ever did, we'd be living in Utopia. I think the punishment was a bit harsh." One of the applicants who searched the site said, "For what we did to be considered unethical, you would think it would have to have done harm to someone or gained an unfair advantage to ourselves."

Sources: Based on material in Philip Delves Broughton, "A Lesson in Moral Leadership," *Financial Times* (April 25, 2005), p. 15; and Jonathan Finer, "MBA Applicants Pay Price for Unauthorized Site Searches," *Washington Post* (March 10, 2005), p. E1.

firm seeking a global Internet strategy. Because global distribution tends to be complicated, there often is a need to outsource tasks.

7-6b The Future of E-Marketing

Here are some projections about the future of E-marketing:

> As a major new technology, the Internet will have a bright future, with some stumbles along the way.

- The impact of the Internet on all parties will be enormous, but somewhat different than originally anticipated. Although Internet-generated revenues will grow, there will be more emphasis on E-marketing (using the Internet to enhance marketing strategies) than on E-commerce (sales from Internet transactions).
- Bricks-and-clicks firms will outperform bricks-and-mortar firms and clicks-only firms. Bricks-and-clicks firms with a bricks-and-mortar background will do the best of all, due to their name recognition, customer following, and established physical presence. See Figure 7-11.

Figure 7-11

Dorothy Lane Market: A Well-Integrated Bricks-and-Clicks Approach

With Dorothy Lane Market's (**http://www.dorothylane.com**) DLM in a Dash program, customers have "the convenience of 24-hour online grocery shopping via a secure Internet ordering system with convenient pick-up service at your favorite store. Enjoy the convenience and save precious time for just $6.95 per order, regardless of order size. To help introduce you to this service, we will waive the $6.95 fee for your first order."

Source: Reprinted by permission of Susan Berry, Retail Image Consulting, Inc.

- The growth of new high-speed transmission modes such as cable and DSL connection services will allow more multimedia capabilities to be incorporated into company Web sites, creating an exciting environment for browsing, entertainment, and shopping by users.
- Business-to-business E-commerce will continue to far outstrip business-to-consumer E-commerce.
- It is forecast that U.S. online retail sales will double between 2006 and 2010.
- Most firms engaged in E-commerce will be profitable, having learned valuable insights over the last several years. See Figure 7-12.
- Internet usage and E-commerce will grow more popular around the world. Figure 7-13 shows current data by region. By 2010, the gap among regions will decline. For example, Internet usage in both Africa and Latin America/Caribbean is expected to grow more than two-and-a-half times as fast as in North America. Internet usage in Asia will rise twice as fast.

Figure 7-12

E*Trade: A Master of Online Marketing

E*Trade (**http://www.etrade.com**) averages more than 125,000 transactions per day and receives an average commission of $10 to $11 per trade. The firm is quite profitable.

Source: Reprinted by permission.

Figure 7-13

Internet Usage in Regions Around the World

Sources: Figure developed by the authors from data reported at http://www.internetworldstats.com (February 21, 2006); and "Forrester Projects $6.8 Trillion for 2004 ($ B)," http://www.global-reach.biz/eng/ed/art/2004.ecommerce.php3 (September 9, 2005).

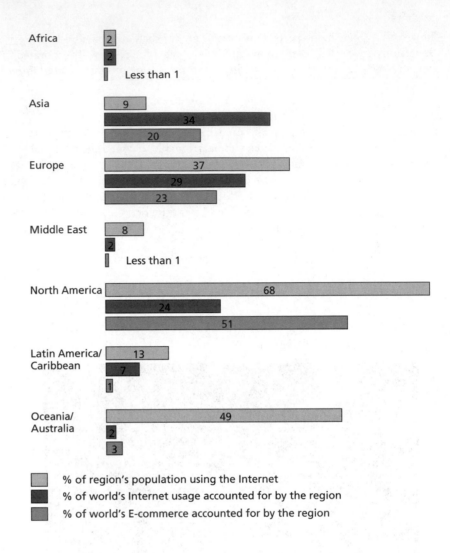

% of region's population using the Internet
% of world's Internet usage accounted for by the region
% of world's E-commerce accounted for by the region

Web Sites You Can Use

Several companies conduct research related to the Internet and provide valuable marketing-related information at their Web sites. These firms include:

- Clickz (**http://www.clickz.com**)—Free articles on all aspects of E-marketing.
- eMarketer (**http://www.emarketer.com/ Newsletter.aspx**)—Sign up for the free daily E-newsletter.
- Forrester Research (**http://www.forrester.com**)—Register as a guest to gain access to free sample reports.

- Internet World Stats (**http:// www.internetworldstats.com/index.html**)—Worldwide Internet usage data.
- Jupiter Research (**http://www.jup.com**)—Register as a guest to gain access to free sample reports.
- Nielsen/Net Ratings (**http://www.nielsen-netratings.com/ news.jsp**)—Click on "NetView Usage Metrics" to see free current data on Internet usage in 10 countries.
- Plunkett Research (**http://www.plunkettresearch.com/ technology/ecommerce_trends.htm**)—Free industry overview.

Summary

1. *To demonstrate why the Internet is a valuable marketing tool* The Internet is a global electronic superhighway of computer networks accessible to people worldwide. The World Wide Web is a way to access the Internet; users see words, colorful charts, pictures, and video, and hear audio. In this chapter (and book), the terms are used interchangeably. E-marketing involves any marketing activity through the Internet. E-commerce refers to sales-generating Internet transactions. E-marketing is the broader concept, and it does not necessarily have sales as the primary goal.

   About 1.35 billion people around the globe use the Web. They surf the Internet for many reasons other than shopping. For instance, they seek out entertainment, financial, sports, and news sites. They do product research. They "talk" to one another. They communicate with firms to register complaints and make suggestions. They send E-mails and greetings cards. Companies also surf the Web for reasons other than shopping. They check what competitors are doing. They read about industry trends and events. They communicate with suppliers. They exchange data among offices anywhere in the world. They monitor inventory. They survey customers. They analyze customer data bases.

   E-marketing is evolving in three phases: (1) traditional bricks-and-mortar firms, (2) clicks-only Internet firms, and (3) bricks-and-clicks firms that combine the other two formats. The trend is more toward bricks-and-clicks firms because they can appeal to multiple market segments, maximize customer contact points, leverage the strengths of each form of business, and enter into new alliances.

   Firms can achieve benefits by using the Internet in marketing. Benefits include communicability, a focus/tailored approach, information, timeliness, cost efficiencies, dynamism/flexibility, global possibilities, multimedia capabilities, interactivity, and sales.

2. *To explore the multifaceted potential marketing roles for the Internet* The Web can serve multiple marketing roles. Each firm must determine which of these roles to pursue and how to prioritize their importance: projecting an image, customer service, channel relations, purchasing and inventory management, information gathering and sharing, data-base development, mass customization (a process by which mass-market goods and services are individualized to satisfy a specific customer need at a reasonable price), advertising and sales promotion, selling, and multichannel marketing.

3. *To show how to develop an Internet marketing strategy* A firm should use a systematic process in forming a proper strategy. The six steps in the process relate to the basic components of an Internet marketing strategy. There are also four outside influences in making strategic decisions.

   (1) Goal categories are set. Both quantitative and qualitative objectives should be stated. (2) The target audience is identified and selected, and its desires studied. (3) Web site attributes are determined. First, the company must decide whether to do Web-related activities itself (insourcing) or to have specialized firms perform some or all Web-related activities for it (outsourcing). Second, the company must choose the scale of its Web presence, especially the importance of the Web site in its overall marketing strategy, the percent of the marketing budget for the Web site, and how the Web site is to be implemented. Third, Web site attributes (address name, home page, etc.) are ascertained.

   (4) Internet-based marketing-mix decisions are made while developing the Web site, consistent with offline marketing decisions. (5) The strategy is implemented. Two factors affect a firm's ability to properly enact its strategy—security and channel relationships—and they must be dealt with well. Once the strategy is enacted, the firm must ensure that it runs smoothly. (6) Performance is assessed and modifications made as necessary.

4. *To illustrate how the Internet is being utilized to enhance marketing strategies* Many firms actively use the Web in their consumer analysis, product planning, distribution planning, promotion planning, and price planning. Several examples are noted.

5. *To consider the challenges of using the Internet in marketing and to forecast the future of E-marketing* Some challenges are rather uncontrollable (such as dial-up connections) and others are self-inflicted by companies. Attention must be paid to consumer shopping resistance, customer service, system breakdowns, site speed, connection costs, legal issues, privacy issues, spamless communications, clutter, a workable business model, expectations of free services, integrating bricks-and-clicks operations, and global issues.

   In the future, Internet usage will continue growing, with E-marketing being even more essential. Bricks-and-clicks firms will succeed best. High-speed connections will lead to more multimedia-rich Web sites. Business-to-business E-commerce will greatly outstrip business-to-consumer E-commerce. There will be a considerable increase in Internet use outside North America.

Key Terms

Internet (p. 185)

World Wide Web (WWW) (p. 185)

E-marketing (p. 185)

E-commerce (p. 185)

bricks-and-mortar firms (p. 187)

clicks-only firms (p. 187)

bricks-and-clicks firms (p. 187)

mass customization (p. 192)

opt-in (permission-based) E-mail (p. 197)

spam (p. 205)

Review Questions

1. Distinguish between E-marketing and E-commerce.
2. Describe the three phases of E-marketing.
3. What cost efficiencies does the Internet offer for companies that use it properly?
4. What is mass customization? Give an example not mentioned in the chapter.
5. Discuss the six basic steps in developing an Internet marketing strategy.
6. Why is it important for a company to monitor the links, both internal and external, at its Web site?
7. Why is opt-in E-mail gaining in popularity with both companies and Internet users?
8. State four major challenges facing E-marketers.

Discussion Questions

1. What can a firm learn by studying Tables 7-1 and 7-2?
2. Visit your school's Web site. Which of the marketing roles cited in this chapter do you think it is performing? Explain your answer.
3. Develop and explain a five-item survey to use in assessing the design of a Web site.
4. What is your favorite Web site? Why?

Web Exercise

eBay (http://www.ebay.com) is the world's most successful online marketer. Its sales have grown by leaps and bounds, and it is quite profitable. As an auction company, eBay has imposed some very strict rules of behavior—which it updates regularly—for both buyers (http://pages.ebay.com/help/policies/buyer-rules-overview.html) and sellers (http://pages.ebay.com/help/policies/seller-rules-overview.html). What are the most important rules for each party to understand? Why do you think that eBay has such formal policies?

Practice Quiz

1. The basic difference between the Internet and the World Wide Web is that only
   a. the Internet is a self-sustaining system.
   b. through the Web can users see graphics and hear audio.
   c. the Internet is a public system.
   d. through the Web can consumers E-mail each other.

2. A consumer request for information on the Web that is helpful in determining the features of a particular refrigerator model is an example of
   a. Hypertext Transfer Protocol (HTTP).
   b. E-commerce.
   c. E-marketing.
   d. electronic data interchange (EDI).

3. Which of these is the broadest concept?
   a. Electronic data interchange
   b. Bricks-and-mortar
   c. E-marketing
   d. E-commerce

4. Which E-marketing format has recently undergone a major shakeup?
   a. Clicks-only firms
   b. Catalogs
   c. TV shopping
   d. Direct mail

5. Which one of the following is *not necessarily* a benefit for a company using the Internet in marketing?
   a. Low system-maintenance costs
   b. Timeliness
   c. 24/7 operations
   d. Global possibilities

6. Which of these Internet attributes relates to the ability of the Internet to have two-way communication?
   a. Hyperactivity
   b. Connectivity
   c. Globalization
   d. Interactivity

7. Which role of the Internet in marketing is best illustrated by a firm maintaining a list of key customers and their purchasing behavior?
   a. Advertising and sales promotion
   b. Data-base development
   c. Channel relations
   d. Customer service

8. The lot size in mass customization is typically
   a. more than 1,000 units.
   b. 100 units.
   c. 10 units.
   d. 1 unit.

9. Multichannel marketing is practiced by a(n)
   a. clicks-only firm.
   b. bricks-and-mortar firm.
   c. bricks-and-clicks firm.
   d. E-commerce firm.

10. What type of Internet shopper knows what he or she wants before going online and to a specific site to shop?
    a. A frugal shopper
    b. An enthusiastic shopper
    c. A convenience shopper
    d. A strategic shopper

11. Which aspect of a Web site includes such topics as company background, financial performance, and an online shopping cart?
    a. Site content
    b. Web address
    c. Links
    d. Home page

12. An Internet retailer respects a consumer's privacy by
    a. using opt-in E-mail.
    b. selling names to mailing-list brokers.
    c. using spam.
    d. trading names and addresses of customers with noncompeting firms.

13. Computing daily Web site traffic, ratings on customer service surveys, and sales revenues are measures to be used in
    a. making promotion decisions.
    b. assessing performance.
    c. making distribution decisions.
    d. enacting trade-off decisions.

14. Which of these factors should *not* be regularly reviewed in evaluating the quality of a Web site?
    a. Download time
    b. Security
    c. Product prices
    d. Currency

15. The large number of search engines, as well as the number of companies that are now online, contribute to
    a. clutter.
    b. the need to outsource Web decision making.
    c. consumer privacy concerns.
    d. system breakdowns.

For the answers to these questions, please visit the online site for this book at **http://www.atomicdog.com.**

2 Short Cases

Case 1: Is Ambush Marketing Going Too Far?[c2-1]

In "ambush marketing," a competitor attends another firm's marketing events without its approval; the latter intends to fool attendees or viewers into thinking that it is the official sponsor of the events. A representative of the ambush firm typically gains access to an event by purchasing tickets, and then erects signs and distributes fliers and merchandise without permission. Ambush marketing is quite popular for some small brands because they can get valuable exposure to a highly targeted audience at a very low cost.

With "guerilla marketing," public spaces and unsponsored events are used to increase awareness or trial of a brand. For example, Red Bull (http://www.redbullusa.com) uses guerilla marketing by giving students a free case of its beverage if they throw a party featuring the energy drink. A common strategy in guerilla marketing is to bypass security guards by befriending the staff or to use disguises to appear to be an authorized entrant (such as a marketer's being dressed up to resemble a student).

Nike (http://www.nike.com) is another firm that has used ambush marketing. In one instance, Nike's ambush marketing was so effective that 22 percent of British consumers thought Nike was the official sponsor of the World Cup taking place in Japan and Korea—in contrast to the 19 percent who knew it was Adidas (the official sponsor). Nike used ambush marketing at the Atlanta Olympics by purchasing all outdoor poster sites and setting up Nike Village directly next to the official Olympic Sponsors' Village.

According to a partner with Nike's promotion agency, "ambush marketing is merely a clever use of locations. Why would Nike spend nearly $20 million sponsoring the Olympics when it can do better free of charge with ambush marketing? Nike's brand reputation is built on making the most of opportunities and playing at the edge to the rules. There's no gentleman's agreement; it's a competitive world. Why should the rest of the marketing community stand aside and let the sponsor and organizer agree to terms for everybody?"

Official sponsors of events need to protect themselves from ambush marketing. One way is to have an ambush-marketing clause in every event or sponsorship contract. This clause requires the event's organizer to police the event and remove unauthorized personnel. Security guards at a recent Wimbledon tennis tournament confiscated water bottles with prominent labels for Colgate-Palmo-

live's (http://www.colgate.com) Aloe Vera deodorant. The guards' actions were designed to protect the "official water" of the event, Nestlé's (http://www.nestle.com) Buxton, as well as other Wimbledon sponsors. In addition, some marketers withhold a percentage of the sponsorship monies from the organizer. If the antiambush terms of the contract are not properly enforced, these funds may be permanently withheld. Some marketers are also trying to limit the opportunity for ambush marketers by closely examining an event's co-sponsors and refusing to co-sponsor events where a known ambush marketer is a participant.

The concern over ambush advertising is so great that the International Olympic Committee (http://www.olympic.org) has asked those countries bidding to host the Olympics to secure sites close to major events to prevent unauthorized outdoor advertising from being shown on television. One critic of ambush advertising says that "sponsors that see the value of their brand consistently diluted by ambush marketing will offer less money for new contracts."

Some advertising agencies and marketers prohibit the use of ambush marketing in their code of ethics. According to one leading observer, an account executive needs to question, "Is the short-term gain worth your job or your reputation to achieve a quick hit win against another brand manager? How would your stable of clients feel about this approach? Is there any potential for lost business?"

Questions

1. Discuss the ethical concerns regarding ambush marketing.
2. Discuss the ethical concerns regarding guerilla marketing.
3. Develop a plan for Olympic Sponsors' Village to prevent ambush advertising by Nike or other firms.
4. As a partner in a major advertising agency, discuss the pros and cons of engaging in ambush advertising for a major client at your agency.

[c2-1] The data in the case are drawn from Graham Medcalf, "Ambush Marketing: Bang, You're Dead," *New Zealand Marketing Magazine Online* (May 2005); and "Ambush Campaigns: When It Pays to Pounce," *Marketing Week* (July 8, 2005), p. 28.

Case 2: City View Center: From Landfill to Retail Shopping Center[c2-2]

John McGill, a real-estate developer, envisioned a Garfield Heights, Ohio, site as an ideal location for a shopping center. The site has excellent visibility (as it was on a hill overlooking an interstate highway) and a steady flow of car traffic—more than 180,000 cars passed the location daily. The site—at the intersection of I-480 and I-77—is a 15- to 20-minute trip to Cleveland and Akron, as well as the Cleveland Hopkins International Airport. The closest other location with large specialty retailers is 10 miles away. Finally, the site is in Cuyahoga County, the state's most populous county. Garfield Heights alone has a population of 30,000.

Although the site had a lot of potential, it also had more than its share of problems:

- The site was a multicounty regional trash dump from the late 1960s through the early 1970s. In total, the EPA had 31 stipulations for its approval to move the waste that accumulated at the former landfill. McGill worked with both government officials and private consultants to resolve this issue. After an 18-month review process, the Ohio Environmental Protection Agency (EPA) (http://www.epa.state.oh.us) approved moving the buried waste.
- A pile of trash that was moved to make space for the shopping center shifted, forcing the developer to construct a $200,000 retaining wall about 10 feet high and a few hundred feet long, as well as to remove the trash. There was a significant problem with odor when the buried garbage was moved. So, the developer had to use an odor control system to limit the smell.
- The center's foundation required additional reinforcement due to soft ground conditions.
- Site development required approval of the Ohio EPA due to the presence of flammable methane gas. The developer had to construct pipes and fans to rid the area of the gas.
- The site had been zoned for office space—not retail—and the former owner wanted to have the property developed as an office complex. This caused the approval process to be even more time consuming. The developer calculates that these problems added $25 per square foot to the center's total costs.

That works out to an additional $16,250,000 on a $70-million project.

Getting around the construction and zoning difficulties, as well as attracting suitable tenants, was a challenge. What made the project doable was the significant experience of the developer. McGill Property, which was founded in 1998 as Heritage Development Company, has built 11 shopping centers. (The company changed its name to McGill Property in August 2004.) It also required a developer with considerable vision, as well as determination. According to John McGill, "I needed to know whether this was a dream that made sense, or if it's something we'd never accomplish." To encourage development of the eyesore, Garfield Heights rezoned the land for retail use. The city also spent $10 million and made necessary improvements in access roads and in utility improvements.

City View Center is now a 650,000-square-foot shopping center on 95 acres with such major tenants as Bed Bath & Beyond, Giant Eagle, Circuit City, Office Max, Dick's Sporting Goods, and Wal-Mart. Plans are also in effect to build about 1 million square feet of office buildings nearby. The retail site is expected to bring in $6 million in property taxes and another $6.4 million in income taxes each year to Garfield Heights. In a city with a general budget of $43 million, these funds are significant. As John McGill says, "we're taking a pile of trash and making it into a treasure for the [area]."

Questions

1. For a developer, describe the pros and cons of reclaiming a site such as the one described in this case versus using a traditional site for a large shopping center.
2. Discuss the additional costs associated with claiming a site from either a landfill or a polluted location.
3. Discuss the practice of reclaiming a site from the perspective of social responsibility.
4. Explain the pros and cons of situating in a reclaimed location from the perspective of a major retail tenant.

[c2-2] The data in the case are drawn from Pat Salemi, "EPA OKs City View," *Sun Newspapers Online* (March 24, 2005); Patrick A. O'Donnell and John C. Kuehner, "Garfield Heights Shopping Center Plans Shift Slightly; Slipping Mound of Trash Will Have to Be Walled Off," *The Plain Dealer* (June 8, 2004), p. B3; and Ian Ritter, "Trash Removal," *Shopping Centers Today* (December 2004), pp. 99–100.

Case 3: American Entrepreneurs Create Fortunes in China[c2-3]

Barrett Comiskey, a Stamford MBA, and his business partner, Andy Mulkerin, a Harvard MBA, have established a company in China for U.S. firms that seek to outsource production to China. Unlike other similar firms, they plan to develop deals with U.S. firms that seek to make nontraditional products in China, such as vending machines and hearing aids.

Although China is now the world's second largest economy (behind the United States) and growing quickly, American entrepreneurs such as Comiskey and Mulkerin need to better understand how to overcome the difficulties associated with doing business there. One reporter put it thusly: "The place is commonly regarded as a mausoleum for the broken dreams of fresh-faced foreign entrepreneurs like Comiskey and Mulkerin—people who caught China fever only to be laid low by the country's impenetrable business culture, its barbed-wire bureaucracy, its endemic corruption."

Even large sophisticated firms with significant experience in global markets have found success to be elusive in China. Pepsi's Chinese operations have never been profitable over its 20-year history. Kraft lost money in a cheese operation there. And Amazon.com, which purchased a Chinese online bookseller in 2004, has warned its investors that success is "many years" away.

Here are five tips for American entrepreneurs aiming to be successful in China:

1. *Court powerful partners, but get out of their way:* Derek Sulger left his job as a Goldman Sachs investment banker to form Linktone, a firm specializing in selling ring-tones and other content to Chinese consumers. Sulger and his American business partner quickly hired Chinese locals who were knowledgeable in local business practices and had strong business contacts. A critical factor in Linktone's success was selling its services to China Mobile's regional divisions before selling to China Mobile's national operations. When Linktone went public in 2004, Sulger's stake was worth about $30 million.

2. *Go native, but think different:* Peter Loehr, a New Yorker, has single-handedly produced the top-three native-language films of all time in China. Loehr's business success is due in large part to his recognizing the value of getting proper distribution for his films. He was also first to promote a film in China using television, radio, and bus billboards.

3. *Try to get rich quick, but prepare to put in the time:* Chris Barclay, an American, had several business failures in China before establishing his current firm in 1995. This company offers management training to Chinese employees of multinational firms such as Adidas, Coca-Cola, and Sun Microsystems. Barclay also owns a resort. The two ventures earn a 20 percent profit rate on sales.

4. *Feel free to change the world, but don't think you can change China:* Terry Rhoads, an Oregon native, was sent to China by Nike to run its marketing operations in 1994. He subsequently started his own company, Zou Marketing, with another former Nike employee. Zou is now China's leading sports marketing firm, with annual revenues of $5 million. According to Rhoads, being pragmatic is essential for doing business in China. Although he is concerned about China's treatment of its athletes, he realizes that he needs to work closely with the Chinese government and does not want to spoil his good relationship.

5. *Focus not on America's cultural values, but on the value of its culture:* Andrew Ballen dropped out of Duke University's law school and went to China. He now operates a weekly hip-hop show in Shanghai. He pays a flat fee for renting out the club and then keeps the $4 admission fee, as well as part of the liquor bill. In four years, his business has grossed close to $2 million.

Questions

1. Comment on the five tips described in this case.
2. Describe the pros and cons of American entrepreneurs using joint ventures with Chinese partners.
3. Evaluate the use of straight extension versus backward invention in marketing U.S.-made products in China.
4. List and discuss the factors to consider in price planning in the Chinese market.

[c2-3] The data in the case are drawn from G. Pascal Zachary, "Making It in China," *Business 2.0* (August 2005), pp. 59–64, 66.

Case 4: The Boom in Online Ticket Sales[c2-4]

According to one estimate, in Great Britain, advance ticket sales for music and sports events generate $2.5 billion in annual revenues. Several firms, such as Clear Channel (http://www.clearchannel.com), Emap (http://www.emap.com), Ticketmaster (http://www.ticketmaster.com), and See Tickets (http://www.seetickets.com), have each invested in developing online ticket sales there.

One of the largest British ventures is Emap's Aloud.com (http://www.aloud.com), with 5 million impressions a month and 750,000 opt-in registered users. Emap generates traffic and provides content for its site, and deals directly with all major promoters. The promoters provide back-end support functions such as handling credit card purchases and ticket delivery support. Revenues for purchases on Aloud.com are split among a number of parties. According to Aloud.com, "Usually, the face value of the ticket price is split between the artist, venue, and promoter." A 10 to 15 percent booking fee is added to the face value of the ticket price as a service charge, and a delivery charge is also added. The credit card company and the online ticketing company also take a percentage of the ticket sales.

Another major online ticket provider in Great Britain is getLIVE.co.uk (http://www.getlive.co.uk), a partnership of Clear Channel and Ticketmaster. getLIVE covers live music events ranging from heavy metal to jazz. Under the partnership agreement, Ticketmaster handles such back-end support functions as processing credit card receipts and mailing tickets to customers. Ticketmaster was launched in Great Britain in 1981 and acquired TicketWeb, an Internet-based ticketing software and services firm, in 1998.

In addition to the large online ticketing firms such as Aloud.com and getLIVE, smaller firms such as eFestivals specialize in ticketing for festivals. As that firm's founder says, "Fans come on to the site to see what the line-up is for festivals and there are easy links for them to buy tickets. This way, tickets are just a click away from news about the festival."

Many events allow consumers to use multiple channels to purchase tickets. For example, an event can use its own box office for ticketing and also allow online and telephone sales through its ticketing agency: "If people are at school, college, or work and want to buy a ticket, then having so many different ways of buying them can only be a good thing."

A number of benefits are associated with the use of online ticketing, for both customers and promoters. Customers have 24/7 access to ticketing, can more easily compare seating and pricing alternatives, and can avoid waiting in long lines for tickets (and then finding themselves sold out of a show). Promoters benefit from their events being more available to a larger audience, faster transaction times, access to the customer data bases the agencies hold, and outsourcing of back-end functions. Online sales are also an effective medium for selling all of a show's tickets: "Where online ticketing really helps is for shows with 1,000 seats, where 990 of the tickets are guaranteed to be sold. It is those last 10 that are the hardest to sell and where an online presence really makes a difference."

Questions

1. What are the opportunities for outsourcing in the music and sports event ticketing business?
2. How can a music and sports event marketer overcome the resistance to online shopping for tickets?
3. Discuss how music and sports events marketers can utilize multichannel marketing.
4. Describe the pros and cons the use of multichannel retailing by a music and sports event marketer.

[c2-4] The data in the case are drawn from "Ticketing Boom Clicks into Place," *Music Week* (July 16, 2005), pp. 9–11.

Enhancing Business Ethics Through Transparency[pc-2]

INTRODUCTION

Herbert M. Baum's career in corporate America is drawing to a close, and the turnaround specialist has some words of advice for those who follow. With contretemps like Enron, MCI WorldCom, Adelphia Communications, and Martha Stewart, it's been a tough century for executive integrity. Corporate chiefs appear more likely to be disciples of Gordon Gekko (of the movie *Wall Street*) than Mr. Rogers (of *Mr. Rogers' Neighborhood*). Was Leo Durocher, the old-time baseball manager, right?—"Do nice guys finish last?" Herb Baum doesn't think so.

Baum is the author of *The Transparent Leader: How to Build a Great Company Through Straight Talk, Openness, and Accountability* (HarperCollins, 2004). In his view, corporate ethics isn't an oxymoron, it's a redundancy. "A self-described goody two-shoes," Baum argues that honesty and openness are not outmoded values but essential elements of a successful organization. It is the corporate leader's responsibility to create a culture that embraces, and even requires, ethical behavior.

Baum also is president and CEO of Dial Corp. (http://www.dialcorp.com), a $1.4 billion consumer packaged goods firm based in Scottsdale, Arizona. A mid-tier player in four business lines—personal cleansing (Dial, Coast), laundry care (Purex, Zout), canned meats (Armour), and air fresheners (Renuzit)—Dial was laden with debt and saddled with poor acquisitions in mid-2000 when Dial's board of directors ousted former CEO Malcolm Jozoff. The directors didn't look far to find a replacement: Baum had been a board member for three years. He also had reversed the fading fortunes of Quaker State (http://www.quakerstate.com) in the 1990s.

The recipe at Dial called for debt reduction, divestiture of underperforming businesses, and a search for a "white knight" with the capital to enable Dial to compete with multibillion-dollar competitors. With Dial's March 2004 acquisition by Dusseldorf, Germany-based Henkel KGaA (http://www.henkel.com), the final reorganization objective was met.

Baum energized Dial with the leadership style he calls transparency. A premium was placed on diversity in the workforce, a focus that has won Dial recognition by groups promoting women and minorities in business. Product innovation was championed in a variety of programs that spurred a doubling of patent filings and 96 innovations in packaging, formulations, and new products in 2004 alone. And a nine-point cultural contract emphasizing ethical behavior, initiative, and respect for all was drafted and embraced.

Baum is winding down half of a century in corporate America. Before returning the keys to the executive washroom, he wanted to leave a book he describes as a cry for a level playing field. *The Transparent Leader* likely will wind up on university reading lists as a teaching tool for tomorrow's business leaders.

Here are the highlights of a recent question-and-answer (Q & A) session between Kevin Higgins, a respected marketing journalist, and Herb Baum.

HERB BAUM: AN EXECUTIVE STAR

Herbert M. Baum is a native of Chicago, where he also began his professional career after graduating with a B.S. degree in business administration from Drake University in Des Moines, Iowa. He spent his first 20 years working in advertising and public relations, beginning with Aaron Cushman and Associates and including stops at Doyle Dane Bernbach and Needham, Harper & Steers. Baum made the transition to the client side in 1978 when he joined Campbell Soup (http://www.campbellsoup.com). He held a number of positions there and was named executive vice-president and acting co-chief executive in 1989. Baum left the food manufacturer to become chairman and chief executive of Quaker State in 1993. He then became president and chief operating officer of toy maker Hasbro (http://www.hasbro.com), before assuming the position of president and chief executive of Dial Corp. in August 2000.

Aside from duties at Dial, Baum serves on four corporate boards: bottler PepsiAmericas (http://www.pepsiamericas.com), publisher Meredith Corp. (http://www.meredith.com), America West Airlines (http://www.americawest.com), and Action Performance Companies (http://www.action-performance.com), a marketer of motor sports merchandise. He is a former board chairman of the Advertising Council, the National Food Processors Association, the Association of National Advertisers, and National Hispanic University. He received the Charles Coolidge Parlin Award from the American Marketing Association in 1992 and was elected to the Sales and Marketing Executives International Hall of Fame in 1998.

A Q & A WITH HERB BAUM

Q: "What is transparency?"
A: "For me, transparency is always telling the truth, being honest and open about how you run your life and business, and 'fessing up when you make mistakes."

[pc-2] Adapted by the authors from Kevin T. Higgins, "A Transparent Legacy," *Marketing Management* (March-April 2005), pp. 18–21. Reprinted by permission of the American Marketing Association.

Q: "How has the book been received?"

A: "You never get comments from people who hate your book. I don't know if there's a group of executives who say: 'That's nice, but it's not how the game is played.' The book is on some business bestseller lists, though I didn't do it for personal gain: I just wanted to tell it like it is. The publisher's advance went to the Juvenile Diabetes Research Foundation (http://www.jdf.org), and any royalties will go to my co-author, Tammy Kling."

Q: "You quote Grantland Rice as saying, 'It's not whether you win or lose but how you play the game.' Vince Lombardi gave us: 'Winning isn't everything, it's the only thing.' Which attitude prevails in corporate America?"

A: "Both. Winning is a value, but you want to do it in an honest and ethical way. I think that's the prevailing view in business. While a few bad apples have polluted the corporate environment and have been caught doing the wrong thing, the great bulk of corporate leadership is very open, honest, and ethical about running businesses."

Q: "Would it be fair to describe the philosophy of transparency as doing well by doing right?

A: "I don't know if I would agree with that. You want to be socially correct in the way you run your business, but at the end of the day, you have to deliver for your shareholders or you won't be in business. We regularly poll our employees on their perceptions of Dial. The highest attributes are that we are honest and we have diversity."

Q: "You write about 'the fine line between what is ethical and what's transparent.' What is that line?"

A: "There are some great businesspeople out there with outstanding reputations, but you wonder if, when push comes to shove, do they cut corners to achieve their objectives? Procter & Gamble [P&G, http://www.pg.com] invented the Swiffer cleaning system. Besides marketing its own Swiffer products, P&G licenses technology to other companies, including Clorox [http://www.clorox.com], which markets ReadyMop. When I was in Wal-Mart last Saturday, I noticed P&G makes a refill that fits the ReadyMop. P&G is collecting a royalty from Clorox, yet it also is competing with Clorox on refills. Is that really ethical? I think P&G is a very ethical company, but sometimes people do questionable things."

Q: "You're very critical of executive compensation. How likely is a moderation in CEO pay packages?"

A: "Audit committees have been under fire. The next big drive is going to be against the compensation committees of boards of directors because, as CEOs, we all make too much money. Some of the paychecks are outrageous. With the federal rules requiring expensing of stock options, that aspect of compensation is going to be reined in. Reducing the use of stock options is one way of putting a lid on corporate compensation. New York's Attorney General launched prosecutions that exhibit almost a need for vengeance. Absolutely, executive compensation needs to be addressed."

Q: "You criticize former American Airlines' (http://www.aa.com) CEO Don Carty of lack of transparency for accepting a retention bonus triple his base salary after winning $1.8 billion in employee wage concessions, then say the bonus could have been explained and justified. What justification exists?"

A: "He was running one of the biggest airlines in the world and probably making less than his counterpart at United Airlines [http://www.united.com]. Anybody who knows Don Carty knows he just missed an opportunity to be transparent. If he had been open and honest, the outcome would have been different. [A week later, American's board dumped Carty.] Granted, if he had been transparent, it would have been unlikely employees would have agreed to the wage cuts. Employee givebacks are very bothersome, but if workers understand that the company has to make a profit or go out of business, they will accept them. Airlines don't control the price of fuel and employee wages are the only place they can effect savings. It's an enigma: Some airlines have taken advantage of the situation to win concessions that weren't needed."

Q: "The CEO salary skew isn't just with the people who do the heavy lifting; it also exists with foreign counterparts. With global companies as likely to be based in Germany as America, how will those CEOs react to U.S. subordinates receiving salaries that, on average, are triple their pay?"

A: "It will certainly help temper the compensation packages. I don't think you'll see a rollback, however. In the case of Dial, if the new owners were to say, 'We've got to establish base compensation packages that are close to what counterparts in Germany make,' Dial would lose people to P&G, Unilever [http://www.unilever.com], and Colgate [http://www.colgate.com]. European perks are never mentioned in comparisons. At Henkel, most top managers have a driver and a company car that's a Mercedes. Other than salespeople, I'm the only employee at Dial with a company car. I choose to drive a VW Beetle, and that means something to the people at Dial."

Q: "You were on Dial's board when the previous CEO was dismissed. Was a lack of transparency a factor?"

A: "Malcolm Jozoff had a 25-year background at P&G and was very successful when he first came to Dial. Then he came up against some big numbers, made some bad acquisitions, and began to load dealers with product to meet short-term sales goals. He also acted opaquely instead of transparently. Employees revolted, and the board ousted him."

Q: "In your second year as CEO, Dial posted a net loss of $132 million. Did critics suggest transparency meant the emperor had no clothes?"

A: "We were very open about how that loss was generated; and in fact, the turnaround outlined in SFX '01 already was well under way. The losses in 2001 were attributable to the sale for pennies on the dollar of bad businesses the previous CEO had bought. A company that Dial paid $200 million to acquire was sold for $6 million. SFX '01 was something I came up with in the shower. It stood for Stabilize good businesses, Fix or jettison the bad, and X meant exploring our options, including finding a buyer for the corporation. When I took over, Dial's shares were selling for $9. Henkel paid $28.75."

Q: "America is hemorrhaging manufacturing jobs. To what degree do corporations move offshore to reduce labor costs and escape worker-safety rules and environmental regulations?"

A: "I would say that is the exception. If you're going to be corporately responsible, you're not going to want to put people out of work just to be the lowest cost operator and have a skeleton staff in the United States. In my five years at Dial, we did not have a layoff. Labor is only 4 to 5 percent of our costs. If companies try to reduce the cost of labor, they typically take away people at the bottom and leave fat salaries at the top. If we were to have a layoff, I would start at the top."

Q: "What impact will the Henkel acquisition have on Dial's marketing strategy?"

A: "It makes us a stronger company in our core businesses. When I became CEO, I realized we needed to be part of a company with greater resources because of the difficulty of competing with very well financed organizations. When we were seeking a buyer, the No. 1 goal was to keep people's jobs. As a result, we soon cut off talks with U.S. buyers, since they were only interested in acquiring our brands. Henkel needed Dial to build its U.S. business. It's the P&G of Europe. We'll take Henkel technology and bring products in under Dial brands for sale here. If it has a glass cleaner that's a great product, we might bring it in under the Purex brand. Henkel's a believer in consumer marketing and we have a value brand company that doesn't do much advertising. We have to convince Henkel that our approach is the way to make money."

Q: "Wal-Mart forced a 17 percent cut in Purex's retail price when it dropped private-label detergent, but Tide's price was unaffected. Wouldn't you be better off with a premium brand position?"

A: "Value brands are the fastest-growing part of the detergent category. P&G spends jillions on advertising for Tide, which is the market leader. We spend nothing on Purex, and we're No. 2. We're about 80 percent of Tide's efficacy at 50 percent of the price. It's possible we'll get into the premium end of the market with some of the Henkel products, but value brands can be very profitable."

Q: "Product innovation has been a priority during your tenure. Has it produced any hits?"

A: "We've done a really good job of generating concepts in the lab but a poor job of executing successful rollouts. We've upgraded our talent, and we're getting better at innovation, but I'm still waiting for the first breakthrough that puts points on the board. One of the first changes I made was to rename the R&D lab the Dial Innovation Center. Our researchers were working on 158 projects, which was simply too much. I told them to limit themselves to three at a time, and each researcher had to come up with two patentable ideas a year. Most manufacturers develop new products based on what they can make, not what consumers want. P&G is a great example of a company that develops products based on what consumers want, and it still does it better than anyone else. The great majority of our managers now are former P&Gers."

Q: "You've reached out to independent inventors with programs like Quest for the Best, which generated thousands of proposals and 10 finalists at a Dial new-product expo. How are those projects panning out?"

A: "It's been very exciting and a highlight of my time here. I'm almost sure the product that finished first in last year's Quest for the Best, a reusable fabric-softener packet, will make it to market. We also encourage employees to submit ideas. We used to stage an inventors' night at Hasbro, and I brought that idea here. Most new toys come from outside the companies in the industry. If we bring any of these products to market, we pay a royalty to the inventors."

Q: "You tell the story of watching shoppers sniffing bottles of detergent at Wal-Mart before buying, a discovery that led to many new scents for Purex. Is trench research part of the transparent leader's duties?"

A: "I just enjoy watching people and how they interact with products, not just products in our categories but those where we have an interest. Lately, I've been spending a lot of time in the insecticide section. Dial is likely to get the Combat line from Henkel. Buyers of insecticide are extraordinary label readers; if the pest they're trying to eliminate isn't prominently cited, they'll read the entire can to see if it's mentioned."

Q: " 'Marketing is the world' is one of your seven principles of a better business life. What do you mean?"

A: "When you ask your wife to marry you, you're marketing yourself. Marketing is my whole life. I was touring a Costco [http://www.costco.com] store with CEO Jim Sinegal. Purex is not in Costco. He was trying to be nice and asked me if I'd like to see Purex in his stores. I said no. The market for Purex is more the Wal-Mart customer, not the Costco customer. Marketing isn't about trying to sell people. You shouldn't try to sell your product to people who don't need or want it."

Q: "You became CEO in 2000, and the board extended your contract to 2006. Why are you violating your five-years-and-out rule for CEOs?"

A: "I became CEO in August 2000, and I will retire as soon as I find my successor. The Henkel people are terrific, but having been a CEO, it's tough to work for someone. Besides, people get stale. Whenever you get fresh blood in the CEO's office, you see an uptick in the organization's performance. The tough part is sustaining it."

Questions

1. Do you think that Herbert M. Baum would have articulated his ethical beliefs as forcefully if he planned on remaining active as a corporate leader? Explain your answer.
2. What should Baum's ethical responsibilities be for the corporate boards on which he sits?
3. What is a "transparent" leader?
4. Can "transparency" be a differential advantage? Should it be? Explain your answers.
5. Why don't more companies practice transparency? What are the risks they face?
6. Why do you think that American business ethics differ from those in other countries?
7. What universal ethical marketing standards should companies apply around the globe?

Consumer Analysis: Understanding and Responding to Diversity in the Marketplace

In Part 3, we see why consumer analysis is essential and discuss consumer characteristics, needs, profiles, and decision making—and how firms can devise marketing plans responsive to today's diverse global marketplace.

8 Final Consumers

This chapter is devoted to final consumer demographics, lifestyles, and decision making. We examine several specific demographics (objective and quantifiable characteristics that describe the population) for the United States and other countries around the globe. By studying final consumer lifestyles and decision making, we can learn about why and how consumers act as they do. Lifestyles encompass various social and psychological factors, many of which we note here. The decision process involves the steps performed as consumers move from stimulus to purchase or nonpurchase.

9 Organizational Consumers

Here, we focus on organizations purchasing goods and services for further production, use in operations, or resale to other consumers—business-to-business marketing. We look at how they differ from final consumers and at their individual characteristics, buying goals, buying structure, constraints on purchases, and decision process.

10 Developing a Target Market Strategy

We now discuss how to plan a target market strategy. Consumer-demand patterns and segmentation bases are examined; and undifferentiated marketing, concentrated marketing, and differentiated marketing are explained and contrasted. The requirements for successful segmentation and the importance of positioning are also considered. We conclude with a discussion of sales forecasting.

After reading Part 3, you should understand element 9 of the strategic marketing plan outlined in Table 3-2 (page 77).

Chapter 8

Final Consumers

Nestlé (**http://www.nestle.com**) is the world's largest food manufacturer. Its Nescafé coffee brand, Perrier bottled water, and Ralston Purina pet foods are the market-share leaders in their respective product categories. Nestlé has traditionally been a global marketer. As early as 1875, it sold its products in 16 countries. Popular globally-based Nestlé brands include Buitoni, Friskies, Magi, and Nestea.

Chocolate has always been vital to Nestlé. The firm began selling chocolate in 1904, and in 1920, it purchased Cailler (the first firm to mass produce chocolate bars) and Swiss General (the inventor of milk chocolate). Nestlé developed its Nestlé Crunch bar in 1938 and it purchased the Butterfinger and Baby Ruth candy brands in the 1990s. Nestlé's chocolate products comprise almost 10 percent of its sales.

To increase its market share in the chocolate business, Nestlé is carefully monitoring the sales of candies to diabetics and the marketing of chocolates to adults. In a sponsorship arrangement with the American Diabetes Association (ADA), the ADA sends information on certain Nestlé products to ADA members and others who seek out dietary advice. Nestlé has also arranged to reduce the sugar content of some of its products to better meet the dietary needs of diabetics. Nestlé's "Carb Select" Crunch bar has no sugar and fewer calories than the regular bar. Reduced-sugar products also appeal to consumers who wish to reduce their carbohydrates through Atkins or South Beach diets. In recognition of the importance of the diabetics market, Hershey Foods has also recently introduced a line of sugar-free chocolates.

Nestlé is shifting more of its chocolate and confectionery advertising from children to adults. Like other chocolate and confectionery manufacturers, Nestlé is increasingly aware that a large portion of its target market consists of adults who either consume the products themselves or who purchase chocolate candy for their children. For example, when a spokesperson for Nestlé was asked who the target market for Baby Ruth chocolate candy bars was, her response was "Definitely adult men." Other chocolate and confection manufacturers report that women aged 18 to 45 years are their key buyers.[1]

In this chapter, we will explore several key consumer demographic and lifestyle trends, as well as the marketing implications of the trends. This will enable us to pinpoint market needs, reasons for purchases, changing lifestyles, and purchase patterns among adult consumers and other market segments.

Chapter Objectives

1. To show the importance and scope of consumer analysis
2. To define and enumerate important consumer demographics for the U.S. population and other countries
3. To show why consumer demographic analysis is not sufficient in planning marketing strategies
4. To define and describe consumer lifestyles and their characteristics, examine selected lifestyles, and consider the limitations of consumer lifestyle analysis
5. To define and describe the final consumer's decision process and consider the limitations of final consumer decision-making analysis

---

[1] Various company and other sources.

8-1 OVERVIEW

The consumer is the central focus of marketing, as discussed in Chapters 1 and 2. To devise good marketing plans, it is essential to study consumer attributes and needs, lifestyles, and purchase processes, and then make proper marketing-mix decisions.

The scope of consumer analysis includes the study of *who* buys, *what* they buy, *why* they buy, *how* they make decisions to buy, *when* they buy, *where* they buy, and *how often* they buy.[2] For example, we might study a college student (who) buying textbooks (what) that are required for various classes (why). The student looks up the book list at the school store and decides whether to buy new or used books for each course (how). Just before the first week of classes (when), the student goes to the school store or online to buy the books (where). This is done three times per year—fall, spring, and summer (how often).

In today's diverse global marketplace, an open-minded, consumer-oriented approach is imperative so a firm can identify and serve its target market, minimize dissatisfaction, and stay ahead of competitors. Why is this important? "If we make customers feel that they are special and unique, we stand a better chance both of retaining their loyalty when they next make a buying decision and of gaining new business through word of mouth and recommendation."[3] See Figure 8-1.

In Chapters 8 to 10, we cover the concepts needed to understand consumers in the United States and other nations, to select target markets, and to relate marketing strategy to consumer behavior. Chapter 8 examines final consumer demographics, lifestyles, and

Figure 8-1

Creatively Appealing to the Customer of Today

Consumers are now more discriminating than ever before. They want superior quality—and a great value (in this case, a free phone), as Sprint (**http://www.sprint.com**) realizes.

Source: Reprinted by permission of Susan Berry, Retail Image Consulting, Inc.

---

[2] Adapted from Leon G. Schiffman and Leslie Lazar Kanuk, *Consumer Behavior*, 8th ed. (Upper Saddle River, N.J: Prentice-Hall, 2004), p. 5.

[3] "Getting Intimate with Customers," **http://www.marketing-magic.biz/archives/archive-marketing/getting-intimate-with-customers.htm** (March 21, 2006).

Final consumers buy for personal, family, or household use; **organizational consumers** buy for production, operations, or resale.

decision making. *Final consumers* buy goods and services for personal, family, or household use. Chapter 9 looks at *organizational consumers*, those buying goods and services for further production, usage in operating the organization, or resale to other consumers. Chapter 10 explains how to devise a target market strategy and use sales forecasts.

8-2 DEMOGRAPHICS DEFINED AND ENUMERATED[4]

Consumer demographics are easily identifiable and measurable.

Consumer demographics are objective and quantifiable population characteristics. They are rather easy to identify, collect, measure, and analyze—and show diversity around the globe. The demographics we discuss here are population size, gender, and age; location, housing, and mobility; income and expenditures; occupations and education; marital status; and ethnicity/race. After studying single factors, a firm can form a consumer demographic profile—a demographic composite of a consumer group. See Figure 8-2. By creating profiles, a firm can pinpoint both opportunities and potential problems.

Several secondary sources offer data on demographics. For U.S. demographics, a key resource is the U.S. Bureau of the Census (**http://www.census.gov**), a federal government agency with considerable national, state, and local data via printed reports, computer tapes, microfiche, CDs, and online data bases. Its American FactFinder Web site (**http://www.factfinder.census.gov**) is quite useful. Many marketing research firms and state data centers arrange census data by ZIP code, make forecasts, and update data. Because complete *Census of Population* data are gathered only once a decade, they must be supplemented by Bureau of the Census estimates (**http://www.census.gov/popest/estimates.php**) and statistics from chambers of commerce, public utilities, and others.

About.com has a section of its Web site (**http://http://geography.about.com/cs/uspopulation**) devoted to "U.S. Population, Census, & Demographics." The annual *Survey of Buying Power* (**http://www.cluster2.claritas.com/MySBP/Default.jsp**) has

Figure 8-2

Factors Determining a Consumer's Demographic Profile

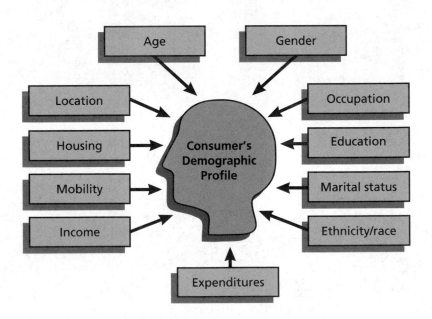

[4] Unless otherwise indicated, the data presented in this chapter are all from the U.S. Bureau of the Census (various publications); the U.S. Bureau of Labor Statistics; the United Nations (various publications); the Organization for Economic Cooperation and Development (various publications); the *CIA World Factbook,* **http://www.odci.gov/cia/publications/factbook** (August 30, 2005); "2005 World Population Data Sheet of the Population Data Sheet," **http://www.prb.org/pdf05/05WorldDataSheet_Eng.pdf**; and authors' estimates and extrapolations.

current U.S. data by metropolitan area and state, including retail sales, income, and five-year estimates. Other valuable U.S. sources are *Editor & Publisher Market Guide* (**http://www.editorandpublisher.com**), *Rand McNally Commercial Atlas & Marketing Guide* (**http://www.randmcnally.com**), *Standard Rate & Data Service* (**http://www.srds.com**), local newspapers, and regional planning boards.

The United Nations (**http://www.un.org**), Euromonitor (**http://www.euromonitor.com**), Organization for Economic Cooperation and Development (**http://www.oecd.org**), and Population Reference Bureau (**http://www.prb.org**) are four excellent sources for international demographics. The UN publishes a *Statistical Yearbook* and numerous other population studies. Euromonitor publishes *International Marketing Data and Statistics*. OECD issues demographic and economic reports on an ongoing basis. The Population Reference Bureau publishes an annual *World Population Data Sheet*. In highly industrialized nations, demographic data are pretty accurate because actual data are regularly collected. In less-developed and developing nations, demographic data are often based on estimates rather than actual data because such data are apt to be collected on an irregular basis.

Information is provided throughout the chapter on both U.S. and worldwide demographics. A broad cross-section of country examples is provided to give a good sense of the diversity around the globe.

8-2a   Population Size, Gender, and Age

The world population is expected to go from 6.45 billion in 2005 to 7.2 billion in 2015, an annual rise of 1.1 percent. Over the same period, the U.S. population will rise from 297 million to 322 million, an annual rise of less than 0.9 percent. The U.S. population will drop from 4.6 percent of world population in 2005 to 4.4 percent in 2015. Figure 8-3 shows world population by region for 2005 and 2015.

Newborns are less than 2 percent of the population (1.4 percent in the United States) in industrialized nations—compared with up to 4 to 5 percent or more in nations such as Afghanistan and the Congo. For the industrialized countries, a large proportion of the births are firstborns.

Males and females comprise equal percentages of the worldwide population. Yet, in many industrialized nations, females are over one-half of the population—mostly due to differences in life expectancy. For newborn females, it is 84 years in Canada, 83 in Italy, 81 in the United States, and 65 in India; it is 77 years for newborn males in Canada, 77 in Italy, 75 in the United States, and 64 in India.

The populations in industrialized nations are older than in less-developed and developing nations. Today, the portion of the population age 14 and under is 14 percent in Italy, 14 percent in Japan, 18 percent in Great Britain, 21 percent in the United States, 21 percent in China, 26 percent in Brazil, 31 percent in Mexico, and 42 percent in Nigeria.

8-2b   Location, Housing, and Mobility

Over the last century, a major move of the world population to large urban areas and surrounding suburbs has taken place. As of 2006, 25 cities and their suburbs had at least 10 million residents each—led by Tokyo and Mexico City. Today, about 80 percent of the U.S. population resides in cities and their suburbs. But, the level of urbanization varies greatly by country. It is 41 percent in China, 34 percent in Pakistan, 19 percent in Laos, and 14 percent in Nepal.

> The world is becoming more urban.

In many parts of the world, the majority of people own the homes in which they reside. Here are some examples: Bangladesh, Finland, Greece, New Zealand, Paraguay, Sri Lanka, and the United States.

The worldwide mobility of the population is high; annually, millions of people emigrate from one nation to another and hundreds of millions move within their nations. Since 1990, roughly 17 million people have legally emigrated to the United States. Overall, nearly one-eighth of those living in the United States were born elsewhere.

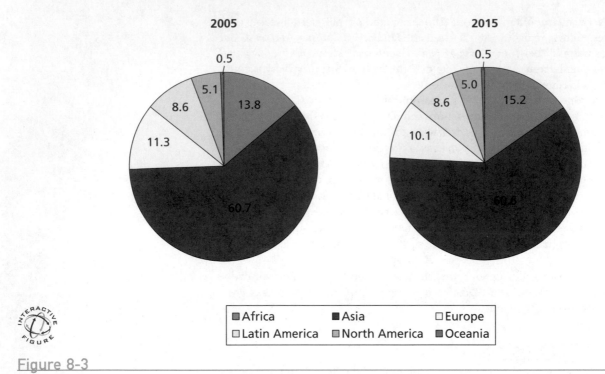

Figure 8-3

The World's Population Distribution, 2005 and 2015

Source: U.S. Bureau of the Census, International Data Base.

Among U.S. residents, about 15 percent of all people move yearly—60 percent within the same county, 80 percent within the same state, and 90 percent within the same region; only 10 percent of moves are to a new region or abroad. Recently, the greatest U.S. population growth has been in Mountain, Pacific, South Atlantic, and Southwest areas.

8-2c   Income and Expenditures

Consumer income and expenditure patterns are valuable demographic factors when properly studied. These points should be kept in mind when examining them:

- Personal income is often stated as GDP per capita—the total value of goods and services produced in a nation divided by population size. This does not report what people really earn, and it inflates per-capita income if a small portion of the population is affluent. A better measure is median income—the income for those at the 50th percentile in a nation; it is a true midpoint. Yet, median incomes are rarely reported outside the United States.
- Personal income can be expressed as family, household, and per capita. Because families are larger than households and per-capita income is on an individual basis, these units are not directly comparable. Income can also be stated in pre-tax or after-tax terms, which are not directly comparable.
- Because prices differ by country, a comparison of average incomes that does not take purchasing power into effect will be inaccurate.
- Economic growth is cyclical. And at any given time, some economies will perform well while others struggle.
- Although the term "poverty" varies greatly by nation, more than 1 billion people in the world are characterized by malnutrition, illiteracy, and disease.

In 2005, the U.S. median household income was between $44,000 and $45,000 (and mean household income was nearly $60,000). Yet, even though the mean income for the top one-fifth of households was $150,000, and 40 percent of U.S. households had incomes of $60,000 or more, the bottom one-fifth accounted for under 3.5 percent of all household income—and 13 percent of U.S. households were at the poverty level. The United States has one of the greatest spreads between high-income and low-income households of any industrialized nation in the world. Furthermore, in terms of purchasing power, U.S. median household income has risen only slightly over the last 25 years.

The slow growth in real U.S. income (after taking inflation into account) has occurred because the increases in household income have been virtually offset by increases in prices. The price increases have led to a higher *cost of living*, the total amount consumers annually pay for goods and services. Over the last 25 years, the greatest price increases have been for medical care, tuition, auto insurance, and tobacco items; the smallest have been for phone services, apparel, video and audio products, and computers.

> Changes in the **cost of living** are measured by a consumer price index.

Many nations monitor their cost of living via a *consumer price index (CPI)*, which measures monthly and yearly price changes (the rate of inflation) for a broad range of consumer goods and services. Since 1983, the overall annual rise in the U.S. CPI (**http://www.bls.gov/cpi/home.htm**) has been less than 5 percent (except for 1990, when it rose by 5.5 percent). In 2005, the CPI rose by 5 percent or less in many countries around the world; it was about 4 percent in the United States.

Global consumption patterns have been shifting. In industrialized nations, the proportion of income that people spend on food, beverages, and tobacco has been declining. The percentage spent on medical care (including insurance), personal business, and recreation has been rising. In less-developed and developing nations, the percentage of spending devoted to food remains high. Americans spend 15 percent of income on food, beverages, and tobacco, while Pakistanis spend nearly one-half of their income on food, beverages, and tobacco.

Disposable income is a person's, household's, or family's total after-tax income to be used for spending and/or savings. *Discretionary income* is what a person, household, or family has available to spend on luxuries after necessities are bought. Classifying some product categories as necessities or luxuries depends on a nation's standard of living. In the United States, autos and home telephones are generally considered necessities; in many less-developed countries, they are often considered luxuries.

> Consumption reflects **disposable income** and **discretionary income**.

8-2d Occupations and Education

The work force in industrialized nations is still moving toward more white-collar and service jobs. In less-developed and developing nations, many jobs still involve manual work and are more often agriculture-based.

The total employed civilian U.S. labor force is 140 million people—compared with Japan, 63 million; Germany, 36 million; Great Britain, 28 million; France, 24 million; and Italy, 22 million. For the last 40 years, the percent of U.S. workers in service-related, technical, and clerical white-collar jobs has risen; the percent as managers, administrators, and sales workers has been constant; and the percent as nonskilled workers has dropped. Only about 2.5 million U.S. workers have an agriculture-related job.

Another change in the labor force around the world has been the increase in working women. Forty years ago, women comprised one-third of the total U.S. labor force. Today, the figure is 47 percent; and 71 percent of adult U.S. women are in the labor force. In Great Britain and Sweden, the percentage is comparable, while 65 percent of Japan's adult women are in the labor force.

> Women are a large and growing percentage of the worldwide labor force.

During 1970, 40 percent of all married U.S. women were in the labor force. Now, nearly two-thirds are. The percent of married women with children under age six in the U.S. labor force has also jumped dramatically, to 60 percent today. Similar rises have also occurred in other nations.

Unemployment rates, which reflect the percentage of adults in the total labor force not working, vary widely by nation. During 2005, the U.S. unemployment rate was 5 percent. In contrast, the rate for the European Union nations averaged 9 percent. Though the U.S. percentage was lower, it still meant millions of people without jobs. Some worldwide unemployment has been temporary, due to weak domestic and international economies. Other times, depending on the nation and industry, many job losses have been permanent. Unemployment is often accompanied by cutbacks in discretionary purchases.

Great strides are being made globally to upgrade educational attainment, but the level of education tends to be much higher in industrialized nations than in less-developed and developing ones. One measure of educational attainment is the literacy rate, the percentage of people in a country who can read and write. In industrialized nations such as the United States, this rate exceeds 97 percent. Here are the rates for some less-developed and developing nations: Bolivia, 87 percent; Chad, 48 percent; Ethiopia, 43 percent; India, 60 percent; Laos, 66 percent; and Saudi Arabia, 79 percent.

Compared to other large industrialized nations, the United States is the most educated. A higher percentage of U.S. adults has finished high school and college as compared to Canada, France, Germany, Great Britain, Japan, and South Korea. As of 2005, 88 percent of U.S. adults 25 years old and older were high school graduates, and 29 percent were college graduates. Figure 8-4. compares U.S. higher education with other nations (based on 2002 data, the latest available).

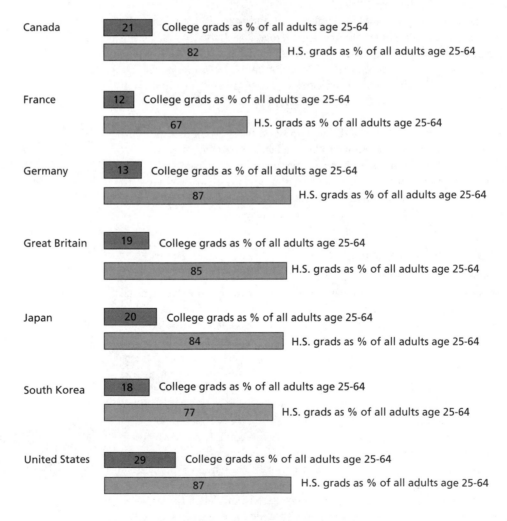

Note: These statistics are from 2002, the latest common date available. The % of high school graduates includes those who also graduated from college.

Figure 8-4

Percentage of Adults Who Have Graduated from High School and College

Source: Organization for Economic Cooperation and Development data, as reported in *Education at a Glance 2004.*

The sharp increase in working women and higher educational attainment have generally contributed to the growing number of people in upper-income brackets; the rather high unemployment rate in some nations and industries, and slow-growth economies, have caused other households to have low incomes.

8-2e Marital Status

Marriage and family are powerful institutions worldwide, but in some nations, they are now less dominant. Although 2.2 million U.S. couples get married each year, only 52 percent of U.S. households contain married couples; the percentage of households with married adults in many other nations is much higher. The median U.S. age at first marriage is 28 years for males and 26 years for females, as people wait to marry and have children. The average U.S. family size is now 3.1. Male and female ages at first marriage are much lower in less-developed and developing nations, and their average family is bigger.

A *family* is a group of two or more persons residing together who are related by blood, marriage, or adoption. A *household* is a person or group of persons occupying a housing unit, whether related or unrelated. In many nations, average household size has been dropping. The U.S. average today is 2.6—due to later marriages, more widows and widowers, a high divorce rate, many couples deciding to have fewer children, and the growth of single-person households. Of the 113 million U.S. households, 26 percent are one-person units. Family households represent 68 percent of U.S. households (down from 85 percent in 1960).

> A **family** has related persons residing together. A **household** has one or more persons who may not be related.

8-2f Ethnicity/Race

From a demographics perspective, *ethnicity/race* should be studied to determine the existence of diversity among and within nations in terms of language and country of origin or race.

More than 250 different languages worldwide are spoken by at least 1 million people each—12 of those are spoken by at least 100 million people (including Mandarin, English, Hindi, and Spanish). Even within nations, there may be diversity as to the languages spoken. Canada (English and French), Chad (French and Arabic), Peru (Spanish and Quechua), and the Philippines (Pilipino and English) all have two official languages. One of the issues facing the European Union in its expansion is the multiplicity of languages spoken.

> **Ethnicity/race** is one measure of a nation's diversity with regard to language, country of origin, or race.

Most nations consist of people representing different ethnic and racial backgrounds. For instance, among those living in the Philippines are Malays, Chinese, Americans, and Spaniards. Sometimes, the people in various groups continue to speak in the languages of their countries of origin, even though they may have resided in their current nations for one or two generations.

The United States is comprised of people from virtually every ethnic and racial group in the world. The Bureau of the Census uses "Black or African-American," "White," "Asian," "Native Hawaiian and Other Pacific Islander," and "American Indian and Alaska Native" to delineate racial groups; "Hispanic" is an ethnic term, denoting people of any race.

As of 2010, the U.S. population will be 75.0 percent White, 13.0 percent Black/African-American, 4.5 percent Asian/Native Hawaiian/Other Pacific Islander, and 0.9 percent American Indian/Alaska Native, with 4.2 percent defined as "Other Race" and 2.4 percent as "Multiracial." Hispanics will be 15.5 percent of the population. In the future, the United States will become even more diverse, due to both higher birth rates and the immigration to the United States by Nonwhites. See Figure 8-5.

8-2g Uses of Demographic Data

As noted at the beginning of the chapter, after studying individual demographics, a firm can form demographic profiles to better focus its marketing efforts. Following are three examples.

Figure 8-5

Marketing to a Diverse Marketplace

More and more companies, such as HSBC (**http://www.hsbc.com**), "the world's local bank," recognize the changing face of the U.S. marketplace and are working hard to appeal to the increasingly diverse consumer population.

Source: Reprinted by permission.

The single-person U.S. household is changing: One-quarter of those living alone are divorced. Sixty percent are over 50 years of age. Only 8 percent of 18- to 34-year-olds live alone, while 30 percent of those 65 and over live alone (39 percent of the women in this age category and 19 percent of the men). One-quarter of those living alone are smokers, 56 percent own a car, 55 percent own their home, and 60 percent have cable TV. It is twice as likely for a person living alone to own a laptop PC than the average household. Forty percent of those living alone use a microwave to do at least one-half of their cooking.[5]

Twenty-one-year-olds have an interesting demographic profile: In the United States, 1 million people turn 21 each year: more than 40 percent of these 21-year-olds live at home, 70 percent have a full- or part-time job, and 93 percent have a credit card. They spend an average of three hours daily surfing the Web, downloading music, and E-mailing friends. They will spend an average of $210,000 over their adult lives on cars.[6]

Demographic profiles of nations, such as Australia and Turkey, can be contrasted. Australia presents better marketing opportunities for firms targeting older, well-educated consumers, and Turkey presents better opportunities for firms marketing to children:[7]

[5] Chris Reynolds, "Me, Myself, and I," *American Demographics* (September 2004), p. D36; and U.S. Bureau of the Census (various publications).

[6] John Fetto "Twenty-One, and Counting," *American Demographics* (September 2003), p. 48.

[7] *CIA World Factbook*, **http://www.odci.gov/cia/publications/factbook**.

	Australia	**Turkey**
Gender ratio (male/female)	0.99/1.00	1.02/1.00
Annual population growth	0.9%	1.1%
Life expectancy	80 years	72 years
Median age	37 years	28 years
Population under 15 years of age	20%	26%
Working women as part of all adult women	66%	27%
Literacy rate	100%	87%

8-2h Limitations of Demographics

These limitations should be noted in applying demographic data: Information may be old; even in the United States, a full census is done once per 10 years and there are time lags before data are released. Data may be limited in some nations, especially less-developed and developing ones. Summary data may be too broad and hide opportunities and risks in small markets or specialized product categories. The psychological or social factors influencing people are not considered. The decision process used in purchasing is not explained. Demographics do not delve into the reasons why people make decisions.

> Demographic data may be dated, unavailable, too general, require profile analysis, and not consider reasons for behavior.

Here are some of the questions not addressed by demographic data:

- Why do consumers act as they do?
- Why do consumers with similar demographic characteristics act differently?
- To whom do consumers look for advice prior to purchasing?
- Under what situations do families (households) use joint decision making?
- Why does status play a large role in the purchase of some products and a small role in others?
- How do different motives affect consumer decisions?
- How does risk affect consumer decisions?
- Why do some consumers act as innovators and buy products before others?
- How important are purchase decisions to consumers?
- What process do consumers use when shopping for various products?
- How long will it take for consumers to reach purchase decisions?
- Why do consumers become brand loyal or regularly switch brands?

Global Marketing in Action

Body Shop: Using "Masstige" Marketing to Attract New Customers

Andy King, Body Shop's (http://www.thebodyshop.com) director of marketing, is presiding over the most far-reaching image change in the history of the firm. The repositioning is based on a new store design, new products (including its best-selling passion fruit body butter product line), extensive use of back-lighting to draw attention to the new products, the introduction of a loyalty card program, and a new corporate slogan, "Made with Passion." As King noted, Body Shop's original store design "served the brand well, but became dark, dated, and cluttered."

The firm's new positioning seeks to both to bring in new customers and to attract the customers who loved Body Shop during the 1980s, the chain's heyday period. Many of these former customers now either purchase discount and private-label brands of cosmetics at supermarkets or use prestige brands such as Clarins (http://www.clarins.com) and Clinique (http://www.clinique.com). King calls his strategy "masstige" positioning, which means carving out a niche by taking sales away from competitors located at both lower and higher price points.

Those who have worked with King understand that he is unforgiving when a retail brand is no longer able to justify its existence. He is also very much concerned about customer service. King says that "I know every retailer talks about this, but it is not always well delivered."

Source: Based on material in Claire Murphy, "Makeover Man—Andy King, Global Marketing Director, The Body Shop," *Marketing Online* (May 11, 2005).

Consumer **lifestyles** describe how people live. In making purchases, people use a decision process with several stages.

To answer these questions, more firms now use demographic data in conjunction with consumer lifestyle and decision-making analysis. A final consumer's *lifestyle* represents the way in which a person lives and spends time and money. It is based on the social and psychological factors that have been internalized by that person, as well as his or her demographic background.[8] These factors overlap and complement each other; they are not independent of one another. The consumer's decision process involves the steps a person uses in buying goods and services. Demographics, social factors, and psychological factors all affect the process.

8-3 CONSUMER LIFESTYLES

The social and psychological characteristics that help form final consumer lifestyles are described next.

8-3a Social Characteristics of Consumers

The final consumer's social profile is based on a combination of culture, social class, social performance, reference groups, opinion leaders, family life cycle, and time expenditures (activities). See Figure 8-6.

Each **culture** transmits acceptable behavior and attitudes. **Social class** separates society into divisions. **Social performance** describes how people fulfill roles.

As discussed in Chapter 6, a *culture* comprises a group of people who share a distinctive heritage, such as Americans or Canadians. People learn about socially proper behavior and beliefs via their culture. The American culture values achievement and success, activity, efficiency and practicality, progress, material comfort, individualism, freedom, external conformity, humanitarianism, youthfulness, and fitness and health.[9]

Cross-cultural differences involving people around the globe must be studied. For instance:

As Americans, we tend to be much more casual and informal when we meet people. Our natural inclination to be familiar can put some people on edge. Germans and Japanese are unlikely to use first names in business. Asians prefer to use less eye and physical contact. Latins

Figure 8-6

Factors Determining a Consumer's Social Profile

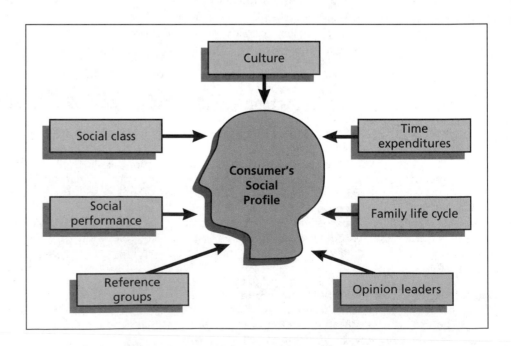

---

[8] "Dictionary of Marketing Terms," **http://www.marketingpower.com/mg-dictionary.php** (May 3, 2006).

[9] Schiffman and Kanuk, *Consumer Behavior*, Chapter 12.

Table 8-1	The Informal Social Class Structure in the United States
Class	**Characteristics**
Upper Americans (nearly one-fifth of population)	
Upper-upper	Social elite; inherited wealth; exclusive neighborhoods; summer homes; children attend best schools; money unimportant in purchases; secure in status; spending with good taste
Lower-upper	Highest incomes; earned wealth; often business leaders and professionals; college educated; seek best for children; active socially; insecure; conspicuous consumption; money unimportant in purchases
Upper-middle	Career-oriented; executives and professionals earning over $75,000 yearly; status tied to occupations and earnings; most educated, but not from prestige schools; demanding of children; quality products purchased; attractive homes; socially involved; gracious living
Middle Americans (nearly two-thirds of population)	
Middle class	Typical Americans; average-earning white-collar workers and the top group of blue-collar workers; many college educated; respectable; conscientious; try to do the right thing; home ownership sought; do-it-yourselfers; family focus
Working class	Remaining white-collar workers and most blue-collar workers; working class lifestyles; some job monotony; job security sought more than advancement; usually high school education; close-knit families; brand loyal and interested in name brands; not status-oriented
Lower Americans (about one-sixth of population)	
Upper-lower	Employed, mostly in unskilled or semiskilled jobs; poorly educated; low incomes; rather difficult to move up the social class ladder; protective against lower-lower class; standard of living at or just above poverty; live in affordable housing
Lower-lower	Unemployed or most menial jobs; poorest income, education, and housing; the bottom layer; present-oriented; impulsive as shoppers; overpay; use credit

Sources: Adapted by the authors from Linda P. Morton, "Upper or Elite Class," *Public Relations Quarterly*, Vol. 49 (Winter 2004), pp. 30-32; Linda P. Morton, "Segmenting Social Classes: The Middle Class," *Public Relations Quarterly*, Vol. 49 (Fall 2004), pp. 46–47; Linda P. Morton, "Segmenting Social Classes: The Working Class," *Public Relations Quarterly*, Vol. 49 (Summer 2004), pp. 45–47; Roger D. Blackwell, Paul W. Miniard, and James F. Engel, *Consumer Behavior*, 9th ed. (Fort Worth, TX: Harcourt, 2001), and Leon Schiffman and Leslie Lazar Kanuk, *Consumer Behavior*, 8th ed. (Upper Saddle River, NJ: Prentice Hall, 2004), Chapter 11.

are prone to touching and to smaller personal space, while Asians and Germans enjoy more distance. The Latin hug ("abrazo") is common between men and men and women and women. At home, the Japanese are more comfortable with a bow from the waist. With Asians and Germans, punctuality is a must! Business cards are treated with more respect by people from other countries, and there is a strong emphasis on titles and positions. It is helpful to have cards printed in their language on the back if you are regularly dealing with a particular country. Germans often include university degrees and the company's founding date on their cards; so you may want to add similar information to yours. Germans, Japanese, and Latins value more formality in manners than Americans. Don't stand with hands on hips or talk with hands in pockets. Be tolerant about smoking, as Japanese and Europeans smoke more than Americans. Avoid speaking in a loud voice. Respect privacy and a sense of order with Germans. Latins enjoy discussing family, whereas Germans and Japanese generally do not.[10]

Social class systems reflect a "status hierarchy by which groups and individuals are classified on the basis of esteem and prestige."[11] They exist all over the globe and divide society into segments, informally or formally grouping those with similar values and lifestyles. Industrialized nations have a larger middle class, greater interchange among classes, and less rigidly defined classes than less-developed and developing nations. Social

[10] Carolyn Luesing, "Appreciating Cultural Differences Makes Good Business Sense," http://www.media3pub.com/bizonline/articles/culture.html (February 11, 2006).

[11] "Dictionary of Marketing Terms," http://www.marketingpower.com/mg-dictionary.php (May 3, 2006).

Ethical Issues in Marketing

Marketing to Children: The Controversy Rages On

The American Psychological Association's Task Force on Advertising to Children (http://www.apa.org) has been pressing for federal restrictions on all advertising to children under the age of 8. According to the six psychologists on the task force, children under this age cannot "recognize persuasive intent."

Government criticism regarding advertising to children dates to 1978, when the Federal Trade Commission (http://www.ftc.gov) sought to ban ads to children under 7 years of age (this was overruled by Congress). Another common area of criticism of marketing to children is based on the widespread use of advertising junk food to children and its effect on childhood obesity.

Some marketers believe that enacting such restrictions is impossible. According to president of an advertising and marketing firm specializing in the children's market, "How can you possibly ban advertising to the 7-year-old who lives with his 9-year-old brother?" Other firms are carefully restructuring their promotions to avoid legal issues. Although character endorsements to children are illegal, Holiday Inn (http://www.holiday-inn.com) makes heavy use of Nickelodeon cartoon characters (to promote its new Nickelodeon Family Suites hotel in Orlando) but does not aim these ads directly at children. The ads are run on television programs that have a large children's audience but are not specifically classified as children's programming. Under a recent Federal Trade Commission ruling, product placements are not considered as advertising. This opens the door for placements to be used in children's programming.

Sources: Based on material in Tiffany Meyers, "*Marketing to Kids Comes Under Fresh Attack,*" *Advertising Age* (February 21, 2005), p. S2; and Janice Healing, "The Ethics of Wooing Kids," *Sunday Times South Africa* (April 24, 2005), p. 6.

---

classes are based on income, occupation, education, and type of dwelling. Each class may represent a distinct target market. Table 8-1 shows the informal U.S. social class system.

Social performance refers to how a person carries out his or her roles as a worker, family member, citizen, and friend. A person may be an executive, have a happy family life, be active in the community, and have many friends. Or he or she may never go higher than assistant manager, be divorced, not partake in community affairs, and have few friends. Many combinations are possible.

> **Reference groups** influence thoughts and behavior. **Opinion leaders** affect others through face-to-face contact.

A *reference group* is one that influences a person's thoughts or actions. Such groups have a large impact on the purchase of many goods and services. Face-to-face reference groups, such as family and friends, have the most effect. Yet, other—more general—groups also affect behavior and may be cited when marketing products. Ads showing goods and services being used by college students, successful professionals, and pet owners often ask viewers to join the "group" and make similar purchases. By pinpointing reference groups that most sway consumers, firms can better aim their strategies.

Firms want to know which persons in reference groups are *opinion leaders*. These are people to whom other consumers turn for advice and information via face-to-face communication. They tend to be expert about a product category, socially accepted, long-standing members of the community, gregarious, active, and trusted, and they tend to seek approval from others. They typically have an impact over a narrow product range and are perceived as more believable than company-sponsored information.

> The **family life cycle** describes life stages, which often use **joint decision making**. The **household life cycle** includes family and nonfamily units.

The *family life cycle* describes how a family evolves through various stages from bachelorhood to solitary retirement. At each stage, needs, experience, income, family composition, and the use of *joint decision making*—the process whereby two or more people have input into purchases—change. The number of people in the various stages can be found from demographic data. Table 8-2 shows a traditional cycle and its marketing relevance. The stages apply to families in all nations—industrialized and less-developed/developing, but opportunities are most applicable for industrialized countries.

When doing life-cycle analysis, the people who do not follow a traditional pattern because they do not marry, do not have children, become divorced, have

Table 8-2 The Traditional Family Life Cycle

Stage in Cycle	Characteristics	Marketing Opportunities
Bachelor, male or female	Independent; young; early in career, low earnings, low discretionary income	Clothing; auto; stereo; travel; restaurants; entertainment; status appeals
Newly married	Two incomes; relative independence; present- and future-oriented	Apartment furnishings; travel; clothing; durables; appeal to enjoyment and togetherness
Full nest I	Youngest child under 6; one to one-and-a-half incomes; limited independence; future-oriented	Goods and services for the child, home, and family; durability and safety; pharmaceuticals; day care; appeal to economy
Full nest II	Youngest child over 6, but dependent; one-and-a-half to two incomes; at least one spouse set in career; future-oriented	Savings; home; education; family vacations; child-oriented products; some luxuries; appeal to comfort and long-term enjoyment
Full nest III	Youngest child living at home, but independent; highest income level; thoughts of future retirement	Education; expensive durables for children; replacement and improvement of parents' durables; appeal to comfort and luxury
Empty nest I	No children at home; independent; good income; thoughts of self and retirement	Vacation home; travel; clothing; entertainment; luxuries; appeal to self-gratification
Empty nest II	Retirement; less income and expenses; present-oriented	Travel; recreation; new home; health-related items; less interest in luxuries; appeal to comfort at a low price
Sole survivor I	Only one spouse alive; actively employed; present-oriented; good income	Immersion in job and friends; interest in travel, clothing, health, and recreation areas; appeal to productive lifestyle
Sole survivor II	Only one spouse alive; retired; some feeling of futility; less income	Travel; recreation; pharmaceuticals; security; appeal to economy and social activity

Table 8-3 The Current Status of U.S. Family and Nonfamily Households

Household Status	Percentage of All U.S. Households	
Family Households	68	
Married couples, no children under age 18		27
Married couples, with children under age 18		25
Other types of families, no children under age 18		7
Other types of families, with children under age 18 [a]		9
Single-Person Households [b]	26	
Age 24 and under		1
Age 25 to 44		8
Age 45 to 64		7
Age 65 and over		10
Other Nonfamily Households	6	
Unmarried couples, no children under age 18		2
Unmarried couples, with children under age 18		2
Other [c]		2
Total	100	100

[a] Includes one-parent families in which married couples are separated but not divorced, one-parent families headed by divorcees, one-parent families headed by widows and widowers, and one-parent families headed by never-married mothers and fathers.
[b] Includes people who have never married, as well as those who are widowed, separated, and divorced.
[c] Includes roommates.

Source: Computed by the authors from *America's Families and Living Arrangements: 2004* (Washington, DC: U.S. Census Bureau, November 2005).

families with two working spouses (even if there are very small children), and so on, should be noted. They are not adequately reflected in Table 8-2, but may represent good marketing opportunities. As a result, the concept of the ***household life cycle***—which incorporates the life stages of both family and nonfamily households—is taking on greater significance. Table 8-3 shows the current status of U.S. family and nonfamily households.

Time expenditures refer to the activities in which a person participates and the time allocated to them. They include work, commuting, personal care, home maintenance, food preparation and consumption, child rearing, social interactions, reading, shopping, self-improvement, recreation, entertainment, vacations, and so on. Though the average U.S. workweek for the primary job has stabilized at 35 to 40 hours, some people work at two jobs. Americans enjoy TV, phone calls, pleasure driving, walking, swimming, sightseeing, bicycling, spectator events, reading, and playing games and sports.

> **Time expenditures** reflect the workweek, family care, and leisure.

8-3b   Psychological Characteristics of Consumers

The final consumer's psychological profile involves his or her personality, attitudes (opinions), class consciousness, motivation, perceived risk, innovativeness, and purchase importance. See Figure 8-7.

A ***personality*** is the sum total of an individual's enduring internal psychological traits that make the person unique. Self-confidence, dominance, autonomy, sociability, defensiveness, adaptability, and emotional stability are selected personality traits. An individual's behavior is strongly affected by his or her personality. As an example, a self-confident and sociable person often will not buy the same goods and services as an inhibited and aloof person. It is necessary to remember that a personality is made up of many traits operating in association with one another.

> A **personality** describes a person's composite internal, enduring psychological traits.

Attitudes (opinions) are an individual's positive, neutral, or negative feelings about goods, services, firms, people, issues, and/or institutions. They are shaped by demographics, social factors, and other psychological traits. One marketing task is to foster favorable attitudes; given the intensive competition in many industries, a firm cannot normally succeed without positive consumer attitudes. When studying attitudes, two concepts should often be measured—the attitude itself and the purchase intention toward a firm's brand. For example: (1) Do you like brand A? Would you buy brand A in the future? (2) How does brand A compare with other brands? Would you buy brand A if it were priced higher than other brands?

> **Attitudes** can be positive, negative, or neutral.

Class consciousness is the extent to which a person seeks social status. It helps determine the interest in social-class mobility, the use of reference groups, and the importance of prestige purchases. Inner-directed people want to please themselves and are often attracted by products that perform well functionally. They are not concerned with social mobility, rely on their own judgment, and do not value prestige items. Outer-directed people want to please others. Upward social mobility, reference group approval, and ownership of prestige items are sought. These people are often attracted by products with social visibility, well-known brands, and uniqueness. Functional excellence may be less important.

> **Class consciousness** is low for inner-directed persons and high for outer-directed individuals.

Motivation involves the positive or negative needs, goals, and desires that impel a person to or away from certain actions, objects, or situations.[12] By identifying and appealing to people's ***motives*** – the reasons for behavior—a firm can produce positive motivation. For example:

Each person has distinct motives for purchases, and these change by situation and over time. Consumers often combine economic (price, durability) and emotional (social acceptance, self-esteem) motives when making purchases.

> **Motivation** is a drive-impelling action; it is caused by **motives**.

[12] "Dictionary of Marketing Terms," http://www.marketingpower.com/mg-dictionary.php (May 3, 2006).

Figure 8-7

**Factors Determining a
Consumer's Psychological Profile**

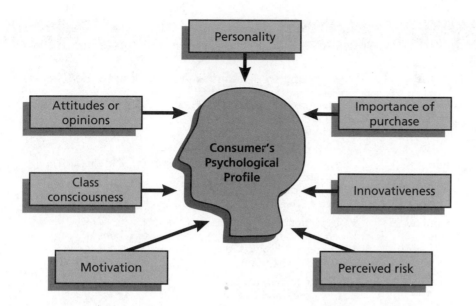

Perceived risk is the uncertainty felt by the consumer about a purchase.

Perceived risk is the level of uncertainty a consumer believes exists as to the outcome of a purchase decision; this belief may or may not be correct. Perceived risk can be divided into six major types:

1. Functional—risk that a product will not perform adequately.
2. Physical—risk that a product will be harmful.
3. Financial—risk that a product will not be worth its cost.
4. Social—risk that a product will cause embarrassment around others.
5. Psychological—risk that one's ego will be bruised.
6. Time—risk that the time spent shopping will be wasted if a product does not perform as expected.[13]

Because high perceived risk can dampen customer motivation, firms must deal with it even if people have incorrect beliefs. Firms can lower perceived risk by giving more information, having a reputation for superior quality, offering money-back guarantees, avoiding controversial ingredients, and so on.

A person willing to try a new good or service that others perceive as risky exhibits *innovativeness*. An innovator is apt to be young and well educated, and to have above-average income for his or her social class. The person is also likely to be interested in

Innovativeness is trying a new product others see as risky.

Motives	Marketing Actions That Motivate
Hunger reduction	Television and radio ads for fast-food restaurants
Safety	Smoke detector demonstrations in stores
Sociability	Perfume ads showing social success due to products
Achievement	Use of consumer endorsements in ads specifying how much knowledge can be gained from a course in real-estate sales
Economy	Newspaper coupons advertising sales
Social responsibility	Package labels that emphasize how easy it is to recycle products

[13] Schiffman and Kanuk, *Consumer Behavior*, Chapter 6.

Table 8-4	Selected Marketing Opportunities of Consumer Lifestyles
Lifestyle Category	**Marketing Opportunities in Appealing to the Lifestyle**
Family values	Family-oriented goods and services Educational devices and toys Traditional family events "Wholesome" entertainment
Voluntary simplicity	Goods and services with quality, durability, and simplicity Environmentally safe products Energy-efficient products Discount-oriented retailing
Getting by	Popular brands and good buys ("value") Video rentals and other inexpensive entertainment Do-it-yourself projects such as "knock-down" furniture Inexpensive child care
"Me" generation	Individuality in purchases Luxury goods and services Nutritional themes Exercise- and education-related goods and services
Blurring of gender roles	Unisex goods, services, and stores Couples-oriented advertising Child-care services Less male and female stereotyping
Poverty of time	Internet and phone sales Service firms with accurate customer appointments Laborsaving devices One-stop shopping
Component lifestyle	Situational purchases Less social class stereotyping Multiple advertising themes Market niches

change, achievement-oriented, open-minded, status-conscious, mobile, and venturesome. Firms need to identify and appeal to innovators when introducing a new good or service.

The ***importance of a purchase*** affects the time and effort a person spends shopping for a product—and the money allotted. An important purchase means careful decision making, high perceived risk, and often a large amount of money. An unimportant purchase means less decision time (an item may be avoided altogether) and low perceived risk, and it is probably inexpensive.

> The **importance of a purchase** determines the time, effort, and money spent.

8-3c Selected Consumer Lifestyles

Many distinct consumer lifestyles will continue, including family values, voluntary simplicity, getting by, "me" generation, blurring of gender roles, poverty of time, and component lifestyles. Their marketing implications are shown in Table 8-4.

A *family values* lifestyle emphasizes marriage, children, and home life. With this lifestyle, people focus on children and their education; family autos, vacations, and entertainment; and home-oriented products. Because the traditional family is becoming less representative of U.S. households, firms must be careful in targeting those following this lifestyle. They should also remember that a family values lifestyle remains the leading one in other nations. For instance, in Italy, far less than one-half of women are in the labor force and the divorce rate is much lower than that of the United States.

> In some households, family values have a great impact.

Voluntary simplicity is a lifestyle in which people have an ecological awareness, seek product durability, strive for self-reliance, and buy technologically simple products. People with this lifestyle are cautious, conservative, and thrifty shoppers. They do not buy expensive cars and clothing, hold on to products for long periods, and rarely eat out or go on pre-packaged vacations. They like going to a park or taking a vacation by car, are more concerned with product toughness than appearance, and believe in conservation. There is an attraction to rational appeals and no-frills retailing.

Getting by is a frugal lifestyle pursued by people due to economic circumstances. They seek product durability, self-reliance, and simple products. Unlike people with voluntary simplicity, they do so because they must. In less-developed and developing nations, most people have this lifestyle; a much smaller proportion has this orientation in industrialized nations. Getting-by consumers are attracted to well-known brands (to reduce perceived risk), do not try new products, rarely go out, and take few vacations. They seek bargains and patronize local stores. They rarely feel they have any significant discretionary income.

A *"me" generation* lifestyle stresses being good to oneself, self-fulfillment, and self-expression. There is less pressure to conform and greater diversity; there is also less interest in responsibilities and loyalties. Consumers with this lifestyle stress nutrition, exercise, and grooming. They buy expensive cars and apparel, and visit full-service stores. These people are more concerned with product appearance than durability. Some place below-average value on conservation if it will negatively affect their lifestyle.

Because many women work, more men are assuming the once-traditional roles of their wives, and vice versa, thus *blurring gender roles*. According to the American Time Use Survey, "On an average day, 84 percent of women and 63 percent of men spend some time doing household activities, such as housework, cooking, lawn care, or financial and other household management. Women spend 2.7 hours on such activities while men spend 2.1 hours. Nineteen percent of men report doing housework—such as cleaning or doing laundry; and 35 percent of men do food preparation or cleanup."[14] See Figure 8-8.

The prevalence of working women, the long distances between home and work, and the large number of people working at second jobs contribute to a *poverty-of-time* lifestyle in many households. For such families, the quest for financial security means less free time. This lifestyle leads people to greater use of time-saving products. Included are convenience foods, quick-oil-change services, microwave ovens, fast-food restaurants, mail-order retailers, one-hour film processing, and professional lawn and household care.

Today, more people employ a *component lifestyle*, whereby their attitudes and behavior depend on particular situations rather than an overall lifestyle philosophy. People may take their children with them on vacation (family values), engage in recycling (voluntary simplicity), look for discounts to save money (getting by), take exercise classes ("me" generation), share shopping chores (blurring gender roles), and eat out on busy nights (poverty of time). As one marketing expert puts it:

> The success of Coach [http://www.coach.com], Burberry [http://www.burberry.com], and Tiffany [http://www.tiffany.com] indicates consumers are more than willing to pay for "new luxury" items in certain categories while at the same time they doggedly shop for deals and wait for items to go on sale in others. What's going on? Consumers are paying close attention to categories that are important to them, making small statements in quality products. An example of this is the higher socioeconomic consumer who appreciates nice furniture, but cannot justify the expense on every piece. He or she will shop at Ikea [http://www.ikea.com] for certain items and then at a high-end store such as Luminaire [http://www.luminaire.com] for others. Or there's the woman who mixes ready-to-wear apparel from Target [http://www.target.com] with her Prada [http://www.prada.com] purse and Manolo Blahnik [http://www.style.com/manolo] shoes.[15]

Voluntary simplicity is based on self-reliance.

When economic circumstances are tough, some people emphasize getting by.

The "me" generation stresses self-fulfillment.

Blurring gender roles involves men and women undertaking nontraditional duties.

A poverty of time exists when a quest for financial security means less free time.

With a component lifestyle, consumer attitudes and behavior vary by situation.

[14] "American Time Use Survey—2004 Results Announced by BLS," http://www.bls.gov/news.release/atus.nr0.htm (September 20, 2005).

[15] Paul Marobella, "Contradictions in Consumer Trends," *Direct* (May 15, 2004), p. 32.

Figure 8-8

Blurring Gender Roles

More men and women are now engaging in nontraditional activities, such as doing grocery shopping together.

Source: Reprinted by permission of Susan Berry, Retail Image Consulting, Inc.

8-3d Limitations of Lifestyle Analysis

Unlike demographics, many of the social and psychological aspects of final consumer lifestyles are difficult to measure, somewhat subjective, usually based on the self-reports of consumers, and sometimes hidden from view (to avoid embarrassment, protect privacy, convey an image, and other reasons). Ongoing disputes continue over terminology, misuse of data, and reliability.

8-4 THE FINAL CONSUMER'S DECISION PROCESS

> The **final consumer's decision process** has many stages and various factors affect it.

The ***final consumer's decision process*** is the way in which people gather and assess information and choose among alternative goods, services, organizations, people, places, and ideas. It comprises the process itself and the factors affecting it. The process has six stages: stimulus, problem awareness, information search, evaluation of alternatives, purchase, and post-purchase behavior. Demographic, social, and psychological factors affect the process. Figure 8-9 shows the total decision-making process.

Whenever a consumer buys a good or service, decides to vote for a political candidate or donate to a charity, and so on, he or she goes through a decision process. Sometimes, all six stages in the process are used; other times, only a few steps are utilized. The purchase of an expensive stereo requires more decision making than the purchase of a new music video.

At *any* point in the decision process, a person may decide not to buy, vote, or donate—and, thereby end the process. A good or service may turn out to be unneeded, unsatisfactory, or too expensive.

A. The Decision Process

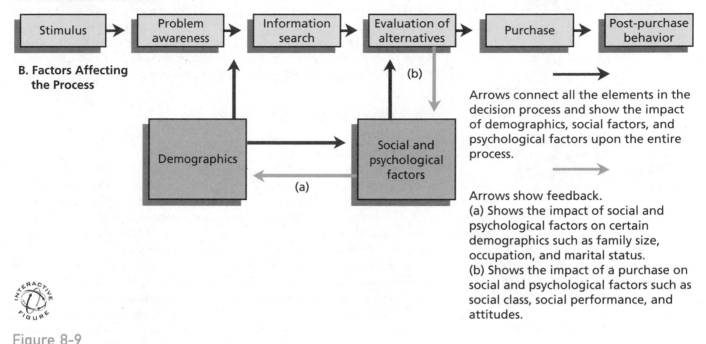

B. Factors Affecting
the Process

Arrows connect all the elements in the decision process and show the impact of demographics, social factors, and psychological factors upon the entire process.

Arrows show feedback.
(a) Shows the impact of social and psychological factors on certain demographics such as family size, occupation, and marital status.
(b) Shows the impact of a purchase on social and psychological factors such as social class, social performance, and attitudes.

Figure 8-9

The Final Consumer's Decision Process

8-4a   Stimulus

A *stimulus* is a cue (social, commercial, or noncommercial) or a drive (physical) meant to motivate a person to act.

A *social cue* occurs when someone talks with friends, family members, co-workers, and others. It is from an interpersonal source not affiliated with a seller. A *commercial cue* is a message sponsored by a seller to interest a person in a particular good, service, organization, person, place, or idea. Ads, personal selling, and sales promotions are commercial cues. They are less regarded than social cues because people know they are seller-controlled. A *noncommercial cue* is a message from an impartial source such as *Consumer Reports* (**http://www.consumerreports.org**) or the government. It has high believability because it is not affiliated with the seller. A *physical drive* occurs when a person's physical senses are affected. Thirst, hunger, and fear cause physical drives.

A person may be exposed to any or all of these stimuli. If sufficiently stimulated, he or she will proceed to the next stage in the decision process. If not, the person will ignore the cue and delay or terminate the decision process for the given good, service, organization, person, place, or idea.

> A **stimulus** is a cue or drive intended to motivate a consumer.

8-4b   Problem Awareness

At the *problem awareness* stage, a consumer recognizes that the good, service, organization, person, place, or idea under consideration may solve a problem of shortage or unfulfilled desire.

Recognition of shortage occurs when a consumer realizes a repurchase is needed. A suit may wear out. A man or woman may run out of razor blades. An eye exam may be needed. A popular political candidate may be up for re-election. It may be time for a charity's annual fundraising campaign. In each case, the consumer recognizes a need to repurchase.

Recognition of unfulfilled desire takes place when a consumer becomes aware of a good, service, organization, person, place, or idea that has not been bought before. Such an item may improve status, appearance, living conditions, or knowledge in a way not

> **Problem awareness** entails recognition of a shortage or an unfulfilled desire.

tried before (luxury car, cosmetic surgery, proposed zoning law, encyclopedia), or it may offer new performance features not previously available (laser surgery, tobacco-free cigarettes). Either way, a person is aroused by a desire to try something new.

Many consumers hesitate to act on unfulfilled desires due to greater risks. It is easier to replace a known product. Whether a consumer becomes aware of a problem of shortage or of unfulfilled desire, he or she will act only if the problem is perceived as worth solving.

8-4c Information Search

An **information search** determines alternatives and their characteristics.

Next, an ***information search*** requires listing the alternatives that will solve the problem at hand and determining the characteristics of each option.

A *list of alternatives* does not have to be written. It can be a group of items a consumer thinks about. With internal search, a person has experience in the area being considered and uses a memory search to list the choices. A person with minimal experience will do an external search to list alternatives; this can involve commercial sources, noncommercial sources, and/or social sources. Often, once there is a list of choices, items (brands, companies, and so on) not on it do not receive further consideration.

The second phase of information search deals with the *characteristics of each alternative*. This information can also be generated internally or externally, depending on the expertise of the consumer and the perceived risk. As risk increases, more information is sought. Once an information search is completed, it must be determined whether the shortage or unfulfilled desire can be satisfied by any alternative. If one or more choices are satisfactory, the consumer moves to the next step. The process is delayed or discontinued when no alternative provides satisfaction.

The Web has become a major source for shopping information. Among the many useful sites are:

- CNET (**http://www.cnet.com**)—"Bringing tech to life."
- Epinions.com (**http://www.epinions.com**)—Helps people make informed purchase decisions."
- mySimon (**http://www.mysimon.com**)—"Price comparison, store & product reviews—compare prices & stores from around the Web."

Marketing and the Web

Blogging: An Emerging Form of Consumer Communications

Blogging involves everyday people developing and updating easy-to-use Web sites where they can share their thoughts and interact with others. Many consumers use blogging as their voice on the Web or as a means of posting their thoughts and opinions.

Adam Seifer, chief executive of a Web site for camera bugs, has been blogging pictures of every meal he has eaten. Sometimes, he uses a pocket camera and other times a camera phone. Although his pictures are often fuzzy with hard-to-read text and typos, mobile bloggers ("mobloggers") such as Seifer can send mundane details of their lives to their friends and family. Mobloggers are also well equipped to send pictures of protests, traffic jams, and natural disasters.

Industry experts believe that a number of technical advances will make moblogging even more popular in the future. New versions of camera phones provide sharper videos and videos. Some camera phone models are even equipped with keyboards to facilitate text entries. And phone companies, such as Verizon (**http://www.verizon.com**), are offering blogging programs on their phones.

Google's Blogger site (**http://www.blogger.com**) enables users to create a free blog in several easy steps, as well as software to post a blog directly from Microsoft Word. Yahoo's Flickr (**http://www.flickr. com**) has over 150,000 phone-produced pictures. It also contains a search engine to find specific photos.

Source: Based on material in Stephen Baker, "Covering the Story of Your Life," *Business Week* (July 4, 2005), pp. 90–91.

- Pricing Central (**http://www.pricingcentral.com**)—"Indexes all the best price search engines and online shopping bots into a comprehensive directory."
- StartSpot (**http://www.shoppingspot.com**)—"Simplifying the search for the best shopping-related content online."
- Yahoo! Shopping (**http://shopping.yahoo.com**)—"Find the lowest total prices, and get recommendations!"

8-4d Evaluation of Alternatives

There is now enough information for a consumer to select one alternative from the list of choices. This is easy if one option is clearly the best across all attributes: A product with excellent quality and a low price will be a sure choice over an average-quality, expensive one. The choice is usually not that simple, and a consumer must carefully engage in an *evaluation of alternatives* before making a decision. If two or more alternatives seem attractive, a person needs to determine which criteria to evaluate and their relative importance. Alternatives would then be ranked and a choice made.

Decision criteria are the features a person deems relevant—such as price, style, quality, safety, durability, status, and warranty. A consumer sets standards for these features and forms an attitude on each alternative according to its ability to meet the standards. In addition, each criterion's importance is set because the multiple attributes of products are usually of varying weight. For example, a consumer may consider shoe prices to be more important than style and select inexpensive, non-distinctive shoes.

A consumer then *ranks alternatives* from most to least desirable and selects one. This may be hard because alternatives might have technical differences or be poorly labeled, new, or intangible (such as two political candidates). On these occasions, options may be ranked on the basis of brand name or price, which is used to indicate overall quality.

In situations where no alternative is satisfactory, a decision to delay or not make a purchase is made.

> **Evaluating alternatives** consists of weighing features and selecting the desired product.

8-4e Purchase

After choosing the best alternative, a person is ready for the *purchase act*: an exchange of money, a promise to pay, or support in return for ownership of a specific good, the performance of a specific service, and so on. Three considerations remain: place of purchase, terms, and availability.

The *place of purchase* is picked the same way as a product: Choices are noted, attributes are detailed, and a ranking is performed. The best locale is chosen. Although most items are bought at stores, some are bought at school, work, and home. *Purchase terms* involve the price and method of payment. Generally, a price is the amount (including interest, tax, and other fees) a person pays to gain ownership or use of a good or service. It may also be a person's vote, time investment, and so on. The payment method is the way a price is paid (cash, short-term credit, or long-term credit). *Availability* refers to the timeliness with which a consumer receives a product that he or she buys. It depends on stock on hand (or service capacity) and delivery. Stock on hand (service capacity) relates to a seller's ability to provide a good or service when requested. For items requiring delivery, the period from when an order is placed by a consumer until it is received and the ease with which an item is transported to its place of use are crucial.

A consumer will purchase if these elements are acceptable. That is why companies such as AutoNation (**http://www.autonation.com**), highlighted in Figure 8-10, want to be seen as consumer friendly. However, sometimes, dissatisfaction with any one of the elements may cause a person to delay or not buy, even though there is no problem with the good or service itself. If a store is closed or a salesperson is unfriendly, the consumer might not come back.

> The **purchase act** means picking where to buy, agreeing to terms, and checking availability.

Figure 8-10

Providing a Satisfying Purchase Experience

AutoNation strives to provide a pleasurable shopping trip for consumers buying new and used cars. Its consumer-oriented philosophy is "Shop. Save. Easy." It wants to encourage further purchases and reduce or eliminate cognitive dissonance.

Source: Reprinted by permission of Retail Planning Associates. Photography by Michael Houghton/STUDIOHIO.

Post-purchase behavior often involves further buying and/or re-evaluation. **Cognitive dissonance** can be reduced by proper consumer after-care.

8-4f   Post-Purchase Behavior

Once a purchase is made, a person may engage in **post-purchase behavior**, via further purchases and/or re-evaluation. Many times, one purchase leads to others: A house purchase leads to the acquisition of fire insurance. A PC purchase leads to the acquisition of computer software. In addition, displaying complementary products near one another may encourage related purchases.

A person may also re-evaluate a purchase after making it: Are expectations matched by performance? Satisfaction often means a repurchase when a good or service wears out, a charity holds a fund raising campaign, and so on, and leads to positive communication with other people interested in the same item. Dissatisfaction can lead to brand switching and negative communication. It is often due to **cognitive dissonance**—doubt that a correct decision has been made. A person may regret a purchase or wish another choice had been made. To overcome dissonance, a firm must realize the process does not end with a purchase. Follow-up calls, extended warranties, and ads aimed at buyers can reassure people.

8-4g   Factors Affecting the Final Consumer's Decision Process

Demographic, social, and psychological factors affect the way final consumers make choices and can help a firm understand how people use the decision process. For example, an affluent consumer would move through the process more quickly than a middle-income one due to less financial risk. An insecure consumer would spend more time making a decision than a secure one.

By knowing how these factors influence decisions, a firm can fine-tune its marketing strategies to cater to the target market and its purchase behavior, and answer these questions: Why do two or more people use the decision process in the same way? Why do two or more people use it differently?

8-4h   Types of Decision Processes

Final consumer decision making can be categorized as **extended, limited,** or **routine**.

Each time a person buys a good or service, donates to a charity, and so on, he or she uses the decision process. This may be done subconsciously, with the person not aware of using it. Some situations let a person move through the process quickly and de-emphasize or skip steps; others require a thorough use of each step. A consumer may use extended, limited, or routine decision making—based on the search, level of experience, frequency of purchase, amount of perceived risk, and time pressure. See Figure 8-11.

With **extended consumer decision making**, a person fully uses the decision process. Much effort is spent on information search and evaluation of alternatives for expensive, complex items with which a person has little or no experience. Purchases are made infrequently. Perceived risk is high, and the purchase is important. A person has time

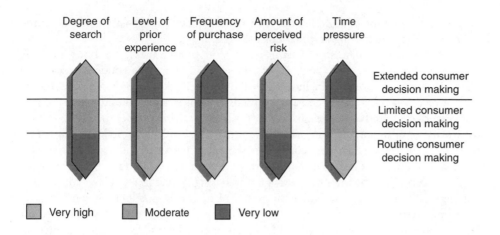

Figure 8-11

The Three Types of Final Consumer Decision Processes

available to make a choice. Purchase delays often occur. Demographic, social, and psychological factors have their greatest impact. Extended decision making is often involved in picking a college, a house, a first car, or a location for a wedding.

Limited consumer decision making occurs when a person uses every step in the purchase process but does not spend a great deal of time on some of them. The person has previously bought a given good or service, but makes fresh decisions when it comes under current purchase consideration—due to the relative infrequency of purchase, the introduction of new models, or an interest in variety. Perceived risk is moderate, and a person is willing to spend some time shopping. The thoroughness with which the process is used depends on the amount of prior experience, the importance of the purchase, and the time pressure facing the consumer. Emphasis is on evaluating a list of known choices, although an information search may be done. Factors affecting the decision process have some impact. A second car, clothing, gifts, home furnishings, and an annual vacation typically need limited decision making.

In *routine consumer decision making*, a person buys out of habit and skips steps in the process. He or she spends little time shopping and often repurchases the same brands (or those bought before). This category includes items with which a person has much experience. They are bought regularly, have little or no perceived risk, and are rather low in price. Once a person realizes a good or service is depleted, a repurchase is made. Time pressure is high. Information search, evaluation, and post-purchase behavior are normally omitted, as long as a person is satisfied. Impulse purchases, where consumers have not thought of particular items until seeing displays for them, are common. Factors affecting the process have little impact because problem awareness usually leads to a purchase. Examples of items routinely purchased are the daily paper, a haircut by a regular stylist, and weekly grocery items.

There are differences between consumers in industrialized nations and those in less-developed and developing ones. Generally, consumers in less-developed and developing countries:

- are exposed to fewer commercial and noncommercial cues.
- have access to less information.
- have fewer goods and services from which to choose.
- are more apt to buy a second choice if the first one is not available.
- have fewer places of purchase and may have to wait on long lines.
- are more apt to find that stores are out of stock.
- have less purchase experience for many kinds of goods and services.
- are less educated and have lower incomes.
- are more apt to repurchase items with which they are moderately satisfied (due to a lack of choices).

Most purchases are made by routine or limited decision making because many consumers—in both industrialized nations and less-developed nations—want to reduce shopping time, the use of complex decision making, and risk. Consumers often employ low-involvement purchasing and/or brand loyalty.

With *low-involvement purchasing*, a consumer minimizes the time and effort expended in both making decisions about and shopping for those goods and services he or she views as unimportant. Included are "those situations where the consumer simply does not care and is not concerned about brands or choices and makes the decision in the most cognitively miserly manner possible. Most likely, low involvement is situation-based, and the degree of importance and involvement may vary with the individual and with the situation."[16] In these situations, consumers feel little perceived risk, are passive about getting information, act fast, and may assess products after (rather than before) buying.

Firms can adapt to low-involvement purchasing by using repetitive ads to create awareness and familiarity, stressing the practical nature of products, having informed salespeople, setting low prices, using attractive displays, selling in all types of outlets, and offering coupons and free samples. Table 8-5 compares the traditional high-involvement view of consumer behavior with the low-involvement view. AdCracker.com has good examples at its Web site (**http://www.adcracker.com/involvement**).

After a consumer tries one or more brands of a good or service, *brand loyalty* – the consistent repurchase of and preference toward a particular brand—may take place. With it, a person can reduce time, thought, and risk whenever buying a given good or service. Brand loyalty can occur for simple items such as gasoline (due to low-involvement purchasing) and for complex items such as autos (to minimize the perceived risk of switching brands).

According to a major study, at least 40 percent of U.S. adults say they prefer one brand or service provider for auto insurance (70 percent), bath soap (49 percent), autos (46 percent), and life insurance (41 percent). However, 20 percent or less prefer one brand or service provider for athletic/leisure wear (10 percent), hotels and motels (12 percent), air travel (18 percent), and auto rentals (19 percent).[17]

How can firms generate and sustain customer loyalty? Here's the way Whirlpool (**http://www.whirlpool.com**), the home appliance company, does it:

> We know that loyal customers are recommending our brands to others, that they are requesting and repurchasing our brands over those of competitors, and that they are beginning to upgrade their appliances because they trust the innovation and value that our brands deliver. Initiatives that lead to higher levels of customer loyalty, such as our innovation process, result in improved revenue growth, margin expansion, and trade support for our brands. Because innovation is such an important driver of customer loyalty, we are expanding our efforts to transfer innovation capabilities and skills to employees everywhere. Innovation is ingrained in the Whirlpool culture, with more than 5,000 employees trained and actively involved in innovation initiatives. Another key aspect of customer loyalty involves the experiences that touch customers before, during, and long after the initial purchase. Each of our brands is putting in place a complete set of experiences—including brand advertising, the in-store purchase, call center interactions, and ongoing customer communications—that will help forge lifelong relationships with our customers.[18]

8-4i Marketing Applications of the Final Consumer's Decision Process

Over the years, the final consumer's decision process has been studied and applied in many settings, as these illustrations indicate:

Low-involvement purchasing occurs with unimportant products.

Brand loyalty involves consistent repurchases of and preferences for specific brands.

---

[16] "Dictionary of Marketing Terms," **http://www.marketingpower.com/mg-dictionary.php** (May 3, 2006).

[17] "Knowledge Networks/Ad Age Survey: CPG Brand Loyalty and In-Store Influencers," **http://www.knowledgenetworks.com/CPGsurvey** (May 5, 2003).

[18] "Building Customer Loyalty," **http://www.whirlpoolcorp.com/about/vision_and_strategy/loyalty.asp** (April 24, 2006).

Table 8-5	High-Involvement View of Active Consumers Versus Low-Involvement View of Passive Consumers

Traditional High-Involvement View of Active Consumers	Newer Low-Involvement View of Passive Consumers
1. Consumers are information processors.	1. Consumers learn information at random.
2. Consumers are information seekers.	2. Consumers are information gatherers.
3. Consumers are an active audience for ads and the effect of ads on them is *weak*.	3. Consumers are a passive audience for ads and the effect of ads on them is *strong*.
4. Consumers evaluate brands before buying.	4. Consumers buy first. If they do evaluate brands, it is done after the purchase.
5. Consumers seek to maximize satisfaction. They compare brands to see which provide the most *benefits* and buy based on detailed comparisons.	5. Consumers seek an acceptable level of satisfaction. They choose the brand least apt to have *problems* and buy based on few factors. Familiarity is key.
6. Lifestyle characteristics are related to consumer behavior because the product is not closely tied to a consumer's identity and belief system.	6. Lifestyle characteristics are not related to consumer behavior because the product is closely tied to a consumer's identity and belief system.
7. Reference groups influence behavior because of the product's importance to group norms.	7. Reference groups have little effect on behavior because the product is unlikely to be related to group norms.

Source: Henry Assael, *Consumer Behavior and Marketing Action*, 6th ed. (Cincinnati: South-Western Publishing, 1998), p. 155. Reprinted by permission.

- More than two-thirds of U.S. consumers shop for clothing for themselves at least once every two to three months, while one-quarter shop for clothing at least once per month. As income increases, so does the frequency of apparel shopping. [19]
- Just over one-half of the respondents age 12 and younger to a recent Harris Interactive YouthPulse survey "said they had to abandon a purchase because of parent interference, making it the top reason for online shopping-cart abandonment in that group." In addition, "27 percent of those age 13 and older said their parents had forced them to abandon an online purchase. But while tween online purchasers might have been stopped in their tracks by parents, the survey also reports that young consumers spend $20 billion a year on shopping sprees that they initially researched online."[20]
- Consumers in India "like to bargain at any store. This seems to be driven by the gratification derived out of 'extracting' a right price from the retailer. During the process of bargaining, the shoppers collect considerable information about merchandise, as well as the store. The current market scenario, where sales promotion is rampant, could also be affecting such an orientation. There is a tendency of shoppers to ask retailers to round off the total bill, which leads to a sort of "cent-off." Thus, the salespersons at the store need to possess good communication and negotiation skills."[21]
- Brand-loyal customers are quite apt to make referrals to their friends. According to a recent Parago *Customer Loyalty Research Report*, "Eighty-two percent of Americans participating in customer loyalty programs have actively referred friends and family to their favorite programs. On average, active members refer about three friends or family members to their favorite programs. High-income earners—household incomes of $125,000 or higher—tend to be the most active in referrals since they are typically more involved in loyalty and rewards programs. Consumers are using

[19] Retail Forward, *ShopperScape Newsletter* (August 2005).

[20] "All in the Family," *Marketing Management* (May-June 2005), p. 4.

[21] Piyush Kumar Sinha, "Shopping Orientation in the Evolving Indian Market," *Vikalpa*, Vol. 28 (April-June 2003), p. 21.

referral and word-of-mouth more than we ever expected. It's clear customers want to be loyal."[22]

- Despite the preceding results, satisfied consumers discuss their experiences with far fewer people than dissatisfied ones. As one insurance expert said, "Word of mouth has always been a powerful force, but never before could it be used so quickly, nor spread so widely as in this age of the digital nervous system. Unfortunately, negative news seems to spread more than positive news. Researchers have found that one offended person can repeat the story of a negative experience to as many as 13 people before either the offended person tires of telling it or runs out of people interested in hearing him or her rant and rave. A person with a positive experience will tell only five people."[23]

8-4j Limitations of the Final Consumer's Decision Process

The limitations of the final consumer's decision process for marketers lie in the hidden (unexpressed) nature of many elements of the process; the consumer's subconscious performance of the process or a number of its components; the impact of demographic, social, and psychological factors on the process; and the differences in decision making among consumers in different countries.

Web Sites You Can Use

One of the best features of the Web is that it gives us access to so much varied information. Thus, there are Web sites devoted to virtually every consumer lifestyle topic imaginable. Just type in a lifestyle topic in your favorite search engine, and away you go. Here is a sampling of the Web sites devoted to mainstream consumer lifestyle topics:

- 360 Youth (**http://www.360youth.com/teens**)—A site focusing on the teenage market.
- American Association of Retired People (**http://www.aarp.org**)—Provides tips for people ages 50 and older.
- Consumer Behavior and Marketing (**http://www.consumerpsychologist.com**)—Focuses on the psychology of consumers.
- Diabetic Lifestyle (**http://www.diabetic-lifestyle.com**)—Geared toward people with diabetes.

- Excel International Sports (**http://www.excelsports.net**)—Offers custom-designed vacation trips to sporting events in Europe.
- Food & Brand Lab (**http://www.consumerpsychology.org**)—Research into why consumers buy what they buy and eat what they eat.
- F.U.N. Place (**http://www.thefunplace.com**)—Devoted, in a colorful way, to parenting.
- Google Groups (**http://groups.google.com**)—Discussion groups on a wide range of lifestyle topics.
- Trendwatching.com (**http://www.trendwatching.com**)—"Scans the U.S., Canada, European Union, Japan, South Korea, India, South Africa, Australia, Brazil, and 70 other nations & regions for hot, emerging consumer and marketing trends."
- Ubercool (**http://www.ubercool.com**)—"Bringing Trends to Life."

Summary

1. *To show the importance and scope of consumer analysis* By analyzing consumers, a firm can better determine the most appropriate audience to which to appeal and the combination of marketing factors to satisfy this audience. This is a critical task given the diversity of the global marketplace. The scope of consumer

analysis includes who, what, why, how, when, where, and how often. Chapter 8 examines final consumers, while Chapters 9 and 10 cover organizational consumers, developing a target market strategy, and sales forecasting.

[22] "Majority of Americans Refer Friends to Favorite Loyalty Programs," http://www.promomagazine.com/premiums/wordofmouth_loyalty_051105 (May 11, 2005).

[23] Jim Cecil, "The Vengeance Factor," *Rough Notes* (January 2001), p. 44.

2. *To define and enumerate important consumer demographics for the U.S. population and other countries* Consumer demographics are objective and quantifiable population statistics. They include population size, gender, and age; population location, housing, and mobility; population income and expenditures; population occupations and education; population marital status; and population ethnicity/race. Profiles can be derived.

The world has nearly 6.5 billion people, rising by 1.2 percent annually. By 2015, the United States will have 322 million people, increasing by less than 0.9 percent each year. In many nations, a large proportion of births involves firstborns. Worldwide, the number of men and women is roughly equal; however, women generally live longer than men. The average age of populations in industrialized nations is higher than in less-developed and developing countries.

Urbanization varies by country, with about four-fifths of the U.S. population living in urban and suburban areas. In many countries, the majority of people own the home in which they live. Each year, millions of people emigrate from one country to another and hundreds of millions move within their countries.

The 2005 U.S. median household income was between $44,000 and $45,000. Many nations measure their cost of living and rate of inflation via a consumer price index. Differences in consumption patterns exist between people in industrialized nations and ones in less-developed and developing countries. When assessing consumption patterns, the distinction between disposable-income spending and discretionary-income expenditures should be kept in mind.

For industrialized nations, the labor force is continuing its movement to white-collar and service occupations; many more jobs in less-developed and developing nations still entail manual work and are agriculture-based. Throughout the world, women comprise a significant part of the labor force. Unemployment varies widely among nations, based on economics and industry shifts. Globally, education has improved in recent decades.

Marriage and family are strong institutions, although less dominant than before for some nations. A family consists of relatives living together. A household consists of a person or persons, related or not, occupying a housing unit. In many nations, both family and household size have declined, due to the growth in single-person households and other factors.

Demographically, ethnicity/race is important as it pertains to the diversity of people among and within nations. Most countries have populations representing different ethnic and racial groups.

3. *To show why consumer demographic analysis is not sufficient in planning marketing strategies* Demographics have limitations: Data may be obsolete; data may be unavailable for some nations; there may be hidden trends or implications; and demographics do not explain the factors affecting behavior, consumer decision making, and motivation.

Because demographic data do not answer such questions as why consumers act as they do, why demographically similar consumers act differently, how motives and risks affect decisions, and how long it takes people to make purchase decisions, many firms now analyze the social and psychological aspects of final consumer lifestyles, as well as the way in which consumers make decisions, in conjunction with demographics.

4. *To define and describe consumer lifestyles and their characteristics, examine selected lifestyles, and consider the limitations of consumer lifestyle analysis* A final consumer's lifestyle is the way in which a person lives and spends time and money. It is a function of the social and psychological factors internalized by that person, along with his or her demographic background. Consumer social profiles consist of several elements, including culture, social class, social performance, reference groups, opinion leaders, the family life cycle, and time expenditures. Psychological profiles are based on a combination of personality, attitudes (opinions), the level of class consciousness, motivation, perceived risk, innovativeness, and purchase importance.

Seven lifestyle types are expected to continue, with their popularity often differing by country: family values, voluntary simplicity, getting by, the "me" generation, blurring gender roles, poverty of time, and component lifestyles.

Many lifestyle concepts are hard to measure, rather subjective, based on consumer self-reports, and sometimes hidden from view. Disputes continue over terms, misuse of data, and reliability.

5. *To define and describe the final consumer's decision process and consider the limitations of final consumer decision-making analysis* Through the decision process, people collect and analyze information and make choices among alternatives. There is the process itself and the factors affecting it (demographic, social, and psychological). A consumer can delay or terminate the process at any point.

The process has six steps: stimulus, problem awareness, information search, evaluation of alternatives, purchase, and post-purchase behavior. There are three types of process: extended, limited, and routine. The way people make decisions varies widely between industrialized nations and less-developed and developing nations. Consumers often reduce shopping time, thought, and risk via low-involvement purchasing and brand loyalty.

The limitations of the decision process for marketers lie in the unexpressed nature of many aspects of the process; the subconscious nature of many consumer actions; the impact of demographic, social, and psychological factors; and the differences between countries in consumer decision making.

Key Terms

final consumers (p. 226)

organizational consumers (p. 226)

consumer demographics (p. 226)

cost of living (p. 229)

disposable income (p. 229)

discretionary income (p. 229)

family (p. 231)

household (p. 231)

ethnicity/race (p. 231)

lifestyle (p. 234)

culture (p. 234)

social class (p. 235)

social performance (p. 236)

reference group (p. 236)

opinion leaders (p. 236)

family life cycle (p. 236)

joint decision making (p. 236)

household life cycle (p. 238)

time expenditures (p. 238)

personality (p. 238)

attitudes (opinions) (p. 238)

class consciousness (p. 238)

motivation (p. 238)

motives (p. 238)

perceived risk (p. 239)

innovativeness (p. 239)

importance of a purchase (p. 240)

final consumer's decision process (p. 242)

stimulus (p. 243)

problem awareness (p. 243)

information search (p. 244)

evaluation of alternatives (p. 245)

purchase act (p. 245)

post-purchase behavior (p. 246)

cognitive dissonance (p. 246)

extended consumer decision making (p. 246)

limited consumer decision making (p. 247)

routine consumer decision making (p. 247)

low-involvement purchasing (p. 248)

brand loyalty (p. 248)

Review Questions

1. How does the use of consumer demographics aid marketing decision making?
2. Cite several reasons why it is difficult to contrast personal income data by country.
3. Why are demographic data alone frequently insufficient for marketing decisions?
4. Distinguish between the traditional family life cycle and the household life cycle.
5. Distinguish between actual risk and perceived risk. How may a firm reduce each type of perceived risk for a new MP3 portable music player?
6. Compare the voluntary simplicity lifestyle with the getting-by lifestyle.
7. What could cause a consumer to *not* make a purchase even when he or she really likes a product?
8. Define low-involvement purchasing and explain its use by consumers. Give an example.

Discussion Questions

1. Develop a demographic profile of the people residing in your state, using the *Census of Population*. What are the marketing overtones of this profile?
2. American culture emphasizes achievement and success, activity, efficiency and practicality, progress, material comfort, individualism, freedom, external conformity, humanitarianism, youthfulness, and fitness and health. What are the implications of this for firms marketing the following goods and services?
   a. Bicycles
   b. Fast food
   c. Personal care products for men
   d. Vacation travel
3. A leading home furnishings designer has hired you as a marketing consultant. It is particularly interested in learning more about the concept of a component lifestyle and developing an appropriate strategy.
   a. Explain the relevance of the component lifestyle concept for the home furnishings industry.
   b. Suggest various ways in which the home furnishings designer can appeal to component lifestyles.
4. How may Kia (http://www.kia.com), the maker of inexpensive autos, reduce both perceived risk *and* cognitive dissonance through its marketing efforts?

Web Exercise

Visit the site of the Jung Typology Test (http://www.humanmetrics.com/cgi-win/JTypes1.htm) for personality assessment and answer the questions. What can a person learn about himself or herself from this site? Do you agree with the profile generated about you from the survey? Explain your answer.

Practice Quiz

1. *Census of Population* data
   a. are gathered annually.
   b. are gathered every 10 years.
   c. include retail sales by merchandise category.
   d. are limited to cities.

2. Projections of the size of the U.S. population reveal that
   a. the number of people is decreasing.
   b. the Northeast is expanding rapidly.
   c. the rate of population growth is slow.
   d. population growth is increasing at a rapid rate.

3. Approximately what percent of people in the United States reside in urban areas and their suburbs?
   a. 80
   b. 60
   c. 50
   d. 45

4. Among U.S. residents, about what percentage of all people move annually?
   a. 50
   b. 35
   c. 25
   d. 15

5. A family is
   a. one or more people residing together.
   b. two or more related people residing together.
   c. a husband, wife, and children, regardless of whether living together.
   d. all relatives, including cousins, regardless of whether living together.

6. According to the U.S. Bureau of the Census, which of the following is *not* a major racial group?
   a. Asian
   b. Hispanic
   c. Black
   d. White

7. Which of the following is *not* an attribute upon which social classes are based?
   a. Culture
   b. Education
   c. Occupation
   d. Type of dwelling

8. The concept of the household life cycle is taking on greater importance because of the
   a. declining number of people who do not have children.
   b. growing number of families with only one working spouse.
   c. growing number of people who do not marry.
   d. declining number of people getting divorced.

9. Self-confidence, dominance, autonomy, sociability, defensiveness, adaptability, and emotional stability are selected
   a. attitudes.
   b. personality traits.
   c. social classes.
   d. stages in the household life cycle.

10. The risk that a product will not perform adequately is an example of which type of perceived risk?
    a. Social
    b. Time
    c. Functional
    d. Financial

11. If a husband stays home and takes care of the children and a wife works full-time outside the home, which type of lifestyle is being exhibited?
    a. Voluntary simplicity
    b. "Me" generation
    c. Blurring of gender roles
    d. Getting by

12. Unlike demographics, many of the social and psychological aspects of consumer lifestyles are
    a. objective.
    b. difficult to measure.
    c. based primarily on observation.
    d. never hidden from view.

13. Listing alternatives that will solve the problem at hand and determining the characteristics of each occurs during which stage of the final consumer's decision process?
    a. Information search
    b. Stimulus
    c. Purchase
    d. Evaluation of alternatives

14. Follow-up telephone and service calls, ads aimed at purchasers, and extended warranties can all be used to help reduce
    a. the time spent on the purchase act.
    b. the number of criteria used in the evaluation of alternatives.
    c. the period from when an order is placed by a consumer until it is received.
    d. cognitive dissonance.

15. In low-involvement purchasing situations, consumers
    a. act slowly.
    b. use extended decision making.
    c. have a relatively high degree of functional perceived risk.
    d. are passive about acquiring information.

For the answers to these questions, please visit the online site for this book at **http://www.atomicdog.com**.

Chapter 9

Organizational Consumers

Even though Boeing (http://www.boeing.com) is the world's largest aerospace firm, it typically is "neck-and-neck" with Airbus (http://www.airbus.com) in market share for commercial jets. Based on orders taken but not yet completed, Airbus has about 55 percent of the large commercial jet business (100-seat-plus planes). In one recent three-year period, Boeing's delivery of commercial jets fell from 527 planes to 285 planes. 2003 was the first year when Airbus outsold Boeing in the number of commercial planes.

The large commercial jet manufacturing business is characterized by slow growth. From 1991 to 2005, deliveries of these planes grew at less than 4 percent per year. Demand is historically affected by airlines' profitability, final consumer demand for air travel, and airlines' retirement cycles for planes. None of these factors suggests high growth: airline profitability has been poor due to high jet fuel costs, and worldwide air travel is growing at an average rate of about 4 percent. One market research firm predicts that world airlines will retire an average of 286 planes per year through 2013.

Commercial airlines generally buy planes from Boeing via long-term fixed-price contracts. The buyer typically pays one-third of the contract price upfront, makes several smaller payments as the planes are being built, and pays the balance upon receipt of the new planes. The fixed-price contract includes escalator clauses tied to labor and materials cost increases over the one-year period it takes to build a commercial plane. Contracts generally specify specific delivery dates. If Boeing cannot deliver the planes on the agreed date, it faces a large penalty. However, if an airline cannot afford to take delivery for all or part of an order, it can defer delivery to a future time period and not forfeit its deposits.

Two of Boeing's most popular commercial planes are its 737 and 787 models. It recently obtained orders for 75 of its 737 model aircraft from Ryanair (http://www.ryanair.com) and for 35 737s from Alaska Airlines (http://www.alaskaair.com). Boeing also got 56 orders for its 787 model aircraft from All Nippon Airways (http://www.fly-ana.com). This was the biggest single order for a new plane in Boeing history.[1]

In this chapter, we will study much more than the characteristics and behavior of organizational (b-to-b) consumers. We will also discuss the different types of b-to-b consumers (including wholesalers and retailers) and their buying objectives, buying structure, and purchase constraints.

Chapter Objectives

1. To introduce the concept of industrial (b-to-b) marketing
2. To differentiate between organizational consumers and final consumers and look at organizational consumers from a global perspective
3. To describe the different types of organizational consumers and their buying objectives, buying structure, and purchase constraints
4. To explain the organizational consumer's decision process
5. To consider the marketing implications of appealing to organizational consumers

---

[1] Various company and other sources.

9-1 OVERVIEW

Organizations purchase goods and services for further production, use in operations, or resale to others—as noted in Chapter 8. In contrast, final consumers buy for personal, family, or household use. Organizational consumers are manufacturers, wholesalers, retailers, and government and other nonprofit institutions. When firms deal with organizational consumers, they engage in *industrial (b-to-b) marketing*. Purchasing executives around the world spend trillions of dollars annually for the goods and services their companies require. Throughout this chapter, we use the term "b-to-b" (business-to-business) to refer to activities and transactions involving organizations. Following are some b-to-b examples.

Calico Cottage (**http://www.calicocottage.com**) is a highly successful company involved in b-to-b marketing. Calico "is the world's largest provider of fudge-making ingredients, equipment, and merchandising expertise—serving customers worldwide, including New Zealand, Australia, Europe, Canada, the Caribbean, and the United States." The firm provides ingredients for more than 400 fudge flavors, offers seasonal packaging and recipes, and has a number of private-label make-at-home mixes—such as brownie mix, hot cocoa mix, and fudge pie mix—that its customers can sell under their own names. Calico customers include gourmet candy stores, local and tourist gift shops, casinos, hotels, and the largest amusement and recreational parks in the world.[2] See Figure 9-1.

The Principal Financial Group, PFG (**http://www.principal.com**), is a leader in financial services for businesses. Its b-to-b insurance division alone serves 74,000

> Firms involved with organizational consumers use **industrial (b-to-b) marketing**.

Calico Cottage, Inc.
210 New Highway • Amityville, NY 11701-1116

631 841-2100
800 645-5345
Fax: 631 841-2401
Click here to contact us.

Home
About Us
Our Program
Our Customers
Our Products
World Record
Success Stories
Local Consultants
Trade Shows
Contact Us

Calico's Program

Opportunity Assessment
We will help you determine whether our program is appropriate for your establishment. We will identify and analyze your key retailing success factors such as traffic count, location, display, signage, flow and dwell time. We will then project your potential sales, profits and return-on-investment from the program.

Differentiation
Only you can offer a product bearing your establishment's name. Our program enables you to create the dramatic sensory impact of a world class, home-made product. It has extraordinary visual appeal and a great aroma. Combine that with unlimited varieties and packaging options and you can create or support a unique theme or personality for your establishment.

Figure 9-1

Calico Cottage: Providing Superior Service to Its Business Customers

Source: Reprinted by permission.

---

[2] "About Fudge and the Calico Cottage Fudge Program," **http://www.calicocottage.com/about_us.shtml** (March 29, 2006).

employers. PFG offers retirement plans (including investment management, employee education, enrollment, comprehensive consulting services, government reporting, compliance testing, and asset allocation), group life and health insurance, business protection plans (in case an owner or key employee dies, becomes disabled, retires, or leaves the client), and employee benefit plans (to help recruit, reward, and retain key employees).[3]

For a long time, Dell (**http://www.dell.com**) earned its reputation, and considerable profits, by making and marketing personal computers for final consumers. But, in recent years, Dell has been placing more emphasis on b-to-b marketing. For instance: "Needing to make complex calculations in a compressed time frame, the Federal Home Loan Bank of Chicago wanted a highly precise, reliable, and scalable solution. In addition, it wanted to offer more choice to users on their Mortgage Partnership Finance Web site and streamline workflow processes." Using advanced Microsoft .NET technologies, Dell developed "a highly interactive Web site and scalable backend applications that enabled the bank to process more mortgage loans. What took hours is now instantaneous."[4]

American Greetings (**http://www.americangreetings.com**) makes cards and other personal-communications products. It is the second-largest firm in the field, behind Hallmark, and markets products in more than 70 nations. Although its products are ultimately sold to final consumers, American Greetings must first get support from organizational consumers—the 125,000 retailers that stock its cards and related items. Accordingly, American Greetings provides research on greeting-cards customers to its retailers, devises and sets up in-store displays, helps computerize transactions, runs special promotions to draw consumers to retail stores, and so on.[5]

Accenture (**http://www.accenture.com**) is a b-to-b consulting firm with annual revenues of $14 billion and more than 115,000 employees in nearly 50 nations. It is "is a global management consulting, technology services, and outsourcing company. Committed to delivering innovation, Accenture collaborates with its clients to help them become high-performance businesses and governments. With deep industry and business process expertise, broad global resources, and a proven track record, Accenture can mobilize the right people, skills, and technologies to help clients improve their performance."[6]

Two emerging trends merit special attention: the growth of the Internet in b-to-b marketing and the rise in outsourcing. As noted in Chapter 7, the b-to-b use of the Internet is having a major impact on the way companies deal with their suppliers and customers. It fosters closer relationships, better communications, quicker transaction times, cost efficiencies, and greater flexibility. Consider the situation at Staples (**http://www.staples.com**), where the Internet is driving its b-to-b efforts:

> StaplesLink.com [**http://www.stapleslink.com**] is our proprietary Web site developed expressly for Staples Contract customers. Created to provide a fast, easy, and cost-effective way to purchase office supplies, this site set the industry standard from day one—and continues to raise the bar today. StaplesLink.com gives you access to over 80,000 products, along with company-specific contract pricing and delivery dates. You can order and return online, minimizing the time and effort spent on procurement. And with StaplesLink.com, you maintain control of the approval and purchasing process. It's no wonder that today more than 66,000 companies and over five million users turn to StaplesLink.com to place 85 percent of their orders.[7]

Outsourcing occurs when one company provides services for another company that could also be or usually have been done in-house by the client firm.[8] Global outsourcing now accounts for hundreds of billions of dollars in annual revenues; and it is gaining

With **outsourcing**, client firms farm out nonessential functions.

[3] "For Businesses," **http://www.principal.com/biz.htm** (March 29, 2006).

[4] "Case Study: Federal Home Loan Bank of Chicago," **http://www.dell.com/downloads/global/casestudies/2005_fed_home_bank_chicago.pdf** (June 2005).

[5] "Investor Relations," **http://www.corporate-ir.net/ireye/ir_site.zhtml?ticker=AM&script=2100** (April 4, 2006).

[6] "Fact Sheet," **http://www.accenture.com/xd/xd.asp?it=enweb&xd=newsroom%5Cfact_sheet.xml** (March 4, 2006).

[7] "Learn About StaplesLink," **http://www.stapleslink.com** (March 4, 2006).

[8] "Outsourcing," **http://searchcio.techtarget.com/sDefinition/0,,sid19_gci212731,00.html** (March 5, 2006).

momentum as companies look to "farm out" to third parties some of the functions that they consider to be nonessential, as highlighted in Figure 9-2. The functions most likely to be outsourced include human resources, information technology, facilities and real-estate management, and accounting. Furthermore, "many companies also outsource customer support and call center functions, manufacturing, and engineering. Outsourcing is characterized by expertise not inherent to the core of the client organization."[9] For more information, visit Outsourcing Center (**http://www.outsourcing-center.com**)—which has a video overview (**http://www.outsourcing-faq.com/1.html**)—and GlobalSources (**http://www.globalservicesmedia.com**).

Next, organizational consumers are distinguished from final consumers and a global perspective is provided. Various b-to-b consumers are described. Key factors in b-to-b consumer behavior are presented. The b-to-b consumer's decision process is outlined. Marketing implications are offered.

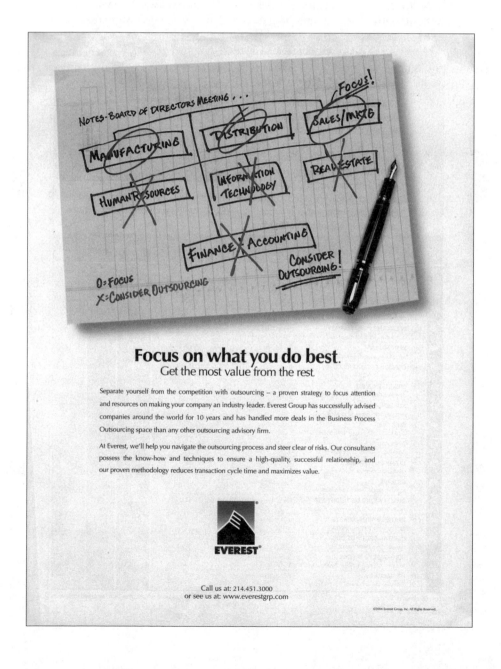

Figure 9-2

The Outsourcing Option for B-to-B Firms

Source: Reprinted by permission.

9-2 THE CHARACTERISTICS OF ORGANIZATIONAL CONSUMERS

In undertaking industrial marketing, a firm must recognize that organizational consumers differ from final consumers in several ways. As shown in Table 9-1, differences are due to the nature of purchases and the nature of the market. A firm must also see that b-to-b consumer characteristics vary by nation.

9-2a Differences from Final Consumers Due to the Nature of Purchases

Organizational and final consumers vary in how they use goods and services and in the items bought. Organizations buy capital equipment, raw materials, semifinished goods, and other products for use in further production or operations or for resale to others. Final consumers usually buy finished items (and are not involved with million-dollar purchases) for personal, family, or household use. Thus, organizations are more apt to use specifications, multiple-buying decisions, value and vendor analysis, leased equipment, and competitive bidding and negotiation than are final consumers.

Many organizations rely on product specifications in purchase decisions and do not consider alternatives unless they meet minimum standards, such as engineering and architectural guidelines, purity, horsepower, voltage, type of construction, and construction materials. Final consumers more often purchase on the basis of description, style, and color.

Table 9-1 Major Differences Between Organizational and Final Consumers

Differences in Purchases

Organizations
1. Buy for further production, use in operations, or resale to others. Final consumers buy only for personal, family, or household use.
2. Commonly purchase installations, raw materials, and semifinished materials. Final consumers rarely purchase these goods.
3. Often buy on the basis of specifications and technical data. Final consumers frequently buy based on description, fashion, and style.
4. Utilize multiple-buying and team-based decisions more often than final consumers.
5. Are more apt to apply formal value and vendor analysis.
6. More commonly lease equipment.
7. More frequently employ competitive bidding and negotiation.

Differences in the Market

Organizations
1. Derive their demand from that of final consumers.
2. Have demand states that are more subject to cyclical fluctuations than final consumer demand.
3. Are fewer in number and more geographically concentrated than final consumers.
4. Often employ buying specialists.
5. Require a shorter distribution channel than do final consumers.
6. May require special relationships with sellers.
7. Are more likely than final consumers to be able to make goods and undertake services as alternatives to purchasing them.

Ethical Issues in Marketing

Nike Promotes the Good Practices of Its Suppliers

Nike (http://www.nike.com) recently decided to publish the names and locations of over 700 of its suppliers. This was an important part of Nike's strategy to highlight the firm's support for ethical working conditions in plants that produce its goods throughout the world. Like other clothing and sportswear manufacturers, Nike has been accused of having some of its products made in sweatshop conditions and of using child labor.

Nike's listing of its suppliers came one month after the company launched Edun (http://www.edun.ie), a brand that focuses on ethical production practices. Edun is seeking to do in the fashion business what Body Shop (http://www.bodyshop.com) has done in beauty and cosmetics (based on its pledge to not test products on animals). Edun, whose fashions are made in Africa, uses nonsubsidized cotton to boost the local economy of developing world nations.

Edun's chief executive says that the "fashion business is uniquely suited to addressing third-world issues because of its increasing reliance on outsourcing. Working conditions can be ethically appraised, and who a brand such as ours conducts business with— and which brands consumers choose to buy—has a significant impact."

Other clothing brands with an ethical orientation include Rogan (http://www.rogannyc.com), which recently introduced a line of organic cotton, and American Apparel (http://www.americanapparelstore. com), which has a "no sweatshops" policy and produces its products in downtown Los Angeles.

Source: Based on material in Meg Carter, "Ethical Business Practices Come into Fashion: Corporate Social Responsibility," *Financial Times* (April 19, 2005), p. 14.

Organizations often use ***multiple-buying responsibility***, whereby two or more employees formally participate in complex or expensive purchase decisions. A decision to buy computerized cash registers may involve input from computer personnel, marketing personnel, the operations manager, a systems consultant, and the controller. The firm's president might make the final choice about system features and the supplier. Although final consumers use multiple-buying responsibility (joint decision making), they employ it less frequently and less formally.

> **Multiple-buying responsibility** may be shared by two or more employees.

Many entities use value analysis and vendor analysis. *In **value analysis**,* organizational consumers thoroughly compare the costs and benefits of alternative materials, components, designs, or processes so as to reduce the cost/benefit ratio of purchases. They seek to answer such questions as: What is the purpose of each good or service under consideration? What are the short-run and long-run costs of each alternative? Is a purchase necessary? Are there substitute goods or services that could be more efficient? How long will a good or service last before it must be replaced? Can uniform standards ease reordering? In ***vendor analysis***, organizational consumers thoroughly assess the strengths and weaknesses of current or new suppliers in terms of quality, customer service, reliability, and price.[10] Satisfaction with current vendors often means customer loyalty. Figures 9-3 and 9-4 illustrate value analysis and vendor analysis.

> **Value analysis** reduces costs; **vendor analysis** rates suppliers.

Organizations of all sizes frequently lease major equipment. The Equipment Leasing Association (**http://www.elaonline.org**) estimates that U.S. firms spend $225 billion each year in leasing equipment (measured by the original cost of the equipment). Commonly leased equipment includes aircraft, computers, office machinery, and trucks and trailers. The worldwide use of commercial leasing is rising rapidly. Final consumers are less involved with leasing; it is most common in apartment and auto leasing.

Organizations often use competitive bidding and negotiation. In ***competitive bidding***, two or more sellers submit independent price quotes for specific goods and/or services to a buyer, which chooses the best offer. In ***negotiation***, a buyer uses bargaining ability and order size to get sellers' best possible prices. Bidding and negotiation most often apply to complex, custom-made goods and services.

> In **competitive bidding**, sellers submit price bids; in **negotiation**, buyers bargain to set prices.

---

[10] "Dictionary of Marketing Terms," **http://www.marketingpower.com/mg-dictionary.php** (May 3, 2006).

Figure 9-3

Value Analysis by a Purchaser of an Electric Pump

	Definitely Yes	Probably Yes	Uncertain	Probably No	Definitely No
• Can plastic pipe be substituted to reduce costs?	_____	_____	_____	_____	_____
• Can a standardized 1/3-horsepower motor be used?	_____	_____	_____	_____	_____
• Can an external float-triggered switch be used instead of an internal one?	_____	_____	_____	_____	_____
• Can a noncorrosive base replace the current base that is easily corroded?	_____	_____	_____	_____	_____
• Is a Westinghouse motor more reliable than a GE motor?	_____	_____	_____	_____	_____
• Is a 5-year warranty acceptable?	_____	_____	_____	_____	_____

9-2b Differences from Final Consumers Due to the Nature of the Market

Derived demand occurs for organizational consumers because the quantity of the items they purchase is often based on the anticipated level of demand by their subsequent customers for specific goods and services. For example, the demand for the precision rivets used in cruise ships is derived from the demand for new cruise ships, which ultimately is derived from the demand for cruises. Firms know that unless demand is generated at the end-user level, distribution pipelines become clogged and resellers will not buy fresh goods and services. Organizational consumers' price sensitivity depends on end-user demand. If end users are willing to pay higher prices, organizations will not object much to increases. If end-user demand is low, organizations will reduce purchases, even if prices to them are lowered. Figure 9-5 illustrates derived demand for major household appliances.

The demand of organizations tends to be more volatile than that of final consumers. A small change in the final demand for highly processed goods and services can yield a large change in organizational consumers' demand. This is due to the ***accelerator principle***, whereby final consumer demand affects many layers of organizational consumers. For example, a drop in auto demand by final consumers reduces dealer demand for cars, auto maker demand for steel, and steel maker demand for iron ore. In addition, capital purchases by organizations are highly influenced by the economy.

> Organizational consumers **derive demand** from their own customers. With the **accelerator principle**, final consumer demand impacts on many organizational consumers.

Figure 9-4

Vendor Analysis of a Sweater Supplier by a Purchaser

	Superior	Average	Inferior
• Speed of normal delivery	_____	_____	_____
• Speed of rush delivery	_____	_____	_____
• Distinctiveness of merchandise	_____	_____	_____
• Availability of styles and colors in all sizes	_____	_____	_____
• Handling of defective merchandise	_____	_____	_____
• Percent of merchandise defective	_____	_____	_____
• Ability for organizational consumer to make a profit when reselling merchandise	_____	_____	_____
• Purchase terms	_____	_____	_____

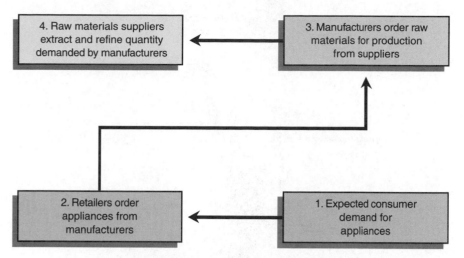

Figure 9-5

Derived Demand for Major Appliances

There are far fewer organizations than final consumers. The United States has 345,000 manufacturing establishments, 440,000 wholesaling establishments (including manufacturer-owned facilities), and 3 million retailing establishments (including small family businesses), as compared with 113 million final consumer households. In some industries, large organizations dominate, and their size and importance give them bargaining power in dealing with sellers.

Organizations tend to be geographically concentrated. For instance, eight states (California, New York, Texas, Ohio, Illinois, Pennsylvania, Michigan, and Florida) contain about half of U.S. manufacturing plants. Some industries (such as steel, petroleum, rubber, auto, and tobacco) are even more geographically concentrated.

Due to their size and the types of purchases, many organizations use buying specialists. These people often have technical backgrounds and are trained in supplier analysis and negotiating. Their full-time jobs are to purchase goods and services and analyze purchases. Expertise is high.

Inasmuch as many organizations are large and geographically concentrated, purchase complex and custom-made goods and services, and use buying specialists, distribution channels tend to be shorter than for final consumers. For example, a laser-printer maker would deal directly with a firm buying 100 printers; a salesperson would call on its purchasing agent. A company marketing printers to final consumers would distribute them via stores and expect final consumers to purchase there.

Organizations may require special relationships. They may expect to be consulted as new products are devised; want extra services, such as extended warranties, liberal returns, and free or inexpensive credit; and want close communications with vendors. That is why firms such as Oracle (**http://www.oracle.com**), the information technology company, devote much attention to their sales force and customer relations.

Systems selling and reciprocity are two specific tactics used in b-to-b marketing. In *systems selling*, a combination of goods and services is provided to a buyer by one vendor. This gives a buyer one firm with which to negotiate and consistency among various parts and components. For example, Fluid Management (**http://www.fluidman.com**) is the worldwide leading maker of mixing and tinting equipment for the paint, coatings, and ink industries. It also markets specialized equipment and engineered systems to other industries, such as food, chemicals, and cosmetics. The firm's products increase the accuracy and efficiency of tinting and mixing paints, inks, and other fluids.[11] See Figure 9-6.

> Organizational consumers tend to be large and geographically concentrated.

> **Systems selling** offers single-source accountability.

---

[11] "About FM," **http://www.fluidman.com/aboutfm/index.asp?page=About** (March 2, 2006).

Figure 9-6

Fluid Management's TintMaster: A Systems Approach

For retailers such as Ace Hardware, "When you're being flooded with large custom paint orders and need to get that long string of tint tasks completed quickly, Fluid Management's TintMaster system gets the job done right the first time, every time."

Source: Reprinted by permission.

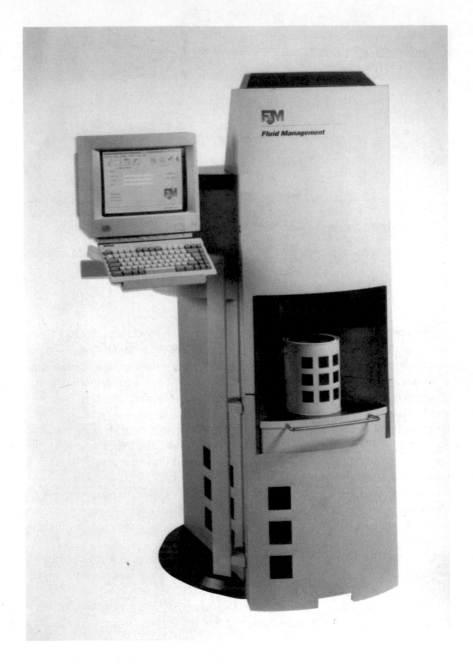

In **reciprocity,** suppliers purchase... as well as sell.

Reciprocity is a procedure by which organizational consumers select suppliers that agree to purchase goods and services, as well as sell them. In the United States, the Justice Department and the FTC monitor reciprocity due to its potential lessening of competition. However, in their international marketing efforts, sellers may sometimes be required to enter into reciprocal agreements—known as "countertrade." Worldwide, countertrade accounts for 15 percent of business transactions between countries; and hundreds of thousands of companies participate in it.[12] The Global Offset and Countertrade Association (**http://www.globaloffset.org**) promotes trade and commerce between companies and their foreign customers who engage in countertrade as a form of doing business.

Last, organizations may produce goods and services themselves if they find purchase terms, the way they are treated, or available choices unacceptable. They may sometimes suggest to suppliers that they will make their own goods or perform services so as to improve bargaining positions.

---

[12] "2004 Global Reciprocal Trade Statistics," **http://www.irta.com/Page.asp?Script=56** (September 28, 2005).

9-2c   A Global Perspective

As with final consumers, dissimilarities exist among organizational consumers around the world, and sellers must understand and respond to them. We discuss these topics here: attitudes to foreign firms as suppliers, the effects of culture on negotiating styles and decision making, the impact of economic development, the need for an adaptation strategy, and the opportunities available due to new technology.

> Foreign organizations must be carefully studied.

Firms doing business in foreign markets need to know how organizations there perceive the goods and services of firms from different countries. The attitudes of purchasing agents in foreign nations toward U.S. products are often quite positive for high-technology items, professional services, and industrial machinery. Likewise, many U.S. firms believe product quality and/or prices for some foreign goods and services are better as compared to American suppliers. That is why Ortho Biotech (**http://www.orthobiotech.com**), a Johnson & Johnson subsidiary, has bought water-purification equipment from Finland and Limited Brands (**http://www.limited.com**) buys clothing from Hong Kong, Taiwan, and other countries.

Nations' cultures have a large impact on the way their organizational consumers negotiate and reach decisions. Here is an illustration:

> Patience is important for successful negotiations with the Chinese. Negotiations there often take time because different Chinese organizations and different departments within one organization tend to be involved in the process, and decision making within the Chinese bureaucracy often takes time. The Chinese will not rush into any serious meetings with someone whom they do not know; trust and a certain feeling of closeness must be in place for negotiation to start. The notions of relationship, face, etiquette, harmony, and so forth, are all time consuming. When mutual trust is not very high and the Chinese are exposed to bureaucratic pressures, tricky situations are common scenes in negotiations.[13]

The stage of economic development in foreign countries affects the types of goods and services bought by organizations there. Many less-developed and developing nations do not yet have the infrastructure (electricity, roads, transportation systems, skilled workers) to properly use state-of-the-art machinery and equipment. In addition, such machinery and equipment may be too expensive for organizations in those markets to afford. On the other hand, there is substantial long-term growth potential in those nations due to their scarcity of industrial goods and services. Firms marketing to less-developed and developing nations need to be understanding and flexible in dealing with organizations.

Firms have to consider how much to adapt their strategies—and their goods and services—to address the unique characteristics and needs of organizations in foreign markets. Because large organizations can account for a significant part of any firm's overall revenues, sellers are often quite willing to be responsive to the organizations' desires—by hiring personnel who fluently speak the language of the foreign markets, utilizing the most appropriate negotiating styles, and adapting product features and customer service as requested. In general, it is more likely that selling firms will engage in meaningful adaptation of their marketing efforts if a potential order is big, the good or service is complex, and the business cultures and stage of economic development in the domestic and foreign markets are dissimilar.

Due to new technology, more opportunities are now available to market to foreign organizational consumers than ever before. The Internet, E-mail, fax machines, satellite TV, and video conferencing all facilitate buyer-seller communications—and tear down the barriers caused by weak technological infrastructures, differences in time zones, and other factors.

---

[13] Pervez Ghauri and Tony Fang, "Negotiating with the Chinese: A Socio-Cultural Analysis," *Journal of World Business*, Vol. 36 (Fall 2001), pp. 320–321.

Marketing and the Web

Designing a Super B-to-B Web Site

Even though a well-designed Web site is often easily remembered, many experts feel that b-to-b sites are generally not designed for maximum impact. According to one consultant, "What you want to do is to take a step back and look at [navigation] from a user's standpoint. Your site is their first impression on how well you understand their needs and how easy you're going to be to do business with."

W.W. Grainger (http://www.grainger.com), which markets maintenance products such as motors and safety gear, originally had a navigation system for its Web site based on its business divisions. It subsequently replaced the older system with one based on consumer behavior. The new design enables users to choose a path using Search or Browse commands.

Here are several tips for creating and maintaining a successful b-to-b Web site:

- Get other Web sites to establish links to your site.
- Obtain feedback about your site from usability studies and focus groups. The site should be organized based on how products are used, not how they are made. Also, watch how typical users attempt to use your site.
- Online chat groups are useful in answering specific questions. They also help move prospective customers closer to making a purchase.
- Organize your site's search engine using terminology used by consumers.

Source: Based on material in Karen J. Bannan, "Sites Designed for Customers," *BtoB's Interactive Marketing Guide* (2005), p. 24.

9-3 | TYPES OF ORGANIZATIONAL CONSUMERS

In devising a marketing plan aimed at organizations, these attributes should be researched: areas of specialization, size and resources, location, and goods and services purchased. As shown in Figure 9-7, organizations can be placed into five broad major categories: manufacturers, wholesalers, retailers, government, and nonprofit.

The *North American Industry Classification System (NAICS)* (http://www.census.gov/epcd/www/naics.html), may be used to derive information about most organizational consumers. The NAICS, which has replaced the outdated Standard Industrial Classification (SIC), was introduced in 1999. The NAICS is the official classification system for the United States, Canada, and Mexico (the members of NAFTA). It assigns organizations to 20 industrial classifications:

> The **North American Industry Classification System (NAICS)** provides information on U.S., Canadian, and Mexican organizations.

- Agriculture, forestry, fishing, and hunting
- Mining
- Utilities
- Construction
- Information
- Finance and insurance
- Real-estate and rental and leasing
- Professional, scientific, and technical services

Figure 9-7

Types of Organizational Consumers

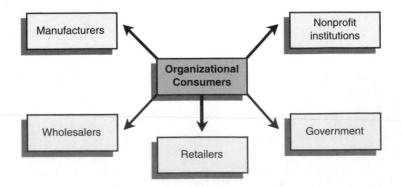

- Management of companies and enterprises
- Administrative and support and waste management and remediation services
- Manufacturing
- Wholesale trade
- Retail trade
- Transportation and warehousing
- Educational services
- Health care and social assistance
- Arts, entertainment, and recreation
- Accommodation and food services
- Other services (except public administration)
- Public administration

Within these groups, 1,150 more specific industry classifications exist, such as farm machinery and equipment manufacturing.

U.S. data by industry code are available from various government and commercial publications. The *U.S. Industry & Trade Outlook* (**http://www.ita.doc.gov/td/industry/ otea/outlook**) and the *Annual Survey of Manufactures* (**http://www.census.gov/prod/ www/abs/industry.html**) are U.S. government reports with data on hundreds of industries. *Standard & Poor's Industry Surveys* (**http://www.standardpoor.com**) and *D&B Reference Book of American Business* (**http://www.dnb.com**) also provide data by industry code and/or geographic area. Data on government institutions are available on a local, state, and federal level from the *Census of Governments* (**http://www.census.gov/govs/ www**).

Although the NAICS is a North American classification system, considerable data on industrial activity and companies in other nations are available in the context of industry codes. The U.S. Department of Commerce's *U.S. Foreign Trade Highlights* (**http://www.ita.doc.gov/td/industry/otea/usfth**) has information on a number of international industries. Dun & Bradstreet's *Principal International Businesses Directory* lists more than 50,000 firms outside the United States.

End-use analysis is one way in which NAICS data can be employed. With it, a seller determines the proportion of sales made to organizational consumers in different industries.[14] Table 9-2 shows end-use analysis for a glue manufacturer (in this case, the seller). First, the firm learns the current relative importance of various categories of customers (section A of Table 9-2.) It then applies end-use analysis to make an overall sales forecast by estimating the expected growth of each customer category in its area (section B of Table 9-2.)

Next, several characteristics of manufacturers, wholesalers, retailers, government, and nonprofit organizations as consumers are described.

> With **end-use analysis**, a seller studies sales made in different industries.

9-3a Manufacturers as Consumers

Manufacturers produce products for resale to other consumers. The NAICS lists three 2-digit industry groups in manufacturing. Each may be divided into 3-digit groups, 4-digit groups, 5-digit groups, and 6-digit groups. Thus, NAICS 33 is a manufacturing classification; 333 refers to machinery manufacturing; 3331 refers to agricultural, construction, and mining machinery manufacturing; 33311 refers to agricultural implement manufacturing; and 333112 refers to farm machinery and equipment manufacturing. Table 9-3 shows the 21 3-digit groups

> **Manufacturers** make items for resale to others.

In the United States, one-third of manufacturers have 20 or more workers. The annual costs of their materials are $2.2 trillion. Their capital expenditures for plant and equipment (from trucks to generator sets) are $150 billion each year. They annually use trillions of BTUs of energy. Annual net sales (including shipments between firms in the

---

[14] See Keith Malo and Mark Marone, "Gather End-User Data and Leverage It to Gain Competitive Edge," *Marketing News* (September 15, 2003), pp. 38–39.

Table 9-2   End-Use Analysis for a Regional Glue Manufacturer

(A) Simple End-Use Analysis

NAICS Code	Industry Classification of Customers	Current Total Sales (in Percent)[a]
321	Wood product manufacturing	25
337	Furniture and related product manufacturing	20
323	Printing and related support activities	17
326	Plastics and rubber products manufacturing	15
316	Leather and allied product manufacturing	10
339	Miscellaneous manufacturing	13
	Total	100

(B) Applying End-Use Analysis to Sales Forecasting

NAICS Code	Industry Classification of Customers	Current Total Sales (in Percent)	Estimated Annual percentage Growth Rate of Industry[b]	Overall Sales Growth Percentage for a Glue Manufacturer[c]
321	Wood product manufacturing	25	+1.8	+0.45
337	Furniture and related product manufacturing	20	+3.2	+0.64
323	Printing and related support activities	17	+1.9	+0.32
326	Plastics and rubber products manufacturing	15	+3.0	+0.45
316	Leather and allied product manufacturing	10	−2.0	−0.20
339	Miscellaneous manufacturing	13	+2.0	+0.26
	Total estimated sales increase			+1.92

[a] Firm examines its sales receipts and categorizes them by NAICS group.

[b] Firm estimates growth rate of each category of customer (in its geographic area) on the basis of trade association and government data.

[c] Firm multiplies percent of current sales in each NAICS group by expected growth rate in each industry to derive its expected sales for the coming year. It expects sales to rise by 1.92 percent during the next year.

Table 9-3	U.S. Manufacturing Industries
NAICS Code	**Industry Name**
31, 32, 33	Manufacturing
311	Food manufacturing
312	Beverage and tobacco product manufacturing
313	Textile mills
314	Textile product mills
315	Apparel manufacturing
316	Leather and allied product manufacturing
321	Wood product manufacturing
322	Paper manufacturing
323	Printing and related support activities
324	Petroleum and coal products manufacturing
325	Chemical manufacturing
326	Plastics and rubber products manufacturing
327	Nonmetallic mineral product manufacturing
331	Primary metal manufacturing
332	Fabricated metal product manufacturing
333	Machinery manufacturing
334	Computer and electronic product manufacturing
335	Electrical equipment, appliance, and component manufacturing
336	Transportation equipment manufacturing
337	Furniture and related product manufacturing
339	Miscellaneous manufacturing

Source: "2002 NAICS Codes and Titles," http://www.census.gov/epcd/naics02/naicod02.htm.

same industry category) are $4 trillion, with the largest 500 industrial firms accounting for 60 percent of the total.

By knowing where different industries are located, a seller can concentrate efforts and not worry about dispersed markets. Because manufacturers' purchasing decisions tend to be made centrally at headquarters or at divisional offices, the seller must identify the location of the proper decision makers.

As consumers, manufacturers buy a variety of goods and services, including land, capital equipment, machinery, raw materials, component parts, trade publications, accounting services, supplies, insurance, advertising, and delivery services. For example, Boeing (http://www.boeing.com) has long- and short-term contracts with suppliers that total several billion dollars; and it buys equipment, raw materials, component parts, finished materials, and services from thousands of subcontractors and other businesses.

9-3b   Wholesalers as Consumers

Wholesalers buy or handle merchandise and its subsequent resale to organizational users, retailers, and other wholesalers. They do not sell significant volume to final users but are involved when services are marketed to organizations. Table 9-4 lists the major industry groups in wholesaling, as well as transportation industries and business services. Chapter 16 has a broad discussion of wholesaling.

Wholesalers buy or handle merchandise and its resale to nonfinal consumers.

Table 9-4	U.S. Wholesaling and Related Industries
NAICS Code	**Industry Name**
42	Wholesale trade
423	Merchant wholesalers, durable goods
424	Merchant wholesalers, nondurable goods
425	Wholesale electronic markets and agents and brokers
48, 49	Transportation and warehousing
481	Air transportation
482	Rail transportation
483	Water transportation
484	Truck transportation
486	Pipeline transportation
488	Support for transportation
491	Postal service
492	Couriers and messengers
493	Warehousing and storage
54	Professional, scientific, and technical services
541	Professional, scientific, and technical services

Source: "2002 NAICS Codes and Titles," http://www.census.gov/epcd/naics02/naicod02.htm.

U.S. wholesalers are most prominent in California, New York, Texas, Florida, Illinois, Pennsylvania, Ohio, and New Jersey. Annual wholesaling and related sales (excluding manufacturer wholesaling) are $4 trillion. Sales are largest for groceries and related products; drugs and related products; professional and commercial equipment and supplies; petroleum products; machinery, equipment, and supplies; motor vehicles and related parts and supplies; electrical goods; lumber and other construction materials; and farm-product raw materials.

As consumers, wholesalers buy or handle many goods and services, including warehouse facilities, trucks, finished products, insurance, refrigeration and other equipment, trade publications, accounting services, supplies, and spare parts. A major task in dealing with wholesalers is getting them to carry the selling firm's product line for further resale, thereby placing items into the distribution system. For new sellers or those with new products, gaining cooperation may be difficult. Even well-established manufacturers may have problems with their wholesalers due to the competitive marketplace, wholesalers' perceptions that they are not being serviced properly, or wholesalers' lack of faith in the manufacturers' products.

9-3c Retailers as Consumers

Retailers sell to the final consumer.

Retailers buy or handle goods and services for sale (resale) to the final (ultimate) consumer. They usually obtain goods and services from both manufacturers and wholesalers. Table 9-5 lists the major industry groups in retailing, as well as several related service businesses that cater to final consumers. Chapter 17 has a broad discussion of retailing.

Annual U.S. retail sales (both store and nonstore) for firms in NAICS codes 44, 45, and 722 are $4.5 trillion. Chains account for about 65 percent of total retail sales. About 750,000 retail stores are operated by franchisees. A large amount of retailing involves auto dealers, general merchandise stores, food and beverage stores, eating and drinking places,

Table 9-5	U.S. Retailing and Retailed Industries
NAICS Code	**Industry Name**
44, 45	Retail trade
441	Motor vehicle and parts dealers
442	Furniture and home furnishings stores
443	Electronics and appliance stores
444	Building materials and garden equipment and supplies dealers
445	Food and beverage stores
446	Health and personal care stores
447	Gasoline stations
448	Clothing and clothing accessories stores
451	Sporting good, hobby, book, and music stores
452	General merchandise stores
453	Miscellaneous store retailers
454	Nonstore retailers
52	Finance and insurance
522	Credit intermediation and related activities
523	Securities, commodity contracts, and other financial investments
524	Insurance carriers and related activities
53	Real-estate and rental and leasing
531	Real-estate
532	Rental and leasing services
71	Arts, entertainment, and recreation
711	Performing arts, spectator sports, and related industries
712	Museums, historical sites, and similar institutions
713	Amusements, gambling, and recreational industries
72	Accommodation and food services
721	Accommodations
722	Food services and drinking places
81	Other services, except public administration
811	Repair and maintenance
812	Personal and laundry services

Source: "2002 NAICS Codes and Titles," http://www.census.gov/epcd/naics02/naicod02.htm.

gas stations, apparel stores, health and personal care stores, and furniture and home furnishings stores.

As consumers, retailers buy or handle a variety of goods and services, including store locations, facilities, interior design, advertising, resale items, insurance, and trucks. Unlike wholesalers, they are usually concerned about both product resale and the composition of their physical facilities (stores)—because final consumers usually shop at stores, whereas wholesalers frequently call on customers. Retailers often buy fixtures, displays, and services to decorate and redecorate stores.

Getting retailers to stock new items or continue handling current ones can be difficult because store and catalog space is limited and retailers have their own goals. Many retail chains have evolved into large and powerful customers, not just "shelf stockers." Some are so powerful that they may even charge *slotting fees* just to carry manufacturers' products in their stores:

> Slotting fees, referring to both upfront fees paid to get products on the shelves and ongoing fees to stay in stores, have become commonplace since they were instituted in supermarkets in the 1980s to cover marketing and other costs. They have since spread to more products, from greeting cards to over-the-counter drugs. Small manufacturers argue that steep payments for shelf placement, mostly hidden from public view, make it difficult to compete with larger, wealthier companies. The Federal Trade Commission estimates that retailers collect $9 billion in the fees annually.[15]

Retailers (wholesalers) sometimes insist that suppliers make items under the retailers' (wholesalers') names. For private-label manufacturers, the continued orders of these customers are essential. If a large retailer (wholesaler) stops doing business with a private-label manufacturer, that firm has to establish its own identity with consumers. It may even go out of business due to the lack of recognition.

9-3d Government as Consumer

> **Government** purchases and uses a variety of routine and complex products.

Government consumes goods and services in performing its duties and responsibilities. Federal (1), state (50), and local (88,000) units together account for the greatest volume of purchases of any consumer group in the United States—with all branches spending $2.2 trillion (excluding employee wages) on goods and services each year. The federal government accounts for 40 percent of that spending. The biggest budget shares (including employee wages) go for operations, capital outlays, military services, postal services, education, highways, public welfare, health care, police, fire protection, sanitation, and natural resources. Data on all levels of U.S. government expenditures are compiled by the Census Bureau (http://www.census.gov/govs/www/index.html). Table 9-6 shows the major NAICS codes for government.

Governmental consumers buy a wide range of goods and services, including food, military equipment, office buildings, subway cars, office supplies, clothing, and vehicles.

Table **9-6**	U.S. Federal, State, and Local Government (Public Administration)
NAICS Code	**Industry Name**
92	Public administration
921	Executive, legislative, and other general government support
922	Justice, public order, and safety activities
923	Administration of human resource programs
924	Administration of environmental quality programs
925	Administration of housing programs, urban planning, and community development
926	Administration of economic programs
927	Space research and technology
928	National security and international affairs

Source: "2002 NAICS Codes and Titles," http://www.census.gov/epcd/naics02/naicod02.htm.

[15] Rachel Brown, "Pay-to-Shelve Grocery Store Practices Called Too Pricey," *Los Angeles Business Journal Online* (April 11, 2005).

Some purchases involve standard products offered to traditional consumers; others, such as highways, are specially made for a government customer. Although many big firms— such as Boeing (**http://www.boeing.com**) and Lockheed Martin (**http://www.lockheed.com**) derive major percentages of their sales from government contracts, small sellers now account for several billion dollars in federal purchases. In fact, one-quarter of federal agency purchase contracts are with small firms.

Some small firms are unaccustomed to the bureaucracy, barriers, political sensitivities, and financial constraints of selling to government consumers. To aid them, the federal General Services Administration operates regional Small Business Utilization Centers (**http://www.gsa.gov/smallbusiness**) to issue directories, reference data, and technical reports on contracts and contracting procedures, bidding documents, and specifications.

9-3e   Nonprofit Institutions as Consumers

Nonprofit institutions act in the public interest or to foster a cause and do not seek financial profits. Public hospitals, museums, most universities, civic organizations, and parks are nonprofit institutions. They buy goods and services in order to run their organizations and also buy items for resale to generate additional revenues to offset costs. Many national and international nonprofit institutions exist, such as the American Cancer Society (**http://www.cancer.org**), the Boy Scouts (**http://www.scouting.org**) and Girl Scouts (**http://www.girlscouts.org**), and the International Committee of the Red Cross (**http://www.icrc.org/eng**). Hospitals, museums, and universities, due to fixed locations, tend to be local nonprofit institutions.

> **Nonprofit institutions** function in the public interest.

No separate NAICS codes exist for nonprofit- versus profit-oriented firms. Yet, firms in these NAICS categories are often nonprofit: 61 (educational services), 62 (health care and social assistance), 712 (museums and similar institutions), and 813 (organizations and associations).

9-4   KEY FACTORS IN ORGANIZATIONAL CONSUMER BEHAVIOR

Organizations' purchase behavior depends on their buying objectives, buying structure, and purchase constraints.

9-4a   Buying Objectives

Organizations have several distinct goals in purchasing goods and services. Generally, these objectives are important: availability of items, reliability of sellers, consistency of quality, delivery, price, and customer service. See Figure 9-8.

> **Organizational buying objectives** relate to availability, reliability, consistency, delivery, price, and service.

Availability means a buyer can obtain items as needed. An organization's production or resales may be inhibited if products are unavailable at the proper times. *Seller reliability* is based on the fairness in allotting items in high demand, nonadversarial relationships, honesty in reporting bills and shipping orders, and reputation. *Consistency of quality* refers to buyers' interest in purchasing items of proper quality on a regular basis. Thus, drill bits should have the same hardness each time they are bought. *Delivery goals* include minimizing the time from ordering to receiving items, minimizing the order size required by the supplier, having the seller responsible for shipments, minimizing costs, and adhering to an agreed-on schedule. *Price considerations* involve purchase prices and the flexibility of payment terms. *Customer service* entails the seller's satisfying special requests, having a staff ready to field questions, promptly solving problems, and having a good relationship. For example, Hewlett-Packard works with small and medium businesses (**http://www.hp.com/sbso**), large businesses (**http://www.hp.com/go/enterprise**), and government, health, and education customers (**http://government.hp.com/index.asp**). See Figure 9-9.

Figure 9-8

Goals of Organizational Consumers

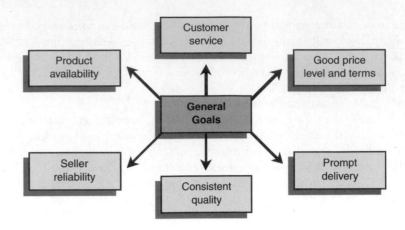

B-to-b marketers must recognize that price is only one of several considerations for organizations. It may be lower in importance than availability, quality, service, and other factors. Consider this: "Everyone thinks you have to offer the lowest prices, but that simply isn't the case. Governments are getting more sophisticated about specifying bids for the lowest total cost of ownership through the product's life cycle, so such things as maintenance and repair costs are major factors."[16]

With regard to more specific goals, manufacturers are concerned about quality standards for raw materials, component parts, and equipment. Some like dealing with many suppliers to protect against shortages, foster price and service competition, and be exposed to new products. Others have been reducing the number of suppliers from which they buy to foster better relationships, cut ordering inefficiencies, and have more clout with each supplier.

> Saleability and exclusivity are keys for wholesalers and retailers.

Wholesalers and retailers consider further saleability (their customers' demand) to be the highest priority. If possible, they seek buying arrangements whereby the number of distribution intermediaries that can carry goods and services in a geographic area is limited. They also seek manufacturers' advertising, transportation, and warehousing support.

Government buyers frequently set exact specifications for some products they purchase; as large-volume buyers, they can secure them. Governments may sometimes consider the economic conditions in the geographic areas of potential sellers. Contracts may be awarded to the firms with higher unemployment in their surrounding communities.

Nonprofits stress price, availability, and reliability. They may seek special terms in recognition of their nonprofit status.

9-4b   Buying Structure

The buying structure refers to the formality and specialization used in the purchase process. It depends on the organization's size, resources, diversity, and format. The structure is apt to be formal (separate department) for a large, corporate, resourceful, diversified, and departmentalized organization. It will be less formal for a small, independently owned, financially limited, focused, and general organization.

> The organization's buying structure depends on its attributes.

Large manufacturers normally have specialized purchasing agents who work with the firms' engineers or production department. Large wholesalers tend to have a purchasing department or a general manager in charge of operations. Large retailers tend to be quite specialized and have buyers for each narrow product category. Small manufacturers, wholesalers, and retailers often have their buying functions completed by the owner-operator.

---

[16] Roger Slavens, "How to Market to Government," http://www.btobonline.com/article.cms?articleId=24152 (May 2, 2005).

If you're not at capacity, don't pay for capacity.

With the new hp superdome, you can pay less when you use less, or buy more when you need more.
By adjusting capacity with a simple phone call, you pay only for what you use—not unlike how you pay for electricity.
You can run IA-64, you can run multiple operating systems, and because comprehensive service is included,
you can run your business instead of your server. hp.com/superdome

hp invent

Figure 9-9

Hewlett-Packard: Striving to Meet Buyers' Objectives

HP really tries to work with its business and government accounts. As this ad for an always-on, high-end computer server states, "You can pay less when you use less, or buy more when you need more. By adjusting capacity with a simple phone call, you pay only for what you use."

Source: Reprinted by permission.

Each government unit (federal, state, and local) typically has a purchasing department. The General Services Administration, or GSA (**http://www.gsa.gov**), is the federal office responsible for centralized procurement and coordination of purchases. Each federal unit may buy via the GSA's Federal Acquisition Service (formerly the Federal Supply Service) or directly from suppliers; either way, it must adhere to printed rules. In a nonprofit organization, there is often one purchasing department or a member of the operations staff performs buying functions.

9-4c Constraints on Purchases

For manufacturers, wholesalers, and retailers, derived demand is the major constraint on purchase behavior. Without the demand of consumers, production halts and sales drop as the backward chain of demand comes into play (final consumers→retailers→wholesalers→manufacturers).

Manufacturers also are constrained by the availability of raw materials and their ability to pay for big-ticket items. Wholesalers and retailers are limited by the funds available to make purchases, as well as by the level of risk they are willing to take. In this case, risk refers to the probability that wholesalers or retailers can sell the products they buy in a reasonable time and at a satisfactory profit. Products such as fashion apparel have higher risks than such staple items as vitamins and disposable diapers.

Government buyers are constrained by the budgeting process. Approval for categories of purchases must normally be secured well in advance, and deviations must be

> Derived demand is the key constraint on organizational purchases.

explained. Budgets must be certified by legislative bodies. For many nonprofit consumers, cash flow (the timing of the money they have coming in versus the money they spend) is the major concern.

9-5 THE ORGANIZATIONAL CONSUMER'S DECISION PROCESS

> An **organizational consumer's decision process** is like that of a final consumer.

Organizations use a decision-making procedure in much the same way as final consumers. Figure 9-10 shows the ***organizational consumer's decision process***, with its four components: expectations, buying process, conflict resolution, and situational factors.[17]

9-5a Expectations

> Expectations are based on buyers' backgrounds, information, perceptions, and experience.

Purchasing agents, engineers, and users bring a set of organizational expectations to any buying situation: "These expectations refer to the perceived potential of alternative suppliers and brands to satisfy a number of explicit and implicit objectives."[18]

For purchases to occur, buyers must have positive expectations about such supplier attributes as product availability and quality, vendor reliability, delivery time, price, and customer service. Expectations are based on the backgrounds of those participating in the buying process, the information received, perceptions, and satisfaction with past purchases.

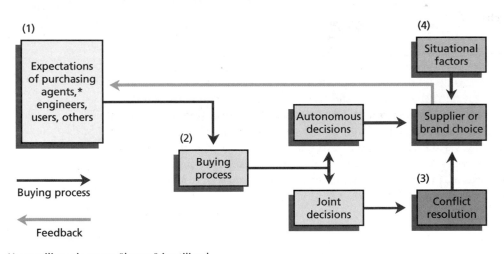

Figure 9-10

The Organizational Consumer's Decision Process

Source: Adapted from Jagdish N. Sheth, "A Model of Industrial Buyer Behavior," *Journal of Marketing*, Vol. 37 (October 1973), p. 51. Reprinted by permission of the American Marketing Association.

---

[17] The material in this section is drawn from Jagdish N. Sheth, "A Model of Industrial Buyer Behavior," *Journal of Marketing*, Vol. 37 (October 1973), pp. 50–56. See also John F. Tanner, Jr., Jeong Eun Park, and Michele Bunn, "Organizational Memory: A New Perspective on the Organizational Buying Process," *Journal of Business & Industrial Marketing*, Vol. 18 (Number 3, 2003), pp. 237–257; and Jeffrey E. Lewin and Naveen Donthu, "The Influence of Purchase Situation on Buying Center Structure and Involvement: A Select Meta-Analysis of Organizational Buying Behavior Research," *Journal of Business Research*, Vol. 58 (October 2005), pp. 1381–1390.

[18] Sheth, "A Model of Industrial Buyer Behavior," p. 52.

9-5b Buying Process

In the buying process, a decision as to whether to consider making a purchase is initiated, information is gathered, alternative suppliers are rated, and conflicts among different buyer representatives are resolved. The process is similar to the final consumer buying process. Because of the Internet, information gathering—at sites such as Grainger.com (**http://www.grainger.com**) and Thomas Register (**http://www.thomasnet.com**)—has been simplified for many buyers.

The buying process may involve autonomous (independent) or joint decisions based on product and company factors. *Product-specific buying factors* include perceived risk, purchase frequency, and time pressure. Autonomous decisions occur mostly with low perceived risk, routine products, and high time pressure. Joint decisions are more likely with high perceived risk, seldom-bought products, and low time pressure. *Company-specific buying factors* are a firm's basic orientation, size, and level of decision-making centralization. Autonomous decisions most often occur with a high technology or production orientation, small organization, and high centralization. Joint decisions are more likely with a low technology or production orientation, large organization, and little centralization in decision making.

As noted earlier, competitive bidding is often used by organizational buyers: Potential sellers specify in writing all terms of a purchase in addition to product attributes; the buyer then selects the best bid. With *open bidding*, proposals can be seen by competing sellers. With *closed bidding*, contract terms are kept secret and sellers are asked to make their best presentation in their first bids. Bidding is used in government purchases to avoid charges of unfair negotiations, and government bids tend to be closed.

> Autonomous or joint decision making is based on product and company buying factors.

9-5c Conflict Resolution

Joint decision making may lead to conflicts due to the diverse backgrounds and perspectives of purchasing agents, engineers, and users. **Conflict resolution** is then needed to make a decision. Four methods of resolution are possible: problem solving, persuasion, bargaining, and politicking.

Problem solving occurs if purchasing team members decide to acquire further information before making a decision. This is the best procedure. *Persuasion* takes place when each team member presents reasons why a given supplier or brand should be picked. In theory, the most logical presentation should be chosen. Yet, the most dynamic (or powerful) person may persuade others to follow his or her lead.

Under *bargaining*, team members agree to support each other in different situations, with less attention paid to the merits of a purchase. One member may select the supplier of the current item; in return, another member would choose a vendor the next time. The last, and least desired, method of conflict resolution is *politicking*. In this method, team members try to persuade outside parties and superiors to back their positions, and seek to win at power plays.

> Problem solving, persuasion, bargaining, and politicking lead to **conflict resolution**.

9-5d Situational Factors

A number of **situational factors** can interrupt the decision process and the actual selection of a supplier or brand. These include "temporary economic conditions such as price controls, recession, or foreign trade; internal strikes, walkouts, machine break-downs, and other production-related events; organizational changes such as merger or acquisition; and ad hoc changes in the marketplace, such as promotional efforts, new-product introduction, price changes, and so on, in the supplier industries."[19]

> **Situational factors** affect organizational consumer decisions.

[19] Ibid., p. 56.

Global Marketing in Action

Specialty Malls for Wholesale Buyers

International Home Deco Park (IHDP) is a 350,000-square-foot business-to-business mall located near Delhi, India. IHDC serves as a center where organizational buyers can visit with permanent exhibitors throughout the year. IHDP caters to each of the major home décor sectors: floor coverings, textiles, gifts and handicrafts, and furniture and fittings. Integral to IHDP's strategy is the space devoted to providers of such support services as a design library, a photo studio, and a service center for packaging, labeling, testing, inspecting, and shipping goods.

Another similar b-to-b mall is Ishanya, which is being marketed as a one-stop shopping mall for interiors and exteriors. The center targets real-estate projects in the western region of India. Ishanya sells such products as furniture, kitchen goods, bathroom accessories, and flooring. The mall also devotes space to specialists in illumination services; landscaping design; heating, ventilating, and air-conditioning (HVAC); and real-estate consultants. In addition to traditional space, this mall has a 750-seat convention center, as well as meeting rooms for seminars and conferences.

These b-to-b malls can be differentiated from trade shows, which use a facility on a temporary basis and do not have adequate space for many samples. Like traditional shopping centers for final consumers, they provide industrial buyers with one-stop shopping and the ability to easily compare offerings.

Source: Based on material in "It's Time for B2B Malls Now," *Financial Express Online* (July 31, 2005).

9-5e Purchase and Feedback

After the decision process is completed and situational factors are taken into account, a purchase is made (or the process terminated) and a product is used or experienced. The level of satisfaction with a purchase is then fed back to a purchasing agent or team, and the data are stored for future use.

To keep customers satisfied and ensure continued purchases, regular service and follow-up calls by sellers are essential:

A beer salesperson became very busy and stopped calling on a small retail chain. The operator called him; the rep said he'd been swamped, but would get to the retailer as soon as he could. Another month passed. Frustrated, the retailer bought a bereavement card, scribbled a message on it, and sent it to the salesperson's boss. The card read: "I know Pat must have either passed away or is in a coma, or he certainly wouldn't have neglected me for so long." The boss was not amused. He called the retailer and said he didn't appreciate the sarcasm. In response, the retailer faxed a copy of a recent letter naming a competitor the chain's "Top Sales Professional" in the beer category. Within minutes, the boss called the retailer back and said, "I can't quarrel with a person who sees both sides of the matter!" The next year, the once-neglectful beer salesperson received the chain's recognition.[20]

9-5f Types of Purchases

Organizational buyers use a **new-task process** for unique items, **modified rebuys** for infrequent purchases, and **straight rebuys** for regular purchases.

A **new-task purchase process** is needed for expensive products an organizational consumer has not bought before. A lot of decision making is undertaken, and perceived risk is high. This is similar to extended decision making for a final consumer. A **modified-rebuy purchase process** is employed for medium-priced products an organizational consumer has bought infrequently before. Moderate decision making is needed. This is similar to limited decision making for a final consumer. A **straight-rebuy purchase process** is used for inexpensive items bought regularly. Reordering, not decision making, is applied because perceived risk is very low. This is similar to a routine purchase for a final consumer.

[20] Barbara Grondin Francella, "The Ties That Bind," *Convenience Store News* (May 5, 2003), p. 31.

9-6 | MARKETING IMPLICATIONS

Although organizations and final consumers have substantial differences in their purchasing behavior (as mentioned earlier), they also have similarities.

- Both can be described demographically; statistical and descriptive data can be gathered and analyzed.
- Both have different categories of buyers, each with separate needs and requirements.
- Both can be defined by using social and psychological factors, such as operating style, buying structure, purchase use, expectations, perceived risk, and conflict resolution.
- Both use a decision process, employ joint decision making, and face various kinds of purchase situations.

> Many similarities, as well as differences, exist between organizational and final consumers.

This means that b-to-b marketers must have plans reflecting the similarities, as well as the differences, between organizations and final consumers. In their roles as sellers, manufacturers and wholesalers may also need two marketing plans: one for intermediate buyers and one for final consumers.

Finally, it must be recognized that purchasing agents or buyers have personal goals, as well as organizational goals. They seek status, approval, promotions, bonuses, and other rewards. And as shown in Figure 9-10, they bring distinct expectations to each buying situation, just as final consumers do.

One leading consultant offers these suggestions for b-to-b marketers:

- *Understand how your customers run their business.*
- *Show how your good or service fits into your customer's business.*
- *Make sure the benefits you sell stay current.*
- *Know how customers buy, and fit your selling to their buying process.*
- *When selling, reach everyone on the customer's side involved in the buying decision.*
- *Communicate to each decider the message that will address his or her chief concerns.*
- *Be the person or firm with whom your customers prefer to have a relationship.*
- *Be sure everything is consistent with your chosen level of quality, service, price, and performance.*
- *Understand your competitors' strengths and weaknesses.*
- *Strive to dominate your niche.*
- *Train your people in each aspect of your business and that of your customers.*
- *Have a distribution system that meets your needs and those of your customers.*
- *Seek new markets and new applications for your existing products.*
- *Enhance your products with customer service.*
- *Have your goals clearly in mind.*[21]

> Industrial marketing strategies should be insightful.

Web Sites You Can Use

Many Web sites are devoted exclusively to industrial marketing. One of the best such sites is BtoBonline.com (http://www.netb2b.com), "the magazine for marketing strategists." It covers a range of topics and has many special sections, including a "Marketers' Resource Guide" (http://www.netb2b.com/pdfs.cms), the "10 Great Web Sites" (http://www.btobonline.com/article.cms?articleId=25424)—which cites 10 outstanding b-to-b Web sites, and "Newsletters" (http://www.btobonline.com/newsletters.cms)—which covers several areas of business-to-business marketing.

---

[21] F. Michael Hruby, "17 Tips (Not Just) for Industrial Marketers," *Sales & Marketing Management* (May 1990), pp. 68–76.

Summary

1. *To introduce the concept of industrial (b-to-b) marketing* When firms market goods and services to manufacturers, wholesalers, retailers, and government and other nonprofit institutions, industrial (b-to-b) marketing is used.

2. *To differentiate between organizational consumers and final consumers and look at organizational consumers from a global perspective* Organizations buy goods and services for further production, use in operations, or resale to others; they buy installations, raw materials, and semifinished materials. They often buy based on specifications, use joint decision making, apply formal value and vendor analysis, lease equipment, and use bidding and negotiation. Their demand is generally derived from that of their consumers and can be cyclical. They are fewer in number and more geographically concentrated. They may employ buying specialists, expect sellers to visit them, require special relationships, and make goods and undertake services rather than buy them.

   There are distinctions among organizational consumers around the globe.

3. *To describe the different types of organizational consumers and their buying objectives, buying structure, and purchase constraints* Organizations may be classified by area of specialization, size and resources, location, and goods and services purchased. Major organizations are manufacturers, wholesalers, retailers, government, and nonprofits. The North American Industry Classification System provides much data on organizations in the United States, Canada, and Mexico.

   B-to-b consumers have general buying goals, such as product availability, seller reliability, consistent quality, prompt delivery, good prices, and superior customer service. They also have more specific goals, depending on the type of firm involved. An organization's buying structure refers to its level of formality and specialization in the purchase process. Derived demand, availability, further saleability, and resources are the leading purchase constraints.

4. *To explain the organizational consumer's decision process* This process includes buyer expectations, the buying process, conflict resolution, and situational factors. Of prime importance is whether an organization uses joint decision making and, if so, how. Some form of bidding may be employed with organizational consumers (most often with government).

   If conflicts arise in joint decisions, problem solving, persuasion, bargaining, or politicking is used to arrive at a resolution. Situational factors can intervene between decision making and a purchase. They include strikes, economic conditions, and organizational changes.

   New task, modified rebuy, and straight rebuy are the different purchase situations facing organizational consumers.

5. *To consider the marketing implications of appealing to organizational consumers* Organizational buyers and final consumers have many similarities and differences. B-to-b marketers must understand them and adapt marketing plans accordingly. Dual marketing campaigns may be necessary for manufacturers and wholesalers that sell to intermediate buyers and have their products resold to final consumers.

   Purchasing agents and buyers have personal goals, such as status, promotions, and bonuses; these may have a large impact on decision making.

   B-to-b marketers can do many things to enhance their chances for success. A number of them are outlined in this chapter.

Key Terms

industrial (b-to-b) marketing (p. 257)

outsourcing (p. 258)

multiple-buying responsibility (p. 261)

value analysis (p. 261)

vendor analysis (p. 261)

competitive bidding (p. 261)

negotiation (p. 261)

derived demand (p. 262)

accelerator principle (p. 262)

systems selling (p. 263)

reciprocity (p. 264)

North American Industry Classification System, NAICS (p. 266)

end-use analysis (p. 267)

manufacturers (p. 267)

wholesalers (p. 269)

retailers (p. 270)

government (p. 272)

nonprofit institutions (p. 273)

organizational consumer's decision process (p. 276)

conflict resolution (p. 277)

situational factors (p. 277)

new-task purchase process (p. 278)

modified-rebuy purchase process (p. 278)

straight-rebuy purchase process (p. 278)

Review Questions

1. Describe five of the most important differences between organizational and final consumers.
2. Distinguish between vendor analysis and value analysis.
3. How is the North American Industry Classification System a useful marketing tool?
4. What are the most important general organizational consumer-buying objectives?
5. For manufacturers, wholesalers, and government, what is the major constraint on their purchase behavior? Why?

6. How do product-specific and company-specific buying factors affect the use of autonomous or joint decision making?

7. Which is the worst form of conflict resolution? The best? Explain your answers.

8. Cite several suggestions that b-to-b marketers should keep in mind when developing and enacting their strategies.

Discussion Questions

1. As a university's purchasing agent, what criteria would you use for competitive bidding in the purchase of new classroom furniture?

2. A packaging firm knows its current sales are allocated as follows: 30 percent to animal food manufacturers (NAICS code 3111), 15 percent to sugar and confectionery products manufacturers (NAICS code 3113), 15 percent to dairy products manufacturers (NAICS code 3115), 20 percent to bakeries (NAICS code 3118), and 20 percent to other food manufacturers (NAICS code 3119). The firm expects next year's industry sales growth in these categories to be as follows: 3111, 3 percent; 3113, 4 percent; 3115, 6 percent; 3118, 0 percent; and 3119, 7 percent. According to end-use analysis, by how much should the packaging firm's sales increase next year? Explain your answer.

3. Describe an auto maker's decision process with regard to what radio manufacturer to use for a new car. Does this process entail a new task, modified rebuy, or straight rebuy? Explain your answer.

4. "The least desired method of conflict resolution is politicking." Comment on this statement.

Web Exercise

Procter & Gamble, the world's largest consumer products firm, has a Web site (**http://pg.com/b2b/index.jhtml**) devoted strictly to b-to-b issues: "Welcome to the P&G Business-to-Business Directory, your source for information on how to conduct business with P&G. Here you will find a variety of information, including pertinent Web sites and other online resources, as well as key P&G contacts." Visit the site and explain how it would be useful for a shampoo buyer working for a small supermarket chain.

Practice Quiz

1. Which of the following is *not* an example of industrial marketing?
   a. A final consumer buying a bathing suit at the end of a season due to an attractive price
   b. A government agency purchasing a police car
   c. A manufacturer leasing personal computers
   d. A retailer buying bathing suits at the end of a season for a special promotion

2. Derived demand tends to be
   a. unrelated to the accelerator principle.
   b. sensitive to price changes.
   c. very volatile.
   d. independent of final consumers.

3. A combination of goods and services is provided to a buyer by a single source in
   a. negotiation.
   b. reciprocity.
   c. conflict resolution.
   d. systems selling.

4. Which statement concerning the North American Industry Classification System (NAICS) is correct?
   a. The NAICS is the official classification system for the members of NAFTA.
   b. The NAICS assigns organizations to 30 industrial classifications.
   c. There is little data on the NAICS outside of the U.S. government.

   d. NAICS data is further classified into over 5,000 more specific classifications.

5. North American Industry Classification System data would most likely be employed in
   a. systems selling.
   b. end-use analysis.
   c. reciprocity.
   d. value analysis.

6. Unlike wholesalers, retailers are more concerned with their
   a. resale items.
   b. trucks.
   c. refrigeration and other equipment.
   d. physical facilities.

7. Which statement about nonprofit institutions is *not* correct?
   a. They buy goods and services in order to run their organizations.
   b. There are few international nonprofit institutions.
   c. They buy items for resale to generate additional revenues.
   d. There are no separate NAICS codes for nonprofit-versus profit-oriented firms.

8. Which of the following is *not* a major component of the organizational consumer's decision process?
   a. Expectations
   b. Conflict resolution

c. Problem awareness
d. Buying process

9. For organizational consumers,
   a. the buying process always involves joint decisions.
   b. vendor reliability is not very important.
   c. satisfaction with past purchases is not important in current purchase decisions.
   d. expectations refer to the perceived potential of alternative suppliers and brands to satisfy a number of explicit and implicit objectives.

10. Product-specific buying factors leading to joint decision making usually include
    a. low perceived risk.
    b. low time pressure for purchases.
    c. routine products.
    d. technology orientation.

11. Which of the following is *not* a method of conflict resolution?
    a. Politicking
    b. Persuasion
    c. Lobbying
    d. Bargaining

12. In which form of conflict resolution does each member of a purchasing team present his or her reasons why a particular supplier or brand should be selected?
    a. Politicking
    b. Persuasion

c. Problem solving
d. Bargaining

13. Reordering, *not* decision making, is usually applied when
    a. a firm has not previously purchased the product.
    b. medium-priced products previously bought infrequently by the firm now need to be purchased.
    c. competitive bidding is used.
    d. perceived risk is very low.

14. Which of the following is *not* a similarity between organizational consumers and final consumers?
    a. They both use a decision process.
    b. They both employ joint decision-making.
    c. They both purchase products for resale to others.
    d. They both can be defined by using social and psychological factors.

15. When dealing with organizational purchasing agents, sellers have to realize that these buyers
    a. rarely get involved with the final purchase decision.
    b. have personal, as well as company, goals.
    c. are only interested in price.
    d. usually have very little technical knowledge.

For the answers to these questions, please visit the online site for this book at **http://www.atomicdog.com.**

Chapter 10

Developing a Target Market Strategy

In 1886, John Pemberton, an Atlanta pharmacist, invented a new soft drink. The beverage was named Coca-Cola (**http://www.coca-cola.com**), based on its two primary ingredients: coca leaves (the product does not have any narcotics) and kola nuts. Coca-Cola expanded its operations overseas and introduced the popular slogans "The Pause that Refreshes" in 1929 and "It's the Real Thing" in 1941.

For decades, Coca-Cola practiced undifferentiated marketing, using one product and brand name throughout the world. This provided Coca-Cola with economies in planning and enacting its marketing program, as well as a uniform image. In 1982, Roberto Goizueta, Coca-Cola's chairman, changed that by introducing Diet Coke. Although prior past Coca-Cola management had refused to use the Coke name on any new product, Diet Coke ultimately became one of the world's most successful new products.

Since then, Coca-Cola has introduced a number of new brands, including caffeine-free versions of Coca-Cola Classic and Diet Coke. Vanilla Coke, introduced in 2002, quickly became the firm's biggest new product venture since New Coke in the 1980s. And in January 2004, Coca-Cola introduced a lime-flavored version of its Diet Coke. In total, Coca-Cola has four diet-based cola products: Tab, Diet Coke, Diet Coke with Splenda, and Coca-Cola Zero. Each of these brands has a different target market and a different ad message. Diet Coke focuses on a late 20s to early 30s audience that is slightly more female than male with an upscale, sophisticated message. Coca-Cola Zero appeals to 18- to 34-year-olds and is promoted as "the pause that lets them re-center in this fast-paced, time-warped world and keep going."

In addition to its cola-based beverages, Coca-Cola owns Mad River Traders (teas, juices, and sodas), as well as Dasani bottled water (the second best-selling water brand in the United States). Coca-Cola also has the exclusive rights to distribute Danone's Evian brand of bottled water in the United States.

Coca-Cola's multibrand, multiflavor, approach has moved the firm to a differentiated marketing strategy. Coca-Cola can now more effectively appeal to multiple consumer groups with distinctive offerings and marketing plans for each group. Differentiated marketing enables the company to control even more of the valuable shelf space in retail stores.[1]

In this chapter, we will examine each step involved in planning a target market strategy, including concentrated versus differentiated marketing. We will also explore the related topic of sales forecasting.

Chapter Objectives

1. To describe the process for planning a target market strategy
2. To examine alternative demand patterns and segmentation bases for both final and organizational consumers
3. To explain and contrast undifferentiated marketing (mass marketing), concentrated marketing, and differentiated marketing (multiple segmentation)
4. To show the importance of positioning in developing a marketing strategy
5. To discuss sales forecasting and its role in target marketing

---

[1] Various company and other sources.

10-1   OVERVIEW

Once a firm has gathered data on consumer traits, desires, and decision making; industry attributes; and environmental factors, it is ready to select the target market(s) to which it will appeal and for which it will develop a suitable strategy. The total *market* for a particular good or service consists of all the people and/or organizations who desire (or potentially desire) that good or service, have sufficient resources to make purchases, and are willing and able to buy. Firms often use *market segmentation*—dividing the market into distinct subsets of customers that behave in the same way or have similar needs. Each subset could possibly be a target market, such as a specialty apparel store catering to young adult women shopping for mid-priced casual clothing.

Developing a *target market strategy* consists of three general phases: analyzing consumer demand, targeting the market, and developing the marketing strategy. This comprises the seven specific steps shown in Figure 10-1 and described in Chapter 10. First, a firm determines the demand patterns for a given good or service, establishes bases of segmentation, and identifies potential market segments. For example, do prospective consumers have similar or dissimilar needs and desires? What consumer characteristics, desires, and behavior types can be best used to describe market segments?

Second, a firm chooses the target market approach and selects its target market(s). It can use *undifferentiated marketing (mass marketing)*—targeting the whole market with a single basic marketing strategy intended to have mass appeal; *concentrated marketing*—targeting one well-defined market segment with one tailored marketing strategy; or *differentiated marketing (multiple segmentation)*—targeting two or more well-defined market segments with a marketing strategy tailored to each segment.[2] DSS Research has a good synopsis of market segmentation at its Web site (**http://www.dssresearch. com/ toolkit/resource/papers/SR01.asp**)

Third, a firm positions its offering relative to competitors and outlines the proper marketing mix(es). Of particular importance here is attaining *product differentiation*, whereby the consumer perceives a product's physical or nonphysical characteristics,

A **market** is all possible consumers for a good or service. Through **market segmentation**, it can be subdivided.

In a **target market strategy**, a firm first studies demand.

Targeting approaches are **undifferentiated**, include **concentrated**, and **differentiated marketing**

The marketing strategy is developed with an emphasis on **product differentiation**.

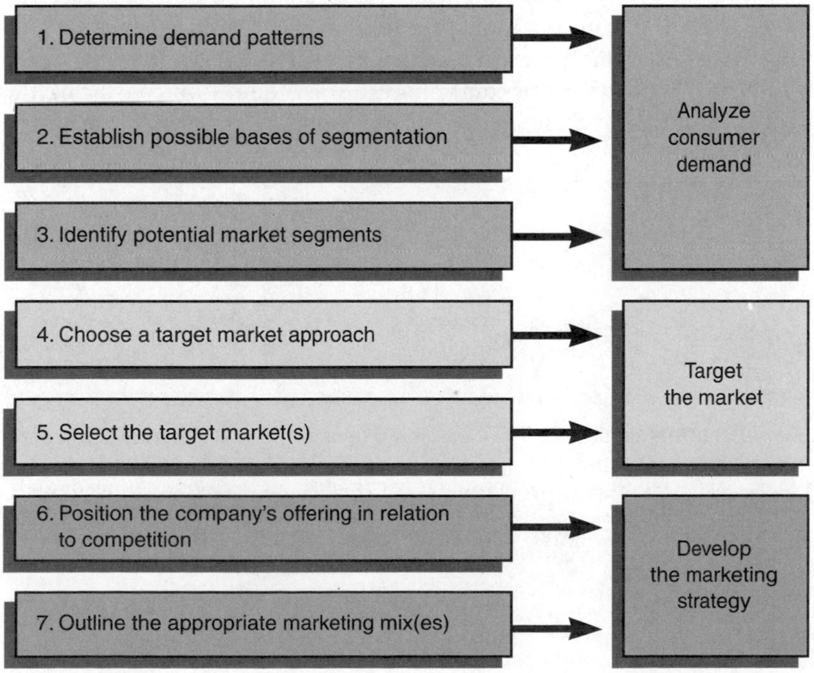

Figure 10-1

The Steps in Planning a Target Market Strategy

1. Determine demand patterns	→	
2. Establish possible bases of segmentation	→	Analyze consumer demand
3. Identify potential market segments	→	
4. Choose a target market approach	→	
5. Select the target market(s)	→	Target the market
6. Position the company's offering in relation to competition	→	
7. Outline the appropriate marketing mix(es)	→	Develop the marketing strategy

---

[2] "Dictionary of Marketing Terms," **http://www.marketingpower.com/mg-dictionary.php** (May 3, 2006).

including price, as differing from competitors. When differentiation is favorable, it yields a competitive advantage. A firm may be able to achieve a key differential advantage by emphasizing how its offering satisfies existing consumer desires and needs better than competitors do. Sometimes, demand patterns may have to be modified for consumers to perceive a firm's product differentiation as worthwhile. Thus, Tylenol (**http://www.tylenol.com**) is promoted as an alternative to aspirin for persons who cannot take aspirin (appealing to existing consumer needs), whereas Dove (**http://www.dove.com**) is marketed as a nonsoap bar cleanser with moisturizing qualities (modifying consumer perceptions of soap's role). If targeted consumers do not believe that moisturizing is a meaningful product attribute, then they will probably not buy Dove—no matter how much better a job of moisturizing it does compared to competing soaps. Because Dove is an industry leader in sales, moisturizing is clearly a desirable attribute.

In this chapter, we detail the steps in a target market strategy as they pertain to final and organizational consumers.[3] Sales forecasting and its role in target marketing are also examined.

10-2   ANALYZING CONSUMER DEMAND

The initial phase in planning a target market strategy (analyzing consumer demand) has three steps: determining demand patterns, establishing possible bases of segmentation, and identifying potential market segments.

10-2a   Determining Demand Patterns

A firm must first determine the **demand patterns**—which indicate the uniformity or diversity of consumer needs and desires for particular categories of goods and services—it faces in the marketplace. A firm would encounter one of the three alternative demand patterns described here for each good or service category it markets. See Figure 10-2.

With **homogeneous demand**, consumers have rather uniform needs and desires for a good or service category. A firm's marketing tasks are straightforward: to identify and satisfy the basic needs of consumers in a superior way. For instance, business customers in the express-mail-delivery market are most interested in rapid, reliable delivery and reasonable prices. UPS (**http://www.ups.com**) appeals to customers by convincing them it is better than competitors in these areas. As competition picks up, firms may try to alter

> **Demand patterns** show if consumer desires are similar for a good or service. People may have **homogeneous, clustered,** or **diffused demand.**

Figure 10-2

Alternative Consumer Demand Patterns for a Good or Service Category

Homogeneous Demand

Consumers have relatively similar needs and desires for a good or service category.

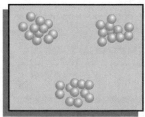

Clustered Demand

Consumer needs and desires can be grouped into two or more identifiable clusters (segments), each with its own set of purchase criteria.

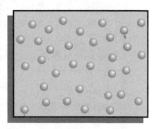

Diffused Demand

Consumer needs and desires are so diverse that no clear clusters (segments) can be identified.

---

[3] An excellent overview of target marketing is Virtual Advisor's "Targeting Your Market," found at **http://va-interactive.com/inbusiness/editorial/sales/ibt/target_market.html**.

consumer demand so new product features become desirable and homogeneous demand turns to clustered demand, with only one or a few firms marketing the new features.

With *clustered demand*, consumer needs and desires for a good or service category can be divided into two or more clusters (segments), each having distinct purchase criteria. A firm's marketing efforts must be geared toward identifying and satisfying the needs and desires of a particular cluster (or clusters) in a superior way. For example, in the golf equipment market, people can be grouped by their interest in performance and price. Thus, Golfsmith (**http://www.golfsmith.com**) sells a Hippo brand set of irons for $200 and a Callaway set of irons for $1,200—with each brand appealing to a particular cluster of consumer needs and desires. Clustered demand is the most prevalent demand pattern.

With *diffused demand*, consumer needs and desires for a good or service category are so diverse that clear clusters (segments) cannot be identified. Marketing efforts are complex because product features are harder to communicate and more product versions may be desired. For example, consumers have diverse preferences for lipstick colors; even the same person may desire several colors, to use on different occasions or to avoid boredom. Thus, cosmetics firms offer an array of lipstick colors. It would be nearly impossible for them to succeed with one color or a handful of colors. To make marketing strategies more efficient, firms generally try to modify diffused demand so clusters of at least moderate size appear.

Firms today often try to perform a balancing act regarding demand patterns. Just as the global marketplace is getting closer due to more open borders and enhanced communications, there is also more information available on marketplace diversity via customer data bases, point-of-sale scanning in stores, and other data-collection techniques. On the one hand, some firms look for demand patterns that let them standardize (perhaps even globalize) their marketing mixes as much as possible—to maximize efficiency, generate a well-known image, and use mass media. On the other hand, some firms search for demand patterns that let them pinpoint more specific market segments—to better address consumer needs. The development of Web sites such as **http://www.pantene.com** ("shampoo and conditioner strength against damage") and **http://www.urbanbearmarketing.com/micromarketing-home.htm** illustrates firms' interest in addressing individual consumer needs. See Figure 10-3.

Figure 10-3

Appealing to Diffused Demand

Through Color Smart technology, Home Depot can offer its customers a virtually limitless choice of paint colors.

Source: Reprinted by permission of Susan Berry, Retail Image Consulting, Inc.

Global Marketing in Action

Japanese Consumers Love U.S.-Made Coach Bags

During one recent five-year period, Coach Inc. (http://www.coach.com) saw its sales in Japan jump by 300 percent. Coach's increased sales can be traced to 2001 when it opened a number of freestanding stores in Japan. Coach now has about 110 retail outlets in Japan versus about 50 for Louis Vuitton (http://www.louisvuitton.com), a competitor. Coach also has worked hard to better understand the preferences of Japanese consumers. For example, Coach changed its image from being a maker of sensible bags for working women to a maker of more fashion-conscious products.

Another part of Coach's Japanese competitive strategy relates to its relatively low prices (for a luxury brand!). Coach pocketbooks typically sell for 40 to 50 percent of the price of Louis Vuitton's. As Coach's chief executive notes, "Unlike the older Japanese cus-tomer who would spend $1,000 on an Hermès [http://www.hermes.com] bag, the younger customer will buy one Coach bag and use the extra money to buy an iPod or go to a day spa. She is much more confident and secure in herself."

Coach forecasts that its share of the Japanese market for imported bags and accessories is about 8 percent as compared with Louis Vuitton's 30 percent market share. Coach's long-time rivalry with Louis Vuitton recently heated up after Coach filed a complaint with Japan's Federal Trade Commission against Vuitton. In its complaint, Coach stated that Vuitton threatened to withdraw its branded merchandise from Japanese stores that stocked Coach goods.

Source: Based on material in Ginny Parker, "A Yen for Coach," *Wall Street Journal* (March 11, 2005), pp. B1, B4.

10-2b Establishing Possible Bases of Segmentation

A firm next studies possible bases for segmenting the market for each product or product line. See Table 10-1. It must decide which of these segmentation bases are most relevant for its particular situation.

> **Geographic demographics** describe towns, cities, states, regions, and countries.

Geographic Demographics *Geographic demographics* are basic identifiable characteristics of towns, cities, states, regions, and countries. A firm may use one or a combination of the geographic demographics cited in Table 10-1 to describe its final or organizational consumers.

Because a segmentation strategy can be geared to geographic differences, it is useful to know such facts as these: Per-capita chocolate consumption in Western Europe is several times that in the United States; and per-capita consumption of bottled water in Italy is many times that in the United States. Germans want laundry detergents that are gentle on rivers, and will pay more for them; Greeks want small packages to keep down the cost per store visit. Canada and Mexico account for more than one-half of steel-mill products exported by U.S. firms. Many Brazilian, German, Korean, and Chinese consumers like to buy books and magazines online.

Here are some geographic household differences in the United States:

- Home ownership—70 percent in the Midwest, 69 percent in the South, 64 percent in the Northeast, and 63 percent in the West.
- At least one vehicle owned or leased—91 percent in the West, 90 percent in the Midwest, 89 percent in the South, and 80 percent in the Northeast.
- Proportion of income spent on housing—31 percent in the West, 27 percent in the Northeast and in the South, and 25 percent in the Midwest.
- Proportion of income spent on transportation—17 percent in the West and in the South, 16 percent in the Midwest, and 13 percent in the Northeast.
- Proportion of income spent on food away from home—4.9 percent in the West, 4.5 percent in the Northeast, and 4.4 percent in the Midwest and in the South.[4]

---

[4] *Consumer Expenditure Survey,* http://www.bls.gov/cex/home.htm (February 25, 2006).

Table 10-1   Possible Bases of Segmentation

Bases	Examples of Possible Segments
Geographic Demographics	
Population (people or organizations)	
Location	North, South, East, West; domestic, global
Size	Small, medium, large
Density	Urban, suburban, rural
Transportation network	Mass transit, vehicular, pedestrian
Climate	Warm, cold
Type of commerce	Tourist, local worker, resident; NAICS codes
Retail establishments	Downtown shopping district, shopping mall
Media	Local, regional, national, global
Competition	Underdeveloped, saturated
Growth pattern	Stable, negative, positive
Legislation	Stringent, lax
Cost of living/operations	Low, moderate, high
Personal Demographics	
A. Final Consumers	
Age	Child, young adult, adult, older adult
Gender	Male, female
Education	than high school, high school, college
Mobility	residence for 2 years, moved in last 2 years
Income	middle, high
Occupation	ue-collar, white-collar, professional
Marital status	Single, married, divorced, widowed
Household size	1, 2, 3, 4, 5, 6, or more
Ethnicity or race	European, American; black, white
B. Organizations	
Industry designation	NAICS codes; end-use analysis
Product use	Further production, use in operations, resale to others
Institutional designation	Manufacturer, wholesaler, retailer, government, nonprofit
Company size	Small, medium, large
Industry growth pattern	Slow, moderate, high
Company growth pattern	Slow, moderate, high
Age of company	New, 5 years old, 10 years old or more
Language used	English, French, Japanese

(continued)

Consumer Lifestyles

Social class (final consumers)	Lower-lower to upper-upper
Family life cycle (final consumers)	Bachelor to solitary survivor
Buying structure	Informal to formal, autonomous to joint
Usage rate	Light, medium, heavy
Usage experience	None, some, extensive
Brand loyalty	None, some, total
Personality	Introverted-extroverted, persuasible-nonpersuasible
Attitudes	Neutral, positive, negative
Class consciousness	Inner-directed, outer-directed
Motives	Benefit segmentation
Perceived risk	Low, moderate, high
Innovativeness	Innovator, laggard
Opinion leadership	None, some, a lot
Importance of purchase	Little, a great deal

Figure 10-4 indicates the population size, urbanization, and per-capita GDP ranking of the 10 most populated nations of the world. Figure 10-5 shows a demographic map of the United States.

Personal Demographics   *Personal demographics* are basic identifiable characteristics of individual final consumers and organizational consumers, and groups of final consumers and organizational consumers. They are often used as a segmentation base because groups of people or organizations with similar demographics may have similar needs and desires that are distinct from those with different backgrounds. Personal demographics may be viewed singly or in combinations.

> **Personal demographics** describe people and organizations. They should be used in studying final and organizational consumers.

Final Consumers   As noted in Table 10-1, several personal demographics for final consumers may be used in planning a segmentation strategy.

Applications of personal demographic segmentation are plentiful, as these examples indicate: In the United States and other Western nations, Clairol and many other companies are now placing greater emphasis on wooing consumers in the early stages of middle age. This group is quite large and particularly interested in slowing the aging process. Procter & Gamble has set up a special Web site for teenage girls (**http://www.beinggirl.com**) sponsored by its feminine care products division. Godiva Chocolatier (**http://www.godiva.com**) has separate Valentine's Day promotions aimed at men and women; in the past, all ads were oriented at gift-giving by men. Nike (**http://www.nike.com**), Reebok (**http://www.reebok.com**), and others are devoting greater advertising to women's sports shoes and apparel. Why? Women annually buy billions of dollars worth of these products—more than men spend![5]

Dollar General (**http://www.dollargeneral.com**), a discount "neighborhood" store chain, attracts value-conscious consumers with low prices; many items are $10 or less. It locates in smaller communities, sells many irregulars and factory overruns, and has few employees per store. In contrast, American Express attracts upper-income consumers with its platinum card (**http://www.americanexpress.com/platinum**). They pay an annual fee

---

[5] Anthony Vagnoni, "Ads Are from Mars, Women Are from Venus," *Print* (March-April 2005), pp. 52-55.

	Total Population	Urbanization Percentage[a]	Top 10 GDP Ranking Per Capita
China	1.3 billion	41	5
India	1.1 billion	29	7
United States	296 million	81	1
Indonesia	242 million	48	6
Brazil	186 million	84	4
Pakistan	162 million	35	8
Bangladesh	144 million	25	9
Russia	143 million	73	3
Nigeria	129 million	48	10
Japan	127 million	66	2

[a] Percent of population living in urban areas.

Figure 10-4

Comparing the 10 Most Populated Countries in the World, 2005

Source: Compiled by the authors from U.S. Bureau of the Census, International Data Base (February 10, 2006); and United Nations, *World Population Prospects*, **http://esa.un.org/unup** (February 10, 2006).

of $395 and charge tens of thousands of dollars per year; in return, they get special services (such as a worldwide valet service to help them shop, plan trips, etc.) and a high credit line.

Several firms have launched major marketing efforts aimed at U.S. ethnic groups, including those in the fast-food industry: "Many of the biggest names, including Burger King [**http://www.burgerking.com**], Chili's Grill & Bar [**http://www.chilis.com**], and Denny's [**http://www.dennys.com**] dedicate resources to reaching key niche markets including African-American, Asian, and Hispanic consumers. 'We have made a concerted effort to focus on these customers because we realize how important they are to business. The multicultural market makes up 40 percent of our business, so in terms of our overall growth it's an important component,' says the manager of multicultural marketing at Burger King, which for more than 15 years has employed ad agencies specializing in reaching black and Hispanic consumers."[6]

Organizational Consumers   Table 10-1 also shows several personal demographics for b-to-b consumers that may be used in planning a segmentation strategy.

The easiest way to segment organizations is by their industry designation. As an illustration, if a firm studies the U.S. consumer goods rental industry sector

[6] Allison Perlik, "Minority Matters," *Restaurants & Institutions* (March 15, 2005), pp. 36–38.

States	Population Ranking	Median Household Income Ranking	Population Density Ranking[a]
Alabama	24	43	26
Alaska	47	4	50
Arizona	17	30	35
Arkansas	32	48	33
California	1	13	11
Colorado	22	10	37
Connecticut	29	5	4
Delaware	45	9	6
Florida	4	37	8
Georgia	9	23	18
Hawaii	42	11	13
Idaho	39	34	44
Illinois	5	17	12
Indiana	14	29	17
Iowa	30	31	34
Kansas	33	22	40
Kentucky	26	39	22
Louisiana	23	47	23
Maine	40	41	38
Maryland	19	2	5
Massachusetts	13	8	3
Michigan	8	19	15
Minnesota	21	6	31
Mississippi	31	49	32
Missouri	18	25	28
Montana	44	46	48
Nebraska	38	20	42
Nevada	35	15	43
New Hampshire	41	3	19
New Jersey	10	1	1
New Mexico	36	45	45
New York	3	27	7
North Carolina	11	40	16
North Dakota	48	38	47
Ohio	7	24	9
Oklahoma	28	44	36
Oregon	27	28	39
Pennsylvania	6	21	10
Rhode Island	43	18	2
South Carolina	25	36	21
South Dakota	46	35	46
Tennessee	16	42	20
Texas	2	33	27
Utah	34	12	41
Vermont	49	26	30
Virginia	12	7	14
Washington	15	16	25
West Virginia	37	50	29
Wisconsin	20	14	24
Wyoming	50	32	49

[a] Population per square mile.

A Demographic Map of the United States, 2005

Source: Compiled by the authors from U.S. Bureau of the Census and U.S. Bureau of Economic Analysis data.

(NAICS code 5322), it would learn the sector comprises 35,000 businesses with 250,000 employees, and generates $20 billion in annual sales. Among the business segments in this category are consumer electronics and appliances rental, formal wear and costume rental, video tape and disc rental, home health equipment rental, and recreational goods rental.[7]

To access potential b-to-b consumers by institutional type, some sellers rely on trade directories—such as the *Blue Book of Building & Construction* (**http://www.thebluebook.com**), with about 1 million U.S. construction firms; *SA Yellow Online* (**http://www.sayellow.com**), with numerous South African listings by business category; *BizEurope*, "Europe's leading import and export directory"; and *Scott's Directories* (**http://www.scottsinfo.com**), with more than 115,000 Canadian manufacturers and service firms. Mailing lists of organizations may also be bought. InfoUSA's (**http://www.infousa.com**) business lists have information on millions of U.S. manufacturers, wholesalers, retailers, professional service businesses, membership organizations, and others.

Organizations may be divided into small, medium, and large categories. Some firms prosper by marketing goods and services to smaller b-to-b customers, whereas others focus on medium and/or large accounts. For example, Brother (**http://www.brother.com**) has a line of inexpensive fax machines for small businesses that cost $150 or less, while Muratec's (**http://www.muratec.com**) top-line fax machines are priced at several thousand dollars; they can store 1,400 pages or more of text in memory, collate, and scan pages in under one second. Blackbourn (**http://www.blackbourn.com**), which makes plastic packaging for audio and video products, has a primary market of large *Fortune 500* companies but also sells to small businesses.

Industry growth patterns may indicate a firm's future potential in marketing to businesses in those industries and provide a good segmentation base. The International Trade Administration of the U.S. Department of Commerce (**http://www.ita.doc.gov**) cites electronic information services, health services, semiconductors, and surgical and medical instruments as fast-growth industries. Paper industries machinery, personal leather goods, farm machinery, and newspapers are low-growth industries.

Consumer Lifestyles Lifestyles are the ways in which people live and spend time and money, and many lifestyle factors can be applied to both final and organizational consumers. Table 10-1 lists several lifestyle segmentation bases; except where indicated, these factors are relevant when segmenting either final or organizational consumer markets.

> Final consumer and organizational consumer segments each can be described on the basis of lifestyle factors.

Applications of lifestyle segmentation are abundant, as these examples show: Final consumers may be segmented by social class and stage in the family life cycle. The posh Four Seasons hotel chain (**http://www.fourseasons.com**) appeals to upper-middle-class and upper-class guests with luxurious accommodations, whereas the Hampton Inn chain (**http://www.hampton-inn.com**) appeals to middle-class and lower-middle-class consumers with low rates and limited services (such as no restaurant). Tiffany (**http://www.tiffany.com**), Bloomingdale's (**http://www.bloomingdales.com**), Williams-Sonoma (**http://www.williamssonoma.com**), Crate and Barrel (**http://www.crateandbarrel.com**), and other retailers offer online wedding registry services for prospective brides and grooms through Wedding Channel.com (**http://www.weddingchannel.com**). To attract families with children, some Club Med resorts (**http://www.clubmed.com**) have day camps.

Final and organizational consumer market segments may be based on their usage rate, the amount of a product they consume. People or organizations can use very little, some, or a great deal. A *heavy-usage segment* (at times known as the *heavy half*) is a consumer group that accounts for a large proportion of a good's or service's sales relative to the size of the market. Women buy 85 percent of all greeting cards. Heavy yogurt

> A **heavy-usage segment** has a rather large share of sales.

---

[7] Current projections estimated by the authors, based on "Consumer Goods Rental," *2002 Economic Census* (Washington, DC: U.S. Bureau of the Census).

consumers eat nearly double the amount as average yogurt consumers. Manufacturers, wholesalers, and retailers account for over 90 percent of all U.S. b-to-b equipment leasing; government and nonprofit organizations make less than 10 percent of equipment leases. Sometimes, a heavy-usage segment may be attractive because of the volume it consumes; other times, the competition for consumers in that segment may make other opportunities more attractive. Consider the case of Kodak:

> When film ruled home photography, women took about two-thirds of all pictures and ordered most of the prints. But things changed when digital cameras began horning in on film's turf. More men got behind the camera—and many of the shots ended up trapped inside a computer. It was a disaster for Eastman Kodak [http://www.kodak.com]. Sales of film and paper, its biggest sources of profit, tumbled. The long-successful strategy of courting women, emphasizing not so much gee-whiz technology as the chance to capture "Kodak moments," was in deep trouble. Today, Kodak is clawing its way to the top of the digital world by catering to its best customers. Starting four years ago, Kodak set out to make digital photography female-friendly. Its research showed that women wanted digital photography to be simple, and they desired high-quality prints to share with family and friends. Kodak revamped its digital cameras, stressing simple controls and larger display screens. It invented a new product category, the compact, stand-alone photo printer, to easily make prints without a PC. And it pushed to make digital-image printing simpler through retail kiosks and an online service. Kodak isn't saying that women lack the aptitude to deal with digital photography. Women simply aren't that interested in fiddling with cables and complex camera-computer interfaces. So Kodak has worked to keep things simple, while most rivals focused on developing high-tech features and marketing them to techies.[8]

> **Benefit segmentation** groups consumers based on their reasons for using products.

Consumer motives may be used to establish benefit segments. *Benefit segmentation* is a procedure for grouping people into segments on the basis of the different benefits sought from a product. It was first popularized when Russell Haley divided the toothpaste market into four segments: sensory—people wanting flavor and product appearance; sociable—people wanting brighter teeth; worrier—people wanting decay prevention; and independent—people wanting low prices. Since then, benefit segmentation has been applied in many final and organizational consumer settings.[9] Figure 10-6 shows how benefit segmentation may be used to market children's toothpaste.

> **VALS** and the **Social Styles model** describe market segments in terms of a broad range of factors.

Blending Demographic and Lifestyle Factors   It is generally advisable to use a mix of demographic and lifestyle factors to set up possible bases of segmentation. A better analysis then takes place. See Figure 10-7. Two broad classification systems are the *VALS (Values and Lifestyles) program*, which divides final consumers into lifestyle categories; and the *Social Styles model*, which divides the personnel representing organizational consumers into lifestyle categories.

In the United States, the current VALS 2 typology (http://www.sric-bi.com/VALS) explains why and how people make purchases, and places them into segments based on resources and innovativeness. Thinkers and believers are guided by their ideals; achievers and strivers are achievement-oriented; and experiencers and makers are guided by a desire for self-expression. People's resources include their education, income, self-confidence, health, eagerness to buy, intelligence, and energy level; and resources rise

[8] William M. Bulkeley, "Softer View: Kodak Sharpens Digital Focus on Its Best Customers: Women," *Wall Street Journal* (July 6, 2005), p. A1.

[9] Russell I. Haley, "Benefit Segments: Backwards and Forwards," *Journal of Advertising Research*, Vol. 24 (February-March 1984), pp. 19–25; P. J. O'Connor and Gary L. Sullivan, "Market Segmentation: A Comparison of Benefits/Attributes Desired and Brand Preference," *Psychology & Marketing*, Vol. 12 (October 1995), pp. 613–635; Rizal Ahmad, "Benefit Segmentation: A Potentially Useful Technique of Segmenting and Targeting Older Consumers," *International Journal of Market Research*, Vol. 45 (Quarter 3, 2003), pp. 373–388; and Erdener Kaynak and Talha D. Harcar, "American Consumers' Attitudes Towards Commercial Banks: A Comparison of Local and National Bank Customers by Use of Geodemographic Segmentation," *International Journal of Bank Marketing*, Vol. 23 (January 2005), pp. 73–89.

from youth to middle age and fall with old age. Here are descriptions of the basic VALS 2 segments (in terms of adult characteristics):

- *Innovators*—successful, sophisticated, take-charge people with high self-esteem. Abundant resources. Can indulge in any of the three primary motivations. Act as change leaders who are most receptive to new things. Active consumers; often interested in upscale, niche goods and services.
- *Thinkers*—Mature, satisfied, comfortable, and reflective. Value order, knowledge, and responsibility. Well educated; actively seek information in decision making. Alert to opportunities to broaden knowledge. Practical consumers interested in durability, functionality, and value.
- *Believers*—Conservative, conventional people with beliefs based on family, religion, community, and the nation. Follow established routines. Choose familiar products and established brands. Favor American products and are generally loyal.
- *Achievers*—Goal-oriented lifestyles and a deep commitment to career and family. Conventional lives, politically conservative, and respectful to authority. Active as consumers and favor established, prestige goods and services that show success to their peers.
- *Strivers*—Trendy and fun loving. Concerned about the opinions and approval of others. Money as a symbol of success. Income not high enough to meet their desires. Active, impulsive consumers who favor stylish products that emulate the purchases of those with more material wealth.
- *Experiencers*—Young and enthusiastic. Quickly become enthusiastic about new possibilities but are equally quick to cool. Seek variety and excitement, the offbeat, and the risky. Socially active. Spend a high proportion of their income on fashion and entertainment.
- *Makers*—Express themselves and experience the world by building a house, raising children, fixing a car, or canning vegetables. Have enough skill and energy to carry out practical projects successfully. Unimpressed by material possessions. Prefer value to luxury.

Figure 10-6

Applying Benefit Segmentation to Children's Toothpaste

Colgate and Oral-B realize that, as with adult toothpaste users, children are attracted to products that offer particular benefits—especially good-tasting flavors and packaging showing their favorite characters.

Source: Reprinted by permission of Retail Forward.

Figure 10-7

Segmentation Based on Both Demographic and Lifestyle Factors

Dove (**http://www.dove.com**) markets its products to various customer segments based on a combination of demographic and lifestyle factors. For example, Dove shampoos come in several types: Dove Beautifully Clean Shampoo, Dove Extra Volume Shampoo, Dove Intensive Moisture Shampoo, Dove Moisture Rich Color Shampoo, and Dove Volumizing Color Shampoo.

Source: Reprinted by permission.

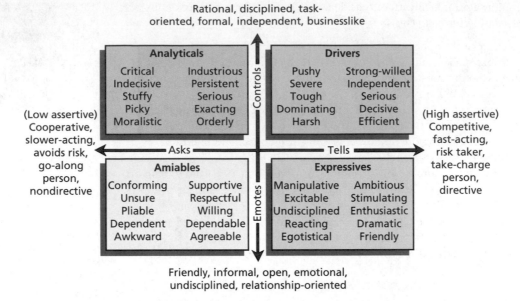

Figure 10-8

The Social Styles Model for Organizational Consumers

Source: Wilson Learning Corporation and Tracom Corporation. Reprinted by permission of Crain Communications Inc., from Tom Eisenhart, "How to Really Excite Your Prospects," *Business Marketing* (July 1988).

- *Survivors*—Narrowly focused. Few resources. Often believe the world is changing too quickly. Comfortable with the familiar and mostly concerned with safety and security. Work to meet needs rather than fulfill desires. Cautious consumers. Loyal to favorite brands.[10]

GeoVALS is a high-tech way to use the U.S. VALS 2 model. Through GeoVALS, the VALS 2 market segments can be broken down by metropolitan area, city, and ZIP code.

The VALS system is so popular that it is also utilized in Japan, and tailored to people there (**http://www.sric-bi.com/VALS/JVALS.shtml**). For example, ryoshiki ("socially intelligent") innovators are career-oriented, middle-aged innovators; ryoshiki adapters are shy and look to ryoshiki innovators; tradition adapters are young and affluent; and low pragmatic are attitudinally negative and oriented to inexpensive products.

The Social Styles model popularized by Wilson Learning (**http://portalcenter. wilsonlearning.com**) and Tracom (**http://www.tracomcorp.com**), shown in Figure 10-8, indicates how social styles affect people's reactions to stimuli on and off the job. The model studies two traits—assertiveness and responsiveness—and divides organizational personnel into analyticals, drivers, amiables, and expressives. Assertiveness is the degree to which a person states views with assurance, confidence, and force, and the extent to which he or she tries to direct others' actions. Responsiveness is the extent to which a person is affected by appeals, influence, or stimulation and how feelings, emotions, or impressions are shown to others:

- *Analyticals*—Low in both assertiveness and responsiveness. Like facts and details. Money- and numbers-oriented. Work well alone. Stay under control. Interested in processes. Risk avoiders.
- *Expressives*—High in both assertiveness and responsiveness. The opposite of analyticals. Use hunches to make decisions. Need to be with people. Focus on

---

[10] SRI Consulting Business Intelligence, "The VALS Segments," **http://www.sric-bi.com/VALS/types.shtml** (May 2, 2006).

generalities. Thrive on freedom from outside control. Risk takers, but seek approval for themselves and their firms.

- *Drivers*—Low responsiveness and high assertiveness. Get right to the point. Limited time. "Hard chargers." Self-motivated and impatient. Work well alone. Risk takers. Success-oriented.
- *Amiables* Low assertiveness and high responsiveness. Team players. Relationship builders. Friendly and loyal. Need support from others. Careful. Less time-oriented. Can be indecisive. Risk avoiders.[11]

The Social Styles model has been used to classify personnel in such industries as banking, computers and precision instruments, chemicals, pharmaceuticals, telecommunications, aerospace, utilities, and industrial and farm equipment. In all cases, the analyticals segment is the largest.

10-2c Identifying Potential Market Segments

Once it has established possible segmentation bases, a firm is ready to construct specific consumer profiles that identify potential market segments for the firm by aggregating consumers with similar traits and needs and separating them from those with different traits and needs. Following are some examples.

> Consumer profiles are used in identifying market segments.

A supermarket can segment female and male shoppers in terms of their in-store behavior. In general, on each visit, women spend more time shopping, buy more items, are more apt to bring children, and more often use a shopping list than men; and they are equally apt to shop in the evening.

In appealing to the "senior" marketplace, "firms need to realize they can't approach them en masse. Firms tend to lump seniors into the 'old-old' category. That's a big mistake. Most observers say mature adults can break down into three different groups: (1) Leading-edge boomers or pre-retirees—younger seniors in their late 40s to late 50s still in the workplace. (2) In-betweeners or active retirees—range from their late 50s to early 70s, often in the beginning stages of retirement. (3) Seniors—'old' defined by most Americans as around the mid-70s (although most 70-year-olds would probably take exception to that)."[12]

A photocopier manufacturer could group the office-copier market into benefit segments, such as: basic copying (satisfied via simple, inexpensive machines that make up to 99 black-and-white copies of a single page at a time); extensive copying (satisfied via mid-priced machines that make up to 100 or more one- or two-sided copies of multiple pages and then collate them); and desktop publishing (satisfied via expensive, sophisticated machines that make high-quality color copies in large quantities).

10-3 TARGETING THE MARKET

The second phase in planning a target market strategy (targeting the market) entails choosing the proper approach and selecting the target market(s).

10-3a Choosing a Target Market Approach

A firm now selects undifferentiated marketing, concentrated marketing, or differentiated marketing. We show these options in Figure 10-9 and Table 10-2, and discuss them next.

[11] Wilson Learning, "Social Styles as a Global Phenomenon," **http://portalcenter.wilsonlearning.com/pls/portal/url/ page/wlc_web_site/resources** (1999); and Tracom, "Social Style Interpersonal Skill Development," **http:// www.tracomcorp.com/article/CA372855.html** (May 2, 2006).

[12] Matt Kinsman, "Forever Young," *Promo* (October 2003), p. 22.

Figure 10-9
Contrasting Target Market Approaches

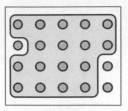

Undifferentiated Marketing (Mass Marketing)
The firm tries to reach a wide range of consumers with one basic marketing plan. These consumers are assumed to have a desire for similar good and service attributes.

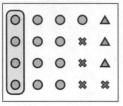

Concentrated Marketing
The firm concentrates on one group of consumers with a distinct set of needs and uses a tailor-made marketing plan to attract this single group.

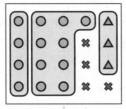

Differentiated Marketing (Multiple Segmentation)
The firm aims at two or more different market segments, each of which has a distinct set of needs, and offers a tailor-made marketing plan for each segment.

> With undifferentiated marketing, a firm appeals to a broad range of consumers with one basic marketing plan.

Undifferentiated Marketing (Mass Marketing) With an undifferentiated marketing (mass marketing) approach, a firm aims at a large, broad consumer market via one basic marketing plan. It believes consumers have very similar desires regarding product attributes or opts to ignore differences among segments. An early practitioner of mass marketing was Henry Ford, who sold one standard car at a reasonable price to many people. The original Model T had no options and came only in black.

Mass marketing was popular when large-scale production started, but the number of firms using a pure undifferentiated marketing approach has declined markedly in recent years. Among the factors behind the drop are the following: competition has grown, consumer demand may be stimulated by appealing to specific segments, improved marketing research can better pinpoint different segments' desires, and total production and marketing costs can be reduced by segmentation.

Before engaging in undifferentiated marketing, a firm must weigh several factors. High total resources are needed to mass produce, mass distribute, and mass advertise. Yet, there may be per-unit production and marketing savings because a limited product line is offered and different brand names are not employed. These savings may allow low competitive prices.

A major goal of undifferentiated marketing is to maximize sales; a firm tries to sell as many units as possible. Regional, national, and/or international goals are set. Diversification is not undertaken.

For a firm to succeed with mass marketing, a large group of consumers must have a desire for the same product attributes (homogeneous demand) so one basic marketing program can be used. Or, demand must be so diffused that it is not worthwhile for a firm to aim marketing plans at specific segments; the firm would try to make demand more homogeneous. In undifferentiated marketing, different consumer groups are not identified and sought. For example, suppose all consumers buy Morton's salt for its freshness, quality, storability, availability, and fair price. Mass marketing is then proper. If various shoppers want attractive decanters, a low-sodium version, larger crystals, and smaller-sized packages (as they now do), then Morton (**http://www.mortonsalt.com**) could not appeal to everyone with one marketing mix.

Table 10-2	Contrasting Target Market Approaches		
	Approaches		
Strategic Factors	**Undifferentiated Marketing**	**Concentrated Marketing**	**Differentiated Marketing**
Target market	Broad range of consumers	One well-defined consumer group	Two or more well-defined consumer groups
Product	Limited number of products under one brand for many types of consumers	One brand tailored to one consumer group	Distinct brand or version for each consumer group
Distribution	All possible outlets	All suitable outlets	All suitable outlets—differs by segment
Promotion	Mass media	All suitable media	All suitable media—differs by segment
Price	One "popular" price range	One price range tailored to the consumer group	Distinct price range for each consumer group
Strategy emphasis	Appeal to a large number of consumers via a uniform, broad-based marketing program	Appeal to one specific consumer group via a highly specialized, but uniform, marketing program	Appeal to two or more distinct market segments via different marketing plans catering to each segment

In undifferentiated marketing, a firm sells via all possible outlets. Some resellers may be displeased if a brand is sold at nearby locations and insist on carrying additional brands to fill out their product lines. It may be hard to persuade them not to carry competing brands. The shelf space a firm gets is based on its brand's popularity and the promotion support it provides.

An undifferentiated marketing strategy should take both total and long-run profits into account. Firms sometimes may be too involved with revenues and lose sight of profits. For example, for several years, A&P's sales rose as it competed with Safeway (**http://www.safeway.com**) for leadership in U.S. supermarket sales. A&P (**http://www.aptea.com**) incurred large losses during that period. Only when it began to close some unprofitable stores and stop pursuing sales at any cost did it regain profitability.

A firm and/or its products can ensure a consistent, well-known image with a mass-marketing approach. Consumers have only one image when thinking of a firm (or a brand), and it is retained for a number of years. Think of Wal-Mart (**http://www.walmart.com**) and Target (**http://www.target.com**), discount department store chains that have a broad customer following.

USA Today (**http://www.usatoday.com**) is an example of undifferentiated marketing in action. As its Web site notes: "*USA Today* is the easy to use, comprehensive source of timely news and information." Its main section provides news and exclusive features and reports: "It's the important news of the day in our 'what it means to me' style of journalism." The business section gives "financial news that's timely and accessible. Coverage includes the day's big business story plus reports on personal finance, investments, technology, advertising/marketing, the latest market updates from around the world." The sports section "delivers every score, every stat, every story, every day. Sports come alive with brilliant photos, ground-breaking graphics, and exclusive interviews." The life section "is full of the latest entertainment, travel, and lifestyle news."

Via concentrated marketing, a firm appeals to one segment with a tailored marketing plan.

Concentrated Marketing A concentrated marketing approach enables a firm to aim at a narrow, specific consumer segment with one specialized marketing plan catering to the needs of that segment. This is proper to consider if demand is clustered or if diffused demand can be clustered by offering a unique marketing mix.

Concentrated marketing has become more popular, especially for smaller firms. A firm does not have to mass produce, mass distribute, or mass advertise. It can succeed with limited resources and abilities by focusing efforts. This method does not usually maximize sales; the goal is efficiency—attracting a large part of one segment at controlled costs. The firm wants recognition as a specialist and does not diversify.

A firm must do better than competitors in tailoring a strategy for its segment if concentrated marketing is used. Areas of competitor strength should be avoided and weaknesses exploited. A new vendor selling standard office stationery would have a harder time distinguishing itself from competitors than a new vendor that provides customers with free recycling services for the stationery it sells.

When there are two or more attractive market segments from which a firm may choose, it should select the one with the greatest opportunity, while being alert to these two factors: (1) The largest segment may not be the best option, due to heavy competition or high consumer satisfaction with competitor offerings. A firm entering this segment may regret it due to the *majority fallacy*, which causes some firms to fail if they go after the largest market segment because competition is intense. See Figure 10-10. (2) A potentially profitable segment may be one ignored by other firms. As an example, Perdue (**http://www.perdue.com**) does well in the poultry business, due to its being the first chicken processor to see a market segment desiring superior quality, an identifiable brand name, and a guarantee—and having a willingness to pay premium prices. Previously, chicken was sold as an unbranded commodity.

To avoid the **majority fallacy**, a company can enter a smaller, but untapped, segment.

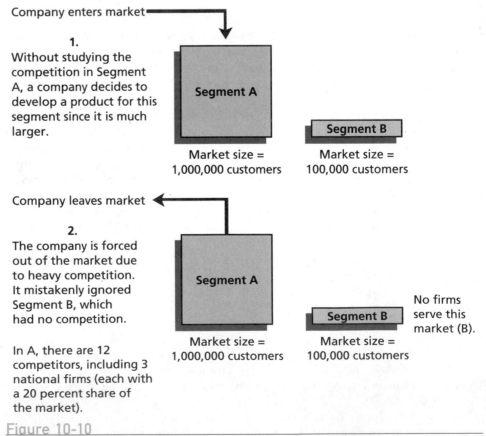

Company enters market

1.
Without studying the competition in Segment A, a company decides to develop a product for this segment since it is much larger.

Segment A

Segment B

Market size = 1,000,000 customers

Market size = 100,000 customers

Company leaves market

2.
The company is forced out of the market due to heavy competition. It mistakenly ignored Segment B, which had no competition.

In A, there are 12 competitors, including 3 national firms (each with a 20 percent share of the market).

Segment A

Segment B

No firms serve this market (B).

Market size = 1,000,000 customers

Market size = 100,000 customers

Figure 10-10

How the Majority Fallacy Occurs

Through concentrated marketing, a firm can maximize per-unit profits, but not total profits, because only one segment is sought. In addition, a firm with low resources can vie effectively for specialized markets. Many local and regional firms profitably compete in their own markets with national and international companies, but they do not have the finances to compete on a larger scale. Furthermore, minor shifts in population or consumer tastes can sharply affect a firm using concentrated marketing.

By carving out a distinct niche via concentrated marketing, a firm may foster a high degree of brand loyalty for a current offering and also be able to develop a product line under a popular name. As long as the firm stays within its perceived area of expertise, the image of one product will rub off on another: Porsche (**http://www.porsche.com**) aims only at the upscale segment of the auto market—people interested in styling, handling, acceleration, and status—even though it makes multiple vehicles (including a new sports utility vehicle). Whole Foods Market (**http://www.wholefoodsmarket.com**) offers products only for consumers interested in natural ingredients. See Figure 10-11.

Differentiated Marketing (Multiple Segmentation)

A firm can utilize differentiated marketing (multiple segmentation) to appeal to two or more distinct market segments, with a different marketing plan for each. This strategy combines the best aspects of undifferentiated marketing and concentrated marketing: A broad range of consumers may be sought and efforts focus on satisfying identifiable consumer segments. Differentiated marketing is appropriate to consider if there are two or more significant demand clusters, or if diffused demand can be clustered into two or more segments and satisfied by offering unique marketing mixes to each one.

> In differentiated marketing, two or more marketing plans are tailored to two or more consumer segments.

Some firms appeal to each segment in the market and achieve the same market coverage as with mass marketing. Kyocera Mita (**http://www.kyoceramita.com**) markets copiers ranging from simple and inexpensive to sophisticated and expensive, thus separately appealing to small and large businesses. Other firms appeal to two or more, but not all, segments. Marriott International (**http://www.marriott.com**) operates Marriott Hotels & Resorts, Fairfield Inn, Courtyard by Marriott, Marriott Vacation Club, Residence Inn, Renaissance Hotels & Resorts, and other hotel chains. It aims at several—but not all—hospitality segments. Switzerland's Swatch Group (**http://www.swatchgroup.com**) markets Swatch watches for teens and young adults, Hamilton watches for adults lured by

Figure 10-11
Concentrated Marketing in Action

Founded in 1980 as one small store in Austin, Texas, Whole Foods Market is the world's largest retailer of natural and organic foods, with 145 North American stores. The firm is very mission driven: "We're highly selective about what we sell, dedicated to stringent quality goals, and committed to sustainable agriculture."

Source: Reprinted by permission of Susan Berry, Retail Image Consulting, Inc.

Figure 10-12

Differentiated Marketing in Action

At Home Depot, "We cater to both do-it-yourselfers and professional customers who serve the home improvement construction and building maintenance market segments."

Source: Reprinted by permission.

classic styles, and upscale Blancpain, Omega, and Tissot brands. Home Depot (**http://www.homedepot.com**) targets to small businesses, other b-to-b customers, and final consumers. See Figure 10-12. Kapers for Kids (**http://www.funsteps.com/Funsteps/features.html**) offers a curriculum with fun and educational activities designed for several settings: family child-care homes, child-care centers, pre-schools, or the home. Its programs are geared to 3- to 5-year-olds.

Firms may use both mass marketing and concentrated marketing in their multiple segmentation strategies. They could have one or more major brands aimed at a wide range of consumers (the mass market) and secondary brands for specific segments. For example, Time Inc. publishes *Time* (**http://www.time.com**) and *People* (**http://www.people.com**) for very broad audiences and *Fortune* (**http://www.fortune.com**) and *Sports Illustrated for Kids* (**http://www.sikids. com**) for more specialized segments.

Differentiated marketing requires thorough analysis. Resources and abilities must be able to produce and market two or more different sizes, brands, or product lines. This can be costly, as with high-tech products. However, if a firm sells similar products under its own and retailer brands, added costs are low.

A firm can attain many goals with differentiated marketing. It can maximize sales: Procter & Gamble (**http://www.pg.com**) is the world leader in laundry products with such brands as Tide, Dreft, Cheer, Gain, Era, and Ivory Snow. Boeing (**http://www.boeing.com**) leads in the global commercial aircraft business—offering planes with different sizes and configurations (including the 737, 747, 757, 767, 777, and 787). Recognition as a specialist can be sustained if a firm has separate brands for distinct segments: Whirlpool has a clear image under its own name (**http://www.whirlpool.com**); few people know it also makes products under Sears' Kenmore brand (**http://www.kenmore.com**). Multiple segmentation lets a firm diversify and minimize risks since all emphasis is not on one segment: Honda's (**http://www.honda.com**) motorcycles and small engines (for lawn mowers and outboard motors) provide an excellent hedge against a drop in the sales of its cars.

Differentiated marketing does not mean a firm has to enter segments where competition is intense and face the majority fallacy. Its goals, strengths, and weaknesses must be weighed against competitors'. A firm should target only segments it can handle. The majority fallacy can work in reverse. If a firm enters a segment before a competitor, it may prevent the latter from successfully entering that segment.

Marketing and the Web

Getting Inside Shoppers' Minds

Coca-Cola's Retailing Research Council (CCRRC) (http://www.ccrrc.org) recently developed a Web-based marketing tool titled "Getting Inside the Minds of Your Shoppers." This tool, which incorporates a 60-item questionnaire, focuses on how a retailer can effectively meet the different need states that shoppers have on different shopping trips. These need states include "care for family," "efficient stock-up," "smart budget-shopping," "discovery," "specific item," "reluctance (don't want to shop, but have to)," "bargain hunting among stores," "small basket grab and go," and "immediate consumption."

Chatham Food Center was able to achieve double-digit annual sales increases in its meat department by using this tool. Through an analysis of its customers' behavior, the Chicago-based chain better understood that the shoppers are family-oriented and appreciate the firm's selection of fresh meat and produce. As a result of the analysis, Chatham began offering family packs for consumers who want to purchase fresh meat, that is not going to be frozen.

Iowa-based Hy-Vee Supermarkets (http://www.hyvee.com) runs its 225 stores as independent units. As a Hy-Vee executive says, "It's [the online tool's] like having a focus group in each individual store. The connectivity between the managers, the various department heads and their employees, and the customers is essential. It all comes down to satisfying customer needs and getting to know your customer base better."

Source: Based on material in Jenny McTaggart, "Focus on the Shopper," *Progressive Grocer* (May 1, 2005), p. 36.

Although differentiated marketing requires the existence of at least two consumer segments (with distinct desires by each), the more potential segments exist, the better the opportunity for multiple segmentation. Firms that start with concentrated marketing often turn to multiple segmentation and pursue other segments after they become established in one segment.

Wholesalers and retailers usually find differentiated marketing by suppliers to be attractive. It lets them reach multiple segments, offers some exclusivity, allows orders to be placed with fewer suppliers, and may enable them to carry their own private brands. For the selling firm, several benefits exist. Items can be placed with competing resellers under different brands. Space is given to display various sizes, packages, and/or brands. Price differentials among brands can be kept. Competitors may be discouraged from entering a channel. Overall, differentiated marketing places the seller in a good bargaining position.

Multiple segmentation can be quite profitable because total profits should rise as a firm increases the number of segments it services. Per-unit profits should also be high if a firm does a good job of enacting a unique marketing plan for each segment. Consumers in each segment would then be willing to pay a premium price for the tailor-made offering.

Although risks from a decline in any one segment are lessened, when a firm serves diverse segments, extra costs may be incurred by making product variations, selling in more channels, and promoting more brands. The firm must weigh the revenues gained from selling to multiple segments against the costs.

A company must be careful to maintain product distinctiveness for each market segment and guard its overall image. Some consumers still perceive various General Motors' divisions as having "look-alike" cars. And IBM's image was affected by its past weak performance in the home PC segment (causing IBM's PC division to be sold to China's Lenovo, **http://www.lenovo.com**).

10-3b Selecting the Target Market(s)

At this point, a firm has these decisions: Which segment(s) offer the best opportunities? How many segments should it pursue? In assessing market segments, goals and strengths, competition, segment size and growth potential, distribution requirements, necessary expenditures, profit potential, company image, ability to create and sustain differential advantages, and other factors should be reviewed.[13]

Based on the approach chosen, a firm would decide whether to pursue one or more segments (or the mass market). Due to the high costs of entering the digital camera market and the existence of well-defined demand clusters, it is most likely that a firm new to that industry would start with concentrated marketing. On the other hand, a new sweater maker could easily use differentiated marketing to target boys, girls, men, and women. Pep Boys (**http://www.pepboys.com**), the auto repair and parts giant, aims to serve two distinct segments: do-it-yourselfers and professional mechanics. It estimates the size of the U.S. do-it-yourself segment at $25 billion per year, and the professional segment is $50 billion.

> A company now chooses which and how many segments to target.

Requirements for Successful Segmentation   For concentrated marketing or differentiated marketing plans to succeed, the selected market segment(s) must meet five criteria:

1. *Differences* must exist among consumers, or mass marketing would be an appropriate strategy.
2. Within each segment, there must be enough consumer *similarities* to develop an appropriate marketing plan for that segment.
3. A firm must be able to *measure* consumer attributes and needs in order to form groups. This may be hard for some lifestyle attributes.
4. A segment must be *large enough* to produce sales and cover costs.
5. The members of a segment must be *reachable* in an efficient way. For example, young women can be reached via *Teen* magazine (**http://www.teenmag.com**). It is efficient because males and older women do not read the magazine.

> Effectiveness requires segments that are distinct, homogeneous, measurable, large enough, and reachable.

Limitations of Segmentation   Segmentation is often consumer-oriented, efficient, and profitable—but it should not be abused. Firms can fall into one or more of these traps, which they should avoid. They may:

> The shortcomings of segmentation need to be considered.

- Appeal to segments that are too small
- Misread consumer similarities and differences
- Become cost inefficient
- Spin off too many imitations of their original products or brands
- Become short-run instead of long-run oriented
- Be unable to use certain media (due to the small size of individual segments)
- Compete in too many segments
- Confuse people
- Become locked into a declining segment
- Be too slow to seek innovative possibilities for new products

10-4   DEVELOPING THE MARKETING STRATEGY

The third phase in planning a target market strategy (developing the marketing strategy) includes these steps: positioning the firm's offering relative to competitors and outlining appropriate marketing mix(es).

---

[13] See Karsten Sausen, Torsten Tomczak, and Andreas Herrmann, "Development of a Taxonomy of Strategic Market Segmentation: A Framework for Bridging the Implementation Gap Between Normative Segmentation and Business Practice," *Journal of Strategic Marketing*, Vol. 13 (September 2005), pp. 151–173; and Sally Dibb, "Market Segmentation Implementation Barriers and How to Overcome Them," *Marketing Review*, Vol. 5 (Spring 2005), pp. 13–30.

Ethical Issues in Marketing

Dr Pepper Recognizes the Importance of the Hispanic Market

The Hispanic market is an important one for soda manufacturers. Hispanics typically consume more fruit-flavored beverages than the general population. Acculturated Hispanics, who speak English and are part of the American mainstream but still identify with their Hispanic heritage, drink 62 percent more Dr Pepper (http://www.drpepper.com) than the general population.

Dr Pepper's marketing challenge is to effectively promote its products to two Hispanic market segments: acculturated Hispanics and recent immigrants. For the recent immigrant market, Dr Pepper is more like a new product. To enhance its marketing strategy, Dr Pepper chose a Hispanic advertising agency, Cartel Group (http://www.thecartel.com), to plan and implement its ad campaign. As the agency's head stated, "We had Dr Pepper lovers [the acculturated Hispanics]

and people with no relationship with the brand [new immigrants]. We had to figure out a bridge to get them together so we could proceed with one target the way it is in the general market." The bridge the agency discovered was Dr Pepper's taste, which both groups could easily distinguish from other cola brands.

The ad agency produced two versions of radio ads—one for each market. In the Spanish-language ad, recent Hispanic immigrants were portrayed as surprised and delighted at Dr Pepper's taste. In the English version, acculturated Hispanics (who are blindfolded) were so confident that they could distinguish Dr Pepper from rival cola brands that they were willing to bet on being correct.

Source: Based on material in Laurel Wentz, "Getting Hispanics to Be a Pepper, Too," *Advertising Age* (June 20, 2005), pp. 27–28.

10-4a Positioning the Company's Offering in Relation to Competition

Once a firm selects its target market(s), it must identify the attributes and image of each competitor and select a position for its own offering.

> A good or service must be carefully positioned against competitors.

For example, a firm considering entry into the office PC market could describe the key strengths of some major competitors as follows:

- Acer—Good pricing, reliability, durability, product variety.
- Apple—Ease of use, graphics, desktop publishing, innovativeness.
- Compaq/Hewlett-Packard—Innovativeness, construction, monitor quality, competitive pricing.
- Dell—Made-to-order products, range of accessories carried, direct marketing experience.

In positioning itself against these competitors, the firm would need to present a combination of customer benefits that are not being offered by them and that are desirable by a target market. Customers must be persuaded that there are clear reasons for buying the new firm's computers. It is not a good idea for the firm to go head on against such big, well-known competitors.

As one alternative, the firm could focus on small businesses that have not yet bought a computer and that need a personal touch during both the purchase process and the initial use of the product. It could thus market fully configured PC systems, featuring Windows-based clones that are installed by the seller (complete with software libraries and customized programs), in-office training of employees, and a single price for a total system. The positioning emphasis would be "to provide the best ongoing, personalized customer service possible to an underdeveloped market segment, small-business owners."

A fuller discussion of product positioning appears in Chapter 11.

10-4b Outlining the Appropriate Marketing Mix(es)

The last step in the target-marketing process is for a firm to outline a marketing-mix plan for each customer group sought. Marketing decisions relate to product, distribution, promotion, and price factors.

> The marketing mix must be attractive to the target market.

Here is a logical marketing-mix plan for a firm newly entering the office PC market and concentrating on small-business owners:

- Product—Good-quality, Windows operating system, Intel Pentium chip, expansion capability; user friendly, simple keyboard layout; high-resolution color monitor; high-speed DVD player/rewriter and suitable speakers; 120-gigabyte hard drive; basic software library; customized software; and more.
- Distribution—Direct calls and installations at customers' places of business; follow-up service calls.
- Promotion—Focus on personal selling and direct mail; hands-on, on-site training; customer referrals.
- Price—Average to above average; customers presented with nonprice reasons to buy; positioning linked to high value for the price; price of computer, software, and service bundled together.

10-5 SALES FORECASTING

> A **sales forecast** predicts company sales over a specified period.

A firm should forecast short-run and long-run sales to the chosen market as it plans a target market strategy. A *sales forecast* outlines expected company sales for a specific good or service to a specific consumer group over a specific period of time under a specific marketing program. By accurately projecting sales, a firm can better set a marketing budget, allot resources, measure success, analyze sales productivity, monitor the environment and competition, and modify marketing efforts.[14]

First, industry forecasts should be studied; they can strongly affect any company's sales. Next, sales potential outlines the upper limit for the firm, based on marketing and production capacity. A sales forecast then enumerates a firm's realistic sales. The forecast is also based on the expected environment and company performance. Figure 10-13 shows this sales forecasting process.

A sales forecast should take into account demographics (such as per-capita income), the economy (such as the inflation rate), the competitive environment (such as promotion levels), current and prior sales, and other factors. When devising a forecast, precision is required. A forecast should break sales down by good or service (model 123), consumer group (adult female), time period (July through September), and type of marketing plan (intensive advertising).

10-5a Data Sources

Several external secondary sources can be consulted to obtain the data needed for a forecast. Government agencies provide data on global, national, regional, and local demographic trends; past sales by industry and product category; and the economy. Trade associations publish statistics and often have libraries. General and specialized media, such as *Business Week* (**http://www.businessweek.com**) and *Ward's Automotive Reports* (**http://www.wardsauto.com**) do forecasts.

A firm can also get data from present and future customers, executives, salespeople, research studies and market tests, and internal records. These data often center on company, not industry, predictions.

---

[14] See Tim Berry, "Creating a Sales Forecast," http://www.entrepreneur.com/article/0,4621,321257,00.html (May 1, 2005); "Sales Forecasting," http://www.tutor2u.net/business/marketing/sales_forecasting.asp (May 6, 2006); "Sales Forecasting Examples," http://www.decisioneering.com/models/sales_forecast.html (May 6, 2006); and "Calculating a Sales Forecast for a Business Plan," http://www.fastlinksolutions.co.uk/calculat.htm (May 6, 2006).

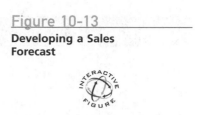

Figure 10-13

Developing a Sales Forecast

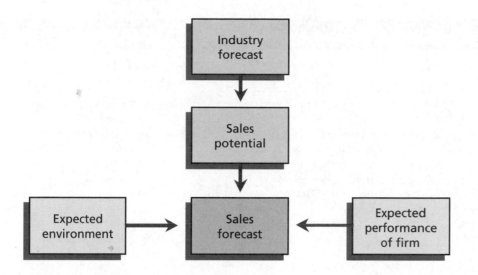

10-5b Methods of Sales Forecasting

Sales forecasting methods range from simple to sophisticated. Among the simple methods are trend analysis, market share analysis, jury of executive (expert) opinion, sales force surveys, and consumer surveys. Among the more complex methods are the chain-ratio technique, market buildup method, and statistical analyses. Table 10-3 illustrates each. By combining two or more techniques, a firm can better forecast and minimize the weaknesses in any one method.

With simple trend analysis, a firm forecasts sales on the basis of recent or current performance. If sales have risen an average of 10 percent annually over the last five years, it will forecast next year's sales to be 10 percent higher than the present year's. Although the technique is easy to use, the problems are that sales fluctuations, changing consumer tastes, changing competition, the economy, and market saturation are not considered. A firm's growth may be affected by these factors.

Market share analysis is similar to simple trend analysis, except that a company assumes that its share of industry sales will be constant. However, all firms in an industry do not progress at the same rate. Market share analysis has the same weaknesses as simple trend analysis, but uses more industry data—and it would let an aggressive or declining firm adjust its forecast and marketing efforts.

A ***jury of executive (expert) opinion*** is used if the management of a firm or other well-informed persons meet, discuss the future, and set sales estimates based on the group's experience and interaction. By itself, this method relies too much on informal analysis. In conjunction with other methods, it is effective because it enables experts to directly interpret and respond to concrete data. Because management lays out goals, sets priorities, and guides a firm's destiny, its input is crucial.

The employees most in touch with consumers and the environment are sales personnel. A sales force survey allows a firm to obtain input in a structured way. Salespeople are often able to pinpoint trends, strengths and weaknesses in a firm's offering, competitive strategies, customer resistance, and the traits of heavy users. They can break sales forecasts down by product, customer type, and area. However, they can have a limited perspective, offer biased replies, and misinterpret consumer desires.

Many marketers feel the best indicators of future sales are consumer attitudes. By conducting consumer surveys, a firm can obtain data on purchase intentions, future expectations, consumption rates, brand switching, time between purchases, and reasons for purchases. Yet, consumers may not reply to surveys and may act differently from what they say.

> A **jury of executive (expert) opinion** has informed people estimate sales.

Table 10-3 Applying Sales Forecasting Techniques		
Technique	**Illustration**	**Selected Potential Shortcomings**
Simple trend analysis	This year's sales = $2 million; company trend is 5% growth per year; sales forecast = $2,100,000.	Industry decline not considered
Market share analysis	Current market share = 18%; company seeks stable market share; industry forecast = $10,000,000; company sales forecast = $1,800,000.	New competitors and greater marketing by current ones not considered
Jury of executive opinion	Three executives see strong growth and three see limited growth; they agree on a 6% rise on this year's sales of $11 million; sales forecast = $11,660,000.	Change in consumer attitudes not uncovered
Jury of expert opinion	Groups of wholesalers, retailers, and suppliers meet. Each group makes a forecast; top management utilizes each forecast in forming one projection.	Different beliefs by groups about industry growth
Sales force survey	Sales personnel report a competitor's price drop of 10% will cause company sales to decline 3% from this year's $7 million; sales forecast = $6,790,000.	Sales force unaware a competitor's price cut will be temporary
Consumer survey	85% of current customers indicate they will repurchase next year and spend an average of $1,000 with the firm; 3% of competitors' customers indicate they will buy from the firm next year and spend an average of $800; sales forecast = $460,000.	Consumer intentions possibly not reflecting real behavior
Chain-ratio method	Unit sales forecast for introductory marketing text = (number of students) × (% annually enrolled in marketing) × (% buying a new book) × (expected market share) = (10,000,000) × (0.07) × (0.87) × (0.11) = 66,990.	Inaccurate estimate of enrollment in introductory marketing course made
Market buildup method	Total sales forecast = region 1 forecast + region 2 forecast + region 3 forecast = $2,000,000 + $7,000,000 + $13,000,000 = $22,000,000.	Incorrect assumption that areas will behave similarly in future
Test marketing	Total sales forecast = (sales in test market A + sales in test market B) × (25) = ($1,000,000 + $1,200,000) × (25) = $55,000,000.	Test areas not representative of all locations
Detailed statistical analyses	Simulation, complex trend analysis, regression, and correlation.	Lack of understanding by management; all factors not quantifiable

> With the **chain-ratio method**, general data are broken down. The **market buildup method** adds segment data.

In the *chain-ratio method*, a firm starts with general market information and then computes a series of more specific information. These combined data yield a sales forecast. A maker of women's casual shoes can first look at a trade association report to learn the industry sales estimate for shoes, the percentage of sales from women's shoes, and the percentage of women's shoe sales from casual shoes. It would then project its own sales of casual women's shoes to its target market. This method is only as accurate as the data plugged in for each market factor. It is useful because it gets management to think through a forecast and obtain different information.

Opposite to the chain-ratio method is the *market buildup method*, by which a firm gathers data from small, separate market segments and aggregates them. This method lets a firm operating in four urban areas devise a forecast by first estimating sales in each area and then adding them. A firm must note that consumer tastes, competition, population growth, and media do differ by area. Equal-size segments may present dissimilar opportunities; they should not be lumped together without careful study.

Test marketing is a form of market buildup analysis in which a firm projects a new product's sales based on short-run, geographically limited tests. With it, a company usually introduces a new product into one or a few markets for a short time and enacts a full marketing campaign there. Overall sales are forecast from test market sales. Yet, test areas may not be representative of all locales, and test-market enthusiasm may not carry into national distribution. Test marketing is discussed more fully in Chapter 13.

Many detailed statistical methods are used for sales forecasting. Simulation lets a firm enter market data into a computer model and forecast under varying conditions and marketing plans. In complex trend analysis, the firm includes past sales fluctuations, cyclical factors (such as economic conditions), and other factors when looking at sales trends. Regression and correlation techniques explore mathematical links between future sales and market factors, such as annual income or derived demand. These methods rely on good data and the ability to use them well. Further discussion is beyond the scope of our text.

10-5c   Additional Considerations

The method and accuracy of sales forecasting greatly depend on the newness of a firm's offering. A forecast for a continuing good or service could be based on trend analysis, market share analysis, executive (expert) opinion, and sales force surveys. Barring major alterations in the economy, industry, competition, or consumer tastes, the forecast should be relatively accurate.

> A forecast for a continuing product should be the most accurate.

A forecast for an item new to the firm but continuing in the industry could be based on trade data, executive (expert) opinion, sales force and consumer surveys, and test marketing. The first year's forecast should be somewhat accurate, the ensuing years more so. It is hard to project first-year sales precisely because consumer interest and competition may be tough to gauge.

A forecast for a good or service new to both the firm and the industry should rely on sales force and consumer surveys, test marketing, executive (expert) opinion, and simulation. The forecast for the early years may be highly inaccurate because the speed of consumer acceptance cannot be closely estimated. Later forecasts will be more accurate. Though an initial forecast may be imprecise, it is still needed for setting marketing plans, budgeting, monitoring the environment and competition, and measuring success.

A firm must consider *sales penetration*—the degree to which a firm is meeting its sales potential—in forecasting sales. It is expressed as:

> **Sales penetration** shows whether a firm has reached its potential. **Diminishing returns** may result if the firm seeks nonconsumers.

Sales penetration = Actual sales/Sales potential

Table 10-4 Illustrating Sales Penetration and Diminishing Returns	
Year 1	**Year 2**
Sales potential = $1,000,000	Sales potential = $1,000,000
Actual sales = $600,000 (60,000 units)	Actual sales = $700,000 (70,000 units)
Selling price = $10/unit	Selling price = $10/unit
Total marketing costs = $100,000	Total marketing costs = $150,000
Total production costs (at $8/unit) = $480,000	Total production costs (at $8/unit) = $560,000
Sales penetration = $\dfrac{\$600{,}000}{\$1{,}000{,}000}$ = 60%	Sales penetration = $\dfrac{\$700{,}000}{\$1{,}000{,}000}$ = 70%
Total profit = $600,000 − ($100,000 + $480,000) = $20,000	Total profit = $700,000 − ($150,000 + $560,000) = −$10,000

In year 1, sales penetration is 60% and the firm earns a $20,000 profit. In year 2, the firm raises marketing expenditures to increase sales penetration to 70%; as a result, it suffers diminishing returns—the additional $100,000 in actual sales is more than offset by a $130,000 rise in total costs (from $580,000 in year 1 to $710,000 in year 2).

A firm with high sales penetration needs to realize that *diminishing returns* may occur if it seeks to convert remaining nonconsumers; the costs of attracting them may outweigh revenues. Other products or segments may offer better potential. Table 10-4 illustrates sales penetration and diminishing returns.

Factors may change and cause a wrong forecast, unless revised. These include economic conditions, industry conditions, firm performance, competition, and consumer tastes.

Web Sites You Can Use

Many valuable Web sites are related to target marketing. Following are several of them:

- Bank of America has an insightful, animated workshop on "Target Marketing" (**http://www.va-interactive.com/ bankofamerica/resourcecenter/workshops/targetmarket/ targetmarket.html**).
- Business Resource Center (**http://www.businessplans.org/ Segment.html**) has a section of its site dedicated to market segmentation.
- Claritas markets lifestyle segmentation programs to business clients. At its Web site, Claritas discusses market segmentation (**http://www.claritas.com**) and enables visitors to try out its PRIZM NE program (**http:// www.claritas.com/MyBestSegments/Default.jsp**). The segments are described at the Web site.
- Easy Analytic Software (**http:// www.easidemographics.com**) makes available a number

of free demographic and lifestyle reports. This enables firms to study consumer backgrounds in different states and communities.

- *Target Marketing* has an online version of its magazine (**http://www.targetonline.com**) devoted to this topic from the perspective of direct marketing.
- The U.S. Small Business Administration has a section of its site devoted to target marketing (**http://www.sba.gov/ starting_business/marketing/target.html**).
- Yankelovich MindBase (**http://www.yankelovich.com/ products/MindBase_PS.pdf**) identifies eight major consumer groups based on attitudes and motivations. Each group is broken down into three distinct subsegments, which enable client firms to create high-impact marketing programs and develop high-value customer relationships. The segments are described at its Web site.

Summary

1. *To describe the process for planning a target market strategy* After collecting information on consumers and the environment, a firm can pick the target market(s) to which to appeal. A potential market has people with similar needs, enough resources, and a willingness and ability to buy.

There are three general phases in developing a target market strategy, with seven specific steps: analyzing consumer demand—determining demand patterns (1), establishing bases of segmentation (2), and identifying potential market segments (3); targeting the market—choosing a target market approach (4) and selecting the target market(s) (5); and developing the marketing strategy—positioning the company's offering relative to competitors (6) and outlining the appropriate marketing mix(es) (7). Of particular importance is product differentiation, whereby a product offering is perceived by the consumer to differ from its competition on any physical or nonphysical product characteristic, including price.

2. *To examine alternative demand patterns and segmentation bases for both final and organizational consumers* Demand patterns indicate the uniformity or diversity of consumer needs and desires for particular categories of goods and services. With homogeneous demand, consumers have

relatively uniform needs and desires. With clustered demand, consumer needs and desires can be classified into two or more identifiable clusters (segments), with each having distinct purchase requirements. With diffused demand, consumer needs and desires are so diverse that clear clusters cannot be identified.

The possible bases for segmenting the market can be placed into three categories: geographic demographics—basic identifiable traits of towns, cities, states, regions, and countries; personal demographics—basic identifiable traits of individual final consumers and organizations and groups of final consumers and organizations; and lifestyles—patterns in which people (final consumers and those representing organizational consumers) live and spend time and money. It is generally advisable to use a combination of demographic and lifestyle factors to form possible segmentation bases. Although the distinctions between final and organizational consumers should be kept in mind, the three broad segmentation bases could be used in both cases.

After establishing possible segmentation bases, a firm is ready to develop consumer profiles, which identify potential market segments by aggregating those with similar attributes and needs.

3. *To explain and contrast undifferentiated marketing (mass marketing), concentrated marketing, and differentiated marketing (multiple segmentation)* Undifferentiated marketing aims at a large, broad consumer market via a single basic marketing plan. In concentrated marketing, a firm aims at a narrow, specific consumer group via a single, specialized marketing plan catering to the needs of that segment. Under differentiated marketing, a firm appeals to two or more distinct market segments, with a different marketing plan for each. When segmenting, a firm must understand the majority fallacy: The largest segment may not offer the best opportunity; it often has the most competitors.

In selecting its target market(s), a firm should consider its goals and strengths, competition, segment size and growth potential, distribution needs, required expenditures, profit potential, company image, and its ability to develop and sustain a differential advantage.

Successful segmentation requires differences among and similarities within segments, measurable consumer traits and needs, large enough segments, and efficiency in reaching segments. It should not be abused by appealing to overly small groups, using marketing inefficiently, overly emphasizing imitations of original company products or brands, confusing consumers, and so on.

4. *To show the importance of positioning in developing a marketing strategy* In positioning its offering against competitors, a firm needs to present a combination of customer benefits that are not being provided by others and that are desirable by a target market. Customers must be persuaded that there are clear reasons for buying the firm's products rather than those of its competitors.

The last step in the target marketing process is for a firm to develop a marketing mix for each customer group to which it wants to appeal.

5. *To discuss sales forecasting and its role in target marketing* Short- and long-run sales should be forecast in developing a target market strategy. This helps a firm compute budgets, allocate resources, measure success, analyze productivity, monitor the environment and competition, and adjust marketing plans. A sales forecast describes the expected company sales of a specific good or service to a specific consumer group over a specific time period under a specific marketing program.

A firm can obtain sales-forecasting data from internal and external sources. Forecasting methods range from simple trend analysis to detailed statistical analyses. The best results are obtained when methods and forecasts are combined. A sales forecast should consider the newness of a firm's offering, sales penetration, diminishing returns, and the changing nature of many factors.

Key Terms

markct (p. 285)

market segmentation (p. 285)

target market strategy (p. 285)

undifferentiated marketing (mass marketing) (p. 285)

concentrated marketing (p. 285)

differentiated marketing (multiple segmentation) (p. 285)

product differentiation (p. 285)

demand patterns (p. 286)

homogeneous demand (p. 286)

clustered demand (p. 287)

diffused demand (p. 287)

geographic demographics (p. 288)

personal demographics (p. 290)

heavy-usage segment (heavy half) (p. 293)

benefit segmentation (p. 294)

VALS (Values and Lifestyles) program (p. 294)

Social Styles model (p. 294)

majority fallacy (p. 300)

sales forecast (p. 306)

jury of executive (expert) opinion (p. 307)

chain-ratio method (p. 308)

market buildup method (p. 308)

sales penetration (p. 309)

diminishing returns (p. 310)

Review Questions

1. Distinguish between the terms "market" and "market segmentation."
2. Explain this comment: "Sometimes a firm can achieve a key differential advantage by simply emphasizing how its offering satisfies existing consumer desires and needs better than its competitors do. Sometimes demand patterns must be modified for consumers to perceive a firm's product differentiation as worthwhile."
3. Differentiate among homogeneous, clustered, and diffused consumer demand. What are the marketing implications of each?
4. Describe five personal demographics pertaining to organizations.
5. What is the majority fallacy? How may a firm avoid it?
6. Cite the five key requirements for successful segmentation.
7. Why is sales forecasting important when developing a target market strategy?
8. Why are long-run sales forecasts for new products more accurate than short-run forecasts?

Discussion Questions

1. How could a global TV maker apply geographic demographic segmentation?
2. Develop a personal-demographic profile of the students at your school. For what goods and services would the class be a good market segment? A poor segment?
3. Describe several potential benefit segments for a firm marketing office furniture to business clients.
4. A firm has a sales potential of $5,000,000 and attains actual sales of $4,000,000. What does this signify? What should the firm do next?

Web Exercise

Claritas helps companies develop and enact target market strategies through its MyBestSegments program (**http://www.claritas.com/MyBestSegments/Default.jsp**): "Think of MyBestSegments as a consumer 'photo album'". Each Claritas segment has its own pages displaying 'snapshots' of the segment's demographic traits, lifestyle preferences, and behavior. Marketers can use MyBestSegments to guide marketing campaigns and media strategies for specific consumer targets by answering: "What are they like? Where can I find them? How can I reach them?" Visit the MyBestSegments Web site, and then click on "Segment Look-Up." Select any three segments, review their characteristics, and explain how a cell phone marketer could use the information in devising its target market strategy.

Practice Quiz

1. When a company strives to appeal to multiple well-defined market segments with a strategy tailored to each segment, it is applying
   a. undifferentiated marketing.
   b. differentiated marketing.
   c. concentrated marketing.
   d. the majority fallacy.

2. Personal demographics include
   a. benefit segments.
   b. usage experience.
   c. gender.
   d. class consciousness.

3. According to Haley's study of benefit segmentation in the toothpaste industry, the consumer group most interested in low prices was known as the
   a. independent segment.
   b. sensory segment.
   c. sociable segment.
   d. worrier segment.

4. According to the VALS 2 typology, within the ideals type are
   a. believers.
   b. achievers.
   c. strivers.
   d. makers.

5. Which of the following is *not* a lifestyle designation of the Social Styles model?
   a. Drivers
   b. Expressives
   c. Strugglers
   d. Amiables

6. In general, female shoppers in supermarkets, as compared to males,
   a. spend less time shopping.
   b. use a shopping list less often.
   c. are less likely to bring children.
   d. buy more items.

7. For a firm with limited resources and abilities, the most promising method of developing a target market is
   a. differentiated marketing.
   b. concentrated marketing.
   c. undifferentiated marketing.
   d. benefit segmentation.

8. Differentiated marketing is appropriate if
   a. benefit segmentation cannot be used.
   b. a firm wishes to maximize per-unit profits by appealing to only one segment.
   c. diffused demand can be clustered into two or more segments and satisfied by offering unique marketing mixes to each.
   d. homogenous demand exists in a particular market.

9. A consumer goods marketer produces multiple brands of shampoo that are positioned for consumers with dyed hair, dandruff, oily hair, or dry hair. This strategy illustrates
   a. concentrated marketing.
   b. undifferentiated marketing.
   c. differentiated marketing.
   d. mass marketing.

10. Wholesalers and retailers usually find differentiated marketing on the part of their suppliers to be attractive because it
    a. can allow them to avoid having to carry their own private brands.
    b. lets them avoid having to reach multiple segments.
    c. means that they cannot concentrate orders with fewer suppliers.
    d. can offer them some brand exclusivity.

11. Which of the following is *not* a criterion for successful market segmentation?
    a. There must be differences among consumers.
    b. Each segment must be located within a small geographic area.
    c. There must be consumer similarities within each segment identified.
    d. A segment must be large enough to cover costs.

12. A firm is abusing segmentation when it
    a. becomes too efficient.
    b. is consumer oriented.
    c. is generating too much profit.
    d. becomes short-run oriented rather than long-run oriented.

13. The upper sales limit for a company is defined as
    a. market segmentation.
    b. market program.
    c. sales potential.
    d. sales forecast.

14. Experience and interaction guide sales forecasting by
    a. juries of executives.
    b. sales force surveys.
    c. consumer surveys.
    d. test marketing.

15. The opposite approach to the market buildup method of sales forecasting is
    a. a sales force survey.
    b. a consumer survey.
    c. simulation.
    d. the chain-ratio method.

For the answers to these questions, please visit the online site for this book at **http://www.atomicdog.com.**

Case 1: J.C. Penney Turns to the "Missing Middle"[c3-1]

J.C. Penney's (http://www.jcpenney.com) core female shoppers can be characterized as "middle market" consumers. They are 35 to 54 years old, have a $69,000 median household income, and are married with children. Penney realizes that while many of its core middle-market consumers continue to shop for housewares and children's clothing at Penney's, this target market is increasingly shopping for ladies' clothing at stores such as Target. As Penney's chief executive says, "This customer is underserved."

Penney has recently launched two new lines of moderate-price clothing, one designed by Nicole Miller and other called "W—Work to Weekend," a private-label brand, to better serve these consumers. The two lines have been introduced as part of Penney's strategy of shedding its dowdy image. Penney initially advertised these brands on the Academy Awards TV show, an event that Penney's marketers call the "Super Bowl for Women."

As part of its turnaround strategy, Penney has upgraded its private-label brands, particularly the Arizona jeans brand, which targets juniors and young men. It also recently added home furnishings products designed by Chris Madden and Colin Cowie (http://www.colincowie.com). Although Penney still sells some major sportswear brands such as Bisou Bisou (http://www.bisou-bisou.com) and Bongo (http://www.bongo.com), it understands that these brands are not purchased by the middle-market consumers it is seeking. Penney was unsuccessful in past efforts to go upscale because several important high-end brands refused to sell their clothing to Penney due to its poor fashion image.

Penney recently conducted a telephone survey of 900 females to better understand their attitudes toward casual clothing. The retailer wanted to learn the shoppers' attitudes toward fashion, determine what kind of clothes they own, and ascertain their feelings about shopping at Penney. The firm videotaped interviews with 30 women that lasted up to six hours each. The respondents were also asked to clip words and images from magazines to express what casual clothing represented to them.

All of the interviews took place in the respondents' homes. Several comments by consumers struck a chord with Penney's management. One was a consumer's concern with the stress asso-ciated with clothing shopping. Pointing to a photo of Sponge Bob SquarePants, with an overstressed expression, the consumer stated, "This is me, my stress with shopping." She continued, "These are the things to stop—short shorts and skirts, exposed midriffs or cleavage, spaghetti straps on tank tops." Another woman said, "You could still be a mom, but you still want to be cute and a little hip." Added another subject, "You're not dead yet, and you're not a grandma—you still want to be in the game."

Penney's research clearly showed that matronly or sex-kitten looks were major "no-nos." Its customers wanted casual clothes that were stylish, but not overly trendy; form fitting, but not too tight. They wanted "dressy-casual" clothing appropriate for work, eating out, and attending children's school activities. Quality was also important, with respondents telling Penney that they carefully look at clothing labels and assess an item's fabric and detail. They stated that they prefer fabrics with a Lycra blend, distinctive buttons, and high-quality stitching. A personal statement was also important.

Penney approached Nicole Miller, a well-regarded designer, and showed her and the chief executive of her firm the videotapes. Penney plans to market the Nicole Miller brand (http://www.nicolemiller.com) as more of a working woman's brand and less as a designer brand. At Penney stores, Nicole Miller photos contain such quotes as "Great designs shouldn't be limited to those who can afford them."

Questions

1. Describe J.C. Penney's target consumer from the perspective of demographics and lifestyles.
2. Discuss the pros and cons of J.C. Penney's repositioning strategy.
3. What are the pros and cons of J.C. Penney's using a private-label strategy?
4. Compare the positioning strategies of J.C. Penney and Target. Refer to secondary sources such as articles and each firm's Web site.

[c3-1] The data in the case are drawn from Ellen Byron, "New Penney: Chain Goes for 'Missing Middle'," *Wall Street Journal* (February 14, 2005), pp. B1, B3.

Case 2: Vendors as B-to-B Partners[c3-2]

Although many business startups begin with innovative approaches to marketing, they often have difficulties in implementing their plans. These startups need to consider how to outsource such business services as technical support, real-estate planning, warehousing, and delivery. Some startups have turned to large corporations for support, whereas others hire smaller firms much like themselves. Let's look at how some entrepreneurial firms have formed collaborative relationships.

Sepaton (http://www.sepaton.com), a data protection firm experiencing rapid growth, found that it had to quickly lease space that was three times larger than its current offices. What added to the difficulty in finding appropriate space was its need for special electrical and air-conditioning facilities due to the nature of its business. Furthermore, Sepaton needed the space in "move-in condition," including furnishing. Sepaton used T3, a buyer's broker that functions much like a real-estate department for high-tech firms. Unlike a typical broker that focuses on finding space and negotiating leases, T3's services include architectural issues and managing contractors. T3 quickly found six spaces that met Sepaton's criteria and Sepaton signed a three-year lease on one of these properties. According to T3's chief executive, "If we can't make the smallest three-person company happy about T3, we've failed."

The Center for Systems Management (CSM) provides consulting services for government agencies (such as NASA), as well as for-profit organizations. When NASA asked CSM to develop an internal marketing campaign—including a video—in 45 days, CSM's project manager was concerned about the ability of its marketing department to undertake that responsibility. CSM hired Technovative Marketing (http://www.technovative.com) to assist with the campaign. Harriet Donnelley, Technovative Marketing's president, personally worked on the video and attended all NASA meetings. Donnelley says, "We represented the project as if we were part of CSM's team, which is what we were. That means behaving as much like a salaried employee as a contractor." Due to the success of the video, CSM has been asked to do additional work by NASA and now markets internal marketing campaigns to other clients.

In January, just at the beginning of tax season, Charles M. Ross, a CPA, realized he had made a major error. He had set up a client's payroll system using incorrect wages and ran it that way for six months. The magnitude of the problem was so great that Ross quickly realized that he could not fix the problem on his own because the W2 forms were due shortly. Ross used PayCycle (http://www.paycycle.com), a payroll services firm, to process payrolls for some of his clients. Ross contacted his PayCycle customer representative, who assured him that the company would quickly resolve his problem. Over the weekend, PayCycle's staff recalculated the payroll error—a task that took almost a day of nonstop work. This level of customer service is not unusual for PayCycle, which expects all of its employees to be able to solve any customer problem. All employees, including the chief executive, spend at least 10 percent of their time answering calls from customers.

Michael Joseph, the chief executive officer of ASI Inc., a medical instruments distributor, did not realize that he was getting much more than a traditional accountant when he hired Skoda Minotti (http://www.skodaminotti.com), a 120-person firm. Joseph routinely calls on Ken Haffney, a Skoda Minotti partner, for advice on strategic planning, benefits packages, and even technology problems. As Joseph acknowledges, "I bring up things that are giving me pain, and I see what he has to say about it. For all intents and purposes, Ken's my CFO [chief financial officer]."

Questions

1. Discuss the pros and cons of outsourcing business services by small firms.
2. Explain the significance of the following statement: "We represented the project as if we were part of CSM's team, which is what we were. That means behaving as much like a salaried employee as a contractor."
3. Comment on PayCycle's customer service philosophy.
4. What is the significance of the following statement? "For all intents and purposes, Ken's my CFO [chief financial officer]."

[c3-2] The data in the case are drawn from Michael Fitzgerald, "Turning Vendors into Partners," *Inc.* (August 2005), pp. 94–100.

Case 3: PRIZM NE: Lifestyle Segmentation[c3-3]

The overriding notion of PRIZM NE is that if marketers can better understand the lifestyle behaviors of their customers, they will know how to better reach them and others with similar characteristics. PRIZM NE is the current version of Claritas Corporation's (http://www.claritas.com) lifestyle segmentation system. With PRIZM NE, Claritas changed its prior version of PRIZM to correspond with the 2000 U.S. Census.

The PRIZM NE system classifies each household into 1 of 66 lifestyle segments. Each segment is defined by product purchases (e.g., food and beverages, clothing, household goods, appliances, electronics, sports equipment, and automobiles), lifestyles (e.g., travel, vacations, hobbies, sports, and music), media used (such e.g., cable, print, outdoor, broadcast television, radio, and Internet), and neighborhoods (maps showing high potential areas and highly penetrated areas).

PRIZM NE links a client's customer data bases with data on a neighborhood's demographics, syndicated research data (from firms such as A.C. Nielsen, J.D. Power, Polk Automotive, and Simmons), and survey research. With this linkage, PRIZM NE determines the types of consumers who are most apt to buy a firm's goods or services. PRIZM NE works with different geographical areas. This enables a marketer to determine where to promote products, where additional stores and distribution centers should be located, and which geographic regions require additional advertising and sales support.

PRIZM NE divides U.S. consumers into 15 different groups and 66 different segments. These groups live in diverse areas ranging from downtown in major cities to suburban and rural areas. Let's compare the characteristics of the midtown mix, middleburbs, and rustic living groups. The midtown mix group is the most ethically diverse, consisting of singles, couples, homeowners, and renters. Households within this group are typically childless couples who pursue active social lives. The group frequents health clubs and restaurants, drives small import cars, and purchases the latest in consumer electronics.

Middleburb consumers comprise five segments that live in middle-class suburban communities. Two of these have very young residents, two have large compositions of seniors, and one is middle-aged. Middleburbs contain a mix of homeowners and renters. With good jobs, middleburbs visit nightclubs and casual dining restaurants, shop at mid-scale department stores, travel across the United States and Canada, and purchase CDs in large quantities.

In contrast, the rustic living group lives in isolated towns and rural villages. As a group, it has modest income, aging homes, and blue-collar occupations. These consumers spend their leisure time fishing, hunting, attending church and veterans club functions, and enjoying country music.

Let's look at how direct marketers can increase the effectiveness of a marketing strategy through PRIZM NE:

- Direct marketers often advertise in traditional media to generate mailing lists for contact via catalog mailings and telephone. PRIZM NE can be used to determine the media patterns of list members. For example, if a ZIP code contains a large proportion of "Winner's Circle" consumers (wealthy suburbanites with a median income of close to $90,000 who live in new-money subdivisions and who like to travel and eat out), appropriate media for advertising would be *Smithsonian Magazine* and the *Wall Street Journal*.
- Direct marketers who use club-based lists (such as college alumni or fraternal organizations) can use PRIZM NE to select the best names for subsequent mailings.
- Direct marketers can use PRIZM NE to prioritize their response times and communication formats to a large number of inquiries. For example, high-priority customers could be contacted through a salesperson's call, whereas lower-priority consumers may be contacted via E-mail.

Questions

1. Discuss the advantages of a retailer's use of PRIZM NE as compared to its using census data that contain detailed demographic data for geographic areas.
2. What goods and services are apt to be heavily used by the midtown mix group? Explain your answer.
3. What goods and services are apt to be heavily used by middleburb consumers? Explain your answer.
4. Describe additional ways that direct marketers can use PRIZM NE.

[c3-3] The data in the case are drawn from "PRIZM NE: Lifestyle Segmentation System," http://www.claritas.com (February 11, 2006); "PRIZM NE: The New Evolution in Segmentation," http://www.claritas.com (February 11, 2006); and "PRIZM NE: Successful Direct Marketing Applications," http://www.claritas.com (February 11, 2006).

Case 4: Searching for Narrower and Narrower Niches[c3-4]

Department stores are broad-based retailers, whereas niche stores selling women's clothing include bridal shops, clothing stores for girls and teenagers, clothing stores that specialize in given price points (such as every item under $10), and stores featuring maternity wear, petite-size clothing, and plus-size clothing. Let's examine the niche strategies of three successful firms: Designing Solutions, TLM Industries (**http://www.tlmind.com**), and Jets International (**http://jets.com**).

Deborah Wiener's company, Designing Solutions, specializes in creating child-proof interiors for her clients' homes. Wiener helps clients choose stain-resistant fabrics, lamps that are less prone to breaking when dropped, and carpeting that can withstand the heavy use of young children. She formed her firm after talking to friends and acquaintances with young children who related that typical interior decorators were either too fancy or not practical enough in their selections. She began writing columns in local publications and advertised in religious organization weeklies to promote her niche-based decorating business.

When Tim Mossberg started TLM Industries (**http://www.tlmind.com**), he focused on distributing screen-printed cups and mugs with logos to convenience stores. Mossberg's clients then told him that they needed uniforms for their employees that would last through several washings. Many of these businesses expressed concern that current suppliers did not stock the larger sizes needed by many of their workers. After Mossberg traveled to clients in five southern states, he decided to switch to supplying uniforms. Mossberg's firm now has 20 employees and annual sales of $2 million, and supplies uniforms to more than 200 convenience-store chains. He also supplies uniforms to supermarkets and fast-food retailers.

Jets International (**http://jets.com**) locates premium jets for its clients using an auction format. The firm's founder, Nathan Kelvey, managed two private jets for three years prior to starting his own company. According to McKelvey, "That was an approximately $2 billion industry that was underserved." The company had 25 employees and $15 million in annual sales revenues.

Ira Davidson, the director of the Small Business Development Center at Pace University, says that niche businesses are growing at the rate of 20 to 25 percent per year: "Niche startups are good in that they offer you a chance to focus all your branding and marketing in one area and expand on those core customers as you grow your company." Another small-business analyst, who is the author of *Niche and Get Rich*, believes that niche companies have a 25 percent better chance of surviving over 10 years than firms that appeal to a broader population. In many cases, niche marketers require less capital because the overall size of the market is smaller. In addition, there may be less competition from major firms.

In developing a marketing plan, care must be taken to properly define the niche. Too narrow a niche may limit demand, tie a business around a technology or product that can become obsolete, or make the firm vulnerable to changes in demand. As one consultant suggests, "You don't want to be so niched that you're the only one out there, and no one quite understands what you're talking about." On the other hand, too broad a definition of a niche would result in a small firm's competing in a general marketplace with many large competitors.

One way of determining if a niche is properly defined is to examine the survival rate for competitors that were priorly established in comparable markets: "A good survival rate could indicate that your idea has lasting potential and is not faddish, which is a danger for overly trendy niche businesses."

Questions

1. What are the pros and cons of pursuing a niche strategy for a small retailer?
2. Discuss the potential pitfalls in defining a niche too broadly.
3. Comment on the potential pitfalls in defining a niche too narrowly.
4. Explain the relationship between niche marketing and concentrated marketing.

[c3-4] The data in the case are drawn from Laura Koss-Feder, "Scratch a Niche," *Entrepreneur* (August 2005), pp. 92–96.

Thinking Outside the Box to Attract Customers[pc-3]

INTRODUCTION

According to conventional wisdom, customers will buy your brand only if it offers them something unique. Further, it is generally assumed that, in today's competitive markets, one can no longer differentiate the basic good or service. Thus, the only ways to differentiate are through branding and emotional values or by "thinking outside the box" and changing the rules of the industry.

We believe that the conventional view is largely wrong and that in reality:

- Customers usually choose the brand that they expect to give them the basics—the generic category benefits—better and more reliably than the competition.
- In most markets, the basics are not a commodity. Product and service quality and reliability still vary significantly between brands. This provides an opportunity for the best firms to differentiate by being "simply better," rather than by trying to be unique.
- Once a brand is simply better than the competition, great branding and extra features can reinforce its advantage. But with a few exceptions in which customers' responses really are strongly influenced by branding (e.g., beers, fragrances, luxury products), the main basis of brand equity and shareholder value is users' experience of how well and how reliably the brand provides the generic category benefits.

BRAND APPEARANCE

Research has long shown that the marketing obsession with unique brand differentiators goes largely unnoticed by customers—and even when noticed, it rarely convinces them. In most categories, consumers don't have strongly differentiated images of the different brands, except for simple descriptive attributes (e.g., Mountain Dew is known for its caffeine intensity) that don't greatly discriminate between people who do and do not buy the brand. For more evaluative attributes that do matter (e.g., "tastes nice"), people are more likely to say these things about the brands they buy. And, partly for this reason, they're more likely to say them about the biggest brands.

The size of a brand is largely a reflection of how many category users believe it delivers the main category benefits. In one of researcher Andrew Ehrenberg's studies of British toothpaste, he reported, "An estimated 55 percent of the customers of the brand

leader, Colgate Dental Cream, thought that it 'promotes strong healthy teeth,' and a very similar 57 percent of customers of the eighth biggest brand, Ultrabrite, thought that about their brand—despite Ultrabrite's radically different positioning based on whiteness." The main explanation for the relative size of each brand (leaving aside the exact causality, which does not affect the argument) was that many more consumers attributed this and other category benefits to Colgate than to Ultrabrite.

In other words, customers either don't notice or, if they do notice, don't care about most of the differentiators that brand marketers often fuss about. The implication is that strategists should not try to make their brand different for the sake of being different. They should focus on providing the benefits that matter to the customer, regardless of the extent to which the competitors provide them, too. This is often more like hard work than adding a unique, trivial differentiator (e.g., making the toothpaste pink), but is usually the only way to create shareholder value through differentiation, as opposed to low price.

Even advocates of strategy based on "unique selling propositions" (USPs) admit—and bemoan—that brands are becoming less differentiated. One of the best-known is Jack Trout, whose apocalyptic book *Differentiate or Die* (John Wiley & Sons, 2000) was dedicated to Rosser Reeves, inventor of the USP strategy. Together with marketing consultant Kevin J. Clancy, Trout asked U.S. consumers if they perceived 46 pairs of leading brands (e.g., Visa/MasterCard, Nike/Adidas, Mobil/Shell) as having become more differentiated or more similar. In 40 out of the 46 categories, the response was that the brands were becoming less distinct.

Clancy and Trout blame marketers for this reduction in perceived differentiation, saying (with some justification) that too many have diverted money away from long-term brand building into short-term price promotions that do nothing for brand equity. In our view, however, the main explanation is simply that consumers are increasingly resistant to marketers' attempts to differentiate their brands through advertising—and in most cases, simply don't care.

DOUBLE JEOPARDY

The lack of perceived differentiation is also reflected in patterns of buyer behavior. There is a myth that through clever targeting, positioning, and advertising, a small brand can create a profitable niche within a category by dominating the category purchases of a small minority of customers. In practice, this never happens. Instead, the pattern is that small brands suffer from the law of double jeopardy: In a given time period, they not only have far fewer buyers than for a big brand, but usually also a slightly lower average purchase rate.

The main difference between big and small brands is that the big brands are bought by many more people over the year. In

[pc-3] Adapted by the authors from Patrick Barwise and Seán Meehan, "Simply Better," *Marketing Research* (Summer 2005), pp. 9–14. Reprinted by permission of the American Marketing Association.

addition, they are on average bought on somewhat more purchase occasions. Most small toothpaste brands aim for a niche positioning, but none of them achieves this in terms of having an especially high average purchase frequency.

This pattern is typical and has been replicated many times. Most so-called niche brands are just small, not different in their purchase patterns. The exceptions are where a brand meets a very specific set of needs that other brands don't meet. For instance, Velux's main product is a particular type of double-glazed window that, when closed, fits flush into a sloping roof, but also hinges in the middle for easy opening. Conceptually, it is better to think of Velux as a big brand in a niche category (roof windows and skylights), rather than as a niche brand in the general window category, because its products have limited substitutability with windows designed for installation in a wall.

In some other categories (e.g., foods, beverages, and many services), these distinctions are less clear-cut. For instance, is lemon-lime soda a separate category? We would argue no, because it is closely substitutable with other sodas. This is a researchable question in each case, but not necessarily crucial: Sprite and 7 UP are both subject to the law of double jeopardy no matter which market definition one chooses.

SIMPLIFYING LIVES

Often, our biggest mistake as managers is believing that customers care a lot about our brand. They rarely do. They care about the benefits our brand and the competitors' brands deliver. All other things being equal (e.g., price and availability), customers usually buy the brand they think will deliver these category benefits the best. The process works like this: Consumers realize they need to make a category purchase—some gasoline, a DVD player, a mortgage, or whatever. The brand they choose is greatly influenced by prior knowledge—hence the importance of brand equity. Many purchases rely so much on what the customer remembers that they require no real thought: You are next to the yogurt section in the store, you need yogurt, you see your favorite brand in its usual place, you put it in a shopping cart, and you're done.

Customers usually have quite limited consideration sets. They rarely bother to use all the available information even about brands they do consider. This means their behavior falls short of economic rationality, which would ordinarily assume that they would use all the information on every brand before making their choice. But time is limited, shopping around is usually a chore, and favorite brands work pretty well, so "routinized" buying behavior seems extremely rational to us. We sometimes do stop and think a little, but our lives are greatly enriched by the fact that, most of the time, it is only a little.

MAJOR PURCHASES

Even major purchases depend on impressions, unconscious memories, and intuition. Buying a home is a huge decision. Yet from the time someone sees a house to the time they decide they would like to buy it often takes just a few seconds. This is followed by a long process of information gathering, reflection, anxiety, discussion, and so on but the final choice is still likely to be strongly influenced by the prospective buyer's reactions during those first few seconds. That's why realtors encourage sellers to spruce up the front garden and the entrance hall.

The same can hold true for organizations buying brain scanners, management consultants, and other corporate brand choices, including recruitment: First impressions matter. The main difference in b-to-b is that the decision makers are spending the organization's money, not their own. The amount involved is typically much larger than for most consumer purchases. The decision process is more formalized and its results are more apt to be explicitly monitored. It may require complex technical and financial evaluation and will likely involve several different individuals. Despite these complexities, the underlying process is the same as in b-to-c purchases: generic category needs, a brand consideration set, and brand choice.

MARKET SHARE DIFFERENCES

If customers rarely perceive brands as strongly differentiated, why do market shares vary so much? It's not at all unusual for the market leader to be 10 times bigger than the number-seven or number-eight brand.

Price

Sometimes, the explanation is price. If two or more acceptable brands are perceived as equally available and equally good but their prices differ (e.g., because one is on special), the customer will usually buy the cheapest. For example: "We'd actually been into the Borders [http://www.bordersstores.com] a few doors down from WH Smith [http://www.whsmith.co.uk] and saw that there were certain books we wanted. We thought we'd try Smith first before buying them and found a few other books in Smith that we wanted." "Why Smith rather than Borders? The price is the same, isn't it?" "No, because Smith is doing a lot of three for less than $20."

But price is also perceived as an indicator of quality, so a customer will sometimes pay more on the assumption that you "get what you pay for." Though Wal-Mart (http://www.walmart.com) got to be the world's biggest retailer with a business model that relentlessly drives down its unit costs and passes most of the benefits on to consumers in lower prices, for every Wal-Mart, there is a Coca-Cola (http://www.cocacola.com), a Microsoft (http://www.microsoft.com), or some other market leader whose prices are as high as or higher than most of its competitors.

In its glory days, IBM (http://www.ibm.com) had a 60 percent share of the world market for mainframe computers. This was certainly not driven by price: It was said that, if an IBM proposal came with a lower price than a competitor's, at least one of them had misunderstood the specification or messed up the quotation. Nokia (http://www.nokia.com), Intel (http://www.intel.com),

Cisco (**http://www.cisco.com**), Procter & Gamble (**http://www.pg.com**), Disney theme parks (**http://www.disney.com**), Mercedes vehicles (**http://www.mercedes-benz.com**), and HBO (**http://www.hbo.com**) did not become leaders by undercutting the competition. Price is rarely the explanation for the huge disparity in market shares.

Distribution

Another factor is distribution. If the customer sees no meaningful differences between several acceptable brands and believes any price differences to be too small to justify the effort of shopping around, he or she will simply buy the first brand seen. In services such as fast food, auto repair, and others, brands can vary a lot in the number of outlets. Similarly, sales of physical products, and even products such as movies and consumer magazines, depend on how widely they are distributed. Distribution is vital for impulse or convenience items, which is why Coca-Cola, Mars (**http://www.mars.com**), Frito-Lay (**http://www.fritolay.com**), Kodak (**http://www.kodak.com**), and Bic (**http://www.bicworld.com**) take trade sales, logistics, and merchandising so seriously. But for established brands within a national market, distribution rarely explains the large long-term differences in market shares.

In the short term, there is a "chicken and egg" relationship between distribution and final sales: You need distribution to get consumer sales and you need consumer sales to persuade stores to stock your brand. But in the long term, it is mainly final customer preferences that determine distribution, not the other way around: If McDonald's (**http://www.mcdonalds.com**) franchisees and the retailers and distributors of Kodak and Frito-Lay did not make money selling these brands, they would switch to selling others. And the reason they make money is final customers' brand choice.

This relationship is especially clear for established brands of packaged goods such as breakfast cereals or toothpaste. Typically, the top brand and the number-five brand are both available in at least 80 to 90 percent of supermarkets, but the first outsells the second by a factor of three or four, and sometimes much more. True, the bigger brand will likely have more shelf space in each outlet, but a customer who wants the niche brand can usually find it with little effort.

Small differences in brand preference can lead to large market share differences. Paradoxically, the lack of strong perceived differentiation means that small differences in brand preference can lead to large differences in market share. If a consumer thinks Colgate Total is 10 percent better than Crest, she won't just buy 10 percent more Colgate than Crest. She will always buy Colgate unless it is out of stock, or Crest is on special, or occasionally just for a change. The relative market shares of Colgate and Crest will largely depend on how many consumers think each brand is a bit better than the other. Neither group's brand preference will be strong: A Crest buyer would be annoyed to run out of toothpaste but quite happy to buy Colgate if it was on special or was all that was available because she knows it will provide similar category benefits to a similar extent.

One manifestation of consumers' lack of interest in the differences between brands, and of the fact that small preference differences can lead to large market share differences, is that market shares can vary enormously between different local markets. Bart J. Bronnenberg, a marketing professor at the University of California, Los Angeles, has found large and persistent market share differences for packaged-goods brands in different local markets in the United States. For instance, two brands might have market shares of 40 percent and 10 percent, respectively, in Los Angeles and 10 percent and 40 percent in New York. Further, these variations are greater for relatively undifferentiated categories (such as mayonnaise) than for more differentiated categories (such as breakfast cereals).

HOW BUYERS CHOOSE

The generic model in Figure 1 depicts what the customer wants, knows, and expects and how he or she chooses. It reflects our

Figure 1

How Buyers Choose and Firms Compete

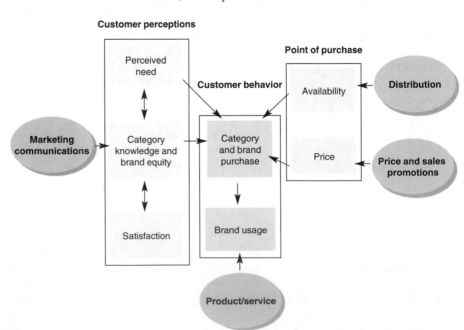

category-first perspective and the impact of customers' simplification processes. It also shows how firms compete to win sales through the marketing mix—activities (the shaded ovals) aimed at encouraging customers to choose their brand.

The key element is the good or service itself. This determines the extent to which the benefits the customer experiences from brand usage meet—or even exceed—the benefits sought and expected when the brand was bought. Was the new car as reliable as claimed? Was it a pleasure to drive? Did the after-sales service meet expectations?

Marketing communications usually focus on building brand equity, although they can also be used to reinforce or trigger a perceived need (e.g., "call stimulation" in telecoms, which encourages customers to use the phone more) or to communicate price or availability ("New York return for only $99," "Delivery guaranteed in 24 hours"). Distribution (including managing the lead times on delivering orders) focuses on availability. Frito-Lay ensures not only that its products are widely available, but also that they are usually fresher than competitors' products. Coke's dominance is also built on a relentless focus on distribution that strongly reinforces its brand awareness and equity around the world. Price includes price promotions, payment terms, and issues such as which TV channels to bundle together at each price point.

Customers' brand knowledge (brand equity) comes from their total brand experience. In addition to brand usage, this also includes their experience of brand communications (advertising, etc.), coverage and word of mouth (reputation), and casual interactions with the brand (such as seeing a new car in the street). In all markets, the challenge is to provide a competitively priced and distributed good or service that is well-supported by marketing communications so that the customer experience reliably meets or exceeds expectations. This should lead to repeat purchases by the same customers and positive word of mouth to others.

DIFFERENT WORLDS

Suppliers and buyers live in different worlds. For the supplier, the only thing that matters on a particular purchase occasion is whether the customer buys the supplier's brand and at what price. This is a winner-take-all game—no prize for coming in second. All the revenue goes to the brand the customer buys, with none going to any other brand. The difference between winning and not winning is everything.

To the customer, the world looks different. Usually, the purchase is triggered by a simple need, such as the need for a small bag of cement for a house extension or a business hotel for two nights in Chicago. The customer meets the need by making a category purchase. What the customer actually buys is a brand, but what he or she wants or needs is the category. If gasoline disappeared, America would grind to a halt. If Exxon (**http://www.exxon.com**) gasoline disappeared, who would lose out? The answer is Exxon employees, dealers, and shareholders. Perhaps this is an extreme case, but the contrast between the importance to customers of the category and the relative unimportance of even the strongest brand is not so very different in other categories such as cars, PCs, fast-food restaurants, strategy consultants, credit cards, and satellite TV. Overstating things a bit, to the supplier the only thing that matters is the brand (how many sales and at what price?), and to the customer the only thing that matters is the category (does it meet my need, is it available, and at what price?).

Questions

1. According to the case, why is the following statement wrong? "It is generally assumed that, in today's competitive markets, one can no longer differentiate the basic good or service."

2. Do you agree or disagree with this statement? "Marketers should focus on providing the benefits that matter to the customer, regardless of the extent to which the competitors provide them, too." Why?

3. If more consumers now consider many brands to be quite similar, then why are they still loyal to some brands in the product categories where brand distinctions are fuzzy?

4. Does this case support or refute the concept of low-involvement purchasing behavior by consumers? Explain your answer.

5. How can brand loyalty be applied as part of a market segmentation strategy?

6. What are the marketing implications of Figure 1?

7. How does the discussion in the case apply to b-to-b marketing, not just consumer marketing?

4

Product Planning

A firm needs a systematic marketing plan if it is going to practice the marketing concept. This plan centers on the four elements of the marketing mix: product, distribution, promotion, and price. We present these elements in Parts 4 through 7, with Part 4 devoted to product planning.

11 Basic Concepts in Product Planning

Here, we define tangible, augmented, and generic products and distinguish among different types of consumer and industrial products (both goods and services). We look at product mix strategies, product management organizations, and product positioning in detail. The roles of branding and packaging in product planning are also covered. The chapter concludes with a look at the global dimensions of product planning.

12 Goods Versus Services Planning

In this chapter, we look at the scope of goods and services, and present a goods/services continuum. We review goods and services classification systems. Then, we study the special considerations in the marketing of services. We also see that service marketing has lagged behind goods marketing and why this is changing. At this point, our discussion turns to nonprofit marketing and its distinction from profit-oriented marketing. We examine how nonprofits can be classified and the role of nonprofit marketing in the economy.

13 Conceiving, Developing, and Managing Products

To conclude Part 4, we look at products from their inception to their removal from the marketplace. We present the concept of the product life cycle and discuss types of new products, reasons for new-product failures, and the new product planning process. We explain the growth of products in terms of the adoption and diffusion processes, and note several methods for extending the lives of mature products. Product deletion strategies are also offered.

After reading Part 4, you should understand element 10 of the strategic marketing plan outlined in Table 3-2 (page 77).

Chapter 11

Basic Concepts in Product Planning

Procter & Gamble (P&G) (**http://www.pg.com**) is the largest manufacturer of household products in the United States. P&G markets 300 or so brands in more than 160 countries. Sixteen of these brands (pre-Gillette merger) have sales of at least $1 billion per year: Actonel, Always/Whisper, Ariel, Bounty, Charmin, Crest, Downy/Lenor, Folgers, Head & Shoulders, Iams, Olay, Pampers, Pantene, Pringles, Tide, and Wella. Other popular P&G brands are Cascade, Cover Girl, Mr. Clean, Scope, and Vicks 44.

P&G constantly adjusts its product mix to reflect industry growth, competitive conditions, and profit prospects. It sold off Spic and Span cleaning products, Jif peanut butter, and Crisco shortening. To increase its presence in beauty care, it bought Wella. In its largest acquisition, P&G bought Gillette (**http://www.gillette.com**) for $57 billion. This purchase adds five more $1 billion brands to P&G: Gillette, Oral-B, Braun, Duracell, and Mach 3—and gives P&G a stronger presence in the male market. The Gillette purchase has the potential for advertising and distribution savings, as well as brand extensions. As P&G's chief executive noted. "I look in the marketplace and see Clinique for men, Nivea for men."

P&G traces its history to 1837, when William Procter, a candle maker, and James Gamble, a soap maker, merged their businesses. By 1859, the company had become one of the largest firms in Cincinnati with annual revenues of $1 million. Among its most successful products and their first introduction are Ivory soap (1879), Crisco shortening (1911), Tide detergent (1946), Crest toothpaste (1955), Charmin Paper (1957), Head & Shoulders shampoo (1961), and Pampers disposable diapers (1961).

P&G has been associated with a number of marketing firsts. These include sponsorship of daytime radio and TV dramas (called soap operas due to P&G's role as advertiser) and the development of the product management organization. When it introduced Camay, a soap with a different target market and features than its popular Ivory Soap (with its 99-and-44-one-hundredths percent pure positioning), P&G was concerned that Camay's marketing plan too closely resembled that of Ivory's. So, in 1927, P&G appointed a separate manager to oversee Camay, and the modern product management system was born.[1]

In this chapter, we will look at the product-planning decisions a firm must make, including product management organizations, product positioning, branding, and packaging strategies.

Chapter Objectives

1. To define product planning and differentiate among tangible, augmented, and generic products
2. To examine the various types of products, product mixes, and product management organization forms from which a firm may select
3. To discuss product positioning and its usefulness for marketers
4. To study branding and packaging, and their roles in product planning
5. To look at the global dimensions of product planning

---

[1] Various company and other sources.

11-1 OVERVIEW

Product planning is systematic decision making relating to all aspects of the development and management of a firm's products, including branding and packaging. Each *product* consists of a bundle of attributes (features, functions, benefits, and uses) capable of exchange or use, usually a mix of tangible and intangible forms. A product "may be an idea, a physical entity, or a service, or any combination of the three. It exists for the purpose of exchange in satisfying individual and organizational objectives."[2]

A well-structured product plan lets a company pinpoint opportunities, develop appropriate marketing programs, coordinate the product mix, maintain successful products as long as possible, reappraise faltering products, and delete undesirable products. A firm should define products in three distinct ways: tangible, augmented, and generic. By considering all three definitions, consumer needs, competitive offerings, and distinctive product attributes can be better identified. This is illustrated in Figure 11-1.

A *tangible product* is a basic physical entity, service, or idea; it has precise specifications and is sold under a given description or model number. Windows XP Professional software (**http://www.microsoft.com/windowsxp/pro**), a Cat 776D Off Highway Tractor (**http://www.cat.com/products**), a 75-minute Circle Line cruise to the Statue of Liberty (**http://www.circleline42.com**), and a proposal to cut state income taxes by 3.5 percent are examples of tangible products. Color, style, size, weight, durability, quality of construction, price, and efficiency in use are some tangible product features.

An *augmented product* includes not only the tangible elements of a product, but also the accompanying cluster of image and service features. One political candidate may receive more votes than another because of charisma (augmented product), despite identical platform issues (tangible product). Rolex watches (**http://www.rolex.com**) are popular chiefly due to the image of luxury and status they convey. At Cummins Engine (**http://www.cummins.com**), offering augmented products means helping customers to succeed, not just selling them quality engines. Cummins uses a value-added package of products, information systems, and support services to enhance customer performance.

> **Product planning** means devising and managing **products** that satisfy consumers.

> A tangible product has precise specifications; an augmented product includes image and service features; and a generic product centers on consumer benefits.

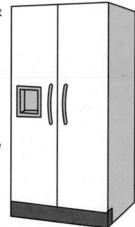

Tangible Product
- Color
- Design
- Quality
- Size
- Weight
- Features
- Materials used in construction
- Efficiency in use
- Power source
- Brand name

Augmented Product
- Image of product and brand
- Status of product and brand
- Guarantee/warranty
- Delivery
- Installation
- Repair facilities
- Instructions and technical advice
- Credit
- Return policy
- Follow-up service

Generic Product
- Stores, preserves, cools, and otherwise helps to satisfy home food-consumption needs

Figure 11-1

Illustrating the Three Product Definitions

---

[2] "Dictionary of Marketing Terms," **http://www.marketingpower.com/mg-dictionary.php** (May 3, 2006).

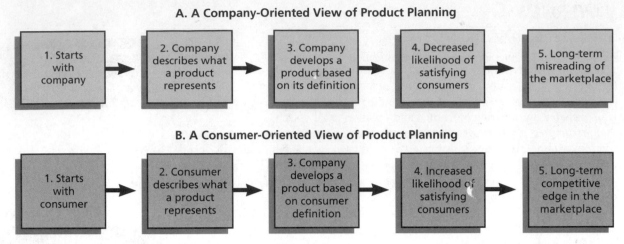

Figure 11-2

Applying the Generic Product Concept

Source: Adapted by the authors from Leon G. Schiffman and Elaine Sherman, "Value Orientations of New-Age Elderly: The Coming of an Ageless Market," *Journal of Business Research,* Vol. 22 (March 1991), p. 193.

A *generic product* focuses on what a product means to the customer, not the seller. It is the broadest definition and is consistent with the marketing concept: "In the factory we make cosmetics, and in the drugstore we sell hope" (Charles Revson, founder of Revlon, **http://www.revlon.com**). "We know our customers come to us to buy more than bearings and steel. They come to us looking for solutions" (Timken Company, **http://www.timken.com**).

Two points should be kept in mind when applying the generic product concept. First, because a generic product is a consumer view of what a product represents, a firm should learn what the product means to the consumer before further planning, as shown in Figure 11-2. Second, inasmuch as people in various nations may perceive the same product (such as a car) in different generic terms (such as basic transportation versus comfortable driving), a firm should consider the impact of this on a global strategy.

Chapter 11 provides an overview of product planning. We study the areas in which a firm makes decisions: product type(s), product mix, product management organization, and product positioning. Branding and packaging, as well as considerations for international marketers, are also considered. Chapter 12 covers goods versus services planning. Chapter 13 discusses how to manage products over their lives, from finding new product ideas to deleting faltering products.

11-2   TYPES OF PRODUCTS

The initial product-planning decision is choosing the type(s) of products to offer. Products can be categorized as goods or services and as consumer or industrial. Classification is important because it focuses on the differences in the characteristics of products and the resulting marketing implications.

11-2a   Fundamental Distinctions Between Goods and Services

> **Goods marketing** relates to selling physical products. **Service marketing** includes rented-goods services, owned-goods services, and nongoods services.

Goods marketing entails the sale of physical products—such as furniture, heavy machinery, food, and stationery. *Service marketing* encompasses the rental of goods, servicing goods owned by consumers, and personal services—such as vehicle rentals, house painting, and accounting services.

Four attributes generally distinguish services from goods: intangibility, perishability, inseparability from the service provider, and variability in quality. Their impact is greatest for personal services—which are usually more intangible, more perishable, more dependent on the skills of the service provider (inseparability), and have more quality variations than rented- or owned-goods services.

The sales of goods and services are frequently connected. For instance, a computer manufacturer may provide—for an extra fee—extended warranties, customer training, insurance, and financing. In goods marketing, goods dominate the overall offering and services augment them. In service marketing, services dominate the overall offering and goods augment them.

The distinctions between goods and services planning are more fully discussed in Chapter 12.

11-2b Consumer Products

Consumer products are goods and services destined for the final consumer for personal, family, or household use. The purpose of a good or service designates it as a consumer product. A calculator, dinner at a restaurant, phone service, and an electric pencil sharpener are consumer products only if bought for personal, family, or household use. Consumer products may be classed as convenience, shopping, and specialty products—based on shoppers' awareness of alternative products and their characteristics prior to a shopping trip and the degree of search people will undertake. Placing a product into one of these categories depends on shopper behavior. See Table 11-1.

Convenience products are those bought with a minimum of effort because a consumer has knowledge of product attributes prior to shopping and/or is pressed for time. The person does not want to search for much information and will accept a substitute, such as Green Giant (**http://www.greengiant.com**) instead of Libby's (**http://consumer.senecafoods.com/product/branded/libby.cfm**) corn, rather than visit more than one store. Marketing tasks center on distribution at all available outlets, convenient store locations and hours, the use of mass advertising and in-store displays, well-designed store layouts, and self-service to minimize purchase time. Resellers often carry many brands

Convenience products include staples, impulse products, and emergency products. Staples are low-priced and routinely purchased on a regular basis, such as detergent and cereal. Impulse products are items or brands a person does not plan to buy on a specific store trip, such as candy or a lottery ticket. Two-thirds of brand decisions at supermarkets and one-half at drugstores are made in-store.[3] Emergency products are bought out of urgent need, such as an umbrella in a rainstorm and aspirin for a headache.

Shopping products are those for which people feel they lack sufficient information about product alternatives and their attributes (or prices), and thus, must acquire more knowledge to make a decision. People exert effort because these products are bought infrequently, are expensive, or require comparisons. The marketing emphasis is on full assortments (many colors, sizes, and options), the availability of sales personnel, the communication of competitive advantages, informative ads, well-known brands (or stores), distributor enthusiasm, and customer warranties and followup service to reduce perceived risk. Shopping centers and downtown business districts ease shopping behavior by having many adjacent stores.

> **Consumer products** are final-consumer goods and services that may be categorized as convenience products, shopping products, and specialty products.

[3] "Knowledge Networks/*Ad Age* survey: CPG Brand Loyalty and In-Store Influencers," http://www.knowledgenetworks.com/CPGsurvey (May 5, 2003); and "Measuring Marketing At-Retail in Chain Drugstores," http://www.popai.com (September 28, 2005).

Table 11-1   Characteristics of Consumer Products

Consumer Characteristics	Type of Product		
	Convenience	Shopping	Specialty
Knowledge prior to purchase	High	Low	High
Effort expended to acquire product	Minimal	Moderate to high	As much as needed
Willingness to accept substitutes	High	Moderate	None
Frequency of purchase	High	Moderate or low	Varies
Information search	Low	High	Low
Major desire	Availability without effort	Comparison shopping to determine best choice	Brand loyalty regardless of price and availability
Examples	(a) Staple: cereal (b) Impulse: candy (c) Emergency: tire repair	(a) Attribute-based: designer clothes (b) Price-based: budget hotel	Hellmann's mayonnaise

Shopping products may be attribute- or price-based. With attribute-based products, consumers get information on features, performance, and so forth. The items with the best combination of attributes are bought. Sony electronics (**http://www.sony.com**) and Tommy Hilfiger clothes (**http://www.tommy.com**) are marketed as attribute-based shopping products. With price-based products, people feel the choices are similar and shop for low prices. Budget hotels and low-end electronics are marketed in this way.

Specialty products are particular brands, firms, and persons to which consumers are loyal. People are fully aware of these products and their attributes prior to making a purchase decision. They make a significant effort to acquire the brand desired and will pay an above-average price. They will not buy if their choice is unavailable: Substitutes are not acceptable. The marketing emphasis is on maintaining the attributes that make products unique to loyal patrons, reminder ads, proper distribution (*Business Week* [**http://www.businessweek.com**] uses home subscriptions for loyal customers), brand extension to related products (such as Hellmann's [**http://www.hellmanns.com**] tartar sauce, in addition to the flagship mayonnaise), product improvements, customer contact (such as opt-in E-mail from the Hilton HHonors program [**http://www.hhonors.com**]), and monitoring reseller performance.

This classification is excellent for segmentation because many people may view the same products differently. Tylenol pain reliever (**http://www.tylenol.com**) is a convenience product for some people (who will buy another brand if Tylenol is unavailable), a shopping product for others (who read ingredient labels), and a specialty product for others (who insist on Tylenol). Johnson & Johnson, maker of Tylenol, understands how Tylenol fits into the various categories and markets accordingly.

11-2c   Industrial Products

Industrial products are organizational consumer goods and services that may be classified as installations, accessory equipment, raw materials, component materials, fabricated parts, industrial supplies, and industrial services.

Industrial products are goods and services purchased for use in the production of other goods or services, in the operation of a business, or for resale to other consumers. Customers are manufacturers, wholesalers, retailers, government entities, and other nonprofit organizations.

Products may be grouped by the level of decision making in a purchase, costs, consumption rapidity, role in production, and change in form. Because industrial-products sellers often visit b-to-b customers, stores may not be not involved. Installations, accessory equipment, raw materials, component materials, fabricated parts, business supplies, and business services are types of industrial products. See Table 11-2.

Installations and *accessory equipment* are capital goods. They are used in the production process and do not become part of the final product. Installations are nonportable, involve considerable decision making (usually by upper-level executives), are expensive, last many years, and do not change form. Key marketing tasks are direct selling to the purchaser, negotiations on features and terms, having complementary services such as maintenance and repair, tailoring products to buyers' desires, and offering technical expertise and team selling (whereby various salespeople have different expertise). Examples are buildings, assembly lines, major equipment, large machine tools, and printing presses.

Accessory equipment consists of movable goods that require moderate decision making, are less costly than installations, last many years, and do not become part of the final product or change form. The key marketing tasks are tying sales to those of installations; providing various choices in price, size, and capacity; having a strong distribution channel or sales force; stressing durability and efficiency; and having maintenance and technical support. Examples are drill presses, trucks, vans, and lathes.

Raw materials, *component materials*, and *fabricated parts* are used up in production or become part of final products. They are expense items. They require limited decision making, have low unit costs, and are rapidly consumed. Raw materials are unprocessed primary materials—such as minerals, coal, and crops. Component materials are semi-manufactured goods that undergo changes in form—such as steel, textiles, and basic chemicals. Fabricated parts are placed in products without changes in form—such as electric motors, thermostats, and microprocessors. Marketing tasks for materials and parts are to ensure consistent quality, continuity in shipments, and prompt delivery; pursue reorders; have fair prices; seek long-term contracts; use assertive distributors or sales personnel; and meet buyer specifications.

Table 11-2 Characteristics of Industrial Products

Characteristics	Installations	Accessory Equipment	Raw Materials	Component Materials	Fabricated Parts	Supplies	Services
Degree of consumer decision making	High	Moderate	Low	Low	Low	Very low	Low to high
Per-unit costs	High	Moderate	Low	Low	Low	Very low	Low to moderate
Rapidity of consumption	Very low	Low	High	High	High	High	Low to high
Item becomes part of final product	No	No	Sometimes	Yes	Yes	No	Sometimes
Item undergoes changes in form	No	No	Yes	Yes	No	No	Sometimes
Major consumer desire	Long-term facilities	Modern equipment	Continuous, low-cost, graded materials	Continuous, low-cost, specified materials	Continuous, low-cost, fabricated materials	Continuous, low-cost, efficient supplies	Efficient, expert services
Examples	Production plant	Forklift truck	Coal	Steel	Thermostat	Light bulb	Accounting

Industrial supplies are convenience goods used in a firm's daily operation. They can be maintenance supplies, such as light bulbs, cleaning materials, and paint; repair supplies, such as rivets, nuts, and bolts; or operating supplies, such as stationery, pens, and business cards. They require little decision making, are very low cost on a per-unit basis, are rapidly consumed, and do not become part of the finished product. Marketing emphasis is on availability, promptness, and ease of ordering.

Industrial services are maintenance and repair services, and business advisory services. Maintenance and repair services (janitorial services and machinery repair) usually involve little decision making, are rather inexpensive, and are consumed quickly. They may become part of a final product (keeping for-sale equipment in good working condition) or involve a change in form (janitorial services converting a dirty office into a clean one). The key marketing thrust is on consistent, efficient service at a reasonable price. Business advisory services (accounting and legal services) may involve a moderate to high level of decision making when first bought. Ongoing costs tend to be low to moderate, while benefits may be long-lasting. These services do not become part of the final product. The major marketing task is to have an image of expertise and convey reasons for clients to use the service.

11-3 ELEMENTS OF A PRODUCT MIX

A **product item** is a specific model; a **product line** has related items; a **product mix** is all a firm's lines.

After determining the type(s) of products to offer, a firm needs to outline the variety and assortment of those products. A **product item** is a specific model, brand, or size of a product that a company sells, such as *Marketing 10e* (**http://www.atomicdog.com**), an Apple iPod Shuffle (**http://www.apple.com/ipodshuffle**), or the Cadillac XLR roadster (**http://www.cadillac.com**). Usually, a firm sells a group of closely related product items as part of a **product line**. In each product line, items have some common characteristics, customers, and/or uses; they may also share technologies, distribution channels, prices, related services, and so on.[4] Revlon (**http://www.revlon.com**) markets lipstick, eye makeup, and other cosmetics. Visa (**http://www.visa.com**) offers several credit cards. Atomic Dog (**http://www.atomicdog.com**) publishes business and economics textbooks. Many local lawn-service firms offer mowing, landscaping, and tree-trimming services.

A **product mix** consists of all the different product lines a firm offers. Heinz (**http://www.heinz.com**) markets ketchup, low-calorie foods, frozen french fries, soup, barbeque sauces, and other food products in more than 200 nations. Metropolitan Life Insurance Company (**http://www.metlife.com**) operates North America's largest life insurer (MetLife), and concentrates on various types of insurance and related services. Tyco International (**http://www.tyco.com**) is a global b-to-b manufacturer with five product lines: electronics, fire and security, health care, plastics and adhesives, and engineered products and services.

A product mix can be described in terms of its width, depth, and consistency. The *width of a product mix* is based on the number of different product lines a company offers. A wide mix lets a firm diversify products, appeal to different consumer needs, and encourage one-stop shopping. A narrow mix requires lower resource investments and does not call for expertise in different product categories.

The *depth of a product mix* is based on the number of product items within each product line. A deep mix can satisfy the needs of several consumer segments for the same product, maximize shelf space, discourage competitors, cover a range of prices, and sustain dealer support. A shallow mix imposes lower costs for inventory, product alterations, and order processing; and there are no overlapping product items.

[4] "Dictionary of Marketing Terms," **http://www.marketingpower.com/mg-dictionary.php** (May 3, 2006).

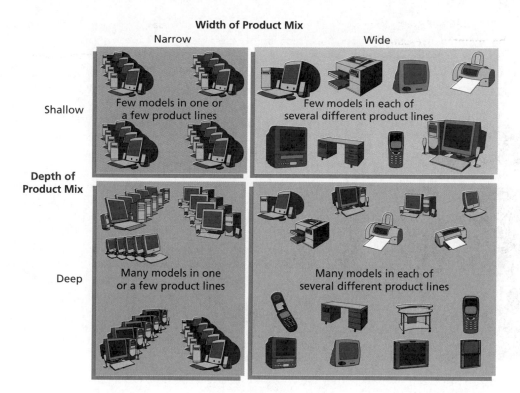

Width of Product Mix

Narrow | Wide

Shallow
- Few models in one or a few product lines
- Few models in each of several different product lines

Depth of Product Mix

Deep
- Many models in one or a few product lines
- Many models in each of several different product lines

Figure 11-3

Product Mix Alternatives

The *consistency of a product mix* is based on the relationship among product lines in terms of their sharing a common end-use, distribution outlets, consumer group(s), and price range. A consistent mix is generally easier to manage than an inconsistent one. It lets a firm focus on marketing and production expertise, create a strong image, and generate good distribution relations. Excessive consistency may leave a firm vulnerable to environmental threats, sales fluctuations, or less growth potential because emphasis is on a limited product assortment. Figure 11-3 shows product mix alternatives in terms of width and depth. Figure 11-4 highlights part of La-Z-Boy's (**http://www.lazboy.com**) product mix.

Product-mix decisions can have positive and negative effects, as these examples demonstrate:

- The highly successful Wrigley (**http://www.wrigley.com**) focuses on chewing gum and confectionary items: "It has been over 110 years since we introduced our first two products, Juicy Fruit and Wrigley's Spearmint gums. Today, our brands are sold in over 180 countries and the product portfolio includes brands that provide consumers with a variety of benefits, including breath freshening, tooth whitening, and vitamin delivery." In recent years, the firm has moved into other confection categories through acquisitions: "Brands such as Altoids, Life Savers, Creme Savers, Pim Pom, and Solano provide consumers with a variety of fun, delicious products in numerous formats and flavors. From mints to candies to lollipops, these products help Wrigley reach consumers of all ages around the world and are a wonderful complement to Wrigley's great-tasting gum products."[5]
- WD-40 (**http://www.wd40.com**) is a powerhouse in its product categories and has added a number of product lines over the past several years to foster further growth: "The same company you've trusted for years now offers a complete line of products to help you accomplish almost any household task, including the clean up afterward.

[5] "About Us," **http://www.wrigley.com/wrigley/about/about_index.asp** (April 29, 2006).

You're the kid
and we're the candy store.

LA**Z**BOY
The new look of comfort

Figure 11-4

La-Z-Boy's Deep Product Mix

Within its furniture product categories, La-Z-Boy (**http://www.lazboy.com**) offers a large selection.

Source: Reprinted by permission.

Whether you're a mechanic, a do-it-yourselfer, an everyday handyperson, or you just want to keep your house clean, we offer the right products to get the job done. Our products are found under the sink, in the garage, and in the toolboxes of the world." Its products include lubricants (WD-40 and 3-IN-ONE Oil), heavy-duty hand cleaners (Lava and Solvol) toilet bowl cleaners (X-14 and 2000 Flushes), bathroom cleaners (X-14), rug and room deodorizers (Carpet Fresh), and carpet stain remover (Spot Shot).[6]

- General Motors (GM) (**http://www.gm.com**) is undergoing a major restructuring: "Facing its worst financial outlook in more than a decade, General Motors has outlined a new product development and sales strategy, saying that from now on Chevrolet and Cadillac would be the only brands to offer a full lineup of vehicles. That means GM's other brands sold in the United States will focus on a narrower selection of segments. GMC and Hummer will sell trucks while Pontiac, Saab, and Saturn will focus on cars and smaller SUVs. Buick will offer some of both." As GM's marketing chief said, "GMC, Pontiac, Buick, Saturn, Saab, and Hummer can

---

[6] "About Us," **http://www.wd40.com/AboutUs** (April 29, 2006); and "Our Brands," **http://www.wd40.com/Brands** (April 29, 2006).

offer very specific vehicles rather than shipping millions of identical vehicles all over the world. Our complementary brands won't succeed as 'Little Chevrolets' or less-expensive Cadillacs. They have to be distinctive, differentiated products."[7]

11-4 PRODUCT MANAGEMENT ORGANIZATIONS

A firm may select from among these organizational forms of product management: marketing manager, product manager, product planning committee, new-product manager, and venture team.[8] See Table 11-3.

Under a ***marketing manager system***, an executive is responsible for overseeing a wide range of marketing functions (such as research, target marketing, planning existing and new products, distribution, promotion, pricing, and customer service) and for coordinating with other departments that do marketing-related activities (such as warehousing, order filling, shipping, credit, and purchasing). It works well for firms with a line of similar products or one dominant product line and for smaller firms that want centralized control of marketing tasks. It may be less successful if there are several product lines that require different marketing mixes—unless there are category marketing managers, each responsible for a broad product line. Pepsi-Cola North America (**http://www.pepsico.com**), Purex (**http://www.purex.com**), and Levi Strauss (**http://www.levi.com**) have used a marketing manager system at one point.

> One person is responsible for a host of marketing tasks, including product planning, with a **marketing manager system.**

With a ***product (brand) manager system***, there is a level of middle managers, each of whom is responsible for planning, coordinating, and monitoring a single product (brand) or a small group of products (brands). Managers handle both new and existing products and are involved with all marketing activities related to their product or product group. The system lets all products or brands get adequate attention. It works well if there are many distinct products or brands, each needing marketing attention. It also has two potential weaknesses: lack of authority for the product manager and inadequate attention to new products. Procter & Gamble (**http://www.pg.com**), Nabisco (**http://www.nabisco.com**), and Black & Decker (**http://www.blackanddecker.com**) have used product managers.[9]

> Middle managers handle new and existing products in a category in the **product (brand) manager system.**

A ***product-planning committee*** is staffed by high-level executives from various functional areas in a firm, such as marketing, production, engineering, finance, and research and development. It handles product approval and development on a part-time basis. Once a product is introduced, the committee usually turns to other opportunities and gives the item over to a product manager. This system lets management have input into decisions; but the committee meets irregularly and passes projects on to line managers. It is best as a supplement to other methods, and is used by many large and small firms.

> A **product-planning committee** has top executives involved part-time.

A ***new-product manager system*** has product managers supervise existing products and new-product managers develop new ones. It ensures the time, resources, enthusiasm, and expertise necessary for new-product planning. Once a product is introduced, it is given to the product manager who oversees existing products of that line (or brand). The system can be costly, incur conflicts, and cause discontinuity when an item is introduced. Kraft Foods (**http://www.kraftfoods.com**), General Electric

> A **new-product manager system** has separate middle managers for new and existing products.

---

[7] Danny Hakim, "G.M.'s Brands to Cut Back on Variety," *New York Times* (May 20, 2005), pp. C1, C7.

[8] The definitions in this section are drawn from "Dictionary of Marketing Terms," **http://www.marketingpower.com/ mg-dictionary.php** (May 3, 2006).

[9] For a good overview of the challenges facing the product (brand) manager system, see James R. Stengel, Andrea L. Dixon, and Chris T. Allen, "Listening Begins at Home," *Harvard Business Review*, Vol. 81 (November-December 2003), pp. 106–115.

Table 11-3 Comparing Product Management Organizations

Organization	Characteristics		
	Staffing	Ideal Use	Permanency
Marketing manager system	Key functional areas of marketing report directly to a senior marketer with a lot of authority.	A company makes one product line, has a dominant line, or uses broad category marketing managers.	The system is ongoing.
Product (brand) manager system	There is a layer of middle managers, with each focusing on a single product or a group of related products.	A company makes many distinct products, each requiring expertise.	The system is ongoing.
Product planning committee	Senior executives from various functional areas participate.	The committee should supplement another product organization.	The committee meets irregularly.
New-product manager system	Separate middle managers focus on new products and existing products.	A company makes several existing new products; and substantial time, resources, and expertise are needed for new products.	The system is ongoing, but new products are shifted to product managers after introduction.
Venture team	An independent group of company specialists guides all phases of a new product's development.	A company wants to create vastly different products than those currently offered, and needs an autonomous structure to aid development.	The team disbands after a new product is introduced, with responsibility going to a product manager.

(http://www.ge.com), and Johnson & Johnson (http://www.jnj.com) have employed new-product managers.

A **venture team** is a small, independent department in a firm that has a broad range of specialists—drawn from that firm's marketing, finance, engineering, and other functional departments—who are involved with a specific new product's entire development process. Team members work full-time and act in a relatively autonomous manner. The team disbands when its new product is introduced, and the product is then managed within the firm's regular management structure. With a venture team, there are proper resources, a flexible environment, expertise, and continuity in new-product planning. It is valuable if a firm wants to be more far-sighted, reach out for truly new ideas, and foster creativity. It is also expensive to form and operate. Xerox (http://www.xerox.com), Monsanto (http://www.monsanto.com), and 3M (http://www.3m.com) are among the firms that have used venture teams.

The correct organization depends on the diversity of a firm's offerings, the number of new products introduced, the innovativeness sought, company resources, management expertise, and other factors. A combination organization may be highly desirable; among larger firms, this is particularly common.

> A **venture team** is an autonomous new-product department.

11-5 PRODUCT POSITIONING

Critical to a firm's product-planning efforts is how the items in its product mix are perceived in the marketplace. The firm must work quite hard to make sure that each of its products is perceived as providing some combination of unique features (product differentiation) and that these features are desired by the target market (thereby converting product differentiation to a differential advantage).

When a product is new, a company must clearly communicate its attributes: What is it? What does it do? How is it better than the competition? Who should buy it? The goal is to have consumers perceive product attributes as the firm intends. When a product has

Ethical Issues in Marketing

Addressing the Flood of Counterfeit Products

The World Customs Organization (http://www.wcoomd.org) estimates that counterfeiting accounts for between 5 and 7 percent of global merchandise trade. And there is a strong chance of finding counterfeit products for such popular items as Callaway golf clubs, Intel computer chips, Nokia cell phone parts, and even Sony PlayStation game controllers. The World Health Organization (http://www.who.int/en) estimates that up to 10 percent of all medicines sold worldwide are counterfeit. A DaimlerChrysler (http://www.chrysler.com; http://www.mbusa.com) executive noted that "Counterfeiting has gone from a local nuisance to a global threat." One estimate is that 30 percent of the market for DaimlerChrysler car parts (anything from fenders to engine blocks) in China, Taiwan, and Korea consists of counterfeit goods.

Many experts view China as the main source of counterfeits, with Chinese counterfeiters becoming increasingly adept at copying holograms, "smart" chips, and other security devices that have traditionally been used to detect fake products. According to a Callaway Golf Co. (http://www.callawaygolf.com) executive, "The Chinese are extremely ingenious, inventive, and scientifically oriented, and they are becoming the world's manufacturer, so back-engineering a golf club is a piece of cake" for them.

Some counterfeit products look so much like the real thing that many company executives cannot distinguish them. "We had to cut them apart or do chemical analysis to tell," says a General Motors executive.

Source: Based on material in Frederik Balfour, "Fakes," *Business Week* (February 7, 2005), pp. 54–64.

---

an established place in the market, a firm must regularly reinforce its image and communicate the reasons for its success. Once consumer perceptions are formed, they may be hard to alter. And it may also be tough later to change a product's niche in the market (for instance, from low price, low quality to high price, high quality).

Through ***product positioning***, a firm can map each of its products in terms of consumer perceptions and desires, competition, other company products, and environmental changes. Consumer perceptions are the images of products, both a firm's and competitors', in people's minds. Consumer desires refer to the attributes that people would most like products to have—their ***ideal points***. If a group of people has a distinctive "ideal" for a product category, that group is a potential market segment. A firm will do well if its products' attributes are perceived by consumers as being close to their ideal.

Competitive product positioning refers to people's perceptions of a firm relative to competitors. The goal is for the firm's products to be viewed as "more ideal" than those of competitors. *Company product positioning* shows a firm how consumers perceive that firm's different brands (items) within the same product line and the relationship of those brands (items) to each other. The goal is for each of the firm's brands to be positioned near an ideal point, yet not clustered near one another in the consumer's mind—the brands should appeal to different ideal points (market segments). A firm must monitor the environmental changes that may alter the way its products are perceived. Such changes could include new technology, changing consumer lifestyles, new offerings by competitors, and negative publicity.

Product positioning is illustrated in Figure 11-5, which depicts the U.S. car marketplace—not including sports utility vehicles—in terms of the consumer desires regarding two key attributes: price and size. In this figure, there are nine ideal points (target markets)—I1 to I9, each associated with a specific type of car. Here is a brief description:

> **Product positioning** maps out consumer perceptions of product attributes. **Ideal points** show the most preferred attributes.

- I_1—*full-size luxury cars.* Large cars typically priced at $40,000 and up. Cadillac DTS (http://www.cadillac.com), Infiniti Q45 (http://www.infiniti.com), and Lincoln Town Car (http://www.lincolnvehicles.com) are in this grouping.
- I_2—*full-size cars.* Large cars typically priced at $20,000 to $30,000. Chevrolet Impala (http://www.chevrolet.com/impala), Buick Lucerne (http://www.buick.com/lucerne), and Mercury Grand Marquis (http://www.mercuryvehicles.com/grandmarquis) are in this category.

- I_3—*full-size economy cars.* Large cars typically priced at less than $20,000. There are currently no significant brands in this category selling in the United States.
- I_4—*midsize luxury cars.* Midsize cars typically priced at $30,000 and up. BMW 3 Series sedans (http://www.bmwusa.com/vehicles), Cadillac STS (http://www.cadillac.com), and Lexus ES 300 (http://www.lexus.com/models/es) are positioned here.
- I_5—*midsize cars.* Midsize cars typically priced from $18,000 to $27,000. Toyota Camry (http://www.toyota.com/camry), Pontiac G6 sedan (http://www.pontiac.com/g6sedan), and Volkswagen Passat (http://www.vw.com/passat) fit here.
- I_6—*midsize economy cars.* Midsize cars typically priced at less than $18,000. Hyundai Sonata GL (http://www.hyundaiusa.com), Saturn L300 sedan (http://www.saturn.com), and Kia Optima (http://www.kia.com/optima) are in this grouping.
- I_7—*small luxury cars.* Small cars typically priced at $30,000 and up. BMW Z4 (http://www.bmw.com), Cadillac SRX (http://www.cadillac.com), and Porsche Boxster (http://www.porsche.com) are in this category.
- I_8—*small cars.* Small cars typically priced between $14,000 and $22,000. Volkswagen New Beetle (http://www.vw.com/newbeetle), Chevrolet Cobalt (http://www.chevrolet.com/cobalt), and Dodge Neon (http://www.dodge.com/neon) are positioned here.
- I_9—*small economy cars.* Small cars typically priced at less than $14,000. Hyundai Accent (http://www.hyundaiusa.com), Saturn Ion sedan (http://www.saturn.com), and Kia Spectra (http://www.kia.com/spectra) are grouped here.

An examination of competitive product positioning reveals that competing products exist in each market niche except for I3 (full-size economy cars). In some instances, the marketplace is saturated. Nonetheless, the companies in the industry have generally done a good job in addressing the needs of the various consumer segments and in differentiating the products offered to each segment.

From an analysis of company product positioning, it is clear that General Motors (http://www.gm.com) serves all of the identified market segments (except I3). The

Figure 11-5

Product Positioning and the Auto Industry

Source: Figure developed by the authors based on data from http://www.wardsauto.com (April 9, 2004).

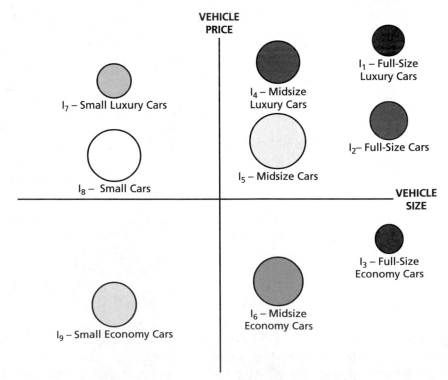

Note: The size of the circles reflects the relative sales volume for each segment (in units).

Cadillac DTS, Chevrolet Impala, Buick Lucerne, Cadillac STS, Pontiac Grand G6 sedan, Saturn L300 sedan, Cadillac SRX, Chevrolet Cobalt, and Saturn Ion sedan are all marketed by General Motors. However, it must continue to differentiate carefully among its various brands to avoid confusion and a "fuzzy" perception by consumers.

By undertaking product-positioning analysis, a company can learn a great deal and plan its marketing efforts accordingly, as these examples indicate:

- "One can easily understand and accept positioning that's embodied in a single word because the positioning is obviously a single concept. In what has to be the quintessential positioning example, Volvo has demonstrated that its own persuasive, enduring positioning can be stated in a single word: safety. Others have succeeded as well—Charmin equals softness; Ivory soap equals purity; Coke equals the real thing (OK, that's three words, but you get the idea). These are simple, singular concepts, well understood and remembered for that very reason. Many marketers fail when it comes to simplicity by injecting multiple concepts into their positioning statement until they've manufactured a multidimensional hodgepodge that isn't positioning at all."[10]
- Upscale Coach (**http://www.coach.com**) has done extremely well with its distinctive positioning approach: "More than 40 years ago, Coach introduced 12 eloquently simple bag designs with classic, well-balanced proportions. Over the years, we have added a multitude of new shapes, styles, and materials, but each collection embodies the same principles of classic design and American style. Every Coach product embodies the perfect balance between aesthetics and functionality. Sizes, shapes, pockets, and straps are carefully considered to provide maximum efficiency, comfort, and convenience. Seams are double-stitched where reinforcement is required. In our glove-tanned pieces, the inside pockets, handles straps, and interior bound edges are all made of the same leather to ensure a consistency of color and texture. Coach selects only the top 10 percent of leathers for their tactile quality, strength, character, and grain. In the tanning process, the untreated leather is rotated for days in large drums where it is softened and enriched with natural treatments drawn from plant extracts, fats and clear aniline dyes. Like fingerprints, no two grain patterns are alike. Our method of slow curing brings natural markings to the surface, making every Coach product original and unique."[11]

Figure 11-6 shows another product positioning example.

11-6   BRANDING

Another key aspect of product planning is branding, the way a firm researches, develops, and implements its brands. A *brand* is a name, term, design, symbol, or any other feature that identifies the goods and services of a seller or group of sellers. The four types of brand designation are as follows:

> **Brands** identify a firm's products.

1. A *brand name* is a word, letter (number), group of words, or letters (numbers) that can be spoken. Examples are Boeing, Century 21, and Lipton Cup-a-Soup.
2. A *brand mark* is a symbol, design, or distinctive coloring or lettering that cannot be spoken. Examples are Lexus' stylized L crest, McDonald's golden arch, and Prudential's rock.
3. A *trade character* is a brand mark that is personified. Examples are Qantas Airlines' koala bear, Met Life's use of Snoopy, the Pillsbury Doughboy, and Kellogg's Tony the Tiger. See Figure 11-7.

> Branding involves **brand names, brand marks, trade characters**, and **trademarks**.

[10] Bill Robertson, "Ten Rules of Product Positioning," *Medical Marketing & Media* (May 2005), pp. 53–54.
[11] "Our Design Philosophy," **http://www.coach.com/about/hist_design.asp** Andy (May 9, 2006).

Figure 11-6

Audi Positioning Message: Power and Styling

Source: Reprinted by permission.

4. A **trademark** is a brand name, brand mark, or trade character or combination thereof that is given legal protection. When used, a registered trademark is followed by ®, such as Scotch Brand ® tape.

Brand names, brand marks, and trade characters do not offer legal protection against use by competitors, unless registered as trademarks (which all of the preceding examples have been). Trademarks ensure exclusivity for their owners or those securing permission, and provide legal remedies against firms using "confusingly similar" names, designs, or symbols. They are discussed more fully later in the chapter.

Worldwide, millions of brand names are in circulation. Each year, firms spend hundreds of billions of dollars worldwide to advertise their brands. Permanent media expenditures (such as company logos, stationery, brochures, business forms and cards, and vehicular and building signs) for brands are another large marketing cost.

Brand loyalty is a key goal. This enables firms to maximize sales and maintain a strong brand image. As two experts noted: "Marketers must understand what brand

Figure 11-7

Tony the Tiger: A Very Popular—and Enduring—Trade Character

Source: Reprinted with permission of Kellogg Company.

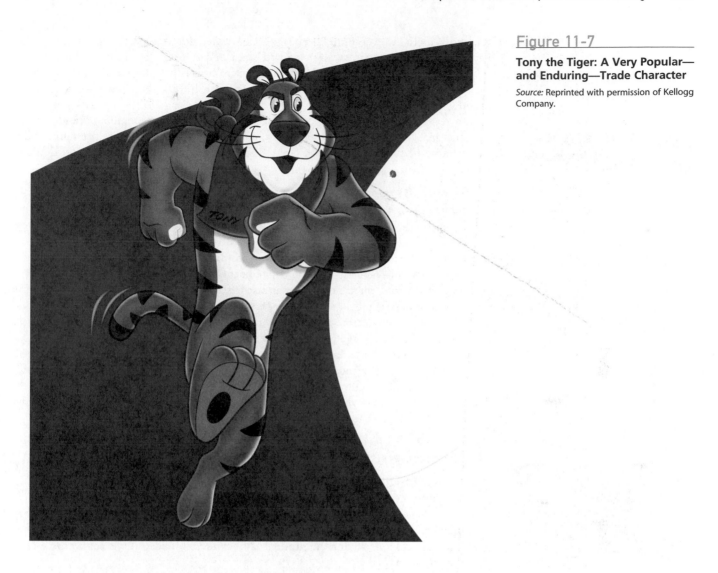

loyalty is, bearing in mind that brand loyalty will be different for each brand managed. Research suggests that customers can demonstrate brand loyalty in a variety of ways. They can demonstrate loyalty by purchasing, by being willing to recommend, by providing advice to the company, and through an intention to repurchase."[12]

Some brands do so well that they gain "power" status—they are well known and highly esteemed. According to one recent study, the world's 10 most valuable brands are (in order) Coca-Cola, Microsoft, IBM, General Electric, Intel, Nokia, Disney, McDonald's, Toyota, and Marlboro. Of the world's 100 most valuable brands, 53 are American, 9 are German, 8 are French, 7 are Japanese, 5 are British, and 5 are Swiss.[13] The use of popular brands can also speed up public acceptance and gain reseller cooperation for new products.

Gaining and maintaining brand recognition and preference are often top priorities: "Why would P&G tinker with Tide? Long the detergent leader, Tide would seem best left alone as a profitable annuity. But P&G has tinkered nonetheless, combining strong technology and consumer research to push sales up in a category that is growing very little. The secret: a widening family of detergents and cleaners

[12] Rebekah Bennett and Sharyn Rundle-Thiele, 'The Brand Loyalty Life Cycle: Implications for Marketers," *Journal of Brand Management*, Vol. 12 (April 2005), p. 258.

[13] Robert Berner and David Kiley, "Global Brands," *Business Week* (August 1, 2005), pp. 86–94. See also "*Brandweek* Customer Loyalty Awards," **http://www.brandkeys.com/awards.**

that now includes everything from Tide Coldwater, for cold-water washing, to Tide Kick, a combination measuring cup and stain penetrator." In addition, the firm has introduced the new Tide StainBrush, an electric brush for removing stains, based on the same basic mechanism as the Crest Spinbrush Pro toothbrush—also a P&G brand."[14]

In recent years, a branding concept that more concretely recognizes brands' worth has emerged. It is known as ***brand equity***, which represents the revenue premium that a brand earns in the marketplace in comparison with an identical, but unbranded, alternative.[15] As one research company noted:

> There are many different definitions of brand equity, but they do have several factors in common: *Monetary Value.* Grocery stores frequently sell unbranded versions of name-brand products. The branded and unbranded products are made by the same companies, but they carry a generic brand or store brand label like Kroger's or Albertson's. Store brands sell for much less than name-brand counterparts, even when the contents are identical. This price differential is the monetary value of a brand name. *Intangibility.* Nike has created many intangible benefits for its products by associating them with star athletes. Children and adults want to wear Nike products to feel some association with these athletes. It is not the physical features that drive demand for Nike products, but the marketing image that has been created. Buyers will pay high price premiums over lesser-known brands which may offer the same, or better, product quality and features. *Perceived Quality.* Mercedes and BMW have established their brands as synonymous with high-quality, luxurious autos. Years of marketing, image building, brand nurturing, and quality manufacturing have led consumers to assume a high level of quality in everything these firms produce. Consumers are likely to perceive Mercedes and BMW as providing superior quality to other brands, even when such a perception is unwarranted.[16]

These reasons summarize why branding is important:

- Product identification is eased. A customer can order a product by name instead of description.
- Customers are assured that a good or service has a certain level of quality and that they will obtain comparable quality if same brand is reordered.
- The firm responsible for the product is known. Unbranded items cannot be as directly identified.
- Price comparisons are reduced when customers perceive distinct brands. This is most likely if special attributes are linked to different brands.
- A firm can advertise (position) its products and associate each brand in the buyer's mind. This aids the consumer in forming a *brand image*, which is the perception a person has of a particular brand.
- Branding helps segment markets by creating tailored images. By using two or more brands, multiple market segments can be attracted.
- For socially visible goods and services, a product's prestige is enhanced via a strong brand name.

Brand equity represents a brand's worth.

Branding creates identities, assures quality, and performs other functions. Brand images are perceptions that consumers have of particular brands.

[14] Nanette Byrnes, Robert Berner, Wendy Zellner, and William C. Symonds, "Branding: Five New Lessons," *Business Week* (February 14, 2005), p. 28.

[15] See Colin Baker, Clive Nancarrow, and Julie Tinson, "The Mind Versus Market Share Guide to Brand Equity," *International Journal of Market Research*, Vol. 47 (Number 5, 2005), pp. 525–542; Angel F. Villarejo-Ramos and Manuel J. Sánchez-Franco, "The Impact of Marketing Communication and Price Promotion on Brand Equity," *Journal of Brand Management*, Vol. 12 (August 2005), pp. 431–444; and Ravi Pappu, Pascale G. Quester, and Ray W. Cooksey, "Consumer-Based Brand Equity: Improving the Measurement—Empirical Evidence," *Journal of Product & Brand Management*, Vol. 14 (Number 3, 2005), pp. 142–154.

[16] "Understanding Brand Equity," **http://www.dssresearch.com/toolkit/resource/papers/SR02.asp** (December 27, 2002).

- People feel less risk when buying a brand with which they are familiar and for which they have a favorable attitude. This is why brand loyalty occurs.
- Cooperation from resellers is greater for well-known brands. A strong brand also may let its producer exert more control in the distribution channel.
- A brand may help sell an entire line of products, such as Kellogg's cereals.
- A brand may help enter a new product category, such as Reese's peanut butter.
- "Consumers decide with their purchases, based on whatever factors they deem important, which brands have more equity than other brands."[17]

There are four branding decisions a firm must undertake, involving corporate symbols, the branding philosophy, choosing a brand name, and using trademarks. See Figure 11-8.

11-6a   Corporate Symbols

Corporate symbols are a firm's name (and/or divisional names), logos, and trade characters. They are key parts of the overall image. When a firm begins a business; merges with another company; reduces or expands product lines; seeks new geographic markets; or finds its name to be unwieldy, nondistinctive, or confusing, it should assess and possibly change its symbols. Here are examples of each situation.

Google (**http://www.google.com**) is a leading search engine company. It is a worldwide phenomenon after just a decade in the marketplace: "Google's name is a play on the

> **Corporate symbols** help establish a company-wide image.

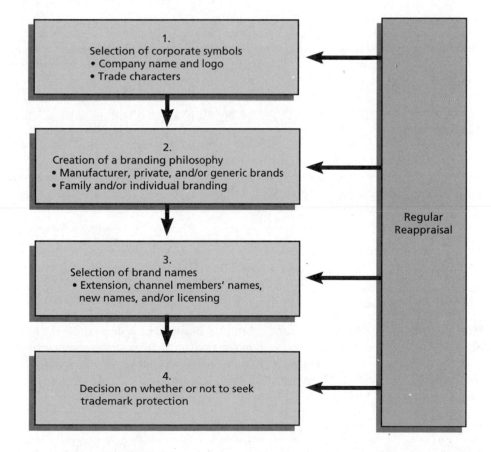

Figure 11-8

Branding Decisions

[17] Steve Hoeffler and Kevin Lane Keller, "The Marketing Advantages of Strong Brands," *Journal of Brand Management,* Vol. 10 (August 2003), p. 421.

word googol, which refers to the number 1 followed by one hundred zeroes." This is appropriate because "Google's index of Web pages is the largest in the world, comprising billions of Web pages. Google searches this immense collection of Web pages often in less than half a second." The firm "receives daily search requests from all over the world, including Antarctica. Users can restrict their searches for content in 35 non-English languages, including Chinese, Greek, Icelandic, Hebrew, Hungarian, and Estonian. To date, no requests have been received from beyond the earth's orbit, but Google has a Klingon interface just in case."[18]

Due to mergers, defense contractors Lockheed and Martin Marietta are now Lockheed Martin (**http://www.lockheedmartin.com**), pharmaceutical firms Glaxo Wellcome and SmithKline Beecham are now GlaxoSmithKline (**http://www.gsk.com**), and auto makers Daimler and Chrysler are now DaimlerChrysler (**http://www.daimlerchrysler.com**).

Because the nature of its business changed, International Harvester is now Navistar International (**http://www.navistar.com**), after selling its farm equipment business, and General Shoe Corporation is Genesco (**http://www.genesco.com**), a diversified retailer. When Andersen Consulting was spun off from Andersen Worldwide, it changed its name to Accenture (**http://www.accenture.com**).

As it expanded into new market areas, Allegheny Airlines was renamed US Airways (**http://www.usairways.com**); the old name suggested a small regional airline. More recently, America West merged with US Airways and the combined firm retained the more national US Airways name. The Exxon (**http://www.exxon.com**) name was developed globally because the firm's regional brands, including Esso and Humble, could not be used nationwide and other brands had unfortunate foreign connotations (for example, Enco means "stalled car" in Japanese).

The National Railroad Passenger Corporation was an unwieldy name; it became Amtrak (**http://www.amtrak.com**). Federal Express now promotes the FedEx name (**http://www.fedex.com**), because it is easier to say. United Telecommunications converted its nondistinctive name to Sprint (**http://www.sprint.com**), in recognition of its leading brand. The upscale Holiday Inn Crowne Plaza was changed to Crowne Plaza (**http://www.ichotelsgroup.com/h/d/cp/1/en/home**) to avoid confusion with the middle-class Holiday Inn name.

Developing and maintaining corporate symbols are not easy. When Nissan (**http://www.nissanusa.com**) changed the name of its U.S. car division from Datsun to Nissan (to have a global brand), sales fell, despite a major ad campaign. It took years for the Nissan name to reach the level of awareness that Datsun had attained. Along the way, Nissan had clashes with dealers not wanting the name change.

11-6b   Branding Philosophy

In preparing a brand strategy, a firm needs to determine its branding philosophy. This outlines the use of manufacturer, private, and/or generic brands, as well as the use of family and/or individual branding.

Manufacturer, Private, and Generic Brands[19]   *Manufacturer brands* use the names of their makers. They generate the vast majority of U.S. revenues for most product categories, including more than 80 percent of food, all autos, 75 percent of major appliances, and more than 80 percent of gasoline. They appeal to a wide range of people who desire good quality, routine purchases, status, convenience, and low risk of poor

---

[18] "Google Fun Facts," **http://www.google.com/press/funfacts.html** (April 27, 2006).

[19] See Jill Jusko, "Consumer Packaged Goods: Muscling In," **http://www.industryweek.com/ReadArticle.aspx? ArticleID=10649** (September 1, 2005); "Private Label Widely Seen as 'Good Alternative' to Other Brands, According to A.C. Nielsen Global Survey," **http://us.acnielsen.com/news/20050811.shtml** (August 11, 2005); and Mary Beth Whitfield, "The Surging Growth of Private Brands," *2005 Strategic Outlook Conference* (Columbus, OH: Retail Forward).

product performance. The brands are often well known and trusted because quality control is strictly maintained. They are identifiable and present distinctive images. Producers may have a number of product alternatives under their brands.

Manufacturers have better channel control over their own brands, which may be sold through many competing intermediaries. Yet, individual resellers can have lower investments if the brands' pre-sold nature makes turnover high—and if manufacturers spend large sums promoting their brands and sponsor cooperative ads with resellers (so costs are shared). Prices are the highest of the three brands, with the bulk going to the manufacturer (which also has the greatest profit). The marketing goal is to attract and retain loyal consumers for these brands, and for their makers to direct the marketing effort for the brands.

Private (dealer) brands use names designated by their resellers, usually wholesalers or retailers—including service providers. They account for sizable U.S. revenues in many categories, such as 50 percent of both apparel and shoes, one-third of tires, one-sixth of food items, and one-quarter of major appliances. Unit market shares are higher. Private brands account for 20 percent of unit sales in supermarkets. Firms such as Limited Brands (**http://www.limitedbrands.com**) and McDonald's (**http://www.mcdonalds.com**) derive most revenues from their own brands. Private-brand foods are more popular in Europe than in the United States. They generate 39 percent of revenues in British food stores and one-quarter in Belgian and German stores.

Private brands appeal to price-conscious people who buy them if they feel the brands offer good quality at a lower price. They accept some risk as to quality, but reseller loyalty causes the people to see the brands as reliable. Private brands often have similar quality to manufacturer brands, with less emphasis on packaging. At times, they are made to dealer specifications. Assortments are smaller and the brands are unknown to people not shopping with a given reseller. Resellers have more exclusive rights for these brands, and are more responsible for distribution and larger purchases. Inventory turnover may be lower than for manufacturer brands; and promotion and pricing are the reseller's job. Due to lower per-unit packaging and promotion costs, resellers can sell private brands at lower prices and still have better per-unit profits (due to their higher share of the selling price). The marketing goal is to attract people who become loyal to the reseller and for that firm to exert control over marketing. Large resellers advertise their brands widely. Some private brands, such as Sears' Kenmore (**http://www.kenmore.com**), are as popular as manufacturer brands; and firms such as Sherwin-Williams (**http://www. sherwin-williams.com**) are manufacturers and retailers. As with all supermarket chains, Stop & Shop (**http://www.stopandshop.com**), which features manufacturer brands, also has its own private brand. Linens 'n Things (**http://www.lnt.com**) has now added an exclusive collection from up-and-coming designer Nate Berkus. See Figure 11-9.

Generic brands emphasize the names of the products themselves and not manufacturer or reseller names. They started in the drug industry as low-cost alternatives to expensive manufacturer brands. Today, generics have expanded into cigarettes, batteries, motor oil, and other products. Nearly half of U.S. prescriptions are filled with generics; but, due to their low prices, this is only 10 to 15 percent or so of prescription-drug revenues. Although 85 percent of U.S. supermarkets stock generic products, they account for under 1 percent of supermarket revenues. Generics appeal to price-conscious, careful shoppers, who perceive them as being a very good value, are sometimes willing to accept lower quality, and often purchase for large families or large organizations.

Generics are seldom advertised and receive poor shelf locations; consumers must search out these brands. Prices are less than other brands by up to 50 percent, due to quality, packaging, assortment, distribution, and promotion economies. The major marketing goal is to offer low-priced, lower-quality items to consumers interested in price savings. Table 11-4 compares the three types of brands.

Many companies—including service firms—use a *mixed-brand strategy*, thereby selling both manufacturer and private brands (and possibly generic brands). This benefits manufacturers and resellers: There is control over the brand bearing each seller's name. Exclusive rights to a brand can be gained. Multiple segments may be targeted. Brand and dealer loyalty are fostered, shelf locations coordinated,

> **Private (dealer) brands** enable channel members to get loyal customers.

> **Generic brands** are low-priced items with little advertising.

> A **mixed-brand strategy** combines brand types.

Figure 11-9

Linens 'n Things: Introducing Nate Berkus

Source: Reprinted by permission of Susan Berry, Retail Image Consulting, Inc.

cooperation in the distribution channel improved, and assortments raised. Production is stabilized and excess capacity used. Sales are maximized and profits are fairly shared. Planning is better. In Japan, Kodak (**http://www.kodak.com**) markets its own brand

Table **11-4**	Manufacturer, Private, and Generic Brands		
	Type of Brand		
Characteristics	**Manufacturer**	**Private**	**Generic**
Target market	Risk avoider, quality-conscious, brand loyal, status-conscious, quick shopper	Price-conscious, comparison shopper, quality-conscious, moderate risk taker, dealer loyal	Price-conscious, careful shopper, willing to accept lower quality, large family or organization
Product	Well known, trusted, best quality control clearly identifiable, deep product line	Same overall quality as manufacturer, less emphasis on packaging, less assortment, not known to nonshoppers of the dealer	Usually less overall quality than manufacturer, little emphasis on packaging, very limited assortment, not well known
Distribution	Often sold at many competing dealers	Usually only available from a particular dealer in the area	Varies
Promotion	Manufacturer-sponsored ads, cooperative ads	Dealer-sponsored ads	Few ads, secondary shelf space
Price	Highest, usually suggested by manufacturer	Moderate, usually controlled by dealer	Lowest, usually controlled by dealer
Marketing focus	To generate brand loyalty and manufacturer control	To generate dealer loyalty and control	To offer a low-priced, lesser-quality item to those desiring it

Global Marketing in Action

Chinese Brands Go Global

WWP Group's Ogilvy & Mather Worldwide (http://www.ogilvy.com), a leading advertising agency, recently interviewed executives at 47 Chinese companies with sales exceeding $100 million each in such categories as telecommunications, consumer electronics, food, pharmaceuticals, and airlines. Based on the interviews, an Ogilvy & Mather executive estimates that within the next 20 years, there will be seven to eight major worldwide Chinese brands similar in scope to Sony and Samsung Electronics.

Executives at 85 percent of the Chinese companies interviewed stated that they currently market their branded products outside China, mainly in Asia (excluding Japan), and 67 percent stated that they have a globally based corporate strategy. About two-thirds of the firms export their brands as a means of enhancing their global reputation.

When Chinese marketers were asked to identify which brands they most admire, only one Chinese brand, Haier (http://www.haieramerica.com), was named. Forty percent of the respondents mentioned Haier as among the top brands they most admire. In contrast, 33 percent mentioned Coca-Cola and 23 percent stated GE as a most admired brand.

Another WWP Group company, Millward Brown (http://www.millwardbrown.com), interviewed 300 U.S., Great Britain, and French consumers about their attitudes toward Chinese brands. Most American and British consumers associated China with low-priced products that have high value. French consumers cited China's large population and rapid economic expansion, but were concerned about its repressive government. Consumers in all three countries were concerned about the quality of Chinese goods.

Source: Based on material in Normandy Madden, "Chinese Marketers Bent on Going Global," *Advertising Age* (March 15, 2005), p.16.

of film and COOP private-brand film (for the 2,500-store Japanese Consumer Cooperative Union, http://www.jccu.coop). It wants to make a dent in Fuji's large percent share of the Japanese market. Kodak does not market private-brand film in the United States.

Manufacturer, private, and generic brands also repeatedly engage in a ***battle of the brands***, in which each strives to gain a greater share of the consumer's dollar, control over marketing strategy, consumer loyalty, product distinctiveness, maximum shelf space and locations, and a large share of profits. In recent years, this battle has intensified.

> In the **battle of the brands**, the three brand types compete.

Family and Multiple Branding

In ***family (blanket) branding***, one name is used for two or more individual products. Many firms selling industrial goods and services such as aircraft manufacturer Boeing (http://www.boeing.com) and global delivery service firm DHL (http://www.dhl.com), as well as those selling consumer services such as Teléfonos de México (http://www.telmex.com.mx), use some form of family branding for all or most of their products. Other companies employ a family brand for each category of products. For example, Sears has Kenmore appliances (http://www.kenmore.com) and Craftsman tools (http://www.craftsman.com). Family branding can be applied to both manufacturer and private brands, and to both domestic and international (global) brands.

> **Family (blanket) branding** uses a single name for many products.

Family branding is best for specialized firms or ones with narrow product lines. Companies capitalize on a uniform, well-known image and promote a name regularly—keeping promotion costs down. The major disadvantages are that differentiated marketing opportunities may be low (if only one brand is used to target all customers), company image may be adversely affected if vastly different products (such as men's and women's cologne) carry one name, and innovativeness may not be projected to consumers.

Brand extension, whereby an established name is applied to new products, is an effective use of family branding. Quick customer acceptance may be gained because people are familiar with existing products having the same name, a favorable brand image can be carried over to a new product, and the risk of a failure is less. Brand extension may have a negative effect if people do not see some link between the original

> **Brand extension** gains quick acceptance.

product and a new one. The majority of new products now use some form of brand extension. See Figure 11-10.

These are examples of situations in which brand extension could be effective:

- Same product in a different form—Jell-O Pudding Pops.
- Distinctive taste/ingredient/component in a new item—Arm & Hammer detergent.
- New companion product—Colgate Plus toothbrush.
- Same customer franchise for a new product (a different product offered to the same target market)—Visa traveler's checks aimed at Visa credit-card customers.
- Expertise conveyed to a new product—Canon laser-jet printers.
- Benefit/attribute/feature conveyed to new product—Ivory shampoo (connoting mildness).
- Designer image/status conveyed to new item—Pierre Cardin sunglasses.[20]

With *individual (multiple) branding*, separate brands are used for different items or product lines sold by a firm. For example, these are just some of the brands in Frito-Lay's (**http://www.fritolay.com**) product mix: Cheetos cheese-flavored snacks, Cracker Jack snacks, Doritos tortilla chips, Fritos corn chips, Funyuns onion flavored rings, Grandma's cookies, Lay's potato chips, Munchies snack mix, Rold Gold pretzels, Ruffles potato chips, and SunChips snacks. This strong brand lineup enables Frito-Lay to dominate the snack food business with a more than 50 percent share of the market.

A firm can create multiple product positions (separate brand images) through individual branding, and thereby attract various market segments, increase sales and marketing control, and offer both premium and low-priced brands. Manufacturers can

> **Individual (multiple) branding** uses distinct brands.

Figure 11-10

A Logical Brand Extension: From Skippy Peanut Butter to Skippy Squeeze Stix

Source: Reprinted by permission of Susan Berry, Retail Image Consulting, Inc.

[20] Edward M. Tauber, "Brand Leverage: Strategy for Growth in a Cost-Controlled World," *Journal of Advertising Research,* Vol. 28 (August-September 1988), pp. 26–30. See also Ingrid M. Martin, David W. Stewart, and Shashi Matta, "Branding Strategies, Marketing Communication, and Perceived Brand Meaning: The Transfer of Purposive, Goal-Oriented Brand Meaning to Brand Extensions," *Journal of the Academy of Marketing Science,* Vol. 33 (Summer 2005), pp. 275–294; and Devon DelVecchio and Daniel C. Smith, "Brand-Extension Price Premiums: The Effects of Perceived Fit and Extension Product Category Risk," *Journal of the Academy of Marketing Science,* Vol. 33 (Spring 2005), pp. 184–196.

also secure greater shelf space in stores. However, each brand requires a promotion budget, and there is no positive brand image rub-off. Economies from mass production may be lessened. New products may not benefit from an established identity. And there may be some cannibalization among company brands. Consumer-products firms are more likely than industrial-products firms to engage in individual branding.

To gain the benefits of family and individual branding, many firms combine the two. A firm may have a flagship brand and secondary brands. A third of Heinz's (**http://www.heinz.com**) sales are from products with the Heinz name; the rest have names such as Ore-Ida and Weight Watchers Foods. A family brand could be used with individual brands. At Honda, upscale Acura (**http://www.acura.com**) and mainstream Honda (**http://www.honda.com**) are the two auto lines. The Honda line includes the Accord, Civic, and Prelude. It has an overall image and targets a specific market. New models gain from the Honda name, and a relationship exists among models. Individual brands are used with each model to highlight differences.

11-6c   Choosing a Brand Name

Several potential sources are considered when a firm chooses brand names:

> Brand sources range from existing names to **licensing agreements** and **co-branding**.

1. Under brand extension, an existing name is used with a new product (Tylenol Arthritis Pain with EZ-Open Cap, **http://www.tylenol.com**).
2. For a private brand, the reseller specifies the name (St. John's Bay—an apparel brand of J.C. Penney, **http://www.jcpenney.com**).
3. If a new name is sought, these alternatives are available:

   a. Initials (HBO, **http://www.hbo.com**).
   b. Invented name (Kleenex, **http://www.kleenex.com**).
   c. Numbers (WD-40, **http://www.wd40.com**).
   d. Mythological character (Samsonite luggage, **http://www.samsonite.com**).
   e. Personal name (Heineken, **http://www.heineken.com**).
   f. Geographical name (Air France, **http://www.airfrance.com**).
   g. Dictionary word (Scope mouthwash, **http://www.scope-mouthwash.com**).
   h. Foreign word (Nestlé, **http://www.nestle.com**).
   i. Combination of words, initials, numbers, and so on (Head & Shoulders shampoo, **http://www.headandshoulders.com**).

4. With a *licensing agreement*, a company pays a fee to use a name or logo whose trademark rights are held by another firm. Due to the high consumer recognition of many popular trademarks, sales for a product may be raised by paying a royalty fee to use one. Examples of names used in licensing are Coca-Cola, Dallas Cowboys, and George Foreman. Salton Inc. (**http://www.esalton.com**) has sold millions of George Foreman grills. Licensing generates a total of $110 billion in yearly U.S. retail sales alone.
5. In *co-branding*, two or more brand names are used with the same product to gain from the brand images of each. Typically, a company uses one of its brands in conjunction with another firm's—sometimes via a licensing agreement. Some examples of co-branding are the GM MasterCard (**http://www.gmcard.com**), Bath and Body Works (**http://www.bbw.com**) toiletries stocked in guest rooms at Renaissance Hotels (**http://www.renaissancehotels.com**), and various PC brands with "Intel Inside" (**http://www.intel.com**).

A good brand name has several attributes, depending on the situation: It suggests something about a product's use or attributes (Liquid-Plumr drain cleaners, **http://www.liquid-plumr.com**). It is easy to spell and recall and pronounceable in only one way (Bic, **http://www.bicworld.com**). It can be applied to a whole line of products (Deere tractors, **http://www.deere.com**). It is capable of legal protection from use by others (Perrier, **http://www.perrierusa.com**). It has a pleasant or at least neutral meaning internationally (Onvia—the b-to-b marketplace, **http://www.onvia.com**). It conveys a differential advantage (Pert Plus, **http://www.pertplus.com**).

As firms expand globally, branding takes on special significance. Regardless of whether brands are "global" or tailored to particular markets, their meanings must not have negative connotations or violate cultural taboos. To make sure that this does not happen, such specialized firms as Namestormers (**http://www.namestormers.com**) can devise names for clients that are acceptable around the world. But outside of the leading power brands, which firms may want to make into global brands, brands often must reflect the cultural and societal diversity in the way products are positioned and used in different nations.

> The **consumer's brand decision process** moves from nonrecognition to insistence (or aversion).

When branding, a firm should plan for the *consumer's brand decision process* as shown in Figure 11-11. For a new brand, a consumer begins with nonrecognition of the name; the seller must make a potential buyer aware of it. He or she then moves to recognition, where the brand and its attributes are known; the seller stresses persuasion. Next, the potential buyer develops a preference (or dislike) for a brand and buys it (or opts not to buy); the seller's task is to gain loyalty. Last, some customers show a brand insistence (or aversion) and become loyal (or never buy); the seller's role is to maintain loyalty. Often, people form preferences for several brands but do not buy or insist upon one brand exclusively.

A brand extension strategy enables a new product to begin at the recognition, preference, or insistence stage of the brand decision process due to the carryover effect of the established name. However, consumers who dislike the existing product line would be unlikely to try a new product under the same name, but they might try another company product under a different brand.

11-6d   The Use of Trademarks

Finally, a firm must decide whether to seek trademark protection. In the United States, it would do so under either the federal Lanham Act (updated by the Trademark Law Revision Act) or state law. A trademark gives a firm the exclusive use of a word, name, symbol, combination of letters or numbers, or other devices—such as distinctive packaging—to identify the goods and services of that firm and distinguish them from others for as long as they are marketed. Both trademarks (for goods) and service marks (for services) are covered by trademark law; and there are 300,000 U.S. filings each year through the U.S. Patent and Trademark Office (**http://www.uspto.gov/main/trademarks.htm**).

Trademarks are voluntary and require registration and implementation procedures that can be time consuming and expensive (challenging a competitor may mean high legal fees and years in court). A global firm must register trademarks in every nation in which it operates; even then, trademark rights may not be enforceable. To be legally

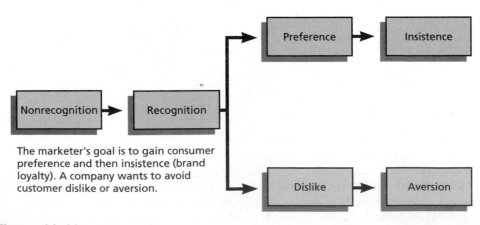

The marketer's goal is to gain consumer preference and then insistence (brand loyalty). A company wants to avoid customer dislike or aversion.

Figure 11-11

The Consumer's Brand Decision Process

protected, a trademark must have a distinct meaning that does not describe an entire product category, must be used in interstate commerce (for federal protection), may not be confusingly similar to other trademarks, and may not imply attributes a product does not have. A surname by itself cannot be registered because any person can generally do business under his or her name; it can be registered if used to describe a specific business (such as McDonald's restaurants). The U.S. Supreme Court has ruled that the color of a product can gain trademark protection, as long as it achieves "secondary meaning," whereby the color distinguishes a particular brand and indicates its "source."

When brands become too popular or descriptive of a product category, they risk becoming public property and losing trademark protection. Brands that have worked hard over the years to remain exclusive trademarks include L'eggs (**http://www.leggs.com**), Rollerblade (**http://www.rollerblade.com**), Formica (**http://www.formica.com**), and Teflon (**http://www.teflon.com**). Former trademarks now considered generic—thus, public property—are cellophane, aspirin, shredded wheat, cola, linoleum, and lite beer.

DuPont has used careful research to retain a trademark for Teflon. Company surveys have shown that most people identify Teflon as a brand name. On the other hand, the U.S. Supreme Court ruled that *Monopoly* was a generic term that could be used by any game maker; and a federal court ruled that Miller could not trademark the single word "Lite" for its lower-calorie beer.

11-7   PACKAGING

Packaging is the part of product planning where a firm researches, designs, and produces package(s). A *package* is a container used to protect, promote, transport, and/or identify a product. It may consist of a product's physical container, an outer label, and/or inserts:

> A **package** involves decisions as to a product's physical container, label, and inserts.

- The physical container may be a cardboard, metal, plastic, or wooden box; a cellophane, waxpaper, or cloth wrapper; a glass, aluminum, or plastic jar or can; a paper bag; styrofoam; some other material; or a combination of these. Products may have more than one container: Cereal is individually packaged in small boxes, with inner waxpaper wrapping, and shipped in large corrugated boxes; watches are usually covered with cloth linings and shipped in plastic boxes.
- The label indicates a product's brand name, the company logo, ingredients, promotional messages, inventory codes, and/or instructions for use.
- Inserts are (1) instructions and safety information placed in drug, toy, and other packages or (2) coupons, prizes, or recipe booklets. They are used as appropriate.

About 10 percent of a typical product's final selling price goes for its packaging. The amount is higher for such products as cosmetics (as much as 40 percent or more). A complete package redesign for a major product might cost millions of dollars for machinery and production. Packaging decisions must serve both resellers and consumers. Plans are often made in conjunction with production, logistics, and legal personnel. Errors in packaging can be costly.

Package redesign is most likely if a firm's current packaging receives a poor response from channel members and customers or becomes too expensive; the firm seeks a new market segment, reformulates a product, or changes or updates its product positioning; there are difficulties in mass producing packages; or new technology is available. For instance,

> Take just one category—pharmaceutical products. There are prescription drugs, over-the-counter drugs, dietary supplements, and traditional and dietary foods. You can find products on the retail shelf that appear to be similar, but they're regulated differently, because one is considered a drug and the other a supplement. Companies constantly seek to expand their product mix. Future packaging will face the problem of differentiating similar products at an increasing rate. One of the biggest tests will be in meeting the needs of the senior market—and that's not even mentioning the approaching deluge of baby boomers. Challenges include

striking the right balance between the ease of opening a bottle and preserving child-resistance; using larger type for the visually impaired, without crowding the package; and using color and warning messages, without turning off other consumers.[21]

The functions of packaging, factors considered when making packaging decisions, and criticisms of packaging are described next.

11-7a   Basic Packaging Functions

The basic *packaging functions* are containment and protection, usage, communication, segmentation, channel cooperation, and new-product planning:

- *Containment and protection*—Packaging enables liquid, granular, and other divisible products to be contained in a given quantity and form. It protects a product while it is shipped, stored, and handled.
- *Usage*—Packaging lets a product be easily used and re-stored. It may even be reusable after a product is depleted. Packaging must also be safe for all, from a young child to a senior.
- *Communication*—Packaging communicates a brand image, provides ingredients and directions, and displays the product. It is a major promotion tool.
- *Segmentation*—Packaging can be tailor-made for a specific market group. If a firm offers two or more package shapes, sizes, colors, or designs, it may employ differentiated marketing.
- *Channel cooperation*—Packaging can address wholesaler and retailer needs with regard to shipping, storing, promotion, and so on.
- *New-product planning*—New packaging can be a key innovation for a firm and stimulate sales.

11-7b   Factors Considered in Packaging Decisions

Several factors must be weighed in making packaging decisions. Because package design affects the image a firm seeks for its products, the color, shape, and material all influence consumer perceptions. For instance: "In a triumph for eye-catching package design, a tired body spray brand aimed at young Australian men that had no ad support and was under threat of being axed was rescued by a packaging makeover that gave the brand a hipper look. PZ Cussons (**http://www.cussons.com**), a $1-billion, British-based consumer-products group, was won over when edgy new packaging designs for its Graphite male body spray and antiperspirant deodorant impressed the trade. The brand is now marketed to 14- to 25-year-old men with sharp, bold images." As an advertising consultant noted: "The designs will jump off the shelves and speak directly to the male teenagers who are just beginning to use these products. These kids are smart, savvy, and hip to anything commercial."[22]

In family packaging, a firm uses a common element on each package in a product line. It parallels family branding. Campbell (**http://www.campbellsoup.com**) has virtually identical packages for its traditional soups, distinguished only by flavor or content identification. Johnson & Johnson (**http://www.jnj.com**), maker of Pepcid AC and Mylanta stomach pain medicine, does not use family packaging with these brands; they have distinct packages to lure different segments.

A global firm must decide if a standardized package can be used worldwide (with only a language change on the label). Standardization boosts global recognition. Thus, Coke and Pepsi have standard packages when possible. Yet, some colors, symbols, and shapes have negative meanings in some nations. For example, white can mean purity or mourning, two vastly different images. As shown in Figure 11-12, Tide

---

[21] "Future Packaging—What's Ahead?" *Brand Packaging Online* (May 2005).

[22] Normandy Madden and Laurel Wentz, "Package Redesign Saves Body Spray in Australia," *Advertising Age* (May 16, 2005), p. 28.

Figure 11-12

Nonstandardized Packaging for Tide

Tide packaging adapts to the markets in which it is sold. In Shanghai, China, it is sold in tough plastic bags and labeled in Chinese.

Source: Reprinted by permission of Retail Forward.

detergent (**http://www.tide.com**) has different packaging in Shanghai, China, than in the United States.

Package costs must be considered on both a total and per-unit basis. As noted earlier, total costs can run into the millions of dollars, and per-unit costs can go as high as 40 percent or more of a product's selling price, depending on the purpose and extent of packaging.

A firm has many packaging materials from which to select, such as paperboard, plastic, metal, glass, styrofoam, and cellophane. In the choice, trade-offs are probably needed: Cellophane allows products to be attractively displayed, but it is highly susceptible to tearing; paperboard is relatively inexpensive, but it is hard to open. A firm must also decide how innovative it wants its packaging to be. Aseptic packaging (for milk and juice boxes) allows beverages to be stored in special boxes without refrigeration. These beverages are more popular in Europe than in the United States. Figure 11-13 shows a typical display at Target (**http://www.target.com**)—with packaging that facilitates both the promotion and storage of products.

> What materials and innovations are right?

A wide range of package features is available from which to choose, depending on the product. These features include pour spouts, hinged lids, screw-on tops, pop-tops, see-through bags, tuck- or seal-end cartons, carry handles, product testers (for items like batteries), and freshness dating. They may provide a firm with a differential advantage.

A firm has to select the specific sizes, colors, and shapes of its packages. In picking a package size, shelf life (how long a product stays fresh), convenience, tradition, and competition must be considered. In the food industry, new and larger sizes have captured high sales. The choice of package color depends on the image sought. Mello Yello, a citrus soft drink made by Coca-Cola (**http://www.cocacola.com**), has a label with bright orange and green lettering on a lemon-yellow background. Package shape also affects a product's image. Hanes (**http://www.hanes.com**) created a mystique for L'eggs pantyhose via the egg-shaped package. The number of packages used with any one product depends on competition and the firm's use of differentiated marketing. By selling small, medium, and large sizes, a firm may ensure maximum shelf space, appeal to different consumers, and make it difficult for a new company to gain channel access.

> What size(s), color(s), and shape(s) are used?

The placement, content, size, and prominence of the label must be set. Both company and brand names (if appropriate) need to appear on the label. The existence of package inserts and other useful information (some required by law) should be noted on the label. Sometimes, a redesigned label may be confusing to customers and hurt a product's sales.

Multiple packaging couples two or more product items in one container. It may involve the same product (such as razor blades) or combine different ones (such as a

Figure 11-13

Packaging Sells at Target

Source: Reprinted by permission of Susan Berry, Retail Image Consulting, Inc.

first-aid kit). The goal is to increase usage (hoarding may be a problem), get people to buy an assortment of items, or have people try a new item (such as a new toothpaste packaged with an established toothbrush brand). Many multiple packs, such as cereal, are versatile—they can be sold as shipped or broken into single units.

Individually wrapping portions of a divisible product may offer a competitive advantage. It may also be costly. Kraft (**http://www.kraftfoods.com**) has done well with its individually wrapped cheese slices. Hammermill (**http://www.internationalpaper. com/Paper/Paper.html**) sells its paper in single packages with 500 sheets each, as well as in boxes with 12,500-sheet packages.

For certain items (such as shirts, magazines, watches, and candy), some resellers want pre-printed prices. They then can charge those prices or adhere their own labels. Other resellers prefer only a space for the price on the package and insert their own price labels automatically. With the growing use of computer technology by resellers in monitoring their inventory levels, more of them are insisting on pre-marked inventory codes on packages. The National Retail Federation (**http://www.nrf.com**) endorses the Universal Product Code (**http://www.gs1us.org/gs1us.html**) as the voluntary U.S. vendor-marking standard.

With the ***Universal Product Code (UPC)***, manufacturers pre-mark items with a series of thick and thin vertical lines. Price and inventory data barcodes are represented by these lines, which appear on outer package labels but are not readable by employees and customers. Lines are "read" by computerized scanning equipment at the checkout counter; the cashier does not have to ring up a transaction manually and inventory data are instantly transmitted to the main computer of the retailer (or manufacturer). In the UPC system, human-readable prices must still be marked, either by the manufacturer or the reseller.

Last, a firm must be sure the package design fits in with the rest of its marketing mix. A prestige perfume may be extravagantly packaged, distributed in select stores, advertised in upscale magazines, and sold at a high price. In contrast, a firm making perfumes that imitate leading brands has more basic packages, distributes in discount stores, does not

Should items be individually wrapped?

Should a package have a pre-printed price and use the Universal Product Code (UPC)?

Marketing and the Web

Using the Internet to Strengthen Brand Popularity

According to a survey of decision makers at 148 companies, "building the brand" is rated as the second most important goal for their business-to-consumer Web site. This same group also says that when considering new content and features for their Web site, alignment with the brand is as important as alignment with user goals, and a close second to usability in their overall rankings.

Forrester Research (http://www.forrester.com), a large Internet-based marketing research firm, recently did a study to determine how well 16 business-to-consumer Web sites in four industries communicated brand image and delivered value to consumers. The Web sites chosen for analysis were from four industries: athletic shoes, credit cards, fast food, and PCs—and included such leading brands as Nike, New Balance, American Express, MasterCard, McDonald's, Wendy's, Hewlett-Packard, and Dell. Analysts eval-

uated each site twice. The first assessment centered on how well a site conveyed the emotional and experiential attributes of the brand's image. The second review looked at the transactional, informational, and usability aspects of the brand.

Even though 6 of the 16 sites passed the research company's brand image tests, only two sites passed the brand action evaluation: Dell and Wendy's. Dell did well based on its detailed product listings, comparison charts, and detailed product photos (which can be seen from several different perspectives). Features were explained in a manner understandable to even novice consumers. Wendy's site clearly explained calorie levels, fat content, and nutritional guidelines.

Source: Based on material in Harley Manning and Bob Chatham, Jim Nail, Michelle Amato, and Elizabeth Backer, "How Brands Succeed Online," *Forrester Research* (June 9, 2005).

---

advertise, and uses low prices. The two brands may cost an identical amount to make, but the imitator would spend only a fraction as much on packaging.

The Business Owner's Toolkit (http://www.toolkit.cch.com/text/P03_5100.asp) has a good discussion on package design, including its relationship with brand positioning, the use of graphics, and reflecting target market values.

> How does the package interrelate with other marketing variables?

11-7c Criticisms of Packaging

The packaging practices of some industries and firms have been heavily criticized and regulated due to their impact (or potential impact) on the environment and scarce resources, the high expenditures on packaging, questions about the honesty of labels and the confusion caused by inconsistent designations of package sizes (such as *large, family, super*), and critics' perceptions of inadequate package safety.

> Packaging is faulted for waste, misleading labels, and so on.

Yet, consumers—as well as business—must bear part of the responsibility for the negative results of packaging. Throwaway bottles (highly preferred by consumers) use almost three times the energy of returnable ones. Shoplifting annually adds to packaging costs because firms must add security tags and otherwise alter packages.

In planning their packaging strategy, firms need to weigh the short-term and long-term benefits and costs of providing environmentally safer ("green"), less-confusing, and more tamper-resistant packages. Generally, firms are responding quite positively to the criticisms raised here. These issues were examined in Chapter 5.

11-8 THE GLOBAL DIMENSIONS OF PRODUCT PLANNING

When a product plan is devised, these points should be kept in mind with regard to international marketing:

> Several factors should be considered with international product planning.

- Although a firm may offer the same products in countries around the globe, those products can have distinct generic meanings in different countries.
- In developing and less-developed countries, product "frills" are often less important than in industrialized countries.

- Due to their intangibility, perishability, inseparability, and variability, the international marketing efforts for services are often more complex than those on behalf of goods.
- The concept of convenience, shopping, and specialty products is less valid in markets where distribution is limited or consumers have few choices.
- Installations and accessory equipment may be hard to ship overseas.
- Marketing all of the items in a wide and/or deep product mix may not be appropriate or economically feasible on a global basis.
- The diversity of international markets may necessitate a decentralized product management organization, with some executives permanently assigned to foreign countries.
- For many products, there are differences in product positioning and consumer ideal points by country or region. Simple positioning messages travel better than more complicated ones.
- Even though global branding and packaging may be desirable, various nations may have special needs or requirements.
- Expectations about goods/services combinations (discussed in the next chapter) may differ by nation.
- A product modification or minor innovation in a home market may be a major innovation internationally, necessitating different marketing approaches.
- The characteristics of the market segments—innovators, early adopters, early majority, late majority, and laggards—in the diffusion process (covered in Chapter 13) often differ by country.
- Some products are in different stages of their life cycles in developing and less-developed countries than in industrialized countries.

Web Sites You Can Use

A number of Web sites provide expert advice on how to properly position company products and brands in the consumer's mind. Here is a sampling:

- "Brand Positioning" (**http://www.s-m-a-r-t.com/Exp_brand pos.htm**) from Strategic Marketing and Research Techniques
- "How to Strengthen Product Positioning" (**http://www.toolkit.cch.com/text/P03_1074.asp**) from Business Owner's Toolkit
- "Market Positioning" (**http://www.marketing.about.com/od/positioning**) from About.com

- "Positioning" (**http://www.quickmba.com/marketing/ries-trout/positioning**) from Quick MBA
- "Positioning: Marketing" (**http://www.en.wikipedia.org/wiki/Positioning_(marketing)**) from Wikipedia
- "Repositioning for a New Market" (**http://www.biz360.com/positioning**), a free positioning guide

Summary

1. *To define product planning and differentiate among tangible, augmented, and generic products*   Through product planning, a firm can pinpoint opportunities, develop marketing programs, coordinate a product mix, maintain successful products, reappraise faltering products, and delete undesirable products.

    A tangible product is a basic physical entity, service, or idea with precise specifications that is offered under a given description or model. An augmented product includes tangible elements and the accompanying image and service features. A generic product focuses on the benefits a buyer desires; this concept looks at what a product means to the consumer rather than the seller.

2. *To examine the various types of products, product mixes, and product management organization forms from which a firm may select*   Goods marketing entails physical products. Service marketing includes goods rental, servicing consumer-owned goods, and personal services. Goods and services often differ in intangibility, perishability, inseparability from the provider, and variability in quality.

    Consumer products can be classified as convenience, shopping, and specialty items—on the basis of consumer awareness of alternatives prior to the shopping trip and the degree of search and time spent shopping. Industrial products include installations, accessory equipment, raw materials, component materials, fabricated parts, business supplies, and business services. They are distinguished on the basis of decision making, costs, consumption, the role in production, and the change in form.

A product item is a model, brand, or size of a product sold by a firm. A product line is a group of closely related items sold by a firm. A product mix consists of all the different product lines a firm offers. Width, depth, and consistency of a product mix are important.

A firm may choose from or combine several product management structures, including marketing manager system, product (brand) manager, product-planning committee, new-product manager system, and venture team. Each has particular strengths and best uses.

3. *To discuss product positioning and its usefulness for marketers* A firm must ensure that each of its products is perceived as providing some combination of unique features and that they are desired by the target market. In product positioning, a firm can map its offerings with regard to consumer perceptions, consumer desires, competition, its own products in the same line, and the changing environment. Competitive positioning, company positioning, and consumers' ideal points are key.

4. *To study branding and packaging, and their roles in product planning* Branding is the procedure a firm follows in planning and marketing its brand(s). A brand is a name, term, design, or symbol (or a combination) that identifies a good or service. A brand name is a word, letter (number), or group of words or letters (numbers) that can be spoken. A brand mark is a symbol, design, or distinctive coloring or lettering. A trade character is a personified brand mark. A trademark is a brand name, brand mark, or trade character given legal protection.

Millions of brand names are currently in circulation worldwide. Ad spending on them is billions and billions of dollars annually. Through strong brands, brand loyalty can be secured. Popular brands also speed up the acceptance of new products. Gaining and keeping brand recognition is essential in the development of brand equity and a brand image. Branding benefits all parties: manufacturers and service providers, distribution intermediaries, and consumers.

Four primary decisions are necessary in branding. First, corporate symbols are determined and, if applicable, revised. Second, a branding philosophy is set, which includes the proper use of manufacturer, private, and/or generic brands, as well as family and/or individual branding. At this stage, a mixed-brand strategy, the battle of the brands, and brand extension (a popular approach) are also assessed. Third, a brand name is chosen from one of several sources, including brand extension from existing names, private brands, licensing a name from another firm, and co-branding. With a new brand, the consumer's brand decision process moves from nonrecognition to recognition to preference (dislike) to insistence (aversion). Fourth, the use of trademarks is evaluated and planned.

Packaging is the procedure a firm follows in planning and marketing product package(s). A package has a physical container, label, and/or inserts. Ten percent of a typical product's final selling price goes for packaging. Packaging has six basic functions: containment and protection, usage, communication, market segmentation, channel cooperation, and new-product planning.

Packaging decisions involve image; family packaging; standardization; package costs; packaging materials and innovativeness; package features; package size, color, and shape; the label and package inserts; multiple packaging; individual wrapping; pre-printed prices and inventory codes (such as the UPC); and integration with the marketing plan. Packaging has been criticized on the basis of environmental, safety, and other issues.

5. *To look at the global dimensions of product planning* If a firm intends to market products internationally, the distinctive generic meanings of products in different nations and the complexity of marketing services in foreign markets should be kept in mind.

Key Terms

product planning (p. 327)

product (p. 327)

goods marketing (p. 328)

service marketing (p. 328)

consumer products (p. 329)

industrial products (p. 330)

product item (p. 332)

product line (p. 332)

product mix (p. 332)

marketing manager system (p. 335)

product (brand) manager system (p. 335)

product-planning committee (p. 335)

new-product manager system (p. 335)

venture team (p. 336)

product positioning (p. 337)

ideal points (p. 337)

brand (p. 339)

brand name (p. 339)

brand mark (p. 339)

trade character (p. 339)

trademark (p. 340)

brand equity (p. 342)

corporate symbols (p. 343)

manufacturer brands (p. 344)

private (dealer) brands (p. 345)

generic brands (p. 345)

mixed-brand strategy (p. 345)

battle of the brands (p. 347)

family (blanket) branding (p. 347)

brand extension (p. 347)

individual (multiple) branding (p. 348)

licensing agreement (p. 349)

co-branding (p. 349)

consumer's brand decision process (p. 350)

package (p. 351)

packaging functions (p. 352)

Universal Product Code (UPC) (p. 354)

Review Questions

1. Why is it so important to understand the concept of a generic product?
2. Distinguish between a consumer product and an industrial product.
3. How can the same product be a convenience, shopping, *and* specialty product? What does this mean to marketers?
4. Under what circumstances is a venture team appropriate? A new-product manager system?
5. What is the role of product positioning for a new product? A continuing product?
6. Why do manufacturer brands have such a large percentage of sales in so many product categories? Will private and generic brands eventually displace manufacturer brands? Explain your answers.
7. What are the three components of a package?
8. Describe the six major functions of packaging. Give an example of each.

Discussion Questions

1. For each of the following, describe the tangible, augmented, and generic product:
   a. A review course for the Graduate Management Aptitude Test (GMAT)
   b. A Sony DVD player
   c. Roofing materials
2. What product positioning would you recommend for a small firm that makes, installs, and services bookcases for offices? Explain your answer.
3. Present two successful and two unsuccessful examples of brand extension. Discuss why brand extension worked or did not work in these cases.
4. Evaluate the recent package redesigns of three products. Base your analysis on several specific concepts covered in this chapter.

Web Exercise

Visit the Web site of Product Development Consulting (**http://www.pdcinc.com/fast**) and explore these three sections of the site: "Cross-Functional Team Management," "Portfolio Management," and "Strategic Business Development." Discuss what you learn from these sections.

Practice Quiz

1. The broadest definition of a product is
   a. generic.
   b. tangible.
   c. convenience.
   d. extended.

2. The marketing emphasis for shopping products is on maintaining
   a. self-service.
   b. intensive distribution.
   c. competitive advantages.
   d. convenient locations.

3. Raw materials are
   a. semimanufactured goods that undergo further changes in form during manufacturing.
   b. convenience goods necessary for the daily operation of the firm.
   c. parts placed in products without further changes in form.
   d. expenses rather than capital items.

4. A narrow/deep mix is characterized by
   a. a small number of product lines and a large number of product items within each line.
   b. a large number of product lines and a small number of product items within each line.
   c. a large number of product lines and a large number of product items within each line.
   d. a small number of product lines and a small number of product items within each line.

5. The product management organizational form that functions best as a supplement to other forms is the
   a. marketing manager system.
   b. product-planning committee.
   c. new-product manager system.
   d. brand manager system.

6. Which is a characteristic of a venture team organization format?
   a. The team disbands when a new product is introduced.
   b. The venture team is ongoing.
   c. Product managers supervise existing products.
   d. One executive oversees a wide range of functions.

7. A trade character is defined as a
   a. symbol or design that is distinctive.
   b. word or letters that can be spoken.
   c. corporate symbol that is legally protected.
   d. brand mark that is personified.

8. Which of the following is *not* a reason why branding is important?
   a. Product identification is eased.
   b. The firm responsible for the product is hidden.

c. Price comparisons are reduced.

d. Consumers' perceived risk is reduced.

9. When manufacturer, private, and generic brands each attempt to gain a greater share of the consumer's dollar, they engage in

   a. a battle of the brands.

   b. a mixed-brand strategy.

   c. family branding.

   d. a licensing agreement.

10. Which of the following is *not* an advantage of family branding?

    a. Maximization of multiple segmentation

    b. Uniformity of a company's image

    c. Lower promotion costs

    d. Ease of introduction of new products

11. Which of the following is *not* an advantage of individual branding?

    a. A firm can create multiple product positions.

    b. A firm can attract multiple market segments.

    c. New products benefit from an established identity.

    d. Manufacturers can secure greater shelf space in retail stores.

12. A new product that is a brand extension is *least* likely to start at which stage of the consumer's brand decision process?

    a. Recognition

    b. Nonrecognition

c. Insistence

d. Preference

13. For a trademark to be legally protected, it must

    a. only imply characteristics that a product actually possesses.

    b. have a distinctive meaning that describes an entire product category.

    c. be used only in intrastate commerce.

    d. be confusingly similar to other trademarks.

14. Multiple packaging often

    a. lengthens shelf life.

    b. gets a consumer to buy an assortment of items.

    c. hurts a brand's image.

    d. reduces consumption.

15. The Universal Product Code

    a. is readable by humans and by machines.

    b. requires prices to be marked on merchandise.

    c. is not endorsed by the National Retail Merchants Association.

    d. is only used in the food industry.

For the answers to these questions, please visit the online site for this book at **http://www.atomicdog.com.**

Chapter 12

Goods Versus Services Planning

Oprah Winfrey (http://www.oprah.com) has built a service empire via her show, magazine, book club, and company's film division. In 2005, *Forbes* magazine listed Oprah as the world's most powerful celebrity, ahead of golf star Tiger Woods (ranked second) and basketball star Shaquille O'Neal (ranked fifth). In a separate story, *Forbes* estimated Oprah Winfrey's wealth at $1.4 billion. Her success is so staggering that she has been called the "most powerful woman on the planet."

Oprah's TV show, *The Oprah Winfrey Show*, the cornerstone of her empire, has been on the air for more than 20 years. It has an audience of nearly 50 million viewers in the United States and is aired in 118 countries worldwide. The show began locally as a Chicago talk program in 1984. In 1986, when the show entered national syndication, it became the highest-rated talk show in the history of television.

Oprah's monthly magazine, *O, the Oprah Magazine*, has a circulation of 3 million readers. In 2004, she launched *O at Home*, a quarterly magazine that focuses on home furnishings.

Like her other ventures, Oprah's Book Club has been a tremendous success: "She [Oprah] has repeatedly proved herself to be the arbiter of literary taste for millions of Americans, turning classics such as John Steinbeck's *East of Eden* into overnight million-sellers and making sensations of lesser-known works." Within four days of Oprah's mentioning his book on her talk show, James Frey sold 85,000 copies of his controversial new book, *A Million Little Pieces*. Another 615,000 copies with Oprah's Book Club logo were available at local bookstores. Within the book club's first year, it became the largest such club in the world, with more than 600,000 members.

In 1988, Oprah started her production company, Harpo ("Oprah" spelled backwards). Oprah was only the third woman to have her own studio (Mary Pickford and Lucille Ball were the others). Harpo Films produced *Beloved* in 1998 and released the *Oprah Winfrey Show: 20th Anniversary DVD Collection*.

Through her foundation, Oprah has given grants to organizations that support education around the world—through scholarships, school development, and funding for libraries and teacher education.[1]

In this chapter, we will study key concepts pertaining to the marketing of services. We will focus on the differences and similarities between goods and services marketing, as well as nonprofit marketing.

Chapter Objectives

1. To examine the scope of goods and services, and explain how goods and services may be categorized
2. To discuss the special considerations in the marketing of services
3. To look at the use of marketing by goods versus services firms and provide illustrations of service marketing
4. To distinguish between nonprofit and profit-oriented marketing
5. To describe a classification system for nonprofit marketing, the role of nonprofit marketing in the economy, and applications of nonprofit marketing

[1] Various company and other sources.

12-1 OVERVIEW

A firm must fully comprehend the distinctions between goods and services when devising and enacting product plans—beyond the brief coverage in Chapter 11. Although the planning process is the same for goods and services, their differences need to be reflected by the decisions made in the process.

Chapter 12 covers the scope of goods and services, a goods/services continuum, goods and services classifications, special considerations in service marketing, and the use of marketing by goods and services firms. We also include information on nonprofit marketing because most nonprofits (such as colleges, health facilities, and libraries) are involved with services.

12-2 THE SCOPE OF GOODS AND SERVICES

As noted in Chapter 11, *goods marketing* entails the sale of physical products. *Durable goods* are physical products that last for an extended period, such as furniture and heavy machinery. *Nondurable goods* are physical products made from materials other than metals, hard plastics, and wood; they are rather quickly consumed or worn out; or they become dated, unfashionable, or otherwise unpopular. Examples are food and office supplies.

Service marketing includes the rental of goods, the alteration or maintenance/repair of goods owned by consumers, and personal services. *Rented-goods services* involve the leasing of goods such as autos, hotel rooms, office space, and tuxedos for a specified time. *Owned-goods services* involve alterations or maintenance/repairs of goods owned by consumers. These services include house painting, clothing alterations, lawn care, and equipment maintenance. *Nongoods services* involve personal service on the part of the seller, such as accounting, legal, and tutoring services; they do not involve goods.

Overall, the value of manufacturers' shipments of U.S.-made durable goods exceeds that of nondurable goods. The leading durable products are transportation equipment, computer and electronic products, fabricated metal products, and machinery. Among U.S. final consumers, nondurables comprise nearly three-quarters of all goods purchases—led by food products. Because nondurables are bought more often and consumed more quickly, revenues are more affected by ads and sales promotions.

In industrialized nations, services account for a substantial share—generally well over one-half—of the gross domestic product. In developing and less-developed nations, services account for a lower share of the GDP; goods production (including agricultural items and extracted resources) is more dominant. Yet, even there, the role of services is growing rapidly.

The United States is the world's leading service economy: Services account for $7.5 trillion in annual spending (including government services). As noted in Chapter 6, on a global level, the United States is by far the biggest service exporter. Seventy percent of U.S. service spending is by final consumers, the rest is by businesses, government, and other nonprofits. Among the leading U.S. service industries are housing and household operations, medical care, personal services, transportation services, and repair services. Nearly 80 percent of the U.S. labor force is in service jobs. Other nations with at least one-half of the labor force in service jobs include Australia, Canada, France, Great Britain, Japan, and Germany.[2]

These reasons have been cited for the global growth of final consumer services: the rising standard of living, the complex goods that require specialized installation and repair, the lack of consumer technical skills, the high purchase prices of items that can be rented rather than bought, and the greater need for health care, child care, and

> **Goods marketing** involves the sale of **durable** and **nondurable goods**.

> **Service marketing** covers **rented-goods, owned-goods**, and **nongoods services**.

> Service marketing is huge in industrialized nations and the United States is the world leader.

---

[2] Estimated by the authors based on data from *Survey of Current Business*, http://www.bea.gov/bea/pub/0905cont.htm (September 2005); and *Comparative Civilian Labor Force Statistics, Ten Countries*, http://www.bls.gov/fls/flslforc.pdf (May 13, 2005).

educational services. In the b-to-b sector, among the services experiencing the greatest growth are business services, computer repair and training, and equipment leasing.

> The **hidden service sector** refers to services offered by goods-oriented firms.

The scope of services is sometimes underestimated because services may be lumped with goods in assigning revenues. The ***hidden service sector*** encompasses the delivery, installation, maintenance, training, repair, and other services provided by firms that emphasize goods sales. For instance, although IBM is considered a manufacturer, its Global Services division (**http://www.ibm.com/services**) now accounts for 48 percent of revenues: "With approximately 190,000 professionals in some 160 countries, IBM Global Services is the world's largest information technology services and consulting provider. Since its inception in 1991, IBM Global Services has grown to become IBM's biggest division."[3]

12-3 CATEGORIZING GOODS AND SERVICES

Goods and services can be categorized in two ways. They can be located on a goods/services continuum and they can be placed into separate classification systems.

12-3a   A Goods/Services Continuum

> Products are positioned from pure goods to pure services in a **goods/services continuum.**

A ***goods/services continuum*** categorizes products along a scale from pure goods to pure services. With pure goods, the seller offers consumers only physical goods without any accompanying services. With pure services, the seller offers consumers only nongoods services without accompanying physical goods. Between the two extremes, the seller would offer good/service combinations.

Figure 12-1 shows a goods/services continuum with four different examples. In each one, a pure good is depicted on the far left and a pure service is depicted on the far right. Moving from left to right, within each example, the combined good/service offerings become more service-oriented. Here is the reasoning behind the continuum examples in Figure 12-1:

- A computer disk is usually sold as a pure good—a product free from defects. With some computer software, a telephone hotline is available for questions. A PC is typically configured by the seller, pre-loaded with software, and accompanied by on-site service. Computer programming involves labor-intensive service on a physical good. Systems design entails professional consultation as to a client's information system needs; the seller offers a pure service and does not sell or service goods.
- When a consumer buys such exercise equipment as a stationary bike, he or she owns a pure good. If a person rents a stationary bike for the home, that individual obtains the use of a physical product. When a person uses a stationary bike at a hotel, he or she obtains the use of a physical product and the related facilities. If a person joins a health-and-fitness club, he or she not only gets to use the physical facilities but also can participate in exercise classes. When a person hires a personal trainer, he or she acquires the pure service of an expert teacher in exercise and motivation.
- Off-the-rack office furniture may be marketed as a pure good—with the buyer responsible for delivery and set-up. Custom-made office furniture is based on buyer specifications and buyer/seller consultations; delivery and set-up are included. Furniture reupholstering involves labor-intensive service on a physical good; the seller markets a service along with a physical good (the fabric used in the reupholstering). Cleaning office furniture is a labor-intensive service on a physical good; the seller markets a service (the value of the cleaning solution is minor). An interior decorator offers professional consultation regarding a client's office furniture, wall coverings, flooring materials, layout, and so on; the seller provides a pure service and does not sell or service goods.

---

[3] "Fast Facts," **http://www.ibm.com/ibm/us** (May 2005).

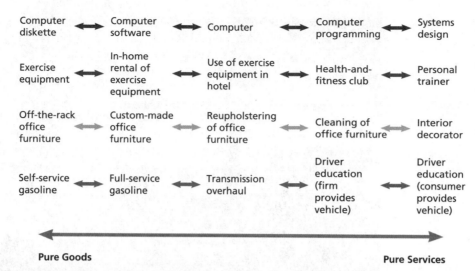

Please note: The above continuum should be viewed from left to right. Within each row, there is a consistent pattern from pure good to pure service. When comparing different rows, there is somewhat less consistency due to the diversity of the examples shown.

Figure 12-1

Illustrating the Goods/Services Continuum

- Self-service gasoline is marketed as a pure good, with no accompanying service. With full-service gasoline, an attendant pumps the gas—sometimes washing the windshield and doing other minor tasks. A transmission overhaul is a labor-intensive service on a physical good; the seller markets both a physical product (new parts) and service. In driver education, where the driving school provides the vehicle, the seller teaches a potential driver how to drive in a school car; the major offering is the education provided. In driver ed, where the trainee supplies his or her own vehicle, the driving school markets a pure service; it is not offering the use of a vehicle.

We can learn several lessons from a goods/services continuum. One, it applies to both final consumer and b-to-b products. Two, most products embody goods/services combinations; the selling firm must remember this. Three, each position along the continuum represents a marketing opportunity. Four, the bond between a goods provider and customers becomes closer as the firm moves away from marketing pure goods. Five, a firm must decide if it is to be perceived as goods- or services-oriented. See Figure 12-2.

Whether a firm is goods- or services-oriented, it must specify which are core services and which are peripheral—and the level of peripheral services to offer. *Core services* are the basic services that firms provide to their customers to be competitive. At Casio (**http://www.casio.com**), core services include prompt delivery, credit, advertising support, and returns handling for the far-flung retailers that carry its products around the globe. At Federal Express (**http://www.fedex.com**), core services involve taking phone orders, picking up packages, tracking them, shipping on time, and providing proof of delivery.

Peripheral services are supplementary (extra) services that firms provide to customers. Casio's peripheral services are extended credit and advice on how to set up displays for retailers, and a toll-free phone number for consumer inquiries. Federal Express' peripheral services include shipping advice for customers, packaging materials, and tracing packages in transit. Although these services may increase costs, require added employee skills, and be time consuming, they may also help a company create and sustain a competitive advantage.

> Firms can create a competitive advantage by adding **peripheral services** to their **core services**.

Figure 12-2

A Goods *and* Services Strategy

Home Depot is steadily moving away from the left side of the goods/services continuum toward the center. It is more heavily involved with the marketing of home improvement services than ever before. The firm hand-picks the licensed and insured contractors it recommends.

Source: Reprinted by permission.

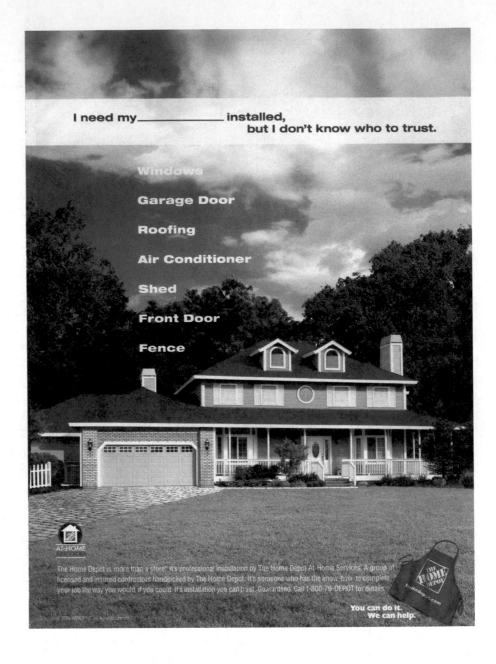

12-3b Goods and Services Classification Systems

Figure 12-3 shows a detailed, seven-way classification system for goods. It highlights the diversity of goods marketing.

In selecting a market segment, a goods seller should remember that final and organizational consumers have similarities and differences. The same good may be offered to each segment. The major distinctions between segments are the reasons for purchases, the amount bought, and the features desired.

Durable-goods firms have a particular challenge. On the one hand, they want to stress the defect-free, long-running nature of their products. On the other hand, inasmuch as they need to generate repeat sales from current customers, they continually try to add unique features and enhance the performance of new models—and then convince people to buy again while the goods they own are still functional. For nondurable-goods firms, the key task is to engender brand loyalty, so consumers rebuy the same brands.

High-value-added goods are those where manufacturers convert raw materials or components into distinctive products. The more value firms add to the goods

> Goods may be classified as to market, durability, value added, goals, regulation, distribution channel, and customer contact.

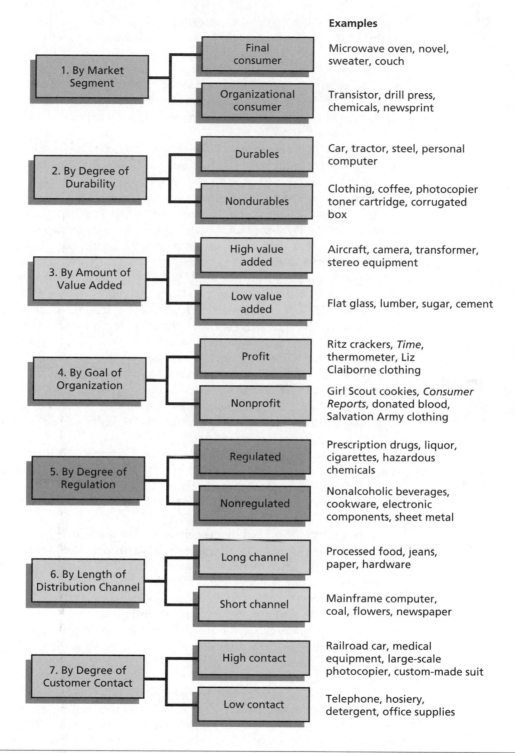

Examples

1. By Market Segment
- Final consumer — Microwave oven, novel, sweater, couch
- Organizational consumer — Transistor, drill press, chemicals, newsprint

2. By Degree of Durability
- Durables — Car, tractor, steel, personal computer
- Nondurables — Clothing, coffee, photocopier toner cartridge, corrugated box

3. By Amount of Value Added
- High value added — Aircraft, camera, transformer, stereo equipment
- Low value added — Flat glass, lumber, sugar, cement

4. By Goal of Organization
- Profit — Ritz crackers, *Time*, thermometer, Liz Claiborne clothing
- Nonprofit — Girl Scout cookies, *Consumer Reports*, donated blood, Salvation Army clothing

5. By Degree of Regulation
- Regulated — Prescription drugs, liquor, cigarettes, hazardous chemicals
- Nonregulated — Nonalcoholic beverages, cookware, electronic components, sheet metal

6. By Length of Distribution Channel
- Long channel — Processed food, jeans, paper, hardware
- Short channel — Mainframe computer, coal, flowers, newspaper

7. By Degree of Customer Contact
- High contact — Railroad car, medical equipment, large-scale photocopier, custom-made suit
- Low contact — Telephone, hosiery, detergent, office supplies

Figure 12-3

A Classification System for Goods

they sell, the better the chance for a goods-based differential advantage. Low-value-added goods are those where manufacturers do little to enhance the raw materials or components they extract or buy. These firms often must compete on price because their goods may be seen as commodities. Superior customer service can be a major differential advantage and enable marketers of low-value-added goods to avoid commodity status.

For the most part, goods-oriented firms are profit-oriented. Sometimes, as noted in Figure 12-3, goods are marketed by nonprofit organizations—usually as a way of generating revenue to support the organizations' activities. Nonprofit marketing is discussed in depth in Section 12-6.

Goods may be grouped by the extent of government regulation. Some items, such as those related to the health and safety of people and the environment, are highly regulated. Others, generally those not requiring special health and safety rules, are subject to less regulation.

Distribution channel length refers to the number of intermediaries between goods producers and consumers. Final consumer goods tend to have more intermediaries than b-to-b goods due to the size and importance of the latter. Furthermore, goods that are complex, expensive, bulky, and perishable are more apt to have shorter channels.

Goods may be classified by the degree of customer contact between sellers and buyers. Contact is greater for sophisticated equipment, items requiring some training, and custom-made goods. In these instances, proper employee training is needed. Low customer contact is required for goods that consumers are able to buy and use with little assistance from sellers.

A good would normally be classified on a combination of the factors in Figure 12-3. *Time* magazine (**http://www.time.com**) appeals to final consumers, is nondurable, has high value added, is profit-oriented, faces few regulations, is sold at newsstands and through home delivery, and has low customer contact.

Figure 12-4 displays a detailed, seven-way classification system for services. It demonstrates the diversity of service marketing.

As with goods, final and organizational consumers have similarities and differences, so the same basic service may be offered to each segment. Both groups can counter high prices or poor service by doing some tasks themselves. The major differences between the segments are the reasons for the service, the quantity of service required, and the complexity of the service performed.

> Services may be classified as to market, tangibility, skill, goals, regulation, labor intensity, and customer contact.

In general, the less tangible a service, the less service marketing resembles goods marketing. For nongoods services, performance can be judged only after the service is completed, and consistency is hard to maintain. Rentals and owned-goods services involve physical goods and may be marketed in a manner somewhat similar to goods.

Services may be offered by persons of varying skills. For those requiring high skill levels, customers are quite selective in picking a provider. That is why professionals often gain customer loyalty. For services requiring low levels of skill, the range of acceptable substitutes is usually much greater.

Service firms may be profit- or nonprofit-oriented. Nonprofit service marketing may be undertaken by government or private organizations. The major distinctions between profit- and nonprofit-oriented marketing are noted in Section 12-6a.

Services may be classed by level of government regulation. Some firms, such as insurance companies, are highly regulated. Others, such as caterers and house painters, are subject to limited regulation.

The traditional view of services has been that they are done by one person for another. Yet, this view is too narrow. Services differ in labor intensity—such as automated versus teller-oriented bank services. Labor intensity rises if skilled personnel are used and/or services must be done at a customer's home or business. Also, do-it-yourself consumers may undertake some services, such as home repair.

Services may be grouped by their degree of customer contact. If contact is high, training personnel in interpersonal skills is essential, in addition to the technical schooling needed to perform a service properly. Such personnel as appliance repairpeople and car mechanics may be the only contact a person has with a firm. If contact is low, technical skills are most essential.

A service would typically be classified on a combination of the factors in Figure 12-4. A firm tutoring students for college entrance exams appeals to final consumers, has an intangible service, requires skill by the service provider, is profit-oriented, is not regulated, has many trainers, and has high customer contact. A company may also operate in

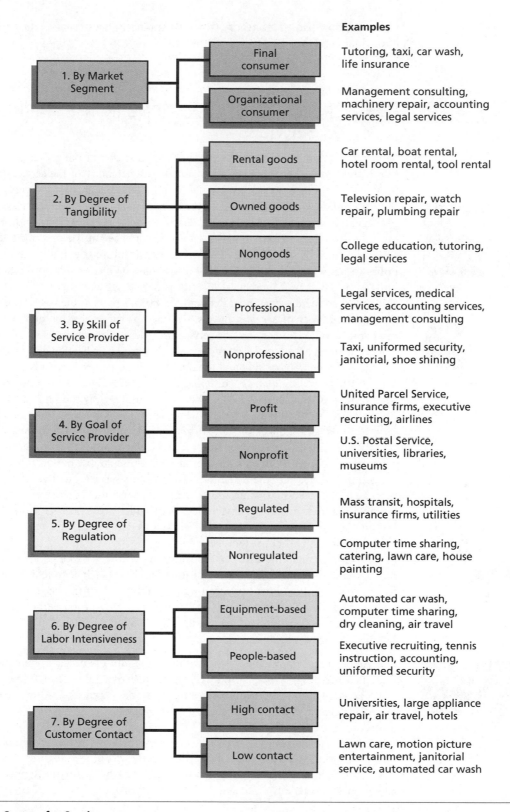

Examples

1. By Market Segment

Final consumer — Tutoring, taxi, car wash, life insurance

Organizational consumer — Management consulting, machinery repair, accounting services, legal services

2. By Degree of Tangibility

Rental goods — Car rental, boat rental, hotel room rental, tool rental

Owned goods — Television repair, watch repair, plumbing repair

Nongoods — College education, tutoring, legal services

3. By Skill of Service Provider

Professional — Legal services, medical services, accounting services, management consulting

Nonprofessional — Taxi, uniformed security, janitorial, shoe shining

4. By Goal of Service Provider

Profit — United Parcel Service, insurance firms, executive recruiting, airlines

Nonprofit — U.S. Postal Service, universities, libraries, museums

5. By Degree of Regulation

Regulated — Mass transit, hospitals, insurance firms, utilities

Nonregulated — Computer time sharing, catering, lawn care, house painting

6. By Degree of Labor Intensiveness

Equipment-based — Automated car wash, computer time sharing, dry cleaning, air travel

People-based — Executive recruiting, tennis instruction, accounting, uniformed security

7. By Degree of Customer Contact

High contact — Universities, large appliance repair, air travel, hotels

Low contact — Lawn care, motion picture entertainment, janitorial service, automated car wash

Figure 12-4

A Classification System for Services

more than one part of a category (this also applies to goods marketers): A CPA may have both final consumer and b-to-b clients.

12-4 SPECIAL CONSIDERATIONS IN THE MARKETING OF SERVICES

Services have four attributes that typically distinguish them from goods (as noted in Chapter 11): higher intangibility, greater perishability, inseparability of the service from the service provider, and greater variability in quality. Their effect is greatest for personal services.

> Services differ from goods in terms of **intangibility, perishability, inseparability,** and **variability.**

Intangibility of services means they often cannot be displayed, transported, stored, packaged, or inspected before buying. This occurs for repair services and personal services; only the benefits derived from the service experience can be described. *Perishability of services* means many of them cannot be stored for future sale. If a painter who needs eight hours to paint a single house is idle on Monday, he or she will not be able to paint two houses on Tuesday; Monday's idle time is lost. A service supplier must try to manage consumers so there is consistent demand for various parts of the week, month, and/or year.

Inseparability of services means a service provider and his or her services may be inseparable. When this occurs, the service provider is virtually indispensable, and customer contact is often an integral part of the service experience. The quality of machinery repair depends on a mechanic's skill and the quality of legal services depends on a lawyer's ability. *Variability in service quality*—differing service performance from one purchase occasion to another—often occurs even if services are completed by the same person. This may be due to a firm's difficulty in problem diagnosis (for repairs), customer inability to verbalize service needs, and the lack of standardization and mass production for many services.

In planning its marketing strategy, a service firm needs to consider how intangible its offering is, how perishable its services are, how inseparable performance is from specific service providers, and the potential variability of service quality. Its goal would be to prepare and enact a marketing strategy that lets consumers perceive its offering in a more tangible manner, makes its services less perishable, encourages consumers to seek it out but enables multiple employees to be viewed as competent, and makes service performance as efficient and consistent as possible.

> Service intangibility makes positioning decisions more complex.

Service intangibility can make positioning harder. Unlike goods positioning, which often stresses tangible factors and consumer analysis (such as touching and tasting) prior to a purchase, much service positioning must rely on performance promises (such as how well a truck handles after a tune-up), which can only be measured once a purchase is made. But, there are ways to use positioning to help consumers perceive a service more tangibly. A firm can:

- Associate an intangible service with tangible objects better understood by the customer. Figure 12-5 shows Hilton (**http://www.hilton.com**) does this.
- Focus on the relationship between the company and its customers. It can sell the competence, skill, and concern of employees.
- Popularize the company name.
- Offer tangible benefits, such as Northwest Airlines' (**http://www.nwa.com**) promoting specific reasons for people to fly with it. See Figure 12-6.
- Achieve a unique product position, such as 24-hour, on-site service for office equipment repair.[4]

---

[4] Gordon H. G. McDougall and Douglas W. Snetsinger, "The Intangibility of Services: Measurement and Competitive Perspectives," *Journal of Services Marketing*, Vol. 4 (Fall 1990), pp. 27-40. See also David D. C. Tarn, "Raising Services' Tangibility in Foreign Markets via Marketing: A Model Construction and a Cross-National Comparative Empirical Survey," *International Marketing Review*, Vol. 22 (Number 3, 2005), pp. 327-352; and Michel Laroche, Gordon H. G. McDougall, Jasmin Bergeron, and Zhiyong Yang, "Exploring How Intangibility Affects Perceived Risk," *Journal of Service Research*, Vol. 6 (May 2004), pp. 373-389.

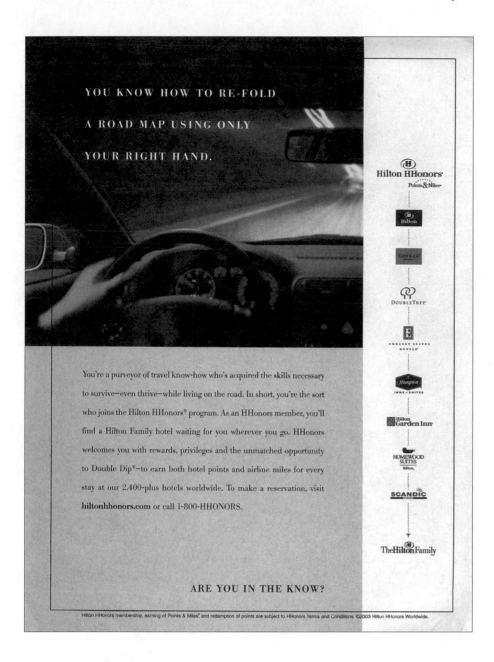

Figure 12-5

How Hilton Hotels Uses Tangible Objects to Create Service Tangibility

By showing the open road in front of a car, Hilton makes the locations of its many nearby hotels more tangible. This ad also promotes the Hilton Honors frequent guest plan with the Hilton logo.

Source: Reprinted by permission.

Service intangibility may be magnified if only a small portion of the service is seen by the consumer. For example, in-shop repairs are normally not viewed by customers. Although a repairperson may spend two hours on an industrial copy machine and insert two parts worth $35, when the customer sees a bill for $195, he or she may not realize the service time involved. Thus, firms must explain how much time is needed for each aspect of service—and the tasks performed—to make the service seem more tangible.

To handle service perishability, a firm must match demand and supply patterns as well as possible. It might have to alter the timing of consumer demand and/or exert better control over the supply of its service offering. As much as possible, situations should be avoided in which excess demand goes unsatisfied and excess capacity causes unproductive resource use. To better match demand with supply, a firm can:

Services often cannot be stored for later sale, so demand must be matched with supply.

- Market similar services to segments having different demand patterns.
- Market new services with different demand patterns from existing services.
- Market new services that complement existing ones.
- Market service "extras" during nonpeak periods.

Figure 12-6

The Tangible Benefits of Northwest's Online Check-In Service

Source: Reprinted by permission.

- Market new services not affected by existing capacity constraints.
- Train personnel to perform multiple tasks.
- Hire part-time employees during peak periods.
- Educate consumers to use services during nonpeak periods.
- Offer incentives and price reductions in nonpeak periods.[5]

The existence of a close service provider/consumer relationship makes employee interpersonal skills important. The work force must be trained to interact well with people in such diverse situations as selling and performing services, handling payments,

> Interpersonal skills are crucial for service businesses.

[5] Leonard L. Berry A. Parasuraman, and Valarie A. Zeithaml, "Synchronizing Demand and Supply in Service Businesses," *Business*, Vol. 34 (October-December 1984), pp. 36–37; James L. Heskett, W. Earl Sasser, Jr., and Christopher W. L. Hart, *Service Breakthroughs* (New York: Free Press, 1990), pp. 135–158; and Donald J. Shemwell, Jr. and J. Joseph Cronin, Jr., "Services Marketing Strategies for Coping with Demand/Supply Imbalances," *Journal of Services Marketing*, Vol. 8 (Number 4, 1994), pp. 14–24. See also Pei-Chun Lai and Tom Baum, "Just-in-Time Labor Supply in the Hotel Sector: The Role of Agencies," *Employee Relations*, Vol. 27 (Number 1, 2005), pp. 86–102.

Global Marketing in Action

The Kenya Tourist Board Ramps Up Its Marketing Efforts

The Kenya Tourist Board (KTB) (http://www.visit-kenya.com) has spent the equivalent of $9 million to promote tourism in such key markets as Great Britain, Western Europe, and the United States. With this increase in promotional support, the head of marketing for Kenya's Tourism Trust Fund (TTF) (http://www.ttfkenya.org) projected that Kenya tourism revenues would be the equivalent of $666 million as of 2006. Much of the revenue increase was from Great Britain, German, the Netherlands, South African, Chinese, and Belgian tourists.

The TTF recently extended its promotion to include new markets in Asia and South Africa. The KTB also was active and established a regional office in the Far East and began promotional activities aimed at Japan and China. As result, the number of tourists from China rose by 85 percent and tourism from Japan increased by 55 percent. The gain from China was due to China's granting Approved Destination Status (ADS) for Kenya; Kenya was the third African country to receive ADS (after Egypt and South Africa).

"Our focus is on attracting high-yield tourists rather than simply high numbers. The challenge is for Kenya to diversify its tourism products even more if we are to encourage tourists to spend more of their dollars," said the KTB's chairman. The KTB is also working on increasing Kenya's number of tourist destinations and diversifying its tourism-based products to encourage more repeat visits.

Source: Based on material in "Kenya to Spend $9 Million in New International Marketing Drive," *Africa News Online* (July 26, 2005); and Derek Otieno, "Kenya: Tourism Bounces Back," *African Business* (March 2005), p. 55.

---

and delivering repaired goods. Generally, more personal involvement, personal contact, and customer input are needed to market services than to market goods. Employee empowerment can be beneficial. At Enterprise Rent-A-Car (http://www.enterprise.com), "Our industry is fiercely competitive. So how is it that we have remained ahead of the pack for so many years? (1) We hire smart, motivated individuals and teach them to run a business by delivering exceptional customer service. (2) Completely satisfied customers come back—and they tell others about us, naturally growing the base of each of our local operations. (3) As business grows, we open more branches, creating new opportunities for employees. Career advancement is tied not only to growth, profitability, and employee development, but, most importantly, to customer service quality. (4) As employees progress through our system, growth drives their financial rewards and opens new opportunities to attract more top talent."[6]

These points should also be considered in planning a service provider/consumer relationship: Customers of personal service firms often become loyal to a particular employee rather than the firm. If that person leaves the firm, he or she may take some customers with him or her. Thus, it is important for a firm to show its customers that multiple employees are equally capable of providing excellent service.

By their nature, many services have the potential for great variability in quality. It is hard for lawn care firms to mow lawns exactly the same way each week, for consultants to make sales forecasts for clients that are always accurate, and for each airline flight to arrive on time. But what service firms can do is strive to make their performance as efficient and consistent as possible. Service reliability can also be improved by setting high-level standards and by tying employee pay and promotions to performance.

One solution to the issue of high costs (inefficiency) and low reliability (performance variability) is the *industrialization of services* by using hard, soft, and hybrid technologies.[7] *Hard technologies* substitute machinery for people, such as utilizing electronic

> The **industrialization of services** can lower inefficiency and excessive variability via hard technologies, soft technologies, or hybrid technologies.

---

[6] "Management Philosophy," http://aboutus.enterprise.com/who_we_are/management_philosophy.html (May 9, 2006).

[7] Theodore Levitt, *The Marketing Imagination* (New York: Free Press, 1983), pp. 50–71; and James S. Hensel, "Service Quality Improvement and Control: A Customer-Based Approach," *Journal of Business Research*, Vol. 20 (January 1990), pp. 43–54. See also Uday Karmarkar, "Will You Survive the Services Revolution?" *Harvard Business Review*, Vol. 82 (Issue 6, June 2004); and David Ticoll, "Service Sector Is on the Eve of a Global Restructuring," http://www.globetechnology.com/servlet/story/RTGAM.20040617.wticoll17_HP/BNStory/davidTicoll/ColumnistSummary (June 17, 2004).

Figure 12-7

Red Box Automated DVD Rentals: Substituting Technology for People

Source: Reprinted by permission of Susan Berry, Retail Image Consulting, Inc.

financial transactions instead of human bank tellers. See Figure 12-7. Hard technologies are not as readily applied to services requiring extensive personal skill and contact—such as medical, legal, and hairstyling services. *Soft technologies* substitute pre-planned systems for individual services. For example, travel agents sell pre-packaged vacation tours to standardize transportation, accommodations, food, and sightseeing. *Hybrid technologies* combine both hard and soft technologies. Examples include muffler repair and quick-oil-change shops.

This is how Hilton (**http://www.hilton.com**) has industrialized more of its service activities:

> Hilton deploys a single, integrated technology platform called OnQ across the entire business. Using OnQ, Hilton owns the customer engagement advantage via a common view of 7 million of our most valuable guests. We will continue to focus on opportunities to leverage our OnQ advantage, through innovative use of new technologies to offer guests more choices and flexibility, further customizing their travel experience when they stay with any of our Hilton family of hotels (Hilton, Doubletree, Embassy Suites Hotels, Hampton Inn, Hampton Inn & Suites, Hilton Garden Inn, and Homewood Suites). New high-tech projects we are working on include eCheck-in, the capability to check-in via the Internet up to 24 hours prior to arrival; transforming the brand Web sites from a distribution channel facilitating the sale of rooms to

a travel planner with the capability to locate and book area events, preview shopping, and make reservations at area restaurants; and expanding our use of wearable computers, such as handheld check-in and check-out devices, to maximize communication between the front desk, housekeeping, and maintenance to expedite turnaround of rooms brands.[8]

To industrialize their services better, many firms use a ***service blueprint***—a visual portrayal of the service process: "It displays each subprocess (or step) in the service system, linking the various steps in the sequence in which they appear. A service blueprint is essentially a detailed map or flowchart of the service process."[9] Figure 12-8 shows how a blueprint can be used in administering an X-ray to a patient.

While planning their marketing strategies, it is also important for firms to understand service quality from a customer perspective. They must try to minimize any possible ***service gap***—the difference between customer expectations and actual service performance.

Consumer expectations regarding service companies cover these 10 areas:

- Tangibles—facilities, equipment, personnel, communication materials.
- Reliability—ability to perform a desired service dependably and accurately.
- Responsiveness—willingness to provide prompt service and assist customers.
- Competence—possession of the necessary skills and knowledge.
- Courtesy—respect, politeness, and friendliness of personnel.
- Credibility—honesty, trustiness, and believability of service performers.
- Security—freedom from risk, doubt, or danger.
- Access—ease of contact.
- Communication—keeping customers informed in a clear manner and listening to comments.
- Understanding—the customer knowing the customer's needs.[10]

> A **service blueprint** enhances productivity. **Service gaps** must be reduced.

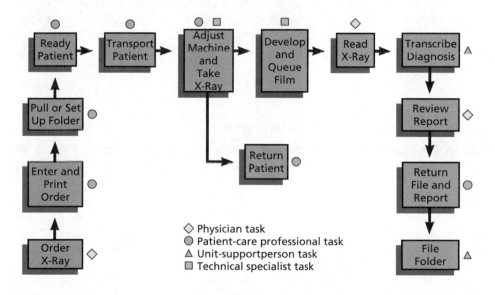

◇ Physician task
○ Patient-care professional task
△ Unit-supportperson task
▢ Technical specialist task

Figure 12-8

A Service Blueprint for an X-Ray

This service blueprint depicts the 13 steps involved in a typical hospital's X-ray process. The steps can be completed in under one hour and they require multiple employees. Without such a blueprint, the X-ray process would probably be less systematic, more time-consuming, and less efficient.

Source: Stephen H. Baum, "Making Your Service Blueprint Pay Off!" *Journal of Services Marketing*, Vol. 4 (Summer 1990), p. 49. Reprinted by permission of MCB University Press Ltd.

[8] Cristina McEachern, "CIOs Plot the Year Ahead," **http://www.varbusiness.com/sections/customer/customer.jhtml?articleId=56700064** (January 05, 2005).

[9] Valarie A. Zeithaml, A. Parasuraman, and Leonard L. Berry, *Delivering Quality Service* (New York: Free Press, 1990), p. 158. See also Ravi Kalakoata and Marcia Robinson, *Services Blueprint: Roadmap for Execution* (Boston: Addison-Wesley, 2003); and Jim Barthold, "Building the Managed Services Blueprint," *Telecommunications—Americas Edition* (September 2005), pp. 8–12.

[10] Zeithaml, Parasuraman, and Berry, *Delivering Quality Service*, pp. 18–22. See also Avinandan Mukherjee and Prithwiraj Nath, "An Empirical Assessment of Comparative Approaches to Service Quality Measurement," *Journal of Services Marketing*, Vol. 19 (Number 3, 2005), pp. 174–184; Zhilin Yang, Shaohan Cai, Zheng Zhou, and Nan Zhou, "Development and Validation of an Instrument to Measure User Perceived Service Quality of Information-Presenting Web Portals," *Information & Management*, Vol. 42 (May 2005), pp. 575–589; and Charilaos Kouthouris and Konstantinos Alexandris, "Can Service Quality Predict Customer Satisfaction and Behavioral Intentions in the Sport Tourism Industry? An Application of the SERVQUAL Model in an Outdoors Setting," *Journal of Sport Tourism*, Vol. 10 (May 2005), pp. 101–111.

12-5 THE USE OF MARKETING BY GOODS AND SERVICES FIRMS

Goods and services firms have differed in their use of marketing, but service firms are now better adapting to their special circumstances than in the past.

12-5a A Transition in the Marketing of Services

> The low use of marketing for services has been due to small firm size, an emphasis on technical expertise, limited competition, negative attitudes, and other factors.

Service firms have lagged behind manufacturers in the use of marketing for several reasons: (1) Many service firms are so small that marketing specialists cannot be afforded. (2) Because manufacturers often have a larger geographic market, they can more efficiently advertise. (3) Many service firms are staffed by people with technical expertise in their fields but limited marketing experience. (4) Strict licensing provisions sometimes limit competition among service firms and the need for marketing; in most industries, manufacturers have faced intense competition for years. (5) Because consumers have held such service professionals as doctors and lawyers in very high esteem, marketing has not been needed. (6) In the past, some professional associations banned ads by members; this was changed by court rulings that now permit it. (7) Some service professionals still dislike marketing, do not understand it, or question the use of marketing practices, such as advertising, in their fields. (8) Some manufacturers have only recently set up services as profit centers.

Today, the marketing of services has expanded greatly, due to a better understanding of the role of customer service in gaining and retaining consumers, worldwide service opportunities, deregulation in numerous service industries, competition among service providers, consumer interest in renting/leasing rather than buying, the aggressive marketing of services by firms that once focused on manufacturing, the advent of high-technology services (such as video conferencing), the growth of do-it-yourselfers due to high service costs, and the number of service professionals with formal business training.

> Service firms' use of marketing practices is expected to continue increasing in the future.

12-5b Illustrations of Service Marketing

This section examines the use of marketing by hotels, auto repair and servicing firms, and lawyers. The examples represent rented-goods services, owned-goods services, and non-goods services. They differ by the degree of tangibility, the service provider skill, the degree of labor intensiveness, and the level of customer contact. But, in all three instances, the use of marketing practices is expanding.

Hotels may target one or more market segments: business travelers, through tourists (who stay one night), regular tourists (who stay two or more nights), extended-stay residents (who stay up to several months or longer), and conventioneers. Each requires different services. The business traveler wants efficiency, a desk and Internet connection in the room, and convenient meeting rooms. A through tourist wants a convenient location, low prices, and quick food service. A regular tourist wants a nice room, recreational facilities, and sightseeing assistance. An extended-stay resident wants an in-room kitchen and other apartment-like amenities. Conventioneers want large meeting areas; pre-planned sightseeing; an in-hotel business center with fax machines, computer access, and printers; and hospitality suites.

To attract and keep customers, hotels are upgrading, adding new services, opening units in emerging markets around the world, and improving marketing efforts. Elaborate, distinctive lobby areas and immaculate grounds are popular with resort hotels. First-run movies that can be viewed in the room, frequent-stay bonus plans, and special promotions are offered. For example, Starwood Hotels & Resorts Worldwide, the parent company of Sheraton, Westin, Four Points, St. Regis, and other hotel chains, has a global

Marketing and the Web

Online Reservations: An Effective Tool for Hotels

About one-half of U.S. adults say that they have booked hotel reservations online, according to the *2005 National Leisure Travel Monitor* study. Let's look at how the most successful hotel chains are maximizing their Web bookings.

Best Western International's Web site (http://www.bestwestern.com) reported an average annual growth rate of 54 percent from 2001 to 2005. Internet bookings now comprise close to one-half of all Best Western reservations. In addition to English, all of the hotel chain's online booking information is available in French, German, Italian, and Spanish. Web pages for some properties are also available in simplified Chinese and Korean. In 2005, Best Western rolled out 360-degree virtual tours to enable a potential guest to more closely examine each hotel property.

Choice Hotels' Web site (http://www.choicehotels.com) recently offered an "Earn Nights or Flights 3X Faster" promotion in which online bookings earned three times its Choice Privileges points or triple airline credits. As with Best Western, Choice guests can book a room in multiple languages including English, French, Spanish, German, and Japanese.

Morgans Hotel Group (http://www.morganshotelgroup.com) has increased its online bookings through special offers to its customer data base, as well as partnerships with sites that drive traffic to Morgans' site. Morgans also seeks to optimize its positioning on search engines whereby a consumer searches for "hotel AND Miami," for example.

Source: Based on material in Derek Gale, "Logging Lower Reservation Costs," *Hotels* (July 2005), pp. 71–72.

frequent-stay program (http://www.starwood.com/preferredguest) with millions of members.

Hotel marketing efforts now rely more on research, public relations, TV ads, well-conceived slogans, guest services, focused product positioning, and better employee training. Canada's Professional Institute of Tourism, in partnership with the Educational Institute of the American Hotel & Motel Association, offers professional certificates (http://www.hospitalitytraining.net/pdit/tourism4RDM.html) for workers who complete courses in any of five key operational departments: rooms management, food and beverage management, marketing and hospitality management, accounting and financial management, and human resource management. Each specialization includes four departmental-specific courses plus a course on supervision in the hospitality industry.

Hotels are even trying to resolve consumer complaints more effectively. For instance, business travelers are quite concerned about overbooking, long waiting lines, late check-in times, and unresponsive or discourteous employees. In response, many hotels arrange for alternative accommodations if they are overbooked, have computerized check-ins, offer express checkout (with bills placed under room doors or mailed to guests' businesses or homes), serve free drinks and provide baggage handling if check-in times are late, and give workers more flexibility. Several hotels have eliminated blackout dates for customers wishing to use their frequent-stay rewards and reduced the amount of points needed to earn rewards.

Repair and servicing firms operate in a variety of product categories, including motor vehicles, computers, TVs and appliances, industrial equipment, watches and jewelry, and a host of others. These firms fix malfunctioning products, replace broken parts, and provide maintenance. Let us highlight the auto repair and servicing industry.

Auto repairs and servicing are carried out at manufacturer-owned or manufacturer-sponsored dealers and independent service centers. New-car dealers generate most of their profits from parts and servicing. In total, more than $200 billion is spent annually on U.S. auto and truck repairs and servicing (including parts and labor)— $85 billion at new-car dealers and the rest at independents.[11] General Motors cars can be repaired and serviced through its Mr. Goodwrench program (**http://www.gmgoodwrench.com**), available at approved GM dealerships; independent repair and maintenance shops; tire, muffler, and battery outlets; mass merchants (such as Sears); and service stations. Independents handle many makes and models. Among the largest independents are Pep Boys (**http://www.pepboys.com**), general service; Jiffy Lube (**http://www.jiffylube.com**), oil and lubricating fluids; Meineke (**http://www.meineke.com**), mufflers; and Aamco (**http://www.aamco.com**), transmissions.

How has the auto repair and servicing business changed? Consider this:

> In recent years, increased competition from independent service stations and quick-lube centers has cut into dealerships' service work, but dealers are fighting back. New-car dealers have made a major investment in service and parts to beef up sales and customer satisfaction. They offer 370,000 service stalls, employ 280,00 technicians, and carry a parts inventory valued at $5.6 billion. To boost customer convenience and make full use of their facilities, 66 percent of dealers offer evening service hours, weekend hours, or both. More dealerships have opted to stay out of the body shop business.[12]

The Internet is also having a major impact. Consider Jonko.com (**http://www.jonko.com**), which "is an automobile reference and opinion site that offers a variety of auto repair tips, tricks, and tutorials. The Jonko.com staff is comprised of a handful of motivated individuals who volunteer their time to create and manage the site. At present, Jonko.com is a completely volunteer effort that pulls together folks who all share a love of cars and the community that can be built on the Web."[13]

About 30 years ago, the U.S. Supreme Court ruled that lawyers could not be barred from advertising. Since then, legal services advertising has risen significantly and many marketing innovations have been enacted. And today, all U.S. professionals are able to advertise their services. As one observer noted: "With thousands of mid-sized law firms and hundreds of thousands of lawyers all competing for the same pool of clients and prospects, differentiation is one of the most important ways to gain recognition and build brand awareness. Communicating your firm's unique characteristics, expertise, strengths, and successes to a large number of prospects can be achieved through advertising. This is not about selling the skill of your firm, but about promoting the qualities that differentiate your firm from so many others. Differentiation is your brand, and advertising is about positioning that brand by promoting and communicating your firm's differentiators to a targeted mass audience."[14]

The American Bar Association (**http://www.abanet.org**) says that two-thirds of its members engage in some form of advertising. Industry experts estimate that 20 to 30 percent of new clients now choose attorneys on the basis of the latter's marketing efforts; the rest rely on personal referrals. Thus, many attorneys advertise in the Yellow Pages and have printed brochures. Some advertise in newspapers and magazines; and certain ones use TV and radio ads. Various law firms send out newsletters, employ public relations firms, and have sessions where partners and associates practice selling services to clients. Many firms hire jury consultants to advise them on the characteristics to look for in potential jurors.

Law clinics and franchised law firms have grown. They concentrate on rather routine legal services. They have large legal staffs, convenient locations (such as in shopping centers), standardized fees and services ($100 or so for a simple will), and plain fixtures. The largest franchised firms have hundreds of attorneys, cover a wide geographic area, advertise heavily, and set fees in advance and in writing.

[11] Bureau of Economic Analysis, U.S. Commerce Department; and *2005 NADA Data* (McLean, VA: National Automobile Dealers Association).

[12] *2005 NADA Data*, p. 52.

[13] "About Jonko," **http://www.jonko.com/about** (May 4, 2006).

[14] Terry Isner, "Creating a Brand Through Advertising," *Law Journal Newsletters Online* (May 2005).

Legal-services marketing has been met with resistance from a number of attorneys. They criticize some advertising for stressing price at the expense of quality and mass-marketing techniques as eliminating personal counseling. They feel the public's confidence in the profession is falling, information in ads may be inaccurate, and overly high consumer expectations are created. A great many lawyers still do not advertise in mass media; they rely totally on referrals.

12-6 NONPROFIT MARKETING

Nonprofit marketing is conducted by organizations and individuals that operate in the public interest or that foster a cause and do not seek financial profits. It may involve organizations (charities, unions, trade associations), people (political candidates), places (resorts, convention centers, industrial sites), and ideas ("stop smoking"), as well as goods and services. See Figure 12-9.

> **Nonprofit marketing** serves the public interest and does not seek financial profits.

LIKE HUMANS, WOLVES LIVE IN FAMILIES.

LIKE HUMANS, WOLVES NEED FRIENDS.

WOLVES DISPLAY A HIGH DEGREE OF INTELLIGENCE,
EXPRESSIVENESS AND OTHER CHARACTERISTICS THAT ENABLE THEM TO
MAINTAIN SOPHISTICATED, FAMILY-BASED SOCIAL BONDS. BUT WITHOUT FRIENDS
LOOKING OUT FOR THEM, THESE FAMILIES WILL BE BROKEN APART. TO LEARN HOW YOU
CAN BECOME A FRIEND AND HELP FRIENDS OF ANIMALS PROTECT ALASKA'S WOLVES,
PLEASE CALL 203.656.1522 OR VISIT WWW.FRIENDSOFANIMALS.ORG.
BE A FRIEND FOR LIFE.

Friends of Animals

Figure 12-9

Illustrating the Breadth of Nonprofit Marketing

Source: Reprinted by permission.

Although nonprofit organizations conduct exchanges, they do not have to be in the form of dollars for goods and services. Politicians request votes in exchange for promises of better government. The U.S. Postal Service (**http://www.usps.com**) wants greater use of ZIP codes in exchange for improved service and fewer rate hikes. The American Red Cross (**http://www.redcross.org**) seeks funds to help victims of disasters.

The prices charged by nonprofit organizations often have no relation to the cost or value of their services. The Girl Scouts of the USA (**http://www.girlscouts.org**) sells cookies to raise funds; only a small part of the price actually goes for the cookies. In contrast, the price of a chest X-ray at an overseas health clinic may be below cost or free.

Due to its unique attributes, marketing by nonprofit organizations rates a thorough discussion from a product-planning perspective. It is important that nonprofit organizations address the following:

> Not enough nonprofit organizations have a comprehensive approach to marketing. While many nonprofits perform one or more marketing functions, few have embraced a marketing approach to operations. People are in charge of many marketing tasks, but their marketing responsibilities are secondary to other priorities. Organizations have added marketing tasks, but envision marketing in narrow terms. A majority of those performing marketing came into their jobs without formal training. While low salaries are a problem in attracting top talent, the larger problem may be nonprofit leaders who do not appreciate marketing as a comprehensive process and are not fully committed to incorporating the marketing approach into their marketing strategies.[15]

Next, nonprofit marketing is examined in terms of a comparison with profit-oriented marketing, a classification system, and its extent in the economy. Three detailed examples are also presented.

12-6a Nonprofit Versus Profit-Oriented Marketing

A number of marketing similarities exist between nonprofit and profit-oriented firms. In today's uncertain and competitive arena, nonprofits must apply appropriate marketing concepts and strategies if they are to generate adequate support—financial and otherwise.

With both nonprofit and profit-oriented organizations, there is usually a choice among competing entities; the benefits provided by competitors differ; consumer segments may have distinct reasons for their choices; people are lured by the most desirable product positioning; and they are either satisfied or dissatisfied with performance. Figure 12-10 shows how a political candidate could seek various voter segments via a well-conceived marketing mix and careful product positioning (party platform, past record, and personal traits). This approach is similar to the one a profit-oriented firm would use.

Doesn't this message from the Dallas Symphony Orchestra (**http://www.dallassymphony.org**) sound like the approach a profit-oriented firm would take?

> At the Dallas Symphony, great music has always been our mission. Thousands of ticket buyers affirm this priority season after season. However, ticket sales only provide half of our operating budget. We depend upon your annual contributions to make up the difference. The symphony recognizes your generosity with priority service in everything from seat assignments to parking. Sign Up for SymphonEmail and get weekly updates, reviews, concert reminders, discounts, and special offers! As a SymphonEmail patron, you will have access to exclusive E-mail offers and priority ordering![16]

There are also some basic differences in marketing between nonprofit and profit-oriented organizations. They are highlighted in Table 12-1 and described next.

Nonprofit marketing includes organizations, people, places, and ideas, as well as goods and services. It is more apt to be involved with social programs and ideas than is

Nonprofit marketing has both similarities with and distinctions from profit-oriented marketing.

---

[15] Don Akchin, "Nonprofit Marketing: Just How Far Has It Come?" *Nonprofit World* (January-February 2001), p. 33.

[16] "About Us," http://www.dallassymphony.com/?crs=ms (April 30, 2006).

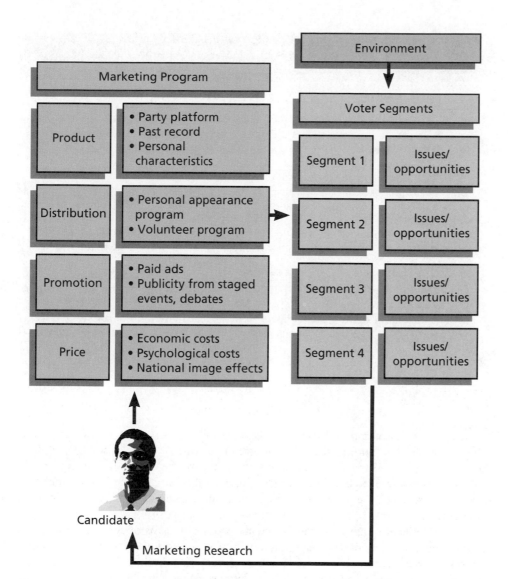

Figure 12-10

The Political Marketing Process

Source: Adapted by the authors from Phillip B. Niffenegger, "Strategies for Success from the Political Marketers," *Journal of Consumer Marketing,* Vol. 6 (Winter 1989), p. 46. Reprinted by permission of MCB University Press Ltd.

profit-oriented marketing. Examples are AIDS prevention, recycling, highway safety, family planning, and conservation. Using marketing to gain the acceptability of social ideas is referred to as *social marketing.* Two good Web sites on this topic are the Social Marketing Institute (**http://www.social-marketing.org**) and "The Social Marketing Concept" (**http://www.novartisfoundation.com/en/projects/access_health/leprosy/social_marketing/social_marketing.htm**).[17]

The nonprofit exchange process can include nonmonetary and monetary transactions. Nonmonetary transactions can be votes, volunteers' time, blood donations, and so forth. Monetary transactions can be contributions, magazine subscriptions, tuition, and so on. Some nonprofit marketing does not generate revenues in daily exchanges, relying instead on infrequent fundraising efforts. A successful marketing campaign may even lose money if services or goods are provided at less than cost. Operating budgets must be big enough to serve the number of anticipated clients, so none are poorly treated or turned away.

> Nonprofit marketing is broad in scope and frequently involved with **social marketing.**

---

[17] See also Carol L. Cone, Mark A. Feldman, and Alison T. DaSilva, "Causes and Effects," *Harvard Business Review,* Vol. 81 (July 2003), pp. 95-101; and Laura McDermott, Martine Stead, and Gerard Hastings, "What Is and What Is Not Social Marketing: The Challenge of Reviewing the Evidence," *Journal of Marketing Management,* Vol. 21 (July 2005), pp. 545-553,

Table 12-1	The Basic Differences Between Nonprofit and Profit-Oriented Marketing
Nonprofit Marketing	**Profit-Oriented Marketing**
1. Nonprofit marketing is concerned with organizations, people, places, and ideas, as well as goods and services.	1. Profit-oriented marketing is largely concerned with goods and services.
2. Exchanges may be nonmonetary or monetary.	2. Exchanges are generally monetary.
3. Objectives are more complex because success or failure cannot be measured strictly in financial terms.	3. Objectives are typically stated in terms of sales, profits, and recovery of cash.
4. The benefits of nonprofit services are often not related to consumer payments.	4. The benefits of profit-oriented marketing are usually related to consumer payments.
5. Nonprofit organizations may be expected or required to serve economically unfeasible market segments.	5. Profit-oriented organizations seek to serve only those market segments that are profitable.
6. Nonprofit organizations typically have two key target markets: clients and donors.	6. Profit-oriented organizations typically have one key target market: clients.

Goals may be complex because success or failure cannot be measured just in financial terms. A nonprofit might have this combination of goals: raise $250,000 from government grants, increase client usage, find a cure for a disease, change public attitudes, and raise $750,000 from private donors. Goals must include the number of clients to be served, the amount of service to be rendered, and the quality of service to be provided.

Consumer benefits may not be related to their payments.

The benefits of nonprofits may not be allotted on the basis of consumer payments. Only a small portion of the population contracts a disease, requires humanitarian services, visits a museum, uses a public library, or goes to a health clinic in a given year; yet, the general public pays to find cures, support fellow citizens, or otherwise assist nonprofit organizations. Many times, those who would benefit most from a nonprofit's activities may be the ones least apt to seek or use them. This occurs for libraries, health clinics, remedial programs, and others. With profit-oriented firms, benefits are usually distributed equitably, based on consumers' direct payments in exchange for goods or services.

Nonprofits may be expected, or required, to serve markets that profit-oriented firms find uneconomical. The U.S. Postal Service must have rural post offices, and Amtrak must offer passenger rail service over some sparsely populated areas. This may give profit-oriented firms an edge; they can concentrate on the most lucrative market segments.

Nonprofit organizations must satisfy clients and donors.

Profit-oriented firms have one major target market—clients (customers)—to whom they offer goods and services and from whom they receive payment; a typical nonprofit has two: *clients*—to whom it offers membership, elected officials, locations, ideas, goods, and services; and *donors*—from whom it receives resources (which may be time from volunteers or money from foundations and individuals). There may be little overlap between clients and donors.

Private nonprofits have been granted many legal advantages. These include tax-deductible contributions, exemptions from most sales and real-estate taxes, and reduced postal rates. Profit-oriented firms often feel they are harmed competitively by these legal provisions.

Ethical Issues in Marketing

Improving the Integrity of Bankers

Roger Steare, a business ethics consultant, and Craig Smith, dean at the London Business School, are attempting to increase the ethical standards of bankers. As part of his training program, Steare administers Giotto, an ethics test, to bankers. Although the results of the test are confidential, they are used to make bankers aware of some of the ethical pitfalls they face on an everyday basis. Steare states that the average score for bankers on this test is 70, versus 84 for compliance officers and 77 for human resource managers.

As part of Smith's training program, bankers are shown photographs of the prison cell that was occupied by Martha Stewart. Smith also discusses a controversial trade by Citibank as an example for bankers specializing in fixed-income securities. As Smith says, "In compliance training, everyone is taught what's legal, but most people don't even bother to ask what's right."

Both Steare and Smith emphasize ethical practices with their banker students by outlining procedures for them to reach ethical decisions. Part of the training program involves empathizing with other parties, analyzing the desired consequences, and considering their obligations. Steare says that he cannot teach people to do the right thing, but he can teach them to ask the right questions. Attendees are given these questions on a small card; many attendees still carry these cards months after their training.

Source: Based on material in Sarah Butcher, "Bankers' Ethics Put to the Test," *eFinancialNews* (March 7, 2005).

12-6b   Classifying Nonprofit Marketing

Nonprofits may be classified in terms of tangibility, structure, goals, and constituency. This is shown in Figure 12-11. An organization would be classed by a combination of factors. For example, postage stamps for collectors are tangible, distributed by the federal government, intended to reduce the Postal Service's deficit, and aimed at the general public.

Nonprofit marketing involves organizations, people, places, ideas, goods, and services. Organizations include foundations, universities, religious institutions, and government; people include politicians and volunteers; places include resorts and industrial centers; ideas include family planning and patriotism; goods include postage stamps and professional journals; and services include medical care and education.

Nonprofits may have a government-affiliated, private, or cooperative structure. The federal government markets military service to recruits, postal services, and other goods and services; state governments market universities and employment services; local governments market colleges, libraries, and sports arenas. Government marketing is also used to increase voter registration, secure bond approval, and gain passage of school budgets. Private organizations market hospitals, charities, social services, and other goods and services. They also use marketing to increase membership and donations. Cooperative organizations (such as the Better Business Bureau, **http://www.bbb.org**) aid consumers and/or businesses; success depends on their securing a large membership base and efficiently performing functions.

Overall nonprofit marketing goals may be divided into health (increase the number of nonsmokers), education (increase usage of the local library), welfare (list more job openings at a state employment office), and other (increase membership in the Boy Scouts) components.

Nonprofits usually require the support of both clients/users and donors. Clients/users are interested in the direct benefits they get by participating in an organization, such as their improved health, education, or welfare. Donors are concerned about the efficiency of operations, success rates, the availability of goods and services, and the recognition of their contributions. For each constituency, an organization must pinpoint its target market. For example, the League of Women Voters (**http://www.lwv.org**) might focus on unregistered voters during an enrollment drive and seek funds from corporate foundations. Figure 12-12 shows some of the differing interests between clients and donors.

> The classification of nonprofit marketing may be based on tangibility, structure, goal, and constituency.

There are millions of
nonprofit organizations in
the world.

Figure 12-11

**A Classification System for
Nonprofit Marketing**

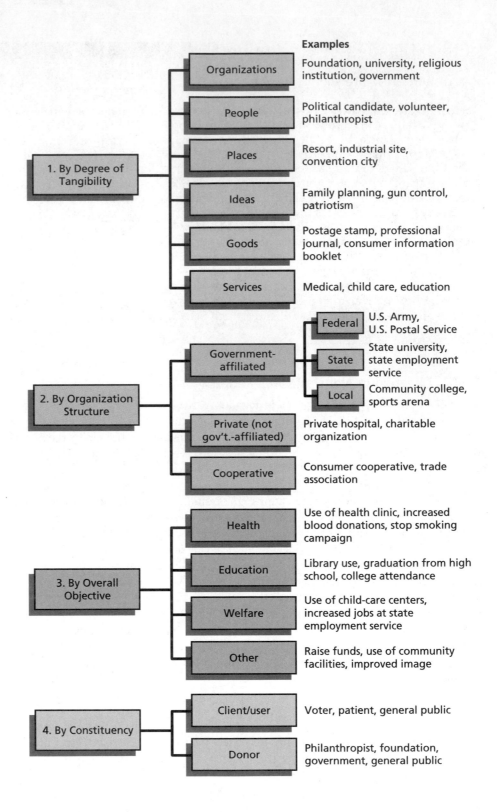

Examples

Organizations — Foundation, university, religious institution, government

People — Political candidate, volunteer, philanthropist

Places — Resort, industrial site, convention city

Ideas — Family planning, gun control, patriotism

Goods — Postage stamp, professional journal, consumer information booklet

Services — Medical, child care, education

1. By Degree of Tangibility

Government-affiliated
- **Federal** — U.S. Army, U.S. Postal Service
- **State** — State university, state employment service
- **Local** — Community college, sports arena

Private (not gov't.-affiliated) — Private hospital, charitable organization

Cooperative — Consumer cooperative, trade association

2. By Organization Structure

Health — Use of health clinic, increased blood donations, stop smoking campaign

Education — Library use, graduation from high school, college attendance

Welfare — Use of child-care centers, increased jobs at state employment service

Other — Raise funds, use of community facilities, improved image

3. By Overall Objective

Client/user — Voter, patient, general public

Donor — Philanthropist, foundation, government, general public

4. By Constituency

12-6c The Extent of Nonprofit Marketing in the Economy

Worldwide, millions of organizations and individuals engage in nonprofit marketing. There are about 1.5 million U.S. nonprofits (30,000 of which are national or international in scope) with millions of paid employees. They annually generate revenues exceeding $2 trillion and receive $250 billion in private contributions, three-quarters from individual donors. Eighty-five percent of U.S. households make a donation each

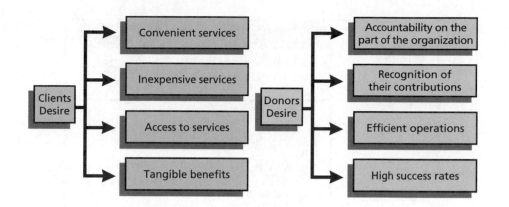

Figure 12-12

Clients Versus Donors

year. The U.S. mass media provide billions of dollars in free advertising space for public-service messages. Half of U.S. adults do some form of volunteer work.[18]

This further demonstrates the scope of nonprofit marketing:

- The American Foundation for Aids Research (amFAR) is just one of the thousands of nonprofit organizations that operates an Internet site (**http://www.amfar.org**). Its site describes the organization, encourages online contributions, and provides a treatment directory.
- Many countries use tourism boards to market foreign travel to those nations. India's Ministry of Tourism (**http://www.tourisminindia.com**) actively promotes visits to that country. Visit Britain (**http://www.visitbritain.com**) works with airlines, hotels, and credit-card firms to create and publicize special offers. The German National Tourist Board (**http://www.germany-tourism.de**) has an elaborate Web site with colorful information on cities throughout the country.
- Newman's Own (**http://www.newmansown.com**), a nonprofit company founded by actor Paul Newman and his business partner A. E. Hotchner, makes and markets salad dressing, popcorn, lemonade, and other food products. All after-tax profits are donated to charities. Since the company's founding in the early 1980s, it has contributed more than $200 million to thousands of charitable groups worldwide.

12-6d Illustrations of Nonprofit Marketing

This section looks at marketing by the U.S. Postal Service (USPS), colleges and universities, and the United Way. The activities differ due to the level of tangibility, structure, objectives, and constituencies.

The U.S. Postal Service (**http://www.usps.com**) is an independent federal agency with 710,000 career employees and yearly revenues of nearly $70 billion. It delivers to more than 142 million homes, offices, and post office boxes, and operates 38,000 post offices.[19] Competition is intense, and it must deliver all mail—no matter how uneconomical. The Postal Service often runs an annual deficit, and all rate increases must be approved by a Board of Governors.

To protect itself against competitors and stimulate consumer demand, the Postal Service has enacted a strong marketing program—comprising a mix of continuing and

---

[18] National Center for Charitable Statistics, "Statistics," **http://nccsdataweb.urban.org/FAQ/index.php?category=44** (May 7, 2006); "Giving USA," **http://www.aafrc.org** (May 7, 2006); Robyn Greenspan, "Direct Mail Best for Charity Awareness," **http://cyberatlas.internet.com/markets/advertising/print/0,,5941_3064601,00.html** (August 15, 2003); and authors' estimates.

[19] "Postal Facts 2005," **http://www.usps.com/communications/organization/postalfacts2005.pdf**.

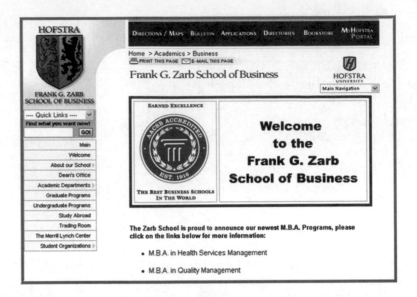

Figure 12-13

The Marketing of Higher Education

Source: Reprinted by permission.

new offerings and extensive advertising. With Express Mail, packages and letters are delivered overnight; the items can be dropped at special boxes or picked up for a small fee. Priority Mail is an inexpensive service, with two- to three-day average delivery anywhere in the United States. ZIP + 4 is an improved ZIP-code service that offers cost savings for both the Postal Service and its business customers, but it has not been used by customers as much as the Postal Service desires. The Postal Service has an agreement with Federal Express for the latter to use its planes to ship USPS Express and Priority Mail.

The Postal Service does hundreds of millions of dollars of business in commemorative stamps each year. It has featured celebrities such as Elvis Presley, sports heroes such as Jackie Robinson, and social marketing causes such as breast cancer awareness. Many post offices now sell hand-held scales, padded envelopes for packages, air mail markers, and devices to adhere stamps to envelopes. Self-service stamp vending machines can be found in shopping centers. Some post offices are "postal stores"—with interior space divided into two sections, one for specialized postal services and one for retail sales. The retail part of the stores carries stamps, envelopes, packing material, posters, T-shirts, coffee mugs, pen-and-pencil sets, and earrings. The Postal Service's annual ad budget is $75 million to $100 million, with large sums going to Express Mail and Priority Mail, direct-mail ads for business accounts, and commemorative stamps.

Colleges and universities know that population trends in many industrialized nations (such as smaller households and a relatively low birthrate) affect their enrollment pools, especially with the number of 18- to 24-year-olds falling in some areas. From 1977 to 1991, the number of U.S. high school graduates fell steadily and did not begin to rise until 1992. Nonetheless, overall U.S. college enrollment has gone up only 1.4 percent annually since 1992. Thus, new markets are being targeted and marketing strategies are being used by more educational institutions than ever before.

Many schools actively seek nontraditional students: Today, 40 percent of U.S. college students attend part-time; and more than one-sixth of college students are at least 35 years old. In addition, millions of people are now in adult higher-education programs at U.S. colleges, universities, and private firms.[20] The adult market needs convenient sites and classes not infringing on work hours. At New York University, the School of Continuing and Professional Studies (**http://www.scps.nyu.edu**) offers 2,500 courses to tens of thousands of students each year.

[20] U.S. Department of Education, National Center for Education Statistics, *Projections of Education Statistics to 2014,* **http://nces.ed.gov/pubs2005/2005074.pdf** (September 2005).

Traditional students are also being sought vigorously. Schools often spend several hundred dollars—or more—on recruitment efforts for each new student who enrolls. Many buy direct-mailing lists of prospective students from the Educational Testing Service (**http://www.ets.org**), which administers college board examinations. A number of colleges distribute recruiting films, videocassettes, or CDs—which cost tens of thousands of dollars (and up) to produce—to high schools. And the vast majority of schools have a significant presence on the Web.

The heightened use of marketing is not limited to poor- or average-quality schools. For example, New York's Hofstra University has an award-winning Web site (**http://www.hofstra.edu**), as highlighted in Figure 12-13. Bryn Mawr, Duke, Harvard, and Stanford are among the huge number of colleges and universities that let prospective students submit applications via the Internet through FastWeb (**http://www.fastweb.com**) software, which enables applicants to enter standardized data just once and add customized information for each college. Johns Hopkins University (**http://www.jhu.edu**) in Maryland offers an online "virtual" college tour: "Our virtual campus tour allows you to get a feel for our campus through photos, descriptions, and 360 degree QuickTime VR panoramic views. Click here to start our virtual tour."[21]

The United Way of America (**http://national.unitedway.org**), with its 1,350 affiliated local organizations and annual fundraising of $4 billion, is one of the leading nonprofit organizations in the world. It supports such groups as Boys and Girls Clubs of America (**http://www.bgca.org**), centers for children with learning disabilities, immigration centers, and mental health and drug rehabilitation programs. Most United Way donations come from deductions made from worker paychecks. In contrast, the Salvation Army USA (**http://www.salvationarmyusa.org**) receives most donations from non-workplace sources. It gets $1.5 billion in yearly contributions (of money and "donations in kind"), and earns hundreds of millions of dollars more from its stores.[22]

For years, the United Way has had an outstanding marketing orientation. It is well known for its long-run association with the National Football League (**http://national.unitedway.org/nfl**) and the touching ads that appear during each game. Employees in affiliated chapters are trained in marketing. Periodic conferences on business topics are held. Affiliated chapters present United Way videos, films, and slide-show programs to potential contributors and volunteers. The United Way even published a book, *Competitive Marketing*, so other charitable groups could learn from its techniques.

Web Sites You Can Use

Service firms cover a very broad spectrum of businesses. Here is a sampling of them—from insurance to PC-based phone calls:

- Aetna (**http://www.aetna.com**)
- H&R Block (**http://www.handrblock.com**)
- Blockbuster Inc. (**http://www.blockbuster.com**)
- Century 21 Real Estate (**http://www.century21.com**)
- Choice Hotels International (**http://www.hotelchoice.com**)
- Club Med (**http://www.clubmed.com**)
- Cort Furniture Rental (**http://www.cort1.com**)
- Jenny Craig (**http://www.jennycraig.com**)
- Discovery Communications (**http://www.discovery.com**)
- ESPN (**http://espn.go.com**)
- E* Trade (**http://www.etrade.com**)
- FedEx Kinko's (**http://www.fedex.com/us/officeprint/main**)
- FTD (**http://www.ftd.com**)
- Hertz (**http://www.hertz.com**)
- Hilton (**http://www.hilton.com**)
- InterContinental Hotels Group (**http://www.ichotelsgroup.com**)
- Jazzercise (**http://www.jazzercise.com**)
- Knott's Berry Farm (**http://www.knotts.com**)
- Madison Square Garden (**http://www.thegarden.com**)
- MapQuest (**http://www.mapquest.com**)

[21] "Virtual Tour," **http://apply.jhu.edu/visit/tour.html** (March 30, 2006).

[22] "About United Way," **http://national.unitedway.org/about/about.cfm** (April 2, 2006); and "Annual Reports," **http://www.salvationarmyusa.org** (April 2, 2006)

- Marriott (http://www.marriott.com)
- MasterCard (http://www.mastercard.com)
- Prudential (http://www.prudential.com)
- Schwab (http://www.charlesschwab.com)
- ServiceMagic (http://www.servicemagic.com)
- Sheraton (http://www.starwood.com/sheraton)
- Sir Speedy (http://www.sirspeedy.com)
- Supercuts (http://www.supercuts.com)

- Thrifty Car Rental (http://www.thrifty.com)
- Ticketmaster.com (http://www.ticketmaster.com)
- Travelocity (http://www.travelocity.com)
- Universal Studios (http://www.universalstudios.com)
- Vindigo (http://www.vindigo.com)
- Visa (http://www.usa.visa.com)
- visitalk.com (http://www.visitalk.com)

Summary

1. *To examine the scope of goods and services, and explain how goods and services may be categorized* Goods marketing encompasses the sales of durable and nondurable physical products; service marketing involves goods rental, goods alteration and maintenance/repair, and personal services. In the United States, the revenues from nondurable goods are higher than those from durable goods—and final consumers spend several times as much on nondurables as on durables. Services account for a very large share of the GDP in industrialized nations, and account for a smaller share in developing and less-developed nations. The United States has the world's largest service economy. Both final consumer and business services have seen significant growth in recent years. The scope of services is sometimes underestimated due to the hidden service sector.

With a goods/service continuum, products can be positioned from pure goods to goods/services combinations to pure services. Much can be learned by studying the continuum, including its use for final consumer and b-to-b products, the presence of unique marketing opportunities, and the changing relationship between sellers and buyers as pure goods become goods/services combinations. Both goods- and services-oriented firms need to identify core and peripheral services.

Goods can be classed by market, product durability, value added, company goal, regulation, channel length, and customer contact. Services can be classed by market, tangibility, service provider skill, service provider goals, regulation, labor intensiveness, and customer contact. A firm would be categorized on the basis of a combination of these factors.

2. *To discuss the special considerations in the marketing of services* Services are generally less tangible, more perishable, less separable from their provider, and more variable in quality than goods that are sold. The effect of these factors is greatest for personal services. Service firms need to enact strategies that enable consumers to perceive their offerings more tangibly, make their offerings less perishable, encourage consumers to seek them out but enable multiple employees to be viewed as competent, and make performance as efficient and consistent as possible. Such approaches as the industrialization of services, the service blueprint, and gap analysis enable service firms to better devise and implement marketing plans by improving their performance.

3. *To look at the use of marketing by goods versus services firms and provide illustrations of service marketing* Many service firms have lagged behind manufacturers in marketing because of their small size, the larger geographic coverage of goods-oriented companies, their technical emphasis, less competition and the lack of need for marketing, the high esteem of consumers for certain service providers, past bans on advertising, a dislike of marketing by some service professionals, and the reluctance of some manufacturers to view services as profit centers. Yet, for a number of reasons, this has been changing, and the marketing of services is now expanding greatly.

The marketing practices of hotels, repair and servicing firms, and lawyers are highlighted.

4. *To distinguish between nonprofit and profit-oriented marketing* Nonprofit marketing is conducted by organizations and individuals operating for the public good or to foster a cause and not for financial profit. It is both similar to and different from profit-oriented marketing. These are some differences: Nonprofit marketing is more apt to involve organizations, people, places, and ideas. Nonprofit exchanges do not have to involve money, and goals can be hard to formulate. The benefits of nonprofit firms may be distributed unequally, and economically unfeasible segments may have to be served. Two target markets must be satisfied by nonprofit organizations: clients and donors.

5. *To describe a classification system for nonprofit marketing, the role of nonprofit marketing in the economy, and applications of nonprofit marketing* Nonprofits can be classed on the basis of tangibility, organization structure, objectives, and constituency. A nonprofit would be categorized by a combination of these factors.

Worldwide, millions of organizations and individuals are engaged in nonprofit marketing. There are 1.5 million nonprofit organizations in the United States, generating greater than $2 trillion in annual revenues (including contributions). Their marketing efforts have increased greatly in a short time, and they play a key role in the U.S. economy. The marketing practices of the U.S. Postal Service, colleges and universities, and the United Way are highlighted.

Key Terms

goods marketing (p. 363)	goods/services continuum (p. 364)	service blueprint (p. 375)
durable goods (p. 363)	core services (p. 365)	service gap (p. 375)
nondurable goods (p. 363)	peripheral services (p. 365)	nonprofit marketing (p. 379)
service marketing (p. 363)	intangibility of services (p. 370)	social marketing (p. 381)
rented-goods services (p. 363)	perishability of services (p. 370)	clients (p. 382)
owned-goods services (p. 363)	inseparability of services (p. 370)	donors (p. 382)
nongoods services (p. 363)	variability in service quality (p. 370)	
hidden service sector (p. 364)	industrialization of services (p. 373)	

Review Questions

1. Differentiate among rented-goods services, owned-goods services, and nongoods services.
2. What is a goods/services continuum? Why should firms be aware of this concept?
3. Distinguish between core and peripheral services. What is the marketing role of each?
4. How can a service be positioned more tangibly?
5. Describe how hard, soft, and hybrid technologies may be used to industrialize services.
6. What are some of the similarities and differences involved in the marketing efforts used by nonprofit and profit-oriented organizations?
7. Discuss the factors that may be used to classify nonprofit marketing.
8. How do the goals of clients and donors differ?

Discussion Questions

1. Present a goods/services continuum related to golf. Discuss the implications of this continuum for a firm interested in developing a golf-related business.
2. State several ways that a university could attract more students during the regular academic year.
3. Draw and discuss a service blueprint for an insurance broker dealing with life insurance for people ages 50 and over.
4. Discuss several innovative fundraising programs that could be used by the ALS Association (**http://www.alsa.org**), the "only national not-for-profit voluntary health organization dedicated solely to the fight against Amyotrophic Lateral Sclerosis (often called Lou Gehrig's disease)."

Web Exercise

Entrepreneur (**http://www.entrepreneur.com**) provides "solutions for growing businesses." Read "Service with a Smile: Not Sure How to Market Your Service Business? Focus on These 5 Tips for Bringing in New Customers, and You'll Be Glad You Did" (**http://www.entrepreneur.com/article/0,4621,320971,00.html**). What are the most important lessons of this article? Why?

Practice Quiz

1. Which of the following is *not* among the leading service industries in terms of revenues generated?
   a. Housing
   b. Medical care
   c. Leisure activities
   d. Transportation services

2. Which of the following is *not* part of the hidden service sector?
   a. Goods sales
   b. Delivery
   c. Repair
   d. Maintenance

3. Peripheral services
   a. are the basic services that companies provide for their customers.
   b. can be used to create and sustain a competitive advantage.
   c. decrease a service firm's investment.
   d. combine hard and soft technologies.

4. Which type of good is characterized by a high level of price competition?
   a. Low-value-added
   b. Nondurable
   c. Durable
   d. High-value-added

5. When services are classified by their degree of customer contact, they are based on
   a. professionals or nonprofessionals.
   b. machinery or people.
   c. final consumers or industrial consumers.
   d. technical or interpersonal skill training.

6. To overcome high costs and low reliability, many firms involved in services rely on
   a. social marketing.
   b. industrialization of services.
   c. peripheral services.
   d. hidden service sectors.

7. An example of a soft technology is the
   a. electronic credit authorization system.
   b. muffler repair shop.
   c. parking service at a hotel.
   d. pre-packaged vacation tour.

8. Which of the following is *not* a reason why service firms have typically lagged behind manufacturing firms in developing marketing plans?
   a. Service firms stress technical expertise.
   b. Many firms are so small that marketing specialists cannot be used.
   c. The customers of service firms tend to reject any marketing efforts.
   d. Strict licensing provisions sometimes limit competition and the need for marketing.

9. Which of the following is *not* a result of the Supreme Court decision that allows attorneys to advertise their services?
   a. The spread of legal clinics
   b. The decline of legal services marketing
   c. The growth of prepaid legal services
   d. The availability of services to new consumer groups

10. Which of the following is often *not* an aspect of nonprofit marketing?
    a. Being in the public interest
    b. Spreading social ideas
    c. Fostering a cause
    d. Relating pricing to costs

11. A municipality developed an advertising campaign designed to increase recycling of newspapers by homeowners. This illustrates
    a. a core service.
    b. the industrialization of services.
    c. social marketing.
    d. service variability.

12. Donors
    a. are those for whom nonprofit organizations provide services.
    b. are those from whom nonprofit organizations receive resources.
    c. do not engage in exchanges with nonprofit organizations.
    d. are most likely to benefit from nonprofit organizations' activities.

13. Which group is most likely to be either a client or a donor to the American Red Cross?
    a. Hurricane victims
    b. Millionaires
    c. Private foundations
    d. Public schools

14. College and university marketing
    a. actively seeks adults.
    b. ignores traditional students.
    c. is confined to average-quality institutions.
    d. is on the decline.

15. Which of the following has published a marketing-oriented book to enable other charitable groups to learn from it?
    a. The U.S. Postal Service
    b. The Girl Scouts
    c. The United Way
    d. The Red Cross

For the answers to these questions, please visit the online site for this book at **http://www.atomicdog.com.**

Chapter 13

Conceiving, Developing, and Managing Products

DuPont (http://www.dupont.com) is the second-largest U.S. chemical manufacturer (after Dow Chemical). DuPont manufactures a variety of products, including automotive finishes, crop-protection chemicals, electronic materials, packaging materials, safety and security materials, and industrial chemicals.

DuPont began in 1802 with a gunpowder plant based in Delaware. Within 10 years, the plant was the largest of its kind in the United States. DuPont added dynamite and nitroglycerine in 1880, guncotton (an explosive substance) in 1892, and smokeless powder in 1894. As of 1906, DuPont controlled most of the market for explosives in the United States. After World War I, DuPont diversified into paints, plastics, and dyes. DuPont's rich history of product innovation continued with its production of neoprene synthetic rubber in 1931, Lucite in 1937, nylon in 1938, Teflon in 1938, Dacron in 1945, and Kevlar in 1965. Among DuPont's current projects are the building of a biorefinery to produce chemicals and biofuels from corn and corn husks and the production of fish food and chemicals from methane gas. In 2004 alone, DuPont invested $1.2 billion in research and development—resulting in 800 new patents.

DuPont's innovations can be classified as either scientific (where the impetus for a new product is based on a laboratory finding) or market-driven (where a new product is based on consumer input that identifies unmet needs). Although scientific innovations can become major marketing successes (such as nylon, Teflon, and Dacron), DuPont must clearly demonstrate the benefits to consumers. Because marketing innovations are often easier to understand by consumers, they may require lower marketing costs.

Let's look at two recent DuPont marketing-based innovations. In cooperation with Procter & Gamble (http://www.pg.com), Dupont developed a water-soluble pouch that combines a powdered dishwasher detergent and a liquid grease cutter in one package. The pouch is used for Cascade's 2 in 1 ActionPac dishwasher detergent. Dupont devised another new bag for Ocean Spray (http://www.oceanspray.com). The bag is divided into two pieces—one with syrup, the other with a juice concentrate. When the bag is squeezed by a consumer, the two liquids form a combination juice flavor such as cranberry-apple.[1]

Next, we will study how new products are developed, the factors causing rapid or slow growth for new products, how to manage mature products, and what to do when existing products falter.

Chapter Objectives

1. To study how products are created and managed, with an emphasis on the product life cycle
2. To detail the importance of new products and describe why new products fail
3. To present the stages in the new-product planning process
4. To analyze the growth and maturity of products, including the adoption process, the diffusion process, and extension strategies
5. To examine product deletion decisions and strategies

---

[1] Various company and other sources.

13-1 OVERVIEW

In this chapter, we discuss the conception and development of new products, the management of growing and mature products through their life cycle, and the termination of undesirable products.

> Product planning involves new and existing products.

Though any product combines tangible and intangible features to satisfy consumer needs, a *new product* involves a modification of an existing product or an innovation the consumer perceives as meaningful. To succeed, a new product must have desirable attributes, be unique, and have its features communicated to consumers. Marketing support is necessary.

Modifications are alterations in or extensions of a firm's existing products and include new models, styles, colors, features, and brands. *Minor innovations* are items not previously marketed by a firm that have been marketed by others (such as the Sony personal computer). *Major innovations* are items not previously sold by any firm (such as the first cell telephone). If a firm works with major innovations, the costs, risks, and time required for profitability all rise. Overall, most new products are modifications; few are major innovations.

> New products may be modifications, minor innovations, or major innovations.

A company may conceive and develop new products by itself or purchase them from another firm. With the latter, a company may buy a firm, buy a specific product, or sign a licensing agreement (whereby it pays an inventor a royalty fee based on sales). Acquisitions may reduce risks and time demands, but they rely on outsiders for innovations and may require large investments.

There is usually strong sales growth early in a product's life, as more people purchase and repurchase. This is an exciting time; and if a product is popular, it can last for quite a while. Next, the market becomes more saturated and competition intensifies. At that point, a firm can keep sales high by adding features that provide convenience and durability, using new materials in construction, offering more models, stressing new packaging, and/or adding customer services. It can also reposition a product, enter untapped geographic markets, demonstrate new uses, offer new brands, set lower prices, use new media, and/or appeal to new segments. For many products, at some point down the road, firms must decide whether those items have outlived their usefulness and should be dropped.

13-2 THE PRODUCT LIFE CYCLE

The *product life cycle* is a concept that seeks to describe a product's sales, competitors, profits, customers, and marketing emphasis from its beginning until it is removed from the market.[2]

> The product life cycle describes each stage in a product's life.

From a product-planning perspective, the product life cycle is valuable for these reasons: (1) Some product lives are shorter than ever. (2) New products often require high marketing and other investments. (3) An understanding of the concept lets a firm anticipate changes in consumer tastes, competition, and support from resellers and adjust its marketing plan accordingly. (4) The concept enables a firm to consider the product mix it should offer; many firms seek a *balanced product portfolio*, whereby a combination of new, growing, and mature products is maintained.

> Companies often desire a balanced product portfolio.

The life-cycle concept can be applied to a product class (watches), a product form (quartz watches), and a brand (Seiko quartz watches). Product forms generally follow the traditional life cycle more faithfully than product classes or brands.

Product life cycles may vary a lot, both in length of time and shape. See Figure 13-1. A *traditional cycle* has distinct periods of introduction, growth, maturity, and decline.

[2] For good overview articles, see Steven Haines, "Determining Where a Product Stands on the Product Life Cycle Curve," http://www.pdma.org/visions/apr05/life.html (April 2005); and Youngme Moon, "Break Free from the Product Life Cycle," *Harvard Business Review*, Vol. 83 (May 2005), pp. 86–94.

Figure 13-1

Selected Product Life-Cycle Patterns

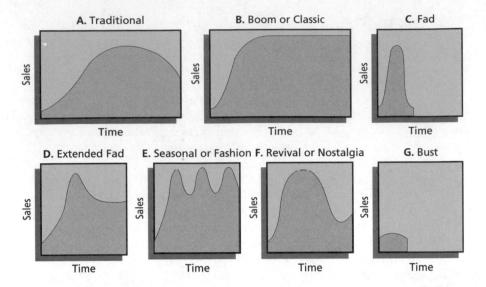

A *boom*, or *classic*, *cycle* describes a very popular product that sells well for a long time. A *fad cycle* represents a product with quick popularity and a sudden decline. An *extended fad* is like a fad, but residual sales continue at a lower level than earlier sales. A *seasonal*, or *fashion*, *cycle* results if a product sells well in nonconsecutive periods. With a *revival*, or *nostalgia*, *cycle*, a seemingly obsolete product achieves new popularity. A *bust cycle* occurs for a product that fails.

13-2a   Stages of the Traditional Product Life Cycle

The stages and characteristics of the traditional product life cycle are shown in Figure 13-2 and Table 13-1, which both refer to total industry performance during the cycle. The performance of an individual firm may vary from that of the industry, depending on its specific goals, resources, marketing plans, location, competitive environment, level of success, and stage of entry.

During the ***introduction stage of the product life cycle***, a new product is introduced to the marketplace and the goal is to generate customer interest. The rate of sales growth depends on a product's newness and desirability. Generally, a product modification gains sales faster than a major innovation. Only one or two firms have entered the market, and competition is minimal. Losses occur due to high production and marketing costs; and cash flow is poor. Initial customers are innovators who are willing to take risks, can afford to take them, and such as the status of buying first. Because one or two firms dominate and costs are high, only one or a few basic product models are sold. For a routine item such as a new cereal, distribution is extensive. For a luxury item like a new boat, distribution is limited. Promotion must be informative, and samples may be desirable. Depending on the product and target market, a firm may start with a high status price or low mass-market price.

In the ***growth stage of the product life cycle***, a new product gains wider consumer acceptance, and the marketing goal is to expand distribution and the range of available product alternatives. Industry sales increase rapidly as a few more firms enter a highly profitable market that has substantial potential. Total and unit profits are high because an affluent (resourceful) mass market buys distinctive products from a limited group of firms and is willing to pay for them. To accommodate the growing market, modified versions of basic models are offered, distribution is expanded, persuasive mass advertising is utilized, and a range of prices is available.

During the ***maturity stage of the product life cycle***, a product's sales growth levels off and firms try to maintain a differential advantage (such as a lower price, improved features, or extended warranty) for as long as possible. Industry sales stabilize as the

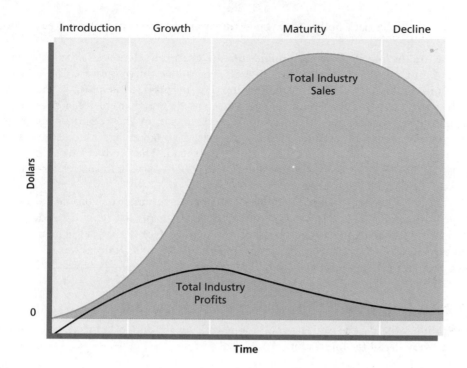

Figure 13-2

The Traditional Product Life Cycle

market becomes saturated and many firms enter to appeal to the still sizable demand. Competition is at its highest. Thus, total industry and unit profits drop because discounting is popular. The average-income mass market makes purchases. A full product

Table 13-1 The Characteristics of the Traditional Product Life Cycle

	Stage in Life Cycle			
Characteristics	**Introduction**	**Growth**	**Maturity**	**Decline**
Marketing goal	Attract innovators and opinion leaders to new product	Expand distribution and product line	Maintain differential advantage as long as possible	(a) Cut back, (b) revive, or (c) terminate
Industry sales	Increasing	Rapidly increasing	Stable	Decreasing
Competition	None or small	Some	Substantial	Limited
Industry profits	Negative	Increasing	Decreasing	Decreasing
Customers	Innovators	Resourceful mass market	Mass market	Laggards
Product mix	One or a few basic models	Expanding line	Full product line	Best-sellers
Distribution	Depends on product	Rising number of outlets/ distributors	Greatest number of outlets/ distributors	Decreasing number of outlets/ distributors
Promotion	Informative	Persuasive	Competitive	Informative
Pricing	Depends on product	Greater price range	Full line of prices	Selected prices

line is available at many outlets (or by many distributors) and at many prices. Promotion is very competitive.

At the ***decline stage of the product life cycle***, a product's sales fall as substitutes enter the market or consumers lose interest. Firms have three options. They can cut back on marketing, thus reducing the number of product items they make, the outlets they sell through, and the promotion used; they can revive a product by repositioning, repackaging, or otherwise remarketing it; or they can drop the product. As industry sales decline, many firms exit the market because customers are fewer and, as a group, they have less money to spend. The product mix emphasizes best-sellers, selected outlets (distributors) and prices, and informative promotion stressing availability and price.

The bulky, electric-powered portable calculator is an example of a product form that moved through the life cycle. It went from an exclusive, expensive item to a widespread, moderately priced item to a mass-marketed, inexpensive item to an obsolete item. Today, earlier versions of the calculator have been replaced by technologically advanced forms—such as credit-card sized, solar-powered calculators.

> **In decline**, firms reduce marketing, revive a product, or drop it.

13-2b Evaluating the Product Life-Cycle Concept

The product life cycle provides a good framework for product planning; but, it has not proven very useful for forecasting:

- The stages, time span, and shape of a cycle (such as flat, erratic, or sharply inclined) vary by product.
- The economy, inflation, consumer lifestyles, and other external factors may shorten or lengthen a product's life cycle.
- A firm may do better or worse than the industry "average" at any stage in the cycle. An industry's being in the growth stage for a product does not mean success for every firm in the market, nor does its being in the decline stage for a product necessarily mean lower sales for every firm.
- A firm may not only be able to manage a product life cycle, it may also be able to extend it or reverse a decline. Effective marketing may lure a new market segment, find a new product use, or foster better reseller support.
- Many firms may engage in a ***self-fulfilling prophecy***, whereby they predict falling sales and then ensure this by reducing or removing marketing support. See Figure 13-3. With proper marketing, some products might not fail.

> A **self-fulfilling prophecy** may occur when a firm reduces marketing.

Figure 13-3

A Self-Fulfilling Prophecy

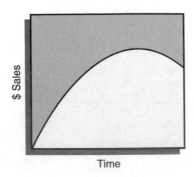

1. A company observes that one of its product's sales are declining.

2. By withdrawing marketing support, the company ensures that sales will fall off drastically.

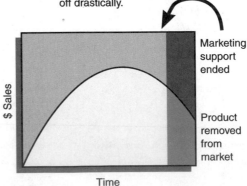

Marketing support ended

Product removed from market

13-3 THE IMPORTANCE OF NEW PRODUCTS

A firm's product policy should be future-oriented and recognize that products, no matter how successful, tend to be mortal—they usually cannot sustain peak sales and profits indefinitely. So, product line additions and replacements should be constantly planned and a balanced product portfolio pursued by both large and small firms. Consider these recent remarks by General Electric's (**http://www.ge.com**) chief executive: "We need to be focused on where customers are going. We should be playing into major demographic trends and the needs of our customers. We want to make it O.K. to take risks and do things that aren't just going to [produce results] this quarter. We're working on a whole new set of leadership traits: decisiveness, imagination and courage, inclusiveness, and domain expertise. We're leaving a period where global economic growth of the developed world was pretty robust. [Traditional] professional management isn't going to give you the kind of growth you need in a slow-growth world."[3]

Introducing new products is important for several reasons. Desirable differential advantages can be attained. Consider the case of the Swiffer (**http://www.swiffer.net**) line of dusters and mops:

> New products offer differential advantages.

> The CarpetFlick, hitting stores just six years after the original Swiffer Sweeper made its debut, is the seventh Swiffer product, joining the "wet jet" mop, the duster, and others in what's considered likely to eventually become a billion-dollar brand for P&G. And Swiffers have also become part of American pop culture. They have shown up everywhere from the cover of *Rolling Stone* to a *Saturday Night Live* "Swiffer Sleepers" spoof, and on a range of other TV shows. "When products hit that kind of status, it's generally because they've fulfilled a unique need for consumers and it really takes off," said a consumer goods specialist with the Kurt Salmon Associates consulting firm. Swiffer is innovative and easy to use; and it has "penetrated across all segments and demographics." Small children can use them and like to play with them, young people use them for inexpensive, quick clean-ups, active families love the convenience, and seniors find them easy on the back.[4]

New products may be needed for continued growth. That is why ESPN created the ESPN Zone (**http://www.espnzone.com**) restaurant chain to capitalize on the cable network's strong brand loyalty among viewers: "ESPN Zone includes several Sports Bars and Restaurants, sport arcade games, and ESPN merchandise to provide an entertainment family fun center and the ultimate sports dining experiences."[5] It is also why Apple recently introduced the iPod Nano (**http://www.apple.com/ipodnano**), a smaller version of the original iPod. See Figure 13-4.

> New products lead to sales growth or stability.

For firms with cyclical or seasonal sales, new products can stabilize revenues and costs. Dow Chemical (**http://www.dow.com**) makes medical-testing equipment, and other stable product categories, to reduce dependence on cyclical chemicals. Black & Decker (**http://www.blackanddecker.com**) has cut back on lawn-care items and looks for opportunities in less seasonal products, such as power tools for the home.

Planning for growth must take into account the total time to move from the idea stage to commercialization. Consider the lengthy process Boeing (**http://www.boeing.com**) must undergo: "Responding to the overwhelming preference of airlines around the world, Boeing Commercial Airplanes has focused its new airplane product development efforts on the Boeing 787 Dreamliner, a super-efficient airplane. The Boeing board of directors granted authority to offer the airplane for sale in late 2003. Program launch occurred in April 2004 with a record order from All-Nippon Airways. Production began in 2006. First flight is expected in 2007 with certification, delivery, and entry into service occurring in 2008."[6]

> New products can take time.

[3] "Bringing Innovation to the Home of Six Sigma," *Business Week* (August 1, 2005), p. 68.

[4] Dan Sewell, "P&G Household Chores Brand Cleans Up," *Associated Press State & Local Wire* (July 31, 2005).

[5] "About ESPN Zone," **http://www.espnzone.com** (May 9, 2006).

[6] "787 Dreamliner," **http://www.boeing.com/commercial/7e7/flash.html** (February 27, 2006).

Figure 13-4

The Growing Family of iPods

Source: Reprinted by permission of Susan Berry, Retail Image Consulting, Inc.

New products can increase profits and control.

New products can lead to larger profits and give a firm more control over its marketing strategy. New luxury car models such as Lincoln (**http://www.lincoln.com**) and Lexus (**http://www.lexus.com**) are often quite popular. When they are popular, the cars sell at or close to the "sticker" price, with dealers earning gross profits of up to $10,000 or more on each car sold. Because there are fewer luxury dealers relative to ones selling lower-priced cars, they do not use as much discounting and have command over their marketing efforts.

Risk may be lessened through diversity.

To limit risk, many firms seek to reduce dependence on one product or product line. Thus, many movie theaters are now multiplexes, so their revenues are not tied to any one film's performance. Hewlett-Packard's (**http://www.hp.com**) offerings span information technology infrastructure, personal computing and access devices, global services, and imaging and printing; and it regularly adds new products. Turtle Wax (**http://www.turtlewax.com**), the world's leader in car-care products, now makes glass cleaners, leather cleaners, carpet cleaners, and upholstery cleaners. It is "not just wax anymore."

New products may improve distribution.

Firms may improve the efficiency of their established distribution systems by placing new products in them. They can then spread advertising, sales, and distribution costs among several products, gain dealer support, and discourage others from entering the market. Manufacturers such as Panasonic (**http://www.panasonic.com**) and Revlon (**http://www.revlon.com**) can place new products in many outlets quickly. Service firms such as the Royal Bank of Canada (**http://www.royalbank.com**) also can efficiently add new products (financial services) into their distribution networks.

Technology can be exploited.

Firms often seek technological breakthroughs. Makers of computer storage devices constantly introduce faster, better products—at lower prices. A Western Digital (**http://www.westerndigital.com**) 15-gigabyte hard drive sold for $200 in 2000. By 2006, the firm was selling 320-gigabyte drives for $180. At All-Clad (**http://www.allclad.com**), new cookware provides "the ideal combination of culinary performance and ease of use." See Figure 13-5. General Electric highlights many of its breakthroughs at the company Web site (**http://www.ge.com/files/usa/commitment/innovation/flash.html**).

Figure 13-5

Capitalizing on New Technology

Source: Reprinted by permission.

Firms sometimes want to find uses for waste materials from existing products—to aid productivity or be responsive to recycling: "Electric utilities are spinning gold out of gunk they once spewed in the air. To comply with the 1970 Clean Air Act, companies have been 'scrubbing' the smoke coming out of their stacks to remove sulfur and fly ash, then dumping the wastes into landfills. Now, they are finding farmers and construction companies will buy the stuff. Near Oak Ridge, Tennessee, a unit of Caraustar Industries [http://www.caraustar.com] built a factory to make wallboard out of sulfur residue produced at the Tennessee Valley Authority power plant next door. Farmers buy sulfur residue—'scrubber sludge'—since it improves soil and boost crop yields. 'Wherever you put that stuff, it just greens up.' By selling what it calls 'coal byproducts,' the TVA [http://www.tva.gov] makes from $6 million to $10 million a year."[7]

> Waste materials can be used.

[7] John J. Fialka, "Once a Pollutant, 'Scrubber Sludge' Finds a Market," *Wall Street Journal* (October 5, 1998), pp. B1-B2.

Ethical Issues in Marketing

Do Consumers Care About "Ethical" Products?

Some marketing experts believe that there has been a recent increase in the availability of ethically made products. Widely distributed ethically made products include Starbucks' (http://www.starbucks.com) coffee produced by coffee farmers who receive higher prices and do not employ child labor, Toyota's Prius hybrid car that runs on a mix of gasoline and electricity, and American Apparel's (http://www.americanapparel.net) clothing line that is produced in nonsweatshop conditions. Analysts trace the increased importance of ethical shopping to Naomi Klein's *No Logo,* a book critical of multinational firms' unethical practices. In addition, the U.S. anti-sweatshop movement has raised ethical awareness to new levels.

Although some marketers such as Starbucks advertise their ethically made products, others do not. Unilever (http://www.unilever.com) does not promote its sustainable fishing program. People Tree (http://www.peopletree.com), which has an ethically made line of clothing, promotes its ethical practices as a secondary message. The firm's founder stated, "We knew we had to make a well-designed, high-quality product, then educate consumers about the environmental cotton and social benefits after purchase."

One marketing research executive feels that there are differences in ethical orientations by market. For example, British consumers are more interested in ethically produced products than Southern Europeans, who are more concerned with how people are treated. In the United States, consumers have increased their purchases of organics and have begun to express concern over child labor issues.

Source: Based on material in "Ethical Marketing: A Question of Ethics," *Brand Strategy Online* (June 9, 2005).

New products respond to consumer needs.

Companies may bring out new products to respond to changing consumer demographics and lifestyles. Single-serving pre-packaged foods are aimed at smaller households. Kodak (http://www.kodak.com) and Fuji (http://www.fujifilm.com) have a full line of single-use disposable cameras that appeal to people interested in convenience. Microsoft (http://www.microsoft.com/hardware) offers computer keyboards that are easier on the wrist. The Hain Celestial Group (http://www.hain-celestial.com) markets foods that appeal to consumers interested in natural, specialty, organic, and snack foods under brand names such as Estee sugar-free foods, Celestial Seasonings teas, and Terra chips.

Government mandates are addressed.

New products may be devised in response to government mandates. To address growing concerns about battery disposal (and the carcinogenic properties of nickel cadmium batteries), battery makers such as Rayovac (http://www.rayovac.com/recharge) have introduced rechargeable batteries that can be recharged up to 25 times or more. With the growing popularity of such power-draining products as digital cameras, rechargeable battery sales are expected to go up greatly in the future.

Good long-run, new-product planning requires systematic research and development—to match the requirements of new-product opportunities with company abilities, to determine consumer desires, to properly allocate time and money, and to consider both defensive and offensive plans. Some criticism exists about the negative effects of many U.S. firms' short-run, bottom-line orientation on their level of innovativeness (and willingness to take risks). A progressive firm accepts that some new products may have problems or even fail; it will take risks: "Dutch Boy [http://www.dutchboy.com], a unit of Sherwin-Williams, recently launched its all-plastic gallon containers with a twist-off lid, side handle, and pour spout. Before launching this innovative packaging, the company had to deal with production problems, like changing from all-magnetic conveyor belts designed for metal cans. It also encountered retail problems, like retrofitting paint shakers in stores to accept the new container. But the efforts are paying off. 'Sales are far exceeding our expectations.' "[8]

---

[8] Lawrence A. Crosby, Sheree L. Johnson, and Karen D. Winslow, "Innovation—Not for the Fainthearted," *Marketing Management* (March-April 2003), pp. 10-11.

13-4 WHY NEW PRODUCTS FAIL

Despite better product-planning practices today than ever before, the failure rate for new products is quite high. According to various sources, 35 percent *or more* of all new industrial and consumer products fail.[9] The marketplace can be quite tough on new products.

We can define product failure in both absolute and relative terms. ***Absolute product failure*** occurs if a firm is unable to regain its production and marketing costs. It incurs a financial loss. ***Relative product failure*** occurs if a firm makes a profit on an item but that product does not reach profit goals and/or adversely affects a firm's image. In computing profits and losses, the impact of the new product on the sales of other company items must be measured. Wikipedia has a detailed list of product failures at its Web site (**http://http://en.wikipedia.org/wiki/List_of_product_failures**).

Even firms with good new-product records have had failures. These include "light" pizza (Pizza Hut), Noxema Skin Fitness (Procter & Gamble), Pepsi Edge (PepsiCo), Bic perfume, McLean Deluxe (McDonald's), Surge (Coca-Cola), Telaction interactive cable-TV shopping service (J.C. Penney), Premier smokeless cigarettes (R.J. Reynolds), and *Gigli* (the Jennifer Lopez and Ben Affleck movie).

Numerous factors may cause new-product failure:

- *Lack of a strong enough differential advantage:* Consumers had little interest in "DIVX (Digital Video Express), an attempt by Circuit City and an entertainment law firm to create an alternative to video rental in the United States. The idea was to sell customers a DIVX disc (similar to a DVD) at a low cost. This disc had a limited viewing period (generally 48 hours) that started after its initial viewing. After this, the disc could be viewed by paying a fee (generally $3.25). DIVX discs could only be played on special DVD players connected to a phone line." Circuit City lost $200 million.[10]
- *Poor planning:* "BarnesandNoble.com, once one of electronic publishing's biggest boosters, shuttered its E-books store. 'Sales did not take off as we and many others expected,' said the general manager of books, music, and video for BN.com. He believed the market failed to grow for a number of reasons, including the lack of a reading device that consumers could embrace. He pointed to the digital music market, praising the iPod, the Macintosh-developed digital music player, calling it 'a real consumer electronics device. We're not at that point with E-books.' He also blamed publishers for not releasing enough E-books and charging too much. 'We think there has to be more flexibility in pricing in order to create an incentive for customers to buy an E-book.'"[11]
- *Poor timing:* "The Apple Pippin was a technology intended to create an inexpensive computer aimed mostly at playing CD-based multimedia titles, especially games, but also functioning as a network computer. Apple never intended to release its own Pippin. It intended to license the technology to third parties; however, the only licensee to release a product was Bandai. By the time the Bandai Pippin was released, the market was already dominated by Nintendo, Sony, and Sega, which had machines which were much more powerful as game machines than the more general purpose Pippin. Bandai's version died quickly, having a relatively limited release in the United States and Japan."[12]

With **absolute product failure**, costs are not regained. With **relative product failure**, goals are not met.

Leading to failure are lack of an advantage, poor planning and timing, and excess enthusiasm.

---

[9] See Richard Osborne, "New Product Development—Lesser Royals," **http://www.industryweek.com/ReadArticle.aspx?ArticleID=1049** (April 1, 2002); "A Creative Corporation Toolbox," **http://images.businessweek.com/ss/05/07/toolbox/index_01.htm** (August 1, 2005); and Rob Smart, "Assuming Doesn't Feed the Bulldog!" **http://www.inventvermont.com/RobSmartPresentation.pdf** (June 9, 2005).

[10] "DIVX," **http://en.wikipedia.org/wiki/DIVX** (April 17, 2006).

[11] Andrew Albanese, "B&N Bows Out of E-Books, But Publishers Upbeat," *Library Journal* (Fall 2003), p. 4.

[12] "Apple Pippin," **http://en.wikipedia.org/wiki/Apple_Pippin** (April 17, 2006).

- *Excessive enthusiasm by the sponsor*: "The XFL was conceived to build on the success of the NFL and professional wrestling. It was hyped as 'real' football without penalties for roughness and with fewer rules in general. The loud games featured players and coaches with microphones and cameras in the huddle and in locker rooms. Although the XFL began with reasonable TV ratings, the audience declined sharply after the first week due to a number of factors including the poor quality of the play. The XFL folded after one season, with one NBC broadcast receiving the lowest-ever market share for a major network prime time show. NBC originally signed a two-year broadcasting contract. The XFL was estimated by both the WWF and NBC to have lost approximately $70 million."[13]

13-5   NEW-PRODUCT PLANNING

> The **new-product planning process** moves from ideas to commercialization.

The **new-product planning process** consists of a series of steps from idea generation to commercialization. A firm generates ideas, evaluates them, weeds out poor ones, gets consumer feedback, devises the product, tests it, and brings it to market. An idea can be terminated at any time; costs rise as the process goes on. The process could be used by any firm, and applies to goods and services. See Figure 13-6. In the United States alone, Marketing Intelligence Service (**http://www.marketingintel.com**) reports that more than 33,000 new products are introduced into supermarkets every year.

Firms need to endeavor to balance competing goals during new-product planning:

- A systematic process should be followed; however, there must be flexibility to adapt to each unique opportunity.
- The process should be thorough, yet not unduly slow down introductions.
- True innovations should be pursued, yet fiscal constraints must be considered.
- An early reading of consumer acceptance should be sought, but the firm must not give away too much information to potential competitors.
- There should be an interest in short-run profitability, but not at the expense of long-run growth.

Many companies do all the new-product planning activities themselves. Others outsource various tasks. A number of consulting firms specialize in this area, such as

Figure 13-6

The New-Product Planning Process

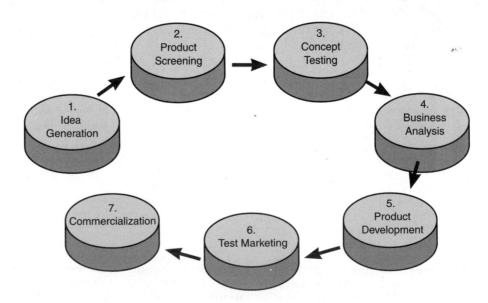

[13] "XFL," **http://en.wikipedia.org/wiki/XFL** (April 17, 2006).

Cheskin (**http://www.cheskin.com**), Ideo (**http://www.ideo.com**), JRC&A (**http://www.jrcanda.com**), and Products 2 Market (**http://www.products2market.com**).

13-5a Idea Generation

Idea generation is a continuous, systematic search for new product opportunities. It involves new-idea sources and ways to generate ideas.

Sources of ideas may be employees, channel members, competitors, outside inventors, customers, government, and others.[14] *Market-oriented sources* identify opportunities based on consumer needs and wants; laboratory research is used to satisfy them. Light beer, many ice cream flavors, and easy-to-open soda cans have evolved from market-oriented sources. *Laboratory-oriented sources* identify opportunities based on pure research (which seeks to gain knowledge and indirectly leads to specific new-product ideas) or applied research (which uses existing scientific techniques to develop new-product ideas). Penicillin, antifreeze, and synthetic fibers have evolved from laboratory sources.

Methods for generating ideas include brainstorming (small-group sessions to come up with a variety of ideas), analyzing current products, reading trade publications, visiting suppliers and dealers, and doing surveys. An open perspective is key: Different people should be consulted; many ideas should be offered; and ideas should not be criticized, no matter how offbeat:

> Revolutionary products and strategies start with the same thing—a brilliant idea. But the smartest, most innovative companies don't stop with one inspiration. They know how to keep churning out new breakthroughs. After all, creativity isn't just a matter of waiting for the muse to strike. The more brainpower you bring to bear on a problem, the smarter the solutions you're likely to get. But that's easier said than done: Nothing stifles creativity faster than a heavy-handed boss who shoots down ideas before they're even properly aired.[15]

> **Idea generation** is the search for opportunities.

13-5b Product Screening

Once a firm spots potential products, it must screen them. In **product screening**, poor, unsuitable, or otherwise unattractive ideas are weeded out from further consideration. Today, many firms use a new-product screening checklist for preliminary analysis. In it, they list the attributes deemed most important and rate each idea on those attributes. The checklist is standardized and allows ideas to be compared.

Figure 13-7 shows a new-product screening checklist with three major categories: general characteristics, marketing characteristics, and production characteristics (which can be applied to both goods and services). Several product attributes must be assessed in each category. They are scored from 1 (outstanding) to 10 (very poor) for each product idea. In addition, the attributes would be weighted because they vary in their impact on new-product success. For every idea, the checklist would yield an overall score. Here is an example of how a firm could develop overall ratings for two ideas. Remember, in this example, the best rating is 1 (so, 3 is worse than 2):

> **Product screening** weeds out undesirable ideas.

1. Idea A gets an average rating of 2.5 on general characteristics, 2.9 on marketing characteristics, and 1.4 on production characteristics. Idea B gets ratings of 2.8, 1.4, and 1.8, respectively.
2. The firm assigns an importance weight of 4 to general characteristics, 5 to marketing characteristics, and 3 to production characteristics. The best overall rating is

[14] See Chris Penttila, "Fantastic Forum," *Entrepreneur* (September 2005), pp. 92–93; Jane M. Howell, "The Right Stuff: Identifying and Developing Effective Champions of Innovation," *Academy of Management Executive*, Vol. 19 (May 2005), pp. 108–119; Robert W. Veryzer and Brigitte Borja de Mozota, "The Impact of User-Oriented Design on New-Product Development: An Examination of Fundamental Relationships," *Journal of Product Innovation Management*, Vol. 22 (March 2005), pp. 128–143; and Melanie Wells, "Have It Your Way," *Forbes* (February 14, 2005), pp. 78–86.

[15] Bridget Finn, "Brainstorming for Better Brainstorming," *Business 2.0* (April 2005), pp. 109–114.

Figure 13-7

A New-Product Screening Checklist

	Rating
General Characteristics of New Product	
Profit potential	_____
Existing competition	_____
Potential competition	_____
Size of market	_____
Level of investment	_____
Patentability	_____
Level of risk	_____
Marketing Characteristics of New Product	
Fit with marketing capabilities	_____
Effect on existing products (brands)	_____
Appeal to current consumer markets	_____
Potential length of product life cycle	_____
Existence of differential advantage	_____
Impact on image	_____
Resistance to seasonal factors	_____
Production Characteristics of New Product	
Fit with production capabilities	_____
Length of time to commercialization	_____
Ease of production	_____
Availability of labor and material resources	_____
Ability to produce at competitive prices	_____

12 $[(1 \times 4) + (1 \times 5) + (1 \times 3)]$. The poorest possible average rating is 120 $[(10 \times 4) + (10 \times 5) + (10 \times 3)]$.

3. Idea A gets an overall rating of 28.7 $[(2.5 \times 4) + (2.9 \times 5) + (1.4 \times 3)]$. B gets an overall rating of 23.6 $[(2.8 \times 4) + (1.4 \times 5) + (1.8 \times 3)]$.

4. Idea B's overall rating is better than A's due to its better marketing evaluation (the characteristics judged most important by the firm).

> A **patent** gives exclusive selling rights to an inventor.

During screening, patentability must often be determined. A ***patent*** grants an inventor of a useful product or process exclusive selling rights for a fixed period. An invention may be patented if it is a "useful, novel, and nonobvious process, machine, manufacture, or composition of matter" and not patented by anyone else. Separate applications are needed for protection in foreign markets. Many nations have simplified matters via patent cooperation treaties; however, some do not honor such treaties. Today, in the United States and the other members of the World Trade Organization, patents last for 20 years from the date that applications are filed. The U.S. Patent and Trademark Office (**http://www.uspto.gov**) receives almost 400,000 patent applications and grants 185,000 patents annually. Nearly one-half of U.S. patents involve foreign firms; in contrast, one-sixth of Japanese patents are held by foreigners.

A firm should answer these questions in screening: Can the proposed new product be patented? Are competitive items patented? When do competitors' patents expire? Are patents on competing items available under a licensing agreement? Would the company be free of patent liability (infringement) if it introduces the proposed new product?

13-5c Concept Testing

> **Concept testing** determines customer attitudes before product development.

Next, a firm needs consumer feedback about the new-product ideas that pass through screening. ***Concept testing*** presents the consumer with a proposed product and measures attitudes and intentions at an early stage of the new-product planning process.

Concept testing is a quick, inexpensive way to assess consumer enthusiasm. It asks potential customers to react to a picture, written statement, or oral product description. This lets a firm learn initial attitudes prior to costly, time-consuming product

A leading music company is considering the introduction of a new online music service. The company would make its whole catalog of 10,000 recorded songs available under two different subscription plans. With plan 1, customers would pay a monthly fee of $10.00 for up to 50 downloads per month. With plan 2, customers would pay a fee of 30 cents for each song that is downloaded. All songs would have the same fee.

1. React to the overall concept described above.
_ _

2. What do you like most about the proposed concept? Why?
_ _

3. What do you like least about the proposed concept? Why?
_ _

4. What suggestions do you have for improving the proposed concept?
_ _

5. What else would you like to know about the proposed concept?
_ _

6. How likely would you be to participate in the proposed music service?
Very likely ____ ____ ____ ____ ____ Very unlikely
Why? _

Figure 13-8

A Brief Concept Test for a Proposed New Online Music Service

development. Heinz (**http://www.heinz.com**), Kodak (**http://www.kodak.com**), Sony (**http://www.sony.com**), and Sunbeam (**http://www.sunbeam.com**) are among the firms using concept testing. Figure 13-8 shows a brief concept test for a proposed fee-based online music service.

Concept testing generally asks consumers these types of questions:

- Is the idea easy to understand?
- Would this product meet a real need?
- Do you see distinct benefits for this product over those on the market?
- Do you find the claims about this product believable?
- Would you buy the product?
- How much would you pay for it?

- Would you replace your current brand with this new product?
- What improvements can you suggest in various attributes of the concept?
- How frequently would you buy the product?
- Who would use the product?[16]

13-5d   Business Analysis

> **Business analysis** looks at demand, costs, competition, and so on.

At this point, a firm does business analysis for the new-product concepts that are deemed attractive. *Business analysis* involves the detailed review, projection, and evaluation of such factors as consumer demand, production costs, marketing costs, break-even points, competition, capital investments, and profitability for each proposed new product. It is much more detailed than product screening.

Here are some considerations at this planning stage:

Criteria	Selected Considerations
Demand projections	Short- and long-run sales potential; speed of sales growth; price/sales relationship; seasonality; rate of repurchases
Production cost projections	Total and per-unit costs; startup versus continuing costs; estimates of raw materials and other costs; economies of scale; break-even points
Marketing cost projections	Product planning (patent search, product development, testing); promotion; distribution; marketing research; break-even points
Competitive projections	Short-run and long-run market shares of company and competitors; competitors' strengths and weaknesses; potential competitors; likely strategies by competitors in response to firm
Capital investment projections	Need for new equipment and facilities versus use of existing facilities and resources
Profitability projections	Time to recoup initial costs; short- and long-run total and per-unit profits; reseller needs; control over price; return on investment; risk

The next step is expensive and time-consuming product development; thus, critical use of business analysis is needed to eliminate marginal items. For an online demonstration of business analysis, go to "New Concept Analysis" (**http://www.businessplansoftware.org/qidemo/qidemo.asp**) and click on the arrow key that appears in the upper right portion of the screen. Keep clicking until you have finished the demonstration.

13-5e   Product Development

> **Product development** focuses on devising an actual product and a broad marketing strategy.

In *product development*, an idea for a new product is converted into a tangible form and a basic marketing strategy is identified. Depending on the product involved, this planning stage encompasses product construction, packaging, branding, product positioning, and consumer attitude and usage testing.

Product construction decisions include the type and quality of materials comprising the product, the method of production, production time, production capacity, the assortment to be offered, and the time needed to move from development to commercialization. Packaging decisions include the materials used, the functions performed, and

---

[16] Adapted by the authors from Philip Kotler and Kevin Lane Keller, *Marketing Management*, 12th ed. (Upper Saddle River, NJ: Pearson Education, 2006).

alternative sizes and colors. Branding decisions include the choice of a name, trademark protection, and the image sought. Product positioning involves selecting a target market and positioning the new good or service against competitors and other company offerings. Consumer testing studies perceptions of and satisfaction with the new product.

Product-development costs may be relatively low with a modification. However, an innovation may be costly (up to several million dollars or more), time consuming (up to four years for a new car), and complex. This is true of services as well as goods: "The doors have just opened on the world's most expensive hotel, the Emirates Palace [**http://www.emiratespalace.com/en/main.htm**], costing £2 billion ($3.5 billion) to build. Its owner, the government of Abu Dhabi, knows the hotel will never make a profit. That doesn't matter. The intent was to impress the world by creating the most lavish experience imaginable. It features an entrance arch which is 40 meters (131 feet) high and 36 meters (118 feet) wide and a lobby atrium with a dome larger than St. Paul's Cathedral, topped by a finial made of solid gold. There are 16 Palace Suites, among the most expensive in the world at £8,000 ($14,200) a night."[17]

Many firms are working diligently to make product development more efficient: "The same special-effects technology used in making *Spiderman* and *Harry Potter* movies is helping auto makers produce vehicles in less time and at lower cost. 'Virtually' building cars eliminates the expensive and time-consuming trial-and-error process of producing prototypes to test how and if they work." This enables the manufacturers to "find and correct problems with parts before they are produced." The firms can "even 'virtually' crash a vehicle to see how it performs." At General Motors (**http://www.gm.com**), the technique has reduced product-development costs by 40 percent.[18]

13-5f Test Marketing

Test marketing involves placing a fully developed new product (a good or service) in one or more selected areas and observing its actual performance under a proposed marketing plan. The purpose is to evaluate the product and planned marketing efforts in a real setting prior to a full-scale introduction. Rather than just study intentions, test marketing lets a firm monitor actual consumer behavior, competitor reactions, and reseller interest. After testing, the firm could go ahead, modify the product and then go ahead, modify the marketing plan and then go ahead, or drop the product. Anheuser-Busch (**http://www.anheuser-busch.com**), Georgia-Pacific (**http://www.gp.com**), John Hancock Funds (**http://www.jhfunds.com**), Home Depot (**http://www.homedepot.com**), Levi Strauss (**http://www.levistrauss.com**), McDonald's (**http://www.mcdonalds.com**), and Procter & Gamble (**http://www.pg.com**) are among the firms that use test marketing. Consumer-products firms are more apt to engage in test marketing than industrial-products firms, which often do product-use testing with key customers.

> **Test marketing** occurs in selected areas and observes real performance.

Test marketing requires several decisions: when to test, where to test, how long to test, what test information to acquire, and how to apply test results. Figure 13-9 shows the criteria in making choices.

Although test marketing has often been beneficial, some firms now question its effectiveness and downplay or skip this stage in new-product planning. Dissatisfaction arises from test marketing's costs, the time delays before full introduction, the information being provided to competitors, the inability to predict national (global) results based on limited test-market areas, and the impact of such external factors as the economy and competition on test results. Test marketing can even allow nontesting competitors to catch up with an innovative firm by the time a product is ready for a full rollout.

Sometimes, consumer panels are used to simulate test market conditions—even online. For example, GlobalTestMarket.com (**http://www.globaltestmarket.com**), "is a world-wide technology leader in global consumer research sponsored by Global Market Insite.

---

[17] "The World's Most Expensive Hotel," *European Business Forum* (Spring 2005), p. 73.

[18] "Build It Faster, Cheaper," *Machine Design* (February 17, 2005), p. 214.

Figure 13-9

Test Marketing Decisions

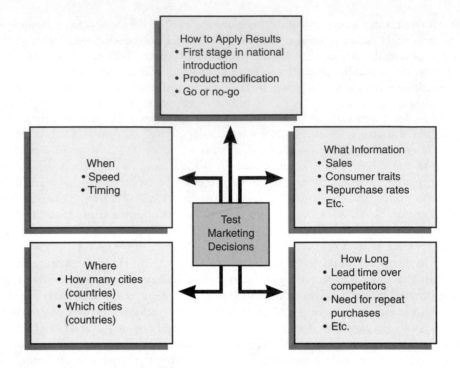

The intention was to develop a global solution for companies who wish to conduct online consumer research across multiple countries. GMI serves more than 300 clients in more than 40 countries. If you are a retailer or manufacturer and are interested in listing a development-stage or new-to-the-world consumer product in one of the online test markets, please contact us."

13-5g Commercialization

At this point, a firm is ready to introduce a new product to its full target market. This involves *commercialization* and corresponds to the introductory stage of the product life cycle. During commercialization, the firm enacts a total marketing plan and works toward production capacity. Among the factors to be considered are the speed of acceptance by consumers and distribution intermediaries, the intensity of distribution (how many outlets), production capabilities, the promotion mix, prices, competition, the time until profitability, and commercialization costs.

Commercialization involves a major marketing commitment.

Commercialization may require large outlays and a long-term commitment. Manufacturers often spend millions of dollars for a typical national rollout in U.S. supermarkets—nearly half on consumer promotion and the rest on product costs, marketing research, and promotions for supermarkets. Yet, commercialization costs can go much higher. When the Venus shaver for women was introduced, it had a $150 million marketing budget—for TV and print ads, a Web site, contests, in-store promotions, and other activities. Look at how sophisticated and detailed the Web site (**http://www.gillettevenus.com/us**) is.

Commercializing a new product sometimes must overcome consumer and reseller reluctance because of ineffective prior company offerings. This occurred with Texas Instruments (**http://www.ti.com**) in the business computer market, after it bowed out of the home computer market. And many resellers were upset with the usually reliable Sony when it was able to ship only 500,000 units of the Sony PlayStation 2 (**http://www.us.playstation.com**) during the new product's North American debut, rather than the 1 million that had been promised.

13-6 GROWING PRODUCTS

Once a product is commercialized, the goal is for consumer acceptance and company sales to rise rapidly. Sometimes, this occurs quickly; other times, it may take a while. The growth rate and total sales of new products rely on two consumer behavior concepts: the adoption process and the diffusion process. In managing growing products, a firm must understand these concepts and plan its marketing efforts accordingly.

The *adoption process* is the mental and behavioral procedure an individual consumer goes through when learning about and purchasing a new product. It consists of these stages:

1. *Knowledge*—A person (firm) learns of a product's existence and gains some understanding of how it functions.
2. *Persuasion*—A person (firm) forms a favorable or unfavorable attitude about a product.
3. *Decision*—A person (firm) engages in actions leading to a choice to adopt or reject a product.
4. *Implementation*—A person (firm) uses a product.
5. *Confirmation*—A person (firm) seeks reinforcement and may reverse a decision if exposed to conflicting messages.[19]

> The **adoption process** explains the new-product purchase behavior of individual consumers.

The speed of adoption depends on consumer traits, the product, and the firm's marketing effort. It is faster if people have high discretionary income and are willing to try new offerings; the product has low perceived risk; the product has an advantage over others on the market; the product is a modification, not an innovation; the product is compatible with current lifestyles or ways of operating a business; product attributes can be easily communicated; product importance is low; the product can be tested before a purchase; the product is consumed quickly; the product is easy to use; mass advertising and distribution are used; and the marketing mix adjusts as the person (organization) moves through the adoption process.

The *diffusion process* describes the manner in which different members of the target market often accept and purchase a product. It spans the time from product introduction through market saturation and affects the total sales level of a product as it moves through the life cycle:

> The **diffusion process** describes when different segments are likely to purchase.

Global Marketing in Action

Brand Extendibility on the Global Stage

Brand extendibility measures the ability of a brand to enter new markets and to add new products under the existing brand designation. Based on survey results from close to 13,000 consumers in 17 countries, Sony (http://www.sony.com), LG (http://www.lge.com), and Wal-Mart (http://www.walmart.com) are leaders in "brand extendibility" rankings. As the chief executive of one of the study's sponsoring firms noted, "Building brand recognition is not enough in any market. It may help defend share, but extending a brand portfolio or moving into new geographic markets requires a brand to create a more active consumer experience."

According to the survey, respondents believed that Wal-Mart could extend its brand name to nearly every category including computers/software, hotels, and kitchen appliances. Similarly, respondents in many countries expressed an interest in LG stores, and Korean respondents showed an interest in LG credit cards, athletic apparel, and an LG airline.

The study also found that over one-half of all respondents prefer global brands across a variety of different product categories such as computers/software, athletic wear, consumer electronics, and automobiles. Significant differences were noted in preferences for global versus local brands by region and age. Latin American and European consumers preferred global brands, whereas U.S. and Asian consumers were split over global and local brands. In terms of age, younger consumers had a higher preference for global brands than older consumers.

Source: Based on material in "Sony, LG, Wal-Mart Among Most Extendible Brands, Global Brand Study Finds," *Business Wire* (June 6, 2005).

---

[19] Everett M. Rogers, *Diffusion of Innovations*, 5th ed. (New York: Free Press, 2003), Chapter 5.

1. *Innovators* are the first to try a new product. They are venturesome, willing to accept risk, socially aggressive, communicative, and worldly. It must be learned which innovators are opinion leaders—those who influence others. This group is about 2.5 percent of the market.

2. *Early adopters* are the next to buy a new product. They enjoy the prestige, leadership, and respect that early purchases bring—and tend to be opinion leaders. They adopt new ideas but use discretion. This group is about 13.5 percent of the market.

3. The *early majority* is the initial part of the mass market to buy. They have status among peers and are outgoing, communicative, and attentive to information. The group is about 34 percent of the market.

4. The *late majority* is the second part of the mass market to buy. They are less cosmopolitan and responsive to change, and include people (firms) with lower economic and social status, those past middle age (or set in their jobs), and skeptics. This group is about 34 percent of the market.

5. *Laggards* purchase last, if at all. They are price-conscious, suspicious of change, low in income and status, tradition bound, and conservative. They do not adopt a product until it reaches maturity. Some sellers ignore them because it can be hard to market a product to laggards. Thus, concentrated marketing may do well by focusing on products for laggards. This group is about 16 percent of the market.[20]

Growth for a major innovation often starts slowly because there is an extended adoption process and the early majority may be hesitant to buy. Sales may then rise quickly. For minor innovations or product modifications, growth is much faster right from the start.

The first high-definition television (HDTV) sets—a major innovation—were marketed in 1996; yet, by the end 2002, only 4 percent of U.S. households had a set. During 2004, only 5 million of the 30 million TV sets purchased were HDTV sets. Consumers were hesitant to buy due to the high initial prices (several thousand dollars), the complexities of HDTV technology, the lack of programming in the HDTV format, and skepticism about how much better HDTV viewing really was. In recent years, sales have risen because of much lower prices, greater programming, and Federal Communications Commission support for the HDTV format. Today, HDTV sets are in more than 13 percent of U.S. households; and one research firm states that HDTV sets will be in 50 million U.S. homes as of 2010.[21] See Figure 13-10.

These products are among those now in the growth stage, and they represent good opportunities for firms: DVD burners; cell phones with colorful displays, text messaging, online access, and camera features; MP3 players; men's personal care products; generic drugs; flat-screen PC monitors; online banking; adult education; self-scanning equipment for retailers, and b-to-b video conferencing services.

13-7 MATURE PRODUCTS

> Proper marketing can let mature products maintain high sales.

Products are in the maturity stage of the life cycle when they reach the late majority and laggard markets. Goals turn from growth to maintenance. Because new products are so costly and risky, more firms are placing marketing emphasis on mature products with steady sales and profits and minimal risk.

When managing mature products, a firm should study the size, attributes, and needs of the current market; untapped market segments; competition; the potential for product modifications; the likelihood of new company products replacing mature ones; profit

---

[20] Ibid, Chapter 7.

[21] *CE Ownership and Market Potential* (Arlington, VA: Consumer Electronics Association, 2005); and Alan Breznick, "Consumer Confusion Hampers Cable's HDTV Sales Drive," **http://www.cabledatacomnews.com/sep05/sep05-3. html** (September 1, 2005).

Figure 13-10

Encouraging Consumers to Want HDTV

Source: Reprinted by permission.

margins; the marketing effort for each sale; reseller attitudes; the promotion mix; the impact of specific products on the product line; each product's effect on company image; the remaining years for the products; and the management effort needed.

A firm can accrue many benefits if it has a popular brand in a mature category: (1) The life cycle may be extended almost indefinitely. Budweiser beer (**http://www.budweiser.com**), Coke soda (**http://www.coke.com**), Goodyear tires (**http://www.goodyeartires.com**), Life Savers candy (**http://www.candystand.com/lifesavers.do**), and Sherwin-Williams paints (**http://www.sherwin-williams.com**) are leaders in their categories; each is over 80 years old.[22] (2) A mature brand has a loyal customer base and a stable, profitable market position. (3) The likelihood of future low demand is reduced; this is a real risk for new products. (4) A firm's overall image is enhanced. This may allow it to extend a popular name to other products. (5) More control exists over marketing and more precise forecasts.

> Popular mature brands offer several benefits for companies.

---

[22] See Jack Trout, "Solid Foundations," *Advertising Age* (March 14, 2005), p. 28.

Figure 13-11

The Everlasting Role of Old English Furniture Polish

Source: Reprinted by permission of Reckitt Benckiser Inc.

(6) Mature products can be cash cows that support new-product spending. Some marketing support must be continued if a mature product is to stay popular.

Successful products can stay in maturity for long periods, as Figures 13-11 and 13-12 and the following illustrate:

- Although the paper clip was invented in 1899 by Norwegian Johan Vaaler, today it is more popular than ever due to its ease of use, flexible applications, and large customer following: "The variety of uses range from bookmark, money clip, and staple remover to the item that holds a hem that needs sewing or serves as a hanger for curtains, lights, and pictures. Because of its price and availability, it is easy to see why the paper clip is one of the most versatile of inventions." It seems that, after more than 100 years, there is still nothing to match a paper clip. Twenty billion are sold yearly.[23]

---

[23] "A History of the Paper Clip," http://www.writeonoffice.com/info/index.asp?page=his_paperclip.asp (April 4, 2006).

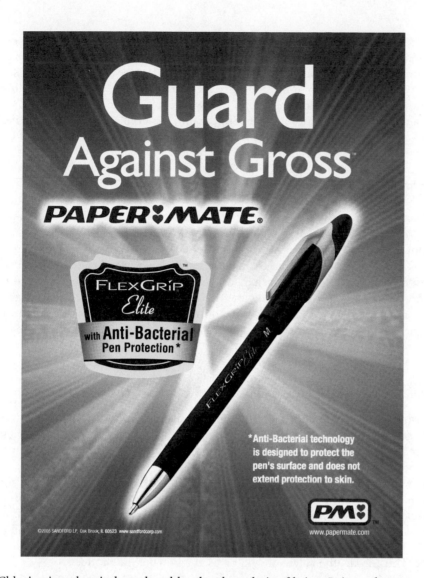

Figure 13-12

Growing the Sales of Papermate After More Than 50 Years on the Market

Source: Reprinted by permission.

- Chlorine is a chemical produced by the electrolysis of brine. It is used to process organic chemicals and in the production of pulp, paper, and other industrial goods. In industrialized nations, chlorine is a mature product—with stable sales in the United States and negative sales growth in Canada, Japan, and Europe. Sales are growing in Asia, Latin America, Africa, and the Middle East. Thus, chlorine producers' marketing efforts are now quite aggressive in developing and less-developed nations. There is even an active trade association, the Chlorine Chemistry Council (**http://www.c3.org**).

- Lycra (**http://www.lycra.com**), the trademark for spandex fiber, began life in the 1950s as a rubber substitute in girdles. After sales stagnated, the fiber gained attention in the 1980s with the advent of cycling pants and leggings, and new technology that let Lycra fibers be used in sheer hosiery. Lycra is now included in all sorts of garments. To ensure continued success, Invista (**http://www.invista.com**)—a company that was spun off from DuPont in 2004—steadily invests in the brand: "Lycra has been able to continuously evolve and grow to meet the demanding needs of the apparel and home interiors industries. In the apparel context, consumers love Lycra for the pure pleasure of the way you look and feel when you wear a garment made with Lycra. In the home interiors context, consumers appreciate that products made with Lycra breathe better, look better, and fit better."[24]

[24] "Lycra: Look Better, Feel Better," **http://www.invista.com/prd_lycra.shtml** (April 2, 2005).

- Since the 1930s, Hormel Foods (**http://www.hormel.com**) has marketed canned chili. To keep the line as the best-selling chili in the United States, the firm regularly introduces new versions—including chilis that are fat-free and that have less sodium, as well as ones in easy-to-open cartons. Its online digital recipe book gives dozens of ways to use chili in casseroles, dips, sandwiches, pizza, and a lot more.
- Campbell's V8 juice (**http://www.v8juice.com**) has been around for several decades. After a lull, Campbell has rejuvenated V8 by promoting it as "unique blend of eight vegetable juices that is vitamin-rich. It provides more than a full serving of vegetables in every nutritious 8-ounce glass for your balanced lifestyle. All this for 50 calories per serving and half the carbs of orange juice."

Many options are available for extending the mature stage of the product life cycle. Table 13-2 shows seven strategies and examples of each.

Not all mature products can be revived or extended. Consumer needs may disappear, as when frozen juice replaced juice squeezers. Lifestyle changes may lead to less interest in products, such as teller services in banks. Better, more convenient products may be devised, such as CD (and now, DVD) players replacing record players. The market may be saturated and marketing efforts may not garner enough sales to justify time and costs, which is why Japan's NEC reduced its consumer electronics presence.

13-8 PRODUCT DELETION

> Products need to be deleted if they have consistently poor sales, tie up resources, and cannot be revived.

Products should be deleted if they offer limited sales and profit potential, reflect poorly on the firm, tie up resources that could be used for other opportunities, involve lots of management time, create reseller dissatisfaction due to low turnover, and divert attention from long-term goals.

However, many points must be weighed before deleting a product: As a product matures, it blends in with existing items and becomes part of the total product line (mix). Customers and distribution intermediaries may be hurt if an item is dropped. A firm may not want competitors to have the only product for customers. Poor sales and profits may be only temporary. The marketing strategy, not the product, may cause the poor results. Thus, in-depth analysis should be used with faltering products.

Marketing and the Web

Photo-Sharing Web Sites Revolutionize Picture Taking

Ofoto (**http://www.ofoto.com**), a division of Kodak, is a photo-sharing Web site that not only develops film but also enables users to scan and post pictures online. Ofoto typically lets consumers store the equivalent of photo albums on its Web site free of charge. Consumers who want reprints simply click on their favorite photos and then enter their credit card number.

Various photo-sharing Web sites have different features. Some allow users to lighten or darken images to correct lighting. Others let users improve their pictures by cropping, changing colors, and adjusting contrast. With one site, Flickr (**http://www.flickr.com**), friends, family, and even strangers can label photos that have been uploaded to its site with key words or notes so that they can be more easily searched or better organized into albums. Users can specify who has access to their pictures.

One potential opportunity for photo sharing is based on the increased popularity of camera phones. Although hundreds of millions of camera phones are now used in the United States, research by Kodak shows that just one-third of camera-phone users upload their pictures to a computer. And just 30 percent send these photos to other phones. Sprint (**http://www.sprint.com**) users can now upload their digital camera photos to a Web site and then send them to a phone or a Fuji (**http://www.fujifilm.com**) photo site for printing.

Sources: Based on material in Brad Smith, "Photo Sharing Starts to Click," *Wireless Week* (June 1, 2005), pp. 30–31; and Cade Metz, "Photo Sharing with a Community Flair," *PC Magazine* (April 26, 2005), p. 36.

Table 13-2 Selected Strategies for Extending the Mature Stage of the Product Life Cycle

Strategy	Examples
1. Develop new uses for products	Jell-O used in garden salads WD-40 used in the maintenance of kitchen appliances
2. Develop new product features and refinements	Zoom lenses for 35mm cameras Battery-powered televisions
3. Increase the market	American Express accounts for small businesses International editions of major magazines
4. Find new classes of consumers for present products	Nylon carpeting for institutional markets Johnson & Johnson's baby shampoo used by adults
5. Find new classes of consumers for modified products	Industrial power tools altered for do-it-yourself market Inexpensive copy machines for home offices
6. Increase product usage among current users	Multiple packages for soda and beer Discounts given for increased long-distance phone calls
7. Change marketing strategy	Greeting cards sold in supermarkets Office furniture promoted via mail-order catalogs

Low-profit or rapidly declining products are often dropped or de-emphasized:

- The once popular VHS tape is in its final days: "The format that debuted in 1977 and created a new industry has been in decline since the arrival of DVD in 1997. With sales dwindling fast, major retailers are getting ready to follow the lead of Best Buy (http://www.bestbuy.com) and Circuit City (http://www.circuitcity.com) and put VHS out to pasture. VHS sales have been falling fast since hitting a high of $6.3 billion in 1998. Sales fell to $1.2 billion in 2004 (from $2.3 billion in 2003), $700 million in 2005, and $400 million in 2006." Although mass merchants were reluctant to set a time for exiting the VHS market, most observers expected them to pull the plug in 2007 or 2008.[25]

- After nearly 90 years, the upscale Helena Rubinstein cosmetics brand was pulled from the U.S. marketplace in 2003. The brand had lost its cachet and distinctiveness; and it was carried by very few stores. Parent company L'Oreal (http://www.loreal.com) decided to place more U.S. emphasis on its other brands: "Given the current economic climate, we have decided to concentrate our efforts and resources in markets where the Helena Rubinstein [http://www.helenarubinstein.com] brand is experiencing exceptional growth (Asia, Europe and South America). Our plan is to return to the North American market in the future with greater resources so that we can offer our customers everything they expect from an international luxury brand. Naturally, we understand how disappointed you may be on learning that products you have enjoyed using and we share your feelings. However, Helena Rubinstein products are still available in over 50 countries around the world, in many duty free shops, and in all countries in the European Union."[26]

- In late 2000, General Motors decided to gradually phase out its then 103-year-old Oldsmobile division (http://www.oldsmobile.com): "Under General Motors [http://www.gm.com], Oldsmobile enjoyed years of success. But the past two decades saw stiff competition and overlapping models for the company, and the brand was eventually phased out. The last Alero that rolled off the assembly

[25] Doug Desjardins, "Retailers and Studios to Bid Farewell to VHS," *DSN Retailing Today* (July 25, 2005), pp. 1, 27.

[26] "Dear Customer," http://www.helenarubinstein.co.uk/_en/_us/whatsnew/whatsnew_edito.aspx (February 19, 2006).

line in Lansing, Michigan, in April 2004 marked the end of the line for Oldsmobile."[27]

- "If business is a jungle, then the rise and fall of the typewriter is a demonstration of evolution, of the little creature that could. When Smith Corona filed for bankruptcy in 1995, one of the final signals in the triumph of PCs and software over the typewriter [originally patented in 1868] was at hand."[28]

> During deletion, customer and distributor needs must be considered.

A firm must decide about replacement parts, the notification time for customers and resellers, and the honoring of warranties/guarantees when discontinuing a product. For example, a company planning to delete its line of office telephones must resolve these questions: (1) Replacement parts—Who will make them? How long will they be made? (2) Notification time—How soon before the actual deletion will an announcement be made? Will distributors be alerted early enough so they can contact other suppliers? (3) Warranties—How will warranties be honored? After they expire, how will repairs be done? [29]

Web Sites You Can Use

These are just a few of the many helpful Web sites dealing with various aspects of product management:

- Idea Site for Business (**http://www.ideasiteforbusiness.com**)
- "Learn More About a Company by Examining Its Products" (**http://www.virtualpet.com/industry/howto/preview.htm**)
- National Inventors Hall of Fame (**http://www.invent.org**)
- "New Product Development" (**http://www.smsource.com/productdevelopment.htm**)

- Product Development & Management Association (**http://www.pdma.org**)
- "Product Life Cycles" (**http://www.marketing-magic.biz/archives/archive-management/product-life-cycles.htm**)
- "Product Management and Packaging" (**http://www.knowthis.com/management/product.htm**)
- Product*News*Network (**http://www.productnews.com**)
- Ready 2 Launch (**http://www.ready2launch.com**)
- *Visions* Magazine (**http://www.pdma.org/visions/backissues.html**)

Summary

1. *To study how products are created and managed, with an emphasis on the product life cycle*   Product management creates and oversees products over their lives. New products are modifications or innovations that consumers see as substantive. Modifications are improvements to existing products. Minor innovations have not been previously sold by the firm but have been sold by others. Major innovations have not been previously sold by anyone.

   The product life cycle seeks to describe a product's sales, competitors, profits, customers, and marketing emphasis from inception until removal from the market. Many firms seek a balanced product portfolio, with

products in various stages of the cycle. The product life cycle has several derivations, from traditional to fad to bust. The traditional cycle consists of four stages: introduction, growth, maturity, and decline. During each stage, the marketing goal, industry sales, competition, industry profits, customers, and marketing mix change. Though the life cycle is useful in planning, it should not be a forecasting tool.

2. *To detail the importance of new products and describe why new products fail*   New products may foster differential advantages, sustain sales growth, require a lot of time for development, generate large profits, enable a firm to diversify, make distribution more efficient, lead to

[27] Adele Woodyard, "Olds Heritage Lives on in Florida," *AutoWeek* (April 25, 2005), p. 24.

[28] Francis X. Clines, "An Ode to the Typewriter," *New York Times* (July 10, 1995), p. D5.

[29] See "Maintain Your Market: Keep Customers Even After You Pull a Product," *Sales & Marketing Management* (May 2005), p. 10.

technological breakthroughs, allow waste products to be used, respond to changing consumers, and address government mandates.

If a firm has a financial loss, a product is an absolute failure. If it has a profit but does not attain its goals, a product is a relative failure. Failures occur due to such factors as a lack of a significant differential advantage, poor planning, poor timing, and excessive enthusiasm by the product sponsor.

3. *To present the stages in the new-product planning process* New-product planning involves a comprehensive, seven-step process. During idea generation, new opportunities are sought. In product screening, unattractive ideas are weeded out via a new-product screening checklist. At concept testing, the consumer reacts to a proposed idea. Business analysis requires a detailed evaluation of demand, costs, competition, investments, and profits. Product development converts an idea into a tangible form and outlines a marketing strategy. Test marketing, a much-debated technique, involves placing a product for sale in selected areas and observing performance under actual conditions. Commercialization is the sale of a product to the full target market. A new product can be terminated or modified at any point in the process.

4. *To analyze the growth and maturity of products, including the adoption process, the diffusion process, and extension strategies* After commercialization, the firm's goal is for consumer acceptance and company sales to rise as rapidly as possible. However, the growth rate and level for a new product are dependent on the adoption process—which describes how a single consumer learns about and purchases a product—and the diffusion process—which describes how different members of the target market learn about and purchase a product. These processes are faster for certain consumers, products, and marketing strategies.

As products mature, goals turn from growth to maintenance. Mature products can provide stable sales and profits and loyal consumers. They do not require the risks and costs of new products. There are several factors to consider and alternative strategies from which to choose when planning to sustain mature products. It may not be possible to retain aging products if consumer needs disappear, lifestyles change, new products make them obsolete, or the market becomes too saturated.

5. *To examine product deletion decisions and strategies* At some point, a firm may have to determine whether to continue a faltering product. Deletion may be hard due to the interrelation of products, the impact on customers and resellers, and other factors. It should be done in a structured manner; and replacement parts, notification time, and warranties should all be considered in a deletion plan.

Key Terms

new product (p. 393)

modifications (p. 393)

minor innovations (p. 393)

major innovations (p. 393)

product life cycle (p. 393)

balanced product portfolio (p. 393)

introduction stage of the product life cycle (p. 394)

growth stage of the product life cycle (p. 394)

maturity stage of the product life cycle (p. 394)

decline stage of the product life cycle (p. 396)

self-fulfilling prophecy (p. 396)

absolute product failure (p. 401)

relative product failure (p. 401)

new-product planning process (p. 402)

idea generation (p. 403)

product screening (p. 403)

patent (p. 404)

concept testing (p. 404)

business analysis (p. 406)

product development (p. 406)

test marketing (p. 407)

commercialization (p. 408)

adoption process (p. 409)

diffusion process (p. 409)

Review Questions

1. Distinguish among a product modification, a minor innovation, and a major innovation. Present an example of each for a hospital.
2. Explain the basic premise of the product life cycle. What is the value of this concept?
3. Give four reasons why new products are important to a company.
4. How does product screening differ from business analysis?
5. What are the pros and cons of test marketing?
6. How can a firm speed a product's growth?
7. Cite five ways in which a firm could extend the mature stage of the product life cycle. Provide an example of each.
8. Why is a product deletion decision so difficult?

Discussion Questions

1. Comment on the following statement: "We never worry about relative product failures because we make a profit on them. We only worry about absolute product failures."
2. Develop a ten-item new-product screening checklist for a sporting goods manufacturer interested in new aluminum baseball bats. How would you weight each item?
3. Differentiate between the commercialization strategies for a minor innovation and a major innovation. Relate your answers to the adoption process and the diffusion process.
4. Select a product that has been in existence for 20 or more years and explain why it has been successful for so long.

Web Exercise

At the Web site of the U.S. Patent and Trademark Office (**http://www.uspto.gov**), a data base of current patents and trademark is available. Go here (**http://www.patft.uspto.gov/netahtml/** search-bool.html) and enter the term "air conditioner." Then, select two patents that you believe have strong sales potential and state why.

Practice Quiz

1. An example of a major product innovation is
   a. Black & Decker's current production of an electric-powered lawn mower.
   b. the minivan produced by Ford (based on Chrysler's success).
   c. the Honda Accord station wagon (introduced in the 1990s).
   d. the first laptop computer that was originally marketed by Tandy.

2. During which stage of the product life cycle does the average-income mass market make purchases?
   a. Maturity
   b. Introduction
   c. Decline
   d. Growth

3. Which of the following is *not* a key point that should be kept in mind when using the product life cycle?
   a. The shape and length of the product life cycle may vary greatly by product.
   b. External factors may have a major impact on the performance of a product and shorten or lengthen its life cycle.
   c. A company may be able to manage the product life cycle and extend it or reverse a decline.
   d. It is useful in forecasting.

4. A major reason for the importance of new products is to
   a. meet foreign competition.
   b. reduce dependence on one product or product line.
   c. copy a competitor's innovation.
   d. match a competitor's prices.

5. Though a firm made a profit with a new product, the new product's return on investment did not meet the firm's targeted level. The new product was subsequently discontinued. The product can be best classified as a(n)
   a. relative product failure.
   b. total product failure.
   c. marginal product failure.
   d. absolute product failure.

6. Which of the following products evolved from laboratory-oriented sources?
   a. Synthetic fibers
   b. Roll-on deodorants
   c. Easy-opening soda cans
   d. Swiss-almond chocolate ice cream

7. Which of these is the *least* expensive stage in new-product development?
   a. Test marketing
   b. Product development
   c. Concept testing
   d. Commercialization

8. In the business analysis stage of the new-product planning process,
   a. consumer acceptance is determined.
   b. the return on investment of the new product is calculated.
   c. a prototype product is developed.
   d. a brand name and product package are determined.

9. Which of the following is *not* a type of decision usually made during the product development stage?
   a. Branding
   b. Product screening
   c. Packaging
   d. Product positioning

10. In test marketing, which of the following is determined?
    a. Consumer attitudes
    b. Product development costs
    c. Consumer and reseller product acceptance
    d. Long-term competitive advantages

11. The commercialization stage corresponds to which stage of the product life cycle?
    a. Maturity
    b. Decline

c. Introduction
d. Growth

12. The rate of adoption is faster if a product
a. is compatible with a consumer's current lifestyle.
b. is a major innovation.
c. has high perceived risk.
d. can be tried in small quantities.

13. In the diffusion process, laggards can be characterized as
a. opinion leaders, and high in income and status.
b. cosmopolitan, and attentive to information cues.
c. tradition bound, and conservative.
d. past middle age, and skeptics.

14. An appropriate marketing goal for a mature product is
a. product deletion.
b. maintenance of product lines.
c. orderly withdrawal from the market.
d. expanding the market.

15. A product should be deleted when it
a. diverts attention from the firm's long-term goals.
b. has a poor outlook for short-run sales and profit.
c. complements other company offerings.
d. attracts a small, loyal market.

For the answers to these questions, please visit the online site for this book at **http://www.atomicdog.com**.

Case 1: Motorola: From Cold to Cool[c4-1]

After a decade of lackluster sales for its cell telephone products, Motorola's (http://www.motorola.com) super-thin clamshell-shaped Razr V3 phone is a hit in both Europe and North America. Motorola estimates that it sold roughly 1.2 million Razr phones in Europe and North America during just the first quarter of 2005. The new phone was responsible for Motorola's 10 percent sales gain from the March 2004 to the March 2005 sales quarters. Motorola's 1.4 percent increase in market share (to 17.1 percent) during the first quarter of 2005 can also be directly traced to the Razr, which is available exclusively from Cingular (http://www.cingular.com) in the United States. In contrast, Nokia (http://www.nokia.com) had a 32 percent market share over the corresponding time period.

Although Motorola has traditionally been associated with technological excellence, many of its products have also been viewed as boring. For much of its history, Motorola was run by executives with engineering backgrounds. As an engineering company, Motorola was a pioneer in the development of car radios in the late 1920s. It invented cellular technology and marketed the first hand-held cell phone in 1983. It also made a number of critical marketing mistakes such as being too slow to change from analog to digital handsets and not considering the potential magnitude of Asian competition for cell phones.

Ed Zander, Motorola's chief executive, is much more consumer focused than Motorola's past senior executives. Zander has continually challenged Motorola to develop products that let customers express who they want to be: "Cool is innovative. I want us to be cool in everything we do, from phones to set-top boxes to public safety systems to telecommunications infrastructure."

In developing the Razr, Zander encouraged the phone's designers to build the product based on their own wish list, not based on consumer focus groups. As a result, the Razr was completed in one year—six months faster than the normal time period. To assure that its plans were not shared with competitors, subcontractors only made small parts of the phone. No single subcontractor made enough of the phone for it to figure out the overall design and features. Motorola executives who worked on the project were also told to keep the plans secret. To add excitement to the phone's marketing program, Motorola promoted Geoffrey Frost, a former Nike executive, to become its chief marketing officer. He prepared a campaign based on a "fashion-meets-functionality" role in the life of a young adult. Frost's initial advertising plan was tied to Nike's notion that its advertising was not about sneakers, but about the wearer.

A key question among marketing analysts is whether one phone model, regardless of its success, is enough to turn Motorola's fortunes around. One industry expert notes that "Cool phones will be the key to Motorola's success at the high end, but the company also faces manufacturers who can and do turn out a lot of low-cost phones." Particularly worrisome to Motorola are the 40 or so million handsets that are now made in China. To compete in this segment, Motorola will sell a new low-cost model in emerging markets for the equivalent of $40.

Motorola has introduced a cell phone in collaboration with Apple that is compatible with iTunes (http://www.apple.com/itunes), Apple's music-playing software. Some naysayers feel that many mobile-phone service providers will not carry this model because they are developing their own music services for sale to consumers. Motorola thinks that the market for this phone will be small service carriers that do not have the resources to build their own music facilities.

Questions

1. How can Motorola continue to make "cool" products?
2. Present a program to ensure confidentiality for Motorola's new products that are in various stages of the new-product planning process.
3. Explain how the success of the Razr can be applied to related products.
4. Discuss the pros and cons of the Razr phone's being so vital to Motorola's success.

[c4-1] The data in the case are drawn from Ted C. Fishman, "How Ed Zander Honed Razr's Edge," *Business 2.0* (June 2005), pp. 47–49.

Case 2: The Changing Role of Private Brands[c4-2]

A common perception is that private brands trade on the success of manufacturer brands. This perspective suggests that private brands are lower-cost, lower-quality alternatives to manufacturer brands and that they are not supported with research and development, marketing, or promotional funds.

Private brands now account for about 15 percent of U.S. retail sales and as much as 40 percent of retail sales in some major European markets. A key factor contributing to the success of private brands is the 25 percent or so price differential with comparable-quality manufacturer brands. According to Jim Jubak, an editor for *MS Money*, the small differences in product quality compared to manufacturer brands no longer can justify the manufacturer's higher price to many consumers. Jubak says that manufacturer brands need to have constant product innovation to continue to enjoy success.

A common error among product managers of manufacturer brands is to assume that their brands are viewed by final consumers as more legitimate than store brands. In reality, private brands such as Craftsman, Gap, and Martha Stewart enjoy significant trust in terms of quality and style that are the envy of many manufacturer brands. The success of major retailers such as Wal-Mart, Target, and Costco is also tied to their strong private brands. Wal-Mart generally positions its private brand next to the strongest-selling manufacturer brand and does not even stock second-level, "me-too" manufacturer brands.

All brands must be managed so that they can connect with consumers on a personal and emotional level. Brands also need to innovate, offer value, establish confidence, and generate pride of ownership. These connections cannot be based on a low price or a brand name alone. Brands have to offer an experience that is both meaningful and differentiated from other brands. This experience bonds a customer to the brand.

One way to determine how well a brand connects with its consumers is to look at its level of customer engagement, which examines what a brand designation means to a customer, not a manufacturer or a retailer. There are four levels of customer engagement: fully engaged, engaged, not engaged, and actively disengaged. These categories apply equally to manufacturer and private brands. Let's examine the characteristics of each of these levels.

Fully engaged customers are extremely loyal to a brand and will not accept a substitute. If a desired brand is not available, this shopper will go elsewhere or elect to buy at a later date. Fully engaged customers tend to be a firm's most profitable customers due to their large purchases on a consistent basis. They also serve as brand ambassadors due to their positive word-of-mouth influence with others.

Even though engaged customers are emotionally attached to a brand, they are not as loyal as fully engaged customers. Though they may like a firm's brands, they may also switch to other brands based on price, convenience, or additional customer service. An example of an engaged customer is one who is loyal to Coca-Cola but will switch to a Pepsi product when it is on sale.

Not engaged customers are disconnected emotionally and are neutral to a brand. They often have a "take-it-or-leave-it" mentality about purchase decisions. Actively disengaged customers are completely detached from a brand. They quickly switch to another brand and may even become angry if switching is difficult or even impossible. Like fully engaged customers, actively disengaged customers often tell others about their experiences with a brand. However, this group will focus on negative experiences.

Questions

1. Explain the significance of this statement: "All brands need to innovate, offer value, establish confidence, and generate pride of ownership. These connections cannot be based on a low price or a brand name alone."
2. Describe your degree of product engagement regarding your choice of soda, bottled water, or prepackaged iced tea. What factors contribute to your degree of engagement?
3. Compare and contrast the degree of product engagement notion described in this case with the consumer's brand decision process covered in Chapter 8.
4. How has Craftsman, Gap, or Martha Stewart built trust among consumers as brand name designations?

[c4-2] The data in the case are drawn from William J. McEwen, "Private Brands Are Brands, Too," *Gallup Management Journal* (June 9, 2005).

Case 3: Creating a Better Screwdriver—and Getting It into Sears[c4-3]

Allen Kenner started developing his "Grip-N-Drive" screwdrivers in 1998. Although the Grip-N-Drive model spins freely in both directions like a typical ratchet screwdriver, it spins faster and more easily with a single twist than a typical screwdriver. Kenner invested about $15,000 to secure the necessary patents and to prepare a working model of his invention.

Kenner believes in simplicity. "People fall in love with inventions that are simple to use, simple to understand, and that work really well." The Grip-N-Drive screwdriver's technology relies on two nylon snap-rings and a rubber grip that is mounted on the screwdriver. To make sure that his new product would be viewed as a significant innovation, Kenner showed his prototype model to friends, spoke to successful businesspeople, and contacted hand-tool industry executives. Kenner always insisted that anyone he discussed the product with sign a nondisclosure agreement. This agreement states that any information obtained from Kenner's discussion would be treated as strictly confidential.

Kenner's marketing strategy was to license Grip-N-Drive to a manufacturer that would then sell the product to Sears (http://www.sears.com). Kenner would receive profits from royalty agreements, giving him a percentage of the product's sales. He chose Sears as an outlet for his invention because of its significant presence in the hand-tool market and its large distribution network. Kenner initially worked with a manufacturer that produced tools sold at Sears, but later switched to Pratt-Read (http://www.pratt-read.com), a leading private label manufacturer, once the original manufacturer found that a design change required by Sears was too costly to implement. The Grip-N-Drive screwdriver was first sold in some Sears stores in October 2004. A national rollout to all Sears stores occurred soon thereafter. Pratt-Read anticipates that Grip-N-Drive will have annual sales of between $1 million and $5 million through the Sears affiliation. Sears currently sells the screwdriver with five screw bits for $19.99 under its Craftsman label.

Inventors can learn a number of lessons from Kenner's experiences:

1. *Protect your idea:* It may be necessary to show the invention to consumers, manufacturers, and other channel members; however, all parties should sign a nondisclosure agreement. Sample agreements may be found at the United Inventors Association Web site (http://www.uiausa.com) and other sites, as well as through attorneys.

2. *Be patient:* Inventors are typically in a rush to market their new products. However, they must recognize that securing the proper design, manufacturer, and reseller are critical tasks. The ultimate goal is to develop a relationship with a manufacturer that has high quality control and customer support levels and to partner with a retailer that has sufficient distribution prowess.

3. *Be careful about agreements:* An inventor should not have to pay a royalty fee to any firm that does not either manufacture or market his or her product. This should be stated in all verbal and written communications.

4. *Deal with trustworthy firms:* Because the design of the Grip-N-Drive was simple, Kenner was concerned that his invention would be copied if it were manufactured overseas. He insisted that it be made in the United States as a way of better protecting his patent.

5. *Know your strengths and weaknesses:* Kenner understood that he did not have the resources, know-how, or depth of management required to produce or market his invention. The licensing arrangement enabled him to outsource these activities while still retaining profits and some control.

6. *Know how to interpret consumers' willingness to buy:* The success of a product is largely based on the manufacturing-to-price ratio. Inventors should work backward from the price a customer is willing to pay to see if there are adequate profits for the retailer and manufacturer—and the inventor.

Questions

1. Kenner's overall new-product planning strategy was to outsource product manufacturing and distribution. Describe the pros and cons of this strategy.
2. Download a sample nondisclosure agreement from the Web. Discuss its key components.
3. Describe the pros and cons of Kenner's use of Sears as a marketing channel for Grip-N-Drive.
4. Prepare a list of additional suggestions for inventors with little marketing experience. Refer to the United Inventors Association Web site (http://www.uiausa.org).

[c4-3] The data in the case are drawn from Don Debelak, "Tool Time," *Entrepreneur* (July 2005), pp. 126, 128.

Case 4: From Startup to Innovative Shoe Line: Nearly an Overnight Success[c4-4]

Footwear companies typically spend as much as 10 months designing a new style. So it may have seemed strange to some observers that Jim Van Dine and his three Keen Footwear (**http://www.keenfootwear.com**) company partners were still fine-tuning a Mary Janes (a popular girl's shoe with a strap-and-buckle design) shoe design just eight weeks prior to needing samples. A major strategic advantage for Keen was that one of its partners had contacts with overseas suppliers and had already reserved manufacturing capacity for large production runs. The firm also had access to independent shoe designers that could develop manufacturing specifications based on the team's drawings.

Two months after its designs were finalized, a Chinese factory began producing 16 styles of shoes: clogs, slip-on models, and of course, the Mary Janes. During the first year, Keen sold $30 million worth of shoes (700,000 pairs). In contrast, it took Teva, another popular brand, three years to reach $1 million in annual sales. "You could say we were birthed full size," stated Van Dine.

Keen Footwear is an example of a small startup firm that has grown into a major competitive force at lightning speed. Other small firms have had similar success in the toy, sporting equipment, apparel, and electronics industries. Many of them owe the fast success to their ability to use innovations in product design, outsource production, and generate sales and publicity through the Internet. Let's examine each of these steps.

Use innovations in product design: Kidrobot (**http://www.kidrobot.com**) is an 11-employee firm that specializes in the sale of collectible dolls on the Web. The firm is on track to attain $5.5 million in annual sales at its retail stores and through a TV cartoon. Its characters are designed with the Adobe Illustrator software package (**http://www.adobe.com/products/illustrator**), which sells for $500. Adobe Illustrator enables Kidrobot's designers to produce six views of each toy, including close-ups of specific details such as eyelashes. It also uses Basecamp software (**http://www.basecamphq.com**) to link its New York designers with its Chinese manufacturers. With Basecamp, factories can make clay or wax models from detailed sketches without the need to send multiple prototypes halfway around the world for preliminary approval. Basecamp, priced at about $100 a month, helped Kidrobot move through the design, manufacture, and marketing cycle in four months. Some established firms such as Mattel and Hasbro require at least a year.

Outsource production: Joyce Yu is an account representative for Union Electric, her family's contract manufacturing business. Union Electric produces singing cake cutters, golf pedometers, and digital recording devices and other products for firms such as Brookstone, Discovery Channel, and Radio Shack. Although there are thousands of contract manufacturers in Asia, the best of them have teams of industrial designers and mechanical and electrical engineers who can translate a design to a finished product in as little as two months.

Generate sales and publicity through the Internet: The existence of online chat groups, bulletin boards, and blogs has reduced the time needed for consumers to research, purchase, and recommend new items to friends and family. At Freebord (**http://www.freebord.com**), a skateboard company founded in 2001, the firm's chief executive received an E-mail concerning the firm's six-wheel rides. After a post from the owner of Coolhunting.com (**http://www.coolhunting.com**), Freebord's Web site traffic increased to fives times its normal level. Freebord still does not advertise and spends its $1,800 marketing budget totally on stickers. The company anticipated 2005 sales to reach $1.5 million. "We weren't very well known, and suddenly everyone was checking us out," said Bayard Winthrop, Freebord's chief executive officer.

Questions

1. Visit the Kidrobot (**http://www.kidrobot.com**), Adobe Illustrator (**http://www.adobe.com/products/illustrator**), and Basecamp (**http://www.basecamphq.com**) Web sites. Explain how one of these software packages could be effectively used by a small innovator.

2. Describe the pros and cons of using a Chinese contractor to outsource a product.

3. Develop a program for generating sales and publicity through the Internet for a new watch maker.

4. What lessons can be derived from Keen Footwear's success that are applicable to other small startups?

[c4-4] The data in the case are drawn from Michael V. Copeland and Andrew Tilin, "The New Instant Companies," *Business 2.0* (June 2005), pp. 82–94.

Using a Cross-Functional Team to Plan a Successful New Product Launch[pc-4]

INTRODUCTION

Implementing a marketing program is still closer to art than science. A case in point is that new-product development (NPD) has witnessed significant progress in developing a systematic process for its front end and middle part. But new-product launch planning (NPLP) still depends in large part on the marketing manager's experience. The new-product launch phase involves the highest costs, resources, and risks of all the phases. It is also the least well-managed. Such high stakes make it imperative for the marketing manager to better understand the inner workings of the launch-planning process. The key question is: How can marketing managers improve the new-product launch planning process and coordination so it results in reduced risk?

To answer this question, I conducted a study with marketing executives of manufacturing companies. Of 250 targeted respondents contacted to participate, 102 executives responded. All were senior managers of marketing, with marketing-sales, and/or product management functions involved in new product development, specifically NPLP decisions within the manufacturing industry. The companies in the study represented five major subcategories, including machinery (e.g., agricultural machinery, machine tools), equipment (e.g., industrial control, material handling equipment), components (e.g., valves, electrical parts), material (e.g., glass, chemical), and processing (e.g., construction, packaging).

COORDINATING NPLP

Only one-fourth (28 percent) of all firms in my study said that their NPLP was carried out well. Three-fourths thought there was room for improving the planning and its coordination. Also, the study revealed that larger firms (those with annual revenues of $500 million or more) carried out the NPLP much better than their smaller counterparts (those with annual revenues of $100 million or less), as shown in Figure 1.

Several reasons were given for the NPLP not necessarily being carried out well, as summarized in Figure 2. "Not well-defined planning steps" was the most often mentioned reason, followed by "weak functional support" and "ineffective communication." Also mentioned were "functional silos" and "poor project management." More than half of the respondents considered functional silos to be the most critical reason that planning coordination was

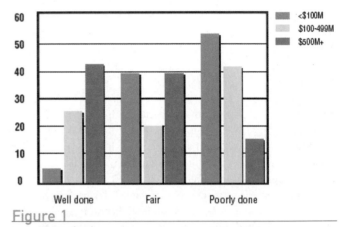

Figure 1

Rated New Product Launch Planning Efforts (in %)

hampered. A much smaller proportion, 10 percent, considered "poor project management" to be most critical.

Compared to smaller firms, a greater proportion of larger firms considered functional silos to be the most significant reason for poor NPLP coordination. Larger firms tend to adopt more formal procedures, including formal planning to improve control. Increased firm size brings greater organizational complexity and

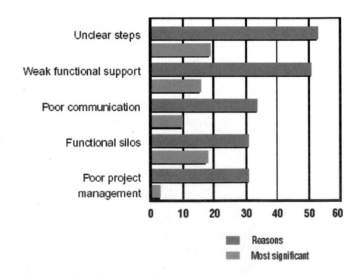

Figure 2

Reasons for Poor Coordination of NPLP

[pc-4] Adapted by the authors from Ken Kono, "Planning Makes Perfect," *Marketing Management* (March-April 2005), pp. 31–35. Reprinted by permission of the American Marketing Association.

carries with it the need for coordination through some mechanism. As a result, functional silos tend to emerge as an organization grows. A marketing vice-president of a medium-size manufacturer commented: "When we were a small company, new products were developed really informally—everyone worked well with one another. As we grew bigger, personal touch was lost, departments got bigger, and people who didn't know each other were thrown into a team. We had to get to know each other quickly. People subtly brought their departments into the team as part of their names like 'John Finance Smith.' "

Mechanisms such as cross-functional teams mitigate functional silos. For cross-functional teams to work effectively, though, they need active support from senior management. The finding that "weak functional support" is another key reason for poor coordination, as shown in Figure 2, speaks loudly about the importance of senior management's commitment to inter-functional coordination. Another respondent echoed this point: "Rather than the executive of interest, a steering committee guides the work of new product [development] teams in my company. The important thing about it, I believe, is not the specific decisions the steering committee makes, but rather how it sets the tone—the environment in which the teams operate."

USING CROSS-FUNCTIONAL TEAMS

As a coordination mechanism, cross-functional teams generally serve well for the front-end and middle part of the NPD process. So would they serve well for the back end? One-third (33 percent) of the companies surveyed used cross-functional teams as the primary coordinator of NPLP, whereas 37 percent of the companies reported no use of them. The remaining 30 percent said that they use cross-functional teams on a case-by-case basis, depending on the relative importance or circumstances of particular projects.

The study observed a much differing level of cross-functional teams' involvement in marketing mix decisions, as shown in Figure 3. Cross-functional teams' involvement was highest for new-product pricing, followed by distribution decisions and marketing communications. Less than 10 percent of the firms used cross-functional teams as the primary vehicle for marketing communications decisions, such as trade promotion, trade shows, publicity, and advertising. But 41 percent of the firms used cross-functional teams as a resource for the primary lead organization charged with marketing communication planning.

Most of the "depends" responses shown in Figure 3 represent a case in which cross-functional teams are used as a resource team. For example, a sales executive works with a cross-functional team before making a decision regarding the choice of distributors. The team offers input as a resource, but the sales executive makes the final decision.

More than half (54 percent) of the respondents indicated that cross-functional teams determined the new-product pricing. This is an interesting observation, given the prevalent notion that an existing function (such as product management) or department (such as finance) often takes over new-product pricing decisions from cross-functional teams. Reflecting on this point, a marketing director of a large manufacturing company commented: "We had no idea at first

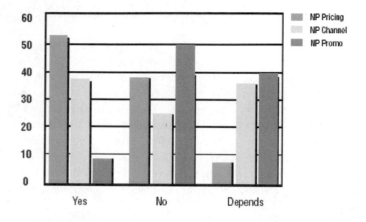

Figure 3

Use of Cross-Functional Teams for Marketing Mix Decisions

how well our [NPLP cross-functional] team could lead the pricing decision by working together with the finance folks. But two members of the team who represented the finance group felt the decisions the team made were really sharp. They thought through unit cost, target margin, and competition carefully without losing sight of [the product's] value. The team's presentation to the finance management was well done—"really convincing."

Regardless of the size of companies, the extent of the use of cross-functional teams was relatively constant with respect to their involvement in marketing communications decisions. However, the extent of cross-functional team involvement differed significantly regarding new-product pricing and channel decisions. Smaller firms (those with an annual revenue of less than $100 million) are less likely to use cross-functional teams for pricing and channel distribution decisions than larger firms (those with an annual revenue of more than $500 million). The use of cross-functional teams for pricing decisions is clear cut—either they do it or they don't. Their use for channel decisions, on the other hand, is less clear-cut in that cross-functional teams often are used as a resource, as indicated by a relatively high percentage of "depends" responses.

Those respondents with "depends" responses were asked to clarify their conditional responses. Their conditional responses meant that cross-functional teams were used as a resource team, making input to key decision maker(s). Other responses indicated whether or not and to what extent the member composition of cross-functional teams is suitable for the specific tasks of NPLP. A remark by a respondent underscores this point: "We used to use original cross-functional teams with most of the core members still staying on through the [new product] launch. For the most part, they served minimally as a resource for promotion planning. A promo manager led the launch prep work. Recently, a few people suggested letting the cross-functional teams lead [launch planning] while a few members need to be replaced with the ones with more experience [in the launch work]."

Regardless of the approach, a majority of respondents said they would like to see cross-functional teams play a larger role, at least as a resource in the channel and in the marketing communications area.

WHAT CAN BE DONE?

One of the key observations in this study is that three-quarters of respondents thought there was room for improving NPLP and its coordination. The most often mentioned reason for this was "not well-defined planning steps." NPLP is creative knowledge work, yet it could benefit from a certain level of structured process. It falls somewhere between two polar positions: the specific activity-defined process approach versus the laissez-faire approach. The implication to management is clear: Give a certain level of structure for NPLP, such as defining a relatively high level of key activity steps and coordination checkpoints. Figure 4 shows four steps for better planning.

For better coordination and execution of NPLP, cross-functional teams need to continue to be involved in decision making. Cross-functional teams carry knowledge about the new product from its inception to its market offering, especially the specific details and nuances specified early on. Specifics of launch tactics are often determined by the front end of product development. For example, the product's newness is determined at the very outset of its development process. It significantly influences how it is launched. Such decisions are determined by the new-product development team. The team provides valuable product knowledge as input to NPLP.

One of the study observations is that management judiciously replaces a few team members with those with NPLP expertise when the team transitions into the NPLP phase. The team should be left intact in terms of its collective memory on earlier tasks on the development process, yet some members' contributions may taper off to little or nil for NPLP. This is because the NPLP requires different skill sets. It is a delicate balancing act to preserve the team's integrity while NPLP task-appropriate skills are brought in. The second managerial implication is then to subtly reconfigure the cross-functional team for the NPLP phase while maintaining the integrity of the original cross-functional team. Make sure the transition is smooth to maintain the team's enthusiasm and momentum.

In an environment where rigid functional silos exist, the cross-functional teams' effectiveness may be less than optimal. Clearly, in such cases, senior management needs to provide strong support to the project manager and his or her team. It is essential to make his project implementation one of the top priorities. Rather than an executive of interest, an executive team that represents key stakeholder functions should guide the cross-functional teams. This sets the tone for interfunctional coordination and signals the project's criticality throughout the organization. The third implication, thus, is that an active steering committee that represents the key stakeholder functions is as critical to NPLP as it is to the front-end and middle part of the new-product development process.

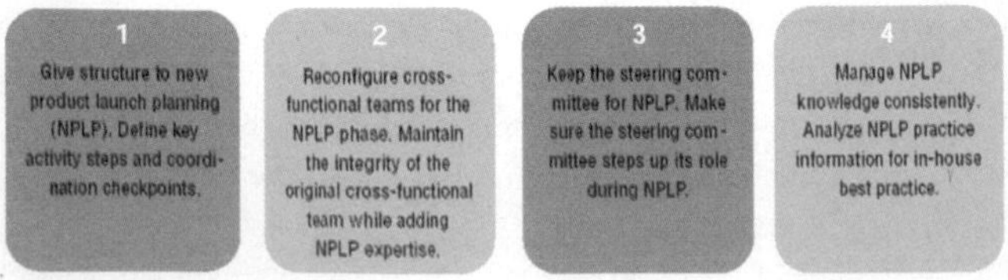

Cross-functional teams, if managed well, could solve some of the NPLP barriers that this study has identified, including, "poorly defined planning steps," "ineffective communications," and "functional silos." (See Figure 2.) With executives' active support, cross-functional teams could define their own NPLP planning steps themselves as they move along. They should be able to do it well, because all key functions that would be involved in NPLP are represented in the teams. Over time, the cross-functional teams accumulate substantial knowledge on planning steps. The knowledge eventually could become in-house NPLP best practices. Hence, the fourth implication is to capture NPLP practice information for each NPLP project, to tease out best practices from the accumulated team information, and to have subsequent teams review and update the practice book.

MORE TO BE DONE

A surprising finding is that there is still much room to improve cross-functional communication and coordination, even though the industry has gone through what Thomas Davenport and J. Short described as the "decade of process management" in their well-known 1990 *Sloan Management Review* article. The process management concept first and foremost attempted to break down functional silos for more effective strategy execution. Cross-functional coordination is critical, particularly during the NPLP phase because all activities need to be synchronized to be effective in NPLP. All functions and their resources need to be made ready for deployment—ranging from production ramp-up to the preparation of channel partners to priming of market demand. Cross-functional teams, by definition, are a direct answer to ineffective communication and functional silos. The very nature of cross-functional teams should directly help marketing implementation.

Figure 4

Four Steps for Success

1	2	3	4
Give structure to new product launch planning (NPLP). Define key activity steps and coordination checkpoints.	Reconfigure cross-functional teams for the NPLP phase. Maintain the integrity of the original cross-functional team while adding NPLP expertise.	Keep the steering committee for NPLP. Make sure the steering committee steps up its role during NPLP.	Manage NPLP knowledge consistently. Analyze NPLP practice information for in-house best practice.

Questions

1. In general, how can marketing managers improve the new-product planning process and coordinate tasks better so there is reduced risk of failure?
2. Comment on the new-product planning findings summarized in Figure 2.
3. What would you recommend to improve the company performance in each of the areas listed in Figure 2?
4. What is the purpose of a cross-functional team in product planning?
5. In practice, what potential problems may exist with a cross-functional team involved in product planning? How would you solve them?
6. As an executive at a small startup firm, what are the most important lessons you garnered from this case?
7. As an executive at a large established firm, what are the most important lessons you garnered from this case? Discuss the differences in your answers to questions 6 and 7.

Distribution Planning

Part 5 deals with distribution, the second major element of the marketing mix.

14 Value Chain Management and Logistics

Here, we study the value chain and value delivery chain, which encompass all activities and parties that create and deliver a given level of customer value. This requires careful planning as to the physical movement and transfer of ownership of a product from producer to consumer. We explore distribution functions, types of channels, supplier/distribution intermediary contracts, channel cooperation and conflict, the industrial channel, and international distribution. We also look at logistics, especially transportation and inventory management issues.

15 Wholesaling

In this chapter, we examine wholesaling—buying and/or handling goods and services and their subsequent resale to organizational users, retailers, and/or other wholesalers. We show wholesaling's impact on the economy, its functions, and its relationships with suppliers and customers. We describe the major company-owned and independent wholesalers and note trends in wholesaling.

16 Retailing

Here, we concentrate on retailing, which consists of those business activities involved with the sale of goods and services to the final consumer. We show retailing's impact on the economy, its functions in distribution, and its relationship with suppliers. We categorize retailers by ownership, store strategy mix, and nonstore operations. We also describe several retail planning considerations and note trends in retailing.

 After reading Part 5, you should understand element 11 of the strategic marketing plan outlined in Table 3-2 (page 77).

Chapter 14

Value Chain Management and Logistics

Dell (**http://www.dell.com**) is the world's largest direct seller of computers. In addition to its desktop and notebook PCs, Dell sells servers, workstations, third-party software, and systems support. Dell has annual revenues of more than $45 billion, a net profit margin of 6.4 percent, and an impressive return on equity.

Twenty-year-old Michael Dell founded PC Limited in 1984, when he started selling computer chips and disk drives from his University of Texas dormitory room. Dell bought these products at cost from retailers who were forced to purchase more units than they could sell due to IBM's quota system. Soon, Dell's computer business was grossing about $80,000 a month due to his ability to underprice traditional dealers by 10 to 15 percent. Dell then dropped out of college and began making IBM clones that he sold directly to consumers at a significant discount from IBM's prices. In 1987, Dell renamed PC Limited "Dell Computer," went public, and added international offices. In 1988, Dell Computer began selling to large corporate customers. In 1999, Dell became the largest marketer on the Web with greater sales than Amazon.com, eBay, and Yahoo! combined. In 2005, *Forbes* magazine ranked Michael Dell as the fourth wealthiest person in the United States, with a net worth of approximately $18 billion.

Much of Dell's initial and continuing success is due to a combination of factors: Dell's direct-to-consumer model, mass customization, sales to large corporate customers, and recognition of consumer value. The direct-to-consumer model gives Dell greater control over pricing and customer service. Mass customization fulfills customers' specific needs while reducing inventory requirements for Dell. Sales to large corporate customers mean lower sales and customer support costs due to large orders and the customers' well-informed information technology staff. Finally, Dell recognizes customer value by installing software and providing the same configuration for all orders from the same corporate customer.

As one analyst remarked, "Before him [Dell], innovation was about well-schooled engineers in pricey research and development labs inventing high-margin products and technologies. Dell instead trained his eye on finding the most efficient way to get tech products into the hands of customers. By perfecting a simple credo—cut out the middleman—he turned the computer business on its head."[1]

In this chapter, we will learn about the decisions made in distribution planning—including direct channels—and the activities involved in physical distribution.

Chapter Objectives

1. To discuss the role of the value chain and the value delivery chain in the distribution process
2. To explore distribution planning and examine its importance, distribution functions, the factors used in selecting a distribution channel, and the different types of distribution channels
3. To consider the nature of distribution intermediary contracts, cooperation and conflict in a channel of distribution, the special aspects of a distribution channel for industrial products, and international distribution
4. To examine logistics and demonstrate its importance
5. To discuss transportation alternatives and inventory management issues

[1] Various company and other sources.

14-1   OVERVIEW

In recent years, the distribution process has witnessed a dramatic transformation, one that is expected to continue in the future. Consider the following:

Best Buy [**http://www.bestbuy.com**] is revamping its processes and systems to improve the flow of goods through its Asian purchasing office and to import more products directly to its U.S. distribution centers and stores. Best Buy's strategy involves sharing its demographic and forecasting information with suppliers overseas and working with them to develop products and track them through various channels. A new purchase-order and inventory system helps Best Buy more closely monitor its assortment and replenishment processes so it can reroute products to prevent running out of an item or take advantage of a spike in demand: "It's all about collaboration among the different pieces of software that we've implemented over the last four to five years."[2]

Your PC may have been designed in Taiwan and assembled in Mexico, with memory chips from South Korea, a motherboard from China, and a hard drive from Thailand. Firms around the world now specialize—as innovators and designers of goods, low-cost producers, specialized assemblers, or marketers and distributors. Countries too are starting to specialize: Mexico and Eastern Europe take advantage of their location to assemble goods destined for the United States and Europe, respectively, and China uses its huge labor pool to be a global base for low-cost manufacturing.[3]

In a recent survey of large firms, nearly all respondents said that improving customer experience is either critical or very important. But too often, their efforts end up as hype-heavy—delivering little improvement to a subpar set of customer interactions. So what's going wrong? **Fragmented responsibilities:** Customers interact with companies across a number of different touchpoints to meet a variety of different needs. And while customers view these interactions as pieces of a single "relationship," companies often don't look at it the same way. **Pushy marketing:** Companies regularly promote their goods and services by creating explicit and implicit promises about their brands. But firms often forget to shift gears and deliver on these promises. Some telltale signs of the problem: Retailers that send coupons for products that are out of stock in the store and Web site home pages overrun with product pictures that obscure the customer's path to achieving her goals.[4]

This chapter presents an in-depth look at the value chain and the value delivery chain, distribution planning, and logistics. Chapter 15 covers wholesaling. Chapter 16 discusses retailing.

14-2   THE ROLE OF THE VALUE CHAIN AND THE VALUE DELIVERY CHAIN IN THE DISTRIBUTION PROCESS[5]

The four stages of the distribution process are depicted in Figure 14-1: goals, value chain and value delivery chain, total delivered product, and level of satisfaction. Here are the key points to consider:

> The distribution process has four stages, from setting goals to the level of satisfaction for each party in the process.

[2] "How Far Can It Go?" *McKinsey Quarterly* (Issue 4, 2003), Special Edition.

[3] Elena Malykhina, "Best Buy Bolsters Supply Chain," *Information Week* (February 7, 2005), p. 43.

[4] Bruce D. Temkin, *The Customer Experience Value Chain* (Cambridge, MA: Forrester Research, March 15, 2005).

[5] The material in this section is loosely adapted by the authors from Joel R. Evans and Barry Berman, "Conceptualizing and Operationalizing the Business-to-Business Value Chain," *Industrial Marketing Management*, Vol. 30 (February 2001), pp. 135–148. Copyright Elsevier Science. Reprinted by permission.

Figure 14-1

The Distribution Process

Source: Loosely adapted by the authors from Joel R. Evans and Barry Berman, "Conceptualizing and Operationalizing the Business-to-Business Value Chain," *Industrial Marketing Management,* Vol. 30 (February 2001), p. 138. Copyright Elsevier Science. Reprinted by permission.

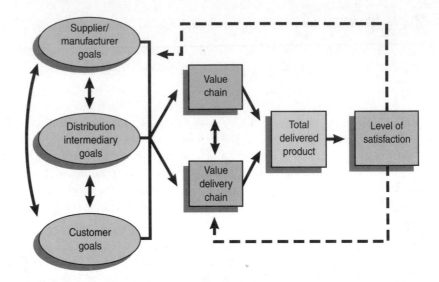

- The goals of the various parties are considered as inputs to the value chain and value delivery chain.
- The value chain and value delivery chain are parallel processes.
- The total delivered product is the *actual* result of the value chain and value delivery chain.
- Satisfaction is based on the *perceived* value received from the value chain and value delivery chain.
- Feedback regarding service gaps and breakdowns must be handled systematically in the process.

Let us now discuss the stages in the distribution process.

14-2a   Goals

The distribution process may be viewed from multiple perspectives, and the goals represented by these perspectives must be in sync for the distribution process to succeed in the long run. Many channels have three basic participants: suppliers/manufacturers, distribution intermediaries, and customers. Before enacting a distribution strategy, the goals of each party must be determined, exchanged, and reconciled. These goals then set the direction for the value chain and value delivery chain. As enumerated in Table 14-1, the three parties typically have distinct distribution goals.

14-2b   Value Chain and Value Delivery Chain

A value chain has two aspects: the value chain itself and the value delivery chain. A *value chain* represents the series of business activities that are performed to design, produce, market, deliver, and service a product for customers.[6] These value chain activities are often performed: order fulfillment, product development, research and development, quality control, cost management,

> The **value chain** consists of activities that design, produce, market, deliver, and service a product for customers. The **value delivery chain** includes all the parties in a value chain.

[6] "Dictionary of Marketing Terms," **http://www.marketingpower.com/mg-dictionary.php** (May 3, 2006).

Table 14-1 Selected Distribution Goals by Party

Party	Distribution Goals
Suppliers/ Manufacturers	To gain access to the distribution channel
	To ensure that all distribution functions are performed by one party or another
	To hold down distribution and inventory costs
	To foster relationship marketing with distribution intermediaries and customers
	To obtain feedback from distribution intermediaries and customers
	To have some control over the distribution strategy
	To optimize production runs and achieve economies of scale
	To secure some exclusivity with distribution intermediaries
	To resist the payment of slotting allowances (the fees charged by some distribution intermediaries to secure shelf space)
	To receive a fair share of profits
Distribution Intermediaries	To have on-time deliveries and quick turnaround time for orders
	To ensure that all distribution functions are performed by one party or another
	To service multiple suppliers/manufacturers in order to present a choice for customers
	To meet customer needs
	To foster relationship marketing with manufacturers/suppliers and customers
	To obtain feedback from distribution manufacturers/suppliers and customers
	To have some control over the distribution strategy
	To be as efficient as possible in shipping and inventory management
	To secure some exclusivity with suppliers/manufacturers
	To receive a fair share of profits
Customers	To have an assortment of products from which to choose
	To have a variety of resellers from which to choose
	To purchase in small quantities
	To shop at convenient locations
	To find items in-stock, including those on sale
	To have a number of payment options
	To be able to easily return products that are unsatisfactory
	To be treated in a respectful manner
	To have enough information to make informed decisions
	To pay fair prices

information interchange, facilities management, customer service, procurement, product commercialization, and returns (reverse logistics). The value chain is task-based.

A **value delivery chain** encompasses all of the parties who engage in value chain activities. It is performer-based and involves three factors: the specific parties in a given value chain, their relationships, and the activities undertaken by each party. The effectiveness of a value chain is greatly affected by the caliber of the value delivery chain. Value is added by each participant, and differentiation is enhanced by the delivery chain, because each party adds something to the mix. A delivery chain is only as strong as its weakest link. If a supplier has quality control problems, this hurts the manufacturer. If a manufacturer is late with shipments, this hurts the wholesaler. If a wholesaler does not keep its facilities well maintained, this hurts the supplier and manufacturer. Win-win-win is a delivery chain goal. For the value delivery chain to work properly, the supplier/manufacturer, distribution intermediary, and customer must each feel its needs are satisfied. Firms must do everything possible to avoid value delivery chain breakdowns.

As an illustration, these are some activities that must be performed in a value chain for fresh-cut flowers: growing and harvesting the flowers, selecting the best flowers and storing them as they await shipment, shipping the flowers to resellers, displaying and preserving the flowers in florists' shops, wrapping flowers for customers, delivering customer orders when requested, and providing instructions for extending the life of the flowers. Through the value delivery chain, the supplier undertakes certain tasks and outsources others, such as using a local delivery firm to ship flowers throughout the city in which it operates and selling at florists rather than at an on-site shop. The consumer is responsible for keeping the flowers in water and making sure they are not in direct sunlight.

14-2c   Total Delivered Product

> The **total delivered product** is the bundle of product attributes actually provided to consumers, and depends on how well distribution functions are performed.

The **total delivered product** comprises the bundle of tangible and intangible product attributes actually provided to consumers through a value chain and its related value delivery chain. This concept reflects how well activities in the distribution process are performed: Is the product shipped on time? Does it arrive intact without breaking or spoiling? Are store shelves fully stocked? Is the product properly price-marked? Is the return policy clearly stated and reasonable? Is the waiting time to make a purchase short enough? In the case of the fresh-cut flowers, the total delivered product is affected by delivery time, the refrigeration of delivery vehicles, the use of proper shipping containers, and other activities. See Figure 14-2.

The Web is a very promising tool for marketers to enhance the total delivered product, sometimes by adding value and other times by reducing costs. Through the Web, firms can access competitive intelligence, better communicate with one another, provide faster customer service, facilitate inventory planning, process orders, and reach channel members around the world.

14-2d   Level of Satisfaction

The last stage in Figure 14-1 is the level of satisfaction with the distribution process, whereby the contentment of each party is determined and related to its goals. When the total delivered product is below expectations, gaps exist—due to poor performance, high prices, low profits, channel conflicts, and other factors. Value gaps should become integrated with future goals (as indicated by the top feedback arrow). If there are breakdowns in the delivery chain, they must be resolved by the parties in the chain (as shown by the bottom feedback arrow) and return policies must be clear. Only in this unlikely scenario would full satisfaction ever be reached: "Someone once described a truly integrated supply chain as one in which any time a Florida customer buys a bag of potato chips, an Idaho farmer plants two potatoes."[7]

---

[7] Joseph Bonney, "Missing Link in Supply Chain," *Journal of Commerce* (February 10, 2003), p. 6.

Figure 14-2

Best Buy: Enhancing the Total Delivered Product

Source: Reprinted by permission of Susan Berry, Retail Image Consulting, Inc.

14-3 DISTRIBUTION PLANNING

Distribution planning is systematic decision making regarding the physical movement of goods and services from producer to consumer, as well as the related transfer of ownership (or rental) of them. It encompasses such diverse functions as transportation, inventory management, and customer transactions.

These functions are carried out by a *channel of distribution*, which comprises all the organizations or people involved in the distribution process. Those organizations or people are known as *channel members* and may include manufacturers, service providers, wholesalers, retailers, marketing specialists, and/or consumers. When the term *distribution intermediaries* is used, it refers to wholesalers, retailers, and marketing specialists (such as transportation firms) that act as facilitators (links) between manufacturers/service providers and consumers.

A channel of distribution can be simple (based on a handshake between a small manufacturer and a local reseller) or complex (requiring detailed written contracts among numerous parties). Some firms seek widespread distribution and need independent wholesalers and/or retailers to carry their merchandise and improve cash flow. Others want direct customer contact and do not use independent resellers. Industrial channels usually have more direct contact between manufacturers/service providers and customers than final consumer channels. International channels also have special needs.

We next discuss the importance of distribution planning, the tasks performed in the distribution process, the criteria to consider in selecting a distribution channel, supplier/distribution intermediary contracts, channel cooperation and conflict, the industrial channel, and international distribution.

14-3a The Importance of Distribution Planning

Distribution decisions have a great effect on a company's marketing efforts. Because intermediaries can perform a host of functions, a firm's marketing plan will differ if it sells direct rather than via intermediaries; and a decision to sell in stores rather than through the mail or the World Wide Web requires a different marketing orientation and tasks.

One of the most critical decisions a firm makes is the choice of a distribution channel. Close ties with intermediaries and/or customers may take time to develop; if there are existing bonds among channel members, it may be hard for a new firm to enter. Once

> **Distribution planning** involves movement and ownership in a **channel of distribution**. It consists of **channel members**.

> **Distribution intermediaries** often have a channel role.

> **Distribution arrangements** vary widely.

Global Marketing in Action

Lenovo's Distribution Network a Key Asset After Acquisition of IBM's PC Division

Lenovo Group (http://www.lenovo.com), a Chinese-based computer manufacturer, recently acquired IBM's (http://www.ibm.com) PC division for $1.25 billion. As a result, Lenovo has annual revenues of about $13 billion from the sales of 14 million PCs. The company is now the world's third-largest PC company. In addition to PCs, Lenovo sells mobile handsets, peripherals, and digital entertainment products.

Lenovo has been the market share leader in PC sales in China for about a decade. Its current market share for all PC segments in China is approximately 33 percent. Lenovo has 4,400 retail outlets in China for its consumer-based PCs. Lenovo has also been the best-selling PC vendor in Asia-Pacific (excluding Japan).

As part of the acquisition agreement, Lenovo's computers are to be marketed through IBM's existing distribution and sales facilities. IBM will continue to market a full complement of information technology solutions to its business clients. IBM will serve as Lenovo's preferred supplier of services and financing, and Lenovo will serve as a preferred supplier of PCs to IBM. Marketing analysts assume that the acquisition has given Lenovo significant access to IBM's distribution facilities, product offerings, and broad geographic coverage.

According to Lenovo's chief executive officer, "Lenovo's leading R&D and product differentiation capabilities, experienced management team, and global distribution network—through our unique alliance with IBM—give us a powerful competitive position in global markets."

Source: Based on material in "Lenovo Group Completes IBM Division Acquisition," *Asia Pulse Online* (May 2, 2005).

> In relationship marketing, firms seek ongoing ties with suppliers, intermediaries, and customers.

alliances are achieved, suitable new products can be put into distribution more easily. Channel members need to act in a coordinated way. Strong resellers enhance manufacturers' marketing abilities. Consumers like to buy products the same way over time.

More firms now recognize the value of good relationships throughout the distribution channel. See Figure 14-3. Thus, many companies engage in relationship marketing and seek to develop and maintain continuous long-term ties with suppliers, distribution intermediaries, and customers. These firms ensure a more consistent flow of goods and services from suppliers, encourage intermediaries to act more as partners than as adversaries, and increase the likelihood of customer loyalty. They foster good employee morale by empowering them to respond positively to reasonable requests from suppliers, intermediaries, and customers. They get earlier and better data on new products and the best strategies for continuing ones. They lower operating and marketing costs, thus improving efficiency. As the supply chain director for Hugo Boss (http://www. hugoboss.com) recently noted: "We think of ourselves as being embedded in a network of supply chain partners, with warehousing operators, logistics service providers, forwarders, and manufacturers. We have to manage that network to get the shortest lead times and the best costs."[8]

This is how effective relationship marketing in a distribution channel may be achieved:

- There should be a continuous and systematic process that incorporates both buyer and seller needs.
- Top management support is required, and relationship marketing principles should permeate a firm's corporate culture.
- At a minimum, a firm needs to understand consumer expectations, build service partnerships, empower employees, and utilize total quality management.
- Suppliers, intermediaries, and customers should be surveyed—by category—to determine the aspects of relationship marketing to be emphasized for them.
- Although increased profitability is a desirable result, other important measures of success are customer satisfaction, customer loyalty, and product quality.

---

[8] "Air Freight Attractive for Hugo Boss," *Supply Chain Europe* (February 2005), p. 36.

Figure 14-3

Piggly Wiggly Supermarkets Progressively Add New Value-Added Elements to the Channel

Source: Reprinted by permission.

- Both positive and negative feedback (going far beyond just passively receiving customer complaints) can provide meaningful information.
- Sellers need to communicate to their customers that relationship marketing involves responsibilities, as well as benefits, for both parties.
- There should be mutually agreeable (by buyer and seller) contingency plans if anything goes awry.[9]

Both costs and profits are affected by the selection of a distribution channel. A firm doing all functions must pay for them itself; in return, it reaps all profits. A firm using intermediaries reduces per-unit distribution costs; it also reduces per-unit profits because those resellers receive their share. With intermediaries, a firm's total profits would rise if there are far higher sales than it could attain itself.

Distribution formats are long-standing in some industries. For example, in the beverage and food industry, manufacturers often sell through wholesalers that then deal with retailers. Auto makers sell through franchised dealers. Mail-order firms line up suppliers, print catalogs, and sell to consumers. As a result, firms must frequently conform to the channel patterns in their industries.

A firm's market coverage is often influenced by the location and number, market penetration, image, product selection, services, and marketing plans of the wholesalers, retailers, and/or marketing specialists with which it deals. In rating its options, a firm should note that the more intermediaries it uses, the less customer contact it has and the lower its control over marketing.

These examples show the scope of distribution planning:

- Sherwin-Williams (**http://www.sherwin-williams.com**) distributes its paints via 3,000 company-owned stores and through independent paint stores, mass merchandisers, auto supply stores, and wholesale distributors. It also has a direct sales force for certain industrial markets, and employs distributors in many foreign nations.[10]

---

[9] Joel R. Evans and Richard L. Laskin, "The Relationship Marketing Process: A Conceptualization and Application," *Industrial Marketing Management*, Vol. 23 (December 1994), p. 451.

[10] *Sherwin-Williams Co. 2005 Annual Report.*

- Shoppers Advantage (**http://www.shoppersadvantage.com**) is a shopping service operating exclusively on the Web: "We're the one-stop shopping site where members and nonmembers can browse diverse superstores to find hundreds of thousands of products, and 1,200 name brands at deep discounts everyday. Members enjoy extra benefits including 3.5% Shoppers Advantage cash back on qualifying purchases, up to a 2-year extended warranty, and a 200% Low Price Guarantee."[11]
- Century 21 (**http://www.century21.com**) is the "franchisor of the world's largest residential real-estate sales organization, with more than 6,600 independently owned and operated franchised broker offices in over 30 countries and territories worldwide."[12]
- Singer N.V. (**http://www.retailholdings.com**) has been "one of the world's leading makers of consumer sewing machines for more than 150 years. Its machines range from basic $150 models to computerized units that start at $3,000. Products are sold in more than 190 countries, through about 1,300 Singer retail outlets, 58,000 independent dealers and mass merchandisers, and a door-to-door sales force of more than 12,000 agents."[13]

14-3b Channel Functions and the Role of Distribution Intermediaries

> Intermediaries can perform **channel functions** and reduce costs, provide expertise, open markets, and lower risks.

The *channel functions* shown in Figure 14-4 must be undertaken for most goods and services. They must be completed somewhere in a distribution channel and responsibility for them must be assigned.

Distribution intermediaries can play a vital role in marketing research. Due to their closeness to the market, they generally have good insights into the characteristics and needs of customers.

In buying products, intermediaries sometimes pay as items are received; other times, they accept items on consignment and do not pay until after sales are made. Purchase terms for intermediaries may range from net cash (payment due at once) to net 60 days (payment not due for 60 days) or more. If intermediaries do not pay until after resale, manufacturers risk poor cash flow, high product returns, obsolescence and spoilage, multiple transactions with intermediaries, and potentially low customer sales.

Manufacturers and service firms often take care of national (international) ads in assigning promotion roles. Wholesalers may coordinate regional promotions among retailers, and motivate and train retail salespeople. Many retailers undertake local ads, personal selling, and events.

Customer services include delivery, credit, in-office and in-home purchases, training, warranties, and return privileges. Again, these services can be offered by one channel member or a combination of them.

Distribution intermediaries can contribute to product planning in several ways. They often provide advice on new and existing products. Test marketing requires their cooperation. And intermediaries can be helpful in positioning products against competitors and suggesting which products to drop.

Wholesalers and retailers often have strong input into pricing decisions. They state their required markups and then price-mark products or specify how they should be marked. Court rulings limit manufacturers' ability to control final prices. Intermediaries thus have great flexibility in setting them.

Distribution involves three major factors: transportation, inventory management, and customer contact. Goods must be shipped from a manufacturer to consumers;

[11] "Customer Center: Who We Are," **http://www.shoppersadvantage.com** (May 11, 2006).

[12] "Learn About the Century 21 System," **http://www.century21.com/learn/tools.aspx** (May 11, 2006).

[13] "Singer N.V.," **http://www.hoovers.com/singer/--ID__42974--/free-co-factsheet.xhtml** (January 29, 2006).

Figure 14-4

Channel Functions

intermediaries often do this. Because production capabilities and customer demand often differ, inventory levels must be properly managed (and items may require storage in a warehouse before being sold). Consumer transactions may require a store or other seller location, long hours of operation, and store fixtures (such as dressing rooms).

Manufacturers typically like to make a limited variety of items in large quantities and have as few transactions as possible to sell their entire output. However, consumers tend to want a variety of brands, colors, sizes, and qualities from which to select—and opt to buy a small amount at a time. Manufacturers might also prefer to sell products from a factory, have 9-to-5 hours and spartan fixtures, and use a limited sales force. Yet, b-to-b customers may want salespeople to visit them and final consumers may want to shop at nearby locales and visit attractive, well-staffed stores on weekends and evenings.

To resolve these differences, intermediaries can be used in the *sorting process*, which consists of four distribution functions: *Accumulation* is collecting small shipments fr[om] several firms so shipping costs are lower. *Allocation* is apportioning items to consumer markets. *Sorting* is separating products into grades, colors, and [...] *Assorting* is offering a range of products so the consumer has choices.

> The **sorting process** coordinates manufacturer and consumer goals.

14-3c   Selecting a Channel of Distribution

Several key factors must be considered in choosing a distributio[n...]

- *The consumer:* (a) characteristics—number, concentration[...] needs—shopping locations and hours, assortment, sales[...] size, purchase behavior.
- *The company itself:* (a) goals—control, sales, profit, t[...] flexibility, service needs; (c) expertise—functions, sp[...] experience—distribution methods, channel relation[s...]
- *The product:* (a) value—price per unit; (b) complex[...] perishability—shelf life, frequency of shipments; (d[...] divisibility.
- *The competition:* (a) characteristics—number, conce[...] (b) tactics—distribution methods, channel relation[...]

> Channel choice depends on consumers, the company, the product, competition, existing channels, and legalities.

- *Distribution channels*: (a) alternatives—direct, indirect; (b) characteristics—number of intermediaries, functions performed, tradition; (c) availability—exclusive arrangements, territorial restrictions.
- *Legalities*: (a) current laws; (b) pending laws.

While it assesses the preceding factors, a firm would decide about the type of channel, contractual arrangements or administered channels, channel length and width, channel intensity, and dual channels.

There are two basic types of channels. A ***direct channel of distribution*** involves the movement of goods and services from producer to consumers without the use of independent intermediaries. An ***indirect channel of distribution*** involves the movement of goods and services from producer to independent intermediaries to consumers. Figure 14-5 shows the transactions necessary for the sale of 200,000 men's umbrellas under direct and indirect channels. Figure 14-6 shows the most common indirect channels for final consumer and organizational consumer products.

If a manufacturer or service provider sells to consumers at company-owned outlets (for example, Shell-owned gas stations), this is a direct channel. In an indirect channel, a manufacturer may use several layers of independent wholesalers (for example, regional, state,

> In a **direct channel**, one firm performs all tasks. An **indirect channel** has multiple firms.

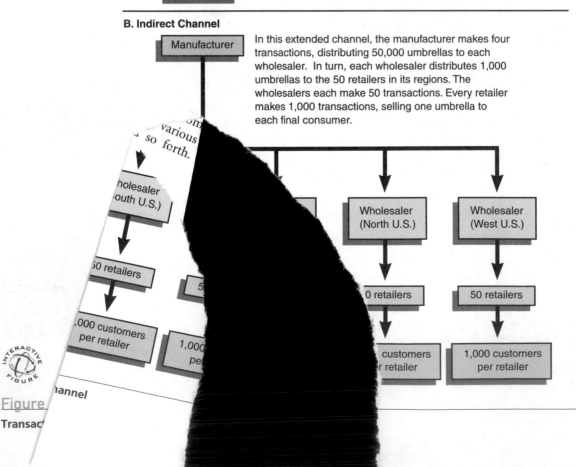

A. Direct Channel

Manufacturer

In this direct channel, an umbrella manufacturer sells directly to final customers. It makes 200,000 separate transactions, one for each customer.

200,000 customers

B. Indirect Channel

Manufacturer

In this extended channel, the manufacturer makes four transactions, distributing 50,000 umbrellas to each wholesaler. In turn, each wholesaler distributes 1,000 umbrellas to the 50 retailers in its regions. The wholesalers each make 50 transactions. Every retailer makes 1,000 transactions, selling one umbrella to each final consumer.

Wholesaler (North U.S.)   Wholesaler (West U.S.)

50 retailers

1,000 customers per retailer

Figure

Transac

Figure 14-6

Typical Indirect Channels of Distribution

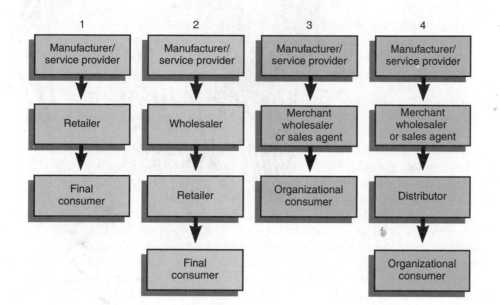

and local) and sell at different kinds of retailers (such as discount, department, and specialty stores). A direct channel is most often used by firms that want control over their entire marketing efforts, desire close customer contact, and have limited markets. An indirect channel is most often used by firms that want to enlarge their markets, raise sales, and give up distribution functions and costs; they will surrender some control and customer contact.

Because an indirect channel has independent members, a method is needed to plan and assign marketing responsibilities. With a *contractual channel arrangement*, all the terms regarding distribution tasks, prices, and other factors are stated in writing for each member. A manufacturer and a retailer could sign an agreement regarding promotion support, delivery and payment dates, and product handling, marking, and displays. In an *administered channel arrangement*, the dominant firm in the distribution process plans the marketing program and itemizes and coordinates each member's duties. Depending on its relative strength, a manufacturer/service provider, wholesaler, or retailer could be a channel leader. Accordingly, a manufacturer with a strong brand could set its image, price range, and selling method.

Channel length refers to the levels of independent members along a distribution channel. In Figure 14-5, *A* is a short channel and *B* is a long channel. Sometimes, a firm shortens its channel by acquiring a company at another stage, such as a manufacturer merging with a wholesaler. This may let the firm be more self-sufficient, ensure supply, control channel members, lower distribution costs, and coordinate timing throughout the channel. Critics of the practice believe it limits competition, fosters inefficiency, and does not result in lower consumer prices.

Channel width refers to the number of independent members at any stage of distribution. In a narrow channel, a manufacturer or service provider sells via few wholesalers or retailers; in a wide channel, it sells via many. If a firm wants to enhance its position at its stage of the channel, it may buy other companies like itself, such as one janitorial services firm buying another. This lets a firm increase its size and market share, improve bargaining power with other channel members, and utilize mass promotion and distribution techniques more efficiently.

A firm must decide on the intensity of its distribution coverage in selecting a channel. A firm severely limits the number of resellers utilized in a geographic area under *exclusive distribution*, perhaps having only one or two resellers within a specific shopping location. It seeks a prestige image, channel control, and high profit margins and accepts lower total sales than in other types of distribution. With *selective distribution*, a

> Channel length describes the levels of independents. Channel width refers to the independents at one level.

> Exclusive, selective, and intensive distribution depend on goals, sellers, customers, and marketing.

firm employs a moderate number of resellers. It wants to combine some channel control and a solid image with good sales volume and profits. A firm uses a large number of resellers in *intensive distribution*. Its goals are wide market coverage, channel acceptance, and high total sales and profits. Per-unit profits are low. It is a strategy aimed at the most consumers. See Table 14-2.

> A dual channel (multichannel distribution) lets a firm reach different segments or diversify.

Some additional factors are noteworthy in selecting a channel. First, a firm may use a *dual channel of distribution* (also known as *multichannel distribution*), whereby it appeals to different market segments or diversifies business by selling through two or more separate channels. A company could use selective distribution for a prestige brand of watches and intensive distribution for a discount brand, or use both direct and indirect channels (such as an insurance firm selling group health insurance directly to large businesses and individual life insurance indirectly to final consumers via independent agents). Consider the strategy of Office Depot (**http://www.officedepot.com**). It has 1,200 stores in 24 nations, annually conducts 1,100 catalog mailings, operates 9 U.S. E-commerce and 33 sites outside the United States, and employs a 2,500-person corporate account sales force. As one observer notes, "Merchants that large and diverse must coordinate their various channels to present an integrated brand and message to customers."[14] At our book Web site, see a multichannel distribution slide show by Retail Forward (**http://www.retailforward.com**).

Second, a firm may go from exclusive to selective to intensive distribution through the product life cycle. Yet, it would be hard to go from intensive to selective to exclusive distribution. Designer jeans moved from prestige stores to better stores to all types of outlets. This process would not have worked in reverse. Third, a firm may distribute products in a new way and achieve great success. See Figure 14-7.

At its Web site (**http://www.toolkit.cch.com/text/P03_6000.asp**), the Business Owner's Toolkit gives some excellent advice for "Choosing Distribution Methods."

Table 14-2 Intensity of Channel Coverage

Attributes	Exclusive Distribution	Selective Distribution	Intensive Distribution
Objectives	Prestige image, channel control and loyalty, price stability and high profit margins	Moderate market coverage, solid image, some channel control and loyalty, good sales and profits	Widespread market coverage, channel acceptance, high volume sales and total profits
Resellers	Few in number, well established, reputable firms (outlets)	Moderate in number, well established, better firms (outlets)	Many in number, all types of firms (outlets)
Customers	Final consumers: fewer in number, trend setters, willing to travel to store, brand loyal B-to-b consumers: focus on major accounts, service expected from manufacturer	Final consumers: moderate in number, brand conscious, somewhat willing to travel to store B-to-b consumers: focus on many types of accounts, service expected from manufacturer or intermediary	Final consumers: many in number, convenience-oriented B-to-b consumers: focus on all types of accounts, service expected from intermediary
Marketing emphasis	Final consumers: personal selling, pleasant shopping conditions, good service B-to-b consumers: availability, regular communications, superior service	Final consumers: promotional mix, pleasant shopping conditions, good service B-to-b consumers: availability, regular communications, superior service	Final consumers: mass advertising, nearby location, items in stock B-to-b consumers: availability, regular communications, superior service
Major weakness	Limited sales potential	May be difficult to carve out a niche	Limited channel control
Examples	Autos, designer clothes, capital equipment, complex services	Furniture, clothing, mechanics' tools, standardized services	Household products, groceries, office supplies, routine services

[14] Brian Quinton, "Office Depot's Multichannel Challenge," *Direct* (May 1, 2005), p. 10.

Figure 14-7

New Forms of Multichannel Distribution at REI

REI (**http://www.rei.com**) has marketed its products through stores for years. Today, it also uses in-store computerized kiosks and a Web site to sell its products.

Source: Reprinted by permission of Retail Forward.

14-3d   Supplier/Distribution Intermediary Contracts

Distribution contracts focus on price policies, conditions of sale, territorial rights, the services/responsibility mix, and contract length and conditions of termination. The highlights of a contract follow.

> Distribution contracts cover prices, sale conditions, territories, commitments, timing, and termination.

Price policies largely deal with the discounts given to intermediaries for their functions, quantity purchases, and cash payments, and with commission rates. Functional discounts are deductions from list prices for performing storage, shipping, and other jobs. Quantity discounts are deductions for volume purchases. Cash discounts are deductions for early payment. Some intermediaries get paid commissions.

Conditions of sale cover price and quality guarantees, payment and shipping terms, reimbursement for unsaleable items, and returns. A guarantee against a price decline protects one intermediary from paying a high price for an item that is then offered to others at a lower price; the original buyer then receives a rebate so its costs are like those of competitors. Otherwise, it could not meet the competitors' resale prices. Suppliers sometimes use full-line forcing and require intermediaries to carry an entire product line. This is legal if they are not prevented from also buying items from other suppliers.

Territorial rights outline the geographic areas (such as greater Paris) in which resellers may operate and/or the target markets (such as small business accounts) they may contact. Sometimes, they have exclusive territories, as with McDonald's (**http://www.mcdonalds.com**) franchisees; in other cases, many firms gain territorial rights for the same areas, as with retailers selling Sharp (**http://www.sharpusa.com**) calculators.

The *services/responsibility mix* describes the role of each channel member. It outlines who delivers products, stores inventory, trains salespeople, writes ad copy, and sets up displays; and it sets performance standards. If included, a hold-harmless clause specifies that manufacturers or service providers—not resellers—are liable in lawsuits arising from poor design or negligence in production.

Contract length and conditions of termination protect an intermediary against a manufacturer or service provider prematurely bypassing it after a territory has been built up. The manufacturer or service provider is shielded by limiting contract duration and stating the factors leading to termination.

Although some firms rely on verbal agreements, without a written contract, there is a danger of misunderstandings as to goals, compensation, tasks performed, and the length of the agreement. A constraint of a written contract may be its inflexibility under changing market conditions.

14-3e Channel Cooperation and Conflict

> Channel-member goals need to be balanced.

All firms in a distribution channel have similar general goals: profitability, access to goods and services, efficient distribution, and customer loyalty. Yet, the way these and other goals are achieved often leads to differing views, even if the parties engage in relationship marketing: How are profits allocated along a channel? How can manufacturers sell products via many competing resellers and expect the resellers not to carry other brands? Which party coordinates channel decisions? To whom are consumers loyal—manufacturers/service providers, wholesalers, or retailers?

Natural differences among the firms in a distribution channel exist by virtue of their channel positions, the tasks performed, and the desire of each firm to optimize its profits and control its strategy. A successful channel maximizes cooperation and minimizes conflict. In the past, manufacturers dominated channels because they had the best market coverage and recognition; resellers were small and local. With the growth of large national (and global) distribution intermediaries, the volume accounted for by them, and the popularity of private brands, the balance of power has shifted more to resellers. Table 14-3 cites causes of conflict. Table 14-4 shows how cooperation can reduce these conflicts.

If conflicts are not resolved cooperatively, confrontations may occur. A manufacturer or service provider may then ship late, refuse to deal with certain resellers, limit financing, withdraw promotional support, or use other tactics. Similarly, a reseller may make late payments, give poor shelf space, refuse to carry items, return many products, and apply other tactics. A channel cannot function well in a confrontational framework. Yet, in some instances, channel conflict seems to be growing:

> Conflict between channels is a perennial issue that every sales group faces and one that is increasingly relevant to high-tech companies. These businesses have traditionally sold their hardware, software, and networking products through a combination of distributors, resellers, and retailers. In recent years, however, sales through direct channels have grown as fast as, and in some cases faster than, those through traditional stores or resellers. Strong online sales by Dell [**http://www.dell.com**] and others have inspired many high-tech vendors to invest in Internet sales channels. Yet, pursuing a direct-sales channel can alienate a firm's sales partners, who see the shift as a threat to them.[15]

A thriving manufacturer or service provider can often secure reseller support and enthusiasm when it introduces new products and continues popular ones. This occurs because resellers know the manufacturer's or service provider's past sales track record,

---

[15] Girish Nair and Darren Pleasance, "Mitigating Channel Conflict," *McKinsey Quarterly* (Number 3, 2005), p. 16.

Table 14-3 Potential Causes of Channel Conflict

Factors	Manufacturer's/Service Provider's Goals	Distribution Intermediary's Goals
Pricing	To establish final prices consistent with product image	To establish final prices consistent with the intermediary's image
Purchase terms	To ensure prompt, accurate payments and minimize discounts	To defer payments as long as possible and secure discounts
Shelf space	To obtain plentiful shelf space with good visibility so as to maximize brand sales	To allocate shelf space among multiple brands so as to maximize total product sales
Exclusivity	To hold down the number of competing brands each intermediary stocks while selling via many intermediaries	To hold down the number of competing intermediaries carrying the same brands while selling different brands itself
Delivery	To receive adequate notice before deliveries are required	To obtain quick service
Advertising support	To secure ad support from intermediaries	To secure ad support from manufacturers/service providers
Profitability	To have adequate profit margins	To have adequate profit margins
Continuity	To receive orders on a regular basis	To receive shipments on a regular basis
Order size	To maximize order size	To have order size conform with consumer demand to minimize inventory investment
Assortment	To offer a limited variety	To secure a full variety
Risk	To have intermediaries assume risks	To have manufacturers/service providers assume risks
Branding	To sell products under the manufacturer's/service provider's name	To sell products under private brands, as well as manufacturers'/service providers' brands
Channel access	To distribute products wherever desired by the manufacturer/service provider	To carry only those items desired by intermediaries
Importance of account	To not allow any one intermediary to dominate	To not allow any one manufacturer/service provider to dominate
Consumer loyalty	To have consumers loyal to the manufacturer/service provider	To have consumers loyal to the intermediary
Channel control	To make key channel decisions	To make key channel decisions

Table 14-4 Methods of Channel Cooperation

Factors	Manufacturer's/Service Provider's Actions	Distribution Intermediary's Actions
New-product introduction	Thorough testing, adequate promotional support	Good shelf location and space, enthusiasm for product, assistance in test marketing
Delivery	Prompt filling of orders, adherence to scheduled dates	Proper time allowed for delivery, shipments immediately checked for accuracy
Marketing research	Data provided to resellers	Data provided to manufacturers/service providers
Pricing	Prices to intermediaries let them gain reasonable profits, intermediary flexibility encouraged	Infrequent sales from regular prices, maintaining proper image
Promotion	Training reseller's salespeople, sales force incentives, developing appropriate ad campaign, cooperative ad programs	Attractive store displays, knowledgeable salespeople, participation in cooperative programs
Financing	Liberal financial terms	Adherence to financial terms
Product quality	Product guarantees	Proper installation and servicing of products for customers
Channel control	Shared and specified decision making	Shared and specified decision making

> In a **pushing strategy**, there is cooperation. With **pulling**, a firm generates demand before channel support.

the promotion support to be provided, and delivery reliability. Thus, a *pushing strategy* is used, whereby the various firms in a distribution channel cooperate in marketing a product. With this approach, relationship marketing is involved.

As a rule, it is harder for a new manufacturer or service provider to break into an existing channel. Resellers are unfamiliar with the firm, not able to gauge its sales potential, and wonder about its support and future deliveries. So, a new firm often needs a *pulling strategy*, whereby it first stimulates consumer demand and then gains dealer support. This means heavy promotion spending, fully paid by the manufacturer or service provider; the firm may have to offer guarantees of minimum sales or profits to resellers—and make up shortfalls. Figure 14-8 contrasts pushing and pulling strategies.

In today's highly competitive marketplace, with so many new domestic and foreign products being introduced each year, even leading firms must sometimes use pulling strategies. They need to convince resellers that demand exists for their products before the resellers will agree to tie up shelf space.

14-3f   The Industrial Channel of Distribution

The distribution channel for industrial (b-to-b) products differs from that for consumer products in these significant ways:

> An industrial channel has unique characteristics.

- Retailers are typically not utilized.
- Direct channels are more readily employed.
- Transactions are fewer and orders are larger.
- Specification selling is more prevalent.
- Intermediaries are more knowledgeable.
- Team selling (two or more salespeople) may be necessary.
- Distinct intermediaries specialize in industrial products.
- Leasing, rather than selling, is more likely.
- Customer information needs are more technical.
- Activities such as shipping and warehousing may be shared.

Industrial Distribution magazine (**http://www.manufacturing.net/ind**) is a good source for further information on this topic. Be sure to take a look at the online version

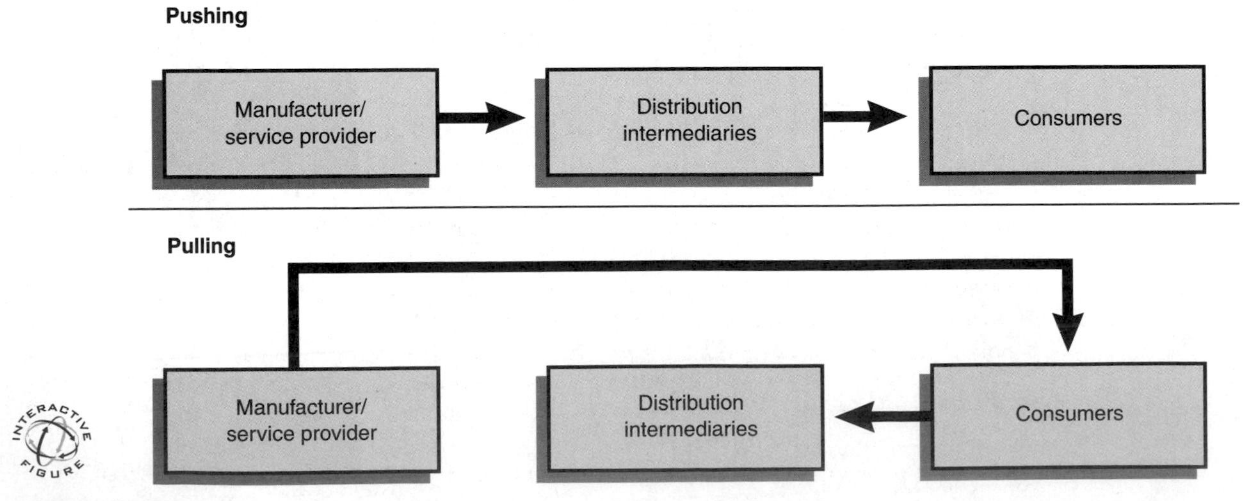

Pushing

Pulling

Figure 14-8

Pushing Versus Pulling Strategies

of the *Annual Survey of Distributor Operations*. Click "Annual Survey" on the left toolbar to view key findings.

14-3g   International Distribution Planning

When devising an international distribution plan, a number of factors should be kept in mind.[16] Following are several of them.

> International distribution requires particular planning.

Channel length often depends on a nation's stage of economic development and consumer patterns. Less-developed and developing nations tend to use shorter, more direct channels than do industrialized ones. They have many small firms marketing goods and services to nearby consumers, and limited transportation and communications networks foster local shopping. At the same time, cultural norms in nations—both developing and industrialized—affect expected interactions between sellers and consumers. For instance, in Japan, people treasure personal attention when making purchases, especially of expensive products. Unlike American shoppers, Japanese consumers are not used to buying by phone.

Distribution practices and formats vary by nation, as these examples show:

- Many European countries have been dominated by independent retailers rather than large chains. However, with the expansion of the European Union, the growth of chains will speed up throughout Europe in the future.
- Some Mexican supermarkets shut off electricity overnight to reduce costs. Perishable items such as dairy products have a shorter shelf life and require more frequent deliveries than in the United States.
- Large Japanese firms often set up *keiretsus*. A vertical keiretsu is an integrated network of suppliers, manufacturers, and resellers. A horizontal keiretsu typically consists of a money-center bank, an insurance company, a trust banking company, a trading company, and several major manufacturers. U.S. firms have some channels that resemble vertical keiretsus, but they do not have networks that emulate horizontal keiretsus.
- Although it has four times as many people as the United States, India has roughly the same number of retail establishments, and just one-quarter of them are in metropolitan areas. The leading retailers are the popular neighborhood grocery and general stores that offer very low prices.

If a firm enters a foreign market for the first time, it must resolve various questions: Should products be made domestically and shipped to the foreign market or made in the foreign market? If products are made domestically, what form of transportation is best? What kind of distribution intermediaries should be used? Which specific intermediaries should be used? The U.S. Department of Commerce runs a Commercial Service division (**http://www.export.gov/comm_svc**) to assist small and medium-size firms seeking advice on international distribution. That division has 107 Export Assistance Centers in the United States and more than other 150 offices globally. Along with Unz & Company (**http://www.unzco.com**), the U.S. Department of Commerce has prepared an online manual that includes "Methods/Channels"—Chapter 4—to use when developing an export strategy (**http://www.unzco.com/basicguide/c4.html**).

Legal requirements for distribution differ by country—some have strict laws as to hours, methods of operation, and sites. In France, there are severe limits on Sunday retail hours. In Germany, there are strict limits on store size and Sunday hours. Many nations have complex procedures for foreign firms to distribute there. Thus, firms interested in standardized (global) distribution may be stymied.

---

[16] See "Checklist for Int'l Distributor Agreements Diminishes Export Risk," *IOMA's Report on Managing Exports* (September 2003), pp. 4-7; and "Checklist: International Distributorship Agreement," http://www.internationalbusiness lawyers.org/distrib-agreement.html (March 29, 2006).

What causes a company to be more or less satisfied with its international distribution channel? If a firm's domestic channel performs better than its international channel, it is likely that the firm will be dissatisfied with the international channel. If a firm has experience and expertise in foreign markets, it is likely that the firm will be satisfied with its international channel. If a firm has several distribution choices in entering a foreign market, it is likely to be more satisfied with the channel it selects. If environmental uncertainty is high, it is likely the firm will be less satisfied with its international channel.

14-4   LOGISTICS

> **Logistics (physical distribution)** involves the location, timing, and condition of deliveries. An order cycle covers many activities.

Logistics (also known as ***physical distribution***) encompasses the broad range of activities concerned with efficiently delivering raw materials, parts, semifinished items, and finished products to designated places, at designated times, and in proper condition. It may be undertaken by any member of a channel, from producer to consumer. Logistics involves such functions as customer service, shipping, warehousing, inventory control, private trucking-fleet operations, packaging, receiving, materials handling, and plant, warehouse, and store location planning. The logistics activities involved in a typical *order cycle*—the period of time that spans a customer's placing an order and its receipt—are illustrated in Figure 14-9.

14-4a   The Importance of Logistics

Logistics is important due to its costs, the value of customer service, and its relationship with other functions. At our book Web site, view the Council of Supply Chain Management Professionals (**http://www.cscmp.org**)—formerly known as the Council of Logistics Management—slide show.

> Cost control is a major goal.

Costs   Logistics costs amount to 9 to 10 percent of the U.S. GDP, with transportation (freight) accounting for about 60 percent of that total.[17] To contain costs, firms have been working hard to improve efficiency. Today, logistics tasks are completed faster, more accurately, and with fewer people than 25 years ago. Due to computerization and improved transportation, firms have reduced their annual inventory levels by tens of billions of dollars, thus saving on warehousing and interest expenses.

Distribution costs vary by industry and company type. Total logistics costs for individual firms depend on the nature of the business, the geographic area covered, the tasks done by other channel members, and the weight/value ratio of the items. While petroleum refiners spend almost one-quarter of their sales just on inbound and outbound transportation, many retailers spend under 5 percent of their sales on

Figure 14-9

Selected Physical Distribution Activities Involved in a Typical Order Cycle

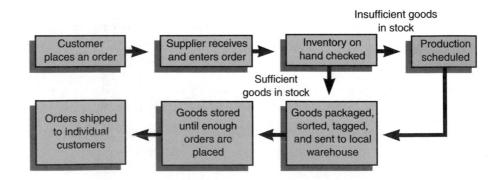

---

[17] "16th Annual State of Logistics Report," *Inbound Logistics* (August 2005), p. 12.

transportation from vendors and receiving, marking, storing, and distributing goods. When the U.S. Postal Service (**http://www.usps.com**) raises rates, shipping costs are affected for all kinds of firms.

Firms must identify the symptoms of poor distribution systems and strive to be more efficient. Up to one-fifth of the perishable items carried by U.S. grocers, such as fish and dairy items, are lost to spoilage due to breakdowns in shipping or too much time on store shelves. To reduce losses, many grocers insist on small, frequent deliveries and have upgraded their storage facilities. Many firms engaged in E-commerce are still finding their way. This is what one firm has done to improve its distribution system:

> Mattel [**http://www.mattel.com**] can better meet toy demand because it has spent the last few years paying attention to software and processes that simplify its supply chain, cut costs, shorten cycle times, and bring more science to the art of meeting customer demand. The firm installed a new transportation-management system that saves it a lot of money by reducing the number of less-than-full truckload shipments and optimizing its shipping networks. And it has gotten forecasting down from "monthly to weekly. We aren't building more stuff than stores need, and they're getting it when they want it."[18]

Table 14-5 shows several cost ramifications of poor distribution.

Customer Service A chief concern in planning a firm's logistics program is the level of customer service it should provide. Decisions involve delivery frequency, speed, and consistency; the use of emergency shipments; whether to accept small orders; warehousing; coordinating assortments; whether to provide order progress reports (and when to do so online); the return policy (known as *reverse logistics*); and other factors. Weak performance may lose customers.

To provide the proper customer service, distribution standards—clear and measurable goals as to service levels in logistics—must be devised. Examples are filling 90 percent of orders from existing inventory, responding to customer requests for order information within two hours, filling orders with 99 percent accuracy, and limiting goods damaged in transit to 1 percent or less.

Table 14-5 Selected Symptoms and Cost Ramifications of a Poor Physical Distribution System	
Symptoms	**Cost Ramifications**
1. Slow-turning and/or too-high inventory	Excessive capital is tied up in inventory. The firm has high insurance costs, interest expenses, and high risks of pilferage and product obsolescence. Merchandise may be stale.
2. Inefficient customer service	Costs are high relative to the value of shipments; warehouses are poorly situated; inventory levels are not tied to customer demand.
3. A large number of interwarehouse shipments	Merchandise transfers raise physical distribution costs because items must be handled and verified at each warehouse.
4. Frequent use of emergency shipments	Extra charges add significantly to physical distribution costs.
5. Peripheral hauls and/or limited backhauling	The firm uses its own trucking facilities; but many hauls are too spread out and trucks may only be full one way.
6. A large number of small orders	Small orders often are unprofitable. Many distribution costs are fixed.
7. Excessive number of returns	The firm incurs high handling costs and may lose disgruntled customers.

[18] Beth Bacheldor, "Steady Supply," *Information Week* (November 24, 2003), p. 36.

The **total-cost approach** considers both costs and opportunities.

One way to set the proper customer service level is the ***total-cost approach***, whereby the distribution service level with the lowest total costs—including freight (shipping), warehousing, and lost business—is the best service level. Figure 14-10 illustrates the total-cost approach. An ideal system seeks a balance between low expenditures on distribution and high opportunities for sales. Seldom will that be at the lowest level of distribution spending; lost sales would be too great.

By offering superior customer service, a firm may establish a significant competitive advantage. The opposite is also true: "Despite the increased use of new technologies intended to improve customer service, such as automated phone systems and live chat over the Internet, poor customer service is the primary reason that consumers switch service providers." About one-third of the respondents to a survey about 10 service-related industries (banking, Internet services, wireless telephone services, home telephone services, utilities, cable/satellite television services, hotels, airlines, life insurance, and retailing) "said that the most important aspect of a satisfying customer service experience is the ability to obtain assistance from a company without being forwarded to multiple representatives."[19]

Logistics must be coordinated with other areas.

Logistics and Other Functional Areas There is an interaction between logistics and every aspect of marketing, as well as other functional areas in the firm, as the following indicate.

Product variations in color, size, features, quality, and style impose a burden on a firm's distribution network. Greater variety means lower volume per item, which increases unit shipping and warehousing costs. Stocking a broader range of replacement parts also becomes necessary.

Logistics planning is related to the overall channel strategy. A firm seeking extensive distribution needs dispersed warehouses. One involved with perishables must be sure that most of a product's selling life is not spent in transit.

Promotion campaigns are often planned well in advance, so it is essential that resellers receive goods at the proper times. Resellers may get consumer complaints for not having sufficient quantities of advertised items, although the manufacturer is really at fault. Some new products fail or lag behind sales projections due to poor initial distribution. As noted in Chapter 13, this occurred when Sony PlayStation 2 (**http://www.us. playstation.com**) was introduced; the firm ran out of merchandise due to a parts shortage.

Logistics plays a part in pricing. A firm with fast, reliable delivery and in-stock replacement parts—that handles small orders and emergency shipments—can charge more than one with less service.

Figure 14-10

An Illustration of the Total-Cost Approach in Distribution

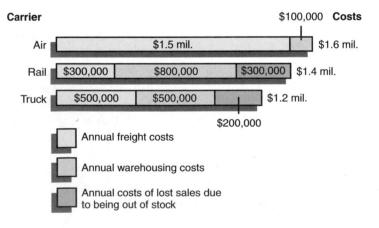

[19] "Poor Customer Service Is Top Reason Consumers Switch Service Providers," *Accenture News Release* (June 26, 2005).

A logistics strategy is linked with production and finance functions. High freight costs motivate firms to put plants closer to markets. Low average inventories in stock allow firms to reduce finance charges. Warehouse receipts may be used as collateral for loans.

Overall, many decisions must be made and coordinated in planning a logistics strategy: the transportation form(s) used, inventory levels and warehouse form(s), and the number and sites of plants, warehouses, and shopping facilities. A strategy can be simple: A firm may have one plant, focus on one geographic market, and ship to resellers or customers without the use of decentralized warehouses. On the other hand, a strategy may include multiple plants, assembly and/or warehouse locations in each market, thousands of customer locations, and several transportation forms.

We now look at two central aspects of a logistics strategy: transportation and inventory management.

14-4a Transportation

Five basic **transportation forms** are used for shipping products, parts, raw materials, and so forth: railroads, motor carriers, waterways, pipelines, and airways. Table 14-6 shows the share of U.S. mileage and revenue for each. Table 14-7 ranks them on seven operating characteristics.

> Transportation is rated on speed, availability, dependability, capability, frequency, losses, and cost. There are five major **transportation forms:** railroads, motor carriers, waterways, pipelines, and airways.

The deregulation of U.S. transportation industries has expanded the competition in and among these industries. Deregulation generally allows transportation firms to have greater flexibility in entering markets, expanding businesses, products carried, price setting, and functions performed. It also means more choice for those shipping. Each transportation form and three transport services are studied next.

Railroads *Railroads* usually carry heavy, bulky items that are low in value (relative to weight) over long distances. They ship items too heavy for trucks. Despite their position in ton-miles shipped, railroads have had problems. Fixed costs are high due to facility investments. Shippers face railroad car shortages in high-demand months for agricultural goods. Some tracks and railroad cars are in need of repair. Trucks are faster, more flexible, and packed more easily. In response, railroads are relying on new shipping techniques, operating flexibility, and mergers to improve efficiency.

Motor Carriers *Motor carriers* mostly transport small shipments over short distances. They handle most of U.S. shipments weighing less than 500 or 1,000 pounds. Seventy percent of all motor carriers are used for local deliveries and two-thirds of total truck miles are local. For these reasons, motor carriers account for a huge share of shipping

Table 14-6	The Relative Share of U.S. Shipping Mileage and Revenue by Transportation Form	
Transportation Form	**Share of Ton-Miles Shipped**	**Share of Shipping Value**[a]
Railroads	41%	6%
Motor carriers	27	85
Waterways	16	2
Pipelines	15	2
Airways	less than 1	5

[a] Does not include multimodal shipping

Source: Computed by the authors from *National Transportation Statistics 2004* (Washington, DC: U.S. Bureau of Transportation Statistics, January 2005).

Table 14-7 The Relative Operating Characteristics of Five Transportation Forms

Operating Characteristics	Ranking by Transportation Form[a]				
	Railroads	Motor Carriers	Waterways	Pipelines	Airways
Delivery speed	3	2	4	5	1
Number of locations served	2	1	4	5	3
On-time dependability[b]	3	2	4	1	5
Range of products carried	1	2	3	5	4
Frequency of shipments	4	2	5	1	3
Losses and damages	5	4	2	1	3
Cost per ton mile	3	4	2	1	5

[a] 1= highest ranking.
[b] Relative variation from anticipated delivery time.

Sources: Adapted by the authors from Donald J. Bowersox, David J. Closs, and M. Bixby Cooper, *Supply Chain Logistics Management* (New York: McGraw-Hill/Irwin, 2002); Ronald H. Ballou, *Business Logistics/Supply Chain Management*, 5th ed. (Upper Saddle River, NJ: Prentice Hall, 2004); James R. Stock and Douglas Lambert, *Strategic Logistics Management*, 4th ed. (New York: McGraw-Hill/Irwin, 2001); and *CSCMP Toolbox* (Oak Brook, IL: Council of Supply Chain Management Professionals, 2003).

revenue. Motor carriers are more flexible than rail because they can pick up packages at a factory or warehouse and deliver them to the customer's door. They often supplement rail, air, and other forms that cannot deliver directly to customers. In addition, trucks are faster than rail for short distances. Like railroads, the trucking industry has been deregulated since 1980. See Figure 14-11.

Waterways U.S. *waterways* are involved with the movement of goods on barges via inland rivers and on tankers and general-merchandise freighters through the Great Lakes, intercoastal shipping, and the St. Lawrence Seaway. They are used mostly for transporting low-value, high-bulk freight (such as coal, iron ore, gravel, grain, and cement). Waterways are slow and may be closed by ice in winter, but rates are quite low. Various improvements in vessel design have occurred over the years. For example, many "supervessels" now operate on the Great Lakes and other waterways. They can each carry up to 60,000 gross tons or more of iron-bearing rock (or similar heavy materials) in one trip. Their conveyor systems are twice as efficient as the ones on older boats. Navigation is computer-controlled.

Figure 14-11

Motor Carriers Drive Many Distribution Channels

Source: Reprinted by permission of Susan Berry, Retail Image Consulting, Inc.

Pipelines Within *pipelines*, there is continuous movement and there are no interruptions, inventories (except those held by a carrier), and intermediate storage sites. Handling and labor costs are minimized. Although pipelines are very reliable, only certain commodities can be moved through them. In the past, emphasis was on gas and petroleum products. Pipelines now handle coal and wood chips, which are sent as semiliquids. Still, the lack of flexibility limits their potential. Some pipelines are enormous. The Trans-Alaska Highway pipeline is 48 inches in diameter and 800 miles long. It carries 25 percent of all the U.S. crude oil produced. It can discharge up to 2 million barrels daily. Oil is loaded from the pipeline to supervessels and then sent by water to the lower 48 states.

Airways *Airways* are the fastest, most expensive transportation form. High-value, perishable, and emergency goods dominate air shipments. Although air transit is costly, it may lower other costs, such as the need for outlying or even regional warehouses. The costs of packing, unpacking, and preparing goods for shipping are lower than for other transportation forms. Airfreight has been deregulated since the late 1970s. So, many firms have stepped up their air cargo operations. Some now use wide-bodied jets for large containers. Modern communications and sorting equipment have also been added to airfreight operations. Firms specializing in air shipments stress speedy, guaranteed service at acceptable prices.

Transportation Services Transportation service companies are marketing specialists that chiefly handle the shipments of small and moderate-sized packages. Some pick up at the sender's office and deliver direct to the addressee. Others require packages to be brought to a service company outlet. The major kinds of transportation service firms are government parcel post, private parcel, and express.

Parcel post from the U.S. Postal Service (**http://www.usps.com**) operates out of post offices and has rates based on postal zones, of which there are eight in the United States. Parcel post can be insured and it can be sent COD (collect on delivery). Regular service is completed in a few days. Special handling (at an extra cost) can expedite shipments. Express mail is available for next-day service from a post office to most addresses.

> These transportation service companies ship packages: government parcel post, private parcel, and express.

Ethical Issues in Marketing

Chargebacks and Markdown Money: An Intensifying Battle Between Channel Members

Chargebacks are deductions that retailers make from suppliers' bills due to missing or incorrectly shipped items, damaged goods, late deliveries, or goods placed on incorrect hangers or packaged with incorrect materials. In a related practice, many retailers require that vendors provide them with markdown money to reimburse them for goods sold below full price.

When used fairly, chargebacks reimburse retailers for extra costs associated with a supplier errors. Markdown monies can be effectively used by a supplier to entice a major retailer to stock an unproven designer's clothing line. However, in practice, chargebacks and markdown monies are often used as a bargaining mechanism by powerful retailers. A number of abuses also are associated with these practices, such as a clothing designer that was charged $750 for shipping goods by FedEx instead of UPS.

Federated Department Stores (**http://www. federated-fds.com**), the largest U.S. department store chain, was accused in a class-action suit of taking unauthorized chargebacks from its suppliers. Federated, which started to reimburse its suppliers for recent chargebacks, plans to defend its past practices. Saks Fifth Avenue (**http://www.saksfifthavenue.com**) had two separate government actions associated with chargebacks and markdown monies. Saks admitted to overcharging its suppliers by $20 million from 1999 to 2003 and is reimbursing the affected suppliers. Saks has also conducted an internal investigation of its actions and recently dismissed three of its top executives.

Sources: Based on material in Tracie Rozhon, "Saks Gets Default Notice on Debt," *New York Times* (June 17, 2005), p. F16; and Robin Gihvan, "The Grim Reality of the Bottom Line," *Washington Post* (May 27, 2005), p. C2.

Private parcel services specialize in small-package delivery, usually less than 50 pounds. Most shipments go from businesses to their customers. Regular service generally takes two to three days. More expensive next-day service is also available from many carriers. The largest firm is United Parcel Service (**http://www.ups.com**), a multibillion-dollar, global company that dominates the Internet delivery business.

Specialized express companies, such as Federal Express (**http://www.fedex.com**), do most of their business by providing guaranteed delivery of small packages within one or two days. The average express delivery is under 10 pounds.

Coordinating Transportation Because a single shipment may involve a combination of transportation forms, a practice known as *intermodal shipping*, coordination is needed. A firm can enhance its ability to coordinate shipments via containerization and freight forwarding.

> **Containerization** and **freight forwarding** simplify intermodal shipping.

With *containerization*, goods are placed in sturdy containers that can be loaded on trains, trucks, ships, or planes. The marked containers are sealed until delivered, thereby reducing damage and pilferage. Their progress and destination are monitored. The containers are mobile warehouses that can be moved from manufacturing plants to receiving docks, where they remain until the contents are needed.

In *freight forwarding*, specialized firms (freight forwarders) collect small shipments (usually less than 500 pounds each) from several companies. They pick up merchandise at each shipper's place of business and arrange for delivery at buyers' doors. Freight forwarders prosper because less than carload (lcl) shipping rates are sharply higher than carload (cl) rates. They also provide traffic management services, such as selecting the best transportation form at the most reasonable rate. The online *Directory of Freight Forwarding Services* (**http://www.forwarders.com**) has a good listing of freight forwarders by name. Menlo Worldwide (**http://www.menloworldwide.com**) is an industry leader in this area of logistics.

The Legal Status of Transportation Firms Transportation firms are categorized as common, contract, exempt, and/or private carriers. *Common carriers* must transport the goods of any company (or individual) interested in their services; they cannot refuse shipments unless their rules are broken (such as packing requirements). Common carriers provide service on a fixed, publicized schedule between designated points. Fees are published. All railroads and petroleum pipelines and some air, motor vehicle, and water transporters are common carriers.

> Carriers are classified as **common, contract, exempt,** or **private.**

Contract carriers provide transportation services to one or more shippers, based on individual agreements. Contract carriers do not have to maintain set routes or schedules and may negotiate rates. Many motor vehicle, inland waterway, and airfreight firms are contract carriers. Firms can operate as both common and contract carriers, depending on their services.

Exempt carriers are excused from legal regulations and must only comply with safety rules. They are specified by law. Some commodities moved by water and most agricultural goods are exempt carriers.

Private carriers are firms with their own transportation facilities. They are subject to safety rules. In the United States, there are more than 100,000 private carriers.

14-4b Inventory Management

The intent of *inventory management* is to provide a continuous flow of goods and to match the quantity of goods kept in inventory as closely as possible with customer demand. When production or consumption is seasonal or erratic, this can be particularly difficult.

> Inventory management deals with the flow and allocation of products.

Inventory management has broad implications: A manufacturer or service firm cannot afford to run out of a crucial part that could halt its business. Yet, inventory on hand should not be too large because the costs of storing raw materials, parts, and/or finished products can be substantial. If models change yearly, as with autos, large

Marketing and the Web

eBay and Its Sellers: Not Always on the Same Page

In January 2005, eBay (http://www.eBay.com) announced fee increases for its services. Beginning February 18, 2005, store owners had to pay eBay an 8 percent commission on each sale, up from 5.25 percent. Immediately, many disgruntled sellers took action.

Some posted comments on community bulletin boards on and off of eBay's site. About 24,000 people signed a petition, and other sellers even debated boycotting eBay. Based on one source, the Power-SellersUnite.com (http://www.powersellersunite.com), more than 7,000 eBay stores were shut down during the five-week period after eBay posted its price increase. Some of these tried to create their own Web sites or use other auction sites. Those who felt particularly angry renamed eBay as "FeeBay" or "GreedBay." Each time over the past five years when

eBay increased its fees (for either listing an item at its auction site or increasing the commission for sold items), sellers reacted with similar actions.

What may be different this time is the concern by some sellers that eBay has continued not to address some major issues. These include the lack of detection of counterfeit merchandise, as well as fewer buyers and a reduced number of bidders per auction. According to one seller, "My complaint with eBay isn't that I'm paying more. The way I look at it, rent goes up. That's just reality. My complaint is that my rent is going up but I'm getting less for my money."

Sources: Based on material in Gary Rivlin, "eBay's Joy Ride: Going Once...," *New York Times* (March 6, 2005), pp. F1, F4; and Mylene Mangalindan, "Some Sellers Leave eBay over New Fees," *Wall Street Journal* (January 31, 2005), pp. B1, B3.

---

inventories can adversely affect new-product sales or rentals. Excessive stock may also lead to stale goods, cause a firm to mark down prices, and tie up funds. Thus, a pulling strategy by a manufacturer may be hard for a reseller to react to quickly.

A lot of companies are now applying either or both of two complementary concepts to improve their inventory management: a just-in-time inventory system and electronic data interchange. With a *just-in-time (JIT) inventory system*, a purchasing firm reduces the amount of inventory it keeps on hand by ordering more often and in lower quantity. This means better planning and data on the part of the buyer, collaborative computer systems, geographically closer sellers, improved buyer-seller relationships, and better production and distribution facilities. To retailers, a JIT system is known as a *quick response (QR) inventory system*—a cooperative effort between retailers and suppliers to reduce retail inventory while providing a merchandise supply that more closely addresses the actual buying patterns of consumers.

> **Just-in-time (JIT)** and **quick response (QR) inventory systems** monitor inventory levels.

JIT and QR systems are being used by virtually all auto makers, Black & Decker (http://www.blackanddecker.com), Boeing (http://www.boeing.com), DuPont (http://www.dupont.com), General Electric (http://www.ge.com), Hewlett-Packard (http://www.hp.com), Levi Strauss (http://www.levistrauss.com), Limited Brands (http://www.limited.com), Motorola (http://www.motorola.com), Wal-Mart (http://www.walmart.com), and numerous other large and small firms. For example, when a Camry (http://www.toyota.com/camry) lands at Toyota's Kentucky paint shop, a seat order—color, fabric, and type (bench or bucket)—is sent by computer to a nearby Johnson Controls (http://www.johnsoncontrols.com) factory. Just hours later, the seat can be installed in the Camry. Johnson Controls provides similar service for a dozen other auto makers.

Through *electronic data interchange (EDI)*, suppliers and their manufacturers/service providers, wholesalers, and/or retailers exchange data via computer linkups. This lets firms maximize revenues, reduce markdowns, and lower inventory-carrying costs by speeding the flow of data and products. For EDI to work well, each firm in a distribution channel must use the Universal Product Code (UPC) and electronically exchange data. To learn more about EDI, visit the IBM Web site (http://www.ibm.com) and type "EDI" in the search box.

> With **electronic data interchange (EDI),** computers are used to exchange information between suppliers and their customers.

Four specific aspects of inventory management are examined next: stock turnover, when to reorder, how much to reorder, and warehousing.

Stock turnover shows the ratio between sales and average inventory.

Stock Turnover *Stock turnover*—the number of times during a stated period (usually one year) that average inventory on hand is sold—shows the relationship between a firm's sales and the inventory level it maintains. It is calculated in units or dollars (in selling price or at cost):

$$\frac{\text{Annual rate of}}{\text{stock turnover}} = \frac{\text{Number of units sold during year}}{\text{Average inventory on hand (in units)}}$$

or

$$= \frac{\text{Net yearly sales}}{\text{Average inventory on hand (valued in sales dollars)}}$$

or

$$= \frac{\text{Cost of goods sold}}{\text{Average inventory on hand (valued at cost)}}$$

For example, in retailing, average annual stock turnover ranges from less than 3 in jewelry stores to 40 or more in gasoline service stations.

A high turnover rate has many advantages: inventory investments are productive, items are fresh, losses from style changes are reduced, and inventory costs (such as insurance, breakage, warehousing, and credit) are lower. Turnover can be improved by reducing assortments, dropping slow-selling items, keeping only small amounts of some items, and buying from suppliers that deliver on time. On the other hand, too high a turnover rate may have adverse effects: small purchases may cause a loss of volume discounts, low assortment may reduce sales volume if consumers do not have enough choice or related items are not carried, discounts may be needed to lift sales, and chances of running out of stock go up if average inventory size is low. Figure 14-12 shows how people can act should a firm run out of stock.

Knowing when to reorder helps protect against stockouts while minimizing inventory investments.

The **reorder point** is based on lead time, usage, and safety stock.

When to Reorder Inventory A firm sets the inventory levels at which to place new orders by having a specified *reorder point* for each of its products (or raw materials or parts). A reorder point depends on order lead time, the usage rate, and safety stock. *Order lead time* is the period from the date of an order until the date items are ready to sell or use (received, checked, and altered, if needed). *Usage rate* is the average unit sales (for a reseller) or the rate at which a product is used in production (for a manufacturer).

Figure 14-12

What Happens When a Firm Has Stock Shortages

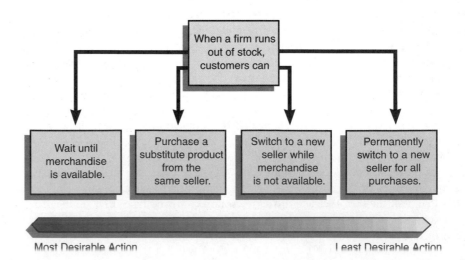

When a firm runs out of stock, customers can

| Wait until merchandise is available. | Purchase a substitute product from the same seller. | Switch to a new seller while merchandise is not available. | Permanently switch to a new seller for all purchases. |

Most Desirable Action → Least Desirable Action

Safety stock is extra inventory to guard against being out of stock due to unexpectedly high demand or production and delivery delays.

The reorder point formula is

$$\text{Reorder point} = (\text{Order lead time} \times \text{Usage rate}) + (\text{Safety stock})$$

A wholesaler that needs 4 days for its purchase orders to be placed and received, sells 10 items per day, and wants to have 10 extra items on hand in case a delivery is delayed by one day, has a reorder point of 50 [(4 × 10) + (10)]. Without safety stock, the firm would lose 10 sales if it orders when inventory is 40 items and the items are received in 5 days.

How Much to Reorder   A firm must decide on its *order size*—the right amount of products, parts, and so on, to buy at one time. This depends on volume discounts, the firm's resources, the stock turnover rate, the costs of processing each order, and the costs of holding goods in inventory. If a firm places large orders, quantity discounts are often available, a large part of its finances are tied up in inventory, its stock turnover rate is relatively low, per-order processing costs are low, and inventory costs are generally high. The firm is also less apt to run out of goods. The opposite is true for small orders.

Many firms seek to balance order-processing costs (filling out forms, computer time, and product handling) and inventory-holding costs (warehouse expenses, interest charges, insurance, deterioration, and theft). Processing costs per unit fall as orders get bigger, but inventory costs rise. The **economic order quantity (EOQ)** is the order volume corresponding to the lowest sum of order-processing and inventory-holding costs. Table 14-8 shows three ways to compute EOQ for a firm with an annual demand of 3,000 units for a product; the cost of each unit is $1; order-processing costs are $3 per order; and inventory-holding costs equal 20 percent of each item's cost. As shown in the table, the economic order quantity is 300 units. Thus, the firm should place orders of 300 units and have 10 orders per year.

> **Economic order quantity (EOQ)** balances ordering and inventory costs.

Warehousing   *Warehousing* involves the physical facilities used to store, identify, and sort goods in expectation of their sale and transfer within a distribution channel. Warehouses can be used to store goods, prepare goods for shipment, coordinate shipments, send orders, and aid in product recalls.

> **Warehousing** involves storing and dispatching goods.

Private warehouses are owned and operated by firms that store and distribute their own products. They are most likely to be used by those with stable inventory levels and long-run plans to serve the same geographic areas.

Public warehouses provide storage and related distribution services to any interested firm or individual on a rental basis. They are used by small firms without the resources or desire to have their own facilities, larger firms that need more storage space (if their own warehouses are full), or any size of firm entering a new area. They offer shipping economies by allowing carload shipments to be made to warehouses in local markets; then short-distance, smaller shipments are made to customers. Firms can also reduce their investments in facilities and maximize flexibility by using public warehouses. If products must be recalled, these warehouses can be used as collection points, where items are separated, disposed of, and/or salvaged. There are thousands of public warehouses in the United States.

Public warehouses can accommodate both bonded warehousing and field warehousing. In bonded warehousing, imported or taxable goods are stored and can be released for sale only after applicable taxes are paid. This enables firms to postpone tax payments until they are ready to make deliveries to customers. Cigarettes and liquor are often stored in bonded warehouses. In field warehousing, a receipt is issued by a public warehouse for goods stored in a private warehouse or in transit to consumers. The goods are put in a special area, and the field warehouser is responsible for them. A firm may use field warehousing because a warehouse receipt serves as collateral for a loan.

The most high-tech distribution center is automated and uses computer technology to replace people with machines. Both private and public warehouses are now more automated.

Table 14-8 Computing an Economic Order Quantity

A.

	Order Quantity (Units)	Average Inventory Maintained (Units)[a]	Annual Inventory-Holding Costs[b]	Annual Order-Processing Costs[c]	Annual Total Costs
	100	50	$10	$90	$100
	200	100	20	45	65
EOQ→	300	150	30	30	60
	400	200	40	24	64
	500	250	50	18	68

B.

EOQ

[Graph: Total costs vs Order quantity (Units). Curves for Total costs, Holding costs, and Order-processing costs.]

C.

$$EOQ = \sqrt{\frac{2DS}{IC}} = \sqrt{\frac{2(3,000)(\$3)}{0.20(\$1)}} = 300$$

where   EOQ = Order quantity (units)

D = Annual demand (units)

S = Costs to place an order ($)

I = Annual holding costs (as a % of unit costs)

C = Unit cost of an item ($)

[a] The average inventory on hand = 1/2 x Order quantity.

[b] Inventory-holding costs = Annual holding costs as a percent of unit cost x Unit cost x Average inventory.

[c] Order-processing costs = Number of annual orders x Costs to place an order. Number of orders = Annual demand/Order quantity.

Web Sites You Can Use

These Web sites offer much information pertaining to the value chain and distribution planning:

- BetterManagement.com (http://www.bettermanagement.com/library/default.aspx): Choose "Supply Chain Management" from the "Topics" toolbar
- *IndustryWeek's Value/Supply Chain* (http://www.industryweek.com/section.aspx?sectionid=11)

- Logistics Online (http://www.logisticsonline.com)
- QuickMBA (http://www.quickmba.com/strategy/value-chain)
- Supply Chain Management articles (http://www.bpubs.com/Management_Science/Supply_Chain_Management)
- *Supply Chain Management Review* (http://www.manufacturing.net/scm)

Summary

1. *To discuss the role of the value chain and the value delivery chain in the distribution process* The distribution process has four stages: goals, value chain and value delivery chain, total delivered product, and level of satisfaction.

   In many channels, there are three participants: suppliers/manufacturers, distribution intermediaries, and customers. The goals of each must be determined, exchanged, and reconciled.

   A value chain has two components: the value chain itself and the value delivery chain. A value chain represents the series of business activities that are performed to design, produce, market, deliver, and service a product for customers. A value delivery chain encompasses all of the parties who engage in value chain activities. It is performer-based and involves three factors: the specific parties in a given value chain, their relationships, and the activities undertaken by each party. A delivery chain is only as strong as its weakest link. Win-win-win is a delivery chain goal.

   The total delivered product comprises the tangible and intangible product attributes that are actually provided to consumers. From a distribution perspective, the total delivered product reflects how well the activities in the distribution process are performed. The Web is a promising tool to enhance the total delivered product, sometimes by adding value and other times by reducing costs.

   The final stage is the level of satisfaction with the distribution process, whereby the satisfaction of each party is determined and related to its goals.

2. *To explore distribution planning and examine its importance, distribution functions, the factors used in selecting a distribution channel, and the different types of distribution channels* Distribution planning systematically deals with the physical movement of goods and services from producer to consumer, as well as the related transfer of ownership (or rental). A channel of distribution consists of the organizations or people—known as channel members or distribution intermediaries—involved in the distribution process.

   Distribution decisions often affect a firm's marketing plans. For many firms, the choice of a distribution channel is one of their most important decisions. More companies now realize the value of relationship marketing and strive for long-term relations with suppliers, intermediaries, and customers. Both costs and profits are affected by the channel chosen. Firms may have to conform to existing channel patterns, and their markets' size and nature are also affected by the channel used.

   No matter who performs them, channel functions include research, buying, promotion, customer services, product planning, pricing, and distribution. Intermediaries can play a key role by doing various tasks and resolving differences in manufacturer and consumer goals via the sorting process.

   These factors must be considered in selecting a method of distribution: the consumer, the company, the product, the competition, the distribution channels themselves, and legal requirements.

   A direct channel requires that one party do all distribution tasks; in an indirect channel, tasks are done by multiple parties. In comparing methods, a firm must weigh its costs and abilities against control and total sales. An indirect channel may use a contractual or an administered agreement. A long channel has many levels of independents; a wide one has many firms at any stage. A channel may be exclusive, selective, or intensive, based on goals, resellers, customers, and marketing. A dual channel (multichannel distribution) lets a company operate via two or more distribution methods.

3. *To consider the nature of distribution intermediary contracts, cooperation and conflict in a channel of distribution, the special aspects of a distribution channel for industrial products, and international distribution* In supplier/distribution intermediary contracts, price policies, sale conditions, territorial rights, the services/responsibility mix, and contract length and termination conditions are specified.

   Cooperation and conflict may occur in a channel. Conflicts must be settled fairly; confrontation can cause hostility and negative acts by all parties. Frequently, a pushing strategy—based on channel cooperation—can be used by established firms. A pulling strategy—based on proving that demand exists prior to gaining intermediary support or acceptance—must be used by many new companies.

   An industrial channel normally does not use retailers; it is more direct, entails larger orders and fewer transactions, requires specification selling and knowing resellers, uses team selling and special intermediaries, includes more leasing, provides more technical data, and embraces shared activities.

   Channel length depends on a nation's stage of economic development and consumer behavior. Distribution practices and structures differ by nation. International decisions must be made as to shipping and intermediaries. Each country has distinct legal provisions pertaining to distribution.

4. *To examine logistics and demonstrate its importance* Logistics (physical distribution) involves efficiently delivering products to designated places, at designated times, and in proper condition. It may be undertaken by any member of a channel, from producer to consumer.

   There are various reasons for studying logistics: its costs, the value of customer service, and its relationship with other functional areas in a firm. With the total-cost approach, the service level with the lowest total cost (including freight, warehousing, and lost business) is the best one. In a logistics strategy, choices are made as to transportation, inventory levels, warehousing, and facility locations.

5. *To discuss transportation alternatives and inventory management issues* Railroads usually carry bulky goods for long distances. Motor carriers dominate small shipments over short distances. Waterways ship low-value freight. Pipelines provide ongoing movement of liquids, gases, and semiliquids. Airways offer fast, costly shipping of perishables and high-value items.

Transportation specialists mostly handle small and medium-sized packages. Coordination can be improved by containerization and freight forwarding. There are common, contract, exempt, and private carriers.

Inventory management needs to provide a continuous flow of goods and match the stock kept in inventory as closely as possible with demand. In a just-in-time (JIT) or quick response (QR) system, the purchasing firm reduces the stock on hand by ordering more often and in lower quantity. With electronic data interchange

(EDI), channel members exchange information via computer linkages.

The interplay between a firm's sales and the inventory level it keeps is expressed by stock turnover. A reorder point shows the inventory level when goods must be reordered. The economic order quantity (EOQ) is the optimal amount of goods to order based on order-processing and inventory-holding costs. Warehousing decisions include selecting a private or public warehouse and examining the availability of public warehouse services.

Key Terms

value chain (p. 432)

value delivery chain (p. 433)

total delivered product (p. 434)

distribution planning (p. 435)

channel of distribution (p. 435)

channel members (p. 435)

distribution intermediaries (p. 435)

channel functions (p. 438)

sorting process (p. 439)

direct channel of distribution (p. 440)

indirect channel of distribution (p. 440)

exclusive distribution (p. 441)

selective distribution (p. 441)

intensive distribution (p. 442)

dual channel of distribution (multichannel distribution) (p. 442)

pushing strategy (p. 446)

pulling strategy (p. 446)

logistics (physical distribution) (p. 448)

total-cost approach (p. 450)

transportation forms (p. 451)

containerization (p. 454)

freight forwarding (p. 454)

common carriers (p. 454)

contract carriers (p. 454)

exempt carriers (p. 454)

private carriers (p. 454)

inventory management (p. 454)

just-in-time (JIT) inventory system (p. 455)

quick response (QR) inventory system (p. 455)

electronic data interchange (EDI) (p. 455)

stock turnover (p. 456)

reorder point (p. 456)

economic order quantity (EOQ) (p. 457)

warehousing (p. 457)

Review Questions

1. Distinguish between the terms *value chain* and *value delivery chain*. Provide an example in your answer.
2. Explain the sorting process. Provide an example in your answer.
3. Which factors influence the selection of a distribution channel?
4. Under what circumstances should a company engage in direct distribution? Indirect distribution?
5. Explain how a product could move from exclusive to selective to intensive distribution.

6. Compare motor carrier and waterway deliveries on the basis of the total-cost approach.
7. The average stock turnover rate in jewelry stores is less than 3. What does this mean? How could a jewelry store raise its turnover rate?
8. Two wholesalers sell identical merchandise. Yet, one plans a safety stock equal to 50 percent of expected sales, while the other plans no safety stock. Comment on this difference.

Discussion Questions

1. What distribution decisions would a new firm that leases PCs to small businesses have to make?
2. Devise distribution channels for the sale of DVD players, fresh fruit, and women's sweaters. Explain your choices.

3. Present a checklist that a firm could use in making international distribution decisions on a country-by-country basis.
4. Develop a list of distribution standards for a firm delivering flowers on Valentine's Day.

Web Exercise

InboundLogistics.com (**http://www.inboundlogistics.com**) calls itself "the Web site for demand-driven logistics." Its mission "is to provide today's business logistics managers with the information they need to speed cycle times, reduce

inventories, and use logistics expertise to get closer to their markets and customers." Visit the site and then describe what kinds of valuable information could be learned by logistics managers.

Practice Quiz

1. Which statement concerning the value chain is correct?
   a. Value does not have to be added by each participant.
   b. A valid delivery chain goal is for one channel participant to win at another participant's expense.
   c. A value delivery chain involves three factors: the parties, their respective goals, and their respective profits.
   d. A value delivery chain is only as strong as its weakest link.

2. A common characteristic of a value chain is
   a. channel conflict among channel members.
   b. outsourcing activities to selected channel members.
   c. a win-lose relationship.
   d. the search for low-cost, low-quality alternatives.

3. Which of the following is *not* an aspect of distribution planning?
   a. Transportation
   b. Inventory management
   c. Manufacturing
   d. Customer transactions

4. Which of the following is the intermediary task of apportioning items to various consumer markets?
   a. Accumulation
   b. Sorting
   c. Allocation
   d. Assorting

5. Direct channels of distribution are most frequently used by firms that
   a. want to increase sales volume.
   b. wish to relinquish customer contact.
   c. give up many distribution costs.
   d. service limited target markets.

6. In describing a channel of distribution, *length* refers to
   a. the levels of independent members along a channel.
   b. the number of independent members that are at any stage of distribution.
   c. ownership of companies at different stages in the channel.
   d. acquisition of businesses at the same stage in the channel.

7. Broadening its distribution channel enables a firm to
   a. increase its market share.
   b. be more self-sufficient.
   c. eliminate intermediary costs.
   d. coordinate the timing of products through the channel.

8. With exclusive distribution, a firm
   a. seeks mass market appeal.
   b. seeks a prestige image.
   c. maximizes total sales.
   d. reduces per-unit profit margins.

9. Logistics costs amount to what percent of the U.S. GDP?
   a. 9–10
   b. 7–8
   c. 4–6
   d. 1–3

10. Many retailers spend what percent of revenues on physical distribution activities?
    a. 31–40
    b. 21–30
    c. 11–20
    d. Under 5

11. Heavy, bulky items that are low in value (relative to their weight) and transported over long distances are usually carried by
    a. trucks.
    b. pipelines.
    c. airways.
    d. railroads.

12. Stock turnover is the balance between
    a. sales and inventory on hand.
    b. reorder point and economic order quantity.
    c. usage rate and order-processing costs.
    d. order lead time and safety stock.

13. Which of these is *not* an advantage of a high inventory turnover rate?
    a. Items are fresh.
    b. Losses from style changes are reduced.
    c. Inventory investments are productive.
    d. The chances of running out of stock are reduced.

14. Which of the following is *not* used in the calculation of a reorder point?
    a. Safety stock
    b. Order size
    c. Order lead time
    d. Usage rate

15. Firms with stable inventory levels and long-run plans to serve the same geographic areas tend to use
    a. public warehousing.
    b. bonded warehousing.
    c. field warehousing.
    d. private warehousing.

For the answers to these questions, please visit the online site for this book at **http://www.atomicdog.com.**

Chapter 15

Wholesaling

McKesson Corporation (http://www.mckesson.com), with annual sales of $75 billion, is the largest and oldest U.S. pharmaceutical distributor. It traces its roots to 1833 when John McKesson opened a drugstore in New York City. McKesson conducts its business in three business groups: pharmaceutical solutions, medical-surgical solutions, and information solutions.

Pharmaceutical solutions accounts for 94 percent of total revenues, serving more than 30,000 locations in all 50 states. To better serve customers, McKesson's distribution centers are all equipped with its proprietary Acumax Plus software system that tracks the receipt of merchandise—as well as orders—using barcode technology, wrist-mounted computer hardware, and radio frequency signals.

McKesson's pharmaceutical segment serves three groups of customers: retail chains (such as drugstores, food/drug combination stores, mail-order pharmacies, and mass merchandisers with drugstores), independent retail pharmacies, and institutional providers (including hospitals, clinics, and long-term care providers). Each segment requires a different combination of services from McKesson. For example, retail chains often want to reduce their labor costs by having prescriptions for multiple stores filled by a pharmacist in a central location. Chains also want to reduce their inventory-carrying costs by using McKesson's sophisticated inventory and automatic replenishment system.

In contrast, independent pharmacies want to (a) combine their purchases to obtain quantity discounts, (b) use McKesson's software to better process managed-care reimbursements, (c) be given a selection of generics from one source at significant savings, and (d) have access to profitability analysis tools. Independents that use McKesson receive signage that identifies their stores as part of McKesson's Value-Rite network. McKesson also offers the pharmacies its Sunmark private-label brand with 1,000 items.

Institutional providers are more concerned with automated inventory reordering and in improving patient health through increased drug safety.

In a recent study, Value-Rite pharmacists earned the highest ratings for customer satisfaction for personal service, convenience, and access to health information.[1]

In this chapter, we will further study wholesalers' relationships with their suppliers and customers. We will also examine the different types of firms that perform wholesaling activities and their strategies.

Chapter Objectives

1. To define wholesaling and show its importance
2. To describe the three broad categories of wholesaling (manufacturer/service provider wholesaling, merchant wholesaling, and agents and brokers) and the specific types of firms within each category
3. To examine recent trends in wholesaling

15-1   OVERVIEW

Wholesaling is the buying/handling of products and their resale to organizational buyers.

Wholesaling encompasses the buying and/or handling of goods and services and their subsequent resale to organizational users, retailers, and/or other wholesalers—but not the sale of significant volume to final consumers. It assumes many functions in a distribution channel, particularly those in the sorting process.

[1] Various company and other sources.

Manufacturers and service providers can be their own wholesalers or employ independent firms. Independents may or may not take title to or possession of products, depending on the type of wholesaling. Some independents have limited tasks; others do many functions.

Industrial, commercial, and government institutions are wholesalers' leading customers, followed closely by retailers. Sales from one wholesaler to another also represent a significant proportion of wholesaling activity. The following list shows the diversity of transactions considered as wholesaling:

- Sales of goods and services to manufacturers, service providers, oil refiners, railroads, public utilities, and government departments
- Sales of office or laboratory equipment, supplies, and services to professionals such as doctors, chiropractors, and dentists
- Sales of materials and services to builders of offices and homes
- Sales to grocery stores, restaurants, hotels, apparel stores, stationery stores, and all other retailers
- Manufacturer/service provider sales to wholesalers, and wholesaler sales to other wholesalers

In this chapter, the importance of wholesaling, the different types of wholesaling, and recent trends in wholesaling are all discussed in depth.

15-2 THE IMPORTANCE OF WHOLESALING

Wholesaling is a vital aspect of distribution because of its impact on the economy, its functions in the distribution channel, and its relationships with suppliers and customers.

15-2a Wholesaling's Impact on the Economy

In the United States, there are about 430,000 wholesale establishments with total annual sales of $5.5 trillion (including manufacturers with wholesale facilities); yet, although wholesale revenues are higher than those in retailing, there are several times as many retail establishments as wholesale.[2] According to the National Association of Wholesaler-Distributors (**http://www.naw.org**), U.S. wholesalers generate one-fifth of their total revenues from foreign markets.

> Wholesale sales are high; and wholesalers greatly affect final prices.

Revenues are high because wholesaling involves any purchases by businesses and other organizations. Some products also move through multiple levels of wholesalers (such as regional and then local); an item can be sold two or three times at the wholesale level. There are far more retailers because they serve individual, dispersed final consumers; wholesalers handle fewer, larger, more concentrated customers.

From a cost perspective, many wholesalers have a big impact on prices. Table 15-1 shows the percent of wholesale selling prices that go to wholesalers to cover operating expenses and pre-tax profits. For example, 27.6 percent of the prices a hardware wholesaler charges its retailers cover that wholesaler's operating expenses and profits. Expenses include inventory charges, sales force salaries, ads, and rent.

Wholesaler costs and profits depend on inventory turnover, the dollar value of products, the functions performed, efficiency, and competition.

---

[2] *Statistical Abstract of the United States 2004-2005* (Washington, DC: U.S. Department of Commerce, 2005).

15-2b   The Functions of Wholesalers

Wholesalers can:

> Wholesalers perform tasks ranging from distribution to risk taking.

- enable manufacturers and service providers to distribute locally without making customer contacts.
- provide a trained sales force.
- provide marketing and research support for manufacturers, service providers, retailers, and other organizations.
- gather assortments for customers and let them make fewer transactions.
- purchase and/or handle large quantities, thus reducing total physical distribution costs.
- provide warehousing and delivery facilities.
- offer financing for manufacturers and service providers (by paying for products when shipped, not when sold) and retailer and other organizations (by granting credit).
- handle financial records.
- process returns and make adjustments for defective merchandise.
- take risks by being responsible for theft, deterioration, and obsolescence of inventory.

Table 15-1 Gross Margin Data for U.S. Wholesalers by Product Category	
Product Category of Wholesaler	**Gross Profit (As % of Sales)[a]**
Total	20.2
Durable goods	24.0
Motor Vehicle and Motor Vehicle Parts and Supplies	19.6
Furniture and Home Furnishings	31.7
Lumber & Other Construction Materials	19.5
Professional and Commercial Equipment and Supplies	25.6
Computer and Peripheral Equipment and Software	18.8
Metals and Minerals, Except Petroleum	21.1
Electrical and Electronic Goods	22.5
Hardware, and Plumbing and Heating Equipment & Supplies	27.6
Machinery, Equipment, and Supplies	27.4
Miscellaneous Durable Goods	26.2
Nondurable goods	16.6
Paper and Paper Products	21.2
Drugs and Druggists' Sundries	10.8
Apparel, Piece Goods, and Notions	29.9
Groceries and Related Products	18.4
Farm Product Raw Materials	10.1
Chemicals and Allied Products	26.2
Petroleum and Petroleum Products	7.6
Beer, Wine, and Distilled Alcoholic Beverages	26.1
Miscellaneous Nondurable Goods	19.5

[a] Total costs of wholesaling, which include expenses and profit.

Source: *Annual Benchmark Report for Wholesale Trade: January 1992 Through January 2005* (Washington, DC: U.S. Census Bureau, March 2005).

Wholesalers that take title to and possession of products usually perform several or all of these tasks. Agents and brokers that facilitate sales, but do not take title or possession, have more limited duties.

Independent wholesalers vary by industry. Most consumer products, food items, replacement parts, and office supplies are sold by independents. Yet, for heavy equipment, mainframe computers, gasoline, and temporary employment, manufacturers and service providers may bypass independent resellers.

Without independent wholesalers, b-to-b consumers have to develop their own supplier contacts, deal with a number of suppliers and coordinate shipments, do more distribution functions, stock greater quantities, and place more emphasis on an internal purchasing agent or department. Many small retailers and other firms might be avoided as customers because they might not be profitably reached by a manufacturer or service provider, and they might not be able to buy necessary items elsewhere.

An illustration of wholesaling's value is the U.S. auto parts industry, in which there used to be thousands of firms making a wide range of products and marketing them through a multitude of sales organizations. At that time, customers (mostly specialty stores and service stations) faced constant interruptions by salespeople, and manufacturers' sales costs were high. A better system exists today with the organized use of a much smaller number of independent distributors.

15-2c Wholesalers' Relationships with Suppliers and Customers

Independent wholesalers are often caught "in the middle," not knowing whether their allegiance is more to manufacturers/service providers or their own customers. This is the challenge wholesalers face: " 'I have a hard time trying to understand the value [wholesalers] are bringing,' says the marketing director at Express Manufacturing [**http://www.eminc.com**], a $50 million (sales) maker of circuit boards for telecom and water systems. Express tried letting a big wholesale distributor (which it won't identify) manage its component inventory on-site but eventually dropped the service because it figured it could manage on its own."[3]

> Wholesalers have obligations to both suppliers and customers.

Many wholesalers feel they get scant support from manufacturers/service providers. They desire training, technical assistance, product literature, and advertising. They dislike it when vendors alter territories, add new distributors to cover an existing geographic area, or decide to change to a direct channel and do wholesale tasks themselves. Wholesalers want manufacturers/service providers to sell *to* them and not *through* them. *Selling to the wholesaler* means a distributor is viewed as a customer to be researched and satisfied. *Selling through the wholesaler* means retailers or consumers are objects of manufacturers'/service providers' interest and wholesalers are less important. See Figure 15-1.

To remedy the situation, the best wholesalers are aggressively adapting to the marketplace:

> If they aren't selling to new markets, chances are distributors [wholesalers] have made themselves invaluable to their existing customer base. That's the case at Consumers Interstate [**http://www.cicgo.com**], a janitorial, safety, paper products, and office supplies distributor based in Connecticut. The company president says his customer base has not changed drastically in recent years, despite the poor health of the manufacturing industry in the United States. Though he has picked up business selling to Connecticut's casinos, which have emerged in the last 10 years or so, manufacturers still remain his company's emphasis: "We've remained focused on the manufacturing industry—and that's been terrible. But there's still a lot of market share for us. We're growing every year, and we're enjoying it." Consumers Interstate has

---

[3] Nelson Brett, "Stuck in the Middle," *Forbes* (August 15, 2005), pp. 88-89.

Marketing and the Web

Electrical Distributors Flock to the Internet

Even though industrial, institutional, and commercial accounts are large users of electrical distributors' Web sites, electrical contractors are much less likely to make Web-based purchases from these sites. Typically, the industrial, institutional, and commercial accounts use standardized purchase orders based on negotiated agreements, whereas the electrical contractors do not.

To highlight the relatively low levels of Web site usage by electrical contractors, a recent study found that 32 percent of the electrical contractors surveyed had not purchased electrical materials online. Forty-four percent of the contractors also purchased less than 10 percent of their materials online. What is particularly disturbing to the electrical distributors is that these contractors account for a large proportion of total sales for many distributors.

One way to increase Web-based sales to electrical contractors is to increase the ease of making online purchases. Web sites can be more effective to this segment by allowing purchasers to verify orders, track back orders, access active links to manufacturer training and contractor resources, download statements and invoices, view their purchase history, and check pricing.

Another way to increase Web sales is to improve the visibility of the Web site to electrical contractors. This can be accomplished by sales force and customer service staff training, promoting the Web site in print newsletters, direct-mail promotions for the Web site, and an E-newsletter tailored to the specific interests of electrical contractors.

Source: Based on material in David Gordon, "Online Ventures," *Electrical Wholesaling* (June 2005), p. 45.

grown because it's found ways to make those customers run more efficiently. The firm has helped manufacturers find better ways of ordering supplies, for one thing—specifically, by using an Internet procurement method that saves time and money. It also has added to its product base, enabling customers to buy more from one source.[4]

See Figure 15-2.

Figure 15-1

Selling *to* Versus Selling THROUGH the Wholesaler

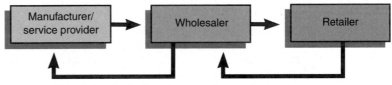

Selling **to** the Wholesaler

The wholesaler is viewed as a customer who is researched and satisfied.

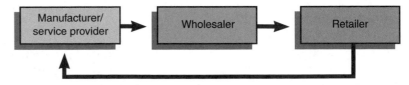

Selling **Through** the Wholesaler

The retailer (or final consumer) is the object of the manufacturer's/service provider's interests. The needs of the wholesaler are considered unimportant.

---

[4] Victoria Fraza Kickham, "Distributors Change with the Times," *Industrial Distribution* (August 2005), pp. 15–16.

<u>Figure 15-2</u>

Maintaining a Strong Wholesaling Business

As Menlo Worldwide (**http://www.menloworldwide.com**) says at its Web site, "Top-tier companies around the world look to Menlo for innovative solutions that help plan business strategies, improve customer service, accelerate order cycle times, and tighten control of the supply chain—all while reducing costs in transportation, inventory, and order fulfillment." Menlo "helps firms attain operational excellence across their global supply chains."

Source: Reprinted by permission.

15-3 TYPES OF WHOLESALING

Figure 15-3 outlines the three broad categories of wholesaling: manufacturer/service provider wholesaling, merchant wholesaling, and agents and brokers. Table 15-2 contains detailed descriptions of every type of independent wholesaler and shows their functions and special features.

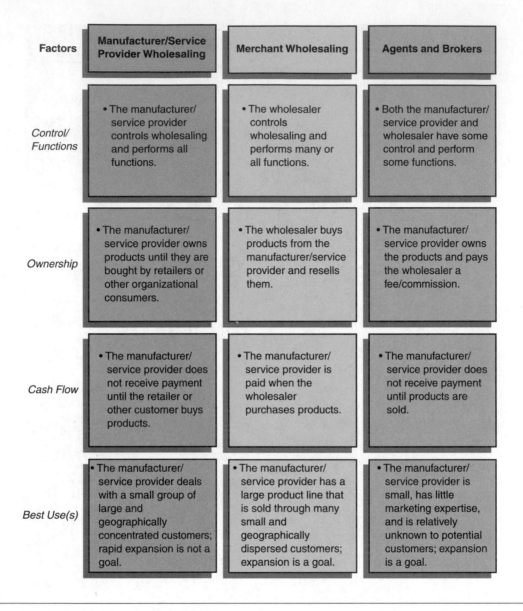

Factors	Manufacturer/Service Provider Wholesaling	Merchant Wholesaling	Agents and Brokers
Control/Functions	• The manufacturer/service provider controls wholesaling and performs all functions.	• The wholesaler controls wholesaling and performs many or all functions.	• Both the manufacturer/service provider and wholesaler have some control and perform some functions.
Ownership	• The manufacturer/service provider owns products until they are bought by retailers or other organizational consumers.	• The wholesaler buys products from the manufacturer/service provider and resells them.	• The manufacturer/service provider owns the products and pays the wholesaler a fee/commission.
Cash Flow	• The manufacturer/service provider does not receive payment until the retailer or other customer buys products.	• The manufacturer/service provider is paid when the wholesaler purchases products.	• The manufacturer/service provider does not receive payment until products are sold.
Best Use(s)	• The manufacturer/service provider deals with a small group of large and geographically concentrated customers; rapid expansion is not a goal.	• The manufacturer/service provider has a large product line that is sold through many small and geographically dispersed customers; expansion is a goal.	• The manufacturer/service provider is small, has little marketing expertise, and is relatively unknown to potential customers; expansion is a goal.

Figure 15-3

The Broad Categories of Wholesaling

15-3a   Manufacturer/Service Provider Wholesaling

In **manufacturer/service provider wholesaling**, a producer does all wholesaling functions itself. This occurs if a firm feels it is best able to reach b-to-b customers by doing wholesaling tasks. The format yields 30 percent of U.S. wholesale revenues and 6 percent of establishments. Manufacturer/service provider wholesalers include Citigroup (**http://www.citigroup.com**), Frito-Lay (**http://www.fritolay.com**), General Motors (**http://www.gm.com**), Hanes (**http://www.hanes.com**), IBM (**http://www.ibm.com**), Pitney Bowes (**http://www.pb.com**), and Prudential (**http://www.prudential.com**).

Wholesale activities by a manufacturer or service provider may be done at sales offices and/or branch offices. A *sales office* is located at a firm's production facilities or close to the market. No inventory is kept there. In contrast, a *branch office* has facilities for warehousing products, as well as for selling them.

Manufacturer/service provider wholesaling works best if independent intermediaries are unavailable, existing intermediaries are unacceptable, the manufacturer or service provider wants control over marketing, customers are few in number and each is a key account, customers desire personal service from the producer, customers are near the

In **manufacturer/service provider wholesaling**, a firm has its own sales or branch offices.

Table **15-2**   Characteristics of Independent Wholesalers

Wholesaler Type	Major Functions						
	Provides Credit	Stores and Delivers	Takes Title	Provides Merchandising and Promotion Assistance	Provides Personal Sales Force	Performs Research and Planning	Special Features
I. _Merchant wholesaler_							
A. Full service							
1. General merchandise	Yes	Yes	Yes	Yes	Yes	Yes	Carries nearly all items a customer usually needs
2. Specialty merchandise	Yes	Yes	Yes	Yes	Yes	Yes	Specializes in a narrow product range, extensive assortment
3. Rack jobber	Yes	Yes	Yes	Yes	Yes	Yes	Furnishes racks and shelves, consignment sales
4. Franchise	Yes	Yes	Yes	Yes	Yes	Yes	Use of common business format, extensive management services
5. Cooperative							
a. Producer-owned	Yes	Yes	Yes	Yes	Yes	Yes	Farmer controlled, profits divided among members
b. Retailer-owned	Yes	Yes	Yes	Yes	Yes	Yes	Wholesaler owned by several retailers
B. Limited service							
1. Cash and carry	No	Stores, no delivery	Yes	No	No	No	No outside sales force, wholesale store for business needs
2. Drop shipper	Yes	Delivers, no storage	Yes	No	Yes	Sometimes	Ships items without physically handling them
3. Truck/wagon	Rarely	Yes	Yes	Yes	Yes	Sometimes	Sales and delivery on same call
4. Mail order	Sometimes	Yes	Yes	No	No	Sometimes	Catalogs used as sole promotion tool
II. _Agents and brokers_							
A. Agents							
1. Manufacturers' (service providers')	No	Sometimes	No	Yes	Yes	Sometimes	Sells selected items for several firms
2. Selling	Sometimes	Yes	No	Yes	Yes	Yes	Markets all the items of a firm

(continued)

3. Commission (factor) merchants	Sometimes	Yes	No	No	Yes	Yes	Handles items on a consignment basis
B. Brokers							
1. Food	No	Sometimes	No	Yes	Yes	Yes	Brings together buyers and sellers
2. Stock	Sometimes	Sometimes	No	Yes	Yes	Yes	Brings together buyers and sellers

firm or clustered, computerized ordering links a firm with customers, and/or laws (particularly in foreign markets) limit arrangements with independent resellers.

For instance, because it seeks close contact with its retailers and control over its marketing strategy, manufacturer wholesaling is a must for Frito-Lay. But, it sure is complex: "Distributing 9 billion bags of snacks a year creates quite a delivery crunch. With net sales exceeding $11 billion annually, Frito-Lay (a PepsiCo division) is the undisputed leader in the salty snack industry. Doritos, Ruffles, and dozens of other well-known Frito-Lay brands command more than half the U.S. snack chip market. Approximately 14,000 Frito-Lay sales and delivery personnel connect 200 distribution centers to hundreds of thousands of retailers. Each delivery generates a proof of delivery receipt, to the tune of 120,000 daily."[5]

15-3b Merchant Wholesaling

> **Merchant wholesalers** buy products and are full or **limited service**.

Merchant wholesalers buy, take title, and take possession of products for further resale. This is the largest U.S. wholesaler type in sales (60 percent of the total) and establishments (84 percent of the total).

As an example, Sysco (**http://www.sysco.com**) is a merchant wholesaler that buys and handles 150,000 products from 3,000 producers of food and related products from around the world. It carries fresh and frozen meats, seafood, poultry, fruits and vegetables, bakery products, canned and dry foods, paper and disposable products, sanitation items, dairy foods, beverages, kitchen and tabletop equipment, and medical and surgical supplies. The firm operates throughout the contiguous United States and in parts of Alaska, Hawaii, and Canada. Sysco has more than 160 distribution facilities, and it serves about 400,000 restaurants, hotels, schools, hospitals, retirement homes, and other locations.[6] See Figure 15-4.

Full-service merchant wholesalers perform a full range of distribution tasks. They provide credit, store and deliver products, offer merchandising and promotion assistance, have a personal sales force, offer research and planning support, pass along information to suppliers and customers, and give installation and repair services. They are prevalent for grocery products, pharmaceuticals, hardware, plumbing equipment, tobacco, alcoholic beverages, and television program syndication.

Limited-service merchant wholesalers do not perform all the functions of full-service merchant wholesalers. They may not provide credit, merchandising assistance, or marketing research data. They are popular for construction materials, coal, lumber, perishables, equipment rentals, and specialty foods.

On average, full-service merchant wholesalers require more compensation than limited-service ones because they perform greater functions.

Full-Service Merchant Wholesalers Full-service merchant wholesalers can be divided into the following types.

---

[5] "HighView at Frito-Lay," **http://www.htech.com/fritopoda.htm** (April 4, 2006).

[6] "Investor Relations," **http://www.sysco.com/investor/investor.html** (April 4, 2006).

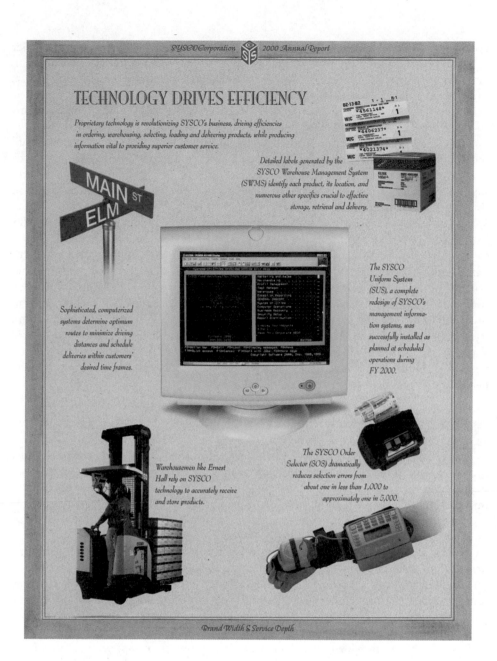

Figure 15-4

A Leader in Merchant Wholesaling

Source: Reprinted by permission.

General-merchandise (full-line) wholesalers carry a wide product assortment— nearly all the items needed by their customers. Some general-merchandise hardware, drug, and clothing wholesalers stock many product lines, but not much depth in any one line. They seek to sell their retailers or other organizational customers all or most of their products and foster strong loyalty and exclusivity.

Specialty-merchandise (limited-line) wholesalers concentrate on a rather narrow product range and have an extensive selection in that range. They offer many sizes, colors, and models—and provide functions similar to other full-service merchant wholesalers. They are popular for health foods, seafood, retail store displays, frozen foods, and video rentals.

Rack jobbers furnish the racks or shelves on which products are displayed. They own the products on the racks, selling them on a consignment basis—so their clients pay after goods are resold. Unsold items are taken back. Jobbers set up displays, refill shelves, price-mark goods, maintain inventory records, and compute the amount due from their customers. Heavily advertised, branded merchandise that is sold on a self-service basis is most often handled. Included are magazines, health and beauty aids, cosmetics, drugs, hand tools, toys, housewares, and stationery.

> **General-merchandise wholesalers** sell a range of items.

> **Specialty-merchandise wholesalers** sell a narrow line.

> **Rack jobbers** set up displays and are paid after sales.

In *franchise wholesaling*, independent retailers affiliate with an existing wholesaler to use a standardized storefront design, business format, name, and purchase system. Suppliers often produce goods and services according to specifications set by a franchise wholesaler. This form of wholesaling is used for hardware, auto parts, and groceries. Franchise wholesalers include Independent Grocers Alliance (IGA, **http://www.iga.com**) and Ben Franklin Stores (**http://www.benfranklinstores.com**).

Wholesale cooperatives are owned by member firms to economize functions and provide broad support. Producer-owned cooperatives are popular in farming. They market, transport, and process farm products—as well as make and distribute farm supplies. These cooperatives often sell to stores under their own names, such as Farmland (**http://www.farmlandfoods.com**), Land O'Lakes (**http://www.landolakes.com**), Ocean Spray (**http://www.oceanspray.com**), Sunkist (**http://www.sunkist.com**), and Welch's (**http://www.welchs.com**). With retailer-owned cooperatives, independent retailers form groups that buy, lease, or build wholesale facilities. The cooperatives own products, handle cooperative ads, and negotiate with suppliers. They are used by hardware and grocery stores. Ace Hardware (**http://www.acehardware.com**), as described at its Web site, "is a cooperative of more than 4,800 independent retail stores. It is committed to providing low upfront costs on merchandise purchases by affiliated retailers from strategically located Ace Hardware retail support centers or through Ace's drop ship and bulletin programs. Retailers are supported by over 65,000 brand name and Ace items, a comprehensive advertising program, sophisticated retail support systems, and headquarters and field staff personnel." See Figure 15-5.

Limited-Service Merchant Wholesalers Limited-service merchant wholesalers can be classified as follows.

In *cash-and-carry wholesaling*, small-business people drive to wholesalers, order products, and take them back to a store or business. These wholesalers offer no credit or delivery, no merchandising and promotion help, no outside sales force, and no research or planning aid. They are good for fill-in items, have low prices, and allow immediate product use. They are used for construction materials, electrical supplies, office supplies, auto supplies, hardware products, and groceries.

Drop shippers (desk jobbers) buy goods from manufacturers or suppliers and arrange for their shipment to retailers or industrial users. They have legal ownership, but do not physically possess products and have no storage facilities. They purchase items, leave them at manufacturers' plants, contact customers by phone, set up and coordinate carload shipments from manufacturers directly to customers, and are responsible for items that cannot be sold. Trade credit, a personal sales force, and some research and planning are provided; merchandising and promotion support are not. Drop shippers are often used for coal, coke, and building materials. These goods have high freight costs, in relation to their value, because of their weight. Thus, direct shipments from suppliers to customers are needed.

Truck/wagon wholesalers generally have a regular sales route, offer items from a truck or wagon, and deliver goods when they are sold. These wholesalers provide merchandising and promotion support; they are considered limited service because they usually do not extend credit and offer little research and planning help. Operating costs are high due to the services performed and low average sales. These wholesalers often deal with goods requiring special handling or with perishables such as bakery products, tobacco, meat, candy, potato chips, and dairy products.

Mail-order wholesalers use catalogs, instead of a personal sales force, to promote products and communicate with customers. They may provide credit but do not generally give merchandising and promotion support. They store and deliver goods, and offer some research and planning assistance. These wholesalers are found with jewelry, cosmetics, auto parts, specialty food product lines, business supplies, and small office equipment.

15-3c Agents and Brokers

Agents and *brokers* perform various wholesale tasks, but do not take title to products. Unlike merchant wholesalers, which make profits on the sales of products they own, they work for commissions or fees as payment for their services. They account for 10 percent of wholesale sales and 10 percent of wholesale establishments. The main difference between agents and brokers is that agents are apt to be used on a permanent basis, whereas brokers often are temporary.

Agents and brokers enable a manufacturer or service provider to expand sales volume despite limited resources. Their selling costs are a predetermined percent of sales, and they have trained salespeople. There are manufacturers'/service providers' agents, selling agents, and commission (factor) merchants.

Manufacturers'/service providers' agents work for several manufacturers/service providers and carry noncompetitive, complementary products in exclusive territories. By selling noncompetitive items, there are no conflicts of interest. By selling complementary items, they stock a fairly complete line of products for their markets. They do not offer credit but may store and deliver products and give limited research and planning

> **Agents** and **brokers** do not take title to products.

> **Manufacturers'/service providers' agents** work for many firms, selling noncompeting items.

Ethical Issues in Marketing

Protecting the Distribution Rights of Legitimate Film Wholesalers

U2 Home Entertainment (U2) is a U.S. distributor of Chinese-language motion pictures. It owns the exclusive rights to import Chinese films into the United States in videocassette, video compact disk, and DVD formats. U2 recently sued the owners of Lai Ying Music & Video Trading (Lai Ying), a New York City-based retail video store, for importing Chinese films that U2 had the exclusive rights to distribute.

This action was not U2's first lawsuit against Lai Ying. In a 2001 action, the U.S. Marshals Service seized unauthorized video compact disk copies from Lai Ying. U2 and Lai Ying also entered into an agreement that included a court order restraining Lai Ying from further purchases of unauthorized copies. In early 2004, U2 became aware that Lai Ying was continuing to sell unauthorized copies of its films. During one seven-month period, the U.S. marshals either seized or purchased 174 unauthorized copies of 49 different U2 film titles from Lai Ying.

U2 sought damages for 47 of the 49 infringed U2 films. It also sought a contempt-of-court finding based on Lai Ying's disregard for the prior injunction. U2 stated that Lai Ying continued to import some of the films that were seized earlier and make illegal copies of other protected films. The Southern District court awarded U2 $7.35 million to compensate it for lost profits, as well as for the harm to its business reputation.

Source: Based on material in "Films' Exclusive Distributor Awarded $7.35 Million for Retailer's Copyright Violations in Importing Films," New York Law Journal (June 2, 2005), p. 21.

---

aid. Merchandising and promotional support are provided. These agents may enhance clients' sales efforts, help introduce new products, enter dispersed markets, and handle items with low average sales. They may carry only some of a firm's products; a manufacturer/service provider may hire many agents. Large firms may hire a separate one for each product line. Agents have little say on marketing and pricing. They earn commissions of 5 to 10 percent of sales, and are popular for auto products, iron, steel, footwear, textiles, and commercial real-estate and insurance. The Manufacturers' Agents National Association (**http://www.manaonline.org**) has 20,000 manufacturers' reps.

> **Selling agents** market all the products of a manufacturer or service provider.

Selling agents are responsible for marketing the entire output of a manufacturer/service provider under a contractual agreement. They become the marketing department for clients and negotiate price and other conditions of sale, such as credit and delivery. They do all wholesale tasks except taking title. Though a firm may use several manufacturers'/service providers' agents, it may hire only one sales agent. These agents are more apt to work for small firms. They are common for textile manufacturing, canned foods, metals, home furnishings, apparel, lumber, and metal products. Because they do more tasks, they often get higher commissions than manufacturers'/service providers' representatives.

> **Commission (factor) merchants** assemble goods from local markets.

Commission (factor) merchants receive goods on consignment, accumulate them from local markets, and arrange for their sale in a central location. They may offer credit; they do store and deliver goods, provide a sales force, and offer research and planning help. They normally do not assist in merchandising and promotion, but can negotiate prices—provided the prices are not below sellers' stated minimums. They may act in an auction setting; commissions vary. These wholesalers are used for agricultural and seafood products, furniture, and art.

Brokers are common in food and financial services. They are well informed about market conditions, terms of sale, sources of credit, price setting, potential buyers and sellers, and the art of negotiating. They do not take title and usually are not allowed to complete a transaction without approval.

> **Food brokers** and **commercial stock brokers** unite buyers and sellers, as well as conclude sales.

Food brokers introduce buyers and sellers of food and related general-merchandise items to one another and bring them together to complete a sale. They operate in specific locales and work for a limited number of food producers. Their sales staff calls on chain-store buyers, store managers, and purchasing agents. They work closely with ad agencies. They often represent the seller, who pays a commission. They do not actually provide credit but may store and deliver. Commissions are typically 3 to 5 percent of sales. Cebco (**http://www.cebco.com**) and Wyman Foorman (**http://www.wymanfoorman.com**) are examples of food brokers with active Web sites.

Global Marketing in Action

Capacitor Industries: Wholesaling Electronic Components from China

Terry Noone is founder and chief executive officer of Capacitor Industries (CI) (**http://www.capacitor industries.com**), a wholesaler of low-cost electronic components made in China. Most of CI's sales come from capacitors, devices that store charges, maintain electrical currents, and protect electrical equipment from power surges. These capacitors are sold primarily to U.S.-based motor manufacturers.

The wholesale capacitor business is a very competitive one. Prices have also historically declined by 5 to 8 percent a year. Noone seeks to remain competitive by keeping an eye on CI's expenses. To reduce fixed costs, CI uses outside sales representatives. To avoid being stuck with unsaleable inventory, Noone actively monitors sales and reduces inventory of slow-selling goods. He also seeks out payment terms of 30 and 60 days, so as to maximize the cash flow of the business.

Increasingly, CI's business relies on custom work. U.S. manufacturers now commonly come to Noone with a custom project, such as a capacitor casing that can cut out a step in the motor-assembly process. He then seeks out a Chinese firm to produce the product and then assists in getting the necessary approval from Underwriters Laboratories (**http://www.ul.com**). Although the custom capacitor work involves much more work than the sale of a standard capacitor, it means less price competition from competitive wholesalers. In addition, CI sells higher-margin capacitors for between $50 and $1,000.

Source: Based on material in Jeff Bailey, "A New Kind of Middleman," *Inc.* (July 2005), pp. 31-32.

Commercial stock brokers are licensed sales representatives who advise business clients, take orders, and then acquire stocks and/or bonds for the clients. They may aid firms selling stocks or bonds, represent either buyers or sellers (with both paying commissions), and offer some credit. While they operate in particular areas, they usually sell stocks and bonds of firms from around the United States—even around the world. They do a lot of business over the phone and may help publicize new stock or bond offerings. Commissions average 1 to 10 percent of sales, based on volume and stock prices.

15-4 RECENT TRENDS IN WHOLESALING

During the last two decades, wholesaling has changed dramatically, with independent wholesalers striving to protect their place in the channel. Among the key trends are those related to the evolving wholesaler mix, productivity, customer service, international opportunities, and target markets.

Since the early 1980s, the proportion of total sales volume contributed by manufacturer wholesaling, merchant wholesaling, and agents and brokers has stayed rather steady. However, manufacturer wholesalers now have fewer establishments (due to the consolidation of facilities) and merchant wholesalers have many more (to provide better customer service). Overall, 250,000 companies currently engage in some form of U.S. wholesaling, down from 364,000 companies in 1987. Today, the average annual sales for the 26,000 U.S. manufacturer wholesaling establishments are $55 million—compared with $9.1 million for the 361,000 merchant wholesaling establishments and $13 million for the 43,000 agent/broker establishments. The trend toward bigger firms is expected to continue well into the future.[7]

> Firms are becoming larger and more cost-conscious.

The Internet is also having a major impact on the wholesaler mix: "The biggest negative influence on wholesalers and the wholesaling industry may be the growth of the Web, which enables sellers and buyers to bypass wholesalers and interface directly with each other. This new medium has been a major factor in products such as books, CDs,

[7] Estimated by the authors.

and airline tickets."[8] Yet, some wholesalers are flourishing on the Web. They understand how to use it to their advantage.

Wholesalers are constantly looking for productivity gains to benefit their customers and themselves, and protect their position in the marketplace. As highlighted in Figure 15-6, consider the approach of United Stationers (**http://www.unitedstationers.com**):

> It's not enough that United Stationers is North America's largest broad line wholesale distributor of business products. Our mission is to become a high performance organization, delivering exceptional value through superior execution of innovative marketing and logistics services. I am pleased to report that we are making progress throughout the company. You can see it in our team structure, which allows us to draw on the expertise of associates at all levels to improve every aspect of our business—from making it easy for customers to work with United, to strengthening our partnerships with suppliers. You can see it in our product

---

[8] "Wholesaling Industry," http://www.activemedia-guide.com/wholesaling_industry.htm (April 6, 2006).

category and channel initiatives, where we are working hard to find products that meet the needs of all of our resellers and designing programs to help our independent resellers more effectively build their businesses. You can see it in our efforts on cost and value leadership, where we are driving operating costs out of our company—to the tune of $20 million a year— while remaining the best value provider of logistical services. You can see it in our use of information technology, as we upgrade our systems platform to do a better job of mining data to improve our business processes while strengthening our service to customers.[9]

Wholesalers know customer service is very important in securing a competitive advantage, developing client loyalty, and attaining acceptable profit margins. Here is what two firms are doing:

- Procter & Gamble (**http://www.pg.com**) often acts as a manufacturer wholesaler: "We provide retailers with consumer and shopper research, supply chain solutions, branding and marketing expertise, and more. This results in stronger retail partnerships. In a recent industry survey of U.S. retailers, P&G was ranked number one in six of eight categories: clearest strategy, most innovative, most helpful consumer and shopper information, best supply chain management, best category management, and best consumer marketing."[10]
- At Grainger (**http://www.grainger.com**), a merchant wholesaler of maintenance, repair, and operating supplies, "we go above and beyond by offering extra-valuable services to you. Call or fax in your order anytime. Go online to view our catalog, place orders, or check order status. Visit your local Grainger branch. If you want, pick up your order at the branch of your choice. Most U.S. orders received within business hours for in-stock items are shipped the same day the order is received, with most items delivered the next day. We'll work with you to find the best way to get your order delivered as quickly as

> Wholesalers are emphasizing customer service and looking to international markets.

Figure 15-7

Supervalu: From Merchant Wholesaling to Retailing

Supervalu is one of the leading food wholesalers in the United States. It provides distribution services to nearly 4,000 stores of all sizes and formats, including regional and national chain supermarkets, mass merchandisers, and E-tailers. It has also become one of the largest U.S. supermarket chains, with more than 1,400 outlets in 40 states. Among the retail stores it operates are Bigg's, Cub Foods, Save-A-Lot, Shop 'n Save (shown here), and Shoppers Food Warehouse.

Source: Reprinted by permission.

[9] "Message from Our President," **http://www.unitedstationers.com/profile/message.html** (April 5, 2006).

[10] *Procter & Gamble 2005 Annual Report*, p. 5.

possible. We accept several methods of payment. We are also pleased to offer open account billing to qualified customers upon credit approval. Enjoy the freedom to place substantial orders without being hindered by your credit card's pre-set limit. Preserve your working capital and get additional purchasing power with our convenient lease program."[11]

More U.S. wholesalers are turning to foreign markets for growth, but many are not necessarily moving quickly enough. Consider this comment from an industry expert:

> European wholesalers are much more interested than their American counterparts in how distributors in other countries do business. They want to know how we do things in the United States. Contrast that with a statement I heard not long ago from a U.S. distributor who said he couldn't be bothered with hearing about what European wholesalers were doing because he didn't plan to open any branches in Paris or Berlin. You don't have to be a company with business interests overseas in Europe or the Far East to be able to take advantage of the exchange of ideas that takes place when meeting with distributors from other parts of the world.[12]

> **Target market strategies are more complex.**

In large numbers, wholesalers are diversifying the markets they serve or the products they carry: Farm and garden machinery wholesalers now sell to florists, hardware dealers, and garden supply stores. Plumbing wholesalers have added industrial accounts, contractors, and builders. Grocery wholesalers deal with hotels, airlines, hospitals, schools, and restaurants. Large food wholesalers such as Supervalu (**http://www.supervalu.com**) have moved more actively into retailing. See Figure 15-7.

Web Sites You Can Use

Here are a variety of useful Web sites related to wholesaling:

- *Annual Wholesale Trade Survey* (**http://www.census.gov/svsd/www/whltable.html**)
- *Electrical Wholesaling* (**http://www.ewweb.com**)
- Healthcare Distribution Management Association (**http://www.healthcaredistribution.org**)

- International Furniture Suppliers Association (**http://www.ifsa-info.com**)
- WholesaleCentral.com (**http://www.sumcomm.com**)
- *Wholesale Source* (**http://www.wsmag.com**)
- Wholesale Trade Definitions (**http://www.census.gov/svsd/www/wnaicsdef.html**)

Summary

1. *To define wholesaling and show its importance* Wholesaling involves the buying and/or handling of goods and services and their resale to organizational users, retailers, and/or other wholesalers—but not the sale of significant volume to final consumers. In the United States, about 430,000 wholesale establishments distribute $5.5 trillion in goods and services annually.

   Wholesale functions encompass distribution, personal selling, marketing and research assistance, gathering assortments, cost reductions, warehousing, financing, returns, and risk taking. They may be assumed by manufacturers/service providers or shared with independent wholesalers. The latter are sometimes in a precarious position because they are located between

manufacturers/service providers and customers and must determine their responsibilities to each.

2. *To describe the three broad categories of wholesaling (manufacturer/service provider wholesaling, merchant wholesaling, and agents and brokers) and the specific types of firms within each category* In manufacturer/service provider wholesaling, a producer undertakes all wholesaling functions itself. This form of wholesaling can be done by sales or branch offices. The sales office has no inventory.

   Merchant wholesalers buy, take title to, and possess products for further resale. Full-service merchant wholesalers gather product assortments, provide trade credit, store and deliver products, offer merchandising and

---

[11] "Services," **http://www.grainger.com/Grainger/static.jsp?page=fos_ordering.html** (May 4, 2006).

[12] John Santa, "Global Learning," **http://ewweb.com/ar/electric_global_learning** (October 2002).

promotion assistance, provide a personal sales force, offer research and planning support, and complete other functions as well. They fall into general merchandise, specialty merchandise, rack jobber, franchise, and cooperative types. Limited-service merchant wholesalers take title to products but do not provide all wholesale functions. They are divided into cash-and-carry, drop shipper, truck/wagon, and mail-order types.

Agents and brokers provide such wholesale tasks as negotiating purchases and expediting sales, but they do not take title. They are paid commissions or fees. Agents are used on a more permanent basis than brokers. Types of agents are manufacturers'/service providers' agents, selling agents, and commission (factor) merchants. Food brokers and commercial stock brokers are two key players in wholesale brokerage.

3. *To examine recent trends in wholesaling*   The nature of wholesaling has been changing. Trends involve the evolving wholesaler mix, productivity, customer service, international openings, and target markets.

Key Terms

wholesaling (p. 464)

manufacturer/service provider wholesaling (p. 470)

merchant wholesalers (p. 472)

full-service merchant wholesalers (p. 472)

limited-service merchant wholesalers (p. 472)

general-merchandise (full-line) wholesalers (p. 473)

specialty-merchandise (limited-line) wholesalers (p. 473)

rack jobbers (p. 473)

franchise wholesaling (p. 474)

wholesale cooperatives (p. 474)

cash-and-carry wholesaling (p. 474)

drop shippers (desk jobbers) (p. 474)

truck/wagon wholesalers (p. 474)

mail-order wholesalers (p. 474)

agents (p. 475)

brokers (p. 475)

manufacturers'/service providers' agents (p. 475)

selling agents (p. 476)

commission (factor) merchants (p. 476)

food brokers (p. 476)

commercial stock brokers (p. 477)

Review Questions

1. Differentiate between selling *to* a wholesaler and selling *through* a wholesaler.
2. Under what circumstances should a manufacturer or service provider undertake wholesaling?
3. Distinguish between a manufacturer's/service provider's branch office and a manufacturer's/service provider's sales office.
4. Which wholesaling functions are performed by merchant wholesalers? Which are performed by agents and brokers?
5. Distinguish between limited-service merchant wholesalers and full-service merchant wholesalers.
6. What are the unique features of cash-and-carry and truck/wagon merchant wholesalers?
7. Why are drop shippers frequently used for coal, coke, and building materials?
8. How do manufacturers'/service providers' agents and selling agents differ?

Discussion Questions

1. "Wholesalers are very much in the middle, often not fully knowing whether their first allegiance should be to the manufacturer/service provider or the customer." Comment on this statement. Can they rectify this situation? Why or why not?
2. The marketing vice-president of Sony (**http://www.sony.com**) has asked you to outline a support program to improve relations with the retailers that see its products. Prepare this outline.
3. Develop a short checklist that a small book publisher could use in determining whether to use merchant wholesalers or agents/brokers in different countries around the world.
4. Discuss how and why a toy maker might use a combination of manufacturer/service provider wholesaling, merchant wholesaling, and agents/brokers.

Web Exercise

The American Wholesale Marketers Association (**http://www.awmanet.org**) "is the only international trade organization working on behalf of convenience distributors in the United States. Its distributor members represent more than $85 billion in U.S. convenience product sales. Associate members include manufacturers, brokers, retailers, and others allied to the convenience product industry." What could a member of this organization learn by visiting its Web site?

Practice Quiz

1. High wholesale sales occur because
   a. there are so many retailers.
   b. items can be sold twice on the wholesale level.
   c. there is only one level of retailing.
   d. wholesalers service small, final consumer groups.

2. Which statement about the functions of wholesalers is false?
   a. They provide a ready-made sales force.
   b. They provide warehouse and delivery facilities.
   c. They process returns and make adjustments for defective merchandise.
   d. They do not allow manufacturers to distribute locally unless the manufacturers make customer contacts.

3. Without independent wholesalers, organizational consumers would have to
   a. deal with a number of suppliers and coordinate shipments.
   b. stock smaller quantities.
   c. place less emphasis on an internal purchasing agent or department.
   d. perform fewer distribution functions.

4. Which statement about wholesalers is false?
   a. Wholesalers want training, technical assistance, product literature, and advertising.
   b. Wholesalers dislike it when vendors alter territory assignments.
   c. Wholesalers want manufacturers to sell through them and not to them.
   d. Wholesalers dislike it when vendors decide to change to a direct channel and perform wholesale functions themselves.

5. The use of sales offices and/or branch offices is associated with which type of wholesaling?
   a. Agents
   b. Merchant wholesalers
   c. Brokers
   d. Manufacturer/service provider wholesalers

6. Channel control is maximized through which form of wholesaling?
   a. Agents
   b. Merchant wholesalers
   c. Brokers
   d. Manufacturer wholesalers

7. The largest category of wholesalers in terms of sales is
   a. manufacturer wholesalers.
   b. merchant wholesalers.
   c. agents.
   d. brokers.

8. Which of the following is *not* a full-service merchant wholesaler?
   a. Rack jobbers
   b. Specialty-merchandise wholesalers

c. Franchise wholesalers
d. Drop shippers

9. Rack jobbers
   a. sell products on a consignment basis.
   b. do not own the merchandise on their racks.
   c. have standardized storefronts, business formats, and purchase systems.
   d. do not take back unsold merchandise.

10. Land O'Lakes, Ocean Spray, Sunkist, and Welch's are all examples of
    a. rack jobbers.
    b. franchise wholesaling.
    c. producer-owned wholesale cooperatives.
    d. cash-and-carry wholesaling.

11. The principal difference between agents and brokers is that
    a. agents take title to goods, whereas brokers do not.
    b. brokers receive profits from the sales of goods they own, whereas agents work for commissions.
    c. agents are more apt to be used on a permanent basis.
    d. agents are very common in the food industry, whereas brokers are not.

12. Which of these is *not* an advantage offered by agents and brokers?
    a. They take title to goods.
    b. They enable a manufacturer or service provider to expand sales volume despite limited resources.
    c. Their selling costs are a predetermined percent of sales.
    d. They have trained salespeople.

13. Commission merchants do *not*
    a. receive goods on consignment from producers.
    b. accumulate goods from local markets.
    c. arrange for the sale of goods in a central market location.
    d. assist in merchandising and promotion.

14. Which statement concerning food brokers is correct?
    a. They work for a large number of competing food producers.
    b. They generally offer credit.
    c. They usually earn commissions in excess of 5 percent of sales.
    d. They often represent the seller.

15. When farm and garden machinery wholesalers begin to sell to florists, hardware dealers, and garden supply stores, which recent trend in wholesaling is being demonstrated?
    a. The decline in the size of independent wholesalers
    b. Gains in productivity
    c. Diversification of the markets served
    d. Emphasis on service

For the answers to these questions, please visit the online site for this book at **http://www.atomicdog.com.**

Chapter 16

Retailing

In 1965, Fred DeLuca and family friend Peter Buck opened Pete's Super Submarines, a hero shop in Bridgeport, Connecticut. DeLuca's main hope was that his small sandwich shop would be profitable enough to pay for his college-related expenses. After struggling for several years, the partners changed the company's name to Subway (**http://www.subway.com**) and began franchising in 1977. The company is still owned by the original founders and is privately held.

As of 2005, Subway had more than 23,000 locations worldwide—18,300 in the United States. Although, McDonald's has more locations than Subway on a worldwide basis, Subway has more U.S. locations than McDonald's. Like other franchisors, Subway operates its stores in a variety of venues. These include freestanding buildings and locations in airports, convenience stores, Wal-Mart stores, and sports facilities. This gives Subway a high degree of flexibility in pursuing growth opportunities.

Unlike many fast-food firms, Subway features a fresh and healthy alternative to hamburgers, french fries, milk shakes, and other food with high fat, salt, and cholesterol content. Subway restaurants offer hot and cold sandwiches, turkey wraps, and salads. To foster its image among consumers, Subway has an exclusive three-year sponsorship with Little League Baseball and Softball. Subway is the only fast-food restaurant with a promotional presence at the Little League World Series. As another part of its promotional efforts, Subway is encouraging young children to be more physically active and to eat more healthy foods. Subway is also a national sponsor of the American Heart Association's Heart Walks.

Virtually all of Subway's locations are franchisee-owned. This means Subway can expand with less company capital, it relies on owners who may be more motivated than managers, and there are fewer conflicts between the company and its franchisees as to whether a prime location should be company- or franchisee-owned. In 2005, *Entrepreneur* cited Subway as the number-one franchise in its *Franchise 500* listing. Subway has held this top position more than a dozen times. The ratings are based on a number of factors, including financial strength and stability, growth rate, size, and years in business. Fred DeLuca was recently inducted into the International Franchise Hall of Fame.[1]

In this chapter, the various types of retailers, considerations in retail planning (including retail franchising), store location, and recent trends in retailing are all discussed in detail.

Chapter Objectives

1. To define retailing and show its importance
2. To discuss the different types of retailers, in terms of ownership, store strategy mix, and nonstore operations
3. To explore five major aspects of retail planning: store location, atmosphere, scrambled merchandising, the wheel of retailing, and technological advances
4. To examine recent trends in retailing

---

[1] Company and various other sources.

16-1 OVERVIEW

Retailing encompasses the business activities involved with the sale of goods and services to the final consumer for personal, family, or household use. It is the final stage in a channel of distribution. Manufacturers, importers, and wholesalers act as retailers when they sell directly to the final consumer.

The average retail sale per shopping trip is small, less than $100 for U.S. department stores and specialty stores. Convenience stores, such as 7-Eleven (**http://www.7-eleven. com**), have average sales of under $10 (not including gasoline). U.S. chain supermarkets average less than $30 per customer transaction. Accordingly, retailers strive to increase their sales volume by using one-stop shopping appeals, broadening merchandise and service assortments, increasing customer shopping frequency, and encouraging more family members to go shopping. Inventory controls, automated merchandise handling, and electronic cash registers enable retailers to reduce their transaction costs.

Despite the low average size of customer transactions, about one-half of sales for such retailers as department stores involve some form of customer credit. This means these retailers must pay a portion of each transaction to a bank or other credit-card service firm or absorb the costs of their own credit programs (in return for increased sales). Even most supermarkets now accept credit cards.

Whereas salespeople regularly visit b-to-b customers to initiate and conclude transactions, most final consumers patronize stores. This makes the location of the store, product assortment, store hours, store fixtures, sales personnel, delivery, customer service, and other factors critical tools in drawing customers to the store. See Figure 16-1.

Final consumers make many unplanned purchases. In contrast, those that buy for resale or use in production (or operating a business) are more systematic in their purchasing. Therefore, retailers need to place impulse items in high-traffic locations, organize store layout, train sales personnel in suggestion selling, place related items next to each other, and sponsor special events to stimulate consumers.

In this chapter, the importance of retailing, the various types of retailers, considerations in retail planning, and recent trends in retailing are all discussed in detail.

16-2 THE IMPORTANCE OF RETAILING

Retailing is a significant aspect of distribution because of its impact on the economy, its functions in the distribution channel, and its relationships with suppliers.

16-2a Retailing's Impact on the Economy

Retail sales and employment are considerable. Annual U.S. retail store sales exceed $4 trillion, an amount that does not include most vending-machine, direct-selling, and direct-marketing revenues or many services. Sales of the world's top 200 retailers (nearly 40 percent from the United States) exceed $3 trillion in annual revenues, and they represent about 20 nations. The largest retailer on the planet, by far, is U.S.-based Wal-Mart (**http://www.walmart.com**)—with total annual domestic and foreign sales of more than $300 billion, 5,600 stores, and multiple store formats (such as Wal-Mart and Sam's Club).[2]

According to U.S. Bureau of Labor Statistics, 25 million people are employed in 3 million U.S. retail establishments. Wal-Mart's work force alone is 1.6 million people (1.1 million in the United States). Industrywide and around the globe, a wide range of retailing career opportunities is available, including store management, merchandising, and owning one's own retail business.[3]

---

[2] Estimated by the authors from data in "2005 Retail Sales," *Monthly Retail Trade Survey* (Washington, DC: U.S. Bureau of the Census, April 2006); *Top 200 Retailers Worldwide, 2004* (Columbus, OH: Retail Forward, October 2005); and "About Wal-Mart," **http://www.walmartstores.com/wmstore/wmstores/Mainnews.jsp** (May 7, 2006).

[3] A discussion of careers in retailing can be found in Barry Berman and Joel R. Evans, *Retail Management: A Strategic Approach*, 10th ed. (Upper Saddle River, NJ: Prentice Hall, 2007), Appendix A.

Figure 16-1

M&M's World: Standing Out in a Crowd

The M&M's World store in Las Vegas is a real crowd pleaser. According to a recent review by **http://www.vegas.com/attractions**: "Four floors of retail space devoted to our favorite chocolate-covered candies? It just doesn't get much better than that! The mouth-watering exhibit features Red, Yellow, and the rest of the brightly colored gang on everything from T-shirts and golf-club covers to calculators and martini glasses. The first floor of the 26,000-square-foot attraction looks like an average gift shop, but as you reach the back and see the escalators climbing toward multiple levels, you realize there is much more than meets the eye. Each floor gets more exciting as you make your way to the top, and just when you think you've seen it all, the folks at M&M World outdo themselves once again. The attraction features a 3-D movie theater; the films rotate, and viewers are rewarded with a surprise treat as they exit. There also is a wall of M&M's, displaying the sweet treat in nearly every color imaginable, from aqua green to gold. But perhaps the most exciting exhibit in the attraction is the M&M Racing Team area. The exhibit is centered on a replica of the M&M's-sponsored race car in the NASCAR Nextel Cup Series."

Source: Reprinted by permission of Susan Berry, Retail Image Consulting, Inc.

From a cost perspective, retailing is a significant field. On average, 30 to 35 cents of every dollar a consumer spends in a traditional U.S. department or specialty store goes to it as compensation for the functions it performs. The corresponding figure is 25 cents for a supermarket. This compensation—known as gross margin—is for rent, taxes, fuel, advertising, management, personnel, and other retail costs, as well as profits. One of the reasons for Wal-Mart's success is that its operating costs are so low (18 percent of sales) compared to other firms. For instance, Federated Department Stores' (**http://www.federated-fds. com**) annual operating costs typically average 30 percent or more of sales.[4]

[4] *2005 Retail Yearbook* (Columbus, OH: Retail Forward, 2005).

Marketing and the Web

The Lifestyle Center: A Bricks-and-Mortar Response to the Internet

Although the Web still accounts for a rather small percentage of total U.S. retail sales, it has had a major impact on retailing beyond Web-based sales revenues.

Many consumers now use the Web to compare a product's features, price, and ratings by other consumers. This reduces the need for shoppers to engage in comparison shopping at multiple stores and the total time spent in major malls. Unfortunately, for mall-based retailers, the reduced time spent at shopping at the mall can result in fewer store-based sales.

One of the major ways that mall developers are reacting to Web purchasers is to build lifestyle centers instead of enclosed malls. Lifestyle centers are smaller than many enclosed malls and have restaurants and movie theaters as leading tenants. Many lifestyle centers have long, landscaped paths to encourage shoppers to stay there longer. Unlike large malls with centralized parking lots, lifestyle centers enable shoppers to quickly park next to a given store and easily purchase exactly what they need based on their Web-based search. Lifestyle centers also cost less to build and maintain than enclosed malls due to lower investment and ongoing costs for air-conditioning and heating. There are already more than 120 U.S. lifestyle centers, while the number of enclosed malls is expected to shrink by 25 percent over the next few years, according to an estimate from the International Council of Shopping Centers (http://www.icsc.org).

Source: Based on material in Joseph Weber and Ann Therese Palmer, "How the Net Is Remaking the Mall," *Business Week* (May 9, 2005), pp. 60–61.

Although comprehensive retail data are not available on a global basis, these statistics indicate the magnitude of retailing around the world: Global retail sales are increasing by a yearly average of 5 percent. Annual retail sales are greater than $3 trillion in Europe and more than $2.5 trillion in Asia.[5] France's Carrefour (**http://www.carrefour.com**) operates 7,000 stores in 28 countries, the Netherlands' Royal Ahold (**http://www.ahold.com**) has 7,300 stores in 20 countries, and Wal-Mart has 1,600 stores in nearly a dozen nations outside the United States.

Current U.S. retail data may be found at the Bureau of the Census' "Retail & Wholesale Trade" Web site (**http://www.census.gov/econ/www/retmenu.html**).

16-2b   Retailing Functions in Distribution

As highlighted in Figure 16-2, retailers generally perform four distinct functions. They:

- engage in the sorting process by assembling an assortment of goods and services from a variety of suppliers and offering them for sale. Width and depth of assortment depend on the retailer's strategy.
- provide information to consumers via ads, displays and signs, and sales personnel. And marketing research support (feedback) is given to other channel members.
- store products, mark prices, place items on the selling floor, and otherwise handle products. Retailers usually pay for items before selling them to final consumers.
- facilitate and complete transactions by having appropriate locations and hours, credit policies, and other services (such as delivery).

> Retailers undertake four key functions.

16-2c   The Relationship of Retailers and Suppliers

Retailers deal with two broad supplier categories: those selling goods or services for use by the retailers and those selling goods or services that are resold by the retailers. Examples of goods and services purchased by retailers for their use are store fixtures, computer equipment, management consulting, and insurance. Resale purchases depend on the lines sold by the retailer.

Suppliers must have knowledge of their retailers' goals, strategies, and methods of business operation to sell and service accounts effectively. Retailers and their suppliers may have divergent viewpoints, which must be reconciled. Here is an example:

---

[5] *Global Retailing: Industry Profile* (New York: Data Monitor, May 2005).

Figure 16-2

Figure 16-2 Key Retailing Functions

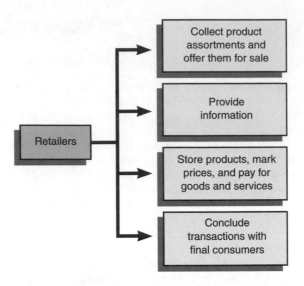

Bicycle manufacturer Pacific Cycle [**http://www.pacific-cycle.com**] spent $700,000 on tags, hardware, and software to test radio frequency identification (RFID) of its products in the last year. Why? Two big customers—Wal-Mart and Target Stores—want to wirelessly track its bikes. But don't expect Pacific Cycle to spend another nickel for a third customer, unless there's a clear return. "Those two are enough for us to handle right now. These things cost money," says the company's director of information technology. Welcome to the conundrum that is RFID. Some large retailers require radio tags to be placed on cases and pallets, but 28 percent of the companies implementing them can't justify the returns, according to recent research.[6]

16-3 TYPES OF RETAILERS[7]

Retailers can be categorized by ownership, store strategy mix, and nonstore operations. See Figure 16-3. The categories overlap; that is, a firm can be correctly placed in more than one grouping. For example, 7-Eleven is a chain, a franchise, and a convenience store. The study of retailers by group provides data on their traits and orientation, and the impact of environmental factors.

16-3a By Ownership

> An **independent retailer** has one store, while a **retail chain** has multiple outlets.

An **independent retailer** operates only one outlet and offers personal service, a convenient location, and close customer contact. About three-quarters of U.S. retail establishments (including those staffed by the owners and their families)—and a higher amount in some foreign nations—are run by independents, including many dry cleaners, beauty salons, furniture stores, gas stations, and neighborhood stores. This large number is due to the ease of entry because various kinds of retailing require low investments and little technical knowledge. So, competition is plentiful. Numerous firms do not succeed due to the ease of entry, poor management skills, and inadequate resources. The U.S. Small

---

[6] Larry Dignan, "Static Returns," *Baseline* (September 7, 2005), p. 21.

[7] Unless otherwise indicated, the statistics in these subsections are the authors' current projections, based on data from "Annual Retail Trade Data," **http://www.census.gov/svsd/www/artstbl.html** (April 29, 2006); "Retailing: General," *Standard & Poor's Industry Surveys* (May 19, 2005); "Retailing: Specialty," *Standard & Poor's Industry Surveys* (July 28, 2005); "State of the Industry," *Chain Store Age* (August 2005), Section Two; *Progressive Grocer*, various issues; *Stores*, various issues; "Annual Industry Report," *DSN Retailing Today* (June 13, 2005); *2005 Vending Times Census of the Industry*; and *2005 Retail Yearbook*.

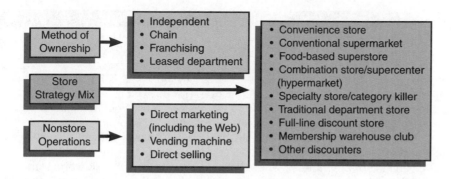

<u>Figure 16-3</u>
Categorizing Retailers

Business Administration says that one-third of new retailers do not last one full year and two-thirds do not make it past three years. About 35 percent of U.S. retail store sales are accounted for by independents.

A *retail chain* involves common ownership of multiple outlets. It usually has central purchasing and decision making. Although independents have simple organizations, chains tend to rely on specialization, standardization, and elaborate control systems. Chains can serve a large, dispersed target market and have a well-known company name. They operate one-quarter of U.S. retail outlets, but account for 65 percent of all retail store sales. Some very big chains have 1,000 or more units; and those chains with at least 100 units generate more than 60 percent of U.S. store sales. Chains are common for department stores, supermarkets, and home improvement stores, among others. Examples are Dillard's (**http://www.dillards.com**), Kroger (**http://www.kroger.com**), and Home Depot (**http://www.homedepot.com**).

Retail franchising is a contractual arrangement between a franchisor (a manufacturer, wholesaler, or service sponsor) and a retail franchisee, which allows the latter to run a certain form of business under an established name and according to specific rules. It is a form of chain retailing that lets owner-operators benefit from the experience, buying abilities, and name of large, multiunit retailers. The franchisee often gets training and engages in cooperative buying and advertising. The franchisor benefits from franchise fees and royalties, faster payments, strict operating controls, consistency among outlets, and motivated owner-operators. Franchises annually account for $1.4 trillion in U.S. retail sales at 750,000 outlets. One-half of U.S. franchisors have stores in foreign markets, a growing number. Franchising is popular for auto dealers, gas stations, fast-food chains, hotels and motels, and service firms. Examples are Chevrolet dealers (**http://www.chevrolet.com**), Pizza Hut (**http://www.pizzahut.com**), and H&R Block (**http://www.hrblock.com**).

> **Retail franchising** uses an established name and operates under certain rules.

A *leased department* is a section of a retail store rented to an outside party. The lessee operates a department—under the store's rules—and pays a percentage of sales as rent. Lessors gain from the reduced risk and inventory investment, expertise of lessees, lucrative lease terms, increased store traffic, and appeal to one-stop shopping. Lessees gain from the location in established stores, lessors' name awareness, overall store traffic, the customers attracted to stores, and the services (such as ads) that lessors provide. Leased departments are popular for beauty salons, jewelry, photo studios, shoes and shoe repairs, and cosmetics. In U.S. department stores, they generate $18 billion in annual sales. Meldisco (**http://www.meldisco.com**) operates leased shoe departments in Kmart (**http://www.kmart.com**) stores nationwide and select Rite Aid Pharmacies (**http://www.riteaid.com**).

> A **leased department** is one rented to an outside party.

Table 16-1 compares the retail ownership forms.

16-3b   By Store Strategy Mix

Firms can be classed by the store strategy mix they undertake. A typical *retail store strategy mix* consists of an integrated combination of hours, location, assortment, service, advertising, prices, and other factors retailers employ. Store strategy mixes vary widely, as the following indicate.

> A **retail store strategy mix** combines the hours, products, and so on, offered.

Global Marketing in Action

Russia: Appealing But Sometimes Scary for Western Retailers

Twenty-four shopping centers, most of them anchored by supermarkets, opened in Russia in 2004. A major real-estate brokerage firm estimates that an additional 43 centers will have opened in Russia during 2005 and 2006. These new shopping centers are adding about 12.5 million square feet of gross leasable space.

Building new retail space in Russia is a very difficult task. Corruption is so rampant at the regional and local levels that a recent Russian government survey found that 71 percent of the 158 foreign companies interviewed cited corruption as the largest single barrier to investing in Russia. "Like all Western companies in Russia, we're subject to blackmail, sabotage, and pressure for bribes. In many cases, we're totally in the hands of local chieftains," said Ikea's (http://www.ikea.com) top

Russian manager. Even though Ikea is Russia's largest foreign retailer, it does not pay bribes.

According to a research report from Retail Forward (http://www.retailforward.com), a prominent consulting company, Russia is the fourth most attractive country in the world for retail expansion (after China, Great Britain, and Thailand), taking into consideration the potential growth and risks. Another report ranks Russia as the top country for retail expansion. According to this study, "With a growth rate of 30 percent for retail trade from 1999 to 2003 and a relatively sparse retail network to serve its growing market, Russia is full of promise."

Source: Based on material in Curt Hazlett, "Wild East," *Shopping Centers Today* (May 2005), pp. 103–108.

Table 16-1 Key Characteristics of Retail Ownership Forms

Ownership Form	Characteristics		
	Distinguishing Features	**Major Advantages**	**Major Disadvantages**
Independent	Operates one outlet, easy entry	Personal service, Convenient location customer contact	Much competition, poor management skills, limited resources
Retail chain	Common ownership of multiple units	Central purchasing, strong management, specialization of tasks, larger market	Inflexibility, high investment costs, less entrepreneurial
Retail franchising	Contractual arrangement between central management (franchisor) and independent businesspersons (franchisees) to operate a specified form of business	To franchisor: investments from franchisees, faster growth, entrepreneurial spirit of franchisees To franchisee: established name, training, experience of franchisor, cooperative ads	To franchisor: some loss of control, franchisees not employees, harder to maintain uniformity To franchisee: strict rules, limited decision-making ability, payments to store
Leased department	Space in a store leased to an outside operator	To lessor: expertise of lessee, little risk, diversification To lessee: lower investment in store fixtures, customer traffic, store image	To lessor: some loss of control, poor performance reflects on store To lessee: strict rules, limited decision-making ability, payments to store

A *convenience store* is usually a well-situated, food-oriented store with long hours and a limited number of items. In the United States, these stores have annual sales of $130 billion, excluding gasoline, and account for 7 to 8 percent of all grocery sales. Annual per-store sales are a fraction of those at a supermarket. Consumers use convenience stores for fill-in items—such as gasoline, milk, groceries, papers, soda, cigarettes, beer, and fast food, often at off-hours. 7-Eleven (**http://www.7-eleven.com**), Circle K (**http://www.circlek.com**), and Speedway SuperAmerica (**http://www.speedway.com**) operate such stores.

A *conventional supermarket* is a departmentalized food store with minimum annual sales of $2 million; it emphasizes a wide range of food and related products—general merchandise sales are limited. It originated many decades ago, when food retailers realized a large-scale operation would let them combine volume sales, self-service, low prices, impulse buying, and one-stop grocery shopping. The car and refrigerator aided the supermarket's success by lowering travel costs and adding to perishables' life spans. These stores account for 26 percent of U.S. supermarket sales (which are $500 billion yearly) and 52 percent of outlets. Kroger (**http://www.kroger.com**), Publix (**http://www.publix.com**), and Safeway (**http://www.safeway.com**) are among the large chains with conventional supermarkets. See Figure 16-4.

A *food-based superstore* is a diversified supermarket that sells a broad range of food and nonfood items. The latter account for 20 to 25 percent of sales. This store usually has greeting cards, floral products, DVDs, garden supplies, some apparel, wine, film developing, and small appliances—in addition to a full line of supermarket items. Whereas a conventional U.S. supermarket has 15,000 to 20,000 square feet of space and annual sales of $6 million to $8 million, a food-based superstore has 25,000 to 50,000 square feet and $20 million to $22 million in sales. About 9,500 superstores account for more than 40 percent of U.S. supermarket sales. Several factors have caused many conventional supermarkets to become superstores: consumer interest in one-stop shopping, the leveling of food sales due to competition from fast-food stores and restaurants, and higher profits on general merchandise. For large chains, the superstore is the preferred format.

A *combination store* unites food/grocery and general merchandise sales in one facility, with general merchandise providing 25 to 40 percent or more of sales. It goes further than a food-based superstore in appealing to one-stop shoppers and occupies

> A **convenience store** stresses fill-in items.

> A **conventional supermarket** is a large, self-service food store.

> A **food-based superstore** stocks food and other products for one-stop shoppers.

> A **combination store** offers a large assortment of general merchandise, as well as food. One type is a **supercenter (hypermarket)**.

Figure 16-4

Kroger: Putting the "Super" in Supermarket

Source: Reprinted by permission of Susan Berry, Retail Image Consulting, Inc.

30,000 to 100,000 square feet or more. It lets a retailer operate efficiently, expand the number of people drawn to a store, raise impulse purchases and the size of the average transaction, sell both high-turnover/low-profit food items and lower-turnover/high-profit general merchandise, and offer fair prices. A *supercenter* (known as a *hypermarket* in Europe) is a combination store that integrates an economy supermarket with a discount department store, with at least 40 percent of sales from nonfood items. It is 75,000 to 150,000 square feet in size or larger and carries 50,000 or more items. Among those with combination stores are Wal-Mart (**http://www.walmartstores.com**), Fred Meyer (**http://www.fredmeyer.com**), and France's Carrefour (**http://www.carrefour.com**).

A *specialty store* concentrates on one product line, such as stereo equipment or hair-care services. Consumers like these stores since they are not faced with racks of unrelated products, do not have to search in several departments, are apt to find informed sales-people, can select from tailored assortments, and may avoid crowding. Specialty stores are quite successful with apparel, appliances, toys, electronics, furniture, personal care products, and personal services. See Figure 16-5. The total annual sales of the 25 largest U.S. specialty chains are hundreds of billion dollars. They include Best Buy (**http://www.bestbuy.com**), Gap (**http://www.gap.com**), and Radio Shack (**http://www.radioshack.com**).

A *category killer* is an especially large specialty store. It features an enormous selection in its product category and relatively low prices, and shoppers are drawn from wide geographic areas. Blockbuster (**http://www.blockbuster.com**), Foot Locker (**http://www.footlocker.com**), Sam Goody (**http://www.samgoody.com**), and Sports Authority (**http://www.sportsauthority. com**) are among the specialty chains largely based on the category-killer store concept.

A department store usually sells a general line of apparel for the family, household linens and textile products, and some mix of furniture, home furnishings, appliances, and consumer electronics. It is organized into functional areas for buying, promotion, service, and control. There are two types: the traditional department store and the full-line discount store.

A *traditional department store* has a great assortment of goods and services, provides many customer services, is a fashion leader, and often serves as an anchor store in a shopping district or shopping center. Prices are average to above average. It has high name recognition and uses all forms of media in ads. In recent years, traditional

> A **specialty store** emphasizes one kind of product, with a **category killer** store being a larger version.

> A **traditional department store** is a fashion leader with many customer services.

Figure 16-5

Build-A-Bear Workshop Specialty Stores

The Build-A-Bear (**http://www.buildabear.com**) chain "is a teddy bear-themed experience retail store that combines the universal appeal of plush animals with an interactive process that allows children from 3 to 103 to create their own huggable companions."

Source: Reprinted by permission of Susan Berry, Retail Image Consulting, Inc.

department stores have set up more boutiques, theme displays, and designer departments to compete better. They face intense competition from specialty stores and discounters. Annual U.S. sales, which have been falling, are $90 billion. Chains include Macy's (**http://www.macys.com**), Bloomingdale's (**http://www.bloomingdales.com**), and Kohl's (**http://www.kohls.com**).

A *full-line discount store* is a department store with lower prices, a broad product assortment, a lower-rent location, more emphasis on self-service, brand-name merchandise, wide aisles, shopping carts, and more goods displayed on the sales floor. U.S. full-line discounters (including supercenters) sell more than $325 billion in goods and services yearly. They are among the largest retailers of apparel, toys, housewares, electronics, health and beauty aids, auto supplies, sporting goods, photographic products, and jewelry. Wal-Mart (**http://www.walmart.com**), Kmart (**http://www.kmart.com**), and Target (**http://www.target.com**) account for three-quarters of U.S. full-line discount store sales. See Figure 16-6.

With a *membership warehouse club*, final consumers and businesses pay small yearly dues for the right to shop in a huge, austere warehouse. Products are often displayed in their original boxes, large sizes are stocked, and some product lines vary by time period (because clubs purchase overruns and one-of-a-kind items that cannot always be replaced). Consumers buy items at deep discounts. In the United States, warehouse clubs generate $40 billion in annual retail sales. The two dominant chains are Costco (**http://www.costco.com**) and Sam's Club (**http://www.samsclub.com**)

Other popular forms of low-price retailing do exist. Among them are warehouse-style food stores, off-price specialty chains, discount drugstore chains, and factory outlet stores. These retailers hold prices down by carrying mostly fast-selling items, using plain fixtures, locating at inexpensive sites, using few ads, and offering less service. They attract price-sensitive shoppers. Examples are Marshalls—an off-price apparel chain (**http://www.marshallsonline.com**)—and Tanger Factory Outlet Centers (**http://www.tangeroutlet.com**), which operates shopping centers with manfacturers' outlet stores in 20 states.

Table 16-2 shows the differences between discount store and traditional department store strategies.

> A **full-line discount store** has self-service and popular brands.

> A **membership warehouse club** offers deep discounts to its member customers.

Figure 16-6

Wal-Mart: The King of All Retailers

To keep growing, Wal-Mart (**http://www.walmart.com**) has recently expanded its emphasis on consumer electronics.

Source: Reprinted by permission of Susan Berry, Retail Image Consulting, Inc.

Table 16-2 Comparing Retail Strategy Mixes: A Discount Store Versus a Traditional Department Store

Discount Store Strategy	Traditional Department Store Strategy
1. Less expensive rental location—lower level of pedestrian traffic. (Note: Some discount stores are using more expensive locations.)	1. More expensive rental location in shopping center or district—higher level of pedestrian traffic.
2. Simpler fixtures, linoleum floor, central dressing room, fewer interior and window displays.	2. More elaborate fixtures, carpeted floor, individual dressing rooms, many interior and exterior displays.
3. Promotional emphasis on price. Some discounters do not advertise brand names, but say "famous brands."	3. Promotional emphasis on full service, quality brands, and store image.
4. Fewer alterations; limited phone orders, delivery, and gift wrapping; less availability of credit.	4. Many alterations included in prices, phone orders accepted, and home delivery at little or no fee; credit widely available.
5. More reliance on self-service, plain displays with piles of merchandise; most merchandise visible.	5. Extensive sales assistance, attractive merchandise displays, a lot of storage in back room.
6. Emphasis on branded products; selection may not be complete (not all models and colors). Some discounters feature "seconds," remove labels from goods if asked by manufacturers, and stock low-price, little-known items.	6. Emphasis on a full selection of branded and privately branded first-quality products; does not stock closeouts, discontinued lines, or seconds.
7. Year-round use of low prices.	7. Sales limited to end-of-season clearance and special events.

16-3c By Nonstore Operations

Nonstore retailing is nontraditional.

With **nonstore retailing**, a firm uses a strategy mix that is not store-based to reach consumers and complete transactions. It does not involve conventional store facilities.

In direct marketing, a seller first communicates with consumers via nonpersonal media.

Direct marketing occurs when a consumer is first exposed to a good or service by a nonpersonal medium (such as direct mail, TV, radio, magazine, newspaper, or PC) and then orders by mail, phone, or PC. The majority of U.S. households do at least some direct shopping each year—mostly due to convenience. The popularity of manufacturer brands and the private brands of direct marketers (and consumer confidence in them), the number of working women, and the belief that direct marketing is a good way to shop all fuel its growth: "Direct marketing lets consumers gather information about goods and services, make educated buying decisions, and acquire the necessities and pleasures of life when and where we decide to do so—even from our kitchen tables at 3 a.m."[8]

Direct marketing provides lower operating costs, a wider geographic area, and new market segments for retailers. It is used both by specialized firms and by store-based retailers that apply it to supplement their regular business. Among the most popular direct-marketing items are books, DVDs and CDs, clothing, magazines, insurance, home accessories, and sports equipment. Yearly U.S. retail sales (including the Web) exceed

[8] "Consumers: A Helpful Guide," http://www.the-dma.org/consumers (May 2, 2004).

$300 billion. Spiegel (**http://www.spiegel.com**), QVC (**http://www.qvc.com**), L.L. Bean (**http://www.llbean.com**), and Netflix (**http://www.netflix.com**) are major direct marketers.

Globally, the United States, Europe, and Japan account for most of the world's mail-order business. The United States alone is responsible for almost one-half of the total. Among the leading Internet retailers are Amazon.com (**http://www.amazon.com**), Buy.com (**http://www.buy.com**), eBay (**http://www.ebay.com**), Dell (**http://www.dell.com**), Gateway (**http://www.gateway.com**), and 1-800-flowers.com (**http://www.800flowers.com**).

A *vending machine* uses coin- or card-operated machinery to dispense goods (such as beverages) or services (such as life insurance policies at airports). It eliminates the need for salespeople, allows 24-hour sales, and can be placed in many nontraditional settings. Beverages and food items account for 95 percent of total U.S. sales. Machines may need intensive servicing due to breakdowns, stock-outs, and vandalism. Newer technology lets vending machines make change for larger bills, "talk" to consumers, use video screens to show products, brew coffee, and so on. Yearly U.S. sales are about $45 billion.

> **Vending machines** allow 24-hour, self-service sales.

Direct selling involves personal contact with consumers in their homes (and other nonstore locations) and phone solicitations initiated by the retailer. Cosmetics, vacuum cleaners, encyclopedias, household services (such as carpet cleaning), dairy products, and newspapers are sometimes marketed via direct selling. In a cold canvass, a salesperson calls people or knocks on doors to find customers. With referrals, past buyers recommend friends to the salesperson. In the party method, one consumer acts as host and invites people to a sales demonstration in his or her home (or other nonstore site). To some consumers, direct selling has a poor image. In addition, sales force turnover is high and many people are not home during the day. To increase business, salespeople for firms such as Avon now target working women via office presentations during breaks and lunch hours. Direct selling has yearly U.S. revenues of $31 billion, and the Worldwide Federation of Direct Selling Associations (**http://www.wfdsa.org**) estimates foreign global sales at $67 billion.[9] Avon (**http://www.avon.com**), Mary Kay (**http://www.marykay.com**), Tupperware (**http://www.tupperware.com**), and Amway (**http://www.amway.com**) are leading direct-selling firms.

> **Direct selling** encompasses personal contacts with consumers in nonstore settings.

16-4   CONSIDERATIONS IN RETAIL PLANNING

Retailers must weigh many factors when devising marketing plans—and manufacturers, service providers, and wholesalers also must keep these factors in mind. Five key factors are store location, atmosphere, scrambled merchandising, the wheel of retailing, and technological advances.

16-4a   Store Location

A retail store's location helps determine the customer mix and competition faced. Once selected, it is also inflexible. The basic forms of store location are the isolated store, the unplanned business district, and the planned shopping center.

An *isolated store* is a freestanding retail outlet located on a highway or street. There are no adjacent stores with which the firm competes, but there are also no stores to help draw shoppers. Customers may hesitate to travel to an isolated store unless it has a good product assortment and an established image. This site may be used by discount stores due to low rent and supplier desires for them to be far enough away from stores selling goods and services at full prices. Some Kmart (**http://www.kmart.com**) and 7-Eleven (**http://www.7-eleven.com**) stores are isolated.

> An **isolated store** is a freestanding outlet on a highway or side street.

An *unplanned business district* exists where multiple stores are located close to one another without prior planning as to the number and composition of stores. The four

> In an **unplanned business district**, stores locate together with no prior planning.

[9] "Direct Selling by the Numbers," **http://www.dsa.org/research/numbers.htm** (May 11, 2006); and "International Direct Selling Statistics," **http://www.wfdsa.org** (May 11, 2006).

unplanned sites are central business district, secondary business district, neighborhood business district, and string.

The hub of retailing in a city is the *central business district (CBD)*, often called "downtown." It has the most commercial, employment, cultural, entertainment, and shopping facilities in a city—with at least one major department store and a broad grouping of specialty and convenience stores. CBDs have had some problems with crowding, a lack of parking, older buildings, limited pedestrian traffic when offices close, nonstandardized store hours, crime, and other elements. Yet, in many urban areas, CBD sales remain strong. Among the tactics being used to strengthen CBDs are modernizing storefronts, improving transportation, closing streets to vehicles, developing strong merchant associations, planting trees to make areas more attractive, and integrating the commercial and residential environment.

A *secondary business district (SBD)* is a shopping area bounded by the intersection of two major streets. Cities tend to have several SBDs, each with at least one branch department store, a variety store, and/or some larger specialty stores, as well as several smaller shops. Compared to a CBD, an SBD has less assortment and a smaller trading area (the geographic area from which customers are drawn), and sells more convenience-oriented items.

A *neighborhood business district (NBD)* satisfies the convenience-shopping and service needs of a neighborhood. It has several small stores, with the major retailer being a supermarket, a large drugstore, or a variety store. An NBD is located on the major street in a residential area.

A *string* typically comprises a group of stores with similar or compatible product lines that situate along a street or highway. Because this location is unplanned, various store combinations are possible. Car dealers, antique stores, and clothing stores are retailers often locating in strings.

> **A planned shopping center is centrally planned and has balanced tenancy.**

A ***planned shopping center*** has centrally owned or managed facilities; it is planned and operated as an entity, ringed by parking, and based on balanced tenancy. With *balanced tenancy*, the number and composition of stores are related to overall shopper needs—stores complement each other in the variety and quality of their offerings. Thus, a center may limit the products a store carries. Planned centers account for 40 percent of total U.S. store sales; unplanned business districts and isolated stores generate the rest. Regional, community, and neighborhood centers exist.

A *regional shopping center* sells mostly shopping goods to a geographically dispersed market. It has at least one or two department stores and up to 100 or more smaller stores. People will drive up to a half-hour to reach such a center. As with CBDs, some regional centers (especially those built a while ago) need renovation. Enhancements include adding new retailers, erecting new store directories, redesigning storefronts, adding trees and plants, and replacing concrete in parking lots. The largest regional center in the United States is Minnesota's Mall of America (**http://www.mallofamerica.com**).

A *community shopping center* has a branch department store and/or a large specialty store as its major retailer, with several smaller stores. It sells both convenience- and shopping-oriented items. A *neighborhood shopping center* sells mostly convenience-oriented goods and services. It has a supermarket and/or drugstore, and a few smaller stores.

As discussed in Chapter 7, one of the biggest challenges facing retailers is the transition to a bricks-and-clicks strategy, whereby firms operate both traditional stores and Web sites. Consider the case of financial services (consumer banking):

> Bricks and clicks coexist in the new world of banking. The branch, historically the foundation of retail banking, is now operating in a more complex context. Newer channels—Internet, phone, ATMs, and point-of-sale transactions—offer the promise of lower costs. Customers, however, continue to rely on the branch for personalized service—as it remains the premier delivery channel for servicing and cross-selling to customers.[10]

---

[10] "Financial Services Industries: Branches," **http://h71028.www7.hp.com/enterprise/cache/80045-0-0-0-121.html** (February 27, 2006).

16-4b   Atmosphere

Atmosphere (also known as *atmospherics*) is the sum total of the physical attributes of a retailer, whether in a store or a nonstore format, that are used to develop an image and draw customers. It affects the target market attracted, the customer's shopping mood and time spent with the retailer, impulse purchases, and retailer positioning; and is related to the strategy chosen.[11] As shown in Table 16-2, a discount store usually has simple fixtures, linoleum floors, and crowded displays. A full-service store usually has elaborate fixtures, carpeted floors, and attractive displays.

A retailer's atmosphere consists of four basic components:

- Exterior—includes the storefront, the marquee, entrances, display windows, store visibility, store design, the surrounding area, and traffic. For a Web retailer, the exterior is the home page.
- General interior—includes flooring, colors, scents, lighting, fixtures, wall textures, temperature, aisle width, vertical transportation, personnel, cash registers, and overall cleanliness. For a Web retailer, the use of colors and descriptive text are quite important, as are the links to product departments.
- Store layout—includes the floor space allotted for customers, selling, and storage; product groupings; and department locations. For a Web retailer, this involves the physical layout of each Web page and the way the customer accesses pages with specific products; the shopping process must also be clear.
- Interior (point-of-sale) displays—includes merchandise cases and racks, mobiles, in-store ads, posters, and mannequins. For a Web retailer, product displays can reflect the choices offered and even rotate items for 360-degree views.

Figure 16-7 highlights the image-oriented interior of a Gap store.

> **Atmosphere (atmospherics)** consists of a retailer's exterior, general interior, layout, and displays.

Figure 16-7

Gap: Using a Welcoming Store Interior to Attract Customers

Source: Reprinted by permission of Susan Berry, Retail Image Consulting, Inc.

[11] For a more in-depth discussion of atmosphere, see Richard Michon, Jean-Charles Chebat, and L. W. Turley, "Mall Atmospherics: The Interaction Effects of the Mall Environment on Shopping Behavior," *Journal of Business Research*, Vol. 58 (May 2005), pp. 576–583; Jacqueline A. Williams, and Helen H. Anderson, "Engaging Customers in Service Creation: A Theater Perspective," *Journal of Services Marketing*, Vol. 19 (January 2005): pp. 13–23; and Steve Greenland and Peter McGoldrick, "Evaluating the Design of Retail Financial Service Environments," *International Journal of Bank Marketing*, Vol. 23 (March 2005), pp. 132–152.

Consider how 70-year-old Longs Drug Stores (**http://www.longs.com**) has carved out a niche based on its distinctive atmosphere:

> Longs Drug Stores started out as a single-store operation that grew into a larger entity. But unlike many chains, Longs has maintained a small-store atmosphere—even with more than 470 stores in six states. Longs set itself apart by opening large stores with a huge variety of general merchandise. At the same time, the stores fine-tuned their merchandise mix to neighborhoods they served, making special orders for customers and earning a reputation for superior service. By early 2002, the chain was ready to make some changes; and Longs' board of directors approved a five-point plan to upgrade and improve store operations. Since then, the chain has upgraded its technology across the board, consolidated buying, and launched the first major store remodel program in its history. In summer 2005, it became the first chain to open walk-in health clinics in stores, once again taking a leadership role in a crowded and competitive market.[12]

16-4c Scrambled Merchandising

A retailer engages in *scrambled merchandising* if it adds goods and services that are unrelated to each other and the firm's original business. Examples are supermarkets adding video rentals, consumer electronics stores offering PCs, drugstores carrying newspapers, and car washes stocking postcards.

Several reasons account for the popularity of scrambled merchandising: Retailers want to make their stores into one-stop shopping centers. Scrambled merchandise is often fast-selling, generates store traffic, and yields high profit margins. Impulse purchasing is increased. Different target markets can be attracted. And the effects of seasonality and competition may be lessened.

On the other hand, scrambled merchandising can spread quickly and cause competition among unrelated firms. When supermarkets branch into nonfood personal-care items, drugstore sales fall. This forces the drugstores to scramble into stationery and other product lines, which has a subsequent impact on specialty store sales. The situation is illustrated in Figure 16-8.

There are limits to how far a firm should go with scrambled merchandising, especially if adding unrelated items would reduce buying, selling, and service effectiveness. Stock turnover might also be low for certain product lines should a retailer enter too many diverse product categories. And, due to scrambled merchandising, a firm's image may become fuzzy to consumers.

> In **scrambled merchandising**, a retailer adds items to obtain one-stop shopping, higher profit margins, and impulse purchases.

Figure 16-8

The Self-Perpetuating Nature of Scrambled Merchandising

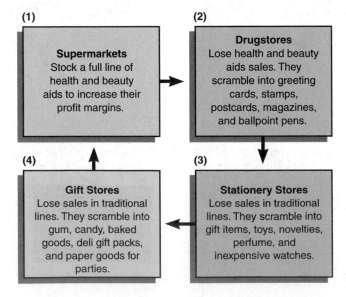

[12] "After 67 Years, Small-Store Atmosphere Survives—Apostrophe Doesn't," *Drug Store News* (September 26, 2005), p. 42.

Figure 16-9

The Wheel of Retailing in Action

Prestige department stores
(e.g., Neiman-Marcus)

Traditional
department
stores (e.g., Macy's)

**High-End
Strategy**

**Low-End
Strategy**

Full-line discount
stores (e.g., Wal-Mart)

Newer discounters
(e.g., Priceline.com)

16-4d   The Wheel of Retailing

The *wheel of retailing* describes how low-end (discount) strategies can evolve into high-end (full service, high price) strategies and thus provide opportunities for new firms to enter as discounters. According to the wheel, retail innovators often begin as low-price operators with low profit-margin requirements and low costs. As time passes, the innovators look to increase their sales and customer base. They upgrade product offerings, facilities, and services and become more traditional. They may expand the sales force, move to better sites, and offer delivery, credit, and alterations. These improvements lead to higher costs, which in turn cause higher prices. As a result, openings exist for a new generation of retailers to emerge by appealing to the price-conscious shoppers who are left behind as existing firms move up the wheel. Figure 16-9 shows the wheel in action.

There are some limitations in applying the wheel-of-retailing theory too literally, these two in particular: (1) many retailers do not follow the pattern suggested and (2) trying to move along the wheel may cause a firm to lose its loyal customers. The best use of the wheel is in understanding that distinct low-end, medium, and high-end strategies can be pursued by retailers.

> The **wheel of retailing** shows how strategies change, leaving opportunities for new firms.

16-4e   Technological Advances

In recent years, many technological advances related to retailing have emerged. The most dramatic involve the Web (which we highlighted in Chapter 7), checkout systems, video kiosks, atmospherics, computer-aided site selection, electronic banking, and enhanced operating efficiency.

Most retailers use a computerized-checkout (electronic point-of-sale) system, whereby a cashier rings up a sale or passes an item over or past an optical scanner; a computerized register instantly records and displays the sale. The customer gets a receipt, and inventory data are stored in a computer memory bank. This reduces checkout time, employee training, misrings, and the need for price markings on all products. It also generates a current list of the items in stock without a physical inventory, improves inventory control, reduces spoilage, and aids ordering. Some retailers are also turning to *self-scanning*, which lets consumers bypass cashiers: "At a growing number of retailers, including gas stations, airports, hotels and even post offices, self-scanning is becoming more popular. Self-scan machines can now be found at Home Depot and Wal-Mart. At Home Depot, nearly two of every five transactions are scanned by shoppers." By 2007, annual U.S. consumer self-checkouts are expected to reach $330 billion.[13]

> Technological advances range from computerized checkout systems to enhanced operating efficiency.

---

[13] "Americans Embrace Self-Scanning Checkout, Other Self-Serve Transactions," **http://www.cstorecentral.com** (February 1, 2005).

Video kiosks let retailers efficiently, conveniently, and promptly present information, receive orders, and process transactions—in a store or nonstore location: "Customers at Virgin Entertainment Group's [**http://www.virgin.com/us/entertainment/default.asp**] completely refurbished flagship Virgin Megastore in Manhattan's Times Square are using 150 of IBM's [**http://www.ibm.com**] latest hands-on, customized kiosks to preview virtually any of the thousands of CDs, DVDs, and console games in the store and gain a world of music information on demand. Virgin promises an 'emotionally exciting' shopping experience in its sprawling, three-level Manhattan store that is America's largest music-entertainment store. The kiosks, built with a sleek and compact design engineered to withstand even the harshest retail environments, give shoppers the ability to sample more than 250,000 CDs, 11,000 DVDs, and 7,000 games."[14]

Technology lets retailers enhance their atmospherics by using electronic point-of-purchase displays with frequently updated scrolling messages, electronic coupons, and video monitors with programming or sales presentations. At Starbucks (**http://www.starbucks.com**), "travel at blazing speeds on the Internet—from the comfort of your favorite cozy chair. Available at thousands of Starbucks locations, T-Mobile HotSpot service [**http://www.t-mobile.com/hotspot**] keeps you connected at speeds of up to 50 times faster than with a dialup internet connection." You can "easily check your E-mail, download that file you need for your next meeting, surf the Web, and get work done in coffeehouse comfort."[15]

The availability of inexpensive, computerized site-selection software is so prevalent that retailers of any size and type can now use it. For as little as a few hundred dollars, a retailer can buy geographic information systems software that graphically depicts population characteristics, location attributes, roadways, and more—for potential or existing store sites. Vendors include Caliper (**http://www.caliper.com**), Claritas (**http://www.claritas.com**), ESRI (**http://www.esri.com**), and Tetrad Computer Applications (**http://www.tetrad.com**). They make their software available through downloads from the Internet or by CD.

Electronic banking involves the use of automatic teller machines (ATMs) and the instant processing of purchases. It provides central record keeping and lets customers conduct transactions 24 hours a day, seven days a week at many bank and nonbank locations (such as supermarkets). Deposits, withdrawals, and other banking and retailing functions can be done. There are 400,000 ATMs in the United States—135,000 at bank locations and 265,000 in shopping centers, stores, airports, and other sites. Each year, Americans engage in billions of ATM transactions.[16] To allow customers to make financial transactions over wider geographic areas, many banks have formed ATM networks—numerous local and regional networks, as well as national (global), locations exist.

As electronic banking spreads, more firms are encouraging *debit transactions*; when purchases are made, the amount is immediately charged against buyer accounts. There is no delayed billing without an interest charge. A debit-card system differs from credit-card policy, in which consumers are sent bills and then remit payment. Debit cards have wide acceptance as a substitute for checks.

Technological advances are also leading to greater retailer efficiency by:

> With debit transactions, payments are immediately deducted from customers' accounts.

- increasing the use of self-service operations by firms marketing gasoline, airline tickets, and rental cars, and for hotel registrations and payment.
- linking manufacturers, warehouses, and transportation firms.
- producing antishopliftin merchandise that sets off an alarm if not properly removed by employees.
- automating energy-control systems to monitor store temperature carefully and reduce fuel costs.
- computerizing in-store promotions.
- enabling touchpad order entry in restaurants.

---

[14] "Virgin Megastore Times Square Features 150 New IBM Anyplace Kiosks That Help Create an 'Emotionally Exciting' Shopping Experience," *Market Wire* (September 20, 2005).

[15] "High-Speed Wireless Internet Access," **http://www.starbucks.com/retail/wireless.asp** (March 11, 2006).

[16] "ATM Industry Statistics," **http://www.atmwarehouse.com/ATMstatistics.htm** (April 30, 2006).

16-5   RECENT TRENDS IN RETAILING

Retailing is in transition, as firms seek to defend or expand their positions in a fast-changing marketplace. Many consumers no longer want to spend as much time shopping as they once did, various retail sectors are saturated, a number of large retailers have heavy debt (typically due to leveraged buyouts or overexpansion), and some retailers—after running frequent sales—find it difficult to maintain "regular prices." This observation about retailing shows where we're at:

> The challenge to compete with giant players in a rapidly changing environment is at the core of an incredible amount of experimentation. Gap Inc. [http://www.gapinc.com] is a prime example. The retailer is looking to expand its reach into an older demographic with the launch of Forth & Towne, the first new concept for the chain since the 1994 introduction of Old Navy. The new strategy will cater to women aged 35 and over. High-flying Abercrombie & Fitch [http://www.abercrombie.com] recently debuted its new retail format, Ruehl, targeting a slightly older demographic than its A&F stores. The move expands the A&F customer while simultaneously introducing higher-priced, higher-margin merchandise. The store-within-a-store concept is going strong. CompUSA [http://www.compusa.com] is rolling out a combination format with its Good Guys subsidiary. Wild Oats Markets (http://www.wildoats.com) opened its first store-within-a-store inside a remodeled Stop & Shop. Retailers are exploring more than just new concepts. Walgreens [http://www.walgreens.com] is a case in point. It is looking to expand its mail-order pharmacy as a response to a movement among big employers (such as General Motors) to mandate mail-order programs. Home Depot [http://www.homedepot.com] is experimenting with gas stations and convenience stores at its home center locations in Nashville.[17]

To succeed in the long run, retailers must respond properly to the trends they face. Among the most prominent are those relating to consumer demographics and lifestyles, competitive forces, operating costs, the labor force, and foreign opportunities. Here is how various retailers are dealing with them.

The aging U.S. population, geographic population shifts, and widespread market saturation have led to innovative retailing actions. In addition to its Web catalog, Wardrobe Wagon (http://www.wardrobewagon.com) uses "traveling clothing stores" to visit nursing homes for the elderly in 16 states. Bloomingdale's (http://www.bloomingdales.com) has stores in California, Florida, Georgia, Illinois, Maryland, Minnesota, Nevada, and Virginia to reduce emphasis on its Northeast base. Nontraditional locales, which have been underserved, are being used—Baskin-Robbins (http://www.baskin-robbins.com) has outlets in U.S. Navy exchanges, and Godiva (http://www.godiva.com) has stores at various airports. See Figure 16-10.

Retailers are adapting to the shopping needs and time constraints of working women and dual-earner households, and the increased consumer interest in quality and customer service. They are stocking such laborsaving products as ready-to-eat foods and pre-loaded PCs; lengthening store hours and opening additional days; expanding Web, catalog, and phone sales efforts; reemphasizing personal selling; prewrapping gift items to eliminate waiting lines; setting up comprehensive specialty boutiques to minimize the number of departments a consumer must visit; including special services, such as fashion coordinators; marketing high-quality private brands; and using more attractive displays.

Retailing's intense competition has led to various company responses. For example, 99 Cents Only (http://www.99only.com) is a "dollar store" chain that has come a long way in a short time: It is a "deep-discount retailer of primarily name-brand consumable general merchandise at an affordable, single-price point. Stores are attractively merchandised, clean, full-service locations that offer customers significant value on everyday household needs. Merchandise encompasses a wide array of name-brand closeout and

---

[17] Ken Clark, "State of the Industry: The Year of the Deal," *Chain Store Age* (August 2005), pp. 22A–23A.

Figure 16-10

The Boom in Airport Retailing

According to *Airport Retail News,* commercial airports now have an average of 50 retail shops and concession stands (for food and related items).

Source: Reprinted by permission of Retail Forward.

regularly available consumable products including food and beverages, health and beauty aids, and household supplies." Pier 1 (**http://www.pier1.com**), the home furnishings and accessories chain, is quicker to freshen its product mix: "Up to 75 percent of our merchandise assortment includes new products each year. After merchandise is developed and packaged, Pier 1's Visual Merchandising team works together to develop strategies that display merchandise in a way that effectively showcases our unique products. The shopping environment found in our stores is one that is distinctly Pier 1 and takes our customers on a path of discovery through one-of-a-kind products from around the world."[18]

Due to competition in many sectors, the price sensitivity of a large segment of consumers, and their interest in improving efficiency (and profit margins), retailers are more concerned with cost control. Several fast-food firms now use a format whereby different outlets occupy the same building (as food courts have done for years in malls). This format allows common costs and some workers to be shared. Most small hardware stores belong to buying cooperatives to get quantity discounts and "buy smarter." Many supermarkets use more bulk selling, by which consumers select items such as candy and dried fruit from open displays. A number of mail-order firms are better targeting customers and containing their catalog costs. Furthermore, the use of self-service in retailing has steadily increased.

Some U.S. retailers have trouble attracting and retaining a quality labor force. According to surveys, retailers rank the labor shortage as one of the most crucial issues for them to address. Among the reasons for the shortage are that the number of interested young people has declined; full-time career opportunities in other industries have lured away a number of part-time retail workers; many retail workers are inexperienced and have overly high job expectations, leading to employee dissatisfaction and turnover; hours can be long and irregular; some people do not like the pressure of interacting with customers on a regular basis; and the pay in other industries has been relatively higher.

Among the actions of retailers to resolve the labor shortage are recruiting more at high schools and colleges, hiring retired persons, offering child care for working mothers, raising starting salaries (sometimes to double the minimum wage), rotating employees among tasks to lessen boredom, rewarding good performance with bonuses, and encouraging the best workers to pursue full-time retailing careers.

---

[18] "99¢ Only Stores—About Our Stores," **http://www.99only.com/about.htm** (May 11, 2006); and "About Us," **http://www.pier1.com/company/aboutus.asp** (May 11, 2006).

Ethical Issues in Marketing

Should Barnes & Noble Have Moved New Writers Off a Power Aisle?

In 1990, Barnes & Noble (http://www.barnesandnoble.com) began its Discover program that featured displays with between 20 and 25 fiction and nonfiction titles by unknown writers in the front of each of its superstores. Discover has been highly regarded in the industry as a sign of the retailer's commitment to new authors. To be eligible for the program, a writer has to have produced fewer than three previously published books, had low sales, and not won any major literary awards.

Many of the books featured through the Discover program have been from small publishers. Being selected as a Discover selection not only helps in increasing orders from wholesalers and other retailers, but also increases the visibility of an author and his or her work. "A Discover selection can bump a first print-

ing from 3,000 to 8,000, which is big for us. No one but a major publisher can buy that kind of space for three months," said an independent publisher.

Recently, Barnes & Noble moved its Discover selections to a secondary location off the "power aisle," so that the titles faced the back wall in many stores. Barnes & Noble now uses the space formerly devoted to the Discover program to promote Barnes & Noble titles, books with large cooperative advertising allowances from publishers, and board games. These products have higher profit margins and higher levels of sales than the books in the Discover program.

Sources: Based on material in Charlotte Abbott, "B&N Pushes New Writers off 'Power Aisle,'" *Publishers Weekly* (April 11, 2005), pp. 5, 8; and "Discover Great New Writers Program," http://www.barnesandnoble.com (April 9, 2006).

For retailers with the proper resources and management prowess, numerous retailing opportunities exist in foreign markets. These are a few examples:

> **Foreign opportunities are plentiful.**

- "Retailers are looking to the Asia-Pacific market as an opportunity to globalize their operations while enhancing sales. Home Depot [http://www.homedepot.com] announced its intentions to foray there with the recent establishment of a development center. With the countries that constituted the former Soviet Union becoming increasingly to market forces, the Eastern European market is also under review by many of the sector's main players. Kingfisher [http://www.kingfisher.co.uk] announced that it was to become the first major British company to enter Russia."[19]
- IGD [http://www.idg.com], the research firm, forecasts that the Chinese grocery market will grow by 65 percent to $456 billion between 2005 and 2010: "Opportunities are great but there are also major challenges in China. The grocery market has been open to foreign retailers since the early 1990s, and until recently, the central government restricted the expansion of international retailers. Most foreign retailers that have entered the market have made huge headway in the primary cities of Shanghai, Beijing, Tianjin, and Guangzhou. The rest of the market outside the primary cities is very fragmented and is dominated by regional domestic retailers who have a strong foothold in their local province."[20]
- Toys "R" Us [http://www2.toysrus.com/our/intl/intlSitemap.cfm] has stores in 27 countries (including several in Eastern and Western Europe, Asia, South Africa and Australia), accounting for one-quarter of total company revenues. It does well in foreign markets because of the wide merchandise selection in its stores, especially compared to local retailers.
- Worldwide, McDonald's [http://www.mcdonalds.com] serves more than 48 million customers each day. One area of growth for the firm is its value orientation: "Value is part of our heritage and an important competitive factor that drives visit frequency. Branded everyday value menus like our PoundSaver Menu in Great Britain, EuroSaver Menu in several European countries, Amazing Value Menu in Asia, and Dollar Menu in the U.S. help capture and retain a larger customer base."[21]

---

[19] *Global Retailing: Industry Profile*, p. 14.

[20] "Grocery Retailing in China," http://www.igd.com/CIR.asp?menuid=51&cirid=1538 (March 18, 2005).

[21] "2005 Fact Sheet," http://www.mcdonalds.com/corp/invest/pub/2005_fact_sheet.html.

Web Sites You Can Use

There are trade associations covering almost every aspect of retailing. Most have detailed Web sites. Here is a sampling of them:

- Direct Marketing Association (**http://www.the-dma.org**)
- Directory of International Retail Trade Associations (**http://www.retailcouncil.org/aboutus/ind_direc.asp**)
- Direct Selling Association (**http://www.dsa.org**)
- International Association of Department Stores (**http://www.iads.org**)
- International Council of Shopping Centers (**http://www.icsc.org**)

- International Franchise Association (**http://www.franchise.org**)
- International Retail Federation (**http://www.nrf.com/irf/directory.asp**)
- National Association of Convenience Stores (**http://www.cstorecentral.com**)
- National Automatic Merchandising Association (**http://www.vending.org**)
- National Retail Federation (**http://www.nrf.com**)
- Retail Industry Leaders Association (**http://www.retail-leaders.org/new/index.aspx**)

Summary

1. *To define retailing and show its importance* Retailing encompasses the business activities involved with selling goods and services to the final consumer for personal, family, or household use. It is the last stage in a distribution channel. Average sales are small, yet use of credit is widespread. Final consumers generally visit a store to make a purchase, and they also make many unplanned purchases.

    Retailing affects the economy due to its total sales and the number of people employed. Retailers provide various functions, including gathering a product assortment, providing information, handling merchandise, and completing transactions. They deal with suppliers that sell products the retailers use in operating their businesses, as well as suppliers selling items the retailers will resell.

2. *To discuss the different types of retailers, in terms of ownership, store strategy mix, and nonstore operations* Retailers may be classified in several ways. Basic ownership formats are independent, a retailer operating one outlet; chain, a retailer operating two or more outlets; franchise, a contractual arrangement between a franchisor and a franchisee; and leased department, a department in a store leased to an outside party. The ease of entry into retailing fosters competition and results in the failure of many new firms.

    Different strategy mixes are used by convenience stores, well-situated, food-oriented retailers; conventional supermarkets, departmentalized food stores with minimum annual sales of $2 million; food-based superstores, diversified supermarkets that sell a broad range of food and nonfood items; combination stores (including supercenters/hypermarkets), outlets that go further than food-based superstores in carrying both food and general merchandise; specialty stores (including category killers), outlets that concentrate on one merchandise or service line; traditional department stores, outlets that have a great assortment, provide customer services, are fashion leaders, often dominate surrounding stores, and have average to above-average prices; full-line discount stores, department stores with a low-price, moderate-service orientation; membership warehouse clubs, stores that offer very low prices in austere settings; and other discounters.

    In nonstore retailing, a firm uses a strategy mix that is not store-based. Direct marketing occurs when consumers are exposed to goods and services through nonpersonal media and then order by mail, phone, or PC. It is now a large part of retailing. Vending machines use coin- or card-operated machinery to dispense goods and services. Direct selling involves both personal contact with consumers in their homes (or other places) and phone solicitations initiated by retailers.

3. *To explore five major aspects of retail planning: store location, atmosphere, scrambled merchandising, the wheel of retailing, and technological advances* A firm may select from three forms of location: an isolated store, a freestanding outlet on a highway or street; an unplanned business district, in which two or more stores locate near one another without prior planning as to their number and composition; and a planned shopping center, which is centrally managed, as well as planned and operated as an entity. Only planned centers utilize balanced tenancy.

    Atmosphere is the sum total of a retailer's physical characteristics that help develop an image and attract customers. It depends on the exterior, general interior, layout, and interior displays.

    In scrambled merchandising, a retailer adds products unrelated to its original business. The goals are to encourage one-stop shopping, increase sales of high-profit items and impulse purchases, attract different target markets, and balance sales throughout the year.

    The wheel of retailing explains low-end and high-end strategies and how they emerge. As low-cost, low-price innovators move along the wheel, they leave opportunities for newer, more cost-conscious firms to enter the market.

    Several technological advances have emerged. These include electronic checkout systems, video kiosks, atmospherics, computer-aided site selection, electronic banking, and enhanced operating efficiency.

4. *To examine recent trends in retailing* The nature of retailing has changed dramatically in recent years. Among the key trends retailers are adapting to are those relating to consumer demographics and lifestyles, competitive forces, operating costs, the labor force, and global opportunities.

Key Terms

retailing (p. 485)

independent retailer (p. 488)

retail chain (p. 489)

retail franchising (p. 489)

leased department (p. 489)

retail store strategy mix (p. 489)

convenience store (p. 491)

conventional supermarket (p. 491)

food-based superstore (p. 491)

combination store (p. 491)

supercenter hypermarket (p. 492)

specialty store (p. 492)

category killer (p. 492)

traditional department store (p. 492)

full-line discount store (p. 493)

membership warehouse club (p. 493)

nonstore retailing (p. 494)

direct marketing (p. 494)

vending machine (p. 495)

direct selling (p. 495)

isolated store (p. 495)

unplanned business district (p. 495)

planned shopping center (p. 496)

atmosphere (atmospherics) (p. 497)

scrambled merchandising (p. 498)

wheel of retailing (p. 499)

Review Questions

1. Describe the four basic functions performed by retailers.
2. What are the disadvantages of an independent retailer in competing with retail chains?
3. What are the benefits of retail franchising to the franchisee? To the franchisor?
4. Compare the strategies of traditional department stores and full-line discount stores.
5. Distinguish between direct marketing and direct selling. Which has greater sales? Why?
6. What are the pros and cons of scrambled merchandising?
7. Explain the wheel of retailing from the perspective of the battle between traditional department stores and full-line discount stores for market share.
8. Differentiate between credit cards and debit cards. What is the benefit of debit cards to retailers?

Discussion Questions

1. As a prospective franchisee for a Lemon Tree beauty salon (http://www.lemontree.com), what criteria would you use in deciding whether Lemon Tree is right for you? What criteria do you think Lemon Tree should use in assessing potential franchisees? Explain the differences in your answers to these two questions.
2. Develop an upscale-store strategy for a furniture store. How would the strategy differ from that for a discount furniture store?
3. Select a planned shopping center near your college or university and evaluate it.
4. How can an online retailer create a good shopping atmosphere for its customers?

Web Exercise

Home Depot is one of the world's leading store-based retailers. Visit the firm's Web site (http://www.homedepot.com) and evaluate it. Compare Home Depot's Web site with that of Lowe's (http://www.lowes.com), a major competitor of Home Depot.

Practice Quiz

1. Which of the following is a characteristic of retailing?
   a. A low percent of consumer sales on credit
   b. Few unplanned purchases by final consumers
   c. Importance of retail location
   d. The high average sale by final consumers
2. Unlike independents, retail chains
   a. operate only one outlet.
   b. have simple organizations.
   c. tend to rely on elaborate control systems.
   d. are the most common form of retail ownership.

3. Conventional supermarkets
   a. emphasize the sale of general merchandise.
   b. have minimum annual sales of $2 million.
   c. originated in the 1800s.
   d. account for a small portion of total U.S. supermarket sales.

4. Which of the following is *not* a reason why many conventional supermarkets are switching to food-based superstores?
   a. The leveling of food sales due to competition from fast-food stores and restaurants
   b. The higher profits on general merchandise
   c. Improved transportation networks
   d. A consumer interest in one-stop shopping

5. Wal-Mart, Fred Meyer, and Carrefour all operate
   a. combination stores.
   b. specialty stores.
   c. convenience stores.
   d. retail cooperatives.

6. Which of the following is *not* true about full-line discount stores?
   a. They are among the largest retailers of apparel, housewares, and electronics.
   b. They offer a broad merchandise assortment.
   c. They emphasize self-service.
   d. They rely more heavily on credit sales than do traditional department stores.

7. Which of these is *not* a form of nonstore retailing?
   a. Vending machine
   b. Direct selling
   c. Membership warehouse club
   d. Direct marketing

8. Where there are no adjacent stores with which a firm competes, the location is most appropriately described as a(n)
   a. string.
   b. planned shopping center.
   c. isolated store.
   d. unplanned business district.

9. A shopping area bounded by the intersection of two major streets is a
   a. central business district.

   b. neighborhood business district.
   c. string.
   d. secondary business district.

10. A regional shopping center sells mostly
    a. convenience products.
    b. discount items.
    c. catalog merchandise.
    d. shopping goods.

11. Atmosphere is most closely related to a store's
    a. interior displays.
    b. nonstore operations.
    c. ownership.
    d. advertisements.

12. Which of the following is *not* a reason for the popularity of scrambled merchandising?
    a. One-stop shopping
    b. Improved store image
    c. High profit margins
    d. Increased impulse purchasing

13. Differences between department-store and discount-store strategies are explained by the
    a. scrambled merchandising concept.
    b. wheel-of-retailing concept.
    c. referral method.
    d. balanced tenancy approach.

14. Computer-based checkouts
    a. increase employee training time.
    b. require price markings on merchandise.
    c. increase checkout time.
    d. improve ordering decisions.

15. Baskin-Robbins outlets in U.S. Navy exchange facilities and Godiva stores at airports are examples of retailers' response to
    a. the saturation of many prime markets.
    b. the slowdown in overall population growth.
    c. time constraints on working women.
    d. increased consumer sophistication about purchases.

For the answers to these questions, please visit the online site for this book at **http://www.atomicdog.com.**

5 Short Cases

Case 1: Making A Multichannel Strategy Work[c5-1]

The year 2004 marked the first time that more U.S. consumers used multichannel shopping than single channel shopping. Forrester Research says that two-thirds of all U.S. shoppers now shop and browse on- and offline. More than one-half of U.S. consumers view themselves as active cross-channel shoppers.

Some marketing analysts believe that although numerous firms offer multichannel shopping, some of them have not developed synergies across the channels. One firm displaying synergy is Saks Fifth Avenue (http://www.saksfifthavenue.com), which uses its Web site to get more information from consumers about their preferences. Gift cards and wedding registries are available online. To encourage cross-shopping, Saks provides its Web customers with an exclusive toll-free service phone number, invitations to in-store events, and free valet parking when they visit a Saks Fifth Avenue store.

Retail banking is another area where a multichannel strategy can be very effective. A study of 2,000 customers of America's top-10 banks, for example, found that 56 percent of the respondents valued online banking and bill payment over services performed at branch locations (which had value for 45 percent of respondents) and ATMs (which had value for 52 percent of respondents). Furthermore, an online transaction costs a bank about 5 cents to process as compared with $1 to $4 for an in-bank transaction.

A significant development is the effort to promote multichannel migration by measuring key customer groups and then influencing each group to interact with the optimal channel. Best Buy (http://www.bestbuy.com), through its multichannel migration strategy, attempts to get last-minute holiday season shoppers to buy goods online due to its large inventories. Best Buy's "Geek Squad" is available to set up or troubleshoot electronics equipment at key customers' homes or offices.

Similarly, Select Comfort (http://www.selectcomfort.com), a Minneapolis mattress retailer, has 370 stores, a contact center, and a sophisticated Web site. Its online site determines which type of mattress a consumer wants based on responses to the chain's sleep personality test. The test asks people a series of questions, such as how long they sleep, what side they sleep on, how much they weigh, and whether they toss and turn. Based on their responses, consumers are referred to a store to try out specific mattresses. Only 4 percent of Select Comfort's sales are made at its Web site. "This is

an experiential product. We want customers to come to the site and spend a lot of time on the site, but then we want them to go to a store and try the mattress out," says a Select Comfort executive.

Customers have to be allowed to use the proper channel based on their individual needs and values. Each company's channel preferences also need be balanced with customer needs. A customer who buys a lot of goods online, for instance, could be encouraged to come to the store for extra customer service. Customers who love online shopping should not be pushed to come to the store (if they truly enjoy the convenience, 24/7 timing, and the ability to more easily research a product through the Web).

A number of potential problems are also associated with the use of multichannels. The American Customer Satisfaction Index (ACSI) (http://www.theacsi.org) recently found that customer satisfaction levels dropped three points from the prior year. ACSI's director believes the "major cause of the plunge in customer satisfaction appears to be problems with servicing a growing volume of shoppers." In addition, a Forrester Research study of consumer satisfaction with multichannels found that many firms had failed to deliver a satisfactory experience in every area from the Internet to E-mail to cross-channel interactions. Only 10 percent of the cross-channel customer experiences reviewed were characterized as satisfactory.

Questions

1. Describe five possible sources of synergies for a small camera shop that offers both a Web site and store facilities for shoppers. The store specializes in the sale of used, high-quality camera equipment.
2. Should a retailer charge the same prices online as compared to in-store? Discuss both sides to this question.
3. Discuss five potential pitfalls associated with a small bricks-and-mortar retailer undertaking a multichannel strategy.
4. Cite five ways that a multichannel retailer can encourage its Web shoppers to visit its stores.

[c5-1] The data in the case are drawn from John Gaffney, "Finding the Right Fit," *1to1* (March 2005), pp. 18–21.

Case 2: Keeping Dunkin' Donuts Fresh—and the Coffee Flowing[c5-2]

Dunkin' Donuts' (http://www.dunkindonuts.com) Mid-Atlantic Distribution Center (MADC) supplies flour, muffin mix, and other ingredients to more than 1,700 Dunkin' Donuts locations in New York, New Jersey, Virginia, West Virginia, Pennsylvania, Delaware, and the eastern parts of Ohio. MADC operates 65 tractors that bring products from such suppliers as Pillsbury, General Goods, and Tropicana and 95 tractors that provide outbound delivery services to Dunkin' Donuts' franchised store units.

A complex issue for MADC relates to the potential impact of such adverse weather conditions as fog, ice, snow, and thunderstorms on its delivery system. MADC uses wireless, satellite, and speech recognition systems to manage the required scheduling changes due to weather and customer demand. MADC uses ResourcePRO scheduling software that assigns routes to trucks and drivers. This software shows arrival times and layovers, as well as wait times. If a manager must change the original route, ResourcePRO calculates a revised schedule and/or advises the manager that a change cannot be done.

ResourcePRO works in conjunction with TerritoryPRO, another application that adjusts and designs territories based on sales volume, the number of stops, and other factors. As Dunkin' Donuts locations are opened or closed, the program recomputes territories that meet its sales criteria. TerritoryPRO also provides drivers with a list of current accounts and a regional map. Other Appian (http://www.appiancorp.com) software programs used by MADC are DirectRoute, an automated route scheduling system that creates optimal routes for drivers, and DR Track, which routes specific trucks to within a very close distance of their current location. MADC managers are able to use this data to update arrival and departure times at each stop and to track each truck's actual versus planned mileage and hours driven.

MADC has seen some major improvements in efficiency as a result of the Appian software. "At certain locations, for example, demand increases during the summer. A route that has one truck at other times of the year will have five or six trucks during the summer," says Tim Kennedy, MADC's director of transportation. Whereas MADC originally had to reroute its trucks manually, this now can be done via the computer programs.

In August 2005, MADC moved to a new 300,000-square-foot distribution center (DC) just a few miles from its previous 125,000-square-foot DC. In addition to space, the new DC offers 134 available shipping doors (up from 22). Although the new DC handles 60,000 cases per day, it has the capacity to handle as many as 280,000 cases per day. A key feature of the new DC is its ability to use wireless technology for its VoiceLogistics voice-based order picking. This technology enables warehouse pickers to control inventory with voice commands. The pickers receive voice instructions on what items to pick and how many items to select. The pickers are then asked to repeat and confirm the instructions. The voice command system should substantially reduce picking errors. In addition, VoiceLogistics has drastically reduced training time. New hires used to need as much as eight weeks to reach MADC's required performance level; now, a new hire with little or no warehouse experience can reach this standard in four weeks or so due to Voice Logistics.

MADC's next step is to link VoiceLogistics software with its accounting, order processing, inventory control, and sales analysis software. The costs for the linkage are being shared by two software vendors. The vendors hope that the new integrated system will serve as a working model for other food distributors.

Questions

1. Describe the unique requirements of Dunkin' Donuts' logistics system.
2. What are the pros and cons of Dunkin' Donuts' use of software solutions versus manual solutions to its logistics problems and opportunities?
3. Analyze the results of Dunkin' Donuts outsourcing its MADC operations.
4. Discuss the pros and cons of Dunkin' Donuts' use of voice-based order picking.

[c5-2] The data in the case are drawn from John Edwards, "Time to Deliver the Donuts," *Inbound Logistics* (April 2005), pp. 100–104.

Case 3: Can Costco's Anti-Wal-Mart Approach Succeed in the Long Run?[c5-3]

Costco (http://www.costco.com) is the nation's leading membership club chain, with about 50 percent of the overall market. This compares favorably with Sam's Club (http://www.samsclub.com), a Wal-Mart subsidiary, which has a 40 percent share. In addition, Costco's U.S.-based stores each average more than $120 million in annual sales versus $70 million for each Sam's Club. Costco has been very successful in attracting and keeping its affluent shopper base. The average household income for a Costco shopper is $74,000, and 31 percent of shoppers have household incomes of over $100,000.

Despite the firm's success, Jim Sinegal—Costco's chief executive—has been criticized by some industry analysts as being overgenerous to both workers (with the company's relatively high salaries and fringe benefits) and its customers (by providing great deals). Costco's average employee earns $17 per hour as compared with Sam's Club's $12 per hour. In addition, Costco's health plan is far better than that of most retailers. Costco workers pay only 8 percent of their total health costs while the average retailer requires a 25 percent payment. Eighty-five percent of Costco's workers have health insurance versus less than one-half at Wal-Mart and Target. Sinegal firmly believes that significant benefits accrue from these compensation practices, including the low rates of employee turnover and theft. In addition, some of Costco's customers shop there due to its fair treatment of employees.

Sinegal rejects analysts' advice to raise prices. Costco uses a 14 percent markup on all of its goods (except for 15 percent on private-label items), while supermarkets have 25 percent markups and department stores use 50 percent or even higher markups. Sinegal is passionate about Costco's pricing: "When I started, Sears was the Costco of the country, but they allowed someone else to come in under them. We don't want to be one of the casualties. We don't want to turn around and say, 'We got so fancy we've raised our prices,' and all of a sudden, a new competitor comes in and beats our prices. We understand that our members don't come and shop with us because of the fancy window displays or the Santa Claus or the piano player. They come and shop with us because we offer great values."

Several key aspects are key to Costco's overall retail strategy: its low building and fixture costs, the low inventory on hand, the relentless search for the best prices, and the "treasure hunts" for shoppers. Costco's warehouse facilities are bare-bone structures with cement floors, high ceilings, visible pallets, and industrial-strength fixtures loaded to the ceiling with merchandise. A Costco store can stock up to 4,000 items and possibly four brands of toothpaste; a Wal-Mart store stocks over 100,000 items and can carry 60 different sizes and brands of toothpaste. Costco's lean stock on hand maximizes its inventory turnover while keeping stockouts low. By concentrating its purchases on fewer items, Costco is also able to receive substantial quantity discounts and purchase special buys.

Sinegal has been known to be a tough negotiator with Costco's suppliers and to warn them of the consequences of selling the same item to competitors at a lower price. When he discovered that a supplier sold frozen foods to Wal-Mart at lower prices, Sinegal dropped the supplier. He also warned Starbucks to reduce its prices, after coffee bean prices were reduced, at the risk of losing Costco's business.

With Costco's treasure hunts, Costco members can purchase items such as Coach leather bags, plasma TVs, and Waterford crystal that are offered on a temporary, "as available" basis. Many of the offers are specifically targeted to Costco's affluent customer base. Because the selection of these items varies daily and cannot be replaced, shoppers are encouraged to return periodically to Costco to take advantage of special offers.

Questions

1. Discuss the benefits of Costco's affluent customer base.
2. Develop a program to enable Costco to further reduce its inventory on hand without having stockouts.
3. Describe the pros and cons of Costco's treasure hunt program.
4. Apply the wheel of retailing to Costco.

[c5-3] The data in the case are drawn from Steven Greenhouse "How Costco became the Anti-Wal-Mart," *New York Times Online* (July 17, 2005).

Case 4: Walgreens: Competing in a Tougher Retail Drugstore Environment[c5-4]

Walgreens is the only *Fortune 500* company other than Wal-Mart that increased its sales and earnings every year from the mid-1970s to the mid-2000s. Walgreens' recent 10-year average shareholder return on investment is 22.4 percent as opposed to 14.0 percent for CVS and 8.2 percent for Longs. Walgreens' same-store sales have also risen steadily (often outperforming Target, Wal-Mart, Rite Aid, and many others). Walgreens currently has about 4,800 drugstores located throughout the United States; these stores serve 4 million customers on a daily basis.

Even though Walgreens has enjoyed a high level of financial performance, some industry analysts are concerned about possible adverse major competitive developments. CVS acquired 1,268 Eckerd stores. CVS' current base of 5,500 stores (including the former Eckerd locations) has the potential to give CVS significant additional bargaining clout with all of its suppliers, including property owners. Furthermore, more than 3,200 Wal-Mart locations now have in-store pharmacies. And Wal-Mart is testing 24-hour pharmacies and offering eye exams in some locations. Walgreens also faces a new competitive threat from mail-order and online pharmacies.

Because mail-order and online pharmacies can be highly automated, can operate in low-cost areas, and do not require a costly store location, they can fill and mail a prescription for as low as $2.50, a 50 percent cost advantage over Walgreens. To save on their health-care costs, 22 percent of employers now require their workers to use "mandatory mail-order plans." A related threat is that mail-order pharmacy customers have less need to visit a Walgreens store at all. Less store traffic can affect Walgreens' sale of highly profitable front-end merchandise (such as health and beauty aids, candy, tobacco, and film products and processing).

Walgreens has drastically underestimated the threat of pharmacy benefit managers (PBMs) such as Medco Health Solutions (http://www.medcohealth.com) and Caremark RX (http://www.caremark.com) that fulfill maintenance prescriptions through mail-order pharmacies. As recently as 2004, Walgreens' annual report did not even mention PBMs. "We were wrong in not seeing mail order. We admit it," stated Walgreens' chief operating officer. According to one benefits consultant, 22 percent of employers either use mandatory mail-order programs or are adopting them, versus 16 percent two years ago.

Walgreens is fighting back against mail-order and online pharmacies. It stopped filling prescriptions from Ohio state employees after the state insisted that its employees use mandatory mail-order pharmacies for certain drugs. Walgreens has also begun to offer 90-day prescriptions through a program called Advantage90. Walgreens claims that this 90-day program is less costly than the typical mail-order pharmacy.

Two of Walgreens' major strategic advantages are its store locations and its constant focus on cost reductions. Walgreens outlets are extremely accessible; the company estimates that close to 50 percent of the U.S. population lives within two miles of a Walgreens store. Still, Walgreens' chief executive, David Bernauer, believes that Walgreens has the potential to open a total of 12,000 stores. Walgreens currently opens a new store every 19 hours; and its site location evaluation process is so exacting that Walgreens has closed only 2 of the 3,600 new stores it has opened in the past 10 years due to poor sales. In addition, many of the stores are drive-in (a significant benefit for a parent with a sick child who does not need to have the child leave the car). Walgreens has more 24-hour stores than all of its competitors combined.

Walgreens' low-cost advantage comes from its ability to fill a prescription at an average cost that is far less than Wal-Mart and CVS. Supply chain management initiatives also let Walgreens reduce its in-store inventory of prescription drugs to only 41 days on average, down from 88 days in 1991.

Questions

1. Describe Walgreens' competitive advantages relative to Wal-Mart.
2. Discuss other ways that Walgreens can fight back against the mail-order pharmacies.
3. Explain how Walgreens can sustain its low-cost advantage.
4. Discuss the pros and cons of Walgreens' Advantage90 program as compared with its developing a mail-order pharmacy.

[c5-4] The data in the case are drawn from Matthew Boyle, "Drug Wars," *Fortune* (June 13, 2005), pp. 79–84.

The Value Chain and Home Improvement Retailing[pc-5]

INTRODUCTION

The good (or potentially bad) news for retailers is that prior customer service experiences impact future shopping decisions. In the past year, however, the perceived level of customer service has improved only minimally. Still, ways exist for retailers to bolster customer service. For installation services, although project incidence is up, the expected drastic shift from DIY (do-it-yourself) to DIFM (do-it-for-me) remains years away. Perceptions about home improvement retailers' installation services are improving.

SHOPPING LEVELS HIGH FOR HOME IMPROVEMENT PRODUCTS

A significant number of shoppers visit an array of stores for home improvement products. In the past six months, a sizable proportion of primary household shoppers have visited a variety of stores for home improvement products. Home Depot (**http://www.home depot.com**) tops the list, followed by its primary competitor Lowe's (**http://www.lowes.com**) and the world's largest retailer, Wal-Mart (**http://www.walmart.com**). In addition to the three largest players in the home improvement industry, many primary household shoppers also shop hardware stores, Sears (**http://www.sears.com**), and Menards (**http://www.menards.com**) for home improvement products.

Comparing the proportion of primary household shoppers who shopped these stores at least a year ago with the percentage who shopped during the past six months, a decrease of several percentage points is typical (for example, from 51 percent to 47 percent for Home Depot). The exception is Sears, where a much smaller proportion of households shopped during the past six months (12 percent) compared with a year ago (19 percent). The decline suggests Sears is losing home improvement customers to competitors.

Within key demographic segments—gender, age, and household income—the incidence of shopping at the leading home improvement retailers varies. Women are more likely than men to shop at Wal-Mart—and to a lesser extent—Menards for home improvement items. By age, 35- to 54-year-olds are the most likely shoppers at most home improvement retailers. Those age 65+ are most likely to shop hardware stores, and shoppers 55+ are most likely to shop Menards. At the aggregate, shoppers ages 18 to 24

are the least likely to shop for home improvement products. As household income grows, shoppers are more likely to shop for home improvement products across most formats. The exception is Wal-Mart—where the lowest-income shoppers are most likely to shop for home improvement products. Overall, shoppers with household incomes less than $25,000 are the least likely to shop for home improvement products.

CUSTOMER SERVICE DRIVES STORE DECISIONS, CAN BE BOLSTERED

For firms that want to improve customer service, the best ways are to have enough salespeople available on the floor and to improve salespeople's knowledge of home improvement products. See Table 1.

Two-thirds of shoppers make home improvement store decisions based on prior customer service experiences, and almost half want to be helped by a salesperson while shopping for home improvement products. Shoppers age 45+ are significantly more likely than shoppers younger than 35 to make future store shopping decisions based on prior customer service experiences. Shoppers with household incomes of $100,000 or more are significantly more likely than shoppers with household incomes less than $50,000 to make future store shopping decisions based on prior customer service experiences. Females are significantly more likely than males to want assistance from a salesperson while shopping for home improvement products. Older shoppers (65+) are significantly more likely than younger shoppers to want assistance from a salesperson while shopping for home improvement products.

Home improvement retailers can improve customer service in several ways: having enough salespeople to help shoppers whenever needed, bolstering salespeople's knowledge about home improvement products and projects, and having salespeople be more proactive in assisting shoppers. Older shoppers (35+) are much more likely than younger shoppers to want enough salespeople available whenever needed. Shoppers with household incomes of $100,000 or more are much more likely than other shoppers to use kiosks in stores to provide information about home improvement products.

LEVEL OF CUSTOMER SERVICE VARIES BY RETAILER

Hardware stores and Lowe's lead the way with regard to perceived level of customer service. Customer service is improving at these

[pc-5] Adapted by the authors from Retail Forward, *Shopper Update: Home Improvement Point of View* (July 2005). Reprinted by permission of Retail Forward, Inc. (**http://www.retailforward.com**).

Table 1 **Ways Stores That Sell Home Improvement Products Could Provide a Better Level of Customer Service—by Demographic Level**

Tactic	Total	Sex		Age						Household Income				
		Females	Males	18-24	25-34	35-44	45-54	55-64	65+	<$25K	$25K-$49.9K	$50K-$74.9K	$75K-$99.9K	$100K+
Have enough salespeople available to help me whenever needed on the sales floor	68%	69%	63%	55%	58%	70%	72%	71%	69%	63%	67%	71%	70%	71%
Train salespeople to have a greater knowledge of home improvement products	60%	60%	58%	52%	54%	61%	64%	64%	59%	58%	61%	59%	62%	61%
Train salespeople to have a greater knowledge of home improvement projects	47%	48%	43%	35%	45%	49%	47%	48%	47%	45%	48%	47%	47%	46%
Have salespeople proactively ask if they can assist me when shopping	32%	32%	31%	27%	25%	33%	35%	31%	36%	32%	31%	33%	28%	33%
Use kiosks in stores to provide information about home improvement products	20%	20%	19%	23%	21%	23%	19%	19%	16%	18%	19%	18%	19%	25%
Have salespeople not bother me unless I ask for assistance	16%	16%	16%	18%	20%	14%	14%	17%	14%	19%	16%	14%	13%	13%

Note: Shaded cells indicate highest level of penetration by demographic factor for each attitude.
Source: Retail Forward ShopperScapeTM, May 2005.

stores, along with Menards, compared with a year ago, while the level of customer service at Home Depot and Sears is basically the same and is declining at Wal-Mart.

Perceived levels of customer service vary significantly by retailer, with hardware stores leading the way and Wal-Mart getting the lowest ranking. One of the few remaining advantages of the hardware store model is a perceived higher level of customer service, likely because it's simply easier for shoppers to locate a customer service associate. Among the leading big-box players, Lowe's gets slightly higher marks than Home Depot. A sizable proportion of Menards shoppers (21 percent) weren't comfortable rating the retailer, which does not represent a show of confidence in the retailer's customer service offering. Shoppers perceive Wal-Mart's customer service to be the lowest, as almost an equal number of shoppers rate the retailer's customer service as "excellent/very good" (44 percent) as "average/fair" (40 percent).

In the last year, there's been minimal movement in shoppers' minds with regard to customer service levels, as the vast majority perceive the level of customer service to be the same today as compared with a year ago. Stores where more shoppers perceive customer service to be better today than worse today compared

with a year ago include: Lowe's (13 percent vs. 7 percent), Menards (13 percent vs. 6 percent), and hardware stores (12 percent vs. 3 percent). Stores where an almost equal proportion of shoppers perceive customer service to be better today than worse today as compared with a year ago include: Home Depot (11 percent vs. 10 percent) and Sears (10 percent vs. 11 percent). Stores where fewer shoppers feel customer service to be better today than worse today as compared with a year ago include only: Wal-Mart (9 percent vs. 16 percent).

HOME IMPROVEMENT PROJECT INCIDENCE INCREASES

Compared with last year at this time, a larger proportion of shoppers initiated a home improvement project during the past 12 months. The increase occurs across most age segments and all household income levels.

At the aggregate, 40 percent of consumers commenced a home improvement project during the past 12 months, inclusive of both DIY and DIFM jobs. Project initiation rates vary by age and household income levels. By age segment, the most significant variation from the prior year is a much higher project incidence rate among shoppers aged 65+—a jump from 32 percent to 45 percent. There are also big increases among baby boomer age segments (35–54), but a slight decline in the 25–34 age bracket. By household income, incidence increases across all income levels but is most dramatic among low-end (less than $25,000) and middle-market ($50,000–$74,999) shoppers.

GENDER ROLE DISAGREEMENTS; MORE MALES TAKING PROJECT LEAD

Males and females have different beliefs about who initiates a home improvement project and purchases home improvement products within the household. This divergence in opinion was not present before. Part of the divergence can be explained by the finding that more males appear to be taking the lead in these activities today compared with the prior year.

A significantly higher proportion of males claim they make the final decision to initiate a home improvement project than females—55 percent vs. 39 percent. A similar gap exists for purchasing home improvement products—65 percent vs. 46 percent. Males and females also have different perceptions with regard to joint decisions, but to a smaller degree (37 percent vs. 43 percent and 29 percent vs. 39 percent). These differences, which were basically nonexistent before, suggest that some males think they play a more critical role in the processes than they actually do, but also that decision-making dynamics appear to be evolving.

HOME IMPROVEMENT PROJECT COMPLETION—DIY STILL LEADING

DIY remains the primary method for getting home improvement projects done today. However, this will change in the future as the population ages and gets wealthier.

A slightly smaller proportion of projects were completed utilizing a complete DIFM solution—one where a contractor buys the materials and completes the work—in 2005 (16 percent) compared with 2004 (18 percent). Just less than one-half (49 percent, down from 50 percent in 2004) used a DIY solution, whereas only a small proportion of consumers bought the materials themselves and then hired a contractor to complete the project (6 percent) or utilized installation services from a store (3 percent, down from 4 percent in 2004). A sizable proportion of respondents (26 percent, up from 22 percent in 2004) didn't know what method was employed for their household's most recent home improvement project. See Table 2.

STORES ASSIST IN PROJECT COMPLETION

Home improvement centers are a destination for shoppers who are completing home improvement projects, though it isn't imperative for retailers that want to sell products for home improvement projects to offer installation services. Compared with last year, fewer shoppers are concerned about the quality of installation services at home improvement retailers that offer services.

More than 70 percent of shoppers purchased the majority of their products for their most recent home improvement project

Table 2	Home Improvement Project Completion Method by Demographic Factor													
		Sex		Age							Household Income				
Factor	Total	Females	Males	18-24	25-34	35-44	45-54	55-64	65+	<$25K	$25K-$49.9K	$50K-$74.9K	$75K-$99.9K	$100K+
Household buys materials, work completed by self/friends	49%	50%	45%	39%	48%	60%	55%	47%	39%	49%	51%	53%	50%	44%
Household buys materials, store arranges installation	3%	3%	4%	4%	3%	2%	3%	4%	5%	2%	3%	4%	3%	5%
Household buys materials, contractor does work	6%	6%	7%	3%	5%	5%	6%	6%	8%	3%	6%	8%	8%	9%
Contractor buys materials, does work	16%	14%	22%	6%	8%	13%	15%	22%	26%	9%	15%	17%	20%	28%

Note: Includes projects initiated by respondent or contractor. Definition for home improvement project is improving, repairing or maintaining one's home or property.
Source: Retail Forward ShopperScape™, May 2005.

from a home improvement center. In the past year, Lowe's increased its share from 23 percent to 25 percent, while Home Depot and Menards remained at 42 percent and 5 percent, respectively. In addition to Lowe's, Wal-Mart (+1 percentage point), lumberyards/building centers (+2 percentage points), and paint/wallpaper stores (+1 percentage point) gained share. One-half of shoppers purchased some products for their latest project from Home Depot, while that metric was 36 percent for Lowe's and 17 percent for Wal-Mart.

Home Depot attracts significantly more project product purchasers with household incomes in excess of $75,000 compared with those who make less money. Almost the exact opposite is true for Wal-Mart, with the retailer disproportionately attracting purchasers with household incomes less than $50,000 compared with purchasers who are more affluent.

Hardware stores and Wal-Mart aren't destinations for home improvement project products; rather, their role is one of "fill-in" product opportunities. This is apparent based on analyzing the ratio of the percent of consumers who purchase the majority of products at a retailer versus the percent of consumers who purchase any products at a retailer. Hardware stores and Wal-Mart are the only retailers where this ratio exceeds 2.0; it is 3.0 for hardware stores (12 percent/4 percent) and 2.1 for Wal-Mart (17percent/8 percent).

A segment of the population prefers to shop for home improvement products at stores that also offer installation services, but fewer shoppers are concerned about the quality of those installation services today compared with a year ago. Compared with last year, a smaller proportion of shoppers either agree or strongly agree with the statement that they are concerned about the quality of installation services at stores that sell home improvement products and offer installation services. That metric declined from 43 percent in 2004 to 38 percent in 2005. Men are significantly more likely than women to be concerned (41 percent vs. 37 percent). Only 36 percent of shoppers either agree or strongly agree with the statement that they prefer to shop for home improvement products at stores that also offer installation services. This result is basically the same as 2004, when 35 percent of shoppers were in agreement with this statement. Women are significantly more likely than men to have this belief (37 percent vs. 31 percent). See Table 3.

Shoppers' perceptions about the size of retailers' installation services offers have eroded in the last year. A smaller percentage of shoppers are in agreement with the statement, "Retailer X offers a large selection of installation services." For Home Depot, Lowe's, and Sears, results declined from 60 percent to 53 percent, 47 percent to 44 percent, and 45 percent to 37 percent, respectively. Lowe's is holding up the best compared with the competition.

ABOUT RETAIL FORWARD'S MONTHLY SHOPPER UPDATE SURVEY

Every month, Retail Forward surveys 4,000 shoppers about their recent and planned spending. Retail forward collects purchasing data for over 150 retailers and more than 100 product categories!

Table 3 Attitudes About Installation Services by Demographic Factor														
		Sex				**Age**					**Household Income**			
Attitude	Strongly Agree/ Agree	Females	Males	18-24	25-34	35-44	45-54	55-64	65+	≤$25K	$25K-$49.9K	$50K-$74.9K	$75K-$99.9K	$100K+
At stores that sell home improvement products and offer installation services, concerned about the quality of installation services	38%	37%	41%	36%	35%	37%	39%	39%	39%	32%	37%	40%	40%	44%
Prefer to shop for home improvement products at stores that also offer installation services	36%	37%	31%	32%	33%	32%	35%	38%	43%	32%	38%	34%	37%	41%
The Home Depot offers a large selection of installation services	53%	53%	54%	42%	47%	55%	52%	57%	56%	43%	50%	59%	62%	63%
Lowe's offers a large selection of installation services	44%	43%	45%	30%	36%	44%	46%	46%	50%	36%	44%	48%	50%	46%
Sears offers a large selection of installation services	37%	36%	43%	28%	28%	32%	40%	43%	48%	33%	37%	39%	41%	39%

Source: Retail Forward ShopperScapeTM, May 2005.

What could you do with this much shopper insight? Retail Forward's Monthly Shopper Update Survey closes the knowledge gap and delivers critical shopping behavior insight down to the category, competitor, and/or consumer segment level. Robust survey data will help you learn:

- Are you gaining or losing shoppers? How you are faring versus your competitors? Who is winning over time? Who is adding loyal, frequent shoppers?
- What categories are shoppers buying from you and your competitors? Is this changing over time? Why are shoppers making these choices?
- Which categories did your customers buy last month? What do they plan to buy next month?
- How much are shoppers spending on these categories at your stores—and at your competitors' stores? How is this changing over time?
- What is most important to shoppers when they are in the market for these categories?
- What are the demographic characteristics of shoppers purchasing these categories—at your store and at your competitors' stores?

1. What are the value chain implications of this case?
2. Describe the value delivery chain for Home Depot and show how it represents a competitive advantage over small hardware stores.
3. What are the implications of Table 1 for a home improvement retailer (or hardware store)?
4. How can a retailer balance the consumers' need for good customer service against its own need for cost containment?
5. To better appeal to female shoppers, what would you suggest to Home Depot?
6. Many consumers purchase installation services from retailers such as Home Depot for complex home improvements. What are the pros and cons of retailers relying on independent service contractors for these services rather than using their own employees?
7. Comment on the data presented in Table 3 regarding attitudes toward installation services. What would you recommend to Home Depot?

Part

6

Part 6 covers promotion, the third major element of the marketing mix.

17 Integrated Marketing Communications

Here, we broadly discuss promotion planning—all communication used to inform, persuade, and/or remind people about an organization's or individual's goods, services, image, ideas, community involvement, or impact on society. We describe the basic types of promotion and the stages in a channel of communication. Next, we present the steps in developing an overall promotion plan. We conclude the chapter with global promotion considerations, and the legal environment and criticisms of promotion.

18 Advertising and Public Relations

In this chapter, we examine two of the four types of promotion: advertising and public relations. Advertising is paid, nonpersonal communication by an identified sponsor, and public relations is any form of image-directed communication by an identified sponsor or the independent media. We detail the scope and attributes of advertising and public relations, and describe the role of publicity. We discuss developing advertising and public relations plans in depth.

19 Personal Selling and Sales Promotion

Now, we focus on the two other key elements of a promotion mix: personal selling and sales promotion. Personal selling is oral communication with one or more prospective buyers by paid representatives for the purpose of making sales, and sales promotion is the paid marketing communication activities (other than advertising, publicity, or personal selling) that stimulate consumer purchases and dealer effectiveness. We describe the scope, characteristics, and stages in planning for both personal selling and sales promotion.

Promotion Planning

After reading Part 6, you should understand element 12 of the strategic marketing plan outlined in Table 3-2 (page 77).

Chapter 17

Integrated Marketing Communications

American Express (AmEx) (**http://www.americanexpress.com**) is the third-largest credit-card firm (after Visa and MasterCard). Its credit-card operations account for more than one-half of revenues, even though AmEx has more than 1,700 locations for its travel agency operations and is the world's largest issuer of traveler's checks. AmEx's credit-card division faces some major challenges.

The U.S. market for credits cards is saturated, with 900-million active credit, charge, and debit cards. And many younger people favor debit cards where funds are instantly drawn from their accounts. Though debit cards account for 60 percent of Visa's transactions, AmEx has no current plans for a debit card.

The three cornerstones of AmEx's credit-card strategy are to: attract and retain more affluent customers, increase the number of firms accepting its cards, and engage in local credit-card programs. The strategy requires a combination of advertising, public relations, personal selling, and sales promotions. To attract wealthy consumers, AmEx has partnerships with financial institutions in 90 countries. These partnerships give AmEx access to the banks' valuable customers.

AmEx understands that it can expand its revenues by increasing the number of establishments that accept its cards. It has directed a substantial amount of advertising and personal selling to increasing the number of gasoline and grocery stores that honor its cards. As a result of this effort, gasoline stations and groceries now account for 60 percent of card spending, compared with 35 percent in 1990.

AmEx also has many local promotions. It sponsors three no-annual-fee special credit cards: IN:New York City, IN:Chicago, and IN:Los Angeles. These cards offer members points that are redeemable for free dining and entertainment. Ninety percent of those signing up never had an AmEx credit card. More than one-half of these cardholders are under 35. This is the youngest age group for any AmEx credit card.

Image-based advertising and public relations are also vital aspects of AmEx's overall promotional strategy. The firm sponsors a number of sporting events (such as NBA games and the U.S. Open series), as well as events such as New York's Tribecca Film Festival.[1]

In this chapter, we will study the many dimensions of promotion planning, including developing an integrated approach to promotion planning.

Chapter Objectives

1. To define promotion planning, show its importance, and demonstrate the value of integrated marketing communications
2. To describe the general characteristics of advertising, public relations, personal selling, and sales promotion
3. To explain the channel of communication and how it functions
4. To examine the components of a promotion plan
5. To discuss global promotion considerations, the legal environment, and criticisms and defenses of promotion

[1] Various company and other sources.

17-1   OVERVIEW

Promotion is any communication used to inform, persuade, and/or remind people about an organization's or individual's goods, services, image, ideas, community involvement, or impact on society. *Promotion planning* is systematic decision making relating to all aspects of an organization's or individual's communications efforts.

Communication occurs through brand names, packaging, company marquees and displays, personal selling, customer service, trade shows, sweepstakes, and messages in mass media (such as newspapers, TV, radio, direct mail, billboards, magazines, and transit). It can be company sponsored or controlled by independent media. Messages may emphasize information, persuasion, fear, sociability, product performance, humor, and/or comparisons with competitors.

In this chapter, we cover the context of integrated promotion planning. Included are discussions on promotion's importance, integrated marketing communications, promotion types, the channel of communication, promotion planning, global considerations, the legal environment, and general criticisms and defenses of promotion. Chapter 18 covers advertising and public relations. Chapter 19 deals with personal selling and sales promotion.

> **Promotion planning** focuses on a total **promotion** effort—informing, persuading, and reminding.

17-2   THE IMPORTANCE OF PROMOTION

Promotion is a vital element of the marketing mix. For new products, people must be informed about items and their features before they can develop favorable attitudes toward them. For products with some consumer awareness, the focus is on persuasion: converting knowledge to liking. For very popular products, the focus is on reminding: reinforcing existing consumer beliefs.

The people and organizations at whom a firm's promotional efforts are aimed may fall into various categories: consumers, stockholders, consumer advocates, government, channel members, employees, competitors, and the public. Communication often goes on between a firm and each group, not just with consumers; and it may differ because the groups have distinct goals, knowledge, and needs.

Within an audience category (such as consumers), a firm needs to identify and appeal to the opinion leaders who influence others' decisions. It also needs to understand *word-of-mouth communication*, the process by which people express opinions and product-related experiences to one another. Unless there is sustained, positive word-of-mouth communication, it is hard to succeed. With such communication, popularity can readily grow:

> **Word-of-mouth communication** occurs as people state opinions to others.

> You could break your small business bank account on flashy ads. Or, you can follow the lead of successful entrepreneurs who know one sure-fire marketing tool: There's no shame in asking a friend to tell a friend. You're encouraging your happiest customers to create a buzz about you. When Mia Jackson, president of Doro Marketing [**http://www.doromarketing. com**]—which produces marketing materials for companies and nonprofit organizations—launched her firm, she counted on friends and former colleagues to chat up her services. As her clientele grew, she began asking her favorites to pass along her name and card to others in need of her expertise. "If you don't have that word of mouth, it's very seldom a brochure will get you the clients you want," says Jackson, who landed her largest client when a woman she once worked with suggested Doro for a marketing project.[2]

> Viral marketing is today's electronic equivalent of word of mouth. It's a strategy that involves creating an online message that's novel or entertaining enough to prompt consumers to pass it on to others—spreading the message across the Web like a virus at no cost to the advertiser. Firms have caught the bug and are increasingly weaving viral components into their marketing

---

[2] Stacy Gilliam, "Closing the Sale," *Black Enterprise* (September 2005), p. 56.

plans. Not only is the approach relatively inexpensive, but also it can sometimes be more believable than standard ads.[3]

These Web sites offer advice on how to stimulate positive word-of-mouth communication among consumers: "Word of Mouth Marketing Articles" (**http://www.mnav.com/womtitlepage.htm**), "How to Promote Your Business by Word of Mouth" (**http://www.smalltownmarketing.com/promoteword.html**), and "Essentials of Word of Mouth Marketing" (**http://www.soho.org/Marketing_Articles/word_of_mouth.htm**).

A company's promotion plan usually stresses individual goods and services, with the intent of moving people from awareness to purchase. Yet, the firm may also convey its overall image (industry innovator), views on ideas (free trade), community service (funding a new hospital), or impact on society (the size of its work force).

A good promotion plan complements the product, distribution, and price aspects of marketing, and it is well designed. Allen Edmonds (**http://www.allenedmonds.com**)—a maker of quality shoes—distributes products at finer stores and sets premium prices. It advertises in such magazines as *GQ* and *Fortune*, and expects retailers to do first-rate personal selling. Ads are in color and stress product features, not prices.

Superior promotion plans are feasible even if companies have limited resources. Here are 10 tips:

1. "Create a brochure for your business. Include testimonials from customers and focus on your unique and special expertise."
2. "Publish a newsletter. Many people will toss out the flyers or advertisements but will take a moment to read an interesting newsletter."
3. "Develop a Web site and get an E-mail address."
4. "Attend trade shows or exhibits related to your industry, product, or business. Bring along your brochures, sales flyers, and newsletters."
5. "Join and participate in community business groups such as your local chamber of commerce."
6. "Write articles for the local paper. Each time one is published, you gain credibility and visibility."
7. "Set up a 'take-one' box in your place of business. Put flyers, brochures, and letters there."
8. "Send out congratulatory notes for customers' personal events such as birthdays."
9. "Ask your customers for referrals."
10. "Send out press releases when you introduce new goods or services."[4]

Promotion's importance is also evident from the spending and jobs in this area. The world's 10 largest ad agencies have overall annual billings of $35 billion. The International Advertising Association (**http://www.iaaglobal.org**) has thousands of members from 90 nations. In the United States alone, each year, auto makers spend $20 billion and retailers spend $17 billion on advertising; 16 million people work in sales; more than 300 billion coupons are given out; and there are several thousand trade shows.[5]

17-3 AN INTEGRATED APPROACH TO PROMOTION PLANNING

> **Integrated marketing communications (IMC)** evaluates the strategic roles of various communication disciplines and combines them for clarity, consistency, and impact.

When it develops and applies a well-coordinated promotion plan, a firm should use *integrated marketing communications (IMC)*. IMC "recognizes the value of a comprehensive plan that evaluates the strategic roles of a variety of communication disciplines—advertising, public relations, personal selling, and sales promotion—and combines them

---

[3] Theresa Howard, "Viral Advertising Spreads Through Marketing Plans," **http://www.usatoday.com/money/advertising/2005-06-22-viral-usat_x.htm php** (June 22, 2005).

[4] Kate Schultz, "Top 10 Tips for Marketing a Small Business," **http://www.marketingsurvivalkit.com/sbmarketing.htm** (May 4, 2006).

[5] "Agency Report," *Advertising Age* (May 2, 2005); "Domestic Spending by Category," *Advertising Age* (June 27, 2005); U.S. Department of Labor, Bureau of Labor Statistics; "Annual Report on the Promotion Industry," *Promo Magazine's SourceBook 2006*; and authors' estimates.

Table 17-1 The Value of Integrated Marketing Communications

Through an integrated marketing communications strategy, a firm can:

- Coordinate all of its promotional activities.
- Establish and maintain a consistent image for the company and its goods and services.
- Communicate the features of goods and services.
- Create awareness for new goods and services.
- Keep existing goods and services popular.
- Reposition the images or uses of faltering goods and services.
- Generate enthusiasm from channel members.
- Note where goods and services can be purchased.
- Persuade consumers to trade up from one product to a more expensive one.
- Alert consumers to sales.
- Justify (rationalize) the prices of goods and services.
- Answer consumer questions.
- Close transactions with customers.
- Provide service for consumers after transactions are completed.
- Reinforce consumer loyalty.
- Place the company and its goods and services in a favorable light, relative to competitors.
- Encourage cross-marketing, whereby each element of the promotion mix reinforces the other (such as including a Web address on shopping bags, in the store, on the sales receipt, and in ads).

to provide clarity, consistency, and maximum communication impact."[6] For example, Frito-Lay (**http://www.fritolay.com**) has a sales force that visits every store stocking its snack food products, advertises in several consumer media, and offers cents-off coupons. Hitachi (**http://www.hitachi.com**) has a technical sales force, advertises in business and trade publications, and sends representatives to trade shows to promote its consumer electronics. Table 17-1 shows the value of integrated marketing communications.

A superior IMC plan properly addresses these points:

- *It is synergistic*, taking into account the multiple ways to reach potential consumers at different points during their decision process.
- *There is tactical consistency*, so various promotion tools complement each other and communicate the same basic themes.
- *There is interactivity with consumers*, so messages are better tailored to specific market segments.
- *Every company message positively influences the target audience*, so each contact builds on the contacts before it.
- *The company's basic promotion themes and differential advantages are clearly understood by all employees who interface with the targeted audience* to avoid the negative impact of misinformed employees passing on the wrong information to potential customers.
- *Advertising, public relations, sales, and sales promotion personnel cooperate with one another*, and view each other as partners rather than as adversaries.
- *Detailed data bases are maintained*, so that promotion efforts can be regularly reviewed.[7]

> IMC efforts should be synergistic, tactically consistent, interactive, positive influences, and so forth.

[6] Adapted by the authors from Janet Smith, "Integrated Marketing," *Marketing Tools* (November–December 1995), p. 64.

[7] Adapted by the authors from Kim Bartel Sheehan and Caitlin Doherty, "Re-Weaving the Web: Integrating Print and Online Communications," *Journal of Interactive Marketing*, Vol. 15 (Spring 2001), pp. 47–59; Anders Gronstedt, *The Customer Century: Lessons from World-Class Companies in Integrated Marketing and Communications* (London: Routledge, 2000); and Michael Render, "IMC Gets Better with Inflow Marketing," *Marketing News* (September 11, 2000), p. 23.

Figure 17-1

Integrated Marketing Communications and FedEx Kinko's

"Make it. Print it. Pack it. Ship it."

Source: Reprinted by permission.

IBM (**http://www.ibm.com**), a leading IMC practitioner, was recently honored by *BtoB* magazine for a major campaign that it ran:

> To underscore its ability to deliver value-added services to a customer, IBM used the metaphor of a help desk across its TV, print, and interactive executions. The first phase of the campaign spoke about how IBM could help the world at large, while the second focused on industry- or customer-specific solutions. Both phases targeted business decision makers. Print ads featured beautiful photos of landscapes. Stylized help desk stickers were applied to each to set up a problem-solution scenario. TV spots had a wry, sometimes comic tone. The help desks appeared in improbable places, such as a golf course where a group of scientists needed help after its solar-powered golf cart runs amok. The centerpiece of the interactive component was an online execution featuring a large white room with classical columns the creative team dubbed "white heaven" because of its almost dreamlike state.[8]

Figures 17-1 and 17-2 highlight the integrated marketing communications approaches of FedEx Kinko's (**http://www.fedexkinkos.com**) and Guess? (**http://www.guess.com**), respectively.

17-4 TYPES OF PROMOTION

Organizations use one or more of four basic types of promotion in their communications programs:

Advertising, public relations (publicity), personal selling, and sales promotion are the four key promotion types.

- *Advertising* is paid, nonpersonal communication regarding goods, services, organizations, people, places, and ideas that is transmitted through various media by business firms, government and other nonprofit organizations, and individuals who are identified in the advertising message as the sponsor. The message is generally controlled by the sponsor.
- *Public relations* includes any communication to foster a favorable image for goods, services, organizations, people, places, and ideas among their publics—such as consumers, investors, government, channel members, employees, and the general public. It may be nonpersonal or personal, paid or nonpaid, and sponsor controlled or not controlled. *Publicity* is the form of public relations that entails nonpersonal

[8] "Integrated Campaign", *BtoB* (October 24, 2005), pp. 30–38.

Figure 17-2

Integrated Marketing Communications and Guess?

The "look" in this Guess? ad is consistent with the fashion-forward, youth-oriented, edgy image that the firm promotes. Visit the Guess? Web site (**http://www.guess.com**) to see a collection of recent ads, all integrated with the "look" sought.

Source: Reprinted by permission. GUESS? Inc. photographer Odette Sugerman and Creative Director Paul Marciano.

communication passed on via various media but not paid for by an identified sponsor. Wording and placement of publicity messages are generally media controlled.

- *Personal selling* involves oral communication with one or more prospective buyers by paid representatives for the purpose of making sales.
- *Sales promotion* involves paid marketing communication activities (other than advertising, publicity, or personal selling) that are intended to stimulate consumer purchases and dealer effectiveness. Included are trade shows, premiums, incentives, giveaways, demonstrations, and various other efforts not in the ordinary promotion routine.[9]

---

[9] Adapted by the authors from "Dictionary of Marketing Terms," http://www.marketingpower.com/mg-dictionary.php (May 3, 2006).

Marketing and the Web

How Spyware and Adware Can Undermine Online Communications Efforts

Spyware and adware consist of programs that can monitor a computer user's behavior without his or her knowledge or permission. Spyware runs on a consumer's PC and displays ads in response to the consumer's Web-based activities. Programs that enable spyware to operate are often bundled with freeware and computer games. The bundled software is typically unknowingly downloaded by a consumer from an adware vendor's site or from an affiliated Web site. When *PC World* recently installed adware monitoring programs on test PCs, it saw ads from such major brands as Chrysler, Expedia, Microsoft, Priceline, and Travelocity.

One firm, DirectRevenue LLC (http://www.direct-revenue.com), has over 20 million adware installations through its instant messaging, Web browser toolbar, and clock and weather programs. Estimates of the revenues from spyware range from $200 million to $2 billion a year based on the number of spyware installations and the amount of money generated by each installation. Among those that profit from spyware are ad brokers, search engines that sell keyword-based ads, and software bundlers that distribute the adware. According to a firm that provided capital to an adware firm, "Adware is here to stay. Privacy for the [Internet] consumer is a lost war."

Two federal anti-spyware bills have been introduced in Congress. Some firms, such as Dell, have also terminated their relationships with firms that placed its ads with several small search engines.

Sources: Based on material in Paul F. Roberts, "The Many Faces of Spyware," *eWeek* (June 20, 2005), pp. 24–28; and Dan Tynan and Tom Spring, "The Hidden Money Trail," *PC World* (November 2005), pp. 71–80.

The general characteristics of each type of promotion are shown in Table 17-2. As discussed later in the chapter, many firms in some way combine them into an integrated promotional blend. This lets them reach their entire target market, present both persuasive and believable messages, have personal contact with customers, sponsor special events, and balance the promotional budget.

Table 17-2 Characteristics of Promotional Types

Factor	Advertising	Publicity Form of Public Relations[a]	Personal Selling	Sales Promotion
Audience	Mass	Mass	Small (one-to-one)	Varies
Message	Uniform	Uniform	Specific	Varies
Cost	Low per viewer or reader	None for media space and time; can be some costs for media releases and publicity materials	High per customer	Moderate per customer
Sponsor	Company	No formal sponsor (media not paid)	Company	Company
Flexibility	Low	Low	High	Moderate
Control over content and placement	High	None (controlled by media)	High	High
Credibility	Moderate	High	Moderate	Moderate
Major goal	To appeal to a mass audience at a reasonable cost, and create awareness and favorable attitudes	To reach a mass audience with an independently reported message	To deal with individual consumers, to resolve questions, to close sales	To stimulate short-run sales, to increase impulse purchases
Example	Television ad for an Apple video iPod	Magazine article describing an an Apple video iPod's unique features	Salesperson explaining how an Apple video iPod works	An Apple video iPod exhibited at trade shows

[a]Please note: When public relations embodies advertising (an image-related message), personal selling (a salesperson describing his or her firm's public service efforts to college students), and/or sales promotion (distributing special discount coupons to low-income consumers), it takes on the characteristics of those promotional types. However, the goal would be more image-related than sales-related.

17-5 THE CHANNEL OF COMMUNICATION

To develop a proper promotion mix and interact effectively with a target audience, the *channel of communication (communication process)* shown in Figure 17-3 must be understood. Through such a channel, a source develops a message, transmits it to an audience via some medium, and gets feedback from the audience. The components of a communication channel are discussed next.

> A message is sent to an audience via a **channel of communication**

17-5a The Source

The *source* of communication is usually a company, an independent institution, or an opinion leader seeking to present a message to an audience. A firm communicates through a(n) spokesperson, celebrity, actor playing a role, representative consumer, and/or salesperson. A company spokesperson is typically a long-time employee who represents the firm in communications. The spokesperson has an aura of sincerity, commitment, and expertise. Sometimes, the spokesperson is a top executive, like Ronco's (**http://www.ronco.com**) Ron Popeil or Ford's (**http://www.ford.com**) William Ford. Other times, front-line workers are used, such as a Verizon (**http://www.verizon.com**) customer service representative or a Sheraton (**http://www.sheraton.com**) hotel chef. In general, this source has been quite effective.

> A **source** presents a message.

A celebrity is used to gain the audience's attention and improve product awareness. Problems can arise if a celebrity is seen as insincere or unknowledgeable. Popular celebrities include George Foreman for the George Foreman brand of grilling machines (**http://www.esalton.com**), Catherine Zeta-Jones for T-mobile (**http://www.tmobile. com**), Snoopy and other *Peanuts* characters for MetLife (**http://www.metlife.com**), and Tiger Woods for Tag Heuer (**http://www.tagheuer.com**). See Figure 17-4.

Many ads have actors playing roles rather than celebrity spokespeople. The emphasis then is on presenting a message about a good, service, or idea rather than on the consumer recognizing a celebrity. The hope is that the consumer will learn more about product attributes.

A representative consumer is one who likes a product and recommends it in an ad. The intent is to present a real consumer in an actual situation, such as Jared Fogle for Subway (**http://www.subway.com**). The person is sometimes shown with his or her name and hometown. A hidden camera or blind taste test may be used with this source. Today, some viewers are skeptical about how "representative" the endorser is.

Finally, a firm may use a salesperson to communicate with consumers. Many salespeople are knowledgeable, assertive, and persuasive. However, consumers may doubt their objectivity and tactics. Auto salespeople rate particularly low in consumer surveys.

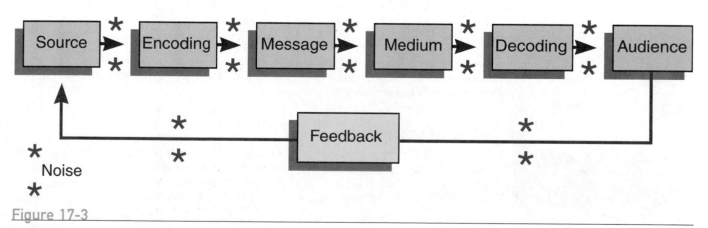

Figure 17-3

A Channel of Communication

Figure 17-4

Tiger Woods: A Tag Heuer Endorser

Source: Reprinted by permission of Susan Berry, Retail Image Consulting, Inc.

An independent institution is not controlled by the firms on which it reports. It presents information in a professional, nonpaid (by the firms) manner. Consumers Union (**http://www.consumersunion.org**), the publisher of *Consumer Reports* (**http://www.consumerreports.org**), and a local newspaper restaurant critic are examples of independent sources. They have great credibility for readers because they discuss both good and bad points, but some segments of the population may not be exposed to these sources. The information presented may differ from that contained in a firm's commercials or sales-force presentations.

An opinion leader has face-to-face contact with and influences potential consumers. Because he or she deals on a personal level, an opinion leader often has strong persuasive impact and believability, and can offer social acceptance for followers. Firms often address initial messages to opinion leaders, who then provide word-of-mouth to others. Many marketers believe opinion leaders not only influence, but also are influenced by, others (opinion receivers); even opinion leaders need approval for their choices.

In assessing a source, these questions are critical: Is he/she believable? Is he/she convincing? Does he/she present an image consistent with the firm? Do consumers value the message of the source? Is he/she seen as knowledgeable? Does the source complement the product he/she communicates about, or does the source overwhelm it? Do significant parts of the market dislike the source?

17-5b Encoding

Encoding is the process whereby a thought or idea is translated into a message by the source. Preliminary decisions are made as to message content, such as the use of symbolism and wording. It is vital that the thought or idea be translated exactly as the source intends. A firm wanting to stress its product's prestige would include the product's status, exclusive ownership, and special features in a message. It would not stress a low price, availability in discount stores, or the millions of people who have already purchased.

> In **encoding**, a source translates a thought into a message.

Figure 17-5

The Inviting Message of Piggly Wiggly

Source: Reprinted by permission.

17-5c   The Message

A *message* is a combination of words and symbols transmitted to an audience. It depends on whether the goal is to inform, persuade, or remind. Almost all messages include some information on the firm's name, the product name, the desired image, differential advantages, and product attributes. A firm would also give information on availability and price at some point in the consumer's decision process. With integrated marketing communications, message consistency is important. As highlighted in Figure 17-5, Piggly Wiggly (**http://www.pigglywiggly.com**) knows this well.

Most communication involves one-sided messages, in which only the benefits of a good, service, or idea are cited. Few firms use two-sided messages, in which both benefits and limitations are noted. Companies are not anxious to point out their shortcomings, although consumer perceptions of honesty may be improved via two-sided messages.

Many messages use symbolism and try to relate safety, social acceptance, or sexual appeal to a purchase. In symbolic messages, a firm stresses psychological benefits rather than tangible product performance. Clothing ads may offer acceptance by peers; toothpaste may brighten teeth and make a person more sexually attractive. One type of symbolism, fear appeals (such as anti-drug ads), has had mixed results. People respond to moderate fear appeals, but strong ones may not be as well received.

A **message** combines words and symbols.

campaignforrealbeauty.com | *Dove*

Say goodbye to stickiness. Say hello to movement.
Turn unruly hair into foxy momma hair. Dove Anti-Frizz Cream with our Weightless Moisturizers™ makes hair smooth, shiny and doesn't leave it greasy. Welcome to blue heaven.

unstick your style.

Figure 17-6

A Clever Use of Humor

Source: Reprinted by permission.

Figure 17-7

Massed Versus Distributed Promotion

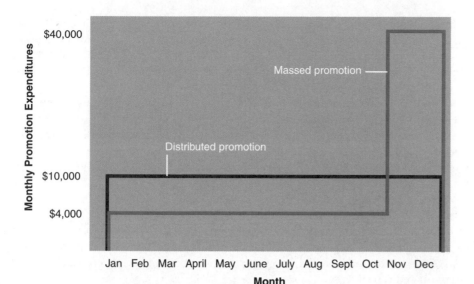

With a total promotion budget of $120,000, a hosiery manufacturer employs distributed promotion and spends $10,000 each month throughout the year. With the same budget, a toy manufacturer uses massed promotion and spends $80,000 from November 1 through December 31 (the remaining $40,000 is spent over the other 10 months). In both cases, monthly promotion expenditures are linked to monthly sales.

Humor may be utilized to gain audience attention and retain it. This has been done quite well by Dove (**http://www.dove.com**), as shown in Figure 17-6. About.com (**http://humor.about.com/cs/advertisinghumor**) has several popular examples and related materials. Yet, a firm needs to be careful to get across the intended message when using humor—which should not make fun of the company, its goods, or its services; and humor should not dominate a message so the brand name or product attributes go unnoticed. Because humor has cultural underpinnings, successful ads in the home country may not work well in another nation:

> Advertising costs are high, and consumer attention spans are low. It's a scary combination that has every business searching for the ad that's not only memorable but also has a measurable impact on the bottom line. The trend has been toward wacky image ads seemingly unrelated to the products they're touting. Other firms have opted for the traditional approach, running "educational" ads with text rather than images or featuring customer testimonials. What will work for *your* business? The good news is, probably any of these strategies will work—*if* you know how to use them.[10]

Comparative messages implicitly or explicitly contrast a firm's offerings with those of competitors. Implicit comparisons use an indirect brand-X or leading-brand approach ("Our industrial glues are more effective than other leading brands"). Explicit comparisons use a direct approach (such as PepsiCo's promoting the "Pepsi Challenge" taste tests in which Pepsi beats Coke). Comparative messages are used in some TV and radio commercials, print ads, and other media, and salespeople often compare their products' attributes with those of competitors. In using comparative messages, a firm must be careful not to turn off consumers, place too much emphasis on a competitor's brand, or lose sight of its own differential advantages to promote.

A message must be presented in a desirable, exclusive, and believable way. The good, service, or idea must be perceived as something worth buying or accepting. It also must be seen as unique to the seller—that is, it cannot be gotten elsewhere. Finally, the message must make believable claims

> **Comparative messages** position a firm versus competitors.

---

[10] Chris Penttila, "Ad It Up," *Entrepreneur* (May 2001), pp. 66–71.

Massed or **distributed promotion** and the **wearout rate** must be carefully planned.

Message timing must also be carefully planned. First, during what times of the year should a firm advertise, seek publicity, add salespeople, or run promotions? In ***massed promotion***, communication efforts are concentrated in peak periods, such as holidays. In ***distributed promotion***, communication efforts are spread throughout the year. Figure 17-7 compares massed and distributed promotion.

Second, the ***wearout rate***—the time it takes for a message to lose effectiveness—must be determined. Some messages wear out quickly; others last for years. Wearout depends on communications frequency, message quality, the number of different messages used, and other factors. Allstate (**http://www.allstate.com**) has done such a good job with its decades-old "You're in good hands" message that it is still popular.

17-5d The Medium

A **medium** is a personal or nonpersonal channel for a message.

The ***medium*** is the personal or nonpersonal means used to send a message. Personal media are company salespeople and other representatives, as well as opinion leaders. Nonpersonal (mass) media include newspapers, television, radio, direct mail, billboards, magazines, and transit.

Personal media offer one-to-one audience contact, are flexible, and can adapt messages to individual needs and handle questions. They appeal to a small audience and are best with a concentrated market. Nonpersonal media have a large audience and low per-customer costs, and are not as flexible and dynamic as one-to-one contacts. They work best with a dispersed target market.

A firm should consider both total and per-unit costs, product complexity, audience attributes, and communication goals in deciding between personal and nonpersonal media. The two kinds of media go well together because nonpersonal media generate consumer interest and personal media help close sales.

17-5e Decoding

In **decoding**, the audience translates the message sent by the source.

Decoding is the process by which a message sent by a source is interpreted by an audience. The interpretation is based on the audience's background, as well as message clarity and complexity. For example, a homemaker and a working woman might have different interpretations of a message on the value of child-care centers. As symbolism and complexity increase, clarity usually decreases. As noted earlier, it is vital that a message be decoded in the manner intended by the source (encoding = decoding): "People have trouble remembering someone's name, let alone a complicated message. Every ad element should support the headline message, whether that message is 'price,' 'selection,' 'quality,' or any other concept. Find a likable style and personality and stay with it for at least a year, to avoid confusing buyers. Be credible. If you say your quality or value is 'best' and it clearly is not, advertising will speed your demise, not increase your business. Identifying and denigrating the competition should also be avoided. It is potentially distracting and may backfire."[11] Is an ad too provocative or merely attention grabbing? Is a serious message buried in the imagery or quite clear to the targeted audience?

Subliminal advertising aims at a consumer's subconscious.

Subliminal advertising is a highly controversial kind of promotion because it does not enable the audience to consciously decode a message. Visual or verbal messages are presented so quickly that they are not consciously seen, heard, or remembered. The assumption is that people will buy products due to subconscious impulses stimulated by the messages. Yet, overwhelming evidence shows that subliminal ads cannot get people to buy items they do not want. And because these ads are often misinterpreted, clearly perceived ads work much better. In the United States, state laws and self-regulation (such as the rules of the National Association of Broadcasters, **http://www.nab.org**) have all but eliminated subliminal ads.

---

[11] Susan Jacksack, "Advertising Ideas on a Small Budget," in *Start, Run & Grow a Successful Small Business—CCH Business Owner's Toolkit Series*, 5th ed. (Riverwoods, IL: CCH Incorporated, 2005).

17-5f   The Audience

An *audience* is the object of a source's message. In marketing, it is generally the target market. However, a source may also want to communicate an idea, build an image, or give information to stockholders, independent media, the public, government officials, and others.

The way a communication channel is used depends on the size and dispersion of the audience, demographic and lifestyle audience traits, and the availability of appropriate media. Because the communication process needs to be keyed to the audience, AIDS prevention organizations have spent a lot of time trying to get their message across to the diverse groups they are targeting. For example:

> The STOP AIDS campaign is a major element in the national Aids prevention strategy being pursued by the Swiss Federal Office of Public Health (SFOPH). It aims to empower people to protect themselves against infection with HIV. The objective of this strategy is to reinforce people's awareness of the risk, to modify their behavior, and to make them protect themselves effectively. In addition, the STOP AIDS campaign promotes solidarity with people affected by HIV and Aids. Information is communicated to the general public through various channels: television and cinema spots, posters, and advertisements; media releases; a Web site; partnership with the Swiss Aids Association and its regional offices; and other partner marketing.[12]

To make matters still tougher for marketers, global consumer surveys have found that many people are rather disapproving of promotion messages. The majority of those questioned believe marketers exaggerate health benefits, do not respect consumers' intelligence, aim too many messages toward children, do not always provide accurate information, and try to make some promotion look like "news."

> The **audience** is usually the target market; but it can also be others.

17-5g   Feedback

Feedback is the response an audience has to a message. It may be a purchase, an attitude change, or a nonpurchase. A firm must realize that all of these responses are possible and devise a way to monitor them.

The most desirable feedback occurs if a consumer buys a good or service (or accepts an idea) after communication with or from a firm. The message is effective enough to stimulate a transaction. A second type of feedback occurs if a firm finds promotion elicits a favorable attitude toward it or its offerings. For new goods or services, positive attitudes must often be formed before purchases (awareness→favorable attitude→purchase). For existing products, people may have bought another brand just before receiving a message or be temporarily out of funds; generating their favorable attitudes may lead to future purchases.

The least desirable feedback is if the audience neither makes a purchase nor develops a favorable attitude. This may happen for one of several reasons: There is no recall of the message. There is contentment with another brand. The message is not believed. No differential advantage is perceived.

> **Feedback** consists of purchase, attitude, or nonpurchase responses to a message.

17-5h   Noise

Noise is interference at any point along a channel of communication. It can cause messages to sometimes be encoded or decoded incorrectly or weak audience responses. Examples are:

- A phone call interrupting a marketing manager while he or she is developing a promotional theme
- A salesperson misidentifying a product and giving incorrect information
- An impatient customer interrupting a sales presentation
- A broken page link at a Web site

> **Noise** may interfere with the communication process at any stage.

[12] "Love Life Stop Aids," http://www.suchtundaids.bag.admin.ch/themen/aids/stopaids/?language=en&schriftgrad (December 9, 2005).

- A conversation between two consumers during a TV commercial
- A direct-mail ad being opened by the wrong person
- A consumer seeing a competitor's item on sale while waiting in line at a checkout counter

17-6 PROMOTION PLANNING

A firm is ready to develop an overall promotion plan once it understands the communication process. Such a plan consists of three parts: objectives, budgeting, and the promotion mix.

17-6a Objectives

Promotion objectives can be divided into two main categories: stimulating demand and enhancing company image.

> The **hierarchy-of-effects model** outlines demand goals.

The **hierarchy-of-effects model** should be used in setting demand goals. It outlines the sequential short-term, intermediate, and long-term promotion goals for a firm to pursue—and works in conjunction with the consumer's decision process we discussed in Chapter 8:

1. *Provide information*—Gain consumer product recognition and then consumer knowledge of product attributes.
2. *Develop positive attitudes and feelings*—Obtain favorable attitudes and then preference for the company's brand(s) over those of competitors.
3. *Stimulate purchases and repeat purchases*—Achieve strong consumer preference toward a good or service and generate purchases; encourage continued purchases (brand loyalty).

> **Primary demand** is for a product category; **selective demand** is for a brand.

By using this approach, a firm can go from informing to persuading and then to reminding consumers about its offerings. When a good or service is little known, **primary demand** should be sought. This is consumer demand for a *product category*. Later, with preference the goal, **selective demand** should be sought. This is consumer demand for a *particular brand*. Sometimes, organizations may try to sustain or revitalize interest in mature products and revert to a primary demand orientation. Thus, the Florida Citrus Growers association (**http://www.floridajuice.com**) sponsors ads to generate primary demand for oranges. On the other hand, sales promotions tend to focus on selective demand.

> **Institutional advertising** is involved with image goals.

With image-related promotion goals, a firm engages in public relations—via suitable advertising, publicity, personal selling, and/or sales promotion (as noted in Table 17-2). **Institutional advertising** is used when the advertising goal is to enhance company image—and not to sell specific goods or services. More than one-half of the leading advertisers in the United States run such ads.

17-6b Budgeting

Five basic methods are used to set a total promotion budget: all-you-can-afford, incremental, competitive parity, percentage-of-sales, and objective-and-task. The choice depends on the individual firm. Budgets often range from 1 to 5 percent of sales for industrial-products firms to up to 20 to 30 percent of sales for consumer-products firms.

> Budgeting methods are **all-you-can-afford, incremental, competitive parity, percentage-of-sales,** and **objective-and-task.**

In the **all-you-can-afford method**, a firm first allots funds for other elements of marketing; any remaining marketing funds then go to the promotion budget. It is the weakest technique and is used most often by small, production-oriented firms. It gives little importance to promotion, spending is not linked to goals, and there is a risk of having no promotion budget if finances are low.

With the **incremental method**, a company bases its new promotion budget on the previous one. A percentage is added to or subtracted from this year's budget to determine next year's. The technique is also used by small firms. It has these advantages: a reference point, a budget based on a firm's feelings about past performance and future trends, and easy calculations. Key disadvantages do exist: budget size is rarely tied to goals, "gut feelings" are overemphasized, and it is hard to evaluate success or failure.

In the ***competitive parity method***, a firm's promotion budget is raised or lowered according to competitors' actions. It is useful to both large and small firms. Benefits are that it is keyed to a reference point, market-oriented, and conservative. Shortcomings are that it is a follower and not a leadership approach, it is difficult to get competitors' promotion data, and there is an assumption of a similarity between the firm and its competitors (as to years in business, goods or services, image, prices, and so on). However, firms usually have basic differences from competitors.

With the ***percentage-of-sales method***, a firm ties its promotion budget to sales revenue. In the first year, a promotion-to-sales ratio is set. During succeeding years, the ratio of promotion to sales dollars is constant. Benefits are the use of sales as a base, the adaptability, and the link of revenues and promotion. However, there is no relation to promotion goals; promotion is a sales follower, not a sales leader; and promotion cuts occur in poor sales periods (when increases could help). The technique yields too large a budget in high sales periods and too small a budget in low sales periods.

Under the ***objective-and-task method***, a firm sets promotion goals, determines the activities needed to satisfy them, and then establishes the proper budget. It is the best method. Advantages are that goals are clearly stated, spending is related to goal-oriented tasks, adaptability is offered, and it is rather easy to evaluate performance. The major weakness is the complexity of setting goals and specific tasks, especially for small firms. Most large companies use some form of objective-and-task technique.

A firm should keep the concept of marginal return in mind during promotional budgeting. The ***marginal return*** is the amount of sales each increment of promotion spending will generate. It tends to be high for a new product because the market is expanding. When a product is established, the marginal return tends to be lower because each additional increment of promotion has less of an impact on sales (due to a saturated target market).

> The **marginal return** refers to the sales generated through incremental promotional spending.

17-6c   The Promotion Mix

After establishing a total promotion budget, a company must determine its ***promotion mix***—the firm's overall and specific communication program, including its involvement with advertising, public relations (publicity), personal selling, and/or sales promotion. Seldom does a firm use just one type of promotion—such as a mail-order firm relying on ads, a hospital on publicity, or a flea-market vendor on selling. A promotion mix is typically used. These Web sites have good online resources regarding the promotion mix: tutor2u (**http://www.tutor2u.net/business/marketing/promotion_mix.asp**) and the Chartered Institute of Marketing (**http://www.cim.co.uk/mediastore/10_minute_ guides/10_min_Promotional_Mix.pdf**).

> A **promotion mix** somehow combines advertising, public relations, personal selling, and/or sales promotion.

Within an integrated marketing communications program, each type of promotion has a distinct function and complements the other types. Ads appeal to big audiences and create awareness; without them, selling is more difficult, time consuming, and costly. Publicity provides credible information to a wide audience, but content and timing cannot be controlled. Selling has one-to-one contact, flexibility, and the ability to close sales; without it, the interest caused by ads might be wasted. Sales promotion spurs short-run sales and supplements ads and selling.

The selection of a promotion mix depends on company attributes, the product life cycle, media access, and channel members. A small firm is limited in the kinds of ads it can afford or use efficiently; it may have to stress personal selling and a few sales promotions. A large firm covering a sizable geographic area could combine many ads, personal selling, and frequent sales promotions. As products move through the life cycle, promotion emphasis goes from information to persuasion to reinforcement; different media and messages are needed at each stage. Some media may not be accessible (no cigarette ads on TV) or require lengthy lead time (Yellow Pages). Channel members may demand special promotions, sales support, and/or cooperative advertising allowances.

Figure 17-8

Contrasting Promotion Mixes

Advertising Dominates When		Personal Selling Dominates When
• The market is large and dispersed, and final consumers are involved.	**Consumers**	• The market is small and concentrated and organizational consumers are involved.
• The budget is large enough to cover regular promotion in mass media.	**Budget**	• The budget is limited or tailored to the needs of specific customers.
• Products are simple and inexpensive, and differential advantages are clear.	**Products**	• Products are complex and expensive, and differential advantages are not obvious.
• Competitors stress it in their promotion mixes.	**Competition**	• Competitors stress it in their promotion mixes.
• A wide range of media are available.	**Media**	• Media are unavailable or inefficient.
• Customers are satisfied with self-service in stores or shop through the mail or the Internet.	**Place of Purchase**	• Customers expect sales assistance and service in stores.

It is the job of a firm's marketing director (or vice-president) to set up a promotion budget and a promotion mix, as well as to allocate resources to each aspect of promotion. In large firms, there may be separate managers for advertising, public relations, personal selling, and sales promotion. They report to, and have their efforts coordinated by, the marketing director.

Figure 17-8 contrasts promotion mixes in which advertising and personal selling would dominate.

Ethical Issues in Marketing

A Failure to Communicate Honestly: Fatal Errors in the Job Search

"Your resumé and its partner, the cover letter, can be either your ticket to an interview or to the recycling bin," stated a vice-president of human resources for CareerBuilder.com (http://www.careerbuilder.com). A recent CareerBuilder.com survey of over 650 hiring managers found that failing to spell-check a resumé, plagiarizing a job posting, and sending multiple employers the same resumé or cover letter are the top ways to get a rejection letter.

Forty-nine percent of hiring managers stated that they would automatically dismiss a resumé or cover letter with spelling or grammatical errors. Forty-eight percent of the hiring managers stated that they would automatically dismiss a resumé or cover letter that has not been customized. Such letters typically start with "Dear Human Resources Department." And 44 percent of the hiring managers said they would automatically pass on a resumé or cover letter that appears to include cut and paste sections of its job posting in the resumé or cover letter. The managers feel that this action questions the professionalism, honesty, and originality of the job applicant.

In contrast, resumés that are concise, demonstrate excitement about a job, and show how a candidate can contribute to a firm's success are more prone to get placed in the "yes" category. Some tips to getting acceptance include stressing team-building and leadership qualities, carefully researching each company, and having at least three people review your resumé and cover letter.

Source: Based on material in "CareerBuilder.com Survey Reveals Top Three Fatal Resumé and Cover Letter Mistakes—and How to Fix Them," *PR Newswire Association* (July 6, 2005).

17-7 GLOBAL PROMOTION CONSIDERATIONS

While preparing a promotion strategy for foreign nations, the channel of communication, promotion goals, budgeting, and the promotion mix should be carefully reviewed as they pertain to each market.

With regard to the channel of communication, a firm should recognize that:

> International promotion decisions should not be made until each market is carefully studied.

- Source recognition and credibility vary by nation or region. As celebrities, golfers such as Annika Sorenstam have high recognition rates around the world. On the other hand, baseball celebrities such as Derek Jeter are mostly popular in the United States.
- Encoding messages can be quite challenging, particularly if the messages must be translated into another language.
- Because the effects of message symbolism depend on the nation or region, care must be taken if fear-related, humorous, and/or sexual messages are used. Themes have to correspond to local customs. French print ads are more apt to have emotional, humorous, and sexual themes than U.S. ones.
- In some locales, few residents have TVs, there are a limited number of newspapers and magazines, and programs (channels) limit or do not accept ads.
- Ensuring that messages are decoded properly can be demanding: Some advertising "can travel across any borders. The categories are simple and obvious: hi-tech products (computers, mobile phones), hi-touch products (beauty, fashion), functional offers (promotions, features), and brands that exploit national heritage (airlines and national icons, for example)." However, "Would you normally try to communicate the same message in the same way to different groups of people who don't speak the same language, don't believe in the same values, don't share cultural or religious roots, don't share the same sense of humor or emotion—and who don't want to be spoken to in the same way?"[13]
- Making assumptions about audience traits in foreign markets without adequate research may lead to wrong assumptions, such as this one: "The Chinese market has huge income divergences between first- and second-tier cities. Let alone the third- and fourth-tier cities and rural areas. The difference exists not only in different areas, but also among different population sectors within a city. These distinctions substantiate one conclusion: do not treat China as one market. Marketing targeted at all consumers is usually short-lived; promotion aimed at particular groups can often break through."[14]
- Global techniques for measuring promotion effectiveness are emerging, particularly on the Web.

In terms of promotion goals, budgeting, and the promotion mix, these points should be considered:

- For nations where a firm and its brands are unknown, there must be a series of promotion goals as people are taken through the hierarchy-of-effects model. For nations in which a product category is new, primary demand must be created before selective demand is gained. To show goodwill, image ads may be even more important in foreign than in domestic markets.
- The promotion budgets in foreign countries must be keyed to the size of the markets and the activities required to succeed there. The objective-and-task method is highly recommended in setting international promotion budgets.
- Due to cultural, socioeconomic, infrastructure, and other differences, promotion mixes must be consistent with the nations served. In Western Europe, Germans listen to the most radio; the Dutch and British watch the most TV.

---

[13] Chris Jaques and David Guerrero, "Do 'Regional' Concepts Exist?" *Media Asia* (June 17, 2005), p. 6.

[14] Miranda Li, "Brand Planning in China," *Brand Strategy* (November 2002), p. 12.

Several Web sites, such as Advertising World International (**http://advertising.utexas.edu/world/index.asp?pageid=International**) and International Advertising Resource Center (**http://www.bgsu.edu/departments/tcom/faculty/ha/intlad1.html**) can help marketers better understand global promotion.

17-8 THE LEGAL ENVIRONMENT OF PROMOTION

Full disclosure, substantiation, cease-and-desist orders, corrective advertising, and fines are major governmental limits on promotion activities.

In the United States and other nations around the globe, federal, state, and local governmental bodies have laws and rules regarding promotion practices. These regulations range from banning billboards in some locales to requiring celebrity endorsers to use products if they say they do. The U.S. agencies most involved with promotion are the Federal Trade Commission (**http://www.ftc.gov**) and the Federal Communications Commission (**http://www.fcc.gov**). Table 17-3 shows selected U.S. regulations.

Five major enforcement tools are used to protect consumers and competing firms from undesirable practices: full disclosure, substantiation, cease-and-desist orders, corrective advertising, and fines.

Full disclosure requires that all data necessary for a consumer to make a safe and informed decision be provided in a promotion message. That is why prescription drugs must indicate possible side effects, and diet products must note how many calories they contain. In this way, consumers can assess the overall benefits and risks of a purchase. Promotion is considered to be deceptive only if claims mislead a "reasonable" person and lead to "injury" (physical, financial, or other). In 2005, the FTC fined Experian North America, a credit-reporting firm, $950,000 and ordered that it repay customers because of an adverting campaign "that promised free credit reports to millions of people." The FTC "alleged that although Consumerinfo.com promised a free credit report, it automatically signed up customers for a credit monitoring service that cost $79.95 a year if they didn't cancel within 30 days. According to the FTC's court complaint, the notice of the yearly fee was in small print buried in the privacy policy notice on the second page of the order form."[15]

Substantiation requires a firm to be able to prove all the claims it makes in promotion messages. This means thorough testing and evidence of performance are needed before making claims. If a tire maker says a brand will last for 70,000 miles, it must be able to verify this with test results. Recently, under a consent decree approved by the FTC, "NBTY, Inc. (NBTY, formerly Nature's Bounty, Inc.), a leading manufacturer and distributor of dietary supplements in the United States and abroad, agreed to pay a $2 million civil penalty to settle charges that it violated the terms of a prior FTC order by making false and misleading health claims about two of its products. The FTC charged that the defendant made unsubstantiated promises that its products would cause consumers to lose weight or cure a variety of health problems."[16]

Under a *cease-and-desist order*, a firm must stop a promotion practice that is deemed deceptive and modify a message accordingly. The firm is often not forced to admit guilt or pay fines, as long as it obeys an order to stop running a particular message. In a 2005 settlement with the FTC, Columbia House (a direct marketer of home entertainment products) agreed to "stop calling any consumer who had previously asked not to be called." Columbia House also agreed not to call "any consumer whose number is registered on the National Do Not Call Registry, unless the company has received a request, in writing, from the consumer permitting future calls; or the company has an established business relationship with the consumer and the consumer has not previously requested to be removed from the company's call list."[17]

---

[15] Michael Fielding, "Law, Regulation & Economy," *Marketing News* (September 15, 2005), p. 4.

[16] "NBTY, Inc. to Pay $2 Million Penalty for Alleged Violations of FTC Order," *State News Service Online* (October 12, 2005).

[17] "Columbia House Settles FTC Charges of Do Not Call Violations," *U.S. Fed News Online* (July 15, 2005).

Table 17-3 Selected U.S. Regulations Affecting Promotion

Factor	Legal Environment
Access to media	Cigarettes and liquor have restricted access. Legal, medical, and other professions have been given the right to advertise.
Deception	It is illegal to use messages that would mislead reasonable consumers and potentially harm them.
Bait-and-switch	It is illegal to lure a customer with an ad for a low-priced item and then, once the customer talks to a salesperson, to use a strong sales pitch intended to switch the shopper to a more expensive item.
Door-to-door selling	Many locales restrict door-to-door sales practices. A cooling-off period allows a person to cancel an in-home sale up to three days after an agreement is reached.
Promotional allowances	Such allowances must be available to channel members in a fair and equitable manner.
Comparative advertisements	Claims must be substantiated. The Federal Trade Commission favors naming competitors in ads (not citing a competitor as brand X).
Testimonials or endorsements	A celebrity or expert endorser must actually use a product if he or she makes such a claim.

Corrective advertising requires a firm to run new ads to correct the false impressions left by previous ones. Although this enforcement tool is not used very often, it has been applied effectively. A few years ago, "the Food and Drug Administration ordered Bristol-Myers Squibb [http://www.bms.com] to pull a print advertising campaign for the anti-cholesterol drug Pravachol that makes what the agency called false claims. 'We asked them to immediately stop running the misleading ads and immediately start running corrections for the false perceptions left by their original promotions,' the FDA Commissioner stated. The FDA asked Bristol-Myers Squibb to respond with a plan of action on two points: the cessation of the ads and promotional materials; and 'prompt

Global Marketing in Action

Cadbury's Dairy Milk: Sending Inconsistent Messages

According to one view, there are two types of brand management: intentional branding and holistic branding. Intentional branding is based on a marketer's use of integrated marketing communications, while holistic branding considers all interactions that consumers have with a brand. Unfortunately, too often, a firm's shortsighted use of intentional branding comes at the expense of holistic branding.

Cadbury (http://www.cadbury.co.uk), a British-based confectionery and beverage manufacturer, recently employed a $24 million advertising campaign that focused on the theme "You dream it, we make it" to stress its chocolate bar's richness. At the same time, Cadbury ran a "buy-one-get-one free" (BOGOF) promotion for its Dairy Milk brand of chocolate at a leading British general merchandise retailer.

The two campaigns had opposite—and somewhat conflicting—goals. While the image-based campaign stressed Cadbury's richness, the BOGOF promotion totally focused on price and value. The BOGOF promotion also had other potential other problems for Cadbury, such as the sales of Dairy Milk declining significantly after the promotion ended. Consumers stocking up on Dairy Milk during the BOGOF promotion would not need to buy additional candy for weeks or even months. In addition, the BOGOF promotion could get other retailers angry with Cadbury as its Dairy Milk products appeared to be drastically overpriced at those stores.

Source: Based on material in Mark Ritson, "Cadbury's Decision to BOGOF Is a Strategic Error," *Marketing* (May 25, 2005), p. 24.

dissemination of accurate and complete information to the audiences that received the misleading messages.' "[18]

The last major remedy is fines, which are dollar penalties for deceptive promotion that are paid to the government or consumers. A short time ago, the FTC and KB Home (the home-building giant) settled a complaint in which the firm was charged with violating a prior agreement regarding its home repair warranties. The firm was required to pay a $2 million civil fine. The new agreement "also bars KB Home from violating the terms of the original order in the future, and requires the company to modify existing home repair warranties to comply with the consent order and extend for one year certain homeowners' two-year warranty coverage for major home components."[19]

Besides government rules, the media have their own voluntary standards for promotion practices. The National Association of Broadcasters (**http://www.nab.org**) monitors TV and radio ads. General industry groups, such as the Better Business Bureau (**http://www.bbb.org**), the American Association of Advertising Agencies (**http://www.aaaa.org**), and the International Advertising Association (**http://www. iaaglobal.org**), also participate in the self-regulation of promotion.

17-9 | CRITICISMS AND DEFENSES OF PROMOTION

> Promotion controversies center on materialism, honesty, prices, symbolism, and consumer expectations.

For many years, industry trade groups have campaigned to improve the overall image of promotion. This is illustrated in Figure 17-9. As the International Advertising Association notes at its Web site: "The IAA works for the freedom of companies to compete through responsible commercial speech, and it fights for consumer choice made possible by commercial speech which informs, inspires, and empowers individuals to raise their sights and reach for the life they want."[20]

Nonetheless, promotion is the most heavily criticized area of marketing. Here are a number of criticisms and the defenses of marketers to them:

Detractors Feel That Promotion	Marketing Professionals Answer That Promotion
Creates an obsession with material possessions.	Responds to consumer desires for material possessions. In affluent societies, these items are plentiful and bought with discretionary income.
Is basically dishonest.	Is basically honest. The great majority of firms abide by all laws and set strict self-regulations. A few dishonest firms give a bad name to all.
Raises the prices of goods and services.	Holds down prices. By increasing consumer demand, promotion enables firms to use mass production and mass distribution and reduce per-unit costs. Employment is higher if demand is stimulated.
Overemphasizes symbolism and status.	Differentiates goods and services by symbolic and status appeals. Consumers desire distinctiveness and product benefits.
Causes excessively high expectations.	Keeps expectations high; it thereby sustains consumer motivation and worker productivity so expectations can be satisfied.

---

[18] Rich Thomaselli and Ira Teinowitz, "FDA Yanks 'Misleading' Pravachol Ads," *Advertising Age* (August 11, 2003), p. 1.

[19] "KB Home to Pay $2 Million Penalty for Alleged Violations of FTC Order," *FTC Press Release* (August 3, 2005).

[20] "About the IAA," **http://www.iaaglobal.org** (May 14, 2006).

We admit it. Advertising has a tremendous impact on prices. But you may be surprised by what *kind* of impact.

In addition to being informative, educational and sometimes entertaining, advertising can actually lower prices.

It works like this: Advertising spurs competition which holds down prices. And since advertising also creates a mass market for products, it can bring down the cost of producing each product, a savings that can be passed on to consumers.

Moreover, competition created by advertising provides an incentive for manufacturers to produce new and better products.

Which means advertising can not only reduce prices, but it can also help you avoid lemons.

ADVERTISING
ANOTHER WORD FOR FREEDOM OF CHOICE.
American Association of Advertising Agencies

Figure 17-9

A Strong Defense of Promotion by the American Association of Advertising Agencies

Sources: Reprinted by permission.

Some people would have you believe that you are putty in the hands of every advertiser in the country.

They think that when advertising is put under your nose, your mind turns to oatmeal.

It's mass hypnosis. Subliminal seduction. Brain washing. Mind control. It's advertising.

And you are a pushover for it.

It explains why your kitchen cupboard is full of food you never eat.

Why your garage is full of cars you never drive.

Why your house is full of books you don't read, TV's you don't watch, beds you don't use, and clothes you don't wear.

You don't have a choice. You are forced to buy.

That's why this message is a cleverly disguised advertisement to get you to buy land in the tropics.

Got you again, didn't we? Send in your money.

ADVERTISING
ANOTHER WORD FOR FREEDOM OF CHOICE.
American Association of Advertising Agencies

Web Sites You Can Use

Many specialized service firms work with clients to devise and enact integrated marketing communications strategies. These service firms help their clients establish goals, coordinate promotion efforts, and devise the best mix of promotion tools. The following integrated marketing communications service firms have attractive Web sites that highlight their capabilities and successes:

- Carbonhouse (**http://www.carbonhouse.com**)
- Godbe Communications (**http://www.godbe.com**)

- Hale! Marketing (**http://www.haleinc.com**)
- Harpell (**http://www.harpell.com**)
- Pacifico (**http://www.pacifico.com**)
- Phelps (**http://www.thephelpsgroup.com/our_work.asp**)
- SGW Integrated Marketing Communications (**http://www.sgw.com**)
- TMP Worldwide (**http://www.integrated.tmp.com**)
- Wallrich Landi (**http://www.wallrichlandi.com**)

Summary

1. *To define promotion planning, show its importance, and demonstrate the value of integrated marketing communications*   Promotion involves any communication that informs, persuades, and/or reminds people about an organization's or individual's goods, services, image, ideas, community involvement, or impact on society. Promotion planning systematically relates to all communication.

   Promotion efforts are needed for both new and existing products. The audience may be consumers, stockholders, consumer advocacy groups, government, channel members, employees, competitors, and the public. Through word of mouth, people express opinions and product-related experiences to one another. A firm may communicate its image, views on ideas, community involvement, or impact on society—as well as persuade people to buy. Good promotion enhances the other elements of the marketing mix. Promotion is a major activity around the world.

   With well-coordinated promotion plans, a firm applies integrated marketing communications. This means the strategic roles of a variety of communication disciplines are evaluated and combined for clarity, consistency, and maximum communication impact. A proper plan is synergistic. It has tactical consistency and fosters interactivity with consumers. Every company message positively influences the target audience. The company's basic promotion themes and differential advantages are clearly understood by all employees who interface with the targeted audience. Promotion personnel cooperate with one another. Data bases are maintained.

2. *To describe the general characteristics of advertising, public relations, personal selling, and sales promotion*   Advertising is paid, nonpersonal communication transmitted through various media by identified sponsors. Public relations includes any communication (paid or nonpaid, nonpersonal or personal, sponsored by a firm or reported by an independent medium) designed to foster a favorable image. Publicity is the nonpaid, nonpersonal,

nonsponsored form of public relations. Personal selling involves oral communication with one or more prospective buyers by paid representatives for the purpose of making sales. Sales promotion involves paid marketing activities to stimulate consumer purchases and dealers.

3. *To explain the channel of communication and how it functions*   A source sends a message to its audience via a channel of communication. A channel consists of a source, encoding, the message, the medium, decoding, the audience, feedback, and noise.

   A source is a company, an independent institution, or an opinion leader that seeks to present a message to an audience. Encoding is the way in which a thought or an idea is translated into a message by the source. A message is a combination of words and symbols transmitted to the audience. A medium is a personal or nonpersonal channel used to convey a message. Decoding is the way in which a message sent by a source is translated by the audience. The audience is the object of a source's message. Feedback is the response the audience makes to a message: purchase, attitude change, or nonpurchase. Noise is interference at any stage.

4. *To examine the components of a promotion plan*   Goals may be demand- or image-oriented. Demand goals should correspond to the hierarchy-of-effects model, moving a consumer from awareness to purchase. Primary demand is total demand for a product category; selective demand refers to interest in a particular brand. Institutional advertising is used to enhance company image.

   Five ways to set a promotion budget are all-you-can-afford (the weakest method), incremental, competitive parity, percentage-of-sales, and objective-and-task (the best method). Marginal return should be considered when budgeting.

   A promotion mix is the overall and specific communication program of a firm, including its use of advertising, public relations (publicity), personal selling, and/or sales promotion. Many factors need to be considered in developing a promotion mix.

5. *To discuss global promotion considerations, the legal environment, and criticisms and defenses of promotion* In devising an international promotion plan, the channel of communication, promotion goals, budgeting, and promotion mix should be studied for and applied to each market.

Many laws and rules affect promotion. The major ways to guard against undesirable promotion are full disclosure, substantiation, cease-and-desist orders, corrective ads, and fines. Critics are strong in their complaints about promotions. Marketers are equally firm in their defenses.

Key Terms

promotion (p. 521)

promotion planning (p. 521)

word-of-mouth communication (p. 521)

integrated marketing communications (IMC) (p. 522)

advertising (p. 524)

public relations (p. 524)

publicitiy (p. 524)

personal selling (p. 525)

sales promotion (p. 525)

channel of communication (communication process) (p. 527)

source (p. 527)

encoding (p. 528)

message (p. 529)

comparative messages (p. 531)

massed promotion (p. 532)

distributed promotion (p. 532)

wearout rate (p. 532)

medium (p. 532)

decoding (p. 532)

subliminal advertising (p. 532)

audience (p. 533)

feedback (p. 533)

noise (p. 533)

hierarchy-of-effects model (p. 534)

primary demand (p. 534)

selective demand (p. 534)

institutional advertising (p. 534)

all-you-can-afford method (p. 534)

incremental method (p. 534)

competitive parity method (p. 535)

percentage-of-sales method (p. 535)

objective-and-task method (p. 535)

marginal return (p. 535)

promotion mix (p. 535)

full disclosure (p. 538)

substantiation (p. 538)

ceasc-and-desist order (p. 538)

corrective advertising (p. 539)

Review Questions

- Why is integrated marketing communications so important?
- Distinguish among advertising, public relations, personal selling, and sales promotion.
- What is a one-sided message? Why do most companies use such messages?
- What should be the relationship between encoding and decoding messages? Why?

- A consumer listens to a sales presentation but does not make a purchase. Has the presentation failed? Explain your answer.
- Explain the hierarchy-of-effects model. How is it related to demand objectives?
- Describe each of the methods of promotional budgeting.
- When should personal selling dominate the promotion mix?

Discussion Questions

1. What are the advantages and disadvantages of changing messages (themes) infrequently?
2. Present a promotion campaign to decrease underage attendance at R-rated movies.
3. As the marketing manager for a small U.S.-based apparel firm that is entering the African market for the first time, devise a promotion budget relying on the objective-and-task method.

4. Develop a promotion mix for:
   a. A global television network.
   b. A stationery store chain.
   c. A four-person medical practice.
   d. A small business software firm.

Web Exercise

Palo Alto Software markets Advertising Plan Pro software to help firms develop integrated marketing communications strategies. Visit the case study section of the Advertising Plan Pro Web site (http://www.paloalto.com/ps/ap/casestudy.cfm) and describe what you learn from looking at the case cited there.

Practice Quiz

1. People express opinions and product-related experiences to one another through
    a. public relations.
    b. verbal media.
    c. marketer-dominated communication.
    d. word-of-mouth communication.

2. An integrated marketing communications plan is based upon which fundamental premise?
    a. Low overall costs
    b. Extensive use of public relations
    c. A well-coordinated promotion plan
    d. An ethical framework

3. Consumers Union and a local newspaper restaurant critic are examples of
    a. opinion leaders.
    b. independent institutions.
    c. representative consumers.
    d. company spokespersons.

4. A firm wanting to stress its product prestige would *not* emphasize
    a. exclusive ownership.
    b. special features.
    c. status.
    d. availability in discount stores.

5. Which promotional concept most closely resembles depreciation?
    a. Decoding
    b. Wearout rate
    c. Lead time
    d. Clutter

6. Which of the following statements about subliminal advertising is false?
    a. It is often misinterpreted.
    b. It does not enable a consumer to consciously decode a message.
    c. Its use has been all but eliminated through self-regulation by advertising associations.
    d. It is effective in getting consumers to buy products they do not want.

7. Which of these statements on consumer attitudes toward promotion is correct?
    a. The majority believe ads do not exaggerate health claims.
    b. The majority believe marketers respect consumers' intelligence.
    c. The majority believe marketers target children too much.
    d. The majority believe marketers give accurate information.

8. Which of the following is *not* an objective found in the hierarchy-of-effects model?
    a. Informing consumers
    b. Persuading consumers
    c. Generating profits
    d. Reminding consumers

9. Which of these is the weakest method for setting a total promotion budget?
    a. All-you-can-afford technique
    b. Incremental technique
    c. Competitive parity technique
    d. Percentage-of-sales technique

10. Which of the following is *not* a benefit of the competitive parity method?
    a. It is market-oriented.
    b. It is useful to both large and small firms.
    c. It is keyed to a reference point.
    d. It recognizes that there are differences between the firm and its competitors.

11. Which of these is the best method for setting a total promotion budget?
    a. Percentage-of-sales
    b. Objective-and-task
    c. Incremental
    d. Competitive parity

12. Which statement about the types of promotion is true?
    a. Sales promotion stimulates long-run sales.
    b. Selling can best be used to reach large audiences with a uniform message.
    c. Without selling, initial interest caused by ads might be wasted.
    d. Advertising can best be used to close sales.

13. A firm must be able to prove its promotional claims under which promotional enforcement rule?
    a. A cease-and-desist order
    b. Substantiation
    c. Corrective advertising
    d. Full disclosure

14. An example of corrective advertising is
    a. Lewis Galoob Toys' agreement not to promote its products as doing things of which they were incapable.
    b. Alka-Seltzer's mentioning that it is an antacid.
    c. Pfizer's payment of a large sum to a number of states.
    d. Listerine's disclaimer that it is not a cold remedy.

15. Which of the following is *not* a common criticism of promotion?
    a. It is basically dishonest.
    b. It underemphasizes symbolism and status.
    c. It creates an obsession with material possessions.
    d. It causes excessively high expectations.

For the answers to these questions, please visit the online site for this book at **http://www.atomicdog.com.**

Chapter 18

Advertising and Public Relations

A "textbook example" of a successful celebrity-based promotion campaign is George Foreman's endorsement of Salton (http://www.salton.com) grilling machines bearing his name. Well over 40 million George Foreman Lean, Mean, Fat-Reducing Grilling Machines have been sold since the mid-1990s. For his part in the firm's success, George Foreman has received an estimated $150 million, more money than he earned in his entire boxing career.

George Foreman, in many ways, was an odd pick for a sports celebrity endorser. Although he earned an Olympic gold metal in 1968 and beat Joe Frazier for the heavy-weight boxing title in 1973, he was not well liked by the public. The turning point for him occurred in 1994, when the 45-year-old Foreman knocked out 26-year-old Michael Moorer and regained his heavyweight title. Foreman's success in the ring, coupled with a new, friendly ("cuddly") persona, made Foreman a highly sought-after endorser.

Under the initial arrangement negotiated with Salton, Foreman would receive 45 percent of the profits on the grill, and Salton would get 40 percent. The balance was to be divided up between a marketing expert and an attorney. Foreman received nothing up front.

In March 1995, five days after the contract was signed, the Gourmet Housewares Show (http://www.thegourmetshow.com) took place in Las Vegas. There, Foreman clearly showed his upbeat personality. Whenever he showed up at the trade show, he was so popular that security personnel had to surround him. Still, the grill did not sell well.

Almost a year later, Foreman went on QVC to sell the grills, and sales took off so rapidly that every available QVC employee was summoned to handle the phone orders. The "magic moment" occurred when the TV audience saw Foreman grab a hamburger from the grill and start eating it. According to Salton's chief executive officer at the time, Leon Dreimann, "It was so spontaneous. It was a real reaction. People saw that he eats what he sells." In 1999, Salton agreed to pay Foreman and his partners $137.5 million over five years for the right to use Foreman's name in perpetuity for cooking appliances.[1]

In this chapter, we will study both the advertising and public relations aspects of promotion, including the use of creative strategies in developing advertisements and the role of advertising agencies.

Chapter Objectives

1. To examine the scope, importance, and characteristics of advertising
2. To study the elements in an advertising plan
3. To examine the scope, importance, and characteristics of public relations
4. To study the elements in a public relations plan

18-1 OVERVIEW

Advertising and public relations are two major forms of promotion.

This chapter covers advertising and public relations. As we defined in Chapter 17, *advertising* is paid, nonpersonal communication regarding goods, services, organizations, people, places, and ideas; it may be used by businesses, government and other nonprofit organizations, and individuals. Its distinguishing features are that a sponsor pays for its message, a set format is sent to an entire audience via mass media, the sponsor's name is clearly presented, and the sponsor controls the message.

---

[1] Various company and other sources.

In contrast, *public relations* involves communication that fosters a favorable image for goods, services, organizations, people, places, and ideas among their various publics. Its unique features are that it is more image- than sales-oriented; it embodies image-oriented advertising, personal selling, and sales promotion; and it often seeks to generate favorable publicity for a firm. As an aspect of public relations, publicity entails nonpersonal communication that is transmitted via mass media but not paid for by an identified sponsor. The media usually control the wording and placement of publicity messages.

The distinctions between advertising and publicity are in part revealed by this statement: "Advertising is paid for, publicity is prayed for." We examine the scope and importance, characteristics, and planning considerations for both advertising and public relations in Chapter 18. InfoTech Marketing has an excellent Web site with resources related to advertising (**http://www.smsource.com/advertis.htm**) and public relations (**http://www.smsource.com/publicrelations.htm**).

18-2 THE SCOPE AND IMPORTANCE OF ADVERTISING

In 2007, more than $550 billion is expected to be spent on advertising globally—one-half in the United States (including direct mail) and the rest elsewhere.[2] Table 18-1 shows global spending by medium, as well as media spending in the United States. Globally, the leading three media account for 80 percent of advertising expenditures. For the United States, the leading three media account for 63 percent of advertising expenditures, due to the level of U.S. media choice. Direct mail is a key U.S. medium; and globally, Internet advertising has gone from virtually zero a decade ago to become a growing presence.

Table **18-1** Global Advertising Expenditures—2007 Projections					
Global Advertising[a]				**U.S. Advertising**	
Region	**Percent of Total Global Ad Expenditures**	**Media**	**Percent of Total Global Ad Expenditures**	**Media**	**Percent of Total U.S. Ad Expenditures**
North America	44.1	Television	37.8	Television	25.9
Europe	24.6	Newspapers	29.3	Direct mail	19.8
Asia/Pacific	20.8	Magazines	13.2	Newspapers	17.7
Latin America	4.5	Radio	8.3	Radio	7.4
Africa/Middle East	6.0	Outdoor	5.4	Yellow Pages	5.3
Total	100.0	Internet	4.4	Magazines	4.7
		Cinema	0.4	Internet	4.5
		Miscellaneous	1.2	Outdoor	2.2
		Total	100.0	Miscellaneous	12.5
				Total	100.0

[a] Includes only the major media shown in the table. A lot of direct-mail advertising is done in the United States, which is not reflected in the table.

Sources: Compiled and estimated by the authors from data reported in "Demand for Traditional Advertising Firm; Internet Up Again," *Zenith Optimedia Press Release* (July 20, 2005); and Jim Conaghan, "Pieces of the Puzzle," **http://www.naa.org/presstime** (September 2005).

[2] Authors' estimate based on a compilation of sources.

The vast majority of U.S. firms spend less than 5 percent of sales on advertising. Ads are most important for standardized products aimed at large markets.

Advertising as a percent of sales varies by industry and firm, and company advertising as a percent of sales is low. During 2005, expenditures were less than 2.5 percent of sales in 57 percent of U.S. industries; 2.5 to 4.9 percent of sales in 25 percent of U.S. industries; and at least 5.0 percent of sales in 18 percent of U.S. industries.[3] Among the leading advertisers, such as Procter & Gamble, the percentages often far exceed industry averages. Table 18-2 shows ad expenditures by selected industry category, and Table 18-3 indicates the highest-spending advertisers in the world.

An advertising emphasis is most likely if products are standardized, have easily communicated features, appeal to a large market, have competitive prices, are marketed via independent resellers, and/or are new. Leading brands often get large ad budgets to hold their positions. At Charles Schwab (**http://www.schwab.com**), the discount stockbroker, ads stress two themes: quality service and competitive prices. It has an in-house ad agency and runs ads on traditional and cable TV, as well as the Internet. By advertising, it has raised awareness and introduced new products.

Consider this: "No, it's not your imagination. The amount of advertising and marketing we are exposed to daily has exploded over the past decade. At the gas pumps, in the movie theater, in a washroom stall, during sporting events—advertising is impossible to avoid. Cars, bicycles, taxis, and buses have become moving commercials. Ads appear on store floors, at gas pumps, on elevator walls, park benches, telephones, fruit, and even pressed into the sand on beaches."[4]

Table 18-2 Advertising in Selected U.S. Industries, 2005

Industry	Advertising as Percent of Sales	Industry	Advertising as Percent of Sales
Food products	11.9	Footwear	4.3
Dolls and stuffed toys	10.9	Household furniture	3.9
Soaps and detergents	10.0	Eating places	2.9
Watches and clocks	9.8	Cable TV services	2.3
Cutlery, hand tools, general hardware	9.1	Household appliances	1.6
Perfume and cosmetics	7.9	Management consulting services	1.5
Books	7.3	Motion picture theaters	1.3
Sugar and confectionary products	5.9	Computer and office equipment	1.2
Jewelry stores	4.9	Auto dealers	1.0
Department stores	4.4	Accident and health insurance	0.4

Source: Derived from "Schonfeld Predicts Continued Ad Spending Increases in 2006," *Schonfeld & Associates Press Release* (June 15, 2005)

[3] Computed by the authors from "Schonfeld Predicts Continued Ad Spending Increases in 2006," *Schonfeld & Associates Press Release* (June 15, 2005).

[4] "Advertising: It's Everywhere," **http://www.media-awareness.ca** (December 9, 2005).

Table **18-3** The Leading 25 Advertisers in the World	
U.S.-Based Firms	**Firms Based Outside the United States**
Procter & Gamble	Unilever (Great Britain/Netherlands)
General Motors	Toyota (Japan)
Ford	DaimlerChrysler (Germany)
Time Warner	L'Oreal (France)
Walt Disney	Nestlé (Switzerland)
Johnson & Johnson	Sony (Japan)
Altria Group (formerly Philip Morris)	Nissan (Japan)
PepsiCo	Honda (Japan)
Pfizer	Volkswagen (Germany)
McDonald's	GlaxoSmithKline (Great Britain)
Coca-Cola	Reckitt Benckiser (Great Britain)
General Electric	Danone (France)
News Corp.	

Source: Table developed by the authors based on worldwide measured media spending data in *Advertising Age 2005 Fact Pack*, p. 29.

These general observations can be made as to the usefulness of advertising:

- When there are low-involvement purchases, consumer behavior may be easier to change than attitudes.
- One ad can have a strong effect on brand awareness.
- By advertising, it is easier to raise people's opinions on a little-known item than a well-known one.
- Effectiveness often rises with long-term campaigns.

18-3 THE CHARACTERISTICS OF ADVERTISING

On the positive side, advertising reaches a large, geographically dispersed market; and, for print media, circulation is supplemented by the passing of a copy from one reader to another. Costs per viewer or listener are low. A single TV ad may cost $360,000 to air and reach 30 million people—a cost of $0.012 per person (for media time). A broad range of media is available: from national (global) TV to local newspapers. Thus, a firm's goals and resources may be matched with the most appropriate medium.

A sponsor can control message content, graphics, timing, and size or length, as well as the audience targeted. A uniform message is sent to the whole audience. With print media, people can study and restudy messages. Editorial content (a news story or segment of a broadcast show) often borders an ad. This can raise readership or viewing/listening, enhance an image, and create the proper mood. A firm may even seek specialized media or sections of media (such as a sports section for a men's clothing ad).

Ads ease the way for personal selling by creating audience awareness and liking for brands. They also enable self-service wholesalers and retailers to operate, and they sustain an industry—mail order. With a pulling strategy, advertising enables a firm to show its resellers that consumer demand exists.

On the negative side, because messages are standardized, they are rather inflexible and not responsive to questions. This makes it hard to satisfy the needs of a diverse

> Advertising attracts an audience, has low per-customer costs, offers varied media, is surrounded by information, and aids selling.

> Advertising is inflexible and can be wasteful, costly, and limit information and feedback.

audience. And because many media appeal to broad audiences, a large portion of viewers or readers may be wasted for a sponsor. A single-unit health spa might find that only one-fifth of a newspaper's readers live in its shopping area.

Advertising sometimes requires high total expenditures, although costs per viewer or reader are low. This may keep smaller firms from using some media. In the example earlier in this section, it was said that a TV ad might cost only $0.012 per viewer. Yet, media time alone for that ad would be $360,000—for one ad, placed once. Also, because high costs lead to brief messages, most ads do not provide much information. TV commercials are short, mostly 15 or 30 seconds; few are as long as one minute. Further, because ads are impersonal, feedback is harder to get and it may not be immediately available.

Mass media are used by many people who do not view or listen to ads. It is estimated that the typical American is exposed to 3,000 to 5,000 advertising messages per day![5] Of added concern to television advertisers is "zapping," whereby a viewer uses a remote-control device to switch programs when an ad comes on. A newer phenomenon, known as the "TiVo (**http://www.tivo.com**) factor," enables consumers to use their personal and digital video recorders (PVRs and DVRs) to skip ads. PVR and DVR owners skip commercials most of the time. As one analyst noted, "In a DVR world, people aren't going to stand around and watch what's irrelevant to them. If they're not buying a car, they're not as tuned in."[6]

18-4 DEVELOPING AN ADVERTISING PLAN

An advertising plan consists of the nine steps shown in Figure 18-1. These steps are now highlighted.

Figure 18-1

Developing an Advertising Plan

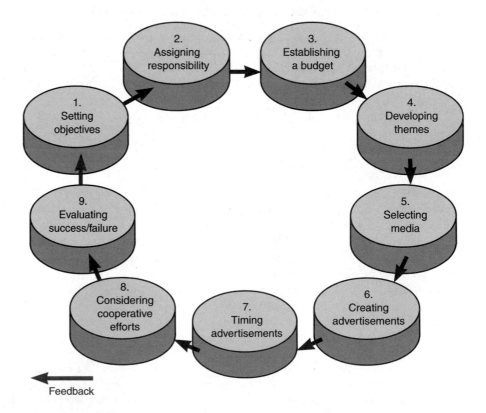

[5] Theresa Howard, "Advertisers Forced to Think Outside the Box," **http://www.usatoday.com/money/advertising/adtrack/2005-06-19-cannes-box_x.htm** (June 19, 2005).

[6] Linda Haugsted, "In DVR Age, Best Keep Promos Snappy," *Multichannel News* (July 11, 2005), p. 17.

18-4a Setting Objectives

Advertising goals can be divided into demand and image types, with image-oriented ads being part of a public relations effort. Table 18-4 cites several goals. Usually, a number of them are pursued.

John Hancock Financial Services (**http://www.johnhancock.com**) recently ran a major ad campaign "to bring attention to its expanded fund lineup and strong brand in the marketplace." The campaign had two targets. The first was sales intermediaries selling Hancock services; the second was people who sought assistance: "For intermediaries, the message was, 'John Hancock now has more innovative investment solutions.' For consumers, it was, 'John Hancock can help me on many aspects of my financial needs, from protecting my family and assets today to managing my financial future tomorrow.'" [7]

18-4b Assigning Responsibility

In assigning advertising responsibility, a firm can rely on its internal marketing personnel, use an in-house advertising department, or hire an outside advertising agency. Although many firms use internal personnel or in-house departments, most companies involved with advertising on a regular or sizable basis hire outside agencies (some in addition to their own personnel or departments). Diversified firms may hire a different agency for each product line. A firm's decision to use an outside agency depends on its own expertise and resources and on the role of advertising for the firm.

An *advertising agency* is an organization that provides a variety of advertising-related services to client firms. It often works with clients in devising their advertising plans—including themes, media choice, copywriting, and other tasks. A large agency may

> An **advertising agency** may work with a firm to develop its ad plan, conduct research, or provide other services.

Table 18-4	Illustrations of Specific Advertising Objectives
Type of Objective	**Illustrations**
Demand-Oriented	
Information	To create target market awareness for a new brand
	To acquaint consumers with new business or store hours
	To reduce the time salespeople take to answer basic questions
Persuasion	To gain brand preference
	To increase store traffic
	To achieve brand loyalty
Reminding (retention)	To stabilize sales
	To maintain brand loyalty
	To sustain brand recognition and image
Image-Oriented	
Industry	To develop and maintain a favorable industry image
	To generate primary demand
Company	To develop and maintain a favorable company image
	To generate selective demand

---

[7] Giselle Abramovich, "John Hancock Advertises Product Range," *Money Management Executive* (November 14, 2005), pp. 1, 12.

also offer market research, product planning, consumer research, public relations, and more. Among the largest U.S.-based ad agencies are Omnicom Group (**http://www.omnicomgroup.com**), Interpublic Group (**http://www.interpublic.com**), and Grey Global (**http://www.greyglobalgroup.com**).

18-4c   Establishing a Budget

After computing overall spending by the all-you-can-afford, incremental, competitive parity, percentage-of-sales, or objective-and-task method, a firm sets a detailed ad budget—to specify the funds for each type of advertising (such as product and institutional messages) and each medium (such as newspapers and radio). Because demand-oriented ads generate revenues, firms should be cautious about reducing these budgets. A better campaign, not a lower budget, may be the answer if goals are not reached.

These points should be addressed: What do various alternatives cost for time or space (a 30-second TV spot versus a full-page magazine ad)? How many placements are needed to be effective (if it takes four telecasts of a single ad to make an impact, a budget must allow four placements)? How have media prices risen recently? How should a firm react during an industry sales slump? What channel members are assigned which promotion tasks? Do channel members require contributions toward advertising? What does it cost to produce an ad? How should a budget be allocated for domestic versus foreign ads? Consider that the cost of producing one 30-second national TV commercial in the United States is now approaching $400,000 (not including the cost for airtime).[8]

From a global perspective, companies can use three major methods to establish their advertising budgets: (1) They can allow personnel in each pan-geographic region to determine their needs and petition headquarters for a budget. (2) They can let each individual market have its own advertising strategy and budget. (3) They can control budgeting decisions from their world headquarters.

18-4d   Developing Themes

> Basic **advertising themes** are product, consumer, and/or institutional appeals.

A firm next develops **advertising themes**, the overall appeals for its campaign. A good or service appeal centers on the item and its attributes. A consumer appeal describes a product in terms of consumer benefits rather than its features. An institutional appeal deals with a firm's image. Table 18-5 presents a full range of advertising themes from which a firm may select. Figures 18-2 and 18-3 show thematic ads for Skinny Cow (**http://www.skinnycow.com**) and Jaguar (**http://www.jaguar.com**).

18-4e   Selecting Media

Many media outlets are available, as noted in Table 18-6. Costs, reach, waste, message permanence, persuasive impact, narrowcasting, frequency, clutter, lead time, and media innovations should be reviewed when choosing among them.

> Advertising media costs include total and per-person costs.

Advertising media costs are outlays for media time or space. They are related to ad length or size, and media attributes. First, the total costs to place an ad in a medium are computed—such as $30,000 for a full-page color magazine ad. Second, per-reader or per-viewer costs are derived (stated in cost per thousand). If a $30,000 ad goes in a magazine with a circulation of 500,000, the cost per thousand is $60.

> **Reach** includes circulation and passalongs.

Reach refers to the number of viewers, readers, or listeners in a medium's audience. For TV and radio, it is the total number of people who watch or listen to an ad. For print

---

[8] American Association of Advertising Agencies, "Results of AAAA 2005 Television Production Cost Survey," **http://www.aaaa.org** (2006).

Marketing and the Web

The Boom in Web-Based Advertising

Web advertising with such features as keyword-based searches and streaming video and audio has begun to challenge traditional media such as television and radio. According to the Interactive Advertising Bureau (http://www.iab.net) and PricewaterhouseCoopers (http://www.pwcglobal.com), firms annually spend $12 billion to $15 billion on Web ads. That's more than a 50 percent increase over the 2003 level and nearly double the Web-based ad 2000 expenditure level. In 2000, most Web advertising was done by venture capital firms. Today, about 30 percent of the expenditures are by *Fortune 500* companies. Nonetheless, Internet advertising still accounts for only 5 percent or so of all U.S. media expenditures.

Three important reasons for the growth of Internet advertising are the greater use of broadband, the ease of targeting an audience, and the ability to track effectiveness. Broadband enables advertisers to use exciting video formats. In some instances, an ad made for television can be broadcast over the Internet. A car dealership ad, for example, can appear at the same time a consumer is searching for a car. And Web marketers typically pay for Web advertising based on dollar sales, not the presentation of the ad.

Because online consumers have more control of the messages that reach them due to ad-blocking software, the online advertising industry is trying to reduce advertising clutter. Many are now using fewer, but more powerful, advertising such as ads that take up the length of a page.

Sources: Based on material in Eileen Colkin Cuneo, "Web Ads Upend Industry Practices," *Information Week* (June 13, 2005), pp. 54, 56.

Table 18-5   Advertising Themes

Theme	Example
Good or Service Related	
Dominant features described	Whirlpool washers emphasize dependability and durability.
Competitive advantages cited	Aiwa stresses the superior quality of its portable stereos.
Price used as dominant feature	Private-label beauty products advertise low prices.
News or information domination	New-model laser printers point out enhancements in color and fonts.
Size of market detailed	Hertz emphasizes its leading position in car rentals.
Primary demand sought	Grapes are advertised.
Consumer Related	
Good or service uses explained	Pillsbury ads have cake recipes.
Cost benefits of good or service shown	Owens-Corning states how consumers reduce heating bills with Fiberglas insulation.
Emphasis on how good or service helps consumer	The Regent Beverly Wilshire hotel says that its customer service is so good that it gives clients complete peace of mind.
Threatening situation	The American Heart Association points out the risks of smoking.
Incentives given to encourage purchases	An ad mentions $1 off a purchase as an introductory offer for a new brand of coffee.
Institutional Related	
Favorable image sought	ExxonMobil explains how it is searching for new energy sources.
Growth, profits, and potential described to attract investors	Companies regularly take out full-page ads in business sections of major newspapers.

media, it has two aspects: *circulation* and *passalong rate*. Circulation is the number of copies sold or distributed to people. The passalong rate is the number of times each copy is read by another reader. For instance, each copy of *Newsweek* is read by several people. The magazine passalong rate is much higher than that for daily papers.

Waste is the audience segment not in the target market.

Waste is the part of a medium's audience not in a firm's target market. Because media appeal to mass audiences, waste can be a big factor. We can show this with the magazine example cited in media costs. If a special-interest magazine with 500,000 readers appeals to amateur photographers, a camera maker knows 450,000 of the readers might be interested in a new digital camera; 50,000 would have no interest. The latter is the wasted audience. The real cost is \$66.67 (\$30,000/450,000 × 1,000 = \$66.67) per thousand readers. The firm also knows a general-interest magazine runs camera ads, attracts 1 million readers, and prices a full-page ad at \$40,000—\$40 per thousand. The firm expects only 200,000 of those readers to be interested in photography. So, the real cost is \$200 (\$40,000/200,000 × 1,000 = \$200) per thousand. See Figure 18-4.

Message permanence srefers to exposures per ad.

Message permanence refers to the number of exposures one ad generates (repetition) and how long it remains available to the audience. Outdoor ads, transit ads, and

Figure 18-3

Jaguar: Showing How a Product Benefits the Consumer

Source: Reprinted by permission of Ford.

phone directories yield many exposures per message; and many magazines are retained by consumers for long periods. On the other hand, radio and TV ads last only 5 to 60 seconds and are over.

Persuasive impact is the ability of a medium to stimulate consumers. TV often has the most persuasive impact because it combines audio, video, color, and action. Magazines and the Internet also have high persuasive impact. Many newspapers have improved their technology so as to feature color ads and increase their persuasive impact.

Narrowcasting—advertising messages presented to rather limited and well-defined audiences—is a way to reduce the audience waste with mass media. It may be done via direct mail, local cable TV, specialty magazines, the Internet, and other targeted media. In narrowcasting, a firm gets less waste in return for a smaller reach. Now that the majority of U.S. homes have cable TV, this medium has great potential for local narrowcasting. As one observer noted: "With the mass media's share of advertising declining, we are seeing more and more marketers boost spending on more tangible 'narrowcast' media. Marketers need to be where the target consumers are and involved in things they value. The big mass marketers increasingly will look to find their target consumers, focus on them, and become relevant to them. They will still be big marketers, but no longer mass marketers."[9]

> **Persuasive impact** is highest for TV.

> In **narrowcasting**, advertisers seek to reduce waste.

[9] Michael C. Bellas, "With Micro-Marketing Comes Narrowcasting," *Beverage World* (June 15, 2005), p. 22.

Table 18-6 Advertising Media

Medium	Market Coverage	Best Uses	Selected Advantages	Selected Disadvantages
Commercial television	Regional, national, or international	Regional, national, and international manufacturers, service firms, and retailers	Reach, low cost per viewer, persuasive impact, creative options, flexible, high frequency, surrounded by programs	High minimum total costs, general audience, lead time for popular shows, short messages, limited availability
Cable television	Local, regional, national, or international	Local, regional, and national manufacturers, service firms, and retailers	More precise audience and more creative than commercial television	Not all consumers hooked up; ads not yet fully accepted on programs
Direct mail	Advertiser selects market	New products, book clubs, financial services, catalog sales	Precise audience, flexible, personal approach, less clutter from other messages	High throwaway rate, receipt by wrong person, low credibility
Daily newspaper	Entire metropolitan area; local editions used sometimes	Medium and large manufacturers, service firms, and retailers	Short lead time, concentrated market, flexible, high frequency, passalongs, surrounded by content	General audience, heavy ad competition, limited color, limited creativity
Weekly newspaper	One community	Local firms	Same as daily	Heavy ad competition, very limited color, limited creativity, small market
Radio	Entire metropolitan area	Local or regional firms	Low costs, selective market, high frequency, immediacy of messages, surrounded by content	No visual impact, commercial clutter, channel switching, consumer distractions
Telephone directories	Entire metropolitan area (with local supplements)	All types of retailers, professionals, service companies, and others	Low costs, permanence of messages, repetition, coverage of market, specialized listings, action-oriented messages	Clutter of ads, limited creativity, very long lead time, low appeal to passive consumers
Magazines	Local, national, or international (with regional issues)	Local service firms and mail-order firms; major manufacturers, service firms, and retailers	Color, creative options, affluent audience, permanence of messages, passalongs, flexible, surrounded by content	Long lead time, poor frequency (if monthly), ad clutter, geographically dispersed audience
Outdoor	Entire metropolitan area or one location	Brand-name products, nearby retailers, reminder ads	Large size, color, creative options, repetition, less clutter, message permanence	Legal restrictions, consumers distractions, general audience, inflexible, limited content, lead time
Internet	Local, national, or international	All types and sizes of firms	Low costs, huge potential audience, vast geographic coverage, amount of information conveyed, interactivity	Clutter of ads, viewed as a novelty by some, goals unclear (advertising vs. entertainment and education), no set rate structure
Business publications	Regional, national, or international	Corporate advertising, b-to-b firms	Selective market, high readability, surrounded by content, message permanence, passalongs	Restricted product applications, may not be read by proper decision maker, not oriented to final consumer
Transit	Urban community with a transit system	Firms located along transit route	Concentrated market, message permanence, repetition, action-oriented messages, color, creative options	Clutter of ads, consumer distractions, geographically limited audience
Flyers	Single neighborhood	Local firms	Low costs, market coverage, little waste, flexible	High throwaway rate, poor image

Figure 18-4
Waste in Advertising

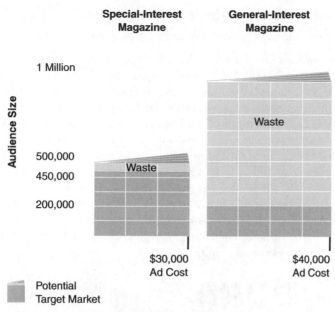

| Special-Interest Magazine | General-Interest Magazine |

Audience Size

1 Million

Waste

500,000
450,000

Waste

200,000

$30,000
Ad Cost

$40,000
Ad Cost

Potential Target Market

Even though the general-interest magazine attracts a much larger overall audience than the special-interest magazine (at little additional cost), a large portion of its audience is wasted—many people are not part of the potential target market.

Frequency refers to how often a medium can be used. It is greatest for the Internet, newspapers, radio, and TV. Different ads may appear daily and a strategy may be easily changed. Phone directories, outdoor ads, and magazines have the worst frequency. A printed Yellow Pages ad can be placed only once per year.

Clutter involves the number of ads found in a single program, issue, and so forth, of a medium. It is low when few ads are presented, such as Hallmark placing only scattered commercials on the TV specials for which it is the sponsor. It is high when there are many ads, such as the large number of supermarket ads in a newspaper's Wednesday issue. Overall, magazines have the most clutter. And TV is criticized for assigning more time per hour to commercials (about 15 to 20 minutes) and for letting firms show very brief messages (15 seconds or shorter). More than one-third of all TV ads are 15-second spots.

Lead time is the period required by a medium for placing an ad. It is shortest for newspapers and longest for magazines and phone directories. Popular TV shows may also require a lengthy lead time because the number of ads they can carry is limited. Because a firm must place ads well in advance, with a long lead time, it risks improper themes in a changing environment.

There have been many media innovations. These include online computer services such as America Google (**http://www.google.com**) and other services that let people "surf the Web" and be exposed to advertising; regional editions and special one-sponsor issues ("advertorials") to revitalize magazines; targeted Yellow Pages; TV ads in supermarkets, movie theaters, and planes; more radio stations handling ads in stereo; better quality in outdoor signs; and full-length advertising programs ("infomercials").

In the United States, "the monthly Internet radio and Internet video audience represents an estimated 55 million consumers. In 2000, 10 percent of Americans had watched Internet video or listened to Internet radio/audio within the last month. By 2005, 22 percent of Americans had watched or listened to Internet broadcasting within the past month."[10]

Frequency is highest for daily media.

Clutter occurs when there are many ads.

Lead time is needed for placing an ad.

[10] Arbitron/Edison Media Research, *Internet and Multimedia 2005: The On-Demand Media Consumer,* http://www.edisonresearch.com/home/archives/Internet%2005Summary%Final.pdf.

18-4f Creating Advertisements

Four Fundamental decisions must be made in creating ads:

> Ad creation involves content, scheduling, media placement, and variations.

1. *Determine message content and devise ads.* Each ad needs a headline or opening to create interest, and copy that presents the message. Content decisions also involve the use of color and illustrations, ad size or length, the source, the use of symbolism, and the adaptations needed for foreign markets. The role of these factors depends on a firm's goals and resources. Figure 18-5 shows a provocative ad from Charles Penzone beauty salons (**http://www.charlespenzone.com**), and Figure 18-6 shows a stylish ad for a new Liz (**http://www.liz.com**) fragrance.
2. *Outline a promotion schedule.* This should allow for all copy and artwork and be based on the lead time needed for the chosen media.
3. *Specify each ad's location in a broadcast program or print medium.* As costs have risen, more firms have become concerned about ad placement.
4. *Choose how many variations of a basic message to use.* This depends on the frequency of presentations and the ad quality.

Figure 18-5

Stopping Traffic

Source: Reprinted by permission of Susan Berry, Retail Image Consulting, Inc.

18-4g Timing Advertisements

Two major decisions must be made about the timing of ads: how often an ad is shown and when to advertise during the year. First, a firm must balance audience awareness and knowledge versus irritation if it places an ad several times in a short period. McDonald's (**http://www.mcdonalds.com**) runs ads often, but changes them repeatedly. Second, a firm must choose whether to advertise over the year or in certain periods. *Distributed ads* hold on to brand recognition and increase sales in nonpeak periods. They are used by many manufacturers, service firms, and general-merchandise retailers. *Massed ads* are used in peak times to foster short-run interest; they ignore nonpeak periods. Specialty and seasonal firms use this method.

Other timing considerations include when to advertise new products, when to stop advertising existing products, how to coordinate advertising and other promotional tools, when to change basic themes, and how to space messages during the hierarchy-of-effects process.

> Timing refers to how often an ad is shown and when to advertise during the year.

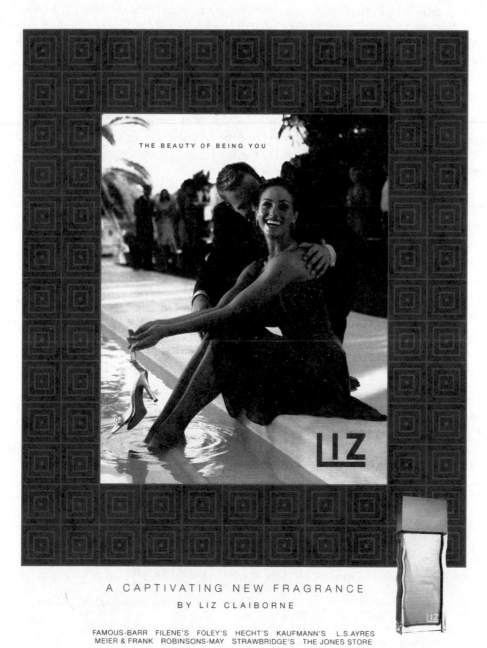

Figure 18-6
A Stylish Ad from Liz Fragrances

Source: Reprinted by permission

18-4h Considering Cooperative Efforts

To stimulate channel member advertising and/or to hold down its own ad budget, a firm should consider cooperative efforts. With **cooperative advertising**, two or more firms share some advertising costs. In *vertical cooperative advertising*, firms at different stages in a distribution channel (such as a manufacturer and a wholesaler) share costs. In *horizontal cooperative advertising*, two or more independent firms at the same stage in a distribution channel share costs (such as retailers in a mall).

Good agreements state the share of costs paid by each party, the functions and responsibilities of each party, the ads covered, and the basis for termination. They benefit all.

Each year, $15 to $20 billion in vertical-cooperative advertising support is made available by manufacturers in the United States. Yet, distribution intermediaries actually use only two-thirds of this amount. The nonuse by so many resellers is due to their perceptions of manufacturer inflexibility with messages and media, the costs of cooperative advertising to the resellers, restrictive provisions (such as high minimum purchases to be eligible), and the emphasis on manufacturer names in ads. To remedy this, manufacturers are more flexible as to the messages and media they support, pay a larger share of advertising costs, have eased restrictive provisions, and feature reseller names more prominently in ads.

18-4i Evaluating Success/Failure

The success of advertising depends on how well it helps to reach promotion goals. Gaining awareness and expanding sales are distinct goals; success or failure in reaching them must be measured differently. Advertising can also be quite difficult to isolate as the one factor leading to a certain image or sales level.

Here are various examples dealing with the evaluation of advertising's success or failure:

- Many "marketers have long known that repetition of an advertisement is critical if people are later to recall the advertised good or service. It also matters, however, how and when an ad is repeated. Spacing the repetitions of an ad, for example, rather than massing them, can increase later recall—and, hence, advertising effectiveness—quite dramatically."[11]

- Humor is often used in ads to final consumers. Yet, its effectiveness is not clear: "Previous studies showed humor to enhance, inhibit, or have no effect on consumer responses to ads. Clearly, there are boundary conditions governing humor. Our study reports a program of experimentation that examines one such contingency—an individual's 'need for humor.' Need for humor (NFH) is a trait that refers to a person's tendency to generate and seek out humor. Humor was manipulated in three studies using print ads and NFH was measured. Results show the impact of humor on attitude toward the ad to be moderated by NFH, such that advertising humor influences only higher-NFH subjects."[12]

- It is crucial for research on the effects of advertising on sales to take into account the activities of competitors. If this does not occur, "advertisers often instinctively match competitors' spending proportionately when it is monitored. The weakness of such a competitive parity approach is that they implicitly assume zero-sum competition only." However, overall sales for all players can rise or fall, depending on the firms' marketing prowess.[13]

---

[11] Sara L. Appleton-Knapp, Robert A. Bjork, and Thomas D. Wickens, "Examining the Spacing Effect in Advertising: Encoding Variability, Retrieval Processes, and Their Interaction," *Journal of Consumer Research*, Vol. 32 (September 2005), p. 266.

[12] Thomas W. Cline, Moses B. Altsech, and James J. Kellaris, "When Does Humor Enhance or Inhibit Ad Responses?" *Journal of Advertising*, Vol. 32 (September 2003), pp. 31–45.

[13] Boonghee Yoo and Rujirutana Mandhachitara, "Estimating Advertising Effects on Sales in a Competitive Setting," *Journal of Advertising Research*, Vol. 43 (September 2003), pp. 310–321.

Global Marketing in Action

Advertising on MTV: Reaching a Worldwide Audience

MTV (http://www.mtv.com), with about 100 channels in 165 territories, is the world's largest television network. MTV has a potential audience of 425 million households worldwide. In second place, CNN (http://www.cnn.com) has 10 networks and services internationally and reaches an audience of 260 million worldwide. MTV's channels include MTV, Music Television, Nick at Nite, Comedy Central, Noggin, and Nickelodeon. In addition to cable television, consumers can watch and listen to MTV via online, broadband, wireless, and interactive television formats.

MTV's success is based on effective localization, "combined with risk-taking, innovative, creative content, and a commitment to maintaining a strong connection with the young and young-minded," said the head of MTV's international marketing partnerships group. An example of the potential impact of MTV Networks was its customized one-hour program of the Live 8 concerts held on July 2, 2005. This concert, whose goal was to reduce poverty in the world's poorest countries, had the potential to reach a worldwide audience of over 1 billion people.

Many global advertisers understand the power of MTV in reaching young audiences. In a recent advertising campaign, McDonald's (http://www.mcdonalds.com) developed a global partnership with MTV in an effort to build closer ties with MTV's youthful audiences. McDonald's is also a sponsor of MTV's *Advance Warning* show in the Asian market. MTV is planning to air the U.S. version in the Asian market and will introduce localized content at a later date.

Sources: Based on material in "Reach the World," *Campaign* (May 27, 2005), pp. 41–42; Atifa Hargrave-Silk, "McDonald's Banks on MTV for Youth Appeal," *Media* (February 25, 2005), p. 6; and "MTV Networks Music Services to Offer Unprecedented Global Platform for Upcoming Live 8 Concerts," *Al Bawaba* (June 29, 2005), p. 1.

- In 25 countries around the world, EFFIE Awards (http://www.effie.org) are presented annually for outstanding ad efforts: "Effective advertising is advertising that sells; advertising that builds market share. The EFFIE award is the symbol of effective advertising and a tribute to the client and agency partnership that strives to create it."[14]

18-5   THE SCOPE AND IMPORTANCE OF PUBLIC RELATIONS

Each firm would like to foster the best possible relations with its publics and receive favorable publicity about its offerings or the firm itself. Sometimes, as with restaurant or theater reviews, publicity can greatly increase sales or virtually put a firm out of business.

In the United States, thousands of firms and hundreds of trade associations have their own public relations departments, and there are 1,800 public relations agencies. The leading U.S. organization in the field is the Public Relations Society of America (http://www.prsa.org), which has almost 20,000 members around the globe. The International Public Relations Association (http://www.ipra.org) has 1,000 members from 96 nations; nevertheless, the role of public relations varies greatly by nation:

Public relations efforts can have a major impact.

> Most PR people get ahead in their careers by making themselves expert in a particular geography, and usually in the nuances of a specific demographic group—for example, the youth market on the West Coast. Yet, today, more clients are looking to their public relations directors and consultancies to coordinate cross-border programs in order to achieve control of messaging, rapid response to issues and crises, best-in-class creative solutions, and insurance against local errors becoming global problems. There is a large and growing demand for professionals who can take responsibility for a multicountry PR program. There is not, however, a large and growing pool of practitioners with the needed experience and training.[15]

The competition to gain media attention for publicity is intense. In the United States, there are rather few national TV networks and less than 100 magazines and

---

[14] "About the EFFIEs," http://www.effie.org/about/awards.html (May 9, 2006).

[15] Adrian Wheeler, "Citizens of the World," http://www.ipra.org/membersfrontline/frontlinejun2005/1.htm (June 2005).

Situation	Poor Response	Good Response
Fire breaks out in company plant	Requests for information by media are ignored.	Company spokesperson explains the fire's causes and the precautions to avoid it, and answers questions.
New product introduced	Advertising is used without publicity.	Pre-introduction news releases, product samples, and testimonials are used.
News story about product defects	Media requests for information are ignored, blanket denials are issued, and there is hostility to reporters.	Company spokesperson says tests are being done, describes the procedure for handling defects, and takes questions.
Competitor introduces new product	A demand-oriented advertising campaign is stepped up.	Extensive news releases, statistics, and spokespeople are made available to media to present firm's competitive features.
High profits reported	Profits are justified and positive effects on the economy are cited.	Profits are explained, comparative data are provided, and profit uses are noted: research and community development.
Overall view of public relations	There is an infrequent need for public relations; crisis fighting is used when bad reports are circulated.	There is an ongoing need for public relations, strong planning, and plans to counter bad reports.

Table 18-7   Public Relations-Related Situations and How a Firm Could Respond to Them

newspapers with circulations of one million or more. However, many opportunities exist for publicity—with 4,700 AM radio stations, 6,000 FM radio stations, 1,650 conventional TV stations, 10,700 newspapers, and 14,000 periodicals around the United States. In addition, there are 10,000 cable TV systems and millions of Web sites.[16]

Some firms have poor policies to deal with their publics and the media, and do not have a sustained public relations approach. Table 18-7 shows public relations–related situations and how a firm could deal with them. Because unfavorable publicity can happen to any firm, a successful one will have a plan to handle it. A firm may foster media fairness by being candid and communicating promptly; media communications may be used to explain complex issues; and preconceived ideas may be dispelled by cooperating with reporters.

The interrelationship of public relations and other promotion forms must be understood. If advertising, personal selling, and sales promotion are image-oriented, public relations is involved. If they are demand-oriented, it is not. Figure 18-7 shows the interface between public relations and other promotion tools. These observations apply to organizations of all sizes and types:

> Every year, firms budget substantial portions of their marketing budgets to traditional advertising venues—print, radio, direct mail and, in some cases, TV—while a possibly more cost-effective way of reaching the masses is left untapped. Public relations is the orphaned child of many companies'

Public relations encompasses image-directed ads, selling, and sales promotion—as well as publicity.

[16] Authors' estimates based on *Statistical Abstract of the United States 2004–2005* (Washington, DC: U.S. Department of Commerce, 2004), various pages.

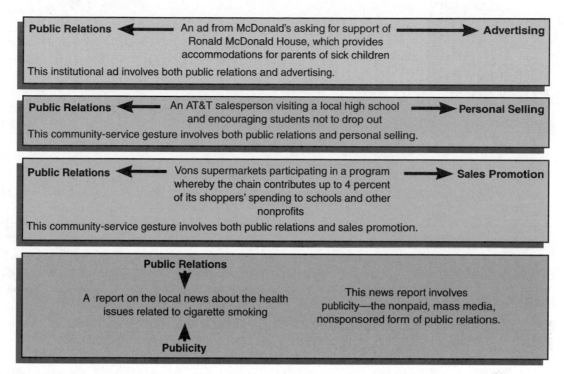

Figure 18-7
The Relationship Between Public Relations and the Other Elements of the Promotion Mix

yearly marketing agenda for reasons ranging from not realizing the importance to not realizing that even the smallest firm has something to share with the public. As one public relations expert says, "Individual firms can become well known by helping the media do the job. Becoming a source for the media and getting that third-party endorsement enhances the brand and is more cost-effective than advertising." Another expert adds, "Effective public relations is done through consistent campaigns that give information people can use. Concentrate on benefits, not features."[17]

18-6 THE CHARACTERISTICS OF PUBLIC RELATIONS

Public relations offers several benefits. Because it is image-oriented, good feelings toward a firm by its external publics can be fostered. In addition, employee morale (pride) is enhanced if the firm is community and civic minded.

When publicity is involved, no costs are incurred for message time or space. A prime-time TV ad may cost $300,000 to $750,000 or more per minute; a five-minute report on a network newscast does not cost anything for media time. Yet, there are costs for news releases, a public relations department, and so on. Publicity reaches a mass audience. In a short time, new products or company policies are well known.

Message believability is higher with publicity because stories are in independent media. A newspaper's movie review is more credible than an ad in that paper—the reader links independence with objectivity. Similarly, people may pay more attention to news than to ads. *Women's Wear Daily* (**http://www.wwd.com**) has both fashion reports and ads; people read the stories, but flip through ads. A dozen or more ads are run in a half-hour TV show, and hundreds in a typical magazine; feature stories are fewer and stand out.

> Public relations engenders good feelings; publicity has no time costs, a large audience, high credibility, and attentiveness.

[17] John Agoglia, "PR, Publicity, and Promotion," *Club Industry* (July 2003): p. 41.

> Public relations may be downplayed by some firms; publicity cannot be controlled or timed accurately by a company.

Compared to other promotion forms, public relations also has limitations. Some firms question the value of image-oriented messages and are disinterested in activities not directly tied to sales and profits. They may give the poor responses that were indicated in Table 18-7.

With publicity, a firm has less control over messages and their timing, placement, and coverage by the media. It may issue detailed press releases and find only parts cited in the media; and media may be more critical than a firm would like. They tend to find disasters, scandals, and product recalls more newsworthy than press releases. This shows how intense bad publicity can be:

Martha Stewart [http://www.marthastewart.com] the brand has set out an ambitious agenda for a comeback following the jail term of Martha Stewart the individual. Stewart plans to issue a home video line, launch a satellite radio network, and expand into the ready-to-assemble furniture business. How she has managed to sign partnerships with top companies so soon after leaving prison is a testament to the cult of celebrity, an indication of the public's love of a good comeback story, or an example of the power of PR—or perhaps all three. Stewart's company, Martha Stewart Living Omnimedia, suffered through some setbacks following the negative publicity surrounding first the government's investigation into her stock trades and then her conviction in 2004 for lying to a grand jury. Her long-running television show was cancelled, and advertising at her flagship magazine declined precipitously. But Stewart might be benefiting from a backlash against what many fans believe was the government's determination to make her a scapegoat for insider trading crimes.[18]

A firm may want publicity during certain periods, because when a new product is introduced or a new store opens, but the media may not provide coverage until much later. Similarly, the media determine a story's placement; it may follow a crime or sports report. Finally, the media choose whether to cover a story at all and the amount of coverage for it. A firm-sponsored jobs program might go unreported or get three-sentence coverage in a local paper.

Publicity may be hard to plan in advance since newsworthy events occur quickly and unexpectedly. Thus, short-run and long-run public relations plans should differ in approach. Publicity must complement advertising and not be a substitute. The assets of each (credibility and low costs for publicity, control and coverage for ads) are needed for a good communications program.

To optimize their public relations efforts, at many companies:

- Public relations personnel have regular access to senior executives.
- The publicity value of annual reports is recognized.
- Public relations messages are professionally prepared (with the same care as used in writing ad copy) and continuously given to media.
- Internal personnel and media personnel interaction is fostered.
- Public-service events are planned to obtain maximum media coverage.
- Part of the promotion budget goes to publicity-generating tasks.
- There is a better understanding of the kinds of stories the media are apt to cover and how to present stories to the media.

18-7   DEVELOPING A PUBLIC RELATIONS PLAN

Developing a public relations plan is much like devising an advertising plan. It involves the steps shown in Figure 18-8 and described next.

[18] Andrew Grossman, "Post-Prison Martha: It's a Good Thing," http://www.chiefmarketer.com/presence/promotion/post_prison_martha_0515 (May 15, 2005).

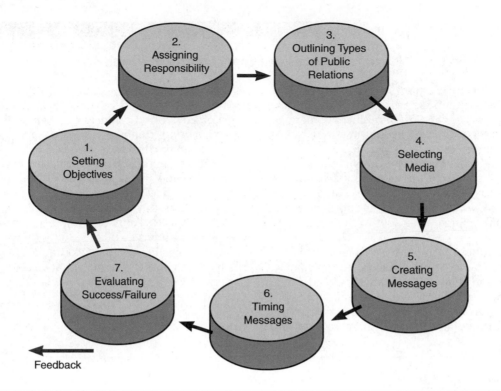

Figure 18-8

Developing a Public Relations Plan

18-7a   Setting Objectives

Public relations goals are image-oriented (firm and/or industry). The choice guides the entire public relations plan. These are some possible goals:

- Gain placement for news releases and appearances for company spokespersons with a variety of media.
- Have the media report on the accomplishments of the company.
- Have the company's viewpoint presented when controversy arises.
- Coordinate publicity with advertising.
- Obtain more media coverage than competitors.
- Sustain favorable publicity as long as possible.
- Reach out to community groups.
- Have publics view the firm and its industry favorably.

In setting goals, this truism should be kept in mind: "While journalists complain that people who work in public relations do not understand news, public relations practitioners complain that sometimes the journalists do not understand well enough the public relations role nor do they understand general business principles."[19]

18-7b   Assigning Responsibility

A firm has three options in assigning public relations responsibility: it may use its existing marketing personnel, an in-house public relations department, or an in-house publicity department; it may have an outside advertising agency handle public relations; or it may hire a specialized public relations firm. Internal personnel or an in-house department ensure more control and privacy. An outside firm often has better contacts and expertise. Each approach is popular, and they may be combined.

> A firm can use a in-house department, hire an outside ad agency, or hire a specialist.

[19] Lee Bollinger, "Public Relations, Business, and the Press," *Public Relations Quarterly*, Vol. 48 (Summer 2003), pp. 20–23.

Ethical Issues in Marketing

Using Ads to Overcome Negative Publicity: A Proper Approach?

What type of publicity program should a firm conduct when one of its key products has been recalled, the financial media accuse the firm of mismanagement, or the company is the subject of a government investigation? Until recently, most firms would not comment on these issues, hoping that the public would soon forget about them. Now, many firms have become more proactive by having their chief executive officers interviewed on key talk shows, increasing their advertising, and sending E-mail messages to their important consumers.

Let's look at how Merck (http://www.merck.com) and Morgan Stanley (http://www.morganstanley.com) have recently handled negative publicity. One of Merck's main products, Vioxx, a painkiller, was linked to users having an increased chance of a heart attack. Vioxx subsequently was withdrawn from the market and subjected to numerous product liability lawsuits. In response to the charges, Merck launched a major advertising campaign to highlight the firm's role in curing childhood diseases and discounting drugs to senior citizens.

Morgan Stanley, a financial services firm, was accused by the media of financial mismanagement. After many of Morgan Stanley's key executives left the firm, the company started a major campaign stressing that its clients come first. To ensure that its new ads would not be placed alongside negative publicity at a specific medium, Morgan Stanley required the media to notify it of any negative Morgan Stanley stories. This enabled it to reschedule ads.

Source: Based on material in Diane Brady, Michael Arndt, and Amy Barrett, "When Your Name Is Mud, Advertise," *Business Week* (July 4, 2005), pp. 56, 58.

Procter & Gamble (http://www.pg.com) has an in-house publicity department and outside public relations agencies. In contrast, some smaller firms rely on specialists, which may charge annual fees of $25,000 to $50,000. Computer software, such as Automated Press Releases (http://www.automatedpr.com) and PR Free (http://www.prfree.com/index.php), also enable small firms to reach media contacts. A wealth of information on the public relations industry may be found at 101publicrelations.com (http://www.101publicrelations.com) and Online Public Relations (http://online-pr.com).

18-7c   Outlining the Types of Public Relations to Be Used

In this step, a firm first chooses the mix of institutional advertising, image-oriented personal selling, image-oriented sales promotion, and publicity to incorporate into an overall promotion plan. Public relations efforts must then be coordinated with the demand-oriented promotion activities of the firm.

Finally, the general **publicity types** must be understood. Each can play a role in an integrated public relations program:

> **Publicity types** include news, features, releases, background material, and emergency information.

- *News publicity* deals with global, national, regional, or local events. Planned releases can be prepared and regularly given out by a firm.
- *Business feature articles* are detailed stories about a firm's offerings that are given to business media.
- *Service feature articles* are lighter stories focusing on personal care, household items, and similar topics that are sent to newspapers, TV stations, magazines, and Internet sites.
- *Finance releases*, such as quarterly earnings, are stories aimed at the business sections of newspapers, TV news shows, magazines, and other media.
- *Product releases* deal with new products and product improvements; they aim at all media forms.
- *Sponsorship releases* report that firms support particular causes or charities.
- *Pictorial releases* are illustrations or pictures sent to the media.
- *Video news releases* are videotaped segments supplied to the media.

- *Background editorial material* is extra information (such as the biography of the chief executive of a firm) given to media writers and editors; it enhances standard releases and provides filler for stories.
- *Crisis publicity* consists of special spontaneous news releases keyed to unexpected events.[20]

18-7d   Selecting the Media for Public Relations Efforts

For institutional ads, personal selling, and sales promotion, traditional nonpersonal and/or personal media would be used. For publicity, a firm would typically focus on newspapers, TV, magazines, radio, business publications, and the Internet. Due to the infrequent nature of many magazines and some business publications, publicity-seeking efforts may be aimed at daily or weekly media.

Public relations executives rank newspapers and business publications the highest. The *Wall Street Journal* (**http://online.wsj.com/public/us**), *New York Times* (**http://www.nytimes.com**), and *USA Today* (**http://www.usatoday.com**) are preferred newspapers. *Business Week* (**http://www.businessweek.com**), *Fortune* (**http://www.fortune.com**), and *Forbes* (**http://www.forbes.com**) are preferred business publications. *Time* (**http://www.time.com**), *Newsweek* (**http://www.newsweek.com**), and *U.S. News & World Report* (**http://www.usnews.com**) are preferred general news magazines.

18-7e   Creating Messages

Public relations messages entails the same factors as other communication—content, variations, and a production schedule. Messages can be sent in one or a combination of forms, such as news conferences, media releases, phone calls or personal contacts, media kits (a group of materials on a story), special events (such as Macy's Thanksgiving Parade—**http://www.nyctourist.com/macys_menu.htm**), or videos.

Because it is essential that the media find a firm to be cooperative and its publicity messages to be useful, these tips should be followed:

1. "Know the reporter and the publication before picking up the phone. First, build a targeted media list of the publications that may have an interest in what you're pitching, and then determine which journalists you should be talking to at those publications."
2. "Always know how and when a reporter wants to be contacted. Some reporters want phone calls, others prefer E-mail, and still others want news the old-fashioned way—by snail mail."
3. "Clarify your message before delivering your pitch. There is nothing worse for a reporter than receiving an E-mail that is a carbon copy of a press release, or getting a call from someone who is not familiar with the company they are pitching or the news they are announcing."
4. In a press release, "it is important to make the reporter's job as easy as possible so make sure to provide the most important news in the first paragraph. You should also include the company's URL, as a reporter will often times visit the company's Web site before calling back."
5. "Never send unsolicited email attachments, as some reporters will be wary of opening them due to virus concerns, and others simply won't take the time."
6. "When calling a reporter, introduce yourself fully, reference previous conversations to jog the reporter's memory on who you are and why you're calling, and ask if this is a good time to talk."

---

[20] Adapted by the authors from Gordon C. Bruner II, "Public Relations," **http://www.cba.siu.edu/osr/Misc/pr/frame.htm** (2002).

7. "When you get a reporter on the phone, ask what they are working on and how you can help."
8. "Never make promises you cannot keep."
9. "Follow up aggressively. Although some reporters will provide coverage after one phone interview, that is often not enough."
10. "Whenever possible, pitch by phone. This will get you better results and allow you to build the relationships you need to ensure consistent success."[21]

18-7f   Timing Messages

Public relations efforts should precede new-product introductions and generate excitement for them. For emergencies, media releases and spokespeople should be immediately available. For ongoing public relations, messages should be properly spaced through the year. As already noted, a firm may find it hard to anticipate media coverage for both unexpected and planned publicity because the media control timing.

18-7g   Evaluating Success/Failure

Several straightforward methods are used to rate a public relations campaign:

- With institutional ads, image-oriented personal selling, and image-oriented sales promotion, a firm can conduct simple surveys to see how well these communications are received and their impact on its image.
- With publicity, a firm can count the stories about it, analyze coverage length and placement, review desired with actual timing of stories, evaluate audience reactions, and/or compute the cost of comparable advertising.
- Firms such as Wal-Mart track the *quality*, as well as the quantity, of media coverage. Wal-Mart classifies items as news stories, letters to the editor, editorials, or opinion articles.
- Through the Internet, companies can track media stories. For example, 1st Headlines (**http://www.1stheadlines.com**) can do a topical search for stories appearing in media around the world.

Web Sites You Can Use

Numerous Web sites provide access to current and past advertisements. Many offer real-time video commercials. Here is a cross-section of sites where you can view or read ads (Please note: TV ads are best viewed through a high-speed connection. The download time may be lengthy with a telephone modem):

- Ad*Access (**http://scriptorium.lib.duke.edu/adaccess**)— Classic print ads from 1911 to 1955
- Adeater (**http://www.adeater.com**)—Click on "The Film Library" to access more than 700,000 TV commercials from around the world
- Adflip (**http://www.adflip.com**)—Print ads

- Advertising Council (**http://www.adcouncil.org/default.aspx?id=15**)—Multimedia public service announcements (PSAs)
- Coca-Cola Television Ads (**http://memory.loc.gov/ammem/ccmphtml/colahome.html**)—50 years of Coke commercials
- Eisner Museum of Advertising & Design (**http://www.eisnermuseum.org/exhibits/index.shtm**)—Multimedia online exhibits
- General Electric TV Commercials (**http://www.ge.com/en/company/companyinfo/advertising/tele_ads.htm**)
- Super Bowl TV Commercials (**http://www.ifilm.com/superbowl**)

---

[21] Peter Granat, "Improve Your Media Relations Skills," **http://aboutpublicrelations.net/ucgranat2a.htm** (May 23, 2006).

Summary

1. *To examine the scope, importance, and characteristics of advertising* Advertising is paid, nonpersonal communication sent through various media by identified sponsors. Worldwide ad spending exceeds $550 billion annually, one-half in the United States, via such media as TV, direct mail, newspapers, radio, Yellow Pages, magazines, outdoor (billboards), the Internet, and business publications. U.S. advertising is under 5.0 percent of sales in four-fifths of industries.

   Ads are most apt with standardized products and when features are easy to communicate, the market is large, prices are low, resellers are used in distribution, and/or products are new. In general, behavior is easier to change than attitudes; one ad can have an impact; ads do well with little-known products; and effectiveness rises during extended campaigns.

   Among advertising's advantages are its appeal to a geographically dispersed audience, low per-customer costs, the availability of a broad variety of media, the firm's control over all aspects of a message, the surrounding editorial content, and how it complements personal selling. Disadvantages include message inflexibility, some viewers or readers not in the target audience, high media costs, limited information provided, difficulty in getting audience feedback, and low audience involvement.

2. *To study the elements in an advertising plan* An advertising plan has nine steps: setting goals—demand and image types; assigning duties—internal and/or external; setting a budget; developing themes—good/service, consumer, and institutional; selecting media—based on costs, reach, waste, message permanence, persuasive impact, narrowcasting, frequency, clutter, lead time, and media innovations; creating ads—including content, placement, and variations; timing ads; considering cooperative efforts—both vertical and horizontal; and evaluating success or failure.

3. *To examine the scope, importance, and characteristics of public relations* Public relations includes any communication that fosters a favorable image among a firm's various publics. It is more image- than sales-oriented; embodies image-oriented ads, personal selling, and sales promotion; and seeks favorable publicity—the nonpersonal communication sent via various media but not paid for by identified sponsors. Thousands of companies have their own public relations departments, and many specialized public relations firms exist. Companies try to get positive publicity and avoid negative publicity. Competition is intense for placing publicity releases. Some firms have ineffective policies to deal with independent media or develop a sustained publicity campaign.

   Among its advantages are the image orientation, the positive effects on employee morale, and—for publicity—the lack of costs for message time, the high credibility, and audience attentiveness. The relative disadvantages of public relations include the lack of interest by some firms in image-oriented communications and the lesser control of publicity placements by the firm, the media interest in negative events, and the difficulty of planning publicity in advance.

4. *To study the elements in a public relations plan* A public relations plan has seven steps: setting goals—company and/or industry; assigning duties—internally and/or externally; outlining types of public relations—the mix of image-oriented promotion forms and the categories of publicity (news publicity, business and service feature articles, finance releases, product and pictorial releases, video news releases, background editorial releases, and emergency publicity); choosing media; creating messages; timing messages; and weighing success or failure.

Key Terms

advertising agency (p. 551)	waste (p. 554)	frequency (p. 557)
advertising themes (p. 552)	message permanence (p. 554)	clutter (p. 557)
advertising media costs (p. 552)	persuasive impact (p. 555)	lead time (p. 557)
reach (p. 552)	narrowcasting (p. 555)	cooperative advertising (p. 560)

Review Questions

1. Explain the statement "Advertising is paid for, publicity is prayed for."
2. List five objectives of advertising and give an example of how each may be accomplished.
3. A large firm has an overall annual budget of $3,000,000 for advertising. What specific decisions must it make in allocating the budget?
4. Differentiate among these advertising concepts: reach, narrowcasting, waste, clutter, and frequency.
5. What are the pros and cons of cooperative advertising?
6. Describe the role of public relations.
7. According to public relations executives, which are the two most preferred media for receiving publicity?
8. State three ways for a firm to evaluate the success or failure of its public relations efforts.

Discussion Questions

1. Devise an advertising plan for generating primary demand for American-made cell phones.
2. A motel chain knows a full-page ad in a general-interest magazine would cost $125,000; the magazine's total audience is 2.5 million—750,000 of whom are part of the chain's target market. A full-page ad in a travel magazine would cost $40,000; its total audience is 375,000—310,000 of whom are part of the chain's target market. Which magazine should be selected? Why?

3. Present and evaluate current examples of companies using institutional advertising, image-oriented personal selling, image-oriented sales promotion, and publicity.
4. How would you obtain publicity for a small company that has developed a "talking" blood pressure machine—one that gives an ongoing pep talk to the user and sets out goals to achieve?

Web Exercise

Go to the Web site of *Advertising Age* (**http://www.adage.com**) and visit the "Data Center." Discuss five interesting facts that you obtain from the Web site and state their implications for marketers.

Practice Quiz

1. Which of the following is common to both advertising and publicity?
   a. Paid presentation
   b. Source control of presentation
   c. Nonpersonal presentation
   d. Known sponsorship of presentation

2. The third-leading medium for U.S. advertising is
   a. magazines.
   b. direct mail.
   c. television.
   d. newspapers.

3. Which of the following is *not* a positive characteristic of advertising?
   a. Low costs per viewer or listener
   b. Control over editorial content
   c. The ability to tailor a message to each reader or viewer
   d. A broad range of media to choose among

4. Which of the following is *not* a negative characteristic of advertising?
   a. It often requires high total expenditures.
   b. Messages are standardized.
   c. Messages in print media can be reread and restudied.
   d. A large portion of viewers or readers may be considered waste for an advertiser.

5. The first step in developing an advertising plan is
   a. assigning responsibility.
   b. developing themes.
   c. setting objectives.
   d. establishing a budget.

6. For print media, reach has two components: circulation and
   a. waste.
   b. passalong rate.

   c. frequency.
   d. clutter.

7. Frequency is greatest for
   a. phone directories.
   b. outdoor ads.
   c. magazines.
   d. radio.

8. The highest level of clutter exists with
   a. television.
   b. telephone directories.
   c. magazines.
   d. newspapers.

9. Which of the following statements concerning distributed ads is correct?
   a. They decrease sales in nonpeak periods.
   b. They are used by most manufacturers.
   c. They decrease brand recognition.
   d. They are more effective than massed ads.

10. Public relations does *not* encompass
    a. personal selling.
    b. demand-oriented advertising.
    c. publicity.
    d. sales promotion.

11. With publicity,
    a. credibility is generally low.
    b. a firm has complete control over messages.
    c. a firm can ensure that the media will cover only positive events.
    d. there are no costs for message time or space.

12. The first step in developing a public relations plan is
    a. setting objectives.
    b. assigning responsibility.
    c. outlining the types of publicity to be used.
    d. selecting media.

13. Assigning public relations responsibility to internal personnel or an in-house department
    a. cannot be combined with any other option for assigning the publicity responsibility.
    b. results in better contacts and expertise than using an outside public relations firm.
    c. is not a popular approach to assigning responsibility.
    d. ensures more control and secrecy.

14. Business feature articles are
    a. stories dealing with finance found in business sections of newspapers and magazines.
    b. concerned with new products and product improvements.
    c. extra information provided to media writers and editors.
    d. detailed stories about a firm's products.

15. Lighter stories focusing on personal care, household items, and similar topics are examples of
    a. service feature articles.
    b. background editorial material.
    c. news releases.
    d. product releases.

For the answers to these questions, please visit the online site for this book at **http://www.atomicdog.com.**

Chapter 19

Personal Selling and Sales Promotion

Anheuser-Busch (A-B) (**http://www.anheuser-busch.com**) is the leading U.S. beer manufacturer, with a market share of about 50 percent. It makes more than 30 beers, including Bud Light, Michelob, and Busch—in addition to Budweiser, the nation's best-selling beer. A large part of its success is due to both the role of its independent sales reps and sales promotions. Let's examine the roles of each of these.

About 93 percent of A-B's beer (as measured by volume) is sold to retailers (stores, bars, restaurants, etc.) through its more than 580 independent wholesalers. Each wholesaler has a written agreement with A-B that covers its territory, the brands it can sell, specific performance standards, and conditions for terminating the agreement. Wholesalers work closely with A-B staff to identify new outlets for their products, increase shelf space in retail stores, and provide and install beer signs in retail outlets.

Each of the wholesalers gets national and local media advertising support, point-of-sale advertising materials, and sales promotional material from A-B. One marketing channel where A-B's sales promotions have been particularly effective is convenience stores. Of the top-10 products sold at convenience stores, beer ranks fourth (with nonalcoholic beverages ranked second and milk eighth), according to the National Association of Convenience Stores (**http://www.nacsonline.com**). In a typical year, A-B sells nearly 40 percent of its products in convenience stores. "We tailor promotions and marketing to every channel. The convenience store is ideal for our 'Freshness' platform, and most convenience stores work with us to use that as a competitive advantage," says an A-B executive. Many sales promotions involve new products such as Budweiser Select, single-serving packaging, and multi-packs. A-B also cross-markets beer via joint promotions with Jack Link's beef jerky and Cape Cod and Pringles snacks.

A-B and its wholesalers have been quite effective in targeting the Hispanic community. In areas with a high Hispanic population, A-B and its wholesalers have recruited bilingual employees and sponsored soccer leagues by providing T-shirts to players, special bags to coaches, special training to coaches, and facilities for coaches. There are about 15,000 players in these sponsored leagues in Florida and Georgia.[1]

Next, we will study the personal selling and sales promotion aspects of promotion and see how these tools can be used effectively.

Chapter Objectives

1. To examine the scope, importance, and characteristics of personal selling
2. To study the elements in a personal selling plan
3. To examine the scope, importance, and characteristics of sales promotion
4. To study the elements in a sales promotion plan

19-1 OVERVIEW

We examine the scope and importance, characteristics, and planning considerations for both personal selling and sales promotion in this chapter.

---

[1] Various company and other sources.

As defined in Chapter 17, *personal selling* involves oral communication with prospective buyers by paid representatives for the purpose of making sales. It relies on personal contact, unlike ads and publicity. Goals are similar to other promotion forms: informing, persuading, and/or reminding.

Sales promotion involves paid marketing communication activities (other than advertising, publicity, or personal selling) that stimulate consumers and dealers. Coupons, trade shows, contests and sweepstakes, and point-of-purchase displays are among the marketing tools classified as sales promotion.

> Personal selling is one-on-one with buyers. Sales promotion includes paid supplemental efforts.

19-2 THE SCOPE AND IMPORTANCE OF PERSONAL SELLING

In the United States, 16 million people work in the sales positions defined by the Department of Labor (**http://www.dol.gov**); millions more in other nations are also employed in sales jobs. Professional salespeople generate new customers, ascertain needs, interact with customers, emphasize knowledge and persuasion, and offer service. They include stockbrokers, insurance agents, manufacturer sales representatives, and real-estate brokers. Top ones can earn well over $100,000 per year. Clerical salespeople answer simple queries, retrieve stock from inventory, recommend the best brand in a category, and complete orders by receiving payments and packing products. They include retail, wholesale, and manufacturer sales clerks.

From a marketing perspective, "personal selling" goes far beyond the people in identified sales positions because every contact between a company representative and a customer entails some personal interaction. Lawyers, hair stylists, and cashiers are not defined as salespeople. Yet, they have lots of customer contact. ConAgra (**http://www.conagra.com**) and Kroger (**http://www.kroger.com**) know the value of customer contact. See Figures 19-1 and 19-2.

In varying situations, a strong personal-selling emphasis may be needed. Large-volume customers require special attention. Geographically concentrated consumers may be more efficiently served by a sales force than with ads in mass media. Custom-made, expensive, and complex goods or services require in-depth consumer information, demonstrations, and follow-up calls. Tangential sales services—like gift wrapping and delivery—may be requested. If ads are not informative enough, questions can be resolved by personal selling. New products may rely on personal selling to gain reseller acceptance. Foreign-market entry may be best handled by personal contacts with prospective resellers and/or consumers. Finally, many b-to-b customers expect a lot of personal contact. Generally, a decision to stress personal selling depends on such factors as costs, audience size and needs, and a desire for flexibility.

> Selling is stressed when orders are large, consumers are concentrated, items are expensive, and service is required.

Selling costs are often greater than advertising costs. Auto parts firms, office and equipment firms, and appliance makers all spend far more on selling than on ads. Direct marketer Fuller Brush's (**http://www.fullerbrush.com**) sales commissions range up to 50 percent or more of sales. The average cost of a single b-to-b field sales call is several hundred dollars; and it may take multiple visits to make a sale.

A number of strategies have been devised to keep selling costs down and improve the efficiency of the sales force, as these examples show:

- Many firms are more effectively routing salespeople to minimize travel time and expenses. Some firms are bypassing smaller customers in their personal selling efforts and specifying minimum order sizes for personalized service. This means opportunities for sellers willing to serve small accounts.
- With **telemarketing**, telephone communications are used to sell or solicit business or to set up an appointment for a salesperson to sell or solicit business. Salespeople can talk to several consumers per hour, centralize operations and lower expenses, screen prospects, process orders and arrange shipments, provide customer service,

> High selling costs have led to a concern for efficiency. In **telemarketing**, phone calls initiate sales or set up sales appointments.

Figure 19-1

Figure 19-1

Personal Selling Throughout the Channel

ConAgra recognizes that it has two customers: the stores that purchase its food products and the final customers who buy them. To enhance its relationship marketing efforts, the firm has increased its in-store sales force. This is part of an overall program to provide greater ordering and display support for resellers, as well as to encourage more frequent communication with store personnel.

Source: Reprinted by permission.

assist the field sales staff, speed communications, and increase repeat business. A lot of companies rely on telephone personnel to contact customers; outside sales personnel (who actually call on customers) are then more involved with customer service and technical assistance. A broad range of small and large firms use some form of telemarketing. The American Teleservices Association (**http://www.ataconnect.org**) is dedicated exclusively to telemarketing issues. One impediment is the "Do Not Call Registry," which prohibits most companies from calling U.S. consumers who list themselves on that registry (**http://www.donotcall. gov**).

- Computerization improves efficiency by providing salespeople with detailed and speedy data, making ordering easier, coordinating orders by various salespeople, and identifying the best prospects and their desires (such as preferred brands)—based on prior purchases. Many salespeople use their laptop computers to communicate with the home office to get the latest product data, learn about inventory status, and so on. Firms are also using the Internet to train salespeople. In nearly every issue, *Sales & Marketing Management* (**http://www.salesandmarketing.com**) reports on computerization and selling.

Figure 19-2

Personal Selling and the Final Customer

Kroger recognizes that every customer contact is important, even if it is not formally called "personal selling."

Source: Reprinted by permission of Susan Berry, Retail Image Consulting, Inc.

- A lot of firms now view computerized customer data bases as among their most valuable sales resources. These data bases enable the firms to focus efforts better, make sure key accounts are regularly serviced, and use direct mailings to complement telephone calls and salesperson visits.

19-3   THE CHARACTERISTICS OF PERSONAL SELLING

On the positive side, personal selling provides individual attention for each consumer and passes on a lot of information. There is a dynamic interplay between buyer and seller. This lets a firm use a *buyer-seller dyad*, the two-way flow of communication between both parties. See Figure 19-3. That is not possible with advertising. Personal selling can be flexible and adapted to specific consumer needs. Thus, a real-estate broker can use one sales presentation with a first-time buyer and another with a person who has already bought a home. A salesperson can also apply as much persuasion as needed and balance it against the need for information.

Through the buyer-seller dyad, *relationship selling* is possible, whereby long-term customer bonds are developed. Consider this example: "The retail banking division of Massachusetts-based Rockland Trust [**http://www.rocklandtrust.com**] has been bustling with new training, coaching practices, and sales and service techniques—aimed at creating a process for boosting customer retention and customer growth." As a Rockland

> Selling uses a **buyer-seller dyad** and is flexible and efficient, closes sales, and provides feedback.

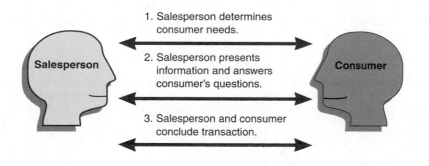

1. Salesperson determines consumer needs.

2. Salesperson presents information and answers consumer's questions.

3. Salesperson and consumer conclude transaction.

Salesperson ↔ Consumer

Figure 19-3

The Buyer-Seller Dyad

executive vice-president puts it, "Our focus is to service customers by satisfying their real financial needs rather than trying to hit sales quotas. The process we use is rooted in good questioning and listening skills and strong, technical product knowledge. Branch staff ask open-ended questions, listen to the answers to understand, and respond by presenting appropriate product recommendations."[2]

Personal selling targets a more defined and concentrated audience, which means less waste than with ads. In addition, people who enter a store or who are contacted by a salesperson are more apt to buy than those watching a TV ad. Because ads stimulate interest, those who make it to the personal selling stage are often in the target market. When unsolicited, direct selling has the most waste in personal selling.

Selling clinches sales and is usually conducted during the purchase stage of the consumer's decision process, taking place after information search. It holds repeat customers and those already convinced by advertising—and resolves any concerns of undecided consumers by answering questions about price, warranty, and other factors. It addresses service issues, such as delivery and installation. Feedback is immediate and clear-cut: Consumers may be asked their feelings about product features or they may complain; and salespeople may unearth a marketing program's strengths and weaknesses.

> **Selling has a limited audience, high costs per customer, and a poor image.**

On the negative side, selling is ineffective for generating awareness because salespeople can handle only a limited number of consumers. A retail furniture salesperson may be able to talk to fewer than 20 people per day if the average length of a customer contact is 15 minutes to a half hour. Sales personnel who call on customers can handle even fewer accounts, due to travel. In addition, many consumers drawn by advertising may want self-service. This is discouraged by some aggressive salespeople.

Personal selling costs per customer can be very high due to the one-on-one nature of selling. An in-store furniture salesperson who talks to 20 customers daily might cost a firm $7 per presentation ($140/day compensation divided by 20), an amount much higher than an ad's cost per-customer contact. For outside salespeople, hotel stays, meals, and transportation can amount to $200 or more—especially in larger cities—daily per salesperson, and compensation must be added to these costs.[3]

Finally, personal selling, especially among final consumers, has a poor image. It needs to overcome criticisms regarding a lack of honesty and pressure tactics:

> The role of selling has never been harder. Many seemingly tried-and-true selling techniques have been rendered virtually ineffective. Schmooze, bluster, and attitude have been replaced by the cold, hard reality of questions like: What can you do for me? How can you help me better than anyone else? How well do you know my business? What will it cost? How soon can you deliver? How do I know I can trust you? To be successful, the answers to these questions can no longer be shrouded in gimmicks and rhetoric. Salespersons must approach each and every meeting with professionalism and courtesy. Savvy is out. Respect is in. Don't pitch. Prepare, explain, listen, be honest, and sell with honor. Honor is synonymous with good reputation, integrity, and the adherence of principles.[4]

This situation can be tackled through better sales-force training and use of consumer-oriented rather than seller-oriented practices. Industry organizations such as the Direct Selling Association (**http://www.dsa.org**), Manufacturers' Agents National Association (**http://www.manaonline.org**), and National Association of Sales Professionals (**http://www.nasp.com**) are also striving to improve the image of personal selling.

---

[2] Rockland Trust Co., "Cross-Selling Is About Relationship Building," *Bank Marketing* (October 2005), p. 36. See also Timothy D. Landry, Todd J. Arnold, and Aaron Arndt, "A Compendium of Sales-Related Literature in Customer Relationship Management: Processes and Technologies with Managerial Implications," *Journal of Personal Selling & Sales Management*, Vol. 25 (Summer 2005), pp. 231–251.

[3] Christine Galea, "Roadblock: High Costs," *Sales & Marketing Management* (September 2005), pp. 31–32.

[4] David Farneti, "Sales with Honor: An Ethical Approach to Successful Business Dealings," *American Salesman* (September 2003), pp. 8–9.

Global Marketing in Action

The Best Salespeople in Hong Kong Are Millionaires

According to Titus Yu Hon-ki, the chairperson of the Sales and Marketing Executives Club of Hong Kong (http://www.sme-dsa.org/english), the most successful young salespeople in such sectors as property and financial products are earning up to $1 million per year. In some cases, these top-performing salespeople have been on their present job for only a few years.

"A lot of university graduates each year, many more than before, are taking sales jobs. Reward in sales is usually based on personal performance, not just job title. Young people want to have a better income, better career growth—and a sales career can give that opportunity," said Hon-ki.

In 2005, 131 salespeople from 50 companies were honored in the 37th Distinguished Salesperson Award

competition. The applicants were required to write an essay outlining their educational and work experience, their contribution to the sales profession, their thoughts on the competition theme, and the role of creativity and innovation in continued sales success. Applicants also had to prepare a sales presentation and conduct a spontaneous sales presentation on a randomly chosen product to a specific target market (such as selling a fish bowl to a disc jockey). Of the 167 people who entered the competition, 131 qualified as winners. The winners sold a variety of products, such as cars, carpeting, credit cards, and condominiums.

Source: Based on material in Victoria Button, "Plugging into Growth," *South China Morning Post Online* (June 3, 2005).

19-4 DEVELOPING A PERSONAL SELLING PLAN

A personal selling plan can be divided into the seven steps shown in Figure 19-4 and highlighted here.

19-4a Setting Objectives

Selling goals can be demand- and/or image-oriented. Image-oriented goals involve public relations. Although many firms have some interest in information, reminder, and image goals, the major goal usually is persuasion: converting consumer interest into a sale. Examples appear in Table 19-1.

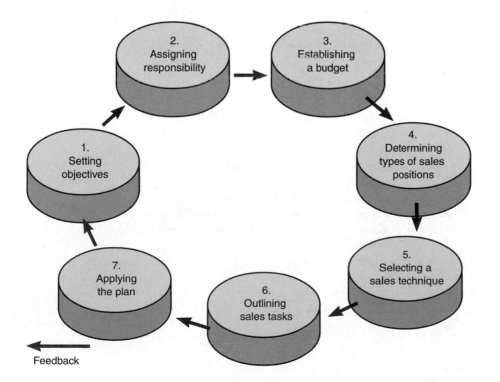

Figure 19-4

Developing a Personal Selling Plan

Table 19-1	Specific Personal Selling Objectives
Type of Objective	**Illustrations**
Demand-Oriented	
Information	Fully explain all attributes of goods and services
	Answer any questions
	Probe for any further questions
Persuasion	Differentiate the attributes of goods or services from those of competitors
	Maximize the number of purchases relative to the presentations made
	Convert undecided consumers into buyers
	Sell complementary items—such as a telephoto lens with a camera
	Placate dissatisfied customers
Reminding	Ensure delivery, installation, etc.
	Follow up after a good or service has been purchased
	Follow up when a repurchase is near
	Reassure previous customers as they make a new purchase
Image-Oriented	
Industry and company	Have a good appearance for all personnel having customer contact
	Follow acceptable (ethical) sales practices
	Be respected by customers, employees, and other publics

19-4b   Assigning Responsibility

The personal selling function may be assigned to a marketing or sales manager who oversees all areas of selling, from planning to sales-force management. A small or specialized firm is likely to have its marketing manager oversee selling or use one general sales manager. A large or diversified firm may have multiple sales managers—assigned by product line, customer type, and/or region.

These are the basic responsibilities of a sales manager:

> A manager must oversee selling functions.

- Understand the firm's goals, strategies, market position, and basic marketing plan and convey them to the sales force.
- Determine and outline a sales philosophy, sales-force characteristics, selling tasks, a sales organization, and methods of customer contact.
- Prepare and update sales forecasts.
- Allocate selling resources based on sales forecasts and customer needs.
- Select, train, assign, compensate, and supervise sales personnel.
- Synchronize selling tasks with advertising, product planning, distribution, marketing research, production, and other activities.
- Assess sales performance by salesperson, product line, customer group, and geographic area.
- Continuously monitor competitors' actions.
- Make sure the sales force acts ethically.
- Convey the image sought by the company.

Table 19-2	An Annual Sales-Expense Budget for a Small Manufacturer Specializing in Business Machinery
Item	**Estimated Annual Costs (Revenues)**
Sales Forecast	$1,950,000
Overhead (1 sales manager, 1 office)	$ 100,000
Sales-force compensation (2 salespeople)	110,000
Sales expenses	50,000
Sales meetings	5,000
Selling aids	20,000
Sales management costs	15,000
Total personal selling budget	$ 300,000
Personal selling costs as a percentage of sales forecast	15.4

19-4c Establishing a Budget

A *sales-expense budget* allots selling costs among salespeople, products, customers, and geographic areas for a given period. It is usually tied to a sales forecast and relates selling tasks to sales goals. It should be somewhat flexible in case expected sales are not reached or are exceeded.

> A **sales-expense budget** assigns spending for a specific time.

These items should be covered in a budget: sales forecast, overhead (manager's compensation, office costs), sales-force compensation, sales expenses (travel, lodging, meals, entertainment), sales meetings, selling aids (including computer equipment), and sales management (employee selection and training) costs. Table 19-2 shows a budget for a small manufacturer of business machinery.

The budget is larger if customers are geographically dispersed and a lot of travel is required. Complex products need costly, time-consuming sales presentations and result in fewer calls per salesperson. An expanding sales force needs expenditures for recruiting and training salespeople.

19-4d Determining the Type(s) of Sales Positions

Salespeople can be broadly classed as order takers, order getters, or support personnel. Some firms employ one type of salesperson; others use a combination.

An *order taker* processes routine orders and reorders. This person does more clerical tasks than creative selling, typically for pre-sold goods or services. He or she arranges displays, restocks items, answers simple questions, writes up orders, and completes transactions. He or she may work in a warehouse (manufacturer clerk) or store (retail clerk) or call on customers (a field salesperson). An order taker has these advantages for a firm: compensation is rather low, little training is required, both selling and nonselling tasks are done, and a sales force can be expanded or contracted quickly. Yet, an order taker is an improper choice for goods and services that need creative selling or extensive information for customers. Personnel turnover is high. Enthusiasm may be limited due to the low salary and routine tasks.

> An **order taker** handles routine orders and sells items that are pre-sold.

An *order getter* generates customer leads, provides information, persuades customers, and closes sales. He or she is the creative salesperson used for high-priced, complex, and/or new products. Less emphasis is placed on clerical tasks. The person may be inside (jewelry store salesperson) or outside (Xerox—**http://www.xerox.com**—salesperson). He or she is expert and enthusiastic, grows sales, and can convince undecided customers to buy or decided customers to add peripheral items—such as appliances along with a

> An **order getter** obtains leads, provides information, persuades customers, and closes sales.

Figure 19-5

Contrasting Order Takers and Order Getters

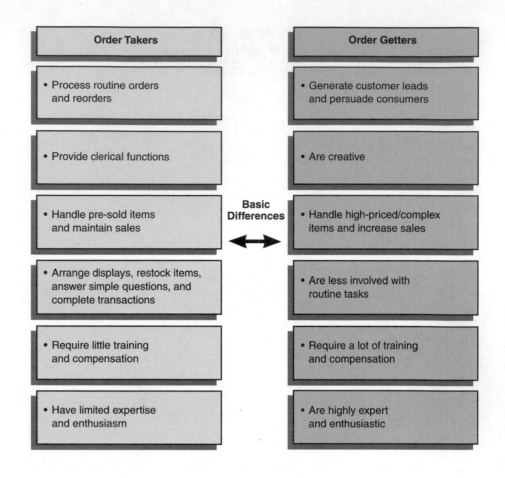

Order Takers	Order Getters
• Process routine orders and reorders	• Generate customer leads and persuade consumers
• Provide clerical functions	• Are creative
• Handle pre-sold items and maintain sales	• Handle high-priced/complex items and increase sales
• Arrange displays, restock items, answer simple questions, and complete transactions	• Are less involved with routine tasks
• Require little training and compensation	• Require a lot of training and compensation
• Have limited expertise and enthusiasm	• Are highly expert and enthusiastic

Basic Differences ←→

newly built house. Yet, for many customers, the order getter has a high-pressure image. He or she may also need expensive training. Such nonsales tasks as writing reports may be avoided because they take away from a salesperson's time with customers and are seldom rewarded. Compensation can be very high for salespersons who are effective order getters. Figure 19-5 contrasts order takers and order getters.

Support personnel supplement a sales force. A ***missionary salesperson*** gives out information on new goods or services. He or she does not close sales but describes items' attributes, answers questions, and leaves written information. This paves the way for later sales and is commonly used with prescription drugs. A ***sales engineer*** accompanies an order getter if a very technical or complex item is involved. He or she discusses specifications and long-range uses, while the order getter makes customer contacts and closes sales. A ***service salesperson*** ordinarily deals with customers after sales. Delivery, installation, and other follow-up tasks are done.

Missionary salespersons, sales engineers, and service salespersons are support personnel.

19-4e   Selecting a Sales Technique

Two basic selling techniques are the canned sales presentation and the need-satisfaction approach. The ***canned sales presentation*** is a memorized, repetitive presentation given to all customers interested in a given item. It does not adapt to customer needs or traits but presumes that a general presentation will appeal to everyone. Though criticized for its inflexibility and a nonmarketing orientation, it does have value for companies that employ inexperienced salespeople and have little time or interest in training them in creative selling techniques. With this approach, salespeople have a consistent sales presentation and a structured order of topics to discuss; basic customer questions-and-answers can be scripted.

The canned sales presentation is memorized and nonadaptive.

The **need-satisfaction approach** is a high-level selling method based on the principle that each customer has different attributes and wants, and therefore the sales presentation should be adapted to the individual consumer. With this technique, a salesperson first asks: What type of product are you looking for? Have you ever bought this product before? What price range are you considering? Then the sales presentation is more responsive to the particular person, and a new shopper is treated differently from an experienced one. The need-satisfaction approach is more customer-oriented; yet, it requires better training and skilled sales personnel. Here are some hints for using this approach:

> The **need-satisfaction approach** adapts to individual consumers.

- "Be sincere with people. Too many salespeople are fake and feign interest in their prospects. People are smart and see right through such insincerity."
- "It is vitally important to constantly hone your sales and communication skills. Continuous growth and training in formal professional selling techniques are also very important."
- "Listen to your customer, understand his or her wants and needs, and then try to learn whether or not you can deliver the goods or services to meet those wants and needs. If you approach a prospect with a solution before understanding the problem, you are apt to be wrong about the solution."
- "The best salespeople ask many questions and genuinely listen to answers before speaking again."
- "Your prospects and customers are all different, so you should treat them differently."
- "The best salespeople listen much more than they talk."
- "If you cannot give your prospects what they want, tell them so and help them find what they are looking for elsewhere."[5]

The canned sales presentation works best with inexpensive, routine items that are heavily advertised and relatively pre-sold. The need-satisfaction approach works best with more expensive, more complex items that have moderate advertising and require substantial additional information for consumers.

19-4f Outlining Sales Tasks

The tasks to be performed by the personal sales force need to be outlined. The **selling process** consists of prospecting for leads, approaching customers, determining consumer wants, giving a sales presentation, answering questions, closing the sale, and following up.[6] See Figure 19-6.

> The **selling process** consists of seven steps.

Outside selling requires a procedure, known as **prospecting**, to generate a list of customer leads. Blind prospecting uses phone directories, the Internet, and other general listings of potential customers; with it, a small percentage of those contacted will be

> **Prospecting** creates customer leads.

Figure 19-6

The Selling Process

---

[5] Dave Dolak, "Sales and Personal Selling," http://www.davedolak.com/psell.htm (March 16, 2006).

[6] For a good checklist of sales tasks, see Barry Farber, "Step by Step," http://www.entrepreneur.com/mag/article/0,1539,306803,00.html (March 2003).

interested in a firm's offering. Lead prospecting depends on past customers and others for referrals; thus, a greater percentage of people will be interested because of the referral from someone they know. Inside selling does not involve prospecting because customers have already been drawn to a store or office through ads or prior purchase experience.

Approaching customers is a two-stage procedure: pre-approach and greeting. During pre-approach, a salesperson tries to get information about the customer from the firm's data base, census materials, and/or other secondary data—as well as from referrals. The salesperson is then better equipped to interact with that customer. Inside retail salespeople may be unable to use a pre-approach; they often know nothing about a consumer until he or she enters the store. During the greeting, a salesperson begins a conversation. The intention is to put the customer at ease and build rapport.

> **The pre-approach and greeting are the two parts of approaching customers.**

The next step is to ascertain customer wants by asking the person a variety of questions regarding past experience with the product category, price, product features, intended uses, and the kinds of information still needed.

The *sales presentation* includes a verbal description of a product, its benefits, options and models, price, associated services such as delivery and warranty, and a demonstration (if needed). A canned sales presentation or need-satisfaction method may be used. The purpose of a sales presentation is to convert an undecided consumer into a purchaser.

> **The sales presentation converts an uncertain consumer.**

After a presentation, the salesperson usually answers consumer questions. They are of two kinds: the first request more information; the second raise objections that must be settled before a sale is made.

Once questions have been answered, a salesperson is ready for *closing the sale*. This means getting a person to agree to a purchase. The salesperson must be sure no key questions remain before trying to close a sale, and the salesperson must not argue with a customer.

> **The closing clinches a sale.**

With a big purchase, the salesperson should follow up after a sale to be sure the customer is pleased. The person is then better satisfied, referrals are obtained, and repurchases are more likely. "Here's the bottom line. You can easily differentiate yourself from your competition by making the effort to follow up with your prospects and customers. Don't take it for granted that they will call you. Be proactive and contact them."[7]

Besides the tasks in the selling process, a firm must clearly enumerate the nonselling tasks it wants sales personnel to perform. Among the nonselling tasks that may be assigned are setting up displays, writing up information sheets, marking prices on products, checking competitors' strategies, doing test marketing analysis and consumer surveys, and training new employees.

19-4g Applying the Plan

Sales management—planning, implementing, and controlling the personal sales function—should be used in applying a personal selling plan. It covers employee selection, training, territory allocation, compensation, and supervision.

> **Sales management tasks range from employee selection to supervision.**

In selecting salespeople, a combination of personal attributes should be assessed: mental (intelligence, ability to plan), physical (appearance, speaking ability), experiential (education, sales/business background), environmental (group memberships, social influences), personality (ambition, enthusiasm, tact, resourcefulness, stability), and willingness to be trained and to follow instructions.[8] What makes a superior sales force?

> (1) *Optimism*—Ever notice how the best reps tend to look on the bright side? Optimism also may determine how resilient a rep will be. (2) *Resilience*—This is the "ability to take 15 no's before you get a yes." (3) *Self-Motivation*—Most managers and experts believe this is a trait that cannot be taught. The best reps tend to have an inherent competitive drive for money or

---

[7] Kelley Robertson, "The Impact of Follow-Up," **http://www.businessknowhow.com/marketing/follow-up.htm** (December 14, 2005).

[8] Adapted by the authors from Rosann L. Spiro, William J. Stanton, and Greg A. Rich, *Management of a Sales Force*, 11th ed. (New York: McGraw-Hill/Irwin, 2003).

recognition or simply pride. (4) *Personability*—You can't sell if your customers don't like you. Being friendly and sociable is a hallmark of reps who maintain long-term customer relationships. (5) *Empathy*—This underlies virtually all other emotional intelligence skills, because it involves truly understanding the customer. Empathetic reps tend to have good listening and communication skills.[9]

The traits of potential salespeople must be compatible with the customers with whom they will interact and the requirements of the good or service being sold. The buyer-seller dyad operates better when there are some similarities in salesperson and customer characteristics. And certain product categories require much different education, technical training, and sales activities than others (such as jewelry versus computer sales).

Once the preceding factors are reviewed, the firm would develop a formal procedure that specifies the personal attributes sought, sources of employees (such as colleges and employment agencies), and methods for selection (such as interviews and testing). It would be based on the overall selling plan.

Salesperson training may take many forms. A formal program uses a trainer, a classroom, lectures, and printed materials. It may also include role playing (in which trainees act out parts) and case analysis. Field trips take trainees on actual calls so they can observe skilled salespeople. On-the-job training places trainees in their own selling situations under the close supervision of a trainer or senior salesperson. Training often covers a range of topics; it should teach selling skills and include information on the firm and its offerings, the industry, and employee duties. For example, Century 21 (**http://www.century21.com**) has a comprehensive sales training initiative called Career Real Estate Agent Training and Education (CREATE 21). It "is a modular 120-hour course for new agents that features a mix of live online and instructor-led training combined with computer-based instruction, in-person broker coaching, and guided, training-specific job tasks called 'revenue-generating homework assignments.'"[10] Besides initial training, continuous training or retraining of sales personnel may be necessary to teach new techniques, explain new products, or improve performance.

Territory size and salesperson allocation are decided next. A ***sales territory*** consists of the geographic area, customers, and/or product lines assigned to a salesperson. If territories are assigned by customer type or product category, two or more salespeople may cover the same area. Territory size depends on customer locations, order size, travel time and expenses, the time per sales call, the yearly visits for each account, and the number of hours per year each salesperson has for selling tasks. The mix of established versus new customer accounts must also be considered. Allocating salespeople to specific territories depends on their ability, the buyer-seller dyad, the mix of selling and nonselling tasks (such as one salesperson training new employees), and seniority. Proper territory size and allocation provide adequate coverage of customers, minimize overlap, recognize geographic boundaries, minimize travel expenses, encourage solicitation of new accounts, provide enough sales potential for good salespeople to be well rewarded, and are fair to everyone. Sales territory software, such as that marketed by Territory Mapper (**http://www.territorymapper.com**) and AlignStar (**http://www.alignstar.com**), can facilitate planning.

Salespeople are compensated by straight salary, straight commission, or a combination of salary and commission or bonus. With a ***straight salary plan***, a salesperson is paid a flat amount per time period. Earnings are not tied to sales. Advantages are that both selling and nonselling tasks can be specified and controlled, salespeople have security, and expenses are known in advance. Disadvantages are the low incentive to increase sales, expenses not being tied to productivity, and the continuing costs even if there are low sales. Order takers are usually paid straight salaries.

> A **sales territory** contains the area, customers, and/or products assigned to a salesperson.

> Sales compensation may be **straight salary, straight commission,** or a **combination** of the two.

---

[9] Julia Chang, "Born to Sell?" *Sales & Marketing Management* (July 2003), p. 36. See also Paul Sloan and Alan Key, "The Sales Force That Rocks," *Business 2.0* (June 2005), pp. 102–107.

[10] Brandon Hall, "Sales Training Makeovers," *Training* (May 2005), pp. 15–22.

With a *straight commission plan*, a salesperson's earnings are directly related to sales, profits, customer satisfaction, or some other performance measure. The commission rate is often keyed to a quota, which is a productivity standard. Advantages of this plan are the use of motivated salespeople, no fixed sales compensation costs, and expenses being tied to productivity. Disadvantages are the firm's lack of control over nonselling tasks, the instability of a firm's expenses, and salesperson risks due to variable pay. Insurance, real-estate, and direct-selling order getters often earn straight commissions. A real-estate salesperson might receive a 3 percent commission of $9,000 for selling a $300,000 house.

To gain the advantages of both salary- and commission-oriented methods, many firms use elements of each in a *combination sales compensation plan*. This balances control, flexibility, and employee incentives; and some firms award bonuses for superior individual or firm performance. All types of order getters work on a combination basis. Two-thirds of U.S. firms compensate sales personnel by some form of combination plan, one-fifth use a straight-salary plan, and the rest use straight commissions. Smaller firms are more apt to use a straight-salary plan and less apt to use a combination plan.

Supervision encompasses four aspects of sales management:

> Supervision involves motivation, performance measures, nonselling tasks, and modifying behavior.

- *Sales personnel must be motivated.* Their motivation depends on such factors as the clarity of the job (what tasks must be performed), the salesperson's desire to achieve, the variety of tasks performed, the incentives for undertaking each task, the style of the sales manager, flexibility, and recognition.
- *Performance must be measured.* To do this, achievements must be gauged against such goals as sales and calls per day. The analysis should take into account territory size, travel time, and experience. Salesperson failure is often related to poor listening skills, the failure to concentrate on priorities, a lack of effort, the inability to determine customer needs, a lack of planning for presentations, promising too much, and inadequate knowledge.
- *The sales manager must ensure that all nonselling tasks are completed,* even if sales personnel are not rewarded for them.
- *Some action may be needed to modify behavior* if performance does not meet expectations.[11]

In sales management, these key factors should also be taken into account: the evolving role of women in selling and the special nature of selling in foreign markets.

> More women are involved in sales than ever before, and international markets require special decisions.

With regard to women in personal selling, a dramatic increase has taken place in the proportion of sales personnel and sales managers who are female. According to the U.S. Bureau of Labor Statistics (**http://www.bls.gov**), women now comprise 50 percent of the total sales force in the United States and nearly 40 percent of sales supervisors (up from 25 percent two decades ago). And as one study found, female sales managers can be quite different from their male counterparts:

> Mixed-gender sales teams led by females display significantly higher levels of job involvement, job satisfaction (with supervision, fellow workers, and customers), as well as lower levels of role ambiguity, job anxiety, and burnout. These teams also display higher levels of organizational commitment and a lower propensity to leave. A tentative yet provocative conclusion is that in a sales force which shows few gender-related differences between salespeople, female managers pursue control strategies of a more behavior-based orientation than do male sales managers, and consequently their sales teams evidence more desirable attitudes, lower stress characteristics, and more positive work outcomes. Symbolically, this suggests that first-line female sales managers do not imitate the behavior of male managers. They exercise latitude via behavior-based control activities.[12]

---

[11] See Chris Lytle, "High-Performing Sales Teams," *American Salesman* (July 2005), pp. 23–27.

[12] Nigel F. Piercy, David W. Cravens, and Nikala Lane, "Sales Manager Behavior Control Strategy and Its Consequences: The Impact of Gender Differences," *Journal of Personal Selling & Sales Management*, Vol. 21 (Winter 2001), pp. 39–49. See also Nikala Lane, "Strategy Implementation: The Implications of a Gender Perspective for Change Management," *Journal of Strategic Marketing*, Vol. 13 (June 2005), pp. 117–131.

When firms go international, sales managers must recognize that sales personnel have to deal with vastly different cultures: "As businesses increasingly seek to market across international borders, they face the challenge of finding people who can successfully communicate to customers of multiple nations. Not only do salespeople need to understand another language, but they must also understand the complex web of social, cultural, and rhetoric features to which customers respond."[13] In particular, the attributes of salespeople; salesperson training, compensation, and supervision; the dynamics of the buyer-seller dyad; and the selling process may need to be tailored to distinct foreign markets.

19-5 THE SCOPE AND IMPORTANCE OF SALES PROMOTION

As a result of intense competition in their industries, numerous firms are aggressively seeking every marketing edge possible. Thus, sales promotion activities worldwide are at their highest level. In the United States alone, spending exceeds $325 billion a year, including some sales promotion activities (such as direct mail and promotion-oriented ads) that may also be viewed as advertising.

> Sales promotion efforts are now quite extensive.

The extent of sales promotion activities can be shown by the following:

- Three-quarters of U.S. households use coupons, half on a regular basis. Each year, about $3 billion worth of coupons are redeemed. Yet, people redeem only a small fraction of distributed coupons.[14]
- Thousands of trade shows take place around the world each year. One is the Automotive Aftermarket Products Expo (AAPEX). It attracts 2,000 exhibitors and 120,000 visitors—including 52,000 b to b customers from 125 countries.[15] The TSNN.com Web site (**http://www.tsnn.com**) contains information on more than 15,000 trade shows and conferences worldwide.
- According to International Events Group (**http://www.sponsorship.com**), firms spend $30 billion annually worldwide (including $12 billion in North America) to sponsor special events—two-thirds on sports-related events. Among the leading sponsors are Anheuser-Busch (**http://www.anheuser-busch.com**), Coca-Cola (**http://www.coca-cola.com**), General Motors (**http://www.gm.com**), and PepsiCo (**http://www.pepsico.com**).[16]
- Safeway (**http://www.safeway.com**), the California-based supermarket chain, has 1.5 million members in its frequent-shopper program. Customers are rewarded with special discounts and Safeway is able to build customer loyalty. Loyalty programs are extremely popular. Figure 19-7 shows a Gap promotion to foster customer loyalty.
- $20 billion is spent on point-of-purchase displays in U.S. stores each year.[17] These displays stimulate impulse purchases and provide information. Besides traditional cardboard, metal, and plastic displays, more stores now use digital electronic signs and video displays.

Several reasons account for sales promotion's strength as a marketing tool. As noted earlier, firms look for any competitive edge they can get, and this often involves some kind of sales promotion. The various forms of sales promotions are more acceptable to firms and consumers than in the past. Rapid results are possible, and numerous firms want to

---

[13] "Global Selling and Sales Management: Cross-Cultural Issues—National Character," *Journal of Personal Selling & Sales Management*, Vol. 22 (Summer 2002), pp. 204–205.

[14] "All About Coupons," **http://www.couponmonth.com/pages/allabout.htm** (January 11, 2006).

[15] "Automobile Aftermarket Products Expo," **http://www.aapexshow.com** (January 29, 2006).

[16] "More for Less," *Promo* (April 2005), p. AR35; and "Learn About Sponsorship," **http://www.sponsorship.com/learn** (February 8, 2006).

[17] "Tuning in at the Shelf," *Promo* (April 2005), pp. AR29, AR32.

improve short-run profits. Today, more shoppers seek promotions before buying, and resellers put pressure on manufacturers for promotions. In economic slowdowns, more shoppers look for value-oriented sales promotions. Due to rising costs, advertising and personal selling have become more expensive relative to sales promotion. Technological advances make aspects of sales promotion, such as coupon redemption, easier to administer.

19-6 THE CHARACTERISTICS OF SALES PROMOTION

Sales promotion lures customers, maintains loyalty, creates excitement, is often keyed to patronage, and appeals to channel members.

Sales promotion has many advantages. It helps attract customer traffic and keep brand or company loyalty: New-product samples and trial offers draw customers. A manufacturer can sustain brand loyalty by giving gifts to regular customers and coupons for its brands. A reseller can retain loyal customers by having incentives for frequent shoppers and using store coupons.

Quick customer responses can be gained. Some promotions provide value and are kept by customers (such as calendars, matchbooks, T-shirts, pens, and posters with the firm's name); they provide a reminder function. Impulse purchases can be stimulated via

Marketing and the Web

Online Coupons Come of Age

As recently as 2004, many retailers were reluctant to place E-coupons on their Web sites. Now, the use of E-coupons from various types of retailers has significantly grown. The increase in E-coupons parallels the overall growth in coupon distribution. Each year, in the United States alone, hundreds of billions of E-coupons are distributed to shoppers.

CoolSavings (http://www.coolsavings.com), a Web site that features E-coupons, works with retailers to target specific groups of customers. Three types of E-coupons are Internet coupons (that are redeemed in a brick-and-mortar store), coupons linked to a loyalty program (that can be automatically redeemed at the cash register), and coupons that are both issued and redeemed online.

Kroger (http://www.kroger.com) uses coupons that are linked to its 2 million-member loyalty pro-gram. Kroger loyalty card members receive selected E-coupon offers. According to CoolSavings' president and chief executive officer, "This method of couponing eliminates the need to clip or carry coupons." The selected discount is automatically deducted at the cash register after the consumer shows his or her loyalty program card.

A common problem among retailers that offer traditional paper-based coupons is that consumers with access to multiple coupons can abuse the coupon offer. Through barcode and other tracking technologies, retailers can control the number of E-coupons that can be printed by a single customer.

Source: Based on material in Katherine Field, "Surfing for Savings," *Chain Store Age* (July 2005), p. 64.

in-store displays. An attractive supermarket display for batteries can dramatically raise sales. In addition, a good display may lead a shopper to buy more than originally intended.

Excitement is created by certain short-run promotions involving gifts, contests, or sweepstakes; and high-value items or high payoffs encourage consumers to participate. Contests offer the further benefit of customer involvement (through the completion of some skill-oriented activity). Many promotions are tied to customer patronage—with coupons, frequent-shopper gifts, and referral gifts directly related to purchases. In these cases, promotions can be a fixed percentage of sales and their costs not incurred until transactions are completed. And resellers may be stimulated if support is provided in the form of displays, manufacturer coupons, manufacturer rebates, and trade allowances.

Sales promotion also has limitations. A firm's image may be lessened if it always runs promotions. People may view discounts as representing a decline in product quality and believe a firm could not sell its offerings without them. Profit margins are often lower for a firm if sales promotion is used. When coupons, rebates, or other special deals are offered frequently, people may not buy when products are sold at regular prices; they will stock up each time there is a promotion. Shoppers may even interpret a regular price as an increase for items that are heavily promoted.

Some promotions shift the marketing focus away from the product itself to secondary factors. People may be lured by calendars and sweepstakes instead of product quality and features. In the short run, this generates consumer enthusiasm. In the long run, it may adversely affect a brand's image and sales because a product-related advantage has not been communicated. Sales promotion should enhance—not replace—advertising, personal selling, and public relations.

> Sales promotion may hurt image, cause consumers to wait for special offers, and shift the focus from the product.

19-7 DEVELOPING A SALES PROMOTION PLAN

A sales promotion plan consists of the steps shown in Figure 19-8 and explained next.

19-7a Setting Objectives

Goals are usually demand-oriented. They may be related to channel members and to consumers.

Figure 19-8

Developing a Sales Promotion Plan

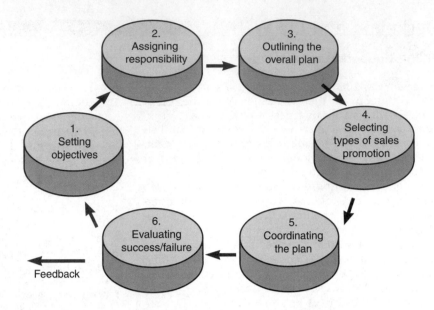

Objectives associated with channel-member sales promotions include gaining distribution, receiving adequate shelf space, increasing dealer enthusiasm, raising sales, and getting cooperation in sales promotion expenditures. Objectives pertaining to consumer sales promotions include boosting brand awareness, increasing product trials, hiking average purchases, encouraging repurchases, obtaining impulse sales, emphasizing novelty, and supplementing other promotional tools.

19-7b   Assigning Responsibility

Duties are often shared by advertising and sales managers, with each directing the sales promotions in his or her area. An advertising manager would work on coupons, customer contests, calendars, and other mass promotions. A sales manager would work on trade shows, cooperative promotions, special events, demonstrations, and other efforts involving individualized attention for channel members or consumers.

Some companies have their own sales promotion departments or hire outside promotion firms, such as PromoWorks (**http://www.promoworkspromotions.com**). Outside firms often work with specific tools—such as coupons, contests, or gifts—and often can devise a sales promotion campaign at less cost than the user company could. These firms offer expertise, swift service, flexibility, and, when requested, distribution.

19-7c   Outlining the Overall Plan

At this juncture, a sales promotion plan should be outlined and include a budget, an orientation, conditions, media, duration and timing, and cooperative efforts. In setting a budget, it is important to include all costs. The average face value of a U.S. coupon is now $1; retailers get a handling fee for each coupon they redeem; and there are costs for printing, mailing, and advertising coupons.

Sales promotion orientation refers to its focus—channel members or consumers—and its theme. Promotions for channel members should improve their product knowledge, provide sales support, offer rewards for selling a promoted product, and foster better cooperation and efficiency. Consumer promotions should induce impulse and larger-volume sales, sustain brand name recognition, and gain participation. A promotion theme refers to its underlying channel member or consumer message—such as a special sale, new-product introduction, holiday celebration, or customer recruitment. See Figure 19-9.

> **Sales promotion orientation** may be toward channel members or final consumers.

Figure 19-9

Making Sales Promotion Special at Target Stores

Source: Reprinted by permission of Susan Berry, Retail Image Consulting, Inc.

Sales promotion conditions are requirements channel members or consumers must meet to be eligible for a specific sales promotion. These may include minimum purchases, performance provisions, and/or minimum age. A channel member may have to stock a certain amount of merchandise to receive a free display case from a manufacturer. A consumer may have to send in proofs of purchase for a refund or gift. In some cases, strict time limits are set as to the closing dates for participation in a promotion.

> **Sales promotion conditions are eligibility requirements.**

Media are the vehicles through which sales promotions reach channel members or consumers. They include direct mail, newspapers, magazines, television, the sales force, trade shows, and group meetings.

A promotion's duration varies, depending on its goals. Coupons usually have short-term closing dates because they are used to increase store traffic. Frequent-shopper points often can be redeemed for at least one year; the goal is to maintain loyalty. As noted earlier, if promotions are lengthy or offered often, consumers may expect them as part of a purchase. Some promotions are seasonal, and for these timing is crucial. They must be tied to such events as fall school openings or model changes.

Finally, the use of shared promotions should be decided. With cooperative efforts, each party pays some costs and gets benefits. Promotions can be sponsored by trade associations, manufacturers and/or service firms, wholesalers, and retailers. Consider this observation about sales promotion in India:

> Collaborative sales promotion agreements are on the rise. This is a trend that began with event sponsorship. World Cup Cricket and Olympics have had multiple noncompeting sponsors for years and this has worked very well for the companies involved. When two or more companies want to reach the same target audience, a collaborative effort amplifies the message they have to send. A Coca-Cola customer is also a Citibank customer, a Nike customer.[18]

19-7d Selecting the Types of Sales Promotion

A wide range of sales promotion tools is available. The attributes of promotion tools oriented to channel members are shown in Table 19-3. The attributes of promotion tools

---

[18] Seema Gupta, "Event Marketing: Issues and Challenges," *Management Review*, Vol. 15 (June 2003), p. 94.

Table 19-3	Selected Types of Sales Promotion Directed at Channel Members	
Type	**Characteristics**	**Illustration**
Trade shows or meetings	One firm or a group of firms invites channel members to attend sessions where products are displayed and explained.	The annual National Hardware Show attracts more than 3,200 exhibitors and tens of thousands of attendees.
Training	A firm provides training for personnel of channel members.	Gateway trains retail salespeople in how to operate and use its computers.
Trade allowances or special offers	Channel members are given discounts or rebates for performing specified functions or purchasing during certain time periods.	A local distributor receives a discount for running its own promotion for GE air conditioners.
Point-of-purchase displays	A firm gives channel members fully equipped displays for its products and sets them up.	Coca-Cola provides display cases with its name on them to retailers carrying minimum quantities of Coca-Cola products.
Push money	Channel members' salespeople are given bonuses for pushing the brand of a certain firm. Channel members may not like this if their salespeople shift loyalty to the supplying firm.	A salesperson in an office-equipment store is paid an extra $50 for every desk of a particular brand that is sold.
Sales contests	Prizes or bonuses are distributed if certain performance levels are met.	A wholesaler receives $2,500 for selling 1,000 microchips in a month.
Free merchandise	Discounts or allowances are provided in the form of merchandise.	A retailer gets one case of ballpoint pens free for every 10 cases purchased.
Demonstration models	Free items are given to channel members for demonstration purposes.	A hospital-bed manufacturer offers demonstrator models to its distributors.
Gifts	Channel members are given gifts for carrying items or performing functions.	During one three-month period, a book publisher gives computerized cash registers to bookstores that agree to stock a specified quantity of its books.
Cooperative promotions	Two or more channel members share the costs of a promotion.	A manufacturer and retailer each pay part of the costs for T-shirts with the manufacturer's and retailer's names embossed.

oriented to consumers are noted in Table 19-4. Examples for each tool are also provided in these tables. The selection of sales promotions should be based on such factors as company image, company goals, costs, participation requirements, and the enthusiasm of channel members or customers.

19-7e   Coordinating the Plan

It is essential for sales promotion activities to be well coordinated with other elements of the promotion mix. In particular:

- Advertising and sales promotion plans should be integrated.
- The sales force should be notified of all promotions well in advance and trained to implement them.
- For special events, such as the appearance of a major celebrity, publicity should be generated.
- Sales promotions should be consistent with channel members' activities.

> Advertising and sales promotion should be integrated.

19-7f   Evaluating Success/Failure

Measuring the success or failure of many sales promotions is straightforward because the promotions may be closely linked to performance or sales. By analyzing before-and-after data, the impact of these promotions is clear. Trade show effectiveness can be gauged by counting the number of leads generated, examining sales from those leads and the cost

> The success or failure of some sales promotions is simple to measure.

Table 19-4	Selected Types of Sales Promotion Directed at Consumers	
Type	**Characteristics**	**Illustration**
Coupons	Firms advertise special discounts for customers who redeem coupons.	P&G mails consumers a 50-cents-off coupon for Sure deodorant, which can be redeemed at any supermarket.
Refunds or rebates	Consumers submit proof purchases (often to the manufacturer) and receive an extra discount.	First Alert provides rebates to consumers submitting proofs of purchase for its fire alarms.
Samples	Free merchandise or services are given to consumers, generally for new items.	Musicmatch offers a free trial of of its Internet services.
Contests or sweepstakes	Consumers compete for prizes by answering questions (contests) or filling out forms for random drawings of prizes (sweepstakes).	Publishers Clearing House sponsors annual sweepstakes and awards cash and other prizes.
Bonus packs or multipacks	Consumers receive discounts for purchasing in quantity.	A furniture store runs a "buy one, get one free" sale on desk lamps.
Shows or exhibits	Many firms co-sponsor exhibitions for consumers.	The Auto Show is annually scheduled for the public in New York.
Point-of-purchase displays	In-store displays remind customers and generate impulse purchases.	*TV Guide* sales in supermarkets are high due to checkout counter displays.
Special events	Firms sponsor the Olympics, fashion shows, and other activities.	Visa USA is a worldwide sponsor of the Olympics.
Product placements	Branded goods and services are depicted in movies and TV shows.	Nike sneakers appear in movies.
Gifts	Consumers get gifts for making a purchase or opening a new account.	Savings banks offer gifts for consumers opening new accounts or expanding existing ones.
Frequent-shopper gifts	Consumers get gifts or special discounts, based on cumulative purchases. Points are amassed and exchanged for gifts or money.	Airline travelers accumulate mileage and receive free trips or gifts when enough miles are earned.
Referral gifts	Existing customers are given gifts for referring their friends to the company.	Tupperware awards gifts to the woman hosting a Tupperware party in her home.
Demonstrations	Goods or services are shown in action.	Different models of barbeque grills are demonstrated in a free lesson.

Ethical Issues in Marketing

Are Frequent Flier Programs a Good Deal for Consumers?

According to some estimates, more than 100 million people are members of frequent flier programs. Yet, despite the popularity of these programs, some experts question their use. These programs are costly for the airlines in that they must first promote membership among consumers and then promote the programs to get members to use their points. In some cases, these promotions stress fringe benefits such as eyeglasses or magazine subscriptions rather than a free flight or an upgrade.

Some consumers have also become less enamored with frequent flier programs. They believe that airline miles are difficult to redeem, causing them to travel at inconvenient times or to make multiple stops, instead of taking direct flights. In comparison to other loyalty programs where the firm provides a customer with a product having a wholesale cost that is high in relation to the retail price, the cost of placing a passenger in an unsold airline seat is very low. A former airline executive stated, "The reality is, very few seats are given away at the expense of a revenue passenger."

Frequent flier programs are highly profitable to the airlines. American Airlines (http://www.aa.com) spends $750,000 in marketing its AAdvantage program to generate revenues exceeding $1 billion. Its revenues come primarily from its nearly 1,200 partners who purchase miles at 1 to 2 cents per mile.

Source: Based on material in Rich Thomaselli, "Who Really Reaps Mileage Rewards?" *Advertising Age* (June 20, 2005), p. 12.

per lead, getting customer feedback about a show from the sales force, and determining the amount of literature given out at a show. Companies can verify sales increases as a result of dealer-training programs. Firms using coupons can review sales and compare redemption rates with industry averages. Surveys of channel members and consumers can indicate satisfaction with promotions, suggestions for improvements, and the effect of promotions on image.

Some sales promotions—such as event sponsorships and T-shirt giveaways—are more difficult to evaluate. Objectives are less definitive.

Here are three examples relating to the effectiveness of sales promotion:

- A well-done contest can win over the media and customers: "TCBY [**http://www.tcby.com**] introduced new frozen-yogurt layer cakes and deep-dish pies with a 'Wish Come True' contest. Entry forms offered contestants a choice of four wishes, ranging from wellness (a year of spa treatments, gym membership, and nutrition counseling) to family fun (a television set, DVD player, and videos). As part of the contest, the chain conducted a national survey to find out what people wish for, when they wish for it, and whether they believe wishes can come true. The campaign was 'a great success on all accounts,' according to TCBY's Dan Martinez. 'It had a newsworthy aspect, and it created customer interest. We got many positive media mentions, with write-ups in local and regional publications.' "[19]

- MasterCard (**http://www.mastercard.com**) recently won four Promo! Awards for its sales promotions: "MasterCard stole the show, hauling away four golds and Best of Show honors. The annual event is produced by the Canadian Association of Promotional Marketing Agencies to celebrate excellence in promotional marketing. Three of the gold awards were for a 'We're at your service' holiday program. It leveraged the firm's partnership with more than 40 retail malls across Canada, offering shoppers who used their MasterCard free services such as coat-check, gift-wrapping, and mall porters."[20]

- How successful is sampling? Not long ago, a research project was undertaken to study the success of samples in magazines. One-half of the respondents received a copy of the magazine with an ad insert and a free sample of a hair care product; the other respondents received just the ad insert: "The results showed that unprompted brand awareness was six times greater with the sample and that prompted awareness was 89 percent higher. Perhaps the most important finding, which appears to confirm sampling's effectiveness in brand building in magazines, is that 60 percent of all respondents were more likely to buy a product if they first used a sample."[21]

Web Sites You Can Use

Looking for a bargain? Try one of these sales promotion Web sites:

- ContestListings.com (**http://contestlistings.com**)
- Cool Savings (**http://www101.coolsavings.com**)
- Coupon Mountain (**http://www.couponmountain.com**)
- Daily eDeals (**http://www.dailyedeals.com**)
- Deal Catcher (**http://www.dealcatcher.com**)
- DealofDay.com (**http://www.dealofday.com**)
- Deals Digger (**http://www.dealsdigger.com**)
- Deals2buy (**http://www.deals2buy.com**)
- FreeClutter.com (**http://www.freeclutter.com**)
- Hot Coupons (**http://www.hotcoupons.com**)
- Loot Deals (**http://www.lootdeals.com**)
- MyCoupons (**http://www.mycoupons.com**)
- MyPoints (**http://www.mypoints.com**)
- StartSampling (**http://www.startsampling.com**)
- UltimateCoupons.com (**http://www.ultimatecoupons.com**)
- Val-Pak (**http://www.valpak.com**)

[19] "Wish Lists," *Restaurants & Institutions* (October 15, 2005), p. 21.

[20] Paul-Mark Rendon, "Promo! Gold," *Marketing* (September 26, 2005), pp. 38–39.

[21] "Sampling the Press," *Soap, Perfumery & Cosmetics* (March 2005). p. 35.

Summary

1. *To examine the scope, importance, and characteristics of personal selling* Personal selling involves oral communication with prospective buyers by paid representatives for the purpose of making sales. About 16 million people work in U.S. selling jobs; millions more work in sales jobs outside the United States. These numbers understate the value of personal selling because every contact between a company employee and a customer involves some degree of selling.

   Selling is used with high-volume clients, geographically concentrated customers, expensive/ complex products, customers wanting sales services, and entries into foreign markets. It also resolves questions and addresses other issues. Selling costs are higher than advertising costs at many firms. Thus, efficiency is important.

   Selling fosters a buyer-seller dyad (a two-way communication flow), is flexible and adaptable, adds to relationships with customers, results in less audience waste, clinches sales, and provides immediate feedback. Yet, personal selling can handle only a limited number of customers, is rather ineffective for creating awareness, and has high costs per customer and a poor image among some shoppers.

2. *To study the elements in a personal selling plan* A selling plan has seven steps: setting goals—demand- and/or image-related; assigning oversight—to one manager or to several managers; setting a budget; choosing the type(s) of sales positions—order takers, order getters, and/or support salespeople; selecting a sales technique—the canned sales presentation or the need-satisfaction approach; outlining tasks—including each of the relevant steps in the selling process and nonselling tasks; and applying the plan— which centers on sales management.

3. *To examine the scope, importance, and characteristics of sales promotion* Sales promotion encompasses paid marketing communication activities (other than advertising, publicity, or personal selling) that stimulate consumer purchases and dealer effectiveness. In the United States, such expenditures exceed $325 billion annually.

   The growth of sales promotion is due to firms looking for a competitive edge, the greater acceptance of sales promotion tools by both firms and consumers, quick returns, the pressure by consumers and channel members for promotions, the popularity during economic downturns, the high costs of other promotional forms, and technological advances.

   A sales promotion helps attract customer traffic and loyalty, provides value and may be retained by people, increases impulse purchases, creates excitement, is keyed to patronage, and improves reseller cooperation. On the other hand, it may hurt a firm's image, encourage consumers to wait for promotions before making purchases, and shift the focus away from product attributes. Sales promotion cannot replace other forms of promotion.

4. *To study the elements in a sales promotion plan* A promotion plan has six steps: setting goals—ordinarily demand-oriented; assigning responsibility—to advertising and sales managers, company departments, and/or outside specialists; outlining the overall plan—including orientation, conditions, and other factors; selecting the types of sales promotion; coordinating the plan with the other elements of the promotion mix; and evaluating success or failure

Key Terms

telemarketing (p. 575)
buyer-seller dyad (p. 577)
sales-expense budget (p. 581)
order taker (p. 581)
order getter (p. 581)
missionary salesperson (p. 582)
sales engineer (p. 582)
service salesperson (p. 582)

canned sales presentation (p. 582)
need-satisfaction approach (p. 583)
selling process (p. 583)
prospecting (p. 583)
approaching customers (p. 584)
sales presentation (p. 584)
closing the sale (p. 584)
sales management (p. 584)

sales territory (p. 585)
straight salary plan (p. 585)
straight commission plan (p. 586)
combination sales compensation plan (p. 586)
sales promotion orientation (p. 590)
sales promotion conditions (p. 591)

Review Questions

1. Under what circumstances should personal selling be emphasized? Why?
2. Draw and explain the buyer-seller dyad.
3. Distinguish among order takers, order getters, and support sales personnel.
4. When is a canned sales presentation appropriate? When is it inappropriate?

5. Outline the steps in the selling process.
6. Why is sales promotion growing as a marketing tool?
7. What are the limitations associated with sales promotion?
8. Differentiate between the orientation and conditions of sales promotions.

Discussion Questions

1. As a telemarketer, how would you deal with the "Do Not Call Registry" (**http://www.donotcall.gov**)?
2. How would you handle these objections raised at the end of a sales presentation for a car?
   a. "I saw the same price at a competing dealer, but that dealer also offered three free years of scheduled maintenance services."
   b. "Your service department is not open on Saturday."
   c. "None of the alternatives you showed me is satisfactory."
3. List several sales promotion techniques that would be appropriate for the American Red Cross. List several that would be appropriate for a community theater group. Explain the differences in your two lists.
4. How could a sales promotion be *too* successful? What are the potential risks with too much success?

Web Exercise

Visit the "Current Issue" section of the *Sales & Marketing Management* Web site (**http://www.salesandmarketing.com**) and read the "In-Depth" article available there. Offer five valuable tips based on the information in the story you read.

Practice Quiz

1. Which of these is *not* a characteristic of personal selling?
   a. Personal selling is usually the last stage in the consumer's decision process.
   b. Personal selling is an ineffective tool for generating consumer awareness.
   c. Personal selling costs per customer can be very high.
   d. There is more waste with most forms of selling than with advertising.

2. Which statement about the drawbacks of personal selling is false?
   a. Only a small number of consumers can be accommodated at a given time.
   b. It is an ineffective tool for generating consumer awareness about a product or service.
   c. Feedback is more difficult to ascertain than with advertising.
   d. It has a poor image in the eyes of a number of consumers.

3. The major goal for personal selling is
   a. information.
   b. persuasion.
   c. reminding.
   d. image.

4. Which of the following is *not* a normal function of an order taker?
   a. Generating customer leads
   b. Writing up orders
   c. Completing transactions
   d. Arranging displays

5. The need-satisfaction approach works best with
   a. complex items that have moderate advertising.
   b. inexpensive items.
   c. items that are pre-sold through heavy advertising.
   d. items for which customers require little additional information.

6. The first stage in the selling process is
   a. approaching customers.
   b. answering questions.
   c. closing the sale.
   d. prospecting for customer leads.

7. Which of the following is *not* a nonselling task that may be carried out by a firm's sales force?
   a. Marking prices on products
   b. Looking through trade publications for customer leads
   c. Writing up information sheets
   d. Checking competitors' strategies

8. Which of the following is *not* a fundamental part of sales management?
   a. Employee selection
   b. Compensation
   c. Marketing research
   d. Territory allocation

9. Earnings are *not* tied to sales with a
   a. straight commission plan.
   b. sales territory assigned on the basis of product type.
   c. combination compensation plan.
   d. straight salary plan.

10. Which of the following is *not* a part of sales supervision?
    a. Assigning sales territories
    b. Motivating sales personnel
    c. Completing nonselling tasks
    d. Modifying behavior changes

11. Which of the following is *not* a contributing factor to the rapid growth of sales promotion as a marketing tool?
    a. More shoppers seek promotions before buying.
    b. Various sales promotions are more acceptable to firms and consumers.

c. Firms are turning away from a short-run orientation and are seeking to improve long-term profits.

d. Advertising and personal selling have become more expensive.

12. Sales promotion may have an adverse effect on
    a. a firm's image.
    b. impulse purchasing.
    c. brand loyalty.
    d. new-product introduction.

13. In contrast to a sales manager, the advertising manager's sales promotion responsibility would focus on
    a. trade shows.
    b. special events.
    c. customer contests.
    d. demonstrations.

14. An example of the conditions of sales promotion is a
    a. direct-mail solicitation.
    b. Thanksgiving theme.
    c. purchase of three bars of soap to get one free.
    d. free sample of a new deodorant.

15. Which is *not* usually a type of promotion directed at channel members?
    a. Coupons
    b. Point-of-purchase displays
    c. Sales contests
    d. Training

For the answers to these questions, please visit the online site for this book at **http://www.atomicdog.com.**

6 Short Cases

Case 1: The Impact of the Web on Advertising[c6-1]

Internet Protocol TV (IPTV) is a new technology that joins television viewing and the Internet. Many different forms of communications-based firms have begun to use IPTV technology, including telecommunications, cable, and satellite companies. For example, cable and satellite companies now offer highly targeted and on-demand advertising through technology contained in viewers' set-top boxes.

IPTV converts video content into digital files and makes television watching an interactive experience. Through IPTV, television viewers can chat on their screens or even use their telephones to remotely program their digital video recorders. Other important capabilities of IPTV include a consumer's ability to watch a baseball game while simultaneously searching the Web for information about a player and the ability to receive videos at a time when they are wanted by viewers, as opposed to when they are aired by a network. IPTV can also target specific audiences with unique ads that best appeal to each group. "IPTV is going to open up the opportunity for more dialog between the marketer and the consumer. For marketers who want to target specific consumers—and what advertiser doesn't? IPTV is going to be a godsend," said a former head of marketing for Coca-Cola and Columbia Pictures.

Because IPTV is a point-to-point service (unlike television, it is not broadcast), every home and even every TV set in a home could receive different advertisements. Through IPTV's interactive capabilities, a consumer can purchase a PC shown in an ad by clicking on a box, instead of having to order the unit via telephone. In addition to the convenience in ordering, a shopper could use IPTV to better understand the options and features available with each model, as well as to gain access to user reviews. Some analysts initially questioned how many consumers would want to pause a show to watch an ad. To its surprise, TiVo (http://www.tivo.com) found that somewhere between 5 and 15 percent of its subscribers watch its mini-infomercials in a typical one-week promotion.

IPTV can be used in conjunction with traditional advertising. Reebok (http://www.reebok.com) shot five hours of footage that featured Allen Iverson, a Philadelphia 76er basketball star. The footage was used to produce both 30- and 60-second traditional television commercials, as well as IPTV. The IPTV version was compiled as a short documentary for Comcast's (http://www.comcast.com) Philadelphia customers.

Some marketing analysts believe that the future of television advertising will be depend on the success of IPTV. One advertising research firm expected television advertising to grow by 1 percent in 2005 versus 8 percent for Internet advertising. Television advertising has been hard hit by TiVo's capability of skipping commercials. And with cable and satellite television stations, a lot more channels are competing for the same viewers.

Television costs have substantially increased on a relative basis. A 30-second spot commercial that reached 88 million viewers on the 2005 Super Bowl cost $2.4 million. Twenty years ago, the same commercial would have cost $900,000 (after adjusting for inflation) and reached 115 million people. IPTV can generate more advertising expenditures due to its highly targeted and interactive nature. One study suggests that advertisers might pay at least 10 to 12 times more for IPTV than for traditional media.

Consumer pricing for IPTV can vary on a customer-to-customer basis due to its customization ability. Some observers believe that sites with a lot of advertising could be free, while other consumers who are not willing to receive banner ads would pay a fee. There could also be a graduated scale for consumers who want different levels of advertising.

Questions

1. Explain the significance of this statement: "Since IPTV is a point-to-point service (unlike television, it is not broadcast), every home and even every TV set in a home could receive different advertisements."
2. Discuss how an IPTV advertiser could best utilize its interactive capabilities.
3. Describe the role of IPTV in a manufacturer's integrated marketing communications (IMC) program.
4. What factors have contributed to the decline in importance of TV advertising over the past 10 years?

[c6-1] The data in the case are drawn from Stephanie N. Mehta, "How the Web Will Save the Commercial," *Fortune* (August 8, 2005), pp. 58–60.

Case 2: Dealing with the 12 Media Myths Affecting Public Relations[c6-2]

As head of a Hong Kong-based Internet service provider, Dan Hoffman has had a number of poor experiences involving interviews with reporters. For example, he would sometimes find that the published interviews had different information than he discussed. Hoffman, now president of an outsourcing telephone systems firm, called his public relations firm to help him better prepare for a television interview. According to the chief of Hoffman's public relations company, a number of pitfalls are commonly made by businesspeople when interviewed by the media. Common errors are not being prepared or having an unclear message.

Here are the 12 most common myths about being media-savvy (based on interviews with public relations executives) and how a marketer can overcome them.

- *Myth 1: Put a Positive Spin on Everything.* Be honest in sharing the necessary information. Recognize that you cannot always put a positive spin on an event.
- *Myth 2: Change the Subject When You Don't Want to Answer a Reporter's Question.* Although you need to answer reporter questions, you can include added information that puts your firm in a positive light. If asked about poor customer service, for example, discuss how the service is being improved.
- *Myth 3: Participate in Every Interview That's Requested of You.* Understand the context before consenting to the interview. Don't agree to participate when there are legal ramifications or where your company will not be cast in a positive light.
- *Myth 4: Reciting How Many Other Media Interviews You've Done.* Many reporters want a fresh perspective and might be turned off by mentions of other interviews. The reporters will be concerned that your interview will not reveal new material.
- *Myth 5: The Best Way to Get Media Attention Is Through a News Release.* A "one-size-fits-all" approach to news releases does not work. Customized letters to individual media are more helpful.
- *Myth 6: Mention Your Company or Product as Often as Possible.* Two to three mentions of a firm or product are instead more appropriate than constantly mentioning the firm or product.
- *Myth 7: Just Say It's "Off the Record," If You Don't Want to Be Quoted.* Journalists are under no obligation not to publish "off-the-record" material. Assume all you say can be published or used by the journalist. "If you say it, it's fair game."

- *Myth 8: Answer Every Question So That You Look Like an Expert.* Reporters may know or later research the facts. You do not want to be caught making an error or be accused of lying. A better response is to call the reporter back after you have researched the correct answer.
- *Myth 9: Advertisers Get Better Media Coverage.* Mentioning your firm's ad spending in a medium may alienate journalists. Ethical journalists are not influenced by advertising expenditures.
- *Myth 10: Bigger Words Make You Sound Smarter.* Use simple words and expressions during an interview. The use of industry terminology or complex words and expressions increases the chance that you will be misunderstood by both the reporter and the media's readers.
- *Myth 11: Never Show Emotion.* The use of emotion during an interview is not a sign of weakness but demonstrates such human qualities as concern, empathy, and humanity. "It's important to appear sincere and believable," says the head of a media training firm.
- *Myth 12: Media Training Is Helpful.* Have a plan in place prior to the interview and stick to it. Adequate preparation for an interview is at least as important as media training.

Questions

1. As director of public relations for a regional home improvement chain, develop an outline for an interview related to your firm's response to a major hurricane. The media have been critical of the firm's inability to reopen several of its stores and of the high prices of plywood.
2. Discuss the pros and cons of outsourcing the public relations function to a specialized firm.
3. As director of public relations for an auto manufacturer, list five situations where you would not agree to be interviewed and explain why.
4. Develop five specific public relations objectives for a retailer that has been criticized by the media for the poor coverage of its health-care program.

[c6-2] The data in the case are drawn from Gwen Moran, "Say It Isn't So!" *Entrepreneur* (August 2005), pp. 64–67.

Case 3: Guitar Center Turns Ex-Rockers into Sales Dudes[c6-3]

Before the doors open at the Guitar Center (**http://www.guitarcenter.com**) each morning, the firm's salespeople get together for a "power huddle," just like athletes do prior to a game. For example, during one "power huddle," the store manager at Guitar Center's Jacksonville, Florida, store, yelled out, "We are the biggest and the baddest. But is that enough? We're about integrity. We're about doing the right thing for our customers. That is how we win." A salesperson then responded, "We're about selling dreams."

Guitar Center is a 150-unit chain that sells electric guitars, keyboards, drums, recording equipment, and amplifiers. The chain's annual sales exceed $1.7 billion. Profits have increased by more than double since 2002. Guitar Center opens new stores on a regular basis.

The profile of Guitar Center's salespeople is quite different from that at most retailers. One-half of its salespeople never held a previous sales job and few have attended college. However, almost all can play music and love musical instruments and accessories. Turnover among salespeople is also very high. "We're just a bunch of busted guitar players with really big dreams," says Larry Thomas, Guitar Center's recently retired co-chief executive.

Four major components comprise Guitar Center's personal selling strategy: fading, take the deal, follow-up, and the use of motivational meetings. Fading is when a salesperson's commissions exceed his or her base salary (which is often minimum wage). At that point, a salesperson is eligible for bonuses. Salespeople are generally not profitable to the company until their commissions exceed their base salary. Salespeople who do not fade for three paychecks are typically terminated.

Although all of Guitar Center's equipment is labeled with a tag stating "guaranteed lowest price," its salespeople are trained to accept any profitable deal and to handle tough negotiators. According to a salesperson at Guitar Center, "No two people ever have to pay the same price, and within reason, you can name your price. Unless it's costing the store money, I've got to take the deal." On the other hand, Guitar Center understands that customers rarely bargain over accessories such as guitar strings and straps that are highly profitable.

Guitar Center's best salespeople call their customers to follow up after a sale. Some even go to customers' homes to help them set up their new equipment. And the top salespeople have a huge file of customers who are called periodically, such as on their birthday or when new equipment comes in.

Slogans such as "Everyone leaves delighted" and "Whatever it takes" are instilled throughout the organization. Guitar Center holds motivational meetings for its store managers three times a year where sales techniques are practiced. In one part of the meetings, called "phone-shopping," a random store is called. The managers listen carefully to determine if the phone is picked up within three rings and if the salesperson understands how to close a sales transaction based on the store's policies. The entire call is broadcast so all store managers can hear it. "If it's your store, you're just praying. It's brutal—a complete public flogging—but very effective. You really see the truth come out," says a Guitar Center store manager.

Guitar Center is working to further reduce the turnover rate among its sales staff. The current turnover rate is 95 percent, down from 160 percent in 2003; the industry average is 60 percent. Guitar Center's high turnover rate means higher training costs, lower sales, and lower levels of customer support. Guitar Center recently expanded its human resources department and is in the process of teaching its sales managers more effective interviewing techniques.

Questions

1. Discuss the pros and cons of the Guitar Center's pricing strategy in terms of its image.
2. Evaluate the pros and cons of the Guitar Center's salesperson compensation program.
3. Discuss what a new car dealer can learn from the Guitar Center's salesperson compensation, motivation, and supervision strategies.
4. Develop a program to reduce the Guitar Center's high salesperson turnover rate.

[c6-3] The data in the case are drawn from Paul Sloan, "The Sales Force That Rocks," *Business 2.0* (July 2005), pp. 102–107.

Case 4: Are Rebates Still Worth the Effort—for Companies and Their Customers?[c6-4]

Rebates are an important part of many firms' marketing strategies. According to NPD, a marketing research firm, about one-third of consumers who purchase a technology product say it comes with a rebate offer. One-fifth of the consumers say they purchase products earlier than they would have otherwise if an offer is available. One-sixth say they spend more money when there is a rebate offer.

Rebates have been increasingly used by some companies. They are a very flexible form of sales promotion that can be adjusted in terms of dollar value, applicable time period, and conditions (such as whether a consumer must buy a printer along with a digital camera to qualify for a $50 rebate). Rebates are an effective means of clearing out old inventory prior to the introduction of a new model. Unlike reductions in a product's list price, rebates provide full profit margins for wholesalers and retailers. Rebates also enable a retailer to record the sales of discounted merchandise based on the product's full price. In this way, rebates do not reduce retailers' total sales, sales per square foot, and same-store sales levels that are closely watched by security analysts and investors. Lastly, cynics feel that some manufacturers develop rebate offers knowing that many purchasers will not redeem them.

Complying with many rebate offers is not most customers' vision of a fun or even enjoyable experience despite the potential savings. Typically, consumers must remove a barcode (remembering to soak the bottle in warm water so that the label comes off in one piece), keep the applicable receipts, fill out the required forms, make copies of all of the materials (in case it gets lost in the mail), and mark the calendar to remember to look out for the check. The process is so time consuming that one study found that one-half of consumers never submit rebate forms.

In another recent study, one-half of the respondents stated that they did not redeem a rebate offer in the year preceding the survey. Forty-one percent said they forgot to redeem the rebate, 25 percent lost some of the forms or labels that were required for redemption, and 20 percent felt that the rebate amount was not worth all of the effort that had to be expended.

Some rebate offers have involved legal actions against manufacturers and retailers. In October 2004, New York State's attorney general stated that Samsung, which limited rebates to one per household, was not fulfilling its rebate offer to consumers in apartment houses if someone else in the same building already received a rebate. Samsung's settlement with the state required that it honor 4,100 rebates ranging in value from $10 to $150. Ohio's attorney general recently sued Office Max, stating that the office supply retailer did not honor rebates, as well as rain checks (for out-of-stock merchandise that was advertised at reduced prices).

In response to consumer concerns, some marketers have dramatically improved their rebate programs. Staples, the office-supply chain, offers Easy Rebates (**http://www.staplesrebates.com**), a simplified rebate redemption program that requires consumers just to enter information from the receipt online (eliminating the need to remove bar codes, photocopy information, and mail items to qualify for a rebate). At Staples, consumers with rebates enter two numbers from their receipt at their home or office computer or at a store's kiosk to qualify. More than one million Staples consumers used the Easy Rebates program during its first four months. To reduce the possibility of a consumer receiving the rebate and then returning the merchandise, Staples mails out the rebate check four to six weeks after receipt. At that time, the store will not accept the item for return. Costco, BJ's Wholesale Club, and Rite Aid now offer similar online redemption programs.

Questions

1. Differentiate between a rebate, a coupon, and a reduction in a manufacturer's suggested list price as sales promotion techniques.
2. Describe the pros and cons of a manufacturer using a rebate versus a coupon offer.
3. Contrast Staples' Easy Rebates (**http://www.staplesrebates.com**) with the typical rebate promotion in terms of ease of use.
4. Why have other retailers not copied Staples' Easy Rebate program?

[c6-4] The data in the case are drawn from Richard J. Dalton, Jr. "Rethinking Rebates," *Newsday* (January 23, 2005), pp. A48–A49.

Segmenting the Sales Force[pc-6]

INTRODUCTION

Attitude is everything. A sales organization's prosperity depends on its success in meeting two objectives: (1) inducing customers to buy its products and (2) motivating its sales force to close the deal. Because the salesperson is such an important link to customers, he or she is just a different kind of customer. While most successful companies employ the strategy of market segmentation to help achieve the first objective, it is rarely used in conjunction with the second.

BACKGROUND

Wendel Smith introduced the market segmentation concept in his landmark 1956 *Journal of Marketing* article, "Product Differentiation and Market Segmentation as an Alternative Marketing Strategy." But it was Philip Kotler who popularized the concept in his classic *Marketing Management* textbook. The 2002 edition of the book spotlights the three steps in the consumer segmentation process:

- Market segmentation groups consumers along some useful criteria, such as needs, wants, and benefits sought in products.
- Target marketing prioritizes the segments according to their attractiveness to the firm.
- Product positioning modifies the organization's marketing mix for each target segment.

Applying this strategy to the sales force also involves three steps:

- Market segmentation involves identifying groups of salespeople that share similar mind-sets and behaviors related to their task of selling and interfacing with customers.
- Prioritization identifies sales-force segments offering the greatest future investment/return ratio for the organization. The idea here is that an organization will want to invest in a segment to affect those attitudes, beliefs, and behaviors that ultimately lead to better performance. Not all sales-force segments will offer the same "return" to an organization.
- Resource distribution involves reallocating and modifying management and training resources and (sometimes) organizational structures to support and cultivate the most attractive sales-force segments and prune reps from the least attractive segments.

[pc-6] Adapted by the authors from Terry Grapentine, "Segmenting the Sales Force," *Marketing Management* (January-February 2005), pp. 29–34. Reprinted by permission of the American Marketing Association.

HOW TO SEGMENT A SALES FORCE

Segmenting your sales force involves specifying the conceptual measures important in describing different sales rep segments, defining these measures operationally in a survey instrument, and conducting the segmentation analysis.

Specify Measures

In "The Control Factor" (*Marketing Management*, January-February 2004), David W. Cravens and his colleagues identified selected constructs that could be important in developing an attitudinal segmentation model for a sales force. These include organizational commitment, job performance, role ambiguity, role conflict, and emotional exhaustion.

Additional factors important in sales-force segmentation studies relate to issues such as these: (1) the marketing orientation of the sales force, (2) the perceived equity between one's job and comparable jobs in the industry, and (3) salespeople's perception of how competitive the firm's products are in the marketplace.

The American Marketing Association's *Marketing Scales Handbook* identifies nearly 60 categories of segmentation constructs, containing hundreds of different scales, under the section titled "Organizational, Sales Force." There is an abundant store of information, from these and other sources in the sales-force management literature, with which to begin developing a survey instrument. However, it's important to realize that the total number of survey measures available is more than can be measured in a single study.

Exploratory Research

To make the task manageable, combine these sources with a qualitative investigation of the sales-force organization itself. Typically, this includes one-on-one and small-group interviews with sales reps and sales management. The purpose of these interviews is to identify and understand important aspects of the organization (e.g., training, culture, management style, attitudes, and skills) that affect how sales reps approach their jobs.

Ideally, an outside party conducts these interviews, and the organization must assure respondents that their comments will remain confidential. Employees must feel comfortable about discussing their views on these issues without fear of exposure to the employer.

The study should include feedback from members of all the relevant organizational functions—sales management, senior management, and sales training—in addition to the sales reps themselves.

Table 1   Constructs Measured in a Sales-Force Segmentation Study

Subject Area	Example Construct Measures
Personal characteristics of sales rep	*Locus of control:* How people define the causes for success or failure in their lives.
Motivation	*Motivation to work:* Desire to be engaged in one's work.
Selling skills	*Customer orientation of salespeople:* Marketing vs. sales orientation of salespeople.
	Salesperson adaptive selling: Ability to adapt sales behaviors in different selling situations.
Aptitude	*General sales aptitude test*
Role perceptions	*Role conflict and ambiguity:* Conflicts between the sales rep and job demands.

Steering Committees

Consider establishing a study steering committee to oversee the research and implementation of the research findings. Generally, a steering committee is formed from the same departments included in the exploratory study. This gets those who are most responsible for implementing the study's findings on board from the beginning.

Members provide their views on the issues they consider to be relevant in explaining sales rep performance and develop hypotheses describing the number and nature of sales-force segments in the organization. These issues and hypotheses are investigated in the exploratory study and should include subjects related to the personal characteristics of sales reps, environmental and organizational variables, motivation, skill levels, aptitude, and role perceptions. See Table 1 for example constructs.

Upon completion of the exploratory interviews, the committee reviews the findings and helps identify the most relevant measures to be included in the quantitative survey instrument. Preferably, an outside party with experience in the field aids in this effort, as well as assists in questionnaire development.

The segmentation study's outcomes should not be a total surprise to the committee, given its knowledge of the organization and the exploratory investigation's findings. Therefore, at the conclusion of the exploratory phase, the committee should begin brainstorming likely implications of the segmentation study and how the company can and cannot act on particular findings. This gets management thinking through the actionability of the segmentation study in advance. If there are limited training resources or if organizational structures inhibit executing changes in the structure and management of a sales force, the committee should address these issues prior to beginning the quantitative phase of the study.

Creating Survey Instruments

Several issues need to be addressed at this stage: how to administer the questionnaire, how to protect employee confidentiality, and how to craft the questions.

Companies with sophisticated intranets administer surveys via a passcode-protected Web site. If this is not feasible, a self-administered questionnaire works well. In both cases, respondents are better able to comprehend and consider the questions, for the following reasons:

- Respondents are giving their answers in private, as opposed to giving them to an interviewer over the telephone.
- Respondents can complete the survey when it is convenient for them to do so.
- Some of the scales used in such studies are best administered in a visual format versus being read to respondents in a telephone interview.

Protecting employee confidentiality is paramount. Having an outside party administer the questionnaire is the only way to ensure employees that their answers and comments will not be linked to them personally.

Typically, these surveys are 8 to 10 pages in length and require 30 to 40 minutes to complete. Drafting the actual survey questions should be the responsibility of someone who has expertise in the sales-force management area and has done similar work in the past.

Data Analysis

Although it is beyond the scope of this case to delve into the statistical algorithms used to cluster-analyze segmentation solutions, here are a few ideas to keep in mind. As with segmenting consumer markets, guidelines exist to help ensure that your segmentation solution will be useful. The segments should be large enough to warrant attention, be differentiable, and be actionable.

The number of segments can range from one (all reps are considered alike) to as many segments as there are reps (each rep answers differently). To be useful, however, we have found that the number of segments generally ranges from four to eight, depending on the unique characteristics of the organization.

The segments should be differentiated from each other along issues related to the kinds of attitudes, beliefs, and behaviors the organization feels define its ideal sales rep. This generally means that sales-force segments are not defined solely on a rep's sales volume because sales volume is not always a good predictor of the ideal sales rep. For example, Rep A may possess more desirable traits than Rep B. Rep B has higher sales only because he works in an older, more established territory.

Two examples of highly differentiated segments that past research has uncovered are "Pacesetters" and "Happy Habituals." Pacesetters most nearly match the profile of an organization's ideal sales rep. They are proactive in serving customers, aggressive at prospecting, and possess (or strive to possess) professional selling skills. In contrast, Happy Habituals are on cruise control. They typically are good performers, but they exhibit no initiative to improve their performance. They are more attuned to harvesting their book of business than aggressively seeking new business opportunities.

Finally, the segmentation scheme needs to be actionable. This means the company can formulate training programs and perhaps make organizational changes in ways that optimize the return on investment that results from working with each of the segments. For example, if one segment is characterized as possessing a below-average level of professional selling skills, the training department can develop educational resources that address these deficiencies.

APPLY SEGMENTATION FINDINGS

Organizations can use the findings from these studies to refine their hiring criteria, develop sales-training tools, improve company-to-sales-force communications, and enhance sales manager leadership training.

Hiring Criteria

Many organizations use some form of aptitude or psychological testing to screen for sales-force job applicants. Some studies have even found that psychological tests are more valid predictors of job performance than other methods.

One of the outputs of a segmentation study is the creation of a formula (decision rule) that allows you to predict segment membership, based on asking a respondent a subset of the questions from the original survey. Because many organizations that hire salespeople often look for those with past sales experience, some of the questions in the segmentation study can be used to project the segment or segments in which an applicant is likely to be.

Clearly, questions need to be reworded to focus on an applicant's most recent sales position, and this method likely will be most valid if he or she comes from a similar sales environment. The results will increase the likelihood that an organization hires people who fall in the most attractive segments (e.g., Pacesetters), thereby helping to reduce the proportion of sales reps in the least desirable segments.

As with all kinds of aptitude and psychological testing programs, one should make hiring decisions based on many indicators of future job performance (e.g., an applicant's employment history, job interviews, and so forth), not solely on a respondent's test results. But using the segmentation model in this way gives sales management one more lens through which to examine a job applicant.

Sales Training Tools

Use segmentation findings to guide the development of training resources in several ways, such as changing behaviors, improving skill competencies, or altering/bolstering the mind-set of the segment.

Not all sales-force segments are equally attractive to an organization. In the hypothetical examples cited here, an organization wants to diminish the number of Happy Habituals and increase the number of Pacesetters. Often, this requires changing or improving specific behaviors or skills inherent in the less attractive segments and reinforcing and augmenting specific behaviors or skills exhibited by the more attractive segments.

For each segment, an organization needs to identify those behaviors and skills that require change or reinforcement. For the Happy Habituals segment, the organization may want to augment its training resources in the areas of time-management skills or effective selling techniques. For the Pacesetters segment, an organization may want to fine-tune prospecting skills. Off-the-shelf training aids, such as video or Web-based training resources, can help a firm build its training resources in these targeted areas.

Additionally, employees who fall in a particular segment possess particular personality traits. Think of it as the gestalt of a segment. Many Happy Habituals, for example, are not highly motivated—they are very comfortable harvesting their book of business. In contrast, Pacesetters are self-starters and are highly proactive in finding new business. Happy Habituals' perspective will not be changed solely by improving their selling or time-management skills. Their attitude of embracing the status quo needs to be changed. In short, they need to be motivated. Training aids that address these psychological dimensions need to be augmented by effective management coaching. Several companies, such as Prime Resource Group (http://www.primeresource.com), offer training tools and consulting that address these gestalt mind sets. Much of this training, tailored to the particular needs of a sales segment, can be delivered over the Web.

Company Communications

Some beliefs held by members of a particular segment might be untrue, such as the belief that the company's products are not competitive. Communicating with the sales force via a newsletter, group meetings, or other appropriate media can go a long way toward correcting such misunderstandings.

One excellent way to improve communications is to create a specially designed Web site for sales reps. One company, HB Communications (http://www.hbcommunications.com), offers Web-based information dissemination and sales training services over the Internet. One of its customers, MCI (http://www.mci.com), has used the Internet to speed product and company communications to the field. According to an MCI spokesperson on HB's Web site: "Not only have we improved our speed to market of a message, product update, corporate change, and shift in our business, but we've also been able to preserve the message itself—the accuracy and consistency of that message."

Sales Manager Leadership

Share the segmentation study's findings with the sales reps. Perhaps in a group setting, a manager can explain the study's objectives and describe the segments. Subsequently, in individual follow-up meetings, managers can review with their reps the segments in which they are classified—the output of the segmentation analysis.

Being able to describe the segments to a rep provides a forum in which the manager can provide valuable coaching skills. In "Making the Grade" (*Sales & Marketing Management*, March 2004), Julia Chang describes some intriguing coaching ideas that sales managers can use in conjunction with a sales-force segmentation study.

Let members of the most desirable segments (e.g., Pacesetters) serve as coaches to members of less attractive segments (e.g., Happy Habituals). Sometimes, this kind of coaching is more effective than having the boss be the coach. Reps are less intimidated when working with a peer. And it also is motivating to the sales reps who are sharing their experiences because other reps look up to them.

Give more freedom to reps in the highly valued segments. "The most successful salespeople don't rely on just their talents, but they will see skills that need to be developed and go after them," Laura Benjamin—a sales consultant in Colorado Springs—told Chang. "They like autonomy, independence, and new and different activities, and they don't like to do the same things over again."

In serving underachieving segments, strive to change their points of view on the job. For example, members of high-achieving segments often are more proactive in serving customers. These reps' "time horizon" is optimizing the long-run relationship with their client. In contrast, the underachiever's time horizon is on the next paycheck. Apex Performance Systems (**http://www.apexperformancesystems. com**) in Madison, Wisconsin, has sales training tools designed just to meet this objective.

VIVE LA DIFFERENCE

Just as customers in a market are not homogeneous, neither are members of a sales force. Each individual comes to the sales job with a unique background and singular attitudes, beliefs, and behaviors. Although sales managers recognize that no two sales reps are alike, organizations rarely invest the time and energy to identify different groups in a formal way. Yet undertaking a sales-force segmentation study can be the first step toward enhancing the productivity of reps. Managers can use the results to devise strategies and tactics for growing the more attractive sales-force segments while simultaneously winnowing the least attractive ones.

Questions

1. What are the implications of this case for a company interested in integrated marketing communications?
2. Why is it important for a company to consider segmenting its sales force? What are the risks if the firm does not do so?
3. Develop a five item sales-force questionnaire based on the subject areas in Table 1.
4. On what demographic and lifestyle basis would you recommend that a company's sales force be segmented? What are the sales management implications of this?
5. How would you supervise a "Pacesetter" differently from a "Happy Habitual?"
6. How could a company properly segment its sales force without alienating any salespeople?
7. Should sales personnel have input into a company's advertising campaign? Explain your answer.

7
Price Planning

Part 7 covers pricing, the fourth and final element of the marketing mix.

20 Considerations in Price Planning

In this chapter, we study the role of price, its importance, and its interrelationship with other marketing variables. Price-based and nonprice-based approaches are contrasted. We also look at each of the factors affecting price decisions in depth: consumers, costs, government, channel members, and competition.

21 Developing and Applying a Pricing Strategy

Here, we explain how to construct and enact a pricing strategy. First, we distinguish among sales, profit, and status quo objectives. Next, the role of a broad price policy is discussed. Then, we introduce three approaches to pricing (cost-, demand-, and competition-based) and show how they may be applied. We also explain why cost-, demand-, and competition-based pricing methods should be integrated. A number of pricing tactics, such as customary and odd pricing, are examined. The chapter concludes by noting methods for adjusting prices.

After reading Part 7, you should understand element 13 of the strategic marketing plan outlined in Table 3-2 (pages 77–78).

Chapter 20

Considerations in Price Planning

Ask many people to identify the most prestigious jewelry stores in the world and the odds are that they will mention Tiffany (**http://www.tiffany.com**) and probably have a tough time thinking about another store.

Tiffany started in New York as Tiffany & Young, a stationery and costume jewelry store, in 1837. Unlike other stores at the time, where bargaining was common, the firm was known for marking all items with specific prices and for its strict one-price policy (no bargaining). During the 1840s, Tiffany & Young started to sell fine jewelry, moved into catalog sales, and expanded into selling silverware, pocket watches, and other high-price, high-quality goods. In 1851, the store was renamed Tiffany & Co., after Charles Lewis Tiffany purchased his partners' shares in the business.

Today, Tiffany operates about 55 branch stores in the United States (in addition to its New York City main store), about 40 stores in Japan, 25 stores in Asia Pacific (excluding Japan), and 12 stores in Europe. About 82 percent of its total sales are from Tiffany & Co. brand jewelry. Despite the notion among many that Tiffany concentrates its jewelry at higher price levels, the firm offers jewelry, sterling silver, china, crystal, stationery, and fragrances over a wide range of prices. However, virtually all of its merchandise is sold at premium prices that reflect its distinctive merchandise, its high product quality, sophisticated upscale image, and high levels of customer service.

To keep its jewelry distinctive, Tiffany is the sole licensee for jewelry designed by Elsa Peretti, Paloma Picasso, and Jean Schlumberger. These designers account for about 20 percent of Tiffany's sales. Tiffany also makes nearly two-thirds of the finished goods it sells in its own plants. And to keep control over the quality of its diamonds, Tiffany has a financial interest in a firm that supplies rough diamonds.

Tiffany's mission is clear: "The Company competes on the basis of reputation for high-quality products, brand recognition, customer service, and distinctive value-priced merchandise and does not engage in price promotional advertising."[1]

In this chapter, we will learn more about the effect of image on price, the importance of price and nonprice approaches to marketing strategy, and the role of consumers in pricing. We will also look at other factors affecting price decisions: costs, government, channel members, and competition.

Chapter Objectives

1. To define the terms *price* and *price planning*
2. To demonstrate the importance of price and study its relationship with other marketing variables
3. To differentiate between price-based and nonprice-based approaches
4. To examine the factors affecting pricing decisions

20-1   OVERVIEW

> Through **price planning**, each **price** places a value on a good or service.

A *price* represents the value of a good or service for both the seller and the buyer. *Price planning* is systematic decision making by an organization regarding all aspects of pricing.

---

[1] Various company and other sources.

The value of a good or service can involve both tangible and intangible factors. A tangible factor is the cost saving a soda distributor obtains from buying a new bottling machine; an intangible factor is a consumer's pride in owning a Jaguar (**http://www.jaguar.com**) rather than another car brand. For an exchange to occur, both the buyer and seller must feel a price represents an equitable ("fair") value. To the buyer, the payment of a price reduces the purchasing power available for other items. To the seller, the receipt of a price is a source of revenue and a key determinant of sales and profit levels.

Many words are substitutes for the term *price*, including *admission fee*, *membership fee*, *rate*, *tuition*, *service fee*, *donation*, *rent*, *salary*, *interest*, *retainer*, and *assessment*. No matter what it is called, a price refers to all terms of purchase: monetary and non-monetary charges, discounts, handling and shipping charges, credit charges and other forms of interest, and late-payment penalties. A nonmonetary exchange would be a department store awarding a gift to a person who gets a friend to shop at that store or an airline offering tickets as payment for advertising space and time. Monetary and nonmonetary exchanges may be combined. This is common with autos, where the buyer gives the seller money plus a trade-in. That combination leads to a lower monetary price.

From a broader perspective, price is the mechanism that allocates goods and services among potential buyers and ensures competition among sellers in an open marketplace. If demand exceeds supply, prices are usually bid up by consumers. If supply exceeds demand, prices are usually reduced by sellers. See Figure 20-1.

In this chapter, we look at the importance of price and its relationship to other marketing variables, price-based and nonprice-based approaches, and the factors affecting price decisions. Chapter 21 deals with devising and enacting a price strategy, and applying techniques for setting prices.

20-2 THE IMPORTANCE OF PRICE AND ITS RELATIONSHIP TO OTHER MARKETING VARIABLES

The importance of price decisions has risen considerably in recent decades: (1) Because price in a monetary or nonmonetary form is a component of the exchange process, it appears in every marketing transaction. More firms now realize the impact of price on image, sales, and profits. (2) Deregulation in several industries has led to more price competition among firms. (3) To increase profit levels, many firms have become more cost-conscious and more focused on operating as efficiently as possible. (4) The growth of the global economy has led to greater interest in currency valuations and exchange rates. Many firms adapt their marketing strategies to reflect international currency fluctuations. (5) The rapid pace of technological advances has caused intense price competition for such products as PCs, printers, and DVD players. (6) Service-based firms are placing more emphasis on how they set prices. (7) In slow economies, it is hard for firms to raise prices.

> The stature of price decisions has risen because more firms recognize their far-reaching impact.

Consider this insightful observation on the complexity of pricing:

> Value, like beauty, is in the eye of the beholder. "Understanding that different customers place different values on the same good or service is the most important concept in pricing. Once you accept this truism of value-based pricing, you expand the function that pricing performs for you—it's not finding a single perfect price number, it's about creating a series of strategies designed to capture the value each customer sets for your good or service. These strategies will uncover your product's hidden profits."[2]

Inasmuch as a price places a value on the overall marketing mix offered to consumers (such as product features, product image, store location, and customer service), pricing

---

[2] Cecil Johnson, "Pricing Strategies Cut Both Ways: Buyers and Sellers Can Profit, Thanks to a New Book," *Ottawa Citizen* (November 19, 2005), p. D12.

Figure 20-1

The Role of Price in Balancing Supply and Demand

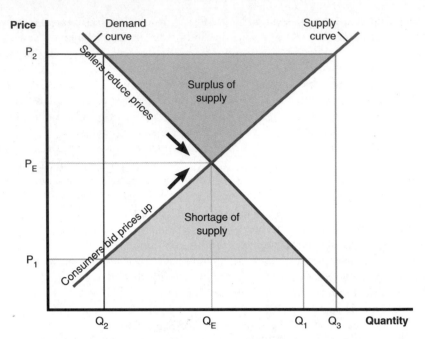

At equilibrium (P_E Q_E), the quantity demanded equals the supply.
At price P_1, consumers demand Q_1 of an item. However, at this price, suppliers will make available only Q_2. There is a shortage of supply of $Q_1 - Q_2$. The price is bid up as consumers seek to buy greater quantities than offered at P_1.
At price P_2, suppliers will make available Q_3 of an item. However, at this price, consumers demand only Q_2. There is a surplus of supply of $Q_3 - Q_2$. Suppliers reduce the price to attract greater consumer demand.

decisions must be made in concert with product, distribution, and promotion plans. Parfums de Coeur (**http://www.parfumsdecoeur.com**) makes imitations of expensive perfumes from Estée Lauder (**http://www.esteelauder.com**), Giorgio (**http://www. giorgiobeverlyhills.com**), and others—and sells them for one-third to one-fifth the price of those perfumes. It uses similar ingredients but saves on packaging, advertising, and personal selling costs. It distributes via such mass merchants as Wal-Mart and online.

These are some basic ways in which pricing is related to other marketing and company variables:

- Prices ordinarily vary over the life of a product category, from high prices to gain status-conscious innovators to lower prices to lure the mass market.
- Customer service is affected because low prices are often associated with less customer service.
- From a distribution perspective, the prices charged to resellers must adequately compensate them for their functions, yet be low enough to be competitive with other brands at the wholesale or retail level.
- There may be conflict in a distribution channel if a manufacturer tries to control or suggest prices.
- Product lines with different features—and different prices—can attract different market segments.
- A sales force may need some flexibility in negotiating prices and terms, particularly with large business accounts.
- The roles of marketing and finance personnel must be coordinated. Marketers often begin with the prices that customers are willing to pay and work backward to ascertain acceptable company costs. Finance people typically start with costs and add desired profits to set prices.
- As costs change, decisions must be made as to whether to pass these changes on to consumers, absorb them, or modify product features.

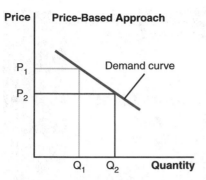

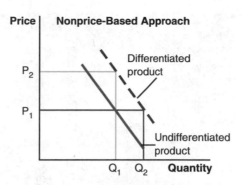

Figure 20-2

Price-Based and Nonprice-Based Approaches

A company operating at P₁ Q₁ may increase sales by lowering its price to P₂. This increases demand to Q₂.

A firm relying on a price-based approach must lower its prices to increase sales.

Through a nonprice-based approach, the firm shifts the consumer demand curve to the right by successfully differentiating its products from competitors. This enables the firm to:

(a) increase demand from Q₁ to Q₂ at price P₁, or

(b) raise the price from P₁ to P₂ while maintaining a demand of Q₁.

If firms market products internationally, they must consider the following: "In what currency will prices be set? What payment options will you offer? How will you clear and collect payments? Whatever your distribution channel, make payment a convenient exercise for your customers."[3] The complexity of pricing in foreign markets is often due to the divergent company goals in different markets, the varying attributes of each market, and other factors. Furthermore, the ability to set prices in foreign markets may be affected by varying government rules, competition, anti-dumping laws, operating costs, the rate of inflation, the standard of living, and so forth.

> Pricing internationally can be quite complicated.

20-3 PRICE-BASED AND NONPRICE-BASED APPROACHES

Sellers influence consumer demand primarily through changes in price levels with a *price-based approach*. Sellers downplay price as a factor in consumer demand by creating a distinctive good or service via promotion, packaging, delivery, customer service, availability, and other marketing factors with a *nonprice-based approach*. The more unique a product offering is perceived by consumers, the greater a firm's freedom to set prices above competitors'. See Figure 20-2.

In a price-based approach, sellers move along a demand curve by raising or lowering prices. This is a flexible marketing technique because prices can be adjusted quickly and easily to reflect demand, cost, or competitive factors. Yet, of all the controllable marketing variables, price is the easiest for a competitor to copy. This may result in "me-too" strategies or even in price wars. Furthermore, the government may monitor anti-competitive aspects of price-based strategies.

In a nonprice-based approach, sellers shift demand curves by stressing the distinctive attributes of products. This lets firms increase unit sales at a given price or sell their original supply at a higher price. The risk is that people may not perceive a seller's product as better than a competitor's. People would then buy the lower-priced item believed to be similar to the higher-priced one.

> A **price-based approach** occurs when sellers stress low prices; a **nonprice-based approach** emphasizes factors other than price.

[3] Renee Frappier, "Hit Close to Home," *Target Marketing* (July 2000), p. 48. See also John Quelch and Gordon Swartz, "Prepare Your Company for Global Pricing," *Sloan Management Review*, Vol. 42 (Fall 2000), pp. 61–70; and Ruth N. Bolton and Matthew B. Myers, "Price-Based Global Market Segmentation for Services," *Journal of Marketing*, Vol. 67 (July 2003), pp. 108–128.

These are examples of price- and nonprice-oriented strategies:

- McDonald's (**http://www.mcdonalds.com**) has been active with a discount price program for a while. It offers "value meals" and other low-priced products to attract price-conscious individuals and their families. See Figure 20-3.
- Since being introduced about 25 years ago, hundreds of millions of low-price Swatch watches (**http://www.swatchgroup.com**) have been sold around the world. They are fashionable, yet have fewer working parts than costlier models. To learn more about the Swatch story, visit the "Brands" section of the Web site (**http://www. swatchgroup.com/brands/brands.php**) and click "Swatch."
- Elara Diamonds (**http://www.elaradiamonds.com**) appeals to upscale shoppers: "An Elara Diamond—as unique as the woman who wears it. The Elara collection of diamond and platinum jewelry has a mystique that appeals to the woman who does not wish to compromise." See Figure 20-4.

Figure 20-4

Elara: A Nonprice-Oriented Upscale Strategy

Source: Reprinted by permission

- Lenox makes fine china and crystal. Ads rarely mention price, but focus on quality and design. As its Web site (**http://www.lenox.com**) notes, "Since 1889, Lenox has created gifts, tableware, and collectibles for U.S. presidents, dignitaries—and families like yours across America. In fact, Lenox was the first American china to be used in the White House. Over the years, our original focus on fine tableware has broadened to include casual collections in stoneware and earthenware, crystal stemware, and flatware. Our gifts in china, crystal, and precious metals have been part of family celebrations for generations. And our collectibles continue to win awards—and the hearts of collectors everywhere."

20-4 FACTORS AFFECTING PRICING DECISIONS

Before developing its pricing strategy (described in Chapter 21), a firm should analyze the outside factors affecting decisions. As with distribution planning, pricing depends heavily on elements external to the company. This contrasts with product and promotion decisions, which are more controlled by a company (except for publicity). Sometimes, outside elements greatly influence the ability to set prices; in other cases, they have little impact. Figure 20-5 outlines the major factors, which are discussed next.

20-4a   Consumers

Company personnel involved with pricing decisions must understand the relationship between price and consumer purchases and perceptions. This relationship is explained by two economic principles—the law of demand and the price elasticity of demand—and by market segmentation.

According to the **law of demand**, consumers usually purchase more units at a low price than at a high price. The **price elasticity of demand** indicates the sensitivity of buyers to price changes in terms of the quantities they will purchase.[4] Price elasticity represents the percentage change in the quantity demanded relative to a specific percentage change in the price charged. This formula shows the percentage change in demand for each 1 percent change in price:

$$\text{Price elasticity} = \frac{\dfrac{\text{Quantity 1} - \text{Quantity 2}}{\text{Quantity 1} + \text{Quantity 2}}}{\dfrac{\text{Price 1} - \text{Price 2}}{\text{Price 1} + \text{Price 2}}}$$

> According to the **law of demand**, more is bought at low prices; **price elasticity** explains reactions to changes.

Because the quantity demanded usually falls as price rises, elasticity is a negative number. However, for purposes of simplicity, elasticity calculations are usually expressed as positive numbers.

Elastic demand occurs if relatively small changes in price result in large changes in quantity demanded. Elasticity is more than 1. Total revenue goes up when prices are decreased and goes down when prices rise. **Inelastic demand** takes place if price changes have little impact on the quantity demanded. Elasticity is less than 1. Total revenue goes up when prices are raised and goes down when prices decline. **Unitary demand** exists if price changes are exactly offset by changes in the quantity demanded, so total sales revenue remains constant. Price elasticity is 1.

> Demand may be **elastic**, **inelastic**, or **unitary**. It depends on the availability of substitutes and urgency of need.

Demand elasticity is based mostly on two criteria: availability of substitutes and urgency of need. If people *believe* there are many similar goods or services from which to choose or have no urgency to buy, demand is elastic and greatly influenced by price changes: Price increases lead to purchases of substitutes or delayed purchases, and decreases expand sales as people are drawn from competitors or move up the date of their purchases. For some people, the airfare for a vacation is highly elastic. If prices go up, they may switch to a cheaper airline, travel to a nearer location by car, or postpone a trip.

If consumers believe a firm's offering is unique or there is an urgency to buy, demand is inelastic and little affected by price changes: Neither price increases nor declines will have much impact on demand. In most locales, when heating oil prices go up or down, demand remains relatively constant because there is often no feasible

Figure 20-5
Factors Affecting Price Decisions

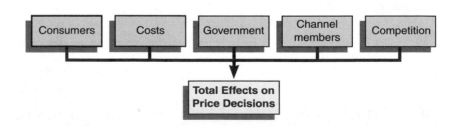

---

[4] For further information, visit these Web sites: "Microeconomics: Elasticity Overview" (http://www.mintercreek.com/micro/overview.html); and "Price Elasticity of Demand" (http://www.quickmba.com/econ/micro/elas/ped.shtml).

substitute and homes and offices must be heated. Brand loyalty also generates inelastic demand; consumers then feel their brands are distinctive and do not accept substitutes. Finally, emergency conditions increase demand inelasticity. A truck driver with a flat tire would pay more for a replacement than one with time to shop around. Figure 20-6 illustrates elastic and inelastic demand.

Elasticity usually varies over a wide range of prices for the same good or service. At very high prices, even revenues for essential goods and services may fall (mass-transit ridership would drop a lot if fares rise from $2 to $4; driving would become a more reasonable substitute). At very low prices, demand cannot be stimulated further; saturation is reached and shoppers may begin to perceive quality as inferior.

Table 20-1 shows elasticity for an office-equipment repair business. A clear relationship exists between price and demand. At the lowest price, $60, daily demand is greatest: 10 service calls. At the highest price, $120, demand is least: 5 service calls. Demand is inelastic between $60 and $84; total service-call revenues rise as price increases. Demand is unitary between $84 and $96; total service-call revenues remain the same ($672). Demand is elastic between $96 and $120; total service-call revenues decline as the price rises within this range. Although a fee of either $84 or $96 yields the highest service-call revenues, $672, other criteria must be evaluated before selecting a price. The repair firm should consider costs per call; the number of servicepeople required at different levels; the overall revenues generated by each service call, including parts and added labor charges; travel time; the percentage of satisfied customers at different prices (expressed by repeat business); and the potential for referrals.

Price sensitivity varies by market segment because all people are not equally price-conscious. Consumers can be divided into such segments as these:

- *Price shoppers*—They are interested in the "best deal" for a product.
- *Brand-loyal customers*—They believe their current brands are better than others and will pay "fair" prices for those products.
- *Status seekers*—They buy prestigious brands and product categories and will pay whatever prices are set; higher prices signify greater status.
- *Service/features shoppers*—They place a great value on customer service and/or product features and will pay for them.
- *Convenience shoppers*—They value ease of shopping, nearby locations, long hours by sellers, and other approaches that make shopping simple; they will pay above-average prices.

> Consumers can be segmented in terms of their price orientation.

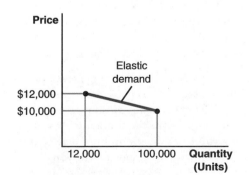

Economy Car (Model A)
The purchasers of an economy car are highly sensitive to price. They perceive many models as interchangeable, and demand will suffer significantly if the car is priced too high. At $10,000, 100,000 models may be sold (revenues are $1 billion). A small increase to $12,000 will cause demand to fall to 12,000 units (revenues are $144 million).

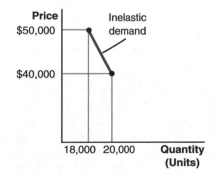

Luxury Car (Model B)
The purchasers of a luxury car have little sensitivity to price. They perceive their model as quite distinctive and will pay a premium price for it. At $40,000, 20,000 models may be sold (revenues are $800 million). A large increase in price, to $50,000, will have only a small effect on demand, reducing it to 18,000 units (revenues are $900 million).

Figure 20-6

Demand Elasticity for Two Models of Automobiles

Table 20-1	Price Elasticity for Service Calls by an Office-Equipment Repair Business			
Price of Service Call	Service Calls Demanded per Day	Revenues from Service Calls	Price Elasticity of Demand[a]	Type of Demand
$ 60.00	10	$600.00		
			0.76	Inelastic
$ 72.00	9	$648.00		
			0.76	Inelastic
$ 84.00	8	$672.00		
			1.00	Unitary
$ 96.00	7	$672.00		
			1.31	Elastic
$108.00	6	$648.00		
			1.73	Elastic
$120.00	5	$600.00		

[a] Expressed as positive numbers.

A firm must decide which segment or segments are represented by its target market and plan accordingly.

The consumer's (market segment's) perception of the price of a good or service as being high, fair, or low—its *subjective price*—may be more important than its actual price. A consumer may feel a low price represents a good buy or inferior quality—or a high price represents status or poor value, depending on his/her perception. Such factors as these affect a consumer's (market segment's) subjective price:

> A consumer's perception of a price level is the **subjective price.**

- *Purchase experience with a particular good or service*—"How much have I paid in the past?"
- *Purchase experience with other, rather similar goods or services*—"What's a fair price for an item in the same or adjacent product category that I bought before?"
- *Self-image*—"How much should a person like me pay for something like this?"
- *Social situation*—"How much do my friends expect me to pay for something like this?"
- *Context of the purchase*—"What should this cost in these circumstances?"[5]

KB Home (http://www.kbhome.com) is a leading U.S. housing developer that strives hard to offer prices perceived as fair by its target market: "A new home from us typically offers more insulation, better energy efficiency (which means lower utility bills), new appliances, and warranties that cover your home from the foundation to the fireplace. Plus, your new KB home is built just for you from the ground up. It reflects your personal tastes, not someone else's. You pay only for what's important to you."[6]

[5] G. Ray Funkhouser, "Using Consumer Expectations as an Input to Pricing Decisions," *Journal of Product & Brand Management*, Vol. 1 (Spring 1992), p. 48. See also Lisa E. Bolton, Luk Warlop, and Joseph W. Alba, "Consumer Perceptions of Price (Un)fairness," *Journal of Consumer Research*, Vol. 29 (March 2003), pp. 474–491 ; and "Shopping Strategies to Get Best Values," *Consumer Reports Buying Guide 2006*, pp. 13–20.

[6] "Home Buying Tips," http://www.kbhome.com/Page~PageID~184.aspx (June 6, 2006).

Global Marketing in Action

EasyGroup: An Anti-Luxury Approach

EasyGroup (http://www.easy.com) is the brainchild of Greek shipping heir Stelios Haji-Ioannou, who initially founded the budget airline EasyJet (http://www.easy jet.com) at the age of 28. According to Haji-Iaonnou, "Easy is a functional brand; it's about value for the many, not the few." In contrast, Virgin, a British brand, evokes sophistication and style to many consumers.

Among the products under the Easy brand umbrella are Easy movie rentals, Easy shaving cream, Easy Internet cafés, and an Easy hotel. Many of these products have been in business for only a few years. Among the EasyGroup's products, EasyJet is highly successful. EasyJet is the fourth largest air carrier as measured by number of passengers carried within Europe, after Lufthansa, Air France, and KLH. In

2005, the airline had profits of $73 million on sales of $1.9 billion.

Let's look at EasyCinema.com (http://www.easy cinema.com), a part of the EasyGroup empire. Begun as a single movie house, the movie theater concept was built on the idea that most theaters sell only 20 percent of their seats. Haji-Ioannou's goal was to have a 50 percent occupancy rate by cutting ticket prices by 50 percent. Customers could pay even less by purchasing tickets well in advance of the movie date. To keep costs low, customers must book their seats over the Web and then print their own tickets. EasyCinema is close to its 50 percent attendance target.

Source: Based on material in Georgia Flight, "Easy Does It All," *Business 2.0* (August 2005), pp. 69–74.

20-4b Costs

The costs of raw materials, supplies, labor, transportation, and other items are commonly beyond a firm's control. Yet, they have a great impact on prices. Since the early 1980s, overall U.S. cost increases have been rather low. Though the 1980 inflation rate was 13.5 percent, the recent annual rate has typically been 3 to 5 percent. This means better cost control and more stable prices for most firms. Nonetheless, the costs of some goods and services have risen rapidly or fluctuated a lot in recent years. For example,

- In 2006, the price for regular unleaded gasoline was about $2.25 to $2.50 per gallon in such cities as San Francisco and Chicago—after reaching more than $3.00 per gallon in the aftermath of Hurricane Katrina.
- The cost of prime-time TV ads for major events has gone up dramatically. A 30-second ad on the 1996 Super Bowl telecast cost $1.3 million. In 2006, the cost was $2.4 million.
- Gold and silver prices have been volatile. Gold went from $325 per ounce in mid-1999 to $250 per ounce in early 2001 to $420 per ounce in 2004 to more than $500 per ounce in 2006. High gold prices adversely affect dentists and jewelers. Silver went from $7.00 per ounce in 1998 to $4.50 an ounce in 2001, back to $6.00 in 2004 and to $8.50 in 2006. The decline had a positive impact on the photography industry, which uses silver as a film ingredient.

During periods of rising costs, firms can react in one or more ways: They can leave products unchanged and pass along all of their cost increases to consumers, leave products unchanged and pass along part of their increases and absorb part of them, modify products to hold down costs and maintain prices (by reducing size, using lesser-quality materials, or offering fewer options), modify products to gain consumer support for higher prices (by increasing size, using better-quality materials, offering more options, or upgrading customer service), and/or abandon unprofitable products:

> When costs rise, companies pass along increases, alter products, or delete some items.

The price increases Target [http://www.target.com] is accepting from many of its suppliers, particularly in food, are being passed along to consumers successfully for the most part: "We've received numerous price increases throughout the year, and they continue to come our way in things like food. As we receive those price increases, we look to pass those on in the marketplace. We pull our prices up to be reflective of what those increases are, and often the price increases stick. But sometimes they don't. It's based on an item-by-item, month-by-month basis. If it is a big price increase, in the range of 10 to 12 percent, it might take a consumer longer than something with a 5 percent increase."[7]

If costs decline, firms can drop prices or raise margins, as these examples show: Using microchips has reduced PC costs by requiring less wiring and assembly time, improving durability, and enlarging information-processing capability. PC prices have gone down steadily, thus expanding the market. On the other hand, low sugar prices let candy makers increase package size (and profits) without raising prices.

> Cost decreases have mostly positive benefits for marketing strategies.

Sometimes, low costs can actually have a negative long-run impact: "Lowering prices is all well and good as long as sales levels remain high, but the problem comes when times become more challenging. Retailers have to sell higher volumes to compensate for lower prices just to maintain the level of cash flowing through their tills. Store owners have to look for even more cost cuts and further efficiencies. There must be concerns about just how much more pressure retailers can put on themselves and their suppliers to gain further price reductions. There are only so many times you can go to the well."[8]

20-4c Government

U.S. government (federal and/or state) actions related to pricing can be divided into the five major areas shown in Figure 20-7 and discussed next.

Price Fixing Both horizontal and vertical price-fixing restrictions exist. *Horizontal price fixing* results from agreements among manufacturers, among wholesalers, or among retailers to set prices at a given stage in a channel of distribution. Such agreements are illegal according to the federal Sherman Antitrust Act and the Federal Trade Commission Act, regardless of how "reasonable" prices are.

> Horizontal price fixing is illegal and results from agreements among companies at the same stage in a channel.

If violations occur, federal penalties may be severe: A firm can be fined up to $10 million per violation, and individuals can be fined up to $350,000 each and imprisoned for up to three years. The Justice Department (**http://www.usdoj.gov/atr/public/ guidelines/guidelin.htm**) investigates and prosecutes price-fixing cases. In late 2005, it reached a plea agreement with Japan's Samsung (**http://www.samsung.com**), whereby the firm was fined $300 million for "conspiring to fix the price of the chips used in personal computers and other electronic devices." Two other firms, Seoul-based Hynix Semiconductor (**http://www.hynix.com**) and Germany's Infineon Technologies (**http:// www.infineon.com**) agreed to pay fines of $185 million and $160 million, respectively.[9]

Figure 20-7

Selected U.S. Government Actions Affecting Price Decisions

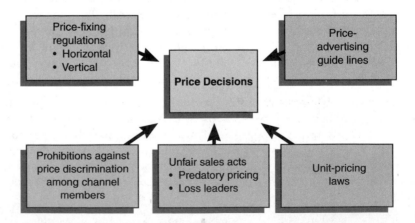

---

[7] Cecile B.Corral, "Target Passes Increases to Consumers," *Home Textiles Today* (November 14, 2005), pp. 1, 27.

[8] Helen Dickinson, "Price Cutters Will Soon Count the Cost," *Marketing* (UK) (October 5, 2005), p. 11.

[9] "Samsung Pleads Guilty to Price Fixing," **http://www.cnn.com/2005/TECH/biztech/12/01/samsung.price.fixing.ap** (December 1, 2005).

Ethical Issues in Marketing

Fighting Against Below-Cost Gas Prices: A Good Idea?

Twenty-four states, including Colorado, have sales-below-cost laws that forbid retailers from selling gasoline below the wholesale cost or require that gasoline stations receive a minimum markup on the sales of gasoline. Many of the laws were originally drafted to protect small retailers from indiscriminate price cutting from larger firms. The laws were based on the fear that rampant price cutting could drive smaller retailers out of business.

In Colorado, large retailers such as Safeway (http://www.safeway.com), Wal-Mart (http://www.walmart.com), and City Market (http://www.citymarket.com), a unit of Kroger, have begun special promotions such as "a 6-cent a gallon discount on gasoline for customers spending $50 on groceries." In a recent legal case, two independent operators of gasoline filed a lawsuit to prevent City Market from selling gasoline below cost. These two retailers claimed that their business was hurt when City Market sold gasoline below cost on numerous occasions in 2003 and 2004. One of these independent operators subsequently went out of business.

City Market stated in court that it needs these incentives to attract and keep grocery shoppers who otherwise would have shopped at Wal-Mart. An economist at a think tank based in Colorado agrees that sales-below-cost laws should be removed from the legal statutes. "I don't think we should be denying people the opportunity to get cheap gas because of some arcane law," he said.

Sources: Based on material in "Smaller Rivals Cry Foul as Retail Giants Lure Consumers with Discounted Gas," *Denver Post Online* (July 3, 2005); and Steve McMillan, "Grocers Accused of Selling Gas Below Cost," *Denver Post Online* (June 9, 2005).

To avoid price-fixing charges, a firm must be careful not to

- coordinate discounts, credit terms, or conditions of sale with competitors.
- talk about price levels, markups, and costs at trade association meetings.
- plan with competitors to issue new price lists on the same date.
- plan with competitors to rotate low bids on contracts.
- agree with competitors to limit production to keep high prices.
- exchange information with competitors, even informally.

Vertical price fixing occurs when manufacturers or wholesalers seek to control the final selling prices of their goods or services. Until 1976, the Miller-Tydings Act allowed these firms to set and strictly enforce resale prices if they so desired. This practice was known as *fair trade*. It protected small resellers and maintained brand images by forcing all resellers within fair-trade states to charge the same price for affected products. The practice was criticized as noncompetitive by consumer groups and many resellers and manufacturers—keeping prices too high, and rewarding reseller inefficiency. The Consumer Goods Pricing Act ended all interstate use of resale price maintenance. Today, resellers cannot be forced to adhere to manufacturer or wholesaler list prices. Most times, they can set their own prices.

> Under **vertical price fixing**, manufacturers or wholesalers try to control resale prices. This practice is now limited.

A manufacturer or wholesaler may control final prices only by one of these methods:

- Manufacturer or wholesaler ownership of sales facilities.
- Consignment selling. The manufacturer or wholesaler owns items until they are sold and assumes costs normally associated with the reseller, such as advertising and selling.
- Careful screening of the channel members that resell goods or services. A supplier can bypass or drop distributors if they are not living up to the supplier's performance standards, as long as there is no collusion between the supplier and other distributors. (A firm must be careful not to threaten channel members that do not adhere to suggested prices.)
- Suggesting realistic selling prices.
- Pre-printing prices on products.
- Establishing customary prices (such as 50 cents for a newspaper) that are accepted by consumers.

Price Discrimination   The ***Robinson-Patman Act*** prohibits manufacturers and wholesalers from price discrimination in dealing with different channel-member purchasers

> The **Robinson-Patman Act** prohibits price discrimination in selling to channel members.

of products with "like quality" if the effect of such discrimination is to injure competition. Covered by the act are prices, discounts, rebates, premiums, coupons, guarantees, delivery, warehousing, and credit rates. Terms and conditions of sale must be made available to all competing channel-member customers on a proportionately equal basis.[10]

The Robinson-Patman Act was enacted in 1936 to protect small retailers from unfair price competition by large chains. It was feared that small firms would be driven out of business due to the superior bargaining power (and the resultant lower selling prices) of chains. This act requires that the price differences charged to competing resellers be limited to the supplier's cost savings in dealing with the different resellers. It remains a legal restraint on pricing.

There are exceptions to the Robinson-Patman Act. Price discrimination within a channel is allowed if each buyer purchases items with substantial physical differences, if noncompeting buyers are involved, if prices do not injure competition, if price differences are justified by costs, if market conditions change (such as production costs rising), or if the seller reduces prices in response to another supplier.

Discounts are permissible if a seller shows they are available to all competing resellers on a proportionate basis, sufficiently graduated so both small and large buyers can qualify, or cost-justified. A seller must also prove that discounts for cumulative purchases (total volume during the year) or multistore purchases by chains are based on cost savings.

Although the Robinson-Patman Act is geared toward sellers, it has specific liabilities for purchasing firms under Section (F): "It shall be unlawful for any person engaged in commerce, in the course of such commerce, knowingly to induce or receive a discrimination in price which is prohibited in this section." Accordingly, resellers should try to get the lowest prices charged to any competitor in their class, but not bargain so hard that their discounts cannot be explained by one of the acceptable exceptions to the act.

> **Unfair-sales acts** protect small firms from **predatory pricing** by large companies and restrict the use of **loss leaders**.

Minimum Prices Many states have ***unfair-sales acts (minimum price laws)*** to prevent firms from selling products for less than their cost plus a fixed percentage that includes overhead and profit. About one-half of the states have unfair-sales acts covering all kinds of products and retail situations; two-thirds have laws involving specific products, such as bread, dairy items, and liquor. These acts are intended to protect small firms from predatory pricing by larger competitors and to limit the use of loss leaders by retailers.

With ***predatory pricing***, large firms cut prices on products to below their cost in selected geographic areas so as to eliminate small, local competitors. At the federal level, predatory pricing is banned by the Sherman and Clayton Acts. Manufacturers, wholesalers, and retailers are all subject to these acts. However, predatory pricing is extremely difficult to prove.[11]

Loss leaders, items priced below cost to attract customers to a seller—usually in a store setting—are also restricted by some state unfair-sales acts. Sellers use loss leaders, typically well-known and heavily advertised brands, to increase their overall sales. They assume customers drawn by loss leaders will also buy nonsale items. Because consumers benefit, loss-leader laws are rarely enforced.

> With **unit pricing**, consumers can compare prices for different-sized packages.

Unit Pricing The lack of uniformity in package sizes has led to unit-pricing legislation in several states.[12] ***Unit pricing*** lets consumers compare price per quantity for competing brands and for various sizes of the same brand.

---

[10] See Roger Dickinson, "The Robinson-Patman Act: An Important Conundrum," *Journal of Macromarketing*, Vol. 23 (June 2003), p. 31–41; and "Robinson-Patman Implications of Dual Distribution of Equipment in the Petroleum Equipment Industry," **http://www.pei.org/FRD/robpat.htm** (May 24, 2006).

[11] See Thomas L.Barton, John B. MacArthur, and Rebecca L. Moore, "BuyGasCo Corporation: The Use of Alternative Costing Methods in a Predatory Pricing Lawsuit," *Issues in Accounting Education*, Vol. 20 (November 2005), pp. 341–357.

[12] See "Unit Pricing," **http://www.fmi.org/consumer/unit** (May 19, 2006); and Kenneth C.Manning, David E. Sprott, and Anthony D. Miyazaki, "Unit Price Usage Knowledge: Conceptualization and Empirical Assessment," *Journal of Business Research*, Vol. 56 (May 2003), pp. 367–377.

Food stores are most affected by unit-pricing laws; they often must show price per unit of measure, as well as total price. For example, through unit pricing, a shopper could learn that a 12-ounce can of soda selling for 40 cents is priced at 3.3 cents per ounce, whereas a 67.6-ounce (2-liter) bottle of the same brand selling for $2.09 is priced at 3.1 cents per ounce. The larger size is cheaper than the smaller one.

Retailers' unit-pricing costs include computing per-unit prices, printing shelf labels, and maintaining computer records. The costs are affected by the number of stores in a chain, the sales per store, the number of items under unit pricing, and the frequency of price changes.

When unit-pricing laws were first enacted 30 years ago, research found that people generally did not use the data and that low-income consumers (for whom the laws were most intended) were unlikely to look at unit prices. Critics felt the laws were costly without providing benefits. More recent research has shown unit pricing to be effective and suggests that consumer learning and the subsequent behavioral changes take time. Upscale suburban residents are still more prone to use the data than others.

Price Advertising Price-advertising guidelines have been set by the FTC (**http:// www.ftc.gov**) and various trade associations, such as the Better Business Bureau (**http://www.bbb.org**). The FTC's guidelines specify standards of permissible conduct in several categories:

> FTC guidelines establish standards for price ads.

- A firm may not claim or imply that a price has been reduced from a former level unless the original price was offered to the public on a regular basis during a reasonable, recent period of time.
- A firm may not claim its price is lower than that of competitors or the manufacturer's list price without verifying, via price comparisons involving large quantities of merchandise, that an item's price at other companies in the same trading area is in fact higher.
- A suggested list price or a pre-marked price cannot be advertised as a reference point for a sale or a comparison with other products unless the advertised product has really been sold at that price.
- Bargain offers ("free," "buy one, get one free," and "half-price sale") are deemed deceptive if terms are not disclosed at the beginning of a sales presentation or in an ad, the stated regular price of an item is inflated to create an impression of savings, or the quality or quantity of a product is lessened without informing consumers. A firm cannot continuously advertise the same item as being on sale.
- *Bait-and-switch advertising* is an illegal practice whereby customers are lured to a seller that advertises items at very low prices and then told the items are out of stock or of poor quality. Salespeople try to switch shoppers to more expensive substitutes, and there is no intent to sell advertised items. Signs of bait-and-switch are refusals to demonstrate sale items, the belittling of sale items, inadequate quantities of sale items on hand, refusals to take orders, demonstrations of defective items, and the use of compensation plans encouraging salespeople to use the tactic.

> Under **bait-and-switch advertising**, sellers illegally draw customers by deceptive pricing.

20-4d Channel Members

Each channel member typically seeks a major role in setting prices so as to generate sales volume, obtain adequate profit margins, have a proper image, ensure repeat purchases, and meet specific goals.

A manufacturer can gain greater control over prices by using an exclusive distribution system or avoiding price-oriented resellers; pre-marking prices on products; owning sales outlets; offering products on consignment; providing adequate margins to resellers; and, most importantly, by having strong brands to which people are brand loyal and for which they will pay premium prices.

Marketing and the Web

Looking for the Best Deal? Check Out Comparison Shopping Web Sites

PriceGrabber (http://www.pricegrabber.com), Shopping.com (http://www.shopping.com), Shopzilla (http://www.shopzilla.com), and Yahoo! Shopping (http://shopping.yahoo.com) are among the online sites that foster comparison shopping. Studies have shown that these sites are used both by online shoppers and by shoppers who wish to be better informed when visiting a traditional bricks-and-mortar store. For example, a store shopper who wants to be knowledgeable about the features of alternative models or prices can access one of these sites prior to going on a traditional shopping trip.

PriceGrabber lets shoppers sort products by their ratings by fellow consumers. For some popular products, it is common for a shopper to review ratings of multiple brands or of multiple models offered by the same manufacturer. Unlike many other sites, PriceGrabber lets consumers download and print all rebate offers.

Shopping.com is the largest online comparison shopping site and the third largest E-commerce site after Amazon.com and eBay. The site offers a multitude of consumer product reviews from Epinions.com (http://www.epinions). It also rates merchants' trustworthiness based on reviewing their return policies.

Shopzilla.com indexes about 30 million products. Unlike other sites, Shopzilla includes professional, as well as consumer reviews.

Yahoo! Shopping is associated with the popular search engine so it includes about 60 million products, more than any other site. It also highlights special offers such as a retailer's free shipping on selected purchases.

Source: Based on material in Sebastian Rupley, "Comparison Shopping," *PC Magazine* (May 10, 2005), pp. 86–87.

> To increase private-brand sales, some channel members **sell against the brand.**

> **Gray market goods** bypass authorized channels.

A wholesaler or retailer can gain better control over prices by stressing its importance as a customer to the supplier, linking resale support to the profit margins allowed by the supplier, refusing to carry unprofitable items, stocking competing items, having strong private brands so people are loyal to the seller and not the supplier, and purchasing outside traditional channels.

Wholesalers and retailers may engage in ***selling against the brand***, whereby they stock well-known brands, place high prices on them, and then sell other brands for lower prices. This is done to increase sales of their private brands and is disliked by manufacturers because sales of their brands decline.

Sometimes, wholesalers and retailers go outside traditional distribution channels and buy ***gray market goods***—foreign-made products imported into countries such as the United States by distributors (suppliers) that are not authorized by the products' manufacturers. Personal stereos, DVD players, car stereos, watches, and cameras are just some of the items handled in this way. If wholesalers and retailers buy gray market goods, their purchase prices are less than they would be otherwise and they have greater control over their own selling prices. The result is often discounted prices for consumers, which may be upsetting to both manufacturers and their authorized dealers.[13]

To maximize channel-member cooperation, these factors should be incorporated in pricing decisions: channel-member profit margins, price guarantees, special deals, and the impact of price increases. Wholesalers and retailers require appropriate profit margins to cover their costs (such as shipping, storage, credit, and advertising) and earn reasonable profits. Thus, the prices charged to them must take these profit margins into account. An attempt to reduce traditional margins for channel members may lose their cooperation and perhaps find them unwilling to carry a product. Pricing through a distribution channel is discussed further in Chapter 21.

Channel members may seek price guarantees to maintain inventory values and profit. Such guarantees assure resellers that the prices they pay are the lowest available. Any discount given to competitors will also be given to the original purchasers.

---

[13] See John P. Koch, "Using Copyright to Police Gray Market Goods in Canada," *Licensing Journal*, Vol. 25 (October 2005), pp. 8–14; and Barry Berman, "Strategies to Combat the Sale of Gray Market Goods," *Business Horizons*, Vol. 47 (July–August 2004), pp. 51–60.

Guarantees are most frequently requested of new firms or new products that want to gain entry into an established channel.

Special deals—consisting of limited-time discounts and/or free products—are often used to stimulate reseller purchases. The deals may require channel members to share their savings with final consumers to increase the latter's demand. For example, soda bottlers normally give retailers large price discounts on new products to encourage them to make purchases and then offer low introductory prices to consumers.

The impact of price increases on channel members' behavior must also be assessed. When firms raise prices to resellers, these increases tend to be passed along to consumers. This practice is more difficult for items with customary prices, such as candy, where small cost rises may be absorbed by the resellers. In any event, cooperation depends on an equitable distribution of costs and profit within the channel.

20-4e   Competition

Another factor contributing to the degree of control a firm has over prices is the competitive environment within which it operates. See Figure 20-8.

A *market-controlled price environment* characterized by a high level of competition, similar goods and services, and little control over prices by individual firms. Those trying to charge much more than the going price would attract few customers because demand for any single firm is weak enough that customers would switch to competitors. There would similarly be little gained by selling for less because competitors would match price cuts.

A *company-controlled price environment* is characterized by moderate competition, well-differentiated goods and services, and strong control over prices by individual firms. Companies can succeed with above-average prices because people view their offerings as unique. Differentiation may be based on brand image, features, associated services, assortment, or other elements. Discounters also can carve out a niche in this environment by attracting consumers interested in low prices.

A *government-controlled price environment* is characterized by prices being set or strongly influenced by some level of government. Examples are public utilities, mass transit, insurance, and state universities. In each case, government bodies determine or affect prices after getting input from relevant firms, institutions, and/or trade associations, as well as other parties such as consumer groups.

Companies may have to adapt to a changing competitive environment in their industries. Firms in the transportation, telecommunications, and financial industries have seen their price environment shift from government- to market-controlled, although some strong firms in these industries have managed to develop a company-controlled price environment.

Because price strategies are rather easy and quick to copy, competitors' reactions are predictable if the firm initiating a price change does well. Thus, marketers must view price from both short- and long-run perspectives. Excessive price competition may lead to lengthy and costly *price wars*, in which various firms continually try to undercut each other's prices to draw customers. These wars often result in low profits or even losses for the participants and in some companies being forced out of business.

> A firm may face a **market-controlled, company-controlled,** or **government-controlled price environment**.

> **Price wars** occur when competitors constantly lower prices.

```
           Market-          ◄──   Type of Pricing   ──►   Government-
          controlled              Environment               controlled
              │                         │
              ▼                         ▼
          Price war                Company-
                                   controlled
```

Figure 20-8

The Competitive Environment of Pricing

In recent years, there have been price wars among some airlines, electronics manu-facturers, PC makers, semiconductor manufacturers, supermarkets, insurance companies, and others. Although price wars have been more common in the United States (due to fierce competition in some industries), they are now spreading overseas—particularly to Europe and, to a lesser extent, to Japan. The impact of price wars can be dramatic:

> It is easy to see the threat that the supermarkets pose to the book industry. They are squeezing everyone in the market and booksellers are fighting back in the worst way. Ever more aggressive discounts not only cut their own throats but also devalue the very product they sell. The time has come for radical thinking. Unless the dynamics of the market are changed now, it will be too late. Booksellers are doing little more than spiraling towards a price war they can't win. Rather than continue to be the whipping boys, the publishers may be the ones who can seize the agenda. They need to start by separating the two retail channels of booksellers and supermarkets. Rather than take a one-size-fits-all approach to publishing, they should be tailoring books (and their production costs) to their markets. For the supermarkets, publishers could create simple versions of their books. Booksellers on the other hand could get "enhanced" books. These would be the same basic product that the supermarkets receive but with added content or production values. They would be sold at a premium and would be available only at booksellers. Suddenly the rules of the market would be changed. The supermarkets and their consumers still get what they want (which is cheap books).[14]

Web Sites You Can Use

As the chief U.S. government agency involved with pricing issues, the Federal Trade Commission's Web site has a lot of excellent information—beneficial for both consumers and businesses:

- At the *For Consumers: Consumer Alerts* section of the site (**http://www.ftc.gov/ftc/consumer/ media_consumeralerts.html**), you will find such reports as "Free and Low-Cost PC Offers. Go Figure," "Holiday Shopping: Is a Sale Price Your Best Deal?" "How to Be Penny Wise, Not Pump Fuelish," "Ads Promising Debt Relief May Be Offering Bankruptcy," "Bogus Medical

Discount Plans: A Bitter Pill," "Computers for Next to Nothing: What's the Deal?" "Long Distance Deals," and "Taking the 'Bait' Out of Rebates."

- At the *For Business: Advertising Guide* section of the site (**http://www.ftc.gov/bcp/guides/guides.htm**), several guides for business are offered, such as "FTC Guides Against Deceptive Pricing," "FTC Guide Concerning the Use of the Word 'Free'," "FTC Guides Against Bait Advertising," "Joint FTC/FCC Guides on Long Distance Advertising," and "Guides for the Jewelry, Precious Metals, and Pewter Industries."

Summary

1. *To define the terms* price *and* price planning A price represents the value of a product for both the seller and the buyer. Price planning is systematic decision making relating to all aspects of pricing by a firm; it involves tangible and intangible factors, purchase terms, and the nonmonetary exchange of goods and services. Exchange does not take place unless the buyer and seller agree that a price represents an equitable value. Price also balances supply and demand.

2. *To demonstrate the importance of price and study its relationship with other marketing variables* Price decisions have become more important to managers. This is due to price (monetary or nonmonetary) being part of every type of exchange, deregulation, cost increases, currency rates, technological advances, the greater emphasis by service

companies, and periodic economic slowdowns.

Price decisions must be made in sync with other marketing-mix elements. And pricing is often related to the product life cycle, customer service levels, and other specific marketing and company variables. In addition, setting prices for foreign markets can be complex and influenced by country factors.

3. *To differentiate between price-based and nonprice-based approaches* Under a price-based approach, sellers influence demand primarily via changes in price levels; they move consumers along a demand curve by raising or lowering prices. With a nonprice-based approach, sellers downplay price and emphasize such other marketing attributes as image, packaging, and features; they shift the

[14] Damian Horner, "It's Time for a Change," *Bookseller* (September 2, 2005), p. 24.

demand curves of consumers by stressing product distinctiveness.

4. *To examine the factors affecting pricing decisions* Several factors affect pricing decisions: consumers, costs, government, channel members, and competition. The law of demand states that consumers usually buy more units at a low price than at a high price. The price elasticity of demand explains the sensitivity of buyers to price changes in terms of the amounts they buy. Demand may be elastic, inelastic, or unitary; and it is impacted by the availability of substitutes and urgency of need. Consumers can be divided into segments based on their level of price sensitivity. Subjective price may be more important than actual price.

The costs of raw materials, supplies, labor, ads, transportation, and other items affect prices. Large increases often lead firms to raise prices, modify products, or abandon some offerings. Cost declines benefit marketing strategies by improving firms' ability to plan prices.

Government restrictions affect a broad variety of pricing areas. Price fixing, both horizontal and vertical, is subject to severe limitations. The Robinson-Patman Act bans most price discrimination to resellers that is not justified by costs. A number of states have unfair-sales acts

(minimum price laws) to protect small firms against predatory pricing. Unit-pricing laws require specified retailers to post prices in terms of quantity. The FTC has a series of guidelines for price advertising.

Often, each channel member seeks a role in pricing. Manufacturers exert control via exclusive distribution, pre-ticketing, opening their own outlets, offering goods on consignment, providing adequate margins, and having strong brands. Resellers exert control by making large purchases, linking sales support to margins, refusing to carry items, stocking competing brands, developing private brands, and purchasing outside traditional channels. Reseller profit margins, price guarantees, special deals, and the ramifications of price increases all need to be considered.

A market-controlled price environment has a lot of competition, similar products, and little control over prices by individual firms. A company-controlled price environment has a moderate level of competition, well-differentiated products, and strong control over prices by individual firms. In a government-controlled price environment, the government sets or influences prices. Some competitive actions may result in price wars, in which firms try to undercut each other's prices.

Key Terms

price (p. 610)

price planning (p. 610)

price-based approach (p. 613)

nonprice-based approach (p. 613)

law of demand (p. 616)

price elasticity of demand (p. 616)

elastic demand (p. 616)

inelastic demand (p. 616)

unitary demand (p. 616)

subjective price (p. 618)

horizontal price fixing (p. 620)

vertical price fixing (p. 621)

Robinson-Patman Act (p. 621)

unfair-sales acts (minimum price laws) (p. 622)

predatory pricing (p. 622)

loss leaders (p. 622)

unit pricing (p. 622)

bait-and-switch advertising (p. 623)

selling against the brand (p. 624)

gray market goods (p. 624)

market-controlled price environment (p. 625)

company-controlled price environment (p. 625)

government-controlled price environment (p. 625)

price wars (p. 625)

Review Questions

1. Explain the role of price in balancing supply and demand. Refer to Figure 20-1.
2. What is the risk with using a price-oriented strategy?
3. Distinguish between elastic and inelastic demand. Why is it necessary for a firm to understand these differences?
4. At a price of $50, a firm could sell 1,000 units. At a price of $35, it could sell 1,750 units. Calculate the elasticity of demand and state what price the firm should charge—and why.

5. If costs fall rapidly, how could a company react?
6. Is horizontal price fixing always illegal? Explain your answer.
7. Does the buyer have any potential liability under the Robinson-Patman Act? Why or why not?
8. How can a firm turn a market-controlled price environment into a company-controlled one?

Discussion Questions

1. How could a firm estimate price elasticity for a new product? A mature product?
2. When would you pass along a cost increase to consumers? When would you not pass the increase along?
3. You are the marketing vice-president of a firm that sells extended warranties for consumer electronics such as DVD

players, stereo systems, television sets, and digital cameras. What would you do to persuade consumers that you offer fair prices?
4. Present five examples of price advertising by a woman's clothing store that would violate FTC guidelines.

Web Exercise

The Marriott Corporation operates more than 2,700 hotels around the world under such names as Marriott Hotels, Renaissance Hotels, Courtyard by Marriott, Residence Inn by Marriott, Fairfield Inn by Marriott, TownePlace Suites, and

Ritz-Carlton (**http://marriott.com/aboutbrands/default.mi**). Visit the firm's Web site and review the prices charged by the various brands. Comment on what you find. Does the firm's strategy make sense to you? Why or why not?

Practice Quiz

1. The one element found in every marketing transaction is
   a. a good.
   b. delivery.
   c. price.
   d. promotion.

2. The law of demand
   a. relates purchase units to price.
   b. defines the sensitivity of buyers to price changes.
   c. concerns nonprice competition.
   d. involves government regulation of price.

3. Brand loyalty tends to generate
   a. elastic demand.
   b. inelastic demand.
   c. price competition.
   d. unitary demand.

4. The type of shopper most interested in the "best deal" for a product is a
   a. status seeker.
   b. price shopper.
   c. service shopper.
   d. convenience shopper.

5. Horizontal price fixing has been outlawed by the
   a. Robinson-Patman Act.
   b. McGuire Act.
   c. Miller-Tydings Act.
   d. Sherman Antitrust Act.

6. Fair trade practices refer to
   a. price controls.
   b. price discrimination.
   c. unfair-sales acts.
   d. vertical price fixing.

7. The Robinson-Patman Act was enacted in 1936 to directly protect
   a. small retailers.
   b. consumers.
   c. large manufacturers.
   d. wholesalers.

8. Which of the following is *not* an exception to the Robinson-Patman Act?
   a. Directly competing buyers are involved.
   b. Each buyer in a channel purchases products with substantial physical differences.

   c. Price differences are justified by costs.
   d. A seller reduces price to meet another supplier's bid.

9. Which of the following statements about loss leaders is *not* correct?
   a. Loss leaders are restricted by some state unfair-sales acts.
   b. Sellers assume customers drawn by loss leaders will also buy nonsale items.
   c. Loss-leader laws are vigorously enforced.
   d. Loss leaders attract customers to a seller.

10. Which of the following statements about price advertising is true?
    a. A firm can claim that a price has been reduced from an original price that was never before offered to the public.
    b. A firm cannot continuously advertise the same item as being on sale.
    c. A suggested list price can be advertised as a reference point for a sale, even though the product was never sold at that price.
    d. A firm cannot claim that its price is lower than that of competitors or the manufacturer's list price, even if it verifies that the price of an item at other companies in the same trading area is in fact higher.

11. When wholesalers and retailers stock well-known brands, place high prices on them, and then sell other brands for lower prices, they engage in
    a. price fixing.
    b. minimum pricing.
    c. selling against the brand.
    d. price discrimination.

12. Price guarantees
    a. bar entry into established channels of distribution.
    b. usually grant discounts to purchasers who are not competitors.
    c. help channel members maintain inventory value and profit.
    d. encourage passing price increases along to consumers.

13. A market-controlled price environment is characterized by
    a. moderate competition.
    b. well-differentiated goods and services.
    c. prices being strongly influenced by some level of government.
    d. little control over prices by individual firms.

14. By attracting consumers interested in low prices, discounters can carve out a niche in a
    a. company-controlled price environment.
    b. market-controlled price environment.
    c. government-controlled price environment.
    d. unitary-demand price environment.

15. Firms in the transportation, telecommunications, and financial industries have seen their price environments shift from

a. government- to market-controlled.
b. market- to company-controlled.
c. company- to market-controlled.
d. market- to government-controlled.

For the answers to these questions, please visit the online site for this book at **http://www.atomicdog.com.**

Chapter 21

Developing and Applying a Pricing Strategy

Club Méditerranée (known by most as Club Med) (**http://www.clubmed.com**) was started in Majorca, Spain in 1950 by a group of vacationers seeking a refuge from war-torn Europe. Even though the vacationers had spartan accommodations (including having to sleep in tents and cook their own food), they enjoyed the community spirit and self-made entertainment. The use of exotic destinations, all-inclusive prices, and simple accommodations has continued at Club Med today.

Club Med has had a colorful history. Polynesian huts replaced tents at the Greece location in 1954, and the firm opened its first ski resort in Switzerland in 1956. Club Med went public in 1966 and rapidly expanded through a number of mergers and acquisitions in the 1970s. Throughout the 1970s and 1980s, Club Med was associated with a "free-wheeling, anything goes" image. In 2002, Club Med bought a chain of 200 fitness clubs that it renamed Club Med Gym. Club Med now has over 1.5 million guests per year at its 150 vacation resorts, which include 120 or so resort villages in over 40 countries, 12 villas, a cruise ship, and a French tour operator. Close to three-fourths of its guests are European.

Club Med is commonly considered to be the originator of the all-inclusive vacation. In typical vacations, consumers are charged separately for meals, beverages, lessons, and equipment usage. In contrast, Club Med's pricing includes continuous buffets, beverages, and a wide variety of leisure, sporting, and recreational activities for the entire family. Club Med's ski programs include lodging, meals, drinks, and snacks, as well as ski lessons and ski passes. To emphasize its all-inclusive pricing, Club Med has declared its 22 villages in the Alps as "cash-free zones" in its ski brochures.

All-inclusive resorts have a number of significant attractions for vacationers. Guests can sample a number of activities such as sailing, snorkeling, or tennis to determine their interest without concern for lesson or equipment usage fees. Vacationers can also better plan their budgets, as well as partake in activities they would ordinarily not conduct. The all-inclusive pricing strategy provides Club Med with a unique pricing strategy among vacation resorts, a high-value-for-the-money image among its guests, and success in reaching and satisfying a target market seeking an active lifestyle vacation.[1]

In this chapter, we will look at the overall process of developing and applying a pricing strategy—including the use of various pricing approaches such as bundled pricing.

Chapter Objectives

1. To present an overall framework for developing and applying a pricing strategy
2. To analyze sales-based, profit-based, and status quo-based pricing objectives, and to describe the role of a broad price policy
3. To examine and apply the alternative approaches to a pricing strategy
4. To discuss several specific decisions that must be made in implementing a pricing strategy
5. To show the major ways that prices can be adjusted

---

[1] Various company and other sources.

21-1 OVERVIEW

A pricing strategy has the five steps shown in Figure 21-1: objectives, broad policy, strategy, implementation, and adjustments. All of them are affected by the outside factors we note in this chapter. Like any planning activity, a pricing strategy begins with a clear statement of goals and ends with an adaptive or corrective mechanism. Pricing decisions are integrated with the firm' s overall marketing program during the broad price-policy step. At the Small Business Administration Web site (**http://www.sba.gov/library/ pubs.html**), you can find an excellent discussion on how to plan and implement a price strategy, complete with checklists and examples. Scroll down to "Startup" and go to "Financial Management Series." Choose "Pricing Your Products and Services Profitably."

Development of a pricing strategy is not a one-time occurrence. The strategy needs to be reviewed when a new product is introduced, an existing product is revised, the competitive environment changes, a product moves through its life cycle, a competitor initiates a price change, costs rise or fall, the firm's prices come under government scrutiny, and/or other events take place.

These are indications a pricing strategy may be performing poorly:

- Prices are changed too frequently.
- The pricing policy is difficult to explain to consumers.
- Channel members complain that profit margins are inadequate.
- Price decisions are made without first conducting adequate marketing research.
- Too many different price options are offered.
- Excessive sales personnel time is spent in bargaining.
- Prices are inconsistent with the target market.

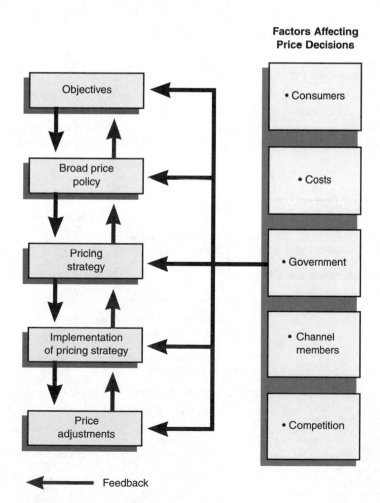

Figure 21-1

A Framework for Developing and Applying a Price Strategy

- A high percentage of goods is marked down or discounted late in the selling season to clear out surplus inventory.
- Too high a proportion of customers is price-sensitive and attracted by competitors' discounts. Demand is elastic.
- The firm has problems conforming with pricing legislation.

This chapter describes in detail the pricing framework outlined in Figure 21-1.

21-2 PRICING OBJECTIVES

A pricing strategy should be consistent with and reflect overall company goals. It is possible for different firms in the same industry to have dissimilar objectives and, therefore, distinct pricing strategies.[2]

Firms may select from three general objectives: sales-based, profit-based, and status quo–based. See Figure 21-2. With sales-based goals, a firm wants sales growth and/or to maximize market share. With profit-based goals, it wants to maximize profit, earn a satisfactory profit, optimize the return on investment, and/or secure an early recovery of cash. With status quo-based goals, it seeks to avoid unfavorable government actions, minimize the effects of competitor actions, maintain good channel relations, discourage the entry of competitors, reduce demands from suppliers, and/or stabilize prices.

A firm may pursue more than one pricing goal, such as increasing sales by 5 to 10 percent each year, achieving a 15 percent return on capital investments, and keeping prices near those of competitors. It may also set distinct short- and long-run goals. In the short run, it may seek high profit margins on new products; in the long run, these profit margins would drop to discourage potential competitors.

21-2a Sales-Based Objectives

> **Sales-based pricing objectives** seek high volume or market share.

A firm with **sales-based pricing objectives** is oriented toward high sales volume and/or expanding its share of sales relative to competitors. The company focuses on sales-based goals for any (or all) of three reasons: (1) It sees market saturation or sales growth as a major step leading to market control and sustained profits. (2) It wants to maximize unit

Figure 21-2

Pricing Objectives

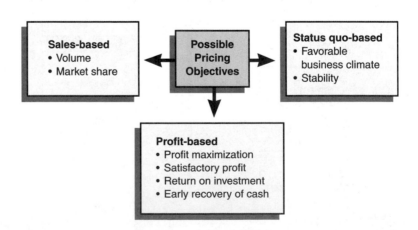

[2] See Richard A. Lancioni, "A Strategic Approach to Industrial Product Pricing: The Pricing Plan," *Industrial Marketing Management*, Vol. 34 (February 2005), pp. 177–183; Melissa Campanelli, "Price Point," *Entrepreneur* (November 2005), pp. 56, 58; and Linda Lisanti, "The Price of Beauty," *Convenience Store News* (November 15, 2005), pp. 59–64.

Marketing and the Web

Online Music Pricing: Pay per Download Versus a Yearly Subscription

Apple Computer, the maker of the iPod music player (http://www.apple.com/ipodstore), has sold several hundred million song downloads through its online iTunes Music Store. To date, Apple has been a clear winner over Napster (http://www.napster.com), AOL (http://www.aol.com), and RealNetworks (http://www.realnetworks.com), which sell subscriptions to download music.

In May 2005, Yahoo! Inc. (http://www.yahoo.com) started its Music Unlimited service, which it offered at $60 a year, about one-third of the price of other subscription services. Many marketing observers believe that it will be very difficult for Yahoo! to earn a profit based on this rate. However, unlike other subscription services, Yahoo! has low marketing costs due to its base of more than 175 million registered users. Yahoo! also has much of the infrastructure to enable shoppers to download the music selections. However, some music labels are concerned that it will be difficult to get consumers attracted by low prices to upgrade or that users will get used to low prices.

There has been no strong incentive for Apple to start a subscription-based service. The sales of iPod players increased from 4.4 million in 2004 to 17.2 million in 2005, while the total number of subscription sales from RealNetworks' Rhapsody division, AOL, Napster, and others were only a fraction of this number. Furthermore, the iPod player is also incompatible with any of the subscription-based services. As one marketing expert said, "There's only one device that matters, and you can't use it with Yahoo's music service."

Source: Based on material in Peter Burrows, Ben Elgin, Ronald Grover, Jay Greene, Heather Green, and Tom Lowry, "Online Music: Rewriting the Score," *Business Week* (May 30, 2005), pp. 34, 36.

---

sales and will trade low per-unit profits for larger total profits. (3) It assumes greater sales will enable it to have lower per-unit costs.

To gain high sales volume, **penetration pricing** is often employed, whereby low prices are used to capture the mass market for a good or service. It is a proper approach if customers are highly sensitive to price, low prices discourage actual and potential competitors, there are economies of scale (per-unit production and distribution costs fall as sales rise), and a large consumer market exists. Penetration pricing also recognizes that a high price may leave a product vulnerable to competition.

> **Penetration pricing** aims at the mass market.

Penetration pricing is used by such firms as NetZero, Malt-O-Meal, and Costco. For $9.95 monthly, NetZero (http://www.netzero.com) markets a dialup Internet connection with these features: E-mail spam protection, E-mail virus protection, 250 mb of E-mail storage, nationwide access, and 24/7 support. Malt-O-Meal (http://www.malt-o-meal.com) makes no-frills cereals and sells many of them in bags rather than boxes. Its prices are far less than those of better-known brands. Kirkland is the low-priced private brand of discounter Costco (http://www.costco.com) that is used with apparel, food, and many other products.

Penetration pricing may even tap markets not originally anticipated. For example, few people forecast that cordless phones would reach the sales attained during their peak. The market expanded rapidly after prices fell below $100. It grew again as new models were introduced for $50 and less.

21-2b Profit-Based Objectives

A firm having **profit-based pricing objectives** orients its strategy toward some type of profit goals. With profit-maximization goals, high dollar profits are sought. With satisfactory-profit goals, stability over time is desired; rather than maximum profits in a given year (which could cause a fall in nonpeak years), steady profits for many years are sought. With return-on-investment goals, profits are related to outlays; these goals are often sought by regulated utilities to justify rate increases. With early-recovery-of-cash goals, high initial profits are sought because firms are short of funds or uncertain about their future.

> **Profit-based pricing objectives** range from maximization of profit to recovery of cash. Goals can be per unit or total.

Profit may be expressed in per-unit or total terms. Per-unit profit equals the revenue a seller receives for one unit sold minus its costs. A product such as custom-made furniture has a high unit profit. Total profit equals the revenue a seller receives for all items sold minus total costs. It is computed by multiplying per-unit profit times the number of units sold. A product such as mass-marketed furniture has a low unit profit; success is based on the number of units sold (turnover). Products with high per-unit profits may have lower total profits than ones with low per-unit profits if the discount prices of the latter generate a much greater level of consumer demand. This depends on the elasticity of demand.

Skimming pricing uses high prices to attract the market segment more concerned with product quality, uniqueness, or status than price. It is proper if competition can be minimized (via patent protection, brand loyalty, raw material control, or high capital requirements), funds are needed for early cash recovery or further expansion, consumers are insensitive to price or willing to pay a high initial price, and unit costs remain equal or rise as sales increase (economies of scale are absent).

Skimming prices are used by such firms as Genentech, Cartier, and British Airways. Genentech (http://www.gene.com) makes Activase, a patented brand of TPA (tissue plasminogen activator), which quickly clears the blood clots associated with heart attacks and effectively treats certain strokes. Activase sells for about $1,700 for one 50-mg dose and $3,400 for one 100-mg dose. One version of Cartier's (http://www.cartier.com) Tank Americaine ladies watch retails for $25,000 or more. This watch has an 18-karat white gold strap in a bracelet design replete with diamonds. It also has a diamond bezel and black roman numerals. British Airways (http://www.britishairways.com) has overhauled its first-class cabins to provide passengers with fully reclining seats ("Our duvets [comforters], crisp linens, and full size pillows encase your 6' 6" bed to ensure your ultimate comfort and a good night's sleep."), greater privacy, and more room. It targets those willing to pay about $13,000 for a roundtrip between London and New York.

Firms may first use skimming pricing and then penetration pricing, or they may market both a premium brand and a value brand. There are many advantages to this:

- High prices are charged when competition is limited.
- High prices help cover development and introductory advertising costs.
- The first group of customers to buy a new product is usually less price-sensitive.
- High initial prices portray a high-quality image.
- Raising initial prices may be resisted by consumers; lowering them is viewed favorably.
- After the initial market segment is saturated, penetration pricing can appeal to the mass market and expand total sales volume.
- Multiple segments can be reached.

> **Skimming pricing** is aimed at the segment interested in quality or status.

21-2c   Status Quo-Based Objectives

Status quo-based pricing objectives are sought by a firm interested in continuing a favorable business climate for its operations or in stability. The pricing strategy is used to minimize the impact of such outside parties as government, competitors, and channel members—and to avoid sales declines.

It should be not inferred that status quo goals require no effort. A firm must instruct salespeople not to offer different terms to competing channel members or it may face a Robinson-Patman Act violation. It may have to match competitors' price cuts to keep customers—while trying to avoid price wars. It may have to accept lower profit margins in the face of rising costs to hold channel cooperation. It may have to charge penetration prices to discourage competitors from marketing certain product lines.

> **Status quo-based pricing objectives** seek good business conditions and stability.

21-3   BROAD PRICE POLICY

A *broad price policy* sets the overall direction (and tone) for a firm's pricing efforts and makes sure pricing decisions are coordinated with the firm's choices as to a target market, an image, and other marketing-mix factors. It includes short- and long-term pricing goals. Pricing can play a passive role—with customer purchases based on service, convenience, and quality—or it can play an active role, with purchases

> A **broad price policy** links prices with the target market, image, and other marketing elements.

based on low prices. A high-income segment buying status brands would expect premium prices. A moderate-income segment buying private brands would expect low prices.

A firm outlines a broad price policy by integrating individual decisions. It then decides on the interrelationship of prices for items within a product line, how often discounts are used, how prices compare to competition, the frequency of price changes, and the method for setting new-product prices.

Utilizing an integrated broad price policy is not effortless:

> As you likely know or suspect, you'll have many motives when deciding the prices for your goods and services, from understanding what the market can bear to figuring out what you can bear. It may be that you want to serve customers with modest incomes or perhaps you aspire to a level of greatness that demands high prices. Watching inflation reports and making sense of what's going on in the market can make new entrepreneurs wonder what they should charge. And they should wonder. If they don't, and they come up with your fees lightly, they may end up paying the hefty price. There is no set formula for price-making, because every single business is unique.[3]

21-4   PRICING STRATEGY

A pricing strategy may be cost-, demand-, and/or competition-based. When these approaches are integrated, combination pricing is involved. See Figure 21-3. Next, we explain each technique and provide illustrations.

21-4a   Cost-Based Pricing

In *cost-based pricing*, a firm sets prices by computing merchandise, service, and overhead costs and then adding an amount to cover its profit goal. Table 21-1 defines the key concepts in cost-based pricing and shows how they may be applied to big-screen television sets.

Cost-based prices are rather easy to derive because there is no need to estimate elasticity of demand or competitive reactions to price changes. There is also greater certainty about costs than demand or competitor responses to prices. Finally, cost-based pricing seeks reasonable profits because it is geared to covering all types of costs. It is often used by firms whose goals are stated in terms of profit or return on investment. A *price floor* is the lowest acceptable price a firm can charge and attain its profit goal.

When used by itself, cost-based pricing does have some significant limitations. It does not consider market conditions, the full effects of excess plant capacity, competitive prices, the product's phase in its life cycle, market share goals, consumers' ability to pay, and other factors.

Sometimes, it is hard to figure how such overhead costs as rent, lighting, personnel, and other general expenses should be allocated. These costs are often assigned in terms of product sales or the personnel time associated with each item. If product A accounts for 10 percent of sales, it may be allotted 10 percent of overhead costs. If product B gets 20 percent of personnel time, it may be allotted 20 percent of overhead costs. Problems may arise because different ways of assigning costs may yield varying results: How are costs allotted if a product yields 10 percent of sales and needs 20 percent of personnel time?

In the following subsections, we cover five cost-based pricing techniques: cost-plus, markup, target, price-floor, and traditional break-even analysis. Figure 21-4 gives a synopsis of each technique. And at the end of these subsections, Table 21-2 contains numerical examples of them.

> Under **cost-based pricing**, expenses are computed, profit is projected, and a **price floor** set.

---

[3] Geoff Williams, "Name Your Price," *Entrepreneur* (September 2005), p. 110.

Figure 21-3

The Alternative Ways of Developing a Pricing Strategy

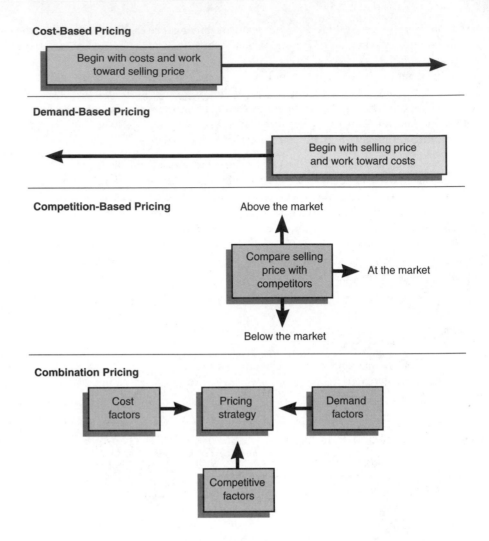

Cost-Based Pricing

Begin with costs and work toward selling price

Demand-Based Pricing

Begin with selling price and work toward costs

Competition-Based Pricing

Above the market

Compare selling price with competitors → At the market

Below the market

Combination Pricing

Cost factors → Pricing strategy ← Demand factors

Competitive factors

> **Cost-plus pricing** is the easiest form of pricing, based on units produced, total costs, and profit.

Cost-Plus Pricing For *cost-plus pricing*, prices are set by adding a predetermined profit to costs. It is the simplest form of cost-based pricing. Generally, the steps for computing cost-plus prices are to estimate the number of units to be produced, calculate fixed and variable costs, and add a desired profit to costs. The formula is

$$\text{Price} = \frac{\text{Total fixed costs} + \text{Total variable costs} + \text{Projected profit}}{\text{Units produced.}}$$

This method is easy to compute; yet, it has shortcomings. Profit is not expressed in relation to sales but in relation to costs, and price is not tied to consumer demand. Adjustments for rising costs are poorly conceived, and there are no plans for using excess capacity. There is little incentive to improve efficiency to hold down costs, and marginal costs are rarely analyzed.

Cost-plus pricing is most effective when price fluctuations have little influence on sales and when a firm is able to control prices. The prices of custom-made furniture, ships, heavy machinery, and extracted minerals typically depend on the costs incurred in producing these items; thus, companies set prices by computing costs and adding a reasonable profit. Cost-plus pricing often allows firms to get consumer orders, produce items, and then derive prices after total costs are known. This protects sellers.

Table **21-1**	Key Cost Concepts and How They May Be Applied to Big-Screen Television Sets			
Cost Concept	**Definition**	**Examples**[a]	**Sources of Information**	**Method of Computation**
Total fixed costs	Ongoing costs not related to volume. They are usually constant over a given range of output for a specified time.	Rent, salaries, electricity, real-estate taxes, plant, and equipment.	Accounting data, bills, cost estimates.	Addition of all fixed cost components.
Total variable costs	Costs that change with increases or decreases in output (volume).	Parts (such as tuners and speakers), hourly employees who assemble sets, and sales commissions.	Cost data from suppliers, estimates of labor productivity, sales estimates.	Addition of all variable cost components.
Total costs	Sum of total fixed and total variable costs.	See above.	See above.	Addition of all fixed and variable cost components.
Average fixed costs	Average fixed costs per unit.	See above under total fixed costs.	Total fixed costs and production estimates.	Total fixed costs/Quantity produced in units.
Average variable costs	Average variable costs per unit.	See above under total variable costs.	Total variable costs and production estimates.	Total variable costs/Quantity produced in units.
Average total costs	Sum of average fixed costs and average variable costs.	See above under total fixed and total variable costs.	Total costs and production estimates.	Average fixed costs + Average variable costs or Total costs/Quantity produced in units.
Marginal costs	Costs of making an additional unit.	See above under total fixed and total variable costs.	Accounting data, bills, cost estimates of labor and materials.	(Total costs of producing current quantity + one unit) − (Total costs of producing current quantity).

[a] Such marketing costs as advertising and distribution are often broken down into both fixed and variable components.

Markup Pricing   A firm uses *markup pricing* when it sets prices by computing the per-unit costs of producing (buying) goods and/or services and then determining the markup percentages needed to cover selling costs and profit. It is most commonly used by wholesalers and retailers, although it is employed by all types of organizations. The formula for markup pricing is:[4]

$$\text{Price} = \frac{\text{Product cost}}{(100 - \text{Markup percent})/100}$$

> **Markup pricing** considers per-unit product costs and the markups required to cover selling costs and profits. Markups should be expressed in terms of price rather than cost.

Several reasons explain why markups are commonly stated in terms of selling price instead of cost: (1) Because expenses, markdowns, and profits are computed as a percentage of sales, when markups are also cited as a percentage of sales, they aid in

---

[4] Markup can be calculated by transposing the formula into

$$\text{Markup percentage} = \frac{(\text{Price} - \text{Product cost})}{\text{Price}} \times 100$$

Figure 21-4

Cost-Based Pricing Techniques

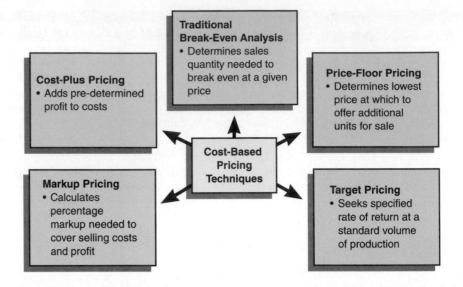

profit planning. (2) Firms quote their selling prices and trade discounts to channel members as percentage reductions from final list prices. (3) Competitive price data are more readily available than cost data. (4) Profitability appears smaller if based on price rather than on cost. This may be useful to avoid criticism over high earnings.

Markup size depends on traditional profit margins, selling and operating expenses, suggested list prices, inventory turnover, competition, the extent to which products must be serviced, and the effort needed to complete transactions. Due to differences in selling costs among products, some firms use a *variable markup policy*, whereby separate categories of goods and services receive different percentage markups. Variable markups recognize that some items require greater personal selling, customer service, alterations, and end-of-season markdowns than others. Expensive cosmetics need more personal selling and customer service than paperback books, suits need greater custom alterations than shirts, and fashion items are marked down more than basic clothing late in the selling season.

Markup pricing, though having many of cost-plus pricing's limitations, is popular. It is fairly simple, especially for firms with uniform markups across several items. Channel members get fair profits. Price competition is less if firms have similar markups. Resellers can show their actual prices compared to suggested prices. Adjustments can be made as costs rise. Variable markups are responsive to selling-cost differences among products or channel members.

Target Pricing In *target pricing*, prices are set to provide a particular rate of return on investment for a standard volume of production—the level of production a firm anticipates achieving. In the paper industry, prices are usually based on the standard volume of production being set at 90 to 92 percent of plant capacity. For target pricing to operate properly, a company must sell its entire standard volume at specified prices.

Target pricing is used by capital-intensive firms (such as auto makers) and public utilities (such as water companies). The prices charged by utilities are based on fair rates of return on invested assets and must be approved by regulatory commissions. Mathematically, a target price is computed as

$$\text{Price} = \frac{\text{Investment costs} \ \times \text{Target return on investment (\%)}}{\text{Standard volume}} + \text{Average total costs (at standard volume)}$$

Target pricing has five major shortcomings: (1) It is not useful for firms with low capital investments; it understates selling price. (2) Because prices are not keyed to

A **variable markup policy** responds to differences in selling costs among products.

Target pricing enables a rate of return on investment to be earned for a standard volume of production.

demand, the entire standard volume may not be sold at the target price. (3) Production problems may hamper output and standard volume may not be attained. (4) Price cuts to handle overstocked inventory are not planned. (5) If the standard volume is reduced due to unexpected poor sales performance, the price would have to be raised.

Price-Floor Pricing A firm's usual goal is to set prices to cover the sum of average fixed costs, average variable costs, and profit per unit. But when a firm has excess (unused) capacity, it may use *price-floor pricing* to find the lowest price at which it is worthwhile to increase the amount of goods or services it makes available for sale. The general principle is that the sale of additional units can be used to increase profits or help pay for fixed costs (which exist whether or not these items are made), as long as marginal revenues are greater than marginal costs. Although a firm cannot survive in the long run unless its average total costs are covered by prices, it may improve performance through price-floor pricing. The formula is

> **Price-floor pricing** may be used if there is excess capacity.

$$\text{Price-floor price} = \text{Marginal revenue per unit} > \text{Marginal cost per unit}$$

Traditional Break-Even Analysis As with target pricing, traditional break-even analysis looks at the relationship among costs, revenues, and profits. Whereas target pricing yields the price that results in a specified return on investment, *traditional break-even analysis* finds the sales quantity in units or dollars that is needed for total revenues (price × units sold) to equal total costs (fixed and variable) at a given price. If sales exceed the break-even quantity, a firm earns a profit. If sales are less than the break-even quantity, it loses money. Traditional break-even analysis does not consider return on investment, but can be extended to take profit planning into account. It is used by all kinds of sellers.

> **Traditional break-even analysis** computes the sales needed to break even at a specific price.

The break-even point can be computed in terms of units or sales dollars:

$$\text{Break-even point (units)} = \frac{\text{Total fixed costs}}{\text{Price} - \text{Variable costs (per unit)}}$$

$$\text{Break-even point (sales dollars)} = \frac{\text{Total fixed costs}}{1 - \dfrac{\text{Variable costs (per unit)}}{\text{Price}}}$$

The preceding formulas are derived from the equation: Price × Quantity = Total fixed costs + (Variable costs per unit × Quantity).

Break-even analysis can be adjusted to take into account the profit sought by a firm:

$$\text{Break-even point (units)} = \frac{\text{Total fixed costs} + \text{Projected profit}}{\text{Price} - \text{Variable costs (per unit)}}$$

$$\text{Break-even point (sales dollars)} = \frac{\text{Total fixed costs} + \text{Projected profit}}{1 - \dfrac{\text{Variable costs (per unit)}}{\text{Price}}}$$

There are limitations to traditional break-even analysis: (1) As with all cost-based pricing, demand is not considered. It is presumed that wide variations in quantity can be sold at the same price; this is highly unlikely. (2) It is assumed that all costs can be divided into fixed and variable categories. Yet, some, such as advertising, are difficult to define; advertising can be fixed or a percent of sales. (3) It is assumed that variable costs per unit are constant over a range of quantities, but purchase discounts or overtime wages may alter the costs. (4) It is assumed that fixed costs remain constant; but increases in production may lead to higher costs for new equipment, new full-time employees, and other items.

By including demand considerations, each of the cost-based techniques can be improved. Demand-based pricing techniques are discussed next.

21-4b Demand-Based Pricing

With **demand-based pricing**, a firm sets prices after studying consumer desires and ascertaining the range of prices acceptable to the target market. This approach is used by firms that believe price is a key factor in consumer decision making. These firms identify a **price ceiling**, which is the maximum amount consumers will pay for a given good or service. If the ceiling is exceeded, consumers will not make purchases. Its level depends on the elasticity of demand (availability of substitutes and urgency of need) and consumers' subjective price regarding the particular good or service.

Demand-based methods require consumer research as to the quantities that will be bought at various prices, sensitivity to price changes, the existence of market segments, and consumers' ability to pay. Demand estimates tend to be less precise than cost estimates. Also, firms that do inadequate cost analysis and rely on demand data may end up losing money if they make unrealistically low cost assumptions.

Under demand-based pricing, very competitive situations may lead to small markups and lower prices because people will buy substitutes; costs must be held down or prices will be too high—as might occur via cost-based pricing. For noncompetitive situations, firms can set large markups and high prices because demand is rather inelastic. Less emphasis is placed on costs when setting prices in these situations. Firms are more apt to set overly low prices in noncompetitive markets with cost-based pricing.

Four demand-based pricing techniques are reviewed next: demand-minus, chain-markup, modified break-even analysis, and price discrimination. Figure 21-5 gives a synopsis of each technique. And at the end of these subsections, Table 21-3 contains numerical examples of them.

Demand-Minus Pricing Through **demand-minus (demand-backward) pricing**, a firm finds the proper selling price and works backward to compute costs. This approach requires that price decisions revolve around consumer demand rather than company operations. It is used by firms selling directly to consumers.

Demand-minus pricing has three steps: Selling price is determined via consumer surveys or other research. The required markup percentage is set based on selling expenses and desired profits. The maximum acceptable per-unit cost for making or buying a product is computed. This formula is used, and it shows that product cost is derived after selling price and markup are set:

$$\text{Maximum product cost} = \text{Price} \times [(100 - \text{Markup percent})/100]$$

The difficulty in demand-minus pricing is that research may be time consuming or complex, especially if many items are involved. Also, new-product pricing research may be particularly inaccurate.

Chain-Markup Pricing **Chain-markup pricing** extends demand-minus calculations all the way from resellers back to suppliers (manufacturers). With it, final selling price is determined, markups for each channel member are examined, and the maximum acceptable costs to each member are computed.

In a typical consumer-goods channel, the markup chain is composed of

1. Maximum selling price to retailer $= \dfrac{\text{Final selling price} \times}{[(100 - \text{Retailer's markup})/100]}$

2. Maximum selling price to wholesaler $= \dfrac{\text{Selling price to retailer} \times}{[(100 - \text{Wholesaler's markup})/100]}$

3. Maximum product cost to manufacturer $= \dfrac{\text{Selling price to wholesaler} \times}{[(100 - \text{Manufacturer's markup})/100]}$

Table 21-2	Examples of Cost-Based Pricing Techniques

Cost-Plus Pricing—A custom-bed maker has total fixed costs of $200,000, variable costs of $1,500 per bed, desires $100,000 in profits, and plans to produce 1,000 beds. What is the selling price per bed?

$$\text{Price} = \frac{\text{Total fixed costs + Total variable costs + Projected profit}}{\text{Units produced}} = \underline{\$1,800}$$

Markup Pricing—A retailer pays $30 for full-featured cordless telephones and wants a markup on selling price of 40 percent (30 percent for selling costs and 10 percent for profit). What is the final selling price?

$$\text{Price} = \frac{\text{Merchandise costs}}{(100 - \text{Markup percent})/100} = \underline{\$50}$$

Target Pricing—A specialty auto maker has spent $160,000,000 for a new plant. It has a 25 percent target return on investment. Standard production volume for the year is 5,000 units. Average total costs, excluding the new plant, are $14,000 for each car (at a production level of 5,000 cars). What is the selling price to the firm's retail dealers?

$$\text{Price} = \frac{\text{Investment costs } \times \text{ Target return on investment (\%)}}{\text{Standard volume}} + \text{Average total costs (at standard volume)} = \underline{\$22,000}$$

Price-Floor Pricing—A big-screen TV manufacturer's plant capacity is 1,000 units. Its total fixed costs are $500,000 and variable costs are $375 per unit. At full production, average fixed costs are $500 per unit. The firm sets a price of $1,100 to retailers and gets orders for 800 TVs at that price. It must operate at 80 percent of capacity, unless it re-evaluates its pricing strategy. With price-floor pricing, it can sell the 200 additional sets to retailers. How?

   The firm could let resellers buy one TV at $425 for every four they buy at $1,100. Then, it earns a profit of $90,000 [revenues of ($1,100 × 800) + ($425 × 200) less costs of ($875 × 1,000)]. If it just makes and sells 800 TVs at full price, it earns $80,000 [revenues of ($1,100 × 800) less variable costs of ($375 × 800) and fixed costs of $500,000]. The higher profits are due to marginal revenue > marginal cost.

Traditional Break-Even Analysis—A small candy maker has total fixed costs of $150,000 and variable costs per unit of $0.25. It sells to retailers for $0.40 per bar. What is the break-even point in units? In sales dollars?

$$\text{Break-even point (units)} = \frac{\text{Total fixed costs}}{\text{Price} - \text{Variable costs (per unit)}} = \underline{1,000,000}$$

$$\text{Break-even point (sales dollars)} = \frac{\text{Total fixed costs}}{1 - \dfrac{\text{Variable costs (per unit)}}{\text{Price}}} = \underline{\$400,000}$$

By using chain-markup pricing, price decisions can be related to consumer demand and each reseller is able to see the effects of price changes on the total distribution channel. The interdependence of firms becomes clearer; they cannot set prices independently of one another.

Modified Break-Even Analysis *Modified break-even analysis* combines traditional break-even analysis with an evaluation of demand at various levels of price. Traditional analysis focuses on the sales needed to break even at a given price. It does not indicate the likely level of demand at that price, examine how consumers respond to different levels of price, consider that the break-even point can vary greatly depending on the price the firm happens to select, or calculate the price that maximizes profits.

Modified analysis reveals the price-quantity mix that maximizes profits. It shows that profits do not inevitably rise as the quantity sold increases because lower prices may be needed to expand demand. It also verifies that a firm should examine various price levels and select the one with the greatest profits. Finally, it relates demand to price, rather than assuming that the same volume could be sold at any price.

> **Modified break-even analysis** melds traditional break-even analysis with demand evaluation at various prices.

Price Discrimination With a *price discrimination* approach, a firm sets two or more distinct prices for a product so as to appeal to different final consumer or organizational consumer segments. Higher prices are offered to inelastic segments and lower prices to

> **Price discrimination** entails setting distinct prices to reach different market segments.

Figure 21-5

Demand-Based Pricing Techniques

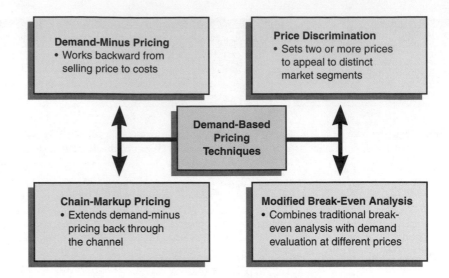

elastic ones. Price discrimination can be customer-based, product-based, time-based, or place-based.[5]

In *customer-based price discrimination*, prices differ by customer category for the same good or service. Price differentials may relate to a consumer's ability to pay (doctors, lawyers, and accountants partially set prices in this manner), negotiating ability (the price of an office building is usually set by bargaining), or buying power (discounts are given for volume purchases).

Through *product-based price discrimination*, a firm markets a number of features, styles, qualities, brands, or sizes of a product and sets a different price for each product version. Price differentials are greater than cost differentials for the various versions. A dishwasher may be priced at $500 in white and $550 in brown, although the brown color costs the manufacturer only $10 more. There is inelastic demand by customers desiring the special color, and product versions are priced accordingly.

Through *time-based price discrimination*, a firm varies prices by day versus evening (movie theater tickets), time of day (telephone and utility rates), or season (hotel rates). Consumers who insist on prime-time use pay higher prices than those who are willing to make their purchases during nonpeak times.

In *place-based price discrimination*, prices differ by seat location (sports events), floor location (office buildings), or geographic location (resort cities). Demand for locations near the field, elevators, or warm climates drives the prices of these locations up. General admission tickets, basement offices, and moderate-temperature resorts are priced lower to attract consumers to otherwise less desirable purchases.

When a firm engages in price discrimination, it should use ***yield management pricing***—whereby it determines the mix of price-quantity combinations that generates the highest level of revenues for a given time. A company should give itself every opportunity to sell as many goods and services at full price as possible, while also seeking to sell as many units as it can. It should not sell so many low-price items that it jeopardizes full-price sales. A 1,000-seat theater offering first-run plays must decide how many tickets to sell as preferred seating (at $75 each) and how many as general admission (at $35 each). If it tries to sell too many preferred seating tickets,

Yield management pricing lets firms optimize price discrimination efforts.

[5] See Romana J. Khan and Dipak C. Jain, "An Empirical Analysis of Price Discrimination Mechanisms and Retailer Profitability," *Journal of Marketing Research*, Vol. 42 (November 2005), pp. 516–524; and Paul W. Dobson and Michael Waterson, "Chain-Store Pricing Across Local Markets," *Journal of Economics & Management Strategy*, Vol. 14 (March 2005), pp. 93–119.

there may be empty seats. If it looks to sell too many general admission tickets, the theater may be full—but total revenues may be unsatisfactory. Yield management pricing is now easier to do because of the availability of inexpensive computer software. It is especially popular with airlines and hotels, and widely used by Internet firms.[6] These Web sites are good sources for information on yield management pricing: Veritec Solutions (**http://www.veritecsolutions.com/Articles.htm**) and Managing Change (**http://www.managingchange.com/dynamic/yieldmgt.htm**).

Before using price discrimination, a firm should address these questions: Are there distinct market segments? Do people talk to each other about prices? Can product versions be differentiated? Will some people choose low-priced versions when they might buy high-priced versions if those are the only ones sold? How do the marginal costs of adding product alternatives compare with marginal revenues? Will channel members stock all models? How hard is it to explain product differences to consumers? Under what conditions is price discrimination legal (so as to not violate the Robinson-Patman Act)?

21-4c   Competition-Based Pricing

Competition-based pricing is involved when a firm uses competitors' prices rather than demand or cost considerations as its primary pricing guideposts. That firm may not respond to changes in demand or costs unless those changes also affect competitors' prices. It can set prices below the market, at the market, or above the market, depending on its customers, image, marketing mix, consumer loyalty, and other factors. This approach is used by firms contending with others selling similar items (or those perceived as similar).

> **Competition-based pricing** is setting prices relative to other firms.

Because it is simple and does not rely on demand curves, price elasticity, or costs per unit, competition-based pricing is popular. The ongoing market price is assumed to be fair for both consumers and companies. Pricing at the market level does not disrupt competition and does not lead to retaliations. It may lead to complacency, and different firms may not have the same demand and cost structures.

We now discuss two aspects of competition-based pricing: price leadership and competitive bidding.

Price Leadership   *Price leadership* exists in situations where one firm (or a few firms) is usually the first to announce price changes and others in the industry follow. The price leader's role is to set prices that reflect market conditions, without disrupting the marketplace—it must not turn off consumers with price increases perceived as too large or precipitate a price war with competitors by excessive price cuts.

> **Price leadership** occurs when one or a few firms initiate price changes in an industry; they are effective when others follow.

Price leaders are often firms with significant market shares, well-established positions, respect from competitors, and a desire to initiate price changes. Consider Southwest Airlines (**http://www.southwest.com**):

> Southwest has the lowest costs on a per mile basis of all the major airlines. Among the factors that contribute to its low cost structure are a single aircraft type and an efficient, high-utilization, point-to-point route structure. Due to a change in passenger profiles, business class and first class seats have suffered declining demand. Many companies have thus been forced to introduce low-cost fares. Since Southwest provides low cost, standardized travel options, it has not had to change its strategy—saving on restructuring costs. It also benefits from a long establishment in the low-cost airline market, allowing the firm to capitalize on significant customer awareness of the brand.[7]

---

[6] See Barry Berman, "Applying Yield Management Pricing to Your Service Business," *Business Horizons*, Vol. 48 (March–April 2005), pp. 169–179.

[7] *Southwest Airlines Co. Company Profile* (New York: Datamonitor USA, May 2005), pp. 5–6.

Global Marketing in Action

The $100 Computer

Rajesh Jain's latest product is an 8-inch by 6-inch computer with a Web browser and E-mail, word processing, and spreadsheet capabilities. What sets the computer apart from its competitors is the price tag of $100—which includes a monitor, keyboard, and mouse, as well as all of the necessary software.

Developing a $100 computer is seen as essential to increase computer usage in countries such as Brazil, China, India, and Russia. Although a 10 percent profit margin on a $100 computer may seem small, the market size is so large that major firms such as Google (http://www.google.com) and Advanced Micro Devices (http://www.amd.com) have partnered with an MIT professor to develop a $100 laptop. For example, in India, a country with more than 1 billion people,

the computer market has a penetration rate of 0.9 percent.

What sets Jain's firm, Novatium (http://www.novatium.com), apart from the others is that its product is similar to a traditional computer at a fraction of the cost. Competitors have attempted to reduce costs by using older and slower microprocessors, less memory, and smaller hard drives. To reduce costs, the Novatium computer uses a network or a USB memory stick to store data instead of a hard drive. And the microprocessor is the same as that used in a wireless phone. To potentially drop its price even lower than $100, Novatium is working to use a household's television set as a monitor.

Source: Based on material in Om Malik, "The Next PC Revolution Will Be Televised," *Business 2.0* (August 2005), pp. 93–95.

Table 21-3 Examples of Demand-Based Pricing Techniques

Demand-Minus Pricing—A hardware manufacturer has done consumer research and found that contractors are willing to spend $60.00 for its flagship electric drill. Selling expenses and profits are expected to be 35 percent of the selling price. What is the maximum the manufacturer can spend to develop and produce each drill?

Maximum merchandise costs = Price $\times$ [(100 − Markup percent)/100] = $39.00

Chain-Markup Pricing—A ladies' shoe maker knows women will pay $100.00 for a pair of its shoes. It sells via wholesalers and retailers. Each requires a markup of 30 percent; the manufacturer wants a 25 percent markup. (a) What is the maximum price that retailers and wholesalers will spend for a pair of shoes? (b) What is the maximum the manufacturer can spend to make each pair of shoes?

(a) Maximum selling price to retailer = Final selling price $\times$ [(100 − Retailer's markup)/100] = $70.00

   Maximum selling price to wholesaler = Selling price to retailer $\times$ [(100 − Wholesaler's markup)/100] = $49.00

(b) Maximum merchandise costs to manufacturer = Selling price to wholesaler $\times$ [(100 − Manufacturer's markup)/100] = $36.75

Modified Break-Even Analysis—An aspirin maker has total fixed costs of $2,000,000 and variable costs of $1.50 per bottle. Research shows the following demand schedule. At what price should the company sell its aspirin?

Selling Price	Quantity Demanded	Total Revenue	Total Cost	Total Profit (Loss)	
$3.00	2,000,000	$6,000,000	$5,000,000	$1,000,000	Maximum
2.50	3,200,000	8,000,000	6,800,000	1,200,000	← profit at
2.00	5,000,000	10,000,000	9,500,000	500,000	price of $2.50

Price Discrimination—A sports team knows people will pay different prices for tickets, based on location. It offers 5,000 tickets at $50 each, 25,000 at $20 each, and 20,000 at $12 each. What are profits if total costs per game are $750,000?

   Profit = (Revenues from segment A + segment B + segment C) − Total costs = $240,000

Today, the role of price leaders has diminished in many industries, including steel, chemicals, glass containers, and newsprint, as more firms have sought greater independence. Many times, an industry leader has announced higher prices, but had to backtrack after competitors decided not to go along.

Announcements of price changes by industry leaders must be communicated through the media. It is illegal for firms in the same industry or in competing ones to confer regarding their prices.

Competitive Bidding Through *competitive bidding* (discussed in Chapter 9), two or more firms independently submit prices to a customer—usually b-to-b—for a specific good, project, and/or service. Sealed bids may be requested by some government or organizational consumers; each seller then has one chance to make its best offer.

Mathematical models have been applied to competitive bidding. All use the expected profit concept, which states that as the bid price increases, the profit to a firm increases but the probability of its winning a contract decreases. The potential profit (loss) at a given bid can usually be estimated accurately, but the probability of getting a contract (underbidding all other qualified competitors) is hard to determine.

21-4d Combination Pricing

Although we have separately discussed cost-, demand-, and competition-based pricing methods, aspects of the three approaches should be integrated into a **combination pricing** approach. This is done often in practice. A cost-based approach sets a price floor and outlines the costs incurred in doing business. It establishes profit margins, target prices, and/or break-even quantities. A demand-based approach finds the prices consumers will pay and the ceiling prices for each channel member. It develops the price-quantity mix that maximizes profits and lets a firm reach different market segments (if it so desires). A competition-based approach examines the proper price level for the firm in relation to competitors.

Critical issues may be overlooked unless the approaches are integrated. Table 21-4 shows a list of questions a firm should consider in setting prices.

> It is essential that companies integrate cost, demand, and competitive pricing techniques via **combination pricing**.

21-5 IMPLEMENTING A PRICING STRATEGY

The implementation of a pricing strategy involves several distinct—but related—specific decisions, in addition to the broader concepts just discussed. Decisions involve whether and how to use customary versus variable pricing, a one-price policy versus flexible pricing, odd pricing, the price-quality association, leader pricing, multiple-unit pricing, price lining, price bundling, geographic pricing, and purchase terms.

21-5a Customary Versus Variable Pricing

Customary pricing occurs when a firm sets prices and seeks to maintain them for an extended time. Prices are not changed during this period. Customary pricing is used for items such as candy, gum, magazines, restaurant food, and mass transit. Rather than modify prices to reflect cost increases, firms may reduce package size, change ingredients, or have a more restrictive transfer policy among bus lines. The assumption is that consumers prefer one of these alternatives to constantly changing prices.

Variable pricing lets a firm intentionally alter prices in response to cost fluctuations or differences in consumer demand. When costs change, prices are lowered or raised; the fluctuations are not absorbed and product quality is not modified to maintain customary prices. Through price discrimination, a firm offers distinct prices

> One price is maintained over an extended period with **customary pricing**. Prices reflect costs or differences in demand under **variable pricing**.

Table 21-4 Selected Issues to Consider When Combining Pricing Techniques

Cost-Based

What profit margin does a particular price level permit?

Do markups allow for differences in product investments, installation and servicing, and selling effort and merchandising skills?

Are there accurate and timely cost data by good, service, project, process, and/or store?

Are cost changes monitored and prices adjusted accordingly?

Are there specific profit or return-on-investment goals?

What is the price-floor price for each good, service, project, process, and/or store?

What are the break-even points for each good, service, project, process, and/or store?

Demand-Based

What type of demand does each good, service, project, process, and/or store face?

Has price elasticity been estimated for various price levels?

Are demand-minus, chain-markup, and modified break-even analyses utilized?

Has price discrimination been considered?

How loyal are customers?

Competition-Based

How do prices compare with those of competitors?

Is price leadership used in the industry? By whom?

How do competitors react to price changes?

How are competitive bids determined?

Is the long-run expected profit concept used in competitive bidding?

---

to appeal to different market segments. The prices charged to diverse consumers are not based on costs, but on consumer price sensitivity. Many firms use some form of variable pricing.

It is possible to combine customary and variable pricing. For example, a magazine may be $3 per single copy and $24 per year's subscription ($2 an issue); two customary prices are charged, and the consumer selects the offer he or she finds most attractive.

21-5b A One-Price Policy Versus Flexible Pricing

A *one-price policy* lets a firm charge the same price to all customers seeking to purchase a good or service under similar conditions. Prices may differ according to the quantity bought, time of purchase, and services obtained (such as delivery and installation), but all consumers are given the opportunity to pay the same price for the same combinations of goods and services. This builds consumer confidence, is easy to administer, eliminates bargaining, and permits self-service and catalog sales. Today, throughout the United States, one-price policies are the rule for most retailers. In industrial marketing, a firm with a one-price policy would not allow sales personnel to deviate from a published price list.

Through *flexible pricing*, a firm sets prices based on the consumer's ability to negotiate or on the buying power of a large customer. People who are knowledgeable

> All those buying the same product pay the same price under a **one-price policy**. Different customers may pay different prices with **flexible pricing**.

or are good bargainers pay less than those who are not knowledgeable or are weaker bargainers. Jewelry stores, car dealers, real-estate brokers, and many industrial marketers tend to use flexible pricing. Commissions may be keyed to profitability to encourage salespeople to obtain higher prices. Flexible prices to resellers are subject to Robinson-Patman limits. Flexible pricing is more likely outside the United States, where "haggling" may be culturally ingrained. To remedy consumer insecurities about bargaining, Web sites now have guides to educate people. The Woman Motorist site (**http://www. womanmotorist.com**) offers a free *New Car Buying Guide* that includes a chapter on "Dealing with Dealers: Negotiating a New Car Purchase," as well as a *Used Car Buying Guide* that has a chapter on "Negotiating a Good Deal." Scroll down to the middle of the Woman Motorist home page to access these guides.

One result of flexible pricing is that some people gather data from full-service sellers, shop for the best price (often on the Internet), and then challenge discount sellers to "beat the lowest price." This practice hurts full-service firms, lets discounters hold down selling costs, and encourages bargaining.

21-5c   Odd Pricing

Odd pricing is used when selling prices are set at levels below even dollar values, such as 49 cents, $4.95, and $199. It is popular for several reasons: People like getting change. Because the cashier must make change, employers ensure that cash sales are recorded and money is placed in the register. Consumers gain the impression that a firm thinks carefully about prices and sets them as low as possible. They may also believe odd prices represent price reductions; a price of $8.95 may be viewed as a discount from $10. See Figure 21-6.

> **Odd prices** are set below even-dollar values.

Odd prices 1 or 2 cents below the next even price (29 cents, $2.98) are common up to $4 or $5. Beyond that point and up to $50 or so, 5-cent reductions from the highest even price ($19.95, $49.95) are more usual. For expensive items, odd endings are in dollars ($499, $5,995).

Odd prices may help consumers stay within their price limits and still buy the best items available. A shopper willing to spend "less than $30" for a tie will be attracted to a $29.95 tie and might be as apt to buy it as a $24 tie since it is within the defined price range. The sales tax in 45 states has the effect of raising odd prices into higher dollar levels and may reduce the impact of odd pricing as a selling tool (**http://www.salestaxinstitute.com/sales_tax_rates.jsp**).

21-5d   The Price-Quality Association

According to the *price-quality association*, consumers may believe high prices represent high quality and low prices represent low quality. This association tends to be most valid when quality is difficult to judge on bases other than price, buyers perceive large differences in quality among brands, buyers have little experience or confidence in assessing quality (as with a new product), high prices exclude the mass market, brand names are unknown, or brand names require certain price levels to sustain their images.[8]

> The **price-quality association** deals with perceptions. **Prestige pricing** indicates that consumers may not buy when a price is too low.

If brand names are well known and/or people are confident of their ability to compare brands on nonprice factors, the price-quality association may be less

[8] See Baba Shiv, Ziv Carmon, and Dan Ariely, "Placebo Effects of Marketing Actions: Consumers May Get What They Pay For," *Journal of Marketing Research*, Vol. 42 (November 2005), pp. 383–393; and Anthony D. Miyazaki, Dhruv Grewal, Ronald C. Goodstein, Dawn Iacobucci, and Kent Monroe, "The Effect of Multiple Extrinsic Cues on Quality Perceptions: A Matter of Consistency," *Journal of Consumer Research*, Vol. 32 (June 2005), pp. 146–153.

Ethical Issues in Marketing

Merchants Take on Visa and MasterCard over Credit-Card Fees

Taylor Bond is president and chief executive officer of Children's Orchard (http://www.childrensorchard.com), a chain of about 100 franchised outlets that specializes in the sale of slightly used children's toys. Bond estimates that the fees for using Visa (http://www.visa.com) and MasterCard (http://www.mastercard.com) have doubled from 1.1 percent to 2.2 percent per transaction.

Two major trade associations, the Food Marketing Institute (FMI) (http://www.fmi.org) and the National Retail Federation (http://www.nrf.com), have railed against a recent increase in credit-card fees. According to the FMI, merchant fees for accepting credit cards increased five times between 1994 and 2005, rising from 1 percent of the transaction amount to 1.65 percent plus a flat fee of 10 cents for the Visa Signa-

ture credit card. Fees for online debit transactions (that require a PIN number entry) also increased from 8 cents to as high as 50 cents. The FMI is concerned that these added fees result in price increases.

Credit card companies have defended the increases based on the necessary investments in technology. Their fees also reflect the value of their cards, which provide access to cardholders, as well as guaranteed payments for authorized purchases. MasterCard and Visa also say that consumers who use their signature cards spend more heavily than their regular credit card users. MasterCard estimates that its premier World card holders use their card six times as often as its Platinum card holders and spend seven times more.

Source: Based on material in Ken Clark, "No Joking Matter," *Chain Store Age* (May 2005), p. 188.

---

valid. Consumers may then be more interested in the perceived value they receive for their money—and not necessarily believe a higher price represents better quality. It is imperative that prices properly reflect both the quality and the image of the firm.

Prestige pricing is a theory drawn from the price-quality association that assumes consumers will not buy goods or services at prices they consider to be too low. Most people set price floors and will not buy at prices below those floors—they feel quality and status would be inferior at extremely low prices. Most people also set ceilings as to the prices they consider acceptable for particular goods or services. Above those ceilings, items are seen as too expensive. For each good or service, a firm should set prices in the target market's acceptable range between the floor and ceiling. See Figure 21-7.

21-5e   Leader Pricing

> **Leader pricing** is used to attract customers to low prices.

A firm uses *leader pricing* to advertise and sell key items in its product assortment at less than usual profit margins. The wholesaler's or retailer's goal is to increase customer traffic. The manufacturer's goal is to gain greater consumer interest in its overall product line. In both cases, it is hoped that consumers will buy regularly priced products in addition to the specially priced items that attract them.

Leader pricing is most used with well-known, high-turnover, frequently bought products. In supermarkets, one best-selling items is soda. To stimulate customer traffic, Coke or Pepsi may be priced very low; in some cases, it is sold at close to cost. Soda is a good item for leader pricing because consumers are able to detect low prices and they are attracted into a store by a discount on the item.

There are two kinds of leader pricing: loss leaders and prices higher than cost but lower than regular prices. As stated in Chapter 20, the use of loss leaders is regulated or illegal in a number of states.

Figure 21-6

Odd Pricing: A Practice Used Around the Globe

Source: Reprinted by permission of Retail Forward.

21-5f Multiple-Unit Pricing

Multiple-unit pricing is a practice whereby a firm offers discounts to consumers to encourage them to buy in quantity, so as to increase overall sales volume. By offering items at two for 89 cents or six for $139, a firm attempts to sell more units than would be sold at 50 cents or $25 each.

Four major benefits arise from multiple-unit pricing: (1) Customers may increase their immediate purchases if they feel they get a bargain. (2) They may boost long-term consumption by making larger purchases, as occurs with soda. (3) Competitors' customers may be attracted by the discounts. (4) A firm may be able to clear out slow-moving and end-of-season merchandise, as wholesaler Liquidity Services does through its Web site (**http://www.liquidation.com**), which sells overstocked and closeout items in bulk.

Multiple-unit pricing will not succeed if shoppers just shift purchases and do not hike consumption. Multiple-unit pricing for Heinz ketchup may not result in consumers using more ketchup with meals. Total revenues would not rise if consumers buy ketchup less often because it can be stored.

> Quantity discounts are intended to result in higher sales volume with **multiple-unit pricing**.

21-5g Price Lining

Price lining involves selling products at a range of prices, with each representing a distinct level of quality (or features). Instead of setting one price for a single version of a good or service, a firm sells two or more versions (with different levels of quality or features) at different prices. Price lining involves two decisions: prescribing the price range (floor and ceiling) and setting specific price points in that range.

A price range may be low, intermediate, or high. Inexpensive radios may be priced from $8 to $20, moderately priced radios from $25 to $50, and expensive radios from $75 to $120. After the range is chosen, a limited number of price points is set. They must be distinct and not too close together. Inexpensive radios could be $8, $12, and $20. They should not be priced at $8, $9, $10, $11, $12, $13, $14, $15, $16, $17, $18, $19, and $20. This would confuse consumers and be inefficient for the firm.

> **Price lining** sets a range of selling prices and price points within that range.

Figure 21-7

Demand for Designer Jeans Under Prestige Pricing

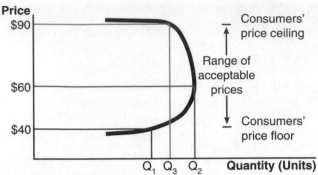

When designer jeans are priced under $40, consumers believe the jeans are labeled incorrectly, are an old style, are seconds, or are of poor quality. Demand is negligible.

When designer jeans are priced at $40, consumer demand is Q_1. A small group of discount-oriented consumers will buy the jeans. This is the minimum price they will pay for a good pair of designer jeans.

As the price goes from $40 to $60, demand rises continuously as more consumers perceive the jeans as a high-quality, status product. At $60, sales peak at Q_2.

As the price goes from $60 to $90, consumer demand drops gradually to Q_3. In this range, some consumers begin to see the jeans as too expensive. But many will buy the jeans until the price reaches $90, their ceiling price.

When designer jeans are priced over $90, consumers believe the jeans are too expensive and demand is negligible.

A firm must consider these factors with price lining: Price points must be spaced far enough apart so customers perceive differences among product versions—otherwise, consumers might view the price floor as the price they should pay and believe there is no difference among models. Price points should be spaced farther apart at higher prices because consumer demand becomes more inelastic. Relationships among price points must be kept when costs rise, so clear differences are retained. If radio costs rise 25 percent, prices should be set at $10, $15, and $25 (up from $8, $12, and $20).

Price lining has benefits for both sellers and consumers. Sellers can offer a product assortment, attract multiple market segments, trade up shoppers within a price range, control inventory by price point, reduce competition by having versions over a price range, and increase overall sales volume. Shoppers are given an assortment from which to choose, confusion is lessened, comparisons may be made, and quality options are available within a given price range.

Price lining can also have constraints: Consumers may feel price gaps are too large—a $25 handbag may be too low, while the next price point of $100 may be too high. Rising costs may squeeze individual prices and make it hard for a firm to keep the proper relationships in its line. Markdowns or special sales may disrupt the balance in a price line, unless all items in the line are proportionately reduced in price.

21-5h Price Bundling

A firm can use **bundled** or **unbundled** pricing.

A firm uses **bundled pricing** to sell a basic product, options, and customer service for one total price. An industrial-equipment manufacturer may have a single price for a drill press, its delivery, its installation, and a service contract. Individual items, such as the drill press, would not be sold separately. With **unbundled pricing**, a firm breaks down prices by individual components and allows the consumer to decide what to purchase. A discount appliance store may have separate prices for a refrigerator, its delivery, its installation, and a service contract. Many firms offer both pricing options and allow a slight discount for bundled pricing. See Figure 21-8.

21-5i   Geographic Pricing

Geographic pricing outlines responsibility for transportation charges. Many times, it is not negotiated but depends on the traditional practices in the industry in which the firm operates, and all companies in the industry normally conform to the same geographic pricing format. Geographic pricing often involves industrial marketing situations.

The most common methods of geographic pricing are:

- *FOB (free-on-board) mill (factory) pricing*—The buyer picks a transportation form and pays all freight charges, the seller pays the costs of loading the goods (hence, "free on board"), and the delivered price to the buyer depends on freight charges.
- *Uniform delivered pricing*—All buyers pay the same delivered price for the same quantity of goods, regardless of their location; the seller pays for shipping.
- *Zone pricing*—This provides for a uniform delivered price to all buyers within a geographic zone; through a multiple-zone system, delivered prices vary by zone.
- *Base-point pricing*—Firms in an industry establish basing points from which the costs of shipping are computed; the delivered price to a buyer reflects the cost of transporting goods from the basing point nearest to the buyer, regardless of the actual site of supply.

> **Geographic pricing** alternatives are FOB mill (factory), uniform delivered, zone, and base-point pricing.

Figure 21-8

Unbundling Prices

To appeal to its price-conscious customers, Ikea (**http://www.ikea. com**) does not include a delivery charge in its basic prices. Delivery is an unbundled add-on for shoppers who want it.

Source: Reprinted by permission of Susan Berry, Retail Image Consulting, Inc.

21-5j Purchase Terms

Purchase terms are the provisions of price agreements. They include discounts, the timing of payments, and credit arrangements.

Discounts are the reductions from final selling prices available to resellers and consumers for doing certain functions, paying cash, buying large amounts, buying in off-seasons, or enhancing promotions. A wholesaler may buy goods at 40 percent off a manufacturer's suggested final selling price. This covers its expenses, profit, and the discount to the retailer. The retailer could buy for 25 percent off list (the wholesaler keeping 15 percent for its costs and profit). Discounts must be proportionately available to all competing channel members to avoid violating the Robinson-Patman Act.

Payment timing must be specified in a purchase agreement. Final consumers may pay immediately or upon delivery. In credit sales, payments are not made until bills are received; they may be made over time. B-to-b consumers negotiate for good terms: "Net 30" means products do not have to be paid for until 30 days after receipt. They must then be paid for in full. With "2/10, net 30," a buyer receives a 2 percent discount if the full bill is paid within 10 days after merchandise receipt. The buyer must pay the face value of a bill within 30 days after the receipt of products. Various time terms are available.

Sellers must sometimes be prepared to wait an extended period to receive payments when marketing internationally. It can take U.S. firms up to 100 days or more—from invoice to payment—to get paid by b-to-b consumers in Iran, Kenya, Argentina, Brazil, Greece, Italy, and elsewhere.

A firm that permits credit purchases may use open accounts or revolving accounts. With an *open credit account*, the buyer receives a monthly bill for the goods and services bought during the preceding month. The account must be paid in full each month. With a *revolving credit account*, the buyer agrees to make minimum monthly payments during an extended period of time and pays interest on outstanding balances. Today, various types of firms (from Xerox to many colleges) offer some form of credit plan. Auto makers provide their own cut-rate financing programs to stimulate sales and leasing.

21-6 PRICE ADJUSTMENTS

Once a price strategy is enacted, it often requires continuous fine-tuning to reflect changes in costs, competitive conditions, and demand. **Price adjustment tactics** include alterations in list prices, escalator clauses and surcharges, added markups, markdowns, and rebates.

List prices are the regularly quoted prices provided to customers. They may be pre-printed on price tags, in catalogs, and in dealer purchase orders. Modifications in list prices are necessary if there are sustained changes in labor costs, raw material costs, and market segments, and as a product moves through its life cycle. If these events are long-term in nature, they enable customary prices to be revised, new catalogs to be printed, and adjustments to be completed in an orderly fashion.

Costs or economic conditions may sometimes be so volatile that revised list prices cannot be printed or distributed efficiently. Escalator clauses or surcharges can then be used. With *escalator clauses*, a firm is contractually permitted to raise prices to reflect higher costs in essential materials without changing printed list prices. It may even be able to set prices at the time of delivery. *Surcharges* are across-the-board published price increases that supplement list prices. These may be used with catalogs because of their simplicity; an insert is distributed with the catalog. Several airlines now impose a fee on paper tickets to encourage travelers to use electronic ticketing (which cuts distribution costs).

When list prices are not involved, *additional markups* can be used to raise regular selling prices if demand is unexpectedly high or costs rise. This involves some risk. For example, supermarkets get bad publicity for relabeling low-cost existing items at higher prices to match those of newer items bought at higher costs.

Markdowns are reductions from items' original selling prices. All types of sellers use them to meet the lower prices of competitors, counteract overstocking of merchandise, clear out shopworn merchandise, deplete assortments of odds and ends, and lift customer traffic.

Although manufacturers regularly give discounts to resellers, they may periodically offer **rebates** to customers to stimulate the purchase of an item or a group of items. Rebates are flexible, do not alter basic prices, involve direct communication between customers and manufacturers (because rebates are usually sent by the manufacturers), and do not affect reseller profits (as regular reductions do). Price cuts by individual resellers may not generate the same kind of consumer enthusiasm. Rebate popularity can be traced to its usage by auto makers to help cut down on inventory surpluses. Rebates are regularly offered by Canon (**http://www.canon.com**), GE Appliances (**http://www.geappliances.com**), Linksys (**http://www.linksys.com**), and others. The major disadvantage is that so many firms use rebates that their impact may be lessened.

Channel members should cooperatively agree on their individual roles whenever adjustments are needed. Price hikes or cuts should not be unilateral.

Web Sites You Can Use

The Business Owner's Toolkit Web site offers a lot of information on price planning. Look at its "Pricing Your Product" section (**http://www.toolkit.cch.com/text/p03_5200.asp**). The Center for Business Planning's Web site (**http://www.businessplans.org/topic71.html**) provides access to a wide range of resources. You can also download a free book, *Make Your Price Sell* (**http://www.thatswise.com/free/e-books/price_sell.html**). For a change of pace, take a look at the Price.com (**http://www.price.com**) and PriceScan.com (**http://www.pricescan.com**) comparison-shopping Web sites.

Summary

1. *To present an overall framework for developing and applying a pricing strategy* The five stages in a pricing strategy are objectives, broad policy, strategy, implementation, and adjustments. These stages are affected by outside factors and must be integrated with a firm's marketing mix.

2. *To analyze sales-based, profit-based, and status quo-based pricing objectives, and to describe the role of a broad price policy* Sales goals center on volume and/or market share. In penetration pricing, low prices capture a mass market. Profit goals focus on profit maximization, satisfactory profits, optimum return on investment, and/or early cash recovery. In skimming pricing, a firm seeks the segment less concerned with price than quality or status. Status quo goals seek to minimize the impact of outside parties and ensure stability. Two or more pricing objectives may be combined.

A broad price policy sets the overall direction for a firm's pricing efforts. Through it, a firm decides if it is price- or nonprice-oriented.

3. *To examine and apply the alternative approaches to a pricing strategy* A price strategy may be cost-based, demand-based, competition-based, or a combination of these.

With cost-based pricing, merchandise, service, and overhead costs are computed and then an amount to cover profit is added. Cost-plus pricing adds costs and a desired profit to set prices. Markup pricing sets prices by calculating the per-unit costs of producing (buying) goods and/or services and then finding the markup percentages to cover selling costs and profit; a variable markup policy has different markups for distinct products. In target pricing, prices provide a rate of return on investment for a standard volume of production. When a firm has excess capacity, it may use price-floor pricing, in which prices are set above variable costs rather than total costs. Traditional break-even analysis determines the sales quantity at which total costs equal total revenues for a chosen price.

With demand-based pricing, prices are set after doing consumer research and learning the range of acceptable prices to the target market. A firm uses demand-minus pricing to find the proper selling price and works backward to set costs. Chain-markup pricing extends demand-minus calculations from resellers back to suppliers (manufacturers). Modified break-even analysis combines traditional break-even analysis with an evaluation of demand at various prices. A firm uses price discrimination to set two or more distinct prices for a product so as to appeal to different market segments.

Competition is the main guidepost in competition-based pricing. Prices may be below, at, or above the market. A firm would see whether it has the ability to be a price leader or price follower. With competitive bidding, two or more firms submit prices in response to precise customer requests.

The three approaches should be integrated via combination pricing, so a firm includes all necessary factors in its pricing strategy. Otherwise, critical decisions are likely to be overlooked.

4. *To discuss several specific decisions that must be made in implementing a pricing strategy*   Enacting a price strategy involves several specific decisions. Customary pricing is used when a firm sets prices for an extended time. In variable pricing, prices coincide with cost or consumer demand fluctuations.

In a one-price policy, all those buying under similar conditions pay the same price. Flexible pricing lets a firm vary prices based on shopper negotiations or the buying power of a large customer.

With odd pricing, amounts are set below even-dollar values. The price-quality theory suggests people may feel there is a relation between price and quality. Prestige pricing assumes people do not buy products at prices that are considered too low. They set price floors, as well as price ceilings.

Under leader pricing, key items are sold at less than their usual amounts to increase consumer traffic. Multiple-unit pricing is a practice that offers discounts to consumers for buying in quantity.

Price lining involves the sale of products at a range of prices, with each embodying a distinct level of quality (or features). In bundled pricing, a firm offers a product, options, and customer service for a total price; unbundled pricing breaks down prices by individual components.

Geographic pricing outlines the responsibility for transportation. Purchase terms are the provisions of price agreements, including discounts, timing of payments, and credit.

5. *To show the major ways that prices can be adjusted*   Once a pricing strategy is enacted, it often needs fine-tuning to reflect cost, competition, and demand changes. Prices can be adjusted by altering list prices, using escalator clauses and surcharges, marking prices up or down, and offering rebates.

Key Terms

sales-based pricing objectives (p. 634)

penetration pricing (p. 635)

profit-based pricing objectives (p. 635)

skimming pricing (p. 636)

status quo-based pricing objectives (p. 636)

broad price policy (p. 636)

cost-based pricing (p. 637)

price floor (p. 637)

cost-plus pricing (p. 638)

markup pricing (p. 639)

variable markup policy (p. 640)

target pricing (p. 640)

price-floor pricing (p. 641)

traditional break-even analysis (p. 641)

demand-based pricing (p. 642)

price ceiling (p. 642)

demand-minus (demand-backward) pricing (p. 642)

chain-markup pricing (p. 642)

modified break-even analysis (p. 643)

price discrimination (p. 643)

yield management pricing (p. 644)

competition-based pricing (p. 645)

price leadership (p. 645)

combination pricing (p. 647)

customary pricing (p. 647)

variable pricing (p. 647)

one-price policy (p. 648)

flexible pricing (p. 648)

odd pricing (p. 649)

price-quality association (p. 649)

prestige pricing (p. 650)

leader pricing (p. 650)

multiple-unit pricing (p. 651)

price lining (p. 651)

bundled pricing (p. 652)

unbundled pricing (p. 652)

geographic pricing (p. 653)

purchase terms (p. 654)

price adjustment tactics (p. 654)

rebates (p. 655)

Review Questions

1. When should a firm pursue penetration pricing? Skimming pricing?
2. Why are markups usually computed on the basis of selling price?

3. A firm requires a 12 percent return on a $1 million investment in order to manufacture a new electric garage-door opener. If the standard volume is 50,000 units, fixed

costs are $500,000, and variable costs are $45 per unit, what is the target price?

4. A company making office desks has total fixed costs of $2 million per year and variable costs of $400 per desk. It sells the desks to retailers for $800 apiece. Compute the traditional break-even point in both units and dollars.

5. Discuss chain-markup pricing from the perspective of a retailer.

6. Contrast customary pricing and variable pricing. How may the two techniques be combined?

7. Under what circumstances is the price-quality association most valid? Least valid?

8. How does price lining benefit manufacturers? Retailers? Consumers?

Discussion Questions

1. A movie theater has weekly fixed costs (land, building, and equipment) of $5,800. Variable weekly costs (movie rental, electricity, ushers, etc.) are $2,500. From a price-floor pricing perspective, how much revenue must a movie generate during a slow week for it to be worthwhile to open the theater? Explain your answer.

2. A retailer determines that customers are willing to spend $21.95 for a new Harry Potter book. The publisher charges the retailer $15.75 for each copy. The retailer wants a 35 percent markup. Comment on this situation.

3. a. A wholesaler of small industrial tools has fixed costs of $250,000, variable costs of $27 per tool, and faces this demand schedule from its hardware-store customers:

Price	Quantity Demanded
$31	100,000
$36	85,000

| $41 | 65,000 |
| $46 | 40,000 |

At what price is profit maximized?

b. If the firm noted in Question 3a decides to sell 40,000 small tools at $36 and 45,000 of these tools at $31, what will its profit be? What are the risks of this approach?

4. A wholesaler of plumbing supplies recently added a new line of kitchen sinks and priced them at $179 each (to plumbers). The manufacturer has just announced a 7 percent price increase on the sinks—due to higher materials and labor costs. Yet, for this wholesaler, the initial response of plumbers to the sinks has been sluggish. Also, some competing wholesalers are selling similar private-label sinks for $149 to plumbers. What should the wholesaler do next?

Web Exercise

ThinkVine, an Ohio-based consulting firm, has prepared a comprehensive report entitled *Pricing and Segmentation*, which is available at its Web site (**http://www.thinkvine.com/**

ThinkVine-Pricing Segmentation.pdf). Download and read the report, and then discuss what a marketing executive could learn by reviewing this information.

Practice Quiz

1. Which statement is *not* true?
   a. A firm may pursue more than one pricing goal at the same time.
   b. A pricing strategy should be consistent and reflect overall company goals.
   c. A firm may set distinct short- and long-run goals.
   d. Different firms in the same industry always have the same pricing strategies.

2. With sales-based objectives, a firm focuses on
   a. optimizing the return on investment.
   b. expanding its market share relative to competitors.
   c. minimizing the effects of competitor actions.
   d. maintaining good channel relations.

3. Firms that desire high initial profits because they are short of funds or uncertain about their future use
   a. return-on-investment goals.
   b. status quo-based goals.
   c. early-recovery-of-cash goals.
   d. satisfactory-profit goals.

4. Which of the following is *not* an advantage to firms that first employ skimming pricing and then apply penetration pricing?
   a. High prices are charged when competition is limited.
   b. Lowering initial prices presents a poor image to the market.
   c. High prices help cover development and introductory advertising costs.
   d. Multiple segments can be reached.

5. The first step in outlining a broad price policy is
   a. examining brand image.
   b. analyzing the marketing mix.
   c. integrating individual decisions.
   d. determining a pricing strategy.

6. Price floors are frequently set in
   a. demand-based strategies.
   b. status quo-based strategies.
   c. cost-based strategies.
   d. competition-based strategies.

7. Price ceilings
   a. do not take demand into account.
   b. depend on the elasticity of demand.
   c. are the lowest acceptable prices firms can set to gain profit goals.
   d. are the minimum amounts consumers will pay for goods or services.

8. Under customary pricing, channel members
   a. modify package size or change ingredients to reflect cost increases.
   b. alter prices to coincide with fluctuations in costs.
   c. adjust prices to levels of demand.
   d. offer discounts to those who buy in quantity.

9. A one-price policy
   a. erodes customer confidence.
   b. encourages bargaining.
   c. is difficult to administer.
   d. permits self-service and catalog sales.

10. With what pricing approach does a firm advertise and sell key items in its product assortment at less than their usual profit margins?
    a. Leader pricing
    b. Customary pricing
    c. Odd pricing
    d. Prestige pricing

11. Which of these is *not* a major reason for employing multiple-unit pricing?
    a. The firm can clear out slow-moving merchandise.
    b. Greater consumption is encouraged.
    c. Competitors' customers may be attracted.
    d. Total dollar sales are maintained.

12. Which of these is *not* a method of geographic pricing?
    a. Multiple-unit pricing
    b. Uniform delivered pricing
    c. Base-point pricing
    d. Zone pricing

13. Purchase terms include discounts, the timing of payments, and
    a. delivery.
    b. installation.
    c. warranty coverage.
    d. credit arrangements.

14. In catalogs, to tie prices to rising costs, it is simplest to
    a. include escalator clauses.
    b. increase markups.
    c. add on surcharges.
    d. change list prices.

15. Which of the following statements about rebates is false?
    a. They help cut down on inventory surpluses.
    b. They affect resellers' profits.
    c. They are flexible.
    d. They increase communication between consumers and manufacturers.

For the answers to these questions, please visit the online site for this book at **http://www.atomicdog.com.**

Case 1: Consumer Electronics: Determining How to Stop Discount Pricing[c7-1]

According to a Brand Keys (http://www.brandkeys.com) research study involving 16,000 respondents, the impact of pricing on the consumer electronics industry is less today than in prior years. The study found that a convenient location and value are still the top-two reasons why consumers choose to shop for consumer electronics. Shopping experience and service are now the third most important factor, versus store reputation in prior years. Let's look at the role of pricing in the sales of PCs, cell phones, and DVD players.

For PCs, pricing has declined to be the fourth most important purchase factor for shoppers after technological advancement, design and added features, and service and support. For cell phones, pricing is also the fourth factor (after connectivity to other products, product design, and product size). Likewise, the importance of pricing has declined to fourth place for DVD players (after picture and sound quality, added features, and connectivity to other equipment).

These findings should be great news to consumer electronics manufacturers and resellers. During the recent period of heavy price competition, manufacturers, as well as retailers, did not earn profits despite high levels of sales. Brand Keys' chief executive says that because technology, design, and connectivity are so important to consumers, marketers need to trade customers up to more desirable and feature-laden products. Although a market still exists for low-priced items, profit margins for these items are generally smaller than for top-of-the-line electronics. Nitlin Gupta, the author of a Yankee Group research study, states, "It is now smart to let the low-end customer go to a competitor (a strategy Best Buy is employing). The value is in building long-term relationships. The margins are higher for high-end customers and the prospects for long-term relationships are greater." This approach questions the strategy of Wal-Mart and Target, which target the price- and convenience-oriented consumer electronics shopper.

The role of price competition in consumer electronics varies by whether a product is relatively new or mature. With new products, such as digital video recorders, issues of connectivity with televisions and surround-sound audio may reduce the effects of price competition. The situation is much different with mature products where there is much less product differentiation. Thus, many consumers view DVD players from different firms as a com-modity—often with similar features and warranties, as well as identical component parts. In an era of more products being classified as commodities, manufacturers and resellers need to resist the temptation for price competition.

One way to reduce price competition in consumer electronics is through nonprice-competition tactics such as customer service. Brand Keys' chief executive says that "retailers and manufacturers should understand that they're no longer selling a box. They're selling the ability to connect products to existing products, and most importantly, they must predict the products that consumers will desire in the future." Similarly, a partner at Peppers & Rogers Group (http://www.1to1.com), a marketing consulting firm, thinks that "once you realize that you can play in the same ballpark as your competitors in terms of pricing and features, you can start to connect to customer needs and values."

Product service and customer support are other forms of nonprice competition. A senior vice-president of sales and marketing for Samsung (http://www.samsung.com) has worked hard to differentiate its products by creating a superior experience for customers. To ensure high levels of customer service, he purchases and uses Samsung's products, calls the customer support center without identifying who he is, and regularly visits and listens to Samsung's distributors and retailers.

Questions

1. Explain the significance of the following statement: "It is now smart to let the low-end customer go to a competitor. The value is in building long-term relationships. The margins are higher for high-end customers and the prospects for long-term relationships are greater."
2. Describe how the manufacturer of DVD players can use a nonprice-based approach to marketing.
3. Develop sales-based, profit-based, and status quo-based objectives for Samsung.
4. Discuss the pitfalls of seeking to build market share based on overreliance on low prices.

[c7-1] The data in the case are drawn from "Consumer Electronics Outgrow Pricing Pains," http://www.1to1.com (March 24, 2005).

Case 2: Does One Price Fit All?[c7-2]

At Kuhlman Co. (http://www.kuhlmancompany.com), a 30-store retailer of men's and women's apparel, items in a given product category sell for a single price—all shirts are $55, all ties are $39, and all suits are $495. Most stores are small (less than 1,000 square feet). Scott Kuhlman, the chain's founder and chief executive, got the idea for the chain while in Europe, which has many small shirt stores. These stores were a few hundred square feet in size and limited their sales to a single item: shirts. His attempts to get department stores to open similar U.S. stores were in vain. Thus, he decided to start the Kuhlman chain.

Kuhlman's main target market is the young professional male in his mid-30s who needs more businesslike apparel than found in stores such as Abercrombie & Fitch (http://www.abercrombie.com). Unlike traditional lines of men's shirts, Kuhlman's shirts are distinctive and have a degree of flair. Its "Maurice" men's shirt, for example, is bright green with a teal-colored crisscross design. According to a vice-president with Retail Forward (http://www.retailforward.com), a consulting firm, Kuhlman's timing is excellent because many employers are tightening up their casual dress codes: "There's a return to a more formal, suit-oriented look in certain industries. Style is [now] a hotter commodity." Men are looking for business apparel with more flair.

Scott Kuhlman and his wife design all of the firm's merchandise and outsource production to plants located in Italy and Turkey. Although the firm's typical order is for 400 to 600 shirts per style, many Turkish manufacturers do not require a minimum order size. In contrast, some Chinese manufacturers require a minimum order of 1,200 shirts per design. The combination of distinctive styling and high-quality fabrics and tailoring make Kuhlman shirts an excellent value. Some people have compared Kuhlman's $55 shirts to those at Thomas Pink (http://www.thomaspink.com), selling for $140 to $170.

Let's look at some pros and cons to Kuhlman's single-price point strategy. These are some pros:

- It speeds the store experience for those men who do not enjoy shopping.
- The one price point facilitates price labeling.
- The one-price point eliminates the need to look up prices when price tickets are missing.

- Price and profit planning is simplified. A cost/sales revenue/profit model can more easily be constructed and better controlled and implemented.
- There is less need for promotional advertising.

These are some cons of the one-price point:

- This approach may be difficult to maintain due to inflation, changes in the value of the U.S. dollar versus foreign currencies, material prices, and so on.
- Despite the existence of a one-price point, there is still a need for price reductions due to markdowns.
- There is no possibility of getting a customer to trade up to a $75 shirt or a $595 suit.
- Kuhlman may have a difficult time keeping its core customer when that customer desires a more costly shirt or acquires more refined tastes.
- The one-price point policy is a direct contrast to one that offers "good," "better," and "best" price points. The same customer may want different price points for different occasions.
- Price is a rationing mechanism. Colors and styles in high demand could sell at a premium price, while slower-selling colors and styles should be reduced in price.
- There is extremely high recognition of Kuhlman's one-price point. Consumers will be aware of any price change.

Questions

1. Present your view of the pros and cons of Kuhlman's one-price point policy.
2. Explain the significance of this statement: "Despite the existence of a one-price point, there is still a need for price reductions due to markdowns."
3. Under what circumstances must Kuhlman's revise its one-price point policy? Explain your answer.
4. Would the one-price point policy work for a retailer with a broader target market? Explain your answer.

[c7-2] The data in the case are drawn from Karen M. Kroll, "One Price Fits All," *Shopping Centers Today* (May 2005), pp. 65–66, 70.

Case 3: Using Price Points to Trade Up Shoppers[c7-3]

The promotional leather sofa segment consists of highly advertised items that are used for starter apartments, and spare rooms, or by retailers seeking to generate store traffic. In many instances, retailers use discount sofa prices in order to trade up customers to more costly, and more profitable, furniture. Currently, the starting retail price points for promotional sofas are between $599 and $999, depending on the importer and the retailer. These price levels represent at least 50 percent of all sofas sold. "There's a large group of consumers interested in leather, but not interested in breaking the bank," says a vice-president of sales for H&S, a Canadian importer of leather furniture.

A common concern among manufacturers, importers, and retailers is selecting the price point most appropriate for promotional pricing. The correct price point gets a consumer to consider purchasing the product, generates store traffic, and creates opportunity for trading the customer up. If the price point is too high, consumers will resist the offering. Too low a price point, on the other hand, can result in the consumer being overly concerned about the product's quality.

Retailers often use a promotional price point to get a consumer into the store and as a starting point in assessing a buyer's needs. Retailers can then determine the buyer's desire for additional features, better construction, and more costly fabrics. A customer examining a $499 promotional sofa might agree to purchase a $799 model due to its higher-quality leather and additional features such as a sofa bed with a high-quality innerspring mattress.

Trading up consumers based on initial promotional pricing is an ethical business practice. However, bait-and-switch advertising is not. In trading up, a retailer ascertains a consumer's needs and may recommend a more costly product that is more suitable to the customer. However, the retailer will gladly sell the promotional product. In contrast, with bait-and-switch advertising, the retailer has no intension of selling the heavily promoted good.

One problem with some popular promotional price points is their impact on profitability. A vice president for Acme Furniture, an importer of Asian-produced furniture, says that, "It's easy to generate business at this [$599] price point, but a struggle to maintain the same price for two years." Competitive pressures may force importers and manufacturers to keep prices low, but they constantly have to be concerned with the impact of cost increases on profitability. In some cases, importers have switched from Italian to Asian manufacturers to keep their promotional price points intact.

Another potential problem is whether the quality of promotionally priced sofas is adequate. Specific aspects of quality relate to the foam fill, the use of hardwood frames, the grade of leather, and the quality of the tanning. According to the president of Leather Italia-USA, the initial price points have changed in the past four years from $499 to $599. However, "they have traded price points for a better starting grade of quality."

There should be some relationship between the starting promotional price point and the trade-up price. It may be difficult to trade a customer up from a $599 sofa to a $1,299 sofa. Both models would usually appeal to different target markets in terms of income and lifestyle or for different purposes (the $599 sofa might be used in a basement, whereas the $1,299 sofa would be placed in the family room).

In additional to promotional pricing, furniture manufacturers use bridge pricing to differentiate low-priced promotional goods from higher-priced merchandise. Part of the logic of bridge pricing is a "good," "better," and "best" pricing model. In this pricing model, "good" represents promotional pricing, "better" can be equated with bridge pricing, and "best" is the top-of-the-line model.

Questions

1. What should be the role of promotional pricing in a retailer's overall pricing strategy?
2. Describe the relationship between trading up and the setting of promotional prices.
3. Discuss how the price-quality association affects promotional pricing.
4. Explain the significance of this statement: "In this pricing model, 'good' represents promotional pricing, 'better' can be equated with bridge pricing, and 'best' is the top-of-the-line model."

[c7-3] The data in the case are drawn from Joan Gunin, "Starting Price Points a Key Element in Leather," *Furniture Today* (February 14, 2005), pp. 12–13; and "Point of Order," *Cabinet Maker* (March 4, 2005), pp. 23–24.

Case 4: Retailers Strive to Cut Down on Their Use of Markdowns^{c7-4}

For years, December 5th marked the day that specialty retailers began to mark down winter coats. What would happen if the date was shifted to January 5th? One possibility is that retailers' gross profit would increase substantially. Although large differences exist in the effectiveness of markdown software, one study reports improvements in a retailer's gross margins of 2 to 10 percent and increases in sales of as high as 6 percent based on the retail industry segment and the merchandise category.

Jo-Ann Stores (http://www.jo-ann.com) is an 850-store arts-and-crafts retailer that has spent millions of dollars generating and maintaining a data base for its 10 million customers. Jo-Ann has hired a team of six analysts (with four additional positions that have not yet been filled) who constantly analyze store data. According to a vice-president of marketing at Jo-Ann, "It's not rocket science anymore, it's mainstream. You've got to be more fact-based in promotions and pricing. You can't just keep sitting on a ton of data."

To aid this analysis, various firms, such as ProfitLogic (http://www.oracle.com/profitlogic), KhiMetrics (http://www.khimetrics.com), and Demand Tec (http://www.demandtec.com), have developed mathematical models to determine the relationship between an item's price, advertising expenditures, and sales. Many of these firms use a regionally based pricing model as opposed to a chain-wide approach.

Among ProfitLogic's retailer clients are Nordstrom, Bloomingdale's, Gap, Sears, Target, and Children's Place. Its data analysis has challenged the conventional wisdom of many "off-the-cuff" pricing decisions. Among upscale apparel retailers, there are two important promotional periods: beginning-of-the-season pricing to establish the product and end-of-the-season pricing to clear out inventory. "We've found the second promotion late in the season actually has very little impact," said ProfitLogic's director of promotional optimization solutions.

Another common error among many retailers is that they may assume that a market is more price sensitive than it really is. "Most managers often make the mistake of interpreting the market as being broadly price sensitive, when, in fact, there are only select segments that are," says one marketing professor. As a result, markdowns are sometimes greater than they need to be to clear out the merchandise. The professor cites a famous case study involving gasoline retailers that showed that only 19 percent of consumers were price sensitive, whereas industry personnel assumed that this segment made up 80 percent of the population.

Most software packages are based on the use of a highly variable pricing strategy in which customers are offered different prices at different times. This enables the retailer to capitalize on changes in supply and demand. The models also allow a retailer to set different price levels on a city, regional, or even store-by-store basis. Many of the models are similar to the yield management pricing models used by airlines, hotels, and car rental firms. In almost all of the markdown software models, a merchandise manager can override the software's recommendations based on his or her knowledge of local conditions. This could include a major storm that is forecast or the opening of a major competitor offering a special store-opening sales event.

One problem with variable pricing is that it violates the customer's notion of fairness. Many customers feel more comfortable with a one-price policy where all consumers pay the same price for purchases made under similar conditions. A second potential problem is the difficulty in applying markdown software at the store level. This relates to getting merchandisers to understand the technology, the need to continually change price tags, and the increased responsibility that store managers have as a result of the software.

Questions

1. Contrast the use of markdown pricing software in retailing with the use of yield management pricing by hotels and airlines.
2. Why are many of the markdown pricing models regional versus chain-wide?
3. List five situations (beyond those mentioned in the case) in which a merchandise manager should override the markdown software's recommendations.
4. Discuss the major implementation difficulties in setting up, maintaining, and using markdown software.

c7-4 The data in the case are drawn from Mya Frazier, "Sales May Go Out Like Last Year's Winter Coat," *Advertising Age* (April 25, 2005), p. 16; and Laurie Sullivan, "Trust Issues: Leading with the Heart and the Head," *Information Week* (August 15, 2005), p. 43.

Making "Cents" of Pricing[pc-7]

INTRODUCTION

Considering all the elements of the marketing mix, price has the most direct effect on profitability. Price is also the most easily controlled of the elements. Yet setting prices and measuring their impact on the entire organization is seldom done properly, or in a manner that optimizes long-term market share and profitability. Pricing strategy must focus on overall category profitability and consider the strategic implications of price changes on brand equity, product positioning, product cannibalization, and competitive response. In addition, the impact of price changes needs to be evaluated in the context of both return on marketing investment and impact on the remaining elements of the marketing mix.

Marketing departments traditionally provide insights into market acceptance of new offerings and prices but have had limited impact on building business cases for changing prices. At a recent American Marketing Association (**http://www.marketingpower. com**) Research Conference, Sally Dancer, a senior practice expert at consulting firm McKinsey & Co. (**http://www.mckinsey.com**), indicated that CEOs want marketing to become a full business partner. She then went on to challenge marketers to become more involved in developing business cases that directly link marketing initiatives with profits.

Based on what Dancer and others are saying, there is a big incentive for marketing departments to expand their traditional role of providing insights and become a more active partner in building a financial model, especially when it comes to developing pricing strategy. In order for marketing departments to make the transition from simply providing business insights to developing full-blown business cases, they need to redesign their research studies to reflect actual marketplace behavior, incorporating inputs for all items in the marketing mix.

CURRENT PARADIGMS

Traditionally, the role of marketing in developing pricing strategy has been the ability to understand market acceptance of price changes to new and existing goods and services. Through the use of various experiments, market researchers have learned about the trade-offs between brands, prices, features, and channels for leveraging customer value propositions and developing pricing strategies. This is valuable information, but this type of research does not do a good job of replicating the complexity of current marketplaces and extracting the real impact of price and price sensitivity. For example, many studies create an artificial marketplace that forces competitive offerings to contain similar features and prices when, in reality, many competitive offerings have features and prices that are unique to a single brand. In addition, some experiments typically underestimate the impact of price and provide price sensitivity in aggregate, rather than by brand.

Pricing research typically focuses on a customer's preference for specific offerings and reports findings in terms of percentages. Given the lack of a complete set of competitive offerings and prices in the marketplace, it's difficult to align preference measures with current market conditions and then accurately project how changes in the marketing mix will affect the marketplace, especially in financial terms. Furthermore, this process tends to lower the value of research because management can only make decisions on a relative "percentage" basis, rather than on an absolute "profit" basis. To develop a meaningful pricing strategy, marketers must integrate customer input on a complete competitive marketplace with all the other business variables that affect pricing decisions.

Many organizations make pricing decisions based on secondary or syndicated data sources, internal costs, or competitive factors. Although each of these items needs to be considered, profit potential and brand equity can erode significantly with strategies based on these items alone. Some companies get input on customers' willingness to pay from measurements based on observed marketplace behavior. Such measurements are limited because they only reflect existing product characteristics. In addition, observational data doesn't involve controls, so it can be difficult to separate the trends and sensitivities in the observed data from external phenomena such as product availability, promotion, and advertising for both the company and competitors.

Because internal costs have a major impact on profitability, not linking them to market input on competitive pricing and customer willingness to pay can affect profits dramatically. It's unwise to develop a reactive pricing strategy based on customers leveraging one supplier over another to get the best possible price. It's equally unwise to develop a pricing strategy in reaction to competitive price changes, internal sales goals, or inventory levels. These factors need to be considered, but basing pricing strategies only on such inputs can damage long-term profitability and product equity. Pricing strategy must also take into account long-term market response and impact on sales channels and profitability.

BUSINESS CASE DEVELOPMENT

Figure 1 shows a comprehensive approach to developing a financial model from market insight. The key is to be able to report the information collected from current and potential customers in the context of overall profitability. Four key components comprise to this approach: (1) Determine the strategic and tactical issues to

[pc-7] Adapted by the authors from David M. Feldman, "Cents of Making Pricing," *Marketing Management* (May-June 2005), pp. 21–25. Reprinted by permission of the American Marketing Association.

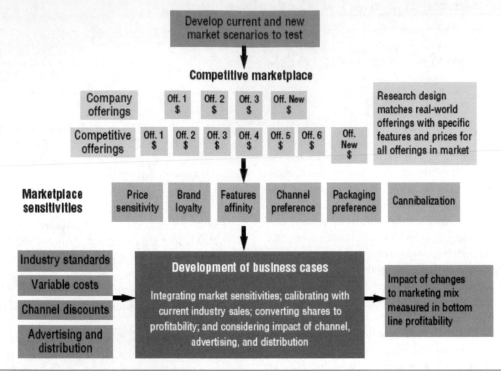

Figure 1

Developing Business Cases from Market Insight

support the business case. (2) Develop a competitive marketplace. (3) Determine marketplace sensitivities. (4) Determine the impact of changes to the marketing mix in terms of profits.

Key Issues

It is extremely important to review with senior management all of the relevant marketing issues that affect costs and profitability before you design the study. Following are examples of the types of questions that need to be considered when reviewing key issues with senior management:

- How do I ensure that my pricing decisions will support the long-term positioning of my product?
- For a specific offering in a category, at what price will I maximize profitability for the entire company offering in the category?
- When introducing a new product or an extension of an existing product, what will be the impact on existing products?
- How can I develop and price bundles of goods/services to enhance overall profitability?
- How do I tailor pricing and bundle offerings to meet the unique needs of my most valuable customers?
- For branded products, how can I effectively compete with value/generic offerings?
- How do I determine the specific benefits for which customers are willing to pay more?
- What will be the impact of competitive responses to my new offerings and how would that change my optimal offering/price?
- If market constraints force downward pressure on prices, how do I price my offerings to minimize the impact on overall positioning and long-term profitability?

COMPETITIVE MARKETPLACE

Once the tactical and strategic issues are defined and prioritized, the research study needs to be carefully designed. When focusing on pricing strategy, the survey instrument must include actual market offerings and prices. The reason for this is twofold. First, it's important to be able to model what the respondents are currently purchasing based on current prices. This base case will be used to calibrate the model and to aid in determining cannibalization. Second, whenever new offerings or prices are considered, the respondent needs to react to them in the context of all the options currently available. Here's where a lot of research studies miss the mark by trying to measure response to new offerings and prices independent of the other alternatives available. By including all company and competitive offerings, the respondent's task of selecting new offerings or prices is more accurate and less subject to survey bias.

To accommodate these types of pricing studies, a custom-designed discrete choice experiment is highly recommended. A discrete choice experiment provides the best analytical methodology for developing pricing strategy. When properly executed, it allows the researcher to present a complete portfolio of goods and services that parallels current marketplace offerings. In addition, combinations of new and existing goods and services can be tested in and out of the current marketplace, changing prices and specific features for any offering in the marketplace.

In general, the key components of a discrete choice design involve multiple price levels for offerings from the company and key competitors, along with testing availability for certain offerings in the marketplace. In addition, offerings need to be tested in and out of the marketplace to determine which offerings will lose share when a new good or service is added and which offerings will gain share when a good or service is no longer in the market. Prices can be different for all goods and services being tested and should reflect current market prices. The ranges of prices to be tested must be wide enough to allow proper sensitivity testing and future use of the market response tool.

It's important to understand how the market values the different components of an offering. For certain studies, part of the design needs to include options for de-bundling an offering, as well as for combining multiple goods and services into a package offering. In both cases, multiple price levels would need to be tested for each de-bundling and package offering. Another consideration for the design is allowing respondent choices to be recorded in a way that matches how customers normally would purchase goods and services. In addition, respondents should indicate not only which offering they would choose but also a volumetric measure, such as "how many" or "how often."

Marketplace Sensitivities

Once the survey has been properly designed and executed, market sensitivities need to be derived from customer input. The modeling of market input must analyze the choices the respondents gave to specific market conditions and convert them into measures of price sensitivity, brand loyalty, feature affinity, channel and packaging preference, and cannibalization. In addition to deriving these sensitivities, such detailed respondent-level choice data will also allow development of segments. Grouping together segments of respondents who exhibit similar market sensitivities will provide a better understanding of the unique needs of target segments. A segment may be defined as customers who prefer a certain brand, feature, channel, or package option—or who have similar price sensitivity.

With these market sensitivities, market share estimates can be produced for new and existing offerings, and the effects of changing prices can be used to update market share estimates. Before these market sensitivities can be used to build a financial model, certain calibrations, conversions, and adjustments need to be made.

Profitability Model

The first step toward building a profitability model is in being able to link survey results to current market size and share. When linking to current market, a base case needs to be developed. The base case is defined as offerings currently in the marketplace, at current prices. The two functions of the base case are replicating known market shares and sizing the overall market in terms of total units sold. The linking is done by calibrating the model's base case with known market shares and market sizes at the same prices and availabilities. This is a very important step in bridging the richness of market input with the accuracy of known market information. No matter how good the sampling or how realistically the survey matches the actual buying experience, this step ensures all projections are based on an agreed-upon starting point. The key for the survey is in deriving sensitivities from market input, putting this information into a context that management can understand, and then using that information to develop an effective pricing strategy.

Once the model has been calibrated and can produce share estimates for alternative scenarios, it needs to report results in profit or contribution. This involves integrating variable costs and relevant channel discounts. In most cases, subtracting the unit cost from the retail selling price will indicate the profit. But sometimes, when a good or service is sold through different channels, a component of the business case involves examining the retail selling price minus the unit cost along with channel discounts. In this case, it would be important to break out the channel discounts so that assumptions on different channel discounts and their effects on channel volumes can be considered.

Before testing the financial impact of various market scenarios, certain adjustments might need to be made. Advertising and distribution are two key areas where adjustments need to be considered. Although there is a big advantage to collecting survey data from a carefully designed, controlled experiment, there also are biases associated with it. By nature of being survey driven, these types of market insights make the assumption that the entire marketplace has complete knowledge about new offerings and changes to prices, as well as 100 percent availability of any goods or services being offered. To adjust for this, the marketing department, working with other departments, must set up a range of awareness levels and associated advertising costs, as well as a range of expected distribution levels. Often, these assumptions follow an "s" curve distribution as they track over time. Thus, it's quite useful to give the financial model a time element so that assumptions for awareness and distribution levels can be tracked over a specified time period. Estimated costs to achieve these levels should also be included in the financial model.

BUILDING BUSINESS CASES

To better understand how developing a financial model can improve marketing strategy, let's consider a case where a company is launching a new offering and wants to know the optimal price. The optimal price is defined as the price that provides the highest contribution for the entire company offering. After collecting and analyzing the market sensitivities, the model first produces market shares based only on existing goods and current prices. These shares

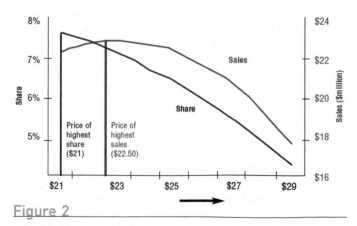

Figure 2

Price Elasticity and Sales

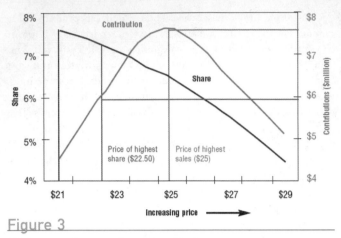

Figure 3

Optimum Price Based on Contribution

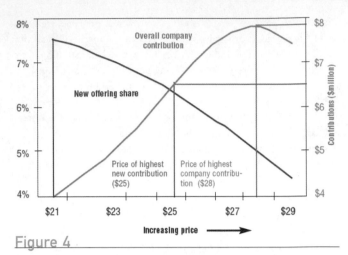

Figure 4

Optimum Price Based on Overall Company Contribution

are calibrated against known market shares to adjust for any sample bias and to ensure that any projections are based on current market shares and sizes.

Next, using the market sensitivities derived from market input, a scenario of the new offering at a specific price is tested. Based on the market sensitivities, the model produces updated market share numbers. Knowing the potential of this new product is very important, but just as important, the model also tells us where that business will come from. For example, if the new offering gets a large share but that new share cannibalizes your existing portfolio, net gains may be very small. It will be much more important to study the effect that price has on the new offering to see if, by changing the price, you can better target the right customers and thus minimize cannibalization and improve overall profitability.

In these types of studies, multiple price points are tested for the new offerin, as well as certain other offerings in the marketplace. Using these multiple price points, the model develops price elasticity curves that show the expected share at different price points.

Figure 2 shows two curves, with the red curve representing share and the green one showing sales at different prices. Looking at the red share curve at a price of $21, projected share is 7.5 percent. If the price was raised to $29, share would drop to 4.5 percent. This does not tell us the optimal price: it only indicates that the lowest price provides the highest share. Figure 2 also indicates that the selling price that maximizes sales for the new offering is $22.50. But this is not the optimal price for the new offering either—it does not factor in the impact of the margin for the new offering.

Figure 3 shows a contribution curve (selling price less unit cost). This suggests that the optimum price to maximize contribution for the new offering is $25. It's interesting to note that even though share drops from 7.5 percent to 6.5 percent when price is raised from $21 to $25, contribution increases from $4.5 million to more than $7.5 million. But $25 is not the optimal price for the new offering either—we must still consider the impact of the new offering on the overall company contribution.

It's necessary to develop one final chart that allows the new offering's price to change, while also showing the effects on the overall company contribution. Figure 4 shows what the total com-

pany contribution will be at various price levels for the new offering. This chart indicates that the optimal selling price for the new offering should be at a higher price of $28. At this price, cannibalization is minimized, with the current offering and company contribution being maximized.

In terms of developing pricing strategy, marketing departments have a real opportunity to elevate themselves and become full business partners with the rest of the organization. This can be accomplished by enhancing their traditional marketing insights into complete business cases. The key for research is to talk about profitability and delete to link pricing studies to business issues in the context of the relevant strategic environment. Success with pricing can only elevate research's positioning in the organization.

Questions

1. If price is the most easily controllable element of the marketing mix, why is properly setting prices and measuring their impact on the entire organization seldom done properly?

2. Comment on this statement: "It's unwise to develop a reactive pricing strategy based on customers leveraging one supplier over another to get the best possible price. It's equally unwise to develop a pricing strategy in reaction to competitive price changes, internal sales goals, or inventory levels."

3. What is the value of Figure 1 to marketers involved in pricing decisions?

4. What is an "optimal price?" Is it possible to determine such a price? Explain your answer.

5. What can be learned by studying Figures 2, 3, and 4?

6. Are the suggestions presented in the case likely to be enacted by a "typical" firm? Explain your answer.

7. Are pricing decisions more complex for manufacturers or retailers? Why?

8
Marketing Management

In Part 8, we tie together the concepts introduced in Chapter 1 through 21 and discuss planning for the future.

22 Pulling It All Together: Integrating and Analyzing the Marketing Plan

We first note the value of developing and analyzing integrated marketing plans. Next, the elements in a well-integrated marketing plan are examined: clear organizational mission, long-term competitive advantages, precisely defined target market, compatible subplans, coordination among SBUs, coordination of the marketing mix, and stability over time. We then study five types of marketing plan analysis: benchmarking, customer satisfaction research, marketing cost analysis, sales analysis, and the marketing audit. These are valuable tools for evaluating the success or failure of marketing plans. We conclude with a look at why and how firms should anticipate and plan for the future.

After reading Part 8, you should understand elements 14 and 15 of the strategic marketing plan outlined in Table 3-2 (page 78).

Chapter 22

Pulling It All Together: Integrating and Analyzing the Marketing Plan

According to a *Business Week* article on the great innovators of the past 75 years, "more than anyone else, he [Bill Gates, Microsoft's founder] can be credited with turning the disorganized PC tribes of the late 1970s into today's huge industry. Gates was among the first to recognize that all sorts of firms and products would be created if a computer's operating system and all the other software programs were separated from the hardware." Gates' most important strategic decision, however, was persuading IBM to allow his firm (Microsoft) to license its MS-DOS computer operations to other manufacturers of PCs.

This gave Microsoft (**http://www.microsoft.com**) a large source of potential revenues. The standardized operating system greatly expanded the market for PCs, as well as peripherals such as disk drives, memory, motherboards, hard drives, and printers. Also contributing to Microsoft's success were the support it gave developers by having technical conferences and its encouragment of software innovation by others to expand the dominance of its operating system. "Microsoft showed amazing determination to make Windows the standard and did everything it could to protect its dominance," said an analyst.

Currently, Microsoft has evolved into selling software for video games, interactive television, tools for software development, cellular phones, and Internet access services. Microsoft is also developing a new operating system for Windows, called Vista. Microsoft anticipates that Vista will have advantages in terms of security, user interfaces, and digital media over Windows XP. Microsoft is also replacing its popular Office XP suite with Office 12, which eliminates menus and toolbars at the top of the screen. Once a user selects a formatting option, Office 12 shows a preview of how the document will look.

In *Forbes'* listing of the world's wealthiest people, Bill Gates, a Harvard dropout, has regularly ranked number one, with a personal worth estimated at $50 billion or more. The Bill & Melinda Gates Foundation, with an endowment of $27 billion, founded by Bill Gates and his wife, aims to address some of the world's most pressing health problems. In one instance, for example, the foundation provided financial incentives to pharmaceutical companies so they would develop vaccines for malaria, hepatitis B, and AIDS. The foundation also provides funding to improve education in high schools.[1]

In this chapter, we will see the value of developing and implementing a clear, forward-looking, cohesive, and adaptable strategy.

Chapter Objectives

1. To show the value of an integrated marketing plan
2. To discuss the elements of a well-integrated marketing plan
3. To present five types of marketing plan analysis: benchmarking, customer satisfaction research, marketing cost analysis, sales analysis, and the marketing audit
4. To see the merit of anticipating and planning for the future

22-1 OVERVIEW

Chapters 1 and 2 introduced basic marketing concepts and described the marketing environment. Chapters 3 and 4 presented the strategic planning process as it applies to

---

[1] Various company and other sources.

marketing and the role of marketing information systems and marketing research. Chapters 5 to 7 broadened our scope to include the societal, ethical, and consumer implications of marketing; global marketing efforts; and marketing applications of the Internet. Chapters 8 to 21 centered on specific aspects of marketing: describing and selecting target markets, and the marketing mix (product, distribution, promotion, and price planning).

We tie things together in this chapter, and describe how a marketing plan can be integrated and assessed. Chapter 22 builds on the strategic planning discussion in Chapter 3—particularly, the total quality approach (whereby a firm strives to fully satisfy customers in an effective and efficient way). With an integrated effort, individual marketing components are synchronized and everyone is "on the same page." When an organization wants to appraise performance, capitalize on strengths, minimize weaknesses, and plan for the future, marketing analysis (including benchmarking and customer satisfaction) is necessary. The overall process is shown in Figure 22-1.

This is the challenge, as one expert sees it:

Strategy is what a firm does, or doesn't do, to fulfill its vision in a competitive marketplace. There are three things you really want to know about strategy: (1) If you know the "who, what, and how," you know strategy. Who are you selling to? (People who value ease of customization and speed of delivery at Dell; customers who value low prices at Southwest). What are you selling? (Dell—reliable computer products; Southwest—convenient travel), How are you selling it? (Focus on logistics and execution at Dell; customer service and speed of airplane turnaround at Southwest). (2) Strategy is just as much about what you decide not to do, as it is what you do. If you do everything, then you don't really have much of a strategy. Dell doesn't sell branded products via resellers; Southwest doesn't offer first-class cabins. This is one of the toughest things for executives to grasp. Sometimes you have to say no. (3) Not all strategies are created equal. They should be based on real internal competence that customers value enough to pay for and that competitors cannot easily replicate. Hewlett-Packard knows how to make PCs, but it loses against Dell because it can't easily switch from a reliance on resellers to a direct-to-customer model. Many established airlines have been unable to weather the post-September 11 storm precisely because their standard operating procedures make it so difficult to take on attributes of the Southwest business model.[2]

Here is what three diverse companies are doing to optimize their marketing strategies:

- Green Hills Farms (**http://www.greenhills.com**) is an independent supermarket in Syracuse, New York. *Inc.* has called it "the best little grocery store in America." It is renowned for its customer loyalty program. The firm tries out all sales promotions on employees before offering them to customers (to see what works best), monitors its customer data base, and exchanges ideas with noncompeting supermarkets. Its strategy is "to offer a wide assortment of specialty, international, gourmet, and high-quality fresh foods in a friendly, courteous shopping environment."[3]
- Japan's Toyota (**http://www.toyota.com**) is widely acknowledged to be one of the leading manufacturers in the world. What makes it tick? "Paranoia, pure and simple." Toyota's paranoia, baked into its corporate mantra of 'continuous improvement,' gives the firm a big edge in product development and operating efficiencies around the world. Toyota's philosophy, known as 'kaizen,' is so ingrained that 'it's almost like a religion.'" "What puts Toyota above everybody? It's the relentless drive to move forward," says the president of Edmunds.com, an independent auto information site. "Toyota's president asks: 'Why would we want to reinvent ourselves when business is good?' He then answers his own question: 'Because any firm not willing to take the risk of reinventing itself is doomed.'"[4]

[2] Sydney Finkelstein, "When Bad Things Happen to Good Companies: Strategy Failure and Flawed Executives," *Journal of Business Strategy*, Vol. 26 (Number 2, 2005), pp. 19–28.

[3] "Our Mission," **http://www.greenhills.com** (May 30, 2006).

[4] Jean Holliday, "Relentless Toyota Thrives on Crisis," *Advertising Age* (February 21, 2005), p. 33.

Figure 22-1

Integrating and Assessing Strategic Marketing Plans

Source: Clark Crouch, "A New Simplified Model for Planning," **http://crouchnet.com/planning.html** (May 5, 2001). Reprinted by permission. Copyright © 1991 by In-Com. Inc. Revision © 1999 by Clark E. Crouch. All Rights reserved.

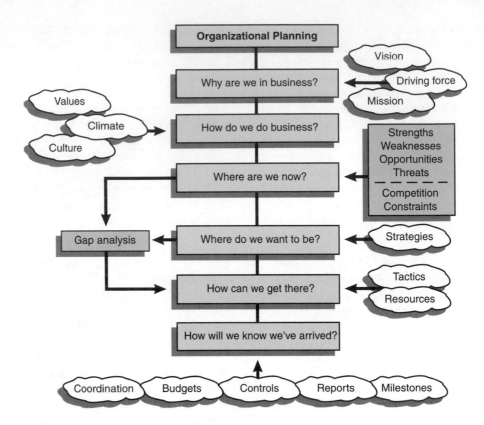

- South Beach Beverage Company (SoBe, **http://www.sobebev.com**) has blossomed into a leader in new-age soft drinks by positioning itself as a healthy refreshment and applying both penetration and expansion strategies: "The company used 'innovative imitation' to learn from Arizona Beverage Co., Snapple, and Mistic Brands." It didn't just copy them, but found out what to avoid. "It also exploited three converging trends: the emphasis on healthier foods and beverages, the growing acceptance of natural or holistic treatments, and the aging of baby boomers. The brand attitude was quite irreverent. Growth was accelerated by line extensions such as herbal tonics that took them toward neutraceuticals. SoBe's initial success made it easier to improve its distribution quality and enter new geographic markets." Since its founding a decade ago, SoBe has expanded its product mix into several new lines, including one that is sugar-free.[5]

22-2 INTEGRATING THE MARKETING PLAN

> From a total quality perspective, the many parts of a marketing plan should be unified, consistent, and coordinated.

When a marketing plan is properly integrated, all its various parts are unified, consistent, and coordinated; and a total quality approach can then be followed. Although this appears to be an easy task, keep in mind that a firm may have long-run, moderate-length, and short-run plans; the different strategic business units in an organization may require separate marketing plans; and each aspect of the marketing mix requires planning:

[5] George S. Day, "Feeding the Growth Strategy," *Marketing Management* (November-December 2003), p. 18; and "Products," **http://www.sobebev.com/product_info** (May 29, 2006).

Ethical Issues in Marketing

Meeting Ethical Responsibilities in a Tough Marketplace

During one recent three-year period, the Securities and Exchange Commission (SEC) (http://www.sec.gov) brought over 1,300 civil cases against businesses, including such high-profile cases as those against Enron, WorldCom, Tyco, and Adelphia. In addition, many major mutual funds have settled SEC actions. No comparable period in history featured as many securities fraud cases. The ethical scandals resulted in many stock market investors being less confident in the trustworthiness of corporate managers.

Jack Guynn, the president and chief executive officer of the Federal Reserve Bank of Atlanta, says that several factors accounted for the large number of ethical lapses. Many of the financial transactions were so complex that some boards of directors and experienced financial analysts had difficulty in fully understanding them. Other firms made use of confusing financial reporting practices to hide their losses or to overstate their performance. Lastly, too many boards of directors did not totally fulfill their responsibilities to stockholders.

The Sarbanes-Oxley Act was designed to prevent unethical behavior by tightening accounting standards and requiring greater disclosure by public companies. Sarbanes-Oxley compliance is costly for a public corporation. One executive at a public company with $12 billion in annual revenues estimates that the cost for his firm to comply is about $40 million per year. Aside from relying on Sarbanes-Oxley, individual investors have the responsibility to be more diligent by carefully reading annual reports and checking out companies through multiple sources.

Source: Based on material in Jack Guynn, "Ethical Challenges in a Market Economy," *Vital Speeches of the Day* (April 15, 2005), pp. 386–390.

- An overall plan would be poorly integrated if short-run profits are earned at the expense of long-term profits. This could occur if marketing research or new-product planning expenditures are reduced to raise profits temporarily. A firm might also encounter difficulties if plans are changed too frequently, leading to a blurred image for consumers and a lack of focus for executives.
- Resources must be allocated among SBUs so funds are given to those with high potential. The target market, image, prices, and so on, of each SBU have to be distinctive, yet not in conflict with one another. Physical distribution and channel member arrangements must be timed so the system and the total quality process are not strained by multiple SBUs making costly demands simultaneously.
- Although a promotion plan primarily deals with one strategic element, it must also be integrated with product, distribution, and pricing plans. It must reflect the proper positioning for a firm's products, encourage channel cooperation, and show that products are worth the prices set.

A well-integrated marketing plan incorporates the elements shown in Figure 22-2. We explain these elements next.

22-2a   Clear Organizational Mission

A clear organizational mission outlines a firm's commitment to a type of business and a place in the market. It directs total quality efforts. The mission is involved whenever a firm seeks new customer groups or abandons existing ones, adds or deletes product lines, acquires other firms or sells part of its own business, does different marketing functions, and/or shifts technological focus (as noted in Chapter 3). See Figure 22-3.

Both top management and marketing personnel must be committed to a mission; and that mission must be communicated to customers, company employees, suppliers, and distribution intermediaries. If the mission is not on target, results can be poor, as Levi Strauss (http://www.levis.com) discovered:

> The long-running woes at Levi Strauss became painfully obvious on December 1, 2003, the day the legendary jeans maker called in the turnaround doctors and replaced its chief financial officer. It'll take a lot to fix what ails Levi's. The story of its slide is a classic case of a powerful

The organizational mission should be clear and directive.

Figure 22-2

Elements Leading to a Well-Integrated Marketing Plan

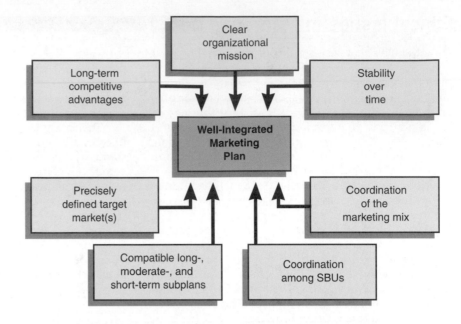

Figure 22-3

The Clear Vision of Build-A-Bear Workshop

As it looks to the future, Build-A-Bear Workshop (**http://www.buildabear. com/aboutus/OurCompany/ franchiseInfo.aspx**) plans to expand internationally in a careful manner: "Our strategy is to grant an exclusive franchise per country (outside the United States, Canada, and Puerto Rico). The franchisee will be responsible for owning and operating all Build-A-Bear Workshop store locations within the country. The preferred franchisee would live in the country of franchise, have experience operating a retail or related service business in that country, and possess an extensive understanding of the culture of that country."

Source: Reprinted by permission of Susan Berry, Retail Image Consulting, Inc.

brand that lost its way. Sales slid from a peak of $7.1 billion in 1996 to about $4 billion in fiscal 2003. For years, Levi's stuck to the middle even as the jeans business became more polarized. Fearful of devaluing the brand, which it sold largely through such mid-market channels as J.C. Penney and Sears, it avoided the discount fray even as its core customers turned to the likes of Wal-Mart, Target, and Kohl's. At the same time, the company was slow to capitalize on the boom in high-fashion denim as new rivals such as Diesel and Lucky piled in. The result: both price- and fashion-conscious buyers abandoned Levi's. Since 2003, Levi's has made improvements in its core segment distribution and product offerings and grown its Levi Strauss Signature and Asia Pacific segments. As a result, revenue increased to $4.1 billion for the 12 months ended August 28, 2005.[6]

Many experts think a firm should reappraise its mission if that company has values that do not fit a changing environment, its industry undergoes rapid changes, its performance is average or worse, it changes size (from small to large or large to small), or opportunities unrelated to its original mission arise. To learn more about devising superior organizational missions, visit the About.com Web site (**http://www.about.com**) and type "mission statement" in the "Search" box.

22-2b   Long-Term Competitive Advantages

Long-term competitive advantages are company, product, and marketing attributes whose distinctiveness and consumer appeal can be maintained over an extended period of time. A firm must capitalize on the attributes that are most important to consumers and prepare competitive advantages accordingly. For advantages to be sustainable, consumers must perceive a consistent positive difference in key attributes between the company's offerings and those of competitors; that difference must be linked to a capability gap that competitors will have difficulty in closing (due to patents, superior marketing skills, customer loyalty, and other factors); and the company's offerings must appeal to an enduring consumer need. This is highlighted in Figure 22-4 for Moen's (**http://www.moen.com**) line of faucets, whose slogan is "Buy it for looks. Buy it for life." While concentrating on its competitive advantages, a company should not lose sight of the role of customer service in a total quality program.

> Competitive advantages should center on company, product, and marketing attributes with long-range distinctiveness.

As Bruce Greenwald and Judd Kahn noted in a recent *Harvard Business Review* article:

> Competitive advantage either generates higher demand or leads to lower costs. "Demand" advantages give firms unequaled access to customers. Also known as customer captivity, this type of advantage generally arises from customers' habits, searching costs, or switching costs. "Cost" (or "supply") advantages almost always come down to a superior technology that competitors cannot duplicate—because it is protected by a patent, for example—or a much larger scale of operation, accompanied by declining marginal costs, that competitors cannot match. These three factors (customer captivity, proprietary technology, and economies of scale) generate most competitive advantages.
>
> Intel [**http://www.intel.com**] benefits from all three factors. Its customers, the PC makers, are reluctant to switch to another supplier due to their long-established relationships with Intel and their customers' preference, thanks in part to the "Intel Inside" campaign. Intel's many patents and years of production experience allow the firm to reach a higher yield rate—fewer defects—in chip production more quickly than its competitors. And because it can spread the fixed costs of R&D for each new generation of chips over many more units than its rivals, it enjoys major economies of scale.[7]

---

[6] Wendy Zellner, "Lessons from a Faded Levi Strauss," *Business Week* (December 15, 2003), p. 44; and "Fitch Upgrades Levi Strauss & Co.; Outlook Is Stable," *Business Wire* (October 28, 2005).

[7] Bruce Greenwald and Judd Kahn, "All Strategy Is Local," *Harvard Business Review*, Vol. 83 (September 2005), pp. 95–104.

Figure 22-4

Moen: Capitalizing on Its Long-Term Competitive Advantages

IF YOU CONSIDER YOURSELF FLASHY

DO TURN THE PAGE.

Because you won't find it here. Only elegant and timeless designs that reflect good taste. Just like yours.

MOEN

Buy it for looks. Buy it for life.®

1-800-BUY-MOEN • www.moen.com

© 2005 Moen Incorporated. All rights reserved.

Smaller firms often cannot compete on the basis of low prices, so they tend to concentrate on other competitive advantages, such as:

- Targeting underserved market niches, including foreign ones.
- Having unique offerings by specializing. Firms can be innovative, process customized orders, or otherwise adapt products for particular customers.
- Emphasizing product quality and reliability to reduce customers' price sensitivity.
- Working harder to attain shopper loyalty. Hands-on customer service is particularly effective.
- Emphasizing relationship marketing, whereby relationships with both suppliers and customers are viewed as important.

When implementing a marketing strategy, a firm should note that its competitive advantages may not apply in all situations. For instance, an advantage can lose its value when transferred to another nation, because it is not relevant in a different context or because it can easily be countered by local competitors.

22-2c   Precisely Defined Target Market(s)

By precisely defining its target market(s), a firm identifies the specific consumers to be addressed in its marketing plans. This guides current marketing efforts and future direction. When a firm engages in concentrated marketing or differentiated marketing, it is essential that each segment be understood. TCF Bank (**http://www.tcfbank.com**) has nearly 450 bank offices in Minnesota, Illinois, Michigan, Wisconsin, Colorado, and Indiana. Although most of its loans are for residential real-estate, TCF also engages in commercial real-estate, business, and consumer loans. The firm offers other services via real-estate, mortgage, and insurance subsidiaries. TCF targets "a broad range of customers, individuals, families, and small to medium-size businesses. We also work to ensure that credit is available to everyone, especially those in low- to moderate-income neighborhoods." The emphasis is on "convenience in banking; we're open 12 hours a day, seven days a week, 364 days per year. We provide customers innovative products through multiple banking channels, including traditional and supermarket branches, TCF Express Teller ATMs, TCF Express Cards, phone banking, and Internet banking."[8]

A firm's target market approach may have to be fine-tuned due to changing demographics and lifestyles—or declining sales. Consider the dinnerware market:

> The consumer market is in transition. Moderate-income shoppers are gravitating to mass merchants and discounters as the preferred shopping venue for tableware and spending less money than in the past. Today's affluent consumers are increasing their spending on dinnerware, not necessarily in the luxury end, but more toward 'casual luxury' that they use and enjoy, not display in cabinets. The new luxury consumers are attracted to new types and brands of dinnerware that offer new experiential attributes besides those provided by fine china and crystal. Pier 1 [**http://www.pier1.com**], Pottery Barn [**http://www.potterybarn.com**], Crate & Barrel [**http://www.crateandbarrel.com**], and many others have discovered a thriving market niche by offering seasonal, casual dinnerware. For $100 to $200, one can set a party table with creative, designer-look, and fully coordinating dishes, glasses, serving dishes, linens, centerpieces, and all the rest that are designed to enhance the moment and are strictly for the here and now. This is dinnerware to use once, twice, maybe three times, then toss it out or recycle it through a local charity. It is fun, frivolous, and total luxury—the equivalent of paper plates and cups for the luxury set.[9]

In this context, a total quality approach is especially crucial in attracting and retaining consumers. This is aided through the use of data-base marketing.

> The target market(s) should be identified precisely.

22-2d   Compatible Long-, Moderate-, and Short-Term Subplans

The long-, moderate-, and short-term marketing subplans of a firm need to be compatible with one another. Long-term plans are the most general and set a broad framework for moderate-term plans. Short-term plans are the most specific, but they need to be derived from both moderate- and long-term plans. Unfortunately, adequate plans and subplans are not always set—or are not communicated to employees.

One important trend among many companies is the shrinking time frame of marketing plans. For example, Tag Heuer (**http://www.tagheuer.com**)

> Long-, moderate-, and short-term subplans must be compatible.

> has always been rooted in sport, but what we've tried to do and have done very successfully is position the brand from sports-inspired to sports- and glamour-directed. With the addition of Uma Thurman and Brad Pitt, we've extended the position to more of a lifestyle position of

---

[8] "About TCF," **http://www.tcfbank.com/About/index.jsp** (May 17, 2006).

[9] Michelle Moran and Pam Danziger, "Heading Toward Casual Luxury," *Gourmet Retailer* (October 2005), pp. 43-46.

active, successful people who want to win in their lives, whatever that means to them. We've also very recently made a much stronger push into the women's business. Tag Heuer was historically known as a male-skewed brand, but we realized through various surveys with consumers that our U.S. women's sales have been growing very fast. We have developed a huge business in the women's category without consciously trying to get that appeal to women in a large way. With Maria Sharapova and Uma Thurman, we think we're making an aggressive push into the women's market.[10]

22-2e   Coordination Among SBUs

Coordination among an organization's SBUs is enhanced when the functions, strategies, and resources allotted to each are described in long-, moderate-, and short-term plans. For big firms, SBU coordination can be challenging. Arcadia Group (**http://www.arcadiagroup.co.uk**) is one of the largest apparel retailers in Great Britain, with more than 2,000 stores. It has a number of store divisions (SBUs), such as Burton for men, Dorothy Perkins for women, Miss Selfridge for women, and many more. Arcadia also owns Zoom (**http://www.zoom.co.uk**), an E-commerce Web site and Internet service provider; and Arcadia is growing internationally. To position its SBUs properly, each division seeks distinct segments. As Arcadia's Web site notes, Burton is "targeted at 25- to 34-year-old men looking for great value with a fashionable edge," Dorothy Perkins attracts the busy 20- to 50-year-old woman who want products "that make her look and feel great and that don't break the bank," and Miss Selfridge appeals to women who are "between 18 and 24, make reference to celebrities and style leaders, but have their own opinions and unique style."

The coordination of SBUs by large multinational firms can be complex. For example, as recently as 2001, ABB (Asea Brown Boveri, **http://www.abb.com**), had 175 global managers at its Swiss headquarters, 200,000 employees, and more than 1,000 companies operating in 140 countries around the globe. Today,

> ABB is a global leader in power and automation technologies that enable utility and industry customers to improve performance while lowering environmental impact. Our 100,000 employees are close to customers in around 100 countries. With our technology leadership, global presence, application knowledge, and local expertise, we offer products, systems, solutions, and services that allow our customers to improve operations—whether they need to increase the reliability of a power grid or raise factory productivity. Focusing on our core strengths in power and automation technologies, we strive for organic profitable growth. Our global manufacturing base ensures consistent top-quality products and systems—made in ABB—for customers around the world. Our customers have easy access to ABB—whether they buy from us or through distributors, wholesalers, system integrators, or other partners. Our people work together seamlessly to deliver customer benefits. Our way of doing business is values-based, leadership-driven, and performance-oriented.[11]

22-2f   Coordination of the Marketing Mix

Marketing mix components (product, distribution, promotion, and price) need to be coordinated and consistent with the organizational mission. JetBlue (**http://www.jetblue.com**) is a discount airline that had its first flight in 2000. Unlike other startup airlines, JetBlue has been very successful. After only six months, it was earning a profit—a feat rarely achieved in the passenger service business. When it began, JetBlue operated one route between New York City and Buffalo, New York. By 2006, it was serving about 35 destinations and had hubs at New York's JFK airport, Long Beach Airport in California, and Boston's Logan Airport. The key to JetBlue's success is a marketing mix that adheres to a total quality philosophy:

[10] Sandra O'Loughlin, "Tag Heuer Makes Time for New Marketing Tactics," *Brandweek* (May 9, 2005), p.16.
[11] "Strategy," **http://www.abb.com** (May 27, 2006).

- Product—To maximize productivity and standardize maintenance, until 2005, JetBlue used just one type of plane, the 156-seat Airbus A320. In 2005, JetBlue also began flying new 100-seat Embraer 190 aircraft to better accommodate shorter flights. The firm flies its fleet up to 14 hours per day. In contrast to most other discount airlines with their no-frills approach, JetBlue flies new planes with leather seats and free onboard television. Yet, it does not offer meals.
- Distribution—JetBlue flies to many underserved destinations, such as Buffalo, Rochester, and Syracuse, New York; Burlington, Vermont; Fort Myers and West Palm Beach, Florida; and Oakland, California. This keeps costs down (airport fees are lower). There is also less competition. Because its planes are relatively quiet, JetBlue gained access to Long Beach Airport that was denied to others.
- Promotion—Although its advertising expenditures are modest, JetBlue runs regular ads in print media and always emphasizes its low prices in the ads. The airline has generated a huge amount of free publicity because of its unique approach, with full-length articles appearing in *USA Today*, *Wall Street Journal*, *Fortune*, and elsewhere.
- Price—JetBlue offers low airfares and special deals. It provides only one class of service; there is no first-class. And the firm actively uses its Web site in its pricing strategy: "JetBlue is committed to offering our customers competitive and low fares. Special fare rates change often and are updated on our SuperFly fares page. To find the lowest JetBlue fares available, click the 'see deals' button."[12]

22-2g   Stability over Time

A marketing plan must have a degree of stability over time to be implemented and evaluated properly. This does not mean it should be inflexible and thus unable to adjust to a dynamic environment. Rather, it means a broad marketing plan, consistent with the firm's mission and total quality approach, should guide long-term efforts and be fine-tuned regularly; the basic plan should remain in effect for a number of years. Short-run marketing plans can be more flexible, as long as they conform to long-term goals and the organizational mission. Low prices might be part of a long-term marketing plan. However, in any particular year, prices might have to be raised in response to environmental forces.

> The stability of the basic plan should be maintained over time.

U.S.-based Staples (highlighted in Figure 22-5) is a firm seeking to maintain a stable, but flexible, strategy. Here is how:

> Staples invented the office superstore concept in 1986 and today is the world's largest office products company. With 65,000 talented associates, the company is committed to making it easy to buy a wide range of office products, including supplies, technology, furniture, and business services. With annual sales of $15 billion, Staples serves consumers and businesses ranging from home-based businesses to *Fortune 500* companies in 21 countries throughout North and South America, Europe, and Asia. Headquartered outside of Boston, Staples operates approximately 1,750 office superstores and also serves its customers through mail order catalog, E-commerce, and contract businesses.[13]

22-3   ANALYZING THE MARKETING PLAN

Marketing plan analysis involves comparing actual performance with planned or expected performance for a specified period of time. If actual performance is unsatisfactory, corrective action may be needed. Also, plans must sometimes be revised due to uncontrollable variables.

> Marketing plan analysis compares actual and targeted achievements.

---

[12] "Fact Sheet," **http://www.jetblue.com/learnmore/factsheet.html** (May 30, 2006); "JetBlue 101," **http://www.jetblue.com/learnmore/air101.html** (May 30, 2006); and "Awards & Accolades," **http://www.jetblue.com/learnmore/awards.html** (May 30, 2006).

[13] "Staples, Inc. Fact Sheet," **http://www.staples.com** (June 2, 2006).

Figure 22-5

Staples: Applying a Consistent, but Evolving, Strategy

Everything that Staples (**http://www.staples.com**) does is intended to grow its business: "Staples Express stores are located in densely populated downtown markets. They can best be described as a smaller version of our familiar Staples superstores. However, small size does not mean small selection; Staples Express stores typically offer over 5,600 of our top-selling office products at Guaranteed Low Prices."

Source: Reprinted by permission.

Five techniques to analyze marketing plans are discussed next: benchmarking, customer satisfaction research, marketing cost analysis, sales analysis, and the marketing audit. Although our discussion relates to these tools' utility in assessing marketing plans, they may also be used in devising and adjusting plans.

22-3a Benchmarking

> In **benchmarking**, a firm sets specific points of comparison so performance can be measured.

A company must set performance standards to properly assess the effectiveness of its marketing plans. That is, it must specify what exactly is meant by "success." One way to do this is to utilize *benchmarking*, whereby a firm sets its own marketing performance standards based on prior actions by the firm itself, the prowess of direct competitors, the competence of the best companies in its industry, and/or the approaches of innovative companies in other industries anywhere around the world. As two observers recently noted: A firm's "capacity to flourish depends in part on its ability to capture and embed best practices from its own and other companies. Without mechanisms that facilitate the sharing of best-practice knowledge—such as visits to exemplar companies and the use of experts—organizations would be consigned to reliving the same mistakes day after day. Searching for and then articulating, refining, and embedding best-practice ideas brings companies in a sector to a level playing field. Those companies that fail to adopt best-practice processes rapidly become complacent laggards."[14] Among the firms that do benchmarking are Best Buy (**http://www.bestbuy.com**), DuPont (**http://www.dupont.com**), Hewlett-Packard (**http://www.hp.com**), IBM (**http://www.ibm.com**), Marriott (**http://www.marriott.com**), and Walt Disney (**http://www.disney.com**). According to a recent global study of senior executives by Bain & Company, about four-fifths of the responding firms regularly do benchmarking.[15]

---

[14] Lynda Gratton and Sumantra Ghoshal, "Beyond Best Practice," *Sloan Management Review*, Vol. 46 (Spring 2005), p. 49.

[15] Darrell Rigby, "Best Tools: Benchmarking," **http://www.bain.com/management_tools/tools_Benchmarking.asp** (December 19, 2005).

There are two main types of external benchmarking—competitive and best practice:

The goal of *competitive benchmarking* is to assess your advantages and disadvantages by comparing them with those of direct competitors. *Best practice benchmarking*, by contrast, is designed to identify world-class performers and the specific underlying best practices they utilize that will enable your company to realize similar world-class results. It is natural for companies to want to benchmark their performance against a handpicked group of major competitors. However, depending on individual objectives and business strategy, different companies, even within the same industry, have different strategic goals. Assessing potentially effective best practices is possible only by looking at companies outside one's own industry to see what innovators are doing elsewhere.[16]

A good benchmarking process comprises these steps:

1. *Plan*: Identify the subject area to benchmark and define the criteria to assess success. Choose the type of benchmarking and develop a project plan. Gain top management support and allot resources.
2. *Collect data and information*: Obtain information and data on performance. Collate the findings to facilitate analysis.
3. *Analyze findings*: Review results and prepare tables and charts to support the analysis. Identify performance gaps and uncover explanations for the gaps. Make sure that comparisons are meaningful and credible. Highlight realistic opportunities to improve. Communicate findings.
4. *Make and enact recommendations*: Present realistic recommendations to upgrade performance. Reach internal company agreement on the most appropriate improvements. Gather the support of key groups for undertaking the proposed changes. Devise and implement an action plan.
5. *Monitor and review*: Regularly assess the benchmarking process and the results of the action plan.[17]

When formulating a program, a company needs to consider the experience it has with benchmarking and act accordingly.[18] A *novice* firm should try to emulate direct competitors, not world-class companies. It should rely on customers for new-product ideas and choose suppliers mostly on price and reliability. The focus should be on cost reduction, with a "don't develop it, buy it" thrust. The firm should look for processes to add value, simplify those processes, and be faster responding to the marketplace.

A *journeyman* firm should encourage workers to find ways to do their jobs better and simplify operations. It should emulate market leaders and selected world-class companies. Consumer input, formal marketing research, and internal ideas should be used in generating new products. The firm should select good-quality suppliers, and then look at their prices. The firm should refine practices to improve value added per employee, time to market, and customer satisfaction.

A *master* firm should rely on self-managed, multiskilled teams that emphasize horizontal processes (such as product development). It should measure its marketing practices against the world's best. Consumer input, benchmarking, and internal research and development should be used in generating new products. The firm should select suppliers that are technologically advanced and offer superior quality. Executive compensation should be linked to teamwork and quality. The firm should continue refining

> There are three rungs in the benchmarking ladder: novice, journeyman, and master.

[16] Richard T. Roth, "Best Practice Benchmarking vs. Competitive Benchmarking," *Financial Executive* (July-August 2005), p. 58.

[17] Adapted by the authors from "The Benchmarking Process," **http://www.benchmarking.gov.uk/about_bench/ theprocess.asp** (June 3, 1006).

[18] Otis Port, John Carey, Kevin Kelly, and Stephanie Anderson Forest, "Quality: Small and Midsize Companies Seize the Challenge—Not a Moment Too Soon," *Business Week* (November 30, 1992), pp. 66–72.

its practices to improve the value added per employee, the time to market, and customer satisfaction.

Two especially useful benchmarks are the Malcolm Baldridge National Quality Award (**http://www.quality.nist.gov**) and *Fortune's* "Most Admired" corporate reputations surveys (one for U.S. firms—**http://money.cnn.com/magazines/fortune/mostadmired**—and one for global firms, including American companies—**http://money.cnn.com/magazines/fortune/globalmostadmired/top50**). A firm does not have to participate in either of these competitions to benefit from the benchmarks. Any organization can internally assess itself and compare its results with others.

The Baldridge Award rates U.S. firms in seven areas: leadership; strategic planning; customer and market focus; measurement, analysis, and knowledge management (such as competitive comparisons); human resource focus; process management; and results. Of the maximum 1,000 points a company can score, a total of 255 are for customer and market focus, customer-focused results, and product and service results. *Fortune's* corporate reputations surveys (one for U.S. firms—**http://www.money.cnn.com/magazines/fortune/mostadmired**—and one for global firms, including American companies—**http://www.money.cnn.com/magazines/fortune/globaladmired/top50**) rate companies in such areas as quality of management; quality of goods and services; innovativeness; long-term investment value; financial soundness; the ability to attract, develop, and keep talented people; responsibility to the community and the environment; and wise use of corporate resources. The global survey also asks about global business acumen. Companies are rated within their own industry.

These four Web sites provide further insights into benchmarking: Benchmark Index (**http://www.benchmarkindex.com**), Benchmarking Exchange (**http://www.benchnet.com**), Benchmarking Network (**http://www.well.com/user/benchmar**), and Best Practices (**http://www.benchmarkingreports.com**).

22-3b   Customer Satisfaction Research

> Research is needed to gauge customer satisfaction. ACSI is a broad project that does so.

As we defined it in Chapter 1, *customer satisfaction* is the degree to which there is a match between a customer's expectations of a good or service and the actual performance of that good or service, including customer service. Today, due to the intensely competitive global marketplace, it is more important than ever that companies regularly—and properly—measure the level of customer satisfaction. Here are some common mistakes that companies make in assessing customer satisfaction:

Asking only about your product. If you ask only about your products, you're likely to miss the little things that actually drive choice in a competitive market. **Asking only about your company.** Customers ultimately choose among competing products. What drives their behavior is not their absolute satisfaction with your company, but their satisfaction relative to the competitive options available. **Asking only about satisfaction.** One of the key assumptions underlying customer satisfaction research is that satisfaction leads to loyalty, but research suggests the strength of this link varies widely across business sectors and customer groups. **Not asking about price.** No matter how wonderful a product may be, price still has a tremendous impact on most customer decisions. This impact may remain hidden unless you ask about price directly. **Asking only your current customers.** If you talk only to current customers, you're likely to get an overly rosy picture of your situation.[19]

The largest ongoing customer satisfaction research project is the American Customer Satisfaction Index (ACSI, **http://www.theacsi.org/overview.htm**) by the University of Michigan, the American Society for Quality (**http://www.asq.org**), and CFI Group (**http://www.cfigroup.com**). To compute ACSI, more than 65,000 consumers are surveyed annually on 200 firm and government agencies in 41 industries: "ACSI is based on modeling of customer evaluations of the quality of goods and services purchased in the

---

[19] Bruce H. Clark, "Bad Examples," *Marketing Management* (November-December 2003), pp. 34–38.

United States and produced by both domestic and foreign firms that have substantial U.S. market shares. ACSI answers these questions: Are customer satisfaction and evaluations of quality improving or declining for the nation's output of goods and services? Are they improving or declining for particular sectors of industry, for specific industries, or for specific companies? Firms can use the data to assess customer loyalty, identify potential barriers to entry within markets, predict return on investments, and pinpoint areas in which customer expectations are not being satisfied." With a maximum score of 100, these were the 2005 ratings for several firms: Heinz (**http://www.heinz.com**), 91; Cadillac (**http://www.cadillac.com**), 86; Coca-Cola (**http://www.cocacola.com**), 84; Procter & Gamble (**http://www.pg.com**), 82; Apple (**http://www.apple.com**), 81; Nike (**http://www.nike.com**), 75; Hyatt (**http://www.hyatt.com**), 74; AOL (**http://www.aol. com**), 71; McDonald's (**http://www.mcdonalds.com**), 62; and United Airlines (**http:// www.ual.com**), 61. The average score for all companies was 73.[20]

Any firm can measure customer satisfaction:

If you have only 20 clients, you can talk to each one personally. Focus groups are good ways to get informal input from a group of customers. You bring in 5 to 10 customers and ask them questions. You have a chance to gather ideas about customer needs, reactions to your company, suggestions for new services, and so forth. One way to get regular input from customers is to put together an advisory group. This can act like a focus group, but is set up to provide input over time. If you create a good group, members may enjoy meeting and interacting with each other. Advisory boards are a much underused way to improve customer service, develop new services, and encourage repeat business. Even the smallest businesses can use them effectively.

Customer surveys with standardized questions insure that you will collect the same information from everyone. Remember that few of your customers will be interested in "filling out a questionnaire." It's work for them without much reward. By casting any survey as an attempt to find out "how we can serve you better," your customers will feel less put upon. Up to about 10 minutes of questions can be done on the phone. By speaking directly with people, you have the flexibility to talk with them. But, of course, it takes more of your time. On a longer survey, here are a few of the possible dimensions you could measure: service quality and speed, pricing, complaints or problems, and your positioning in customers' minds. If you have a simple survey, E-mail can be the way to go.[21]

The Edward Lowe Foundation Web site (**http://www.edwardlowe.org**) has an excellent discussion about customer satisfaction measurement. At the site, choose "Defining and Serving a Market" under "Entrepreneur's Resource Center," click on "Customer Feedback," and then choose "How to Measure Customer Satisfaction."

22-3c   Marketing Cost Analysis

Marketing cost analysis is used to evaluate the cost efficiency of various marketing factors, such as different total quality configurations, product lines, order sizes, distribution methods, sales territories, channel members, salespersons, advertising media, and customer types. Even if a firm is very profitable, it is unlikely that all products, distribution methods, and so on are equally cost efficient (or profitable). In the early 2000s, "marketing spending grew dramatically. It rose at a rate that was nearly four times the inflation rate—as firms placed bigger bets on marketing to address their growth needs. Now, as the economy awakens from the longest period of post-war expansion into a new, leaner age, firms are taking a look at their marketing spending and asking, 'Where did the money go?' "[22]

> Cost efficiency is measured in **marketing cost analysis**.

---

[20] "FAQ's," **http://www.theacsi.org/faq.htm** (January 5, 2006); and "Scores by Industry," **http://www.theacsi.org/ industry_scores.htm** (January 5, 2006).

[21] Rick Crandall, "Why Measure Customer Satisfaction?" **http://www.hostedsurvey.com/article-measure-survey.html** (February 28, 2006).

[22] Chris Halsall and Gary Singer, "Doing More," *Marketing Management* (January-February 2003), p. 31.

Global Marketing in Action

Maintaining a Leading Position Around the Globe

Let us summarize some of the views of leading chief marketing executives with major global brands regarding how to maintain their current lead position in the market.

When asked about the most important challenge facing his brand, Andrea Ragnatti, the chief marketing officer of Philips (http://www.philipsusa.com), says that it needs to make the world marketplace better aware of its corporate mission. Although many people associate Philips with televisions and home theaters, the company needs to make the public aware of the other industries in which it is engaged (everything from light bulbs to life-support equipment).

Michael Renz, the global marketing director for Audi (http://www.audi.com), says that Audi's biggest challenge is to become a true global brand with a single image worldwide. Even though Audi is very strong in

Europe, the marketing director acknowledges that Audi needs to do a lot of work in both Asia and the United States.

Larry Light, McDonald's (http://www.mcdonalds.com) global chief marketing director, says that the firm's "I'm Lovin' It" campaign was highly successful on a global basis. The campaign marked the first time that McDonald's used a global campaign that focused on young adults. McDonald's challenge is to sustain the energy of the campaign. "It's a bit like making the sequel to a great movie," Light notes.

Colin Green, Land Rover's (http://www.landrover.com) global marketing director, says his brand's challenge is to modernize the Land Rover brand while being careful to be faithful to its brand image.

Source: Based on material in "When the World Is Your Market," *Campaign* (May 27, 2005), pp. 46–47.

With marketing cost analysis, a firm can determine which factors (classifications) are the most efficient and which are the least efficient, and make appropriate adjustments. It can also generate information that may be needed to substantiate price compliance with the Robinson-Patman Act.

For this type of analysis to work properly, a firm needs to obtain and use continuous and accurate cost data. Table 22-1 presents several examples of marketing cost analysis.

Marketing cost analysis consists of three steps: studying natural account expenses, reclassifying natural accounts into functional ones, and allocating functional accounts by marketing classification.

> **Natural accounts** are reported as salaries, rent, insurance, and other expenses.

Studying Natural Account Expenses The first step is to determine the level of expenses for all *natural accounts*, which report costs by the names of the expenses and not by their purposes. Expense categories include salaries and fringe benefits, rent, advertising, supplies, insurance, and interest. These are the names most often entered in accounting records. Table 22-2 shows a natural-account expense classification.

> **Functional accounts** denote the purpose or activity of expenditures.

Reclassifying Natural Accounts into Functional Accounts In the second step, natural accounts are reclassified into *functional accounts*, which indicate the purposes or activities for which expenditures have been made. These costs include marketing administration, personal selling, advertising, transportation, warehousing, marketing research, and general administration. Table 22-3 reclassifies the natural accounts of Table 22-2 into functional ones.

Once functional accounts are set, cost analysis is clearer. For instance, if salaries and fringe benefits increase by $25,000 from the prior year, natural account analysis cannot allocate the rise to a functional area. Functional account analysis can pinpoint the areas of marketing having higher personnel costs.

> **Functional costs** are assigned with each marketing classification becoming a profit center.

Allocating Functional Accounts by Marketing Classification The third step assigns functional costs by product, distribution method, customer, or other marketing classification. Each classification is reported as a profit center. Table 22-4 shows how costs can be allocated to different products, using the data in Tables 22-2 and 22-3. From Table 22-4, it is obvious that product A has the highest sales and total profit. Product C has the greatest profit as a percent of sales.

Table 22-1 Examples of Marketing Cost Analysis

Marketing Factor	Strategy/Tactics Studied	Problem/ Opportunity Discovered	Action Applied
Customer type	What are the relative costs of selling X-rays to dentists, doctors, and hospitals?	Per-unit costs of hospital sales are lowest (as are prices); per-unit costs of dentist and doctor sales are highest (as are prices).	Current efforts are maintained. Each customer is serviced.
Product	Should a manufacturer accept a retailer's offer that it make 700,000 private-label sneakers?	A lot of excess capacity exists; the private label would require no additional fixed costs.	A contract is signed. Different features for private and manufacturer labels are planned.
Distribution	Should a men's suit maker sell direct to consumers, as well as through normal channels?	Startup and personal selling costs would be high. Additional sales would be minimal.	Direct sales are not undertaken.
Order size	What is the minimum acceptable order size for a hardware manufacturer?	Orders below $50 are not profitable; they are too costly to process.	Small orders are discouraged by surcharges and minimum order size.
Advertising media	Which is more effective, TV or magazine advertising?	TV ads cost 5 cents for every potential customer reached; magazine ads cost 7 cents.	TV ads are increased.
Personal selling	What are the costs of making a sale?	15 percent of sales covers compensation and selling expenses, 2 percent above the industry average.	Sales personnel are encouraged to phone customers before visiting them, to confirm appointments.

These two points should be kept in mind in assigning functional costs. One, assigning some costs—such as marketing administration—to different products, customers, or other classifications is often somewhat arbitrary. Two, the elimination of a poorly performing classification would lead to overhead costs—such as general administration—being allotted among the remaining product or customer categories. This may lead to lower overall total profit. A firm should distinguish between the separable costs directly associated with a given classification category that can be eliminated if a category is dropped and the common costs shared by various categories that cannot be eliminated if one is dropped.

Before making strategic changes suggested by marketing cost analysis, a firm must be sure its cuts do not damage the value (price-quality) proposition offered to customers: "Many companies take a quick-fix approach by cutting costs to save this quarter's profit margin. This can cause permanent harm due to lost know-how and less control over innovation and quality. The puzzle is how to do more for less."[23]

[23] Geoffrey Somary, "Cutting Costs While Doing More—Is It Possible?" *Industrial Paint & Powder* (November 2003), p. 10.

Table 22-2 A Natural-Account Expense Classification

Net sales (after returns and discounts)	$1,000,000	
Less: Costs of goods sold	450,000	
Gross profit		$550,000
Less: Operating expenses (natural account expenses)		
Salaries and fringe benefits	220,000	
Rent	40,000	
Advertising	30,000	
Supplies	6,100	
Insurance	2,500	
Interest expense	1,400	
Total operating expenses		300,000
Net profit before taxes		$250,000

22-3d Sales Analysis

Sales analysis is the detailed study of sales data to appraise the appropriateness and effectiveness of a marketing strategy. Without it, a poor response to the firm's total value chain may not be seen early enough, the strength of certain market segments and territories may be overlooked, sales effort may be poorly matched with market potential, trends may be missed, or support for sales personnel may not be forthcoming. Sales analysis enables plans to be set in terms of revenues by product, product line, salesperson, region, customer type, time period, price line, method of sale, and so on. It also compares actual sales against planned sales. More firms engage in sales analysis than in marketing cost analysis.

The main source of sales analysis data is the sales invoice, which may be written, typed, or computer generated. An invoice may contain such data as the customer's name and address, the quantity ordered, the price paid, purchase terms, all the different items bought at the same time, the order date, shipping arrangements, and the salesperson. Summary data are generated by adding invoices. Computerized marking, cash register, and inventory systems speed data recording and improves accuracy.

Proper control units must be selected in conducting sales analysis. *Control units* are the sales categories for which data are gathered, such as boys', men's, girls', and women's

> **Sales analysis** looks at sales data to assess the effectiveness of a marketing strategy.

> **Control units** are an essential aspect of sales analysis.

Table 22-3 Reclassifying Natural Accounts into Functional Accounts

		Functional Accounts						
Natural Accounts	**Total**	**Marketing Administration**	**Personal Selling**	**Advertising**	**Transportation**	**Warehousing**	**Marketing Research**	**General Administration**
Salaries and fringe benefits	$220,000	$30,000	$50,000	$15,000	$10,000	$20,000	$30,000	$65,000
Rent	40,000	3,000	7,000	3,000	2,000	10,000	5,000	10,000
Advertising	30,000			30,000				
Supplies	6,100	500	1,000	500			1,100	3,000
Insurance	2,500		1,000			1,200		300
Interest expense	1,400							1,400
Total	$300,000	$33,500	$59,000	$48,500	$12,000	$31,200	$36,100	$79,700

Table 22-4	Allocating Functional Expenses by Product			
	Total	**Product A**	**Product B**	**Product C**
Net sales	$1,000,000	$500,000	$300,000	$200,000
Less: Cost of goods sold	450,000	250,000	120,000	80,000
Gross profit	$550,000	$250,000	$180,000	$120,000
Less: Operating expenses (functional account expenses)				
Marketing administration	33,500	16,000	10,000	7,500
Personal selling	59,000	30,000	17,100	11,900
Advertising	48,500	20,000	18,000	10,500
Transportation	12,000	5,000	5,000	2,000
Warehousing	31,200	20,000	7,000	4,200
Marketing research	36,100	18,000	11,000	7,100
General administration	79,700	40,000	23,000	16,700
Total operating expenses	300,000	149,000	91,100	59,900
Net profit before taxes	$250,000	$101,000	$ 88,900	$ 60,100
Profit as percent of sales	25.0	20.2	29.6	30.1

clothing. Although a marketing executive can broaden a control system by adding sales categories together, wide categories cannot be broken down into components. Thus, a narrow sales category is preferable to one that is too wide. It is also helpful to select control units consistent with other company, trade association, and government data. A stable classification system is necessary to compare data from different time periods.

A key concept when undertaking sales analysis is that summary data, such as overall sales or market share, are usually insufficient to diagnose a firm's strength and weakness. More intensive investigation is needed. Two techniques that offer in-depth probing are the 80-20 principle and sales exception reporting.

According to the *80-20 principle*, in many organizations, a large proportion of total sales (profit) is likely to come from a small proportion of customers, products, or territories. To function as efficiently as possible, firms need to determine sales and profit by customer, product, or territory. Marketing efforts can then be allocated accordingly. Firms err if they do not isolate and categorize data, and they then may place equal effort into each sale instead of concentrating on key accounts. These errors are due to a related concept, the *iceberg principle*, which states that superficial data are insufficient to make sound evaluations. This is how Illinois Tool Works (http://www.itw.com) applies the 80-20 principle:

> The **80-20 principle** notes that a large share of sales (profits) often comes from few customers, products, or territories. Analysis errors may be due to the **iceberg principle**.

ITW has assembled a comprehensive 80-20 body of knowledge which touches all parts of our businesses. Put simply, too often companies do not spend enough time on the critical 20 percent of their key customers and products and spend too much time on the less important 80 percent. Our process is really about simplifying and focusing on the key parts of business. Simplicity focuses action, while complexity often blurs what is important. In the process of simplification, we view all aspects of the business on an 80-20 basis. This includes finding ways to simplify our product lines, customer and supply base, and business processes and systems. In the end, 80-20 improves quality, productivity, delivery, innovation, market penetration, and ultimately, customer satisfaction.[24]

[24] "About 80/20," http://www.itw.com/80_20/about_80_20.html (May 23, 2006).

Sales exception reporting centers on unmet goals or special opportunities.

Sales exception reporting, which highlights situations where goals are not met or opportunities are present, can further enhance analysis. The firm can evaluate the validity of forecasts and make the proper modifications in them. A slow-selling item report cites products whose sales are below forecasts. It could suggest such corrective actions as price reductions, promotions, and sales incentives to increase sales. A fast-selling item report cites items whose sales exceed forecasts. It points out opportunities, as well as items that need more inventory to prevent stockouts. Figure 22-6 presents examples of the 80-20 principle, the iceberg principle, and sales exception reporting.

Organizations also may use sales analysis to identify and monitor consumer buying patterns by answering such questions as these:

- *Who purchases?* B-to-b versus final consumer, geographic region, end use, purchase history, customer size, customer demographics
- *What is sold?* Product line, price, brand, country of origin, package size, options purchased
- *Where are sales made?* Place of customer contact, purchase location, warehouse location
- *How are items sold?* Form of payment, billing terms, delivery form, packaging technique
- *When are sales heaviest and lightest?* Season, day of week, time of day
- *How much is sold?* Unit sales volume, dollar sales volume, profit margin
- *What types of promotion get the best sales results?* Advertising, personal selling, sales promotion
- *What prices do customers pay?* List prices versus discounted prices

22-3e The Marketing Audit

A marketing audit examines a firm in a systematic, critical, and unbiased manner.

A *marketing audit* is a systematic, critical, impartial review and appraisal of the basic goals and policies of the marketing function, and of the organization, methods, procedures, and personnel employed to implement the policies and achieve the goals. The purpose of a marketing audit is to determine (1) how well a firm's marketing efforts are being conducted and (2) how they can be improved. Audits should be conducted on a regular basis.[25]

The marketing audit process involves the six steps shown in Figure 22-7:

1. A marketing audit may be conducted by company specialists, by company division or department managers, or by outside specialists. Expertise, access to information, costs, and potential biases are some of the factors to be considered when choosing audit personnel.
2. An audit may be undertaken at the end of a calendar year, at the end of a firm's annual reporting year, or when conducting a physical inventory. It should be done at least annually, although some firms prefer more frequency. The same time period should be used each year to allow comparisons. Unannounced audits may be useful to keep employees alert and to ensure spontaneous answers.

A horizontal audit studies overall marketing performance; a vertical audit analyzes one aspect of marketing.

3. A *horizontal audit* (a marketing-mix audit) studies the overall marketing performance of a firm with particular emphasis on the interrelationship of variables and their relative importance. A *vertical audit* (a functional audit) is an in-depth analysis of one aspect of a firm's marketing strategy, such as product planning. The two audits should be used in conjunction with one another because a horizontal audit often reveals areas needing further study.
4. Audit forms list the topics to be examined and the exact information required to evaluate each topic. Forms usually resemble questionnaires, and they

---

[25] See Geril Clarke, "International Marketing Environment Analysis," *Marketing Review*, Vol. 5 (Summer 2005), pp. 159–173; and "How to Conduct a Marketing Audit," http://www.tri-media.com/en/about/article_details.php?id=20 (December 31, 2004).

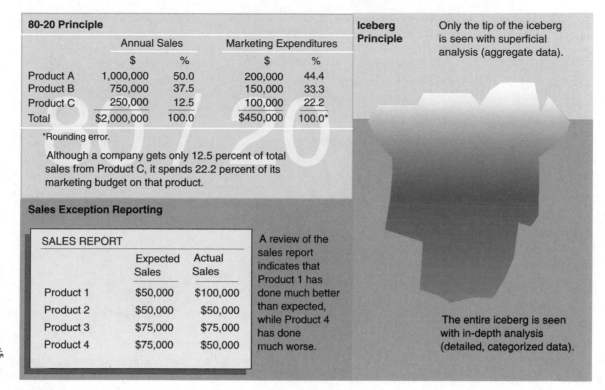

Figure 22-6

Sales Analysis Concepts

are completed by the auditor. Examples of audit forms are shown in Figures 22-8 and 22-9.

5. When implementing an audit, decisions need to be made as to its duration, whether employees are to be aware of the audit, whether the audit is performed while a firm is open or closed for business, and how the final report is to be prepared.

6. The last step is to present findings and recommendations to management. However, the auditing process is complete only after suitable responses are taken by management. It is the responsibility of management, not the auditor, to determine these responses.

Despite the merits, many firms still do not use formal marketing audits. Three factors mostly account for this. One, success or failure is difficult to establish in marketing. A firm may have poor performance despite the best planning if environmental factors intervene; and good results may be based on a firm's being at the right place at the right time. Two, if marketing audits are done by company personnel, they may not be detailed enough to be considered audits. Three, the pressures of other activities often mean that only a small part of a marketing strategy is audited or that audits are done infrequently.

22-4 ANTICIPATING AND PLANNING FOR THE FUTURE

The future promises to be complex for firms around the globe as they try to anticipate trends and plan their long-run marketing strategies. On the positive side, there should be greater consumer affluence in many countries, advances in technological capabilities, expanded worldwide markets, further industry deregulation, and other opportunities. On the negative side, there will probably be greater competition among firms based in different countries, relatively moderate growth in U.S. and European markets, some resource instability, and an uncertain worldwide economy, among other potential problems.

Figure 22-7

The Marketing Audit Process

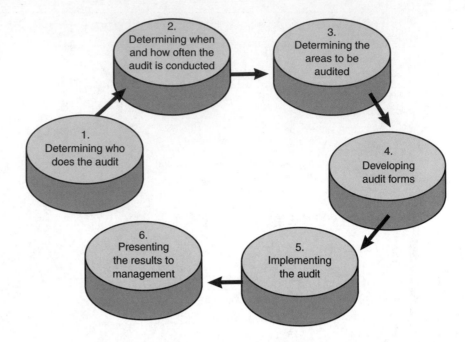

Long-range plans must take into account both the external factors a firm faces and its capacity for change. What variables will affect the firm? What trends are forecast for these variables? Is the firm able to respond to these trends because it has the needed resources and lead time? For example, manufacturers that have recognized the retailing trend toward self-service have successfully redesigned their packaging to provide more information for shoppers.

A firm that does not anticipate and respond to future trends has a good possibility of falling into the marketing myopia trap and losing ground to more farsighted competitors:

> Suppose you work at a firm that has been in business for years. Sometimes you "pulled yourself up by your own bootstraps" to survive. In other cases, you worked your way up through the ranks. You have an employee base that can be as small as one person or as large as thousands of people. You represent the many faces of success in your profession—and you are ripe for failure. Success breeds arrogance, and arrogance leads to complacency. Complacency can come in many forms. One is the one-trick pony: You ride your success well beyond the effective lifespan. For example, why deal with all of that confusing Internet and E-commerce stuff when you have done just fine without it? Why think of the impact of diversity on your service, product selection, or store layout? Why change now? Great question. The key to getting beyond the one-trick pony is to be honest with yourself and recognize that, possibly, the way you conduct business is out of date. Perhaps customers would like services you don't provide. Join the club. To remain the same (successful!), we must all change.[26]

To prepare for the future, organizations can engage in the following:

- *Company vision planning* articulates the firm's future mission.
- *Scenario planning* identifies the range of events that may occur in the future.
- *Contingency planning* prepares alternative strategies, each keyed to a specific scenario.
- *Competitive positioning* outlines where a firm will be positioned versus competitors.
- *Competitive benchmarking* keeps a firm focused on how well it is doing versus competitors.
- *Ongoing marketing research* entails consumer and other relevant research.[27]

Planning efforts for the future must consider external factors and company abilities.

---

[26] Doug Lipp, "Why Change?" *Leadership Excellence* (April 2005), p. 15.

[27] Adapted by the authors from Bernard Taylor, "The New Strategic Leadership: Driving Change, Getting Results," *Long Range Planning*, Vol. 28 (No. 5, 1995), pp. 71–81.

Does Your Department, Division, or Firm...	Answer Yes or No to Each Question
Planning, Organization, and Control	
1. Have specific objectives?	_ _ _ _ _
2. Devise objectives to meet changing conditions?	_ _ _ _ _
3. Study customer needs, attitudes, and behavior?	_ _ _ _ _
4. Organize marketing efforts in a systematic way?	_ _ _ _ _
5. Have a market planning process?	_ _ _ _ _
6. Engage in comprehensive sales forecasting?	_ _ _ _ _
7. Integrate buyer behavior research in market planning?	_ _ _ _ _
8. Have strategy and tactics within the marketing plan?	_ _ _ _ _
9. Have clearly stated contingency plans?	_ _ _ _ _
10. Monitor environmental changes?	_ _ _ _ _
11. Incorporate social responsiblity as a criterion for decision making?	_ _ _ _ _
12. Control activities via marketing cost analysis, sales analysis, and the marketing audit?	_ _ _ _ _
Marketing Research	
13. Utilize marketing research for planning, as well as problem solving?	_ _ _ _ _
14. Have a marketing information system?	_ _ _ _ _
15. Give enough support to marketing research?	_ _ _ _ _
16. Have adequate communication between marketing research and line executives?	_ _ _ _ _
Products	
17. Utilize a systematic product-planning process?	_ _ _ _ _
18. Plan product policy relative to the product life-cycle concept?	_ _ _ _ _
19. Have a procedure for developing new products?	_ _ _ _ _
20. Periodically review all products?	_ _ _ _ _
21. Monitor competitive developments in product planning?	_ _ _ _ _
22. Revise mature products?	_ _ _ _ _
23. Phase out weak products?	_ _ _ _ _
Distribution	
24. Motivate channel members?	_ _ _ _ _
25. Have sufficent market coverage?	_ _ _ _ _
26. Periodically evaluate channel members?	_ _ _ _ _
27. Evaluate alternative shipping arrangements?	_ _ _ _ _
28. Study warehouse and facility locations?	_ _ _ _ _
29. Compute economic order quantities?	_ _ _ _ _
30. Modify channel decisions as conditions warrant?	_ _ _ _ _
Promotion	
31. Have an overall promotion plan?	_ _ _ _ _
32. Balance promotion components within the plan?	_ _ _ _ _
33. Measure the effectiveness of advertising?	_ _ _ _ _
34. Seek out favorable publicity?	_ _ _ _ _
35. Have a procedure for recruiting and retaining sales personnel?	_ _ _ _ _
36. Analyze the sales-force organization periodically?	_ _ _ _ _
37. Moderate the use of sales promotions?	_ _ _ _ _
Prices	
38. Have a pricing strategy that is in compliance with government regulations?	_ _ _ _ _
39. Have a pricing strategy that satisfies channel members?	_ _ _ _ _
40. Estimate demand and cost factors before setting prices?	_ _ _ _ _
41. Plan for competitive developments?	_ _ _ _ _
42. Set prices that are consistent with image?	_ _ _ _ _
43. Seek to maximize total profits?	_ _ _ _ _

Figure 22-8

A Horizontal Marketing Audit Form

As we look ahead, it is clear that the role of marketing will take on greater importance at many forward-looking companies: "Marketing has changed. Once upon a time, you could utilize 'seat of the pants marketing' with some success. However, with the speed of change in demands and budgets, a well-defined plan must be in place to increase the chances of success. Because you will hit some home runs and you will strike out sometimes, it is crucial to develop, at least once a year, an aggregate roadmap for

Figure 22-9

A Total-Quality Vertical-Audit Form

Source: Dick Berry, "How Healthy Is Your Company?" *Marketing News* (February 15, 1993), p. 2. Reprinted by permission of the American Marketing Association.

Total Quality Health Check-up Questionnaire

After filling out questionnaire, return to: _____

   The purpose of this questionnaire is to provide a means for companies to conduct a study of their employees, to determine the degree of involvement and commitment to the principles and practices of Total Quality Management.

   The questionnaire is based on the criteria embodied in the Baldridge Quality Award categories (being employed by many companies as an integrated management system and to conform to requirements in attaining the award).

INDIVIDUAL INSTRUCTIONS

   Identify your position title and company department in the spaces below, then respond to each of the following ten statements, indicating your personal opinion as to the degree of compliance with the criteria in company operations. When completed, return to the individual identified at the top of the sheet for tabulation and reporting of results.

Your Position: _____   Department: _____

QUALITY HEALTH CRITERIA (Circle numbers at right to indicate agreement)	HOW ARE WE DOING? Not true → Very true
1. External customer expectations define the quality of our goods and services.	0 1 2 3 4 5
2. Cross-functional and inter-departmental cooperation are encouraged and supported.	0 1 2 3 4 5
3. There is active leadership for quality improvement at all levels of management.	0 1 2 3 4 5
4. Employees have the authority to act on goods and service quality problems.	0 1 2 3 4 5
5. A team approach is used to solve quality problems and to meet customer expectations.	0 1 2 3 4 5
6. Measures of internal and external customer expectations are well understood.	0 1 2 3 4 5
7. Employees are brought into decisions that affect the quality of their work.	0 1 2 3 4 5
8. There is major emphasis on the prevention and solving of quality problems.	0 1 2 3 4 5
9. Individuals and teams are given recognition for contributions to quality improvement.	0 1 2 3 4 5
10. Systems are in place to assess and respond to changing customer expectations.	0 1 2 3 4 5

---

marketing; and regular adjustments should be made."[28] For instance, with the use of advanced computer data bases, market segmentation efforts will be even more focused and responsive than ever before.

---

[28] David G. Malkowski, "Planning Well: Creating a Marketing Plan," *Rural Telecommunications* (July-August 2003), pp. 34–38.

Marketing and the Web

Benchmarking E-Commerce

Prism Business Media (http://www.prismb2b.com) recently completed a research study of subscribers of its *Multichannel Merchant* magazine for its *Benchmark Report on E-Commerce*. The report examines the practices and performance data for both business-to-consumer (b-to-c) and businesss-to-business (b-to-b) Web sites.

Here are some of the findings of the study:

- The Web is viewed as a complement to other company marketing channels, rather than as a competitor. Fewer than one-quarter of survey respondents had separate online and catalog divisions in 2005 versus close to 31 percent in 2004. Furthermore, 66 percent of respondents used the same pricing and promotions in all of their channels. Eighty-one percent of b-to-b firms versus 64 percent of b-to-c firms had consistent policies across channels.

- The typical firm spent $181,071 on annual site maintenance, while the average for small and large companies was $43,955 and $321,250, respectively. Average site maintenance costs for b-to-c marketers was $136,272 versus $129,015 for b-to-b marketers.
- Although 35 percent of the smallest companies offered online tracking, this service was offered by 70 percent of the largest firms.
- Two-thirds of firms outsourced the hosting server functions. Other Web management tasks and the percent of firms outsourcing them were search engine optimization (31 percent), maintenance/page updates (18 percent), affiliate marketing (16 percent), and back-end operations (13 percent).

Source: Based on material in Margery Weinstein, "Benchmark Report on E-Commerce," *Multichannel Merchant Online* (June 1, 2005).

Web Sites You Can Use

Here are several good Web sites related to the integration and assessment of marketing strategies:

- Business Owner's Toolkit—*Small Business Tools* (http://www.toolkit.cch.com/tools/tools.asp)
- *Finding Hidden Profits Using a Marketing Audit* (http://www.wilsonconsultants.com/Articles/marketing_audit.htm)
- *Free Marketing Audit* (http://www.sms-direct.com/marketingaudits.htm)

- InfoTech Marketing—*Strategy* (http://www.infotechmarketing.net/strategy.htm)
- Maritz Loyalty Marketing—*Why Loyalty Marketing* (http://www.maritzloyalty.com/loyalty-why.html)
- *The Marketing Audit* (http://www.marketingaudit.com)
- PlanMagic Marketing 6.0 (http://planmagic.com/tourmar/tourmar.htm)

Summary

1. *To show the value of an integrated marketing plan* Integrated planning builds on a firm's strategic planning efforts and its use of a total quality approach. Thus, everyone is "on the same page." With an integrated marketing plan, all of its various parts are unified, consistent, and coordinated.
2. *To discuss the elements of a well-integrated marketing plan* A clear organizational mission outlines a firm's commitment to a type of business and a place in the

market. Long-term competitive advantages are company, product, and marketing attributes—whose distinctiveness and appeal to consumers can be maintained over an extended period of time. A precisely defined target market enables a firm to identify the specific consumers it addresses in a marketing plan. Long-, moderate-, and short-term marketing subplans need to be compatible with one another. Coordination among SBUs is enhanced when the functions, strategies, and resources of each are

...onitored by top management. Marketing ...need to be coordinated within each SBU. ...e a certain degree of stability over time.

...es of marketing plan analysis:
...omer satisfaction research, marketing
...les analysis, and the marketing audit
...marketing plan analysis compares a firm's actual performance with planned or expected performance for a specified period of time. If actual performance is unsatisfactory, corrective action may be needed. Plans may have to be revised because of the impact of uncontrollable variables.

Through benchmarking, a company can set its own marketing performance standards by studying the best firms in its industry, innovative firms in any industry, direct competitors, and/or itself. There are process benchmarks and strategic benchmarks. In general, firms progress through three stages as they engage in benchmarking: novice, journeyman, and master. The Malcolm Baldridge National Quality Award and *Fortune's* corporate reputations surveys are good benchmarking tools.

In customer satisfaction research, a firm determines the degree to which customer expectations regarding a good or service are actually satisfied. The largest research project in this area is the American Customer Satisfaction Index (ACSI), which rates thousands of goods and services. In 2005, the average ACSI score for all companies was 73 (out of 100).

Marketing cost analysis evaluates the efficiency of various marketing factors, such as different total quality configurations, product lines, order sizes, distribution methods, sales territories, channel members, salespersons, advertising media, and customer types. Continuous and accurate cost data are needed. Marketing cost analysis involves studying natural account expenses, reclassifying natural accounts into functional accounts, and allocating accounts by marketing classification.

Sales analysis is the detailed study of sales data to appraise the appropriateness and effectiveness of a marketing strategy. It enables plans to be set in terms of revenues by product, product line, salesperson, region, customer type, time period, price line, or method of sale. It also monitors actual sales against planned sales. More firms use sales analysis than marketing cost analysis. The main source of sales data is the sales invoice; control units must be specified. Sales analysis should take the 80-20 principle, the iceberg principle, and sales exception reporting into account.

The marketing audit is a systematic, critical, impartial review and appraisal of a firm's marketing objectives, strategy, implementation, and organization. It has six steps: determining who does the audit, establishing when and how often the audit is conducted, deciding what the audit covers, developing audit forms, implementing the audit, and presenting the results. A horizontal audit studies the overall marketing performance of a firm. A vertical audit is an in-depth analysis of one aspect of marketing strategy.

4. *To see the merit of anticipating and planning for the future* Long-range plans must take into account both the external variables facing a firm and its capacity for change. A firm that does not anticipate and respond to future trends has a good chance of falling into the marketing myopia trap—which should be avoided.

Key Terms

marketing plan analysis (p. 679)
benchmarking (p. 680)
marketing cost analysis (p. 683)
natural accounts (p. 684)
functional accounts (p. 684)

sales analysis (p. 686)
control units (p. 686)
80-20 principle (p. 687)
iceberg principle (p. 687)
sales exception reporting (p. 688)

marketing audit (p. 688)
horizontal audit (p. 688)
vertical audit (p. 688)

Review Questions

1. Explain Figure 22-1, which deals with a well-integrated marketing plan.
2. Why might competitive advantages not travel well internationally?
3. What is benchmarking? How should a *journeyman* firm use it differently from a *master* firm?
4. Explain the American Customer Satisfaction Index (**http://www.theacsi.org/overview.htm**).

5. Why is functional-account cost analysis more useful than natural account analysis?
6. Distinguish between marketing cost analysis and sales analysis.
7. Differentiate between a vertical and a horizontal marketing audit.
8. What are some of the positive and negative trends firms are likely to face over the coming decade?

Discussion Questions

1. Do you think your college or university is applying an integrated marketing approach? Why or why not? What marketing recommendations would you make for your school?
2. Develop a customer satisfaction survey for a local shopping center. Discuss the kinds of information you are seeking.
3. Develop a vertical marketing audit form for Sony to appraise its relationship with the retailers that carry its products.
4. As the marketing vice-president for a small furniture manufacturer, how would you prepare for the future? What key trends do you foresee over the next decade? How would you address them?

Web Exercise

Explore the iSixSigma Web site on benchmarking (**http://www.isixsigma.com/me/benchmarking**). Visit at least three of the sites that are described there, and discuss what you learn from these sites. How is this information useful to marketers?

Practice Quiz

1. Organizational mission is *least* likely to be reappraised when
   a. the industry undergoes rapid changes.
   b. company values suit a changing environment.
   c. the firm's performance is average or worse.
   d. new opportunities arise.

2. Smaller firms *cannot* usually compete on the basis of
   a. specialization.
   b. gaining customer loyalty.
   c. low prices.
   d. enhanced product quality.

3. Which of the following statements about marketing subplans is *not* correct?
   a. Long-, moderate-, and short-term subplans need to be compatible with one another.
   b. Adequate plans are always communicated to employees.
   c. Long-term plans set a broad framework for moderate-term plans.
   d. Short-term plans are the most specific.

4. For it to be implemented and evaluated properly, a marketing plan must
   a. be inflexible.
   b. be narrow.
   c. concern the short run.
   d. have stability.

5. Which of the following is *not* a technique used to analyze marketing plans?
   a. Marketing cost analysis
   b. Differentiated marketing
   c. Marketing audit
   d. Sales analysis

6. As it relates to benchmarking, which type of firm should emulate market leaders and selected world-class companies?
   a. A novice firm
   b. A journeyman firm
   c. A master firm
   d. A technological firm

7. The final step in marketing cost analysis is
   a. monitoring results of marketing costs through natural accounts.
   b. assigning natural accounts to functional accounts.
   c. allocating functional accounts by marketing classification.
   d. determining natural account expenses.

8. Which of the following is *not* an example of a functional expense?
   a. Salaries
   b. Marketing administration
   c. Personal selling
   d. Warehousing

9. The main source of sales analysis data is the
   a. control unit.
   b. functional account.
   c. sales invoice.
   d. horizontal audit.

10. Sales categories for which data are gathered are known as
    a. order-processing costs.
    b. functional accounts.
    c. control units.
    d. SBUs.

11. According to the 80-20 principle, firms should
    a. determine sales and profit by customer, product, and territory.
    b. allocate revenues according to how items relate to sales forecasts.
    c. place equal effort into every sale.
    d. use total sales data to diagnose their strengths and weaknesses.

12. The first step in a marketing audit is
    a. determining areas to be audited.
    b. developing audit forms.
    c. determining when the audit is done.
    d. deciding who does the audit.

lete after

is prepared.

onds.

ives the findings and

...ions.

14. Situations where sales forecasts are exceeded are reported in
a. fast-selling item reports.
b. natural account expenses.
c. sales invoices.
d. functional accounts.

15. Which of the following is *not* a reason why formal marketing audits have been adopted by relatively few firms?
a. Many companies do not label their analyses as audits.
b. Marketing audits conducted by company personnel may not be detailed enough to be considered audits.
c. Success or failure is difficult to determine.
d. Company personnel do not have time for audits.

For the answers to these questions, please visit the online site for this book at **http://www.atomicdog.com.**

Case 1: **Can Apple Stay on a Roll?**[c8-1]

When Steve Jobs retook control as Apple's (http://www.apple.com) chief executive in 1997, the firm was in poor financial condition. However, ever since Apple introduced its first iPod in late 2001, the firm has been doing extremely well. From 2002 to 2005, Apple literally changed the way in which consumers purchase, record, and listen to music. And its sales revenues have grown from $5.7 billion in fiscal year 2002 to $13.4 billion in fiscal year 2005.

As one reporter says, "The iPod ranks as one of the greatest consumer electronics scores of all time—and may stand as the ultimate champ before all is said and done." Apple's sales of about 10 million iPods during its first three years after introduction were more than three times greater than Sony's sales of its Walkman in a comparable three-year time period. Several hundred million songs have also been downloaded from Apple's iTunes (http://www.itunes.com) online music warehouse. Both iPod and iTunes have more than a two-thirds market share in their respective markets. Apple is in the process of expanding its iTunes music store to Europe, Canada, and Japan. The European and Canadian markets alone are expected to add 190 million customers.

Some marketing analysts question whether Apple can continue its momentum. iPod's sales growth will probably drop because buyers are increasingly purchasing the least costly $99 model. These analysts also suggest that Apple's share of the iPod market will decrease as the market matures. Lastly, Apple's Macintosh line of computers was forecast to grow by only about 6 percent in 2005.

Based on interviews with past and current Apple executives, suppliers, and patent applications that have been filed, Apple is likely to develop a large number of blockbuster products based on the iPod. These include wireless iPods that could communicate with each other and a video iPod (vPod) model that plays both music and home movies, as well as an all-in-one model that could be used in a person's home and car.

Let's look at some of the expected features of the newer wireless and video iPods. The wireless iPod could use Bluetooth technology that synchronizes with a user's computer without needing a docking station. With Wi-Fi capability, users could purchase and download music from any public network. Apple's patent filing application also suggests that the wireless unit could even send content from one device to selected remote recipients. Through this technology, an iPod could play music from another unit.

Apple recently introduced an iPod that can play videos, as well as music. The company made available movies from Pixar's library (a firm also headed by Jobs) and secured a deal with Disney to offer popular TV shows such as *Desperate Housewives* and *Lost* shortly after they appeared on Disney's ABC network. As Apple co-founder Steve Wozniak pointed out, the only reason that Apple was hesitant about the video iPod is that "they hadn't found the right product yet—and Jobs isn't willing to make a mediocre product."

To increase growth for its Macintosh computer line, Apple is now using PowerPC chips made by Intel instead of those used in past computers that were made by IBM and Freescale Semiconductor. Intel's chips are faster, and the use of Intel chips could give Apple access to Intel's technology. Apple's most costly laptop computer currently has a 1.67-gigahertz (gHz) per second chip speed versus 2.21-gHz with an Intel chip. Apple gets 43 percent of its overall sales from its computer notebooks and the increased speed is critical for corporate and power users. The association with Intel could also help in resolving technical difficulties in an Apple computer running Windows along with the Apple operating system.

Questions

1. Outline Apple's short-term and long-term competitive advantages.
2. Discuss how Apple can better coordinate its iPod, iTunes, and PC businesses.
3. Describe how Apple can use benchmarking.
4. Develop a vertical marketing audit to assess Apple's new-product planning efforts.

[c8-1] The data in the case are drawn from Peter Burrows, "Silicon Valley: Tougher Days, Bolder Apple," *Business Week* (June 20, 2005), pp. 38, 40; and Paul Sloan and Paul Kaihla, "What's Next for Apple," *Business 2.0* (April 2005), pp. 69–72.

Case 2: VF: The Apparel Juggernaut Plans Ahead[c8-2]

Since 1986, Vanity Fair (VF) (http://www.vfc.com) has purchased such famous brands as Gitano, Nautica (http://www.nautica.com), and Wrangler (http://www.wrangler.com). Its annual sales of $7 billion from clothing make it the world's largest apparel manufacturer. Due to its huge size, VF is able to gain access to the best global clothing manufacturers, as well as effectively deal with the bargaining power of huge retailers such as Wal-Mart. With a best-in-industry operating margin of 12.8 percent, VF's profitability is worthy of benchmarking by competing firms.

VF has historically been a jeans and underwear company, but its sales began to level off in 2000. At that time, Mackey McDonald, VF's chief executive, decided to seek out a lifestyle brand acquisition. He sought a brand that could be applied to multiple clothing lines and accessories. McDonald acquired North Face (http://www.thenorthface.com), an outdoor apparel, ski gear, and tent company, for $135 million. Although North Face had an excellent reputation among consumers, it was notorious for shipping incorrect and late orders (so that retailers received the order at or near the end of the selling season).

North Face had outsourced its distribution and did not have accurate information as to shipment times to stores. VF quickly placed North Face into its supply chain system that accurately tracks over 500 million items made by 1,000 contract and company-owned factories around the world. North Face was also integrated into the VF sourcing group, which has a reputation as being among the best in the world. Many of North Face's down jackets, for example, are filled with 900-fill down, a high grade that is produced only in Hungary. VF now supplies the fill down based on its supply chain.

The transformation was so rapid that North Face returned to profitability within a year of the time of its purchase by VF. In the five years of VF's ownership, North Face went from a net loss of $100 million on sales of $238 million (year 2000 data) to sales of $500 million and a net operating margin of 13 percent (VF does not provide net profit data on its individual brands).

The Nautica acquisition in 2003 also worked out extremely well for VF. However, Nautica represented a different set of opportunities and problems. In contrast to North Face, Nautica had grown too much and suffered from a blurred image with its target market. According to VF's consumer research, "At one point, it [Nautica] was European contemporary. Then it was rugged outdoor." VF quickly bought out Nautica's lead designer, who had spread the Nautica brand too far out. VF then reduced Nautica's offerings to include only sweaters, shirts, and slacks. It also used its manufacturing expertise to reestablish the brand's reputation through better tailoring and materials. Although Nautica's initial sales were down 6 percent after VF's acquisition (due to the trimming of Nautica's lines), Nautica's operating margins have more than doubled to reach 12 percent.

In 2004, VF purchased Vans (http://www.vans.com), a footwear company. As with North Face and Nautica, in the year prior to VF's acquisition, Vans had sales of $330 million and a net operating loss of 10 percent. In 2005, it was expected to have sales of $350 million and an operating margin of 7 percent. VF is now seeking to purchase a women's sportswear brand. According to Mackey McDonald, "We have our game plan, and we have our targets."

Questions

1. Outline VF's short-term and long-term competitive advantages.
2. What are the pros and cons of VF seeking a lifestyle brand acquisition?
3. Discuss how VF can use marketing cost analysis in developing and controlling its marketing plans.
4. How can VF use sales analysis in developing and controlling its marketing plans?

[c8-2] The data in the case are drawn from Michael V. Copeland, "Stitching Together an Apparel Powerhouse," *Business 2.0* (April 2005), pp. 52, 54.

Get Results with the New Marketing Mix^{pc-8}

INTRODUCTION

The traditional view of marketing assumes that a firm should start with its customers, learn their needs, and then try to fill those needs—profitably and on an ongoing basis. But that's not the way it works today.

Marketing, as it has evolved over the past half-century, has not been developed to satisfy customer wants and needs. Instead, in too many cases, it has been used to assist firms in disposing of goods and services they have manufactured, created, developed, or simply wanted to vend at a profit. As a result, most marketing concepts and techniques have focused almost exclusively on new customer acquisition and on generating profitable transactions through cross-selling and up-selling, rather than on building long-term relationships with customers over time.

In today's interactive, networked, and customer-controlled marketplace, we attribute much of marketing's inability to live up to the stated goals of "identifying and satisfying customer needs and wants," the most common of all marketing management concepts, the managerial rubric of the four Ps—the focus on product, price, place, and promotion. We believe it's time for marketers to learn to implement a new marketing mix—time to take a different view of the value creation process in organizations by first building a customer-centric view and then integrating internal activities and processes. In an earlier article, we proposed a new marketing mix, one that reflected the customer's point of view rather than viewpoint of the supplier or producer. Instead of defining marketing in terms of what it does, we defined it in terms of what customers expect. We built a new mix based on our demand-based approach and called it SIVA—an acronym for these new customer-centric competencies and the order of their use: solutions, information, value, and access. The four imperatives we proposed are: develop and manage solutions not just products, offer information instead of simply promoting, create value instead of obsessing with price, and provide access wherever, whenever, and however the customer wants to experience your solution rather than thinking merely of where to place products. This approach suggests new opportunities, leads to different conclusions, and changes the way you relate to customers.

Some marketers recognize the change and get it. Others don't. A recent full-page ad in the *Wall Street Journal* for SAP AG (**http://www.sap.com**) bore the headline: "Your Customers Expect Your Entire Enterprise to Revolve Around Them." That's impossible in a four Ps-driven, supply-chain-led environment, but it's critically

^{pc-8} Adapted by the authors from Chekitan S. Dev and Don E. Schultz, "Simply SIVA," *Marketing Management* (March-April 2005), pp. 36–41. Reprinted by permission of the American Marketing Association.

important if a firm is to meet customer demand. Further, the four Ps are grounded in a manufacturing mind-set and need to be adapted to reflect the service economy. Thus, the question for most marketing organizations is not "should we change?" but rather "what should we change, when, and how?"

VALUE CREATION CYCLE

If one were to visualize the way in which organizational managers generally use the four Ps, it might look something like Figure 1. Using the four Ps, the marketing manager would start with the evaluation of an organization's asset base. Clearly, if an organization lacks assets, it most likely will be unable to develop any type of marketing activity. We therefore assume the firm has assets it can leverage in some way.

The assets available to the marketing manager typically include facilities, financial resources, raw materials, intellectual capital, and the like. Such resources allow a company to create something of value that it believes can be exchanged in the marketplace at a profit. Using the four Ps, the marketing manager takes an "inside-out" or "here's-what-we-can-do" approach to marketplace entry and development.

Four steps or stages commonly are used, starting with the identification of the corporate goals or what the management of the firm wants to achieve. Goals are usually set in terms of marketplace results or returns the firm wants to receive based on the use of its assets. Commonly, the second step is to identify the organizational resources that can or should be used to achieve the firm's goals. The third step is where the four Ps start to emerge in earnest: Here, the organization develops and distributes its products and services, making choices that involve the product, the place or distribution, the promotion, and the price. The final step in this internally oriented, marketer-driven system is, of course, how the organization measures the success or results of its program and the returns it generates for its owners and shareholders.

This approach fits the four Ps perspective. It is based on an internally driven system in which the marketer controls all the assets, all the resources, and all the power. In short, the marketer controls the system, sets the objectives, and determines the goods and services and how and in what way to distribute them. Most important, the marketer measures the returns. So far, there's not a customer in sight. In fact, if the marketing organization manages its four Ps-related resources right, customers never enter into the equation. They are superfluous and just get in the way.

Consider the alternative externally focused approach, shown in Figure 2. This, we argue, is the way marketing in a 21st-century organization should be developed and implemented. The marketing

Figure 1

An Asset-Based Organizational View

Source: Adapted from Cranfield University.

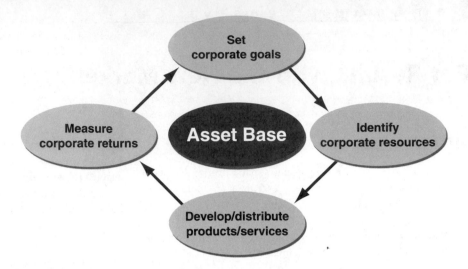

manager in our approach starts with the same asset base or the same resources shown in Figure 1. The difference, however, is that he or she would take a market-driven rather than a firm-driven approach.

The first step in a true market-driven approach is to understand the market and the customers based on true and deep customer insights. From that point, the goal would be to identify and clarify what customers value and determine whether the firm could create those values using the organization's assets and resources. The second step involves identifying or creating various customer value propositions. That is, the marketing organization attempts to determine what customers want, need, and value, and then focuses its resources and asset base on fulfilling those wants and needs. The third step is just as simple. Rather than focusing on goods and services that could be made, assembled, or developed, the organization finds ways to deliver the value customers seek. The fourth step is, then, almost a naturally occurring event in which the organization measures the extent to which the customer value was delivered, not just the returns to the corporation or marketing firm.

Looking at this rather simplistic example, four Ps proponents will argue that focusing on the customer and meeting customer needs and wants is inherent in the traditional four Ps process. They will say that research with customers must be done before products

can be made or that distribution channels must be selected that fit a customer's requirements. And, though this rhetoric is good, in practice, the four Ps approach generally never gets started or implemented in a customer-focused way.

Our comparison of the two approaches shows that the four Ps approach is internally driven, organizationally focused, and ignores customers. The four Ps approach does not reflect the marketing concept—it is simply a managerial tool that is driven by a manufacturer-driven concept that cannot be supported in the much more customer-oriented marketplace that exists today.

Stemming customer turnover has become the new marketing mantra, and yet with the four Ps approach, that can never happen. Taking a new approach to building the business for and around the customer must become one of the firm's core competencies. Marketing must become a process in which all the customer-touching elements are connected and aligned.

INTERNAL ACTIVITIES AND PROCESSES

We have known all along that marketing efforts manage only a portion of the customer experience. In most organizations, the sales force, customer service personnel, and frontline, customer-facing

An Asset-Based Customer View

Source: Adapted from Cranfield University.

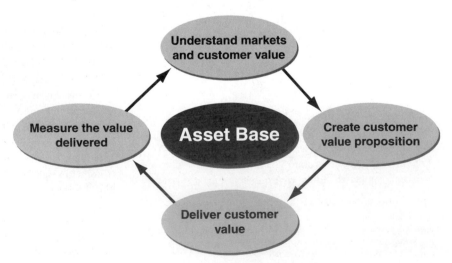

people do not report to marketing; in fact, most do not consider themselves to be involved in the marketing process. Yet, the quality of the experience customers have with a good or service, not just the quality of the good itself or the delivery of the service, has much to do with whether or not they return and repurchase. So, yes, marketing is responsible for retention but not for the retention-generating activities of the organization. And that's part of the organizational problem of the four Ps.

Internal marketing, internal alignments, and internal systems are the tasks of the new organization. Today, much internal marketing activity either doesn't occur or falls between the cracks in the firm—between marketing and human relations for example, or between marketing and information systems or between marketing and operations. One of the greatest challenges to marketing is to align and integrate the entire organization through processes and systems, particularly the employees, channels, business associates, and other stakeholders who really deliver the solutions the customers believe they are buying.

Finding the better, faster, cheaper, smarter way to get the solution in the customer's hands becomes the key imperative. Once this thinking is in place, the employees of the firm then need to be trained as problem solvers and value deliverers with support from the marketers, who in turn need to become knowledge providers and access creators.

JUST DO IT

Clearly, the question arises: Is SIVA just another clever marketing term that reiterates what marketers are already doing or have done in the past? We believe SIVA supports and builds on the true marketing concept—finding customer needs, wants, or desires and fulfilling them at a profit to the marketing organization. The reason? SIVA suggests a radically different approach to think, plan, and develop marketing programs. A case example of SIVA in action illustrates the point.

Southern LINC is a division of Southern Co. (http://www.southerncompany.com), the parent company of several electric utilities operating in the Southeast. Southern LINC grew out of a set of tools and technologies originally developed by Motorola (http://www.motorola.com) and chosen for use by Southern Co. to replace aging dispatch systems being used by utility companies.

Recognizing the need for a highly reliable communication network for the utility operations, the Motorola iDEN (Integrated Digital Enhanced Network) technology was chosen as the solution for a mobile communication system for its own internal use. The iDEN technology combines two-way radio, cellular, paging, and Internet access through one integrated handset. Southern Co. recognized that the iDEN technology could provide more capacity than its operating companies required. This would allow it to sell the additional capacity to provide a communication solution that would meet the needs of other business and government users, providing additional revenue to Southern Co. The system was built to cover 127,000 square miles across four states and designed to withstand adverse weather conditions and to cover both the metropolitan and rural areas that the electric utilities served.

Like many other technology-driven organizations, initially the Southern LINC focus was on the goods and services, not on the customer benefits that the service provided. As with most other telecommunications organizations, Southern LINC was organized and operated on functional lines. That enabled the firm to develop areas such as technology, finance, operations, marketing, sales, and so on quickly and efficiently. Although the functional managers worked well together horizontally (i.e., technology managers met with and worked directly with customer service and the financial team worked directly with the various product managers), the chief executive felt the firm was missing something. The group held an annual meeting where all functional groups came together to plan the coming year, but the focus was still on trying to sell what Southern LINC had to offer.

Starting in 1998, the firm's vice-president of marketing began to organize the annual planning meeting around team-building and cross-functional team interactions. That brought the group together and created a common ground for product and service development and delivery. But a sense remained that the organization was missing a customer orientation. The problem was that the functional groups lacked a framework to help them start with customers, rather than with goods and services.

Southern LINC had discovered what so many other marketing organizations were learning, that the four Ps is an internally oriented approach to marketing. It focuses on what the company wants to do, not what customers need or want. No matter how much better Southern LINC got at managing the various marketing activities, their processes always started with goods and services, not with customers.

"At our annual planning meeting, we met as a group. We worked together. We identified the common problems that needed to be solved. We got the functional groups to agree on what needed to be done. We generated a number of solutions but, when it came time for implementation, something was missing," said the vice-president of marketing.

The marketing vice-president decided to use the SIVA framework for the annual Southern LINC planning meeting. In the opening sessions, Southern LINC functional managers were immersed in the approach as the model for future planning. The impact was almost immediate. Southern LINC's chief executive said he saw it in the discussions in the planning sessions at the meeting: Rather than talking about product improvements and enhancements, the managers of the various functional groups began to talk about customer needs. What are those needs? How are they currently being met? By whom, if not Southern LINC? What does the firm need to do to solve customer problems and provide solutions?

According to the firm's vice-president of sales and distribution, "We began to look for ways to provide what customers wanted and needed, not to just find new or different or better ways to tell prospects about the nifty new features that Southern LINC was developing." Customer problems and solutions became the issues for the discussion during the intensive three-day planning program.

A key element to emerge from the 2003 planning meeting was the group consensus that, despite the improvements in product offerings—such as enhancements in customer service and expansions of the network—the theme running through all the discussions was: "We have to make it easier for customers to do business with us." Overall, the feeling was: "We're still too hard to do business with. We've developed truly novel and efficient systems that serve our internal needs, but we may have made it too complicated for customers. We're not sufficiently customer-focused or customer-oriented. We're better than before, but to compete as a regional player against multinational competitors' pockets, we have to be a firm that anticipates customer needs and steps up to meet them across the whole range of service delivery points."

These themes framed the objectives for 2004. Using SIVA, six groups were formed to tackle key strategic initiatives designed to:

- understand the service needs of specific geographic and industry segments and develop goods/services accordingly. (S and I)
- improve network coverage where needed. (S and V)
- provide outstanding value by managing processes to deliver excellent service at a reasonable cost. (S and V)
- develop a long-term, integrated multichannel distribution strategy. (I and A)
- improve business process from a customer perspective. (S, I, and V)
- launch new goods and services. (S, I, V, and A)

The six groups set about following the SIVA process. Starting with customers, they identified the solutions customers wanted. They then looked at how well Southern LINC provided those solutions. Next, they determined the information customers wanted Southern LINC to supply and the form and manner in which those customers wanted it available and delivered, not merely how Southern LINC wanted to distribute it. Then, they looked at value, not in the sense of cost benefit, but in terms of customer experiences. What was Southern LINC doing that created customer problems or customer concerns or questions? How could it reduce those problems or issues, whether they came in the form and format in which billing was done to the number of rings customer service set as a goal for answering incoming customer telephone service requests?

The total customer experience became the beacon for the Southern LINC managers, more than the network or system or reliability of the service. By looking at customers first, Southern LINC managers began to imagine new ways to expand and extend its services. And, of course, access became a key issue. It was not just a case of how Southern LINC wanted to reach their customers and prospects, it was how the customer wanted to access the information and material they needed from the organization. It was also about how the customer wanted to be served or the type of relationship the customer wanted, not how Southern LINC wanted to deliver the service or relationship.

The SIVA approach turned the organization upside down, but not in a destructive, change-management sense. SIVA provided the process Southern LINC managers needed to understand their customers, to really know what they wanted, needed, required, and would be willing to pay for. Best of all, SIVA provided the framework for a horizontal planning system in which marketing became

something the entire organization did, not something a group of functional marketing managers did.

Is the SIVA system completed at Southern LINC? Not by a long shot. During 2003, the Southern LINC managers identified dozens of issues to address. Some were capital intensive. Some were cultural. Some were simply things that had developed as policies and procedures as the company had developed and grown that had never been questioned. And, some were holdovers from the regulatory environment at the roots of the communication and utility organization. All had to be rethought and reappraised—not in terms of "how can we fix them?" Instead, they should be thought of in terms of "what solutions, information, value, and access do customers want, and how can we provide them?"

The SIVA approach continues to serve its purpose at Southern LINC. It has helped a technologically driven company move from a goods and services focus to a customer orientation. It has brought the organization together horizontally. Although the organization is still functionally organized, as it likely should be, it has helped provide a horizontal process that allows various functional managers and functional specialists to work across the organization to solve customer problems efficiently and effectively. From a management view, it has helped the middle managers identify the changes that need to be made. It has allowed them to take on board, identify, value, and prioritize the recommendations they now present to senior management for funding.

Most of all, SIVA has provided the catalyst for a strong firm to move to the next level of marketing thinking by building a better model. It allowed the organization to escape the restraints of the internally focused methodology of the four Ps and move to the customer-oriented SIVA approach better suited to the realities of the 21st-century marketplace.

Questions

1. Discuss whether or not you agree with this statement: "The traditional view of marketing assumes that a firm should start with its customers, learn their needs, and then try to fill those needs—profitably and on an ongoing basis. But that's not the way it works today."

2. What are the pros and cons of the organizational view presented in Figure 1?

3. How does the customer view presented in Figure 2 differ from the organizational view in Figure 1?

4. Do these two approaches conflict with or complement each other? Explain your reasoning.

5. Why is internal marketing so important? What would you recommend to encourage more internal marketing at a company?

6. What is the goal of the SIVA approach described in the case?

7. How would you answer this question posed in the case: "Is SIVA just another clever marketing term that reiterates what marketers are already doing or have done in the past?"

Appendix A

Careers in Marketing

Marketing career opportunities are extensive and diverse. Many marketing positions give a lot of responsibility to people early in their careers. For example, within six months to one year of being hired, assistant retail buyers are usually given budget authority for purchases involving hundreds of thousands of dollars. Beginning salespeople typically start to call on accounts within several weeks of being hired. Marketing research personnel actually develop preliminary questionnaires, determine sampling procedures, and interpret study results within a short time after their initial employment. A marketing career is excellent preparation for a path to top management positions in all types of organizations.

Marketing positions are often highly visible. These include salespeople, sales managers, retail buyers, brand managers, industrial traffic managers, credit managers, and advertising and public relations personnel. For instance, a bank manager of deposits development at Canadian Imperial Bank (http://www.cibc.com), one of North America's largest banks, develops localized marketing strategies within bank branches. Such a manager trains branch personnel in identifying market opportunities, using bank data bases, seeking prospects, telemarketing, and writing marketing letters. In general, because marketing positions are visible, effective persons can be readily recognized, promoted, and well compensated.

Marketing offers career opportunities for people with varying education. An associate's or a bachelor's degree is often needed for management training positions in retailing, inventory management, sales, public relations, and advertising. A master's degree is usually necessary for marketing research, consulting, brand management, marketing management, and industrial sales jobs. Consultants, research directors, and marketing professors frequently have Ph.D. degrees in marketing or related subjects.

A marketing background can also train a person to operate his or her own business. Among the entrepreneurial opportunities available are careers as retail store owners, manufacturers' agents, wholesalers, insurance and real-estate brokers, marketing consultants, marketing researchers, and freelance advertising illustrators or copywriters.

Table 1 contains a detailed listing of jobs in marketing. Overall, these jobs are growing more rapidly than those in other occupational categories—and this is expected to continue. For example, today, there are nearly 30 million people working in U.S. retailing and wholesaling activities, representing more than one-fifth of all civilian employees 16 years old and older. And according to U.S. Bureau of Labor Statistics (http://www.bls.gov) projections, employment in marketing, marketing research, advertising, sales, and public relations occupations will increase faster than average between now and the year 2014.

The strong demand for marketing personnel is based on several factors. More service firms, nonprofit institutions, political candidates, and others are applying marketing principles. The deregulation of several industries (such as banking, communication, and transportation) has encouraged firms in these industries to increase their marketing efforts. Although production can be mechanized and automated, many marketing activities require personal contact. The rise in foreign competition, the attraction of many international markets, and the maturity of several market segments in the United States are causing more U.S. firms to expand and upgrade their marketing programs.

Such new technologies as electronic checkouts, marketing-based computer software, data-base marketing techniques, and E-marketing are creating marketing opportunities for firms. The changes in U.S. and foreign societies (such as blurring gender roles, recreational activities, and the rise in single-person households) need to be monitored through marketing research and marketing information systems, and adapted to via careful marketing planning.

Figure 1 shows four potential marketing career paths. They are general and intended to give you a perspective about "moving up the ladder." Individual firms have their own versions of these career paths. Specialized opportunities also exist in each area shown (such as sales training, support sales, and final consumer versus organizational consumer sales in the sales area); and these are not revealed in Figure 1.

Starting salaries for marketing personnel range from $18,000 to $30,000 for those with an associate's degree, $25,000 to $45,000 for those with a bachelor's degree, and $50,000 to $85,000+ for those with a master of business administration degree. In addition to salary, some marketing positions (especially in sales) provide a company car, bonus, and/or expense account that are not common to other professions.

Worldwide, and especially in the United States, marketing executives often become chief executive officers (CEOs) of major industrial and nonindustrial corporations. They each typically earn at least several hundred thousand dollars per year plus bonuses.

Table 2 shows the types of firms that employ people in marketing positions. Table 3 presents salary ranges for a number of marketing positions (with a focus on entry-level, middle-management, and top management jobs). Table 4 gives the Web site addresses of several sources with useful information relating to marketing careers.

Table 1   Selected Jobs in Marketing

Job Title	Description
Account executive	Liaison between an ad agency and its clients. This person is employed by the agency to study clients' promotion goals and create promotion programs (including messages, layout, media, and timing).
Advertising copywriter	Creator of headlines and content for ads.
Advertising layout person	Producer of illustrations or one who uses other artists' materials to form ads.
Advertising manager	Director of a firm's ad program. He or she determines media, copy, budget size, ad frequency, and the choice of an ad agency.
Advertising production manager	Person who arranges to have an ad filmed (for TV), recorded (for radio), or printed (for newspaper, magazine, Internet, etc.).
Advertising research director	Person who researches markets, evaluates alternative ads, assesses media, and tests reactions.
Agent (broker)	Wholesaler who works for a commission or fee.
Catalog manager	Person who determines target market, products, copy, displays, and pricing for sales catalogs.
Commercial artist	Creator of ads for TV, print media, the Internet, and product packaging. This artist selects photos and drawings, and determines the layout and type of print used in newspaper and magazine ads. Sample scenes of TV commercials are sketched for clients.
Consumer affairs specialist (customer relations specialist)	Firm's contact with consumers. The person handles consumer complaints and attempts to have the firm's policies reflect customer needs. Community programs, such as lectures on product safety, are devised.
Credit manager	Supervisor of the firm's credit process, including eligibility for credit, terms, late payments, consumer complaints, and control.
Customer service	Person responsible for order status inquiries, expediting deliveries, representative field sales support, and returns and claims processing.
Direct-to-home (or office) salesperson	Person who sells goods and services to consumers by personal contact at the consumer's home or office.
Display worker	Person who designs and sets up retail store displays.
Exporter	Individual who arranges for foreign sales and distribution, mostly for domestic firms having a small presence internationally.
Fashion designer	Designer of such apparel as beachwear, pants, dresses, scarves, shoes, and suits.
Franchisee	Person who leases or buys a business with many outlets and a popular name. A franchisee often has one outlet and engages in cooperative planning and ads. The franchisor sets operating rules for all.
Franchisor	Person who develops a company name and reputation and then leases or sells parts of a firm to independent businesspeople. The franchisor oversees the firm, sets policy, and often trains franchisees.
Freight forwarder	Wholesaler who consolidates small shipments from many companies.
Industrial designer	Person who enhances the appearance and function of machine-made products.
Industrial traffic manager	Arranger of transportation to and from firms and customers for raw materials, fabricated parts, finished goods, and equipment.
International marketer	Person who works abroad or in the international department of a domestic firm and is involved with some aspect of marketing. Positions are available in all areas of marketing.
Inventory manager	Person who controls the level and allocation of merchandise throughout the year. This manager evaluates and balances inventory amounts against the costs of holding merchandise.
Life insurance agent (broker)	Person who advises clients on the policy types available relative to their needs. Policies offer insurance and/or retirement income.
Manufacturers' representative (agent)	Salesperson representing several, often small, manufacturers that cannot afford a sales force. The person often sells to wholesalers and retailers.

(continued)

Marketing manager (vice-president)	Executive who plans, directs, and controls all of a firm's marketing functions. He or she oversees marketing decisions and personnel.
Marketing research project supervisor	Person who develops the research methodology, evaluates the accuracy of different sample sizes, and analyzes data.
Media analyst	Person who evaluates the characteristics and costs of available media. He or she examines audience size and traits, legal restrictions, types of messages used, and other factors. The effectiveness of company messages is also measured.
Media director (space or time buyer)	Person who determines the day, time (for radio and TV), media, location, and size of ads. The goal is to reach the largest desirable audience efficiently. This person negotiates contracts for ad space or air time.
Missionary salesperson	Support salesperson who provides information about new and existing products.
Order-fulfillment manager	Supervisor responsible for shipping merchandise. He or she verifies orders, checks availability of goods, oversees packing, and requests delivery.
Packaging specialist	Person responsible for package design, durability, safety, appeal, size, and cost. This specialist must be familiar with all key laws.
Political consultant	Person who advises political candidates on media relations, opinion polling, fundraising, and overall campaign strategy.
Pricing economist	Specialist who studies sources of supply, consumer demand, government restrictions, competition, and costs and then offers short-run and long-run pricing recommendations.
Product manager (brand manager)	Person who supervises the marketing of a product or brand category. In some firms, there are product (brand) managers for existing items and new-product (brand) managers for new items. For a one-brand or one-product firm, this manager is really the marketing manager.
Property and casualty insurance agent (broker)	Person who evaluates client risks from such perils as fire, burglary, and accidents; assesses coverage needs; and sells policies to indemnify losses.
Public relations director	Manages a firm's efforts to keep the public aware of its societal accomplishments and to minimize negative reactions to its policies and activities. He or she constantly measures public attitudes and seeks to keep a favorable public opinion of a firm.
Purchasing agent	Buyer for a manufacturer, wholesaler, or retailer. He or she purchases the items necessary for operating the firm and usually buys in bulk, seeks reliable suppliers, and sets precise specifications.
Real-estate agent (broker)	Liaison who brings together a buyer and a seller, lessor and lessee, or landlord and tenant. This salesperson receives a commission.
Retail buyer	Person responsible for purchasing items for resale. The buyer normally concentrates on a product area and develops a plan for proper styles, assortments, sizes, and quantities.
Retail department manager	Supervisor of one retail department, often at a branch store. This is often the first job a college graduate gets after initial training.
Retail merchandise manager	Supervisor of several buyers. He or she sets the retailer's direction in terms of styles, product lines, image, pricing, and other factors and allocates budgets among buyers.
Retail salesperson	Salesperson for a firm that sells to final consumers.
Retail store manager	Supervisor of day-to-day operations of a store. All in-store personnel report to this manager.
Sales engineer	Support salesperson involved with technical goods or services.
Sales manager	Sales force supervisor who is responsible for recruitment, selection, training, motivation, evaluation, compensation, and control.
Salesperson	Company representative who interacts with consumers. He or she may require limited or extensive skills, deal with final or organizational customers, work from an office or go out in the field, and be a career salesperson or progress in management.
Sales promotion director	Person involved with supplementary promotional activities, such as frequent-shopper programs, coupons, contests, and free samples.

(continued)

Securities salesperson (commodities broker)	Salesperson involved with buying and selling stocks, bonds, government securities, mutual funds, and other financial transactions.
Traffic manager	Supervisor of the purchase and use of alternative transportation methods. This manager routes shipments and monitors performance.
Warehouser	Person responsible for storage and movement of goods within a firm's warehouse facilities. He or she keeps inventory records and makes sure older items are shipped before newer ones (rotating stock).
Wholesale salesperson	Salesperson representing a wholesaler to retailers and other firms.

Figure 1

Selected Marketing Career Paths

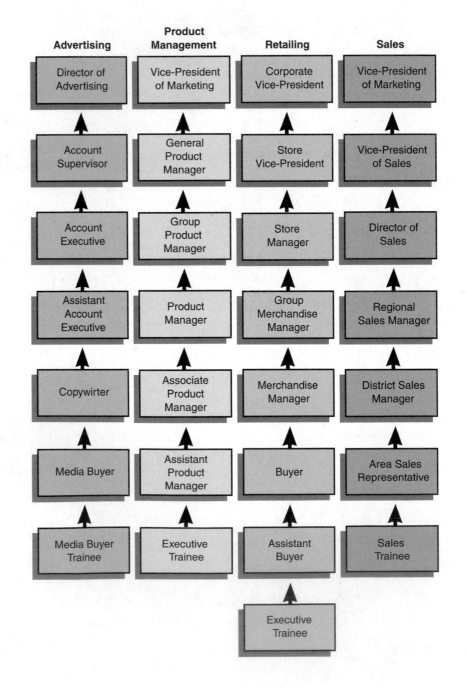

Table 2	Selected Employers of Marketing Personnel

Advertising agencies	Internet companies
Agents and brokers	Manufacturers
Common carriers	Marketing research firms
Computer service bureaus	Marketing specialists
Consulting firms	Media firms
Credit bureaus	Multinational firms
Delivery firms	Nonprofit institutions
Direct marketing businesses	Product-testing laboratories
Educational institutions	Public relations firms
Entertainment firms	Raw material extractors
Exporting companies	Real-estate firms
Financial institutions	Retailers
Franchisees	Self-employed
Franchisors	Service firms
Fundraising organizations	Shopping centers
Government agencies	Sports teams
Health-care firms	Transportation firms
Industrial firms	Warehousers
International firms	Wholesalers

Table 3	Annual Compensation for Personnel in Selected Marketing Positions (Including Bonus)

Advertising Positions	Compensation
Assistant media planner	$ 25,000-$ 40,000+
Media planner	$ 40,000-$ 70,000+
Chief copywriter	$ 50,000-$ 90,000+
Creative director	$ 75,000-$150,000+
Marketing Research Positions	**Compensation**
Junior analyst	$ 30,000-$ 45,000+
Senior analyst/project director	$ 45,000-$ 85,000+
Research director	$ 80,000-$150,000+
Product Management Positions	**Compensation**
Senior marketing analyst	$ 35,000-$ 60,000+
Product manager	$ 65,000-$110,000+
Group product manager	$ 85,000-$175,000+
Public Relations Positions	**Compensation**
Account executive	$ 30,000- $45,000+
Account supervisor	$ 55,000- $80,000+
Retailing Positions	**Compensation**
Assistant buyer	$ 28,000-$ 40,000+
Buyer	$ 45,000-$ 90,000+
General merchandise manager	$ 90,000-$200,000+

(continued)

Sales Positions	Compensation
Sales trainee	$ 25,000-$ 45,000+
Real-estate agent (broker)	$ 35,000-$100,000+
Regional sales manager	$ 75,000-$135,000+
Miscellaneous Marketing Positions	**Compensation**
Customer service representative	$ 25,000-$ 35,000+
Customer service supervisor	$ 35,000-$ 65,000+
Distribution general manager	$ 45,000-$100,000+
Sales promotion director	$ 55,000-$100,000+
International general sales executive	$ 75,000-$125,000+
Top Marketing Positions	**Compensation**
Branch office manager—advertising agency	$ 70,000-$200,000+
Senior public relations executive	$ 75,000-$175,000+
Senior sales executive	$ 85,000-$175,000+
President—distributor	$ 85,000-$200,000+
Executive vice-president—advertising agency	$ 90,000-$200,000+
Vice-president of sales	$100,000-$275,000+
Vice-president of marketing	$100,000-$500,000+
President—advertising agency	$125,000-$500,000+

Source: Compiled by the authors from various publications.

Table 4   Selected Online Sources of Marketing Career Information

Source	Web Address
Abbott, Langer & Associates Salary Survey	http://www.abbott-langer.com/amasumm.html
About Marketing Careers and Training	http://marketing.about.com/od/careersinmarketing
American Marketing Association	http://www.marketingpower.com/content966.php
Career Magazine	http://www.careermag.com
Careers in Marketing	http://www.careers-in-marketing.com
CollegeGrad.com Marketing and Sales Careers	http://www.collegegrad.com/career/marketingcareer.shtml
Direct Marketing Association Job Bank	http://www.the-dma.org/jobbank
Hot Jobs: Marketing	http://hotjobs.yahoo.com/marketingjobs
InfoTech's Marketing Careers Center	http://www.smsource.com/careers.htm
KnowThis.com's Careers in Marketing	http://www.knowthis.com/careers/careersmkt.htm
Marketing Careers Overview	http://www.careeroverview.com/marketing-careers.html
MarketingHire.com	http://www.marketinghire.com
MarketingJobs.com	http://www.marketingjobs.com
Monster Sales	http://sales.monster.com
NationJob's Marketing and Sales Job Page	http://www.nationjob.com/marketing
Occupational Outlook Handbook	http://www.bls.gov/oco
Salary Wizard	http://www.salary.com/salary/layoutscripts/sall_display.asp
TigerJobs.com	http://www.tigerjobs.com
TopUSAJobs.com Sales/Marketing	http://www.topjobsusa.com/jobs-by-cat/sales
True Careers	http://www.truecareers.com

Appendix B

Marketing Mathematics

To properly design, implement, and review marketing programs, it is necessary to understand basic business mathematics from a marketing perspective. Accordingly, this appendix describes and illustrates the types of business mathematics with which marketers should be most familiar: the profit-and-loss statement, marketing performance ratios, pricing, and determining an optimal marketing mix.

The crucial role of marketing mathematics can be seen from the following:

- By utilizing marketing mathematics well, a firm can evaluate monthly, quarterly, and annual reports; and study performance on a product, market, SBU, division, or overall company basis.
- Marketing plans for all types of channel members (manufacturers, wholesalers, and retailers) and all time periods (short term through long term) should be based on marketing mathematics.
- Both small and large, goods and services, and profit and nonprofit organizations need to rely on marketing mathematics in making decisions.
- Marketing mathematics provide a systematic basis for establishing standards of performance, reviewing that performance, and focusing attention on opportunities and problem areas.
- By comprehending marketing mathematics, better marketing mix decisions can be made.
- By grasping marketing mathematics, decision making with regard to entering or withdrawing from a market, budgeting expenditures, and the deployment of marketing personnel can be aided.

The Profit-and-loss Statement

The **profit-and-loss (income) statement** presents a summary of the revenues and costs for an organization over a specific period of time. Such a statement is generally developed on a monthly, quarterly, and yearly basis. The profit-and-loss statement enables a firm to examine overall and specific revenues and costs over similar time periods (for example, July 1, 2006 to June 30, 2007 versus July 1, 2005 to June 30, 2006), and to analyze its profitability. Monthly and quarterly statements enable a firm to monitor progress toward goals and revise performance estimates.

The profit-and-loss statement consists of these major components:

- **Gross sales**—The total revenues generated by a firm's goods and services.

- **Net sales**—The revenues received by a firm after subtracting returns and discounts (such as trade, quantity, cash, and special promotional allowances).
- **Cost of goods sold**—The cost of merchandise sold by a manufacturer, wholesaler, or retailer.
- **Gross margin (profit)**—The difference between net sales and the cost of goods sold; consists of operating expenses plus net profit.
- **Operating expenses**—The cost of running a business, including marketing.
- **Net profit before taxes**—The profit earned after all costs have been deducted.

When examining a profit-and-loss statement, it is important to recognize a key difference between manufacturers and wholesalers or retailers. For manufacturers, the cost of goods sold involves the cost of producing products (raw materials, labor, and overhead). For wholesalers or retailers, the cost of goods sold involves the cost of merchandise purchased for resale (purchase price plus freight charges).

Table 1 shows the projected fiscal 2007 annual profit-and-loss statement (in dollars) for a manufacturer, the General Toy Company. From this table, these observations can be made:

- Total company sales for fiscal year 2007 are $1 million. However, the firm gives refunds worth $20,000 for returned merchandise and allowances. Discounts of $50,000 are also provided. This leaves the firm with actual (net) sales of $930,000.
- As a manufacturer, General Toy computes its cost of goods sold by adding the cost value of the beginning inventory on hand (items left in stock from the previous period) and the merchandise manufactured during the time period (costs included raw materials, labor, and overhead), and then subtracting the cost value of the inventory remaining at the end of the period. For General Toy, this is $450,000 ($100,000 + $400,000 - $50,000).
- The gross margin is $480,000, calculated by subtracting the cost of goods sold from net sales. This sum is used for operating expenses, with the remainder accounting for net profit.
- Operating expenses involve all costs not considered in the cost of goods sold. Operating expenses for General Toy include sales force compensation, advertising, delivery, administration, rent, office supplies, and miscellaneous costs, a total of $370,000. Of this amount, $225,000 is directly allocated for marketing costs (sales force, advertising, delivery).

Table 1   General Toy Company, Projected Profit-and-Loss Statement for the Fiscal Year July 1, 2006 through June 30, 2007 (in Dollars)

Gross sales			$1,000,000
Less: Returns and allowances		$ 20,000	
Discounts		50,000	
Total sales deductions			70,000
Net sales			$ 930,000
Less cost of goods sold:			
Beginning inventory (at cost)		$100,000	
New merchandise (at cost)[a]		400,000	
Merchandise available for sale		$500,000	
Ending inventory (at cost)		50,000	
Total cost of goods sold			450,000
Gross margin			$ 480,000
Less operating expenses:			
Marketing expenses			
Sales force compensation	$125,000		
Advertising	75,000		
Delivery	25,000		
Total marketing expenses		$225,000	
General expenses			
Administration	$ 75,000		
Rent	30,000		
Office supplies	20,000		
Miscellaneous	20,000		
Total general expenses		145,000	
Total operating expenses			370,000
Net profit before taxes			$ 110,000

[a]For a manufacturer, new-merchandise costs refer to the raw materials, labor, and overhead costs incurred in the production of items for resale. For a wholesaler or retailer, new-merchandise costs refer to the purchase costs of items (including freight) bought for resale.

- General Toy's net profit before taxes is $110,000, computed by deducting operating expenses from gross margin. This amount is used to cover federal and state taxes as well as company profits.

Performance Ratios

Performance ratios are used to measure the actual performance of a firm against company goals or industry standards. Comparative data can be obtained from trade associations, Dun & Bradstreet (**http://www.dnb.com**), Risk Management Association (**http://www.rmahq.org**), and other sources. Among the most valuable performance ratios for marketing analysis are the following:

$$(1)\ \text{Sales efficiency ratio (percentage)} = \frac{\text{Net sales}}{\text{Gross sales}}$$

The **sales efficiency ratio (percentage)** compares net sales against gross sales. The highest level of efficiency is 1.00; in that case, there would be no returns, allowances, or discounts. General Toy has a sales efficiency ratio of 93 percent ($930,000/$1,000,000) in fiscal 2007. This is a very good ratio; anything greater would mean General Toy is too conservative in making sales.

$$(2)\ \text{Cost-of-goods-sold ratio (percentage)} = \frac{\text{Cost of goods sold}}{\text{Net sales}}$$

The **cost-of-goods-sold ratio (percentage)** indicates the portion of net sales used to manufacture or purchase the goods sold. When the ratio is high, a firm has little revenue left to use for operating expenses and net profit. This could mean costs are too high or selling price is too low. In fiscal 2007, General Toy has a cost-of-goods-sold ratio of 48.4 percent ($450,000/$930,000), a satisfactory figure.

(3) Gross margin ratio (percentage) $= \dfrac{\text{Gross margin}}{\text{Net sales}}$

The **gross margin ratio (percentage)** shows the proportion of net sales allotted to operating expenses and net profit. If the ratio is high, a firm has substantial revenue left for these items. During fiscal 2007, General Toy has a gross margin ratio of 51.6 percent ($480,000/$930,000), a satisfactory figure.

(4) Operating expense ratio (percentage) $= \dfrac{\text{Operating expenses}}{\text{Net sales}}$

The **operating expense ratio (percentage)** expresses these expenses in terms of net sales. When the ratio is high, a firm is spending a large amount on marketing and other operating costs. General Toy has an operating expense ratio of 39.8 percent in fiscal 2007 ($370,000/$930,000), meaning that almost 40 cents of every sales dollar goes for operations, a moderate amount.

(5) Net profit ratio (percentage) $= \dfrac{\text{Net profit before taxes}}{\text{Net sales}}$

The **net profit ratio (percentage)** indicates the portion of each sales dollar going for profits (after deducting all costs). The net profit ratio varies a lot by industry. For example, in the supermarket industry, net profits are about 2 percent of net sales; in the industrial chemical industry, net profits are about 5 percent of net sales. The fiscal 2007 net profit for General Toy is 11.8 percent of net sales ($110,000/$930,000), well above the industry average.

(6) Stock turnover ratio $= \dfrac{\text{Net sales (in units)}}{\text{Average inventory (in units)}}$

or

$\dfrac{\text{Net sales (in sales dollars)}}{\text{Average inventory (in sales dollars)}}$

or

$\dfrac{\text{Cost of goods sold}}{\text{Average inventory (at cost)}}$

The **stock turnover ratio** shows the number of times during a specified period, usually one year, that average inventory on hand is sold. It can be calculated in units or dollars (in selling price or at cost).

In the case of General Toy, the fiscal 2007 stock turnover ratio can be calculated on a cost basis. The cost of goods sold during fiscal 2007 is $450,000. Average inventory at cost $=$ (Beginning inventory at cost + Ending inventory at cost)/2 $=$ ($100,000 + $50,000)/2 $=$ $75,000. The stock turnover ratio is ($450,000/75,000) $=$ 6. This compares favorably with the industry average which means General Toy sells its goods more quickly than competitors.

(7) Return on investment $= \dfrac{\text{Net sales}}{\text{Investment}} \times \dfrac{\text{Net profit before taxes}}{\text{Net sales}}$

$= \dfrac{\text{Net profit before taxes}}{\text{Investment}}$

The **return on investment (ROI)** compares profitability with the investment necessary to manufacture or distribute merchandise. For a manufacturer, this investment includes land, plant, equipment, and inventory costs. For a wholesaler or retailer, it involves inventory, the costs of land, the outlet and its fixtures, and equipment. To find General Toy's return on investment, total investment costs are culled from its **balance sheet**, which lists the assets and liabilities of a firm at a particular time.

There are two components to the return on investment measure—investment turnover ratio and net profit ratio (percentage):

Investment turnover ratio $= \dfrac{\text{Net sales}}{\text{Investment}}$

Net profit ratio (percentage) $= \dfrac{\text{Net profit before taxes}}{\text{Net sales}}$

The investment turnover ratio computes the sales per dollar of investment. The General Toy management calculates that an overall investment of $550,000 is needed to yield fiscal 2007 net sales of $930,000. Thus, its investment turnover ratio is 1.7 times ($930,000/$550,000). Because General Toy's net profit ratio is 11.8 percent ($110,000/$930,000), the firm's return on investment equals 20.1 percent (1.7 x .118). This figure is above the industry norm.

Table 2 shows a percentage profit-and-loss statement for the General Toy Company, using the same period as in Table 1. All figures in the table are computed on the basis of net sales equaling 100 percent. This table allows a firm to quickly observe such performance measures as the cost-of-goods-sold percentage, operating expense percentage, and net profit percentage.

Table 2	General Toy Company, Projected Profit-and-Loss Statement for the Fiscal Year July 1, 2006 through June 30, 2007 (in Percent, with Net Sales = 100.0)	
Net sales		100.0
Less cost of goods sold		48.4
Gross margin		51.6
Less operating expenses:		
Marketing expenses	24.2	
General expenses	15.6	
Total operating expenses		39.8
Net profit before taxes		11.8

Pricing

The material here complements Chapters 20 and 21. Five specific aspects of pricing are examined: price elasticity, fixed versus variable costs, markups, markdowns, and profit planning using markups and markdowns.

Price Elasticity

As defined in Chapter 20, **price elasticity** refers to the buyer sensitivity to price changes in terms of the quantities they will purchase. It is based on the availability of substitutes and the urgency of need, and expressed as the percentage change in quantity demanded divided by the percentage change in price:

$$\text{Price elasticity} = \frac{\dfrac{\text{Quantity 1} - \text{Quantity 2}}{\text{Quantity 1} + \text{Quantity 2}}}{\dfrac{\text{Price 1} - \text{Price 2}}{\text{Price 1} + \text{Price 2}}}$$

For purposes of simplicity, elasticity is often shown as a positive number (as it will be in this section).

Table 3 shows a demand schedule for women's blouses at several different prices. When selling price is reduced by a small percentage, from $40 to $35, the percentage change in quantity demanded rises materially, from 120 to 150 units. Maxine's Blouses then gains a strong competitive advantage. Demand is highly elastic (price sensitive). As price is reduced, total revenues go up:

$$\text{Price elasticity} = \frac{\dfrac{120 - 150}{120 + 150}}{\dfrac{\$40 - \$35}{\$40 + \$35}} = 1.7 \text{ (expressed as a positive number)}$$

At a price of $25, the market becomes more saturated—the percentage change in price, from $25 to $20, is directly offset by the percentage change in quantity demanded, from 240 to 300 units:

$$\text{Price elasticity} = \frac{\dfrac{240 - 300}{240 + 300}}{\dfrac{\$25 - \$20}{\$25 + \$20}} = 1.0 \text{ (expressed as a positive number)}$$

Total revenues remain the same at a price of $25 or $20. This is unitary demand, whereby total revenues stay constant as price changes.

At a price of $20, the market becomes extremely saturated, and further price reductions have little impact on demand. A large percentage change in price, from $20 to $15, results in a small percentage change in quantity demanded, from 300 to 350 units. Maxine's is able to sell relatively few additional blouses. Demand is inelastic (insensitive to price changes):

$$\text{Price elasticity} = \frac{\dfrac{300 - 350}{300 + 350}}{\dfrac{\$20 - \$15}{\$20 + \$15}} = 0.5 \text{ (expressed as a positive number)}$$

Total revenue falls as demand goes from elastic to inelastic; at this point, price cuts are not effective.

Total revenue is maximized at the price levels where price and demand changes directly offset each other (in this example, $25 and $20). How does a firm choose between those prices? It depends on the marketing philosophy. At a price of $25, profit will probably be higher because the firm needs to produce and sell fewer products, thus reducing some costs. At a price of $20, more units are sold; this may increase the customer base for other products the firm offers and raise overall company sales and profits.

Figure 1 graphically depicts demand elasticity for Maxine's Blouses. This figure indicates that a demand curve is not necessarily straight and that a single demand schedule has elastic, unitary, and inelastic ranges.

Remember: Elasticity refers to percentage changes, not to absolute changes. A demand shift from 120 to 150 units involves a greater

Selling Price	Quantity Demanded	Elasticity[a]	Total Revenue[b]
$40	120		$4,800
		1.7	
35	150		5,250
		1.5	
30	190		5,700
		1.3	
25	240		6,000 ← Maximum total
		1.0	
20	300		6,000 ← revenue
		0.5	
15	350		5,250
		0.3	
10	390		3,900

Table 3   Maxine's Blouses—A Demand Schedule

[a]Expressed as positive numbers.
[b]Total revenue = Selling price × Quantity demanded.

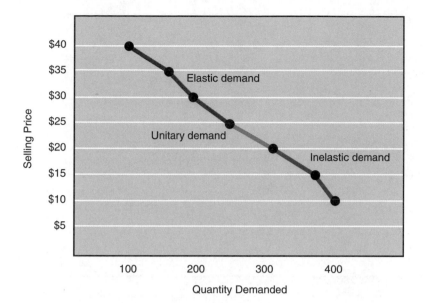

Figure 1

Maxine's Blouses, Demand Elasticity

percentage change than one from 300 to 350 units. In addition, each product or brand faces a distinct demand schedule. Milk and magazines have dissimilar schedules, despite similar price ranges, due to different availability of substitutes and urgency of need.

Fixed Versus Variable Costs

In making pricing decisions, it is essential to distinguish between fixed and variable costs. **Fixed costs** are ongoing costs that are unrelated to production or sales volume; they are generally constant for a given range of output for a specific period. In the short run, fixed costs cannot usually be changed. Examples are rent, full-time employee salaries, physical plant, equipment, real-estate taxes, and insurance.

Variable costs are directly related to production or sales volume. As volume increases, total variable costs increase; as volume declines, total variable costs decline. Per-unit variable costs often remain constant over a given range of volume (e.g., total sales commissions go up as sales rise, while sales commissions as a percent of sales remain constant). Examples are raw materials, sales commissions, parts, salaries of hourly employees, and product advertising.

Figure 2 shows how fixed, variable, and total costs vary with production or sales for Eleanor's Cosmetics, a leased-department operator selling popular-priced cosmetics in a department store. Total fixed costs are $10,000. Variable costs are $5.00 per unit. Figure 2A depicts total costs: as volume rises, total fixed costs are constant at $10,000, while total variable costs and total costs go up by $5.00 per unit. At 1,000 units, total fixed costs are $10,000, total variable costs are $5,000, and total costs are $15,000. At 5,000 units, total fixed costs are $10,000, total variable costs are $25,000, and total costs are $35,000.

Figure 2B depicts average costs: as volume increases, average fixed costs and average total costs decline (because fixed costs are spread over more units), while average variable costs remain the same. At 1,000 units, average fixed costs are $10.00 ($10,000/1,000 units), average variable costs are $5.00, and average total costs are $15.00. At 5,000 units, average fixed costs are $2.00 ($10,000/5,000 units), average variable costs are $5.00, and average total costs are $7.00.

By knowing the relationship between fixed and variable costs, firms are better able to set prices. They recognize that average total costs usually decline as sales volume expands, which allows them to set skimming prices when volume is low and penetration prices when volume is high. They also realize that losses can be reduced with selling prices that are lower than average total costs—as long as prices are above average variable costs, transactions will contribute toward the payment of fixed costs. Finally, the break-even point can be shown on a total-cost curve graph. See Figure 3.

With a selling price of $10.00 per unit, Eleanor's Cosmetics loses money unless 2,000 units are sold. At that amount, the firm breaks even. For all sales volumes above 2,000 units, the company earns a profit of $5.00 per unit, an amount equal to the difference between selling price and average variable costs (fixed costs are assumed to be "paid off" when sales reach 2,000 units). A sales volume of 5,000 units returns a profit of $15,000 (total revenues of $50,000 - total costs of $35,000).

Markups

A **markup** is the difference between merchandise cost and selling price for each channel member. Markup is usually expressed as a percentage:

$$\text{Markup percentage (on selling price)} = \frac{\text{Selling price} - \text{Merchandise cost}}{\text{Selling price}}$$

$$\text{Markup percentage (at cost)} = \frac{\text{Selling price} - \text{Merchandise cost}}{\text{Merchandise cost}}$$

Table 4 shows markup percentages on selling price and at cost for an item selling for $10.00 under varying costs. Because firms often consider a markup percentage as the equivalent of the gross margin percentage discussed earlier in this appendix, they use the markup percentage on selling price in their planning. As with gross margins, firms use their markups to cover operating expenses and net profit.

Channel members need to be aware of the discounts given to them by vendors (suppliers). Besides markups for providing regular

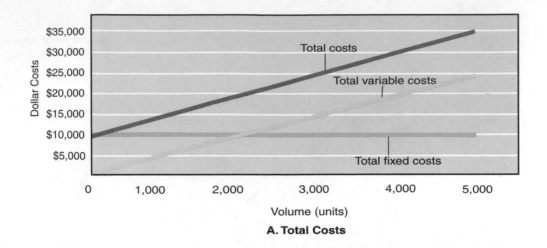

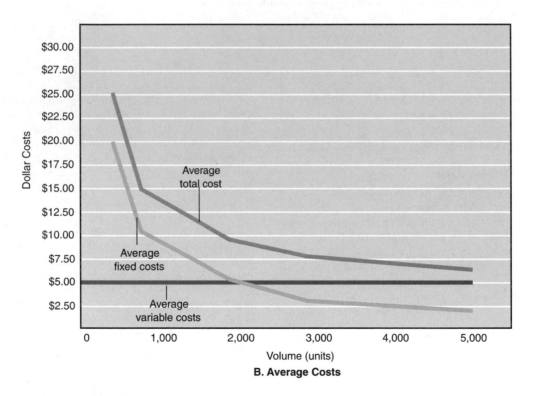

Figure 2

Fixed and Variable Costs for Eleanor's Cosmetics

marketing functions, they may also get quantity, cash, seasonal, and/or promotional discounts. Transportation costs are added to the price; they are not discounted.

Table 5 shows the computation of a purchase price by a TV retailer, based on a functional markup of 40 percent and individual discounts of 10 (quantity), 2 (cash), 5 (seasonal), and 5 (promotional) percent. The discounts do not total 62 percent off final selling price. They total 52.2 percent because the discounts are computed upon successive balances. For example, the 10 percent quantity discount is computed on $165, which is the purchase price after deducting the functional markup allowed by the vendor.

Markdowns

A key price adjustment made by most firms is a **markdown**, which is a reduction in the original selling price of an item so as to sell it. Markdowns are due to slow sales, model changes, and other factors.

Markdown percentages can be computed in either of two ways:

$$\text{Markdown percentage (off-original price)} = \frac{\text{Original selling price} - \text{Reduced selling price}}{\text{Original selling price}}$$

$$\text{Markdown percentage (off-sale price)} = \frac{\text{Original selling price} - \text{Reduced selling price}}{\text{Reduced selling price}}$$

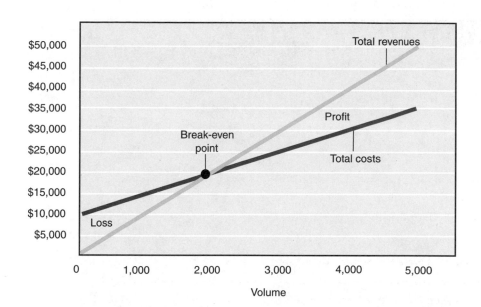

Figure 3

Break-Even Analysis for Eleanor's Cosmetics

The off-original markdown percentage for an item that initially sold for $20 and has been marked down to $15 is ($20 − $15)/$20 = 25. The off-sale markdown percentage is ($20 − $15)/$15 = 33. The off-original percentage is more accurate for price planning, but the off-sale percentage shows a larger price reduction to consumers and may generate increased interest.

Profit Planning Using Markups and Markdowns

Although lower markups (higher markdowns) generally result in higher unit sales and higher markups (lower markdowns) generally result in lower unit sales, it is essential that a firm determine the effect of a change in selling price on its profitability. The impact of a price adjustment on total gross profit (also known as gross margin) can be determined through the use of this formula:

$$\begin{array}{l}\text{Unit sales required to earn} \\ \text{the same total gross profit} \\ \text{with a price adjustment}\end{array} = \frac{\text{Original markup (\%)}}{\begin{array}{l}\text{Original markup (\%)} \\ \text{+/− Price change (\%)}\end{array}} \times \begin{array}{l}\text{Expected unit} \\ \text{sales at original} \\ \text{price}\end{array}$$

If a wholesaler pays $7 to buy one unit of an item and decides to reduce that item's selling price by 10 percent—from an original price of $10 to $9—its markup on selling price drops from 30 percent ($3/$10) to 22.2 percent ($2/$9). Because the wholesaler

Table 4	Markups on Selling Price and at Cost		
Selling Price	**Merchandise Cost**	**Markup (% on Selling Price)**	**Markup (% at Cost)**
$10.00	$9.00	10	11
10.00	8.00	20	25
10.00	7.00	30	43
10.00	6.00	40	67
10.00	5.00	50	100
10.00	4.00	60	150
10.00	3.00	70	233
10.00	2.00	80	400
10.00	1.00	90	900

Formulas to convert markup percentages:

$$\begin{array}{l}\text{Markup percentage} \\ \text{(on selling price)}\end{array} = \frac{\text{Markup percentage (at cost)}}{100\% + \text{Markup percentage (at cost)}}$$

$$\begin{array}{l}\text{Markup percentage} \\ \text{(at cost)}\end{array} = \frac{\text{Markup percentage (on selling price)}}{100\% - \text{Markup percentage (on selling price)}}$$

Table 5   A TV Retailer's Final Purchase Price, After Deducting All Discounts—Model 123

Discounts Offered by Manufacturer (in %)

Functional	40
Quantity	10
Cash	2
Seasonal	5
Promotional	5

Suggested Final Selling Price	$275.00
Shipping Charges	$15.30

Computation of Purchase Price Paid by Retailer

List price	$275.00
Less functional markup ($275.00 X 0.40)	110.00
Balance	$165.00
Less quantity discount ($165.00 X 0.10)	16.50
Balance	$148.50
Less cash discount ($148.50 X 0.02)	2.97
Balance	$145.53
Less seasonal discount ($145.53 X 0.05)	7.28
Balance	$138.25
Less promotional discount ($138.25 X 0.05)	6.91
Balance after all discounts	$131.34
Plus shipping charges	15.30
Price to TV retailer	$146.64
Total of Discounts	$143.66
Total Discount % ($143.66/$275)	52.2

originally planned to sell 1,000 units at $10, it must now sell 1,500 units at $9 to keep the same gross profitability (30/20 x 1,000). Conversely, if it decides to raise its price by 10 percent—to $11—its new markup on selling price is 36.4 percent ($4/$11), and it must sell only 750 units to keep the original gross profit level (30/40 x 1,000).

Determining an Optimal Marketing Mix

When devising, enacting, and assessing a marketing plan, a firm should consider alternative marketing mixes and find the most effective one. Because many marketing costs (such as packaging, distribution, advertising, and personal selling) can be both order generating and variable, marketers need to estimate and compare sales for various combinations at various levels of costs. Table 6 shows how a firm could set prices and allot its $3 million annual marketing budget among product, distribution, advertising, and personal selling—so as to maximize profit. In this situation, the firm would choose a mass marketing mix resulting in a low price, a lower-quality product, extensive distribution, and an emphasis on advertising.

The concepts of opportunity costs and sales response curves provide valuable information in determining an optimal marketing mix. **Opportunity costs** measure the foregone revenues (profit) from not using the optimal marketing mix. For example, it may be possible for a firm to sell an additional 10,000 units in a selective marketing strategy by raising advertising expenditures by $100,000 and reducing distribution expenditures by $100,000. A firm that is unaware of this option would have opportunity costs—in terms of profit—of $110,000:

$$
\begin{aligned}
\text{Opportunity costs} &= (\text{Foregone unit sales} \times \text{Selling price}) - (\text{Added costs}) \\
&= (10,000 \times \$29.00) - (10,000 \times \$18.00) \\
&= \$110,000
\end{aligned}
$$

At its optimal marketing strategy, a firm's opportunity costs equal zero.

| Table 6 | Determining an Optimal Marketing Mix for a Company with a $3 Million Annual Marketing Budget |

Alternative Marketing Mix	Selling Price	Unit Sales	Sales Revenue	Total Product Costs[a]	Advertising	Personal Selling Costs	Distribution Costs	Total Costs	Profit
Mass marketing	$11.00	2,507,000	$27,577,000	$22,563,000	$1,400,000	$ 300,000	$1,300,000	$25,563,000	$2,014,000
Selective marketing	29.00	432,000	12,528,000	7,776,000	900,000	1,200,000	900,000	10,766,000	1,762,000
Exclusive marketing	43.00	302,000	12,986,000	9,966,000	600,000	1,850,000	550,000	12,966,000	20,000

[a]Mass marketing = $9.00 per unit for labor, materials, and other production costs; selective marketing = $18.00 per unit for labor, materials, and other production costs; and exclusive marketing = $33.00 per unit for labor, materials, and other production costs.

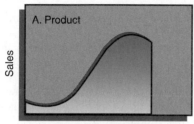

With limited depth in the product line, consumers have few choices and many find none satisfactory. As the firm adds new brands, styles, options, etc., sales increase because customers have a better variety from which to choose. At some point, consumers believe there are enough choices and will not increase purchases if new brands/models are introduced.

Figure 4

Selected Sales Response Curves for Marketing Mix Functions

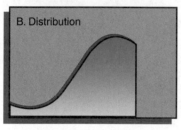

With products distributed through too few outlets in a given area, many consumers find it inconvenient to shop for or purchase the firm's items. As the number of outlets increases, sales rise because it is easier for consumers to shop and purchase. At some point, there is saturation, as stores only draw each other's customers not new ones for the firm's products.

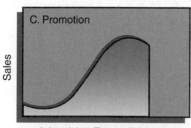

With too little advertising, there is inadequate awareness of the firm's products. As advertising increases, more people become aware of and develop a preference toward the firm. At some point, there is saturation as media coverage is duplicated and ads are repeated too frequently.

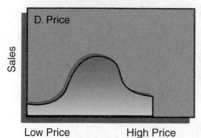

With a low price, many consumers believe the firm's offering is of poor quality. At a medium price, many consumers feel there is a good value for their money. At a high price, many consumers think there is poor value for their money and consider other alternatives.

Figure 5

Sales Response Curves and Product/Market Maturity

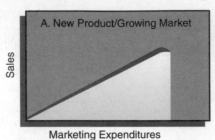

A. New Product/Growing Market

Due to product/market newness, marketing expenditures have a large impact on sales. By adding product features, increasing distribution and promotion, and offering special credit terms or special introductory prices, sales will rise dramatically.

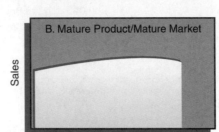

B. Mature Product/Mature Market

When a product/market is mature, marketing expenditures have a limited impact on sales. With no or little marketing effort, brand-loyal consumers continue to purchase. With extensive marketing effort, a small number of consumers may switch from competitors, buy earlier than intended, or increase consumption.

Sales response curves show the expected relationships between sales revenue and functional marketing efforts. These curves are estimated on the basis of executives' judgment, surveys, industry data, and/or experiments (whereby marketing mix factors are systematically varied in a controlled way).

Figure 4 shows sales response curves for a firm examining four aspects of its marketing effort: depth of product line, number of outlets carrying products, advertising expenditures, and price level. For each of these factors, the expected impact of a strategy change on sales is shown; it is clear that different actions will result in different sales responses.

When using sales response curves, these points should be considered:

- Sales responsiveness may vary by product and by market segment. Marketing expenditures have a much greater influence on new products/growing markets than on mature products/mature markets. See Figure 5.
- The range of efficient marketing efforts must be determined. At low levels, marketing activities may be insufficient to generate consumer interest. At high levels, these activities may be redundant and appeal to a saturated market. The range of marketing efforts having the greatest impact on sales is the appropriate one. See Figure 6.
- Sales response curves are related to the combination of marketing mix factors employed by a firm. To determine its overall sales response curve, a company would combine all the

individual curves shown in Figure 4 (or use all the data in Table 6).
- Sales response curves examine revenue fluctuations. Before making marketing decisions, profit response curves should also be studied.
- Sales response curves should be projected under different conditions, such as good economy/poor economy or heavy competition/light competition.

Questions

1. What information can a firm obtain from a profit-and-loss statement (in dollars)?

2. Develop a profit-and-loss statement for The Flying Carpet, a retail store, based on the following:

Beginning inventory (at cost)	$ 800,000
New merchandise (at cost)	750,000
Ending inventory (at cost)	600,000
Gross sales	2,100,000
Returns and allowances	220,000
Marketing expenses	440,000
General expenses	300,000

Figure 6

Optimal Marketing Expenditures

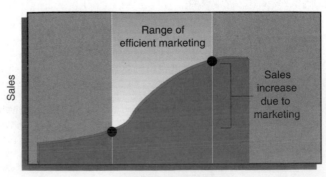

3. Using the profit-and-loss statement from Question 2, calculate:
   a. Return on investment. (Assume that investment equals $500,000 plus average inventory.)
   b. Stock turnover ratio.
   c. Net profit ratio (percentage).
   d. Operating expense ratio (percentage).
   e. Gross margin ratio (percentage).
   f. Cost-of-goods-sold ratio (percentage).
   g. Sales efficiency ratio (percentage).

4. How would The Flying Carpet Company determine whether its performance ratios are satisfactory?

5. a. What is the impact on return on investment if a firm increases its investment turnover from four times to six times?
   b. List five ways for a firm to increase its investment turnover.

6. A wholesaler estimates that it can sell 12,000 DVD players at $60 each or 7,500 at $95 each. The CD changers cost the wholesaler $45 each.
   a. Calculate the price elasticity between the $60 and $95 price levels.
   b. What factors should determine the price to be set?

7. A full-service car wash has done research on customer sensitivity to price. These are the results:

Price	Number of Car Washes Demanded in Market Area per Year
$5.25	75,000
5.75	65,000
6.25	55,000
6.75	30,000
7.25	20,000
7.75	10,000

   a. Calculate price elasticity for all price levels.
   b. At what price is total revenue maximized?
   c. What price should be set? Why?
   d. What other information, not given in this question, is important in setting price?
   e. Which expenses for a car wash are fixed? Which expenses are variable?

8. The car wash in Question 7 can accommodate up to 30,000 cars per year with fixed costs of $75,000. Above 30,000 cars, fixed costs rise to $90,000. Variable costs are $3.00 per car wash.
   a. Compute average fixed costs, average variable costs, and average total costs for the car wash at each price.
   b. Why might the car wash set a price that does not maximize profit?

9. A tire manufacturer has fixed costs of $1,500,000 and variable costs of $47.00 per tire.

   a. Calculate total costs for volumes of 10,000, 25,000, and 50,000 tires.
   b. Calculate average total, fixed, and variable costs for the same volumes.
   c. At a volume of 50,000 tires, would the firm make a profit or loss with a wholesale selling price of $71.00? What is the total profit or loss?

10. A supermarket retailer sells medium-sized shaving cream containers for $1.49; they are purchased for $1.07. Large-sized containers sell for $2.09; they are purchased for $1.65.
    a. For each size container, determine the markup percentage on selling price and at cost.
    b. Why would the retailer use a different markup percentage for medium containers from that for large containers?
    c. If a shaving cream manufacturer offers the supermarket a 25 percent markup on selling price for medium-sized containers, as well as a cash discount of 2 percent and a quantity discount of 5 percent, what is the purchase price to the supermarket? What is the overall discount? There are no transportation costs.

11. A wholesaler requires a 35 percent markup on selling price for profit projections to be met. The merchandise costs $42.00.
    a. What must the selling price be for the wholesaler to meet its markup goal?
    b. What would be the minimum selling price if the wholesaler has a markup goal of 40 percent on selling price?

12. Convert the following markups from selling price to cost:
    a. 20 percent markup on selling price.
    b. 35 percent markup on selling price.
    c. 70 percent markup on selling price.

13. Convert the following markups from cost to selling price:
    a. 100 percent markup at cost.
    b. 125 percent markup at cost.
    c. 175 percent markup at cost.

14. An auto parts distributor is offered the following discounts: functional markup, 45 percent; quantity discount, 5 percent; cash discount, 2 percent; and seasonal discount, 3 percent. If the suggested final selling price of the total order is $1,000 and shipping charges are $60.00, compute the total order cost to the firm.

15. A glove manufacturer originally sold suede gloves for $39 per pair. An end-of-season sale has reduced the price of these gloves to $22.
    a. Compute the off-original and off-sale markdown percentages.
    b. Why is there a difference in these calculations?

16. a. A firm expects to sell 1,000 notebook PCs yearly at a price of $875 per system (including color monitor, DVD-RW drive, 80-gigabyte hard drive, 2.5 gigabyte processor chip, printer, keyboard, and graphics board). At the $875 price, the company's markup is 18 percent. How many units would the firm need to sell to earn the same gross profit at a selling price of $990 as it would at a selling price of $875?

b. How many units must the firm sell to earn the same gross profit at a selling price of $825 as it would at a selling price of $875?

17. A manufacturer estimates the following relationship between marketing expenses and sales:

Marketing Expenses	Unit Sales
$100,000	235,000
200,000	285,000
300,000	335,000
400,000	385,000
500,000	410,000

If a product has a gross profit of $5 per unit and general operating expenses are constant at $100,000, at what marketing expenditure level is profit maximized?

18. Calculate the opportunity costs associated with each marketing expenditure level in Question 17.

19. a. Why do most sales response curves have "S" shapes?
    b. Under what conditions would sales response curves have different shapes?
    c. Draw sales response curves based on the information in Table 6.

Appendix C

Computer-Based Marketing Exercises

An accompanying computer program enables you to engage in marketing decision making under simulated conditions and apply many of the concepts studied during your principles of marketing course. The exercises described in this appendix are designed to reinforce text material; to have you manipulate controllable marketing factors and see their impact on costs, sales, and profits; to have you better understand the impact of uncontrollable factors; and to have you gain experience using a computer to assess marketing opportunities and solve marketing problems. All 18 exercises are designed to be handed in for class assignments or for your own use. They are balanced in terms of subject and level.

Please note: A separate, more-detailed computer exercise, entitled *StratMktPlan*, covers the basic elements of a strategic marketing plan. It is tied to all eight parts in *Marketing*. An overview of this exercise is presented at the end of Chapter 3 ("Developing and Enacting Strategic Marketing Plans"). That exercise may be accessed from your Backpack at our Web site.

How to Use the Computer-Based Exercise Program

Program Downloading and Operation Using a Computer with a Hard Drive

This section explains how to install and operate your copy of *Computer-Based Marketing Exercises*—and how to permanently place your name, class, and section on your copy (so that assignments may be submitted with your name printed on them).

To run *Computer-Based Marketing Exercises,* you must first download the compressed installation program from your Backpack at the text's Web site. Save this program in a folder on your hard drive. It is recommended that you save this program in a folder labeled as TEMP. If you do not have this folder, make one with this title. (Because this program is compressed and then extracted, it cannot be run from a traditional 3-1/2-inch disk.) You must also download a program to unzip these compressed files. Download WINZIP Evaluation version 10.0 (or later) from **http://www.winzip.com**. The evaluation version is for a 45-day trial period; a license fee is required for continued use beyond 45 days.

Complete the following steps to extract the installation program and install the exercise program on your hard drive:

1. Go to the TEMP file and highlight "ExerZip.zip."
2. Open the zip file by clicking on it or by using the Run utility on your Start Menu. (See instructions below to use the Run utility.)

3. Activate the "Extract" function by clicking the "Extract" button or the "Unzip or Install" button on the Actions menu.
4. A dialog screen should appear providing actions for extraction. Select the drive and folder in which you would like to save the extracted files. The default drive and folder is C:\EXERCISE.
5. Complete the extraction by clicking "Extract," "Continue," or "OK."
6. The extracted files should be downloaded in the folder you specified.
7. Click on the set.up file to install the program.

If you prefer to open the zip file by using the Run utility, click the Start menu and select "Run." You can browse for the zip file or type in C:\TEMP\ExerZip.zip and press "OK." Then go to step 3 above.

You are now ready to run *Computer-Based Marketing Exercises* from your hard drive. If you are still in the Windows environment, follow the screen prompts for the *Computer-Based Marketing Exercises* program. If you have exited your computer and then return at another time, initialize the Windows environment. Then, simply adhere to the preceding instructions 3 to 5.

The first time you run *Computer-Based Marketing Exercises*, the program requires you to insert your name, class, and section to identify your responses. If necessary, enter this information by choosing the Rest Name button. Once you enter this information, it will appear on each computer screen and printout—and become a permanent part of your exercise program. It will not have to be repeated. The program will do the rest and guide you to the main menu.

After running *Computer-Based Marketing Exercises,* you may wish to delete the "ExerZip.zip" file from your "TEMP" folder. The file was used in installation and will not be needed in the future. Some versions of WinZip will automatically delete the file and others will not.

Running the Program from a Network

Some colleges and universities have PC networks for student use. Because there are many differences in the way these networks are set up and operated, please consult with your professor or someone in the computer lab with regard to using *Computer-Based Marketing Exercises*.

The Main Menu

When running *Computer-Based Marketing Exercises*, all exercises can be accessed from the MAIN MENU. Use your mouse or trackball to select an exercise. You can also choose an exercise by repeatedly pressing the Tab key until the desired exercise is

MAIN MENU

highlighted and then pressing the Enter key. Selecting Exit will enable you to quit the program.

The menu shown above is arranged in the order the topics appear in the text.

How to Operate Each Exercise

At the bottom of each exercise screen, a number of commands appear. They include the Exit button [E] to quit the program, the Menu button [M] to return to the main menu, the Next button [N] to proceed to the following screen, the Back button [B] to return to the prior screen, the Objectives button [O] to go to the Objectives section, the Questions button [Q] to go to the first page of the questions, the Print Screen button [P], and the Analysis button [A]. All commands can be executed by either clicking your mouse (or trackball) or by holding down the [ALT] key and then pressing the respective letter key.

How to Print from the Exercise Program

While using the exercise program, you may print any screen for your own reference or for the submission of an assignment. Simply turn on the printer connected to the computer you are using. Then, click the Print Screen button at the bottom of each exercise screen (or hold down the [Alt] key and then press the [P] key). The screen appearing on your computer monitor will automatically be printed—including your name, class, and section. The printing option should not be selected if no printer is available.

The Exercises

In the following sections, the basic premise of each exercise is described.

Exercise 1: Marketing Orientation

As the owner of a local florist, a table allows you to enter your degree of agreement with 10 statements (on a five-point scale ranging from strongly agree to strongly disagree). Statements relate to such areas as the importance of various markets, planning for seasonality, the impact of the Web, forecasting sales and profits, assessing customer needs, understanding competitors' strategies, and selling flowers with a limited shelf life. The exercise is keyed to "The Marketing Concept" in Chapter 1, pages 10–12 in the printed text.

Exercise 2: Boston Consulting Group Matrix

As a marketing executive for Packard Athletic Shoe Company, a table allows you to enter revised values for the relative market shares and industry growth rates for any or all of Packard's product categories (SBUs). The products are then displayed in a Boston Consulting Group matrix. The exercise is keyed to "The Boston Consulting Group Matrix" in Chapter 3, pages 67–69 in the printed text.

Exercise 3: Questionnaire Analysis

In this exercise, you are a market researcher who is requested to collect data for a consumer survey on boom boxes (portable self-contained stereos with multiple speakers). The exercise screens explain how blank copies of the survey may be printed, as well as how the survey may be administered at the computer. The exercise is keyed to "Data Analysis" in Chapter 4, page 107 in the printed text.

Exercise 4: Ethics in Action

As a marketing executive for an industrial-goods manufacturer, a table allows you to enter your degree of agreement with statements (on a five-point scale ranging from strongly agree to strongly disagree). These statements present a variety of ethical situations relating to salespersons, marketing managers, buyers, retailers, and importers. The exercise is keyed to "Ethics" in Chapter 5, pages 135–137 in the printed text.

Exercise 5: Standardizing Marketing Plans

By answering a series of questions, you—as an international marketing consultant—are able to make decisions regarding the level of standardization for five factors: a product's brand name, its design, its manufacturing process, its advertising, and its pricing. You can vary each factor from pure standardized (global) to glocal to non-standardized. The exercise is keyed to "Standardizing Plans" in Chapter 6, pages 173–174 in the printed text.

Exercise 6: Vendor Analysis

As the purchasing director for a firm, you are to assign weights to eight important vendor attributes: delivery speed, delivery reliability, product quality, quality of final customer support, quality of intermediate customer support, purchase terms, pricing, and availability of styles and colors in all sizes. The exercise is keyed to "Differences from Final Consumers Due to Nature of Purchases" in Chapter 9, pages 260–262 in the printed text.

Exercise 7: Segmentation Analysis

A table allows you, the vice-president of marketing for a medium-sized local company, to allocate a $3 million annual marketing budget between final and organizational market segments. By varying the budget, unit sales, sales revenues, manufacturing costs, total costs, and profit are affected. Different levels of marketing expenditures are required to be successful in each market segment. The exercise is keyed to "Targeting the Market" in Chapter 10, pages 297–304 in the printed text.

Exercise 8: Product Positioning

A product positioning map lets you—acting as an outside consultant—evaluate Hewlett Packard's (HP's) personal computer positioning relative to other major brands (Dell, Compaq, Gateway, IBM, and NEC). By rating HP's updated image on the basis of a series of statements, a revised product-positioning map for HP and five other brands is generated and displayed. In addition, the computer program calculates revised market shares for HP and the other brands, leading to an adjusted market-share table. The exercise is keyed to "Product Positioning" in Chapter 11, pages 336–339 in the printed text.

Exercise 9: Services Strategy

By making a number of marketing decisions, you—as a manager of a hotel chain—are able to develop an overall services strategy. You are seeking to increase your hotel's occupancy rate and profits by offering free breakfasts, exercise facilities, and the use of a print shop. Each of these strategies can be offered at four different levels; cost data are provided for each level. By varying the level of each strategy, total revenues, costs, operating profit, and the hotel's occupancy rate are affected. You can revise your overall strategy by re-entering a new strategy. This exercise is keyed to "Special Considerations in the Marketing of Services" in Chapter 12, pages 370–375 in the printed text.

Exercise 10: Product Screening Checklist

A new-product screening checklist lets you—acting as an outside consultant who specializes in new-product concepts—weight the importance of various general, marketing, and production characteristics, and then rate a new product idea in terms of each of these characteristics. The computer program then computes separate indexes for general, marketing, and production factors—as well as an overall evaluation index. The exercise is keyed to "Product Screening" in Chapter 13, pages 403–404 in the printed text.

Exercise 11: Economic Order Quantity

As the purchasing manager for a firm, you can determine its economic order quantity under various assumptions by answering questions about expected annual demand for a product, its unit cost at wholesale, order-processing costs, and inventory-holding costs (as a percentage of a unit's wholesale cost). The computer program uses the EOQ formula, and a screen graphically displays the results. The exercise is keyed to "How Much to Reorder" in Chapter 14, page 457 in the printed text.

Exercise 12: Wholesaler Cost Analysis

As a consultant for a manufacturer, you have been retained to review that firm's selection of manufacturer wholesaling versus merchant wholesaling. The total costs of each wholesaling alternative differ on the basis of sales. The exercise is keyed to "Manufacturer/Service Provider Wholesaling" in Chapter 15, pages 470–472 in the printed text.

Exercise 13: Advertising Budget

As advertising director for Sunshine Cruise Lines, a leading cruise ship operator, one of your tasks is to allocate the firm's ad budget among various magazines via a computerized spreadsheet table. The exercise is keyed to "Establishing a Budget" in Chapter 18, page 552 in the printed text.

Exercise 14: Salesperson Deployment

As a regional sales manager, one of your more important responsibilities is to determine the required number of salespeople in your territory. Your firm has four types of industrial accounts ("A," "B," "C," and "D"). "A" accounts are key customers, "B" accounts have high potential but only moderate sales, "C" accounts are smaller firms with lower sales potential, and "D" are the smallest accounts. The exercise is keyed to "Establishing a Budget" in Chapter 19, page 581 in the printed text.

Exercise 15: Price Elasticity

As the owner-operator of an auto repair firm specializing in quick oil changes, you are concerned about what price to charge for an oil change. First, you answer a series of questions about the price range to be considered and the expected average amount of consumer demand (which may be expressed in fractions) at various prices. The computer program then calculates elasticity of demand for the various price intervals and graphically displays it. The exercise is keyed to "Consumers" in Chapter 20, pages 616–618 in the printed text.

Exercise 16: Key Cost Concepts

As a pricing consultant for Ultimate Audiovision, you answer questions about the fixed and variable costs of making the home-entertainment system at various production levels. Ultimate

Audiovision contains a state-of-the-art 55-inch rear-projection TV, a hi-fi stereo VCR, a DVD player, a 500-watt digital receiver, and a six-speaker home theater stereo package. The exercise is keyed to "Cost-Based Pricing" in Chapter 21, page 637 in the printed text.

Exercise 17: Performance Ratios

As a General Toy Company executive vice-president, you are quite interested in using performance ratios to measure your company's relative success or failure across several criteria. The pre-set data in this exercise (those programmed into the exercise) are drawn from Appendix B in the text. By entering new data onto a profit-and-loss screen, you can see the impact of changes in General Toy's sales efficiency, cost of goods sold, gross margin, operating expenses, net profit, stock turnover, and return on investment on the company's related performance ratios. For example, what would happen to ROI if General Toy's assets rise by 5 percent? The exercise is keyed to "Performance Ratios" in Appendix B, pages A-8–A-9 in the printed text.

Exercise 18: Optimal Marketing Mix

A table allows you—the marketing director for a small industrial manufacturer—to make decisions regarding your firm's $3 million annual marketing budget. You have the ability to make decisions regarding the expenditures for advertising, personal selling, and distribution and to set the price for your product for each of three strategy alternatives: mass marketing, selective marketing, and exclusive marketing. Thus, you are involved with two distinct areas of decision making: (1) For each strategy alternative (mass marketing, selective marketing, and exclusive marketing), what is the best marketing mix? (2) Which strategy alternative should your firm pursue? Once you enter decisions, the computer program automatically calculates and displays unit sales, revenues, total product costs, total costs, and profit. The results will differ substantially for the three alternative strategies. The exercise is keyed to "Determining an Optimal Marketing Mix" in Appendix B, page A-14 in the printed text.

Appendix D

Glossary

A

Absolute Product Failure Occurs if a firm is unable to regain its production and marketing costs. The firm incurs a financial loss.

Accelerator Principle States that final consumer demand affects many layers of organizational consumers.

Adaptation A firm's responses to the surrounding environment, while continuing to capitalize on differential advantages, including looking for new opportunities and responding to threats.

Adoption Process The mental and behavioral procedure an individual consumer goes through when learning about and purchasing a new product. It consists of five stages: knowledge, persuasion, decision, implementation, and confirmation.

Advertising Paid, nonpersonal communication regarding goods, services, organizations, people, places, and ideas that is transmitted through various media by business firms, government and other nonprofit organizations, and individuals who are identified in the advertising message as sponsors.

Advertising Agency An organization that provides a variety of advertising-related services to client firms. It often works with clients in devising their advertising plans – including themes, media choice, copywriting, and other tasks.

Advertising Media Costs Outlays for media time or space. They are related to ad length or size, as well as media attributes.

Advertising Themes The overall appeals for a campaign. Themes can be good or service, consumer, or institutional.

Agents Wholesalers that do not take title to products. They work for commissions or fees as payment for their services and are comprised of manufacturers'/service providers' agents, selling agents, and commission (factor) merchants.

All-You-Can-Afford Method A promotional budget method in which a firm first allots funds for every element of marketing except promotion; remaining marketing funds go to the promotion budget.

Approaching Customers The stage in the selling process that consists of the pre-approach and greeting.

Atmosphere (Atmospherics) The sum total of the physical attributes of a retailer, whether in a store or a nonstore format, that are used to develop an image and draw customers.

Attitudes (Opinions) An individual's positive, neutral, or negative feelings about goods, services, firms, people, issues, and/or institutions.

Audience The object of a source's message in a channel of communication.

B

Backward Invention An international product-planning strategy in which a firm appeals to developing and less-developed nations by making products less complex than those sold in its domestic market.

Bait-and-Switch Advertising An illegal practice whereby customers are lured to a seller that advertises items at very low prices and then told the items are out of stock or of poor quality. There is no intent to sell advertised items.

Balanced Product Portfolio A strategy by which a firm maintains a combination of new, growing, and mature products.

Barter Era Earliest use of the exchange process. With barter, people trade one resource for another.

Battle of the Brands Manufacturer, private, and generic brands each striving to gain a greater share of the consumer's dollar, control over marketing strategy, consumer loyalty, product distinctiveness, maximum shelf space and locations, and a large share of profits.

Benchmarking A procedure used by a firm to set its marketing performance standards based on prior actions by the firm itself, the prowess of direct competitors, the competence of the best companies in its industry, and/or the approaches of innovative companies in other industries anywhere around the world.

Benefit Segmentation A procedure for grouping consumers into segments on the basis of the different benefits sought from a product.

Blanket Branding See Family Branding.

Boston Consulting Group Matrix Lets a firm classify each strategic business unit (SBU) in terms of market share relative to major competitors and annual industry growth. The matrix identifies four types of SBUs: star, cash cow, question mark, and dog, and offers strategies for them.

Brand A name, term, design, symbol, or any other feature that identifies the goods and services of one seller from those of other sellers.

Brand Equity A branding concept that recognizes the worth of brands. It reflects the revenue premium that a brand earns in the marketplace in comparison with an identical, but unbranded alternative.

Brand Extension A strategy by which an established brand name is applied to new products.

Brand Loyalty The consistent repurchase of and preference toward a particular brand. With it, people can reduce time, thought, and risk.

Brand Manager System See Product Manager System.

Brand Mark   A symbol, design, or distinctive coloring or lettering that cannot be spoken.

Brand Name   A word, letter (number), group of words, or letters (numbers) that can be spoken.

Bricks-and-Clicks Firms   Companies that operate in both a traditional setting and on the Internet.

Bricks-and-Mortar Firms   Traditional companies that have not gotten involved with the Internet.

Broad Price Policy   Sets the overall direction (and tone) for a firm's pricing efforts and makes sure pricing decisions are coordinated with the choices as to a target market, an image, and other marketing-mix factors. It incorporates short- and long-term pricing goals, and the role of pricing.

Brokers   Temporary wholesalers, paid by a commission or fee, who introduce buyers and sellers and help complete transactions.

B-to-B Marketing   See Industrial Marketing.

Bundled Pricing   An offering of a basic product, options, and customer service for one total price.

Business Analysis   The stage in the new-product planning process that involves the detailed review, projection, and evaluation of such factors as consumer demand, production costs, marketing costs, break-even points, competition, capital investments, and profitability for each new proposed product.

Buyer-Seller Dyad   A two-way flow of communication between buyer and seller.

C

Canned Sales Presentation   A memorized, repetitive presentation given to all customers interested in a given item. It does not adapt to customer needs or traits but presumes a general presentation will appeal to everyone.

Cash-and-Carry Wholesaling   A limited-service merchant wholesaler format in which people from small businesses drive to wholesalers, order products, and take them back to a store or business. No credit, delivery, merchandise, and promotional assistance are provided.

Category Killer   An especially large specialty store that features an enormous selection in its product category and relatively low prices.

Cause-Related Marketing   A somewhat controversial practice in which profit-oriented firms contribute specific amounts to given nonprofit organizations for each consumer purchase of certain goods and services during a special promotion.

Cease-and-Desist Order   A consumer-protection legal concept that requires a firm to discontinue a promotion practice that is deemed deceptive and modify a message accordingly.

Chain-Markup Pricing   A form of demand-based pricing in which final selling price is determined, markups for each channel member are examined, and maximum acceptable costs to each member are computed. It extends demand-minus calculations from resellers back to suppliers (manufacturers).

Chain-Ratio Method   A method of sales forecasting in which a firm starts with general market data and then computes a series of more specific information. These combined data yield a sales forecast.

Channel Functions   The functions completed by some member of a channel: marketing research, buying, promotion, customer services, product planning, pricing, and distribution.

Channel Members   Those organizations or people participating in the distribution process. They may be manufacturers, service providers, wholesalers, retailers, and/or consumers.

Channel of Communication (Communication Process)   The mechanism by which a source develops a message, transmits it to an audience via some medium, and gets feedback from the audience.

Channel of Distribution   Composed of all the organizations or people in the distribution process.

Class-Action Suit   A legal action on behalf of many affected consumers.

Class Consciousness   The extent to which a person seeks social status.

Clicks-Only Firms   Companies that do business just online. They do not have traditional facilities.

Clients   The constituency for which a nonprofit organization offers membership, elected officials, locations, ideas, goods, and services.

Closing the Sale   The stage in the selling process that means getting a person to agree to a purchase. The salesperson must be sure no major questions remain before trying to close a sale.

Clustered Demand   A demand pattern in which consumer needs and desires for a good or service category can be classified into two or more clusters (segments), each with distinct purchase criteria.

Clutter   Involves the number of ads found in a single program, issue, and so forth of a medium.

Co-Branding   A strategy in which two or more brand names are used with the same product to gain from the brand images of each.

Cognitive Dissonance   Doubt that a correct purchase decision has been made. To overcome dissonance, a firm must realize that the decision process does not end with a purchase.

Combination Pricing   A pricing approach whereby aspects of cost-, demand-, and competition-based pricing methods are integrated.

Combination Sales Compensation Plan   A format that uses elements of both salary and commission methods. Such plans balance company control, flexibility, and employee incentives.

Combination Store   Unites food/grocery and general merchandise sales in one facility, with general merchandise providing 25 to 40 percent or more of sales.

Commercial Data Bases   Contain information on population traits, the business environment, economic forecasts, industry and companies' performance, and other items.

Commercialization   The final stage in the new-product planning process in which the firm introduces a product to its full target market. This corresponds to the introductory stage of the product life cycle.

Commercial Stock Brokers   Licensed sales representatives who advise business clients, take orders, and then acquire stocks and/or bonds for the clients. They may aid the firms selling the stocks or bonds, represent either buyers or sellers, and offer some credit.

Commission (Factor) Merchants   Agents that receive goods on consignment, accumulate them from local markets, and arrange for their sale in a central location.

Common Carriers   Companies that must transport the goods of any company (or individual) interested in their services; they cannot refuse any shipments unless their rules are broken. They provide service on a fixed and publicized schedule between designated points. A fee schedule is published.

Communication Process   See Channel of Communication.

Company-Controlled Price Environment Characterized by moderate competition, well-differentiated goods and services, and strong control over prices by individual firms.

Comparative Advantage A concept in international marketing that states that each country has distinct strengths and weaknesses based on its natural resources, climate, technology, labor costs, and other factors. Nations can benefit by exporting the goods and services with which they have relative advantages and importing the ones with which they have relative disadvantages.

Comparative Messages Implicitly or explicitly contrast a firm's offerings with those of competitors.

Competition-Based Pricing A pricing strategy approach whereby a firm uses competitors' prices rather than demand or cost considerations as its primary pricing guideposts. A firm can set prices below the market, at the market, or above the market.

Competitive Bidding A situation in which two or more sellers submit independent price quotes for specific goods and/or services to a buyer, which chooses the best offer.

Competitive Parity Method A method by which a firm's promotion budget is raised or lowered according to competitors' actions.

Concentrated Marketing Exists when a company targets one well-defined market segment with one tailored marketing strategy.

Concept Testing The stage in the new-product planning process that presents the consumer with a proposed product and measures attitudes and intentions at an early stage of the process.

Conclusive Research The structured collection and analysis of data about a specific issue or problem.

Conflict Resolution A procedure in organizational buying for resolving disagreements in joint decision making. The methods of resolution are problem solving, persuasion, bargaining, and politicking.

Consumer Bill of Rights A statement by President Kennedy saying that all consumers have four basic rights: to information, to safety, to choice in product selection, and to be heard.

Consumer Demand Refers to the attributes and needs of final consumers, industrial consumers, wholesalers and retailers, government institutions, international markets, and nonprofit institutions.

Consumer Demographics Objective and quantifiable population characteristics. They are rather easy to identify, collect, measure, and analyze—and show diversity around the globe.

Consumerism Encompasses the wide range of activities of government, business, and independent organizations designed to protect people from practices that infringe upon their rights as consumers.

Consumer Products Goods and services destined for the final consumer for personal, family, or household use.

Consumer's Brand Decision Process Consists of nonrecognition, recognition, preference (or dislike), and insistence (or aversion) stages that consumers pass through.

Containerization A coordinated transportation practice in which goods are placed in sturdy containers that can be loaded on trains, trucks, ships, or planes. The containers are mobile warehouses.

Continuous Monitoring Used to regularly study a firm's external and internal environment.

Contract Carriers Provide transportation services to shippers, based on individual agreements. Contract carriers do not have to maintain set routes or schedules and may negotiate rates.

Controllable Factors Decision elements internally directed by an organization and its marketers. Some of these factors are directed by top management; others are directed by marketers.

Control Units The sales categories for which data are gathered, such as boys', men's, girls', and women's clothing.

Convenience Store A retail store that is usually well situated and food-oriented; with long hours and a limited number of items. Consumers shop there for fill-in merchandise, often at off-hours.

Conventional Supermarket A departmentalized food store with minimum annual sales of $2 million that emphasizes a wide range of food and related products.

Cooperative Advertising Allows two or more firms to share some advertising costs. It can be vertical or horizontal.

Core Services The basic services that firms provide to their customers to be competitive.

Corporate Culture The shared values, norms, and practices communicated to and followed by those working for a firm.

Corporate Symbols A firm's name (and/or divisional names), logos, and trade characters. They are significant parts of an overall company image.

Corrective Advertising A consumer-protection legal concept that requires a firm to run new ads to correct the false impressions left by previous ones.

Cost-Based Pricing A pricing strategy approach whereby a firm sets prices by computing merchandise, service, and overhead costs and then adding an amount to cover its profit goal.

Cost of Living The total amount consumers annually pay for goods and services.

Cost-Plus Pricing A form of cost-based pricing in which prices are set by adding a pre-determined profit to costs. It is the simplest form of cost-based pricing.

Culture Consists of a group of people sharing a distinctive heritage.

Customary Pricing Occurs when a firm sets prices and seeks to maintain them for an extended time.

Customer Satisfaction The degree to which there is a match between a customer's expectations of a good or service and the actual performance of that good or service, including customer service.

Customer Service Involves the identifiable, but rather intangible, activities undertaken by a seller in conjunction with the basic goods and/or services it offers.

D

Data Analysis The coding, tabulation, and analysis of marketing research data.

Data-Base Marketing A computerized technique that compiles, sorts, and stores relevant information about customers and potential customers; uses that information to highlight opportunities and prioritize market segments; and enables the firm to profitably tailor marketing efforts for specific customers or customer groups

Data Mining An in-depth, computerized search of available information to find profitable marketing opportunities that may otherwise be hidden.

Data Warehousing Involves retaining all types of relevant company records (sales, costs, personnel performance, etc.), and information collected by continuous monitoring and marketing research.

Decline Stage of the Product Life Cycle The period during which industry sales decline and many firms exit the market since customers are fewer and they have less money to spend.

Decoding The process in a channel of communication by which a message sent by a source is interpreted by an audience.

Dealer Brands See Private Brands.

Demand-Backward Pricing See Demand-Minus Pricing.

Demand-Based Pricing A pricing strategy approach whereby a firm sets prices after studying consumer desires and ascertaining the range of prices acceptable to the target market.

Demand-Minus (Demand-Backward) Pricing A form of demand-based pricing whereby a firm finds the proper selling price and works backward to compute costs.

Demand Patterns Indicate the uniformity or diversity of consumer needs and desires for particular categories of goods and services.

Derived Demand Occurs for organizational consumers because the quantity of the items they buy is often based on anticipated demand by their subsequent customers for specific goods and services.

Desk Jobbers See Drop Shippers.

Developing Countries Have a rising education level and technology, but a per-capita gross domestic product of about $4,000 to $9,000.

Differential Advantages The unique features in a firm's marketing program that cause consumers to patronize that firm and not its competitors.

Differentiated Marketing (Multiple Segmentation) Exists when a company targets two or more well-defined market segments with a marketing strategy tailored to each segment.

Diffused Demand A demand pattern in which consumer needs and desires for a good or service category are so diverse that clear clusters (segments) cannot be identified.

Diffusion Process Describes the manner in which different members of the target market often accept and purchase a product. It spans the time from product introduction through market saturation.

Diminishing Returns May occur in a firm with high sales penetration if the firm seeks to convert remaining nonconsumers because the costs of attracting them may outweigh revenues.

Direct Channel of Distribution Involves the movement of goods and services from producer to consumers without the use of independent intermediaries.

Direct Marketing Occurs when a consumer is first exposed to a good or service by a nonpersonal medium (direct mail, TV, radio, magazine, newspaper, PC, etc.) and orders by mail, phone, or PC.

Direct Ownership A form of international marketing company organization in which a firm owns production, marketing, and other facilities in one or more foreign nations without any partners. The firm has full control over its international operations in those nations.

Direct Selling A nonstore retail operation that involves both personal contact with consumers in their homes (and other nonstore locations) and phone solicitations initiated by the retailer.

Discretionary Income What a person, household, or family has available to spend on luxuries, after necessities are purchased.

Disposable Income A person's, household's, or family's total after-tax income to be used for spending and/or savings.

Distributed Promotion Communication efforts spread throughout the year.

Distribution Intermediaries Wholesalers, retailers, and marketing specialists (such as transportation firms) that are facilitators (links) between manufacturers/service providers and consumers.

Distribution Planning Systematic decision making about the physical movement of goods and services from producer to consumer, and the related transfer of ownership (or rental) of them. It encompasses such diverse functions as transportation, inventory management, and customer transactions.

Domestic Marketing Encompasses a firm's efforts in its home country.

Donors The constituency from which a nonprofit organization receives resources.

Drop Shippers (Desk Jobbers) Limited-service merchant wholesalers that buy goods from manufacturers or suppliers and arrange for their shipment to retailers or industrial users. They have legal ownership, but do not take physical possession of products and have no storage facilities.

Dual Channel of Distribution (Multichannel Distribution) A strategy whereby a firm appeals to different market segments or diversifies business by selling through two or more separate channels.

Dumping Selling a product in a foreign country at a price much lower than that prevailing in the exporter's home market, below the cost of production, or both.

Durable Goods Physical products that last for an extended period.

E

E-commerce Revenue-generating Internet transactions.

Economic Community Promotes free trade among its member nations—but not necessarily with nonmember nations.

Economic Order Quantity (EOQ) The order volume corresponding to the lowest sum of order-processing and inventory-holding costs.

EDI See Electronic Data Interchange.

80-20 Principle States that in many organizations, a large proportion of total sales (profit) is likely to come from a small proportion of customers, products, or territories.

Elastic Demand Occurs if relatively small price changes result in large changes in quantity demanded.

Electronic Data Interchange (EDI) Allows suppliers and their manufacturers/service providers, wholesalers, and/or retailers to exchange data via computer linkups.

E-marketing Any marketing activity that is conducted through the Internet, from customer analysis to marketing-mix components.

Embargo A form of trade restriction that disallows entry of specified products into a country.

Empowering Employees When companies give their workers broad leeway to satisfy customer requests. Employees are encouraged and rewarded for showing initiative and imagination.

Encoding The process in a channel of communication whereby a thought or idea is translated into a message by the source.

End-Use Analysis   The process by which a seller determines the proportion of its sales made to organizational consumers in different industries.

EOQ   See Economic Order Quantity.

Ethical Behavior   Based on honest and proper conduct.

Ethnicity/Race   Should be studied from a demographics perspective to determine the existence of diversity among and within nations in terms of language and country of origin or race.

European Union (EU)   Also known as the Common Market. Rules call for no trade restrictions among members; uniform tariffs with nonmembers; common product standards; and a free flow of people and capital.

Evaluation of Alternatives   The stage in the final consumer's decision process in which criteria for a decision are set and alternatives ranked.

Exchange   The process by which consumers and publics give money, a promise to pay, or support for the offering of a firm, institution, person, place, or idea.

Exclusive Distribution   A policy in which a firm severely limits the number of resellers utilized in a geographic area, perhaps having only one or two within a specific shopping district.

Exempt Carriers   Transporters that are excused from legal regulations and must only comply with safety rules. Exempt carriers are specified by law.

Experiment   A type of research in which one or more factors are manipulated under controlled conditions. Experiments are able to show cause and effect.

Exploratory Research   Used when a researcher is uncertain about the precise topic to be investigated, or wants to informally study an issue.

Exporting   A form of international marketing company organization in which a firm reaches international markets by selling products made in its home country directly through its own sales force or indirectly via foreign merchants or agents. An exporting structure requires minimal investment in foreign facilities.

Extended Consumer Decision Making   Occurs when a person fully uses the decision process. Much effort is spent on information search and evaluation of alternatives for expensive, complex items with which a person has little or no experience.

F

Factor Merchants   See Commission Merchants.

Family   Two or more persons residing together who are related by blood, marriage, or adoption.

Family (Blanket) Branding   A strategy in which one name is used for two or more individual products. It can be applied to both manufacturer and private brands, and to both domestic and international (global) brands.

Family Life Cycle   Describes how a family evolves through various stages from bachelorhood to solitary retirement. At each stage, needs, experience, income, family composition, and the use of joint decision making change.

Feedback (Channel of Communication)   The response an audience has to a message.

Feedback (Uncontrollable Environment)   Information about the uncontrollable environment, the organization's performance, and how well the marketing plan is received.

Final Consumers   Buy goods and services for personal, family, or household use.

Final Consumer's Decision Process   The way in which people gather and assess information and choose among alternative goods, services, organizations, people, places, and ideas. It has six stages: stimulus, problem awareness, information search, evaluation of alternatives, purchase, and post-purchase behavior. Demographic, social, and psychological factors affect this process.

Flexible Pricing   Allows a firm to set prices based on the consumer's ability to negotiate or on the buying power of a large customer.

Food-Based Superstore   A diversified supermarket that sells a broad range of food and nonfood items.

Food Brokers   Introduce buyers and sellers of food and related general-merchandise items to one another and bring them together to complete a sale.

Forward Invention   An international product-planning strategy in which a company develops new products for its international markets.

Franchise Wholesaling   A full-service merchant wholesaler format whereby independent retailers affiliate with an existing wholesaler to use a standardized storefront design, business format, name, and purchase system.

Freight Forwarding   A transportation service in which specialized firms (freight forwarders) collect small shipments (usually less than 500 pounds each) from several companies. They pick up merchandise at each shipper's place of business and arrange for delivery at buyers' doors.

Frequency   How often a medium can be used.

Full Disclosure   A consumer-protection legal concept that requires that all data necessary for a consumer to make a safe and informed decision be provided in a promotion message.

Full-Line Discount Store   A department store with lower prices, a broad product assortment, a lower-rent location, more emphasis on self-service, brand-name merchandise, wide aisles, shopping carts, and more goods displayed on the selling floor.

Full-Line Wholesalers   See General-Merchandise Wholesalers.

Full-Service Merchant Wholesalers   Perform a full range of distribution tasks. They provide trade credit, store and deliver products, offer merchandising and promotion assistance, have a personal sales force, offer research and planning support, pass along information to suppliers and customers, and give installation and repair services.

Functional Accounts   Occur when natural account expenses are reclassified by function to indicate the purposes or activities for which expenditures have been made. Included as functional expenses are marketing administration, personal selling, advertising, transportation, warehousing, marketing research, and general administration.

G

GDP   See gross domestic product.

General Electric Business Screen   Categorizes strategic business units and products in terms of industry attractiveness and company business strengths.

General-Merchandise (Full-Line) Wholesalers   Full-service merchant wholesalers that carry a wide product assortment—nearly all the items needed by their customers.

Generic Brands   Emphasize names of the products themselves and not manufacturer or reseller names.

Geographic Demographics   Basic identifiable characteristics of towns, cities, states, regions, and countries.

Geographic Pricing   Outlines responsibility for transportation charges. The most common methods of geographic pricing are FOB (free on board) mill pricing, uniform delivered pricing, zone pricing, and base-point pricing.

Global Marketing   An advanced form of international marketing in which a firm addresses global customers, markets, and competition.

Global Marketing Approach   See Standardized Marketing Approach.

Glocal Marketing Approach   An international marketing strategy in which combining standardized and nonstandardized efforts lets a firm attain production efficiencies, have a consistent image, have some home-office control, and still be sensitive and responsive to local needs.

Goods Marketing   Entails the sale of physical products.

Goods/Services Continuum   Categorizes products along a scale from pure goods to pure services.

Government   Consumes goods and services in performing its duties and responsibilities. There are 1 federal, 50 state, and 87,000 local governmental units.

Government-Controlled Price Environment   Characterized by prices being set or strongly influenced by some level of government.

Gray Market Goods   Foreign-made products imported into countries such as the United States by distributors (suppliers) that are not authorized by the products' manufacturers.

Gross Domestic Product (GDP)   The total annual value of goods and services produced in a country less net foreign investment.

Growth Stage of the Product Life Cycle   The period during which industry sales increase rapidly as a few more firms enter a highly profitable market that has substantial potential.

H

Heavy Half   See Heavy-Usage Segment.

Heavy-Usage Segment (Heavy Half)   A consumer group that accounts for a large proportion of a good's or service's sales relative to the size of the market.

Hidden Service Sector   Encompasses the delivery, installation, maintenance, training, repair, and other services provided by firms that emphasize goods sales.

Hierarchy-of-Effects Model   Outlines the sequential short-term, intermediate, and long-term promotion goals for a firm to pursue—and works in conjunction with the consumer's decision process.

Homogeneous Demand   A demand pattern in which consumers have rather uniform needs and desires for a good or service category.

Horizontal Audit   Studies the overall marketing performance of a firm with particular emphasis on the interrelationship of variables and their relative importance. It is also called a marketing-mix audit.

Horizontal Price Fixing   Results from agreements among manufacturers, among wholesalers, or among retailers to set prices at a given stage in a channel of distribution. Such agreements are illegal according to the federal Sherman

Antitrust Act and the Federal Trade Commission Act, regardless of how "reasonable" prices are.

Household   A person or group of persons occupying a housing unit, whether related or unrelated.

Household Life Cycle   Incorporates the life stages of both family and nonfamily households.

Hypermarket   The European term for a Supercenter.

I

Iceberg Principle   States that superficial data are insufficient to make sound marketing evaluations.

Idea Generation   The stage in the new-product planning process that involves the continuous, systematic search for product opportunities. It involves new-idea sources and ways to generate ideas.

Ideal Points   The combinations of attributes that people would most like products to have.

IMC   See Integrated Marketing Communications.

Importance of a Purchase   Related to the degree of decision making, level of perceived risk, and amount of money to be spent/invested. The level of importance of a purchase affects the time and effort a person spends shopping for a product—and the money allotted.

Incremental Method   A promotional budget method in which a firm bases a new budget on the previous one. A percentage is added to or subtracted from this year's budget to determine next year's.

Independent Media   Communication vehicles not controlled by a firm; yet, they influence government, consumer, and publics' perceptions of that firm's products and overall image.

Independent Retailer   Operates only one outlet and offers personal service, a convenient location, and close customer contact.

Indirect Channel of Distribution   Involves the movement of goods and services from producer to independent intermediaries to consumers.

Individual (Multiple) Branding   Separate brands used for different items or product lines sold by a firm.

Industrial (B-to-B) Marketing   Occurs when firms deal with organizational consumers.

Industrialization of Services   Improves service efficiency and variability by using hard, soft, and hybrid technologies.

Industrialized Countries   Have high literacy, modern technology, and per-capita income of several thousand dollars.

Industrial Products   Goods and services purchased for use in the production of other goods or services, in the operation of a business, or for resale to other consumers.

Inelastic Demand   Takes place if price changes have little impact on the quantity demanded.

Information Search   The stage in the final consumer's decision process that requires listing the alternatives that will solve the problem at hand and determining the characteristics of them. Information search may be either internal or external.

Innovativeness   The willingness to try a new good or service that others perceive as risky.

Inseparability of Services   Means a service provider and his or her services may be inseparable. Customer contact is often considered an integral part of the service experience.

Institutional Advertising   Used when the advertising goal is to enhance company image—and not to sell specific goods or services.

Intangibility of Services   Means that services often cannot be displayed, transported, stored, packaged, or inspected before buying.

Integrated Marketing Communications (IMC)   Recognizes the value of a comprehensive plan that evaluates the strategic roles of a variety of communication disciplines—advertising, public relations, personal selling, and sales promotion—and combines them to provide clarity, consistency, and maximum communication impact.

Intensive Distribution   A policy in which a firm uses a large number of resellers in order to have wide market coverage, channel acceptance, and high total sales and profits.

International Marketing   Involves marketing goods and services outside a firm's home country, whether in one or several markets.

Internet   A global electronic superhighway of computer networks—a network of networks in which users at one computer can get information from another computer (and sometimes talk directly to users at other computers).

Introduction Stage of the Product Life Cycle   The period during which only one or two firms have entered the market, and competition is limited. Initial customers are innovators.

Inventory Management   Involved with providing a continuous flow of goods and matching the quantity of goods kept in inventory as closely as possible with customer demand.

Isolated Store   A freestanding retail outlet located on a highway or street.

Issue (Problem) Definition   A statement of the topic to be looked into via marketing research. It directs the research process to collect and analyze appropriate data for the purpose of decision making.

Item Price Removal   A practice whereby prices are marked only on store shelves or aisle signs and not on individual items.

J

JIT Inventory System   See Just-in-Time Inventory System.

Joint Decision Making   The process whereby two or more people have input into purchases.

Joint Venture (Strategic Alliance)   A form of international marketing company organization in which a firm agrees to combine some aspect of its manufacturing or marketing efforts with those of a foreign company so as to share expertise, costs, and/or connections with important persons.

Jury of Executive (Expert) Opinion   A method of sales forecasting by which the management of a firm or other well-informed persons meet, discuss the future, and set sales estimates based on the group's experience and interaction.

Just-in-Time (JIT) Inventory System   A procedure by which a purchasing firm reduces the amount of inventory it keeps on hand by ordering more often and in lower quantity.

L

Law of Demand   States that consumers usually purchase more units at a low price than at a high price.

Leader Pricing   A firm's advertising and selling key items in its product assortment at less than their usual profit margins. For a wholesaler or retailer, the goal is to increase customer traffic. For a manufacturer, the goal is to gain greater consumer interest in its overall product line.

Lead Time   The period required by a medium for placing an ad.

Leased Department   A section of a retail store rented to an outside party. The lessee operates a department—under the store's rules—and pays a percentage of sales as rent.

Less-Developed Countries   Have low literacy, limited technology, and per-capita gross domestic product typically below $2,000 (sometimes less than $1,000).

Licensing Agreement   A situation in which a company pays a fee to use a name or logo whose trademark rights are held by another firm.

Lifestyle   Represents the way in which a person lives and spends time and money. It is based on the social and psychological factors that have been internalized by that person—as well as his or her demographic background.

Limited Consumer Decision Making   Occurs when a person uses every step in the purchase process but does not spend a great deal of time on some of them. The person has previously bought a given good or service, but makes fresh decisions when it comes under current purchase consideration.

Limited-Line Wholesalers   See Specialty-Merchandise Wholesalers.

Limited-Service Merchant Wholesalers   Buy and take title to products, but do not perform all the functions of full-service merchant wholesalers. They may not provide credit, merchandising assistance, or marketing research data.

Line of Business   Refers to the general goods/service category, functions, geographic coverage, type of ownership, and specific business of a firm.

Local Content Laws   Require foreign firms to set up local plants and use locally made components. The goal of these laws is to protect the economies and domestic employment of the nations involved.

Logistics (Physical Distribution)   Encompasses the broad range of activities concerned with efficiently delivering raw materials, parts, semifinished items, and finished products to designated places, at designated times, and in proper condition.

Loss Leaders   Items priced below cost to attract customers to a seller—usually in a store setting.

Low-Involvement Purchasing   Occurs when a consumer minimizes the time and effort expended in both making decisions about and shopping for those goods and services he or she views as unimportant.

M

Macroenvironment   Encompasses the broad demographic, societal, economic, political, technological, and other factors that an organization faces.

Mail-Order Wholesalers   Limited-service merchant wholesalers that use catalogs, instead of a personal sales force, to promote products and communicate with customers.

Major Innovations   Items not previously sold by any firm.

Majority Fallacy   Concept stating that firms may fail when they go after the largest market segment because competition is intense. A potentially profitable segment may be one ignored by other firms.

Manufacturer Brands Use the names of their makers and generate the vast majority of U.S. revenues for most product categories. The marketing goal for manufacturer brands is to attract and retain loyal consumers, and for their makers to direct the marketing effort for the brands.

Manufacturers Produce products for resale to other consumers.

Manufacturer/Service Provider Wholesaling Occurs when a producer does all wholesaling functions itself. It may be carried out via sales offices and/or branch offices.

Manufacturers'/Service Providers' Agents Agents who work for several manufacturers/service providers and carry noncompetitive, complementary products in exclusive territories. A manufacturer/service provider may use many agents.

Marginal Return The amount of sales each increment of promotion spending will generate.

Market Consists of all the people and/or organizations who desire (or potentially desire) a good or service, have sufficient resources to make purchases, and are willing and able to buy.

Market Buildup Method A method of sales forecasting in which a firm gathers data from small, separate market segments and aggregates them.

Market-Controlled Price Environment Characterized by a high level of competition, similar goods and services, and little control over prices by individual firms.

Marketing The anticipation, management, and satisfaction of demand through the exchange process.

Marketing Audit A systematic, critical, impartial review and appraisal of the basic goals and policies of the marketing function, and of the organization, methods, procedures, and personnel employed to implement the policies and achieve the goals.

Marketing Company Era Recognition of the central role of marketing. The marketing department is the equal of others in the company. Company efforts are well integrated and regularly reviewed.

Marketing Concept A consumer-oriented, market-driven, value-based, integrated, goal-oriented philosophy for a firm, institution, or person.

Marketing Cost Analysis Used to evaluate the cost efficiency of various marketing factors, such as different total quality configurations, product lines, order sizes, distribution methods, sales territories, channel members, salespersons, advertising media, and customer types.

Marketing Department Era Stage during which the marketing department shares in company decisions but remains in a subordinate position to the production, engineering, and sales departments.

Marketing Environment Consists of controllable factors, uncontrollable factors, the organization's level of success or failure in reaching its objectives, feedback, and adaptation.

Marketing Functions Include environmental analysis and marketing research, broadening the scope of marketing, consumer analysis, product planning, distribution planning, promotion planning, price planning, and marketing management.

Marketing Information System (MIS) A set of procedures and methods designed to generate, analyze, disseminate, and store anticipated marketing decision information on a regular, continuous basis.

Marketing Intelligence Network The part of a marketing information system that consists of continuous monitoring, marketing research, and data warehousing.

Marketing Manager System A product management organizational format under which a company executive is responsible for overseeing a wide range of marketing functions and for coordinating with other departments that perform marketing-related activities.

Marketing Mix The specific combination of marketing elements used to achieve objectives and satisfy the target market. It encompasses decisions regarding four major variables: product, distribution, promotion, and price.

Marketing Myopia A shortsighted, narrow-minded view of marketing and its environment.

Marketing Organization The structural arrangement that directs marketing functions. It outlines authority, responsibility, and tasks to be done.

Marketing Performers The organizations or individuals that undertake one or more marketing functions. They include manufacturers and service providers, wholesalers, retailers, marketing specialists, and organizational and final consumers.

Marketing Plan Analysis Involves comparing actual performance with planned or expected performance for a specified period of time.

Marketing Research Involves systematically gathering, recording, and analyzing information about specific issues related to the marketing of goods, services, organizations, people, places, and ideas.

Marketing Research Process Consists of a series of activities: defining the issue or problem to be studied; examining secondary data; generating primary data, if necessary; analyzing information; making recommendations; and implementing findings.

Marketing Strategy Outlines the way in which the marketing mix is used to attract and satisfy the target market(s) and achieve an organization's goals.

Market Segmentation Involves subdividing a market into clear subsets of customers that act in the same way or that have comparable needs.

Markup Pricing A form of cost-based pricing in which a firm sets prices by computing the per-unit costs of producing (buying) goods and/or services and then determining the markup percentages needed to cover selling costs and profit.

Mass Customization A process by which mass-market goods and services are individualized to satisfy a specific customer need, at a reasonable price.

Massed Promotion Communication efforts that are concentrated in peak periods, like holidays.

Mass Marketing See Undifferentiated Marketing.

Maturity Stage of the Product Life Cycle The period during which industry sales stabilize as the market becomes saturated and many firms enter to capitalize on the still sizable demand. Companies seek to maintain a differential advantage.

Medium The personal or nonpersonal means in a channel of communication used to send a message.

Membership Warehouse Club A retailing format in which final consumers and businesses pay small yearly dues to shop in a huge, austere warehouse. Consumers buy items at deep discounts.

Merchant Wholesalers   Buy, take title, and take possession of products for further resale. Merchant wholesalers may be full or limited service.

Message   A combination of words and symbols sent to an audience via a channel of communication.

Message Permanence   Refers to the number of exposures one ad generates (repetition) and how long it remains available to the audience.

Microenvironment   Encompasses the forces close to an organization that have a direct impact on its ability to serve customers, including distribution intermediaries, competitors, consumer markets, and the capabilities of the organization itself.

Minimum Price Laws   See Unfair-Sales Acts.

Minor Innovations   Items not previously marketed by a firm that have been marketed by others.

MIS   See Marketing Information System.

Missionary Salesperson   A type of sales support person who gives out information on new goods or services. He or she does not close sales, but describes items' attributes, answers questions, and leaves written matter.

Mixed-Brand Strategy   Occurs when a combination of manufacturer and private brands (and maybe generic brands) are sold by manufacturers, wholesalers, and retailers.

Modifications   Alterations in or extensions of a firm's existing products. They include new models, styles, colors, features, and brands.

Modified Break-Even Analysis   A form of demand-based pricing that combines traditional break-even analysis with an evaluation of demand at various levels of price. It reveals the price-quantity mix that maximizes profits.

Modified-Rebuy Purchase Process   A moderate amount of decision making undertaken in the purchase of medium-priced products that an organizational consumer has bought infrequently before.

Monitoring Results   Involves comparing the actual performance of a firm, business unit, or product against planned performance for a specified period.

Monopolistic Competition   A situation in which there are several firms in an industry, each trying to offer a unique marketing mix—based on price or nonprice factors.

Monopoly   A situation in which just one firm sells a given good or service and has a lot of control over its marketing plan.

Motivation   Involves the positive or negative needs, goals, and desires that impel a person to or away from certain actions, objects, or conditions.

Motives   The reasons for behavior.

Multichannel Distribution   See Dual Channel of Distribution.

Multiple Branding   See Individual Branding.

Multiple-Buying Responsibility   Two or more employees formally participating in complex or expensive purchase decisions.

Multiple Segmentation   See Differentiated Marketing.

Multiple-Unit Pricing   A practice whereby a firm offers discounts to consumers to encourage them to buy in quantity, so as to increase overall sales volume.

N

NAFTA   See North American Free Trade Agreement.

NAICS   See North American Industry Classification System.

Narrowcasting   Presenting advertising messages to rather limited and well-defined audiences. It is a way to reduce the audience waste with mass media.

Nationalism   Refers to a country's efforts to become self-reliant and raise its stature in the eyes of the world community. At times, a high degree of nationalism may lead to tight restrictions on foreign firms to foster the development of domestic industry at their expense.

Natural Accounts   Costs that are reported by the names of the expenses and not by their purposes. Such expense categories include salaries, rent, advertising, supplies, insurance, and interest.

Need-Satisfaction Approach   A high-level selling method based on the principle that each customer has different attributes and wants; thus the sales presentation should adapt to the individual consumer.

Negotiation   A situation in which a buyer uses bargaining ability and order size to get sellers' best possible prices.

New Product   A modification of an existing product or an innovation the consumer sees as meaningful.

New-Product Manager System   A product management organizational format that has product managers to supervise existing products and new-product managers to develop new ones. Once a product is introduced, it is given to the product manager.

New-Product Planning Process   Involves a series of steps from idea generation to commercialization. The firm generates ideas, evaluates them, weeds out poor ones, obtains consumer feedback, develops the product, tests it, and brings it to market.

New-Task Purchase Process   A large amount of decision making undertaken in the purchase of an expensive product an organizational consumer has not bought before.

Noise   Interference at any point along a channel of communication.

Nondurable Goods   Physical products made from materials other than metals, hard plastics, and wood; are rather quickly consumed or worn out; or become dated, unfashionable, or otherwise unpopular.

Nongoods Services   Involve personal service on the part of the seller. They do not involve goods.

Nonprice-Based Approach   A pricing strategy in which sellers downplay price as a factor in consumer demand by creating a distinctive good or service via promotion, packaging, delivery, customer service, availability, and other marketing factors.

Nonprofit Institutions   Act in the public interest or to foster a cause and do not seek financial profits.

Nonprofit Marketing   Conducted by organizations and individuals that operate in the public interest or that foster a cause and do not seek financial profits. It may involve organizations, people, places, and ideas, as well as goods and services.

Nonstandardized Marketing Approach   An international marketing strategy in which a firm sees each nation or region as distinct, and requiring its own marketing plan.

Nonstore Retailing   Occurs when a firm uses a strategy mix that is not store-based to reach consumers and complete transactions.

North American Free Trade Agreement (NAFTA)   An agreement that created an economic community linking the United States, Canada, and Mexico. It will remove tariffs and trade restrictions among the three countries over the next several years.

North American Industry Classification System (NAICS)   A coding system that may be used to derive information about most organizational consumers. The NAICS is the official classification system for the United States, Canada, and Mexico. It uses 20 industry categories.

O

Objective-and-Task Method   A promotional budget method in which a firm sets promotion goals, determines the activities needed to satisfy them, and then establishes the proper budget.

Observation   A research method whereby present behavior or the results of past behavior are observed and noted. People are not questioned and cooperation is unnecessary.

Odd Pricing   Used when selling prices are set below even dollar values, such as 49 cents and $199.

Oligopoly   A situation in which a few firms—usually large ones—account for most industry sales and would like to engage in nonprice competition.

One-Price Policy   Lets a firm charge the same price to all customers seeking to purchase a good or service under similar conditions.

Opinion Leaders   People to whom other consumers turn for advice and information via face-to-face communication. They normally have an impact over a narrow product range.

Opinions   See Attitudes.

Opt-In (Permission-Based) E-mail   A Web-based promotion tool whereby Internet users agree to receive targeted E-mail from a firm.

Order Getter   A type of salesperson who generates customer leads, provides information, persuades customers, and closes sales.

Order Taker   A type of salesperson who processes routine orders and reorders. The order taker typically handles goods and services that are pre-sold.

Organizational Consumers   Buy goods and services for further production, usage in operating the organization, or resale to other consumers.

Organizational Consumer's Decision Process   Consists of expectations, the buying process, conflict resolution, and situational factors.

Organizational Mission   A long-term commitment to a type of business and a place in the market. It can be expressed in terms of the customer group(s) served, the goods and services offered, the functions performed, and/or the technologies utilized.

Outsourcing   When one company provides services for another company that could also be or usually have been done in-house by the client firm.

Owned-Goods Services   Involve alterations or maintenance/repairs of goods owned by consumers.

P

Package   A container used to protect, promote, transport, and/or identify a product.

Packaging Functions   Containment and protection, usage, communication, segmentation, channel cooperation, and new-product planning.

Patent   Grants an inventor of a useful product or process exclusive selling rights for a fixed period.

Penetration Pricing   Uses low prices to capture the mass market for a good or service.

Perceived Risk   The level of uncertainty a consumer believes exists as to the outcome of a purchase decision; this belief may or may not be correct. Perceived risk can be divided into six major types: functional, physical, financial, social, psychological, and time.

Percentage-of-Sales Method   A promotional budget method in which a firm ties its promotion budget to sales revenue.

Peripheral Services   Supplementary (extra) services that firms provide to customers.

Perishability of Services   Means that many services cannot be stored for future sale. A service firm must try to manage consumer usage so there is consistent demand over various times.

Permission-Based E-mail   See Opt-In E-mail.

Personality   The sum total of a person's enduring internal psychological traits making the person unique.

Personal Demographics   Basic identifiable characteristics of individual final consumers and organizational consumers and groups of final consumers and organizational consumers.

Personal Selling   Involves oral communication with one or more prospective buyers by paid representatives for the purpose of making sales.

Persuasive Impact   The ability of a medium to stimulate consumers.

Physical Distribution   See Logistics.

Planned Obsolescence   A marketing practice that capitalizes on short-run material wearout, style changes, and functional product changes.

Planned Shopping Center   A retail location that consists of centrally owned or managed facilities. It is planned and operated as an entity, ringed by parking, and based on balanced tenancy. The three types of planned center are regional, community, and neighborhood.

Porter Generic Strategy Model   Identifies two key marketing planning concepts and the options available for each: competitive scope (broad or narrow target) and competitive advantage (lower cost or differentiation).

Post-Purchase Behavior   The stage in the final consumer's decision process when further purchases and/or re-evaluation of the purchase are undertaken.

Predatory Pricing   An illegal practice in which large firms cut prices on products to below their cost in selected geographic areas so as to eliminate small, local competitors.

Prestige Pricing   Assumes consumers will not buy goods or services at prices they consider too low.

Price   Represents the value of a good or service for both the seller and the buyer.

Price Adjustment Tactics   Alterations in list prices, escalator clauses and surcharges, added markups, markdowns, and rebates.

Price-Based Approach   A pricing strategy in which sellers influence consumer demand primarily through changes in price levels.

Price Ceiling   The maximum amount customers will pay for a given good or service.

Price Discrimination   A form of demand-based pricing in which a firm sets two or more distinct prices for a product so as to appeal to different final consumer or organizational consumer segments. Price discrimination can be customer-, product-, time-, or place-based.

Price Elasticity of Demand   Indicates the sensitivity of buyers to price changes in terms of the quantities they will purchase. It is computed by dividing the percentage change in quantity demanded by the percentage change in price charged.

Price Floor   The lowest acceptable price a firm can charge and attain its profit goal.

Price-Floor Pricing   A form of cost-based pricing whereby a firm determines the lowest price at which it is worthwhile to increase the amount of goods or services it makes available for sale.

Price Leadership   A form of competition-based pricing in which one firm (or a few firms) is usually the first to announce price changes and others in the industry follow.

Price Lining   Involves selling products at a range of prices, with each representing a distinct level of quality (or features).

Price Planning   Systematic decision making by an organization regarding all aspects of pricing.

Price-Quality Association   A concept stating that consumers may believe high prices represent high quality and low prices represent low quality.

Price Wars   Situations in which firms continually try to undercut each other's prices to draw customers.

Primary Data   Consist of information gathered to address a specific issue or problem at hand.

Primary Demand   Consumer demand for a product category.

Private (Dealer) Brands   Use names designated by their resellers, usually wholesalers or retailers, and account for sizable U.S. revenues in many product categories. Resellers have more exclusive rights for these brands, and are more responsible for distribution and larger purchases.

Private Carriers   Shippers with their own transportation facilities.

Problem Awareness   The stage in the final consumer's decision process during which a consumer recognizes that the good, service, organization, person, place, or idea under consideration may solve a problem of shortage or unfulfilled desire.

Problem Definition   See Issue Definition.

Process-Related Ethical Issues   Involve the unethical use of marketing strategies or tactics.

Product   A bundle of attributes capable of exchange or use, usually a mix of tangible and intangible forms. It may be an idea, a physical entity, or a service, or any combination of the three.

Product Adaptation   A product planning strategy in which domestic products are modified to meet foreign language needs, taste preferences, climates, electrical requirements, laws, and other factors.

Product Development Stage of New-Product Planning   Converts an idea for a new product into a tangible form and identifies a basic marketing strategy.

Product Differentiation   Occurs when a product offering is perceived by the consumer to differ from its competition on any physical or nonphysical product characteristic, including price.

Production Era   Devotion to physical distribution of products due to high demand and low competition. Consumer research, product modifications, and adapting to consumer needs are not needed.

Product Item   A specific model, brand, or size of a product that a company sells.

Product Life Cycle   A concept that seeks to describe a product's sales, competitors, profits, customers, and marketing emphasis from its beginning until it is removed from the market. It is divided into introduction, growth, maturity, and decline stages.

Product Line   A group of closely related product items.

Product (Brand) Manager System   A product management organizational format under which there is a level of middle managers, each of whom is responsible for planning, coordinating, and monitoring the performance of a single product (brand) or a small group of products (brands). The managers handle both new and existing products and are involved with all the marketing activities related to their product or group of products.

Product/Market Opportunity Matrix   Identifies four alternative marketing strategies to maintain and/or increase sales of business units and products: market penetration, market development, product development, and diversification.

Product Mix   All the different product lines a firm offers. It can be described in terms of its width, depth, and consistency.

Product Planning   Systematic decision making relating to all aspects of the development and management of a firm's products, including branding and packaging.

Product Planning Committee   A product management organizational format with high-level executives from various functional areas in a firm, such as marketing, production, engineering, finance, and R&D. It does product approval, evaluation, and development on a part-time basis.

Product Positioning   Enables a firm to map each of its products in terms of consumer perceptions and desires, competition, other company products, and environmental changes.

Product Recall   The primary enforcement tool of the Consumer Product Safety Commission, whereby the CPSC asks or orders firms to recall and modify (or discontinue) unsafe products.

Product-Related Ethical Issues   Involve the ethical appropriateness of marketing certain products.

Product Screening   The stage in the new-product planning process when poor, unsuitable, or otherwise unattractive ideas are weeded out from further consideration.

Profit-Based Pricing Objectives   Those that orient a firm's pricing strategy toward some type of profit goals: profit maximization, satisfactory profit, return on investment, and/or early recovery of cash.

Promotion   Any communication used to inform, persuade, and/or remind people about an organization's or individual's goods, services, image, ideas, community involvement, or impact on society.

Promotion Mix   A firm's overall and specific communication program, including its involvement with advertising, public relations (publicity), personal selling, and/or sales promotion.

Promotion Planning   Systematic decision making relating to all aspects of an organization's or individual's communications efforts.

Prospecting   The stage in the selling process that generates a list of customer leads. It is common with outside selling, and can be blind or lead in orientation.

Publicity   The form of public relations that entails nonpersonal communication passed on via various media but not paid for by an identified sponsor.

Publicity Types   News publicity, business feature articles, service feature articles, finance releases, product releases, pictorial releases, video news releases, background editorial material, and emergency publicity.

Public Relations Includes any communication to foster a favorable image for goods, services, organizations, people, places, and ideas among various publics—such as consumers, investors, government, channel members, employees, and the general public.

Publics' Demand The attributes and needs of employees, unions, stockholders, the general public, government agencies, consumer groups, and other internal and external forces that affect a company.

Pulling Strategy Occurs when a firm first stimulates consumer demand and then gains dealer support.

Purchase Act The stage in the final consumer's decision process in which there is an exchange of money, a promise to pay, or support in return for ownership of a specific good, the performance of a specific service, and so on.

Purchase Terms The provisions of price agreements.

Pure Competition A situation in which many firms sell virtually identical goods or services and they are unable to create differential advantages.

Pushing Strategy Occurs when various firms in a distribution channel cooperate in marketing a product.

Q

Quick Response (QR) Inventory System A cooperative effort between retailers and suppliers to reduce retail inventory while providing a merchandise supply that more closely addresses the actual buying patterns of consumers.

R

Rack Jobbers Full-service merchant wholesalers that furnish the racks or shelves on which products are displayed. They own the products on the racks, selling them on a consignment basis.

Reach Refers to the number of viewers, readers, or listeners in a medium's audience. For TV and radio, it is the total number of people who watch or listen to an ad. For print media, it has two aspects: circulation and passalong rate.

Real Income The amount of income earned in a year adjusted by the rate of inflation.

Rebates A form of price adjustment in which refunds are given directly from the manufacturer to the customer to stimulate the purchase of an item or a group of items.

Reciprocity A procedure by which organizational consumers select suppliers that agree to purchase goods and services, as well as sell them.

Reference Group A group that influences a person's thoughts or actions.

Relationship Marketing Exists when marketing activities are performed with the conscious intention of developing and managing long-term, trusting relationships with customers.

Relative Product Failure Occurs if a firm makes a profit on an item but that product does not reach profit goals and/or adversely affects a firm's image.

Rented-Goods Services Involve the leasing of goods for a specified time.

Reorder Point Sets an inventory level at which new orders must be placed. It depends on order lead time, the usage rate, and safety stock.

Research Design Outlines the procedures for collecting and analyzing data. It includes decisions relating to the person collecting data, data to be collected, group of people or objects studied, data-collection techniques employed, study costs, method of data collection, length of study period and time, and location of data collection.

Retail Chain Involves common ownership of multiple outlets.

Retailers Buy or handle goods and services for sale (resale) to the final (ultimate) consumer.

Retail Franchising A contractual agreement between a franchisor (a manufacturer, wholesaler, or service sponsor) and a retail franchisee, which allows the latter to run a certain form of business under an established name and according to specific rules.

Retailing Encompasses those business activities involved with the sale of goods and services to the final consumer for personal, family, or household use. It is the final stage in a channel of distribution.

Retail Store Strategy Mix An integrated combination of hours, location, assortment, service, advertising, prices, and other factors retailers employ.

Robinson-Patman Act Prohibits manufacturers and wholesalers from price discrimination in dealing with different channel-member purchasers of products with "like quality" if the effect of such discrimination is to injure competition.

Routine Consumer Decision Making Occurs when a person buys out of habit and skips steps in the decision process. In this category are items with which a person has much experience.

S

Sales Analysis The detailed study of sales data for the purpose of appraising the appropriateness and effectiveness of a marketing strategy.

Sales-Based Pricing Objectives Goals that orient a company's pricing strategy toward high sales volume and/or expanding its share of sales relative to competitors.

Sales Engineer A type of sales support person who accompanies an order getter if a very technical or complex item is being sold. He or she discusses specifications and long-range uses.

Sales Era Involves hiring a sales force and sometimes advertising to sell inventory, after production is maximized. The goal is to make consumer desires fit the features of the products offered.

Sales Exception Reporting Highlights situations where sales goals are not met or sales opportunities are present.

Sales-Expense Budget Allots selling costs among salespeople, products, customers, and geographic areas for a given period.

Sales Forecast Outlines expected company sales for a specific good or service to a specific consumer group over a specific period of time under a specific marketing program.

Sales Management Planning, implementing, and controlling the personal sales function. It covers employee selection, training, territory allocation, compensation, and supervision.

Sales Penetration The degree to which a firm is meeting its sales potential: Sales penetration = Actual sales/Sales potential

Sales Presentation The stage in the selling process that includes a verbal description of a product, its benefits, options and models, price, associated services like delivery and warranty, and a demonstration (if needed).

Sales Promotion Involves paid marketing communication activities (other than advertising, publicity, or personal selling) that are intended to stimulate consumer purchases and dealer effectiveness. Included are trade shows, premiums, incentives, giveaways, demonstrations, and various other efforts not in the ordinary promotion routine.

Sales Promotion Conditions Requirements channel members or consumers must meet to be eligible for a specific sales promotion.

Sales Promotion Orientation Refers to its focus—channel members or consumers—and its theme.

Sales Territory The geographic area, customers, and/or product lines assigned to a salesperson.

Sampling The analysis of selected people or objects in a designated population, rather than all of them.

SBU See Strategic Business Unit.

Scientific Method A research philosophy incorporating objectivity, accuracy, and thoroughness.

Scrambled Merchandising Occurs if a retailer adds goods and services that are unrelated to each other and the firm's original business.

Secondary Data Consist of information not collected for the issue or problem at hand but for some other purpose. The two sources of secondary data are internal and external.

Selective Demand Consumer demand for a particular brand.

Selective Distribution A policy in which a firm employs a moderate number of resellers.

Self-Fulfilling Prophecy A situation in which a firm predicts falling sales and then ensures this by reducing or removing marketing support.

Selling Against the Brand A practice used by wholesalers and retailers, whereby they stock well-known brands, place high prices on them, and then sell other brands for lower prices.

Selling Agents Responsible for marketing the entire output of a manufacturer/service provider under a contractual agreement. They perform all wholesale tasks except taking title to products.

Selling Process Consists of prospecting for leads, approaching customers, determining consumer wants, giving a sales presentation, answering questions, closing the sale, and following up.

Semantic Differential A survey technique using rating scales of bipolar (opposite) adjectives. An overall company or product profile is then devised.

Service Blueprint A visual portrayal of the service process by a firm. It is a detailed map or flowchart.

Service Gap The difference between customer expectations and actual service performance.

Service Marketing The rental of goods, servicing goods owned by consumers, and personal services.

Service Salesperson A type of sales support person who ordinarily deals with customers after sales. Delivery, installation, and other follow-up tasks are done.

Simulation A computer-based method to test the potential effects of various marketing factors via a software program rather than real-world applications.

Single-Source Data Collection Allows research firms to track the activities of individual consumer households from the programs they watch on TV to the products they purchase at stores.

Situational Factors Those that can interrupt the organizational consumer's decision process and the selection of a supplier or brand. They include strikes, machine breakdowns, etc.

Situation Analysis Identifies an organization's internal strengths and weaknesses and external opportunities and threats. It seeks to answer: Where is a firm now? In what direction is it headed?

Skimming Pricing Uses high prices to attract the market segment more concerned with product quality, uniqueness, or status than price.

Social Class A status hierarchy by which groups and individuals are classified on the basis of esteem and prestige. Social classes are based on income, occupation, education, and type of dwelling.

Social Marketing The use of marketing to increase the acceptability of social ideas.

Social Performance How one carries out his/her roles as a worker, family member, citizen, and friend.

Social Responsibility A concern for the consequences of a person's or firm's acts as they might affect the interests of others. Corporate social responsibility balances a company's short-term profit needs with long-term societal needs.

Social Styles Model A classification system for segmenting organizational consumers in terms of a broad range of demographic and lifestyle factors. The model divides the personnel representing those consumers into lifestyle categories.

Socioecological View of Marketing Considers all the stages in a product's life span in developing, selling, purchasing, using, and disposing of that product. It incorporates the interests of everyone affected by a good's or service's use.

Sorting Process The distribution activities of accumulation, allocation, sorting, and assorting. Through this process, intermediaries can resolve the differences in the goals of manufacturers and consumers.

Source A company, an independent institution, or an opinion leader seeking to present a message to an audience. It is part of the channel of communication.

Spam Unsolicited and unwanted E-mail.

Specialty-Merchandise (Limited-Line) Wholesalers Full-service merchant wholesalers that concentrate on a rather narrow product range and have an extensive selection in that range.

Specialty Store A retailer that concentrates on one product line.

Standardized (Global) Marketing Approach A marketing strategy in which a firm uses a common marketing plan for all nations in which it operates—because it assumes worldwide markets are more homogeneous due to better communications, more open borders, free-market economies, etc.

Standard of Living Refers to the average quantity and quality of goods and services that are owned and consumed in a given nation.

Status Quo-Based Pricing Objectives Sought by a firm interested in continuing a favorable business climate for its operations or in stability.

Stimulus A cue (social, commercial, or noncommercial) or a drive (physical) meant to motivate a person to act.

Stock Turnover The number of times during a stated period (usually one year) that average inventory on hand is sold. Stock turnover is calculated in units or dollars (in selling price or at cost).

Straight Commission Plan A sales compensation plan in which a salesperson's earnings are directly related to sales, profits, customer satisfaction, or some other type of performance.

Straight Extension   An international product-planning strategy in which a firm makes and markets the same products for domestic and foreign sales.

Straight-Rebuy Purchase Process   Routine reordering by organizational consumers for the purchase of inexpensive items bought regularly.

Straight Salary Plan   A sales compensation plan in which a salesperson is paid a flat amount per period.

Strategic Alliance   See Joint Venture.

Strategic Business Plan   Describes the overall direction an organization will pursue within its chosen environment and guides the allocation of resources and effort. It integrates the perspectives of functional departments and operating units.

Strategic Business Unit (SBU)   A self-contained division, product line, or product department in an organization with a specific market focus and a manager with complete responsibility for integrating all functions into a strategy.

Strategic Marketing Plan   Outlines the marketing actions to undertake, why they are needed, who carries them out, when and where they will be completed, and how they will be coordinated.

Strategic Planning Process   Consists of seven interrelated steps: defining organizational mission, establishing strategic business units, setting marketing objectives, performing situation analysis, developing marketing strategy, implementing tactics, and monitoring results.

Subjective Price   A consumer's perception of the price of a good or service as being high, fair, or low.

Subliminal Advertising   A highly controversial kind of promotion because it does not enable the audience to consciously decode a message.

Substantiation   A consumer-protection legal concept that requires a firm to be able to prove all the claims it makes in promotion messages. This means thorough testing and evidence of performance are needed before making claims.

Supercenter (Hypermarket)   A combination store that integrates an economy supermarket with a discount department store, with at least 40 percent of sales from nonfood items.

Survey   Gathers information by communicating with respondents in person, by phone, or by mail.

Systems Selling   A combination of goods and services provided to a buyer by one vendor. This gives the buyer one firm with which to negotiate, as well as consistency among various parts and components.

T

Tactical Plan   Specifies the short-run actions (tactics) that a firm undertakes in implementing a given market strategy.

Target Market   The particular group(s) of customers a firm proposes to serve, or whose needs it proposes to satisfy, with a particular marketing program.

Target Market Strategy   Comprises three general phases: analyzing consumer demand, targeting the market, and developing the marketing strategy.

Target Pricing   A form of cost-based pricing in which prices are set to provide a particular rate of return on investment for a standard volume of production—the level of production a firm anticipates achieving.

Tariff   The most common form of trade restriction, in which a tax is placed on imported products by a foreign government.

Technology   Refers to developing and using machinery, products, and processes.

Telemarketing   An efficient way of operating, whereby telephone communications are used to sell or solicit business or to set up an appointment for a salesperson to sell or solicit business.

Test Marketing   The stage in the new-product planning process that involves placing a fully developed new product (a good or service) in one or more selected areas and observing its actual performance under a proposed marketing plan.

Time Expenditures   The activities in which a person participates and the time allocated to them.

Total-Cost Approach   Determines the distribution service level with the lowest total costs—including freight (shipping), warehousing, and lost business. An ideal system seeks a balance between low expenditures on distribution and high opportunities for sales.

Total Delivered Product   The bundle of tangible and intangible product attributes that are actually provided to consumers through a value chain and its related value delivery chain.

Total Quality   A process- and output-related philosophy, whereby a firm strives to fully satisfy customers effectively and efficiently. It requires a customer focus; top management commitment; an emphasis on continuous improvement; and support from employees, suppliers, and intermediaries.

Trade Character   A brand mark that is personified.

Trade Deficit   The amount by which the value of imports exceeds the value of exports for a country.

Trademark   A brand name, brand mark, or trade character or combination thereof with legal protection.

Trade Quota   A restriction that sets limits on the amounts of products imported into a country.

Trade Surplus   The amount by which the value of exports exceeds the value of imports for a country.

Traditional Break-Even Analysis   Finds the sales quantity in units or dollars that is needed for total revenues to equal total costs at a given price.

Traditional Department Store   A department store that has a great assortment of goods and services, provides many customer services, is a fashion leader, and often serves as an anchor store in a shopping district or shopping center.

Transportation Forms   The modes for shipping products, parts, raw materials, and so forth. These include railroads, motor carriers, waterways, pipelines, and airways.

Truck/Wagon Wholesalers   Limited-service merchant wholesalers that generally have a regular sales route, offer items from a truck or wagon, and deliver goods when they are sold.

U

Unbundled Pricing   Breaks down prices by individual components and allows the consumer to decide what to purchase.

Uncontrollable Factors   The external elements affecting an organization's performance that cannot be fully directed by that organization and its marketers. These include consumers, competition, suppliers and distributors, government, the economy, technology, and independent media.

Undifferentiated Marketing (Mass Marketing)   Exists when a company targets the whole market with a single basic marketing strategy intended to have mass appeal.

Unfair-Sales Acts (Minimum Price Laws)   Legislation in a number of states that prevents firms from selling products for less than their cost plus a fixed percentage that includes overhead and profit.

Unitary Demand   Exists if price changes are exactly offset by changes in the quantity demanded, so total sales revenue remains constant.

Unit Pricing   Lets consumers compare price per quantity for competing brands and for various sizes of the same brand. With it, prices are shown per unit of measure, as well as by total price.

Universal Product Code (UPC)   A series of thick and thin vertical lines used to pre-mark items. Price and inventory data are represented by the lines, but are not readable by employees and customers.

Unplanned Business District   A retail location form that exists where multiple stores are located close to one another without prior planning as to the number and composition of stores. The unplanned sites are central business district, secondary business district, neighborhood business district, and string.

UPC   See Universal Product Code.

V

VALS (Values and Lifestyles) Program   A classification system for segmenting consumers via a broad range of demographic and lifestyle factors. It divides final consumers into lifestyle categories.

Value Analysis   A comparison of the costs and benefits of alternative materials, components, designs, or processes so as to reduce the cost/benefit ratio of purchases.

Value Chain   Represents the series of business activities that are performed to design, produce, market, deliver, and service a product for customers.

Value Delivery Chain   Encompasses all of the parties who engage in value chain activities.

Values and Lifestyles Program   See VALS Program.

Variability in Service Quality   Differing service performance from one purchase occasion to another. Variations may be due to the service firm's difficulty in problem diagnosis (for repairs), customer inability to verbalize service needs, and the lack of standardization and mass production.

Variable Markup Policy   Cost-based markup pricing whereby separate categories of goods and services receive different percentage markups. Variable markups recognize that some items require greater personal selling, customer service, alterations, and end-of-season markdowns than others.

Variable Pricing   Allows a firm to intentionally alter prices in response to cost fluctuations or differences in consumer demand.

Vending Machine   A nonstore retail operation that uses coin- or card-operated machinery to dispense goods or services. It eliminates the need for salespeople, allows 24-hour sales, and can be placed outside rather than inside a store.

Vendor Analysis   An assessment of the strengths and weaknesses of current or new suppliers in terms of quality, customer service, reliability, and price.

Venture Team   A product management organizational format in which a small, independent department with a broad range of specialists is involved with a specific new product's entire development process. Team members work on a full-time basis and act in a relatively autonomous manner.

Vertical Audit   An in-depth analysis of one aspect of a firm's marketing strategy. It is also known as a functional audit.

Vertical Price Fixing   When manufacturers or wholesalers seek to control the final selling prices of their goods or services.

W

Warehousing   Involves the physical facilities used to store, identify, and sort goods in expectation of their sale and transfer within a distribution channel.

Warranty   An assurance to consumers that a product meets certain standards.

Waste   The part of a medium's audience not in a firm's target market.

Wearout Rate   The time it takes for a message to lose its effectiveness.

Wheel of Retailing   Describes how low-end (discount) strategies can evolve into high-end (full service, high price) strategies and thus provide opportunities for new firms to enter as discounters.

Wholesale Coopcratives   Full-service merchant wholesalers owned by member firms to economize functions and provide broad support. There are producer-owned and retailer-owned cooperatives.

Wholesalers   Buy or handle merchandise and its subsequent resale to organizational users, retailers, and other wholesalers.

Wholesaling   Includes buying and/or handling goods and services, and their subsequent resale to organizational users, retailers, and/or other wholesalers—but not the sale of significant volume to final consumers.

Word-of-Mouth Communication   The process by which people express opinions and product-related experiences to one another.

World Trade Organization (WTO)   An organization whose mission is to open up international markets even further and promote a cooperative atmosphere around the globe.

World Wide Web (WWW)   Comprises all of the resources and users on the Internet using the Hypertext Transfer Protocol (HTTP). It is a way of accessing the Internet, whereby people work with easy-to-use Web addresses and pages. Users see words, colorful charts, pictures, and video, and hear audio.

WTO   See World Trade Organization.

WWW   See World Wide Web.

Y

Yield Management Pricing   A form of demand-based pricing whereby a firm determines the mix of price-quantity combinations that generates the highest level of revenues for a given period.

Company Index

Name Index

Subject Index